19th Annual Meeting of the Special Interest Group on Discourse and Dialogue (SIGDIAL 2018)

Melbourne, Australia
12 – 14 May 2018

ISBN: 978-1-5108-6854-0

19th Annual Meeting of the Special Interest Group on Discourse and Dialogue

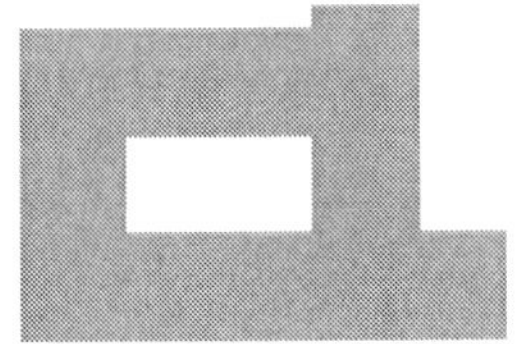 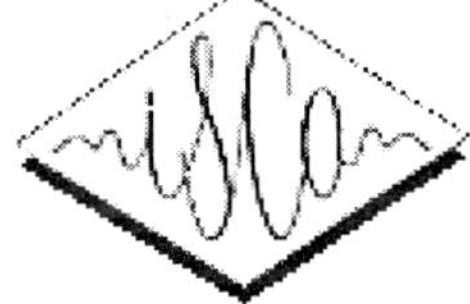 

Proceedings of the Conference

12-14 July 2018
Melbourne, Australia

In cooperation with:
Association for Computational Linguistics (ACL)
International Speech Communication Association (ISCA)
Association for the Advancement of Artificial Intelligence (AAAI)

We thank our sponsors:

Honda Research Institute Japan
Adobe Research
Nextremer
Educational Testing Service (ETS)
Monash University
RMIT University

Interactions
Amazon

Tricorn (Beijing) Technology
PolyAI

Microsoft Research
Apple

Toshiba Research Europe

Platinum

Gold

Silver

Bronze

In cooperation with

Association for Computational Linguistics (ACL)
209 N. Eighth Street
Stroudsburg, PA 18360
USA
Tel: +1-570-476-8006
Fax: +1-570-476-0860
acl@aclweb.org

Introduction

We are excited to welcome you to this year's SIGdial Conference, the 19th Annual Meeting of the Special Interest Group on Discourse and Dialogue. We are pleased to hold the conference in Melbourne, Australia, on July 12-14th, in close proximity to both ACL 2018 (the 56th Annual Meeting of the Association for Computational Linguistics) and YRRSDS 2018 (the 14th Young Researchers' Roundtable on Spoken Dialogue Systems).

The SIGdial conference remains a premier publication venue for research in discourse and dialogue. This year, the program includes 3 keynote talks, 5 oral presentation sessions, 3 poster sessions including 1 demo session, and a special session entitled "Physically Situated Dialogue."

We received 111 submissions this year, almost identical to the 113 received in 2017 (which was the 2nd largest number of submissions to SIGdial in its history). Of the 111 submissions, there were 67 long papers, 39 short papers, and 5 demo papers. All submissions received at least 3 reviews. We carefully considered both the numeric ratings and the tenor of the comments, both as written in the reviews and as submitted in discussions, in making our selections for the program. Overall, the members of the Program Committee did an excellent job in reviewing the submitted papers. We thank them for their important role in selecting the accepted papers and for helping to come up with a high quality program for the conference. In line with the SIGdial tradition, our aim has been to create a balanced program that accommodates as many favorably rated papers as possible. We accepted 52 papers: 36 long papers, 12 short papers, and 4 demo papers. These numbers give an overall acceptance rate of 47%. The rates separately for types of papers are 54% for long papers, 31% for short papers, and 80% for demo papers. After acceptance, 3 papers (2 long and 1 demo) that had also been submitted to other conferences were withdrawn. Of the long papers, 19 were presented as oral presentations. The remaining long papers and all the short papers were presented as posters, split across three poster sessions.

This year SIGdial has a special session on the topic "Physically Situated Dialogue", organized by Sean Andrist, Stephanie Lukin, Matthew Marge, Jesse Thomason, and Zhou Yu. The special session brings diverse paper submissions on a topic of growing interest to our technical program, with 7 of the accepted long papers part of this special session. The special session also features a panel discussion and late-breaking presentations, allowing for active engagement of the conference participants.

This year's SIGdial conference runs 3 full days, following the precedent set in 2017. One keynote and one poster session is held each day, with the remaining time given to oral presentations, demos, and the special session.

A conference of this scale requires advice, help and enthusiastic participation of many parties and we have a big 'thank you' to say to all of them.

Regarding the program, we thank our three keynote speakers, Mari Ostendorf (University of Washington, USA), Manfred Stede (Potsdam University, Germany), and Ingrid Zukerman (Monash University, Australia), for their inspiring talks on socialbots, automated arguing, and interpretation in physical settings, which cover many modern aspects of research in both discourse and dialogue. We also thank the organizers of the special session who designed the schedule for their accepted papers, and organized the session with a panel and late-breaking presentations at the venue. We are grateful for their smooth and efficient coordination with the main conference. We in addition thank Alex Papangelis, Mentoring Chair for SIGdial 2018, for his dedicated work on the mentoring process. The goal of mentoring is to assist authors of papers that contain important ideas but lack clarity. In total, 6 of the accepted papers received mentoring and we would like to thank our mentoring team for their excellent advice and support to the respective authors.

We extend special thanks to our Local Chair, Lawrence Cavedon, and his team. SIGdial 2018 would not have been possible without their effort in arranging the conference venue and accommodations, handling registration, making banquet arrangements, and numerous preparations for the conference. The student volunteers for on-site assistance also deserve our sincere appreciation.

Mikio Nakano, our Sponsorship Chair, has conducted the massive task of recruiting and liaising with our conference sponsors, many of whom continue to contribute year after year. Sponsorships support valuable aspects of the program, such as lunches and the conference banquet. We thank him for his dedicated work and coordination in conference planning. We gratefully acknowledge the support of our sponsors: (Platinum level) Honda Research Institute Japan, Interactions, and Microsoft Research; (Gold level) Adobe Research, Amazon, Apple, and Nextremer; (Silver level) Educational Testing Service (ETS) and Tricom (Beijing) Technology; (Bronze level) Monash University, PolyAI, and Toshiba Research Europe. We also thank RMIT University for their generous sponsorship as host.

We thank the SIGdial board, especially current and emeritus officers Kallirroi Georgila, Vikram Ramanarayanan, Ethan Selfridge, Amanda Stent, and Jason Williams, for their advice and support from beginning to end. We also thank Priscilla Rasmussen at the ACL for tirelessly handling the financial aspects of sponsorship for SIGdial 2018, and for securing our ISBN.

We once again thank our program committee members for committing their time to help us select a superb technical program. Finally, we thank all the authors who submitted to the conference and all the conference participants for making SIGdial 2018 a grand success and for growing the research areas of discourse and dialogue with their fine work.

Kazunori Komatani
General Chair

Diane Litman and Kai Yu
Program Co-Chairs

SIGDIAL 2018

General Chair:

Kazunori Komatani, Osaka University, Japan

Technical Program Co-Chairs:

Diane Litman, University of Pittsburgh, USA
Kai Yu, Shanghai Jiao Tong University, China

Mentoring Chair:

Alex Papangelis, Toshiba Research, UK

Local Chair:

Lawrence Cavedon, RMIT University, Australia

Sponsorship Chair:

Mikio Nakano, Honda Research Institute Japan, Japan

SIGdial Officers:

President: Jason Williams, Apple, USA
Vice President: Kallirroi Georgila, University of Southern California, USA
Secretary: Vikram Ramanarayanan, Educational Testing Service (ETS) Research, USA
Treasurer: Ethan Selfridge, Interactions, USA
President Emeritus: Amanda Stent, Bloomberg, USA

Program Committee:

Stergos Afantenos, IRIT and CNRS, University of Toulouse, France
Masahiro Araki, Kyoto Institute of Technology, Japan
Ron Artstein, USC Institute for Creative Technologies, USA
Rafael E. Banchs, Institute for Infocomm Research, Singapore
Timo Baumann, Carnegie Mellon University, USA
Frederic Bechet, Aix Marseille Universite, France
Steve Beet, Aculab plc, UK
Jose Miguel Benedi, Universitàt Politècnica de València, Spain
Nate Blaylock, Nuance Communications, USA
Johan Boye, KTH, Sweden
Jill Burstein, ETS, USA
Hendrik Buschmeier, Bielefeld University, Germany
Giuseppe Carenini, University of British Columbia, Canada
Christophe Cerisara, CNRS, France
Joyce Chai, Michigan State University, USA
Mark Core, University of Southern California, USA
Heriberto Cuayahuitl, University of Lincoln, UK
Nina Dethlefs, University of Hull, UK
David DeVault, University of Southern California, USA
Barbara Di Eugenio, University of Illinois at Chicago, USA
Maxine Eskenazi, Carnegie Mellon University, USA
Keelan Evanini, Educational Testing Service, USA
Mauro Falcone, Fondazione Ugo Bordoni, Italy

Raquel Fernández, University of Amsterdam, Netherlands
Kotaro Funakoshi, Honda Research Institute Japan Co., Ltd., Japan
Jianfeng Gao, Microsoft Research Redmond, USA
Milica Gasic, University of Cambridge, UK
Kallirroi Georgila, University of Southern California, USA
Jonathan Ginzburg, Université Paris-Diderot (Paris 7), France
Ivan Habernal, Technische Universität Darmstadt, Germany
Dilek Hakkani-Tur, Google Research, USA
Helen Hastie, Heriot-Watt University, UK
Xiaodong He, JD AI Research, China
Ryuichiro Higashinaka, NTT Media Intelligence Labs, Japan
Keikichi Hirose, University of Tokyo, Japan
David M. Howcroft, Saarland University, Germany
David Janiszek, Université Paris Descartes, France
Kristiina Jokinen, the University of Helsinki, Finland
Pamela Jordan, University of Pittsburgh, USA
Tatsuya Kawahara, Kyoto University, Japan
Simon Keizer, Vrije Universiteit Brussel, Belgium
Casey Kennington, Boise State University, USA
Norihide Kitaoka, Tokushima University, Japan
Stefan Kopp, Bielefeld University, Germany
Kornel Laskowski, Carnegie Mellon University, USA
Fabrice Lefevre, Univ. Avignon, France
James Lester, North Carolina State University, USA
Junyi Jessy Li, University of Texas at Austin, USA
Pierre Lison, Norwegian Computing Centre, Norway
Eduardo Lleida Solano, University of Zaragoza, Spain
José Lopes, Heriot-Watt University, UK
Ramon Lopez-Cozar, University of Granada, Spain
Matthew Marge, Army Research Laboratory, USA
Teruhisa Misu, Honda Research Institute USA, USA
Nasrin Mostafazadeh, University of Rochester, USA
Satoshi Nakamura, Nara Institute of Science and Technology, Japan
Mikio Nakano, Honda Research Institute Japan Co., Ltd., Japan
Shashi Narayan, University of Edinburgh, UK
Vincent Ng, University of Texas at Dallas, USA
Douglas O'Shaughnessy, Univ. of Quebec, Canada
Shereen Oraby, University of California Santa Cruz, USA
Alexandros Papangelis, Toshiba Cambridge Research Lab, UK
Rebecca J. Passonneau, The Pennsylvania State University, USA
Laura Perez-Beltrachini, University of Edinburgh, UK
Volha Petukhova, Saarland University, Germany
Paul Piwek, The Open University, UK
Rashmi Prasad, Interactions Corporation, USA
Matthew Purver, Queen Mary University of London, UK
Vikram Ramanarayanan, Educational Testing Service (ETS) Research, USA
Norbert Reithinger, DFKI GmbH, Germany
Giuseppe Riccardi, University of Trento, Italy
Sophie Rosset, Université Paris-Saclay, France

Sakriani Sakti, Nara Institute of Science and Technology, Japan
Niko Schenk, Goethe University Frankfurt am Main, Germany
David Schlangen, Bielefeld University, Germany
Björn Schuller, University of Augsburg / Imperial College London, Germany/UK
Ethan Selfridge, Interactions Corp, USA
Gabriel Skantze, KTH Speech Music and Hearing, Sweden
Manfred Stede, University of Potsdam, Germany
Georg Stemmer, Intel Corp., Germany
Matthew Stone, Rutgers University, USA
Svetlana Stoyanchev, Interactions Corporation, USA
Kristina Striegnitz, Union College, USA
Maite Taboada, Simon Fraser University, Canada
António Teixeira, University of Aveiro, Portugal
Joel Tetreault, Grammarly, USA
Simone Teufel, University of Cambridge, UK
Takenobu Tokunaga, Tokyo Institute of Technology, Japan
David Traum, University of Southern California, USA
Gokhan Tur, Uber, USA
Stefan Ultes, University of Cambridge, UK
David Vandyke, Apple, UK
Hsin-Min Wang, Academia Sinica, Taiwan
Nigel Ward, University of Texas at El Paso, USA
Jason Williams, Apple, USA
Zhou Yu, University of California Davis, USA
Jian Zhang, Dongguan University of Technology; Hong Kong University of Science and Technology, China
Ming Zhou, Microsoft Research Asia, China

Mentors:

Dimitrios Alikaniotis, Grammarly, USA
Hendrik Buschmeier, Bielefeld University, Germany
Helen Hastie, Heriot-Watt University, UK
Shereen Oraby, University of California Santa Cruz, USA
Stefan Ultes, University of Cambridge, UK
David Vandyke, Apple, UK

Invited Speakers:

Mari Ostendorf, University of Washington, USA
Manfred Stede, University of Potsdam, Germany
Ingrid Zukerman, Monash University, Australia

Table of Contents

Conference Program

13:30–14:30   Poster 1

14:30–15:00   *Coffee Break*

July 13 (continued)

11:00–12:15   **Oral 2 - Generation 2**

Unsupervised Counselor Dialogue Clustering for Positive Emotion Elicitation in Neural Dialogue System
Nurul Lubis, Sakriani Sakti, Koichiro Yoshino and Satoshi Nakamura

Discovering User Groups for Natural Language Generation
Nikos Engonopoulos, Christoph Teichmann and Alexander Koller

Controlling Personality-Based Stylistic Variation with Neural Natural Language Generators
Shereen Oraby, Lena Reed, Shubhangi Tandon, Sharath T.S., Stephanie Lukin and Marilyn Walker

12:15–13:30   *Lunch*

13:30–15:00   **Poster 2 and Interactive demos**

A Context-aware Convolutional Natural Language Generation model for Dialogue Systems
Sourab Mangrulkar, Suhani Shrivastava, Veena Thenkanidiyoor and Dileep Aroor Dinesh

A Unified Neural Architecture for Joint Dialog Act Segmentation and Recognition in Spoken Dialog System
Tianyu Zhao and Tatsuya Kawahara

Cost-Sensitive Active Learning for Dialogue State Tracking
Kaige Xie, Cheng Chang, Liliang Ren, Lu Chen and Kai Yu

Discourse Coherence in the Wild: A Dataset, Evaluation and Methods
Alice Lai and Joel Tetreault

Neural Dialogue Context Online End-of-Turn Detection
Ryo Masumura, Tomohiro Tanaka, Atsushi Ando, Ryo Ishii, Ryuichiro Higashinaka and Yushi Aono

Spoken Dialogue for Information Navigation
Alexandros Papangelis, Panagiotis Papadakos, Yannis Stylianou and Yannis Tzitzikas

15:00–15:30   ***Coffee Break***

15:30–17:10   **Oral 3 - Dialogue**

18:15–21:00   ***Banquet***

July 14

09:30–10:30   *Keynote 3*
               Ingrid Zukerman

10:30–11:00   **Coffee Break**

11:00–12:15   **Oral 4 - Discourse**

               Fine-Grained Discourse Structures in Continuation Semantics
               Timothée Bernard

               Automatic Extraction of Causal Relations from Text using Linguistically Informed Deep Neural Networks
               Tirthankar Dasgupta, Rupsa Saha, Lipika Dey and Abir Naskar

               Toward zero-shot Entity Recognition in Task-oriented Conversational Agents
               Marco Guerini, Simone Magnolini, Vevake Balaraman and Bernardo Magnini

12:15–13:30   *Lunch*

13:30–14:30   **Poster 3**

               Identifying Explicit Discourse Connectives in German
               Peter Bourgonje and Manfred Stede

               Feudal Dialogue Management with Jointly Learned Feature Extractors
               Iñigo Casanueva, Paweł Budzianowski, Stefan Ultes, Florian Kreyssig, Bo-Hsiang Tseng, Yen-chen Wu and Milica Gasic

               Variational Cross-domain Natural Language Generation for Spoken Dialogue Systems
               Bo-Hsiang Tseng, Florian Kreyssig, Paweł Budzianowski, Iñigo Casanueva, Yen-chen Wu, Stefan Ultes and Milica Gasic

               Coherence Modeling Improves Implicit Discourse Relation Recognition
               Noriki Nishida and Hideki Nakayama

Zero-Shot Dialog Generation with Cross-Domain Latent Actions

Tiancheng Zhao and Maxine Eskenazi
Language Technologies Institute
Carnegie Mellon University
Pittsburgh, Pennsylvania, USA
{tianchez, max+}@cs.cmu.edu

Abstract

This paper introduces *zero-shot dialog generation* (ZSDG), as a step towards neural dialog systems that can instantly generalize to new situations with minimal data. ZSDG enables an end-to-end generative dialog system to generalize to a new domain for which only a domain description is provided and no training dialogs are available. Then a novel learning framework, Action Matching, is proposed. This algorithm can learn a cross-domain embedding space that models the semantics of dialog responses which, in turn, lets a neural dialog generation model generalize to new domains. We evaluate our methods on a new synthetic dialog dataset, and an existing human-human dialog dataset. Results show that our method has superior performance in learning dialog models that rapidly adapt their behavior to new domains and suggests promising future research.[1]

1 Introduction

The generative end-to-end dialog model (GEDM) is one of the most powerful methods of learning dialog agents from raw conversational data in both chat-oriented and task-oriented domains (Serban et al., 2016; Wen et al., 2016; Zhao et al., 2017). Its base model is an encoder-decoder network (Cho et al., 2014) that uses an encoder network to encode the dialog context and generate the next response via a decoder network. Yet prior work in GEDMs has overlooked an important issue, i.e. the data scarcity problem. In fact, the data

scarcity problem is extremely common in most dialog applications due to the wide range of potential domains that dialog systems can be applied to. To the best of our knowledge, current GEDMs are data-hungry and have only been successfully applied to domains with abundant training material. This limitation prohibits the possibility of using the GEDMs for rapid prototyping in new domains and is only useful for domains with large datasets.

The key idea of this paper lies in developing domain descriptions that can capture domain-specific information and a new type of GEDM model that can generalize to a new domain based on the domain description. Humans exhibit incredible efficiency in achieving this type of adaptation. Imagine that a customer service agent in the shoe department is transferred to the clothing department. After reading some relevant instructions and documentation, this agent can immediately begin to deal with clothes-related calls without the need for any example dialogs. We also argue that it is more efficient and natural for domain experts to express their knowledge in terms of domain descriptions rather than example dialogs. This is because creating example dialogs involves writing down imagined dialog exchanges that can be shared across multiple domains and are not relevant to the unique proprieties of a specific domain. However, current state-of-the-art GEDMs are not designed to incorporate such knowledge and are therefore incapable of adapting its behavior to unseen domains.

This paper introduces the use of *zero-shot dialog generation* (ZSDG) in order to enable GEDMs to generalize to unseen situations using minimal dialog data. Building on zero-shot classification (Palatucci et al., 2009), we formalize ZSDG as a learning problem where the training data contains dialog data from source domains along with domain descriptions from both the source and tar-

---

[1] Code and data are avaliable at https://github.com/snakeztc/NeuralDialog-ZSDG

Proceedings of the SIGDIAL 2018 Conference, pages 1–10,
Melbourne, Australia, 12-14 July 2018. ©2018 Association for Computational Linguistics

get domains. Then at testing time, ZSDG models are evaluated on the target domain, where no training dialogs were available. We approach ZSDG by first discovering a dialog policy network that can be shared between the source and target domains. The output from this policy is distributed vectors which are referred to as *latent actions*. Then, in order to transform the latent actions from any domain back to natural language utterances, a novel Action Matching (AM) algorithm is proposed that learns a cross-domain latent action space that models the semantics of dialog responses. This in turns enables the GEDM to generate responses in the target domains even when it has never observed full dialogs in them.

Finally the proposed methods and baselines are evaluated on two dialog datasets. The first one is a new synthetic dialog dataset generated by Sim-Dial, which was developed for this study. Sim-Dial enables us to easily generate task-oriented dialogs in a large number of domains, and provides a test bed to evaluate different ZSDG approaches. We further test our methods on a recently released multi-domain human-human corpus (Eric and Manning, 2017b) to validate whether performance can generalize to real-world conversations. Experimental results show that our methods are effective in incorporating knowledge from domain descriptions and achieve strong ZSDG performance.

2   Related Work

Perhaps the most closely related topic is zero-shot learning (ZSL) for classification (Larochelle et al., 2008), which has focused on classifying unseen labels. A common approach is to represent the labels as attributes instead of class indexes (Palatucci et al., 2009). As a result, at test time, the model can first predict the semantic attributes in the input, then make the final prediction by comparing the predicted attributes with the candidate labels' attributes. More recent work (Socher et al., 2013; Romera-Paredes and Torr, 2015) improved on this idea by learning parametric models, e.g. neural networks, to map the label and input data into a joint embedding space and then make predictions. Besides classification, prior art has explored the notion of task generalization in robotics, so that a robot can execute a new task that was not mentioned in training (Oh et al., 2017; Duan et al., 2017).

In this case, a task is described by a demonstration or a sequence of instructions, and the system needs to learn to break down the instructions into previously learned skills. Also generating out-of-vocabulary (OOV) words from recurrent neural networks (RNNs) can be seen as a form of ZSL, where the OOV words are unseen labels. Prior work has used delexicalized tags (Zhao et al., 2017) and copy-mechanism (Gu et al., 2016; Merity et al., 2016; Elsahar et al., 2018) to enable RNN output words that are not in its vocabulary.

Finally, ZSL has been applied to individual components in the dialog system pipeline. Chen et al. (Chen et al., 2016) developed an intent classifier that can predict new intent labels that are not included in the training data. Bapna et al. (Bapna et al., 2017) extended that idea to the slot-filling module to track novel slot types. Both papers leverage a natural language description for the label (intent or slot-type) in order to learn a semantic embedding of the label space. Then, given any new labels, the model can still make predictions. There has also been extensive work on learning domain-adaptable dialog policy by first training a dialog policy on previous domains and testing the policy on a new domain. Gasic et al. (Gasic and Young, 2014) used the Gaussian Process with cross-domain kernel functions. The resulting policy can leverage experience from other domains to make educated decisions in a new one.

In summary, past ZSL research in the dialog domain has mostly focused on the individual modules in a pipeline-based dialog system. We believe our proposal is the first step in exploring the notion of adapting an entire end-to-end dialog system to new domains for domain generalization.

3   Problem Formulation

We begin by formalizing zero-shot dialog generation (ZSDG). Generative dialog models take a dialog context $\mathbf{c}$ as input and then generate the next response $\mathbf{x}$. ZSDG uses the term *domain* to describe the difference between training and testing data. Let $D = D_s \bigcup D_t$ be a set of domains, where D_s is a set of source domains, D_t is a set of target domains and $D_s \cap D_t = \emptyset$. During training, we are given a set of samples $\{\mathbf{c}^{(n)}, \mathbf{x}^{(n)}, d^{(n)}\} \sim p_{\text{source}}(\mathbf{c}, \mathbf{x}, d)$ drawn from the *source domains*. During testing, a ZSDG model will be given a dialog context $\mathbf{c}$ and a domain d drawn from the *target domains* and must generate the correct response $\mathbf{x}$. Moreover, ZSDG assumes that every domain d has its own domain description $\phi(d)$ that is available at training for both source and target domains. The primary goal is to learn a generative dialog model $\mathcal{F} : C \times D \to X$ that can perform well in a target domain, by relating the unseen target domain description to the seen descriptions of the source domains. Our secondary goal is that $\mathcal{F}$ should perform similarly to a model that is designed to operate solely in the source domains. In short, the problem of ZSDG can be summarized as:

$$\text{Train Data: } \{\mathbf{c}, \mathbf{x}, d\} \sim p_{\text{source}}(\mathbf{c}, \mathbf{x}, d)$$
$$\{\phi(d)\}, d \in D$$
$$\text{Test Data: } \{\mathbf{c}, \mathbf{x}, d\} \sim p_{\text{target}}(\mathbf{c}, \mathbf{x}, d)$$
$$\text{Goal: } \mathcal{F} : C \times D \to X$$

4 Proposed Method

4.1 Seed Responses as Domain Descriptions

The design of the domain description ϕ is a crucial factor that decides whether robust performance in the target domains is achievable. This paper proposes *seed response* (SR) as a general-purpose domain description that can readily be applied to different dialog domains. SR needs for the developers to provide a list of example responses that the model can generate in this domain. SR's assumption is that a dialog model can discover analogies between responses from different domains, so that its dialog policy trained on source domains can be reused in the target domain. Without losing generality, SR_d defines $\phi(d)$ as $\{\mathbf{x}^{(i)}, \mathbf{a}^{(i)}, d\}_{\text{seed}}$ for domain d, where $\mathbf{x}$ is a seed response and $\mathbf{a}$ is its annotations. Annotations are salient features that help the system in infer the relationship amongst responses from different domains. This may be difficult to achieve using only words in $\mathbf{x}$, e.g. two domains with distinct word distributions. For example, in a task-oriented weather domain, a seed response can be: *The weather in New York is raining* and the annotation is a semantic frame that contains domain general dialog acts and slot arguments, i.e. *[Inform, loc=New York, type=rain]*. The number of seed responses is often much smaller than the number of potential responses in the domain so it is best for SR to cover more responses that are unique to this domain. SRs assume that there is a discourse-level pattern that can be shared between the source and target domains, so that a system only needs

sentence-level knowledge to adapt to the target. This assumption holds in many slot-filling dialog domains and it is easy to provide utterances in the target domain that are analogies to the ones from the source domains.

4.2 Action Matching Encoder-Decoder

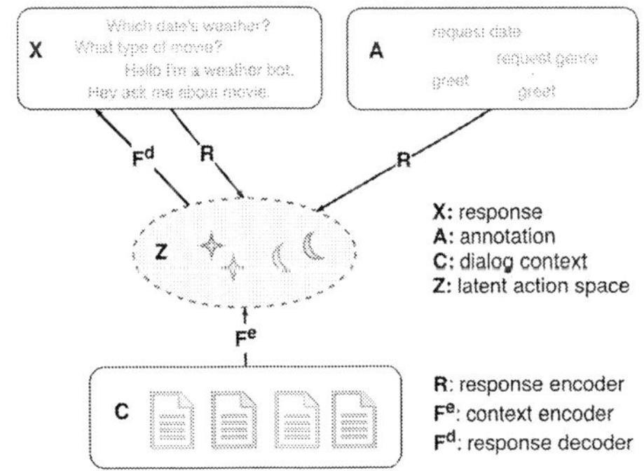

Figure 1: An overview of our Action Matching framework that looks for a latent action space Z shared by the response, annotation and predicted latent action from $\mathcal{F}^e$.

Figure 1 shows an overview of the model we use to tackle ZSDG. The base model is a standard encoder-decoder $\mathcal{F}$ where an encoder $\mathcal{F}^e$ maps $\mathbf{c}$ and d into a distributed representation $\mathbf{z_c} = \mathcal{F}^e(\mathbf{c}, d)$ and the decoder $\mathcal{F}^d$ generates the response $\mathbf{x}$ given $\mathbf{z_c}$. We denote the embedding space that $\mathbf{z_c}$ resides in as the *latent action* space. We follow the KB-as-an-environment approach (Zhao and Eskenazi, 2016) where the generated $\mathbf{x}$ include both system verbal utterances and API queries that interface with back-end databases. This base model has been proven to be effective in human interactive evaluation for task-oriented dialogs (Zhao et al., 2017).

We have two high-level goals: (1) learn a cross-domain $\mathcal{F}$ that can be reused in all source domains and potentially shared with target domains as well. (2) create a mechanism to incorporate knowledge from the domain descriptions into $\mathcal{F}$ so that it can generate novel responses when tested on the target domains. To achieve the first goal, we combine $\mathbf{c}$ and d by appending d as a special word token at the beginning of every utterance in $\mathbf{c}$. This simple approach performs well and enables the context encoder to take the domain into account when processing later word tokens. Also, this context domain integration can easily scale to dealing with a large number of domains. Then we encourage $\mathcal{F}$

to discover reusable dialog policy by training the same encoder decoder on dialog data generated from multiple source domains at the same time, which is a form of multi-task learning (Collobert and Weston, 2008). We achieve the second goal by projecting the response $\mathbf{x}$ from all domains into the same latent action space Z. Since $\mathbf{x}$ alone may not be sufficient to infer its semantics, we rely on their annotations $\mathbf{a}$ to learn meaningful semantic representations. Let $\mathbf{z_x}$ and $\mathbf{z_a}$ be the projected latent actions from $\mathbf{x}$ and $\mathbf{a}$. Our method encourages $\mathbf{z}_{\mathbf{x}_1}^{d_1} \approx \mathbf{z}_{\mathbf{x}_2}^{d_2}$ when $\mathbf{z}_{\mathbf{a}_1}^{d_1} \approx \mathbf{z}_{\mathbf{a}_2}^{d_2}$. Moreover, for a given $\mathbf{z}$ from any domain, we ensure that the decoder $\mathcal{F}^d$ can generate the corresponding response $\mathbf{x}$ by training on both SR_d for $d \in D$ and source dialogs.

Specifically, we propose the Action Matching (AM) training procedure. We first introduce a recognition network $\mathcal{R}$ that can encode $\mathbf{x}$ and $\mathbf{a}$ into $\mathbf{z_x} = \mathcal{R}(\mathbf{x}, d)$ and $\mathbf{z_a} = \mathcal{R}(\mathbf{a}, d)$ respectively. During training, the model receives two types of data. The first type is domain description data in the form of $\{\mathbf{x}, \mathbf{a}, d\}_{seed}$ for each domain. The second type of data is source domain dialog data in the form of $\{\mathbf{c}, \mathbf{x}, d\}$. For the first type of data, we update the parameters in $\mathcal{R}$ and $\mathcal{F}^d$ by minimizing the following loss function:

$$\begin{aligned}
\mathcal{L}_{\mathrm{dd}}(\mathcal{F}^d, \mathcal{R}) = & -\log p_{\mathcal{F}^d}(\mathbf{x}|\mathcal{R}(\mathbf{a}, d)) \\
& + \lambda \mathbb{D}[\mathcal{R}(\mathbf{x}, d)\|\mathcal{R}(\mathbf{a}, d)]
\end{aligned} \quad (1)$$

where λ is a constant hyperparameter and $\mathbb{D}$ is a distance function, e.g. mean square error (MSE), that measures the closeness of two input vectors. The first term in $\mathcal{L}_{\mathrm{dd}}$ trains the decoder $\mathcal{F}^d$ to generate the response $\mathbf{x}$ given $\mathbf{z_a} = \mathcal{R}(\mathbf{a}, d)$ from all domains. The second term in $\mathcal{L}_{\mathrm{dd}}$ enforces the recognition network $\mathcal{R}$ to encode a response and its annotation to nearby vectors in the latent action space from all domains, i.e. $\mathbf{z}_\mathbf{x}^d \approx \mathbf{z}_\mathbf{a}^d$ for $d \in D$.

Moreover, just optimizing $\mathcal{L}_{\mathrm{dd}}$ does not ensure that the $\mathbf{z_c}$ predicted by the encoder $\mathcal{F}^e$ will be related to the $\mathbf{z_x}$ or $\mathbf{z_a}$ encoded by the recognition network $\mathcal{R}$. So when we receive the second type of data (source dialogs), we add a second term to the standard maximum likelihood objective to train $\mathcal{F}$ and $\mathcal{R}$.

$$\begin{aligned}
\mathcal{L}_{\mathrm{dialog}}(\mathcal{F}, \mathcal{R}) = & -\log p_{\mathcal{F}^d}(\mathbf{x}|\mathcal{F}^e(\mathbf{c}, d)) \\
& + \lambda \mathbb{D}(\mathcal{R}(\mathbf{x}, d)\|\mathcal{F}^e(\mathbf{c}, d))
\end{aligned} \quad (2)$$

The second term in $\mathcal{L}_{\mathrm{dialog}}$ completes the loop by encouraging $\mathbf{z}_\mathbf{c}^d \approx \mathbf{z}_\mathbf{x}^d$, which resembles the regularization term used in variational autoencoders (Kingma and Welling, 2013). Assuming that annotation $\mathbf{a}$ provides a domain-agnostic semantic representation of $\mathbf{x}$, then $\mathcal{F}$ trained on source domains can begin to operate in the target domains as well. During training, our AM algorithm alternates between these two types of data and optimizes $\mathcal{L}_{\mathrm{dd}}$ or $\mathcal{L}_{\mathrm{dialog}}$ accordingly. The resulting models effectively learn a latent action space that is shared by the the response annotation $\mathbf{a}$, response $\mathbf{x}$ and predicted latent action based on $\mathbf{c}$ in all domains. AM training is summarized in Algorithm 1.

Algorithm 1: Action Matching Training

Initialize weights of $\mathcal{F}^e, \mathcal{F}^d, \mathcal{R}$;
Data $= \{\mathbf{c}, \mathbf{x}, d\} \bigcup \{\mathbf{x}, \mathbf{a}, d\}_{seed}$
while *batch* $\sim$ *Data* **do**
    if *batch in the form* $\{\mathbf{c}, \mathbf{x}, d\}$ **then**
      | Backpropagate loss $\mathcal{L}_{\mathrm{dialog}}$
    else
      | Backpropagate loss $\mathcal{L}_{\mathrm{dd}}$
    end
end

4.3 Architecture Details

We implement an AMED for later experiments as follows:

Distance Functions: In this study, we assume that the latent actions are deterministic distributed vectors. Thus MSE is used: $\mathbb{D}(\mathbf{z}, \hat{\mathbf{z}}) = \frac{1}{L} \sum_l^L (\mathbf{z}_l - \hat{\mathbf{z}}_l)^2$, where L is the dimension size of the latent actions. Also, L_{dialog} and L_{dd} use the same distance function.

Recognition Networks: we use a bidirectional GRU-RNN (Cho et al., 2014) as $\mathcal{R}$ to obtain utterance-level embedding. Since both $\mathbf{x}$ and $\mathbf{a}$ are sequences of word tokens, we combine them with the domain tag by appending the domain tag in the beginning of the original word sequence, i.e. $\{\mathbf{x}, d\}$ or $\{\mathbf{a}, d\} = [d, w_1, ...w_J]$, where J is the length of the word sequence. Then the $\mathcal{R}$ will encode $[d, w_1, ...w_J]$ into hidden outputs in forward and backward directions, $[(\overrightarrow{h_0}, \overleftarrow{h_J}), ...(\overrightarrow{h_J}, \overleftarrow{h_0})]$. We use the concatenation of the last hidden states from each direction, i.e. $\mathbf{z_x}$ or $\mathbf{z_a} = [\overrightarrow{h_J}, \overleftarrow{h_J}]$ as utterance-level embedding for $\mathbf{x}$ or $\mathbf{a}$ respectively.

Dialog Encoders: a hierarchical recurrent encoder (HRE) is used to encode the dialog context, which handles long contexts better than non-

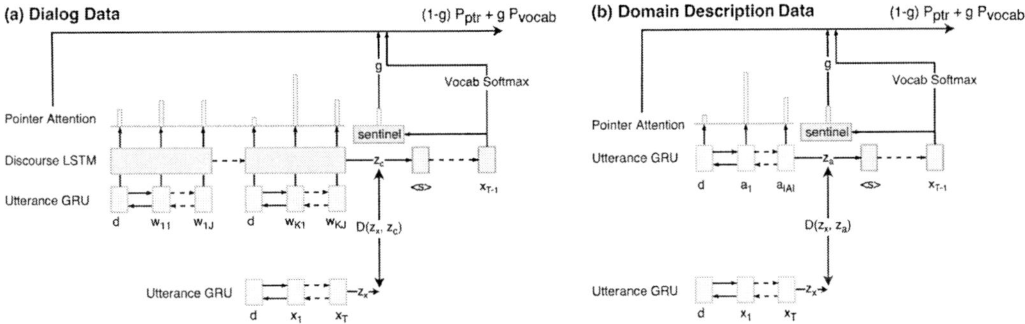

Figure 2: Visual illustration of our AM encoder decoder with copy mechanism (Merity et al., 2016). Note that AM can also be used with RNN decoders without the copy functionality.

hierarchical ones (Li et al., 2015). HRE first uses an utterance encoder to encode every utterance in the dialog and then uses a discourse-level LSTM-RNN to encode the dialog context by taking output from the utterance encoder as input. Instead of introducing a new utterance encoder, we reuse the recognition network $\mathcal{R}$ described above as the utterance encoder, which serves the purpose perfectly. Another advantage is that using $\mathbf{z_x}$ predicted by $\mathcal{R}$ as input enables the discourse-level encoder to use knowledge from latent actions as well. Our discourse-level encoder is a 1-layer LSTM-RNN (Hochreiter and Schmidhuber, 1997), which takes in a list of output $[\mathbf{z}_1, \mathbf{z}_2..\mathbf{z}_K]$ from $\mathcal{R}$ and encodes them into $[v_1, v_2, ...v_K]$, where K is the number of utterances in the context. The last hidden state v_K is used as the predicted latent action $\mathbf{z}_c$.

Response Decoders: we experiment with two types of LSTM-RNN decoders. The first is an RNN decoder with an attention mechanism (Luong et al., 2015), enabling the decoder to dynamically look up information from the context. Specifically, we flatten the dialog context into a sequence of words $[w_{11}, ...w_{1J}...w_{KJ}]$. Using output from the $\mathcal{R}$ and the discourse-level LSTM-RNN, each word here is represented by $m_{kj} = h_{kj} + W_v v_k$. Let the hidden state of the decoder at step t be s_t, then our attention mechanism computes the Softmax output via:

$$\alpha_{kj,t} = \text{softmax}(m_{kj}^T \tanh(W_\alpha s_t)) \quad (3)$$

$$\tilde{s}_t = \sum_{kj} \alpha_{kj,t} m_{kj} \quad (4)$$

$$p_{\text{vocab}}(w_t|s_t) = \text{softmax}(\text{MLP}(s_t, \tilde{s}_t)) \quad (5)$$

The second type is the LSTM-RNN with a copy

mechanism that can directly copy words from the context as output (Gu et al., 2016). Such a mechanism has already exhibited strong performance in task-oriented dialogs (Eric and Manning, 2017a) and is well suited for generating OOV word tokens (Elsahar et al., 2018). We implemented the Pointer Sentinel Mixture Model (PSM) (Merity et al., 2016) as our copy decoder. PSM defines the generation of the next word as a mixture of probabilities from either the Softmax output from the decoder LSTM or the attention Softmax for words in the context: $p(w_t|s_t) = g p_{\text{vocab}}(w_t|s_t) + (1 - g)p_{\text{ptr}}(w_t|s_t)$, where g is the mixture weight computed from a sentinel vector u with s_t.

$$p_{\text{ptr}}(w_t|s_t) = \sum_{kj \in I(w,\mathbf{x})} \alpha_{kj,t} \quad (6)$$

$$g = \text{softmax}(u^T \tanh(W_\alpha s_i)) \quad (7)$$

5 Datasets for ZSDG

Two dialog datasets were used for evaluation.

5.1 SimDial Data

We developed SimDial[2], which is a multi-domain dialog generator that can generate realistic conversations for slot-filling domains with configurable complexity. See Appendix A.3 for details. Compared to other synthetic dialog corpora used to test GEDMs, e.g. bAbI (Dodge et al., 2015), SimDial data is significantly more challenging. First since SimDial simulates communication noise, the dialogs that are generated can be very long (more than 50 turns) and the simulated agent can carry out error recovery strategies to correctly infer the users' goals. This challenges end-to-end models

[2]https://github.com/snakeztc/SimDial

to model long dialog contexts. SimDial also simulates spoken language phenomena, e.g. self-repair, hesitation. Prior work (Eshghi et al., 2017) has shown that this type of utterance-level noise deteriorates end-to-end dialog system performance.

Data Details

SimDial was used to generate dialogs for 6 domains: restaurant, movie, bus, restaurant-slot, restaurant-style and weather. For each domain, 900/100/500 dialogs were generated for training, validation and testing. On average, each dialog had 26 utterances and each utterance had 12.8 word tokens. The total vocabulary size was 651. We split the data such that the training data included dialogs from the restaurant, bus and weather domains and the test data included the restaurant, movie, restaurant-slot and restaurant style domains. This setup evaluates a ZSDG system from the following perspectives:

Restaurant (in domain): evaluation on the restaurant test data checks if a dialog model is able to maintain its performance on the source domains. **Restaurant-slot (unseen slots)**: restaurant-slot has the same slot types and natural language generation (NLG) templates as the restaurant domain, but has a completely different slot vocabulary, i.e. different location names and cuisine types. Thus this is designed to evaluate a model that can generalize to unseen slot values. **Restaurant-style (unseen NLG)**: restaurant-style has the same slot type and vocabulary as restaurant, but its NLG templates are completely different, e.g. "which cuisine type?" $\rightarrow$ "please tell me what kind of food you prefer". This part tests whether a model can learn to adapt to generate novel utterances with similar semantics. **Movie (new domain)**: movie has completely different NLG templates and structure and shares few common traits with the source domains at the surface level. Movie is the hardest task in the SimDial data, which challenges a model to correctly generate next responses that are semantically different from the ones in source domains.

Finally, we obtain SRs as domain descriptions by randomly selecting 100 unique utterances from each domain. The response annotation is a response's internal semantic frame used by the SimDial generator. For example, "I believe you said Boston. Where are you going?" $\rightarrow$ [implicit-confirm loc=Boston; request location].

5.2 Stanford Multi-Domain Dialog Data

The second dataset is the Stanford multi-domain dialog (SMD) dataset (Eric and Manning, 2017b) of 3031 human-human dialogs in three domains: weather, navigation and scheduling. One speaker plays the role of a driver. The other plays the car's AI assistant and talks to the driver to complete tasks, e.g. setting directions on a GPS. Average dialog length is 5.25 utterances; vocabulary size is 1601. We use SMD to validate whether our proposed methods generalize to human-generated dialogs. We generate SR by randomly selecting 150 unique utterances for each domain. An expert annotates the seed utterances with dialog acts and entities. For example "All right, I've set your next dentist appointment for 10am. Anything else?" $\rightarrow$ [ack; inform goal event=dentist appointment time=10am ; request needs]. Finally, in order to formulate a ZSDG problem, we use a leave-one-out approach with two domains as source domains and the third one as the target domain, which results in 3 possible configurations.

6 Experiments and Results

The baseline models include 1. hierarchical recurrent encoder with attention decoder (+Attn) (Serban et al., 2016). 2. hierarchical recurrent encoder with copy decoder (Merity et al., 2016) (+Copy), which has achieved very good performance on task-oriented dialogs (Eric and Manning, 2017a). We then augment both baseline models with the proposed cross-domain AM training procedure and denote them as +Attn+AM and +Copy+AM.

Evaluating generative dialog systems is challenging since the model can generate free-form responses. Fortunately, we have access to the internal semantic frames of the SimDial data, so we use the automatic measures used in (Zhao et al., 2017) that employ four metrics to quantify the performance of a task-oriented dialog model. **BLEU** is the corpus-level BLEU-4 between the generated response and the reference ones (Papineni et al., 2002). **Entity F_1** checks if a generated response contains the correct entities (slots) in the reference response. **Act F_1** measures whether the generated responses reflect the dialog acts in the reference responses, which compensates for BLEU's limitation of looking for exact word choices. A one-vs-rest support vector machine (Scholkopf and Smola, 2001) with bi-gram features is trained to tag the dialogs in a response. **KB F_1** checks all the key words in a KB query that the system issues to the KB backend. Finally, we introduce **BEAK** $= \sqrt[4]{\text{bleu} \times \text{ent} \times \text{act} \times \text{kb}}$, the geometric mean of these four scores, to quantify a system's overall performance. Meanwhile, since the oracle dialog acts and KB queries are not provided in the SMD data (Eric and Manning, 2017b), we only report BLEU and entity F_1 results on SMD.

6.1 Main Results

In domain	+Attn	+Copy	+Attn +AM	+Copy +AM
BLEU	59.1	**70.4**	67.7	70.1
Entity	69.2	70.5	74.1	**79.9**
Act	94.7	92.0	94.1	**95.1**
KB	94.7	96.1	95.2	**97.0**
BEAK	77.2	81.3	81.9	**84.7**
Unseen Slot	+Attn	+Copy	+Attn +AM	+Copy +AM
BLEU	24.9	45.6	47.9	**68.5**
Entity	56.0	68.0	53.1	**74.6**
Act	90.9	91.8	86.0	**94.5**
KB	78.1	89.6	81.0	**95.3**
BEAK	56.1	71.1	64.8	**82.3**
Unseen NLG	+Attn	+Copy	+Attn +AM	+Copy +AM
BLEU	15.8	36.9	43.5	**70.1**
Entity	61.7	68.9	63.8	**72.9**
Act	91.5	92.2	89.3	**95.2**
KB	66.2	94.6	93.1	**97.0**
BEAK	49.3	65.9	69.3	**82.9**
New domain	+Attn	+Copy	+Attn +AM	+Copy +AM
BLEU	13.5	24.6	36.7	**54.6**
Entity	23.1	40.8	23.3	**52.6**
Act	82.3	85.5	84.8	**88.5**
KB	43.5	67.1	67.0	**88.2**
BEAK	32.5	48.8	46.8	**68.8**

Table 1: Evaluation results on test dialogs from SimDial Data. Bold values indicate the best performance.

Table 1 shows results on the SimDial data. Although the standard +Attn model achieves good performance in the source domains, it doesn't generalize to target domains, especially for entity F_1 in the unseen-slot domain, BLEU score in the unseen-NLG domain, and all new domain metrics. The +Copy model has better, although still limited, generalization to target domains. The main benefit of the +Copy model is its ability to directly copy and output words from the context, reflected in its strong entity F_1 in the unseen slot domain. However, +Copy can't generalize to new domains where utterances are novel, e.g. the unseen NLG or the new domain. However, our AM algorithm substantially improves performance of both decoders (Attn and Copy). Results show that the proposed AM algorithm is complementary to decoders with a copy mechanism: HRED+Copy+AM model has the best performance on all target domains. In the easier unseen-slot and unseen-NLG domains, the resulting ZSDG system achieves a BEAK of about 82, close to the in-domain BEAK performance (84.7). Even in the new domain (movie), our model achieves a BEAK of 67.2, 106% relative improvement w.r.t +Attn and 38.8% relative improvement w.r.t +Copy. Moreover, our AM method also improves performance on in-domain dialogs, suggesting that AM exploits the knowledge encoded in the domain description and improves the models' generalization.

Navigate	Oracle	+Attn	+Copy	+Copy +AM
BLEU	13.4	0.9	5.4	**5.9**
Entity	19.3	2.6	4.7	**14.3**
Weather	Oracle	+Attn	+Copy	+Copy +AM
BLEU	18.9	4.8	4.4	**8.1**
Entity	51.9	0.0	16.3	**31.0**
Schedule	Oracle	+Attn	+Copy	+Copy +AM
BLEU	20.9	3.0	3.8	**7.9**
Entity	47.3	0.4	17.1	**36.9**

Table 2: Evaluation on SMD data. The bold domain title is the one that was excluded from training.

Table 2 summarizes the results on the SMD data. We also report the oracle performance, obtained by training +Copy on the full dataset. The AM algorithm can significantly improve Entity F_1 and BLEU from the two baseline models. +Copy+AM also achieves competitive performance in terms of Entity F_1 compared to the oracle scores, despite the fact that no target domain data was used in training.

6.2 Model Analysis

Various types of performance improvement were also studied. Figure 3 shows the breakdown of the BLEU score according to the dialog acts of reference responses. Models with +Copy decoder can improve performance for all dialog acts except for the *greet* act, which occurs at the beginning of a dialog. In this case, the +Copy decoder has no context to copy and thus cannot generate any novel responses. This is one limitation of +Copy decoder since in real interactive testing with humans,

Type	Reference	+Attn	+Copy	+Copy+AM
General Utts	See you next time.	Goodbye.	See you next time.	See you next time.
Unseen Slots	Do you mean romance movie?	Do you mean Chinese food.	Do you mean **romance** food?	Do you mean **romance** movie?
Unseen Utts	Movie 55 is a great movie.	Bus 12 can take you there.	Bus **55** can take you there.	Movie **55** is a great movie.

Table 3: Three types of responses and generation results (tested on the new movie domain). The text in bold is the output directly copied from the context by the copy decoder.

each system utterance must be generated from the model instead of copied from the context. However, models with AM training learn to generate novel utterances based on knowledge from the SR, so +Copy+AM can generate responses at the beginning of a dialog.

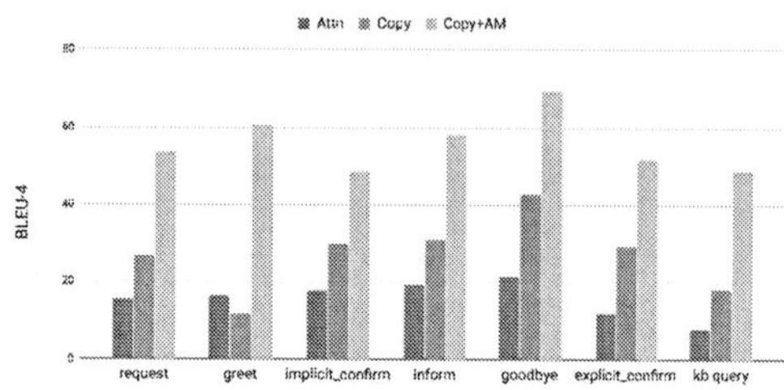

Figure 3: Breakdown BLEU scores on the new domain test set from SimDial.

A qualitative analysis was conducted to summarize typical responses from these models. Table 3 shows three types of typical situations in the Sim-Dial data. The first type is **general utterance** utterances, e.g. "See you next time" that appear in all domains. All three models correctly generate them in the ZSDG setting. The second type is utterances with **unseen slots**. For example, explicit confirm "Do you mean xx?". +Attn fails in this situation since the new slot values are not in its vocabulary. +Copy still performs well since it learns to copy entity-like words from the context, but the overall sentence is often incorrect, e.g. "Do you mean romance food". The last one is **unseen utterance** where both +Attn and +Copy fail. The two baseline models can still generate responses with correct dialog acts, but the output words are in the source domains. Only the models trained with AM are able to infer that "Movie xx is a great movie" serves a function similar to "Bus xx can take you there", and generates responses using the correct words from the target domain.

Finally we investigate how the the size of SR affects AM performance. Figure 4 shows results in the SMD schedule domain. The number of seed

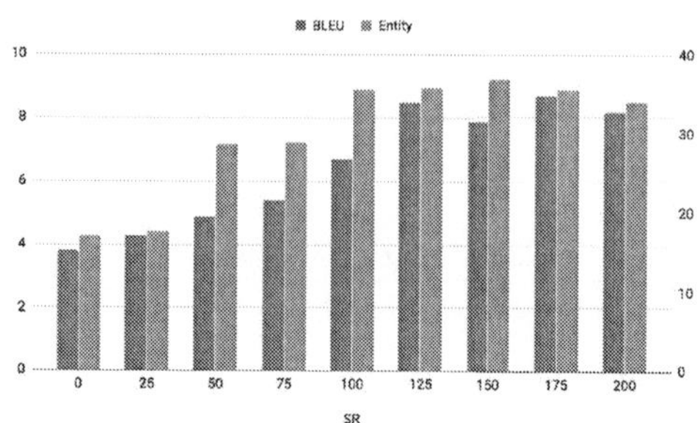

Figure 4: Performance on the schedule domain from SMD while varying the size of SR.

responses varies from 0 to 200. Performance in the target domains is positively correlated with the number of seed responses. We also observe that the model achieves sufficient SR performance at 100, compared to the ones trained on all of the 200 seed responses. This suggests that the amount of seeding needed by SR is relatively small, which shows the practicality of using SR as a domain description.

7 Conclusion and Future Work

This paper introduces ZSDG, dealing with neural dialog systems' domain generalization ability. We formalize the ZSDG problem and propose an Action Matching framework that discovers cross-domain latent actions. We present a new simulated multi-domain dialog dataset, SimDial, to benchmark the ZSDG models. Our assessment validates the AM framework's effectiveness and the AM encoder decoders perform well in the ZSDG setting.

ZSDG provides promising future research questions. How can we reduce the annotation cost of learning the latent alignment between actions in different domains? How can we create ZSDG for new domains where the discourse-level patterns are significantly different? What are other potential domain description formats? In summary, solving ZSDG is an important step for future general-purpose conversational agents.

References

Ankur Bapna, Gokhan Tur, Dilek Hakkani-Tur, and Larry Heck. 2017. Towards zero-shot frame semantic parsing for domain scaling. *arXiv preprint arXiv:1707.02363* .

Yun-Nung Chen, Dilek Hakkani-Tür, and Xiaodong He. 2016. Zero-shot learning of intent embeddings for expansion by convolutional deep structured semantic models. In *Acoustics, Speech and Signal Processing (ICASSP), 2016 IEEE International Conference on*. IEEE, pages 6045–6049.

Kyunghyun Cho, Bart Van Merriënboer, Caglar Gulcehre, Dzmitry Bahdanau, Fethi Bougares, Holger Schwenk, and Yoshua Bengio. 2014. Learning phrase representations using rnn encoder-decoder for statistical machine translation. *arXiv preprint arXiv:1406.1078* .

Ronan Collobert and Jason Weston. 2008. A unified architecture for natural language processing: Deep neural networks with multitask learning. In *Proceedings of the 25th international conference on Machine learning*. ACM, pages 160–167.

Jesse Dodge, Andreea Gane, Xiang Zhang, Antoine Bordes, Sumit Chopra, Alexander Miller, Arthur Szlam, and Jason Weston. 2015. Evaluating prerequisite qualities for learning end-to-end dialog systems. *arXiv preprint arXiv:1511.06931* .

Yan Duan, Marcin Andrychowicz, Bradly Stadie, Jonathan Ho, Jonas Schneider, Ilya Sutskever, Pieter Abbeel, and Wojciech Zaremba. 2017. One-shot imitation learning. *arXiv preprint arXiv:1703.07326* .

Hady Elsahar, Christophe Gravier, and Frederique Laforest. 2018. Zero-shot question generation from knowledge graphs for unseen predicates and entity types. *arXiv preprint arXiv:1802.06842* .

Mihail Eric and Christopher D Manning. 2017a. A copy-augmented sequence-to-sequence architecture gives good performance on task-oriented dialogue. *arXiv preprint arXiv:1701.04024* .

Mihail Eric and Christopher D Manning. 2017b. Key-value retrieval networks for task-oriented dialogue. *arXiv preprint arXiv:1705.05414* .

Arash Eshghi, Igor Shalyminov, and Oliver Lemon. 2017. Bootstrapping incremental dialogue systems from minimal data: the generalisation power of dialogue grammars. *arXiv preprint arXiv:1709.07858* .

Milica Gasic and Steve Young. 2014. Gaussian processes for pomdp-based dialogue manager optimization. *IEEE/ACM Transactions on Audio, Speech, and Language Processing* 22(1):28–40.

Jiatao Gu, Zhengdong Lu, Hang Li, and Victor OK Li. 2016. Incorporating copying mechanism in sequence-to-sequence learning. *arXiv preprint arXiv:1603.06393* .

Sepp Hochreiter and Jürgen Schmidhuber. 1997. Long short-term memory. *Neural computation* 9(8):1735–1780.

Diederik Kingma and Jimmy Ba. 2014. Adam: A method for stochastic optimization. *arXiv preprint arXiv:1412.6980* .

Diederik P Kingma and Max Welling. 2013. Auto-encoding variational bayes. *arXiv preprint arXiv:1312.6114* .

Hugo Larochelle, Dumitru Erhan, and Yoshua Bengio. 2008. Zero-data learning of new tasks. In *AAAI*. 2, page 3.

Jiwei Li, Minh-Thang Luong, and Dan Jurafsky. 2015. A hierarchical neural autoencoder for paragraphs and documents. *arXiv preprint arXiv:1506.01057* .

Minh-Thang Luong, Hieu Pham, and Christopher D Manning. 2015. Effective approaches to attention-based neural machine translation. *arXiv preprint arXiv:1508.04025* .

Stephen Merity, Caiming Xiong, James Bradbury, and Richard Socher. 2016. Pointer sentinel mixture models. *arXiv preprint arXiv:1609.07843* .

Junhyuk Oh, Satinder Singh, Honglak Lee, and Pushmeet Kohli. 2017. Zero-shot task generalization with multi-task deep reinforcement learning. *arXiv preprint arXiv:1706.05064* .

Mark Palatucci, Dean Pomerleau, Geoffrey E Hinton, and Tom M Mitchell. 2009. Zero-shot learning with semantic output codes. In *Advances in neural information processing systems*. pages 1410–1418.

Kishore Papineni, Salim Roukos, Todd Ward, and Wei-Jing Zhu. 2002. Bleu: a method for automatic evaluation of machine translation. In *Proceedings of the 40th annual meeting on association for computational linguistics*. Association for Computational Linguistics, pages 311–318.

Bernardino Romera-Paredes and Philip Torr. 2015. An embarrassingly simple approach to zero-shot learning. In *International Conference on Machine Learning*. pages 2152–2161.

Bernhard Scholkopf and Alexander J Smola. 2001. *Learning with kernels: support vector machines, regularization, optimization, and beyond*. MIT press.

Iulian Vlad Serban, Alessandro Sordoni, Ryan Lowe, Laurent Charlin, Joelle Pineau, Aaron Courville, and Yoshua Bengio. 2016. A hierarchical latent variable encoder-decoder model for generating dialogues. *arXiv preprint arXiv:1605.06069* .

Richard Socher, Milind Ganjoo, Christopher D Manning, and Andrew Ng. 2013. Zero-shot learning through cross-modal transfer. In *Advances in neural information processing systems*. pages 935–943.

Tsung-Hsien Wen, Milica Gasic, Nikola Mrksic, Lina M Rojas-Barahona, Pei-Hao Su, Stefan Ultes, David Vandyke, and Steve Young. 2016. A network-based end-to-end trainable task-oriented dialogue system. *arXiv preprint arXiv:1604.04562* .

Wojciech Zaremba, Ilya Sutskever, and Oriol Vinyals. 2014. Recurrent neural network regularization. *arXiv preprint arXiv:1409.2329* .

Tiancheng Zhao and Maxine Eskenazi. 2016. Towards end-to-end learning for dialog state tracking and management using deep reinforcement learning. *arXiv preprint arXiv:1606.02560* .

Tiancheng Zhao, Allen Lu, Kyusong Lee, and Maxine Eskenazi. 2017. Generative encoder-decoder models for task-oriented spoken dialog systems with chatting capability. *arXiv preprint arXiv:1706.08476* .

A   Supplemental Material

A.1   Seed Response Creation Process

We follow the following process to create SR in a new slot-filling domain. First, we collect seed responses (including user/system utterances, KB queries and KB responses) from each source domain and annotate them with dialog acts, entity types and entity values. Then human experts with knowledge about the target domain can write up seed responses for the target domain by drawing ideas from the sources. For example, if the source domain is restaurants and the target domain is movies. The source may contain a system utterance with its annotation: "I believed you said Pittsburgh, what kind of food are you interested in? → *[implicit-confirm, loc=Pittsburgh, request food type]*". Then the expert can come up with a similar utterance from the target domain, e.g. "Alright, Pittsburgh. what type of movie do you like? → *[implicit-confirm, loc=Pittsburgh, request movie type]*". In this way, our proposed AM training can leverage the annotations to match these two actions as analogies in the latent action space. Another advantage of this process is that human experts do not have to directly label whether two utterances from two domains are direct analogies; this could be ambiguous and challenging. Instead, human experts only create domain shareable annotations and leave the difficult matching problem to our models.

A.2   Model Details

For all experiments, we use a word embedding with size 200. The recognition network uses bidirectional GRU-RNN with hidden size 256 for each direction. The discourse-level LSTM-RNN and the decoder have hidden size 512. The models are trained with Adam (Kingma and Ba, 2014) with learning rate 0.001. All weights are initialized from uniform distribution between +/- 0.08. 30% dropouts are applied at the input and output of recurrent neural networks (Zaremba et al., 2014). For decoders with copy mechanisms, we also use the pointer loss proposed in (Merity et al., 2016) which minimizes $-\log(g + \sum_{kj \in I(\mathbf{x},\mathbf{c})} \alpha_{kj})$, where I results in all positions of output $\mathbf{x}$ in the attention context.

A.3   SimDial Details

To generate data, SimDial expects: a *domain specification* (DS) and a *complexity specification* (CS). DS defines the content of the domain, e.g. restaurant or weather and CS defines complexity of dialogs for three aspects:

Environmental: the complexity level of the communication channel, e.g. automatic speech recognition (ASR) error rate.

Propositional: the complexity level in the propositional content of user utterances, e.g. the chance that a user will give multiple slot values in one utterance.

Interaction: the complexity level in terms of real-time interaction, e.g. the percentage of self-repair.

The following is an example dialog generated for the restaurant domain with all of the above complexity turned on. The number at the end of the speaker turn indicates ASR confidence.

Domain: Restaurant
Sys: Welcome to the restaurant recommendation system. What do you need?
User (0.83): Hello robot. I am looking for a restaurant.
Sys: Which city are you interested in?
User (0.75): I am in San Jose. And Korean. Uhm sorry. I am interested in Chinese food.
Sys: I believe you said San Jose. I believe you said Chinese.
Sys: QUERY goal: restaurant food-pref: Chinese location: San Jose
KB: RET restaurant: 17
Sys: Restaurant 17 is a good choice. What else can I do for you?
User (0.6): Not done yet. Is that restaurant open now?
Sys: QUERY goal: open restaurant: 17 food-pref: Chinese location: San Jose
KB: RET open: yes
Sys: Yes, it is open right now. What else?
User (0.69): No more questions. Thanks.
Sys: Bye.

Table 4: An example dialog generated from SimDial.

Changing the Level of Directness in Dialogue using Dialogue Vector Models and Recurrent Neural Networks

Louisa Pragst
Ulm University
Albert-Einstein-Allee 43
Ulm, Germany
`louisa.pragst@uni-ulm.de`

Stefan Ultes
Cambridge University
Trumpington Street
Cambridge, UK
`su259@cam.ac.uk`

Abstract

In cooperative dialogues, identifying the intent of ones conversation partner and acting accordingly is of great importance. While this endeavour is facilitated by phrasing intentions as directly as possible, we can observe in human-human communication that a number of factors such as cultural norms and politeness may result in expressing one's intent indirectly. Therefore, in human-computer communication we have to anticipate the possibility of users being indirect and be prepared to interpret their actual meaning. Furthermore, a dialogue system should be able to conform to human expectations by adjusting the degree of directness it uses to improve the user experience. To reach those goals, we propose an approach to differentiate between direct and indirect utterances and find utterances of the opposite characteristic that express the same intent. In this endeavour, we employ dialogue vector models and recurrent neural networks.

1 Introduction

An important part of any conversation is understanding the meaning your conversation partner is trying to convey. If we do not obscure our intent and phrase it as directly as possible, our conversation partner will have an easier time to recognise our goal and cooperate in achieving it. Thereby, we can enable a successful conversation. Nevertheless, there are countless instances in which humans choose to express their meaning indirectly, as evidenced by the work of Searle (1975) and Feghali (1997), among others. Answering the question 'How is the weather?' with 'Let's rather stay inside.' gives no concrete in-

formation about the weather conditions, but is commonly understood. There are several reasons why humans could choose to express their intent indirectly, such as cultural preferences, politeness, embarrassment, or simply using common figures of speech such as 'Can you tell me the time?'. Considering the frequency of indirectness in human-human communication, we need to anticipate the use of indirectness in human-computer communication and enable dialogue systems to handle it.

In this work, we introduce an approach to exchanging utterances with others that express the same intent in the dialogue but exhibit a differing level of directness. More concretely, our approach would replace the second utterance of the exchange 'What pizza do you want?' - 'I want a vegetarian pizza.' with an utterance like 'I don't like meat'. To this end, we employ models that can estimate the level of directness of an utterance on the one hand and the degree to which utterances express the same intent on the other.

Our approach can be applied to solve two challenges of indirectness for dialogue systems: On the side of the language analysis, the true intent of the user needs to be recognised so that the dialogue system can react in an appropriate, cooperative manner. If the language analysis is able to not only recognise the user's intended meaning, but also when the user is being indirect, this information can further be utilised by the dialogue manager, e.g. by scheduling a confirmation if the user is believed to have used indirectness. Our approach estimates the level of directness of an utterance as a first step. If the utterance is classified as indirect, this information can be provided to the dialogue manager. Furthermore, our approach exchanges the indirect utterance for a direct counterpart that more accurately reflects the users intent, thereby facilitating the task of the lan-

Proceedings of the SIGDIAL 2018 Conference, pages 11–19,
Melbourne, Australia, 12-14 July 2018. ©2018 Association for Computational Linguistics

guage analysis. The second area of dialogue system that can benefit from taking into account indirectness is the language generation. Studies could show that under specific circumstances indirectness is preferred not only from human conversation partners, but also in human-computer interaction (e.g. (Miehle et al., 2016; Pragst et al., 2017)). Therefore, dialogue systems that can adjust the level of directness in their output to the user and their circumstances should be able to provide an improved user experience. If a certain level of directness is determined to be desirable with regards to the current circumstances, our algorithm can determine whether the utterance chosen as system output possesses the targeted level of directness and exchange it for a more suitable alternative if it does not.

In the following, we will discuss related work, before presenting our general approach and its concrete implementation. This approach is evaluated in Section 4. Here, we introduce the dialogue corpus we created to obtain a reliable ground truth and discuss the results of our evaluation. Finally, we draw a conclusion in Section 5.

2   Related Work

Allen and Perrault (1980) propose a plan-based approach to understanding the intention of the speaker, explicitly mentioning indirect speech acts as application. Similarly, Briggs and Scheutz (2013) address both the understanding and the generation of indirect speech acts. Their approach combines idiomatic and plan-based approaches. In plan-based approaches, a planning model that contains potential goals as well as actions with pre-and post conditions needs to be defined manually in order to anticipate the user's plan and thereby identify the intent of an utterance. Our approach aims to eliminate the explicit preparation of the planning model, and instead relies on patterns learned from a large amount of examples.

In our work, we utilise a Dialogue Vector Model (DVM) (Pragst et al., 2018) to assess whether two utterances express the same intent in a dialogue. A number of different approaches to the representation of sentences in vector space have been proposed, e.g. utilising recurrent neural networks (Sutskever et al., 2014; Palangi et al., 2016; Tsunoo et al., 2017), convolutional neural networks (Shen et al., 2014; Kalchbrenner et al., 2014; Hu et al., 2014) and autoencoders (Socher

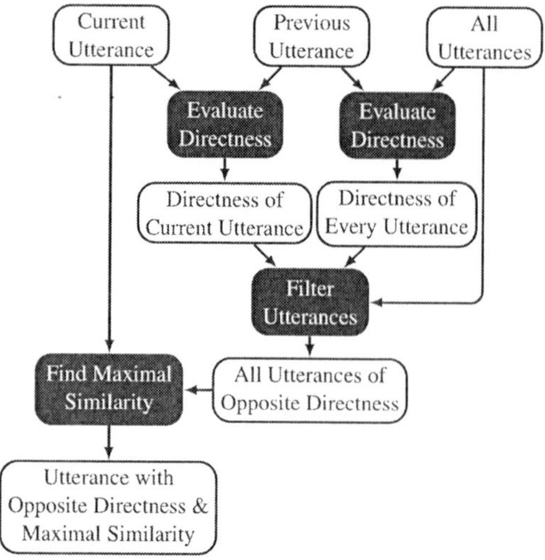

Figure 1: Flow chart of the steps taken to exchange an utterance with another one that is functionally similar and of the opposite directness.

et al., 2011). However, those approaches rely on the words in the sentence only to generate a vector representation. As a consequence, sentences that have the same meaning, but do not share the same words (which is often the case for utterances with different levels of directness) are not mapped in the vicinity of each other. In contrast, DVMs map functionally similar sentences close to each other and are therefore better suited for our needs.

Skip thought vectors (Kiros et al., 2015) are sentence embeddings that are generated in a similar manner as word vector representations, and therefore similar to dialogue vector models. Rather than using the words in the sentence itself as basis to create a vector representation, those vectors are generated taking into account surrounding sentences. However, this representation is trained on novels rather than dialogue, as opposed to DVMs, which focus specifically on dialogue and its peculiarities.

3   Changing the Level of Directness

Our work is concerned with the exchange of utterances for functionally similar ones with differing levels of directness. We define functional similarity as the degree to which two utterances can be used interchangeably in a dialogue as they express the same meaning. Substituting a direct/indirect utterance with its respective counterpart can be achieved by performing the following steps:

Algorithm 1: Pseudocode for exchanging one utterance for another that is functionally similar and of the opposite directness.

Data: $origU$, the utterance to be exchanged
$prvU$, the utterance occurring previous to $origU$
$allU$, the set of all available utterances
DVM, a function that maps an utterance to its corresponding dialogue vector
evalInd, a function that returns the estimated level of directness, ranging from one to three
Result: $excU$, the substitute for $origU$

$origDirectness \longleftarrow$ evalInd$(prvU, origU)$;
if $origDirectness \leq 1$ **then**
   | $oppU \longleftarrow \{u \in allU : $ evalInd$(prvU, u) > 1\}$;
else
   | $oppU \longleftarrow \{u \in allU : $ evalInd$(prvU, u) \leq 1\}$;
$excU \longleftarrow$
argmin$_{u \in oppU}$ euclDist$($DVM$(origU),$ DVM$(u))$;

---

1. Determine the level of directness of the utterance.

2. Gather the remaining known utterances that are of the opposite directness level.

3. From those, choose the utterance that is functionally most similar to the original utterance.

Figure 1 shows this procedure on an abstract level, while a more detailed pseudo-code is depicted in Algorithm 1. Two challenges need to be addressed in order to perform this approach: The first one is to correctly determine the level of directness of an utterance, the second one is to identify utterances that perform a similar semantic functionality in a dialogue. To solve those challenges, we utilise established approaches, namely recurrent neural networks (RNN) and dialogue vector models (DVM). In the following, we take a closer look at how we apply those approaches to solve the presented challenges.

To determine which utterances can be exchanged without altering the intended meaning, a suitable similarity measure is needed. In our work, we utilise DVMs (Pragst et al., 2018) to that end. DVMs are representations of sentences as vectors that captures their semantic meaning in the dialogue context. They are inspired by word vector models (Mikolov et al., 2013a) and generated in a similar manner: The mapping of utterances to their vector representations is trained akin to autoencoding. However, rather than training against the input utterance itself, utterances are trained against their adjacent utterances in the input corpus, either using the utterance to predict its

context or using the context to predict the utterance. The resulting vector representation groups sentences that are used in a similar context and therefore likely to fulfil the same conversational function in close vicinity to each other, as could be shown by Pragst et al. (2018). Therefore, DVMs are well suited to determine whether utterances perform a similar function in a dialogue. Our algorithm calculates the euclidean distance between the dialogue vector representations of two utterances and chooses the utterance with the minimal distance as the most functionally similar.

For the estimation of the level of directness an utterance possesses, we choose a supervised learning approach with a RNN. RNNs are a popular supervised machine learning approach to find complex relationships in large amounts of sequential data. As indirectness relies on the context of the conversation, the use of RNNs seems promising for the estimation the level of directness an utterances possess. The architecture of our RNN is depicted in Figure 2. It is a time delay network that uses the previous input in addition to the current one. To obtain a numerical representation of an utterance that can be used as input to the network, we utilise word vector models (Mikolov et al., 2013a) and DVMs (Pragst et al., 2018). The input for an utterances then consists of its dialogue vector representation and the sum of the word vector representations of its words. Furthermore, the word and dialogue vectors of the previous utterance are provided as recurrent data to reflect the dialogue context. The target value is given by corpus annotations of the level of directness of the utterance. As we are trying to solve a classification problem, the network is designed to provide the probability that the utterance belongs to each of the classes as its result. After training, the network constitutes the core part of the function that estimates the level directness of an utterance.

4 Evaluation

This section presents the evaluation of the proposed approach. We first introduce a dialogue corpus that is suitable to train the required models and provides a reliable ground truth to compare the results of our approach to. Afterwards, the setup of the evaluation is described and its results presented and discussed.

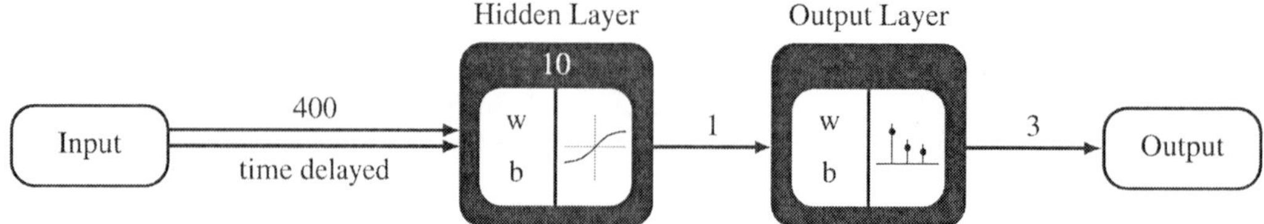

Figure 2: The architecture of the RNN used for the estimation of directness. It is a time-delay network with a one step delay from the input layer to the hidden layer, which contains ten nodes. The output layer gives the probability that the input belongs to a class for each of the three classes.

4.1 Dialogue Corpus

Our approach requires a dialogue corpus for several task: as a source for alternative utterances, as training data for the directness classifier, as training data for the DVM and as ground truth for the evaluation. To fulfil those tasks, the employed corpus has to meet two requirements: it needs to contain a sufficient amount of examples for functionally similar direct and indirect utterances, and the utterances need to be annotated with their dialogue act and level of directness.

We considered several existing dialogue corpora, none of which suited our needs. Furthermore, we dismissed the option to collect and annotate a dialogue corpus ourselves, considering the difficulty to make sure that speakers would use different levels of directness for the same purpose without inhibiting the naturalness of the dialogues. Instead, we decided to generate a suitable dialogue corpus automatically.

The advantages an automatically generated corpus offers for our work are the certainty that it contains a number of examples for functionally similar direct and indirect variants, as well as a dependable ground truth for the evaluation. However, automatically generated corpora come with certain limitations. After introducing our dialogue corpus in the following, we will discuss the potential advantages and limitations of automatically generated corpora.

4.1.1 Description of the Dialogue Corpus

Our corpus contains dialogues with two different tasks: ordering pizza and arranging joint cooking. Example dialogues can be found in Figure 3. The dialogues incorporate typical elements of human conversation: different courses of the dialogue, over-answering, misunderstandings as well as requests for confirmation and corrections, among others. The example dialogues also show

instances of different wordings for the same purpose, such as several indirect variants of 'Yes.', such as 'Great.', 'I'm looking forward to it.' and 'That sounds delicious.' that can be found across the dialogues, and the direct 'I would like to order pizza.' in Dialogue 3 that is exchanged for the indirect 'Can I order pizza from you?' in Dialogue 4. Additionally, the same utterance can have a different level of directness depending on the context: in Dialogue 1, the utterance 'I haven't planned anything.' as response to 'Do you have time today?' is indirect, whereas it is direct as response to 'Do you have plans today?' in Dialogue 2. Overall, the corpus contains more than 400000 different dialogue flows and about four wordings per dialogue action.

As first step of the corpus generation, we defined a dialogue domain in a similar manner to the ones often employed by dialogue managers (e.g. OwlSpeak (Ultes and Minker, 2014)). It contains all system and user actions foreseen for the dialogues, and defines rules about feasible successions of those. Furthermore, each system and user action is assigned a number of different utterances that can be used to express their intent. Each utterance incorporates a level of directness ranging from one to three, with one being direct (e.g. 'I want vegetarian pizza.') and three indirect (e.g. 'I don't like meat.'). A rating of two is assigned if the utterance is indirect, but still very close to the direct one, or a common figure of speech (e.g 'Can I get vegetarian pizza?'). The directness level depends not only on the utterance itself, but also on the dialogue context. Therefore, the utterance 'I have time today.' receives a rating of three if the previous utterance was 'Do you have plans today?', and a rating of one if the previous utterance was 'Do you have time today?'.

In the next step, all dialogue flows are generated by recursively picking a dialogue action, gen-

Dialogue 1

SPEAKER 1: Hello.
SPEAKER 2: Hello.
SPEAKER 1: Do you have time today?
SPEAKER 2: I haven't planned anything.
SPEAKER 1: How hungry are you?
SPEAKER 2: Just a little.
SPEAKER 1: Would you share some food with me?
SPEAKER 2: Yes.
SPEAKER 1: Do you have any food preferences?
SPEAKER 2: I like pineapple.
SPEAKER 1: You probably would like pineapple salad.
SPEAKER 2: Great.
SPEAKER 1: We could cook that together.
SPEAKER 2: I'm looking forward to it.
SPEAKER 1: Byebye.
SPEAKER 2: Byebye.

Dialogue 2

SPEAKER 1: Hello.
SPEAKER 2: Hello.
SPEAKER 1: Do you have plans today?
SPEAKER 2: I haven't planned anything.
SPEAKER 1: What did you eat today?
SPEAKER 2: Just a little.
SPEAKER 1: Would you share some food with me?
SPEAKER 2: I don't need much.
SPEAKER 1: Which food do you like?
SPEAKER 2: I don't like meat.
SPEAKER 1: You probably would like pineapple salad.
SPEAKER 2: That sounds delicious.
SPEAKER 1: We could cook that together.
SPEAKER 2: Great.
SPEAKER 1: Byebye.
SPEAKER 2: Byebye.

Dialogue 3

SPEAKER 1: Hello.
SPEAKER 2: I am listening.
SPEAKER 1: I would like to order pizza.
SPEAKER 2: We offer different sizes.
SPEAKER 1: A small one sounds good.
SPEAKER 2: I have noted a small pizza.
SPEAKER 1: Great.
SPEAKER 2: What would you like on top?
SPEAKER 1: I like pineapple.
SPEAKER 2: You're getting a Hawaiian pizza.
SPEAKER 1: I don't like meat.
SPEAKER 2: Do you want a salad?
SPEAKER 1: You can't live just on pizza.
SPEAKER 2: So you want a small vegetarian pizza with a salad?
SPEAKER 1: That sounds delicious. Byebye.
SPEAKER 2: Byebye.
SPEAKER 1: Byebye.

Dialogue 4

SPEAKER 1: Hello.
SPEAKER 2: Hello. Is there anything I can help you with?
SPEAKER 1: Can I order pizza from you?
SPEAKER 2: We offer Hawaiian, peperoni and vegetarian.
SPEAKER 1: I choose peperoni pizza. I love salad. I'm thinking about a large one.
SPEAKER 2: I have noted a large pepperoni pizza with a salad.
SPEAKER 1: This is going to be good.
SPEAKER 2: Byebye.
SPEAKER 1: Byebye.

Figure 3: Example dialogues from the automatically generated corpus. The dialogues encompass different tasks, over-answering, misunderstandings, confirmations and corrections. Furthermore, they contain several examples of exchangeable utterances with differing directness levels, as well as examples of the same utterances changing its level of directness due to the dialogue context.

erating a list of its possible successors as stated by the rules in the dialogue domain and repeating the procedure for each of the successors. If a dialogue action does not have successor, the sequence of dialogue actions that have been chosen to get to that point are saved as a complete dialogue. The wording is chosen randomly from the utterances associated with the respective dialogue action.

4.1.2 Discussion of Automatically Generated Corpora

The use of automatically generated corpora is not widely adopted in the research community of human-computer interaction. Due to their artificial nature, they have obvious limitations: they possess less flexibility than natural conversations, regarding both the dialogue flow and the different wordings. As a result, both dialogue flow and wording are much more predictable for automatically generated corpora and it is highly likely that machine learning approaches and similar procedures will perform better on generated dialogues than they would on natural ones. Nevertheless, we believe that generated dialogues have their benefits: they should not be used to gauge the actual performance of approaches in an applied spoken dialogue system, but rather to appraise their potential.

The comparison of natural and automatically generated dialogue corpora bears parallels to the discussion regarding laboratory experiments and field experiments, and their respective advantages and limitations (as discussed by Berkowitz and Donnerstein (1982), Harrison and List (2004) and Falk and Heckman (2009), among others). While natural dialogues more accurately represent conversations in the real world, automatically generated dialogues offer more control. In particular, that means specific questions can be tested in a structured and systematic manner, the generation ensuring that relevant data is incorporated in the corpus and irrelevant data that might interfere with the experiments is excluded, as well as the presence of a dependable ground truth. Therefore, we can reliably assess whether an approach is viable to solve a given task.

Additionally, by being able to provide the complete data set for a smaller scale use case as defined by the dialogue domain, we can get an idea about the potential performance of an approach given a large amount of data that approaches the state of total coverage. While this amount of data

is usually unobtainable for most researchers, large companies have the resources to collect a suitably big corpus and are likely already working towards it. Therefore, it is beneficial to examine the full potential of a given approach. However, in our considerations regarding the availability of large amounts of data we need to take into account that even large companies typically do not have access to a large amount of *annotated* data.

In summary, we believe that automatically generated dialogues, while not providing us with an accurate performance measure of an approach in the real world, can help us to assess its general viability to solve a specific task and to estimate its performance given enough data.

4.2 Setup of the Evaluation

For the evaluation of our approach we determine its accuracy in finding an utterance that shares the dialogue action with the original utterance and is of the opposite level of directness. The ground truth for both criteria is given by the previously presented dialogue corpus. In addition, we also evaluate the performance of the trained classifier and investigate how it influences the overall performance. As the ability of DVM to group utterances that share a dialogue action has already been shown in (Pragst et al., 2018), it will not be part of this evaluation.

To investigate the effects of the amount of available data, we use several DVMs that are trained on only a fraction of the complete corpus. Corpus sizes of 0.1, 0.2, 0.4, 0.6, 0.8 and of course the full corpus are considered. The dialogues that are part of the reduced corpora are chosen at random.

Another aspect we study is the impact of the amount of available annotated training data for the classifier on its performance. As usual, we use ten-fold cross-validation in our evaluation. However, instead of only using 90% of the utterances for training and 10% for testing, we also evaluate our approach using 10% of the utterances for training and 90% for testing. With this, we want to investigate how our approach performs given only a limited amount of annotated data.

Finally, we compare the performance of the classifier when using only dialogue vectors as input and when using both dialogue vectors and the sum of word vectors. As DVMs map functionally similar utterances in close vicinity to each other, direct and indirect utterances should be hard to

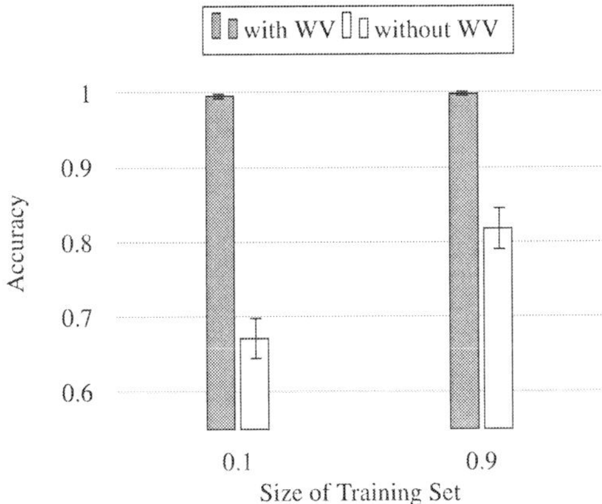

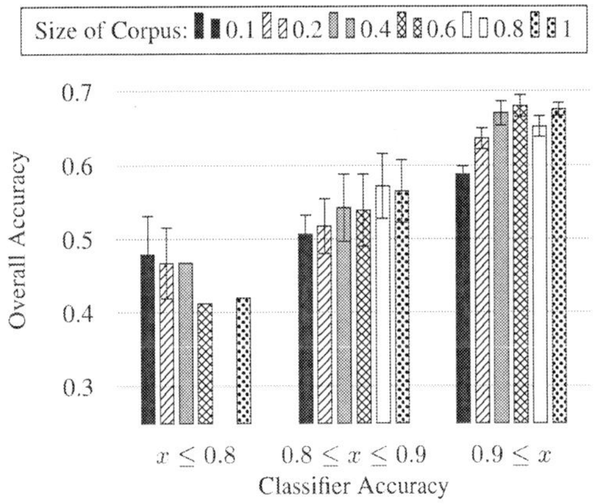

Figure 4: The mean accuracy and SD achieved by different classifiers.

Figure 5: The mean accuracy and SD achieved by with different DVMs and Classifiers.

distinguish with just the information from those models. On the other hand, the sum of word vectors might be missing important context information for the identification of the directness level. We believe that the combination of both the sum of word vectors and dialogue vectors will improve the performance of the classifier.

The DVMs we utilise in our evaluation as similarity measure and as input to the RNN are trained on the presented dialogue corpus. The network additionally receives the sum of the word vectors of an utterance, based on the Google News Corpus model (Mikolov et al., 2013b), as input.

4.3 Results

Overall, our results show that the proposed approach has a high potential. The best mean accuracy reaches a value of 0.68, and the classifier predicts the right class with 0.87 accuracy on average. In the following, we discuss the results and their implications in more detail, starting with the results of the classifier, before assessing the overall performance.

4.3.1 Classification of Directness

The baseline performance our classifier should surpass the prediction of the majority class. With the given data, such a classifier can achieve an accuracy of 0.5291. Our trained classifier achieves a significantly better accuracy of 0.8710 ($t(203) = 35.366$, $p < .001$) averaged over all test cases. Even the worst classifier, with an accuracy of 0.6354, performs more than 10% better than choosing the majority class.

As expected, significant differences exist for the size of the training set ($t(159.425) = -4.008$, $p < .001$), with a larger training set leading to better results. Furthermore, adding the linear combination of the word vectors as input improves the performance of the classifier significantly ($t(101.347) = 32.434$, $p < .001$). The mean performances can be seen in Figure 4. The corpus size the DVMs were trained on does not have a significant impact.

Those results suggest that the amount of labelled training data greatly affects the performance of a classifier using RNN. If the goal is a large scale application, the necessary amount of labelled data might be difficult to achieve. Future work should therefore consider the possibility of unsupervised training approaches or approaches with better scalability. In addition to a larger amount of training data, using the sum of word vectors as additional input greatly improves the performance. As a number of extensive word vector models exist for several languages (e.g. (Bojanowski et al., 2016)), this data is easily available irrespective of the scale of the targeted dialogue domain.

4.3.2 Exchange of Utterances

Our approach for choosing a valid replacement for an utterance was able to achieves a high accuracy of 0.70 at its best performance. However, this performance is significantly influenced by both the accuracy of the classifier for the level of directness ($F(2, 29.090) = 141.564$, $p < .001$) and the amount of data the DVM was trained on ($F(5, 52.864) = 4.304$, $p < .003$). Depending on the quality of the employed components, the accuracy ranges from 0.41 to 0.70. A graphical representation can be found in Figure 5.

The results show the high potential of our approach, but also emphasize the importance of both a good classifier to estimate the level of directness and a good measure of the functional similarity of utterances. If either component under performs, the accuracy declines to undesirable levels. DVMs depend on a large amount of data being available. However, this data does not need to be annotated. Hence, suitable DVMs for our approach can be trained with the amount of data usually available to big companies. Training a good classifier presents a more severe challenge, as annotated data is needed. An unsupervised approach to the training of a classifier for the level of directness would therefore be highly beneficial for the viability of our approach.

4.4 Limitations of the Evaluation

The evaluation of our approach yields promising results and shows its high potential. However, we need to take into account that those results were achieved using an artificially generated corpus. Furthermore, we tested the performance of our approach in a theoretical setting, not its impact in an actual application. This section discusses the limitations of our evaluation.

Natural dialogue possess a greater variability than automatically generated dialogue, and therefore finding reliable patterns in them is a more difficult task. It is likely that the quality of both the classifier and the DVMs decreases if they are trained on a comparable amount of natural dialogue data compared to artificially generated data. We could show in the evaluation that the quality of the classifier and DVM has a major impact on the performance of our approach. This implies that more data is needed for natural dialogues than for automatically generated dialogues to achieve comparable results.

One of the main reasons to use an automatically generated dialogue corpus was to ensure the presence of pairs of direct and indirect utterances. This is important not only for the training of the classifier and DVM, but also to ensure that a suitable substitute is known. As our approach searches for a replacement in a set of established utterances, it can only be successful if the set does contain a suitable utterance. While the likelihood for the

presence of a suitable substitute increases with the size of the dialogue corpus, it cannot be guaranteed that a replacement is present in natural dialogues. When transferring our approach to actual applications, this might present a challenge. To address this challenge, the generation of suitable utterances rather than their identification should be investigated.

While our evaluation shows what accuracy our approach can achieve given different circumstances, we did not yet investigate what accuracy it needs to achieve in actual applications to positively impact the user experience. Without this information, it is difficult to estimate which level of accuracy should be targeted and, as a consequence, the amount of training data needed.

5 Conclusion

In this work, we introduced an approach to exchange utterances that express the same meaning in the dialogue, but possess a differing level of directness. In this endeavour, we utilised supervised training with RNNs for the estimation of directness levels, and DVMs as basis for the similarity measure of the meaning of two utterances in a dialogue. A dialogue corpus that provides a sufficient amount of direct/indirect utterance pairs as well as annotations of the dialogue act and level of directness was generated automatically and utilised to show the high potential of our approach in an evaluation.

Although the results seem promising overall, we identified several challenges that need to be addressed in future work. The chosen classifier for the level of directness relies on a large amount of annotated data. Unsupervised learning approaches will be investigated to eliminate this need. Our evaluation did not incorporate the variability of natural dialogues. We will test our approach on natural dialogues to verify its applicability on more noisy data than an automatically generated corpus provides. Furthermore, the presence of direct/indirect pairs in natural dialogue corpora cannot be guaranteed. It might become necessary to explore the generation of suitable utterances if we find that natural dialogue data does not contain a sufficient amount of direct/indirect utterance pairs. Finally, the integration of our approach in an actual dialogue systems can confirm its beneficial effects on the user satisfaction.

References

James F Allen and C Raymond Perrault. 1980. Analyzing intention in utterances. *Artificial intelligence* 15(3):143–178.

Leonard Berkowitz and Edward Donnerstein. 1982. External validity is more than skin deep: Some answers to criticisms of laboratory experiments. *American psychologist* 37(3):245.

Piotr Bojanowski, Edouard Grave, Armand Joulin, and Tomas Mikolov. 2016. Enriching word vectors with subword information. *arXiv preprint arXiv:1607.04606* .

Gordon Michael Briggs and Matthias Scheutz. 2013. A hybrid architectural approach to understanding and appropriately generating indirect speech acts. In *AAAI*.

Armin Falk and James J Heckman. 2009. Lab experiments are a major source of knowledge in the social sciences. *science* 326(5952):535–538.

Ellen Feghali. 1997. Arab cultural communication patterns. *International Journal of Intercultural Relations* 21(3):345–378.

Glenn W Harrison and John A List. 2004. Field experiments. *Journal of Economic literature* 42(4):1009–1055.

Baotian Hu, Zhengdong Lu, Hang Li, and Qingcai Chen. 2014. Convolutional neural network architectures for matching natural language sentences. In *Advances in neural information processing systems*. pages 2042–2050.

Nal Kalchbrenner, Edward Grefenstette, and Phil Blunsom. 2014. A convolutional neural network for modelling sentences. *arXiv preprint arXiv:1404.2188* .

Ryan Kiros, Yukun Zhu, Ruslan R Salakhutdinov, Richard Zemel, Raquel Urtasun, Antonio Torralba, and Sanja Fidler. 2015. Skip-thought vectors. In *Advances in neural information processing systems*. pages 3294–3302.

Juliana Miehle, Koichiro Yoshino, Louisa Pragst, Stefan Ultes, Satoshi Nakamura, and Wolfgang Minker. 2016. Cultural communication idiosyncrasies in human-computer interaction. In *Proceedings of the 17th Annual Meeting of the Special Interest Group on Discourse and Dialogue (SIGDIAL)*. Association for Computational Linguistics, Los Angeles, USA.

Tomas Mikolov, Kai Chen, Greg Corrado, and Jeffrey Dean. 2013a. Efficient estimation of word representations in vector space. *arXiv preprint arXiv:1301.3781* .

Tomas Mikolov, Ilya Sutskever, Kai Chen, Greg S Corrado, and Jeff Dean. 2013b. Distributed representations of words and phrases and their compositionality. In *Advances in neural information processing systems*. pages 3111–3119.

Hamid Palangi, Li Deng, Yelong Shen, Jianfeng Gao, Xiaodong He, Jianshu Chen, Xinying Song, and Rabab Ward. 2016. Deep sentence embedding using long short-term memory networks: Analysis and application to information retrieval. *IEEE/ACM Transactions on Audio, Speech and Language Processing (TASLP)* 24(4):694–707.

Louisa Pragst, Wolfgang Minker, and Stefan Ultes. 2017. Exploring the applicability of elaborateness and indirectness in dialogue management. In *Proceedings of the 8th International Workshop On Spoken Dialogue Systems (IWSDS)*.

Louisa Pragst, Niklas Rach, Wolfgang Minker, and Stefan Ultes. 2018. On the vector representation of utterances in dialogue context. In *Proceedings of the Eleventh International Conference on Language Resources and Evaluation (LREC 2018)*. European Language Resources Association (ELRA), Paris, France.

John R Searle. 1975. *Indirect speech acts*. na.

Yelong Shen, Xiaodong He, Jianfeng Gao, Li Deng, and Grégoire Mesnil. 2014. A latent semantic model with convolutional-pooling structure for information retrieval. In *Proceedings of the 23rd ACM International Conference on Conference on Information and Knowledge Management*. ACM, pages 101–110.

Richard Socher, Jeffrey Pennington, Eric H Huang, Andrew Y Ng, and Christopher D Manning. 2011. Semi-supervised recursive autoencoders for predicting sentiment distributions. In *Proceedings of the conference on empirical methods in natural language processing*. Association for Computational Linguistics, pages 151–161.

Ilya Sutskever, Oriol Vinyals, and Quoc V Le. 2014. Sequence to sequence learning with neural networks. In *Advances in neural information processing systems*. pages 3104–3112.

Emiru Tsunoo, Peter Bell, and Steve Renals. 2017. Hierarchical recurrent neural network for story segmentation. *Proc. Interspeech 2017* pages 2919–2923.

Stefan Ultes and Wolfgang Minker. 2014. Managing adaptive spoken dialogue for intelligent environments. *Journal of Ambient Intelligence and Smart Environments* 6(5):523–539.

Modeling Linguistic and Personality Adaptation for Natural Language Generation

Zhichao Hu[1], Jean E. Fox Tree[2] and Marilyn A. Walker[1]

Natural Language and Dialogue Systems Lab, Computer Science Department[1]
Spontaneous Communication Laboratory, Psychology Department[2]
University of California Santa Cruz, Santa Cruz, CA 95064, USA
`{zhu, foxtree, mawalker}@ucsc.edu`

Abstract

Previous work has shown that conversants adapt to many aspects of their partners' language. Other work has shown that while every person is unique, they often share general patterns of behavior. Theories of personality aim to explain these shared patterns, and studies have shown that many linguistic cues are correlated with personality traits. We propose an adaptation measure for adaptive natural language generation for dialogs that integrates the predictions of both personality theories and adaptation theories, that can be applied as a dialog unfolds, on a turn by turn basis. We show that our measure meets criteria for validity, and that adaptation varies according to corpora and task, speaker, and the set of features used to model it. We also produce fine-grained models according to the dialog segmentation or the speaker, and demonstrate the decaying trend of adaptation.

1 Introduction

Every person is unique, yet they often share general patterns of behavior. Theories of personality aim to explain these patterns in terms of personality traits, e.g. the Big Five traits of extraversion or agreeableness. Previous work has shown: (1) the language that people generate includes linguistic features that express these personality traits; (2) it is possible to train models to automatically recognize a person's personality from his language; and (3) it is possible to automatically train models for natural language generation that express personality traits (Pennebaker and King, 1999; Mairesse et al., 2007; Mairesse and Walker, 2011; Gill et al., 2012).

A distinct line of work has shown that people adapt to one another's conversational behaviors and that conversants reliably re-use or mimic many

Speaker (Utterance #): Utterance
F97: okay I'm on pacific avenue and plaza
D98: okay so you just take a right once your out of pacific lane you go wait no to late to your left.
F98: okay
D99: and I think. it's right ther- alright so I'm walking down pacific okay so it's right before the object it's right before the mission and pacific avenue intersection okay it's like umm almost brown and kinda like tan colored
F99: is it tan
D100: yeah it's like two different colors its like dark brown and orangey kinda like gold color its kinda like um
F100: okay is it kinda like a vase type of a thing
D101: yeah it has yeah like a vase

Figure 1: Dialog excerpt from the ArtWalk Corpus.

different aspects of their partner's verbal and non-verbal behaviors, including lexical and syntactical traits, accent, speech rate, pause length, etc. (Coupland et al., 1988; Willemyns et al., 1997; Brennan and Clark, 1996; Branigan et al., 2010; Coupland et al., 1988; Parent and Eskenazi, 2010; Reitter et al., 2006a; Chartrand and Bargh, 1999; Hu et al., 2014). Previous work primarily focuses on developing methods on measuring adaptation in dialog, and studies have shown that adaptation measures are correlated with task success (Reitter and Moore, 2007), and that social variables such as power affect adaptation (Danescu-Niculescu-Mizil et al., 2012).

We posit that it is crucial to enable adaptation in computer agents in order to make them more human-like. However, we need models to control the amount of adaptation in natural language generation. A primary challenge is that dialogs exhibit many different types of linguistic features, any or all of which, in principle, could be adapted. Previous work has often focused on individual features when measuring adaptation, and referring expressions have often been the focus, but the conversants in the dialog in Figure 1 from the ArtWalk Corpus appear to be adapting to the discourse marker *okay* in D98 and F98, the hedge *kinda like* in F100, and to the adjectival phrase *like a vase* in D101.

Proceedings of the SIGDIAL 2018 Conference, pages 20–31,
Melbourne, Australia, 12-14 July 2018. ©2018 Association for Computational Linguistics

Therefore we propose a novel adaptation measure, Dialog Adaptation Score (DAS), which can model adaptation on any subset of linguistic features and can be applied on a turn by turn basis to any segment of dialog. Consider the example shown in Table 1, where the context (prime) is taken from an actual dialog. A response (target) with no adaptation makes the utterance stiff (DAS = 0), and too much adaptation (to all four discourse markers in prime, DAS = 1) makes the utterance unnatural. Our hypothesis is that we can learn models to approximate the appropriate amount of adaptation from the actual human response to the context (to discourse marker "okay", DAS = 0.25).

Conversants in dialogs express their own personality and adapt to their dialog partners simultaneously. Our measure of adaptation produces models for adaptive natural language generation (NLG) for dialogs that integrates the predictions of both personality theories and adaptation theories. NLGs need to operate as a dialog unfolds on a turn-by-turn basis, thus the requirements for a model of adaptation for NLG are different than simply measuring adaptation.

Context: *okay alright so yeah Im looking at 123 Locust right now*
Linguistic Features:
Discourse markers: okay, alright, so, yeah
Referring expressions: 123 Locust
Syntactic structures: VP->VBP+VP, VP->VBG+PP+ADVB ...

Adaptation Amount	Response	Adapted Features	DAS
None	*it should be some-where*	None	0
Too much	*okay alright so yeah it should be somewhere*	okay, alright, so, yeah	1
Moderate	*okay I mean it should be some-where*	okay	0.25

Table 1: Linguistic adaptation example: no adaptation, too much adaptation, and moderate adaptation (human response from ArtWalk Corpus).

We apply our method to multiple corpora to investigate how the dialog situation and speaker roles affect the level and type of adaptation to the other speaker. We show that:

- Different feature sets and conversational situations can have different adaptation models;
- Speakers usually adapt more when they have the initiative;
- The degree of adaptation may vary over the course of a dialog, and decreases as the adaptation window size increases.

2 Method and Overview

Our goal is an algorithm for adaptive natural language generation (NLG) that controls the system output at each step of the dialog. Our first aim therefore is a measure of dialog adaptation that can be applied on a turn by turn basis as a dialog unfolds. For this purpose, previous measures of dialog adaptation (Stenchikova and Stent, 2007; Danescu-Niculescu-Mizil et al., 2011) have two limitations: (1) their calculation require the complete dialog, and (2) they focus on single features and do not provide a model to control the interaction of multiple parameters in a single output, while our method measures adaptation with respect to any set of features. We further compare our method to existing measures in Section 6.

Measures of adaptation focus on prime-target pairs: (p, t), in which the prime contains linguistic features that the target may adapt to. While linguistic adaptation occur beyond the next turn, we simplify the calculation by using a window size of 1 for most experiments: for every utterance in the dialog (prime), we consider the next utterance by a different speaker as the target, if any. We show the decay of adaptation with increasing window size in a separate experiment. When generating (p, t) pairs, it is possible to consider only speaker A adapting to speaker B (target=A), only speaker B adapting to speaker A (target=B), or both at the same time (target=Both). In the following definition, $FC_i(p)$ is the count of features in prime p of the i-th (p, t) pair, n is the total number of prime-target pairs in which $FC_i(p) \neq 0$, similarly, $FC_i(p \wedge t)$ is the count of features in both prime p and target t. We define Dialog Adaptation Score (DAS) as:

$$DAS = \frac{1}{n} \sum_{i=1}^{n} \frac{FC_i(p \wedge t)}{FC_i(p)}$$

Within a feature set, DAS reflects the average probability that features in prime are adapted in target across all prime-target pairs in a dialog. Thus our Dialog Adaptation Score (DAS) models adaptation with respect to feature sets, providing a whole-dialog adaptation model or a turn-by-turn adaptation model. The strength of DAS is the ability to model different classes of features related to individual differences such as personalities or social variables of interest such as status.

DAS scores measured using various feature sets can be used as a vector model to control adaptation in Natural Language Generation (NLG). Although we leave the application of DAS to NLG to future work, here we describe how we expect to use it. We consider the use of DAS with three NLG architectures: Overgeneration and Rank, Statistical Parameterized NLG, and Neural NLG.

Overgenerate and Rank. In this approach, different modules propose a possibly large set of next utterances in parallel, which are then fed to a (trained) ranker that outputs the top-ranked utterance. Previous work on adaptation/alignment in NLG has made use of this architecture (Brockmann, 2009; Buschmeier et al., 2010). We can rank the generated responses based on the distances between their DAS vectors and learned DAS adaptation model. The response with the smallest distance is the response with the best amount of adaptation. We can also emphasize specific feature sets by giving weights to different dimensions of the vector and calculating weighted distance. For instance, in order to adapt more to personality and avoid too much lexical mimicry, one could prioritize related LIWC features, and adapt by using words from the same LIWC categories.

Statistical Parameterized NLG. Some NLG engines provide a list of parameters that can be controlled at generation time (Paiva and Evans, 2004; Lin and Walker, 2017). DAS scores can be used as generation decision probabilities. A DAS score of 0.48 for the LIWC feature set indicates that the probability of adapting to LIWC features in discourse context (prime) is 0.48. By mapping DAS scores to generation parameters, the generator could be directly controlled to exhibit the correct amount of adaptation for any feature set.

Neural NLG. Recent work in Neural NLG (NNLG) explores controlling stylistic variation in outputs using a vector to encode style parameters, possibly in combination with the use of a context vector to represent the dialog context (Ficler and Goldberg, 2017; Oraby et al., 2018). The vector based probabilities that are represented in the DAS adaptation model could be encoded into the context vector in NNLG. No other known adaptation measures could be used in this way.

We hypothesize that different conversational contexts may lead to more or less adaptive behavior, so we apply DAS on four human-human dialog corpora: two task-oriented dialog corpora that were designed to elicit adaptation (ArtWalk and Walking Around), one topic-centric spontaneous dialog corpus (Switchboard), and the MapTask Corpus used in much previous work. We obtain linguistic features using fully automatic annotation tools, described in Section 4. We learn models of adaptation from these dialogs on various feature sets. We first validate the DAS measure by showing that DAS distinguishes original dialogs from dialogs where the orders of the turns have been randomized. We then show how DAS varies as a function of the feature sets used and the dialog corpora. We also show how DAS can be used for fine-grained adaptation by applying DAS to individual dialog segments, and individual speakers, and illustrating the differences in adaptation as a function of these variables. Finally, we show how DAS scores decrease as the adaptation window size increases.

3   Corpora

We develop models of adaptation using DAS on the following four corpora.

ArtWalk Corpus (AWC).[1] Figure 1 provides a sample of the Artwalk Corpus (Liu et al., 2016), a collection of mobile-to-Skype conversations between friend and stranger dyads performing a real world-situated task that was designed to elicit adaptation behaviors. Every dialog involves a stationary director on campus, and a follower downtown. The director provided directions to help the follower find 10 public art pieces such as sculptures, mosaics, or murals in downtown Santa Cruz. The director had access to Google Earth views of the follower's route and a map with locations and pictures of art pieces. The corpus consists of transcripts of 24 friend and 24 stranger dyads (48 dialogs). In total, it contains approximately 185,000 words and 23,000 turns, from conversations that ranged from 24 to 55 minutes, or 197 to 691 turns. It includes referent negotiation, direction-giving, and small talk (non-task talk).[2]

Walking Around Corpus (WAC).[3] The Walking Around Corpus (Brennan et al., 2013) consists of spontaneous spoken dialogs produced by 36 pairs of people, collected in order to elicit adaptation behaviors, as illustrated by Figure 2. In each dialog, a director navigates a follower using a mobile phone to 18 destinations on a medium-sized campus. Directors have access to a digital map marked with

---

[1] https://nlds.soe.ucsc.edu/artwalk

[2] For AWC and WAC, we remove annotations such as speech overlap, noises (laugh, cough) and indicators for short pauses, leaving only clean text. If more than one consecutive dialog turn has the same speaker, we merge them into one dialog turn.

[3] https://catalog.ldc.upenn.edu/ldc2015s08

Speaker (Utterance #): Utterance
D137: and. you know on the uh other side of the math building like theres the uh, theres this weird, little concrete, structure that is sticking up out of the bricks, dont make any sense.
F138: uh.
D139: yeah youll see it when you get over there.
F140: okay.
D141: so just keep going and then uh. when you get around the building make a left. and you should be.
F142: when I get around the Physics building make a left?
D143: yeah yeah when you get around to the end here.

Figure 2: Dialog excerpt from the Walking Around Corpus.

Speaker (Utterance #): Utterance
D7: and below the graveyard below the graveyard but above the carved wooden pole.
F8: oh hang on i don't have a graveyard.
D9: okay. so you don't have a graveyard. do you have a fast flowing river.
F10: fast running creek.
D11: ehm mm don't know yeah it could be could be.
F12: is that to the right that'll be to my right to my right.
D13: to your. right uh-huh.
F14: right. so i continue and go below the fast running creek.
D15: no. go just until you go go below the diamond mine until just before the fast fast flowing river.

Figure 3: Dialog excerpt from the Map Task Corpus.

Speaker (Utterance #): [Tag] Utterance
B14: [b] Yeah. [sv] Well that's pretty good if you can do that. [sd] I know. [sd] I have a daughter who's ten [sd] and we haven't really put much away for her college up to this point [sd] but, uh, we're to the point now where our financial income is enough that we can consider putting some away
A15: [b] Uh-huh.
B16: [sd] for college [sd] so we are going to be starting a regular payroll deduction
A17: [%] Um.
B18: [sd] in the fall [sd] and then the money that I will be making this summer we'll be putting away for the college fund.
A19: [ba] Um. Sounds good. [%] Yeah [sd] I guess we're, we're just at the point, uh [sd] my wife worked until we had a family [sd] and then, you know, now we're just going on the one income [sv] so it's
B20: [b] Uh-huh.
A21: [sv] a lot more interesting trying to. uh [sv] find some extra payroll deductions is probably the only way we will be able to, uh, do it. [sd] You know, kind of enforce the savings.
B22: [b] Uh-huh.

Figure 4: Dialog excerpt from the Switchboard Dialog Act Corpus.

target destinations, labels (e.g. "Ship sculpture"), photos and followers' real time location. Followers carry a cell phone with GPS, and a camera in order to take pictures of the destinations they visit. Each dialog ranges from 175 to 885 turns. The major differences between AWC and WAC are (1) in order to elicit novel referring expressions and possible linguistic adaptation, destinations in AWC do not have provided labels; (2) AWC happens in a more open world setting (downtown) compared to WAC (university campus).

Map Task Corpus (MPT).[4] The Map Task Corpus (Anderson et al., 1991) is a set of 128 cooperative task-oriented dialogs involving two participants. Each dialog ranges from 32 to 438 turns. A director and a follower sit opposite one another. Each has a paper map which the other cannot see (the maps are not identical). The director has a route marked on their map, the follower has no route. The participants' goal is to reproduce the director's route on the follower's map. All maps consist of line drawing landmarks labelled with their names, such as "parked van", "east lake", or "white mountain". Figure 3 shows an excerpt from the Map Task Corpus.

Switchboard Corpus (SWBD).[5] Switchboard (Godfrey et al., 1992) is a collection of two-speaker telephone conversations from all areas of the United States. An automatic operator handled the calls (giving recorded prompts, selecting and dialing another speaker, introducing discussion topics and recording the dialog). 70 topics were provided, for example: pets, child care, music, and buying a car. Each topic has a corresponding prompt message played to the first speaker, e.g. "find out what kind of pets the

other caller has." A subset of 200K utterances of Switchboard have also been tagged with dialog act tags (Jurafsky et al., 1997). Each dialog contains 14 to 373 turns. Figure 1 provides an example of dialog act tags, such as b - Acknowledge (Backchannel), sv - Statement-opinion, sd - Statement-non-opinion, and % - Uninterpretable. We focus on this subset of the corpus.

Dialogs in SWBD have a different style from the three task-oriented, direction-giving corpora. Figure 4 illustrates how the SWBD dialogs are often lopsided: from utterance 14 to 18, speaker B states his opinion with verbose dialog turns, whereas speaker A only acknowledges and backchannels; from utterance 19 to 22, speaker A acts as the main speaker, whereas speaker B backchannels. Some theories of discourse define dialog turns as extending over backchannels, and we posit that this

[4] http://groups.inf.ed.ac.uk/maptask/
[5] https://catalog.ldc.upenn.edu/ldc97s62

would allow us to measure adaptation more faithfully, so we utilize the SWBD dialog act tags to filter turns that only contain backchannels, keeping only dialog turns with tags `sd` (Statement-non-opinion), `sv` (Statement-opinion), and `bf` (Summarize/reformulate).[6] We then merge consecutive dialog turns from the same speaker.

4   Experimental Setup

We consider the following feature sets: unigram, bigram, referring expressions, hedges/discourse markers, and Linguistic Inquiry and Word Count (LIWC) features. Previous computational work on measuring linguistic adaptation in textual corpora have largely focused on lexical and syntactical features, which are included as baselines. Referring expressions and discourse markers are key features that are commonly studied for adaptation behaviors in task-oriented dialogs, which are often hand annotated. Here we automatically extract these features by rules. To model adaptation on the personality level, we draw features that correlate significantly with personality ratings from LIWC features. We hypothesize that our feature sets will demonstrate different adaptation models.

We lemmatize, POS tag and derive constituency structures using Stanford CoreNLP (Manning et al., 2014). We then extract the following linguistic features from annotations and raw text. The following example features are based on D137 in Figure 2.

Unigram Lemma/POS. We use lemma combined with POS tags to distinguish word senses. E.g., `lemmapos_building/NN` and `lemmapos_brick/NNS` in D137.

Bigram Lemma. E.g., `bigram_the-brick` and `bigram_side-of` in D137.

Syntactic Structure. Following Reitter et al. (2006b), we take all the subtrees from a constituency parse tree (excluding the leaf nodes that contain words) as features. E.g., `syntax_VP->VBP+PP` and `syntax_ADJP-> DT+JJ` in D137. The difference is that we use Stanford Parser rather than hand annotations.

Referring Expression. Referring expressions are usually noun phrases. We start by taking all constituency subtrees with root `NP`, then map the subtrees to their actual phrases in the text and remove all articles from the phrase, e.g., `referexp_little-concrete`

and `referexp_math-building` in D137.

Hedge/Discourse Marker. Hedges are mitigating words used to lessen the impact of an utterance, such as "actually" and "somewhat". Discourse markers are words or phrases that manage the flow and structure of discourse, such as "you know" and "I mean". We construct a dictionary of hedges and discourse markers, and use string matching to extract features, e.g., `hedge_you-know` and `hedge_like` in D137.

LIWC. Linguistic Inquiry and Word Count (Pennebaker et al., 2001) is a text analysis program that counts words in over 80 linguistic (e.g., pronouns, conjunctions), psychological (e.g., anger, positive emotion), and topical (e.g., leisure, money) categories. E.g., `liwc_second-person` and `liwc_informal` in D137. Because DAS features are binary, features such as Word Count and Number of New Lines are excluded.

Personality LIWC. Previous work reports for each LIWC feature whether it is significantly correlated with each Big Five trait (Mairesse et al., 2007) on conversational data (Mehl et al., 2006). For each trait, we create feature sets consisting of such features. See Table 2.

Personality	#	Example Features
Extraversion	15	Positive Emotion, Swear Words
Emotional Stability	14	Anger, Articles
Agreeable	16	Assent, Insight
Conscientious	17	Fillers, Nonfluencies
Open to Experience	12	Discrepancy, Tentative

Table 2: Number of LIWC features for each personality trait and example features.

5   Experiments on Modeling Adaptation

In this section, we apply our DAS measure on the corpora introduced in Section 3.

5.1   Validity Test: Original vs. Randomized Dialogs

We first establish that our novel DAS measure is valid by testing whether it can distinguish dialogs in their original order vs. dialogs with randomly scrambled turns (the order of dialog turns are randomized within speakers), inspired by similar approaches in previous work (Gandhe and Traum, 2008; Ward and Litman, 2007; Barzilay and Lapata, 2005). We calculate DAS scores for original dialogs and randomized dialogs using target—Both

---

[6]The filtering process removes 48.1% original dialog turns, but only 12.6% of the words. Filtered dialogs have 3 to 85 dialog turns each.

	#	Feature Sets	Original	Random
AWC	48	Unigram + Bigram	**0.10**	**0.07**
		All but LIWC	**0.13**	**0.10**
		LIWC	**0.48**	**0.46**
WAC	36	Unigram + Bigram	**0.22**	**0.19**
		All but LIWC	**0.18**	**0.16**
		LIWC	**0.55**	**0.54**
MPT	128	Unigram + Bigram	**0.27**	**0.24**
		All but LIWC	**0.20**	**0.18**
		LIWC	0.54	0.54
SWBD	1126	Unigram + Bigram	**0.18**	**0.17**
		All but LIWC	**0.20**	**0.19**
		LIWC	**0.67**	**0.66**

Table 3: Number of dialogs in four corpora, and average DAS scores of different feature sets for original and randomized dialogs. Bold numbers indicate statistically significant differences ($p < 0.0001$) between DAS scores for original and randomized dialogs in paired t-tests .

Row	Feature Sets	AWC	WAC	MPT	SWBD
1	Lemma/POS	0.14	0.15	0.29	0.28
2	Bigram	0.04	0.04	0.01	0.07
3	Syntax	0.17	0.14	0.11	0.28
4	ReferExp	0.03	0.03	0.01	0.01
5	Hedge	0.17	0.19	0.18	0.25
6	LIWC	0.48	0.55	0.53	0.71
7	Extra	0.40	0.46	0.30	0.58
8	Emot	0.48	0.50	0.38	0.72
9	Agree	0.47	0.51	0.44	0.71
10	Consc	0.38	0.44	0.20	0.55
11	Open	0.44	0.44	0.31	0.73

Table 4: Average DAS scores for each feature set.

(Sec. 2) to obtain overall adaptation scores for both speakers.

We first test on lexical features (unigram and bigram) as in previous work. Then we add additional linguistic features (syntactic structure, referring expression, and discourse marker). These five features (see Section 4) are referred to as "all but LIWC". Finally, we test DAS validity using the higher level LIWC features.

We perform paired t-tests on DAS scores for original dialogs and DAS scores for randomized dialogs, pairing every original dialog with its randomized dialog. Table 3 shows the number of dialogs in each corpus, the average DAS scores of all dialogs within the corpus and p-values of corresponding t-tests. Although the differences between the average scores are relatively small, the differences in almost all paired t-tests are extremely statistically significant (cells in bold, $p < 0.0001$). The paired t-test on MPT using LIWC features shows a significant difference between the two test groups ($p < 0.05$). The original dialog corpora achieve higher average DAS scores than the randomized corpora for all 12 original-random pairs. The results show that DAS measure is sensitive to dialog turn order, as it should be if it is measuring dialog coherence and adaptation.

5.2 Adaptation across corpora and across features

This experiment aims to broadly examine the differences in adaptation across different corpora and feature sets. We first compute DAS on the whole dialog level for each feature set from Section 4, and then calculate the average across the corpus. We use target=Both (Sec 2) to obtain an overall measure of adaptation and leave calculating fine-grained DAS measures to Section 5.3. Table 4 provides results. We will refer to features in row 1 to 6 as "linguistic features" and row 7 to 11 as "personality features".

Comparing columns, we first examine the DAS scores across different corpora. All p-values reported below are from paired t-tests. The two most similar corpora, the AWC and WAC, show no significant difference on linguistic features ($p = 0.43$). At the same time, the AWC and WAC do differ from the other two corpora. This demonstrates that the DAS reflects real similarities and differences across corpora. MPT shows lower DAS scores on all linguistic features except for lemma (word repetition), where it achieves the highest DAS score. With respect to personality features, WAC has significantly higher DAS scores than AWC ($p < 0.05$), possibly because of the different experiment settings: college student participants are more comfortable around their own campus than in downtown. MPT shows significantly lower DAS scores on personality features than AWC and WAC ($p < 0.05$). This may be because the MPT setting is the most constrained of the four corpora: being fixed in topic and location means dialogs are less likely to be influenced by environmental factors or to contain social chit chat. SWBD has the highest DAS scores in all feature sets except for referring expression. The higher DAS in non-referring features could be because the social chit chat allows more adaptation to occur. In addition, the dialogs we measure in SWBD are backchannel-filtered. The lower referring expression (respective to other SWBD scores) could be because SWBD does not require the referring expressions necessary for the other three task-related corpora. We posit that the DAS adaptation models we present can be used in existing NLG architectures, described in Sec. 2. The AWC column in Table 4 shows adaptation model in the form of a DAS vector obtained from the ArtWalk Corpus.

Comparing rows, we then examine DAS scores among different features sets. LIWC has the highest DAS score among linguistic features, ranging from 0.48 to 0.71. While other linguistic features are largely content-specific, LIWC consists of higher level features that cover broader categories, thus its high DAS scores are expected. The DAS scores for the lemma feature range from 0.14 to 0.29, followed by Syntactic Structure (0.11 to 0.28), Hedge (0.17 to 0.25) and Bigram (0.01 to 0.07). Referring Expression has the lowest DAS score (0.01 to 0.03), possibly because our automatic extraction of referring expressions creates numerous subsets of one referring expression. Among personality features, Emotion Stability, Agreeableness, and Openness to Experience traits are adapted more than Extraversion and Conscientiousness. We leave to future work the question of why these traits have higher DAS scores.

5.3 Adaptation by Dialog Segment and Speaker

Our primary goal is to model adaptation at a fine-grained level in order to provide fine-grained control of an NLG engine. To that end, we report results for adaptation models on a per dialog-segment and per-speaker basis.

Reliable discourse segmentation is notoriously difficult (Passonneau and Litman, 1996), thus we heuristically divide each task-oriented dialog into segments based on number of destinations on the map: this effectively divides the dialog into subtasks. Since each dialog in SWBD only has one topic, we divide SWBD into 5 segments.[7] We compute DAS for each segment, and take an average across all dialogs in the corpus for each segment.

We compare all LIWC features vs. extraversion LIWC features because they provide high DAS scores across corpora. We also aim to explore the dynamics between two conversants on the extraversion scale. Figure 5 in Appendix illustrates how DAS varies as a function of speaker and dialog segment. In AWC, scores for all LIWC features

slightly decrease as dialogs progress (Fig. 5(a)), while extraversion features show a distinct increasing trend with correlation coefficients ranging from 0.7 to 0.86 (Fig. 5(b)), despite being a subset of all LIWC features.[8] Average DAS displays the same decreasing trend in all and extraversion LIWC features for SWBD (Fig. 5(g) and 5(h)). We speculate that this might be due to the setup of SWBD: as the dialogs progress, conversants have less to discuss about the topic and are less interested. We also calculate per segment adaptation in WAC and MPT, but their DAS scores do not show overall trends across the length of the dialog (Fig. 5(c) to 5(f)).

We also explore whether speaker role and initiative affects adaptation. We use target=Both, target=D, and target=F to calculate DAS for each target.[9] We hypothesize that directors and followers adapt differently in task-oriented dialogs. In all task-oriented corpora (AWC, WAC, and MPT), we observe generally higher DAS scores with target=D, indicating that in order to drive the dialogs, directors adapt more to followers. In SWBD, the speaker initiating the call (who brings up the discussion topic and may therefore drive the conversation) generally exhibits more adaptation.

5.4 Adaptation on Different Window Sizes

This experiment aims to examine the trend of DAS scores as the window size increases. We begin with a window size of 1 and gradually increase it to 5. For a window size of n, the target utterance t is paired with the n-th utterance from a different speaker preceding t, if any. For example, in Figure 1, when window size is 3, target D100 is paired with prime F97; target D99 does not have any prime, thus no pair is formed.

Similar to Sec. 5.1, we compare DAS scores between dialogs in their original order vs. dialogs with randomly scrambled turns. We hypothesize that similar to the results of repetition decay measures (Reitter et al., 2006a; Ward and Litman, 2007; Pietsch et al., 2012), the DAS scores of original dialogs would decrease as the window size increases. We use target=both to obtain overall adaptation scores involving both speakers, and calculate DAS with all but the Personality LIWC feature sets introduced in Sec. 4. We first compute DAS on the whole dialog level for each window size, and then calculate the average DAS for each window size

---

[7]To ensure two way adaptation exists in every segment (both speaker A adapting to B, and B adapting to A), the minimum length (number of turns) of each segment is 3. Thus we only work with dialogs longer than 15 turns in SWBD.

[8]Using Simple Linear Regression in Weka 3.8.1.

[9]In task-oriented dialogs, D stands for Director, F for Follower. In SWBD, D stands for the speaker initiating the call.

across the corpus.

Results show that DAS scores for the original dialogs in all corpora decrease as window size increases, while DAS scores for the randomized dialogs stay relatively stable. Figure 6 in Appendix shows plots of average DAS scores on different window sizes for original and randomized dialogs. Plots of the AWC and WAC show similar trends. Experiments with larger window sizes show that the original and random scores meet at window size 6 - 7 (with different versions of randomized dialogs). In MapTask, the original and random scores meet at window size 3 - 4. In SWBD, original and random scores meet at window size 2.

6 Related Work

Recent measures of linguistic adaptation fall into three categories: probabilistic measures, repetition decay measures, and document similarity measures (Xu and Reitter, 2015). Probabilistic measures compute the probability of a single linguistic feature appearing in the target after its appearance in the prime. Some measures in this category focus more on comparing adaptation amongst features and do not handle turn by turn adaptation (Church, 2000; Stenchikova and Stent, 2007). Moreover, these measures produce scores for individual features, which need aggregation to reflect overall adaptivity (Danescu-Niculescu-Mizil et al., 2011, 2012). Document similarity measures calculate the similarity between prime and target by measuring the number of features that appear in both prime and target, normalized by the size of the two text sets (Wang et al., 2014). Both probabilistic measures and document similarity measures require the whole dialog to be complete before calculation.

Repetition decay measures observe the decay rate of repetition probability of linguistic features. Previous work has fit the probability of linguistic feature repetition decrease with the distance between prime and target in logarithmic decay models (Reitter et al., 2006a,b; Reitter, 2008), linear decay models (Ward and Litman, 2007), and exponential decay models (Pietsch et al., 2012).

Previous work on linguistic adaptation in natural language generation has also attempted to use adaptation models learned from human conversations. The alignment-capable microplanner SPUD *prime* (Buschmeier et al., 2009, 2010) uses the repetition decay model from Reitter (2008) as part of the activation functions for linguistic structures. However, the parameters are not learned from real data. Repetition decay models do well in statistical parameterized NLG, but is hard to apply to overgenerate and rank NLG. Isard et al. (2006) apply a pre-trained n-grams adaptation model to generate conversations. Hu et al. (2014) explore the effects of adaptation to various features by human evaluations, but their generator is not capable of deciding which features to adapt based on input context. Dušek and Jurčíček (2016) use a seq2seq model to generate responses adapting to previous context. They utilize an n-gram match ranker that promotes outputs with phrase overlap with context. Our learned adaptation models could serve as a ranker. In addition to n-grams, DAS could produce models with any combinations of feature sets, providing more versatile adaptation behavior.

7 Discussion and Future Work

To obtain models of linguistic adaptation, most measures could only measure an individual feature at a time, and need the whole dialog to calculate the measure (Church, 2000; Stenchikova and Stent, 2007; Danescu-Niculescu-Mizil et al., 2012; Pietsch et al., 2012; Reitter et al., 2006b; Ward and Litman, 2007). This paper proposes the Dialog Adaptation Score (DAS) measure, which can be applied to NLG because it can be calculated on any segment of a dialog, and for any feature set.

We first validate our measure by showing that the average DAS of original dialogs is significantly higher than randomized dialogs, indicating that it is sensitive to dialog priming as intended. We then use DAS to show that feature sets such as LIWC, Syntactic Structure, and Hedge/Discourse Marker are adapted more than Bigram and Referring Expressions. We also demonstrate how we can use DAS to develop fine-grained models of adaptation: e.g. DAS applied to model adaptation in extraversion displays a distinct trend compared to all LIWC features in the task-oriented dialog corpus AWC. Finally, we show that the degree of adaptation decreases as the window size increases. We leave to future work the implementation and evaluation of DAS adaptation models in natural language generation systems.

Acknowledgement

This research was supported by NSF CISE RI EAGER #IIS-1044693, NSF CISE CreativeIT #IIS-1002921, NSF CHS #IIS-1115742, Nuance Foundation Grant SC-14-74, and auxiliary REU supplements.

References

Anne H Anderson, Miles Bader, Ellen Gurman Bard, Elizabeth Boyle, Gwyneth Doherty, Simon Garrod, Stephen Isard, Jacqueline Kowtko, Jan McAllister, Jim Miller, et al. 1991. The hcrc map task corpus. *Language and speech* 34(4):351–366.

Regina Barzilay and Mirella Lapata. 2005. Collective content selection for concept-to-text generation. In *Proceedings of the conference on Human Language Technology and Empirical Methods in Natural Language Processing*. Association for Computational Linguistics, pages 331–338.

H.P. Branigan, M.J. Pickering, J. Pearson, and J.F. McLean. 2010. Linguistic alignment between people and computers. *Journal of Pragmatics* 42(9):2355–2368.

Susan E Brennan and Herbert H Clark. 1996. Conceptual pacts and lexical choice in conversation. *Journal of Experimental Psychology: Learning, Memory, and Cognition* 22(6):1482.

Susan E Brennan, Katharina S Schuhmann, and Karla M Batres. 2013. Entrainment on the move and in the lab: The walking around corpus. In *Proc. of the 35th Annual Conference of the Cognitive Science Society. Austin, TX: Cognitive Science Society*.

Carsten Brockmann. 2009. *Personality and Alignment Processes in Dialogue: Towards a Lexically-Based Unified Model*. Ph.D. thesis, University of Edinburgh, School of Informatics.

Hendrik Buschmeier, Kirsten Bergmann, and Stefan Kopp. 2009. An alignment-capable microplanner for natural language generation. In *Proceedings of the 12th European Workshop on Natural Language Generation*. Association for Computational Linguistics, pages 82–89.

Hendrik Buschmeier, Kirsten Bergmann, and Stefan Kopp. 2010. Modelling and evaluation of lexical and syntactic alignment with a priming-based microplanner. *Empirical methods in natural language generation* 5980.

Tanya L Chartrand and John A Bargh. 1999. The chameleon effect: The perception–behavior link and social interaction. *Journal of personality and social psychology* 76(6):893.

Kenneth W Church. 2000. Empirical estimates of adaptation: the chance of two noriegas is closer to p/2 than p 2. In *Proc. of the 18th conference on Computational linguistics-Volume 1*. pages 180–186.

N. Coupland, J. Coupland, H. Giles, and K. Henwood. 1988. Accommodating the elderly: Invoking and extending a theory. *Language in Society* 17(1):1–41.

Cristian Danescu-Niculescu-Mizil, Michael Gamon, and Susan Dumais. 2011. Mark my words!: linguistic style accommodation in social media. In *Proceedings of the 20th international conference on World wide web*. ACM, pages 745–754.

Cristian Danescu-Niculescu-Mizil, Lillian Lee, Bo Pang, and Jon Kleinberg. 2012. Echoes of power: Language effects and power differences in social interaction. In *Proceedings of the 21st international conference on World Wide Web*. ACM, pages 699–708.

Ondřej Dušek and Filip Jurčíček. 2016. A context-aware natural language generator for dialogue systems. In *Proceedings of the SIGDIAL 2016 Conference*. Association for Computational Linguistics, pages 185–190.

Jessica Ficler and Yoav Goldberg. 2017. Controlling linguistic style aspects in neural language generation. *arXiv preprint arXiv:1707.02633* .

Sudeep Gandhe and David Traum. 2008. An evaluation understudy for dialogue coherence models. In *Proceedings of the 9th SIGdial Workshop on Discourse and Dialogue*. Association for Computational Linguistics, pages 172–181.

Alastair J Gill, Carsten Brockmann, and Jon Oberlander. 2012. Perceptions of alignment and personality in generated dialogue. In *Proc. of the Seventh International Natural Language Generation Conference*. pages 40–48.

John J Godfrey, Edward C Holliman, and Jane McDaniel. 1992. Switchboard: Telephone speech corpus for research and development. In *Acoustics, Speech, and Signal Processing, 1992. ICASSP-92., 1992 IEEE International Conference on*. IEEE, volume 1, pages 517–520.

Zhichao Hu, Gabrielle Halberg, Carolynn R Jimenez, and Marilyn A Walker. 2014. Entrainment in pedestrian direction giving: How many kinds of entrainment? In *Situated Dialog in Speech-Based Human-Computer Interaction*, Springer, pages 151–164.

Amy Isard, Carsten Brockmann, and Jon Oberlander. 2006. Individuality and alignment in generated dialogues. In *Proceedings of the Fourth International Natural Language Generation Conference*. Association for Computational Linguistics, pages 25–32.

Dan Jurafsky, Elizabeth Shriberg, and Debra Biasca. 1997. Switchboard swbd-damsl shallow-discourse-function annotation coders manual. *Institute of Cognitive Science Technical Report* pages 97–102.

Grace Lin and Marilyn Walker. 2017. Stylistic variation in television dialogue for natural language generation. In *EMNLP Workshop on Stylistic Variation*.

Kris Liu, Jean E Fox Tree, and Marilyn A Walker. 2016. Coordinating communication in the wild: The artwalk dialogue corpus of pedestrian navigation and mobile referential communication. In *LREC*.

François Mairesse, Marilyn A. Walker, Matthias R. Mehl, and Roger K. Moore. 2007. Using linguistic cues for the automatic recognition of personality in conversation and text. *Journal of Artificial Intelligence Research (JAIR)* 30:457–500.

Francois Mairesse and Marilyn A. Walker. 2011. Controlling user perceptions of linguistic style: Trainable generation of personality traits. *Computational Linguistics* .

Christopher D. Manning, Mihai Surdeanu, John Bauer, Jenny Finkel, Steven J. Bethard, and David McClosky. 2014. The Stanford CoreNLP natural language processing toolkit. In *Proceedings of 52nd Annual Meeting of the Association for Computational Linguistics: System Demonstrations*. pages 55–60. http://www.aclweb.org/anthology/P/P14/P14-5010.

Matthias R. Mehl, Samuel D. Gosling, and James W. Pennebaker. 2006. Personality in its natural habitat: Manifestations and implicit folk theories of personality in daily life. *Journal of Personality and Social Psychology* 90:862–877.

Shereen Oraby, Lena Reed, Shubhanghi Tandon, Sharath T.S., Stephanie Lukin, and Marilyn Walker. 2018. Controlling personality-based stylistic variation with neural natural language generators. In *Proceedings of the SIGDIAL 2018 Conference: The 19th Annual Meeting of the Special Interest Group on Discourse and Dialogue*. Association for Computational Linguistics.

Daniel S. Paiva and Roger Evans. 2004. A framework for stylistically controlled generation. In Anja Belz, Roger Evans, and Paul Piwek, editors, *Natural Language Generation, Third Internatonal Conference, INLG 2004*. Springer, number 3123 in LNAI, pages 120–129.

Gabriel Parent and Maxine Eskenazi. 2010. Lexical entrainment of real users in the lets go spoken dialog system. In *Proceedings Interspeech*. pages 3018–3021.

Rebecca J. Passonneau and Diane Litman. 1996. Empirical analysis of three dimensions of spoken discourse: Segmentation, coherence and linguistic devices. In Donia Scott and Eduard Hovy, editors, *Computational and Conversational Discourse: Burning Issues - An Interdisciplinary Account*, Springer-Verlag, Heidelberg, Germany, pages 161–194.

J. W. Pennebaker, M. E. Francis, and R. J. Booth. 2001. *Inquiry and Word Count: LIWC 2001*. Lawrence Erlbaum, Mahwah, NJ.

J. W. Pennebaker and L. A. King. 1999. Linguistic styles: Language use as an individual difference. *Journal of Personality and Social Psychology* 77:1296–1312.

Christian Pietsch, Armin Buch, Stefan Kopp, and Jan de Ruiter. 2012. Measuring syntactic priming in dialogue corpora. *Empirical Approaches to Linguistic Theory: Studies in Meaning and Structure* 111:29.

David Reitter. 2008. *Context effects in language production: models of syntactic priming in dialogue corpora*. Ph.D. thesis, University of Edinburgh. http://www.david-reitter.com/pub/reitter2008phd.pdf.

David Reitter, Frank Keller, and Johanna D Moore. 2006a. Computational modelling of structural priming in dialogue. In *Proceedings of the Human Language Technology Conference of the NAACL, Companion Volume: Short Papers*. Association for Computational Linguistics, pages 121–124.

David Reitter and Johanna D Moore. 2007. Predicting success in dialogue. In *Annual Meeting-Association for Computational Linguistics*. volume 45, page 808.

David Reitter, Johanna D. Moore, and Frank Keller. 2006b. Priming of syntactic rules in task-oriented dialogue and spontaneous conversation. In *Proceedings of the 28th Annual Conference of the Cognitive Science Society*. Cognitive Science Society, Vancouver, Canada, pages 685–690. http://www.david-reitter.com/pub/reitter2006priming.pdf.

Svetlana Stenchikova and Amanda Stent. 2007. Measuring adaptation between dialogs. In *Proc. of the 8th SIGdial Workshop on Discourse and Dialogue*.

Yafei Wang, David Reitter, and John Yen. 2014. Linguistic adaptation in online conversation threads: analyzing alignment in online health communities. In *Proceedings of the Fifth Workshop on Cognitive Modeling and Computational Linguistics (at ACL)*. Baltimore, Maryland, USA, pages 55–62. http://www.david-reitter.com/pub/yafei2014cmcl.pdf.

Arthur Ward and Diane Litman. 2007. Automatically measuring lexical and acoustic/prosodic convergence in tutorial dialog corpora. In *Proc. of the SLaTE Workshop on Speech and Language Technology in Education*.

Michael Willemyns, Cynthia Gallois, Victor J Callan, and Jeffery Pittam. 1997. Accent accommodation in the job interview impact of interviewer accent and gender. *Journal of Language and Social Psychology* 16(1):3–22.

Yang Xu and David Reitter. 2015. An evaluation and comparison of linguistic alignment measures. In *Proc. Cognitive Modeling and Computational Linguistics*. Association for Computational Linguistics, Denver, CO, pages 58–67. http://www.david-reitter.com/pub/xu2015evaluation-alignment.pdf.

Appendix

Figure 5 and Figure 6.

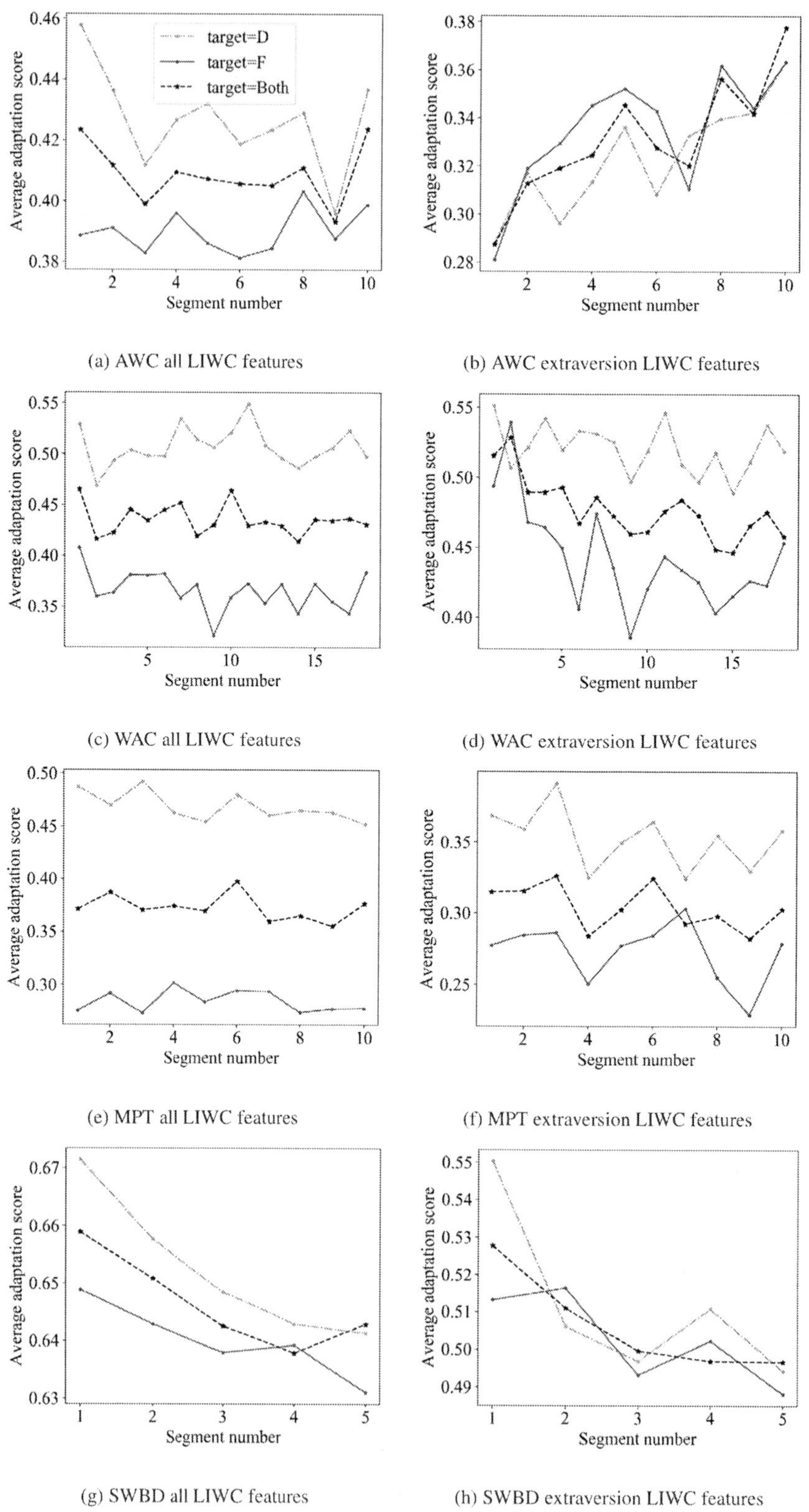

(a) AWC all LIWC features

(b) AWC extraversion LIWC features

(c) WAC all LIWC features

(d) WAC extraversion LIWC features

(e) MPT all LIWC features

(f) MPT extraversion LIWC features

(g) SWBD all LIWC features

(h) SWBD extraversion LIWC features

Figure 5: Plots of average DAS as the dialogs progress, using all LIWC features vs. extraversion LIWC features.

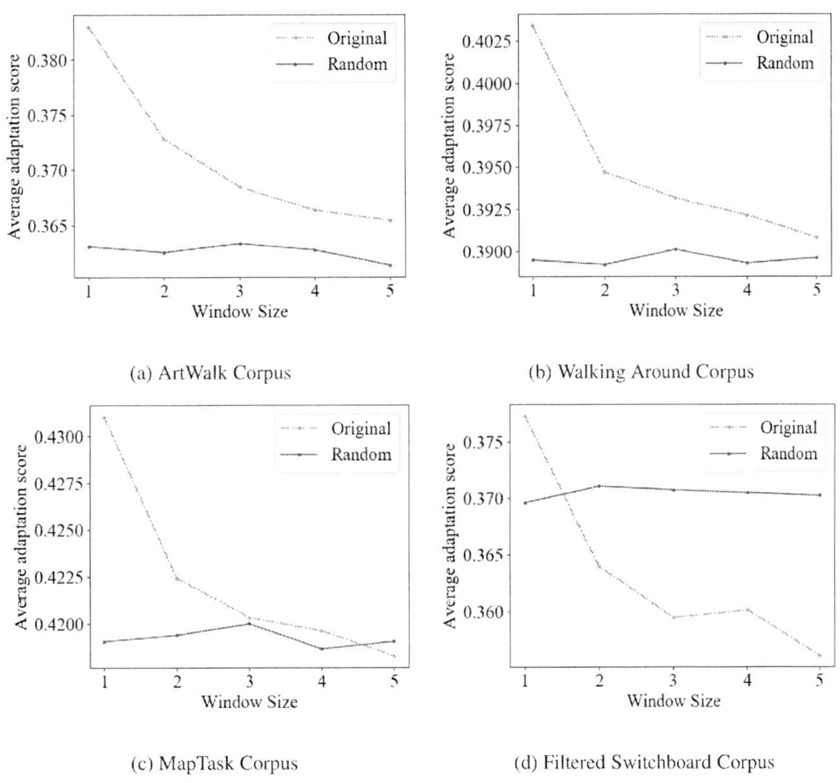

(a) ArtWalk Corpus

(b) Walking Around Corpus

(c) MapTask Corpus

(d) Filtered Switchboard Corpus

Figure 6: Plots of average DAS on different window sizes (1 to 5) for original dialogs vs. randomized dialogs, using all feature sets except Personality LIWC.

Estimating User Interest from Open-Domain Dialogue

Michimasa Inaba   **Kenichi Takahashi**

Hiroshima City University

3-4-1 Ozukahigashi, Asaminami-ku, Hiroshima, Japan

{inaba, takahashi}@hiroshima-cu.ac.jp

Abstract

Dialogue personalization is an important issue in the field of open-domain chat-oriented dialogue systems. If these systems could consider their users' interests, user engagement and satisfaction would be greatly improved. This paper proposes a neural network-based method for estimating users' interests from their utterances in chat dialogues to personalize dialogue systems' responses. We introduce a method for effectively extracting topics and user interests from utterances and also propose a pre-training approach that increases learning efficiency. Our experimental results indicate that the proposed model can estimate user's interest more accurately than baseline approaches.

1 Introduction

Chat is a very important part of human communication. In fact, it has been reported that it makes up about 62% of all conversations (Koiso et al., 2016). Since chat is also important for human-to-machine communication, studies of dialogue systems that aim to enable open-domain chat have received much attention in recent years (Ritter et al., 2011; Higashinaka et al., 2014; Sordoni et al., 2015; Vinyals and Le, 2015; Zhao et al., 2017). In these studies, dialogue personalization is an important issue: if such systems could consider users' experiences and interests when engaging them in a conversation, it would greatly improve user satisfaction. To this end, Hirano et al. extracted predicate-argument structures (Hirano et al., 2015), Zhang and Chai focused on conversational entailment (Zhang and Chai, 2009, 2010) and Bang et al. extracted entity relationships (Bang et al., 2015). These studies aimed to employ users' utterance histories to generate personalized responses.

In contrast, this study aims to estimate the user's interest in particular topics (e.g., music, fashion, or health) to personalize the dialogue system's responses based on these interests. This would allow it to focus on topics the user is interested in and avoid topics they dislike, enhancing user engagement and satisfaction.

This paper therefore proposes a neural network-based method for estimating users' interests using their utterances in chat dialogues. Our method estimates their levels of interest not only in topics that appear in the dialogues, but also in other topics that have not appeared. Even if a user enjoys talking about the current topic, they will get bored if the system talks about it endlessly. By gauging the user's potential interest in topics that have not directly appeared in the dialogue, the system can expand the discussion to other topics before the user gets bored.

In this study, we use data from human-to-human dialogues because the current performance of chat-oriented dialogue systems is not sufficient for them to talk with humans naturally. We also use textual dialogue data to avoid speech recognition issues. In addition, to estimate the target user's interests independently of the dialogue system's utterances, we only consider their own utterances and ignore those of their dialogue partner.

This paper brings three main contributions, as follows. 1. We propose a topic-specific sentence attention approach that enables topics and user interests to be efficiently extracted from utterances. 2. We develop a method for pre-training our model's utterance encoder, so it learns what topics are related to each target user's utterance. 3. We show experimentally that the proposed sentence attention and pre-training methods can provide high performance when used together.

Proceedings of the SIGDIAL 2018 Conference, pages 32–40,
Melbourne, Australia, 12-14 July 2018. ©2018 Association for Computational Linguistics

2 Related Work

Many studies related to estimating user interest from text data have targeted social network services (SNS), especially Twitter users. For example, Chen et al. proposed a method of modeling interest using the frequencies of words in tweets by the target user and followers (Chen et al., 2010). Some methods have also been proposed that consider superordinate concepts acquired from knowledge bases. For example, Abel et al. modeled Twitter users using the appearance frequencies of certain named entities (e.g., people, events, or music groups), acquired using OpenCalais [1] (Abel et al., 2011). In addition, some methods have used categories from Wikipedia (Michelson and Macskassy, 2010; Kapanipathi et al., 2014; Zarrinkalam et al., 2015) or DBPedia (Kapanipathi et al., 2011). Several methods have also been proposed that use topic models, such as latent dirichlet allocation (LDA) (Weng et al., 2010; Bhattacharya et al., 2014; Han and Lee, 2016). However, it is difficult to apply such methods directly to dialogue because they assume that users are posting about subjects they are interested in. This is a reasonable assumption for SNS data, but in conversations, people do not always limit themselves to topics they are interested in. For instance, people will play along and discuss subjects the other persons are interested in, even if they are not interested in them, as well.

Other studies have attempted to estimate users' levels of interest (LOI) from dialogues. Schuller et al. tackled the task of estimating listeners' interest in a product from dialogues between them and someone introducing a particular product, proposing a support vector machine (SVM)-based method incorporating acoustic and linguistic features (Schuller et al., 2006)· In 2010, LOI estimation was selected as a sub-challenge of the INTERSPEECH Paralinguistic Challenge (Schuller et al., 2006), but there the focus was on single-topic (product) interest estimation from spoken dialogue, not open-domain estimation. In addition, that task considered business dialogues, not chats.

3 Model Architecture

The task considered in this paper is as follows. Given an utterance set $U_s = (u_1, u_2, ..., u_n)$ ut-

[1]http://www.opencalais.com/

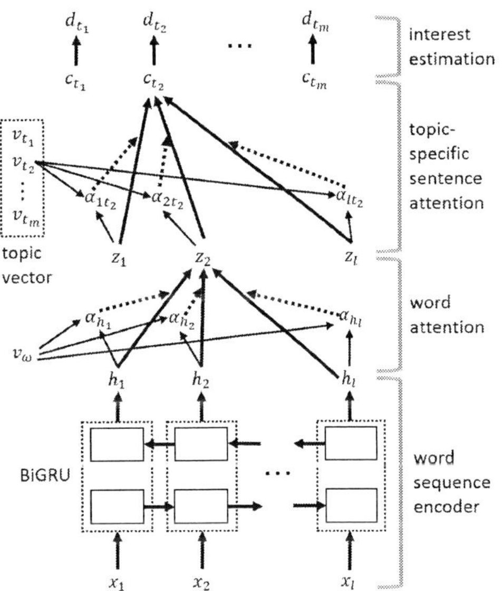

Figure 1: Overview of the proposed interest estimation model.

tered by a speaker s during dialogues with other speakers, we estimate their degrees of interest $Y_s = (y_1, y_2, ..., y_m)$ in topics in a given topic set $T = (t_1, t_2, ..., t_m)$. Here, the t_i correspond to concrete topics, such as movies or travel while y_i indicates the speaker's level of interest in t_i, on the three-point scale used for the LOI estimation task described in the previous section. Using this scale, the y_i can take the values 0 (disinterest, indifference and neutrality), 1 (light interest), or 2 (strong interest).

To accurately gauge the speaker's interest from their utterances, we believe it is important to extract the following two types of information efficiently.

- The topic of each utterance

- How interested the speaker is in the topic

Our proposed interest estimation model extracts this information efficiently and uses a pre-training method to improve learning. Figure 1 presents an overview of our neural network model, which first encodes the word sequence, applies word attention and topic-specific sentence attention, and finally estimates the degrees of interest $D_s = (d_{t_1}, d_{t_2}, ..., d_{t_m})$. The proposed pre-training method is used for the word sequence encoder. The model is described in detail below.

3.1 Word Sequence Encoder

The word sequence encoder converts utterances into fixed-length vectors using a recurrent neural network (RNN). First, the words in each utterance are converted into word vectors using Word2vec (Mikolov et al., 2013), giving word vector sequences $x = (x_1, x_2, ..., x_l)$. The RNN encoder uses a hidden bidirectional-GRU (BiGRU) layer, which consists of a forward GRU that reads from x_1 to x_l in order and a backward GRU that reads from x_l to x_1 in reverse order. The forward GRU computes the forward hidden states $\overrightarrow{h_i}$ as follows.

$$\overrightarrow{h_i} = \overrightarrow{GRU}(x_i, \overrightarrow{h_{i-1}}) \qquad (1)$$

The backward GRU calculates the backward hidden states $\overleftarrow{h_i}$ in a similar way. By combining the outputs of both GRUs, we obtain the objective hidden state h_i:

$$h_i = [\overrightarrow{h_i} : \overleftarrow{h_i}] \qquad (2)$$

where $[:]$ represents vector concatenation.

3.2 Topic Classification Pre-Training

Estimating the user's level of interest in each topic requires first assessing the topic of each utterance. Since this is not given explicitly, the model must infer this information from the utterance set and degrees of interest in each topic, so the learning difficulty is high. In this study, based on the idea of pre-training (Erhan et al., 2010), we introduce a new pre-training method for the sentence topic classification task to the word sequence encoder. The important point to note about this task is that the topic classes involved are identical to those in the topic set Y_s. This helps to reduce the difficulty of learning to estimate the relationships between utterances and topics and allows the model to focus on interest estimation during the main training phase.

During pre-training, the classification probability p for each topic is calculated as follows, based on the output h_l of the BiGRU after inputting the last word vector x_l. (Word attention, as described in the next section, is not used in pre-training.)

$$p = softmax(W_c h_l + b_c) \qquad (3)$$

where W_c and b_c are parameters for topic classification. The cross-entropy is used as the loss function during pre-training.

3.3 Word Attention

Based on an idea from Yang et al., we also included word attention in our model (Yang et al., 2016). Word attention is based on the idea that all words do not contribute equally to the desired result and involves using an attention mechanism to weight each word differently. The resulting utterance vector z is obtained as follows.

$$v_{hi} = tanh(W_\omega h_i + b_\omega) \qquad (4)$$

$$\alpha_{hi} = \frac{\exp(v_{hi}^{\mathrm{T}} v_\omega)}{\sum_i \exp(v_{hi}^{\mathrm{T}} v_\omega)} \qquad (5)$$

$$z = \sum_i \alpha_{hi} h_i \qquad (6)$$

where W_ω and b_ω are parameters. Unlike the original attention mechanism used in neural translation (Bahdanau et al., 2015) and neural dialogue (Shang et al., 2015) models, the word attention mechanism uses a common parameter, called context vector v_ω to calculate weight α_i for each hidden state. v_ω is a high-level representation for calculating word importance and, like the model's other parameters, is randomly initialized and then optimized.

3.4 Topic Specific Sentence Attention

Our model uses a word sequence encoder with word attention to convert the utterance set $U_s = (u_1, u_2, ..., u_n)$ into the utterance vector set $Z_s = (z_1, z_2, ..., z_n)$. It then extracts information for estimating the level of interest in each topic from Z_s, but, as with word attention, not all utterances contribute equally. Yang et al. proposed a sentence attention mechanism that takes the same approach as for word attention, but, since it uses only one parameter to calculate sentence importance (similar to the context vector v_ω for word attention), it is not capable of topic-specific estimation. This is because the important utterances in a given utterance set differ from topic to topic. For example, "I jog every morning" is probably useful for estimating interest in topics, such as sports or health, but not in, say, computers or vehicles.

In this study, we therefore propose a new topic-specific sentence attention approach. The topic vector v_{t_i} represents the importance of each sentence for topic t_i, and the associated content vector c_{t_i} is calculated as follows.

$$v_j = tanh(W_r z_j + b_r) \qquad (7)$$

$$\alpha_{jt_i} = \frac{\exp(v_j^\mathrm{T} v_{t_i})}{\sum_j \exp(v_j^\mathrm{T} v_{t_i})} \qquad (8)$$

$$c_{t_i} = \sum_j \alpha_{jt_i} z_j \qquad (9)$$

Here, W_r and b_r are shared, topic-independent parameters. The topic vector v_{t_i} is randomly initialized and then optimized during training.

3.5 Interest Estimation

We then use the content vector c_{jt_i} to compute the degree of interest d_{t_i} in topic t_i as follows.

$$d_{t_i} = tanh(W_{t_i} c_{t_i} + b_{t_i}) + 1 \qquad (10)$$

Here, the parameters W_{t_i} and b_{t_i} estimate the overall degree of interest in the topics t_i, and it is different for each topic after optimization. Finally, one is added, so that d_{t_i} uses the same 0 to 2 range as the correct values y_i.

During training, we use the mean squared error (MSE) between the correct answer y_i and d_{t_i} as the loss function:

$$L = \frac{1}{n} \sum_i^n (y_i - d_{t_i})^2 \qquad (11)$$

4 Experiments

We conducted a series of experiments to evaluate the proposed method's performance. For these, we created a dataset based on logs of one-to-one text chats between human subjects and the results of questionnaires answered by each subject. We also tested several baseline methods for comparison purposes.

4.1 Datasets

We asked each subject to first fill out a questionnaire about their interests and then engage in text chats in Japanese with partners they had not previously been acquainted with. We recruited 163 subjects via the CrowdWorks[2] crowd-sourcing site. The subjects were asked to rate their levels of interest in the 24 topic categories shown in Table 1 using a three-point scale discussed in Section 3. These topics were selected based on the categories used by Yahoo! Chiebukuro[3], a Japanese question-and-answer site, focusing on topics that are likely to appear in one-to-one dialogues between strangers.

[2] https://crowdworks.jp/
[3] https://chiebukuro.yahoo.co.jp/

Table 1: Topic Categories

Travel	Movies	Celebrities
Music	Reading	Anime / Manga
Games	Computers	Home Appliances
Beauty	Fashion	Sports / Exercise
Health	School	Outdoor Activities
Housing	Housekeeping	Marriage / Love
Animals	Family	Cooking / Meal
Vehicles	History	Politics / Economy

Table 2: Example dialogue (translated by authors)

A	Let's start a conversation. Nice to meet you.
B	Hi, nice to meet you.
A	What are your hobbies?
B	Currently, I am living a pet-centered lifestyle. So, raising pets is my hobby.
A	Which pets do you have?
B	I have three cats and they are lively.
A	Three cats. That sounds great! Are they mixed breed?
B	Yes, they are all mixed breed cats. They are low-maintenance and easy to keep. Do you have any animals?

Each dialogue lasted for one hour and was conducted via Skype instant messaging. We only instructed the subjects to "Please try to find things you and your partner are both interested in and then try to broaden your conversation about these subjects." We gave the subjects no specific instructions as to the intended content or topics of their conversations. Table 2 shows an example dialogue between subject A and B.

All the utterances in the chat data were then classified by subject. Each data point consisted of all the data about one subject, namely their chat ut-

Table 3: Data Statistics

Number of users (data points)	163
Number of dialogues	408
Number of utterances	49029
Avg. number of strong interest topics	11.48
Avg. number of light interest topics	7.30
Avg. number of neutral topics	5.21

terances and questionnaire responses (correspond to U_s and Y_s defined in Section 3). The data was evaluated using 10-fold cross-validation and their statistics are shown in Table 3.

4.2 Settings

Word2Vec (Mikolov et al., 2013) was trained using 100 GB of Twitter data with 200 embedding cells, a minimum word frequency of 10, and a skip-gram window size of 5.

The word sequence encoder was a single-layer BiGRU RNN with 200 input cells and 400 output cells. The word and sentence attention layers had 400 input and output cells while the estimation layer had 400 input cells and 1 output cell. The model was trained using Adam (Kingma and Ba, 2015).

During pre-training, we used questions and answers from the Yahoo! Chiebukuro Data (2nd edition))[4] for each topic. All topics were equally covered, and a total of 770k sentences were used for training while 2400 sentences (100 for each topic) were used for testing. After pre-training, the topic classification accuracy for the test data was 0.755.

4.3 Evaluation

When using the proposed method as part of a dialogue system, it is effective to select the best topic from those available for the system to generate an appropriate response. Therefore, in this experiment, each topic was ranked based on the estimated degree of interest d_{t_i}, and the methods were evaluated based on whether the topics the user was interested in should have been ranked higher or the other topics ranked lower. The rankings were evaluated using the normalized discounted cumulative gain ($NDCG$), a widely used metric in the field of information retrieval. This gives values between 0 and 1, with higher values indicating more accurate

ranking predictions and is calculated as follows.

$$NDCG@k = \frac{DCG_k}{IDCG_k} \quad (12)$$

$$DCG_k = rel_i + \sum_{i=2}^{K} \frac{rel_i}{log_2 i} \quad (13)$$

Here, k is the number of top-ranked objects used for the $NDCG$ calculation, and rel_i is the graded relevance of the result at position i, which was given by the degree of interest Y_s in this experiment. The ideal DCG ($IDCG$) is the DCG if the ranking list had been correctly ordered by relevance.

In addition, to evaluate the accuracy of the estimated degrees of interest in each topic, we also calculated the MSEs between the results of each method and the correct answers.

4.4 Baseline Methods

To evaluate the proposed model, we also conducted experiments using the following three modified models.

Without Pre-Training · ·

To evaluate the effectiveness of topic classification pre-training, we tested our model without this step. Instead, the word sequence encoder was randomly initialized and then trained. This model was otherwise identical to the proposed method.

Without Sentence Attention · ·

To evaluate the effectiveness of topic-specific sentence attention, we tried instead using max-pooling to obtain the content vector. Again, this model was identical to the proposed method.

Without Pre-Training or Sentence Attention

This model combined the two modifications mentioned above: it did not use topic classification pre-training and used max-pooling to obtain the content vectors, but was otherwise identical to the proposed method.

We also compared our model's performance to those of the following two baseline methods.

Topic Frequency · ·

The first baseline was based on a method, proposed by Abel et al., that identifies the named entities (such as people, events, or

<hr>

[4]http://www.nii.ac.jp/dsc/idr/yahoo/chiebkr2/Y_chiebuku ro.html

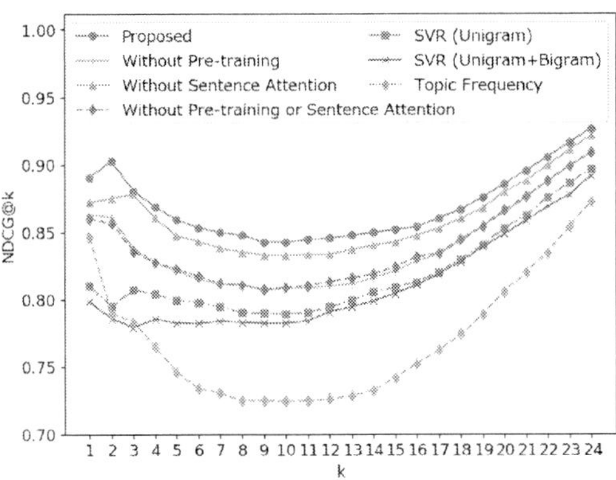

Figure 2: NDCG@k results for all methods, for k between 1 and 24.

Table 4: Mean Squared Error

Proposed	**0.533**
Without Pre-Training	0.580
Without Sentence Attention	0.561
Without Pre-Training or Sentence Attention	0.568
SVR (unigram)	0.597
SVR (unigram + bigram)	0.611

music groups) associated with words in the user's tweets using OpenCalais and models the user's interests using a named entity frequency vector (Abel et al., 2011). However, as we used Japanese dialogues, we could not use OpenCalais, so we instead used the topic classifier described in Section 3.2. Since this classifier is trained for classification for sentences and not for words, we employed sentence level topic frequency. The topic frequency was used to gauge the user's interest, and the topics were ranked in frequency order.

SVR · ·

The second baseline method used support vector regression (SVR) to estimate the degree of interest. We conducted experiments using only unigrams, and using both unigrams and bigrams. We used the RBF kernel function. The SVR models were trained for each topic individually and then used to estimate the degrees of interest.

4.5 Results

Figure 2 shows the $NDCG$ results for the topics ranked in the top k. These indicate that the proposed method performed better than the other methods for all values of k. Comparing the performances of the methods that used pre-training ("Proposed" and "Without Sentence Attention") with those of the ones that did not ("Without Pre-Training" and "Without Pre-Training or Sentence Attention") indicates that the proposed pre-training step was effective. On the other hand, a method that used sentence attention ("Without Pre-Training") showed nearly the same results as one that did not ("Without Pre-Training or Sentence Attention"), although the latter did achieve higher NDCGs for $k \geq 5$. This indicates that using sentence attention alone does not improve performance. However, the proposed method performed better than the method without sentence attention, confirming that sentence attention is useful, but only if it is used in conjunction with pre-training.

Turning now to the SVR-based methods, we observe that using only unigram features worked better than using both unigrams and bigrams, although both methods were still inferior to the neural network-based methods, including the proposed method.

When $k = 1$, the topic frequency baseline achieved higher $NDCG$s than the SVR-based methods, because it correctly noted that users were strongly interested in the topics they spoke about most frequently. However, these results were still inferior to those of the neural network-based methods. Furthermore, it presented the worst $NDCG$ results among all the methods for $k \geq 4$, due to speakers sometimes talking about subjects they were not interested in, as discussed in Section 2.

Table 4 shows the MSEs between the degree of interest results for each method and the correct answers (excluding Topic Frequency, which cannot output the degree of interest). The proposed method gave significantly smaller MSE value, indicating that its estimates were the most accurate. In addition, the "Without Pre-Training" method showed the lowest performance of all the neural network-based methods, also indicating that the proposed sentence attention approach is not effective without also using pre-training.

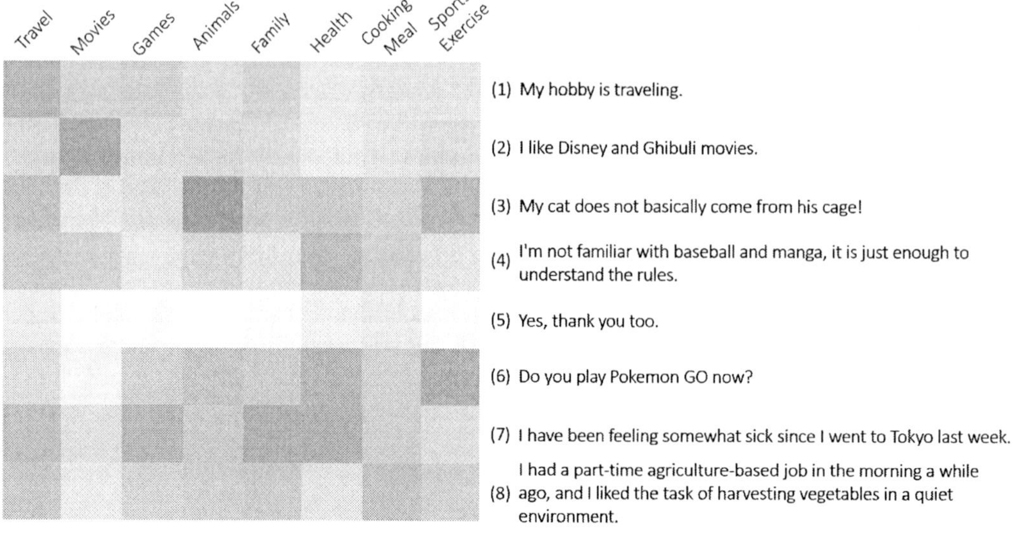

Figure 3: Visualization of Attention (Proposed)

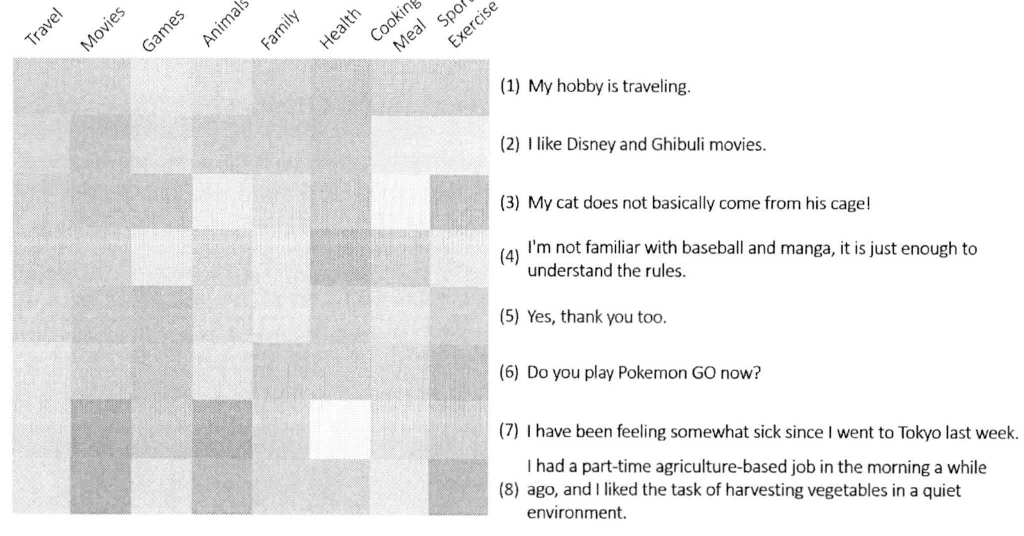

Figure 4: Visualization of Attention (Without Pre-Training)

4.6 Discussion

The experimental results discussed in the previous section indicate that it is important to use the proposed pre-training and sentence attention steps together. To analyze the sentence attention mechanism further, we visualized the sentence weights α_{jt_i} given by equation (8) for selected topics and utterances. Figures 3 and 4 show the sentence weights with and without pre-training, respectively. Here, darker cells indicate higher α_{jt_i} values.

Figure 3 shows that the sentence weights for the topics corresponding to the actual meaning of the sentence are high. (1), (2) and (3) are easy-to-understand examples. The topics related to each utterance take the highest weights. In addition, utterance (4) includes sports-related words, such as "baseball" and "rule", but the weight of the "Sports / Exercise" topic is not high because the utterance did not indicate such an interest on the part of the speaker. Thus, the sentence weights do not simply reflect the topics of the words, but also the user's level of interest in the topic. Interestingly, although the utterance (6) refers to the smartphone game "Pokemon GO", the weight of the "Game" topic is not very high, but those of the "Sports/Exercise" and "Health" topics are both high. Pokemon GO is interesting to people who do not usually play games, and this appears to be reflected in the results. On the other hand, utterance (7) shows high weights for several topics that intuitively appear to be unrelated to the utterance itself.

The sentence weights shown in Figure 4 often do not correspond to the topics or meanings of the utterances. For example, utterance (5) is not important for interest estimation and its weights in Figure 3 are small. However, in Figure 4, all weights are relatively high. Similarly, utterances (7) and (8) show high weights for unrelated topics.

The above results confirm that the pre-training step is important for learning the topic-specific sentence attention correctly. Without pre-training, the model must learn the relationships between utterances and topics by starting from a clean slate, and the difficulty of this task makes harder to determine the appropriate results. The experimental results in the previous section show that pre-training makes this task easier and improves performance. With proper training, topic-specific sentence attention then enabled the proposed method to achieve the best performance.

5 Conclusion

In this paper, we have presented a neural network-based method for estimating users' levels of interest in a pre-determined list of topics based on their utterances in chat dialogues. The proposed method first encodes utterances by using BiGRU and considering word attention, a set of utterance vectors was obtained. It then uses these to generate content vectors corresponding to each topic via topic-specific sentence attention. Finally, it uses the content vectors to estimate the user's degree of interest in each topic. The utterance encoder is pre-trained to classify sentences by topic before the whole model is trained. Our experimental results showed that the proposed method can estimate degrees of interest in topics more accurately than baseline methods. In addition, we found that it was most effecting to use topic-specific sentence attention and topic classification pre-training in combination.

In future work, we plan to apply the proposed method to a dialogue system and conduct dialogue experiments with human users. Even if we can estimate which topics a user is interested in, generating and selecting concrete utterances remains a challenging problem. For example, users who are interested in sports are not equally interested in all of them: someone may be interested in football but not in golf, for instance. We therefore plan to develop an appropriate way of incorporating the proposed method into such a system.

Acknowledgements

The Yahoo! Chiebukuro Data (2nd edition) provided to National Institute of Informatics by Yahoo Japan Corporation was used in this study.

This study received a grant of JSPS Grants-in-aid for Scientific Research 16H05880.

References

Fabian Abel, Qi Gao, Geert-Jan Houben, and Ke Tao. 2011. Analyzing user modeling on twitter for personalized news recommendations. *User Modeling, Adaption and Personalization* pages 1–12.

Dzmitry Bahdanau, Kyunghyun Cho, and Yoshua Bengio. 2015. Neural machine translation by jointly learning to align and translate. *Proc. ICLR* .

Jeesoo Bang, Hyungjong Noh, Yonghee Kim, and Gary Geunbae Lee. 2015. Example-based chat-oriented dialogue system with personalized long-term memory. In *IEEE International Conference on Big Data and Smart Computing (BigComp)*. pages 238–243.

Parantapa Bhattacharya, Muhammad Bilal Zafar, Niloy Ganguly, Saptarshi Ghosh, and Krishna P Gummadi. 2014. Inferring user interests in the twitter social network. In *Proceedings of the 8th ACM Conference on Recommender systems*. ACM, pages 357–360.

Jilin Chen, Rowan Nairn, Les Nelson, Michael Bernstein, and Ed Chi. 2010. Short and tweet: experiments on recommending content from information streams. In *Proceedings of the SIGCHI Conference on Human Factors in Computing Systems*. ACM, pages 1185–1194.

Dumitru Erhan, Yoshua Bengio, Aaron Courville, Pierre-Antoine Manzagol, Pascal Vincent, and Samy Bengio. 2010. Why does unsupervised pre-training help deep learning? *Journal of Machine Learning Research* 11(Feb):625–660.

Jonghyun Han and Hyunju Lee. 2016. Characterizing the interests of social media users: Refinement of a topic model for incorporating heterogeneous media. *Information Sciences* 358:112–128.

Ryuichiro Higashinaka, Kenji Imamura, Toyomi Meguro, Chiaki Miyazaki, Nozomi Kobayashi, Hiroaki Sugiyama, Toru Hirano, Toshiro Makino, and Yoshihiro Matsuo. 2014. Towards an open-domain conversational system fully based on natural language processing. In *COLING*. pages 928–939.

Toru Hirano, Nozomi Kobayashi, Ryuichiro Higashinaka, Toshiro Makino, and Yoshihiro Matsuo. 2015. User information extraction for personalized dialogue systems. *The 19th Workshop on the Semantics and Pragmatics of Dialogue (SemDial)* pages 67–75.

Pavan Kapanipathi, Prateek Jain, Chitra Venkataramani, and Amit Sheth. 2014. User interests identification on twitter using a hierarchical knowledge base. In *European Semantic Web Conference*. Springer, pages 99–113.

Pavan Kapanipathi, Fabrizio Orlandi, Amit P Sheth, and Alexandre Passant. 2011. Personalized filtering of the twitter stream pages 6–13.

Diederik P Kingma and Jimmy Ba. 2015. Adam: A method for stochastic optimization. *Proceedings of the 3rd International Conference on Learning Representations* .

Hanae Koiso, Tomoyuki Tsuchiya, Ryoko Watanabe, Daisuke Yokomori, Masao Aizawa, and Yasuharu Den. 2016. Survey of conversational behavior: Towards the design of a balanced corpus of everyday japanese conversation. In *LREC 2016*.

Matthew Michelson and Sofus A Macskassy. 2010. Discovering users' topics of interest on twitter: a first look. In *Proceedings of the fourth workshop on Analytics for noisy unstructured text data*. ACM, pages 73–80.

Tomas Mikolov, Ilya Sutskever, Kai Chen, Greg S Corrado, and Jeff Dean. 2013. Distributed representations of words and phrases and their compositionality. In *Advances in neural information processing systems*. pages 3111–3119.

Alan Ritter, Colin Cherry, and William B Dolan. 2011. Data-driven response generation in social media. In *Proceedings of the conference on empirical methods in natural language processing*. pages 583–593.

Björn W Schuller, Niels Köhler, Ronald Müller, and Gerhard Rigoll. 2006. Recognition of interest in human conversational speech. In *INTERSPEECH*.

Lifeng Shang, Zhengdong Lu, and Hang Li. 2015. Neural Responding Machine for Short Text Conversation. *Proceedings of the 53th Annual Meeting of Association for Computational Linguistics and the 7th International Joint Conference on Natural Language Processing* pages 1577–1586.

Alessandro Sordoni, Michel Galley, Michael Auli, Chris Brockett, Yangfeng Ji, Margaret Mitchell, Jian-Yun Nie, Jianfeng Gao, and Bill Dolan. 2015. A neural network approach to context-sensitive generation of conversational responses. In *Proceedings of NAACL-HLT*.

Oriol Vinyals and Quoc Le. 2015. A neural conversational model. In *Proceedings of the ICML Deep Learning Workshop*. pages 1–7.

Jianshu Weng, Ee-Peng Lim, Jing Jiang, and Qi He. 2010. Twitterrank: finding topic-sensitive influential twitterers. In *Proceedings of the third ACM international conference on Web search and data mining*. ACM, pages 261–270.

Zichao Yang, Diyi Yang, Chris Dyer, Xiaodong He, Alexander J Smola, and Eduard H Hovy. 2016. Hierarchical attention networks for document classification. In *HLT-NAACL*. pages 1480–1489.

Fattane Zarrinkalam, Hossein Fani, Ebrahim Bagheri, Mohsen Kahani, and Weichang Du. 2015. Semantics-enabled user interest detection from twitter. In *Web Intelligence and Intelligent Agent Technology (WI-IAT), 2015 IEEE/WIC/ACM International Conference on*. IEEE, volume 1, pages 469–476.

Chen Zhang and Joyce Y Chai. 2009. What do we know about conversation participants: Experiments on conversation entailment. In *Proceedings of the SIGDIAL 2009 Conference*. pages 206–215.

Chen Zhang and Joyce Y Chai. 2010. Towards conversation entailment: An empirical investigation. In *Proceedings of the 2010 Conference on Empirical Methods in Natural Language Processing*. pages 756–766.

Tiancheng Zhao, Ran Zhao, and Maxine Eskenazi. 2017. Learning discourse-level diversity for neural dialog models using conditional variational autoencoders. In *Proceedings of the 55th Annual Meeting of the Association for Computational Linguistics (Volume 1: Long Papers)*. Association for Computational Linguistics, pages 654–664.

Does Ability Affect Alignment in Second Language Tutorial Dialogue?

Arabella Sinclair   **Adam Lopez**
Christopher G. Lucas
University of Edinburgh
s0934062@sms.ed.ac.uk
{alopez,clucas2}@inf.ed.ac.uk

Dragan Gasevic
Monash University
dragan.gasevic@monash.edu

Abstract

The role of alignment between interlocutors in second language learning is different to that in fluent conversational dialogue. Learners gain linguistic skill through increased alignment, yet the extent to which they can align will be constrained by their ability. Tutors may use alignment to teach and encourage the student, yet still must push the student and correct their errors, decreasing alignment. To understand how learner ability interacts with alignment, we measure the influence of ability on lexical priming, an indicator of alignment. We find that lexical priming in learner-tutor dialogues differs from that in conversational and task-based dialogues, and we find evidence that alignment increases with ability and with word complexity.

1 Introduction

The *Interactive Alignment Model* (Pickering and Garrod, 2004) suggests that successful dialogue arises from an alignment of representations (including phonological, lexical, syntactic and semantic), and therefore of speakers' situation models. This model assumes that these aspects of the speakers' language will align automatically as the dialogue progresses and will greatly simplify both production and comprehension in dialogue.

In a Second Language (L2) learning setting, a learner will have a more limited scope for alignment due to their situational understanding, and their proficiency will dictate to what extent they are capable of aligning lexically, syntactically and semantically (Pickering and Garrod, 2006). Even once a situational alignment is reached (i.e. the learner understands the context of their interlocutor's interaction with them) there remains the question of the learners *receptive* vs. *productive* vocabulary knowledge (words they understand when others use them vs. words they can use themselves), both of which are active in L2 dialogues (Takač, 2008) and constrain their scope for alignment. Student alignment therefore will also be influenced by the tutor's strategy; or by how much of the student's receptive language the tutor produces which facilitates the student productive ability in this context.

We expect that alignment within L2 learner dialogue will differ from alignment in fluent dialogues due to the different constraints mentioned above (Costa et al., 2008). We also expect learners to align to their interlocutor to a comparatively greater degree than found in native dialogue. This is both because of the difficulty of the task leading to a greater need for alignment (Pickering and Garrod, 2006), and because we know that an L2 learner's lexical complexity increases in a dialogue setting due to the shared context words within that dialogue, compared to the level at which they are capable of expressing themselves in monologue (Robinson, 2011).

In order to find out whether ability affects alignment in L2 dialogue, we investigate *lexical priming* effects between L2 learner and tutor. *Priming* is a mechanism which brings about alignment and entrainment, and when interlocutors use the same words, we say they are *lexically entrained* (Brennan and Clark, 1996). We compare the effects against two different corpora: task-based (Anderson et al., 1991) and conversational (Godfrey et al., 1992), and between different levels of L2 student competency. We expect that alignment of tutor to student and vice versa will be different, and that the degree of alignment at a higher level of L2 learner competence will be more similar to that of conversational dialogue than that at a lower level

Proceedings of the SIGDIAL 2018 Conference, pages 41–50,
Melbourne, Australia, 12-14 July 2018. ©2018 Association for Computational Linguistics

(Sinclair et al., 2017). We are interested in the difference between tutor-to-student (TS) and student-to-tutor (ST) alignment, as there are various factors which could contribute to both increased and decreased alignment to that existing between two fluent interlocutors (Costa et al., 2008).

1.1 Motivation

By examining alignment differences, we aim to better understand the relationship between tutor adaptation and L2 learner production. This understanding can inform analysis of *"good"* tutoring moves, leading to the creation of either an L2 tutoring language model or more informed L2 dialogue agent design, which can exploit this knowledge of effective tutor alignment strategy to contribute to improved automated L2 tutoring. The potential benefits of automated tutoring for L2 dialogue[1] have already been seen through the success of apps such as Duolingo[2] bots which allow the user to engage in instant-messaging style chats with an agent to learn another language. *Adaption* of agent to learner however is an ongoing research task, although outside L2 tutoring, is a well-explored area (Graesser et al., 2005). Alignment, or *"more lexical similarity between student and tutor"* has been shown to be more predictive of increased student motivation (Ward et al., 2011), and agent alignment to students' goals can improve student learning (Ai et al., 2010). We build on previous research by investigating lexical priming effects for *each interlocutor* in dialogue both within- and between-speaker, and at *different ability levels in L2 dialogue*. This adds the dimension of lexical priming and individual speaker interactions to the work of Reitter and Moore (2006) and the inspection of student to tutor, and within-speaker priming to that of Ward and Litman (2007b). By also making comparisons across L2 ability levels, we can now analyse priming effects in terms of L2 acquisition. Similar work in this area outside the scope of this paper includes work analysing alignment of *expressions* in a task-based dialogue setting (Duplessis et al., 2017) and the analysis of alignment-capable dialogue generation (Buschmeier et al., 2009).

In addition to informing dialogue tutoring agent design, this work has potential to augment existing measures of linguistic sophistication predic-

tion (Vajjala and Meurers, 2016) to better deal with individual speakers within a dialogue, using alignment as a predictor of learner ability as has been suggested by Ward and Litman (2007a). Dialogue is inherently sparse, particularly when considering the lexical contribution of a single speaker. Accordingly, alignment could be a useful predictor of student receptive and productive knowledge when in combination with lexical complexity of the shared vocabulary.

1.2 Research Questions

We present evidence which strengthens our hypothesis that tutors take advantage of the natural alignment found in language, in order to better introduce, or *ground*[3] vocabulary to the student; in other words, *scaffolding*[4] vocabulary from receptive to productive practice in these dialogues.

Our work investigates the following research questions:

RQ1 How does L2 dialogue differ from task-based and conversational in terms of alignment?
  We find ST alignment has the strongest effect within L2 dialogue.

RQ2 Does alignment correlate with ability in L2 dialogue?
  We find priming effects are greater at higher levels of student ability.

RQ3 Does linguistic sophistication of the language used influence alignment of speakers at different ability levels in L2 dialogue?
  We find the more complex the word, the greater the likelihood of alignment within L2 dialogue.

2 Corpora

We compare the alignment present within three dialogue corpora: *L2-tutoring, conversational and task-based*. A summary of the corpora is presented in Table 1. The Barcelona English Language Corpus (BELC) (Muñoz, 2006) was gathered at four different periods over the course of

---

[1] Also know as *Dialogue-based Computer Assisted Language Learning (CALL)*

[2] bots.duolingo.com

[3] Grounding in dialogue consists of the participants establishing a common basis, or ground, on which their communication takes place. This can be viewed as a strategy for managing uncertainty and therefore error handling in dialogue (Skantze, 2007).

[4] Scaffolding (Wood et al., 1976) provides a metaphor to the kind of temporary support at successive levels of development needed to construct knowledge, or to support learning.

Corpus	Type	English	Dialogues
BELC	L2 tutoring	non-native (levels 1-4)	118
Switchboard	conversational	fluent	1155
Map Task	task-based	fluent	128

Table 1: Corpora types and details. *Map Task* is referred to in later diagrams as MT, *Switchboard* as SB. The levels in BELC indicate increasing learner ability, with 1 indicating the lowest ability level and 4 the highest.

three years, with the students involved receiving approximately one school year of weekly English tuition between sessions. Table 2 shows a short 20-utterance long extract from a dialogue. The Switchboard Corpus is conversational dialogue over telephone between two fluent English speakers (*A* and *B*), and MapTask is a task-based dialogue where the *instruction-Giver (G)* directs the *instruction-Follower (F)* from a shared start point to an end point marked on *G*'s map but which is unknown to *F*, who also has access to a similar map, although some features may only be present on one of the interlocutors' copies.

3 Methods

To address *RQ1* and *RQ2*, section 3.1 discusses how we measure lexical priming so that we can compare priming effects in different situations. Section 3.2 discusses the measure we use for word complexity in order to address *RQ3*, so that we can use this as an additional parameter in our model.

3.1 Lexical Convergence

Lexical priming predicts that a given word (*target*) occurs more often closely after a potential *prime* of the same word than further away. In order to measure lexical convergence, we count each word used by the speaker being considered as a potential prime. Following Ward and Litman (2007b), who measure the lexical convergence of student to tutor in physics tutorial dialogues, we only count words as primes if in WordNet (Miller, 1995), the word has a non-empty synset[5] e.g. if there was a choice of potential words and the speaker used the same word as their interlocutor, this can be counted as a prime, since it was not simply used because it was the only choice.

Since the learning content of L2 dialogues is the

Tutor	Student
do you have a bedroom for just you ?	
	yes .
ok .	
how many beds are there in your room ?	
	two .
two <u>beds</u> .	
	***<u>two</u> beds** .*
ok one for you...	
	*... and his **friend** algúns amigos .*
*and a **friend** that's good .*	
hmm what is the <u>room</u> like ?	
	hmm...
tell me about your <u>room</u> .	
	*my **room** ?*
uhhuh .	
describe it .	
	*<u>my **room**</u> is...*
there's <u>two beds</u>...	
	...very big...
uhhuh .	

Table 2: Example of lexical alignment in BELC dialogue. *room*, *beds* and *friend* are examples of lexical alignment from student to tutor and from tutor to student respectively. <u>*Underlined*</u> text indicates within-speaker (*TT* or *SS*) alignment, and **bold** text indicates between-speaker (*TS* or *ST*) alignment (*algúns amigos* means *some friends*).

language itself, we group the words into *word families*, which is a common method used to measure L2 student vocabulary (Graves et al., 2012). We do this by lemmatizing[6] the words in a text, and counting *lemmas* used by the speaker as prime. Thus, we count the forms *want, wants, wanted & wanting* as a single word.

We also distinguish between the speakers when looking at between-speaker, or *comprehension-production* (CP) priming where the speaker first comprehends the prime (uttered by their interlocutor) and then produces the target, and within-speaker or *production-production* (PP) priming, where both the prime and the target are produced by the same speaker. Since we are also interested in tutor *T* behaviour vs. student *S* in these interactions we map PP priming to *TT* and *SS* respectively and CP to *TS* and *ST*.

---

[5]This also has the effect of removing function words from consideration.

[6]Using NLTK (Loper and Bird, 2002)

Lexical Repetition

In our data, each repetition of an occurrence of a word W at distance n is counted as *priming*[7] where W has a non-empty synset, and is of the same *word-family* as its prime (section 3.1). Each case where W occurs but is not primed n units beforehand in the dialogue, is counted as *non-priming*. Our goal is to model $\hat{p}(prime|target, n)$, that is the sampling probability that a *prime* is present in the n-th word before *target* occurs. Without lexical priming's effect on the dialogue, we would assume that

$$\hat{p}(prime|target, n) = \hat{p}(prime|target).$$

The distance n between stimulus and target is counted in words, as this has the advantage over utterances for capturing within-utterance priming and is less sensitive to differences in average utterance length between corpora when comparing priming effects. *Words* were chosen as the closest approximate available to *time in seconds* as measured in Reitter and Moore (2006). We look for repetitions within windows of 85 words[8].

Generalized Linear Mixed Effects Regression

For the purposes of this study, following Reitter and Moore (2006), we use a Generalized Linear Mixed Effects Regression Model (GLMM). In all cases, a word instance t is counted as a repetition at distance d if at d there is a token in the same word-family as t. To measure speaker-speaker priming effects, we record both the prime and target producers at d. GLMMs with a binary response variable such as ours can be considered a form of logistic regression.We model the number of occurrences $prime = target|d \leq n$ (where n is window size) of priming being detected[9]. We model this as binomial, where the success proba-

bility depends on the following explanatory variables: *Categorical: corpus choice, priming type from speaker role, ability level;* and *Ordinal: word frequency,* as explained in Section 3.2. The model will produce coefficients β_i, one for each explanatory variable i. β_i expresses the contribution of i to the probability of the outcome event, in our case, successful priming, referred to as *priming effect size* in the following sections. For example, the β_i estimates allow us to predict the decline of repetition probability with increasing distance between *prime* and *target*, and the other explanatory variables we are interested in; we refer to this as the *probability estimates* in in subsequent sections. The model outputs a statistical significance score for each coefficient, these are reported under each figure where relevant.

3.2 Complexity Convergence

To capture *linguistic complexity* within the priming words, we use Word Occurrence Frequency (WOF) as a predictor of the relative difficulty of the words used. We use $log(WOF)$ to normalise the deta before using it as a factor in our model. WOF has been found to predict L2 vocabulary acquisition rates - the higher frequency of a word, the more exposure a student has had to it, the more likely they are to learn it faster (Vermeer, 2001). Word Frequency has also been shown to act as a reasonable indication of word 'difficulty' (Chen and Meurers, 2017). We therefore expect a negative correlation between learner level and frequency of vocabulary used, given a certain prime window. We gathered frequency counts from the Google News Corpus introduced by Mikolov et al. (2013), for its size and diverse language.

4 Results

4.1 Lexical Convergence Cross Corpora

To find how L2 dialogue differs from task-based and conversational in terms of alignment *(RQ1)*, we investigate the priming effects present across corpora of different speaker roles. Figure 1 shows that the BELC corpus has a similar asymmetry in speaker alignment to MT, and that the alignment of speakers in SB is more symmetrical, mirroring the speakers' equal role in the dialogue. This can be seen in the different priming effects between speakers in BELC and MT, and the same effects between speakers in SB. Figure 2 shows the different decay of repetition probability with window

---

[7]The use of *priming* is not intended to imply that priming is the only explanation for lexical repetition

[8]We chose this window size based on Reitter and Moore (2006) using an utterance window of 25 and a time window of 15 seconds. We calculated the average number of words to occur in the utterance window chosen, and the average number of words which are spoken in the 15 second window and chose the average of the two as our window.

[9]For example, if we were only interested in priming within a window size of *3* words, In table 2, for the student's first use of the word *beds* we would record 3 data points: (window:1, target:bed, role:SS, prime=target:0), (window:2, target:bed, role:ST, prime=target:1), (window:3, target:bed, role:ST, prime=target:0) indicating there is a prime for our target *beds* at distance 2. The number of trials = target words $\times$ window size.

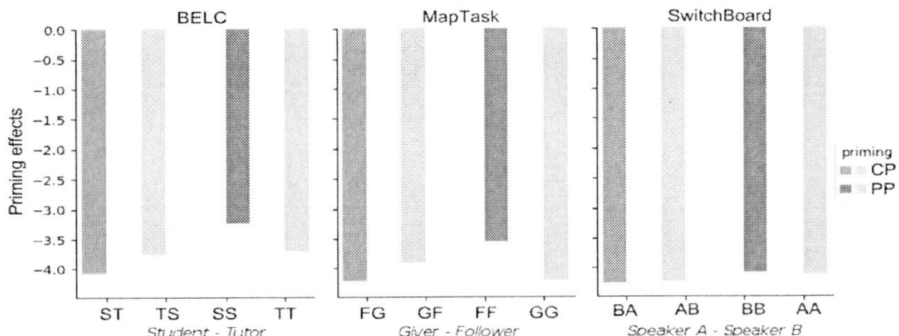

Figure 1: Priming effects of distance across Corpora for different speaker roles. *S:Student, T:Tutor, F:Follower, G:Giver, A& B:Speaker A& B.* AB indicates alignment of *A* to *B*. *CP: comprehension-production,* or between-speaker priming, PP: *production-production,* or within-speaker priming. The results are all significant with ($p < 0.0001$) except *BB* within Switchboard, with ($p < 0.01$).

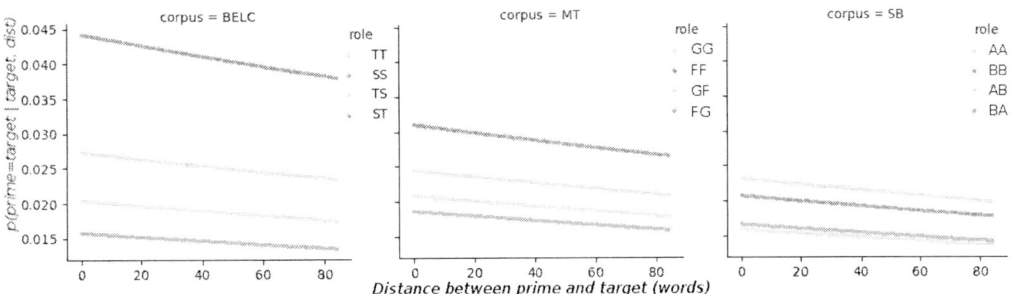

Figure 2: Decaying probability estimates for window lengths for different speaker roles across corpora. $Formula : lemma\_occ{\sim}window + role * corpus$

size for the different roles for all three corpora. This shows the same symmetry and asymmetry of between- and within-speaker repetition decay probability as Figure 1.

4.2 Lexical Convergence by Level

We investigate priming effects within BELC between levels to find whether alignment correlates with ability in L2 dialogue *(RQ2)*. Figure 3 shows the strong student-tutor priming occurring at each ability level, and the general increase in priming effect size as ability level increases for all priming types. When comparing both Figure 1 and 3, we see that as ability level increases, BELC priming effect sizes tend towards those seen in Switch-Board, particularly those of ST and TS, the effect size of which also becomes more symmetrical with ability level, although the imbalance between SS and TT priming remains similar to that of Map-Task.

We also examine the model predictions for different window sizes for different conditions. Figures 4 and 5 describe the relationship between role and ability level on the probability of seeing a prime word at different window sizes. Figure 4 shows a sharper decay in the probability of tutor to student (TS) priming than in student to tutor (ST) priming. Figure 5 shows that tutor self-priming is more probable at lower ability levels, and that ST alignment at lower levels is less likely than at higher levels of ability.

4.3 Linguistic Complexity Convergence

Exploring the question of whether linguistic sophistication of the language used influences alignment of speakers at different ability levels in L2 dialogue *(RQ3)*; we find $log(WOF)$ to have a significant negative correlation ($p < 0.0001$) with priming effects. Thus the more complex the word (as measured by a lower WOF), the greater the likelihood of alignment. Figure 6 shows the priming effects of WOF. It shows that priming effects of WOF are stronger for *ST* and *TT*, than for the other roles, but this difference is less pronounced at higher levels than it is for lower levels of ability. The *ST* shows the most marked difference in

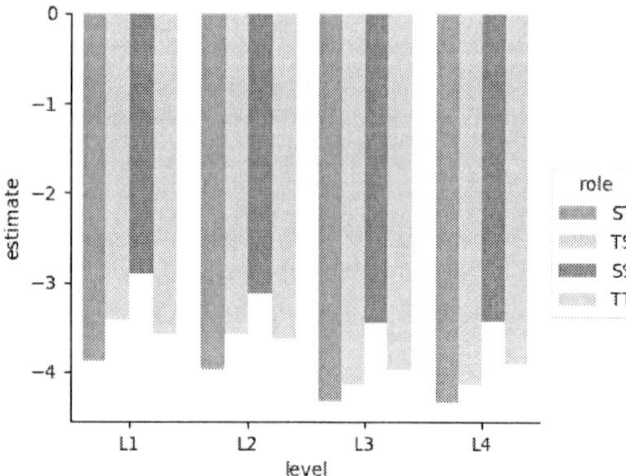

Figure 3: Priming effect sizes under different speaker role situations, across levels in BELC. Effects estimated from separately fitted nested regression models for each subset of BELC split by level(1-4). The results are all significant ($p < 0.0001$).

effect between low and high levels, lowest at the highest ability. Per role, priming effect is generally smaller at higher ability levels than lower.

Figures 7 and 8 show the effects of WOF on level and role respectively. In Figure 7, lower $log(WOF)$ values are indicative of more complex words. In such cases (see Figure 7, column 1), the repetition probability is higher for high ability students, compared to low ability students. This stands in contrast to higher $log(WOF)$ values, indicative of less complex words, where the repetition probability is now lower for high ability students compared to low ability students (see Figure 7, column 6). Figure 8 shows differences in self-priming and within speaker priming, in that for both TS and ST, the probability of repetition is greater for higher frequency words, while for *TT* and *SS*, the probability of repetition is higher for lower frequency words.

5   Discussion

The three spoken dialogue corpora we investigated demonstrate a significant effect of distance between prime and target in lexical repetition, providing evidence of a lexical priming effect on *word family* use. We also found evidence of priming for each interlocutor in both between-speaker and within-speaker roles.

ST alignment has the strongest effect within L2 dialogue. To find how L2 dialogue differs from our other two corpora in terms of role *(RQ1)*, we measured the priming effects for Tutors (TT, TS) and Students (SS, ST) and find it asymmetric in the same manner as for the task-based dialogue MT. This is in contrast to the symmetric effects in the conversational dialogue of SB (Figure 1). ST alignment also has the greatest priming effect compared to the other roles in BELC, which supports our hypothesis that *student-to-tutor* alignment is an artefact of both tutor scaffolding, and students' productive range benefiting from the shared dialogue context.

When considering within-speaker priming, it is also interesting to note that TT priming has a more marked effect than SS priming, similar to the relationship between GG and FF in Map Task. We interpret this similarly to Reitter and Moore's (2006) comparison of Map Task and Switchboard, in that since the task-based or tutoring nature of the dialogue is harder, the leading speakers use more consistent language in order to reduce the cognitive load of the task (tutoring/instruction-giving).

Priming effects are greater at higher levels of student ability. In order to investigate our main hypothesis, that ability *does* affect alignment *(RQ2)*, we measured priming effects in different ability levels of L2 tutorial dialogue (Figure 3), and found that priming effects are greater at higher levels of student ability, which provides evidence that as ability increases, dialogues have more in common with conversational dialogue. We also measured how role influences these priming effects (Figures 4 and 5) and hypothesise that the faster decay of TS repetition probability (Figure 5) is an indication that the tutor is using the immediate encouraging backchanneling seen in the repetition in Table 2. We note (Figure 4) that tutor-to-tutor repetition is more probable at lower levels, which supports the above hypothesis. Additionally, student-to-tutor repetition probability is more likely at higher levels which is a good indication that student ability is higher, since we argue that they are now *able* to align to their interlocutor.

The more complex the word, the greater the likelihood of alignment within L2 dialogue. Lastly, to find whether linguistic sophistication of language aligned to is affected by ability *(RQ3)*, we investigated the influence of word frequency on alignment within BELC. Figure 7 shows that at lower $log(WOF)$ values (which we use to in

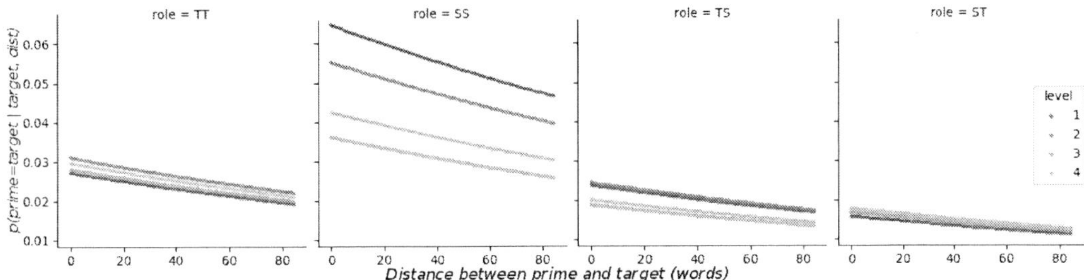

Figure 4: Decaying repetition probability estimates depending on the increasing distance between prime and target, contrasting different speaker roles at different levels.
*Formula : lemma_occ~window + role * categorical_level*

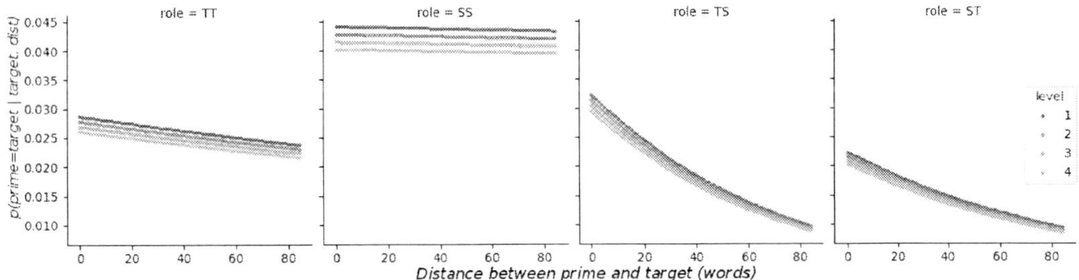

Figure 5: Decaying repetition probability estimates depending on the increasing distance between prime and target, contrasting different speaker roles at different levels.
*Formula : lemma_occ~window * role + categorical_level*

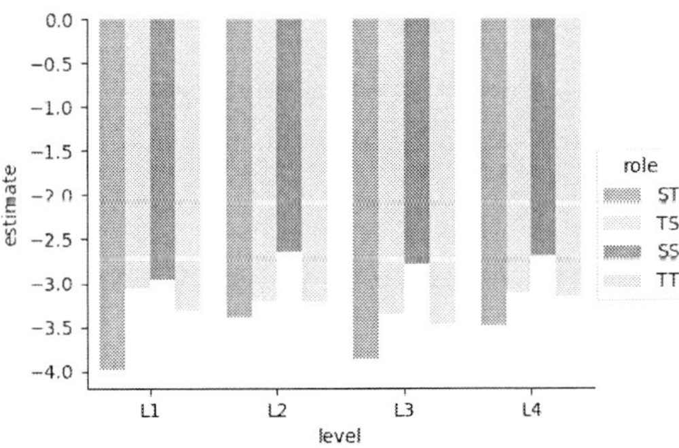

Figure 6: Word Occurrence Frequency Priming effects under different selections of role and level situations in BELC. Each model was separately fitted on the relevant subset of data to show the priming effect sizes for *Word Occurrence Frequency*. (L1:SS, L2:TS and L3:ST are insignificant, all other results are significant with at least $p < 0.001$ and most with $p < 0.0001$.

dicate more complex words), repetition probability is higher in the higher ability levels compared to the lower levels, and at higher $log(WOF)$, the repetition probability of the higher ability levels is now *lower* than at the lower levels. This has interesting implications for using these results as features for student alignment ability prediction. This fits with the Interactive Alignment Model (Pickering and Garrod, 2004), which suggest that alignment will happen more with greater cognitive load, and (Reitter and Moore, 2006), who find stronger priming for less frequent syntactic rules which supports the cognitive-load explanation. The stronger priming effect identified for less frequent vocabulary also supports this hypothesis. Figure 6 shows the priming effects are slightly smaller at higher ability levels. $Log(WOF)$ has a negative correlation, meaning there is more likely to be alignment the lower the WOF. The results at each level have a similar priming effect distribution over role, with the most marked difference in priming effect being for ST (Student to Tutor alignment), which shows a decrease in priming effect for harder words at higher ability levels. This provides an interesting first indication that there is a measurable effect of student leveraging contextual vocabulary to augment their productive reach in L2 dialogue.

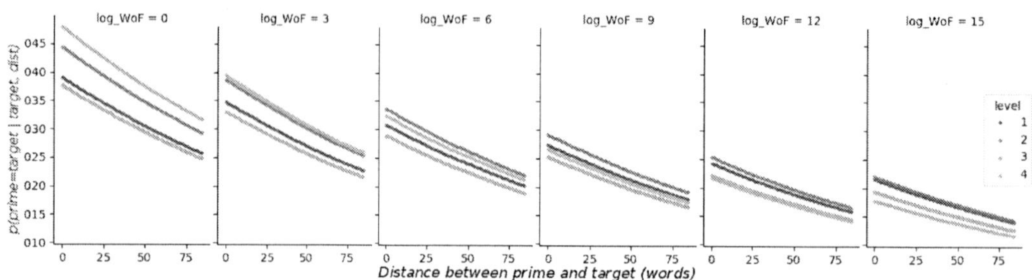

Figure 7: Decaying repetition probabilities of different $log(WOF)$ values on probability of word occurrence by level. Lower $log(WOF)$ values correspond to *lower* frequency, an indication of *more* complex words, and *higher* frequency as *less* complex words.

$Formula : lemma\_occ \sim window + log(WOF) * categorical\_level$

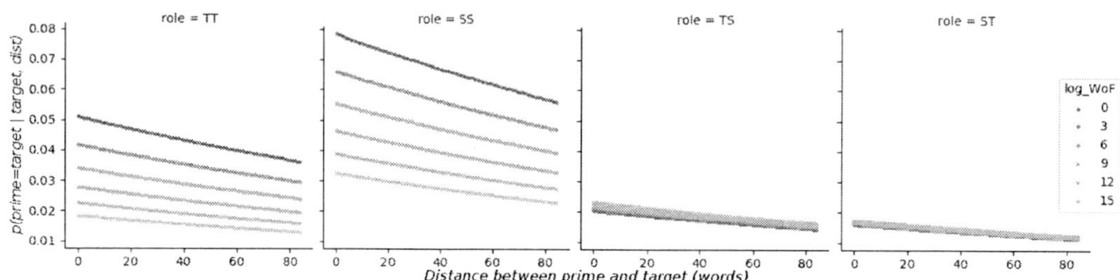

Figure 8: Decaying repetition probabilities of different $log(WOF)$ values on probability of word occurrence by role. *Higher* $log(WOF)$ indicates *easier* words.

$Formula : lemma\_occ \sim window + log(WOF) * role$

6 Conclusions and Future Work

We see these results as an indication that measuring lexical alignment combined with lexical sophistication of vocabulary has potential as a predictor of student competency. We also hypothesise that measurements of *'good tutoring'* actions could consist of how and to what extent tutors adapt interactively to individual students' needs in terms of their conversational ability. Tutor self-priming seems to be an interesting possible feature for measuring this adaption. We want to further investigate different measures of alignment and both lexical and syntactic complexity to inform systems that aim to automate L2 tutoring. We plan to consider which speaker *introduces* the word being aligned to, in order to better understand the relationship between productive and receptive vocabulary of the student in dialogue settings. It is also important to separate the effects of priming per se from other factors that can influence lexical convergence, such as differences in vocabulary and topic specificity. As a first step toward that goal, we plan to compare lexical convergence in the original corpus with convergence in matched baselines of randomly ordered utterances (Duplessis et al., 2017), which will account for vocabulary effects and corpus-specific factors. To explore more measures of word complexity in addition to simple *WOF*, we will further investigate measures specific to L2 dialogue, such as the English Vocabulary Profile (EVP) (Capel, 2012), with word lists per CEFR[10] level, or measures such as counts of word sense per word, or whether a word is *concrete* or *abstract*[11], exploiting existing readability features (Vajjala and Meurers, 2014).

Acknowledgements

Thanks to Amy Isard, Maria Gorinova, Maria Wolters, Federico Fancellu, Sorcha Gilroy, Clara Vania and Marco Damonte as well as the three anonymous reviewers for their useful comments in relation to this paper. A. Sinclair especially acknowledges the help and support of Jon Oberlander during the early development of this idea.

---

[10]The Common European Framework of Reference (CEFR) defines the 6 levels of english proficiency in ascending order as: A1, A2, B1, B2, C1, C2.

[11]Using WordNet or other word/lemma concreteness rating database.

References

Hua Ai, Rohit Kumar, Dong Nguyen, Amrut Nagasunder, and Carolyn P Rosé. 2010. Exploring the effectiveness of social capabilities and goal alignment in computer supported collaborative learning. In *International Conference on Intelligent Tutoring Systems*, pages 134–143. Springer.

Anne H Anderson, Miles Bader, Ellen Gurman Bard, Elizabeth Boyle, Gwyneth Doherty, Simon Garrod, Stephen Isard, Jacqueline Kowtko, Jan McAllister, Jim Miller, et al. 1991. The hcrc map task corpus. *Language and speech*, 34(4):351–366.

Susan E Brennan and Herbert H Clark. 1996. Conceptual pacts and lexical choice in conversation. *Journal of Experimental Psychology: Learning, Memory, and Cognition*, 22(6):1482.

Hendrik Buschmeier, Kirsten Bergmann, and Stefan Kopp. 2009. An alignment-capable microplanner for natural language generation. In *Proceedings of the 12th European Workshop on Natural Language Generation*, pages 82–89. Association for Computational Linguistics.

Annette Capel. 2012. Completing the english vocabulary profile: C1 and c2 vocabulary. *English Profile Journal*, 3:e1.

Xiaobin Chen and Detmar Meurers. 2017. Word frequency and readability: Predicting the text-level readability with a lexical-level attribute. *Journal of Research in Reading*, pages n/a–n/a. JRIR-2017-01-0006.R1.

Albert Costa, Martin J Pickering, and Antonella Sorace. 2008. Alignment in second language dialogue. *Language and cognitive processes*, 23(4):528–556.

Guillaume Dubuisson Duplessis, Chloé Clavel, and Frédéric Landragin. 2017. Automatic measures to characterise verbal alignment in human-agent interaction. In *18th Annual Meeting of the Special Interest Group on Discourse and Dialogue (SIGDIAL)*, pages 71–81.

John J Godfrey, Edward C Holliman, and Jane McDaniel. 1992. Switchboard: Telephone speech corpus for research and development. In *Acoustics, Speech, and Signal Processing, 1992. ICASSP-92., 1992 IEEE International Conference on*, volume 1, pages 517–520. IEEE.

Arthur C Graesser, Patrick Chipman, Brian C Haynes, and Andrew Olney. 2005. Autotutor: An intelligent tutoring system with mixed-initiative dialogue. *IEEE Transactions on Education*, 48(4):612–618.

Michael F. Graves, Diane August, and Jeannette Mancilla-Martinez. 2012. *Teaching Vocabulary to English Language Learners*. TESOL Press/Teachers College Press.

Edward Loper and Steven Bird. 2002. Nltk: The natural language toolkit. In *Proceedings of the ACL-02 Workshop on Effective tools and methodologies for teaching natural language processing and computational linguistics-Volume 1*, pages 63–70. Association for Computational Linguistics.

Tomas Mikolov, Kai Chen, Greg Corrado, and Jeffrey Dean. 2013. Efficient estimation of word representations in vector space. *arXiv preprint arXiv:1301.3781*.

George A Miller. 1995. Wordnet: a lexical database for english. *Communications of the ACM*, 38(11):39–41.

Carmen Muñoz. 2006. *Age and the rate of foreign language learning*, volume 19. Multilingual Matters.

Martin J Pickering and Simon Garrod. 2004. Toward a mechanistic psychology of dialogue. *Behavioral and brain sciences*, 27(2):169–190.

Martin J Pickering and Simon Garrod. 2006. Alignment as the basis for successful communication. *Research on Language and Computation*, 4(2-3):203–228.

David Reitter and Johanna D Moore. 2006. Priming of syntactic rules in task-oriented dialogue and spontaneous conversation. In *Proceedings of the Annual Meeting of the Cognitive Science Society*, volume 28.

P. Robinson. 2011. *Second Language Task Complexity: Researching the Cognition Hypothesis of Language Learning and Performance*. Task-based language teaching : issues, research and practice. John Benjamins Publishing Company.

Arabella Sinclair, Jon Oberlander, and Dragan Gasevic. 2017. Finding the zone of proximal development: Student-tutor second language dialogue interactions. *SEMDIAL 2017 SaarDial*, page 134.

Gabriel Skantze. 2007. *Error Handling in Spoken Dialogue Systems-Managing Uncertainty, Grounding and Miscommunication*. Gabriel Skantze.

Višnja Pavičić Takač. 2008. *Vocabulary learning strategies and foreign language acquisition*. Multilingual Matters.

Sowmya Vajjala and Detmar Meurers. 2014. Exploring measures of readability for spoken language: Analyzing linguistic features of subtitles to identify age-specific tv programs.

Sowmya Vajjala and Detmar Meurers. 2016. Readability-based sentence ranking for evaluating text simplification. *arXiv preprint arXiv:1603.06009*.

Anne Vermeer. 2001. Breadth and depth of vocabulary in relation to l1/l2 acquisition and frequency of input. *Applied Psycholinguistics*, 22(2):217234.

Arthur Ward and Diane Litman. 2007a. Dialog convergence and learning. In *Proceedings of the 2007 conference on Artificial Intelligence in Education: Building Technology Rich Learning Contexts That Work*, pages 262–269. IOS Press.

Arthur Ward and Diane Litman. 2007b. Measuring convergence and priming in tutorial dialog. *University of Pittsburgh*.

Arthur Ward, Diane Litman, and Maxine Eskenazi. 2011. Predicting change in student motivation by measuring cohesion between tutor and student. In *Proceedings of the 6th Workshop on Innovative Use of NLP for Building Educational Applications*, pages 136–141. Association for Computational Linguistics.

David Wood, Jerome S Bruner, and Gail Ross. 1976. The role of tutoring in problem solving. *Journal of child psychology and psychiatry*, 17(2):89–100.

Just Talking - Modelling Casual Conversation

Emer Gilmartin
ADAPT Centre
Trinity College Dublin
gilmare@tcd.ie

Carl Vogel
Computational Linguistics Group
Trinity College Dublin
vogel@tcd.ie

Christian Saam
ADAPT Centre
Trinity College Dublin
saamc@cs.tcd.ie

Nick Campbell
SCL
Trinity College Dublin
nick@tcd.ie

Vincent Wade
ADAPT Centre
Trinity College Dublin
vwade@adaptcentre.ie

Abstract

Casual conversation has become a focus for dialogue applications. Such talk is ubiquitous and its structure differs from that found in the task-based interactions that have been the focus of dialogue system design for many years. It is unlikely that such conversations can be modelled as an extension of task-based talk. We review theories of casual conversation, report on our studies of the structure of casual dialogue, and outline challenges we see for the development of spoken dialog systems capable of carrying on casual friendly conversation in addition to performing well-defined tasks.

1 Introduction

People talk. Human society depends on spoken (or written) interaction. Instrumental or task-based conversation is the medium for practical activities such as service encounters (shops, doctor's appointments), information transfer (lectures), or planning and execution of business (meetings). Much daily talk does not seem to contribute to a clear short-term task, but builds and maintains social bonds, and is described as 'interactional', social, or casual conversation. Casual conversation happens in a wide variety of settings, including 'bus-stop' conversations between strangers, gossipy tea break chats between workmates, family and friends 'hanging out' at home or in cafes and bars engaged in Schelgoff's 'continuing state of incipient talk' (Schegloff and Sacks, 1973), or indeed in stretches of smalltalk and chat preceding or punctuating business interactions. Much research is focused on dyadic task based dialogue interactions. Early dialogue system researchers recognised the complexity of dealing with social talk (Allen et al., 2000), and initial prototypes concentrated on practical tasks such as travel bookings or logistics (Walker et al., 2001; Allen et al., 1995). Implementation of artificial task-based dialogues is facilitated by a number of factors. In these tasks, the lexical content of utterances drives successful completion of the task, conversation length is governed by task-completion, and participants are aware of the goals of the interaction. Such dialogues have been modelled as finite state and later slot-based systems, first using hand-written rules and later depending on data-driven stochastic methods to decide the next action. Task-based systems have proven invaluable in many practical domains. However, dialog technology is quickly moving beyond short task-based interactions, and interest is focussing on realistic artificial dialog for roles such as social companions, educators, and helpmates. To model and generate a wider variety of social talk and indeed to improve the quality and user engagement of task-oriented interactions, there is a need for understanding of social conversation. Stochastic models require appropriate data. This paper provides an overview of our recent work in this area, based on corpus studies of casual conversation. Below we describe the concept of social talk and previous work in the area. We then describe our dataset, annotation and the results of our preliminary analyses, discussing how these may aid the design of conversational agents.

2 Casual Conversation

Social talk or casual conversation, 'talk for the sake of talking', or 'phatic communion' has been described as an emergent behaviour whenever humans gather (Malinowski, 1936), and there are theories which posit that such talk is an 'unmarked case' or base form for human spoken interaction

Proceedings of the SIGDIAL 2018 Conference, pages 51–59,
Melbourne, Australia, 12-14 July 2018. ©2018 Association for Computational Linguistics

(Dunbar, 1998). Examples of such talk include short conversations when people meet, intermittent talk between workers on topics unrelated to the job in hand throughout the workday, or longer dinner table or pub conversations. Subgenres of casual conversation include smalltalk, gossip, and conversational narrative. The duration of such interactions can vary from short 'bus stop' conversations to ongoing interactions which lapse and start again over the course of several hours. Researchers have theorized that such talk functions to build social bonds and avoid unfriendly or threatening silence, as in the phatic component in Jakobson's model of communication (Jakobson, 1960), distinctions between interactional and instrumental language (Brown and Yule, 1983), and theories that language evolved to maintain social cohesion (Dunbar, 1998). Social talk differs in many ways from task-based conversations. A chat between a concierge of an apartment building and a tenant about football differs in many respects from a customer ordering pizza from an employee. In the chat there is no important information exchanged which is vital to the success of a short-term task, the topic could be the weather or football. In the pizza ordering scenario, information on the type of pizza and the price are vital to a successful transaction, and the goal – sale of a pizza – is short-term, achievable within the conversation, and known to both parties. In the chat, the goal could be described as the maintenance of a social relationship – fulfillment of this goal is a process which extends past the temporal boundaries of the current conversation. Casual conversation seems to be based on avoidance of silence and engagement in unthreatening but entertaining verbal display and interaction, as observed by Schneider (Schneider, 1988), who noted 'idling' – sequences of repetitions of agreeing tails such as 'Yes, of course' or 'MmHmm', which seem to keep the conversation going rather than add any new information. He proposed a set of maxims peculiar to this genre, concentrated on the importance of avoiding silence and maintaining politeness. While instrumental talk is often dyadic, casual conversation is very often multiparty. In terms of function, Slade and Eggins view casual conversation as the space in which people form and refine their social reality (Eggins and Slade, 2004) citing gossip between workmates, where participants reaffirm their solidarity, and dinner table talk between friends. In task-based encounters, participants have clear predefined roles ('customer-salesperson', 'teacher-student') which can strongly influence the timing and content of their contributions to the exchange. However, in casual talk, all participants have equal speaker rights and can contribute at any time (Wilson, 1989) (Cheepen, 1988). The form of such talk is also different to that of task-based exchanges - there is less reliance on question-answer sequences and more on commentary, storytelling, and discussion (Thornbury and Slade, 2006; Wilson, 1989). Instead of asking each other for information, participants seem to collaborate to fill the floor and avoid uncomfortable silence. Topics are managed locally – a meeting has an agenda and chairperson to impose the next topic, while casual topics are often introduced by means of a statement or comment by a participant which may or may not be taken up by other participants. Instrumental and interactional exchanges differ in duration; task-based conversations are bounded by task completion and tend to be short, while casual conversation can go on indefinitely. There are a number of syntactical, lexical, and discourse differences between (casual) conversation and more formal spoken and written genres (Biber et al., 1999). Our work explores the architecture of casual talk.

3   The Architecture of Casual Talk

Casual conversation is not a simple sequence of adjacency pairs, but proceeds in distinct phases. Laver concentrated on the 'psychologically crucial margins of interaction', conversational openings and closings in particular, suggesting that small talk performs a transitional function from initial silence through stages of greeting, to the business or 'meat' of the interaction, and back to closing sequences and to leave taking (Laver, 1975). Ventola concentrated on longer conversations, identifying distinct phases. Such conversations often begin with ritualised opening greetings, followed by approach segments of light uncontroversial small talk, and in longer conversations leading to more informative centre phases (consisting of sequential but overlapping topics), and then back to ritualised leave-takings (Ventola, 1979). Ventola described several structural elements or phases (listed below), which could be combined to form conversations ranging from minimal exchanges of greetings to long group interactions such as dinner party conversations.

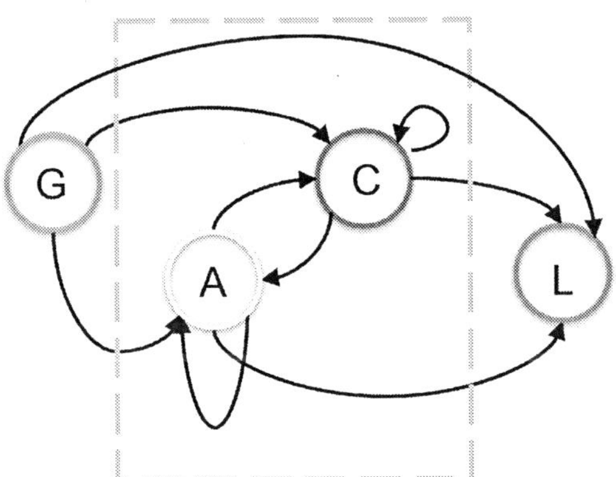

Figure 1: A simplified view of the phases of casual talk described by Ventola - Greeting, Approach, Centre, and Leavetaking.

G   Greeting.

Ad   Address. ("Hello, **Mary**")

Id   Identification (of self)

Ap   Approach. Smalltalk. Direct (ApD) – asking about interactants themselves, or indirect (ApI) – talking about immediate situation (weather, surroundings).

C   Centring. Participants fully involved in conversation, talking at length.

Lt   Leave-taking. Signalling desire or need to end conversation.

Gb   Goodbye. Can be short or extended.

In this model, lighter talk in the form of Approach phases occurs not only at the extremes of conversations, but can recur between Centring phases throughout a longer conversation. Figure 1 shows a simplified schematic of the main phases described by Ventola.

Another model is provided by Slade and Eggins, who contend that casual talk can be seen as sequences of 'chat' and 'chunk' elements (Eggins and Slade, 2004, p. 230). Chunks are segments where (i) 'one speaker takes the floor and is allowed to dominate the conversation for an extended period', and (ii) the chunk appears to move through predictable stages – that is, it is generic. 'Chat' segments, on the other hand, are highly interactive and appear to be managed locally, unfolding move by move or turn by turn. In a study of three hours of conversational data collected during work coffee breaks, Slade found that around fifty percent of all talk was chat, while the rest comprised longer form chunks from the following genres: storytelling, observation/comment, opinion, gossip, joke-telling and ridicule. In chat phases, several participants contribute utterances with many questions and short comments. Chat is highly interactive with frequent turn changes, and often occurs at the start of an interaction. The conversational floor is shared among the participants and no single participant dominates for extended periods. Chat is often used to 'break the ice' among strangers involved in casual talk (Laver, 1975). As the conversation progresses, chat phases are interspersed with chunk phases. The 'ownership' of chunks seems to pass around the participants in the talk, with chat linking one chunk to the next (Eggins and Slade, 2004). Figure 2 shows examples drawn from our data of typical chat and chunk phases in a 5-party conversation.

Both Ventola's and Slade and Eggins' models treat conversation as composed of phases, with parallels between Ventola's approach phases and Slade and Eggins' chat phases. It is likely that the various conversational phases are subject to different norms of turntaking and that phenomena such as laughter or disfluency may appear in different distributions in different phases. Although Ventola's and Slade and Eggins' respective work is based on real dialogue in the form of orthographic transcripts, analyses of longer casual talk have been largely theoretical or based on qualitative descriptions. Our work aims to expand our knowledge of the form of these phases so that they can be modelled for artificial dialogue. In our investigations, we first segmented our data into chat and chunk phases to analyse the characteristics of these two types of talk, and in later work plan to refine our analysis by further segmenting our data into Ventola's phases. Below we outline the limitations of available corpora for work on longer form multiparty casual talk, describe our dataset, annotation, and experiments.

4 Corpora used for Casual Conversation Research

Relevant corpora of human interaction are essential to understanding different genres of spoken dialogue. Dialog corpora have been created of the same spoken task by different subjects, or of inter-

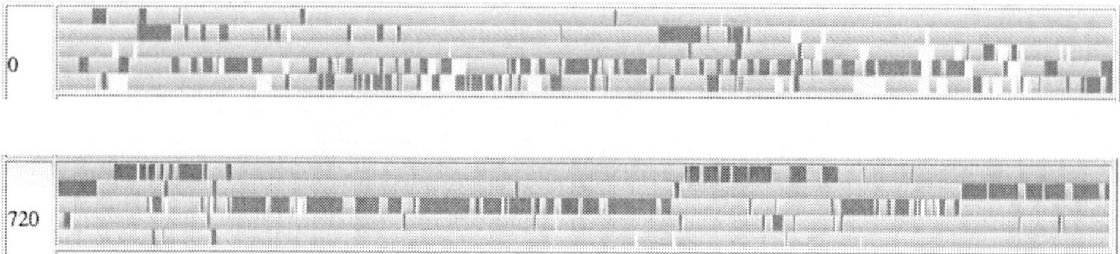

Figure 2: Examples of chat (top) and chunk (bottom) phases in two stretches from a 5-party conversation. Each row denotes the activity of one speaker across 120 seconds. Speech is dark grey, and laughter is white on a light grey background (silence).The chat frame, taken at the beginning of the conversation, can be seen to involve shorter contributions from all participants with frequent laughter. The chunk frame shows longer single speaker stretches.

actions specific to particular domains where lexical content was fundamental to achievement of a practical goal. Such corpora include information gap dialogs such as the HCRC MapTask corpus of dyadic information gap task-based conversations (Anderson et al., 1991) or the LUCID DiaPix corpus of 'spot the difference' games (Baker and Hazan, 2011), as well as real or staged meetings (e.g., ICSI and AMI multiparty meeting corpora (Janin et al., 2003; McCowan et al., 2005)) or genres such as televised political interviews (Beattie, 1983). Because of their task-focused nature, these data, while spontaneous and conversational, cannot be considered true casual talk, and results obtained from their analysis may not generalize to casual conversations.

There are some corpora of casual talk, including telephonic corpora (SWITCHBOARD (Godfrey et al., 1992) and the ESP-C collection of Japanese telephone conversations (Campbell, 2007)), and face-to-face talk datasets (e.g., Santa Barbara Corpus (DuBois et al., 2000), and sections of the ICE corpora (Greenbaum, 1991) and British National Corpus (BNC-Consortium, 2000)). These corpora are audio only and thus cannot be used to inform research on facial expression, gestural or postural research.

Several multimodal corpora of mostly dyadic 'first encounters' have appeared recently, where strangers are recorded engaged in casual conversation for periods of 5 to 20 minutes or so (Edlund et al., 2010; Aubrey et al., 2013; Paggio et al., 2010) in several languages including Swedish, Danish, Finnish, and English. These corpora are very valuable for the study of dyadic interaction, particularly at the opening and early stages of in-teraction. However, the substance of longer casual conversation beyond these first encounters or approach stages has not been focused on in the field.

5 Dataset and Annotation

We compiled a dataset of six informal multiparty conversations, each around an hour long. The requirements for the data were that participants could speak freely, that there was no task or topic imposed by the experimenter, and that recordings were multimodal so that analyses of visual cues could be carried out on the same data and used to build a more comprehensive understanding of multimodal face-to-face interaction. Suitable conversations were drawn from three multimodal corpora, d64, DANS, and TableTalk (Oertel et al., 2010; Hennig et al., 2014; Campbell, 2008). In each of these, participants were recorded in casual conversation in a living room setting or around a table, with no instructions on topic of type of conversation to be carried out - participants were also clearly informed that they could speak or stay silent as the mood took them. Table 1 shows details of participant numbers, gender, and conversation duration for each of the six conversations.

5.1 Data Preparation

The audio recordings included near-field chest or adjacent microphone recordings for each speaker. These were found to be unsuitable for automatic segmentation as there were frequent overlaps and bleedover from other speakers. The audio files were segmented manually into speech and silence intervals using Praat (Boersma and Weenink, 2010). The segmentation was carried out at the intonational phrase level (IP), rather than a more

Table 1: Source corpora and details for the conversations used in dataset

Corpus	Participants	Gender	Duration (s)
D64	5	2F/3M	4164
DANS	3	1F/2M	4672
DANS	4	1F/3M	4378
DANS	3	2F/1M	3004
TableTalk	4	2F/2M	2072
TableTalk	5	3F/2M	4740

coarse and theory dependent utterance or inter-pausal unit (IPU) level. Labels covered speech (SP), silence (SL), coughs (CG), breaths (BR), and laughter (LG). The speech label was applied to verbal and non-verbal vocal sounds (except laughter) to include contributions such as filled pauses, short utterances such as 'oh' or 'mmhmm', and sighs. Laughter was annotated inline with speech. Annotators worked on 10 second and four-second Praat windows of the audio. Doubtful cases were resolved using Elan (Wittenburg et al., 2006) with the video recordings. Manual segmentation into speech and silence can be problematic, as humans listening to speech can miss or indeed imagine the existence of objectively measured silences of short duration (Martin, 1970), and are known to have difficulty recalling disfluencies from audio they have heard (Deese, 1980). However these results were based on speakers timing pauses with a stopwatch in a single hearing. In the current work, using Praat and Elan, speech could be slowed down and replayed and, by using the four-second window, annotators could see silences or more accurately differences in amplitude on the speech waveform and spectrogram. Although breath is extremely interesting as a feature of conversation (Wlodarczak et al., 2015), it was not possible to annotate breath accurately for all participants and thus the breath intervals annotated were converted to silence for the purposes of this study. Similarly, coughs were relabelled as silence for the current work. After segmentation, the data were transcribed, and marked into chat and chunk phases as described below.

5.2 Annotation of Chat and Chunk Phases

Chat and chunk phases were marked using an annotation scheme devised from the definitions of chat and chunk phases given in Slade and Eggins work (Eggins and Slade, 2004; Slade, 2007).

For an initial classification, conversations were divided by first identifying the chunks and considering everything else chat. In the first instance, this was done using the first, structural part of Slade and Eggins' definition of a chunk as 'a segment where one speaker takes the floor and is allowed to dominate the conversation for an extended period'(Eggins and Slade, 2004). The following guidelines were created to aid in the placing of chat/chunk boundaries.

Start   A chunk starts when a speaker has established himself as leading the chunk.

Stop   To avoid orphaned sections, a chunk is ended at the moment the next element (chunk or chat) starts.

Aborted   In cases where a chunk is attempted, but aborted before it is established, this is left as chat. In cases where there is a diversion to another element mid-chunk and a return later, all three elements are annotated as though they were single chunks/stretches of chat.

Overlap   When a new chunk begins where a previous chunk is still tailing off, the new chunk onset is the marker of interest and the old chunk is finished at the onset of the new one.

Once the chunk was identified, it could be classified by genre. For annotation, a set of codes for the various types of chunk and chat was created. Each code is a hyphen-separated string containing at least a Type signifier for chat or chunk, an Ownership label, and optional sub-elements further classifying the chunks with reference to Slade and Eggins taxonomy. A total of 213 chat and 358 chunk phases were identified across the six conversations.

6   Results

Our analysis of social talk focuses on a number of dimensions; chat and chunk duration, laughter and overlap in chat and chunk phases, distribution of chat and chunk phases across conversations, and turntaking/utterance characteristics.

6.1   Chat and Chunk Duration

Preliminary inspection of chat and chunk duration data showed that the distributions were unimodal

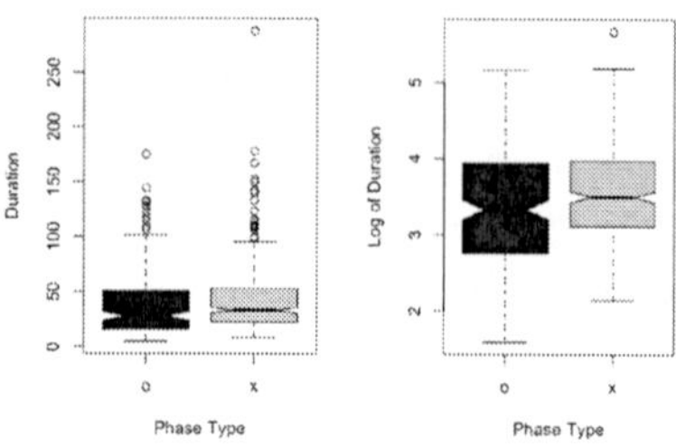

Figure 3: Boxplots of phase duration in Chat (grey) vs Chunk (black) in raw and log transformed data

but heavily right skewed. It was decided to use geometric means to describe central tendencies in the data. The antilogs of geometric means for duration of chat and chunk phases in the dataset were 28.1 seconds for chat and 34 seconds for chunks.

The chat and chunk phase durations (raw and log) are contrasted in the boxplots in Fig 3, where it can be seen that there is considerably more variance in chat durations.

6.2 Speaker, Gender, and Conversation Effects

The raw chunk data were checked for speaker dependency using the Kruskal-Wallis rank sum test, a non-parametric alternative to a one-way analysis of variance (ANOVA), and no significant difference in means due to speaker was found (Kruskal-Wallis chi-squared = 36.467, df = 24, p-value = 0.04941). Wilcoxon Rank Sum tests on chunk duration data showed no significant difference between duration distributions for chunks owned by male or female participants (W = 17495, p-value = 0.1073). Kruskal-Wallis rank sum tests on chunk duration showed no significant difference between duration distributions for chunks from different conversations (Kruskal-Wallis chi-squared = 9.2077, df = 5, p-value = 0.1011). However, the Kruskal-Wallis rank sum tests applied to chat duration showed significant differences between duration distributions for chats from different conversations (Kruskal-Wallis chi-squared = 15.801, df = 5, p-value = 0.007436).

6.3 Laughter Distribution in Chat and Chunk phases

Comparing the production by all participants in all conversations, where a participant may produce either laughter or speech, laughter accounts for approximately 9.5% of total duration of speech and laughter production in chat phases and 4.9% of total duration of speech and laughter production in chunk phases.

6.4 Chunk owner vs Others in Chunk

In the chunks overall, the dominant speakers or chunk owners produced 81.81% (10753.12s) of total speech and laughter, while non-owners produced 18.19% (2390.7s).

6.5 Overlap

There is considerable overlapping of speech in the corpora. For the purposes of this analysis laughter was treated as silence and overlap considered as overlapping speech only. Table 2 and Fig 4 show the occupancy of the conversational floor for all conversations in chat and chunk phases. The number of speakers ranges from 0 (global silence), 1 (single speaker), 2 (2 speakers in overlap) to 3+ (3 or more speakers in overlap).

No. Speaking	Chat	Chunk
0	25.75	22.14
1	61.58	72.27
2	11.88	5.25
3+	0.73	0.42

Table 2: Floor occupancy (%) in chat and chunk for all conversations

It can be seen that overlap is twice as common in chat as in chunk phases, and that silence is slightly more common in chat phases.

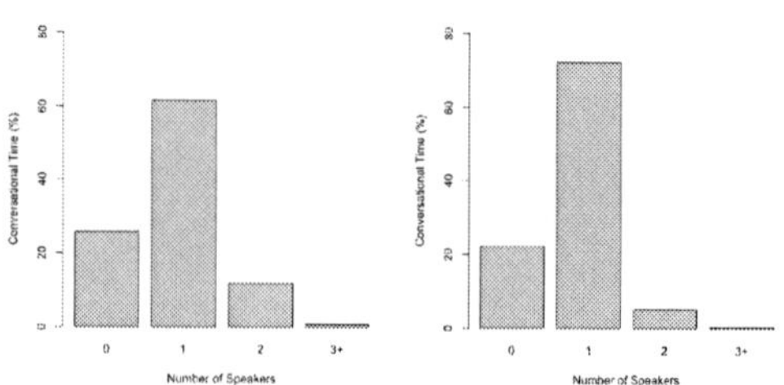

Figure 4: Distribution of the floor in terms of % duration in chat (left) and in chunk (right) phases. X-axis shows number of speakers (0,1,2,3+) speaking concurrently.

6.6 Chat and Chunk Position

Chat predominates for the first 8-10 minutes of conversations. However, as the conversation de-

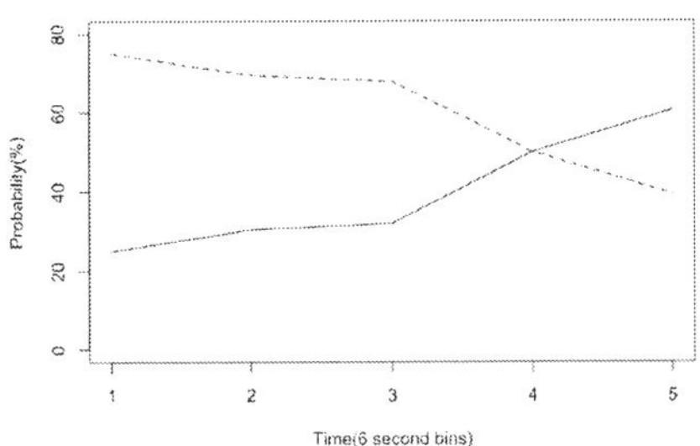

Figure 5: Probability of chunk-chunk transition (solid) and chunk-chat transition (dotted) as conversation elapses (x-axis = time) for the first 30 minutes of conversation

velops, chunks start to occur much more frequently, and the structure is an alternation of single-speaker chunks interleaved with shorter chat segments. Figure 5 shows the probability of a chunk phase being followed by chat or by chunk as conversation continues. It can be seen that there is a greater tendency for the conversation to go directly from chunk to chunk the longer the conversation continues.

6.7 Utterances and Turntaking

We are studying the patterning of speaker contributions in both phases. Overall we have found that utterances cluster into two groups: short utterances with a mean of around 300ms and longer utterances with mean around 1.4s. In chunk owner speech, utterance mean is higher than utterance means in chat.

We performed a prosodic analysis of phrase final intonation in a subset of the data using the IViE annotation system, finding that falling nuclei (H*+L%,!H*+L%) dominated across the data, and particularly in chunks, with relatively few fall-rise tones (H*+LH%) and small numbers of other tunes.

7 Discussion

We have found differences in the distributions of durations of chat and chunk phases, with chat durations varying more while chunk durations have a more consistent clustering around the mean. Chat phase durations tend to be shorter than chunk durations. These findings are not speaker or gender specific in our preliminary experiments and may indicate a natural limit for the time one speaker should dominate a conversation. The dimensions of chat and chunk durations observed would indicate that social talk should 'dose' or package information to fit chat and chunk segments of roughly these lengths. In particular, the tendency towards chunks of around half a minute could help in the design of narrative or education-delivering speech applications, by allowing designers to partition content optimally. Both laughter and overlap are far more prevalent in chat than in chunk phases, reflecting their light and interactive nature. Interestingly, the rarity of more than two speakers talking concurrently was noted in recent work on turn distribution in multiparty storytelling (Rühlemann and Gries, 2015) – our results would seem to show the same phenomenon in casual conversation, where it much more likely for a speaker to be overlapped by one other speaker than by two or more others. Laughter has previously been shown to appear more often in social talk than in meeting data, and to happen more around topic endings/topic changes [self]. This is consistent our with observations on chat and chunk phases – laughter is more common in chat phases – which provide a 'buffer' between single speaker (and topic) chunks.

Chat is more common at the start of multiparty conversations. Although our sample size is small, this observation conforms to descriptions of casual talk in the literature, and reflects the structure of 'first encounter' recordings. Chunk phases become more prominent later. The larger number of chunk phases in the data compared to Slade's findings on work break conversations may be due to the length of the conversations examined here - we found several instances of sequential chunks where the long turn passed directly to another speaker without intervening chat, perhaps reflecting 'story swapping' directly without need for chat as the conversation evolves. While the initial extended chat segments can be used to model 'getting to know you' sessions, and will therefore be useful for familiarisation with a digital companion, it is clear that we need to model the chunk heavy central segments of conversation if we want to create systems which form a longer-term dialogic relationship with users. As chunks are generic (narrative, gossip..), it may be fruitful to consider modelling extended casual talk as a series of 'mini-dialogs' of different types modelled on different corpora – how to convincingly join these sections is an interesting research question.

We have noted that many between speaker silences (pauses) during chunk owner speech in chunks are shorter than between speaker silences in chat, probably due to backchannelling in chunks, this would pose a problem for endpointing in dialog systems which relied simply on speaking at a certain delay after detection of silence, as the system would butt in during chat or wait too long during chunks depending on the time delay set. The majority of phrase final intonation curves are the same for chat and chunk reflecting the nature of casual conversation where utterances are predominantly comments or statements rather than question/answer pairs, exacerbating the endpointing/turntaking problem. Knowledge of the type of phase the dialog is in would allow systems to use more nuanced endpointing and turntaking mechanisms. A major limitation of the current work is the scarcity of data. Data for casual conversations which are longer than 15 minutes are hard to find. We hope that the current study will encourage the production of corpora of longer form casual conversation. We are currently extending our explorations to dyadic conversations, and also working on a dialog act annotation scheme for non-task based talk.

8   Conclusions

There is increasing interest in spoken dialogue systems that act naturally and perform functions beyond information search and narrow task-based exchanges. The design of these new systems needs to be informed by relevant data and analysis of human spoken interaction in the domains of interest. Many of the available multiparty data are based on meetings or first encounters. While first encounters are very relevant to the design of human machine first encounters, there is a lack of data on longer human conversations. We hope that the encouraging results of our analysis of casual social talk will help make the case for the creation and analysis of corpora of longer social dialogues. We also hope that our further explorations into the architecture of longer form conversation will add to this body of knowledge.

Acknowledgments

This work is supported by the European Coordinated Research on Long-term Challenges in Information and Communication Sciences and Technologies ERA-NET (CHISTERA) JOKER project, JOKe and Empathy of a Robot/ECA: Towards social and affective relations with a robot, and by Science Foundation Ireland (Grant 13/RC/2106) and the ADAPT Centre (www.adaptcentre.ie) at Trinity College, Dublin.

References

J. Allen, D. Byron, M. Dzikovska, G. Ferguson, L. Galescu, and A. Stent. 2000. An architecture for a generic dialogue shell. *Natural Language Engineering*, 6(3&4):213–228.

James F. Allen, Lenhart K. Schubert, George Ferguson, Peter Heeman, Chung Hee Hwang, Tsuneaki Kato, Marc Light, Nathaniel Martin, Bradford Miller, Massimo Poesio, and David R. Traum. 1995. The trains project: a case study in building a conversational planning agent. *Journal of Experimental & Theoretical Artificial Intelligence*, 7(1):7–48.

A.H. Anderson, M. Bader, E.G. Bard, E. Boyle, G. Doherty, S. Garrod, S. Isard, J. Kowtko, J. McAllister, J. Miller, et al. 1991. The HCRC map task corpus. *Language and Speech*, 34(4):351–366.

A. J. Aubrey, D. Marshall, P. L. Rosin, J. Vandeventer, D. W. Cunningham, and C. Wallraven. 2013. Cardiff Conversation Database (CCDb): A Database of Natural Dyadic Conversations. In *Computer Vision and Pattern Recognition Workshops (CVPRW), 2013 IEEE*, pages 277–282.

Rachel Baker and Valerie Hazan. 2011. DiapixUK: task materials for the elicitation of multiple spontaneous speech dialogs. *Behavior research methods*, 43(3):761–770.

Geoffrey Beattie. 1983. *Talk: An analysis of speech and non-verbal behaviour in conversation*. Open University Press.

Douglas Biber, Stig Johansson, Geoffrey Leech, Susan Conrad, Edward Finegan, and Randolph Quirk. 1999. *Longman Grammar of Spoken and Written English*, volume 2. Longman London.

BNC-Consortium. 2000. British national corpus. *URL http://www. hcu. ox. ac. uk/BNC.*

Paul Boersma and David Weenink. 2010. *Praat: doing phonetics by computer [Computer program], Version 5.1. 44.*

Gillian Brown and George Yule. 1983. *Teaching the Spoken Language*, volume 2. Cambridge University Press.

N. Campbell. 2008. Multimodal processing of discourse information; the effect of synchrony. In *Universal Communication, 2008. ISUC'08. Second International Symposium on*, pages 12–15.

Nick Campbell. 2007. Approaches to conversational speech rhythm: Speech activity in two-person telephone dialogues. In *Proc XVIth International Congress of the Phonetic Sciences, Saarbrucken, Germany*, pages 343–348.

Christine Cheepen. 1988. *The predictability of informal conversation*. Pinter London.

James Deese. 1980. *Pauses, prosody, and the demands of production in language*. Mouton Publishers.

John W. DuBois, W. L. Chafe, C. Meyer, and S. A. Thompson. 2000. *Santa Barbara Corpus of Spoken American English. CD-ROM. Philadelphia: Linguistic Data Consortium*.

R. Dunbar. 1998. *Grooming, gossip, and the evolution of language*. Harvard Univ Press.

Jens Edlund, Jonas Beskow, Kjell Elenius, Kahl Hellmer, Sofia Strömbergsson, and David House. 2010. Spontal: A Swedish Spontaneous Dialogue Corpus of Audio, Video and Motion Capture. In *LREC*.

S. Eggins and D. Slade. 2004. *Analysing Casual Conversation*. Equinox Publishing Ltd.

John J. Godfrey, Edward C. Holliman, and Jane McDaniel. 1992. SWITCHBOARD: Telephone speech corpus for research and development. In *Acoustics, Speech, and Signal Processing, 1992. ICASSP-92., 1992 IEEE International Conference on*, volume 1, pages 517–520.

Sidney Greenbaum. 1991. ICE: The international corpus of English. *English Today*, 28(7.4):3–7.

Shannon Hennig, Ryad Chellali, and Nick Campbell. 2014. The D-ANS corpus: the Dublin-Autonomous Nervous System corpus of biosignal and multimodal recordings of conversational speech. Reykjavik, Iceland.

R. Jakobson. 1960. Linguistics and poetics. In Th. A. Sebeok, editor, *Style in language*, pages 350–377. MA: MIT Press, Cambridge.

Adam Janin, Don Baron, Jane Edwards, Dan Ellis, David Gelbart, Nelson Morgan, Barbara Peskin, Thilo Pfau, Elizabeth Shriberg, and Andreas Stolcke. 2003. The ICSI meeting corpus. In *Acoustics, Speech, and Signal Processing, 2003. Proceedings.(ICASSP'03). 2003 IEEE International Conference on*, volume 1, pages I–364.

John Laver. 1975. Communicative Functions of Phatic Communion. In Adam Kendon, Richard M. Harris, and Mary R. Key, editors, *Organization of behavior in face-to-face interaction*, pages 215–238. Mouton, Oxford, England.

Bronislaw Malinowski. 1936. The Problem of Meaning in Primitive Languages. In *The meaning of meaning: a study of the influence of language upon thought and of the science of symbolism*, 4th ed. rev edition, pages 296–336. Kegan Paul, Trench, Trübner, London.

James G. Martin. 1970. On judging pauses in spontaneous speech. *Journal of Verbal Learning and Verbal Behavior*, 9(1):75–78.

Iain McCowan, Jean Carletta, W. Kraaij, S. Ashby, S. Bourban, M. Flynn, M. Guillemot, T. Hain, J. Kadlec, and V. Karaiskos. 2005. The AMI Meeting Corpus. In *Proceedings of the 5th International Conference on Methods and Techniques in Behavioral Research*, volume 88.

Catharine Oertel, Fred Cummins, Jens Edlund, Petra Wagner, and Nick Campbell. 2010. D64: A corpus of richly recorded conversational interaction. *Journal on Multimodal User Interfaces*, pages 1–10.

Patrizia Paggio, Jens Allwood, Elisabeth Ahlsén, and Kristiina Jokinen. 2010. The NOMCO multimodal Nordic resource–goals and characteristics.

Christoph Rühlemann and Stefan Gries. 2015. Turn order and turn distribution in multi-party storytelling. *Journal of Pragmatics*, 87:171–191.

E.A. Schegloff and H. Sacks. 1973. Opening up closings. *Semiotica*, 8(4):289–327.

Klaus P. Schneider. 1988. *Small Talk: Analysing Phatic Discourse*, volume 1. Hitzeroth Marburg.

Diana Slade. 2007. *The texture of casual conversation: A multidimensional interpretation*. Equinox.

Scott Thornbury and Diana Slade. 2006. *Conversation: From description to pedagogy*. Cambridge University Press.

Eija Ventola. 1979. The Structure of Casual Conversation in English. *Journal of Pragmatics*, 3(3):267–298.

Marilyn A. Walker, Rebecca Passonneau, and Julie E. Boland. 2001. Quantitative and qualitative evaluation of darpa communicator spoken dialogue systems. In *Proceedings of the 39th Annual Meeting on Association for Computational Linguistics*, ACL '01, pages 515–522, Stroudsburg, PA, USA. Association for Computational Linguistics.

John Wilson. 1989. *On the boundaries of conversation*, volume 10. Pergamon.

Peter Wittenburg, Hennie Brugman, Albert Russel, Alex Klassmann, and Han Sloetjes. 2006. Elan: a professional framework for multimodality research. In *Proceedings of LREC*, volume 2006.

Marcin Wlodarczak, Mattias Heldner, and Jens Edlund. 2015. Communicative needs and respiratory constraints. ISCA.

Neural User Simulation for Corpus-based Policy Optimisation for Spoken Dialogue Systems

Florian L. Kreyssig, Iñigo Casanueva
Paweł Budzianowski and **Milica Gašić**
Cambridge University Engineering Department,
Trumpington Street, Cambridge, CB2 1PZ, UK
`{flk24,ic340,pfb30,mg436}@cam.ac.uk`

Abstract

User Simulators are one of the major tools that enable offline training of task-oriented dialogue systems. For this task the Agenda-Based User Simulator (ABUS) is often used. The ABUS is based on hand-crafted rules and its output is in semantic form. Issues arise from both properties such as limited diversity and the inability to interface a text-level belief tracker. This paper introduces the Neural User Simulator (NUS) whose behaviour is learned from a corpus and which generates natural language, hence needing a less labelled dataset than simulators generating a semantic output. In comparison to much of the past work on this topic, which evaluates user simulators on corpus-based metrics, we use the NUS to train the policy of a reinforcement learning based Spoken Dialogue System. The NUS is compared to the ABUS by evaluating the policies that were trained using the simulators. Cross-model evaluation is performed i.e. training on one simulator and testing on the other. Furthermore, the trained policies are tested on real users. In both evaluation tasks the NUS outperformed the ABUS.

1 Introduction

Spoken Dialogue Systems (SDS) allow human-computer interaction using natural speech. Task-oriented dialogue systems, the focus of this work, help users achieve goals such as finding restaurants or booking flights (Young et al., 2013).

Teaching a system how to respond appropriately in a task-oriented setting is non-trivial. In state-of-the-art systems this *dialogue management* task is often formulated as a reinforcement learning (RL) problem (Young et al., 2013; Roy et al., 2000; Williams and Young, 2007; Gašić and Young, 2014). In this framework, the system learns by a *trial and error* process governed by a *reward function*. User Simulators can be used to train the policy of a *dialogue manager* (DM) without real user interactions. Furthermore, they allow an unlimited number of dialogues to be created with each dialogue being faster than a dialogue with a human.

In this paper the Neural User Simulator (NUS) is introduced which outputs natural language and whose behaviour is learned from a corpus. The main component, inspired by (El Asri et al., 2016), consists of a feature extractor and a neural network based sequence-to-sequence model (Sutskever et al., 2014). The sequence-to-sequence model consists of a recurrent neural network (RNN) encoder that encodes the dialogue history and a decoder RNN which outputs natural language. Furthermore, the NUS generates its own goal and possibly changes it during a dialogue. This allows the model to be deployed for training more sophisticated DM policies. To achieve this, a method is proposed that transforms the goal-labels of the used dataset (DSTC2) into labels whose behaviour can be replicated during deployment.

The NUS is trained on dialogues between real users and an SDS in a restaurant recommendation domain. Compared to much of the related work on user simulation, we use the trained NUS to train the policy of a reinforcement learning based SDS. In order to evaluate the NUS, an Agenda-Based User-Simulator (ABUS) (Schatzmann et al., 2007) is used to train another policy. The two policies are compared against each other by using *cross-model* evaluation (Schatztmann et al., 2005). This means to train on one model and to test on the other. Furthermore, both trained policies are tested on real users. On both evaluation tasks the NUS outperforms the ABUS, which is currently one of

60

the most popular off-line training tools for reinforcement learning based Spoken Dialogue Systems (Koo et al., 2015; Fatemi et al., 2016; Chen et al., 2017; Chang et al., 2017; Casanueva et al., 2018; Weisz et al., 2018; Shah et al., 2018).

The remainder of this paper is organised as follows. Section 2 briefly describes task-oriented dialogue. Section 3 describes the motivation for the NUS and discusses related work. Section 4 explains the structure of the NUS, how it is trained and how it is deployed for training a DM's policy. Sections 5 and 6 present the experimental setup and results. Finally, Section 7 gives conclusions.

2 Task-Oriented Dialogue

A Task-Oriented SDS is typically designed according to a structured *ontology*, which defines what the system can talk about. In a system recommending restaurants the ontology defines those attributes of a restaurant that the user can choose, called *informable slots* (e.g. different food types, areas and price ranges), the attributes that the user can request, called *requestable slots* (e.g. phone number or address) and the restaurants that it has data about. An attribute is referred to as a *slot* and has a corresponding *value*. Together these are referred to as a *slot-value pair* (e.g. `area`=north).

Using RL the DM is trained to act such that is maximises the cumulative future reward. The process by which the DM chooses its next action is called its *policy*. A typical approach to defining the reward function for a task-oriented SDS is to apply a small per-turn penalty to encourage short dialogues and to give a large positive reward at the end of each successful interaction.

3 Motivation and Related Work

Ideally the DM's policy would be trained by interacting with real users. Although there are models that support on-line learning (Gašić et al., 2011), for the majority of RL algorithms, which require a lot of interactions, this is impractical. Furthermore, a set of users needs to be recruited every time a policy is trained. This makes common practices such as hyper-parameter optimization prohibitively expensive. Thus, it is natural to try to learn from a dataset which needs to be recorded only once, but can be used over and over again.

A problem with learning directly from recorded dialogue corpora is that the state space that was visited during the collection of the data is limited; the size of the recorded corpus usually falls short of the requirements for training a statistical DM. However, even if the size of the corpus is large enough the optimal dialogue strategy is likely not to be contained within it.

A solution is to transform the static corpus into a dynamic tool: a *user simulator*. The user simulator (US) is trained on a dialogue corpus to learn what responses a real user would provide in a given dialogue context. The US is trained using supervised learning since the aim is for it to learn *typical* user behaviour. For the DM, however, we want *optimal* behaviour which is why supervised learning cannot be used. By interacting with the SDS, the trained US can be used to train the DM's policy. The DM's policy is optimised using the feedback given by either the user simulator or a separate evaluator. Any number of dialogues can be generated using the US and dialogue strategies that are not in the recorded corpus can be explored.

Most user-simulators work on the level of user semantics. These usually consist of a *user dialogue act* (e.g. inform, or request) and a corresponding slot-value pair. The first statistical user simulator (Eckert et al., 1997) used a simple bi-gram model $P(a_u | a_m)$ to predict the next user act a_u given the last system act a_m. It has the advantage of being purely probabilistic and domain-independent. However, it does not take the full dialogue history into account and is not conditioned on a goal, leading to incoherent user behaviour throughout a dialogue. Scheffler and Young (2000, 2001) attempted to overcome goal inconsistency by proposing a graph-based model. However, developing the graph structure requires extensive domain-specific knowledge. Pietquin and Dutoit (2006) combined features from Sheffler and Young's work with Eckert's Model, by conditioning a set of probabilities on an explicit representation of the user goal and memory. A Markov Model is also used by Georgila et al. (2005). It uses a large feature vector to describe the user's current state, which helps to compensate for the Markov assumption. However, the model is not conditioned on any goal. Therefore, it is not used to train a dialogue policy since it is impossible to determine whether the user goal was fulfilled. A hidden Markov model was proposed by Cuayáhuitl et al. (2005), which was also not used to train a policy. Chandramohan et al. (2011) cast user simulation as an inverse reinforcement learning problem where the user is modelled as a decision-making agent. The model did not incorporate a user goal and was hence not used to train a policy. The most prominent user model for policy optimisation is the Agenda-Based User Simulator (Schatzmann et al., 2007), which represents the user state elegantly as a stack of necessary user actions, called the *agenda*. The mechanism that generates the user response and updates the agenda does not require any data, though it can be improved using data. The model is conditioned on a goal for which it has update rules in case the dialogue system expresses that it cannot fulfil the goal. El Asri et al. (2016) modelled user simulation as a sequence-to-sequence task. The model can keep track of the dialogue history and user behaviour is learned entirely from data. However, goal changes were not modelled, even though a large proportion of dialogues within their dataset (DSTC2) contains goal changes. Their model outperformed the ABUS on statistical metrics, which is not surprising given that it was trained by optimising a statistical metric and the ABUS was not.

The aforementioned work focuses on user simulation at the semantic level. Multiple issues arise from this approach. Firstly, annotating the user-response with the correct semantics is costly. More data could be collected, if the US were to output natural language. Secondly, research suggests that the two modules of an SDS performing Spoken Language Understanding (SLU) and belief tracking should be jointly trained as a single entity (Mrkšić et al., 2017; Sun et al., 2016, 2014; Zilka and Jurcicek, 2015; Ramadan et al., 2018). In fact in the second Dialogue State Tracking Challenge (DSTC2) (Henderson et al., 2014), the data of which this work uses, systems which used no external SLU module outperformed all systems that only used an external SLU Module[1]. Training the policy of a DM in a simulated environment, when also using a joint system for SLU and belief tracking is *not possible* without a US that produces natural language. Thirdly, a US is sometimes augmented with an error model which generates a set of competing hypotheses with associated confidence scores trying to replicate the errors of the speech recogniser. When the error model matches the characteristics of the speech recogniser more accurately, the SDS performs better (Williams, 2008). However, speech recogni-

tion errors are badly modelled based on user semantics since they arise (mostly) due to the phonetics of the spoken words and not their semantics (Goldwater et al., 2010). Thus, an SDS that is trained with a natural language based error model is likely to outperform one trained with a semantic error model when tested on real users. Sequence-to-sequence learning for word-level user simulation is performed in (Crook and Marin, 2017), though the model is not conditioned on any goal and hence not used for policy optimisation. A word-level user simulator was also used in (Li et al., 2017) where it was built by augmenting the ABUS with a natural language generator.

4 Neural User Simulator

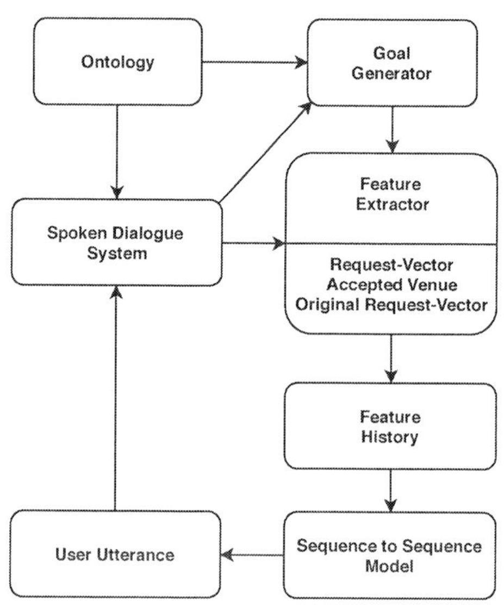

Figure 1: General Architecture of the Neural User Simulator. The System Output is passed to the Feature Extractor. It generates a new feature vector that is appended to the Feature History, which is passed to the sequence-to-sequence model to produce the user utterance. At the start of the dialogue the Goal Generator generates a goal, which might change during the course of the dialogue.

An overview of the NUS is given in Figure 1. At the start of a dialogue a random goal G_0 is generated by the *Goal Generator*. The possibilities for G_0 are defined by the *ontology*. In dialogue turn T, the output of the SDS (da_T) is passed to the NUS's *Feature Extractor*, which generates a feature vector $\mathbf{v}_T$ based on da_T, the current user goal, G_T, and parts of the dialogue history. This

---

[1]The best-performing models used both.

vector is appended to the *Feature History* $\mathbf{v}_{1:T} = \mathbf{v}_1...\mathbf{v}_T$. This sequence is passed to the *sequence-to-sequence* model (Fig. 2), which will generate the user's length n_T utterance $\mathbf{u}_T = w_0...w_{n_T}$. As in Figure 2, words in $\mathbf{u}_T$ corresponding to a slot are replaced by a slot token; a process called *delexicalisation*. If the SDS expresses to the NUS that there is no venue matching the NUS's constraints, the goal will be altered by the Goal Generator.

4.1 Goal Generator

The Goal Generator generates a random goal $G_0 = (C_0, R)$ at the start of the dialogue. It consists of a set of *constraints*, C_0, which specify the required venue e.g. (food=Spanish, area=north) and a number of *requests*, R, that specify the information that the NUS wants about the final venue e.g. the address or the phone number. The possibilities for C_t and R are defined by the *ontology*. In DSTC2 C_t can consist of a maximum of three constraints; food, area and pricerange. Whether each of the three is present is independently sampled with a probability of 0.66, 0.62 and 0.58 respectively. These probabilities were estimated from the DSTC2 data set. If no constraint is sampled then the goal is re-sampled. For each slot in C_0 a value (e.g. north for area) is sampled uniformly from the ontology. Similarly, the presence of a request is independently sampled, followed by re-sampling if zero requests were chosen.

When training the sequence-to-sequence model, the Goal Generator is not used, but instead the goal labels from the DSTC2 dataset are used. In DSTC2 one goal-label is given to the entire dialogue. This goal is always the *final* goal. If the user's goal at the start of the dialogue is (food=eritrean, area=south), which is changed to (food=spanish, area=south), due to the non-existence of an Eritrean restaurant in the south, using only the final goal is *insufficient* to model the dialogue. The final goal can only be used for the requests as they are not altered during a dialogue. DSTC2 also provides turn-specific labels. These contain the constraints and requests expressed by the user up until and including the current turn. When training a policy with the NUS, such labels would not be available as they "predict the future", i.e. when the turn-specific constraints change from (area=south) to (food=eritrean, area=south) it

means that the user will inform the system about her desire to eat Eritrean food in the current turn.

In related work on user-simulation for which the DSTC2 dataset was used, the final goal was used for the entire dialogue (El Asri et al., 2016; Serras et al., 2017; Liu and Lane, 2017). As stated above, we do not believe this to be sufficient. The following describes how to update the turn-specific constraint labels such that their behaviour can be replicated when training a DM's policy, whilst allowing goal changes to be modelled. The update strategy is illustrated in Table 1 with an example. The final turn keeps its constraints, from which we iterate *backwards* through the list of DSTC2's turn-specific constraints. The constraints of a turn will be set to the *updated* constraints of the succeeding turn, besides if the same slot is present with a *different* value. In that case the value will be kept. The behaviour of the updated turn-specific goal-labels can be replicated when the NUS is used to train a DM's policy. In the example, the food type changed due to the SDS expressing that there is no restaurant serving Eritrean food in the south. When deploying the NUS to train a policy, the goal is updated when the SDS outputs the canthelp dialogue act.

4.2 Feature Extractor

The Feature Extractor generates the feature vector that is appended to the sequence of feature vectors, here called *Feature History*, that is passed to the sequence-to-sequence model. The input to the Feature Extractor is the output of the DM and the current goal G_t. Furthermore, as indicated in Figure 1, the Feature Extractor keeps track of the currently accepted venue as well as the current and initial *request-vector*, which is explained below.

The feature vector $\mathbf{v}_t = [\mathbf{a}_t \ \mathbf{r}_t \ \mathbf{i}_t \ \mathbf{c}_t]$ is made up of four sub-vectors. The motivation behind the way in which these four vectors were designed is to provide an embedding for the system response that preserves all necessary *value-independent* information.

The first vector, *machine-act vector* $\mathbf{a}_t$, encodes the dialogue acts of the system response and consists of two parts; $\mathbf{a}_t = [\mathbf{a}_t^1 \ \mathbf{a}_t^2]$. $\mathbf{a}_t^1$ is a binary representation of the system dialogue acts present in the input. Its length is thus the number of possible system dialogue acts. It is binary and not one-hot since in DSTC2 multiple dialogue acts can be in the system's response. $\mathbf{a}_t^2$ is a binary represen-

C_t	Original	Updated
C_0	(food=eritrean)	(area=south, food=eritrean, pricerange=cheap)
C_1	(area=south, food=eritrean)	(area=south, food=eritrean, pricerange=cheap)
C_2	(area=south, food=spanish)	(area=south, food=spanish, pricerange=cheap)
C_3	(area=south, food=spanish, pricerange=cheap)	(area=south, food=spanish, pricerange=cheap)

Table 1: An example of how DSTC2's turn-specific constraint labels can be transformed such that their behaviour can be replicated when training a dialogue manager.

tation of the slot if the dialogue act is `request` or `select` and if it is `inform` or `expl-conf` together with a *correct* slot-value pair for an informable slot. The length is four times the number of informable slots. $\mathbf{a}_t^2$ is necessary due to the dependence of the sentence structure on the exact slot mentioned by the system. The utterances of a user in response to `request(food)` and `request(area)` are often very different.

The second vector, *request-vector* $\mathbf{r}_t$, is a binary representation of the requests that have not yet been fulfilled. It's length is thus the number of requestable slots. In comparison to the other three vectors the feature extractor needs to remember it for the next turn. At the start of the dialogue the indices corresponding to requests that are in R are set to 1 and the rest to 0. Whenever the system informs a certain request the corresponding index in $\mathbf{r}_t$ is set to 0. When a new venue is proposed $\mathbf{r}_t$ is reset to the original request vector, which is why the Feature Extractor keeps track of it.

The third vector, *inconsistency-vector* $\mathbf{i}_t$, represents the inconsistency between the system's response and C_t. Every time a slot is mentioned by the system, when describing a venue (`inform`) or confirming a slot-value pair (`expl-conf` or `impl-conf`), the indices corresponding to the slots that have been misunderstood are set to 1. The length of $\mathbf{i}_t$ is the number of informable slots. This vector is necessary in order for the NUS to correct the system.

The fourth vector, $\mathbf{c}_t$, is a binary representation of the slots that are in the constraints C_t. It's length is thus the number of informable slots. This vector is necessary in order for the NUS to be able to inform about its preferred venue.

4.3 Sequence-To-Sequence Model

The sequence-to-sequence model (Figure 2) consists of an RNN encoder, followed by a fully-connect layer and an RNN decoder. An RNN can be defined as:

$$(\mathbf{h}_t, \mathbf{s}_t) = \text{RNN}\left(\mathbf{x}_t, \mathbf{s}_{t-1}\right) \quad (1)$$

At time-step t, an RNN uses an input $\mathbf{x}_t$ and an internal state $\mathbf{s}_{t-1}$ to produce its output $\mathbf{h}_t$ and its new internal state $\mathbf{s}_t$. A specific RNN-design is usually defined using matrix multiplications, element-wise additions and multiplications as well as element-wise non-linear functions. There are a plethora of different RNN architectures that could be used and explored. Given that such exploration is not the focus of this work a single layer LSTM (Hochreiter and Schmidhuber, 1997) is used for both the RNN encoder and decoder. The exact LSTM version used in this work uses a forget gate without bias and does not use peep-holes.

The first RNN (shown as white blocks in Fig. 2) takes one feature vector $\mathbf{v}_t$ at a time as its input ($\mathbf{x}_t^E = \mathbf{v}_t$). If the current dialogue turn is turn T then the final output of the RNN encoder is given by $\mathbf{h}_T^E$, which is passed through a fully-connected layer (shown as the light-grey block) with linear activation function:

$$\mathbf{p}_T = W_p \mathbf{h}_T^E + \mathbf{b}_p \quad (2)$$

For a certain encoding $\mathbf{p}_T$ the sequence-to-sequence model should define a probability distribution over different sequences. By sampling from this distribution the NUS can generate a diverse set of sentences corresponding to the same dialogue context. The conditional probability distribution of a length L sequence is defined as:

$$P(\mathbf{u}\,|\,\mathbf{p}) = P(w_0\,|\,\mathbf{p})\prod_{t=1}^{L} P(w_t\,|\,w_{t-1}...w_0, \mathbf{p}) \quad (3)$$

The decoder RNN (shown as dark blocks) will be used to model $P(w_t\,|\,w_{t-1}...w_0, \mathbf{p})$. It's input at each time-step is the concatenation of an embedding $\mathbf{w}_{t-1}$ (we used 1-hot) of the previous word w_{t-1} ($\mathbf{x}_t^D = [\mathbf{w}_{t-1}\,\mathbf{p}]$). For $P(w_0\,|\,\mathbf{p})$ a *start-of-sentence* (`<SOS>`) token is used as w_{-1}. The

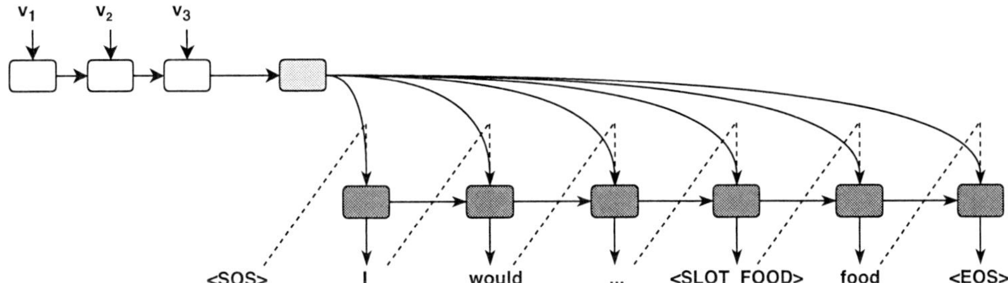

Figure 2: Sequence-To-Sequence model of the Neural User Simulator. Here, the NUS is generating the user response to the third system output. The white, light-grey and dark blocks represent the RNN encoder, a fully-connected layer and the RNN decoder respectively. The previous output of the decoder is passed to its input for the next time-step. $\mathbf{v}_{3:1}$ are the first three feature vectors (see Sec. 4.2).

end of the utterance is modelled using an *end-of-sentence* (<EOS>) token. When the decoder RNN generates the *end-of-sentence* token, the decoding process is terminated. The output of the decoder RNN, $\mathbf{h}_t^D$, is passed through an affine transform followed by the softmax function, *SM*, to form $P(w_t \,|\, w_{t-1}...w_0, \mathbf{p})$. A word w_t can be obtained by either taking the word with the highest probability or sampling from the distribution:

$$P(w_t \mid w_{t-1}...w_0, \mathbf{p}) = SM(W_w \mathbf{h}_t^D + \mathbf{b}_w) \quad (4)$$

$$w_t \sim P(w_t \mid w_{t-1}...w_0, \mathbf{p}) \quad (5)$$

During training the words are not sampled from the output distribution, but instead the true words from the dataset are used. This a common technique that is often referred to as *teacher-forcing*, though it also directly follows from equation 3.

To generate a sequence using an RNN, beam-search is often used. Using beam-search with n beams, the words corresponding to the top n probabilities of $P(w_0 \,|\, \mathbf{p})$ are the first n beams. For each succeeding w_t, the n words corresponding to the top n probabilities of $P(w_t \,|\, w_{t-1}...w_0, \mathbf{p})$ are taken for each of the n beams. This is followed by reducing the number of beams from now n^2 down to n, by taking the n beams with the highest probability $P(w_t w_{t-1}...w_0 \,|\, \mathbf{p})$. This is a deterministic process. However, for the NUS to always give the same response in the same context is not realistic. Thus, the NUS cannot cover the full breadth of user behaviour if beam-search is used. To solve this issue while keeping the benefit of rejecting sequences with low probability, a type of beam-search with sampling is used. The process is identical to the above, but n words per beam are sampled from the probability distribution. The

NUS is now non-deterministic resulting in a diverse US. Using 2 beams gave a good trade-off between reasonable responses and diversity.

4.4 Training

The neural sequence-to-sequence model is trained to maximize the log probability that it assigns to the user utterances of the training data set:

$$\mathcal{L} = \sum_{n=1}^{N} \log P(w_0 \,|\, \mathbf{p}) \sum_{t=1}^{L_n} \log P(w_t \,|\, w_{t-1:0}, \mathbf{p}) \quad (6)$$

The network was implemented in Tensorflow (Abadi et al., 2015) and optimized using Tensorflow's default setup of the Adam optimizer (Kingma and Ba, 2015). The LSTM layers and the fully-connected layer had widths of 100 each to give a reasonable number of overall parameters. The width was not tuned. The learning rate was optimised on a held out validation set and no regularization methods used. The training set was shuffled at the dialogue turn level.

The manual transcriptions of the DSTC2 training set (not the ASR output) were used to train the sequence-to-sequence model. Since the transcriptions were done manually they contained spelling errors. These were manually corrected to ensure proper delexicalization. Some dialogues were discarded due to transcriptions errors being too large. After cleaning the dataset the training set consisted of 1609 dialogues with a total of 11638 dialogue turns. The validation set had 505 dialogues with 3896 dialogue turns. The maximum sequence length of the delexicalized turns was 22, including the end of sentence character. The maximum dialogue length was 30 turns.

5   Experimental Setup

The evaluation of user simulators is an ongoing area of research and a variety of techniques can be found in the literature. Most papers published on user simulation evaluate their US using *direct* methods. These methods evaluate the US through a statistical measure of similarity between the outputs of the US and a real user on a test set. Multiple models can outperform the ABUS on these metrics. However, this is unsurprising since these user simulators were trained on the same or similar metrics. The ABUS was explicitly proposed as a tool to train the policy of a dialogue manager and it is still the dominant form of US used for this task. Therefore, the only fair comparison between a new US model and the ABUS is to use the *indirect* method of evaluating the policies that were obtained by training with each US.

5.1   Training

All dialogue policies were trained with the PyDial toolkit (Ultes et al., 2017), by interacting with either the NUS or ABUS. The RL algorithm used is GP-SARSA (Gašić and Young, 2014) with hyperparameters taken from (Casanueva et al., 2017). The reward function used gives a reward of 20 to a successfully completed dialogue and of -1 for each dialogue turn. The maximum dialogue length was 25 turns. The presented metrics are success rate (SR) and average reward over test dialogues. SR is the percentage of dialogues for which the system satisfied both the user's constraints and requests. The final goal, after possible goal changes, was used for this evaluation. When policies are trained using the NUS, its output is parsed using PyDial's regular expression based semantic decoder. The policies were trained for 4000 dialogues.

5.2   Testing with a simulated user

In Schatzmann et. al (2005) *cross-model evaluation* is proposed to compare user simulators. First, the user simulators to be evaluated are used to train N policy each. Then these policies are tested using the different user simulators and the results averaged. Schatztmann et al. (2005) showed that a strategy learned with a good user model still performs well when tested on poor user models. If a policy performs well on all user simulators and not just on the one that it was trained on, it indicates that the US with which it was trained is diverse and realistic, and thus the policy is likely to perform better on real users. For each US five policies ($N = 5$), each using a different random seed for initialisation, are trained. Results are reported for both the best and the average performance on 1000 test dialogues. The ABUS is programmed to always mention the new goal after a goal change. In order to not let this affect our results we implement the same for the NUS by re-sampling a sentence if the new goal is not mentioned.

5.3   Testing with real users

Though the above test is already more indicative of policy performance on real users than measuring statistical metrics of user behaviour, a better test is to test with human users. For the test on human users, two policies for each US that was used for training are chosen from the five policies. The first policy is the one that performed best when *tested on the NUS*. The second is the one that performed best when *tested on the ABUS*. This choice of policies is motivated by a type of overfitting to be seen in Sec. 6.1. The evaluation of the trained dialogue policies in interaction with real users follows a similar set-up to (Jurčíček et al., 2011). Users are recruited through the Amazon Mechanical Turk (AMT) service. 1000 dialogues (250 per policy) were gathered. The learnt policies were incorporated into an SDS pipeline with a commercial ASR system. The AMT users were asked to find a restaurant that matches certain constraints and find certain requests. Subjects were randomly allocated to one of the four analysed systems. After each dialogue the users were asked whether they judged the dialogue to be successful or not which was then translated to the reward measure.

6   Experimental Results

6.1   Cross-Model Evaluation

Table 2 shows the results of the cross-model evaluation after 4000 training dialogues. The policies trained with the NUS achieved an average success rate (SR) of 94.0% and of 96.6% when tested on the ABUS and the NUS, respectively. By comparison, the policies trained with the ABUS achieved average SRs of 99.5% and 45.5% respectively. Thus, training with the NUS leads to policies that can perform well on both USs, which is not the case for training with the ABUS. Furthermore, the best SRs when tested on the ABUS are similar at 99.9% (ABUS) and 99.8% (NUS). When tested on the NUS the best SRs were 71.5% (ABUS) and

Train. Sim.	Eval. Sim.			
	NUS		ABUS	
	Rew.	Suc.	Rew.	Suc.
NUS-best	13.0	98.0^{V_1}	13.3	99.8
ABUS-best	1.53	71.5^{A_1}	13.8	99.9^{A_2}
NUS-avg	12.4	96.6	11.2	94.0
ABUS-avg	-7.6	45.5	13.5	99.5

Table 2: Results for policies trained for 4000 dialogues on NUS and ABUS when tested on both USs for 1000 dialogues. Five policies with different initialisations were trained for each US. Both average and best results are shown.

Train. Sim.	Eval. Sim.			
	NUS		ABUS	
	Rew.	Suc.	Rew.	Suc.
NUS-best	12.2	95.9	13.9	99.9^{N_2}
ABUS-best	-4.0	54.8	13.2	99.0
NUS-avg	12.0	95.4	12.2	97.3
ABUS-avg	-9.48	42.3	12.8	98.4

Table 3: As Table 2 but trained for 1000 dialogues.

98.0% (NUS). This shows that the behaviour of the Neural User Simulator is realistic and diverse enough to train policies that can also perform very well on the Agenda-Based User Simulator.

Of the five policies, for each US, the policy performing best on the NUS was not the best performing policy on the ABUS. This could indicate that the policy "overfits" to a particular user simulator. Overfitting usually manifests itself in worse results as the model is trained for longer. Five policies trained on each US for only 1000 dialogues were also evaluated, the results of which can be seen in Table 3. After training for 1000 dialogues, the average SR of the policies trained on the NUS when tested on the ABUS was 97.3% in comparison to 94.0% after 4000 dialogues. This behaviour was observed for all five seeds, which indicates that the policy indeed overfits to the NUS. For the policies trained with the ABUS this was not observed. This could indicate that the policy can learn to exploit some of the shortcomings of the trained NUS.

6.2 Human Evaluation

The results of the human evaluation are shown in Table 4 for 250 dialogues per policy. In Table 4 policies are marked using an ID ($\mathcal{U}_\alpha$) that translates to results in Tables 2 and 3. Both policies trained with the NUS outperformed those trained

Training Simulator	Human Evaluation	
	Rew.	Suc.
NUS - $\mathcal{N}_1$	13.4	91.8
NUS - $\mathcal{N}_2$	13.8	93.4
ABUS - $\mathcal{A}_1$	13.3	90.0
ABUS - $\mathcal{A}_2$	13.1	88.5

Table 4: Real User Evaluation. Results over 250 dialogues with human users. $\mathcal{N}_1$ and $\mathcal{A}_1$ performed best on the NUS. $\mathcal{N}_2$ and $\mathcal{A}_2$ performed best on the ABUS. Rewards are not comparable to Table 2 and 3 since all user goals were achievable.

on the ABUS in terms of both reward and success rate. The best performing policy trained on the NUS achieves a 93.4% success rate and 13.8 average rewards whilst the best performing policy trained with the ABUS achieves only a 90.0% success rate and 13.3 average reward. This shows that the good performance of the NUS on the cross-model evaluation transfers to real users. Furthermore, the overfitting to a particular US is also observed in the real user evaluation. For not only the policies trained on the NUS, but also those trained on the ABUS, the best performing policy was the policy that performed best on the other US.

7 Conclusion

We introduced the Neural User Simulator (NUS), which uses the system's response in its semantic form as input and gives a natural language response. It thus needs *less labelling* of the training data than User Simulators that generate a response in semantic form. It was shown that the NUS learns realistic user behaviour from a corpus of recorded dialogues such that it can be used to optimise the policy of the dialogue manager of a spoken dialogue system. The NUS was compared to the Agenda-Based User Simulator by evaluating policies trained with these user simulators. The trained policies were compared both by testing them with simulated users and also with real users. The NUS excelled on both evaluation tasks.

Acknowledgements

This research was partly funded by the EPSRC grant EP/M018946/1 Open Domain Statistical Spoken Dialogue Systems. Florian Kreyssig is supported by the Studienstiftung des Deutschen Volkes. Paweł Budzianowski is supported by the EPSRC and Toshiba Research Europe Ltd.

References

Martín Abadi, Ashish Agarwal, Paul Barham, Eugene Brevdo, Zhifeng Chen, Craig Citro, Greg S. Corrado, Andy Davis, Jeffrey Dean, Matthieu Devin, Sanjay Ghemawat, Ian Goodfellow, Andrew Harp, Geoffrey Irving, Michael Isard, Yangqing Jia, Rafal Jozefowicz, Lukasz Kaiser, Manjunath Kudlur, Josh Levenberg, Dandelion Mané, Rajat Monga, Sherry Moore, Derek Murray, Chris Olah, Mike Schuster, Jonathon Shlens, Benoit Steiner, Ilya Sutskever, Kunal Talwar, Paul Tucker, Vincent Vanhoucke, Vijay Vasudevan, Fernanda Viégas, Oriol Vinyals, Pete Warden, Martin Wattenberg, Martin Wicke, Yuan Yu, and Xiaoqiang Zheng. 2015. TensorFlow: Large-scale machine learning on heterogeneous systems. Software available from tensorflow.org.

Iñigo Casanueva, Paweł Budzianowski, Pei-Hao Su, Nikola Mrkšić, Tsung-Hsien Wen, Stefan Ultes, Lina Rojas-Barahona, Steve Young, and Milica Gašić. 2017. A benchmarking environment for reinforcement learning based task oriented dialogue management. In *NIPS Deep Reinforcement Learning Symposium*.

Iñigo Casanueva, Paweł Budzianowski, Pei-Hao Su, Stefan Ultes, Lina Rojas-Barahona, Bo-Hsiang Tseng, and Milica Gašić. 2018. Feudal reinforcement learning for dialogue management in large domains. In *Proc. NAACL 2018*.

Senthilkumar Chandramohan, Matthieu Geist, Fabrice Lefevre, and Olivier Pietquin. 2011. User simulation in dialogue systems using inverse reinforcement learning. In *Proceedings of the Twelfth Annual Conference of the International Speech Communication Association*.

Cheng Chang, Runzhe Yang, Lu Chen, Xiang Zhou, and Kai Yu. 2017. Affordable on-line dialogue policy learning. In *Proceedings of the 2017 Conference on Empirical Methods in Natural Language Processing*, pages 2200–2209.

Lu Chen, Xiang Zhou, Cheng Chang, Runzhe Yang, and Kai Yu. 2017. Agent-aware dropout dqn for safe and efficient on-line dialogue policy learning. In *Proceedings of the 2017 Conference on Empirical Methods in Natural Language Processing*, pages 2454–2464.

Paul Crook and Alex Marin. 2017. Sequence to sequence modeling for user simulation in dialog systems. In *Proceedings of the 18th Annual Conference of the International Speech Communication Association*.

Heriberto Cuayáhuitl, Steve Renals, Oliver Lemon, and Hiroshi Shimodaira. 2005. Human-computer dialogue simulation using hidden markov models. In *Automatic Speech Recognition and Understanding, 2005 IEEE Workshop on*, pages 290–295. IEEE.

Wieland Eckert, Esther Levin, and Roberto Pieraccini. 1997. User modeling for spoken dialogue system evaluation. In *Automatic Speech Recognition and Understanding, 1997. Proceedings., 1997 IEEE Workshop on*, pages 80–87. IEEE.

Layla El Asri, Jing He, and Kaheer Suleman. 2016. A sequence-to-sequence model for user simulation in spoken dialogue systems. *Proceedings of the 17th Annual Conference of the International Speech Communication Association*, pages 1151–1155.

Mehdi Fatemi, Layla El Asri, Hannes Schulz, Jing He, and Kaheer Suleman. 2016. Policy networks with two-stage training for dialogue systems. In *Proceedings of the 17th Annual Meeting of the Special Interest Group on Discourse and Dialogue*, pages 101–110.

Milica Gašić and Steve Young. 2014. Gaussian processes for pomdp-based dialogue manager optimization. *IEEE/ACM Transactions on Audio, Speech, and Language Processing*, 22(1):28–40.

M. Gašić, F. Jurčíček, B. Thomson, K. Yu, and S. Young. 2011. On-line policy optimisation of spoken dialogue systems via live interaction with human subjects. In *Automatic Speech Recognition and Understanding, 2011 IEEE Workshop on*.

Kallirroi Georgila, James Henderson, and Oliver Lemon. 2005. Learning user simulations for information state update dialogue systems. In *Ninth European Conference on Speech Communication and Technology*.

Sharon Goldwater, Dan Jurafsky, and Christopher D Manning. 2010. Which words are hard to recognize? prosodic, lexical, and disfluency factors that increase speech recognition error rates. *Speech Communication*, 52(3):181–200.

Matthew Henderson, Blaise Thomson, and Jason D Williams. 2014. The second dialog state tracking challenge. In *Proceedings of the 15th Annual Meeting of the Special Interest Group on Discourse and Dialogue (SIGDIAL)*, pages 263–272.

Sepp Hochreiter and Jürgen Schmidhuber. 1997. Long short-term memory. *Neural computation*, 9(8):1735–1780.

Filip Jurčíček, Simon Keizer, Milica Gašić, Francois Mairesse, Blaise Thomson, Kai Yu, and Steve Young. 2011. Real user evaluation of spoken dialogue systems using amazon mechanical turk. In *Proceedings of the Twelfth Annual Conference of the International Speech Communication Association*.

Diederik P Kingma and Jimmy Ba. 2015. Adam: A method for stochastic optimization.

Sangjun Koo, Seonghan Ryu, and Gary Geunbae Lee. 2015. Implementation of generic positive-negative tracker in extensible dialog system. In *Automatic Speech Recognition and Understanding (ASRU), 2015 IEEE Workshop on*, pages 798–805. IEEE.

Xiujun Li, Yun-Nung Chen, Lihong Li, Jianfeng Gao, and Asli Celikyilmaz. 2017. End-to-end task-completion neural dialogue systems. In *Proceedings of the Eighth International Joint Conference on Natural Language Processing (Volume 1: Long Papers)*, pages 733–743, Taipei, Taiwan. Asian Federation of Natural Language Processing.

Bing Liu and Ian Lane. 2017. Iterative policy learning in end-to-end trainable task-oriented neural dialog models. In *2017 IEEE Automatic Speech Recognition and Understanding Workshop, ASRU*, pages 482–489.

Nikola Mrkšić, Diarmuid Ó Séaghdha, Tsung-Hsien Wen, Blaise Thomson, and Steve Young. 2017. Neural belief tracker: Data-driven dialogue state tracking. In *Proceedings of the 55th Annual Meeting of the Association for Computational Linguistics (Volume 1: Long Papers)*, volume 1, pages 1777–1788.

Olivier Pietquin and Thierry Dutoit. 2006. A probabilistic framework for dialog simulation and optimal strategy learning. *IEEE Transactions on Audio, Speech, and Language Processing*, 14(2):589–599.

Osman Ramadan, Paweł Budzianowski, and Milica Gašić. 2018. Large-scale multi-domain belief tracking with knowledge sharing. In *Proceedings of the 56th Annual Meeting of the Association for Computational Linguistics (Volume 2: Short Papers)*. Association for Computational Linguistics.

Nicholas Roy, Joelle Pineau, and Sebastian Thrun. 2000. Spoken dialogue management using probabilistic reasoning. In *Proceedings of the 38th Annual Meeting on Association for Computational Linguistics*, pages 93–100. Association for Computational Linguistics.

Jost Schatzmann, Blaise Thomson, Karl Weilhammer, Hui Ye, and Steve Young. 2007. Agenda-based user simulation for bootstrapping a pomdp dialogue system. In *Human Language Technologies 2007: The Conference of the North American Chapter of the Association for Computational Linguistics; Companion Volume, Short Papers*, pages 149–152. Association for Computational Linguistics.

Jost Schatztmann, Matthew N Stuttle, Karl Weilhammer, and Steve Young. 2005. Effects of the user model on simulation-based learning of dialogue strategies. In *Automatic Speech Recognition and Understanding, 2005 IEEE Workshop on*, pages 220–225. IEEE.

Konrad Scheffler and Steve Young. 2000. Probabilistic simulation of human-machine dialogues. In *Acoustics, Speech, and Signal Processing, 2000. ICASSP'00. Proceedings. 2000 IEEE International Conference on*, volume 2, pages II1217–II1220. IEEE.

Konrad Scheffler and Steve Young. 2001. Corpus-based dialogue simulation for automatic strategy learning and evaluation. In *Proc. NAACL Workshop on Adaptation in Dialogue Systems*, pages 64–70.

Manex Serras, María Inés Torres Torres, and Arantza del Pozo. 2017. Regularized neural user model for goal oriented spoken dialogue systems. In *International Workshop on Spoken Dialogue Systems*. Association for Computational Linguistics.

Pararth Shah, Dilek Hakkani-Tür, Gokhan Tür, Abhinav Rastogi, Ankur Bapna, Neha Nayak, and Larry Heck. 2018. Building a conversational agent overnight with dialogue self-play. *arXiv preprint arXiv:1801.04871*.

Kai Sun, Lu Chen, Su Zhu, and Kai Yu. 2014. The sjtu system for dialog state tracking challenge 2. In *Proceedings of the 15th Annual Meeting of the Special Interest Group on Discourse and Dialogue (SIGDIAL)*, pages 318–326.

Kai Sun, Qizhe Xie, and Kai Yu. 2016. Recurrent polynomial network for dialogue state tracking. *Dialogue & Discourse*, 7(3):65–88.

Ilya Sutskever, Oriol Vinyals, and Quoc V Le. 2014. Sequence to sequence learning with neural networks. In *Advances in neural information processing systems*, pages 3104–3112.

Stefan Ultes, Lina M. Rojas Barahona, Pei-Hao Su, David Vandyke, Dongho Kim, Iñigo Casanueva, Paweł Budzianowski, Nikola Mrkšić, Tsung-Hsien Wen, Milica Gašić, and Steve Young. 2017. PyDial: A Multi-domain Statistical Dialogue System Toolkit. In *Proceedings of ACL 2017, System Demonstrations*, pages 73–78, Vancouver, Canada. Association for Computational Linguistics.

Gellért Weisz, Paweł Budzianowski, Pei-Hao Su, and Milica Gašić. 2018. Sample efficient deep reinforcement learning for dialogue systems with large action spaces. *arXiv preprint arXiv:1802.03753*.

Jason D Williams. 2008. Evaluating user simulations with the cramér–von mises divergence. *Speech communication*, 50(10):829–846.

Jason D Williams and Steve Young. 2007. Partially observable markov decision processes for spoken dialog systems. *Computer Speech & Language*, 21(2):393–422.

Steve Young, Milica Gašić, Blaise Thomson, and Jason D Williams. 2013. Pomdp-based statistical spoken dialog systems: A review. *Proceedings of the IEEE*, 101(5):1160–1179.

Lukas Zilka and Filip Jurcicek. 2015. Incremental lstm-based dialog state tracker. In *Automatic Speech Recognition and Understanding (ASRU), 2015 IEEE Workshop on*, pages 757–762. IEEE.

Introduction method for argumentative dialogue using paired question-answering interchange about personality

Kazuki Sakai[1], Ryuichiro Higashinaka[2], Yuichiro Yoshikawa[1],
Hiroshi Ishiguro[1], and Junji Tomita[2]
[1]Osaka University / JST ERATO
[2]NTT Media Intelligence Laboratories, NTT Corporation
[1]{sakai.kazuki,yoshikawa,ishiguro}@irl.sys.es.osaka-u.ac.jp
[2]{higashinaka.ryuichiro,tomita.junji}@lab.ntt.co.jp

Abstract

To provide a better discussion experience in current argumentative dialogue systems, it is necessary for the user to feel motivated to participate, even if the system already responds appropriately. In this paper, we propose a method that can smoothly introduce argumentative dialogue by inserting an initial discourse, consisting of question-answer pairs concerning personality. The system can induce interest of the users prior to agreement or disagreement during the main discourse. By disclosing their interests, the users will feel familiarity and motivation to further engage in the argumentative dialogue and understand the system's intent. To verify the effectiveness of a question-answer dialogue inserted before the argument, a subjective experiment was conducted using a text chat interface. The results suggest that inserting the question-answer dialogue enhances familiarity and naturalness. Notably, the results suggest that women more than men regard the dialogue as more natural and the argument as deepened, following an exchange concerning personality.

1 Introduction

Argumentation is a process of reaching consensus through premises and rebuttals, and it is an important skill required in daily life (Scheuer et al., 2010). Through argumentation, we can not only reach decisions, but also learn what others think. Such decision-making and the interchange of views are one of the most important and advanced parts of human activities. If an artificial dialogue system can argue on certain topics with us, this can both help us to work efficiently and establish a close relationship with the system.

Recently, there have been some studies concerning argumentative dialogue systems. Higashinaka et al. developed an argumentative dialogue system that can discuss certain topics by using large-scale argumentation structures (Higashinaka et al., 2017). However, this system could not provide all users with a satisfactory discussion experience, even though it could appropriately respond to their opinions. One possible reason for this is that some users are not necessarily motivated to argue on the topics suggested by the system.

We aim to improve an argumentative dialogue system by adding a function to motivate a user to participate in an argumentative dialogue. To increase the user's motivation to participate in the argumentative dialogue, we focus on small talk. Small talk can help participants build certain relationships before they enter the main dialogue (Zhao et al., 2014). In negotiation and counseling, a close relationship between two humans can improve the performance of certain tasks (Drolet and Morris, 2000; Kang et al., 2012). Relationships between a user and system are important for reaching a consensus though dialogue (Katagiri et al., 2013) Thus, it is considered to be possible for a user to be naturally guided into an argumentative dialogue by performing small talk.

In practice, we adopted a question-answering dialogue, where users are casually asked about their personal experiences or ideas. This was implemented by using what we call a personal database (hereafter PDB), which involves pairs consisting of a personal question and a corresponding example answer, which are likely to appear in human-human conversation. When asked about personal issues, users are expected to feel interested in the system, and then be induced to feel open and close to the system. Meanwhile, the system provides its own answers to the questions

Proceedings of the SIGDIAL 2018 Conference, pages 70–79,
Melbourne, Australia, 12-14 July 2018. ©2018 Association for Computational Linguistics

by using the PDB. From the answers of the user and the system, users are expected to gain an idea of what is common and different between them, a requirement which has been suggested to be important for humans to be motivated to understand one another (Uchida et al., 2016).

In this research, we extend the argumentative dialogue system described in (Higashinaka et al., 2017) to add a function that can smoothly introduce argumentative dialogue by inserting a question-answering dialogue using the PDB (hereinafter referred to as PDB-QA dialogue). It is considered that users of the proposed system can be expected to be motivated to partake in the argumentative dialogue, and that they can then partake in a deep discussion with the system. To verify the effectiveness of this system, we conducted a subjective experiment using a text chat interface.

The remainder of this paper is organized as follows. In Section 2, we describe related work. In Section 3, we describe our proposed method, including how to develop the question-answering dialogue and how to integrate this into an existing argumentative dialogue system. In Section 4, we describe an experiment we conducted, in which human subjects expressed their impressions of the dialogue through a text chat interface. We summarize the paper and discuss future work in Section 5.

2 Related work

Although there is little work on an automated system that can perform discussion with users, recently, there has been a great deal of work aimed at automatically extracting premises and conclusions from text; argumentation mining has been applied to various data, including legal text (Moens et al., 2007), newswire text (Bal and Saint-Dizier, 2010), opinions in discussion forums (Rosenthal and McKeown, 2012), and varied online text (Yanai et al., 2016).

There has been some research concerning the introduction of a dialogue. Rogers et al. showed that it became easier for two people to talk during the first meeting by using an application that can share their opinions on a display (Rogers and Brignull, 2002). Patricia et al. reported that small talk in an initial discourse improved the interaction in a business situation (Pullin, 2010). Inaguma et al. analyzed the prosodic features of shared laughter as an icebreaker in initial dialogues (Inaguma et al., 2016).

However, it is unclear how to develop an initial dialogue for smoothly introducing a discussion.

It is known that people interact with artificial constructions such as dialogue systems, virtual agents, and robots in the same manner as they interact with other humans (Reeves and Nass, 1996). Schegloff et al. showed that human conversation usually interleaves the contents of a task-oriented dialogue with social contents (Schegloff, 1968). Jiang et al. showed that 30% of all utterances of Microsoft Cortana, a well-known task-oriented dialogue system, consist of social contents (Jiang et al., 2015). It is considered that performing small talk can be natural in argumentative dialogue systems.

There have been many studies on dialogue systems that include small talk. Bechberger et al. developed a dialogue system that conveys news text and performs small talk related to the news (Bechberger et al., 2016). Kobori et al. showed that inserting small talk improved the impressions of an interview system (Kobori et al., 2016). Bickmore et al. showed that the task success rate was improved by constructing a trust relationship using small talk (Bickmore and Cassell, 2005). Tina et al. developed a dialogue system that included the function of interacting using small talk (Klüwer, 2015). We consider that argumentative dialogues may be performed deeply since small talk can improve the trust relationship.

Related to the studies dealing with multiple dialogue strategies including argumentative and social dialogues, there are several works concerning hybrid dialogue systems that integrate task-oriented and chat-oriented dialogue systems. Papaioannou et al. proposed a method to acquire dialogue strategies for hybrid systems in a robot using reinforcement learning (Papaioannou and Lemon, 2017). Yu et al. showed that multiple dialogue systems can interact using appropriate dialogue strategies learned through reinforcement learning (Yu et al., 2017). Akasaka et al. demonstrated a classification method for input utterances to select what dialogue systems are used (Akasaki and Kaji, 2017). However, in initial dialogue, it is unclear which dialogue strategies can be employed to smoothly introduce an argumentative dialogue.

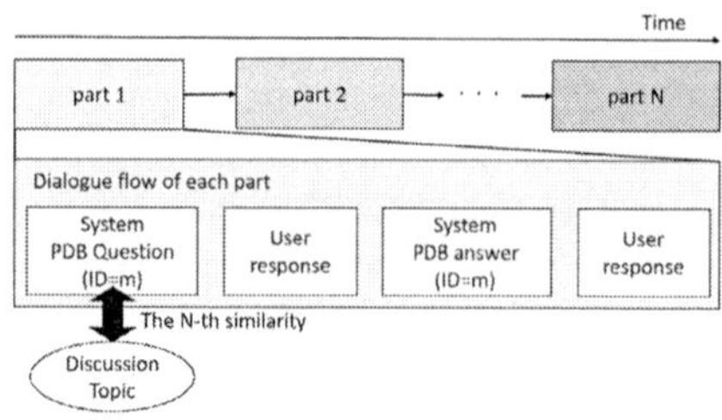

Figure 1: Flow of PDB-QA dialogue. Each part contains two system utterances and two user utterances. We used questions in an order based on the similarity between the dialogue topic and question text.

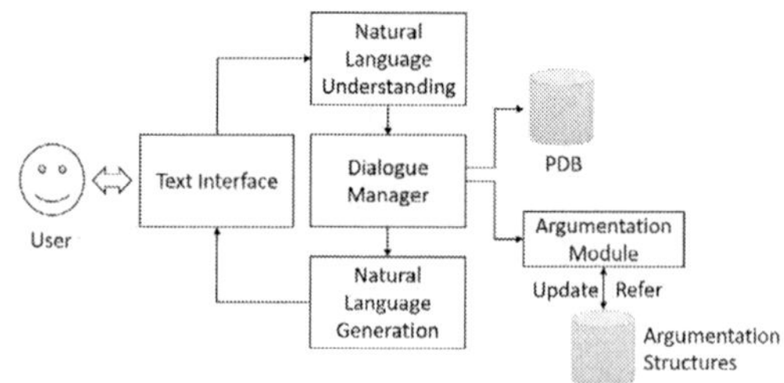

Figure 2: Architecture of developed dialogue system.

3 Proposed method

We propose a method for introducing an argumentative dialogue using the PDB-QA dialogue, which is a question-answering dialogue concerning personality. We then describe some existing argumentative dialogue systems. Next, we explain how to develop an extended argumentative dialogue system using the PDB-QA dialogue.

3.1 PDB-QA dialogue by using question-answering pair about personality

The PDB consists of personal questions and example answers and is used to ask the interlocutor for detailed information (Tidwell and Walther, 2002). Such questions may be asked even when the interlocutor is a dialogue system (Nisimura et al., 2011). In this study, we used the PDB described in (Sugiyama et al., 2014). This PDB is a large-scale database of pairs of questions and answers related to personal information. Questions included in the PDB involved various personal questions, question categories, answer examples, and topics attached to each question. Based on the degree of overlap of questions, question-answer pairs frequently encountered during conversation are extracted. The PDB includes personal questions such as "what dishes do you like?" and "which places have you visited?"

We explain the procedure for generating a PDB-QA dialogue using this PDB. As shown in Figure 1, the PDB-QA dialogue consists of several parts. Each part consists of four utterances: the system's question using the PDB, the user's response, the system's answer, and the user's response to this. To determine the order in which

to ask multiple questions, we used the similarity between the topic of argument and the question text, calculated by Word2vec (Mikolov et al., 2013). From parts 1 to N, we used questions in an order starting from the highest similarity, i.e., part 1 uses a question with the N-th highest similarity and part N uses another question that has the highest similarity. This is because it is considered that approaching the topic gradually is natural as a dialogue structure. Through this process, we can perform N parts of the PDB-QA dialogue.

3.2 Argumentative dialogue system

We used the argumentative dialogue system described in (Higashinaka et al., 2017). This system can generate appropriate argumentative dialogue text based on large-scale knowledge structures, called argumentation structures, which are constructed manually. An argumentation structure is represented by a graph structure, composed of nodes that represent premises and edges representing support or nonsupport relationships, based on an extended version of Walton's model (Walton, 2013).

A user utterance is input into two modules: dialogue act estimation and proposition identification. The dialogue act estimation module estimates four dialogue-act types: assertion, question, concession, and retraction. The proposition identification module determines the argumentation node that contains the content closest to the input user utterance. The discussion manager updates the argumentation structure on the basis of the understanding result, which checks whether the corresponding node is already mentioned. Then the dialogue manager retrieves premises that can be used for support or rebuttal based on traversing along with argumentation structures. The system outputs a supportive or nonsupportive response to

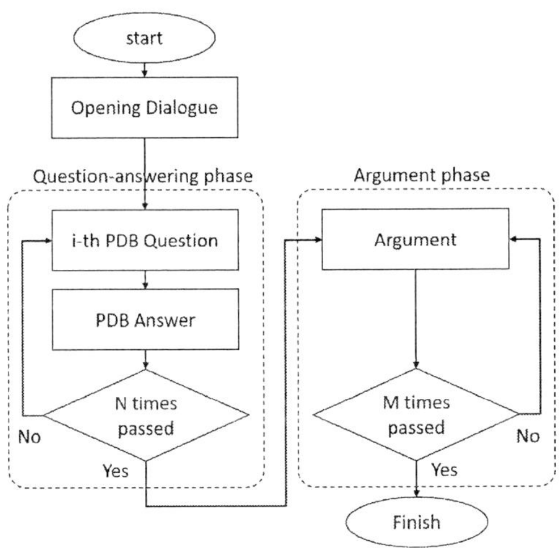

Figure 3: Flow in the dialogue manager.

the user's utterance.

3.3 Integration of argumentation dialogue system and PDB-QA dialogue

Figure 2 illustrates the architecture of our argumentative dialogue system. The user interacts with the system through the text chat interface on the browser. The natural language understanding module has two modules related by the argumentative dialogue system. Note that this module is only used in the argument phase described as follows. The dialogue manager manages two dialogue states. One is the question-answering phase, and the other is the argument phase. Figure 3 illustrates the flow of dialogue managed by the dialogue manager. First, the dialogue manager initiates the opening dialogue, such as by asking the user her name. Then, it begins the question-answering phase. In this phase, the PDB-QA dialogue is performed, as described in Section 3.1. The PDB-QA dialogue is a predefined question-answering dialogue, regardless of user utterances. The answer of the system for a PDB question is prepared by the experimenter in advance. The natural language generation module changes the system response such as adding conjunctions and changing the end of the sentences using a dialogue act. Later, the dialogue manager begins the argument phase. In the argument phase, the utterances of the system are premises that can be used for support or rebuttal, and they consist of the results of the argumentative dialogue system.

Line	Speaker	Utterance
1	S	Do you like trips?
2	U	Yes, I do.
3	S	I see. I like them too. I want to go on a trip during the weekend.
4	U	I also want to go during the weekend.
5	S	Where do you want to go for a trip?
6	U	I want to go abroad.
7	S	Me too. I want to go to France if I have the time.
8	U	French dishes seem great.
9	S	Which is the better place to travel in Japan, Hokkaido or Okinawa?
10	U	I want to go to Okinawa.
11	S	You can enjoy unique dishes in Okinawa.
12	U	I think goya-champuru (a traditional Okinawa dish) is delicious.
13	S	But Hokkaido also has delicious dishes, such as Genghis Khan.
14	U	I see. Hokkaido has more delicious food.

Figure 4: An example of the dialogue. The topic is that of which place the better to travel to in Japan: Hokkaido or Okinawa. Lines 1 ~ 8 are part of the PDB question dialogue, and lines 9 ~ 14 are part of the argumentative dialogue. Speaker S and U represent the system and user, respectively.

Figure 4 shows an example of the dialogue we performed. The topic is as follows: which is the better place to travel to in Japan: Hokkaido or Okinawa? Lines 1 ~ 8 are a part of the PDB question dialogue, and lines 9 ~ 14 are a part of the argumentative dialogue. Speakers S and U represent the system and the user, respectively.

4 Experiment

In this section, we describe a subjective experiment to verify the effect of inserting the PDB-QA dialogue. We compared the subjects' evaluations and behavior for two types of dialogue: one with PDB-QA and the other without it. The hypothesis is that by inserting the PDB-QA dialogue in advance, users are motivated to partake in the argumentative dialogue and can then discuss deeply with the system. To verify this hypothesis, subjects communicated with the argumentative dialogue system through a text chat interface on a browser, and then recorded their impressions in a questionnaire. We quantitatively evaluated the average number of words per utterance of the user in the argument phase. It is expected that the number of words per user's utterance in our argumentative dialogue system should be relatively lower than that in the previous system, because when a

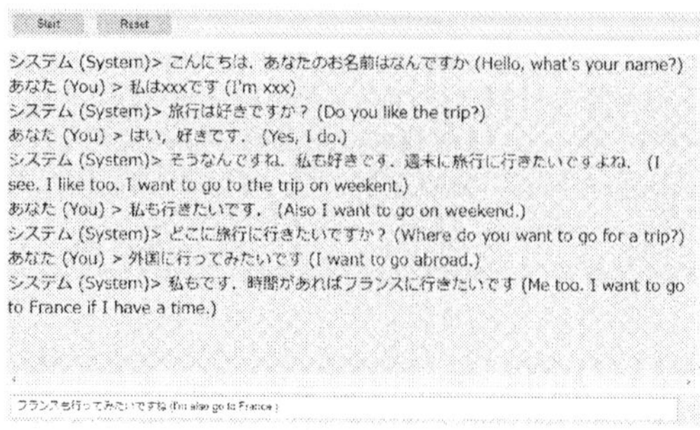

Figure 5: Screenshot of the text chat interface.

user builds a relationship with the system, the user expresses own ideas with fewer words.

4.1 Method

4.1.1 Subjects

Thirty-two Japanese adults (16 males and 16 females, with an average age of 20.3 years) participated as subjects. Half of the subjects participated with the PDB condition, and the other half without it. The ratio of males to females in each condition was the same. One male with the PDB condition and two males without were excluded because of system failures, and the utterances of the remaining 29 people were analyzed.

4.1.2 Apparatus

The experiment was conducted in a space separated by curtains. A laptop PC was placed on the table, and the PC displayed a web browser to show the text chat interface, as shown in Figure 5. Note that the dialogue in the experiment was performed in Japanese. The dialogue text of the interaction between the system and the subject was displayed in the middle part of the browser, and a text box for the subject to input his/her own utterances was displayed at the lower part of the browser. Note that we call the sentence displayed in the interface an "utterance." In other words, sentences produced by the system and input by the user with a keyboard are called the system's and user's utterances, respectively.

4.1.3 Stimuli

In this experiment, we compared two conditions: with and without the PDB. The condition with PDB included two phases of dialogue: a question-answering phase and an argument phase. The condition without PDB included one phase of dialogue: the argument phase. In this experiment, the subject and the system alternately provided utterances. Each pair of such utterances is referred to as one turn. Both conditions included two turns of opening dialogue, such as asking the subject's name and a greeting. The question-answering phase consisted of three parts, each of which included two turns of dialogue. In total, six turns of dialogue were performed. The argument phase contained six turns of dialogue. We prepared five discussion topics and assigned any of these to the subject at random: (1) the pros and cons of driving automobiles, (2) benefits of living in the countryside vs. living in the city, (3) which is the better place to travel to in Japan between Hokkaido and Okinawa, (4) which is the better breakfast between bread and rice, and (5) which is the better theme park betweenTokyo Disney Resort and Universal Studios Japan.

4.1.4 Procedure

This experiment was conducted according to the following procedure. First, the experimenter gave a subject the instructions for the experiment. The contents of the instructions were that the subject interacts with the system through the text chat interface on the browser, interacts only once, and answers the questionnaire after the dialogue. Next, the experimenter asked the subject to read the questionnaire in advance. After that, interaction was started. After completing the dialogue, the experimenter asked the subject to answer the questionnaire.

4.1.5 Measurement

The items of the questionnaire regarding impressions were the same for both conditions, and there were eleven items in total. These included questions related to the overall impression of the dialogue system, the argumentative dialogue, and the user's motivation for conversing with the dialogue system. The items concerning the impression of the dialogue consisted of the following five:

Q1 The utterances of the system are correct in Japanese,

Q2 The dialogue with the system is easy to understand,

Q3 The dialogue with the system is familiar,

Q4 The dialogue with the system has a lot of content, and

Q5 The dialogue with the system is natural.

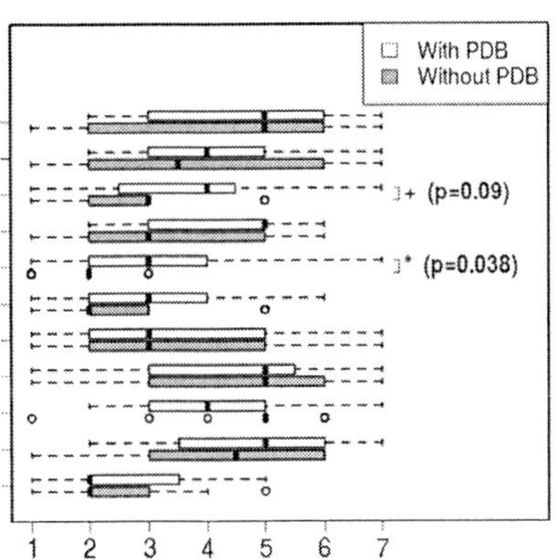

Figure 6: Box plots of the results of the questionnaire.

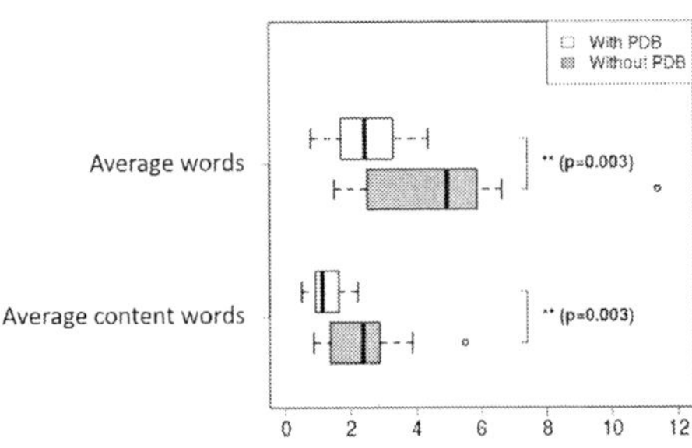

Figure 7: Box plots of results for the average numbers of words and content words (nouns, verbs, adjectives, conjunctions, and interjections) per utterance in the argument phase. We used MeCab to tokenize Japanese words.

The items concerning the impression of the argument dialogue were the following two:

Q6 You can deeply discuss the topic of X, and

Q7 You can smoothly enter the argumentative dialogue about X,

where X is the actual topic (e.g., which is the better place to travel to in Japan between Hokkaido and Okinawa). The items related to motivation for the dialogue were the following four:

Q8 You want to convey your opinions,

Q9 You want to understand the system's opinions,

Q10 You feel that the system wants to convey its opinions, and

Q11 You feel that the system wants to understand your opinions.

A Likert scale was used to elicit the subjects' impressions. We used a seven-point scale that ranged from a value of 1, corresponding to "strongly disagree," to 7, corresponding to "strongly agree." The midpoint value of 4 corresponded to "undecided."

We also counted the average number of words per user utterance and the average number of content words (nouns, verbs, adjectives, conjunctions, and interjections) in the argument phase. We used MeCab to tokenize the words and label the Japanese parts of speech.

4.2 Result

Figure 6 presents the box plots of the answers to the questionnaire. A Mann-Whitney U test was used to compare the scores on the Likert scale. For Q3, namely "the dialogue with the system is familiar," the median score for the condition with PDB was found to be marginally significantly higher than that for the condition without PDB ($W = 143$, $p < 0.1$). For Q5, namely "the dialogue with the system is natural," the median score for the condition with PDB was found to be significantly higher than that for the condition without PDB ($W = 149.5$, $p < 0.05$). For other questions, no significant differences between the two conditions were detected.

As shown in Figure 6, we did not directly confirm an improvement concerning the smooth introduction to the argumentative dialogue by inserting the PDB-QA dialogue. However, this figure suggests that it is possible for the user to feel that the dialogue is familiar and more natural when the PDB-QA dialogue is inserted. This result may be because the system performs in the manner in which a human usually does, and a certain rela-

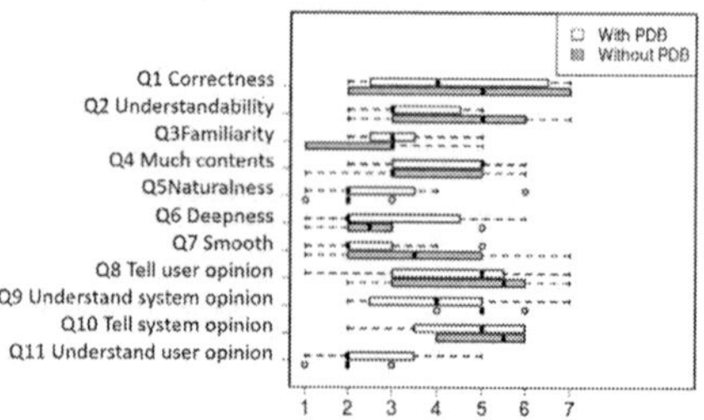

Figure 8: Box plots of results of the questionnaire for male users.

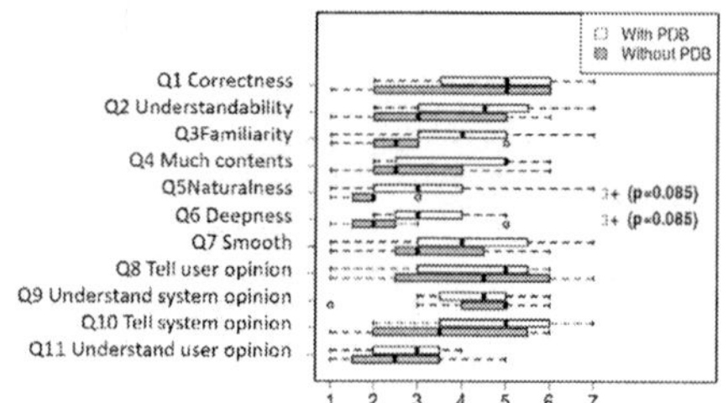

Figure 9: Box plots of female results of the questionnaire for female users.

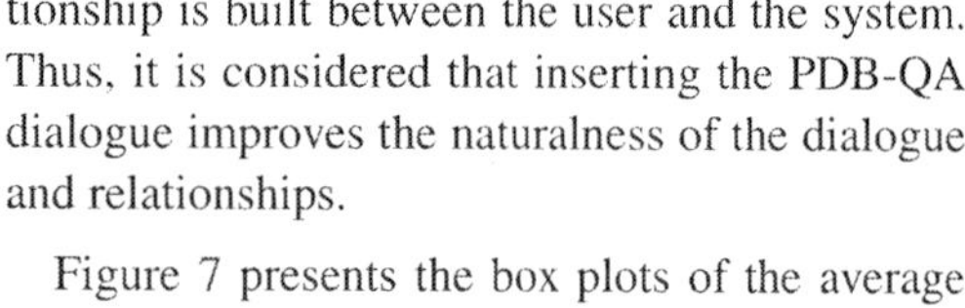

Figure 10: Box plots of results for male users for the average number of words and content words per utterance in the argumentation phase.

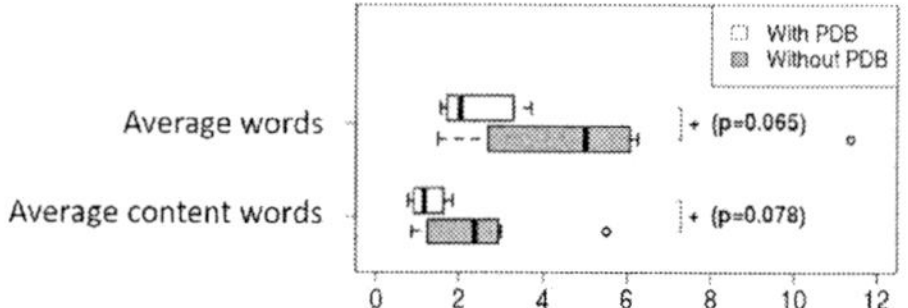

Figure 11: Box plots of results for female users for the average number of words and content words per utterance in the argumentation phase.

tionship is built between the user and the system. Thus, it is considered that inserting the PDB-QA dialogue improves the naturalness of the dialogue and relationships.

Figure 7 presents the box plots of the average numbers of words and content words per user utterance. For the average number of words, the median score for the condition with PDB was found to be significantly less than that for the condition without PDB ($W = 40$, $p < 0.01$). Concerning the average number of content words, the median score for the condition with PDB was also found to be significantly less than that for the condition without PDB ($W = 40$, $p < 0.01$).

As shown in Figure 7, it was found that the average numbers of words and content words in the condition with PDB were significantly less than those in the condition without PDB. These results suggest that when the relationship between the user and the system is not close, the users may express their opinions using a larger number of words, to correctly convey their own message; on the other hand, when the relationship is close, the users may express their opinions using fewer words.

In general, it is known that there are some differences in purposes of conversation owing to gender differences (Tannen, 2001). In this study, we suppose that the different purposes of conversation resulting from gender differences may affect our results. Therefore, we analyzed the effects of gender. We divided the data by gender, and then plotted each result. In the result for male users, shown in Figure 8, no significant differences between the two conditions were detected. On the other hand, in the result for female users, shown in Figure 9, we observe some significant differences between the two conditions. According to this figure, for Q5, namely "the dialogue with the system is natural," the median score for the condition with PDB was found to be marginally significantly higher than that for the condition without PDB ($W = 49$, $p < 0.1$). For Q6, namely "you can deeply discuss the topic," the median score for the condition with PDB was also found to be marginally significantly higher than that for the condition without PDB ($W = 49$, $p < 0.1$). In addition, we compared males' and females' data under the conditions with and without PDB. As a result, for Q7, namely "you can smoothly enter the argumentative dialogue," the median score with PDB for females was found to be marginally significantly higher than that with PDB for males ($W = 13.5$, $p < 0.1$). These results suggest that it is possible that females may feel that the PDB-QA dialogue inserted before the argumentative dialogue is more natural, and this may lead to the result that females feel the argumentative dialogue is deepened more. Thus, it is suggested that inserting the PDB-QA dialogue in our proposed method may be more effective for females.

In addition, Figures 10 and 11 show the results for male and female users for words and content words, respectively. As shown in Figure 10, for male users, the average number of content words for the condition with PDB was found to be significantly less than that without PDB ($W = 7$, $p < 0.05$). This result may be because of their degree of motivation, but the actual reason is unknown. On the other hand, as shown in Figure 11, for female users, the average numbers of words and content words with PDB were found to be marginally significantly less than those without PDB ($W = 14$, $p < 0.1$, $W = 15$, $p < 0.1$, respectively). These results suggest that females may use fewer words when they feel familiarity with the interlocutor.

5 Summary and future work

We proposed a PDB-QA dialogue method to smoothly introduce an argumentative dialogue. We conducted an evaluation experiment to verify the effectiveness of inserting the PDB-QA dialogue. The results suggest that the impressions of the dialogue, such as familiarity and naturalness, may be improved by inserting the PDB-QA dialogue. Specifically, we found that females may perceive a PDB-QA dialogue inserted before an argumentative dialogue as more natural, and this may lead to the result that the argumentative dialogue can be deepened. We also found that when the relationship between the user and the system is not close, the users may express their opinions using a larger number of words, whereas when the relationship is close, the users may express their opinions with fewer words.

We can improve the performance of the dialogue system by adjusting several parameters of PDB dialogue, which were fixed in the experiment for the sake of control. For example, we can adjust how questions are chosen (the degree of similarity of questions to be selected), the order of questions, the number of questions, and the amount of information to be presented in an answer to a question. It may be possible to improve the performance if we select better parameters depending on a user's preferences or the context of a conversation.

For further improvement, we can consider animacy, which is another element that may be important. Animacy describes the characteristic of being like a living being, in other words, the characteristic of whether a human can relate to mind and will in an object. We suppose that in a dialogue, it is important for the user to feel animacy toward the interlocutor, because it is important for the user to recognize the dialogue system as a special target with which they can form a certain relationship. As a preliminary experiment, we measured the psychological indicators for mind perception (Gray et al., 2011). This scale can measure how much agency (capacity for self-control, planning, and memory) and experience (capacity for pleasure, fear, and hunger) the subject feels the target has. Analyzing how impressions of agency and experience might affect the answers to the questionnaire or the behavior of users will be an important aspect of future work.

In this paper, we compared the conditions with and without PDB. Comparing the two conditions, we surmise that at least three factors exist that affect the results: whether utterances are in the form of a question, whether they contain personal content, and whether they are related to the topic of the argumentative dialogue. For the first factor, we suppose that a question form can explicitly reveal common and differing sentiments in the answer to the question. It is considered that this makes it easy for the user to become interested. For the second aspect, we suppose that asking a question concerning personality can make it possible to construct a certain relationship more easily. As regards the final point, we feel this prevents a sudden change of topic. We suppose that this makes it possible for the user to enter the argumentative dialogue more smoothly. Investigating the kinds of factors that affect a natural introduction into the argumentative dialogue will be a topic of future work.

Acknowledgments

This work was supported by JST ERATO Grant Number JPMJER1401, Japan.

References

S. Akasaki and N. Kaji. 2017. Chat detection in an intelligent assistant: Combining task-oriented and non-task-oriented spoken dialogue systems. In *ACL*.

B. K. Bal and P. Saint-Dizier. 2010. Towards building annotated resources for analyzing opinions and argumentation in news editorials. In *Proceedings of the language resources and evaluation conference.*

L. Bechberger, M. Schmidt, A. Waibel, and M. Federico. 2016. Personalized news event retrieval for small talk in social dialog systems. In *Proceedings of Speech Communication; 12. ITG Symposium.*

T. Bickmore and J. Cassell. 2005. *Social Dialongue with Embodied Conversational Agents.* Advances in Natural Multimodal Dialogue Systems.

A. L. Drolet and M. W. Morris. 2000. Rapport in conflict resolution: Accounting for how face-to-face contact fosters mutual cooperation in mixed-motive conflicts. *Journal of Experimental Social Psychology*, 36(1):26–50.

K Gray, AC Jenkins, AS Heberlein, and DM Wegner. 2011. Distortions of mind perception in psychopathology. In *Proceedings of the National Academy of Sciences of the United States of America*, pages 477–479.

R. Higashinaka, K. Sakai, H. Sugiyama, H. Narimatsu, T. Arimoto, T. Fukutomi, K. Matsui, Y. Ijima, H. Ito, S. Araki, Y. Yoshikawa, H. Ishiguro, and Y. Matsuo. 2017. Argumentative dialogue system based on argumentation structures. In *Proceedings of the 21st Workshop on the Semantics and Pragmatics of Dialogue*, pages 154–155.

H. Inaguma, K. Inoue, S. Nakamura, K. Takanashi, and T. Kawahara. 2016. Prediction of ice-breaking between participants using prosodic features in the first meeting dialogue. In *Proceedings of the 2Nd Workshop on Advancements in Social Signal Processing for Multimodal Interaction*, pages 11–15.

J. Jiang, A. H. Awadallah, R. Jones, U. Ozertem, I. Zitouni, R. G. Kulkarni, and O. Z. Khan. 2015. Automatic online evaluation of intelligent assistants. In *Proceedings of the 24th International Conference on World Wide Web*, pages 506–516.

S. Kang, J. Gratch, C. Sidner, R. Artstein, L. Huang, and L. Morency. 2012. Towards building a virtual counselor: Modeling nonverbal behavior during intimate self-disclosure. In *Proceedings of 11th International Conference on Autonomous Agents and Multiagent Systems.*

Y. Katagiri, K. Takanashi, M. Ishizaki, Y. Den, and M. Enomoto. 2013. Concern alignment and trust in consensus-building dialogues. In *Proceedings of the 9th International Conference on Cognitive Science*, pages 422–428.

T. Klüwer. 2015. *Social talk capabilities for dialogue systems.* universaar.

T. Kobori, M. Nakano, and T. Nakamura. 2016. Small talk improves user impressions of interview dialogue systems. In *Proceedings of the 17th Annual Meeting of the Special Interest Group on Discourse and Dialogue*, pages 370–380.

T. Mikolov, I. Sutskever, K. Chen, G. Corrado, and J. Dean. 2013. Distributed representations of words and phrases and their compositionality. In *Advances in Neural Information Processing System*, pages 3111–3119.

M. Moens, E. Boiy, R. M. Palau, and C. Reed. 2007. Automatic detection of arguments in legal texts. In *Proceedings of the 11th international conference on Artificial intelligence and law*, pages 225–230.

R. Nisimura, Y. Nishihara, R. Tsurumi, A. Lee, H. Saruwatari, and K. Shikano. 2011. Takemaru-kun: Speech-oriented information system for real world research platform. In *Proceedings of the 2011 Conference on Empirical Methods in Natural Language Processing*, pages 583–593.

I. Papaioannou and O. Lemon. 2017. Combining chat and task-based multimodal dialogue for more engaging hri: A scalable method using reinforcement learning. In *Proceedings of the Companion of the 2017 ACM/IEEE International Conference on Human-Robot Interaction*, pages 365–366.

P. Pullin. 2010. Small talk, rapport, and international communicative competence: Lessons to learn from belf. *The Journal of Business Communication*, 47(4):455–476.

B. Reeves and C. Nass. 1996. *How people treat computers, television, and new media like real people and places.* CSLI Publications and Cambridge university press.

Y. Rogers and H. Brignull. 2002. Subtle ice-breaking: encouraging socializing and interaction around a large public display. In *In Workshop on Public, Community. and Situated Displays.*

S. Rosenthal and K. McKeown. 2012. Detecting opinionated claims in online discussions. In *Proceedings of the 6th IEEE International Conference on Semantic Computing*, pages 30–37.

E. A Schegloff. 1968. Sequencing in conversational openings. *American anthropologist*, 70(6):1075–1095.

O. Scheuer, F. Loll, N. Pinkwart, and B. M. McLaren. 2010. Computer–supported argumentation: A review of the state of the art. *International Journal of Computer-Supported Collaborative Learning*, 5(1):43–102.

H. Sugiyama, T. Meguro, and R. Higashinaka. 2014. Large-scale collection and analsis of personal question-answer pairs for conversational agents. In *Proceedings of Intelligent Virtual Agents*, pages 420–433.

D. Tannen. 2001. *You junst don't understand: women and men in conversation.* New York: HarperCollins.

L. C Tidwell and J. B. Walther. 2002. Computer-mediated communication effects on disclosure, impressions, and interpersonal evaluations. *Human Communication Research*, 28(3):317–348.

T. Uchida, T. Minato, and H. Ishiguro. 2016. Does a conversational robot need to have its own values? a study of dialogue strategy to enhance people's motivation to use autonomous conversational robots. In *Proceedings of the 4th annual International Conference on Human-Agent Interaction*, pages 187–192.

D. Walton. 2013. *Methods of argumentation*. Cambridge University Press.

K. Yanai, Y. Kobayashi, M. Sato, T. Yanase, Miyoshi T, Y. Niwa, and H. Ikeda. 2016. Debating artificial intelligence. *Hitachi Review*, 65(6):151.

Z. Yu, A. W. Black, and A. I. Rudnicky. 2017. Learning conversational systems that interleave task and non-task content. In *Proceedings of International Joint Conference on Artificial Intelligence*.

R. Zhao, A. Papangelis, and J. Cassell. 2014. Towards a dyadic computational model of rapport management for human-virtual agent interaction. In *Proceedings of International Conference on Intelligent Virtual Agents*, pages 514–527.

Automatic Token and Turn Level Language Identification for Code-Switched Text Dialog: An Analysis Across Language Pairs and Corpora

Vikram Ramanarayanan
Educational Testing Service R&D
90 New Montgomery St, #1500
San Francisco, CA
vramanarayanan@ets.org

Robert Pugh
Educational Testing Service R&D
90 New Montgomery St, #1500
San Francisco, CA
rpugh@ets.org

Abstract

We examine the efficacy of various feature–learner combinations for language identification in different types of text-based code-switched interactions – human-human dialog, human-machine dialog, as well as monolog – at both the token and turn levels. In order to examine the generalization of such methods across language pairs and datasets, we analyze ten different datasets of code-switched text. We extract a variety of character- and word-based text features and pass them into multiple learners, including conditional random fields, logistic regressors, and recurrent neural networks. We further examine the efficacy of character-level embedding and GloVe features in improving performance and observe that our best-performing text system significantly outperforms the majority vote baseline across language pairs and datasets.

1 Introduction

Code-switching refers to multilingual speakers' alternating use of two or more languages or language varieties within the context of a single conversation or discourse in a manner consistent with the syntax and phonology of each variety (Milroy and Muysken, 1995; Wei, 2000; MacSwan, 2004; Myers-Scotton, 2006). Increasing globalization and the continued rise of multilingual societies around the world makes research and development of automated tools for the processing of code-switched speech a very relevant and interesting problem for the scientific community. In our case, an important additional motivating factor for studying and developing tools to elicit and process code-switched or crutched[1] language comes from the education domain, specifically language learning. Recent findings in the literature suggest that strategic use of code-switching of bilinguals' L1 and L2 in instruction serves multiple pedagogic functions across lexical, cultural, and cross-linguistic dimensions, and could enhance students' bilingual development and maximize their learning efficacy (Wheeler, 2008; Jiang et al., 2014). This seems to be a particularly effective strategy especially when instructing low proficient language learners (Ahmad and Jusoff, 2009). Therefore, the understanding of code-switched dialog and development of computational tools for automatically processing code-switched conversations would provide an important pedagogic aid for teachers and learners in classrooms, and potentially even enhance learning at scale and personalized learning.

Automated processing of code-switched text dialog poses an interesting, albeit challenging problem for the scientific community. This is because the hurdles observed during traditional dialog processing tasks such as spoken language understanding (SLU), natural language generation (NLG) and dialog management (DM) are exacerbated in the case of code-switched text where the language the speaker is using at any given instant is not known apriori. Integrating an explicit *language identification* (or LID) step into the processing pipeline can potentially alleviate these issues. Take for example a use case of designing conversational applications for non-native English language learners (ELLs) from multiple native language (or L1) backgrounds. Many such learners tend to "crutch" on their L1 while speaking in the target language (or L2) that they are learning, es-

---

[1] Crutching refers to language learners relying on one language to fill in gaps in vocabulary or knowledge in the other (OConnor and Crawford, 2015).

Proceedings of the SIGDIAL 2018 Conference, pages 80–88,
Melbourne, Australia, 12-14 July 2018. ©2018 Association for Computational Linguistics

pecially if they are low proficiency learners (Little-wood and Yu, 2011), resulting in mixed-language speech. In such a case, LID becomes particularly important for SLU and DM, where the dialog designer/language expert may want the conversational agent to perform different dialog actions depending on whether the speaker used his/her L1 alone, the L2 alone, or a mixture of both during the previous turn.

Researchers have made significant progress in the automated processing of code-switched text in recent years (Solorio et al., 2014; Bali et al., 2014; Molina et al., 2016). While Joshi (Joshi, 1982) had already proposed a formal computational linguistics framework to analyze and parse code-switched text in the early eighties, it was not until recently that significant strides were made in the large-scale analysis of code-switched text. These have been facilitated by burgeoning multilingual text corpora (thanks largely to the rise of social media) and corpus analysis studies (see for example Solorio et al., 2014; Bali et al., 2014; Molina et al., 2016), which have in turn facilitated advances in automated processing. Particularly relevant to our work is prior art on predicting code-switch points (Solorio and Liu, 2008) and language identification (Barman et al., 2014; King and Abney, 2013). Researchers have made much progress on LID in code-switched text (tweets, in particular) thanks to recent workshops dedicated to the topic (Solorio et al., 2014; Molina et al., 2016). One of the top-performing systems used character n-gram, prefix and suffix features, letter case and special character features and explored logistic regression and conditional random field (CRF) learners to achieve the best performance for Spanish-English codeswitched text (Shirvani et al., 2016). Yet another successful system leveraged bi-directional long short term memory networks (BLSTMs) and CRFs (along with word and character embedding features) on both Spanish-English and Standard Arabic-Egyptian language pairs (Samih et al., 2016).

While there is comparatively less work in the literature on automated analysis of code-switched speech and dialog, the number of corpora and studies is steadily growing in several language pairs – for instance, Mandarin-English (Li et al., 2012; Lyu et al., 2015), Cantonese-English (Chan et al., 2005) and Hindi-English (Dey and Fung, 2014). As far as

dialog is concerned, the Bangor Corpus consists of human-human dialog conversations in Spanish–English, Welsh–English and Spanish–Welsh (Donnelly and Deuchar, 2011). More recently, Ramanarayanan and Suendermann-Oeft (2017) also proposed a multimodal dialog corpus of human-machine Hindi–English and Spanish–English code-switched data. In order to understand how turn-level LID systems for dialog perform across different languages and corpora, this paper explores the efficacy of different *text*-based features on multiple human–human and human–machine dialog corpora of code-switched data in multiple language pairs. To that end, this paper builds on other recent work that examined this phenomenon for the Bangor Miami Corpus of English–Spanish human–human dialog (Ramanarayanan et al., 2018) and expands it significantly (note however, that this study does not examine speech data). To our knowledge, this is the first such comprehensive exploration of turn-level LID performance in human-human code-switched text dialog. With that in mind, the specific contributions of this paper are to examine:

1. The performance of: (i) a range of text features (including word- and character-level embedding features) for (ii) both word-level and turn-level LID;

2. How generalizable these features are across different datasets comprising different language pairs and styles of codeswitched text – human-human dialog, human-machine dialog and monolog (tweets);

3. Turn-level LID performance by (i) using word-level LID followed by aggregation over the entire turn v.s. (ii) directly training classifiers at the turn-level.

The rest of this paper is organized as follows: Section 2 describes the various corpora used for our turn-level LID experiments. We then elucidate the various featuresets and learners we explored in Sections 3 and 4 respectively, followed by details of the experimental setup in Section 5. Next, Section 6 presents the results of our LID experiments as well as analyses of performance numbers across featureset-learner combinations, language pairs and dataset style. Finally, we conclude with a discussion of current observations and an outlook for future work in Section 7.

2 Data

We used a total of ten code-switched corpora for our experiments across language pairs and interaction type, summarized briefly below. Note that although some of these corpora contain speech as well, we only consider the text transcripts for the purposes of this paper.

- Bangor University in Wales has assembled three corpora of *human-human code-switched dialog*[2]: (i) The Miami corpus of code-switched English and Spanish, (ii) the Siarad corpus of English and Welsh, and (iii) the Patagonia corpus of Spanish and Welsh.

- The SEAME corpus[3] comprises approximately 192 hours of Mandarin-English code-switching *human-human dialog* from 156 speakers with associated transcripts (Lyu et al., 2015). The speakers were gender-balanced (49.7% female, 50.3% male) and between 19 and 33 years of age. Over 60% of the speakers were Singaporean; the rest were Malaysian.

- The HALEF corpora of code-switched *human-machine dialog* comprise English–Hindi and English–Spanish language pairs. In each language pair, bilingual human participants were encouraged to use code-switched speech as they interacted with a cloud-based multimodal dialog system to order food and drink from a virtual coffee shop barista. For more details, see Ramanarayanan and Suendermann-Oeft (2017).

- Finally, in addition to these dialog corpora, we also used monolog corpora for comparison – four Twitter datasets used in the 1st shared task on language identification held at EMNLP 2016 (Solorio et al., 2014). These consisted of code-switched tweets in the following language pairs: English–Spanish, English–Mandarin, English–Nepalese, and Modern Standard Arabic–Egyptian Arabic.

The transcripts were processed by performing whitespace tokenization on each turn, and removing event descriptions (such as "&=laugh") and

---

[2] http://bangortalk.org.uk/
[3] https://catalog.ldc.upenn.edu/ldc2015s04

Table 1: *Statistics of the different code-switching corpora considered in this paper. Note that H2H stands for human-to-human while H2M stands for human-to-machine.*

Language Pair	ENG-SPA			ENG-CHI		ENG-WEL	WEL-SPA	ENG-HIN	ENG–NEP	MSA–EGY
Corpus Name	Bangor	HALEF	Twitter	SEAME	Twitter	Bangor	Bangor	HALEF	Twitter	Twitter
Type of interaction	H2H dialog	H2M dialog	Text monolog	H2H dialog	Text monolog	H2H dialog	H2H dialog	H2M dialog	Text monolog	Text monolog
Number of turns collected	39660	582	10491	110145	910	61002	34436	727	9662	5115
Utterance-level language use or codeswitching percentage	ENG: 65% SPA: 29% CS: 6%	ENG: 36% SPA: 51% CS: 13%	ENG: 54% SPA: 18% CS: 28%	ENG: 26% CHI: 20% CS: 54%	ENG: 7% CHI: 40% CS: 53%	ENG: 3% WEL: 86% CS: 11%	WEL: 77% SPA: 18% CS: 5%	ENG: 32% HIN: 35% CS: 33%	ENG: 12% NEP: 15% CS: 73%	MSA: 74% EGY: 6% CS: 20%

unintelligible tokens. For the Twitter datasets, in order to enable cross-dataset comparison, we normalized the tag sets by creating an "other" class that included all tokens not belonging to either of the two relevant languages (NEs, ambiguous tokens, etc).

3   Feature Extraction

3.1   Low-Level Text Features

Following earlier work (Shirvani et al., 2016; Samih et al., 2016), we experimented with the following low-level binary text features that capture the presence or absence of the following:

- **Word n-grams**: We used a bag-of-words representation, trying uni- and bi-grams.

- **Character n-grams**: The set of unique character n-grams ($1 \leq n \leq 4$), without crossing word-boundaries. For example, the word sequence "la sal" would produce the following character n-grams {'l', 'a', 's', 'al', 'la', 'sa', 'sal'}.

- **Character Prefixes/Suffixes**: All affixes with length ≤ 3. For example, the word "intricate" would have prefixes {"i", "in", "int"}, and suffixes {"ate", "te", and "e"}.

- **Dictionary Lookup**: We examine whether each word exists in a dictionary for either one of the code-switched languages. Dictionaries for English, Spanish, and Welsh, were sourced from GNU Aspell[4]. Dictionaries from other languages were not used either because they were not available or the dictionary's orthography differed from that used in our data.

We also extracted turn length (in number of words) and used that as an additional feature.

3.2   Embedding Features

We also examined the utility of different combinations of the following embedding features:

- **word2vec** based pre-trained word embeddings (Mikolov et al., 2013). These models are shallow, two-layer neural networks that represent (embed) words in a continuous vector space where semantically similar words are embedded close to each other. In order

to pre-train word2vec models while analyzing the code-switched corpus of a particular language pair, we utilized other corpora (if they existed) for that same language pair (in other words, we were not able to analyze the effect of these features for language pairs that had just one exemplar corpus, like English–Welsh).

- **char2vec** based pre-trained character embeddings. These features are similar to word2vec, but are applied at the character level. In order to generate these embeddings, we run standard Word2Vec with skip-grams, except characters take the place of words and words take the place of sentences, enabling us to learn character contexts within words. Jaech et al. (2016) used a similar feature they termed "char2vec", which is however different from our implementation; it involves learning a character-based word vector using a convolutional neural network.

- **GloVe** based pre-trained word embeddings (Pennington et al., 2014). GloVe is an unsupervised learning algorithm for obtaining vector representations for words, which capture linear substructures of interest in the word vector space. It is a global log bilinear regression model that combines the advantages of the two major methods: matrix factorization of global corpus co-occurence statistics and local context window methods. As in the *word2vec* case, to obtain pre-trained vectors for a corpus in a given language pair, we used the other corpora for that pair to train aggregated global word-word co-occurrence statistics.

- **GloVe** based pre-trained character embeddings. This is the GloVe algorithm applied at the character level. To our knowledge, our paper is the first such application of these features for language identification.

- **No pre-training**: In this case, we learned word and/or character embeddings from scratch, i.e., we randomly initialized the vectors and trained these embeddings using the training partition of the data for each cross-validation fold.

---

[4]http://aspell.net/

4 Machine Learning Methods

Following previous work in this area, we examined the utility of the following learners:

- **Logistic Regression**: The simplest method we investigated was just logistic regression with L2-regularization to generate language label probabilities using the various combinations of the features described in Section 3.1.

- **CRFs**: In this case, instead of modeling language tagging decisions for each word independently, we model them jointly using a conditional random field or CRF (Lafferty et al., 2001).

- **Bidirectional LSTMs**: Long short term memory networks or LSTMS are a special kind of recurrent neural network that is capable of learning long-term dependencies (Hochreiter and Schmidhuber, 1997). They do so using several gates that control the proportion of the input to give to the memory cell, and the proportion from the previous state to forget[5]. We implemented the Stack LSTM architecture first proposed by Dyer et al. (2015), in which the LSTM is augmented with a "stack pointer." While sequential LSTMs model sequences from left to right, Stack LSTMs permit embedding of a stack of objects that are both added to (using a push operation) and removed from (using a pop operation). This allows the Stack LSTM to work like a stack that maintains a "summary embedding" of its contents. In our case, we use this architecture to model a summary embedding of characters within an model of word embedding sequences. In addition to this Stack BiLSTM, following Lample et al. (2016), we used a combination of a Stack BiLSTM with a CRF, where instead of directly using the softmax output from the Stack BiLSTM, we use a CRF to predict the final language tag for each word by taking into account neighboring tags.

An novel feature of our experiments is the examination of the utility of pre-trained *GloVe* and *char2vec* in improving performance of the system proposed for named entity recognition in Lample et al. (2016).

---

[5]Also see http://colah.github.io/posts/2015-08-Understanding-LSTMs

5 Experiments

We conducted 10-fold cross-validation experiments for all datasets. For each dataset, we first extracted the word and character level features described in Section 3. We then tried the following approaches to predicting one of 3 classes – English, Spanish or Code-switched – at the turn-level: (i) Used a CRF to make word-level predictions, and aggregated them to form a turn-level prediction; (ii) aggregated the features at the turn level and try a variety of learners, including logistic regression and deep neural networks to make language predictions at the turn level; (iii) fed word- and character-embedding combinations (both with and without pre-training) to a Stacked-BiLSTM-CRF system and made an LID prediction for each turn. We experimented with different learner configurations and parameter settings and summarize the best performing featureset and learner combination in the Results section. We used a grid search method to find optimal character embedding size for each dataset (among values of 25, 50 and 100). For the Stack-BiLSTM system, given the large number of architectural parameters to optimize (number of LSTM layers and recurrent units, type of optimizer, dropout, gradient clipping/normalization, minibatch size, to name a few), we chose to use the choices recommended by Reimers and Gurevych (2017), who evaluated over 50,000 different setups and found that some parameters, like pre-trained embeddings or the last layer of the network, have a large impact on the performance, while other parameters, like the number of LSTM layers or the number of recurrent units, are of relatively minor importance. We set the word-embedding size to 100 and used 25 and 100 recurrent units in the character-level and word-level BiLSTMs, respectively, following Lample et al. (2016).

6 Observations and Analysis

Table 2 lists the best performing *turn*-level LID systems, including the feature sets and model details. In each cell of the table, the top value indicates the overall weighted average F1 score, while the bottom value (in parentheses) indicates the F1 score of the code-switched class. We decided to list the latter value since this class is easily confusable with the other two, and better F1 scores for this class might give an insight into which algorithms are better at capturing the characteristics

System — Weighted Average F1 Scores for Each Dataset

Featureset	Machine Learner	ENG-SPA Bangor	ENG-SPA HALEF	ENG-SPA Twitter	ENG-CHI SEAME	ENG-CHI Twitter	ENG-WEL Bangor	WEL-SPA Bangor	ENG-HIN HALEF	ENG-NEP Twitter	MSA-EGY Twitter
Word n-grams, Char n-grams, Affixes, Length & Dictionary lookup	Logistic Regression	0.9525 (0.6820)	0.9324 (0.7576)	0.8143 (0.6839)	0.9931 (0.9937)	0.5786 (0.6272)	0.9647 (0.8531)	0.9706 (0.6762)	0.8765 (0.8235)	0.8442 (0.9023)	0.7556 (0.4511)
Word n-grams, Char n-grams, Affixes, Length & Dictionary lookup	CRF aggregated to turn	**0.9696** (0.8381)	0.9584 (0.8874)	0.8912 (0.8247)	0.9977 (0.9979)	0.7393 (0.7457)	**0.9676** (0.8639)	**0.9800** (0.7982)	**0.9022** (0.8553)	**0.9367** (0.9568)	0.7280 (0.3216)
Word and Char Embeddings (both from scratch)	Stacked Bi-LSTM + CRF	0.966 (0.8345)	0.9759 (0.9560)	0.884 (0.8256)	0.999 (0.9991)	**0.742** (0.7268)	0.9606 (0.8469)	0.977 (0.7828)	0.894 (0.8536)	0.932 (0.9525)	0.747 (0.4227)
Pre-trained Word Embeddings ('word2vec' in blue, otherwise 'GloVe') and Char Embeddings (from scratch)	Stacked Bi-LSTM + CRF	0.9671 (0.8438)	0.9708 (0.9308)	0.8950 (0.8421)	0.999 (0.9987)	0.7270 (0.7104)	— —	— —	— —	— —	— —
2 Pre-trained Word and Char Embeddings ('word2vec' in blue, otherwise 'GloVe')	Stacked Bi-LSTM + CRF	**0.9692** (0.8506)	0.976 (0.9560)	**0.8953** (0.8424)	0.999 (0.9992)	0.7332 (0.7173)	— —	— —	— —	— —	— —
Best-performing turn predictions	Stacked Bi-LSTM	0.9621 (0.7962)	0.9394 (0.8235)	0.8587 (0.7770)	— —	0.6089 (0.6821)	0.9485 (0.7869)	0.9501 (0.7277)	0.8514 (0.7889)	0.7906 (0.8710)	**0.7564** (0.5280)
Majority Baseline		0.49	0.34	0.38	0.38	0.37	0.79	0.67	0.18	0.61	0.63
Random Baseline		0.38	0.34	0.35	0.35	0.37	0.43	0.41	0.34	0.39	0.40
Best performance on 1st codeswitching challenge		—	—	0.822	—	0.894	—	—	—	0.977	0.417
Best performance on 2nd codeswitching challenge		—	—	0.913	—	—	—	—	—	—	0.83

Table 2: Weighted average F1 scores obtained by different featureset–learner combinations on each codeswitching dataset. Notice that datasets are organized first by language pair, and then according to type of interaction (human-human vs. human-machine vs. Twitter). Each cell of the table contains two numbers: the overall weighted F1 score on top and the F1 score of the code-switched class in parentheses at the bottom. Note that we obtained performance numbers for pre-trained word and character embeddings only for language pairs with more than one dataset, i.e., ENG-SPA and ENG–CHI. Also shown for benchmarking purposes are the best tweet-level performance numbers from the 1st and 2nd codeswitching challenges for some of the Twitter datasets. However, note that this is *not* a completely fair comparison, because the train-test partitions in our case are different: we used only the train data from the 1st code-switching challenge in order to perform 10-fold cross-validation experiments. Also see the text for more details.

System — Weighted Average Token-Level F1 Scores for Each Dataset

Featureset	Machine Learner	ENG-SPA Bangor	ENG-SPA HALEF	ENG-SPA Twitter	ENG-CHI SEAME	ENG-CHI Twitter	ENG-WEL Bangor	WEL-SPA Bangor	ENG-HIN HALEF	ENG-NEP Twitter	MSA-EGY Twitter
Word n-grams, Char n-grams, Affixes, Length & Dictionary lookup	CRF	0.9774	0.9772	0.9111	0.9989	**0.9513**	**0.9824**	0.9774	**0.9343**	**0.9601**	**0.5804**
Word and Char Embeddings (both from scratch)	Stacked Bi-LSTM + CRF	**0.9883**	0.9721	0.9394	0.9993	0.9476	0.9820	**0.9922**	0.9290	0.9579	0.5791
Pre-trained Word Embeddings ('word2vec' in blue, otherwise 'GloVe') and Char Embeddings (from scratch)	Stacked Bi-LSTM + CRF	0.9814	0.9784	**0.9437**	0.9992	0.9429	—	—	—	—	—
Pre-trained Word and Char Embeddings ('word2vec' in blue, otherwise 'GloVe')	Stacked Bi-LSTM + CRF	0.9819	0.9788	0.9370	0.9993	0.9478	—	—	—	—	—
Best performance on 1st codeswitching challenge		—	—	0.94	—	0.892	—	—	—	0.959	0.936
Best performance on 2nd codeswitching challenge		—	—	0.973	—	—	—	—	—	—	0.876

Table 3: Weighted average F1 scores for token-level predictions after 10-fold crossvalidation. Also shown for benchmarking purposes are the best token-level performance numbers from the 1st and 2nd codeswitching challenges. However, note that this is *not* a fair comparison, because the train-test partitions in our case are different: we used only the train data from the 1st code-switching challenge in order to perform 10-fold cross-validation experiments. Also see the text for more details.

of this class. At the outset, we observe that all text systems significantly outperform the majority vote baseline (where we assign the language labels of all turns in the test set to the majority class) and the random baseline (where the language labels of all test set turns are assigned at random) by a huge margin.

One of the primary research questions we wanted to study (see the penultimate paragraph of Section 1) was how different featureset-learner combinations performed across different language pairs. We see that no particular featureset-learner combination dominated overall performance-wise, with results varying depending on the dataset and language pair in question. Interestingly, in the case of English–Spanish, where there were 3 different datasets of code-switched text, using pre-trained word and character embeddings performed at or above par all other systems. In other words, in the presence of sufficient amounts of data for pre-training, using pre-trained embedding-based systems yields the best results. Even though the overall F1 score of all embedding-based Stack Bi-LSTM systems is similar, notice that the F1 score of the code-switched class improves when we use both pre-trained word *and* character embeddings. This suggests that pretrained character embeddings are particularly useful in capturing the characteristics of code-switched language. While GloVe-based character embeddings were more useful for the human-human (Bangor) and monolog (Twitter) datasets, word2vec was better for the HALEF dataset of human-machine dialog. For English–Mandarin corpora, on the other hand, while the embedding–Stack BiLSTM–CRF combination still performed best, using pre-trained embeddings did not seem to make any significant additional impact.

Another research question of interest dealt with whether we obtained a better turn-level LID performance by (i) using word-level LID followed by aggregation over the entire turn, or (ii) directly training classifiers at the turn-level. Our results seem to suggest that the former is better than the latter across all code-switched text datasets with one notable exception. In the case of the Modern Standard Arabic–Egyptian Arabic Twitter dataset, using a Stacked BiLSTM with embedding features and a direct softmax layer for turn-level predictions (i.e., without an additional CRF aggregation step) performed best.

For all other remaining language pairs (each of which had just one dataset), the simpler CRF classifier (where predictions were aggregated to a turn) with a more standard featureset (word and character n-grams, affixes, turn length and dictionary lookup) yielded the best results. That this simpler CRF system performed competently even in the other cases relative to the Stack-BiLSTM systems suggests that the former is perhaps a better choice when one does not have large amounts of training data, particularly for pre-training. On a related note, it is also worth pointing out that unsurprisingly, performance numbers across the board are influenced by the amount of data in each dataset, i.e., more data leads to higher F1 scores.

Yet another research question dealt with the performance across datasets for human–human dialog vs. human–machine dialog vs. monolog tweets. We observe, in general, a decrease in overall weighted F1 score as one moves from human–human dialog to human–machine dialog to monolog tweet data. One possible reason for this is that Twitter data in particular consists of many "other" non-language tokens (such as named entities, ambiguous tokens, etc.), which, on removal or non-consideration, might lead to different phrase structures in the resulting data[6].

The final question we asked was to examine token-level prediction performance, in order to benchmark ourselves against prior art in this area. Table 3 lists these results. We find that performance trends in this case roughly mirror those observed at the turn-level.

Performances from the 1st and 2nd Code-switching Workshop Challenge results are provided in each table to provide some comparison with our systems. However, it should be noted that these comparisons are not exact. Our results are from 10-fold cross-validation on the training data used in the Workshop challenge, not on the held-out test sets. Additionally, because we pulled the data from Twitter years after the 1st Workshop, some of the tweets initially intended for the dataset were no longer available. For the tweet-level performance, we report results on three-class

---

[6]A big part of the errors made by crowd-sourcing annotators who assigned tag labels for the Twitter datasets involve named entities, probably because the annotators do not take the context into account in an effort to be fast and collect money quickly. The problem is exacerbated in the MSA-EGY set due to the fact that there is inherently considerable amount of data overlap due to homographs between the two varieties of the language (Molina et al., 2016).

classification (language 1 vs. language 2 vs. code-switched), whereas the Code-switching Workshop performances are based on binary classification (monolingual vs. code-switched). Furthermore, as mentioned earlier, in order to enable cross-dataset comparison, we normalized the tag sets by creating an "other" class that included all tokens not belonging to either of the two relevant languages (NEs, ambiguous tokens, etc). Taking these points into consideration, our systems perform competitively with the submissions to the Code-switching Workshop Challenges. The only exception is in the case of the MSA-EGY dataset, where while our tweet-level performance is competitive, our token-level performance far underperforms the state-of-the-art. We suspect that dataset imbalance could play a role, as well as the fact that we didn't use any external resources for this language pair.

7   Discussion and Outlook

We have presented an experimental evaluation of different text-based featuresets in performing language identification (LID) at both the turn and token levels in code-switched text interactions. We studied the generalizability of various systems both across language pair and dataset type— human–human, human–machine and monolog— by examining 10 different datasets of code-switched text. While our best text-based systems performed either at or above par with the state of the art in the field, we found that the use of both pre-trained word and character-based embedding features, and the latter in particular (either through *char2vec* or *GloVe*), were particularly useful at capturing the characteristics of code-switched speech (with the caveat that the feature extraction process requires sufficient data for pre-training). We further observed that a performance drop depending on the style of interaction, as we move from human–human dialog to human–machine dialog to monolog tweets.

Going forward, we will explore a number of potential avenues for improving the performance of the text-based LID systems. Chief among these is to investigate strategies for dealing with little or no code-switched data (or indeed, overall training data) for a given language pair, and how to improve the performance of deep learning algorithms for such datasets. In addition, we would like to perform a deeper error analysis of the al-

gorithms on different featuresets to obtain a better understanding of how best to select a feature-learner combination for the LID task.

Finally, as mentioned earlier, one of the key exciting R&D directions that this work informs is in building code-switching dialog systems. For instance, integrating an explicit language identification step into the spoken language understanding (SLU) could help enhance the system performance. Over and above such applications, such an LID module might also help inform pragmatic considerations during dialog management and the language generation module for the generation of appropriate mixed-language output.

8   Acknowledgements

We would like to thank Julia Hirschberg and other attendees at the Interspeech 2018 Special Session on Speech Techologies for Code-switching in Multilingual Communities for useful discussions and illuminating ideas on the processing of code-switched speech, including available datasets.

References

Badrul Hisham Ahmad and Kamaruzaman Jusoff. 2009. Teachers code-switching in classroom instructions for low english proficient learners. *English Language Teaching* 2(2):49.

Kalika Bali, Yogarshi Vyas, Jatin Sharma, and Monojit Choudhury. 2014. i am borrowing ya mixing? an analysis of english-hindi code mixing in facebook. *Proceedings of the First Workshop on Computational Approaches to Code Switching, EMNLP 2014* page 116.

Utsab Barman, Amitava Das, Joachim Wagner, and Jennifer Foster. 2014. Code mixing: A challenge for language identification in the language of social media. *EMNLP 2014* 13.

Joyce YC Chan, PC Ching, and Tan Lee. 2005. Development of a cantonese-english code-mixing speech corpus. In *INTERSPEECH*. pages 1533–1536.

Anik Dey and Pascale Fung. 2014. A hindi-english code-switching corpus. In *LREC*. pages 2410–2413.

Kevin Donnelly and Margaret Deuchar. 2011. The bangor autoglosser: a multilingual tagger for conversational text. *ITA11, Wrexham, Wales* .

Chris Dyer, Miguel Ballesteros, Wang Ling, Austin Matthews, and Noah A Smith. 2015. Transition-based dependency parsing with stack long short-term memory. *arXiv preprint arXiv:1505.08075* .

Sepp Hochreiter and Jürgen Schmidhuber. 1997. Long short-term memory. *Neural computation* 9(8):1735–1780.

Aaron Jaech, George Mulcaire, Mari Ostendorf, and Noah A Smith. 2016. A neural model for language identification in code-switched tweets. In *Proceedings of The Second Workshop on Computational Approaches to Code Switching*. pages 60–64.

Yih-Lin Belinda Jiang, Georgia Earnest García, and Arlette Ingram Willis. 2014. Code-mixing as a bilingual instructional strategy. *Bilingual Research Journal* 37(3):311–326.

Aravind K Joshi. 1982. Processing of sentences with intra-sentential code-switching. In *Proceedings of the 9th conference on Computational linguistics-Volume 1*. Academia Praha, pages 145–150.

Ben King and Steven P Abney. 2013. Labeling the languages of words in mixed-language documents using weakly supervised methods. In *HLT-NAACL*. pages 1110–1119.

John D Lafferty, Andrew McCallum, and Fernando CN Pereira. 2001. Conditional random fields: Probabilistic models for segmenting and labeling sequence data. In *Proceedings of the Eighteenth International Conference on Machine Learning*. Morgan Kaufmann Publishers Inc., pages 282–289.

Guillaume Lample, Miguel Ballesteros, Sandeep Subramanian, Kazuya Kawakami, and Chris Dyer. 2016. Neural architectures for named entity recognition. In *Proceedings of NAACL-HLT*. pages 260–270.

Ying Li, Yue Yu, and Pascale Fung. 2012. A mandarin-english code-switching corpus. In *LREC*. pages 2515–2519.

William Littlewood and Baohua Yu. 2011. First language and target language in the foreign language classroom. *Language Teaching* 44(1):64–77.

Dau-Cheng Lyu, Tien-Ping Tan, Eng-Siong Chng, and Haizhou Li. 2015. Mandarin–english code-switching speech corpus in south-east asia: Seame. *Language Resources and Evaluation* 49(3):581–600.

Jeff MacSwan. 2004. Code switching and grammatical theory. *The handbook of bilingualism* 46:283.

Tomas Mikolov, Kai Chen, Greg Corrado, and Jeffrey Dean. 2013. Efficient estimation of word representations in vector space. *arXiv preprint arXiv:1301.3781* .

Lesley Milroy and Pieter Muysken. 1995. *One speaker, two languages: Cross-disciplinary perspectives on code-switching*. Cambridge University Press.

Giovanni Molina, Nicolas Rey-Villamizar, Thamar Solorio, Fahad AlGhamdi, Mahmoud Ghoneim, Abdelati Hawwari, and Mona Diab. 2016. Overview for the second shared task on language identification in code-switched data. *EMNLP 2016* page 40.

Carol Myers-Scotton. 2006. Codeswitching with english: types of switching, types of communities. *World Englishes: Critical Concepts in Linguistics* 4(3):214.

Brendan H OConnor and Layne J Crawford. 2015. An art of being in between: The promise of hybrid language practices. In *Research on Preparing Inservice Teachers to Work Effectively with Emergent Bilinguals*, Emerald Group Publishing Limited, pages 149–173.

Jeffrey Pennington, Richard Socher, and Christopher Manning. 2014. Glove: Global vectors for word representation. In *Proceedings of the 2014 conference on empirical methods in natural language processing (EMNLP)*. pages 1532–1543.

Vikram Ramanarayanan, Robert Pugh, Yao Qian, and David Suendermann-Oeft. 2018. Automatic Turn-Level Language Identification for Code-Switched Spanish-English Dialog. In *Proc. of the IWSDS Workshop 2018, Singapore*.

Vikram Ramanarayanan and David Suendermann-Oeft. 2017. Jee haan, I'd like both, por favor: Elicitation of a Code-Switched Corpus of Hindi–English and Spanish–English Human–Machine Dialog. *Proc. Interspeech 2017* pages 47–51.

Nils Reimers and Iryna Gurevych. 2017. Optimal hyperparameters for deep lstm-networks for sequence labeling tasks. *arXiv preprint arXiv:1707.06799* .

Younes Samih, Suraj Maharjan, Mohammed Attia, Laura Kallmeyer, and Thamar Solorio. 2016. Multilingual code-switching identification via lstm recurrent neural networks. *EMNLP 2016* page 50.

Rouzbeh Shirvani, Mario Piergallini, Gauri Shankar Gautam, and Mohamed Chouikha. 2016. The howard university system submission for the shared task in language identification in spanish-english codeswitching. In *Proceedings of The Second Workshop on Computational Approaches to Code Switching*. pages 116–120.

Thamar Solorio, Elizabeth Blair, Suraj Maharjan, Steven Bethard, Mona Diab, Mahmoud Gohneim, Abdelati Hawwari, Fahad AlGhamdi, Julia Hirschberg, Alison Chang, et al. 2014. Overview for the first shared task on language identification in code-switched data. In *Proceedings of the First Workshop on Computational Approaches to Code Switching*. Citeseer, pages 62–72.

Thamar Solorio and Yang Liu. 2008. Learning to predict code-switching points. In *Proceedings of the Conference on Empirical Methods in Natural Language Processing*. Association for Computational Linguistics, pages 973–981.

Li Wei. 2000. *The bilingualism reader*. Psychology Press.

Rebecca S Wheeler. 2008. Code-switching. *EDUCATIONAL LEADERSHIP* .

A Multimodal Dialogue System for Learning Structural Concepts in Blocks World

Ian Perera[1], James F. Allen[1,2], Choh Man Teng[1], Lucian Galescu[1]
[1]Institute for Human and Machine Cognition, Pensacola, FL 32502 USA
[2]University of Rochester, Department of Computer Science, Rochester, NY 14627 USA
`iperera@ihmc.us, jallen@ihmc.us, cmteng@ihmc.us, lgalescu@ihmc.us`

Abstract

We present a modular, end-to-end dialogue system for a situated agent to address a multimodal, natural language dialogue task in which the agent learns complex representations of block structure classes through assertions, demonstrations, and questioning. The concept to learn is provided to the user through a set of positive and negative visual examples, from which the user determines the underlying constraints to be provided to the system in natural language. The system in turn asks questions about demonstrated examples and simulates new examples to check its knowledge and verify the user's description is complete. We find that this task is non-trivial for users and generates natural language that is varied yet understandable by our deep language understanding architecture.

1 Introduction

Current artificial intelligence systems, even dialogue agents, tend to play the role of a tool in real-world or even simulated tasks. Often the human user must be given an artificial handicap to create a situation where the system can play a role as a collaborator rather than a tool with interface commands simply replaced by natural language equivalents (Brooks et al., 2012). We work towards a natural language dialogue agent that we hope will eventually become a collaborator rather than a tool by focusing on knowledge transfer through natural language and determining areas where a dialogue agent's proactive nature is a benefit to learning. To this end, we apply deep language understanding techniques in the situated Blocks World environment, where a user can teach the system physical,

possibly compositional concepts to aid in development of natural language understanding without significant existing domain knowledge needed.

2 The Structure Learning Task

Many natural language dialogue tasks in a Blocks World environment focus on querying the environment (Winograd, 1971), block placement (Bisk et al., 2016; She et al., 2014), or training visual classifiers and grounding perception (Matuszek et al., 2012; Mast et al., 2016; Perera and Allen, 2015). Reference resolution has also been extensively studied in this environment and statistical methods show strong performance in quickly learning referring expressions (Kennington et al., 2015). However, our focus is exploring collaborative concept transfer with the goal of having situated agents learn from natural language dialogue and physical interaction to become better collaborators. With the goal of the system as a collaborator, we find it is important that the task carried out be non-trivial for the user. However, more difficult tasks can have drawbacks – they involve larger amounts of background knowledge and reasoning, progress can be difficult to evaluate, and often the language and concepts learned do not extend easily to other real world applications.

With these constraints in mind, we use a physical Bongard problem (Bongard et al., 1970; Weitnauer and Ritter, 2012) task for evaluating our system in a situated Blocks World environment. The user is provided with a set of visual examples, some positive and some negative, and must determine the constraints on the class of structure that allows the positive examples (and perhaps others) while avoiding any negative examples (Figure 1). By providing only visual clues, we leave the generation of the constraints entirely up to the user. The user then begins interacting with the system

Proceedings of the SIGDIAL 2018 Conference, pages 89–98,
Melbourne, Australia, 12-14 July 2018. ©2018 Association for Computational Linguistics

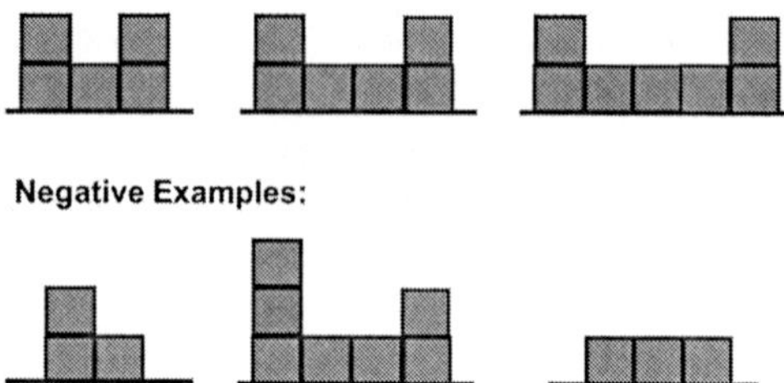

Figure 1: An example of the set of images provided to a participant for teaching the system a "U" shape. The user is tasked with explaining the underlying concept to the system such that the system correctly identifies the positive examples while rejecting the negative examples.

to describe the structure. During this time, the system is able to ask questions, check its model with demonstrations, and ask for the user to present examples. While this problem has been explored in the context of cognitive architectures (Foundalis, 2006) and reinforcement learning (Ramon et al., 2007), we are unaware of any prior work in the context of dialogue systems.

We believe this task addresses a number of issues with previous tasks in evaluating a system that can learn new concepts and structures. Participants typically spent two to three minutes going over the examples, showing that there was some thought required to correctly understand the structure on their part. Furthermore, often the constraints users provided were underspecified – they described what structures would be allowed, but sometimes failed to provide sufficient restrictions to avoid the negative examples. The system is then able to find gaps in the user's description by presenting examples following the current description so far – bringing the system's state in the dialogue from being solely a student to contributing to the task in a meaningful way.

In addition, this task can be scaled in difficulty or extended to other domains. Difficulty scaling can be achieved by using compositional constraints that build on existing knowledge (e.g., "Build a U shape, but make one column taller than the other") or by creating more difficult structures to learn. The task could be adapted to other domains by augmenting the ontology and designing a new reasoning agent that could integrate assertions into its model, while retaining similar interactions and the domain-generic modules.

2.1 Challenges

One of the primary challenges in this task is the wide variety of ways in which a user might describe or teach a class of structures. For example, they might describe necessary features or prohibited features. They may view possibilities as movement, saying "The columns have a row between them wherever they move." They may present negative examples for the system to avoid. Some users describe a particular arrangement of blocks that should or should not appear (e.g., "There is never two blocks on top of each other"), while others describe a more holistic conception (e.g. "The maximum height is one block"). While we do not succeed in interpreting all such description modalities, we believe our current methods handle a large range of possible explanations and are amenable to advancements to understand a greater number of explanation types in the future.

3 Environment and Apparatus

Our system operates in a Blocks World environment consisting of 6-inch cubes placed on a table. Although the cubes have distinct images for identification and colored sides, we do not use this information in our current version – blocks can only be referred to using descriptions of their location in the environment. We use two Kinect 2.0's to detect the blocks, with the separate perspective aiding in avoiding issues with occlusion. On the opposite side of the user is a monitor with a 3D avatar that speaks the system's generated text and also has non-verbal communication capabilities such as nodding, pointing, and other more complex gestures. The environment is calibrated such that these gestures can point to the location of a block for communicating about it. The apparatus with the avatar is shown in Figure 2.

The apparatus has no physical means for the system to move blocks. However, during interaction the system we find it important for the system to build structures to test its knowledge. To do this, we generate a 3D image in a virtual representation of the current environment showing the blocks that the system wants to place as an example for the user. This can be sent to a separate tablet such that an assistant can place the blocks, or displayed on the screen for the user to evaluate themselves.

Figure 2: The apparatus and the environment containing the blocks used, with the screen displaying the avatar and 3D visualization of the environment.

User input is currently carried out by keyboard entry by the user or dictation by an assistant. We are currently implementing speech recognition to enable more natural communication. Towards this end we focus on finite state machine language models given the nature of assertions our system understands, but we may have to consider more flexible corpus-based models in the future, aided by transcripts of previous trials.

4 System Architecture

The heart of the dialogue management is the TRIPS architecture (Allen et al., 2001), which connects a number of components through KQML message passing (Finin et al., 1994), with each component augmented with domain-specific knowledge to varying extents. This dialogue management component, including parser, a generic ontology, and an API for interacting with a domain-specific module is open-source and available for download [1]. As opposed to other dialogue management systems like OpenDial (Lison and Kennington, 2016) or POMDP dialogue systems (Williams and Young, 2007), this dialogue management system is primarily suited for collaborative tasks where there is little to no knowledge of what dialogue state typically follows from the previous one – the user can move from statements about goals to assertions to questions in any order, determined primarily by the speech act detected in their utterance. For semantic language understanding and speech act interpretation of the user's utterances, the domain-generic

[1] https://github.com/wdebeaum/cogent

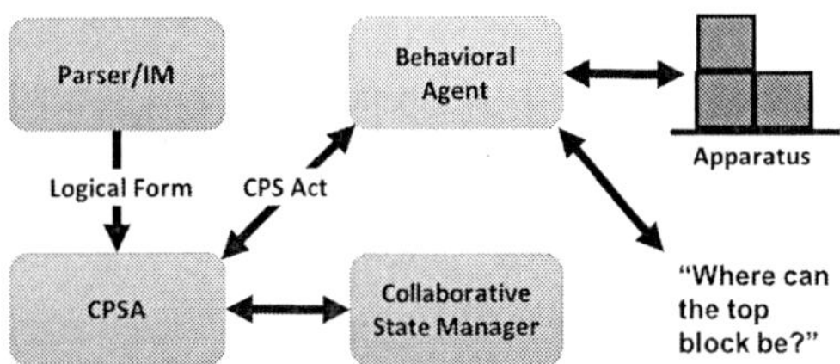

Figure 3: The TRIPS collaborative problem solving architecture adapted to this task. Only the Behavioral Agent and apparatus are specifically designed for this task – the other components are adapted only through additions to the ontology.

TRIPS parser (Allen et al., 2008) generates logical forms and speech act possibilities backed by a domain-augmented ontology. The relevant speech act is then determined by the Interpretation Manager (IM), which also fills in remaining context-dependent references before sending this information to the Collaborative Problem Solving Agent (CPSA). The CPSA facilitates communication between the parser/IM, Collaborative State Manager (CSM) and the Behavioral Agent (BA) as Collaborative Problem Solving (CPS) Acts. These acts include adopting, selecting, proposing, and rejecting goals, queries to the user or the system, and reporting the current status of a given module. The overall architecture is shown in Figure 3.

4.1 Collaborative State Manager

The Collaborative State Manager stores and responds to queries regarding the systems goal state and facilitates decisions based on goal context. As opposed to the CPSA, the CSM does not have a notion of dialogue context, but does respond to speech acts that require the system to generate a response based on the systems state and knowledge. It also is responsible for generating the necessary clarification messages to continue with dialogue, and for managing initiative in mixed-initiative tasks based on a changing domain-specific environment.

To make these decisions, the CSM is designed with a combination of domain-independent behavior and domain-specific knowledge supplied at a broad level. Such knowledge takes the form of a specification of which types of goals might be considered goals in their own right (e.g.,teaching the system a concept, building a structure), and which are considered subgoals (e.g., showing an example, adding a constraint to the system's structure model). The goal hierarchy consists of one or more top-level goals, with sub-goals, queries, and assertions added as child nodes to create a tree structure. With this structure, the user and the system can resolve sub-goals and blocking actions such as goal failures and rejected goals without losing the overall goal context. The system works with the user to ensure that there is a top-level goal when beginning the dialogue to ensure the proper context is available for the system, offering possible top-level goals based on the action or assertion the user provides.

The CSM uses a light, domain-specific knowledgebase of top-level goals, subgoals, and related speech acts to infer the users intentions and goals based on the incoming speech acts. For example, the statement "The top block must be on the leftmost column" would yield a proposed subgoal in a structure building task, but should be resolved as an assertion to be added to the BA's model during the structure learning task. If there is no top-level goal, the system would ask the user about the top-level goal (e.g."Are you trying to teach me something?" in response to an assertion) to establish one. When the CSM is unable to resolve ambiguity given the information it has, it will generate a response that indicates the system needs more information from the user, and will provide possible solutions such that other modules can generate responses to try to provide efficient communication.

4.2 Behavioral Agent

The BA is the domain-specific aspect of the system dealing with interaction with and reasoning over the environment. In this system, we also relegate language generation to this component. To design a BA in this architecture, one creates a module that accepts a set of incoming messages, dealing with goal proposals, requests for execution status (i.e, finished a task, waiting for the user, or currently acting), queries about the environment or model, in addition to a "what-next" message that serves to provide dialogue initiative to the system. As the BA receives goals, it determines whether they are achievable and accepts them, and then proposes the next goal – for example, a teaching goal will be responded with a subgoal to describe an aspect of the structure. As assertions are processed, they will be added to the model, rejected if not understood in context, or clarified with a query in the case of ambiguous statements.

4.3 Goal Management

The base TRIPS architecture provides some means for the user to respond to errors through dialogue, and provides flexibility in goal management. For example, if the user wants to continue the dialogue in a different way, they can reject it by responding "No" to the BA's goal proposal, or they can continue to provide assertions or ask questions even when the system has proposed the goal. This flexibility is essential to reduce user frustration when coming up against obstacles and ensure that the user feels a sense of control even when the BA is proactive in dialogue.

5 Constraint Processing

Constraints are processed as assertions that are interpreted as holding generally during the structure learning process, rather than relying on the identity of any one particular block or group of blocks. Therefore, the utterance, "The top block has to be on the left" may or may not currently be true about a particular example, but nevertheless should hold in all positive instances of a structure class.

Constraints can be general properties about the structures, such as the maximum/minimum height or width, or they can refer to particular blocks or groups of blocks. All non-general constraints must contain a referring expression, which consists of a referred object or arrangement (i.e., blocks, rows, columns, or spaces) and optionally a location description to pick out a particular object. The assertion can assert that such a referent exists in the structure, constrain a particular feature of the referent, (e.g., width, height, the number of blocks it contains), or dictate its location relative to the rest of the blocks or a particular set of blocks denoted by another referring expression. We also have limited support for compositional referents in referring expressions, picking out certain aspects of a structure (e.g., "the ends of the row").

A constraint can be designated as exclusive, which means that only one instance of a particular object can have that property (e.g. "Only the leftmost column has more than 2 blocks"). Currently we take an object-type scoping for this restriction. In addition, we handle negations at certain scopes, such as disallowing a particular arrangement (e.g. "There are no columns of height greater than 2") or location (e.g. "There is no block next to a column"). An example of some utterances understood by the system is shown in Figure 4.

> "The leftmost column's height is 3 blocks."
> "The height is 3."
> "The height of the leftmost column is less than the height of the rightmost column."
> "There is a column with at least 3 blocks."
> "There is a space between the top 2 blocks."
> "The bottom row is connected."
> "The top block is always on the left."
> "The top block can be anywhere."

Figure 4: Examples of understood constraints.

5.1 Constraint Extraction

To extract constraints, we primarily depend upon the logical form structure of the TRIPS parser, which allows direct extraction of the types of constraints we are interested in due to its argument structure of concepts. We first determine all referring expressions by finding mentions of blocks or arrangements. Then we add any modifiers to their location. Once the referring expressions are found, we construct a constraint, which consists of the subject (the :figure argument in the TRIPS logical form), the reference object or property (the :ground argument), and the feature of comparison (e.g., height, width, count) or a predicate constraining the location of the subject relative to some reference set. Figure 5 shows an example of structures extracted from a logical form.

5.2 Constraint Evaluation

When the system is asked to evaluate an example or create its own, it evaluates all current constraints by finding referents for each referring expression according to the object type and predicate. Predicates are calculated using predefined rules, either specifying constraints that apply to individual blocks or using axis-aligned bounding boxes. These rules have built-in tolerances of a half-block width to account for noise or imprecise placement. We then calculate the features and predicates in the constraint for the resolved reference and return a value for each constraint.

Initial versions of the system primarily built up constraints from a sequence of user utterances. When performing Wizard of Oz studies, we found that an issue with this method is that it can sometimes be difficult for users to formulate and describe a concise, consistent model without any direction. This can lead to run-on sentences which are difficult to parse, or, if parsed, difficult to interpret as constraints. We believe one reason for this

is that, while the system provides affirmation at the end of an utterance entered by keyboard, it does not give non-verbal or verbal cues of understanding during speech recognition. Therefore, the user sometimes continues explaining in various ways looking for a signal that the system understands.

To address this issue, we designed our system to take a more proactive role in conversation. While the system still takes a free-form description or constraint at the beginning of the conversation, it then begins to ask questions about the structure class, ask for examples, present examples, and respond to the user's questions about examples. The system can choose a feature of the structure that has not been described (to ensure the user feels that the system has understood the structure so far) and generate a query to send to the user. An unfilled version of the constraint is sent to the CPSA to aid in resolving the query, and the TRIPS parser is able to handle user responses fragments to fill in the constraint. The strategies to generate these utterances are described in Section 5.3.

The system generates its own examples of structures given its current knowledge as well. The BA will generate random arrangements of blocks in a grid structure until the current constraints have been satisfied, and then return a new structure as an example. This allows the user to see the result of the constraints and refine their constraints, while also providing more evidence that the system is understanding what is being said.

At any time, the user can ask whether a particular example is correct given the constraints provided so far. The system enumerates the constraints and can then state whether each constraint is satisfied and why or why not. If there are many constraints, the system will summarize the positive constraints (e.g., "The width is right" rather than "The width is greater than 2") while focusing on the negative constraints to avoid long-winded explanations and provide a more natural response.

5.3 Learning Strategies

We designed the system to follow, with some deviations, a general strategy for learning based on our initial Wizard of Oz tests (Dahlbäck et al., 1993), such that the system can build up knowledge in a way that supports the interactions between different types of knowledge learned throughout an interaction. The system first asks the user for an aspect of the structure, discouraging long-winded

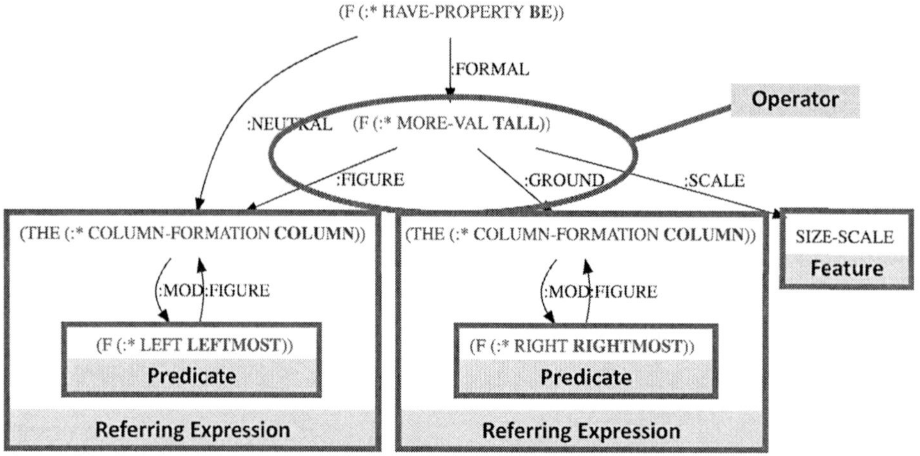

Figure 5: An example of constraint extraction from the TRIPS logical form for the utterance "The left-most column is taller than the rightmost column"

descriptions that can overwhelm the parser and tend to be less structured. With a constraint learned, the system then asks for an example. While the system cannot currently learn from the block positions themselves, it uses the example to generate a pertinent referring expression (e.g., "the top block") that can then be used to ask about a constraint. This query guides the user to thinking about the structure in a concrete and specific way to aid in generating descriptions.

Because the system likely has two or more constraints at this point, it will then generate an example of its own based on its learned constraints and check for correctness. This allows the user to focus on aspects that are explicitly disallowed, since the system's random generation process often reveals when constraints are underspecified. These learning strategies then continue until the user is satisfied that the system understands the structure. A sample dialogue showing the system's abilities is given in Figure 6.

6   Wizard of Oz Experiments

Before developing our system, we carried out several Wizard of Oz experiments to aid in development of the TRIPS parser, ensure that our system had capabilities suited to the dialogue of a naïve user, and determine which interaction strategies of the system would be most effective for learning and most natural for the user. So far we have conducted 3 tasks each with 3 participants who were unaware of the details of the project, yielding 90

user utterances. Two of the participants were familiar with natural language processing research, while one was not.

> **User:** I want to teach you a mountain shape.
> **System:** Okay. Can you describe an aspect of the structure?
> **U:** Yes. The rightmost column has 3 blocks.
> **S:** Ok. What is the greatest the height can be?
> **U:** 3.
> **S:** Ok, got it. Can you show me an example?
> **U:** Yes. This is an example. ⟨shows example⟩
> **S:** Okay.
> **U:** Is this right? ⟨shows example⟩
> **S:** I think so, because the height is less than or equal to 3 and the right column's number is equal to 3.
> **U:** The left column has 2 blocks.
> **S:** Ok.
> **U:** Is this right? ⟨shows example⟩
> **S:** I don't think so, because the height is less than or equal to 3 but the left column's number is not equal to 2 even though the right column's number is equal to 3.

Figure 6: An example dialogue showing interaction with the system.

To ensure the closest approximation to the actual system, we used a tablet for the researcher standing in for the system. Because of the design of the apparatus where the system generates 3D images (and presumably diagnostic data), the participants believed it was actually the system performing the dialogue and interpreting the user's utterances, and the researcher was simply an assistant. In fact, the tablet served as a method for the researcher to respond with predetermined phrases, including acceptances, requests for examples, and questions about the structure. These phrases were then sent through the speech generation component of the system.

We found several advantages of users believing that the system was actually engaging in dialogue. First, the users used simpler language than they might have with a person, while still providing sufficient variation for exploring possible utterances. Second, users sometimes provided their own thoughts aside to the researcher, allowing a specific glimpse into users' responses to certain utterances or tasks. For example, once when the system asked, "How tall can the structure be?", the participant said as an aside, "It can be any height," and then responded to the system "At least two blocks." Finally, we could evaluate how the dialogue might progress without being interrupted by failures of the system at the parsing or interpretation level. We processed the Wizard of Oz dialogues with the TRIPS parser and correctly parsed 89% of the utterances. 90% of these correct parses also yielded the correct constraint when interpreted by the current state of the system.

6.1 Description Modalities

We recognized several different description modalities participants used when describing the structure without responding to a particular feature query. When the system asked questions, typically the user responded directly to the question, reducing the utterance complexity. However, these variations on the expected descriptions reveal interesting insight into how users generate representations of the concepts they are provided.

Basic Constraints – "The height of the leftmost column is greater than 2" – These descriptions are the simplest to interpret and make up the majority of user utterances, especially when the system is proactive in dialogue.

Arrangement Constraint – "The column can be either second in the row or third in the row." Here the definite article conveys that there should be a single instance of a column, and the ordinal reference to the row constrains its position – even though in certain cases a row might be considered to be a line of blocks only a single block high.

We handle such cases by inferring a sequence of columns left to right, and then processing ordinal references to enforce constraints.

Movement Modality – "This top block can move wherever." – These descriptions, using movement as a surrogate for possibility, are slightly more difficult to interpret, but can often be handled by our loose interpretation of logical forms that focuses on referring expressions ("the top block") and predicates ("wherever") without focusing on the event term of "moving".

Transformation Modality – "The left block is a column." – The difficulty in parsing a constraint described in this way is that a particular type of object ("the left block") is picked from the structure with the goal of changing it to another arrangement ("a column", presumably with more than one block). This can also be viewed as an explicit bridge between the current and desired state to fulfill the constraints. Currently we encourage users to describe the structure in a general way – however, this type of utterance demonstrates an example where a specific error or instance applies generally enough to serve as a constraint.

Procedural/Construction Modality – "No, you're missing a row. Subtract by one every time you go up." – Here the user is describing the structure by providing the process for creating it. While our current system does not understand these types of utterances, we are working on a similar task in parallel with this environment that can be leveraged to understand this modality (Perera et al., 2018). The key aspect of understanding this type of utterance is the compositionality of primitive concepts, namely a row, its length, and the sequence of rows that will presumably be placed by the agent building the structure.

A common property of these more complex modalities is the awareness of and reliance on the composition of primitive concepts, such as elements, order, and placement, when referring to more complex concepts such as rows and columns, which can have multiple attributes and purposes when describing a structure. We believe that a system to interpret these types of expressions and extend to other domains must therefore have a compositional model that allows complex concepts to be built from primitive concepts that are simpler to detect or identify. This compositional aspect of concepts used in communication has both informed the design of the system and inspired this task which makes use of such modalities.

6.2 Preliminary Evaluations

Alongside adapting the system to handle our existing Wizard of Oz dialogues, we have begun preliminary user evaluations, primarily for testing for robustness and unforeseen methods of communicating constraints to the system. An example dialogue with a user is shown in Figure 7.

> **User:** I want to teach you a shape.
> **System:** Okay. Can you tell me something about the structure?
> **U:** The bottom row must be at least 2.
> **S:** Hmm, I didn't quite get that.
> **U:** The bottom row has at least 2 blocks.
> **S:** Ok. What is the greatest the width can be?
> **U:** 5.
> **S:** Ok, got it. Can you show me an example?
> **U:** Yes. This is an example. ⟨*shows example*⟩
> **S:** Okay. Where can the top block be?
> **U:** The top block is always on the left.
> **S:** Okay.
> **U:** ⟨*user builds example*⟩ Is this right?
> **S:** I think so, because the bottom row's number is greater than or equal to 2 and the width is less than or equal to 5 and the top block is on the left.

Figure 7: A taken from initial runs of the evaluation with the autonomous system and a user unfamiliar with the system.

Failures of the system are handled by the dialogue manager, with unparsable user utterances causing the system to continue with a question where the response is easy for the system to handle, such as asking for the maximum height or width, or by asking the user to rephrase. In initial trials, users were often able to rephrase constraints in a way the system could understand. Furthermore, users reported that the difficulty of the task made dialogue setbacks seem like a complementary challenge of clearly expressing an idea rather than an obstacle to an otherwise simple task.

To track development of the system, we will evaluate according to several metrics along with user surveys. The first measure will be the number of positive examples successfully recognized by the trained system and the number of negative examples successfully rejected. Next, we plan to track robustness by determining the number of cancellations, undos, or restarts by user, as well as the efficacy of extracting constraints from user assertions. In addition, a final task which ensures that communication is two-way will be to reverse roles and have the system explain the concept to the user based on what it has learned from prior interactions with a different user.

7 Conclusion

We believe our system shows promise in the task of teaching a system new concepts in Blocks World in an manner extendable to multiple types of descriptions and with applications to multiple domains. While our first priority is to handle the most common description modalities of users to ensure broader coverage, we also begin the process of using this system as a stepping stone for language understanding and dialogue in other domains by mapping our concepts and predicates into a database to be used by our collaborators in this and related projects. With multiple definitions of features and predicates, we plan to use these concrete physical representations as proxies for more abstract and metaphorical reasoning capabilities to be developed in other systems.

Because the rules and interpretation are handcrafted, brittleness can be an issue but is partially mitigated through dialogue repair. Given the primarily symbolic nature of the system and the difficulty of specifying composition with statistical models or neural networks, we focus our efforts on building rules to understand conceptual composition rather than processing utterances using statistical techniques. However, development of a broader range of understood constraint modalities can extend this dialogue system to other domains that involve a direct or indirect spatial or temporal component – such as scheduling, building graphical models, or directing scenes of a movie. Finally, we believe the compositionality inherent in the type of communication captured requires background knowledge about the conceptual structures we inherently use in discussing complex ideas.

8 Acknowledgements

This work is supported by the DARPA CwC program and the DARPA Big Mechanism program under ARO contract W911NF-14-1-0391. Special thanks to SRI for their work in developing the physical apparatus, including block detection and avatar software.

References

J. Allen, Mary Swift, and Will de Beaumont. 2008. Deep Semantic Analysis of Text. In *Symposium on Semantics in Systems for Text Processing (STEP)*, pages 343–354, Morristown, NJ, USA. Association for Computational Linguistics.

James Allen, George Ferguson, and Amanda Stent. 2001. An architecture for more realistic conversational systems. In *Proceedings of the 6th international conference on Intelligent user interfaces - IUI '01*, pages 1–8.

Yonatan Bisk, Deniz Yuret, and Daniel Marcu. 2016. Natural Language Communication with Robots. *Proceedings of the 2016 Conference of the North American Chapter of the Association for Computational Linguistics: Human Language Technologies*, pages 751–761.

M. M. (Mikhail Moiseevich) Bongard, Joseph K. Hawkins, and Theodore Cheron. 1970. *Pattern recognition*. Spartan Books.

Daniel J Brooks, Constantine Lignos, Cameron Finucane, Mikhail S Medvedev, Ian Perera, Vasumathi Raman, Hadas Kress-gazit, Mitch Marcus, and Holly a Yanco. 2012. Make It So : Continuous , Flexible Natural Language Interaction with an Autonomous Robot. In *AAAI Workshop on Grounding Language for Physical Systems*.

N. Dahlbäck, A. Jönsson, and L. Ahrenberg. 1993. Wizard of Oz studies - why and how. *Knowledge-Based Systems*, 6(4):258–266.

Tim Finin, Richard Fritzson, Don Mckay, and Robin Mcentire. 1994. KQML as an Agent Communication Language. In *Proceedings of the Third International Conference on Information and Knowledge Management*. ACM Press.

Harry Foundalis. 2006. *Phaeaco: A Cognitive Architecture Inspired By Bongard's Problems*. Ph.D. thesis.

Casey Kennington, Livia Dia, and David Schlangen. 2015. A Discriminative Model for Perceptually-Grounded Incremental Reference Resolution. In *Proceedings of the 11th International Conference on Computational Semantics*, 2002, pages 195–205, Beijing, China.

Pierre Lison and Casey Kennington. 2016. OpenDial: A Toolkit for Developing Spoken Dialogue Systems with Probabilistic Rules. *Proceedings of the 54th Annual Meeting of the Association for Computational Linguistics*, pages 67–72.

V Mast, Z Falomir, and D Wolter. 2016. Probabilistic Reference and Grounding with PRAGR for Dialogues with Robots. *Journal of Experimental & Theoretical Artificial Intelligence*, 28(in press).

Cynthia Matuszek, N FitzGerald, Luke Zettlemoyer, Liefeng Bo, and Dieter Fox. 2012. A Joint Model of Language and Perception for Grounded Attribute Learning. In *Proceedings of the International Conference on Machine Learning (ICML)*.

Ian Perera and James Allen. 2015. Quantity, Contrast, and Convention in Cross-Situated Language Comprehension. *Proceedings of the Nineteenth Conference on Computational Natural Language Learning*, pages 226–236.

Ian Perera, James F. Allen, Choh Man Teng, and Lucian Galescu. 2018. Building and Learning Structures in a Situated Blocks World Through Deep Language Understanding. In *SPLU 2018: Proceedings of the HLT-NAACL Workshop on Spatial Language Understanding*, New Orleans, Louisiana. Association for Computational Linguistics.

Jan Ramon, Kurt Driessens, and Tom Croonenborghs. 2007. Transfer Learning in Reinforcement Learning Problems Through Partial Policy Recycling. *Lecture Notes in Computer Science*, 4701:699–707.

Lanbo She, Shaohua Yang, Yu Cheng, Yunyi Jia, Joyce Y Chai, and Ning Xi. 2014. Back to the Blocks World: Learning New Actions through Situated Human-Robot Dialogue. In *Proceedings of the SIGDIAL 2014 Conference*, June, pages 89–97.

Erik Weitnauer and Helge Ritter. 2012. Physical Bongard Problems. In *IFIP Advances in Information and Communication Technology*, volume 381 AICT, pages 157–163.

Jason D. Williams and Steve Young. 2007. Partially observable Markov decision processes for spoken dialog systems. *Computer Speech and Language*, 21(2):393–422.

Terry Winograd. 1971. Procedures as a Representation for Data in a Computer for Understanding Natural Language. Technical report, Massachusetts Institute of Technology Artificial Intelligence.

Concept	Lemmas
ABOVE	above
HIGHER	higher
BELOW	below, beneath, under, underneath
LOWER	lower
ADJACENT	adjacent (to), next to, beside, by, contiguous (with), flush
CONNECTED	abut, adjoin, connect, touch
TOGETHER	together
ON	on, on top of
LEVEL	level with
TOP-LOC...	top
MIDDLE-LOC	middle
BOTTOM-LOC	bottom
BETWEEN	(in) between
CENTER	center
LEFT-LOC	left, lefthand, leftmost
RIGHT-LOC	right, righthand, rightmost
ANYWHERE	anywhere

Table 1: The list of predicates understood by the system, with their concept in the ontology, and matching lemmas that can resolve to that concept.

Ontological Concept	Data Type
ONT::WIDTH-SCALE	real+, count
ONT::HEIGHT-SCALE	real+, count
ONT::LENGTH-SCALE	real+, count
ONT::CENTER	point
ONT::LOCATION	point
ONT::STARTPOINT	point
ONT::ENDPOINT	point
ONT::TOP-LOC...	point
ONT::BOTTOM-LOC...	point
ONT::NUMBER	count
ONT::COL-FORMATION	column
ONT::ROW-FORMATION	row
ONT::DIRECTION	vector
ONT::HORIZONTAL	(real+)
ONT::VERTICAL	(real+)
ONT::LINE	(real+)

Table 2: Some of the features generated by the system for blocks, sets of blocks, and sequences, listed by their concept in the TRIPS ontology and the resulting data type. A data type in parentheses indicates the value is not presented to the user but is used in comparisons against other sets of blocks.

Pardon the Interruption: Managing Turn-Taking through Overlap Resolution in Embodied Artificial Agents

Felix Gervits and Matthias Scheutz

Human-Robot Interaction Laboratory

Tufts University

Medford, MA 02155

{felix.gervits,matthias.scheutz}@tufts.edu

Abstract

Speech overlap is a common phenomenon in natural conversation and in task-oriented interactions. As human-robot interaction (HRI) becomes more sophisticated, the need to effectively manage turn-taking and resolve overlap becomes more important. In this paper, we introduce a computational model for speech overlap resolution in embodied artificial agents. The model identifies when overlap has occurred and uses timing information, dialogue history, and the agent's goals to generate context-appropriate behavior. We implement this model in a Nao robot using the DIARC cognitive robotic architecture. The model is evaluated on a corpus of task-oriented human dialogue, and we find that the robot can replicate many of the most common overlap resolution behaviors found in the human data.

1 Introduction

Efficient turn-taking is at the heart of human social interaction. The need to fluidly and quickly manage turns-at-talk is essential not only for task-oriented dialogues but also in everyday conversation. Speech overlap is also a ubiquitous feature of natural language dialogue, and serves various supportive functions that people utilize to manage turn-taking (Jefferson, 2004). As spoken dialogue systems continue to advance, it is important that they support increasingly natural interactions with human interlocuters involving both turn-taking and overlap resolution.

Research in the field of HRI has generally overlooked the supportive role of overlap and the ways in which it affects coordination. However, robots are envisioned to serve as teammates in complex domains that involve a great deal of communication with humans (Fong et al., 2003). This requires nuanced methods to handle fluid turn-taking and overlap, especially because the frequency of overlap is higher in task-oriented settings involving remote communication (Heldner and Edlund, 2010).

In this work, we present a formal framework and computational model for overlap identification and resolution behavior in embodied, artificial agents. The present focus is on mechanisms to allow an agent to handle being overlapped on its turn. The model is based on empirical work in a search and rescue domain, and utilizes a variety of features including overlap timing and dialogue context to resolve overlap in real-time in a human-like manner. We implement the model in the DIARC cognitive robotic architecture (Scheutz et al., 2007) and demonstrate its performance on various overlap classes from the behavioral data.

2 Related Work

Below we present some of the relevant theoretical and computational background literature that has informed our work.

2.1 Turn-Taking and Speech Overlap

There has been a great deal of empirical work on both turn-taking and overlap phenomena (De Ruiter et al., 2006; Jefferson, 1982, 2004; Levinson and Torreira, 2015; Magyari and de Ruiter, 2012). Many of these approaches lend support to the model of turn-taking organization proposed by Sacks et al. (1974). On this view, turns-at-talk are separated by a transition-relevance place (TRP), which is located after a complete[1] segment of speech, and represents a point at which a speaker change can "legally" occur. The claim is that people can readily predict

---

[1] "Complete" in this sense refers to syntactic, pragmatic, and prosodic features of the turn in progress.

Proceedings of the SIGDIAL 2018 Conference, pages 99–109,
Melbourne, Australia, 12-14 July 2018. ©2018 Association for Computational Linguistics

the location of a TRP and thus aim to start their turn around that point. However, since natural language is fast-paced and complex, sometimes people miss the TRP, resulting in overlap..

Using this model, Jefferson (1986) identified several types of overlap based on their location relative to the TRP (before, during, slightly after, and much after; see Fig. 1). These overlap types have been systematically examined over the years and have been shown to capture a large range of human overlap phenomena (Jefferson, 2004). Importantly, such an account suggests that overlap is not to be confused with *interruption* (Drew, 2009). While interruption implies a kind of intrusion into the turn, overlap is oftentimes affiliative in nature. For example, people may start their turn slightly before their interlocuter has reached a TRP in order to minimize the gap between turns. This is known as *Last-Item overlap*, and can be accomplished by projecting the end of the first starter's turn. The second starter can also come in slightly after the TRP in order to respond to the content of the first starter's prior turn; such late entry is known as *Post-Transition overlap*. Additionally, the second starter can come in mid-turn (far from the TRP) as a kind of "recognitional" overlap in order to repair, clarify, or otherwise respond to the content of the first starter's turn in progress - this is known as an *Interjacent overlap*. Overlap can also be unintentional, as in *Transition-Space overlap*. This type usually involves simultaneous turn start-up wherein two people both take the turn at the TRP. In sum, because overlap is classified into these functional categories (largely based on timing), it is possible to identify the function of an overlap in a particular context as well as the behaviors that people use to manage and resolve overlap (see Gervits and Scheutz (2018)). These properties make overlap identification and resolution appealing targets for the design of more natural spoken dialogue systems.

2.2 Speech Overlap in Dialogue Systems

While overlap resolution is important in human conversation, it has not historically received the same treatment in dialogue systems. One reason for this may be that it is seen as interruption, and thus not worthy of additional study. Many systems actually ignore overlap altogether, and simply continue speaking throughout the overlapping segment (e.g., Allen et al. (1996)). While such systems may be effective for certain applications (e.g., train booking), they are not sufficient for dialogue with social agents in collaborative task environments. On top of being less fluid and natural, these systems also present problems for grounding. If the system produces an utterance in overlap, it may not be clear that a person understood or even heard what was said.

An alternative approach, and a popular one used by some commercial dialogue systems that handle overlap, is one wherein the agent responds to overlap by simply dropping out (see e.g., Raux et al. (2006)). Apart from the fact that such a system may drop its turn when detecting ambient microphone noise, another problem is that it ignores the supportive benefit that overlap can provide. An example of this is a second starter coming in at the Last-Item position in order to minimize inter-turn gaps (see Dialog *1* below[2]). Since these overlaps are among the most common, it is very inefficient for a system to abandon an utterance at the Last-Item point. Since neither of the above-mentioned approaches can address the challenges at hand, a more nuanced approach is clearly necessary.

Recently, there have been more advanced attempts at modeling overlap behavior (DeVault et al., 2009; Selfridge and Heeman, 2010; Zhao et al., 2015). Many of these approaches involve incremental parsing to build up a partial understanding of the utterance in progress and identify appropriate points to take the turn (e.g., Skantze and Hjalmarsson (2010)). Such incremental models have been used for the generation of collaborative completions (Baumann and Schlangen, 2011; DeVault et al., 2009) and feedback (DeVault et al., 2011; Skantze and Schlangen, 2009) during a human's turn. While these computational approaches tend to focus on overlapping the human, it is also important to handle overlap when the system/agent has been overlapped. Relatively little work has been done to this end, and there remain many open questions about how to interpret the function of overlap as well as how to respond. Moreover, overlap management for HRI is an under-explored area, and one which presents additional challenges for dealing with situated, embodied interaction. The present work attempts to tackle some of these challenges.

---

[2]All dialogs in the paper are from human interactions in the CReST corpus. *S* represents the Searcher role and *D* represents the Director. Overlap is shown in brackets.

3 Framework Description

As a framework for classifying overlap, we use the scheme from Gervits and Scheutz (2018) which includes categories from Eberhard et al. (2010), Jefferson (1986), and Schegloff (2000) as well as our own analyses. Included in this framework is a set of categories for identifying overlap (onset point, local dialogue history) and overlap management behavior. We provide formal definitions of the various categories of the scheme below, and in Section 5 we show how a model using this framework was integrated in a robotic architecture.

An utterance in our scheme is represented as follows: $U_{agent} = SpeechAct(\alpha, \beta, \sigma, \chi, \Omega, \pi)$, where agent can be the human or robot, α represents the speaker, β represents the recipient, σ represents the surface form of the utterance, χ represents the dialogue context, Ω represents a set of four time intervals corresponding to possible overlap onset points (see below), and π represents a boolean priority value (see Section 5.2). The surface form of an utterance, σ is an ordered set of lexical items in the utterance: $\sigma = \{item_{initial}, ..., item_{final}\}$. Dialogue context, χ, can be realized in various ways, but here we assume it to be a record with at least one field to represent the previous utterance and one field to represent the current dialogue sequence. Every utterance also has a speech act type associated with it to denote the underlying communicative intention. These include various types of questions, instructions, statements, acknowledgments, and others from Carletta et al. (1997).

We also include the following components (see Section 3.2 for more detail): 1) a set of competitive overlap resolution behaviors, **C**, which include {*Continue, Disfluency, Self-repair*}, and 2) a set of non-competitive overlap resolution behaviors, **NC**, which include {*Drop Turn, Single Item, Wrap Up, Finish Turn*}. Operational definitions for these behaviors can be found in Gervits and Scheutz (2018).

3.1 Overlap Onset Point

Onset point is the key feature for classifying the function of an overlap, and refers to the window of time in which the overlap occurred (see Jefferson (2004)). There are four types in the scheme (see Fig. 1), and these are represented as elements of Ω, where $\Omega = \{\Omega_{TS}, \Omega_{PT}, \Omega_{IJ}, \Omega_{LI}\}$, and each element is a bounded time interval specifying a

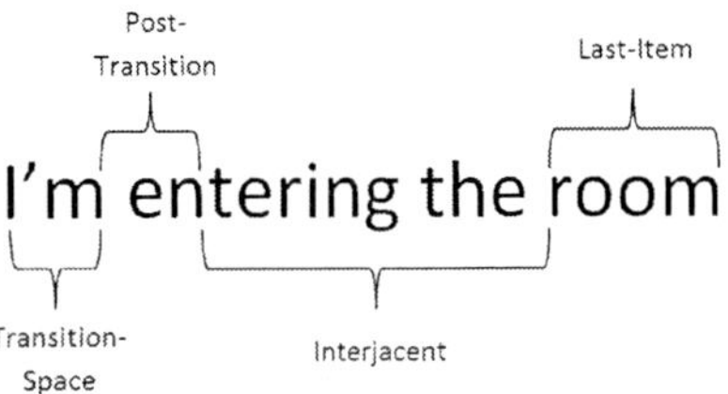

Figure 1: Key overlap onset points.

lower and an upper bound. The first overlap interval, *Last-Item* (see Dialog *1*) refers to overlap occurring on the last word or lexical item[3] before a TRP. Last-Item overlap is defined in our scheme as an interval containing the range of time from the onset to the offset of the final lexical item in the utterance: $\Omega_{LI}(U_{agent}) = [|onset(item_{final}) + 1|, |offset(item_{final})|]$. These values can be obtained from the speech synthesizer or estimated from syllable count.

1)   *D: ...one yellow block . per blue b[ox]*
     S: [o k]ay

Two other overlap types in our scheme are the *Transition-Space* (see Dialog 2) and *Post-Transition* (see Dialog 3). *Transition-Space* overlaps are characterized by simultaneous turn startup, and occur when overlap is initiated within a conversational beat (roughly the length of a spoken syllable) after the first starter began their turn. While the length of a conversational beat varies depending on the rate of speech, it has been estimated to be around 180 ms so this is the value we have implemented (see Wilson and Wilson (2005)). Transition space is thus defined as the following interval: $\Omega_{TS}(U_{agent}) = [|onset(item_{initial})|, |len(beat)|]$, or [1, 180].

2)   *S: Yes*
     (0.5)
     D: [So is]-
     S: A[n d I] just leave that there correct?

The Post-Transition case is similar to Transition-Space except that here the timing window is offset by an additional conversational beat (see Dialog *3*. Note that the TRP here is between the words "sure" and "where"). The interval is defined in our scheme as: $\Omega_{PT}(U_{agent}) = [|len(beat) + 1|, |2(len(beat))|]$, or [181, 360] using 180 ms as the length of a beat.

3)   *S: Is there a time limit?*

---

[3]Note that lexical items need not be single words, but may also be collocations such as "traffic light".

D: I'm- I'm not sure whe[re are you?]
S: [o   k   a   y]

The final overlap type is the *Interjacent* (see Dialog *4*). This type of overlap occurs when the second starter comes in during the middle of the first starter's turn, i.e., not directly near a TRP. In our scheme, Interjacent overlap is defined as an interval specifying a range from the offset of the Post-Transition window (361 ms) to the onset of the Last-Item window: $\Omega_{IJ}(U_{agent}) = [|2(len(beat)) + 1|, |onset(item_{final})|]$.

4) *D: Okay maybe that was a-*
    (0.5)
    D: like they said th[e r e w a s]- [oka]y
    S: [it was a pin]k b[o x]

3.2 Overlap Management Behaviors

The overlap management category describes various ways in which overlap can be resolved[4]. We distinguish between non-competitive behaviors, which do not involve an intent to take the turn, and competitive behaviors, which involve a "fight" for the turn. Non-competitive behaviors include simply dropping out, or uttering a single word or lexical item (e.g., "okay"). *Wrap Up* is a specific non-competitive behavior which involves briefly continuing one's turn ("wrapping up") after being overlapped and then stopping at the next TRP. Wrap Up is performed by a speaker when the overlap occurs near the end of their planned turn (within 4 beats, or 720 ms of the TRP). *Finish Turn* similarly involves reaching the TRP, but this behavior only involves a completion of the word or lexical item on which the overlap occurred (as in Last-Item). Both are considered non-competitive because the intent is to relinquish the turn.

In contrast, the competitive behaviors involve maintaining one's turn during overlap. One such behavior is *Continue*, in which the overlapped speaker simply continues their turn. This differs from Wrap Up in that the speaker continues beyond the next TRP, and so is not relinquishing the turn. Other competitive behaviors include disfluencies and self-repairs from Lickley (1998), which are only marked as competitive if they occurred within two conversational beats of the point of overlap (following Schegloff (2000)) and no other behavior was performed. These categories include

silent/filled pauses, prolongations, various types of self-repairs, and combinations of all of these.

4 Collaborative Remote Search Task

Our task domain is a search and rescue scenario in which human dyads perform a collaborative, remote search task (CReST) in a physical environment (Eberhard et al., 2010). In the task, one person is designated the *director*, and sits in front of a computer monitor that displays a map of the search environment (see Fig. 2). The other person is the *searcher* and is physically situated in the search environment. The two teammates communicate with a remote headset and must locate a variety of colored blocks scattered throughout the environment within an 8-minute time limit. We are interested in how people communicate in this domain so as to inform dialogue and coordination mechanisms for more natural and effective HRI.

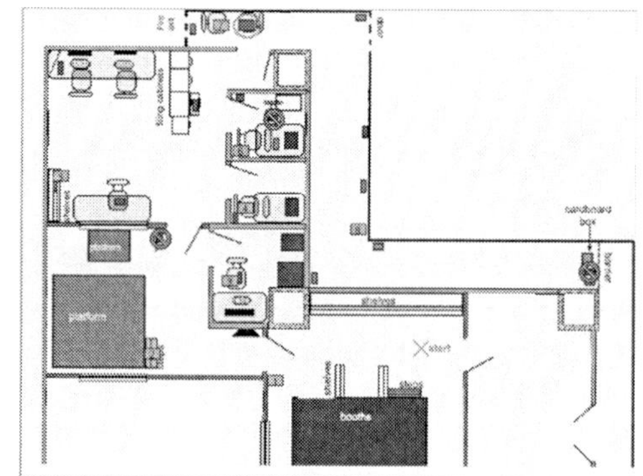

Figure 2: Map of environment from the Collaborative Remote Search Task (CReST).

Language data from 10 dyads performing this task (2712 utterances and 15194 words) was previously transcribed and annotated for a number of features, including: syntax, part-of-speech, utterances, words, disfluencies, conversational moves, and turns (Gervits et al., 2016a,b). Instances of overlap in the CReST corpus were also categorized according to their onset point and other features. (Gervits and Scheutz, 2018). There were a total of 541 overlaps in the 10 teams that we analyzed, with Transition-Space and Last-Item overlaps being the most frequent (see Table 1).

5 Model Implementation

To demonstrate our proposed model, we implemented it in the natural language pipeline of the

---

102

Table 1: Distribution of overlap onset points in the CReST corpus.

Overlap onset	Frequency
Transition-Space	35%
Post-Transition	15%
Interjacent	15%
Last-Item	35%

DIARC cognitive robotic architecture (Scheutz et al., 2007). The architecture was integrated in a SoftBank Robotics Nao robot and evaluated on the CReST corpus data. Although the CReST task was intended for a robot to fill the role of the searcher, we provide examples in which the robot can fill either role. Currently, we have implemented all of the non-competitive behaviors from the scheme, and two of the competitive behaviors (Continue and Repetition). A full implementation of all the behaviors is ongoing work.

5.1 Dialogue Management in the DIARC Architecture

The DM in DIARC is a plan-based system that allows the agent to reason over the effects of utterances and actions based on its goals. Such a system is capable of not just responding to human-initiated dialogue, but also initiating its own speech actions to accomplish goals. The DM receives utterances from the Natural Language Understanding (NLU) component that are represented using the formalism described above: $U_{agent} = SpeechAct(\alpha, \beta, \sigma, \chi, \Omega, \pi)$. Utterances of this form are also generated by the DM, and sent to the Natural Language Generation (NLG) component as output. The flow of dialogue is handled in our system through explicit exchange sequences which are stored in the dialogue context, χ. An example of such a sequence is: $AskYN(A, B) \Rightarrow ReplyY(B, A) \Rightarrow Ack(A, B)$. This represents a sequence involving a yes-no question, followed by a reply-yes, followed by an acknowledgment. A list of known sequences is provided to the system, and the current sequence is represented in a stack called Exchanges. The system always prioritizes the latest exchange added, which becomes important for managing several cases of overlapping speech (see Section 5.3 for more details).

5.2 Model Configuration

Several additional components are needed to implement the model described above. First, we require a mechanism to determine whether to compete for the turn or not. This decision is partly determined by dialogue history (e.g., previous speaker in the Post-Transition case) but also by utterance priority. As a result, a boolean priority value, π, is assigned to every utterance that a system running the model produces in a given context, χ: $\pi(U_{agent})$. This represents the urgency of that utterance at that point in the dialogue, and is used as a tiebreaker in several of the cases to determine whether to hold the turn or not.

We also need specific behaviors for managing turn-taking and dialogue context in the face of overlap. Since the DM in our architecture is a plan-based system, utterances can be thought of as (speech) actions performed to achieve a goal of the agent. As a result, dropping out of a turn (even when appropriate) should not result in the utterance being indefinitely abandoned. Thus, we need a mechanism whereby the system can store a dropped utterance and produce it later. A question then arises about exactly when is appropriate to produce the stored utterance. Our method for addressing these problems involves storing a dropped utterance in a priority queue called NLGrequests, and removing it from the current Exchanges stack. With this method, the system responds to the exchange that the human's overlapped utterance produces until it is resolved. At this point, the system will initiate utterances stored in NLGrequests, in order of priority.

One remaining topic to discuss is how to handle different kinds of feedback in overlap. Given that acknowledgments come in many varieties depending on context (Allwood et al., 1992), we distinguish between several different functions of acknowledgments in our system. Specifically, *continuers*, sometimes known as backchannel feedback, are distinguished from affirmations related to perception or understanding. This is accomplished using the onset point at which these acknowledgments occur. Acknowledgments during the Interjacent position are treated as continuers so that the agent does not attempt to drop out, compete for the turn, or add this feedback to the exchange. On the other hand, acknowledgments occurring at the Last-Item position are treated differently, and are included in the current exchange.

For identifying acknowledgments, we use a simple filter that includes several of the most common feedback words, including "okay", "yeah", "right", and "mhm".

5.3 An Algorithm for Overlap Resolution

We now turn to the task of selecting the appropriate behavior for detecting and resolving speech overlap (see Algorithm 1). A key design goal for the algorithm was speed. It is important that overlap is detected, identified, and resolved within a few hundred milliseconds in order to accommodate human expectations.

The algorithm described here operates during the robot's turn, checking for an overlapping utterance by the human. Since we are modeling remote communication, the robot transmits its speech directly to a headset worn by the human (i.e., it does not hear its own voice). In this way, we avoid the problem of disambiguating multiple simultaneous speech streams, and allow the robot to parse the human's utterance during overlap. For the algorithm, both overlapped utterances, U_{human} and U_{robot}, as well as the overlap onset point, are taken as input. The main flow of the algorithm involves using this onset point in a switch statement to decide which case to enter, and consequently, which resolution behavior to perform. The algorithm output is a behavior that corresponds to the function of the overlap.

The first step in the procedure, before considering the various cases, is to check if U_{robot} is a Single Item or Wrap Up (see Alg. 1, line 3). We have found that people do not typically compete for such utterances, so the robot's behavior here is to just finish its turn. Both utterances are then added to the Exchanges stack in the local dialogue context, χ.

If U_{robot} is not a Single Item or Wrap Up, then the algorithm checks the onset point and goes into the respective case for each type. Each case is handled in a unique way in order to select the proper competitive or non-competitive behavior based on the "function" of that overlap type. For example, because Transition-Space overlap is characterized by simultaneous startup, it uses the priority of the robot's utterance, $\pi(U_{robot})$, to determine whether to hold the turn or not (see Alg. 1, line 7). If priority is low, then it drops the turn; otherwise it competes for the turn. Post-transition overlap uses a similar mechanism, but first checks

the previous speaker (see Alg. 1, line 16). This is done to give the human a chance to respond if the robot had the prior turn. Likewise, if the human had the prior turn, the robot is given a chance to respond, but only if $\pi(U_{robot})$ is high. Interjacent overlap also uses the priority mechanism, but first checks if U_{human} is a backchannel (see Alg. 1, line 31); if so, it will continue the turn. Finally, Last-Item overlap involves finishing the current turn and adding both overlapping utterances to the Exchanges stack. This means that if an acknowledgment occurs in this position, it is treated as part of the exchange rather than as backchannel feedback.

In all cases in which a turn is dropped (see e.g., Alg. 1, line 8), this involves not just abandoning U_{robot} immediately, but also storing it for later in the NLGrequests priority queue. The system simultaneously parses the ongoing U_{human} and adds this to the top of the Exchanges stack.

Competing for the turn (e.g., Alg. 1, line 12) involves producing one of the competitive behaviors from **C**, including *Continue*, *Disfluency*, and *Self-Repair*. Selecting which behavior to employ is a challenging problem due to its stochastic nature, and one which remains elusive even in the empirical literature (but see Schegloff (2000) for some ideas). Our approach is based largely on our analysis of the CreST corpus, specifically on the frequency of the various overlap management behaviors for each overlap type. We use a proportion-based selection method[5] which assigns a probability for a behavior to be selected, p_b, based on its frequency (in the corpus) over the sum of the frequency of all behaviors, f_i, where $|\mathbf{C}|$ is the number of competitive behaviors:

$$p_b = \frac{f_b}{\sum_{i=1}^{|\mathbf{C}|} f_i}$$

As an example, we found that for Transition-Space overlaps, Continues were used 24% of the time in resolution, and Repetition were used 3% of the time. Since we only have these two competitive behaviors currently implemented ($|\mathbf{C}| = 2$), the algorithm will produce a Continue about 89% of the time and a Repetition about 11% of the time for Transition-Space overlaps in which it is competing for the turn. These probabilities vary depending on the overlap type.

---

[5]This is analogous to the fitness proportionate selection operator for genetic algorithms - see Back (1996)

6 Evaluation

Below we present the results of a qualitative evaluation on the CReST corpus data.

6.1 Results

To evaluate our algorithm, we demonstrate that it can handle the main classes of overlap observed in the corpus data[6]. These include the four main overlap types (see Fig. 1), the resolution behaviors, and the additional features from Section 5.2, including handling feedback and restarting abandoned utterances.

Transition-Space overlap (simultaneous startup) is handled by using the priority of the robot's utterance to modulate behavior. If we set $\pi(U_{robot}) =$ low, then it will drop the turn, as the director does in Dialog 2. On the other hand, if priority is high, then it will maintain the turn as the searcher does in the same example with a Continue. We have also implemented the Repetition behavior, which the director performs to maintain the turn in Dialog 5. The Repetition is maintained until the other speaker stops talking. Note that, as in the corpus, these competitive behaviors are not invoked during the production of a single word or lexical item. See Dialog 3 for an example where the searcher produces "okay" in overlap.

5)　　*D: Can you hold on a second?*
　　　 D: They'[re- they're] giving me instructions
　　　 S:　　[y e a h]

Post-transition overlap is characterized by a late entry by the second starter. The algorithm handles this case by checking the previous speaker and dropping out if the robot had the prior turn. Otherwise, it uses priority as a tiebreaker as in the Transition-Space case. Dialog 6 below shows an example of prior speaker being used to resolve overlap. The behavior of the director in this example is demonstrative of the algorithm's performance. On the third line, the director says "I'm not sure" which ends in a TRP. They then continued their turn with "I - I don't..." at which point the searcher overlaps to respond to the previous utterance and the director drops out mid-turn.

6)　　*S: Do I just take-*
　　　 D: There's other things in the box too um .
　　　 D: I'm not sure I- [I don't know what they]-
　　　 S:　　　　　[o k a y .　I'm just tak]ing

---

[6]There is an accompanying video showing some of the algorithm behaviors. It can be found at: `https://vimeo.com/260654351`

everything in the box

Interjacent overlap is handled solely through the use of the priority mechanism to determine turn-holding or turn-yielding behavior. As demonstrated above, both of these cases are readily handled by the algorithm, and only require that $\pi(U_{robot})$ be reasonably set.

Last-Item overlap is handled by finishing the turn, and adding U_{human} to the current exchange, as in Dialog 1. Here, the algorithm replicates the director's behavior of finishing the turn and treating the searcher's feedback as an acknowledgment in the current exchange.

Handling different kinds of feedback is another important component of our approach. In Section 5.2 we showed that continuers at the Interjacent point are handled differently than those at the Last-Item point. In Dialog 7 below, the director produces a continuer ("yeah") at the Interjacent point, followed by a "got that" at the last item position. The continuer is identified by the algorithm as such (and effectively ignored), whereas the Last-Item acknowledgment is added to the current exchange: $Stmt(A, B) \Rightarrow Ack(B, A)$.

7)　　*S: like . um . there's a green box number*
　　　 t[wo o]n the st[a　i　r]s
　　　 D: [yeah]　　[got that]

Wrap Up is another class of overlap behavior that was observed in the corpus. We handle these cases by checking the remaining length of U_{robot} after the overlap onset. If the utterance is within 4 conversational beats (720 ms) of completion then the robot will simply finish it, as seen in Dialog 8. Otherwise, resolution is handled based on the time window in which the overlap occurred.

8)　　*D: ... but was there? O[r was there not?]*
　　　 S:　　　　　　[n　o:::　]

Finally, resolving the effect of overlap on the current dialogue sequence represents a common pattern seen in the corpus. The algorithm handles this differently depending on whether the robot held the turn or dropped out. If the robot held the turn, then U_{robot} is used as the next element in the exchange. Otherwise, the robot drops the turn, and stores U_{robot} in NLGrequests to be uttered after the current exchange is complete. An example of this behavior can be seen in Dialog 9 from the corpus. Our algorithm behaves as the director in this case. It drops the "go down" utterance to quickly handle the new $Stmt(A, B) \Rightarrow Ack(B, A)$ exchange introduced by the searcher in the second line. The

105

abandoned utterance is now at the top of the NL-Grequests stack, so it is restarted once the prior exchange is complete.

9) *D: G[o d o w n]-*   *[yeah yeah ok]ay*
   S: *[there's lik]e boxes all ov[er the place]*
   D: Go down
   S: Okay
   D: And turn- turn right

6.2 Discussion

We have show that the categories of our formal framework are robust and can account for much of human overlap behavior in task-oriented remote dialogue. This model represents a step towards the goal of more natural and effective turn-taking for HRI. A main advantage of our approach is that it enables robots running the model to manage overlap in human-like ways, at human-like timescales, and at minimal computational cost. By handling the different kinds of overlap, robots can produce a wide range of supportive behaviors, including: maintaining dialogue flow during overlap, allowing people to start their turn early for more efficient turn transitions, supporting recognitional overlap during the robot's turn, dropping out to allow a human to clarify or respond, prioritizing urgent messages by holding the turn, and handling simultaneous startup.

One potential issue is that, with only two of the competitive turn-holding behaviors implemented, the current system will tend to produce continues most of the time when competing for the turn. As mentioned previously, this can be problematic because continues present ambiguity in grounding. We will need to conduct empirical studies using our model to explore the grounding cost of different competitive turn-holding behaviors and establish which are the most effective. It is likely that trade offs between model accuracy and usability will be necessary moving forward. For example, in order to maintain grounding, the system may need to prolong its turn-holding behavior until the human stops talking. This is not necessarily what we find in the human data, but nevertheless it may be crucial for a dialogue system.

7 Future Work and Conclusion

7.1 Future Work

While we have demonstrated that our model can handle various classes of behaviors found in the corpus, other components of the system still need to be considered for future evaluation. The components described in Section 5.2 such as priority modulation, feedback handling, delaying abandoned utterances, sequence organization (using the Exchange stack), and behavior selection will need to be separately evaluated in future work. Moreover, a comparison of this system with "non-humanlike" dialogue systems (e.g., Funakoshi et al. (2010) and Shiwa et al. (2009)) will inform whether naturalness and responsiveness are desirable components in a dialogue system.

The other main direction of future work is extending the model to produce overlap on a human's turn. This will require a fully incremental system to predict potential turn completion points. By building up a partial prediction of the utterance in progress, the system will be able to generate backchannel feedback, recognitional overlap, collaborative completions, and other instances of intentional overlap. It will also be able to engage in fluid turn-taking to avoid accidental overlap altogether, and to recover quickly when it happens.

7.2 Conclusion

We have introduced a formal framework and computational model for embodied artificial agents to recover from being overlapped while speaking. The model is informed by extensive empirical work both from the literature as well as from our own analyses. We have integrated the model in the DIARC cognitive robotic architecture and demonstrated how an agent running this model recovers from common overlap patterns found in a human search and rescue domain. The utility of the model is that it can quickly identify and resolve overlap in natural and effective ways, and at minimal computational cost. This project is a step in a larger effort to model various aspects of human dialogue towards the goal of developing genuine robot teammates that can communicate and coordinate effectively in a variety of complex domains.

Acknowledgments

This work was funded by a NASA Space Technology Research Fellowship under award 80NSSC17K0184. We would like to thank Shereen Oraby and the anonymous reviewers for their helpful contributions.

References

James F Allen, Bradford W Miller, Eric K Ringger, and Teresa Sikorski. 1996. A robust system for natural spoken dialogue. In *Proceedings of the 34th annual meeting on Association for Computational Linguistics*, pages 62–70. Association for Computational Linguistics.

Jens Allwood, Joakim Nivre, and Elisabeth Ahlsén. 1992. On the semantics and pragmatics of linguistic feedback. *Journal of semantics*, 9(1):1–26.

Thomas Back. 1996. *Evolutionary algorithms in theory and practice: evolution strategies, evolutionary programming, genetic algorithms*. Oxford university press.

Timo Baumann and David Schlangen. 2011. Predicting the micro-timing of user input for an incremental spoken dialogue system that completes a user's ongoing turn. In *Proceedings of the SIGDIAL 2011 Conference*, pages 120–129. Association for Computational Linguistics.

Jean Carletta, Stephen Isard, Gwyneth Doherty-Sneddon, Amy Isard, Jacqueline C Kowtko, and Anne H Anderson. 1997. The reliability of a dialogue structure coding scheme. *Computational linguistics*, 23(1):13–31.

Jan-Peter De Ruiter, Holger Mitterer, and Nick J Enfield. 2006. Projecting the end of a speaker's turn: A cognitive cornerstone of conversation. *Language*, 82(3):515–535.

David DeVault, Kenji Sagae, and David Traum. 2009. Can i finish?: learning when to respond to incremental interpretation results in interactive dialogue. In *Proceedings of the SIGDIAL 2009 Conference: The 10th Annual Meeting of the Special Interest Group on Discourse and Dialogue*, pages 11–20. Association for Computational Linguistics.

David DeVault, Kenji Sagae, and David Traum. 2011. Detecting the status of a predictive incremental speech understanding model for real-time decision-making in a spoken dialogue system. In *Twelfth Annual Conference of the International Speech Communication Association*.

Paul Drew. 2009. Quit talking while I'm interrupting: a comparison between positions of overlap onset in conversation. In *Talk in Interaction: Comparative Dimensions*, pages 70–93.

Kathleen M Eberhard, Hannele Nicholson, Sandra Kübler, Susan Gundersen, and Matthias Scheutz. 2010. The indiana "cooperative remote search task"(crest) corpus. In *Proceedings of the 11th edition of the Language Resources and Evaluation Conference (LREC)*.

Terrence Fong, Charles Thorpe, and Charles Baur. 2003. Collaboration, dialogue, human-robot interaction. In *Robotics Research*, pages 255–266. Springer.

Kotaro Funakoshi, Mikio Nakano, Kazuki Kobayashi, Takanori Komatsu, and Seiji Yamada. 2010. Non-humanlike spoken dialogue: a design perspective. In *Proceedings of the 11th Annual Meeting of the Special Interest Group on Discourse and Dialogue*, pages 176–184. Association for Computational Linguistics.

Felix Gervits, Kathleen Eberhard, and Matthias Scheutz. 2016a. Disfluent but effective? a quantitative study of disfluencies and conversational moves in team discourse. In *Proceedings of COLING 2016, the 26th International Conference on Computational Linguistics: Technical Papers*, pages 3359–3369.

Felix Gervits, Kathleen Eberhard, and Matthias Scheutz. 2016b. Team communication as a collaborative process. *Frontiers in Robotics and AI*, 3:62.

Felix Gervits and Matthias Scheutz. 2018. Towards a conversation-analytic taxonomy of speech overlap. In *Proceedings of the 11th edition of the Language Resources and Evaluation Conference (LREC)*.

Mattias Heldner and Jens Edlund. 2010. Pauses, gaps and overlaps in conversations. *Journal of Phonetics*, 38(4):555–568.

Gail Jefferson. 1982. Two explorations of the organization of overlapping talk in conversation. In *Tilburg Papers in Language and Literature 28*. University of Tilburg.

Gail Jefferson. 1986. Notes on 'latency' in overlap onset. *Human Studies*, 9(2-3):153–183.

Gail Jefferson. 2004. A sketch of some orderly aspects of overlap in natural conversation. *Pragmatics and Beyond New Series*, 125:43–62.

Stephen C Levinson and Francisco Torreira. 2015. Timing in turn-taking and its implications for processing models of language. *Frontiers in psychology*, 6:731.

Robin J Lickley. 1998. HCRC disfluency coding manual. In *Technical Report HCRC/TR-100*. Human Communication Research Centre, University of Edinburgh.

Lilla Magyari and Jan P de Ruiter. 2012. Prediction of turn-ends based on anticipation of upcoming words. *Frontiers in psychology*, 3:376.

Antoine Raux, Dan Bohus, Brian Langner, Alan W Black, and Maxine Eskenazi. 2006. Doing research on a deployed spoken dialogue system: One year of let's go! experience. In *Ninth International Conference on Spoken Language Processing*.

Harvey Sacks, Emanuel A Schegloff, and Gail Jefferson. 1974. A simplest systematics for the organization of turn-taking for conversation. *Language*, pages 696–735.

Emanuel A Schegloff. 2000. Overlapping talk and the organization of turn-taking for conversation. *Language in society*, 29(1):1–63.

Matthias Scheutz, Paul Schermerhorn, James Kramer, and David Anderson. 2007. First steps toward natural human-like hri. *Autonomous Robots*, 22(4):411–423.

Ethan O Selfridge and Peter A Heeman. 2010. Importance-driven turn-bidding for spoken dialogue systems. In *Proceedings of the 48th Annual Meeting of the Association for Computational Linguistics*, pages 177–185. Association for Computational Linguistics.

Toshiyuki Shiwa, Takayuki Kanda, Michita Imai, Hiroshi Ishiguro, and Norihiro Hagita. 2009. How quickly should a communication robot respond? delaying strategies and habituation effects. *International Journal of Social Robotics*, 1(2):141–155.

Gabriel Skantze and Anna Hjalmarsson. 2010. Towards incremental speech generation in dialogue systems. In *Proceedings of the 11th Annual Meeting of the Special Interest Group on Discourse and Dialogue*, pages 1–8. Association for Computational Linguistics.

Gabriel Skantze and David Schlangen. 2009. Incremental dialogue processing in a micro-domain. In *Proceedings of the 12th Conference of the European Chapter of the Association for Computational Linguistics*, pages 745–753. Association for Computational Linguistics.

Margaret Wilson and Thomas P Wilson. 2005. An oscillator model of the timing of turn-taking. *Psychonomic bulletin & review*, 12(6):957–968.

Tiancheng Zhao, Alan W Black, and Maxine Eskenazi. 2015. An incremental turn-taking model with active system barge-in for spoken dialog systems. In *Proceedings of the 16th Annual Meeting of the Special Interest Group on Discourse and Dialogue*, pages 42–50.

Algorithm 1 Speech Overlap Management

1: **procedure** MANAGEOVERLAP(U_{human}, U_{robot}, onset point)   ▷ Input: Human and robot utterances in context χ, where $U_{agent} = SpeechAct(\alpha, \beta, \sigma, \chi, \Omega, \pi)$; onset point is the timing of the overlap. Output: Resolution behavior
2:    **while** robot speaking **do**
3:        **if** $\sigma(U_{robot}) = Single\ Item$ or length($\sigma(U_{robot})$) - onset point < 720 **then**
4:            Finish Turn(U_{robot})   ▷ Single Item or Wrap Up. Stop at the next TRP
5:            Exchanges.push(U_{robot}, U_{human})
6:        **else if** onset point $\in \Omega_{TS}$ **then**   ▷ Transition-space case. 180 ms of start of U_{robot}
7:            **if** $\pi(U_{robot})$ = low **then**   ▷ Low priority utterance. Non-competitive resolution.
8:                Drop Turn(U_{robot})
9:                NLGrequests.push(U_{robot})   ▷ Store utterance for later
10:                Exchanges.push(U_{human})   ▷ Add human's utterance to current exchange
11:            **else**   ▷ High priority utterance. Maintain turn.
12:                Compete(U_{robot})   ▷ Perform one of the competitive resolution behaviors
13:                Exchanges.push(U_{robot})
14:            **end if**
15:        **else if** onset point $\in \Omega_{PT}$ **then**   ▷ Post-transition case. 180-360 ms of start of U_{robot}
16:            **if** $\chi(U_{robot})$.previous_speaker = robot **then**   ▷ Drop turn to allow for response
17:                Drop Turn(U_{robot})
18:                NLGrequests.push(U_{robot})
19:                Exchanges.push(U_{human})
20:            **else if** $\chi(U_{robot})$.previous_speaker = human **then**   ▷ Use priority to determine behavior
21:                **if** $\pi(U_{robot})$ = low **then**
22:                    Drop Turn(U_{robot})
23:                    NLGrequests.push(U_{robot})
24:                    Exchanges.push(U_{human})
25:                **else**
26:                    Compete(U_{robot})
27:                    Exchanges.push(U_{robot})
28:                **end if**
29:            **end if**
30:        **else if** onset point $\in \Omega_{IJ}$ **then**   ▷ Interjacent case. Mid-turn overlap.
31:            **if** $\sigma(U_{human}) \in \{Backchannels\}$ **then**
32:                Continue(U_{robot})   ▷ Allow backchannel feedback
33:                Exchanges.push(U_{robot})
34:            **else if** $\pi(U_{robot})$ = low **then**
35:                Drop Turn(U_{robot})
36:                NLGrequests.push(U_{robot})
37:                Exchanges.push(U_{human})
38:            **else**
39:                Compete(U_{robot})
40:                Exchanges.push(U_{robot})
41:            **end if**
42:        **else if** onset_point $\in \Omega_{LI}$ **then**   ▷ Last-Item case. End of turn.
43:            Finish_Turn(U_{robot})
44:            Exchanges.push(U_{robot}, U_{human})
45:        **end if**
46:    **end while**
47: **end procedure**

Consequences and Factors of Stylistic Differences
in Human-Robot Dialogue

Stephanie M. Lukin[1], Kimberly A. Pollard[1], Claire Bonial[1], Matthew Marge[1],
Cassidy Henry[1], Ron Artstein[2], David Traum[2] and Clare R. Voss[1]

[1]U.S. Army Research Laboratory, Adelphi, MD 20783
[2]USC Institute for Creative Technologies, Playa Vista, CA 90094
`stephanie.m.lukin.civ@mail.mil`

Abstract

This paper identifies stylistic differences in instruction-giving observed in a corpus of human-robot dialogue. Differences in verbosity and structure (i.e., single-intent vs. multi-intent instructions) arose naturally without restrictions or prior guidance on how users should speak with the robot. Different styles were found to produce different rates of miscommunication, and correlations were found between style differences and individual user variation, trust, and interaction experience with the robot. Understanding potential consequences and factors that influence style can inform design of dialogue systems that are robust to natural variation from human users.

1 Introduction

When human users engage in spontaneous language use with a dialogue system, a variety of naturally occurring language is observed. A persistent challenge in the development of dialogue systems is determining how to handle this diversity. One strategy is to limit diversity and maximize the system's natural language understanding by training users *a priori* on what language and syntax is valid. However, these constraints could potentially yield inefficient interactions, e.g., the user may incur greater task and cognitive load trying to remember the proper phrasing needed by the system, worrying whether or not their speech will be understood if they do not get it exactly right. A broader approach to dealing with diversity is to develop more robust systems that can respond appropriately to different styles of language. A set of dialogue system policies that takes into account natural stylistic variations in users' speech would

Figure 1: Dialogues between Users (U) and a Robot, exemplifying stylistic differences

provide for a more nuanced, adaptable, and user-focused approach to interaction.

Rather than constrain users or develop a generalized dialogue system that attempts to cover all variations in the same way, we focus on analytic understanding of differences in observed language behavior, as well as possible causes of these differences and implications of misunderstanding. This work is a first step towards a more nuanced and flexible dialogue policy that can be sensitive to individual and situational differences, and adapt appropriately. This paper introduces a taxonomy of stylistic differences in instructions that humans issue to robots in a dialogue. The taxonomy consists of two classes: *verbosity* and *structure*. Verbosity is measured by number of words in an instruction. Dialogues 1 and 2 in Figure 1 show contrasting verbosity levels. Structure concerns the number of intents issued in an instruction: Minimal if it contains a single intent (Dialogue 3 in Figure 1 has

Proceedings of the SIGDIAL 2018 Conference, pages 110–118,
Melbourne, Australia, 12-14 July 2018. ©2018 Association for Computational Linguistics

two Minimal) or Extended if it contains more than one intent (Dialogue 4). Understanding stylistic differences can support the development of dialogue systems with strategies that tailor system responses to the user's style, rather than constrain the user's style to the expected input. The taxonomy is described in more detail in Section 3.

We observe and analyze these stylistic differences in a corpus of human-robot direction-giving dialogue from Marge et al. (2017). These styles are not unique to this corpus; they emerge in other human-robot and human-human dialogue, such as TeamTalk (Marge and Rudnicky, 2011) and SCARE (Stoia et al., 2008). The corpus contains 60 dialogues from 20 participants (Section 4). The robot dialogue management in the corpus is controlled by a Wizard-of-Oz experimenter, allowing for the study of users' style with a fluent and naturalistic partner (i.e., with an approximation of an idealized automated system).

In Section 5, we investigate possible consequences and implications of these categorized styles in this corpus. We examine the relationship of style and miscommunication frequency, applying an existing taxonomy for miscommunication in human-agent conversational dialogue (Higashinaka et al., 2015a) to this human-robot corpus. We explore the relationship between stylistic differences and other dialogue phenomena described in Section 6, specifically whether:

- The rate of miscommunication is related to verbosity (H_1) and structure (H_2);
- Latent user differences are related to verbosity (H_3) and structure (H_4);
- Trust in the robot is related to verbosity (H_5) and structure (H_6);
- Time/experience with the robot is related to verbosity (H_7) and structure (H_8).

Finally, we speculate about how knowledge of style, miscommunication, individual differences, trust, and experience might be leveraged to implement targeted and personalized dialogue management strategies and offer concluding remarks on future work (Sections 7 and 8).

2 Related Work

A number of human-human direction-giving corpora exist, among them, ArtWalk (Liu et al., 2016), CReST (Eberhard et al., 2010), SCARE (Stoia et al., 2008), and SaGA (Lücking et al., 2010). The majority of existing analyses on these corpora focus on the vocabulary of referring expressions and entrainment. While variations in instruction-giving verbosity and structure are evident in these human-human interactions, the goal of this work is to improve human-robot communication. Humans have different assumptions about how robots communicate and behave, and may speak differently to robots than they do to other humans. We therefore chose a human-robot corpus for our style analysis that uses a Wizard-of-Oz for dialogue management. This allowed us specifically to isolate the style usage and miscommunication errors of the human partner (because the Wizard makes very few errors on the robot's end).

Studies of human-robot automated systems tend to focus on the miscommunication errors of the dialogue system (i.e., the robot itself), rather than the miscommunication or style of the human partner. In conversational agents, the research focus is also primarily to categorize errors made by the agent, not the human, including errors in ASR, surface realization, or appropriateness of the response (e.g., Higashinaka et al. (2015b); Paek and Horvitz (2000)). The more generic task-oriented and agent-based response-level errors from Higashinaka et al. (2015a) map well to the user miscommunication in the corpus we examine, including excess/lack of information, nonunderstanding, unclear intention, and misunderstanding. Works that focus specifically on miscommunication from the user when interacting with a robot include those categorizing referential ambiguity and impossible to execute commands (Marge and Rudnicky, 2015). These categories are common in the data we examine as well.

In this analysis, we predict that trust will have an effect on stylistic variations. Factors of trust in co-present and remote human-robot collaboration has been studied with respect to engagement with the robot, and memory of information from the robot (Powers et al., 2007).

3 Stylistic Differences

We describe two classes of stylistic differences for instruction-giving: differences in the verbosity of an instruction, and in the structure of the instruction. These styles emerge when decomposing a high-level plan or intent (e.g., exploring a physical space) into (potentially, but not necessarily) low-level instructions (e.g., how to explore the space, where to move, how to turn).

3.1 Verbosity

Verbosity is a continuous measure of the number of words per instruction. Compare the instruction in Dialogue 1 in Figure 1 "take pictures in all four directions" (6 words) with the instruction in Dialogue 2 "robot face north, take a picture, face south, take a picture, face east, take a picture" (16 words). Both issue the same plan (with the exception of a picture towards the west in Dialogue 2), yet Dialogue 1 condenses the instruction and assumes that the robot can unpack the higher-level plan. Dialogue 2 is more verbose and low-level, making reference to individual cardinal directions. Verbosity alone does not capture all style differences; additional categorization is needed.

3.2 Structure of Instructions

We define a *Minimal* instruction as one containing a single intent (e.g., "turn", "move", or "request image"). A sequence of Minimal instructions often reveals the higher-level plan of the user. In Dialogue 3, the user issues a single instruction "go through the other door" and waits until the instruction has been completed. Upon receiving completion feedback from the robot ("executing" and "done" responses), the next instruction, "take a picture", is issued. Compare this with Dialogue 4, where the intents "face your starting position" and "send a picture" are compounded together and issued at the same time. This is classified as an *Extended* intent structure: instructions that have more than one expressed intent. These structural definitions were first described in Traum et al. (2018) to classify the composition of an instruction. In this work, we use these definitions to classify the style of the user.

4 Human-Robot Dialogue Corpus

We examine these styles in a corpus of human-robot dialogue collected from a collaborative human-robot task (Marge et al., 2017). The user and the robot were not co-present. The user instructed the robot in three remote, search-and-navigation tasks: a Training trial and two Main trials (M1 and M2). During Training, users got used to speaking to the robot. Main trials lasted for 20 minutes each, and users were given concrete goals for each exploration, including counting particular objects (e.g., shoes) and making deductions (e.g., if the space could be a headquarters environment).

Users spoke instructions into a microphone while looking at a live 2D-map built from the robot's LIDAR scanner. A low bandwidth environment was simulated by disabling video streaming; instead, photos could be captured on-demand from the robot's front-facing camera. To allow full natural language use, users were not provided example commands to the robot, though they were provided with a list of the robot's capabilities which they could reference throughout the trials. Well-formed instructions (unambiguous, with a clear action, end-point, and state) could be executed without any additional clarification (e.g., all dialogues in Figure 1). The robot responded with status updates to the user to make it known when an instruction was heard and completed. When necessary, the robot requested instruction clarification. A human Wizard experimenter stood in for the robot's speech recognition, natural language understanding, and language production capabilities, which were guided by a response protocol.

4.1 Corpus Statistics

The corpus contains 3,573 utterances from 20 users, totaling 18,336 words. 1,981 instructions were issued. The least verbose instruction observed is 1 word ("stop"), and the most verbose is 59 words (mean 7.3, SD 5.8). Of the total instructions, 1,383 are of the Minimal style, and 598, Extended. A moderate, positive correlation exists between higher verbosity and the Extended style in this corpus ($r_s(1969) = .613, p < .001$), supporting an intuition that more words would be found in Extended instructions. That this correlation is not stronger, however, may suggest that the verbosity metric is insufficient to capture critical elements of stylistic variation of structure. Number of words does not completely map onto the complexity or the "packed" nature of instructions. For example, the Minimal but highly verbose instruction from in corpus "continue down the hallway to the first entrance on the left first doorway on the left" is 16 words, but the Extended instruction "stop. take a picture" is only 4.

5 Stylistic Differences and Miscommunication

A user's utterance is classified as a miscommunication if the following robot utterance is a request for clarification or indicates inability to comply; this occurred at least once in 216 (16%) of the instructions in the corpus. We hypothesize that different instruction styles will differ in their overall rates of miscommunication, i.e., that miscommunication rates are related to verbosity (H_1) and structure (H_2).

If a scarcity of words leads to ambiguity or missing information, we would predict that verbosity and miscommunication rate would be negatively correlated. However, if more words simply yield more opportunities for erroneous or contradictory information, then we would predict a positive correlation between verbosity and miscommunication. We assessed this using binary logistic regression of verbosity on overall miscommunication presence (H_1). Results revealed that miscommunication significantly increases with verbosity (verbosity as a continuous independent variable, with model $\chi^2 = 55.94$, $p < .001$, with Wald $= 56.67$, $p < .001$, Nagelkerke $R^2 = .06$)

If having more intents in a single instruction leaves more opportunities for mistakes, then we would predict that greater use of Extended structure would be positively related to miscommunication rates. To examine this relationship, we compared overall miscommunication rates and use of different instruction structures (H_2). The overall miscommunication rate for Minimal instructions is 8%, while Extended is 18%; we confirmed that Extended instructions were significantly more likely to have miscommunication (structure as a categorical independent variable, with Chi-square test, $\chi^2(1, N = 1969) = 40.91$, $p < .001$).

5.1 Miscommunication Types

While overall miscommunication rate differed significantly among styles, it would be useful to understand whether different styles are associated with different types of miscommunication, as this may inform what error-handing algorithms the system should favor. Following Higashinaka et al. (2015a), we categorize miscommunication in the corpus according to Response-level and Environmental-level ontologies. Though this ontology was designed to categorize errors made by a virtual agent dialogue system, a number of categories are applicable to communicative errors committed by human users in situated dialogues. Figure 2 shows examples of user-miscommunication errors from the human-robot corpus and the robot response. Further explanation and expected relationships are below.

Dialogue 5: Response, Missing Information
U: leave the room and go to your left
Robot: How far left should I go?

Dialogue 6: Response, Unclear Instruction
U: go into the center of the first room on your left and then take a picture at the west north east and south position
Robot: Can you repeat the positions you'd like photos from?

Dialogue 7: Environment, Ambiguous Reference
U: can you move forward to take a picture of the object
Robot: I'm not sure which object you are referring to. Can you describe it another way?

Dialogue 8: Environment, Impossible Instruction
U: move around the cone into the next room turn right ninety degrees
Robot: There is not enough space for me to move around the cone and enter the room ahead. Would you like me to get as close as possible to the room?

Dialogue 9: Environment, Misunderstand Capabilities
U: okay turn to your right forty five degrees and turn on video camera
Robot: Our bandwidth will currently not support the video feed. Would you like me to send a photo?

Figure 2: Dialogues between Users (U) and Robot with different miscommunications types

Response-level, Missing Information instructions lack information required for execution (Dialogue 5). We expected that lower verbosity instructions would be more likely to lead to this type of miscommunication due to a lack of specificity, as measured by fewer words, e.g., "turn right" is missing how many degrees to turn. On the other hand, we might expect that Extended instructions would be more likely to lead to this type because with multiple intent comes a compounding potential for lack of specificity.

Response-level, Unclear Instructions are unclear due to phrasing or order of information presented (Dialogue 6). More verbose instructions were expected to be more prone to this type of miscommunication because more information, measured as words, has a higher potential to be misconstrued (e.g., it is unclear if "north east" is "north" and "east" or "north-east"). However, increased information may provide additional context required for specification, the opposite relationship. Due to compounding potential, we expected Extended style would lead to more Unclear type errors.

Environment-level, Ambiguous Reference instructions include an ambiguous referent in the environment, potentially due to a lack of common ground (Dialogue 7). We expected that lower verbosity instructions, with less information (words) would have more Ambiguous miscommunication (e.g., "go to the doorway" versus "go to the doorway furthest from you"). For Extended style, we hypothesize more Ambiguous type errors due to compounding potential.

Environment-level, Impossible instructions are impossible to execute in the physical space in terms of distance and dimension (Dialogue 8). We expected that overspecified instructions (higher verbosity or Extended) might be more likely to be Impossible (e.g., in the more verbose, Extended instruction "move up two feet, turn right ninety degrees, move forward seven feet", it is not possible for the robot to move 7 feet after completing the first two actions).

Environment-level, Misunderstood Capabilities instructions are those in which the user misunderstands the robot's capabilities (Dialogue 9). We expect verbosity and structure to affect Misunderstood rates much as they affect Impossible miscommunication rates.

Logistic regression revealed that verbosity does not significantly correlate with any type of miscommunication that occurred ($\chi^2 = 4.89$, $p = .298$). To examine this result in more detail, we conducted binomial logistic regression on each miscommunication type separately, asking, e.g., does verbosity predict whether the miscommunication is of the Ambiguous type or not? None of these results were significant.

With regard to structure, a Chi-square test showed a non-significant trend, suggesting there may be a possible influence of structure on miscommunication type ($\chi^2(4, N = 216) = 8.71$, $p = .065$). We explored this result in more detail, looking at each miscommunication type separately, asking, e.g., does structure predict whether the miscommunication is of the Ambiguous type or not? Results were significant for Ambiguous miscommunication type ($\chi^2(1, N = 216) = 4.01$, $p = .045$) and a trend toward significance for Unclear miscommunication type ($\chi^2(1, N = 216) = 3.34$, $p = .067$) With Minimal styles, miscommunications that arise are more likely to be Ambiguous type. With Extended styles, miscommunication that arise may tend to be Unclear type. Counts of miscommunication types for each structure style are shown in Figure 3.

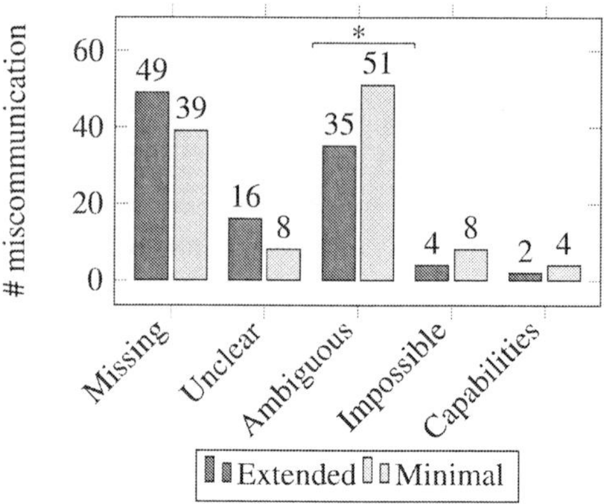

Figure 3: Miscommunication types observed in structures style (* $p < 0.05$)

6 Factors related to Style Differences

Knowing that stylistic differences are observed in unconstrained dialogue and the relationship of these differences to miscommunication rates, it is important to assess factors of these differences in the first place. We examine latent individual differences, as well as trust and interaction time with the robot, which may influence style.

6.1 Individual Differences

A broad-use dialogue system can expect to receive instructions from different individuals. The dialogue system must therefore be robust to a range of individuals who will bring different speaking styles to the interaction. We hypothesized that individual users differ in their verbosity (H3) and structure (H4).

We first examined whether individual user identity predicted verbosity (H3). The ANOVA assumption of homogeneity of variances was violated, so a Kruskal-Wallis H test was used, supporting H3 with significant difference in verbosity across individual participants ($\chi^2(19, N = 1969) = 422.53$, $p < .001$). The most verbose user used an average of 15 words per instruction, and the least verbose used an average of 4 words.

Chi-square tests revealed that individual users also vary in structure (H4; $\chi^2(19, N = 1969) = 511.70$, $p < .001$). Figure 4 graphs the percentage of structural style employed by users (sorted from smallest to largest percent of Extended usage). Some users seem to simply prefer the Minimal style (Users 1, 2, 3) while other users employed a majority of Extended (Users 19, 20). Others are almost evenly split (Users 13, 14, 15).

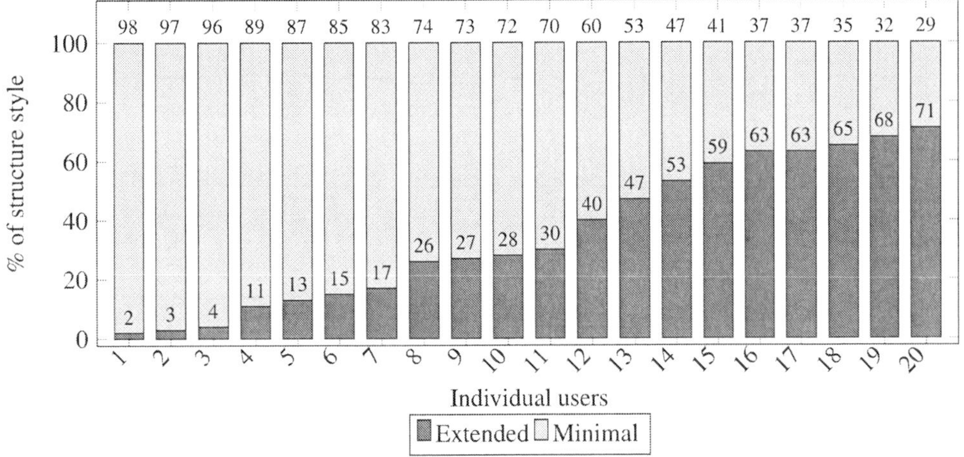

Figure 4: Percent distribution of instruction structure between users (sorted smallest to largest Extended)

6.2 Trust in the Robot

User trust in the robot may be a factor in how the user realizes their instructions, e.g., because the user may have different levels of confidence in the robot's abilities. Users completed the Trust Perception Scale-HRI (Schaefer, 2016) after M1, and again after M2. The Trust Perception Scale-HRI is a 40-item scale designed to measure an individual's subjective perception of trust in a robot.

We hypothesized that trust in the robot would be related to verbosity (H₅) and structure (H₆). If reported trust is indicative of a user's comfort with speaking more with the robot, and/or if trust is indicative of having higher confidence in the robot's ability to process many words, then we would predict a positive relationship between trust and verbosity. On the other hand, if trust scores reflect confidence that the robot will understand instructions without need for additional words or explanations, then we would predict a negative relationship between trust and verbosity.

To assess whether and how trust levels are related to verbosity (H₅), we compared trust levels for a trial to the verbosity in that trial (there were not enough data points to control for individual user ID in a regression). Spearman correlation was significant, with higher trust correlating with greater verbosity ($r_s(38) = .33, p = .035$).

If higher trust scores indicate user confidence that the robot can understand, parse, and execute complex instructions, then we predict that more Extended instructions would be observed. To assess this relationship (H₆), trust levels measured for each trial were compared to the proportion of Extended instructions used in that trial. Spearman correlation revealed a nonsignificant trend for higher trust to correlate with more use of the Extended structure ($r_s(38) = .29, p = .07$).

6.3 Time and Experience

As time passes and experience grows, people are known to interact differently with technology and with communication partners. We thus hypothesize that time/experience with the robot would be related to verbosity (H₇) and structure (H₈), i.e., as the user progresses from Training to M1 and M2, instruction-giving style may change.

If it is the case that users become more comfortable or confident as they gain more experience, we predict that verbosity should increase over time/experience (H₇). Indeed, verbosity increased across trials from an average of 6.1 words in Training, to 7.3 average words in M1, to 8.1 average words in MP2. A one-way repeated measures ANOVA was conducted to determine whether verbosity differed by trial (repeated measures analysis effectively controls for user ID). Trial was significantly related to verbosity, (F(2,38) = 13.45, $p < .001$), and post-hoc LSD t-tests indicated that each trial had significantly more verbose instructions than previous trials (Training vs. M1 $p = .003$; Training vs. M2 $p = .001$; M1 vs. M2 $p = .020$).

Figure 5 shows the percentage of structural style in each trial. There is a general upward trend in use of the Extended style as users engage in successive trials. A one-way repeated measures ANOVA was used to determine whether structure

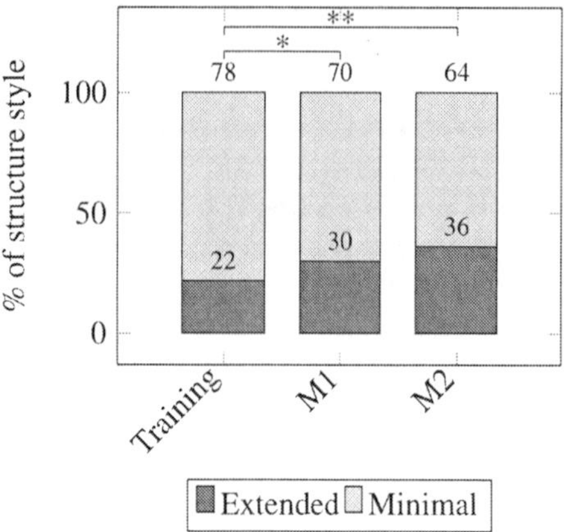

Figure 5: Percent distribution of instruction structure between trials (* $p < 0.05$; ** $p < 0.01$)

usage differed by trial (H₈). Results showed significant differences among trials ($F(2,38) = 8.26$, $p = .001$), with post-hoc LSD t-tests revealing greater Extended structure use in M1 and M2 as compared to Training (Training vs. M1 $p = .014$; Training vs. M2 $p = .002$). Structural usage between M1 and M2 was not significantly different (M1 vs. M2 $p = .190$).

7 Discussion

7.1 Miscommunication

Styles differ in the overall frequency of miscommunication they engender, but these differences are not consistent across all miscommunication types. Among miscommunication-producing instructions, we found no correlation between verbosity and what type of miscommunication was produced (H₁). Future analyses that look at additional linguistic features may help reveal what is happening at a level of specificity beyond a simple word count. We can speculate that this may be because user misunderstandings of the robot or environment exist regardless of how many words it takes the user to express these misunderstandings (Impossible, Misunderstood Capabilities), or because Ambiguous, Unclear, or Missing Information miscommunication can result either from too few words, or from cases where the participant adds more words and commits more miscommunication with those words. This raises the question of what it is that is being added with more verbose instructions, if not clarification information. Future research can aim to address this.

Our analyses revealed an effect of structure on miscommunication types (H₂). Minimal structure

had a greater tendency to yield Ambiguous miscommunications. This may be because additional intents in an instruction offer opportunities to correct ambiguity in the first intent. For example, if the robot is told to go through the door and take a photo of the chair, the robot can use the presence or absence of a chair to settle any ambiguity about which door to go through. Without the additional intent packed into the instruction, this would remain ambiguous. Extended style additionally showed a nonsignificant trend toward yielding more response-level Unclear miscommunication types, which may result because Extended instructions are packed, sequentially-ordered instructions and thus have the ability to introduce miscommunication in the *order* of information presented. Missing Information, Impossible Instructions, and Misunderstood Capabilities were not significantly related to structure. These miscommunication types might not arise from the structural style, but instead stem from a fundamental misunderstanding on the user-end. Further analysis of the content of the instructions, rather than only the structure, may uncover if content is a factor.

7.2 Individual Differences

Our analysis revealed that latent differences among individuals appear to yield differences in verbosity and structure style (H₃ and H₄). Future analysis may aim to identify these latent differences. Possibilities include variations in potential for introspection, personality, perspective-taking ability, and other differences. Regardless of the underlying factors that cause individual differences, dialogue systems must be robust to a range of individuals who bring with them different stylistic tendencies.

7.3 Varying Degrees of Trust

We found that higher trust was related to higher verbosity. We speculate that this may be because when a user trusts in the robot's competence and capabilities, they are more likely to feel comfortable enough to speak more and be confident that the robot can parse longer instructions. Users' propensity for trust was not measured during the experimental collection, which may be an unobserved factor in this analysis. Future analysis will incorporate this additional information about users' latent traits.

If trust is measured in questionnaires, or gauged by other means, this information could be incorporated as feedback for the dialogue system to appropriately adjust dialogue management strategies; as the users' trust in the robot is gauged during an interaction, the system will know to expect adjustments to verbosity and structure, so it can offer more appropriate and tailored responses to the user's style. Furthermore, providing feedback that encourages trust (or discourages it) may be a gentle, minimally obtrusive way of guiding a user to employ a different style to avoid particular miscommunication types, if working with a less robust dialogue system.

7.4 Effect of Interaction Time

Users increased their verbosity (H_7) and use of the Extended style (H_8) when progressing from Training to M1 (and verbosity again when progressing from M1 to M2). We speculate that starting with lower verbosity and Minimal style during the Training trial might suggest users initially are hesitant or do not have a strong sense for the robot's language processing capabilities. Users may be learning from the training and growing in comfort level over interaction time and experience with the robot, and are willing to use more verbose or Extended instructions in successive trials. Another possible explanation might be that users face a more difficult task in the main trials as compared to training; when pressed for time in a more challenging task, users may use more words and be more prone to combine intents together. Future studies can aim to disentangle these effects.

We observed an increase in Extended style use between M1 and M2, but it did not reach statistical significance. This might suggest that any learning or strategy convergence in terms of structure that occurred from training to M1 may have mostly settled by M1. It is possible that future work with a greater sample size will reveal that Extended style use continues to grow across trials. An understanding of interaction time or experience effects can be incorporated in the dialogue system to better support the change of user styles that emerge with repeated interactions.

8 Conclusion and Future Work

This paper defines two classes of stylistic differences: verbosity and structure, and examines these styles in a corpus of human-robot dialogue with no constraints on how robot-directed instructions were formulated. We show that stylistic differences are linked to different rates and types of miscommunication (H_2), that latent individual differences exist (H_3 and H_4), and that there is a relationship between style and trust (H_5 and H_6), and style and interaction time (H_7 and H_8).

By understanding the effects of stylistic differences used in instruction-giving, we are posed to implement adjusting dialogue systems to the expectations of styles to increase user interaction and system performance. Tapus et al. (2008) has shown that users prefer a robot that tailors encouragement strategies according to users' personality (introverted or extroverted). Torrey et al. (2006) found that users prefer robots that tailor their speech to the human's level of expertise. We posit that dialogue systems could similarly be crafted to support and interact with different verbosity and structural styles. Future dialogue systems might adjust to the verbosity style by, for example, providing system feedback in more or less verbose styles, which may make the interaction feel more like a natural conversation. A system can adjust to the structural style by providing incremental feedback to users issuing Extended instructions to capture miscommunications early, as well as provide feedback that the system understood the compound instruction. The monitoring of trust and interaction time can be incorporated as feedback for the dialogue system to offer more appropriate responses or attentive repair strategies in advance of miscommunication being made.

This investigation of style warrants further turn-by-turn analysis to better understand *where* style shift occurs during an interaction, and *why* particular styles are subject to increased rates of miscommunication. A future robot may be able to propose alternate courses of action for certain miscommunication types (e.g., the suggestion to offer the user a picture of the room in Dialogue 9). These propositions may be difficult for other miscommunication styles, which require contextual, environment information and specification directly from the user. Future work will investigate these alternative suggestions to study if a users' style would shift around the alternate action (e.g., reducing Minimal structure usage for Ambiguous instructions), or if the user would adapt the alternate action into their own style (e.g., continuing to use Minimal, but not repeating the same mistake).

References

Kathleen M Eberhard, Hannele Nicholson, Sandra Kübler, Susan Gundersen, and Matthias Scheutz. 2010. The Indiana "Cooperative Remote Search Task" (CReST) Corpus. In *Proceedings of the International Conference on Language Resources and Evaluation*.

Ryuichiro Higashinaka, Kotaro Funakoshi, Masahiro Araki, Hiroshi Tsukahara, Yuka Kobayashi, and Masahiro Mizukami. 2015a. Towards Taxonomy of Errors in Chat-oriented Dialogue Systems. In *Proceedings of the Special Interest Group on Discourse and Dialogue*. pages 87–95.

Ryuichiro Higashinaka, Masahiro Mizukami, Kotaro Funakoshi, Masahiro Araki, Hiroshi Tsukahara, and Yuka Kobayashi. 2015b. Fatal or Not? Finding Errors that Lead to Dialogue Breakdowns in Chat-Oriented Dialogue Systems. In *Proceedings of Empirical Methods for Natural Language Processing*. pages 2243–2248.

Kris Liu, Jean E Fox Tree, and Marilyn A Walker. 2016. Coordinating Communication in the Wild: The Artwalk Dialogue Corpus of Pedestrian Navigation and Mobile Referential Communication. In *Proceedings of the International Conference on Language Resources and Evaluation*.

Andy Lücking, Kirsten Bergmann, Florian Hahn, Stefan Kopp, and Hannes Rieser. 2010. The Bielefeld Speech and Gesture Alignment Corpus (SaGA). In *Proceedings of the International Conference on Language Resources and Evaluation workshop: Multimodal corpora–advances in capturing, coding and analyzing multimodality*.

Matthew Marge, Claire Bonial, Ashley Foots, Cory Hayes, Cassidy Henry, Kimberly Pollard, Ron Artstein, Clare Voss, and David Traum. 2017. Exploring Variation of Natural Human Commands to a Robot in a Collaborative Navigation Task. In *Proceedings of the First Workshop on Language Grounding for Robotics*. pages 58–66.

Matthew Marge and Alexander Rudnicky. 2011. The TeamTalk Corpus: Route Instructions in Open Spaces. In *Proceedings of the Workshop on Grounding Human-Robot Dialog for Spatial Tasks.*.

Matthew Marge and Alexander Rudnicky. 2015. Miscommunication Recovery in Physically Situated Dialogue. In *Proceedings of the Special Interest Group on Discourse and Dialogue*. pages 22–31.

Tim Paek and Eric Horvitz. 2000. Conversation as Action under Uncertainty. In *Proceedings of the Sixteenth conference on Uncertainty in artificial intelligence*. Morgan Kaufmann Publishers Inc., pages 455–464.

Aaron Powers, Sara Kiesler, Susan Fussell, and Cristen Torrey. 2007. Comparing a Computer Agent with a Humanoid Robot. In *Proceedings of Human-Robot Interaction (HRI), 2007 2nd ACM/IEEE International Conference on*. IEEE, pages 145–152.

Kristin E Schaefer. 2016. Measuring Trust in Human Robot Interactions: Development of the "Trust Perception Scale-HRI". In *Proceedings of Robust Intelligence and Trust in Autonomous Systems*, Springer, pages 191–218.

Laura Stoia, Darla Magdalena Shockley, Donna K Byron, and Eric Fosler-Lussier. 2008. SCARE: a Situated Corpus with Annotated Referring Expressions. In *Proceedings of the International Conference on Language Resources and Evaluation*.

Adriana Tapus, Cristian Ţăpuş, and Maja J Matarić. 2008. User-Robot Personality Matching and Assistive Robot Behavior Adaptation for Post-Stroke Rehabilitation Therapy. In *Intelligent Service Robotics* 1(2):169.

Cristen Torrey, Aaron Powers, Matthew Marge, Susan R Fussell, and Sara Kiesler. 2006. Effects of adaptive robot dialogue on information exchange and social relations. In *Proceedings of the First ACM SIGCHI/SIGART Conference on Human-Robot Interaction*. Association for Computing Machinery, pages 126–133.

David Traum, Cassidy Henry, Stephanie Lukin, Ron Artstein, Felix Gervits, Kimberly Pollard, Claire Bonial, Su Lei, Clare Voss, Matthew Marge, Cory Hayes, and Susan Hill. 2018. Dialogue Structure Annotation for Multi-Floor Interaction. In *Proceedings of the International Conference on Language Resources and Evaluation*.

Turn-Taking Strategies for Human-Robot Peer-Learning Dialogue

Ranjini Das and **Heather Pon-Barry**
Department of Computer Science
Mount Holyoke College
South Hadley, MA 01075
{das22r,ponbarry}@mtholyoke.edu

Abstract

In this paper, we apply the contribution model of grounding to a corpus of human-human peer-mentoring dialogues. From this analysis, we propose effective turn-taking strategies for human-robot interaction with a teachable robot. Specifically, we focus on (1) how robots can encourage humans to present and (2) how robots can signal that they are going to begin a new presentation. We evaluate the strategies against a corpus of human-robot dialogues and offer three guidelines for teachable robots to follow to achieve more human-like collaborative dialogue.

1 Introduction

Grounding is the process by which two parties coordinate to come to a joint understanding or common ground in a joint project. This involves assuming mutual knowledge, beliefs, and assumptions (Clark, 1996). Since humans use grounding to collaborate in dialogue interactions, robots can look to human grounding patterns to mimic collaboration in a human-like way. In human-robot dialogue with a *teachable* robot, the robot often wants the human to take initiative in presenting material; at the same time, the robot wants to ensure that it can steer the conversation in a natural way. By analyzing a human-human peer-mentoring corpus, we identify turn-level grounding patterns that help achieve these two goals.

First, we observe peer-learning dialogues in a human-human corpus to model how human teachers and learners signal presentation and understanding. In this corpus, both teachers and learners alternately take the floor to offer presentations. While one speaker presents, the other speaker accepts the presentation by displaying evidence of understanding. Our first goal is to understand how

a speaker signals to the other speaker to take the floor, such as a teacher encouraging a learner to present an idea, or a learner asking a question that leads the teacher to present an explanation.

Second, speakers may need to shift the floor towards themselves during a conversation. For example, a teacher may have a plan to offer feedback on the learner's work, or a learner may need to explain a problem that confused them. Therefore, our second goal is to understand how a speaker can effectively signal that they are taking the floor.

These two goals are also relevant to human-robot dialogue with a teachable robot: a robot who acts as a peer to a student and prompts the student to teach them the material (Jacq et al., 2016; Lubold et al., 2018b). Because humans engage more deeply with material when they teach it to someone else (Roscoe and Chi, 2007), we want a teachable robot to encourage humans to present material. At the same time, especially when interacting with children, the robot may not always understand or be able to process the human's speech and actions. To handle unexpected, degraded, or out-of-vocabulary input, the robot will sometimes need to take the floor and steer the conversation.

In Section 2 of this paper, we discuss related work. We introduce a human-human peer-mentoring corpus and detail our annotation process in Section 3. In Section 4, we analyze human-human grounding patterns with respect to the two goals: encouraging humans to present, and taking the floor. In Section 5, we introduce and analyze grounding in a corpus of dialogues with a teachable robot. We discuss similarities and differences in the two corpora in Section 6, and offer suggestions for improving human-robot dialogue.

2 Related Work

The **contribution model** of Clark and Schaefer is a widely-used theory of conversational ground-

Proceedings of the SIGDIAL 2018 Conference, pages 119–129,
Melbourne, Australia, 12-14 July 2018. ©2018 Association for Computational Linguistics

ing (Clark and Schaefer, 1989; Clark, 1996). The model proposes that collaborative conversations be analyzed in terms of *contribution* units, where each contribution consists of a *presentation phase* followed by an *acceptance phase*. In the presentation phase, Speaker A, the presenter, presents a signal to Speaker B, the acceptor. In the acceptance phase, B, the acceptor, acknowledges that they have understood the signal. This requires positive evidence of understanding from B. The speakers signal back and forth until they have received closure—a sense of mutual understanding.

Traum (1994, 1999) reformulated the contribution model for real-time use by collaborative dialogue agents. In this model, the units of analysis—grounding acts—occur at the utterance level. In human-robot dialogues, Liu et al. (2013) found that incorporating an 'agent-present human-accept' dialogue pattern based on the contribution model into its grounding algorithm led to improved reference resolution. Graesser et al. (2014) used a 'pump-hint-prompt-assertion' dialogue pattern in an intelligent tutoring system, finding learning outcomes comparable to those of human tutors.

Turn-taking in human-robot interaction involves understanding the cues that signal when it is appropriate for a robot to take a turn (Meena et al., 2014). Integrating factors such as robot gaze, head movement, parts of speech, and semantics into turn-taking models is an active area of research (Chao et al., 2011; Andrist et al., 2014; Johannson and Skantze, 2015), informed by studies of turn-taking in human-human dialogue (Gravano and Hirschberg, 2011). In human-human interaction, turn-taking behaviors vary considerably depending on the task. A better understanding of turn-taking in peer-learning dialogue will help inform the design of effective peer-learning robots.

Robot learning companions have the potential to teach broad populations of learners but an important challenge is maintaining engagement and effectiveness over multiple sessions (Kanda et al., 2004). Social robotic learning companions can motivate students, encourage them to persist with a task, and even promote a growth mindset (Park et al., 2017). Recently, *teachable* robots have flipped the traditional teacher-learner roles, with the goal of improving learning and motivation (Hood et al., 2015). Most of the these robots use spoken utterances as output but do not engage in conversational interaction around the human

partner's utterances, if any exist. One exception is a robot that encourages students to think aloud, finding greater long-term learning gains when students articulate their thought process (Ramachandran et al., 2018).

Robots that are physically present have advantages over virtually-present robots and virtual agents. For example, in a game-playing setting with children, a co-present robot companion was found to be more enjoyable and have greater social presence than a virtual version of the same robot (Leite et al., 2008). In a puzzle-solving setting, students learned more with a co-present robot tutor than with a virtual version of the same robot (Leyzberg et al., 2012). A survey by Li (2015) found that in 73% of human-robot interaction studies surveyed, co-present robots were more persuasive, received more attention, and were perceived more positively than virtually-present robots and virtual agents. There may be trade-offs to physical presence; in an interview setting, co-present robots were liked better than virtual agents, but participants disclosed less and remembered less with the co-present robot (Powers et al., 2007). Overall, the literature suggests that physically co-present robots are preferable for relationship-oriented tasks, for interaction with children, and for learning.

3 Peer-Mentoring Dialogue Corpus and Annotation

To develop dialogue strategies for a robot peer-learner to effectively shift the conversational floor, we examine the grounding patterns of human peer-teachers and peer-learners.

Corpus. The human-human peer-mentoring dialogue dataset consists of fifty 10-minute conversations, totaling approximately nine hours. Table 1 summarizes the conversation durations and

Peer-mentoring corpus statistics	Median
Dialogue duration (sec)	596.0
Total turns per dialogue	153.5
Teacher turns per dialogue	76.5
Learner turns per dialogue	76.0
Words per teacher turn	8.0
Words per learner turn	3.0

Table 1: Median duration, number of turns, and turn length data for the corpus of human-human peer-mentoring dialogues (N=50).

Grounding label	Definition	Speaker role
Presentation	A signal or piece of information offered by the presenter	presenter
Probe	Questions such as "When are we meeting?", or a signal made without certainty of positive evidence from the other speaker, such as "You know that assignment..."	either
Backchannel	A short turn to signal understanding, such as "Mm-hmm", "Yeah", and in some cases, laughter	acceptor
Uptake	The acceptor's next relevant turn	acceptor
Answer	A signal to display understanding of the presenter's probe	acceptor
Repetition	A signal to confirm understanding	acceptor
Paraphrase	A signal to confirm understanding	acceptor
Closure	Evidence of the conclusion of a joint project	either

Table 2: Definitions of grounding labels and their associated roles.

turn lengths in this dataset. Audio recordings were collected of conversations between undergraduate computer science students as part of a near-peer mentorship program. The mentees were enrolled in an introductory computer science course. The mentors were mid- and upper-level computer science students. Mentors had multiple mentees and met with each mentee individually each week over the course of a semester to give feedback on completed programming assignments. Because mentors received training on giving effective feedback and encouraging mentees to reflect on their work, we assume that all conversations are examples of effective mentoring. The dataset used in this paper is part of a ongoing data collection project with over 250 dialogues.

The audio recordings of the dialogues were manually transcribed by a commercial transcription service. An excerpt below illustrates an interaction between a mentor and mentee, who we will refer to in this paper as 'teachers' and 'learners' (punctuation is added for clarity).

> TEACHER: So then you might have like a Point2D trunk start which would then update within that method down below
> LEARNER: What do you mean by . . .
> TEACHER: So like up here instead of putting say like public int tx1 you might write something like—
> LEARNER: Oh you mean in uh as a parameter——
> TEACHER: Yeah like just put 'public Point2D trunk start' and then you just end it
> LEARNER: Yeah yeah I got that

Annotation. Our approach to annotation is motivated by the grounding actions proposed in Clark's model of collaborative dialogue (Clark, 1996), and also by the turn-level unit of analysis in Traum's model (see Section 2). The set of grounding labels, shown in Table 2, is designed to be applicable to both human-human and human-robot corpora. The annotation guidelines and the annotated data are publicly available [1].

In our annotation model, at any time, one speaker has the presenter role, and the other is the acceptor. The roles are associated with a set of grounding actions, which characterize individual dialogue turns. Only the presenter's turns can be labeled as *presentation*[2]. Labels such as *uptake, answer,* and *backchannel*[3] typically indicate shorter signals to confirm understanding, and occur in turns by the acceptor. Two labels can occur with both presenters and acceptors: *probe* and *closure*. Each turn is labeled with one or sometimes two grounding labels.

We manually annotated each dialogue turn in the peer-mentoring corpus with one or two grounding labels as well as the identity of the current presenter. This annotation was performed by a single annotator. The counts of each grounding label for teachers and for learners are shown in Table 3. We note that presentation is the most frequent label for teachers, while backchannel is the most frequent label for learners.

---

[1] http://www.ponbarry.com/ PeerLearningDialogueGrounding/

[2] This differs from Clark's model, where contributions in the acceptance phase can also be presentations.

[3] We consider spoken backchannels to be dialogue turns to minimize complexity in the human-robot setting, where we consider all robot utterances to be dialogue turns.

Grounding label	Teacher	Learner
presentation	2475	999
probe	517	507
backchannel	957	1793
uptake	356	701
answer	125	357
repetition	12	26
paraphrase	7	16
closure	205	214
TOTAL	4654	4613

Table 3: Grounding label counts for teacher turns and learner turns in the human-human peer-mentoring corpus.

4 Peer-Mentoring Dialogue Analysis

To support our goal of designing effective turn-taking strategies for a teachable robot, we use the corpus of human-human peer-mentoring dialogues to answer two questions: (1) how do humans encourage their partners to present? and (2) how do humans signal that they are going to shift the floor towards themselves? To frame the decision of whether to focus on teacher strategies, learner strategies, or both, we begin by examining initiative patterns in the corpus.

4.1 Initiative and presentation

Expecting that perceived initiative is closely related to the number of presentation turns, we label each dialogue in the peer-mentoring corpus with a perceived initiative score from 1 to 5 (1=high learner-initiative; 5=high teacher-initiative). We compare the initiative ratings with the count of each speaker's presentation turns as a proportion of their total turns in the dialogue. This is shown in Figure 1. For learners, the proportion of presentation turns is highest when they are perceived to have high initiative. However, teachers present for roughly the same proportion of turns regardless of initiative label. This analysis suggests that learners might assume greater initiative if they are encouraged to present.

4.2 Encouraging partner to present

To analyze how one speaker encourages their partner to present, we consider two cases: (a) when the partner does *not* currently have the floor, and (b) when the partner does currently have the floor.

To understand how human mentors and mentees encourage their partners to present when that part-

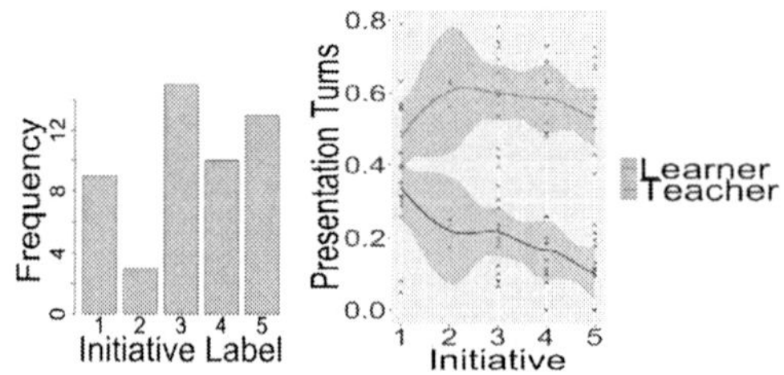

Figure 1: (left) Distribution of initiative labels. (right) Proportion of presentation turns in the conversation compared with conversation initiative.

ner **does not hold the floor** (i.e., to take the floor), we identify all turns with a presentation label that are at the start of a floor shift. A floor shift occurs when a presentation turn shifts the presenter role from one speaker to the other. We examine what the partner's grounding label was in the preceding turn. In other words, if Speaker B has taken the floor by beginning a presentation, what was Speaker A's last grounding action? An annotated example exchange is shown below.

> **A:** But don't put it off because it's a big project *(presentation)*
> **B:** I can tell cause it's broken down into two parts *(uptake/presentation)*
> **A:** Mh-mmm *(backchannel)*

We find that when a speaker takes the floor, their partner is most frequently presenting in the preceding turn: 0.554 and 0.618 for teachers and learners, respectively. The next most frequent grounding label is probe (see all values in Table 4, section (a)).

To understand how human mentors and mentees encourage their partners to present when that partner **already has the floor** (i.e., to continue presenting), we identify all turns with a presentation label that are *not* at the at start of a floor shift. We examine what the partner's grounding label was in the preceding turn. In other words, if Speaker B already has the floor and then has a presentation turn, what is Speaker A doing before B's presentation that encourages B to continue to present? An annotated example exchange is shown below.

> **B:** It'll be the same problems *(presentation)*
> **A:** Mh-mmm *(backchannel)*
> **B:** So you should prepare in the same way you did last semester *(presentation)*

	N	present.	probe	backch.	uptake	ans.	clos.
(a) Encourage presentation - at shift in floor							
Grounding by T before partner presentation	139	**0.554**	0.266	0.122	0.000	0.035	0.024
Grounding by L before partner presentation	136	**0.618**	0.162	0.140	0.015	0.050	0.015
(b) Encourage presentation - no shift in floor							
Grounding by T before partner presentation	995	0.089	0.125	**0.542**	0.181	0.035	0.024
Grounding by L before partner presentation	2453	0.046	0.104	**0.604**	0.166	0.056	0.015
(c) Signal a shift in floor							
Grounding by T at floor shift	136	1.00	0.132	0.007	**0.596**	0.257	0.007
Grounding by L at floor shift	139	1.00	0.115	0.007	**0.547**	0.317	0.014

Table 4: Normalized frequencies of grounding turn labels for teachers (T) and learners (L); for (a) grounding preceding a presentation by partner at a shift in floor, (b) grounding preceding a presentation by partner, with no shift in floor, and (c) grounding accompanying a presentation at a shift in floor. Presentations are most frequent for (a), backchannels are most frequent for (b), and uptakes are most frequent for (c), as indicated by bolded values. Paraphrases and repetitions have values < 0.01 and are omitted from the table.

When there is no floor shift, we find, unsurprisingly, that the most frequent grounding label preceding presentation turns is a backchannel: 0.542 of the turns for teachers, 0.604 of the turns for learners. The next most frequent labels are uptakes and probes (see all values in Table 4, section (b)).

This data suggests that a robot should consider presenting or probing to encourage a partner who does not have the floor to present, and should consider backchannels to encourage a partner who already has the floor to continue presenting. We note, however, that the overall label frequencies are a factor. After considering next-turn probabilities conditioned on the preceding labels, we expect that probes might be more effective than presentations at encouraging a partner to take the floor.

4.3 Signaling taking the floor

To understand how human mentors and mentees naturally take the floor and become the presenter, we look at the grounding labels of dialogue turns at shifts in the conversational floor. All floor shifts begin with a *presentation* turn; most also have a second grounding label. If there is no accompanying grounding label, we report the grounding label of the speaker's previous turn.

We find that when a speaker takes the floor, the grounding label most frequently accompanying the presentation label is uptake: 0.596 and 0.547 for teachers and learners, respectively. The next most frequent grounding labels are answer and probe (see all values in Table 4, section (c)). This suggests that a robot that wants to take the

floor might consider an uptake, answer, or probe in conjunction with their presentation.

5 Comparison with Human-Robot Dialogue Interaction

To understand if the grounding strategies we observed in the human-human corpus are effective in human-robot interaction, we perform a preliminary empirical analysis using dialogue data from a teachable robot interaction experiment conducted in a Wizard-of-Oz (WOZ) style. Section 5.1 describes the dialogue data; Section 5.2 presents our empirical analysis.

5.1 Human-robot dialogue data

The human-robot dialogue data consists of transcripts from a teachable robot interaction experiment where the robot was operated by a human Wizard. In this WOZ experiment, human students interacted in a learning-by-teaching context (Ploetzner et al., 1999) with Nico, a social, teachable, NAO robot. The human participants were peer teachers while Nico behaved as a peer learner, working to solve mathematics word problems.

The human-robot corpus includes dialogue transcripts from twenty college-age participants who each engaged in four problem-solving dialogues with Nico in the WOZ experiment (Chaffey et al., 2018). Table 5 summarizes the dialogue durations and turn lengths in this human-robot dialogue corpus.

The WOZ experiment aided in the development of an autonomous version of the teachable robot

Human-robot corpus statistics	Median
Total turns per dialogue	202.5
Human teacher turns per dialogue	101.5
Robot learner turns per dialogue	100.0
Words per human turn	10.0
Words per robot turn	5.0

Table 5: Median number of turns and turn lengths for the corpus of teachable robot (WOZ experiment) dialogues (N=20).

aimed at middle-school students (Lubold et al., 2018a,b).

WOZ experiment overview. Participants were told that their goal was to help Nico solve a set of mathematics problems. Prior to the interaction, they received worked-out problem solutions. During the interaction, a tablet user interface displayed the problem, highlighting one step at time. Nico, controlled by the Wizard, took initiative in leading the dialogue, asking for help about how to approach the problem sub-parts (e.g., *"How do I figure out how much paint to mix?"*). Participants responded by explaining their reasoning (e.g., *"We want to have six cans of green paint so we mix three cans of yellow paint and three cans of blue paint because..."*). Nico's actions included text-to-speech output, gestures such as scratching its head, and updates to values in the tablet interface. Figure 2 shows a student teaching Nico.

Figure 2: Nico, a teachable robot, being taught by a student.

Wizard behavior. A human Wizard operated Nico behind the scenes, selecting dialogue responses and corresponding gesture movements from a pre-defined set. If necessary, they had the ability to input additional phrases. If the participant did not explain their reasoning, the Wizard prompted them to try again (e.g., *"Could you explain that better?"*). The Wizard was not instructed to model specific grounding behaviors.

5.2 Empirical analysis

We analyze the human-robot dialogue transcripts asking the same questions as in Section 4, but from the robot perspective: (1) how does the robot encourage the human to present, and (2) how does the robot signal that it is taking the floor?

5.2.1 Encouraging partner to present

Based on our analysis of the human-human dialogues, we hypothesize that effective strategies for a robot to use when encouraging their partner to present, e.g., to elaborate or to explain, are: *presentation* and *probe* if their partner does not have floor, and *backchannel* if their partner already has the floor.

To evaluate the extent to which the human-robot dialogues reflect these strategies, we identify the following robot dialogue phrases (fixed phrases or templates, available to the Wizard):

- presentation: "Okay, we [perform math operation][4]", "So now we [perform math operation]?"

- probe: "How did we get that number?", "What do we do next?", "Could you give me a hint?"

- backchannel: "Okay"

For each grounding category (presentation, probe, and backchannel) we manually annotate 50 dialogue exchanges surrounding the queried phrases. Each exchange is five turns in length. We label each turn in the exchange with one or more grounding labels, as we did for the human-human corpus. For presentations and probes, the dialogue exchanges are in contexts where the human partner does not have the floor in the preceding turn. Two examples are shown in Appendix A. We test if presentations and probes result in the human partner taking the floor. For backchannels, the dialogue exchanges are in contexts where the human partner has the floor in the preceding turn. We test if backchannels result in the human partner keeping the floor.

Following presentations, 36% of the exchanges had a presentation in the human's first turn after the robot presentation. Following probes, 74% of the exchanges had a presentation in the human's first turn after the robot probe. Following backchannels, 68% of the exchanges had a presentation in the human's first turn after the robot

---

[4]{add/subtract/multiply/divide} x {and/from/with/by} y.

	Partner turn is presentation	Median turn length (num words)
Following robot presentation		
on the 1st turn	36.0%	13.0
on the 2nd turn	20.0%	19.5
Following robot probe		
on the 1st turn	74.0%	25.0
on the 2nd turn	18.0%	30.0
Following robot backchannel		
on the 1st turn	68.0%	20.0
on the 2nd turn	20.0%	30.0

Table 6: Success in encouraging human to present in the first turn, or second turn following robot presentations, probes, and backchannels; median human turn lengths for presentations.

backchannel. Table 6 summarizes this data, reports turn lengths, and reports on occurence of presentations in the subsequent turn (if the first turn was not a presentation). Not only are probes more effective than presentations at getting the human to present, the subsequent human presentation turns are also longer.

5.2.2 Taking the floor

Based on our analysis of the human-human dialogues, we hypothesize that effective strategies for a robot to use when taking the floor from their partner are: *uptake*, *answer*, and *probe*.

To evaluate the extent to which the human-robot dialogues utilize these grounding acts, we identify four dialogue phrases that the robot uses to take the floor and steer the conversation. The first two selected phrases are navigation instructions, labelled as uptakes. In these, the robot takes the floor to explicitly steer the conversation towards the next problem step. We did not find any suitable robot phrases at floor shifts that we considered to be answers. The second two phrases are questions about the partner's attitudes towards the material. These are labelled as probes, and serve to indirectly steer the conversation away from the previous topic. The dialogue phrases are as follows:

- uptake: "Please tap the 'next' button for me so we can move on to the next step", "Please press the 'back' button"
- probe: "Do you like math?", "Have you done problems like this before?"

We manually annotate 45 dialogue exchanges surrounding each of the queried categories. As above, we label each turn in the exchange with one or more grounding labels. Two examples are shown in Appendix A.

We find that navigation instruction uptakes succeed in taking the floor immediately in 97.8% of the exchanges. For the probes about attitudes towards math, we evaluate their success in shifting the floor by reporting how long the partner continues answering the question that the robot posed, and how verbose those answers are (see Table 7). We find that in 35% of the exchanges, partners continue to answer the question for only one turn; in 60% of the exchanges they stay on-topic for two turns. The average length of these turns is 5.5 and 8.0, respectively.

6 Discussion

In the human-human peer-mentoring dialogue corpus, we find that human speakers encourage partners to take the floor most frequently via presentations or probes. In the human-robot dialogue corpus, we find that probes are more successful than presentations in getting partners to take the floor and also result in longer turn lengths. We note that our analysis is limited by the set of robot phrases queried. To more accurately assess the success of probes versus presentations in human-robot dialogue, we would need to annotate all instances of these two grounding actions in the corpus.

Speakers in the peer-mentoring dialogue corpus encourage partners to keep the floor most frequently by backchanneling. Therefore, it seems that providing a simple acknowledgement of the partner's signal is an effective way to ensure that they continue to present. In the human-robot

	Partner accepts floor shift	Median turn length (num words)
Following robot instruction about UI navigation		
on the 1st turn	97.8%	19.5
on the 2nd turn	0.02%	20.0
Following robot probe about math attitudes		
on the 1st turn	35%	5.5
on the 2nd turn	60%	8.0

Table 7: Success in getting human to accept floor shift following robot instructions about user interface (UI) navigation and probes about math attitudes; median human turn lengths if floor shift is accepted.

dialogue corpus, we find that backchannels are successful in encouraging a partner to hold the floor. Partners present within the next two turns 88% of the time. However, we find that the robot backchannels occur on average in 8.9% of its total turns in a conversation, whereas learners in human-human conversations backchannel for 40.8% of their turns. By incorporating more backchannels in the robot's dialogues (see Kawahara et al. (2016)), we could encourage presentations more often, and also make the robot's dialogue more similar to that of human learners. Backchannels could also take non-verbal form, such as nodding. However, we should be cautious of using backchannels too liberally if they are not a result of true understanding, since they could break down trust between robot and human.

In the human-human corpus, we find that speakers use uptakes, answers, and probes as signals that they are taking the floor. Uptakes are the most frequently used grounding label in this regard. This reinforces the idea that speakers take more initiative when taking the floor because they must produce a relevant turn without being explicitly prompted for it.

In the human-robot dialogue corpus, we find that uptakes in the form of instructions to the human partner are successful in shifting the floor. Due to the nature of the human-robot dialogue, we could not find instances of the robot using answers at floor shifts. Instead, the robot used probes to take the conversation floor. These are less successful than instructions in immediately shifting the floor, but this may be due to the unexpectedness of these questions; participants may have been caught off guard.

To achieve more human-like collaborative dialogue, we suggest that teachable robots consider using the following turn-taking strategies:

- When human partners are not taking initiative, probe partners to encourage them to talk more and take the floor.

- Backchannel more frequently while human partners are presenting to encourage partners to talk more and to better articulate their thoughts and explanations.

- Use uptakes, answers, and probes to take the floor. These can be useful when the conversation has gotten off-course and the robot wants to steer it to a different topic.

7 Conclusion

To inform turn-taking strategies for teachable robots, we annotate and analyze grounding patterns in a corpus of human-human peer-mentoring dialogues and a corpus of human-robot dialogues (Wizard-controlled). In the human-human dialogues, we identify grounding actions that may encourage dialogue partners to take initiative in teaching, while steering the conversation naturally. We find that some of these grounding actions are present in the corpus of human-robot dialogues, but that others are absent, or present to a lesser degree. This suggests future research to investigate whether student outcomes might improve if robot interactions could be designed to encourage more human-like collaborative dialogue.

Acknowledgments

The authors wish to thank Tricia Chaffey, Hyeji Kim, and Emilia Nobrega for their contributions as well as Nichola Lubold and the anonymous SIGDIAL reviewers for their thoughtful feedback. This material is based upon work supported by the National Science Foundation under Grant No. IIS-1637947.

References

Sean Andrist, Xiang Zhi Tan, Michael Gleicher, and Bilge Mutlu. 2014. Conversational gaze aversion for humanlike robots. In *HRI '14 Proceedings of the 2014 ACM/IEEE International Conference on Human-Robot Interaction*, pages 25–32. ACM.

Tricia Chaffey, Hyeji Kim, Emilia Nobrega, Nichola Lubold, and Heather Pon-Barry. 2018. Dyadic stance in natural language communication with a teachable robot. In *HRI '18 Companion: 2018 ACM/IEEE International Conference on Human-Robot Interaction Companion*, pages 85–86. ACM.

Crystal Chao, Jinhan Lee, Momotaz Begum, and Andrea L Thomaz. 2011. Simon plays simon says: The timing of turn-taking in an imitation game. In *Proceedings of RO-MAN*, pages 235–240. IEEE.

Herbert H. Clark. 1996. *Using Language*. Cambridge University Press.

Herbert H Clark and Edward F Schaefer. 1989. Contributing to discourse. *Cognitive Science*, 13(2):259–294.

Arthur C. Graesser, Haiying Li, and Carol Forsyth. 2014. Learning by communicating in natural language with conversational agents. *Current Directions in Psychological Science*, 23(5):374–380.

Agustín Gravano and Julia Hirschberg. 2011. Turn-taking cues in task-oriented dialogue. *Computer Speech & Language*, 25(3):601–634.

Deanna Hood, Séverin Lemaignan, and Pierre Dillenbourg. 2015. When children teach a robot to write: An autonomous teachable humanoid which uses simulated handwriting. In *HRI '15: Proceedings of the Tenth Annual ACM/IEEE International Conference on Human-Robot Interaction*, pages 83–90. ACM.

Alexis Jacq, Severin Lemaignan, Fernando Garcia, Pierre Dillenbourg, and Ana Paiva. 2016. Building successful long child-robot interactions in a learning context. In *HRI '16: Proceedings of the Eleventh Annual ACM/IEEE International Conference on Human-Robot Interaction*, pages 239–246. ACM.

Martin Johannson and Gabriel Skantze. 2015. Opportunities and obligations to take turns in collaborative multi-party human-robot interaction. In *Proceedings of the 16th Annual Meeting of the Special Interest Group on Discourse and Dialogue*, pages 305–314. Association for Computational Linguistics.

Takayuki Kanda, Children A. Field Trial, Takayuki K, Hiroshi Ishiguro, Takayuki Hirano, and Daniel Eaton. 2004. Interactive robots as social partners and peer tutors for children: A field trial. *Human-Computer Interaction*, 19(1):61 84.

Tatsuya Kawahara, Takashi Yamaguchi, Koji Inoue, Katsuya Takanashi, and Nigel G. Ward. 2016. Prediction and generation of backchannel forms for attentive listening systems. In *Proceedings of Interspeech*.

Iolanda Leite, Andre Pereira, Carlos Martinho, and Ana Paiva. 2008. Are emotional robots more fun to play with? In *Proceedings of the 17th IEEE International Symposium on Robot and Human Interactive Communication*, pages 77–82.

Daniel Leyzberg, Samuel Spaulding, Mariya Toneva, and Brian Scassellati. 2012. The physical presence of a robot tutor increases cognitive learning gains. *Proceedings of the Annual Meeting of the Cognitive Science Society*, 34(34).

Jamy Li. 2015. The benefit of being physically present: A survey of experimental works comparing copresent robots, telepresent robots and virtual agents. *International Journal of Human-Computer Studies*, 77:23–37.

Changsong Liu, Rui Fang, Lanbo She, and Joyce Chai. 2013. Modeling collaborative referring for situated referential grounding. In *Proceedings of the SIGDIAL 2013 Conference*, pages 78–86. Association for Computational Linguistics.

Nichola Lubold, Erin Walker, Heather Pon-Barry, Yuliana Flores, and Amy Ogan. 2018a. Using iterative design to create efficacy-building social experiences with a teachable robot. In *Proceedings of the International Conference for the Learning Sciences (ICLS 2018)*.

Nichola Lubold, Erin Walker, Heather Pon-Barry, and Amy Ogan. 2018b. Automated pitch convergence improves learning in a social, teachable robot for middle school mathematics. In *Proceedings of the 19th International Conference on Artificial Intelligence in Education (AIED 2018)*.

Raveesh Meena, Gabriel Skantze, and Joakim Gustafson. 2014. Data-driven models for timing feedback responses in a map task dialogue system. *Computer Speech & Language*, 28(4):903–922.

Hae Won Park, Rinat Rosenberg-Kima, Maor Rosenberg, Goren Gordon, and Cynthia Breazeal. 2017. Growing growth mindset with a social robot peer. In *HRI '17: Proceedings of the 2017 ACM/IEEE International Conference on Human-Robot Interaction*, pages 137–145. ACM.

Rolf Ploetzner, Pierre Dillenbourg, Michael Praier, and David Traum. 1999. Learning by explaining to oneself and to others. In Pierre Dillenbourg, editor, *Collaborative-learning: Cognitive and computational approaches*, pages 103–121. Elsevier.

Aaron Powers, Sara Kiesler, Susan Fussell, and Cristen Torrey. 2007. Comparing a computer agent with a humanoid robot. In *HRI '07: Proceedings of the ACM/IEEE International Conference on Human-Robot Interaction*, pages 145–152. ACM.

Aditi Ramachandran, Chien-Ming Huang, Edward Gartland, and Brian Scassellati. 2018. Thinking aloud with a tutoring robot to enhance learning. In *HRI '18: Proceedings of the 2018 ACM/IEEE International Conference on Human-Robot Interaction*, pages 59–68. ACM.

Rod D. Roscoe and Michelene T.H. Chi. 2007. Understanding tutor learning: Knowledge-building and knowledge-telling in peer tutors explanations and questions. *Review of Educational Research*, 77(4):534–574.

David Traum. 1994. *A Computational Theory of Grounding in Natural Language Conversation*. Ph.D. thesis, Computer Science Dept., University of Rochester.

David R Traum. 1999. Computational models of grounding in collaborative systems. In *AAAI Fall Symposium on Psychological Models of Communication in Collaborative Systems*, pages 124–131.

Example 1: Robot presentation (see 2nd turn)

HUMAN:	Correct so what would you be multiplying by?	*probe*
ROBOT:	We multiply two-point-five and fifty	*presentation*
HUMAN:	Very good so what does that produce?	*probe*
ROBOT:	The answer is one-fifty	*presentation*
HUMAN:	Very good good job	*uptake*

Example 2: Robot probe (see 2nd turn)

HUMAN:	Yes	*answer*
ROBOT:	How did we get that number?	*probe*
HUMAN:	Sixty times two-point-five is one-fifty	*answer/presentation*
ROBOT:	Hmm why did we do that?	*probe*
HUMAN:	Because we knew how many miles he goes in one one hour and we wanted to know how many miles he goes in two hours	*presentation*

Example 3: Robot uptake - navigation instruction (see 2nd turn)

HUMAN:	Mh-mmm	*backchannel*
ROBOT:	Please tap the next button for me so we can move on to the next step	*uptake/presentation*
HUMAN:	Okay now we're gonna work on your torso	*uptake/presentation*
ROBOT:	Hmmm that part seems complicated to me can you explain that again?	*probe*
HUMAN:	So we know that with a surface area of six the volume is two	*presentation*

Example 4: Robot probe - attitude question (see 2nd turn)

HUMAN:	That is correct	*presentation*
ROBOT:	Do you like math?	*probe*
HUMAN:	Eh sometimes	*answer*
ROBOT:	Was it hard when you first started?	*probe*
HUMAN:	Oh yeah it took me a long time to get multiplications right I was a late bloomer	*answer*

Predicting Perceived Age:
Both Language Ability and Appearance are Important

Sarah Plane, Ariel Marvasti, Tyler Egan and **Casey Kennington**
Speech, Language & Interactive Machines Group
Boise State University
Boise, Idaho, U.S.A.
`firstnamelastname@boisestate.edu`

Abstract

When interacting with robots in a situated spoken dialogue setting, human dialogue partners tend to assign anthropomorphic and social characteristics to those robots. In this paper, we explore the age and educational level that human dialogue partners assign to three different robotic systems, including an un-embodied spoken dialogue system. We found that how a robot speaks is as important to human perceptions as the way the robot looks. Using the data from our experiment, we derived prosodic, emotional, and linguistic features from the participants to train and evaluate a classifier that predicts perceived intelligence, age, and education level.

1 Introduction

Co-located, face-to-face spoken dialogue is the primary and basic setting where humans learn their first language (Fillmore, 1981) partly because dialogue participants (i.e., caregiver and child) can denote objects in their shared environment which is an important developmental step in child language acquisition (McCune, 2008). This setting motivates human-robot interaction tasks where robots acquire semantic meanings of words, and where part of the semantic representation of those words is *grounded* (Harnad, 1990) somehow in the physical world (e.g., the semantics of the word *red* is grounded in perception of color vision). Language grounding for robots has received increased attention (Bansal et al., 2017) and language learning is an essential aspect to robots that learn about their environment and how to interact naturally with humans.

However, humans who interact with robots often assign anthropomorphic characteristics to

robots depending on how they perceive those robots; for example stereotypical gender (Eyssel and Hegel, 2012), social categorizations (Eyssel and Kuchenbrandt, 2012) stereotypical roles (Tay et al., 2014), as well as intelligence, interpretability, and sympathy (Novikova et al., 2017). This has implications for the kinds of tasks that we ask our robots to do and the settings in which robots perform those tasks, including tasks where language grounding and acquisition is either a direct or indirect goal. It is important not to assume that humans will perceive the robot in the "correct" way; rather, the age and academic level appropriateness needs to be monitored, particularly in a grounding and first-language acquisition task. The obvious follow-up question here is: *Do robots need to acquire language as human children do?* Certainly, enough functional systems exist that show how language can be acquired in many ways. The motivation here, however, is that those systems could be missing something in the language acquisition process that children receive because of the way they are perceived by human dialogue partners. We cannot tell until we have a robot that is shown as being perceived as a child (current work) and use that robot for language learning tasks (future work).

We hypothesize in this paper that how a robot looks and acts will not only affect how humans perceive that robot's intelligence, but it will also affect how humans perceive that robot's age and academic level. In particular, we explore how humans perceive three different systems: two embodied robots, and one a spoken dialogue system (explained in Section 3). We show through an experiment that human perception of robots, particularly in how they perceive the robots' intelligence, age, and academic level, is due to how the robot appears, but also due to how the robot uses speech to interact.

Proceedings of the SIGDIAL 2018 Conference, pages 130–139,
Melbourne, Australia, 12-14 July 2018. ©2018 Association for Computational Linguistics

2   Related Work

Several areas of research play into this work including seminal (Roy and Reiter, 2005) and recent work in grounded semantic learning in various tasks and settings, notably learning descriptions of the immediate environment (Walter et al., 2014); navigation (Kollar et al., 2010); nouns, adjectives, and relational spatial descriptions (Kennington and Schlangen, 2015); spatial operations (Bisk et al., 2018), and verbs (She and Chai, 2016). Previous work has also focused on multimodal aspects of human-robot interaction, including grounded semantics (Thomason et al., 2016), engagement (Bohus and Horvitz, 2009), and establishing common ground (Chai et al., 2014). Others have explored how robots are perceived differently by different human age groups such as the elderly (Kiela et al., 2015), whereas we are focused on the perceived age of the robot by human dialogue partners. Moreover, though we do not design our robots for deliberate affective grounding (i.e., the coordination effect of building common understanding of what behaviors can be exhibited, and how beahvior is interpreted emotionally) as in Jung (2017), we hypothesize that how our robots behave effects how they are perceived.

Kiela et al. (2015) compared tutoring sequences in parent-child and human-robot interactions with varying verbal and demonstrative behaviors, and Lyon et al. (2016) brought together several areas of research relating to language acquisition in robotics. We differ from this previous work in that we do not explcitely tell our participants to interact with the robots as they would a child, effectively removing the assumption that participants will treat robots in an age-appropriate way. Another important difference to their work is that we opted not to use an anthropomorphically realistic child robot because such robots often make people feel uncomfortable (Eberle, 2009). Our work is similar in some ways to, but different from work in paralinguistics where recognition of age given linguistic features is a common task (Schuller et al., 2013) in that we are make use of exra-linguistic features. Our work primarily builds off of Novikova et al. (2017) who used multimodal features derived from the human participants to predict perceived likability and intelligence of a robot. We use similar multimodal features to predict the perceived age and academic level. An important difference to their work is that we designed

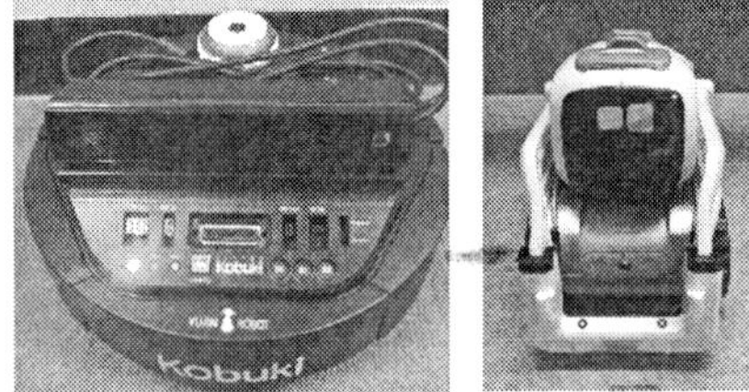

Figure 1: The two physical robots in our study: KOBUKI with a mounted MS Kinect and COZMO.

the experiment with three robots to vary the appearance and two language settings to vary the behavior and linguistic factors of the robots.

3   Experiment

The primary goal of our experiment is to determine what factors play into how humans perceive a robot's age and academic level. We used the three following robotic systems in our experiment:

- Kobuki Base Robot with a Microsoft Kinect on top (denoted as KOBUKI)

- Anki Cozmo robot (denoted as COZMO)

- Non-physical "robot" (i.e., a non-embodied spoken dialogue system) which was just a camera and speaker (denoted as SDS)

Robot Appearance   The COZMO has a head and animated eyes and is noticeably smaller than the KOBUKI. The robots did not move during the experiments, though they were clearly activated (e.g., the KOBUKI had a small light and COZMO's eyes were visible and moved at random intervals, which is the default setting). Figure 1 shows the KOBUKI and COZMO robots as seen by the participants. We chose these three robots because they were available to us and we assume that, based solely on appearance, participants would perceive the robots differently. We chose a spoken dialogue system (SDS) as one of the "robots" because we wanted to explore how participants perceive a system that is unembodied in direct comparison to embodied systems.

Robot Behavior   The COZMO robot has a built-in speaker with a young-sounding synthetic voice. We used two adult voices for the KOBUKI and SDS robots from the Amazon Polly system (the Joey and Joanna voices) which we played on a small speaker.[1] We vary the language setting of the robots by assigning each robot one of two possible settings: *high* and *low*. In the high setting,

---

[1] https://aws.amazon.com/polly/

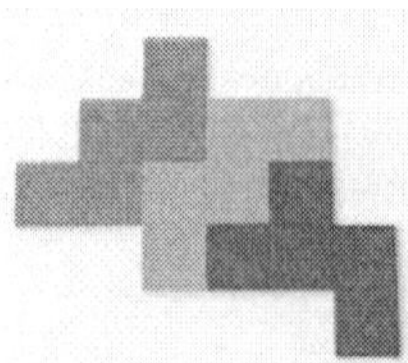

Figure 2: Example puzzle made up of three colored pentomino tiles with a specified name.

the following responses were possible: *sure*; *okay*; *yeah*; *oh*; *I see*; *uh huh*; ___ (where the robot repeats a word spoken by the participant) and any combination of those responses in a single uttered response; and for the low setting, the following responses were possible: *yes*; *okay*; *uh*; ___ (where the robot repeats a word spoken by the participant). In the high setting, the robot would produce responses more often than in the low setting. These responses are characteristic of different levels of *feedback*; the high setting contains feedback strategies that signaled understanding to the participant, whereas the low setting only signaled phonetic receipt. This corresponds to previous work (Stubbe, 1998) which investigated various feedback strategies employed in human-human dialogue termed *neutral minimal responses* (corresponding to our low setting) and *supportive minimal responses* (corresponding to our high setting).

With this setup, there are 6 possible settings: high and low for each of the three robots. Our hypothesis is that participants will perceive KOBUKI as older and more intelligent than COZMO overall (in both high and low settings) despite being less anthropomorphic, perceive COZMO as very young in the low setting, and that SDS will be perceived as older than COZMO in the high setting, but similar to COZMO in the low setting.

3.1 Task and Participants

The experimenter gave each participant consent and instruction forms to complete before the experiment. The participant was then given three colored pentomino puzzle tiles and a sheet of paper with three goal shapes (example in Figure 2), each composed from the corresponding tiles. The experimenter instructed the participant to sit at a table where they would see a robot. Their task was to explain to the robot how to use the tiles to construct the three goal shapes and tell the robot the name of each shape. The experimenter did

Figure 3: Example setting using the KOBUKI robot. The participants were to show the robot how to construct the three goal objects on the paper using the corresponding physical tiles. The additional cameras were used to record audio and video of the participant.

not specify how to accomplish this task or give examples of the kinds of things that the robot might understand. The experimenter then left the room, leaving the participant with the robot to complete the task. The robots only responded verbally in the *low/high* setting as explained above and their responses were controlled by the experimenter (i.e., in a Wizard-of-Oz paradigm). The robots produced no physical movement. When the participant completed each task, they uttered a keyword (i.e., *done*), then the experimenter returned and administered a questionnaire. This process was followed for each of the three robots.

The following aspects of the experiment were randomly assigned to each participant: the order of robot presentation, the puzzle tiles and corresponding goal shapes for each robot, the language setting (i.e., *high* or *low*) which remained the same for all three robot interactions for each participant, and for KOBUKI and SDS the adult voice (either Joey or Joanna). We recruited 21 English-speaking participants (10 Female, 11 Male), most of whom were students of Boise State University. The interaction generally took about 30 minutes; participants received $5 for their participation.

3.2 Data Collection

We recorded the interactions with a camera that captured the face and a microphone that captured the speech of each participant. We automatically transcribed the speech using the Google Speech API (we manually checked an accented female

 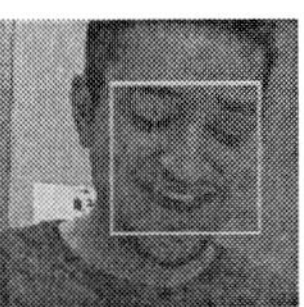 

anger	0.02	anger	0.036	anger	0.031
contempt	0.009	contempt	0.019	contempt	0.182
disgust	0.009	disgust	0.018	disgust	0.04
fear	0.002	fear	0.005	fear	0.000
happiness	0.005	happiness	0.831	happiness	0.066
neutral	0.909	neutral	0.006	neutral	0.649
sadness	0.03	sadness	0.093	sadness	0.027
surprise	0.011	surprise	0.006	surprise	0.002

Figure 4: Examples of results as processed by the MS Emotions API.

voice which achieved an estimated WER of 30.0) and segmented transcriptions into sentences after 1 second of detected silence, which is a longer pause duration than the average pause duration for adult-adult conversation (though adults tend to take longer pauses when interacting with children (DePaulo and Coleman, 1986)). This resulted in video, audio, and transcriptions for each participant, for each robot interaction. We also collected 58 questionnaires (we had to remove several because they were missing data; i.e., some participants did not answer some of the questionnaire questions), one for each robot interaction, from each participant.

4 Data Analysis

Using the data collected from the experiment, we derived subjective measures from the questionnaires and we derived a number of objective measures from the video, audio, and transcriptions. In this section, we explain what methods we used to derive and analyze those measures.

Emotion Features Using the video feed of the participants, we extracted an image of the participants' faces every 5 seconds. We used the Microsoft Emotion API for processing these images to calculate an average distribution over 8 possible emotion categories for each image: *happiness, sadness, surprise, anger, fear, contempt, disgust,* and *neutral.* Figure 4 shows an example of face snapshots taken from the video in the task setting and the corresponding distributions over the emotions as produced by the API.

Prosodic Features From the audio, we calculated the average fundamental frequency of speech (F0) of the participant over the entire interaction

between the participant and the robot for each robot setting.

Linguistic Features Using the automatically transcribed text, we follow directly from Novikova et al. (2017) to derive several linguistic measures, with the exception that we did not derive dialogue-related features because, though our robots were engaging in a kind of dialogue with the participants, they weren't taking the floor in a dialogue turn; i.e., our robots were only providing feedback to signal either phonetic receipt or semantic understanding (*low* and *high* settings, respectively). We used the Lexical Complexity Analyser (Lu, 2009, 2012), which yields several measures, two of which we leverage here: lexical diversity (LD) and the mean segmented type-token ratio (MSTTR), both of which measure diversity of tokens; the latter averaging the diversity over segments of a given length (for all measures, higher values denote more respective diversity and sophistication in the measured text). The Complexity Analyser also produces a lexical sophistication (LS) measure, also known as lexical rareness which is the proportion of lexical word types that are not common (i.e., not the 2,000 most frequent words in the British National Corpus).

For syntactic variation, we applied the D-Level Analyser (Lu, 2009) using the D-Level scale (Lu, 2014). This tool builds off of the Stanford Part-of-Speech Tagger (Toutanova and Manning, 2000) and the Collins Parser (Collins, 2003) and produces a scaled analysis. The D-Level scale counts utterances belonging to one of 8 levels (Levels 0-7), where lower levels such as 0-1 include simple or incomplete sentences; the higher the level, the more complex the syntactic structure. We report each of these levels along with a mean level.

Godspeed Questionnaire We used the Godspeed Questionnaire (Bartneck et al., 2009) which consists of 21 pairs of contrasting characteristics in areas of anthropomorphism (e.g., *artificial* vs. *lifelike*), likability (e.g., *unfriendly* vs. *friendly*), intelligence (e.g., *incompetent* vs. *competent*), and interpretabilitiy (e.g., *confusing* vs. *clear*) each with a 5-point scaling between them. In addition to those questions, we included the following:

- Have you ever interacted with a robot before participating in this study?

- If you could give the robot you interacted

with a human age, how old would you say it was?

- What level of education would be appropriate for the robot you interacted with?

For the question asking about human age, answers could be selected from a set of binned ranges (under 2 years, 2-5, 6-12, 13-17, 18-24, 25-34, 35 and older), and for the education question, answers could be selected from preschool, kindergarten, 1-12 (each grade could be selected), undergraduate, graduate, post-graduate.

4.1 Analysis

In this section, we analyze the results of the data for the emotional, prosodic, and linguistic measures. We also provide correlations between those measures and the Godspeed Questionnaire. At the end of this section, we provide a discussion of the overall analysis.

Emotion Analysis The most common emotional response as produced by the MS Emotions API was *neutral* for all settings, ranging from 73-87% (avg 81%). The next most common emotions were *happiness* (avg 11.1%), *sadness* (avg 3.7%), *surprise* (2%), and *contempt* (avg 1%). We show in Figure 5 the average distribution over those four emotions for all of our settings. All other emotions were negligible.

Prosodic Analysis Table 1 shows the the average F0 scores for each setting. In general, in the low linguistic setting participants averaged a higher F0 across all robots. This was the case also for individual robots. By a wide margin, COZMO

	cozmo	kobuki	noRob	all
low	173.39	164.32	158.49	164.32
high	166.86	153.18	153.15	157.73
both	170.28	157.32	155	

Table 1: Prosodic analysis: average F0 values for each setting.

setting	LD	LS	MSTTR
low	0.45	0.32	0.62
high	0.48	0.34	0.64
cozmo	0.46	0.29	0.62
noRob	0.45	0.3	0.63
kobuki	0.46	0.28	0.63
cozmo low	0.46	0.23	0.61
noRob low	0.45	0.26	0.62
kobuki low	0.45	0.26	0.63
cozmo high	0.47	0.27	0.66
noRob high	0.47	0.27	0.63
kobuki high	0.49	0.23	0.64

Table 2: Linguistic analysis: LD, LS, and MSTTR values for all settings.

averaged a higher F0 than the other two robots under both low and high settings.

Linguistic Analysis Table 2 shows the results of the linguistic analysis. The LD (lexical diversity) scores show that, on average, participants used more LD in the high settings. Figure 6 shows the results of the D-Level analysis. Level0 (i.e., short utterances) was by far the most common level which accounted for 66% of all utterances for all participants. The second most common was Level7, the level representing the most complex types of utterances. This is no surprise, as Level7 accounts for longer utterances above some threshold; i.e., all utterances of a certain length and complexity or higher fit under Level7. The *low* setting had a Level7 value of 17%, and the *high* setting had a Level7 value of 11%. This may seem surprising, but it follows previous research which has shown that, when a speaker receives fewer responses, they draw out their turns, which result longer utterances (Stubbe, 1998).

Questionnaire Analysis We calculated (Spearman) correlations between the prosodic, emotional, and linguistic features, and the questionnaire responses with the *low/high* settings and the robot settings. Table 3 shows the results where the correlation had a strength of 0.5 or higher. Fig

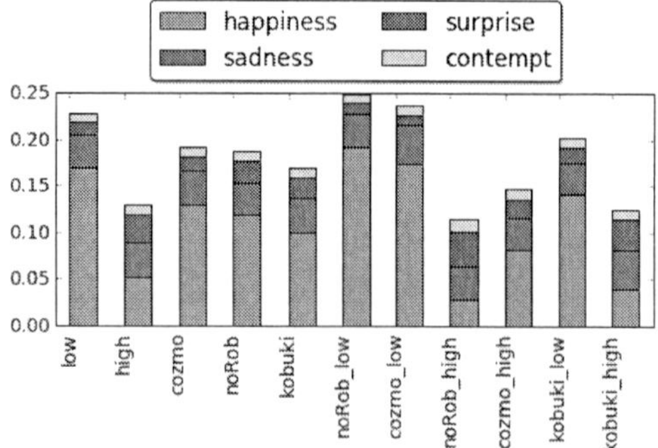

Figure 5: Average emotion (happiness, sadness, surprise, contempt) values for all settings.

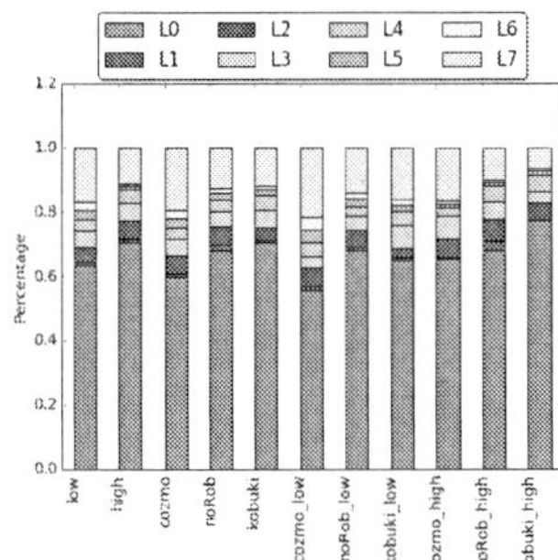

Figure 6: Percentage results for Level0-Level7 for all settings.

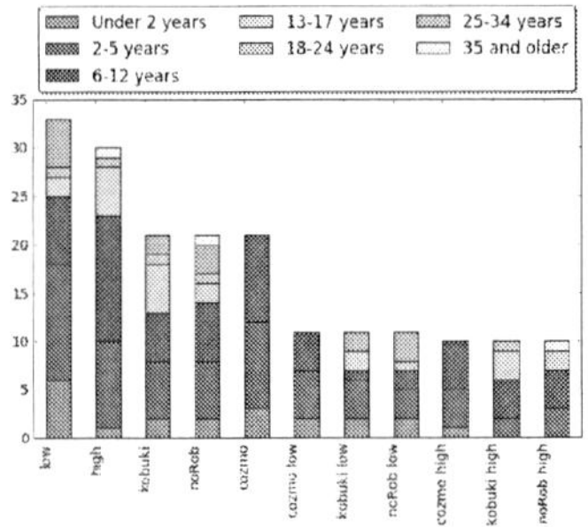

Figure 7: Questionnaire responses (raw scores) for ages.

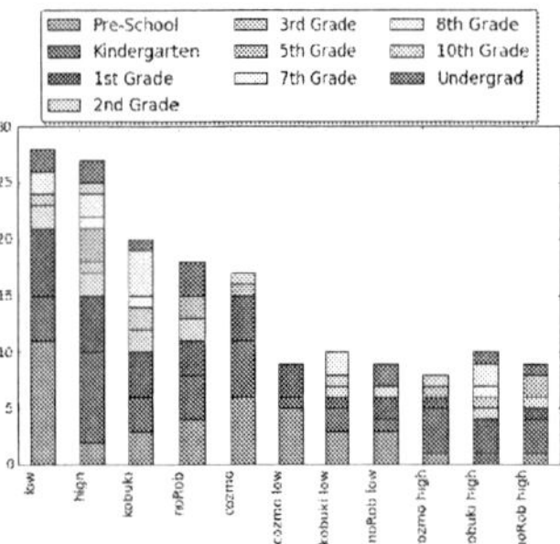

Figure 8: Questionnaire responses for academic grades.

ures 7 and 8 respectively show the age groups and academic years that the participants perceived for each robot in each setting. Overall, participants assigned low age and academic level to all robots when they produced feedback that did not signal semantic understanding (i.e., the low setting). They also assigned a lower age and academic level to COZMO for all settings (with the exception of one 10th grade assignment).

Our results confirm the Novikova et al. (2017) result which showed a strong correlation between F0 and *knowledgeable*. Interestingly, F0 only correlated knowledge with the physical robots and the SDS robot in the low setting. There is more to the F0 correlations: F0 in the low setting correlates with *conscious*, in the high setting correlates with *natural* and *human-like*, and in the COZMO robot setting with *lifelike*. There were some correlations with age and academic level: LS in the high setting correlated with the robot being perceived as age 18-24 and when interacting with COZMO, a higher F0 correlated with a perception of COZMO being 6-12 years old and in the 4th grade. Lexical diversity correlates with *sadness* and *contempt*, which indicates that participants use more diverse language (i.e., they continue speaking) when they are frustrated with the interaction (Stubbe, 1998); particularly in the high setting when they expect more from the robots. However, they increase their LS also in the high setting because they perceive the robot as more intelligent.

Discussion Taken together, the emotional, prosodic, and linguistic analyses show that participants treated the low setting with a higher average F0, less linguistic complexity, and a greater display of happiness in their facial emotions. This is useful knowledge: the way a robot speaks has an impact on the perception of that robot by the human users, regardless of whether or not that robot is embodied. Moreover, despite the fact that the robots only produced feedback as the only system behavior, the participants tended to assign a younger age and academic level to the COZMO robot. There were subtle differences in how the participants perceived the KOBUKI and SDS robots. In general, the participants seemed to perceive the SDS as being older and as having a higher academic level in the emotion, prosodic, and linguistic modalities, though those differences were small. This leads us to postulate that anthropomorphic physical features do not automatically denote intelligence in the same way as perceived ability to comprehend language. In general, participants assigned younger ages and lower academic levels for the low setting, and higher ones for the high setting. Moreover, participants generally assigned COZMO lower ages, including the most for Under 2 years. Of note is that no participant assigned COZMO an age of above 6-12 years for either of the low/high settings. The highest assigned academic level was undergrad, which was never assigned to COZMO. The KOBUKI and SDS robots were both variously assigned comparable older ages and average academic levels under all settings.

5 Prediction Tasks

Using the measures we derived from the collected data, we attempted to determine if we could predict the perceived age and academic level of the robots. We used the emotional features (*happiness, sadness, surprise, anger, fear, contempt, disgust,* and *neutral*), the prosody (F0 average), and the linguistic features (LS, LD, MSTTR) to predict

low/high	feature	correlated feature	corr
low	(P) F0 avg	(Q) knowledgeable	0.65
		(Q) conscious	0.53
		(Q) friendly	0.55
		(Q) intelligent	0.57
		(Q) kind	0.55
	(L) LS	(Q) friendly	0.51
high	(P) F0 avg	(Q) natural	0.53
		(Q) human-like	0.5
		(Q) enjoyable	0.51
		(Q) nice	0.57
		(Q) sensible	0.66
	(L) LD	(E) sadness	0.68
		(E) contempt	0.53
	(L) LS	(Q) age 18-24	0.56
		(Q) meets expect.	0.63
		(Q) sensible	0.62
		(Q) knowledgeable	0.63
		(Q) responsive	0.64

robot	feature	correlated feature	corr
COZMO	(P) F0 avg	(Q) age 6-12	0.51
		(Q) 4th grade	0.53
		(Q) lifelike	0.62
		(Q) knowledgeable	0.81
		(Q) competent	0.64
		(Q) intelligent	0.68
	(L) MSTTR	(E) sadness	-0.55
KOBUKI	(P) F0 avg	(Q) knowledgeable	0.52
	(L) MSTTR	(Q) age 2-5	-0.53
SDS	(P) F0 avg	(Q) liked	0.51

Table 3: Spearman correlations between linguistic (L), prosodic (P), emotional (E), and questionnaire (Q) measures.

both the age and the academic level as separate classification tasks. We also predict intelligence, likability, and interpretability in order to compare to previous work.

5.1 Predicting the Perceived Age & Academic Level of Robots

Data & Task For predicting both age and academic level, we used the 58 data points from the participants for each interaction with each robot and applied those points to a 5-fold cross validation. We used a logistic regression classifier to perform the classification using the Python scikitlearn library. We report accuracy for our metric.

Age We ran the cross validation for two different settings when predicting age. In particular, we varied the labels that could be classified. We conducted a first task which treated all of the 7 possible outcomes for age as individual labels (i.e., under 2 years, 2-5, 6-12, 13-17, 18-24, 25-34, 35 and older) and a second task splitting at age 18 (i.e., younger than 18 is one label; 18 & older is the other label). The respective random baselines are 14% and 50%.

age	acc
7 labels	22%
2 labels ($<$, $>=18$)	87%
academic level	**acc**
14 labels	27%
2 labels ($<$, $>=$ preschool)	78%

Table 4: Accuracies for predicting age and academic level.

Academic Levels Similar to age, we ran the cross validation for two different settings when predicting for perceived academic level. The first task treated all of the 14 possible outcomes for academic level as individual labels (preschool, kindergarten, 1-11, undergraduate; we leave out graduate and post-graduate because they were never selected in the questionnaires, nor was 12th grade), the second task treated treated preschool and beyond preschool as a binary classification task. The respective random baselines are 7% and 50%.

Results The results of this prediction task are in Table 4. As might be expected, when attempting to predict using many labels, the classification task is challenging with so little data. However, the classifiers beat their respective random baselines. When classifying for age, the best performing task was a binary task splitting on 18 years at 87%, effectively making it a classifier that can determine if a human user perceives the robot as an adult or as a minor. The best performing task for the academic level classification was treating preschool and above preschool as a binary classifier. Though the data is sparse, these classifiers give us useful information: a robot can use these classifiers to determine if they are perceived as an adult by human dialogue partners, and, more importantly for our purposes, as a preschool aged child, which is the age range in which we are interested for language acquisition tasks.

5.2 Predicting Intelligence, Likability, and Interpretability

Data & Task To directly compare with Novikova et al. (2017), we also predicted perceived intelligence, likability, and interpretability using a ridge regression classifier (which is optimized to reduced standard error) while considering only certain subsets of out our feature set. We evaluated when only considering emo-

group	emot.	pros.	non-ling.	ling.	all
like	1.08	**0.94**	**0.94**	1.02	**0.94**
intel	1.95	1.44	1.44	**0.84**	1.44
interp	0.67	0.7	0.7	**0.61**	0.7

Table 5: Performance of prediction calculated with RMSE for likability, intelligence, and interpretability. Bold denotes the smallest RMSE for a particular feature subset (emotion, prosody, non-linguistic, linguistic, and all).

tional features, prosody, non-linguistic (in our case, emotions and prosody), linguistic, and all combined features. Our metric was root mean square error (RMSE). We average the RMSE over a 5-fold cross-validation.

Results   Table 5 shows the results of this prediction task. We found that likability is predicted best by prosody, perceived intelligence is predicted best by linguistic features, and interpretability is predicted best by also using linguistic features. One big difference between our experiment data and that of previous work is that we did not consider dialogue features (e.g., number of turns, speech duration, number of self-repetitions, etc.), which they termed as non-linguistic features. Those features were important in predicting perceived intelligence and interpretability in their work; here, linguistic and prosodic features were the most effective in predicting all three human perceptions of the robots. This confirms the work of Novikova et al. (2017) that linguistic features are a good predictor of interpretability.

6   Discussion & Conclusion

In this paper, we have investigated how human dialogue partners perceive the age and academic level of three robotic systems, two of which were embodied (albeit not particularly anthropomorphically), and one unembodied spoken dialogue system. We collected data from participants as they interacted with the three robotic systems then derived prosodic, emotional, and linguistic features from that participant data, and found that those features correlate with certain age and academic perceptions of those robots, as well as a number of other subjective measures from the Godspeed Questionnaire. This work confirms what previous work has shown: that humans tend to perceive robots differently depending on different factors; in our case, varying the look and spoken reposes determined how the human participants perceived the age and academic levels, as well as intelligence, likability, and interpretability of those robots. We were then able to use these features to automatically predict perceived age (i.e., adult or minor), perceived academic level (i.e., preschool or above) and perceived intelligence, likability, and interpretabilitiy. One important result of our experiment was that human dialogue partners perceive the unembodied robot (i.e., SDS) in similar ways to embodied robots; that is, the way a robot or system speaks (i.e., in our case, produces feedback by signaling either phonetic receipt or semantic understanding) is as important to human perceptions of intelligence and likability as visual characteristics.

We cannot not simply assume that human dialogue partners would treat a robot as they would a child, which is an important aspect of tasks with realistic first-language acquisition settings. The work presented here shows that those interacting with a robot like COZMO will more likely treat COZMO as a learning child instead of as an adult. This is an important result because for future work we plan on using the COZMO robot as a platform for first language acquisition research, where the setting will be more similar to first language acquisition in humans than common language grounding tasks. The COZMO robot is an afforable way for reseachers to couple spoken dialogue systems with a robotic system; it has a Python SDK which allows researchers to access its sensors (including a color camera) and control its wheel and arm movements, as well as its speech and animated face. Our results show that human users generally like COZMO, find COZMO lifelike, competent, and intelligent; i.e., COZMO may be treated as a child, but it has potential to learn.

In future work, we will apply a model of grounded semantics in a co-located dialogue setting where COZMO can learn the semantics of words as it interacts with human dialogue partners.

Acknowledgements   This work was supported in part by the Boise State University HERC program. We would like to thank the anonymous reviewers for their comments, Hoda Mehrpouyan for use of her Kobuki robot, and the Mary Ellen Ryder Linguistics Lab at Boise State University for use of their lab for the data collection. This work was approved by Boise State University IRB 131-SB17-043.

References

Mohit Bansal, Cynthia Matuszek, Jacob Andreas, Yoav Artzi, and Yonatan Bisk, editors. 2017. *Proceedings of the First Workshop on Language Grounding for Robotics*. Association for Computational Linguistics, Vancouver, Canada.

Christoph Bartneck, Dana Kulić, Elizabeth Croft, and Susana Zoghbi. 2009. Measurement instruments for the anthropomorphism, animacy, likeability, perceived intelligence, and perceived safety of robots. *International journal of social robotics*, 1(1):71–81.

Yonatan Bisk, Kevin Shih, Yejin Choi, and Daniel Marcu. 2018. Learning Interpretable Spatial Operations in a Rich 3D Blocks World. In *Proceedings of the Thirty-Second Conference on Artificial Intelligence (AAAI-18)*, New Orleans, USA.

Dan Bohus and Eric Horvitz. 2009. Models for Multi-party Engagement in Open-World Dialog. In *Computational Linguistics*, September, pages 225–234, London, UK. Association for Computational Linguistics.

Joyce Y Chai, Lanbo She, Rui Fang, Spencer Ottarson, Cody Littley, Changsong Liu, and Kenneth Hanson. 2014. Collaborative effort towards common ground in situated human-robot dialogue. In *Proceedings of the 2014 ACM/IEEE international conference on Human-robot interaction*, pages 33–40, Bielefeld, Germany.

Michael Collins. 2003. Head-Driven Statistical Models for Natural Language Parsing. *Computational Linguistics*, 29(4):589–637.

Bella M DePaulo and Lerita M Coleman. 1986. Talking to children, foreigners, and retarded adults. *Journal of Personality and Social Psychology*, 51(5):945–959.

Scott G Eberle. 2009. Exploring the Uncanny Valley to Find the Edge of Play. *American Journal of Play*, 2(2):167–194.

Friedericke Eyssel and Frank Hegel. 2012. (S)he's Got the Look: Gender Stereotyping of Robots1. *Journal of Applied Social Psychology*, 42(9):2213–2230.

Friederike Eyssel and Dieta Kuchenbrandt. 2012. Social categorization of social robots: Anthropomorphism as a function of robot group membership. *British Journal of Social Psychology*, 51(4):724–731.

Charles J. Fillmore. 1981. Pragmatics and the description of discourse. *Radical pragmatics*, pages 143–166.

Stevan Harnad. 1990. The symbol grounding problem. *Physica D: Nonlinear Phenomena*, 42(1-3):335–346.

Malte F Jung. 2017. Affective Grounding in Human-Robot Interaction. In *Proceedings of HRI'17*.

Casey Kennington and David Schlangen. 2015. Simple Learning and Compositional Application of Perceptually Grounded Word Meanings for Incremental Reference Resolution. In *Proceedings of the 53rd Annual Meeting of the Association for Computational Linguistics and the 7th International Joint Conference on Natural Language Processing (Volume 1: Long Papers)*, pages 292–301, Beijing, China. Association for Computational Linguistics.

Douwe Kiela, Luana Bulat, and Stephen Clark. 2015. Grounding Semantics in Olfactory Perception. In *Proceedings of the 53rd Annual Meeting of the Association for Computational Linguistics and the 7th International Joint Conference on Natural Language Processing (Volume 2: Short Papers)*, pages 231–236, Beijing, China. Association for Computational Linguistics.

Thomas Kollar, Stefanie Tellex, Deb Roy, and Nicholas Roy. 2010. Toward understanding natural language directions. *Human-Robot Interaction (HRI), 2010 5th ACM/IEEE International Conference on*, page 259.

Xiaofei Lu. 2009. Automatic measurement of syntactic complexity in child language acquisition. *International Journal of Corpus Linguistics*, 14(1):3–28.

Xiaofei Lu. 2012. The Relationship of Lexical Richness to the Quality of ESL Learners' Oral Narratives. *Modern Language Journal*, 96(2):190–208.

Xiaofei Lu. 2014. *Computational methods for corpus annotation and analysis*.

Caroline Lyon, Chrystopher L Nehaniv, Joe Saunders, Tony Belpaeme, Ambra Bisio, Kerstin Fischer, Frank Förster, Hagen Lehmann, Giorgio Metta, Vishwanathan Mohan, Anthony Morse, Stefano Nolfi, Francesco Nori, Katharina Rohlfing, Alessandra Sciutti, Jun Tani, Elio Tuci, Britta Wrede, Arne Zeschel, and Angelo Cangelosi. 2016. Embodied Language Learning and Cognitive Bootstrapping: Methods and Design Principles. *International Journal of Advanced Robotic Systems*, 13(105).

Lorraine McCune. 2008. *How Children Learn to Learn Language*. Oxford University Press.

Jekaterina Novikova, Christian Dondrup, Ioannis Papaioannou, and Oliver Lemon. 2017. Sympathy Begins with a Smile, Intelligence Begins with a Word: Use of Multimodal Features in Spoken Human-Robot Interaction. In *Proceedings of the First Workshop on Language Grounding for Robotics*, pages 86–94.

Deb Roy and Ehud Reiter. 2005. Connecting language to the world. *Artificial Intelligence*, 167(1-2):1–12.

Björn Schuller, Stefan Steidl, Anton Batliner, Felix Burkhardt, Laurence Devillers, Christian Müller, and Shrikanth Narayanan. 2013. Paralinguistics in speech and language—State-of-the-art and the challenge. *Computer Speech & Language*, 27:4–39.

Lanbo She and Joyce Y Chai. 2016. Incremental Acquisition of Verb Hypothesis Space towards Physical World Interaction. *Proceedings of the 54th Annual Meeting of the Association for Computational Linguistics (ACL 2016)*, pages 108–117.

Maria Stubbe. 1998. Are you listening? Cultural influences on the use of supportive verbal feedback in conversation. *Journal of Pragmatics*, 29(3):257–289.

Benedict Tay, Younbo Jung, and Taezoon Park. 2014. When stereotypes meet robots: The double-edge sword of robot gender and personality in human-robot interaction. *Computers in Human Behavior*.

Jesse Thomason, Jivko Sinapov, Maxwell Svetlik, Peter Stone, and Raymond J Mooney. 2016. Learning MultiModal Grounded Linguistic Semantics by Playing " I Spy ". In *Proceedings of IJCAI*, pages 3477—-3483.

Kristina Toutanova and Christopher D. Manning. 2000. Enriching the knowledge sources used in a maximum entropy part-of-speech tagger. In *Proceedings of the 2000 Joint SIGDAT conference on Empirical methods in natural language processing and very large corpora held in conjunction with the 38th Annual Meeting of the Association for Computational Linguistics -*, volume 13, pages 63–70.

Matthew R Walter, Sachithra Hemachandra, Bianca Homberg, Stefanie Tellex, and Seth Teller. 2014. A framework for learning semantic maps from grounded natural language descriptions. *The International Journal of Robotics Research*, 33(9):1167–1190.

Multimodal Hierarchical Reinforcement Learning Policy for Task-Oriented Visual Dialog

Jiaping Zhang
University of California, Davis
jpzhang@ucdavis.edu

Tiancheng Zhao
Carnegie Mellon University
tianchez@cs.cmu.edu

Zhou Yu
University of California, Davis
joyu@ucdavis.edu

Abstract

Creating an intelligent conversational system that understands vision and language is one of the ultimate goals in Artificial Intelligence (AI) (Winograd, 1972). Extensive research has focused on vision-to-language generation, however, limited research has touched on combining these two modalities in a goal-driven dialog context. We propose a multimodal hierarchical reinforcement learning framework that dynamically integrates vision and language for task-oriented visual dialog. The framework jointly learns the multimodal dialog state representation and the hierarchical dialog policy to improve both dialog task success and efficiency. We also propose a new technique, state adaptation, to integrate context awareness in the dialog state representation. We evaluate the proposed framework and the state adaptation technique in an image guessing game and achieve promising results.

1 Introduction

The interplay between vision and language has created a range of interesting applications, including image captioning (Karpathy and Fei-Fei, 2015), visual question generation (VQG) (Mostafazadeh et al., 2016), visual question answering (VQA) (Antol et al., 2015), and reference expressions (Hu et al., 2016). Visual dialog (Das et al., 2017b) extends the VQA problem to multi-turn visual-grounded conversations without specific goals. In this paper, we study the task-oriented visual dialog setting that requires the agent to learn the multimodal representation and dialog policy for decision making. We argue that a task-oriented visual intelligent conversational system should not only acquire vision and language understanding but also make appropriate decisions efficiently in a situated environment. Specifically, we designed a 20 images guessing game using the Visual Dialog dataset (Das et al., 2017a). This game is the visual analog of the popular 20 question game. The agent aims to learn a dialog policy that can guess the correct image through question answering using the minimum number of turns.

Previous work on visual dialogs (Das et al., 2017a,b; Chattopadhyay et al., 2017) focused mainly on vision-to-language understanding and generation instead of dialog policy learning. They let an agent ask a fixed number of questions to rank the images or let humans make guesses at the end of the conversations. However, such setting is not realistic in real-world task-oriented applications, because in task-oriented applications, not only completing the task successfully is important but also completing it efficiently. In addition, the agent should also be informed of the wrong guesses, so that it becomes more aware of the vision context. However, solving such real-world setting is a challenge. The system needs to handle the large dynamically updated multimodal state-action space and also leverage the signals in the feedback loop coming from different sub-tasks.

We propose a *multimodal hierarchical reinforcement learning* framework that allows learning visual dialog state tracking and dialog policy jointly to complete visual dialog tasks efficiently. The framework we propose takes inspiration from feudal reinforcement learning (FRL) (Dayan and Hinton, 1993), where levels of hierarchy within an agent communicate via explicit goals in a top-down fashion. In our case, it decomposes the decision into two steps: a first step where a master policy selects between verbal task (information query) and vision task (image retrieval), and a second step where a primitive action (question or im-

Proceedings of the SIGDIAL 2018 Conference, pages 140–150,
Melbourne, Australia, 12-14 July 2018. ©2018 Association for Computational Linguistics

age) is chosen from the selected task. Hierarchical RL that relies on space abstraction, such as FRL, is useful to address the challenge of large discrete action space and has been shown to be effective in dialog systems, especially for large domain dialog management(Casanueva et al., 2018). Besides, we propose a new technique called *state adaptation* in order to make the multimodal dialog state more aware of the constantly changing visual context. We demonstrate the efficacy of this technique through ablation analysis.

2   Related Work

2.1   Visual Dialog

Visual dialog requires the agent to hold a multi-turn conversation about visual content. Several visual dialog tasks have been developed, including image grounded conversation generation (Mostafazadeh et al., 2017). Guess What?! (De Vries et al., 2017) involves locating visual objects using dialogs. VisDial (Das et al., 2017a) situates an answer-bot (A-Bot) to answer questions from a question-bot (Q-Bot) about an image. Das et al. (2017b) applied reinforcement learning (RL) to the VisDial task to learn the policies for the Q/A-Bots to collaboratively rank the correct image among a set of candidates. However, their Q-Bot can only ask questions and cannot make guesses. Chattopadhyay et al. (2017) further evaluated the pre-trained A-bot in a similar setting to answer human generated questions. Since humans are tasked to ask questions, the policy learning of Q-Bot is not investigated. Finally, (Manuvinakurike et al., 2017) proposed a incremental dialogue policy learning method for image guessing. However, their dialog state only used language information and did not include visual information. We build upon prior works and propose a framework that learns an optimal dialog policy for the Q-Bot to perform both question selection and image guessing through exploiting multimodal information.

2.2   Reinforcement Learning

RL is a popular approach to learn an optimal dialog policy for task-oriented dialog systems (Singh et al., 2002; Williams and Young, 2007; Georgila and Traum, 2011; Lee and Eskenazi, 2012; Yu et al., 2017). The deep Q-Network (DQN) introduced by Mnih et al. (2015) achieved human-level performance in Atari games based on deep neural networks. Deep RL was then used to jointly learn the dialog state tracking and policy optimization in an end-to-end manner (Zhao and Eskenazi, 2016). In our framework, we use a DQN to learn the higher level policy for question selection or image guessing. Van Hasselt et al. (2016) proposed a double DQN to overcome the overestimation problem in the Q-Learning and Schaul et al. (2015) suggested prioritized experience replay to improve the data sampling efficiency for training DQN. We apply both techniques in our implementation. One limitation of DQNs is that they cannot handle unbounded action space, which is often the case for natural language interaction. He et al. (2015) proposed Deep Reinforcement Relevance Network (DRRN) that can handle inherently large discrete natural language action space. Specifically, the DRRN takes both the state and natural language actions as inputs and computes a Q-value for each state action pair. Thus, we use a DRRN as our question selection policy to approximate the value function for any question candidate.

Our work is also related to hierarchical reinforcement learning (HRL) which often decomposes the problem into several sub-problems and achieves better learning convergence rate and generalization compared to flat RL (Sutton et al., 1999; Dietterich, 2000). HRL has been applied to dialog management (Lemon et al., 2006; Cuayáhuitl et al., 2010; Budzianowski et al., 2017) which decomposes the dialog policy with respect to system goals or domains. When the system enters a sub-task, the selected dialog policy will be used and continue to operate until the sub-problem is solved, however the terminate condition for a subproblem has to be predefined. Different from prior work, our proposed architecture uses hierarchical dialog policy to combine two RL architectures within a control flow, i.e., DQN and DRRN, in order to jointly learn multimodal dialog state representation and dialog policy. Note that our HRL framework resembles the FRL hierarchy (Dayan and Hinton, 1993) that exploits space abstraction, state sharing and sequential execution.

3   Proposed Framework

Figure 2 shows an overview of the multimodal hierarchical reinforcement learning framework and the simulated environment. There are four main modules in the framework. The **visual dialog semantic embedding** module learns a multimodal dialog state representation to support the **visual**

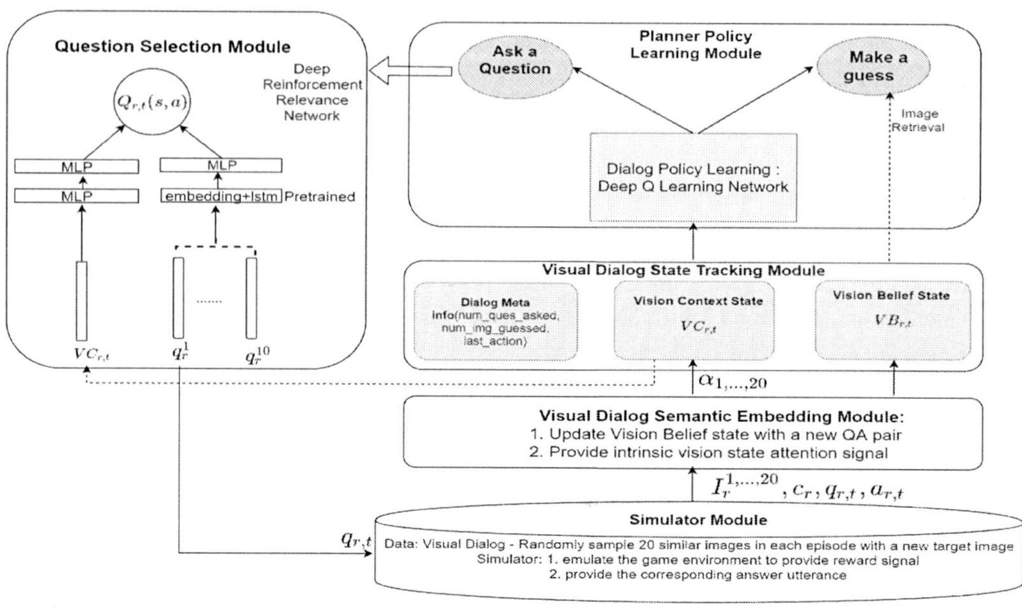

Figure 1: The information flow of the multimodal hierarchical reinforcement learning framework

dialog state tracking module with attention signals. Then the **hierarchical policy learning** module takes the visual dialog state as the input to optimize the high-level control policy between **question selection** and image retrieval.

3.1 Visual Dialog Semantic Embedding

This module learns the multimodal representation for the downstream visual dialog state tracking. Figure 3 shows the network architecture for pretraining the visual dialog semantic embedding. A VGG-19 CNN (Simonyan and Zisserman, 2014) and a multilayer perceptron (MLP) with L2 normalization are used to encode visual information (images) as a vector $I \in R^k$. We use a dialog-conditioned attentive encoder (Lu et al., 2017) to encode textual information as a vector $T \in R^k$ where k is the joint embedding size. The image caption(c) is encoded with a LSTM to get a vector m^c and each QA pair $(H_0, ..., H_t)$ is encoded separately with another LSTM as $M_t^h \in R^{d \times t}$ where t is the turn index and d is the LSTM embedding size. Conditioned on the image caption embedding, the model attends to the dialog history:

$$z_t^h = w_a^T \tanh(W_h M_t^h + (W_c m_t^c)\mathbb{1}^T) \quad (1)$$

$$\alpha_t^h = \mathrm{softmax}(z_t^h) \quad (2)$$

where $\mathbb{1}$ is a vector with all elements set to 1, $W_h, W_c \in R^{t \times d}$ and $w_a \in R^k$ are parameters to be learned. $\alpha \in R^k$ is the attention weight over history. The attended history feature $\hat{m}_t^h$ is the weighted sum of each column of M_t^h with α_t^h. Then $\hat{m}_t^h$ is concatenated with m^c and encoded via MLP and $l2$ norm to get the final textual embedding (T). We train the network with pairwise ranking loss (Kiros et al., 2014) on cosine similarities between the textual and visual embedding. The pretraining step allows the module to have better generalization and improve convergence performance in the RL training.

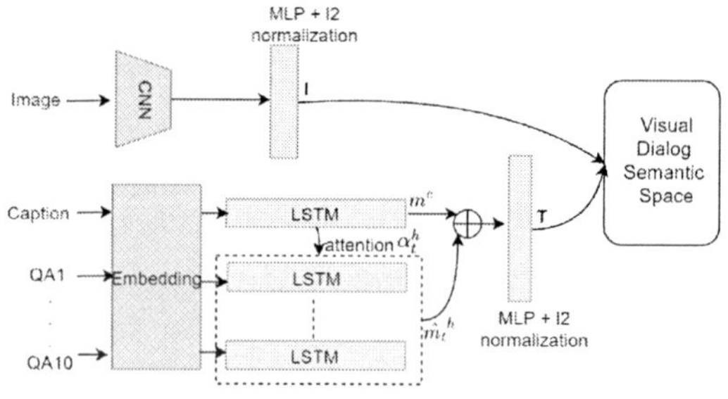

Figure 2: Pretraining scheme of the visual dialog semantic embedding module

Given the QA pairs from the simulated environ

ment, the output of this module can also be used for the image retrieval sub-task. To verify the quality of this module, we perform a sanity check on an image retrieval task, similar to (Das et al., 2017b). We used the output of the module to rank the 20 images in the game setting. Among 1000 games, we achieved 96.8% accuracy for recall@1 (the target image ranked the highest), which means that this embedding module can provide reliable reward signal in an image retrieval task for the RL training if given the relevant dialog history.

3.2 Visual Dialog State Tracking

This module utilizes the output from the visual dialog semantic embedding to formulate the final dialog state representation. We track three types of state information, the dialog meta information ($META$), the vision belief (VB) and the vision context (VC). The dialog meta information includes the number of questions asked, the number of images guessed and the last action. The vision belief state is the output of the visual dialog semantic embedding module, which captures the internal multimodal information of the agent. We initialize the VB with only the encoding of the image caption and update it with each new incoming QA pair. The vision context state represents the visual information of the environment. In order to make the agent more aware of the dynamic visual context and which images to attend more, we introduce a new technique called *state adaptation* as it updates the vision context state with the attention scores. The VC is initialized as the average of image vectors and updated as follows:

$$\alpha_{r,t,i} = \text{sigmoid}(\text{VB}_{r,t} \cdot I_{r,i}) \tag{3}$$

$$\text{VC}_{r,t} = \frac{\sum_{i=1}^{20} \alpha_{r,t,i} I_{r,i}}{\sum_{i=1}^{20} \alpha_i} \tag{4}$$

where r, t and i refer to episode, dialog turn and image index. The VC is then adjusted based on the attention scores (see equation 4). The attention scores calculated by dot product in the equation 3 represent the affinity between the current vision belief state and each image vector. In the case of wrong guesses (informed by the simulator), we set the attention score for that wrong image to zero. This method is inspired by Tian et al. (2017) who explicitly weights context vectors by context-query relevance for encoding dialog context. The question selection sub-task also takes the vision context state as input and the vision belief state is used in the image retrieval sub-task.

3.3 Hierarchical Policy Learning

The goal is to learn a dialog policy that makes decisions based on the current visual dialog state, i.e, asking a question about the image or making a guess about the image that the user is thinking of. As the agent is situated in a dynamically changing vision context to update its internal decision-making model (approximated by the belief state) with new dialog exchange, we treat such environment as a Partially Observable Markov Decision Process (POMDP) and solve it using deep reinforcement learning. We now describe the key components:

Dialog State comes from the visual dialog state tracking module as mentioned in Section 3.2

Policy Learning: Given the above dialog state, we introduce a hierarchical dialog policy that contains a high-level control policy and a low-level question selection policy. We learn the control policy with a Double DQN that decides between "question" or "guess" at a game step.

If the high-level action is a "question", then the control is passed over to the low-level policy, which needs to select a question. One challenge is that the list of candidate questions are different for every game, and the number of candidate questions for different images is also different as well. This prohibits us using a standard DQN with fixed number of actions. He et al. (2015) showed that modeling state embedding and action embedding separately in DRRN has superior performance than per-action DQN as well as other DQN variants for dealing with natural language action spaces. Therefore, we use the DRRN to solve this problem, which computes a matching score between the shared current vision context state and the embedding of each question candidate. We use a softmax selection strategy as the exploration policy during the learning stage. The hierarchical policy learning algorithm is described in the Appendix *Algorithm* 1.

If the high-level action is "guess", then an image is retrieved using cosine distance between each image vector and the vision belief vector. It is worth mentioning that although the action space of the image retrieval sub-task can be incorporated into a flat DRRN combined with text-based inputs,the training is unstable and does not converge within this flat RL framework. We suspect this is due to the sample efficiency problem with large multimodal action space for which the question action or guess action typically results in different reward signals. Therefore, we did not compare our proposed method against a flat RL model.

Rewards: The reward function is decomposed as $R = R_G + R_Q + R_I$ where R_G means the final game reward(win/loss$= \pm 10$), R_I refers to wrong guess penalty (-3). We define R_Q as the pseudo reward for the sub-task of question selection as

$$R_Q = A_t - A_{t-1} \tag{5}$$

$$A_t = \mathrm{sigmoid}(\mathrm{VB}_{r,t} \cdot I_{target}) \tag{6}$$

where t refers to the dialog turn and *affinity scores* (A_t and A_{t-1}) are the outputs of the sigmoid function that scales the similarity score (0-1) of the vision belief state and the target image vector. The intuition is that different questions provide various information gains for the agent. The integration of R_Q is a *reward shaping* (Ng et al., 1999) technique that aims to provide immediate rewards to make the RL training more efficient. At each turn, if the verbal task (question selection) is chosen, the R_Q would serve as immediate reward for training the DQN and DRRN while if the vision task (image retrieval) is chosen, only the R_I is available for training DQN. At the end of a game, the reward function varies based on the primitive action and the final game result.

3.4 Question Selection

The question selection module selects the best question in order to acquire relevant information to update the image belief state. As discussed in Section 3.3, we used a discriminative approach to select the next question for the agent by learning the policy in a *DRRN*. It leverages the existing question candidate pool that is constructed differently with respect to different experiment settings in Section 4.4. Ideally we would like to generate realistic questions online towards a specific goal (Zhang et al., 2017) and we leave this generative approach for future study.

4 Experiments

We first describe the simulation of the environment. Then, we talk about different dialog policy models and implementation details. Finally, we discuss three different experimental settings to evaluate the proposed framework.

4.1 Simulator Construction

We constructed a simulator for 20 images guessing game using the *VisDial* dataset. Each image corresponds to a dialog consisting of ten rounds of question answering generated by humans. To make the task setting meaningful and the training time manageable, we pre-process and select 1000 sets of games consisting of 20 similar images. The simulator provides the reward signals and answers related to the target image. It also tracks the internal game state. A game is terminated when one of the three conditions is fulfilled: 1) the agent guesses the correct answer, 2) the max number of guesses is reached (three guesses) or 3) the max number of dialog turns is reached. The agent wins the game when it guesses the correct image. If the agent wins the game, it gets a reward of 10, and if the agent loses the game, it gets a reward of -10. The agent also receives a -3 penalty for each wrong guess.

4.2 Policy Models

To evaluate the contribution of each technique in the multimodal hierarchical framework: the hierarchical policy, the state adaptation, and the reward shaping, we evaluate five different policy models and perform ablation analysis. We describe each model as follows:

- *Random Policy (Rnd)*: The agent randomly selects a question or makes a guess at any step.
- *Random Question+DQN (Rnd+DQN)*: The agent randomly selects a question but a DQN is used to optimize the hierarchical decision of making a guess or asking a question.
- *DRRN+DQN (HRL)*: Similar to Rnd+ DQN, except that a DRRN is used to optimize the question selection process
- *DRRN+DQN+State Apdation (HRL+SA)*: Similar to HRL, except incorporating the state adaptation, which is similar to the attention re-weighting concept in the vision context state.
- *DRRN+DQN+State Apdation+Reward Shaping (HRL+SAR)*: Similar to HRL+SA, except that reward shaping is applied.

4.3 Implementation Details

The details about data pre-processing and training hyper-parameters are described in the Appendix. During the training, the DQN uses the ϵ-greedy policy and the DRRN uses the softmax policy for exploration, where ϵ is linearly decreased from 1 to 0.1. The resulting framework was trained up to 20,000 iterations for Experiment 1 and 95,000 iterations for Experiment 2 and 3, and evaluated at every 1000 iterations with greedy policy. At each evaluation we record the performance of different models with a greedy policy for 100 independent games. The evaluation metrics are the *win rate* and the *average number of dialog turns*.

4.4 Experimental Setting

We conduct three sets of experiments to explore the effectiveness of the proposed multimodal hierarchical reinforcement learning framework in a real-world scenario step by step. The first experiment constrains the agent to select among the 10 human generated question-answer pairs. This setting enables us to assess the effectiveness of the framework in a less error-prone setting. The second experiment does not require a human to generate the answer to emulate a more realistic environment. Specifically, we enlarge the number of questions by including 200 human generated questions for the 20 images, and use a pre-trained visual question answer model to generate answers with respect to the target image. In the last experiment, we further automate the process by generating questions given the 20 images using a pre-trained visual question generation model. So the agent does not require any human input with respect to any image for training.

5 Results

We evaluate the models described in Section 4.2 under the settings described in Section 4.4 and report results as following.

5.1 Experiment 1: Human Generated Question-Answer Pairs

The agent selects the next question among the 10 question-answer pairs human generated and want to identify the targeted image accurately and efficiently through natural language conversation. We terminate the dialog after ten turns. Each model's performance is shown in Table 1. *HRL+SAR* achieves the best win rate with statistical significance. The *HRL+SAR* policy model performs much better than methods without hierarchical control structure and state adaptation. The learning curves in Figure 4 and 5 reveal that the *HRL+SAR* converges faster. We further perform bootstrap tests by resampling the game results

from each experiment with replacement 1,000 times. Then we calculate the probability of significance level for the difference of average win rates or average turn length to check whether the relative performance improvement from the last baseline is statistically significant. The result shows that the *question selection (DRRN)* and *state adaptation* bring the most significant performance improvements ($p < 0.01$) while *reward shaping* has less impact ($p < 0.05$). We also observe that the average number of turns with hierarchical policy learning (*HRL*) is slightly longer than that of *Rnd+DQN* but with less statistically significant difference. This is probably because this setting provides the 10 predefined question-answer pairs with a smaller action space, the *DQN* model tends to encourage the agent to make guesses quicker, while policy models with hierarchical structures tends to optimize the overall task completion rate.

	Win Rate(%)	Avg Turn
Random Policy	28.3	5.13
Random Question + DQN	42.7 ***	6.68 ***
DRRN + DQN	51.5 ***	6.97 *
DRRN + DQN + State adaptation	71.3 ***	7.12
DRRN + DQN + State adaptation + Reward Shaping	**76.3** **	7.22

***($p < 0.01$), **($p < 0.05$) and *($p < 0.1$)

Table 1: Model Performance in Experiment 1

Figure 3: Learning curves of win rates for five different policy policies in Experiment 1

We find that RL methods (DQN & DRRN) significantly improve the win rate as they learn to select the optimal list of questions to ask. We also observe that our proposed state adaptation method

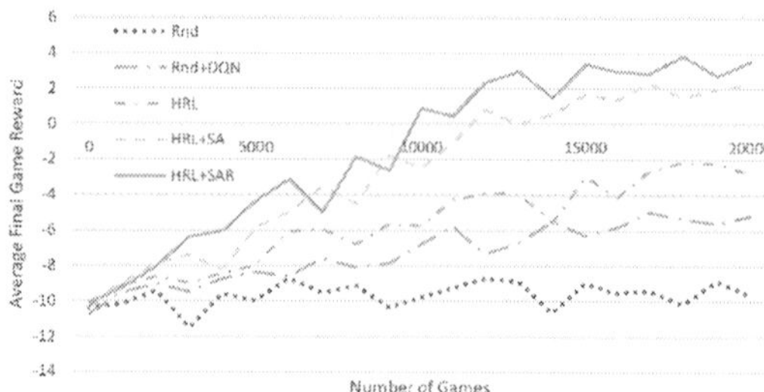

Figure 4: Learning curves of final rewards for five different dialog policies in Experiment 1

for vision context state helps achieve the largest performance improvement. The hierarchical control architecture and the state abstraction sharing (Dietterich, 2000) also improve both learning speed and agent performance. This aligns with the observation in Budzianowski et al. (2017).

Moreover, on average, we observe that after seven turns, the agent was able to select the target image with a sufficiently high success rate. We further explore if the proposed hierarchical framework enables efficient decision-making when compared to the agent that keeps asking questions and only makes the guess at the end of the dialog. We refer to such models as the oracle baselines. For example, the Oracle@7 makes the guess at the 7th turn based on the previous dialog history with the correct order of question-answer pairs in the dataset. The oracle baselines are strong, since they represent the best performance the model can get given the optimal question order provided by human.

	number of rounds	win rate(%)
Oracle Baselines	7	**69.7**
	8	**77.5**
	9	87.8
	10	92.4

Table 2: Oracle baselines Performance

Table 2 shows the performance of the oracle baselines with various fixed turns. We performed significance tests between each oracle baseline and the hierarchical framework. Since our hierarchical framework requires on average 7.22 turns to complete, so we compared it with Oracle@7 and Oracle@8. We found that the proposed method outperforms Oracle@7 with $p - value < 0.01$, and similar to Oracle@8 (significant difference $(p - value > 0.1)$. The reason that the hierarchical framework can outperform Oracle@7 is that it learns to make a guess whenever the agent is confident enough, therefore achieving better win rate. Oracle@8 in general receives more information as the dialogs are longer, therefore has an advantage over the hierarchical method. However, it still performs similar to the proposed method, which demonstrates that by learning the hierarchical decision, it enables the agent to achieve the goal more efficiently. One thing we need to point out is that the proposed method also received extra information about whether the guess is correct or not from the environment. Oracle baselines do not have such information, as it can only make a guess at the end of the dialog. Oracle@9 and @10 are better than the hierarchical framework statistically, because they acquire much more information by having longer turns.

5.2 Experiment 2: Questions Generated by Human and Answers Generated Automatically

To make the experimental setting more realistic, we select 200 questions generated by a human with respect to 20 images provided and create a user simulator that generates the answers related to the target image. Here, as the questions space is larger, we terminate the dialog after 20 turns. We follow the supervised training scheme discussed in (Das et al., 2017b) to train the visual question generation module offline.

	Win Rate(%)	Avg Turn
Random Policy	15.6	5.67
Random Question + DQN	34.8 ***	18.81 ***
DRRN + DQN	48.7 ***	18.78
DRRN + DQN + State adaptation	62.4 ***	16.93 **
DRRN + DQN + State adaptation + Reward Shaping	**67.3 ****	**16.68**

$***(p < 0.01)$, $**(p < 0.05)$ and $*(p < 0.1)$

Table 3: Model Performance in Experiment 2

Results in Table 3 indicate that *HRL+SAR* significantly outperforms *Rnd* and *Rnd+DQN* in both win rate and average number of dialog turns. The setting in Experiment 2 is more challenging than that of Experiment 1, because the visual question module introduces noise that can influence the policy learning. However, the noise also simulates the real-world scenario that a user might have an implicit goal that may change within the task. A user can also accidentally make errors in answering the question. The proposed hierarchical framework (*HRL+SAR*) with state adaptation and reward shaping achieves the best win rate and the least number of dialog turns in this noisy experiment setting. As compared to Experiment 1, the policy models with hierarchical structures can both optimize the overall task completion rate and the dialog turns. We did not report oracle baselines results, since the oracle order of all the questions (ideally generated by humans) was not available.

5.3 Experiment 3: Question-Answer Pairs Generated Automatically

In this setting, both questions and answers are generated automatically through pre-trained visual question and answer generation models (Das et al., 2017b). Such setting enables the agent to play the guessing game given *any* image as no human input of the image is needed. Notice that the answers should be generated with respect to a target image for our task setting. In this setting, we also set the maximum number of dialog turns to be 20.

	Win Rate(%)	Avg Turn
Random Policy	12.4	5.79
Random Question + DQN	18.4 **	19.43 ***
DRRN + DQN	35.6 ***	19.33
DRRN + DQN + State adaptation	44.8 **	18.84 *
DRRN + DQN + State adaptation + Reward Shaping	**48.3** **	**18.77**

$***(p < 0.01)$, $**(p < 0.05)$ and $*(p < 0.1)$

Table 4: Model Performance in Experiment 3

The results in Table 4 show that the performance of the three policies significantly dropped compared to Experiment 2. Such observation is expected, as the noise coming from both the visual question and answer generation module increases the task difficulty. However, the proposed *HRL+SAR* is still more resilient to the noise and achieves a higher win rate and less average number of turns compared to other baselines. Figure 5 from the Appendix shows that in Experiment 2

the agent tends select relevant questions faster to ask although the answers can be misleading. On the other hand, in Experiment 3, the agent reacts to the generated question and answers slower to complete the task. The model performance decreases when we increase the task difficulty in order to emulate the real-world scenarios. It hints that there is a possible limitation of using the *VisDial* dataset, because the dialog is constructed by users who casually talk about MS COCO images (Chen et al., 2015) instead of exchanging with an explicit contextual goal in the dialog.

6 Discussion and Future Work

We develop a framework for task-oriented visual dialog systems and demonstrate the efficacy of integrating multimodal state representation with hierarchical decision learning in an image guessing game. We also introduce a new technique called state adaptation to further improve the task performance through integrating context awareness. We also test the proposed framework in various noisy settings to simulate real-world scenarios and achieve robust results.

The proposed framework is practical and extensible for real-world applications. For example, the designed system can act as a fashion shopping assistant to help customers pick clothes through strategically inquiring their preferences while leveraging vision intelligence. In another application, such as criminology practice, the agent can communicate with witnesses to identify suspects from a large face database.

Although games provide a rich domain for multimodal learning research, admittedly it is challenging to evaluate a multimodal dialog system due to the data scarcity problem. In future work, we would like to extend and apply the proposed framework for human studies in a situated real-world application, such as a shopping scenario. We also plan to incorporate domain knowledge and database interactions into the system framework design, which will make the dialog system more flexible and effective. Another possible extension of the framework is to update the off-line question and answer generation modules with an online generative version and retrain the module with reinforcement learning.

References

Stanislaw Antol, Aishwarya Agrawal, Jiasen Lu, Margaret Mitchell, Dhruv Batra, C Lawrence Zitnick, and Devi Parikh. 2015. Vqa: Visual question answering. In *Proceedings of the IEEE International Conference on Computer Vision*, pages 2425–2433.

Pawel Budzianowski, Stefan Ultes, Pei-Hao Su, Nikola Mrksic, Tsung-Hsien Wen, Inigo Casanueva, Lina Rojas-Barahona, and Milica Gasic. 2017. Subdomain modelling for dialogue management with hierarchical reinforcement learning. *arXiv preprint arXiv:1706.06210*.

Iñigo Casanueva, Paweł Budzianowski, Pei-Hao Su, Stefan Ultes, Lina Rojas-Barahona, Bo-Hsiang Tseng, and Milica Gašić. 2018. Feudal reinforcement learning for dialogue management in large domains. *arXiv preprint arXiv:1803.03232*.

Prithvijit Chattopadhyay, Deshraj Yadav, Viraj Prabhu, Arjun Chandrasekaran, Abhishek Das, Stefan Lee, Dhruv Batra, and Devi Parikh. 2017. Evaluating visual conversational agents via cooperative human-ai games. *arXiv preprint arXiv:1708.05122*.

Xinlei Chen, Hao Fang, Tsung-Yi Lin, Ramakrishna Vedantam, Saurabh Gupta, Piotr Dollár, and C Lawrence Zitnick. 2015. Microsoft coco captions: Data collection and evaluation server. *arXiv preprint arXiv:1504.00325*.

Heriberto Cuayáhuitl, Steve Renals, Oliver Lemon, and Hiroshi Shimodaira. 2010. Evaluation of a hierarchical reinforcement learning spoken dialogue system. *Computer Speech & Language*, 24(2):395–429.

Abhishek Das, Satwik Kottur, Khushi Gupta, Avi Singh, Deshraj Yadav, José MF Moura, Devi Parikh, and Dhruv Batra. 2017a. Visual dialog. In *Proceedings of the IEEE Conference on Computer Vision and Pattern Recognition*, volume 2.

Abhishek Das, Satwik Kottur, José MF Moura, Stefan Lee, and Dhruv Batra. 2017b. Learning cooperative visual dialog agents with deep reinforcement learning. *arXiv preprint arXiv:1703.06585*.

Peter Dayan and Geoffrey E Hinton. 1993. Feudal reinforcement learning. In *Advances in neural information processing systems*, pages 271–278.

Harm De Vries, Florian Strub, Sarath Chandar, Olivier Pietquin, Hugo Larochelle, and Aaron Courville. 2017. Guesswhat?! visual object discovery through multi-modal dialogue. In *Proc. of CVPR*.

Thomas G Dietterich. 2000. Hierarchical reinforcement learning with the maxq value function decomposition. *J. Artif. Intell. Res.(JAIR)*, 13(1):227–303.

Kallirroi Georgila and David Traum. 2011. Reinforcement learning of argumentation dialogue policies in negotiation. In *Twelfth Annual Conference of the International Speech Communication Association*.

Ji He, Jianshu Chen, Xiaodong He, Jianfeng Gao, Lihong Li, Li Deng, and Mari Ostendorf. 2015. Deep reinforcement learning with a natural language action space. *arXiv preprint arXiv:1511.04636*.

Ronghang Hu, Huazhe Xu, Marcus Rohrbach, Jiashi Feng, Kate Saenko, and Trevor Darrell. 2016. Natural language object retrieval. In *Computer Vision and Pattern Recognition (CVPR), 2016 IEEE Conference on*, pages 4555–4564. IEEE.

Andrej Karpathy and Li Fei-Fei. 2015. Deep visual-semantic alignments for generating image descriptions. In *Proceedings of the IEEE conference on computer vision and pattern recognition*, pages 3128–3137.

Ryan Kiros, Ruslan Salakhutdinov, and Richard S Zemel. 2014. Unifying visual-semantic embeddings with multimodal neural language models. *arXiv preprint arXiv:1411.2539*.

Sungjin Lee and Maxine Eskenazi. 2012. Pomdp-based let's go system for spoken dialog challenge. In *Spoken Language Technology Workshop (SLT), 2012 IEEE*, pages 61–66. IEEE.

Oliver Lemon, Xingkun Liu, Daniel Shapiro, and Carl Tollander. 2006. Hierarchical reinforcement learning of dialogue policies in a development environment for dialogue systems: Reall-dude. In *BRANDIAL06, Proceedings of the 10th Workshop on the Semantics and Pragmatics of Dialogue*, pages 185–186.

Jiasen Lu, Anitha Kannan, Jianwei Yang, Devi Parikh, and Dhruv Batra. 2017. Best of both worlds: Transferring knowledge from discriminative learning to a generative visual dialog model. In *Advances in Neural Information Processing Systems*, pages 313–323.

Ramesh Manuvinakurike, David DeVault, and Kallirroi Georgila. 2017. Using reinforcement learning to model incrementality in a fast-paced dialogue game. In *Proceedings of the 18th Annual SIGdial Meeting on Discourse and Dialogue*, pages 331–341.

Volodymyr Mnih, Koray Kavukcuoglu, David Silver, Andrei A Rusu, Joel Veness, Marc G Bellemare, Alex Graves, Martin Riedmiller, Andreas K Fidjeland, Georg Ostrovski, et al. 2015. Human-level control through deep reinforcement learning. *Nature*, 518(7540):529.

Nasrin Mostafazadeh, Chris Brockett, Bill Dolan, Michel Galley, Jianfeng Gao, Georgios P Spithourakis, and Lucy Vanderwende. 2017. Image-grounded conversations: Multimodal context for natural question and response generation. *arXiv preprint arXiv:1701.08251*.

Nasrin Mostafazadeh, Ishan Misra, Jacob Devlin, Margaret Mitchell, Xiaodong He, and Lucy Vanderwende. 2016. Generating natural questions about an image. *arXiv preprint arXiv:1603.06059*.

Andrew Y Ng, Daishi Harada, and Stuart Russell. 1999. Policy invariance under reward transformations: Theory and application to reward shaping. In *ICML*, volume 99, pages 278–287.

Tom Schaul, John Quan, Ioannis Antonoglou, and David Silver. 2015. Prioritized experience replay. *arXiv preprint arXiv:1511.05952*.

Karen Simonyan and Andrew Zisserman. 2014. Very deep convolutional networks for large-scale image recognition. *arXiv preprint arXiv:1409.1556*.

Satinder Singh, Diane Litman, Michael Kearns, and Marilyn Walker. 2002. Optimizing dialogue management with reinforcement learning: Experiments with the njfun system. *Journal of Artificial Intelligence Research*, 16:105–133.

Richard S Sutton, Doina Precup, and Satinder Singh. 1999. Between mdps and semi-mdps: A framework for temporal abstraction in reinforcement learning. *Artificial intelligence*, 112(1-2):181–211.

Zhiliang Tian, Rui Yan, Lili Mou, Yiping Song, Yansong Feng, and Dongyan Zhao. 2017. How to make context more useful? an empirical study on context-aware neural conversational models. In *Proceedings of the 55th Annual Meeting of the Association for Computational Linguistics (Volume 2: Short Papers)*, volume 2, pages 231–236.

Hado Van Hasselt, Arthur Guez, and David Silver. 2016. Deep reinforcement learning with double q-learning. In *AAAI*, volume 16, pages 2094–2100.

Jason D Williams and Steve Young. 2007. Partially observable markov decision processes for spoken dialog systems. *Computer Speech & Language*, 21(2):393–422.

Terry Winograd. 1972. Understanding natural language. *Cognitive psychology*, 3(1):1–191.

Zhou Yu, Alan W Black, and Alexander I Rudnicky. 2017. Learning conversational systems that interleave task and non-task content. *IJCAI*.

Junjie Zhang, Qi Wu, Chunhua Shen, Jian Zhang, Jianfeng Lu, and Anton van den Hengel. 2017. Asking the difficult questions: Goal-oriented visual question generation via intermediate rewards. *arXiv preprint arXiv:1711.07614*.

Tiancheng Zhao and Maxine Eskenazi. 2016. Towards end-to-end learning for dialog state tracking and management using deep reinforcement learning. *arXiv preprint arXiv:1606.02560*.

A   Data Pre-Processing and Training Details

After data pre-processing, we had a vocabulary size of 8,957 and image vector dimension of 4,096. To pre-train the visual dialog semantic embedding, we used the following parameters: the size of word embedding is 300; the size of LSTMs is 512; 0.2 dropout rate and the final embedding size 1024 with MLP and l2 norm. We fixed the visual dialog semantic embedding during the RL training. The high-level policy learning module - Double DQN was trained with the following hyperparameters: three MLP layers of sizes 1000, 500 and 50 with tanh activation respectively. For hyper-parameters of DQN, the behavior network was updated every 5 steps and the interval for updating the target network is 500. ϵ-greedy exploration was used for training, where ϵ is linearly decreased from 1 to 0.1. The question selection module - DRRN encodes the context vector and question vector separately with two MLP layers of sizes 256 and 128 and dot product was used as the interaction function. The experience replay buffer sizes are 25,000 for DQN and 50,000 for DRRN. Both RL networks were trained through RMSProp with batch size 64. Bootstrapping and prioritized replay were also used to facilitate RL training. The reward discount factor was set to be 0.99.

B   Sample Dialog

See Figure 5.

C   Hierarchical Policy Learning Algorithm

See Algorithm 1.

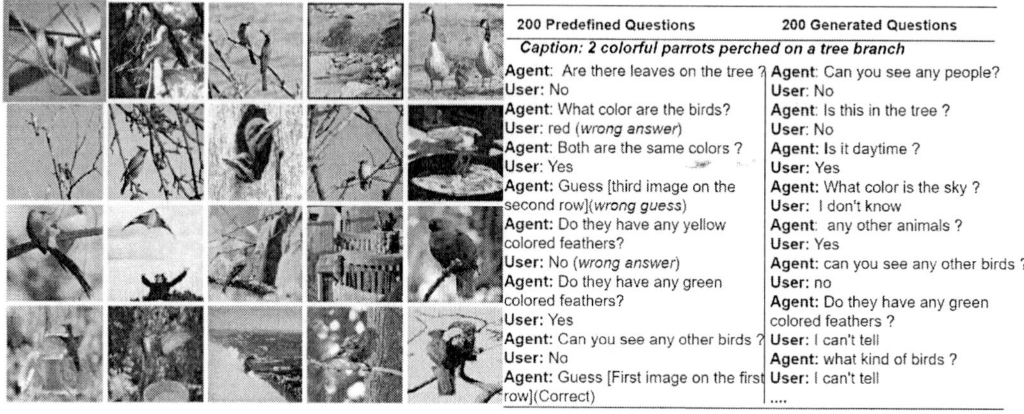

200 Predefined Questions	200 Generated Questions
Caption: 2 colorful parrots perched on a tree branch	
Agent: Are there leaves on the tree ?	**Agent**: Can you see any people?
User: No	**User**: No
Agent: What color are the birds?	**Agent**: Is this in the tree ?
User: red (*wrong answer*)	**User**: No
Agent: Both are the same colors ?	**Agent**: Is it daytime ?
User: Yes	**User**: Yes
Agent: Guess [third image on the second row](*wrong guess*)	**Agent**: What color is the sky ?
Agent: Do they have any yellow colored feathers?	**User**: I don't know
User: No (*wrong answer*)	**Agent**: any other animals ?
Agent: Do they have any green colored feathers?	**User**: Yes
User: Yes	**Agent**: can you see any other birds
Agent: Can you see any other birds ?	**User**: no
User: No	**Agent**: Do they have any green colored feathers ?
Agent: Guess [First image on the first row](Correct)	**User**: I can't tell
	Agent: what kind of birds ?
	User: I can't tell
	....

Figure 5: A successful dialog from Experiment 2 and a failure dialog from Experiment 3

Algorithm 1 Hierarchical Policy Learning

1: Initialize Double DQN(online network parameters θ and target network parameters θ^-) and DRRN(network parameters θ^+) with small random weights and corresponding replay memory E_{DQN} and E_{DRRN} to capacity N.

2: Initialize game simulator and load dictionary.

3: **for** *episode* r = 1, ..., M **do**

4:     Restart game simulator.

5:     Receive image caption and candidate images from the simulator, and convert them to representation via pre-trained visual dialog semantic embedding layer, denoted as initial state $S_{r,0}$

6:     **for** t = 1, ..., T **do**

7:         sample high-level action from DQN, $A_t \sim \pi_{DQN}(S_{r,t})$

8:         **if** $A_{r,t} = $ Q(asking a question) **then**

9:             Compute $Q(VC_t, q^i)$ for the list of questions $Q_{r,t}$ using DRRN forward activation and select the question $q_{r,t}$ with the max *Q-value*, and keep track the next available question pool $Q_{r,t+1}$

10:         **if** $A_{r,t} = $ G (guessing an image) **then**

11:             Select the image $g_{r,t}$ with the smallest cosine distance between an image vector I^i and current image belief state $VB_{r,t}$

12:         Execute action $q_{r,t}$ or $g_{r,t}$ in the simulator and get the next visual dialog state representation $S_{r,t+1}$ and reward signal $R_{r,t}$

13:         Store the transition $(S_{r,t}, A_{r,t}, S_{r,t+1}, R_{r,t})$ into E_{DQN} and if asking a question, also store the transition $(VC_{r,t}, q_{r,t}, VC_{r,t+1}, R_{r,t}, Q_{r,t+1})$ into E_{DRRN}

14:         Sample random mini-batch of transitions (S_k, A_k, S_{k+1}, R_k) from E_{DQN}

15:         Set $y_{DQN} = \begin{cases} R_k & \text{if terminal state} \\ R_k + \gamma Q_{DQN}(S_{k+1}, argmax_{a'}Q(S_{k+1}, a'; \theta); \theta^-) & \text{if } else \end{cases}$

16:         Sample random mini-batch of transitions $(VC_l, q_l, VC_{l+1}, R_l, Q_{l+1})$ from E_{DRRN}

17:         Set $y_{DRRN} = \begin{cases} R_l & \text{if terminal state} \\ R_l + \gamma max_{a' \in Q_{l+1}} Q_{DRRN}(VC_{l+1}, a'; \theta^+) & \text{if } else \end{cases}$

18:         Perform gradient steps for DQN with loss $\| y_{DQN} - Q_{DQN}(S_k, A_k; \theta) \|^2$ with respect to θ and DRRN with loss $\| y_{DRRN} - Q_{DRRN}(VC_l, q_l; \theta^+) \|^2$ with respect to θ^+

19:         Replace target parameters $\theta^- \leftarrow \theta$ for every N steps.
    end for
end for

Language-Guided Adaptive Perception for Efficient Grounded Communication with Robotic Manipulators in Cluttered Environments

Siddharth Patki
University of Rochester
Rochester, NY, 14627, USA
spatki@ur.rochester.edu

Thomas M. Howard
University of Rochester
Rochester, NY, 14627, USA
thoward@ece.rochester.edu

Abstract

The utility of collaborative manipulators for shared tasks is highly dependent on the speed and accuracy of communication between the human and the robot. The run-time of recently developed probabilistic inference models for situated symbol grounding of natural language instructions depends on the complexity of the representation of the environment in which they reason. As we move towards more complex bi-directional interactions, tasks, and environments, we need intelligent perception models that can selectively infer precise pose, semantics, and affordances of the objects when inferring exhaustively detailed world models is inefficient and prohibits real-time interaction with these robots. In this paper we propose a model of language and perception for the problem of adapting the configuration of the robot perception pipeline for tasks where constructing exhaustively detailed models of the environment is inefficient and inconsequential for symbol grounding. We present experimental results from a synthetic corpus of natural language instructions for robot manipulation in example environments. The results demonstrate that by adapting perception we get significant gains in terms of run-time for perception and situated symbol grounding of the language instructions without a loss in the accuracy of the latter.

1 INTRODUCTION

Perception is a critical component of an intelligence architecture that converts raw sensor observations to a suitable representation for the task that the robot is to perform. Models of environments vary significantly depending on the application. For example, a robotic manipulator may need to model the objects in its environment with their six degree-of-freedom pose for grasping and dexterous manipulation tasks, whereas a self-driving car may need to model the dynamics of the environment in addition to domain-specific semantics such as stop signs, sidewalks and pedestrians etc. to safely navigate through the environment.

The ability of robots to perform complex tasks is linked to the richness of the robot's world model. As inferring exhaustively detailed world representations is impractical, it is common to infer representations which are highly specific to the task that the robot is to perform. However, in collaborative domains as we move towards more complex bi-directional interactions, manipulation tasks, and the environments, it becomes unclear how to best represent the environment in order to facilitate planning and reasoning for a wide distribution of tasks. As shown in the Figure 1, modeling the affordance between the chips can and its lid would be unnecessary for the task of picking up the mustard sauce bottle and vice versa. Inferring exhaustively detailed models of all of the objects in the environment is computationally expensive and inconsequential for the individual tasks, and inhibits real-time interaction with these collaborative robots.

The utility of collaborative manipulators is also highly dependent on the speed and accuracy of communication between the human operator and the robot. Natural language interfaces provide intuitive and muti-resolution means to interact with the robots in shared realms. In this work, we propose learning a model of language and perception that can adapt the configurations of the perception pipeline according to the task in order to infer representations that are necessary and suffi-

Proceedings of the SIGDIAL 2018 Conference, pages 151–160,
Melbourne, Australia, 12-14 July 2018. ©2018 Association for Computational Linguistics

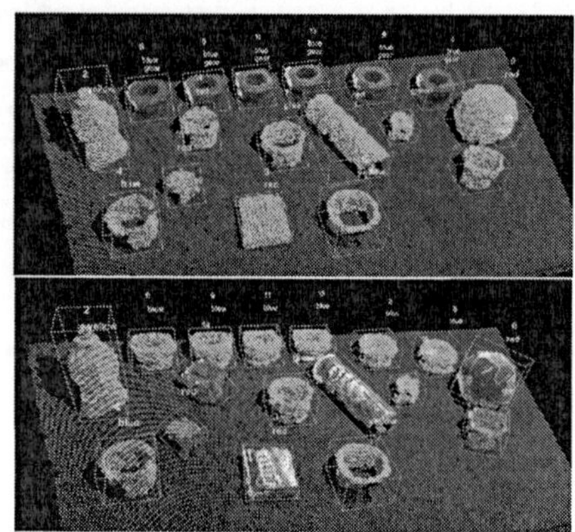

Figure 1: On the left is an image showing the Baxter Research Robot in a cluttered tabletop environment in the context of collaborative human-robot tasks. A perception system that does not use the context of the instruction when interpreting the observations would inefficiently construct detailed world model that is only partially utilized by the symbol grounding algorithm. On the right are the adaptively inferred representations using our proposed language perception model for the instructions, "pick up the leftmost blue gear" and "pick up the largest red object" respectively.

cient to facilitate planning and grounding for the intended task. e.g. the top-right image in the Figure 1 shows the adaptively inferred world model pertaining to the instruction "pick up the leftmost blue gear" which is different than the one inferred for the instruction "pick up the largest red object".

2 BACKGROUND

The algorithms and models presented in this paper span the topics that include robot perception and natural language understanding for human-robot interaction. Perception is a central problem in the the field of situated robotics. Consequently, a plenty of research has focused on developing representations that can faciliate planning and reasoning for highly specific situated tasks. These representations vary significantly depending on the application, from two-dimensional costmaps (Elfes, 1987), volumetric 3D voxel representations (Hornung et al., 2013, 2010), primitive shape based object approximations (Miller et al., 2003; Huebner and Kragic, 2008) to more rich representations that model high level semantic properties (Galindo et al., 2005; Pronobis and Jensfelt, 2012), 6 DOF pose of the objects of interest (Hudson et al., 2012) or affordances between objects (Daniele et al., 2017). Since inferring exhaustively detailed world models is impractical, one solution is to design perception pipelines that infer task relevant world models (Eppner et al., 2016; Fallon et al., 2014). Inferring efficient models that can support reason-

ing and planning for a wide distribution of tasks remains an open research question.

Natural language interfaces provides intuitive and multi-resolution means to interact with the collaborative robots. Contemporary models (Tellex et al., 2011; Howard et al., 2014; Boularias et al., 2015; Matuszek et al., 2013) frame the problem of language understanding as a symbol grounding problem (Harnad, 1990). Specifically, of inferring correspondences between the linguistic constituents of the instruction and the symbols that represent perceived entities in the robot's environment such as objects and regions or desired actions that the robot can take. (Howard et al., 2014) frames this problem as one of inference in a probabilistic graphical model called a Distributed Correspondence Graph (DCG). This model leverages the hierarchical structure of the syntactically parsed instruction and conditional independence assumptions across constituents of a discrete symbol space to improve the run-time of probabilistic inference. Other variations include the Hierarchical DCG (Propp et al., 2015) and Adaptive DCG (Paul et al., 2016) to further improve the run-time performance in cluttered environments with known environment models. Recently, these models have been used to augment perception and representations. (Daniele et al., 2017) uses DCG for supplementing perception with linguistic information for efficiently inferring kinematic models of articulated objects. (Duvallet et al., 2014;

Hemachandra et al., 2015) use DCG to augment the representations by exploiting information in language instruction to build priors over the unknown parts of the world. A limitation of current applications of probabilistic graphical models for natural language symbol grounding is that they do not consider how to efficiently convert observations or measurements into sufficiently detailed representation suitable for inference. We propose to use DCG for the problem of adapting the perception pipelines for inferring task optimal representations.

Our work is most closely related to that of (Matuszek et al., 2013). Their work presents an approach for jointly learning the language and perception models for grounded attribute learning. Their model infers the subset of objects based on color and shape which satisfy the attributes described in the natural language description. Similarly, (Hu et al., 2016) proposes deep learning based approach to directly segment objects in RGB images that are described by the instruction. We differentiate our approach by expanding the diversity and complexity of perceptual classifiers, enabling verbs to modify object representations, and presenting an end-to-end approach to representation adaptation and symbol grounding using computationally efficient probabilistic graphical models. In the following sections we introduce our approach to adapting perception pipelines, define our experiments, and present results against a suitable baseline.

3 TECHNICAL APPROACH

We describe the problem of understanding natural language instructions as one of probabilistic inference where we infer a distribution of symbols that express the intent of the utterance. The meaning of the instruction is taken in the context of a symbolic representation (Γ), observations ($\mathbf{z}_t$) and a representation of the language used to describe the instruction (Λ). A probabilistic inference using a symbolic representation that is described by the space of trajectories $\mathbf{X}(t)$ that the robot may take takes the form of equation:

$$\mathbf{x}(t)^* = \arg\max_{\mathbf{x}(t) \in \mathbf{X}(t)} p(\mathbf{x}(t)|\Lambda, \mathbf{z}_t) \qquad (1)$$

Solving this inference problem is computationally intractable when the space of possible trajectories is large. Contemporary approaches (Tellex

et al., 2011; Howard et al., 2014) frame this problem as a symbol grounding problem, i.e. inferring the most likely set of groundings (Γ^{s*}) given a syntactically parsed instruction $\Lambda = \{\lambda_1, ..., \lambda_m\}$ and the world model Υ.

$$\Gamma^{s*} = \arg\max_{\gamma_1 ... \gamma_n \in \Gamma^s} p(\gamma_1 ... \gamma_n|\Lambda, \Upsilon) \qquad (2)$$

Here, the world model Υ is a function of the constructs of the robot's perception pipeline (P), and the raw observations $\mathbf{z}_t$.

$$\Upsilon \approx f(P, \mathbf{z}_t) \qquad (3)$$

The groundings Γ^s are symbols that represent objects, their semantic properties, regions derived from the world model, and robot actions and goals such as grasping the object of interest or navigating to a specific region in the environment. The set of all groundings $\Gamma^s = \{\gamma_1, \gamma_2, ..., \gamma_n\}$ is called as the *symbol space*. Thus the symbol space forms a finite space of interpretations in which the instruction will be grounded. The DCG is a probabilistic graphical model of the form described in equation 2. The model relates the linguistic components $\lambda_i \in \Lambda$ to the groundings $\gamma_j \in \Gamma^s$ through the binary correspondence variables $\phi_{ij} \in \Phi$. DCG facilitates inferring the groundings at a parent phrase in the context of the groundings at its child phrases Φ_{ci}. Formally, DCG searches for the most likely correspondence variables Φ^* in the context of the groundings γ_{ij}, phrases λ_i, child correspondences Φ_{ci} and the world model Υ by maximizing the product of individual factors.

$$\Phi^* = \arg\max_{\phi_{ij} \in \Phi} \prod_{i=1}^{|\Lambda|} \prod_{j=1}^{|\Gamma^s|} p(\phi_{ij}|\gamma_{ij}, \lambda_i, \Phi_{ci}, \Upsilon) \quad (4)$$

Inferred correspondence variables Φ^* represent the expression of the most likely groundings Γ^{s*}. The factors in the equation 4 are approximated by log-linear models Ψ:

$$\Phi^* = \arg\max_{\phi_{ij} \in \Phi} \prod_{i=1}^{|\Lambda|} \prod_{j=1}^{|\Gamma^s|} \Psi(\phi_{ij}, \gamma_{ij}, \lambda_i, \Phi_{ci}, \Upsilon)$$
$$(5)$$

Model training involves learning the log-linear factors from the labeled data relating phrases with true groundings. Inference process involves searching for the set of correspondence variables that satisfy the above equation. The run-time performance of probabilistic inference with the DCG is positively correlated with the complexity of the world model Υ. This is because the size of the symbolic representation Γ^s increases with the number of objects in the environment representation. Recognizing that some objects (and the symbols based on those objects) are inconsequential to the meaning of the instruction, we consider the optimal representation of the environment Υ^* as one which is necessary and sufficient to solve equation 5. Thus we hypothesize that the time to solve equation 6 will be less than that for the equation 5.

$$\Phi^* = \underset{\phi_{ij} \in \Phi}{\arg\max} \prod_{i=1}^{|\Lambda|} \prod_{j=1}^{|\Gamma^s|} \Psi(\phi_{ij}, \gamma_{ij}, \lambda_i, \Phi_{ci}, \Upsilon^*) \tag{6}$$

Typically the environment model Υ is computed by a perception module P from a set of observations $\mathbf{z}_{1:t} = \{\mathbf{z}_1 \ldots \mathbf{z}_t\}$. In cluttered environments we assume that inferring an exhaustively detailed representation of the world that satisfies all possible instructions is impractical for real-time human-robot interactions. We propose using language as mean to guide the generation of these necessary and sufficient environment representations Υ^* in turn making it a task adaptive process. Thus we define Υ^* inferred from a single observation as:

$$\Upsilon^* \approx f(P, \mathbf{z}_t, \Lambda) \tag{7}$$

where P denotes the perception pipeline of the robotic intelligence architecture. We adapt DCG to model the above function by creating a novel class of symbols called as perceptual symbols Γ^P. Perceptual symbols are tied to their corresponding elements in the perception pipeline. i.e. to the vision algorithms. Since this grounding space is independent of the world model Υ, the random variable used to represent the environment is removed from equation 5. We add a subscript p to denote that we are reasoning in the perceptual grounding space.

$$\Phi^* = \underset{\phi_{ij} \in \Phi}{\arg\max} \prod_{i=1}^{|\Lambda|} \prod_{j=1}^{|\Gamma^P|} \Psi(\phi_{ij}, \gamma_{ij}, \lambda_i, \Phi_{c_i}) \tag{8}$$

Equation 8 represents the proposed model which we refer to as the language-perception model (LPM). It infers the symbols that inform the perception pipeline configurations given a natural language instruction describing the task. The space of symbols Γ^P describe all possible configurations of the perception pipeline. For example, as shown in the Figure 1, for the instruction "pick up the leftmost blue gear", we may need elements in our pipeline that can detect blue objects and gears. Detecting green objects, spherical shapes, or six-dimensional pose of the chips can object would not be necessary to generate the symbols necessary for the robot to perform the instruction.

We assume that the perception pipeline (P) is populated with a set of elements $E = \{E_1, \ldots, E_n\}$ such that each subset $E_i \in E$ represents a set of algorithms that are responsible for inferring a specific property of an object. e.g. a red color-detection algorithm would be a member of the color detector family responsible for inferring the semantic property "color" of the object. While a six degree-of-freedom (DOF) pose detection algorithm would be a member of the pose detector family. More generally, E can be defined as: $E = \{e_1, e_2, \ldots, e_m\}$. With these assumptions, we define our independent perceptual symbols as:

$$\Gamma^{ID}_P = \{\gamma_{e_i} | e_i \in E\} \tag{9}$$

We can imagine that these symbols would be useful to ground simple phrases such as "the red object" or "the ball" etc. where the phrases refer to a single property of the object. In the more complicated phrases such as "the red ball" or "the blue box" we have a joint expression of properties. i.e. we are looking for objects which maximize the joint likelihood $p(red, sphere|o)$. Since these properties are independent we can infer them separately for every object $o_k \in O$. However, we can represent the above joint likelihood expression as $p(red, sphere) = p(red)p(sphere|red)$. In this case, it allows conditioning the evaluation of sphere detection on only a subset of objects which were classified as being red by the red detector. To add this degree of freedom in the construction of the perception pipeline, we define additional set of symbols which we refer to as conditionally dependent perceptual symbols:

$$\Gamma^{CD}_P = \{\gamma_{e_i, e_j} | e_i, e_j \in E \; ; \; i \neq j\} \tag{10}$$

The expression of the symbol γ_{e_i, e_j} refers to running the element e_i from the perception pipeline on the subset of objects which were classified positive by the element e_j. Finally the complete perceptual symbol space is:

$$\Gamma^P - \{\Gamma^{ID}_P \cup \Gamma^{CD}_P\} \tag{11}$$

4 EXPERIMENTAL DESIGN

Herein with our experiments we demonstrate the utility of our language perception model for the task of grounded language understanding of the manipulation instructions. As shown in Figure 3 the process involves two distinct inferences: Inferring the perceptual groundings given a language instruction (eq. 8), and inferring high level motion planning constraints given the language and the generated world model (eq. 5 and eq. 6). In this section we describe our assumptions, and define the distinct symbolic representations used in our experiments for each of the above tasks. We then discuss our instruction corpus and the details of the individual experiments.

Robot and the Environment

For our experiments a Rethink Robotics Baxter Research Robot is placed behind a table. The robot is assumed to perceive the environment using a head-mounted RGB-D sensor. Robot's work space is populated using objects from the standard YCB dataset (Berk Calli, 2017), custom 3D printed ABS plastic objects, and multicolored rubber blocks. We define the world complexity in terms of the number of objects present on the table in the robot's field of view. The world complexity ranges from 15 to 20 in our experiments.

Symbolic Representation

The symbolic representation defines the space of symbols or *meanings* in which the natural language instruction will be grounded or *understood*. As mentioned before we define two distinct sets of symbols in our experiments. Γ^P defines the set of perceptual symbols which are used by the language perception model, and Γ^S defines the set of symbols which are used by the symbol grounding model.

Γ^P is a function of the elements E of the perception pipeline. The elements $e_i \in E$ in our perception pipeline are selected such that they can model the robot's environment with a spectrum of semantic and metric properties which will be necessary towards performing symbol grounding and planning for all of the instructions in our corpus. In our experiment we define E as:

$$E = \{ C \cup G \cup L \cup B \cup R \cup \mathcal{P} \} \tag{12}$$

Here, C is a set of color detectors, G is a set of geometry detectors, L is a set of object label detectors, B is a set of bounding box detectors, R is a set of region detectors, and $\mathcal{P}$ is a set of pose detectors.

$$
\begin{aligned}
C &= \{ \, cd_i \mid i \in color \} \\
G &= \{ \, gd_i \mid i \in geometry \} \\
L &= \{ \, ld_i \mid i \in label \} \\
B &= \{ \, bd_i \mid i \in bbox \} \\
R &= \{ \, rd_i \mid i \in region \} \\
\mathcal{P} &= \{ \, pd_i \mid i \in pose \}
\end{aligned} \tag{13}
$$

where *color* = {red, green, blue, white, yellow, orange}, *geometry* = {sphere, cylinder, cuboid}, *label* = {crackers box, chips can, pudding box, master chef can, bleach cleanser, soccer ball, mustard sauce bottle, sugar packet}, *bbox* = {non-oriented, oriented }, *region* = {left, right, center}, *pose* = { 3 DOF, 6 DOF }. Given the perception elements defined in the equation 13, we define the independent perceptual groundings (Γ_P^{ID}) previously defined in equation 9 as follows:

$$
\begin{aligned}
\Gamma^C &= \{ \gamma_{cd_i} \mid cd_i \in C \} \\
\Gamma^G &= \{ \gamma_{gd_i} \mid gd_i \in B \} \\
\Gamma^L &= \{ \gamma_{ld_i} \mid ld_i \in L \} \\
\Gamma^B &= \{ \gamma_{bd_i} \mid bd_i \in B \} \\
\Gamma^R &= \{ \gamma_{rd_i} \mid rd_i \in R \} \\
\Gamma^P &= \{ \gamma_{pd_i} \mid pd_i \in \mathcal{P} \}
\end{aligned} \tag{14}
$$

$$\Gamma_P^{ID} = \{ \, \Gamma^C \cup \Gamma^G \cup \Gamma^L \cup \Gamma^B \cup \Gamma^R \cup \Gamma^P \} \tag{15}$$

We define the conditionally dependent perceptual groundings (Γ_P^{CD}) previously defined in equation 10 as following:

$$
\begin{aligned}
\Gamma^{GC} &= \{ \gamma_{(gd_i, cd_j)} \mid gd_i \in G, cd_j \in C \} \\
\Gamma^{LC} &= \{ \gamma_{(ld_i, cd_j)} \mid ld_i \in L, cd_j \in C \} \\
\Gamma^{PC} &= \{ \gamma_{(pd_i, cd_j)} \mid pd_i \in \mathcal{P}, cd_j \in C \} \\
\Gamma^{PG} &= \{ \gamma_{(pd_i, gd_j)} \mid pd_i \in \mathcal{P}, gd_j \in G \} \\
\Gamma^{PL} &= \{ \gamma_{(pd_i, ld_j)} \mid pd_i \in \mathcal{P}, ld_j \in L \}
\end{aligned} \tag{16}
$$

$$\Gamma_P^{CD} = \{ \, \Gamma^{GC} \cup \Gamma^{LC} \cup \Gamma^{PC} \cup \Gamma^{PG} \cup \Gamma^{PL} \} \tag{17}$$

These symbols provide us the ability to selectively infer desired properties in the world. Above presented independent and conditionally dependent symbols together cover the complete space of perceptual symbols used by the LPM:

$$\Gamma^P = \{ \Gamma_P^{ID} \cup \Gamma_P^{CD} \} \tag{18}$$

Algorithmic details of the percepion elements are as follows : A single RGB point cloud is fed in as a raw sensor observation to the pipeline. A RANSAC (Fischler and Bolles, 1981) based 3D plane detection technique is used for segmenting the table-top and the objects. HSV colorspace is used for detecting colors. RANSAC based model fitting algorithms form the core of the geometry detectors. A 4 layer (256 - 128 - 64 - 32) feed forward neural network is trained to infer the semantic labels of the objects. It takes in a 32 x 32 RGB image and infers a distribution over 8 unique YCB object classes. A PCA based oriented bounding box estimation algorithm is used to approximate the 6 DOF pose for the individual objects. Algorithms are implemented using OpenCV and PCL library (Rusu and Cousins, 2011).

The space of symbols for the symbol grounding model is similar to the representation defined in (Paul et al., 2016). This space uses symbols to represent objects in the world model ($\Gamma^{\mathcal{O}}$), semantic object labels ($\Gamma^{\mathcal{L}}$), object color($\Gamma^{\mathcal{C}}$), object geometry($\Gamma^{\mathcal{G}}$) regions in the world($\Gamma^{\mathcal{R}}$), spatial relationships ($\Gamma^{\mathcal{SR}}$) and finally high level planning constraints that define the end goal ($\Gamma^{\mathcal{PC}}$). The inferred constraints forms an input to a planning algorithm that can then generate trajectories to accomplish the desired task. Thus the complete symbol space for the symbol grounding model is:

$$\Gamma^{S} = \{ \Gamma^{\mathcal{O}} \cup \Gamma^{\mathcal{L}} \cup, \Gamma^{\mathcal{C}} \cup \Gamma^{\mathcal{G}} \cup \Gamma^{\mathcal{R}} \cup \Gamma^{\mathcal{SR}} \cup \Gamma^{\mathcal{PC}} \} \quad (19)$$

Corpus

For training and testing the performance of the system we generate an instruction corpus using the linguistic patterns similar to that described in (Paul et al., 2016). The corpus used in our experiments consists of 100 unique natural language instructions. Details of the grammar extracted from this corpus is described in the appendix. Each instruction describes a manipulation command to the robot while referring to the objects of interest using their semantic or metric properties. e.g. "pick up the green cup" or "pick up the biggest blue object". If multiple instances of the same objects are present in the robot's work space then the reference resolution is achieved by using spatial relationships to describe the object of interest. e.g."the leftmost blue cube" or "rightmost red object" etc.

As shown in Figure 2, the instructions in the corpus are in the form of syntactically parsed trees.

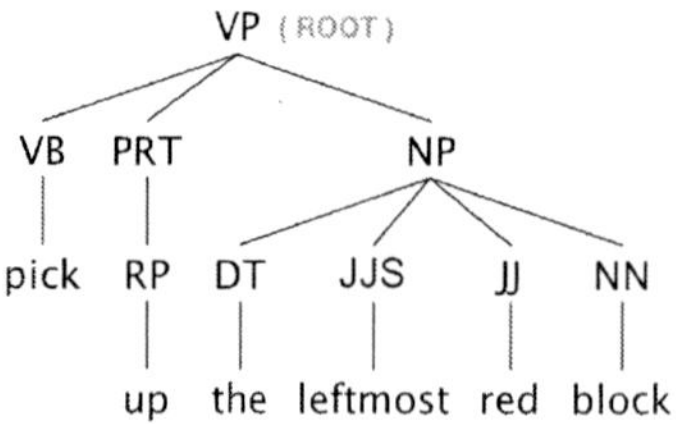

Figure 2: Syntactically parsed tree for the instruction "pick up the leftmost red block".

Each instruction is generated in the context of a specific table-top object arrangement. Thus each instruction is associated with a pair of RGB-D image. A total of 10 unique table-top arrangements are used to generate the set of 100 instructions.

One copy of the corpora is annotated for training LPM using (Γ^{P}) while another for training the symbol grounding model using (Γ^{S}). The annotations for LPM corpus are selected such that that the perception pipelines configured using the annotated groundings would generate the optimal world representations that are necessary and sufficient to support grounding and planning for the given tasks.

We have instructions with varying complexity in our corpus. The instruction complexity from the perception point of view is quantified in terms of the total number of perceptual groundings expressed at the root level. e.g. "pick up the ball" is relatively a simple instruction with only single grounding expressed at the root level, while "pick up the blue cube and put the blue cube near the crackers box" is a more complicated instruction having seven groundings expressed at the root level. This number was found to vary in the range of one to seven in our corpus.

Experiments and Metrics

We structure our experiments to validate two claims. The first claim is that adaptively inferring the task optimal representations reduce the perception run-time by avoiding exhaustively detailed uniform modeling of the world. The second claim is that reasoning in the context of these optimal representations also reduces the inference run-time of the symbol grounding model. An outline of our experiments is illustrated in Figure 3. In the first experiment, we study the root-level inference accuracy of LPM (groundings expressed at the root level of the phrase) as a function of the gradual increase in the training fraction. For each

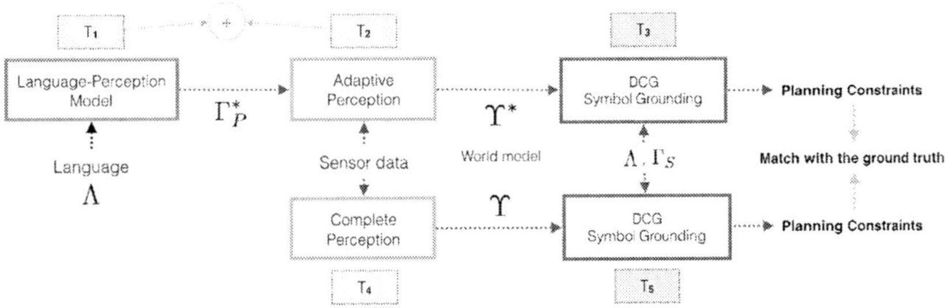

Figure 3: Comparative Experiments: Boxes in the bottom half denote the baseline framework whereas the boxes in the top half represent the proposed framework. Filled boxes enclose the variables that are compared in the experiments.

value of training fraction in the range [0.2 , 0.9] increasing with a step of 0.1, we perform 15 validation experiments. The training data is sampled randomly for every individual experiment. Additionally, we perform a leave-one-out cross validation experiment. We use the inferences generated by the leave-one-out cross validation experiments as inputs to drive the adaptive perception for each instruction.

In the second experiment, we compare the cumulative run-time of LPM inference (eq. 8) and adaptive perception ($T_1 + T_2$) against the run-time for complete perception (T_4) - our baseline, for increasingly complex worlds.

In the third experiment, we compare the inference time of the symbol grounding model reasoning in the context of the adaptively generated optimal world models (T_3, eq. 6) against the inference time of the same model but when reasoning in the context of the complete world models (T_5, eq. 5). We also check whether the planning constraints inferred in both cases match the ground truth or not. Experiments are performed on a system running a 2.2 GHz Intel Core i7 CPU with 16 GB RAM.

5 RESULTS

This section presents the results obtained for the above mentioned three experiments. Specifically, the learning characteristics of LPM, the impact of LPM on the perception run-time, and the impact the adaptive representations on the symbol grounding run-time.

Leftmost graph in the Figure 4 shows the results of the first experiment. We can see that the inference accuracy grows as a function of a gradual increase in the training data. A growing trend is an indicator of the language diversity in the corpus.

Mean inference accuracy starts at 39.25%±5 for k = 0.2 and it reaches 84% for leave-one-out cross validation experiment (k = 0.99).

Middle graph in the Figure 4 shows the result of the second experiment. We can clearly see that the run-time for complete perception grows with the world complexity while the run-time of adaptive perception stays nearly flat and is significantly lower in all cases. Since the adaptive perception run-time varies according to the task, we see bigger error bars. The drop in the complete perception run-time for world complexity of 20 is justifiable as the run-time of our geometry detection algorithm was proportional to the size of the individual objects, and all of the objects for that example world were smaller than other examples.

World Complexity	T_4 (sec) baseline	$T_1 + T_2$ (sec) proposed
15	4.40 ± 0.05	0.96 ± 0.07
16	4.99 ± 0.02	1.33 ± 0.34
17	5.40 ± 0.06	1.11 ± 0.11
18	5.82 ± 0.18	1.51 ± 0.26
20	4.17 ± 0.05	1.11 ± 0.25
Mean	**5.03 ± 0.07**	**1.20 ± 0.21**

Table 1: Adaptive perception run-time compared against complete perception run-time. Deviation measures are 95% confidence interval values.

Rightmost graph in the Figure 4 shows the result of the third experiment. It shows that the symbol grounding run-time when reasoning in the context of detailed world models(Υ) grows as a function of the world complexity. However, it is significantly lower when reasoning in the context of adaptively generated world models (Υ^*) and is independent of the world complexity.

The achieved run-time gains are meaningful

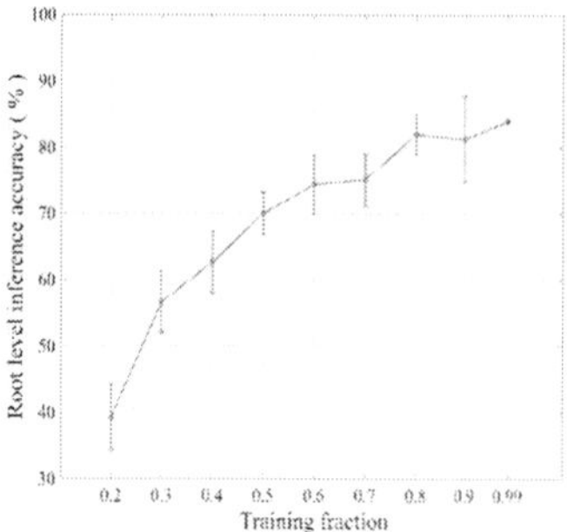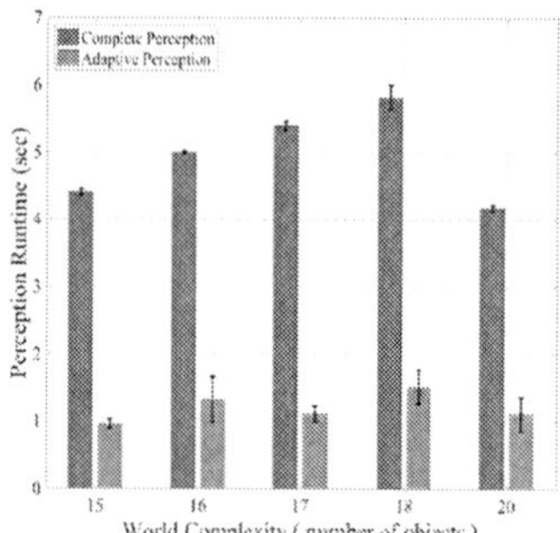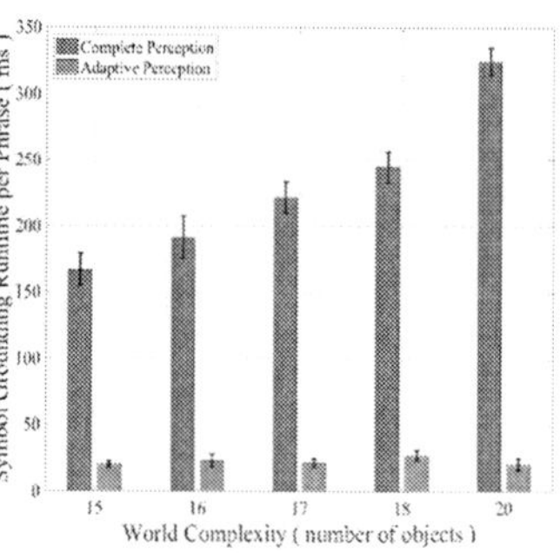

Figure 4: Graph on the left shows the LPM inference accuracy as a function of gradual increase in the training fraction. In the middle is the bar chart comparing the run-time for complete perception (T_4) against the cumulative run-time of LPM inference and adaptive perception ($T_1 + T_2$). Finally, on the right is a bar chart comparing the run-time of symbol grounding when reasoning in the context of the adaptively generated optimal representations (T_3) against when reasoning in the context of exhaustively detailed world models (T_5). The error bars indicate 95% confidence intervals.

World complexity	T_5 (ms) baseline	T_3 (ms) proposed
15	167 ± 12	21 ± 2
16	191 ± 16	23 ± 5
17	222 ± 12	22 ± 3
18	245 ± 12	27 ± 4
20	325 ± 10	20 ± 5
Mean	**214 ± 12**	**23 ± 4**

Table 2: Per phrase symbol grounding run-time in ms (rounded to the nearest integer) using adaptive representations compared against the same when using complete representations. Deviation measures are 95% confidence interval values.

only if we do not incur a loss in the symbol grounding accuracy. Table 3 shows the impact of LPM on SG accuracy and summarizes the gains.

Perception Type	Avg. T_P (sec)	Avg. T_{SG} (ms)	SG Acc.
Complete	5.03 ± 0.07	214 ± 12	**63%**
Adaptive	1.20 ± 0.21	23 ± 4	**66%**
Ratio	**4.19**	**9.30**	

Table 3: Impact of LPM on average perception run-time per instruction (T_P), average symbol grounding run-time per instruction (T_{SG}), and the symbol grounding accuracy.

6 CONCLUSIONS

Real-time human-robot interaction is critical for the utility of the collaborative robotic manipulators in shared tasks. In scenarios where inferring exhaustively detailed models of all the objects is prohibitive, perception represents a bottleneck that inhibits real-time interactions with collaborative robots. Language provides an intuitive and multi-resolution interface to interact with these robots. While recent probabilistic frameworks have advanced our ability to interpret the meaning of complex instructions in cluttered environments, the problem of how language can channel the interpretation of the raw observations to construct world models which are necessary and sufficient for the symbol grounding task is not extensively studied. Our proposed DCG based Language Perception Model, demonstrates that we can guide perception using language to construct world models which are suitable for efficiently interpreting the instruction. This provides run-time gains in terms of both perception and symbol grounding, thereby improving the speed with which collaborative robots can understand and act upon human instructions. In ongoing and future work we are exploring how language can aid efficient construction of global maps for robot navigation and manipulation by intelligently sampling relevant observations from a set of observations.

7 ACKNOWLEDGMENTS

This work was supported in part by the National Science Foundation under grant IIS-1637813 and the New York State Center of Excellence in Data Science at the University of Rochester.

References

James Bruce Aaron Walsman Kurt Konolige Siddhartha Srinivasa Pieter Abbeel Aaron M Dollar Berk Calli, Arjun Singh. 2017. Yale-cmu-berkeley dataset for robotic manipulation research. volume 36, page 261 268.

Abdeslam Boularias, Felix Duvallet, Jean Hyaejin Oh, and Anthony (Tony) Stentz. 2015. Grounding spatial relations for outdoor robot navigation. In *2015 IEEE International Conference on Robotics and Automation (ICRA)*.

Andrea F. Daniele, Thomas M. Howard, and Matthew R. Walter. 2017. A multiview approach to learning articulated motion models. In *Proceedings of the International Symposium of Robotics Research (ISRR)*.

F. Duvallet, M.R. Walter, T.M. Howard, S. Hemachandra, J. Oh, S. Teller, N. Roy, and A. Stentz. 2014. A probabilistic framework for inferring maps and behaviors from natural language. In *Proceedings of the 14th International Symposium on Experimental Robotics*.

A Elfes. 1987. Sonar-based real-world mapping and navigation. *IEEE Journal of Robotics and Automation*, 3(3).

Clemens Eppner, Sebastian Höfer, Rico Jonschkowski, Roberto Martín-Martín, Arne Sieverling, Vincent Wall, and Oliver Brock. 2016. Lessons from the amazon picking challenge: Four aspects of building robotic systems. In *Proceedings of Robotics: Science and Systems*, AnnArbor, Michigan.

Maurice Fallon, Scott Kuindersma, Sisir Karumanchi, Matthew Antone, Toby Schneider, Hongkai Dai, Claudia Prez D'Arpino, Robin Deits, Matt DiCicco, Dehann Fourie, Twan Koolen, Pat Marion, Michael Posa, Andrs Valenzuela, KuanTing Yu, Julie Shah, Karl Iagnemma, Russ Tedrake, and Seth Teller. 2014. An architecture for online affordancebased perception and wholebody planning. *Journal of Field Robotics*, 32(2):229–254.

Martin A. Fischler and Robert C. Bolles. 1981. Random sample consensus: A paradigm for model fitting with applications to image analysis and automated cartography. *Commun. ACM*, 24(6):381–395.

C. Galindo, A. Saffiotti, S. Coradeschi, P. Buschka, J. A. Fernandez-Madrigal, and J. Gonzalez. 2005. Multi-hierarchical semantic maps for mobile robotics. In *2005 IEEE/RSJ International Conference on Intelligent Robots and Systems*, pages 2278–2283.

Stevan Harnad. 1990. The symbol grounding problem. In *Physica D: Nonlinear Phenomena*, volume 42, pages 335 346.

S. Hemachandra, F. Duvallet, T.M. Howard, N. Roy, A. Stentz, and M.R. Walter. 2015. Learning models for following natural language directions in unknown environments. In *Proceedings of the IEEE International Conference on Robotics and Automation*. IEEE.

A. Hornung, K. M. Wurm, and M. Bennewitz. 2010. Humanoid robot localization in complex indoor environments. In *2010 IEEE/RSJ International Conference on Intelligent Robots and Systems*, pages 1690–1695.

Armin Hornung, Kai M. Wurm, Maren Bennewitz, Cyrill Stachniss, and Wolfram Burgard. 2013. Octomap: an efficient probabilistic 3d mapping framework based on octrees. *Autonomous Robots*, 34(3):189–206.

T.M Howard, S. Tellex, and N. Roy. 2014. A natural language planner interface for mobile manipulators. In *Proceedings of the IEEE International Conference on Robotics and Automation*, pages 6652–6659. IEEE.

Ronghang Hu, Marcus Rohrbach, and Trevor Darrell. 2016. Segmentation from natural language expressions. In *European Conference on Computer Vision*, pages 108–124. Springer.

N. Hudson, T.M. Howard, J. Ma, A. Jain, M. Bajracharya, S. Myint, L. Matthies, P. Backes, P Hebert, T. Fuchs, and J. Burdick. 2012. End-to-end dexterous manipulation with deliberative interactive estimation. In *Proceedings of the 2012 IEEE International Conference on Robotics and Automation*.

K. Huebner and D. Kragic. 2008. Selection of robot pre-grasps using box-based shape approximation. In *2008 IEEE/RSJ International Conference on Intelligent Robots and Systems*, pages 1765–1770.

Cynthia Matuszek, Evan Herbst, Luke Zettlemoyer, and Dieter Fox. 2013. *Learning to Parse Natural Language Commands to a Robot Control System*. Springer International Publishing, Heidelberg.

Andrew T. Miller, Steffen Knoop, Henrik I. Christensen, and Peter K. Allen. 2003. Automatic grasp planning using shape primitives. In *ICRA*.

R. Paul, J. Arkin, N. Roy, and T.M. Howard. 2016. Efficient grounding of abstract spatial concepts for natural language interaction with robot manipulators. In *Proceedings of the 2016 Robotics: Science and Systems Conference*.

A. Pronobis and P. Jensfelt. 2012. Large-scale semantic mapping and reasoning with heterogeneous modalities. In *2012 IEEE International Conference on Robotics and Automation*, pages 3515–3522.

O. Propp, I. Chung, M.R. Walter, and T.M. Howard. 2015. On the performance of hierarchical distributed correspondence graphs for efficiency symbol grounding of robot instructions. In *Proceedings of the 2015 IEEE/RSJ International Conference on Intelligent Robots and Systems*.

Radu Bogdan Rusu and Steve Cousins. 2011. 3D is here: Point Cloud Library (PCL). In *IEEE International Conference on Robotics and Automation (ICRA)*, Shanghai, China.

Stefanie Tellex, Thomas Kollar, Steven Dickerson, Matthew Walter, Ashis Banerjee, Seth Teller, and Nicholas Roy. 2011. Understanding natural language commands for robotic navigation and mobile manipulation.

A Grammar and Lexicon of the Corpus

We list the grammar rules and the lexicon for our corpus to demonstrate the diversity of the instructions. Following table lists the words scraped from the instructions in our corpus. We have a total of 56 unique words.

$$
\begin{aligned}
\text{VB} &\rightarrow \{\text{pick}|\text{put}\} \\
\text{RP} &\rightarrow \{\text{up}\} \\
\text{DT} &\rightarrow \{\text{the}|\text{all}\} \\
\text{CC} &\rightarrow \{\text{and}\} \\
\text{VBZ} &\rightarrow \{\text{is}\} \\
\text{WDT} &\rightarrow \{\text{that}\} \\
\text{VB} &\rightarrow \{\text{near}|\text{in}|\text{on}\} \\
\text{PRP} &\rightarrow \{\text{your}\}
\end{aligned}
$$

$$
\text{NN} \rightarrow \left\{
\begin{array}{l}
\text{cup}|\text{pudding}|\text{box}|\text{cube}| \\
\text{object}|\text{ball}|\text{master}| \\
\text{chef}|\text{can}|\text{soccer}| \\
\text{gear}|\text{mustard}|\text{sauce}|\text{bottle}| \\
\text{sugar}|\text{packet}|\text{block}| \\
\text{cleanser}|\text{middle}|\text{left}| \\
\text{right}|\text{crackers}|\text{cheezit}| \\
\text{cleanser}|\text{packet}|\text{block}
\end{array}
\right\}
$$

$$
\text{NNS} \rightarrow \left\{
\begin{array}{l}
\text{cups}|\text{chips}|\text{cubes}| \\
\text{objects}|\text{balls}
\end{array}
\right\}
$$

$$
\text{JJ} \rightarrow \left\{
\begin{array}{l}
\text{blue}|\text{green}|\text{yellow}| \\
\text{red}|\text{white}
\end{array}
\right\}
$$

$$
\text{JJS} \rightarrow \left\{
\begin{array}{l}
\text{nearest}|\text{rightmost}|\text{leftmost}| \\
\text{farthest}|\text{biggest}|\text{smallest}| \\
\text{largest}|\text{closest}
\end{array}
\right\}
$$

Table 4: The words scraped from the corpus of annotated examples

Following table lists the grammar rules scraped from the instructions in our corpus. We have a total of 23 unique grammar rules.

$$
\begin{aligned}
\text{SBAR} &\rightarrow \text{WHNP S} \\
\text{S} &\rightarrow \text{VP} \\
\text{VP} &\rightarrow \text{VB PRT NP} \\
\text{VP} &\rightarrow \text{CC VP VP} \\
\text{VP} &\rightarrow \text{VB NP PP} \\
\text{VP} &\rightarrow \text{VBZ PP} \\
\text{WHNP} &\rightarrow \text{WDT} \\
\text{PRT} &\rightarrow \textit{RP} \\
\text{PP} &\rightarrow \text{IN NP} \\
\text{NP} &\rightarrow \text{DT JJ NN} \\
\text{NP} &\rightarrow \text{DT NN NN} \\
\text{NP} &\rightarrow \text{DT JJS JJ NN} \\
\text{NP} &\rightarrow \text{NP PP} \\
\text{NP} &\rightarrow \text{DT} \\
\text{NP} &\rightarrow \text{DT JJ NNS} \\
\text{NP} &\rightarrow \text{DT NN} \\
\text{NP} &\rightarrow \text{DT NN NN NN} \\
\text{NP} &\rightarrow \text{DT JJ NN NN} \\
\text{NP} &\rightarrow \text{DT JJS NN} \\
\text{NP} &\rightarrow \text{DT NNS NN} \\
\text{NP} &\rightarrow \text{PRP NN} \\
\text{NP} &\rightarrow \text{NP SBAR} \\
\text{NP} &\rightarrow \text{DT NNS}
\end{aligned}
$$

Table 5: The grammar rules scraped from the corpus of annotated examples

Unsupervised Counselor Dialogue Clustering for Positive Emotion Elicitation in Neural Dialogue System

Nurul Lubis, Sakriani Sakti, Koichiro Yoshino, Satoshi Nakamura
Information Science Division,
Nara Institute of Science and Technology, Japan
{nurul.lubis.na4, ssakti, koichiro, s-nakamura}@is.naist.jp

Abstract

Positive emotion elicitation seeks to improve user's emotional state through dialogue system interaction, where a chat-based scenario is layered with an implicit goal to address user's emotional needs. Standard neural dialogue system approaches still fall short in this situation as they tend to generate only short, generic responses. Learning from expert actions is critical, as these potentially differ from standard dialogue acts. In this paper, we propose using a hierarchical neural network for response generation that is conditioned on 1) expert's action, 2) dialogue context, and 3) user emotion, encoded from user input. We construct a corpus of interactions between a counselor and 30 participants following a negative emotional exposure to learn expert actions and responses in a positive emotion elicitation scenario. Instead of relying on the expensive, labor intensive, and often ambiguous human annotations, we unsupervisedly cluster the expert's responses and use the resulting labels to train the network. Our experiments and evaluation show that the proposed approach yields lower perplexity and generates a larger variety of responses.

1   Intoduction

Emotionally intelligent systems has high potential as assistive technology in various affective tasks, such as caring for the elderly, low-cost ubiquitous chat therapy, or providing emotional support in general. Two of the most studied emotional competences for agents are *emotion recognition*, which allows a system to discern the user's

emotions and address them in giving a response (Forbes-Riley and Litman, 2012; Han et al., 2015; Tielman et al., 2014), and *emotion simulation*, which helps convey non-verbal aspects to the user for a more believable and human-like interaction, for example to show empathy (Higashinaka et al., 2008) or personality (Egges et al., 2004). Acosta and Ward (2011) have attempted to connect the two competences to build rapport, by recognizing user's emotion and reflecting it in the system response. Although these competences address some of the user's emotional needs (Picard and Klein, 2002), they are not sufficient to provide emotional support in an interaction.

Recently, there has been an increasing interest in eliciting user's emotional response via dialogue system interaction, i.e. *emotion elicitation*. Skowron et al. (2013) have studied the impact of different affective personalities in a text-based dialogue system, while Hasegawa et al. (2013) constructed translation-based response generators with various emotion targets. Despite the positive results, these approaches have not yet paid attention to the emotional benefit for the users. Our work aims to draw on an important overlooked potential of emotion elicitation: its application to improve emotional states, similar to that of emotional support between humans. This can be achieved by actively eliciting a more positive emotional valence throughout the interaction, i.e. *positive emotion elicitation*. This takes form as a chat-oriented dialogue system interaction that is layered with an implicit goal to address user's emotional needs.

With recent advancements in neural network research, end-to-end approaches have been reported to show promising results for non-goal oriented dialogue systems (Vinyals and Le, 2015; Serban et al., 2016; Nio et al., 2016). However, application of this approach towards positive emotion elicitation is still very lacking. Zhou et al. (2017)

Proceedings of the SIGDIAL 2018 Conference, pages 161–170,
Melbourne, Australia, 12-14 July 2018. ©2018 Association for Computational Linguistics

have investigated 6 categories to emotionally color the response via the internal state of the decoder. However, this study has not yet considered user's emotion in the response generation process, nor attempted improve emotional experience of user.

Towards positive emotion elicitation, Lubis et al. (2018) have recently proposed a model that encodes emotion information from user input and utilizes it in generating response. However, the resulting system is still limited to short and generic responses with positive affect, echoing the long standing lack-of-diversity problem in neural network based response generation (Li et al., 2016). Furthermore, the reported system has not learn about positive emotion elicitation strategies from an expert as the corpus construction relied on crowd-sourcing workers.

This points to another problem: the lack of data that shows positive emotion elicitation or emotion recovery in everyday situations. Learning from expert responses and actions are essential in such a scenario as these potentially differ from standard chat-based scenarios. With scarcity of large-scale data, additional knowledge from higher level abstraction, such as dialogue action labels, may be highly beneficial. However, such high-level information must rely on human annotations, which are expensive, labor intensive, and often ambiguous.

To answer these challenges, first, we construct a corpus containing recordings of a professional counselor and 30 participants in a positive emotion elicitation scenario. Second, we extract higher level information from the expert's responses via unsupervised clustering and use the resulting labels to train a neural dialogue system. Lastly, we propose a hierarchical neural dialogue system which considers 1) expert's action, 2) dialogue context, and 3) user emotion, in generating a response by encoding them from user input. Our evaluations show that the proposed method yields lower perplexity, elicits a positive emotional impact, and generates longer responses that improves subjective engagement.

2 Corpus Construction: Positive Emotion Elicitation by an Expert

Even though various affective conversational scenarios have been considered (McKeown et al., 2012; Gratch et al., 2014), there is still a lack of resources that show common emotional problems in everyday social settings. Furthermore, a great majority of existing corpora does not involve any professional who is an expert in handling emotional reactions in a conversation.

To fill these gaps, we design our corpus to 1) contain recordings of spontaneous dyadic interactions before and after a negative emotion exposure, and 2) involve a professional counselor as an expert. In each interaction, a negative emotion inducer is shown to the dyad, and the goal of the expert is to aid emotion processing and elicit a positive emotional change through the interaction. From this point, we will refer to this corpus as the counseling corpus.

2.1 Negative Emotion Inducer

To induce negative emotion, we opt for short video clips which are a few minutes in length. This method is well established and has been studied for several decades (Gross and Levenson, 1995; Schaefer et al., 2010). One study shows that amongst a number of techniques, the use of video clips is the most effective way to induce both positive and negative emotional states (Westermann et al., 1996). It also offers easy replication in constrained environmental settings, such as the recording room.

However, in contrast to previous works (Schaefer and Philippot, 2005), we look for clips that depict real life situations and issues, i.e., non-fiction and non-films. We select short video clips of news reports, interviews, and documentary films as emotion inducers to avoid the unpredictability of subjective emotional response to fictional clips. Non-fictional inducer also reflects real everyday situations better. We ensure that the clips contain enough information and context to serve as conversation topic throughout the recording session.

We target two emotions with negative valence: anger and sadness. First, we manually selected 34 of videos with varying relevant topics that are provided freely online. Two human experts are then asked to rate them in terms of intensity and the induced emotion (sadness or anger). Finally, we selected 20 videos, 10 of each emotion with varied intensity level where the two human ratings agree.

2.2 Data Collection

We arrange for the dyad to consist of an *expert* and a *participant*, each with a distinct role. The roles are based on the "social sharing of emotion" scenario, which argues that after an emotional event, a person is inclined to initiate an interaction which centers on the event and their reactions to it (Rime et al., 1991; Luminet IV et al., 2000). This form of social sharing is argued to be integral in processing the emotional event (Rime et al., 1991).

In the interactions, the *expert* plays the part of the external party who helps facilitate this process following the emotional response of the *participant*. We recruit a professional counselor as the *expert* in the recording, an accredited member of the British Association for Counseling and Psychotherapy with more than 8 years of professional experience. As *participants*, we recruit 30 individuals (20 males and 10 females) that speak English fluently as first or second language.

A session starts with an opening talk as a neutral baseline conversation. Afterwards, we induce negative emotion by showing an emotion inducer to the dyad. This is followed by a discussion that targets at emotional processing and recovery, during which the expert is given the objective to facilitate the processing of emotional response caused by the emotion induction, and to elicit a positive emotional change.

In total, we recorded 60 sessions of interactions, 30 with "anger" inducer and 30 with "sadness". The combined duration of all sessions sums up to 23 hours and 41 minutes of material. The audio and video recordings are transcribed, including a number of special notations for non-speech sounds such as laughter, back-channels, and throat noise.

2.3 Emotion Annotation

We follow the *circumplex model of affect* (Russell, 1980) in annotating emotion occurrences in the recordings. Two dimensions of emotion are defined: *valence* and *arousal*. Valence measures the positivity or negativity of emotion; e.g., the feeling of joy is indicated by positive valence while fear is negative. On the other hand, arousal measures the activity of emotion; e.g., depression is low in arousal (passive), while rage is high (active).

For each recording, the participants self report their emotional state using the FEELtrace system (Cowie et al., 2000) immediately after the interaction. While an annotator is watching a target person in a recording, he or she is moving a cursor along a linear scale on an adjacent window to indicate the perceived emotional aspect (e.g., valence or arousal) of the target. This results in a sequence of real numbers ranging from -1 to 1 with a constant time interval, called a *trace*. Statistical analyses of validation experiments have confirmed the reliability and indicated the precision of the FEELtrace system (Cowie et al., 2000).

2.4 Dialogue Triples

Throughout the study and experiments, we utilize the dialogue triple format, i.e. a sequence of three dialogue turns. It has been previously utilized for considering dialogue context (Sordoni et al., 2015), filtering multi-party conversation (Lasguido et al., 2014), and observing emotion appraisal (Lubis et al., 2017). In this study, we exploit it to provide both past and future contexts of an emotion occurrence

We extend and adapt the two-hierarchy view of dialogue (Serban et al., 2016). We view a dialogue D as a sequence of dialogue turns of arbitrary length M between two speakers, i.e. $D = \{U_1, ..., U_M\}$. Each utterance in the m-th dialogue turn is a sequence of tokens of arbitrary length N_m, i.e. $U_m = \{w_{m,1}, ..., w_{m,N_m}\}$. In a triple, $D = \{U_1, U_2, U_3\}$, where U_1 and U_3 are uttered by speaker A, and U_2 by speaker B. In particular, we are interested in triturns with counselor-participant-counselor speaker sequence. It is practical to view U_1, U_2, and U_3 as dialogue *context*, *query*, and *response*, respectively. U_1 and U_3 are the contexts of the emotion occurrence in U_2.

We define the end of a dialogue turn as either 1) natural end of the sentence, or 2) turn taking by the other speaker, whichever comes first. Back channels in the middle of a speaker's utterance are not considered as turn taking since they instead signal active listening. This also prevents overly fragmented dialogue turns. The backchannels are instead appended into the next dialogue turn once one of the criteria above is met. We extract a total of 6,064 dialogue triples from the collected data. All U_2 are aligned with self-report emotion annotation by the participants.

3 Recurrent Encoder-Decoder for Dialogue Systems

A recurrent neural network (RNN) is a neural network variant that can retain information over sequential data. In response generation, first, an *encoder* summarizes an input sequence into a vector representation. An input sequence at time t is modeled using the information gathered by the RNN up to time $t - 1$, contained in the hidden state h_t. Afterwards, a *decoder* recurrently predicts the output sequence conditioned by h_t and its output from the previous time step. This architecture was previously proposed as neural conversational model in (Vinyals and Le, 2015).

Based on the two-hierarchy view of dialogue, the hierarchical recurrent encoder-decoder (HRED) extends the sequence-to-sequence architecture (Serban et al., 2016). It consists of three RNNs. An *utterance encoder* recurrently processes each token in the utterance, encoding it into a vector respresentation h_{utt}. This information is then passed on to the *dialogue encoder*, which encodes the sequence of dialogue turns into h_{dlg}. The *utterance decoder*, or the response generator, takes h_{dlg}, and then predicts the probability distribution over the tokens in the next utterance.

Recently, the HRED architecture has been extended to Emo-HRED for the positive emotion elicitation task, exploiting the hierarchical view of dialogue to observe the conversational context of an emotion occurrence (Lubis et al., 2018). Emo-HRED incorporates an *emotion encoder* which predicts user emotional state and passes this information to the response generation process. The emotion encoder is placed in the same hierarchy as the dialogue encoder, capturing emotion information at dialogue-turn level h_{emo} and maintaining the emotion context history throughout the dialogue. Improved naturalness and a more positive emotional impact were reported in the evaluations of Emo-HRED, however the resulting system is still limited to short and generic responses with positive affect. This echoes the long standing lack-of-diversity problem in neural network based response generation (Li et al., 2016), which is also shared by other models previously discussed.

4 Proposed Method

4.1 Unsupervised Clustering of Counselor Dialogue

In constructing an emotionally intelligent system, learning from expert actions and responses are essential. Although statistical learning from raw data has been shown to be sufficient in some cases, it might not be so for positive emotion elicitation task. Due to the absence of large scale data, additional knowledge from higher level abstraction, such as dialogue action labels, may be highly beneficial. We hypothesize that these labels will reduce data sparsity by categorizing counselor responses and emphasizing this information in the

training and generation process.

However, procuring such labels is not a trivial task. Human annotation is not a practical solution as it is expensive, time-consuming, and labor intensive. Especially with subjective aspects such as dialogue act labels, they are often less reliable due to low annotator agreement. On the other hand, training an automatic classifier from data with standard dialogue act labels will not cover actions with specific emotion-related intent that are present in the collected data. For example, empathy towards negative affect ("That's sad.") and positive affect ("I'm happy to hear that.").

We propose unsupervised clustering of counselor dialogue to obtain dialogue act labels of expert responses. We collected a total of 6384 counselor utterances from the counseling corpus. We transform the utterances into vectors by obtaining the embeddings of the words in the utterance and averaging them. We use a word2vec model pretrained on 100 billion words of Google News (Mikolov et al., 2013). The word and utterance embeddings are of length 300. We then apply two clustering methods to the vectorized utterances: K-Means and Dirichlet process Gaussian mixture model (DPGMM).

With K-means, we perform hierarchical clustering, starting with an initial K of 8. We perform K-means clustering the second time on the clusters which are larger than half the full data size. In contrast, DPGMM is a non-parametric model, i.e. it attempts to represent the data without prior definition of the model complexity. We use the stick-breaking construction for the DPGMM. A new data point would either join an existing cluster or start a new cluster following some probabilities. We use diagonal covariance matrices to compensate for the limited amount of data. Henceforth, we refer to the result of the clustering as *cluster label*.

Cluster Analysis

We visualize the found clusters using T-SNE in Figure 1. K-Means clustering shows distinct dialogue acts characteristic in a number of clusters it found. For example, cluster 0 in Figure 1(a) consists of various utterances signaling active listening, such as follow up questions and short back channels. On the other hand, cluster 2 and 6 contains utterance showing confirmation or agreement, such as utterances containing the words "yeah," "right," and "yes." We also obtain

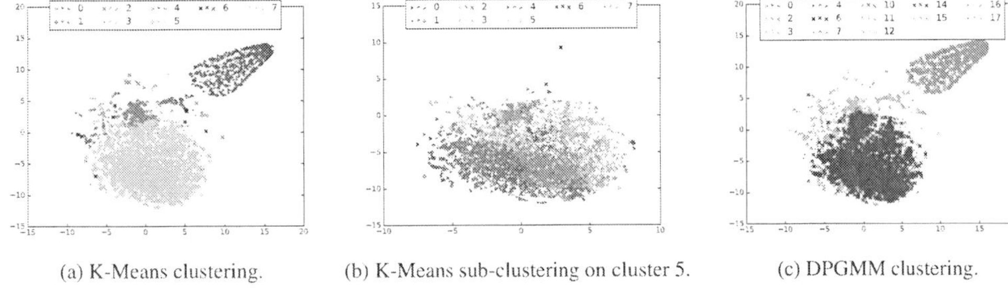

(a) K-Means clustering.   (b) K-Means sub-clustering on cluster 5.   (c) DPGMM clustering.

Figure 1: T-SNE Representation of the clustering results.

smaller clusters for appreciation or thanking and non-speech sounds, such as laughter and breathing. The rest of the utterances which are relatively longer are grouped together in a very large cluster with 4220 members (cluster 5 in Figure 1(a)).

Second clustering on cluster 5 group these utterances into smaller sub-clusters (Figure 1(b)). "I" is the most frequent word in sub-cluster 0, and "you" in sub-cluster 1. Some of the actions from the first clustering are re-discovered during the second clustering, such as thanking and appreciation in sub-cluster 7, and confirmation in sub-cluster 6. The largest sub-cluster is sub-cluster 2 with 1324 members which contain longer utterances, a combination of opinion, questions, and other sentences. In total, we obtained 15 clusters from K-means clustering.

On the other hand, the DPGMM clustering results in 13 clusters. DPGMM clustering yield a similar result, giving one huge cluster for longer sentences and smaller clusters populated with for back channel, non-speech sounds, thank you, and agreement. However, there are several differences between the results from DPGMM and K-means that are worth mentioning. First, we notice that the characteristic of each cluster is less salient compared to that of K-Means; e.g. numerous back channels can be found in several other clusters. Second, the class size distribution is more uneven: there are 6 clusters with less than 100 members, in contrast to only 1 with K-Means. Third, unlike K-Means, re-clustering of the biggest cluster is not possible as it is already represented by one component in the model.

4.2 Hierarchical Neural Dialogue System with Multiple Contexts

We propose providing higher level knowledge about the response to the model, in form of response cluster labels (Section 4.1), to aid its re-sponse generation. We propose a neural dialogue system which generate response based on multiple dialogue contexts: 1) dialogue history, 2) user emotional state, and 3) expert's action label. Henceforth we call this model the multi-context HRED (MC-HRED)

The information flow of the MC-HRED is as follows. After reading the input sequence $U_m = \{w_{m,1}, ..., w_{m,N_m}\}$, the dialogue turn is encoded into utterance representation h_{utt}.

$$h_{utt} = h_{N_m}^{utt} = f(h_{N_m-1}^{utt}, w_{m,N_m}). \quad (1)$$

h_{utt} is then fed into the dialogue encoder to model the sequence of dialogue turns into dialogue context h_{dlg}.

$$h_{dlg} = h_m^{dlg} = f(h_{m-1}^{dlg}, h_{utt}). \quad (2)$$

In MC-HRED, the h_{dlg} is then fed into the emotion and action encoders, which will then be used to encode the emotion context h_{emo} as well as the expert action label h_{act}.

$$h_{enc} = f(h_{m-1}^{enc}, h_{enc}), \quad (3)$$

where $enc = \{emo, act\}$.

The generation process of the response, U_{m+1}, is conditioned by the concatenation of the three contexts: dialogue history, emotion context, and the expert action label.

$$P_\theta(w_{n+1} = v | w_{\leq n}) = \frac{\exp(g(\text{concat}(h_{dlg}, h_{emo}, h_{act}), v))}{\sum_{v'} \exp(g(\text{concat}(h_{dlg}, h_{emo}, h_{act}), v'))}. \quad (4)$$

Figure 2 shows a schematic view of this architecture. For each the emotion and action encoders, we consider an RNN with gated recurrent unit (GRU) cells and sigmoid activation function.

165

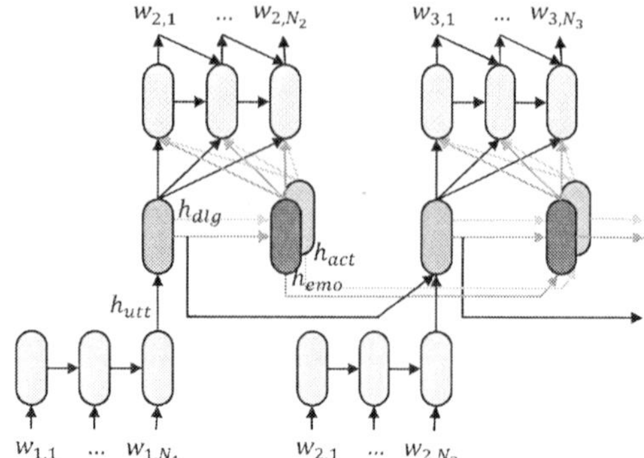

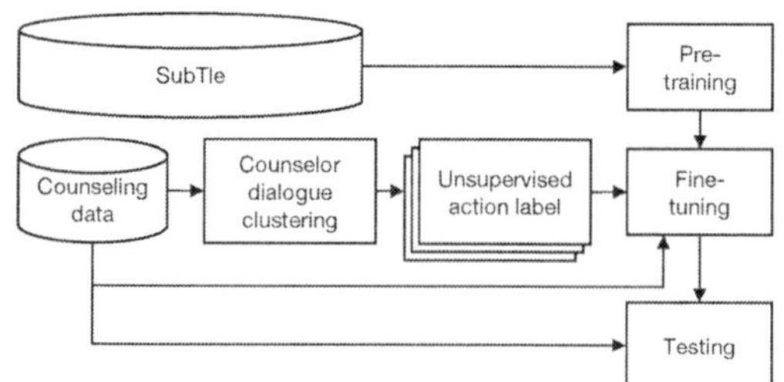

Figure 3: The flow of the experiment.

Figure 2: MC-HRED architecture. Emotion encoder is shown in dark blue, and action encoder in dark yellow. Blue NNs are relating to input, and yellow NNs to response.

Both encoders are trained together with the rest of the network. Each encoder has its own target vector, which is the emotion label of the currently processed dialogue turn U_m^{emo} and expert action label of the target response U_m^{act}. We modify the definition of the training cost to incorporate the cross entropy losses of the emotion and action encoders.

$$cost_{enc} = ((1 - U_m^{enc}) \cdot \log(1 - f(h_{enc})))$$
$$- (U_m^{enc} \cdot \log f(h_{enc})), \quad (5)$$

where $enc = \{emo, act\}$.

The training cost of the MC-HRED is a linear interpolation between the response generation error $cost_{utt}$ (i.e. negative log-likelihood of the generated response) and the prediction errors of the encoders $cost_{emo}$ and $cost_{act}$ with weights α and β which decays after every epoch.

$$cost = (1 - \alpha - \beta) \cdot cost_{utt}$$
$$+ \alpha \cdot cost_{emo} + \beta \cdot cost_{act}. \quad (6)$$

The final cost is then propagated to the network and the parameters are optimized as usual with the optimizer algorithm.

5 Experimental Set Up

Figure 3 illustrates the experimental set up of this work. Each of the steps will be explained in this section. The scope of this study is limited to text data.

5.1 Pre-trained model

Previous works have demonstrated the effectiveness of large scale conversational data in improving the quality of dialogue systems (Banchs and Li, 2012; Ameixa et al., 2014; Serban et al., 2016). In this study, we make use of SubTle (Ameixa et al., 2014), a large scale conversational corpus collected from movie subtitles, to learn the syntactic and semantic knowledge for response generation. The use of movie subtitles is particularly suitable as they are available in large amounts and reflecting natural human communication.

In our experiments, we utilize the HRED trained on the SubTle corpus as our starting model. We follow the data pre-processing method in (Serban et al., 2016). The processed SubTle corpus contained 5,503,741 query-answer pairs in total. The triple format is forced onto the pairs by treating the last dialogue turn in the triple as empty. We select the 10,000 most frequent token from the combination of SubTle and the counseling data as system vocabulary. The purpose is twofold: to help widen the intersection of words between the two corpora, and to preserve special token from the counselor corpus such as laughter and other non-speech sounds.

The model is pre-trained by feeding the SubTle dataset sequentially into the network until it converges, taking approximately 2 days to complete. In addition to the model parameters, we also learn the word embeddings of the tokens. We used word embeddings with size 300, utterance vectors of size 600, and dialogue vectors of size 1200. The parameters are randomly initialized, and then trained to optimize the log-likelihood of the training triples using the Adam optimizer.

5.2 Fine-tuning

All the models considered in this study are the result of fine-tuning the pre-trained model with the counseling corpus (Section 2). The triples from the corpus are fed sequentially into the network. To investigate the effectiveness of the proposed methods, we train multiple models with combinations of set ups.

We consider two different models: Emo-HRED as baseline model and MC-HRED as the proposed model. Emo-HRED considers only dialogue history and emotional context during the response generation, while MC-HRED considers expert action context in addition to the dialogue history and emotional context. For completeness, we also train a model that only utilized dialogue history and action context, which we will call Clust-HRED for convenience.

As emotional context, we encode the self-report emotion annotation into a one-hot vector as follows. We first obtain the average valence and arousal values of an utterance. We then discretize these values respectively into three classes: positive, neutral, and negative. The intervals for the classes are $[-1, -0.07]$ for negative, $(-0.07, 0.07)$ for neutral, and $[0.07, 1]$ for positive. We then encode this class information into a one-hot vector of length 9, one element for each of the possible combinations of valence and arousal classes, i.e. positive-positive, positive-neutral, neutral-negative, etc. Preliminary experiments showed that on the counselor corpus, this representation leads to a better performance compared to fixed-length sampling of the emotion trace.

As action context, we simply encode the cluster label of U_3, obtain as in Section 4.1, into a one-hot vector. We experimented with two cluster label sets, one produced by hierarchical K-Means clustering (15 clusters), and one by DPGMM clustering (13).

To accommodate this additional information during fine-tuning, we append new randomly initialized parameters to the utterance decoder. These parameters are trained exclusively during the fine-tuning process. All models are fine-tuned selectively. That is, we fix the utterance and dialogue encoders parameters, and selectively train only the proposed encoders as well as the decoder. This has been shown to result in a more stable model when fine-tuning with a small amount of data (Lubis et al., 2018).

We partitioned the counseling corpus into 50 recording sessions (5053 triples) for training, 5 (503) for validation, and 5 (508) for testing.

6 Evaluation and Analysis

6.1 Perplexity

We calculate model perplexity, which measures the probability of exactly regenerating the reference response in a triple. Since the target responses are assumed to be expert's response, its reproduction by the model is desirable. Perplexity has also been previously recommended for evaluating generative dialogue systems (Pietquin and Hastie, 2013).

We compute the perplexity for each triple and average it to obtain model perplexity. The model perplexities are summarized in Table 1. We compute the average test triple length (59.6 tokens), and group the test triples into two: those with below average length as "short" (294 triples), and those above as "long" (186). Average perplexities are shown for the entire test set (all), the short group, and the long group, separately.

Model	Emo.	Action	Perplexity		
			all	short	long
Emo-HRED	Yes	No	42.60	35.74	61.17
Clust-HRED	No	K-Means	39.57	32.30	57.37
		DPGMM	30.57	24.79	42.25
MC-HRED	Yes	K-Means	**29.57**	**23.23**	**38.73**
		DPGMM	32.04	25.00	42.34

Table 1: Model Perplexity of different architectures.

We obtain model with the lowest perplexity when emotion and K-Means labels are both utilized in the training and response generation process. For all models, the perplexity of long triples is consistently higher than that of short ones. More significant improvement is observed on long test triples.

Looking at the perplexity on all test triples, interestingly, the two cluster labels are affected in starkly different ways when combined with emotion labels: K-Means gain significant improvement, while DPGMM slightly suffers. We found that on long triples, Clust-HRED and MC-HRED yield similar performances when using the DPGMM cluster label. In contrast, when using K-means label, MC-HRED shows further improvement from Clust-HRED.

We separate the test triples based on the average model perplexity to analyze their properties.

Aside from triple length, no other significant difference was observed. This signals that the ability to capture context is one of the defining characteristic of a strong model for this task.

6.2 Human Subjective Evaluation

We present human judges with a dialogue triple and ask them to rate the response in terms of three criteria: 1) naturalness, which evaluates whether the response is intelligible, logically follows the dialogue context, and resembles real human response, 2) emotional impact, to measure whether the response elicits a positive emotional impact or promotes an emotionally positive conversation, and 3) engagement, to evaluate whether the proposed response shows involvement in the dialogue and promotes longer conversation by inviting more response.

We evaluate Emo-HRED and the best performing MC-HRED utilizing K-Means clustering labels. We evaluate 100 triples from the full test set, where each is judged by 20 human evaluators. Each triple is presented in A-B-A format, the first two dialogue turns are held fixed according to the test set, and the last turn is the response generated by the evaluated model. Evaluators are asked to judge the responses by stating their agreement to three statements: 1) A gives a natural response, 2) A's response elicits a positive emotional impact in B, and 3) A's response in engaging. The agreement is given using a Likert scale, ranging from 1 (strongly disagree) to 5 (strongly agree). Figure 4 summarizes the subjective evaluation result.

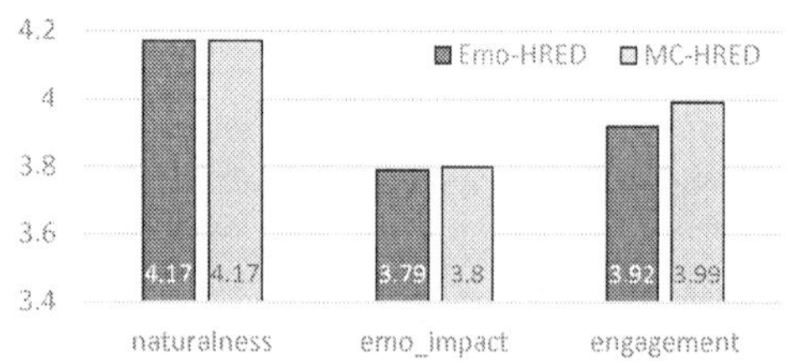

Figure 4: Human subjective rvaluation result.

We observe slight improvement on MC-HRED in the emotional impact and a more notable one in the engagement metric. On average, the responses generated by MC-HRED are 2.53 words longer compared to that of Emo-HRED. From the ratings, we also found that engagement is moderately correlated with response length, with an average Pearson r of 0.41. This signals that MC-

HRED is able to produce longer sentences which results in higher engagement, while still maintaining naturalness and emotional impact. Dialogue samples comparing the systems responses are included in Table 2.

Table 2: Comparison of system responses for two triples in test set.

U_1	oh how do you feel about that one.
U_2	yes i heard the story.
U_3 (Target)	you heard it before.
Emo-HRED	right.
MC-HRED	it's a big thing.
U_1	are you a student here?
U_2	uh yes, actually I just got, er that's my lab over there in social computing yes (laughter).
U_3 (Target)	oh really. so you've been watching us going by.
Emo-HRED	oh okay.
MC-HRED	(laughter) it's nice to meet you.

7 Conclusion

We construct a corpus containing recordings of a counselor and 30 participants following a negative emotional exposure to learn expert responses in a positive emotion elicitation scenario. We unsupervisedly cluster the expert's responses and use the resulting labels to train a dialogue system. We proposed a novel hierarchical neural architecture for response generation that is conditioned on 1) expert's action, 2) dialogue context, and 3) user emotion, encoded from user input.

The objective evaluation we conducted show that the proposed model yields lower perplexity on a held-out test set. Subsequent human subjective evaluation shows that MC-HRED is able to produce longer sentences which improve engagement while still maintaining response naturalness and emotional impact. In the future, we would like to consider emotional impact explicitly for the emotion elicitation in lieu of a data-driven approach of positive emotion elicitation. We would also like to consider other modalitiesm such as speech, for a richer emotion encoding. We acknowledge that evaluation through real user interaction needs to be carried in the future to test the system in a more realistic scenario.

Acknowledgements

Part of this work was supported by JSPS KAKENHI Grant Numbers JP17H06101 and JP17K00237.

References

Jaime C Acosta and Nigel G Ward. 2011. Achieving rapport with turn-by-turn, user-responsive emotional coloring. *Speech Communication*, 53(9-10):1137–1148.

David Ameixa, Luisa Coheur, Pedro Fialho, and Paulo Quaresma. 2014. Luke, i am your father: dealing with out-of-domain requests by using movies subtitles. In *International Conference on Intelligent Virtual Agents*, pages 13–21. Springer.

Rafael E Banchs and Haizhou Li. 2012. Iris: a chat-oriented dialogue system based on the vector space model. In *Proceedings of the ACL 2012 System Demonstrations*, pages 37–42. Association for Computational Linguistics.

Roddy Cowie, Ellen Douglas-Cowie, Susie Savvidou, Edelle McMahon, Martin Sawey, and Marc Schröder. 2000. 'FEELTRACE': An instrument for recording perceived emotion in real time. In *ISCA tutorial and research workshop (ITRW) on speech and emotion*.

Arjan Egges, Sumedha Kshirsagar, and Nadia Magnenat-Thalmann. 2004. Generic personality and emotion simulation for conversational agents. *Computer animation and virtual worlds*, 15(1):1–13.

Kate Forbes-Riley and Diane Litman. 2012. Adapting to multiple affective states in spoken dialogue. In *Proceedings of the 13th Annual Meeting of the Special Interest Group on Discourse and Dialogue*, pages 217–226. Association for Computational Linguistics.

Jonathan Gratch, Ron Artstein, Gale M Lucas, Giota Stratou, Stefan Scherer, Angela Nazarian, Rachel Wood, Jill Boberg, David DeVault, Stacy Marsella, et al. 2014. The distress analysis interview corpus of human and computer interviews. In *LREC*, pages 3123–3128. Citeseer.

James J Gross and Robert W Levenson. 1995. Emotion elicitation using films. *Cognition & emotion*, 9(1):87–108.

Sangdo Han, Yonghee Kim, and Gary Geunbae Lee. 2015. Micro-counseling dialog system based on semantic content. In *Natural Language Dialog Systems and Intelligent Assistants*, pages 63–72. Springer.

Takayuki Hasegawa, Nobuhiro Kaji, Naoki Yoshinaga, and Masashi Toyoda. 2013. Predicting and eliciting addressee's emotion in online dialogue. In *Proceedings of Association for Computational Linguistics (1)*, pages 964–972.

Ryuichiro Higashinaka, Kohji Dohsaka, and Hideki Isozaki. 2008. Effects of self-disclosure and empathy in human-computer dialogue. In *Proceedings of Spoken Language Technology Workshop*, pages 109–112. IEEE.

Nio Lasguido, Sakriani Sakti, Graham Neubig, Tomoki Toda, and Satoshi Nakamura. 2014. Utilizing human-to-human conversation examples for a multi domain chat-oriented dialog system. *Transactions on Information and Systems*, 97(6):1497–1505.

Jiwei Li, Michel Galley, Chris Brockett, Jianfeng Gao, and Bill Dolan. 2016. A diversity-promoting objective function for neural conversation models. In *Proceedings of NAACL-HLT*, pages 110–119.

Nurul Lubis, Sakriani Sakti, Koichiro Yoshino, and Satoshi Nakamura. 2017. Eliciting positive emotional impact in dialogue response selection. In *Proceedings of International Workshop on Spoken Dialogue Systems Technology*.

Nurul Lubis, Sakriani Sakti, Koichiro Yoshino, and Satoshi Nakamura. 2018. Eliciting positive emotion through affect-sensitive dialogue response generation: A neural network approach. In *Proceedings of The Thirty-Second AAAI Conference on Artificial Intelligence*. Association for the Advancement of Artificial Intelligence.

Olivier Luminet IV, Patrick Bouts, Frédérique Delie, Antony SR Manstead, and Bernard Rimé. 2000. Social sharing of emotion following exposure to a negatively valenced situation. *Cognition & Emotion*, 14(5):661–688.

Gary McKeown, Michel Valstar, Roddy Cowie, Maja Pantic, and Marc Schroder. 2012. The SEMAINE database: Annotated multimodal records of emotionally colored conversations between a person and a limited agent. *Transactions on Affective Computing*, 3(1):5–17.

Tomas Mikolov, Ilya Sutskever, Kai Chen, Greg S Corrado, and Jeff Dean. 2013. Distributed representations of words and phrases and their compositionality. In *Advances in neural information processing systems*, pages 3111–3119.

Lasguido Nio, Sakriani Sakti, Graham Neubig, Koichiro Yoshino, and Satoshi Nakamura. 2016. Neural network approaches to dialog response retrieval and generation. *IEICE Transactions on Information and Systems*.

Rosalind W Picard and Jonathan Klein. 2002. Computers that recognise and respond to user emotion: theoretical and practical implications. *Interacting with computers*, 14(2):141–169.

Olivier Pietquin and Helen Hastie. 2013. A survey on metrics for the evaluation of user simulations. *The knowledge engineering review*, 28(1):59–73.

Bernard Rime, Batja Mesquita, Stefano Boca, and Pierre Philippot. 1991. Beyond the emotional event: Six studies on the social sharing of emotion. *Cognition & Emotion*, 5(5-6):435–465.

James A Russell. 1980. A circumplex model of affect. *Journal of personality and social psychology*, 39(6):1161.

Alexandre Schaefer, Frédéric Nils, Xavier Sanchez, and Pierre Philippot. 2010. Assessing the effectiveness of a large database of emotion-eliciting films: A new tool for emotion researchers. *Cognition and Emotion*, 24(7):1153–1172.

Alexandre Schaefer and Pierre Philippot. 2005. Selective effects of emotion on the phenomenal characteristics of autobiographical memories. *Memory*, 13(2):148–160.

Iulian V Serban, Alessandro Sordoni, Yoshua Bengio, Aaron Courville, and Joelle Pineau. 2016. Building end-to-end dialogue systems using generative hierarchical neural network models. In *Thirtieth AAAI Conference on Artificial Intelligence*.

Marcin Skowron, Mathias Theunis, Sebastian Rank, and Arvid Kappas. 2013. Affect and social processes in online communication–experiments with an affective dialog system. *Transactions on Affective Computing*, 4(3):267–279.

Alessandro Sordoni, Michel Galley, Michael Auli, Chris Brockett, Yangfeng Ji, Margaret Mitchell, Jian-Yun Nie, Jianfeng Gao, and Bill Dolan. 2015. A neural network approach to context-sensitive generation of conversational responses. *arXiv preprint arXiv:1506.06714*.

Myrthe Tielman, Mark Neerincx, John-Jules Meyer, and Rosemarijn Looije. 2014. Adaptive emotional expression in robot-child interaction. In *Proceedings of the 2014 ACM/IEEE international conference on Human-robot interaction*, pages 407–414. ACM.

Oriol Vinyals and Quoc Le. 2015. A neural conversational model. *arXiv preprint arXiv:1506.05869*.

Rainer Westermann, Gunter Stahl, and F Hesse. 1996. Relative effectiveness and validity of mood induction procedures: analysis. *European Journal of social psychology*, 26:557–580.

Hao Zhou, Minlie Huang, Tianyang Zhang, Xiaoyan Zhu, and Bing Liu. 2017. Emotional chatting machine: Emotional conversation generation with internal and external memory. *arXiv preprint arXiv:1704.01074*.

Discovering User Groups for Natural Language Generation

Nikos Engonopoulos and **Christoph Teichmann** and **Alexander Koller**
Saarland University
{nikos|cteichmann|koller}@coli.uni-saarland.de

Abstract

We present a model which predicts how individual users of a dialog system understand and produce utterances based on user groups. In contrast to previous work, these user groups are not specified beforehand, but learned in training. We evaluate on two referring expression (RE) generation tasks; our experiments show that our model can identify user groups and learn how to most effectively talk to them, and can dynamically assign unseen users to the correct groups as they interact with the system.

1 Introduction

People vary widely both in their linguistic preferences when producing language and in their ability to understand specific natural-language expressions, depending on what they know about the domain, their age and cognitive capacity, and many other factors. It has long been recognized that effective NLG systems should therefore *adapt* to the current user, in order to generate language which works well for them. This adaptation needs to address all levels of the NLG pipeline, including discourse planning (Paris, 1988), sentence planning (Walker et al., 2007), and RE generation (Janarthanam and Lemon, 2014), and depends on many features of the user, including level of expertise and language proficiency, age, and gender.

Existing techniques for adapting the output of an NLG system have shortcomings which limit their practical usefulness. Some systems need user-specific information in training (Ferreira and Paraboni, 2014) and therefore cannot generalize to unseen users. Other systems assume that each user in the training data is annotated with their group, which allows them to learn a model from the data of each group. However, hand-designed user groups may not reflect the true variability of the data, and may therefore inhibit the system's ability to flexibly adapt to new users.

In this paper, we present a user adaptation model for NLG systems which induces user groups from training data in which these groups were not annotated. At training time, we probabilistically assign users to groups and learn the language preferences for each group. At evaluation time, we assume that our system has a chance to interact with each new user repeatedly – e.g., in the context of a dialogue system. It will then calculate an increasingly accurate estimate of the user's group membership based on observable behavior, and use it to generate utterances that are suitable to the user's true group.

We evaluate our model on two tasks involving the generation of referring expressions (RE). First, we predict the use of spatial relations in human-like REs in the GRE3D domain (Viethen and Dale, 2010) using a log-linear production model in the spirit of Ferreira and Paraboni (2014). Second, we predict the comprehension of generated REs, in a synthetic dataset based on data from the GIVE Challenge domain (Striegnitz et al., 2011) with the log-linear comprehension model of Engonopoulos et al. (2013). In both cases, we show that our model discovers user groups in the training data and infers the group of unseen users with high confidence after only a few interactions during testing. In the GRE3D domain, our system outperformed a strong baseline which used demographic information for the users.

2 Related Work

Differences between individual users have a substantial impact on language comprehension. Factors that play a role include level of expertise and spatial ability (Benyon and Murray, 1993); age (Häuser et al., 2017); gender (Dräger and Koller,

Proceedings of the SIGDIAL 2018 Conference, pages 171–179,
Melbourne, Australia, 12-14 July 2018. ©2018 Association for Computational Linguistics

2012); or language proficiency (Koller et al., 2010).

Individual differences are also reflected in the way people produce language. Viethen and Dale (2008) present a corpus study of human-produced REs (GRE3D3) for simple visual scenes, where they note two clearly distinguishable groups of speakers, one that always uses a spatial relation and one that never does. Ferreira and Paraboni (2014) show that a model using speaker-specific information outperforms a generic model in predicting the attributes used by a speaker when producing an RE. However, their system needs to have seen the particular speaker in training, while our system can dynamically adapt to unseen users. Ferreira and Paraboni (2017) also demonstrate that splitting speakers in predefined groups and training each group separately improves the human likeness of REs compared to training individual user models.

The ability to adapt to the comprehension and production preferences of a user is especially important in the context of a dialog system, where there are multiple chances of interacting with the same user. Some methods adapt to dialog system users by explicitly modeling the users' knowledge state. An early example is Paris (1988); she selects a discourse plan for a user, depending on their level of domain knowledge ranging between novice and expert, but provides no mechanism for inferring the group to which the user belongs. Rosenblum and Moore (1993) try to infer what knowledge a user possesses during dialogue, based on the questions they ask. Janarthanam and Lemon (2014) adapt to unseen users by using reinforcement learning with simulated users to make a system able to adjust to the level of the user's knowledge. They use five predefined groups from which they generate the simulated users' behavior, but do not assign real users to these groups. Our system makes no assumptions about the user's knowledge and does not need to train with simulated users, or use any kind of information-seeking moves; we instead rely on the groups that are discovered in training and dynamically assign new, unseen users, based only on their observable behavior in the dialog.

Another example of a user-adapting dialog component is SPaRKy (Walker et al., 2007), a trainable sentence planner that can tailor sentence plans to individual users' preferences. This requires training on separate data for each user; in contrast to this, we leverage the similarities between users and can take advantage of the full training data.

3 Log-linear models for NLG in dialog

We start with a basic model of the way in which people produce and comprehend language. In order to generalize over production and comprehension, we will simply say that a human language user exhibits a certain *behavior* b among a range of possible behaviors, in response to a *stimulus* s. The behavior of a speaker is the utterance b they produce in order to achieve a communicative goal s; the behavior of a listener is the meaning b which they assign to the utterance s they hear.

Given this terminology, we define a basic log-linear model (Berger et al., 1996) of language use as follows:

$$P(b|s; \rho) = \frac{\exp(\rho \cdot \phi(b, s))}{\sum_{b'} \exp(\rho \cdot \phi(b', s))} \qquad (1)$$

where ρ is a real-valued parameter vector of length n and $\phi(b, s)$ is a vector of real-valued *feature functions* $f_1, ..., f_n$ over behaviors and stimuli. The parameters can be trained by maximum-likelihood estimation from a corpus of observations (b, s). In addition to maximum-likelihood training it is possible to include some prior probability distribution, which expresses our belief about the probability of any parameter vector and which is generally used for regularization. The latter case is referred to as *a posteriori* training, which selects the value of ρ that maximizes the product of the parameter probability and the probability of the data.

In this paper, we focus on the use of such models in the context of the NLG module of a dialogue system, and more specifically on the generation of referring expressions (REs). Using (1) as a *comprehension* model, Engonopoulos et al. (2013) developed an RE generation model in which the stimulus $s = (r, c)$ consists of an RE r and a visual context c of the GIVE Challenge (Striegnitz et al., 2011), as illustrated in Fig. 1. The behavior is the object b in the visual scene to which the user will resolve the RE. Thus for instance, when we consider the RE $r =$"the blue button" in the context of Fig. 1, the log-linear model may assign a higher probability to the button on the right than to the one in the background. Engonopoulos and Koller (2014) develop an algorithm for generating the RE r which maximizes $P(b^*|s; \rho)$, where b^* is the intended referent in this setting.

Conversely, log-linear models can also be used to directly capture how a human speaker would refer to an object in a given scene. In this case, the stimulus $s = (a, c)$ consists of the target object a and

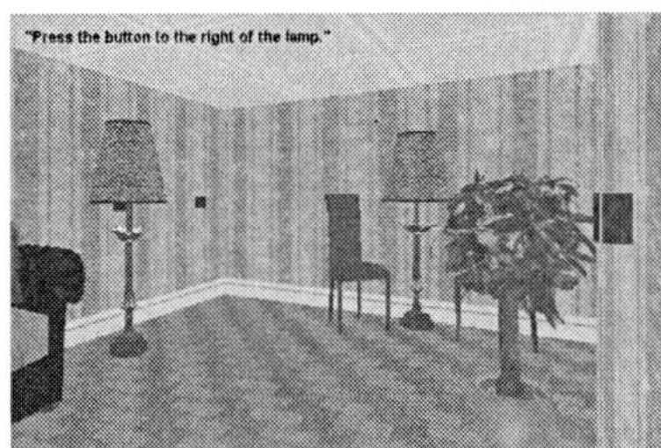

Figure 1: A visual scene and a system-generated instruction from the GIVE challenge.

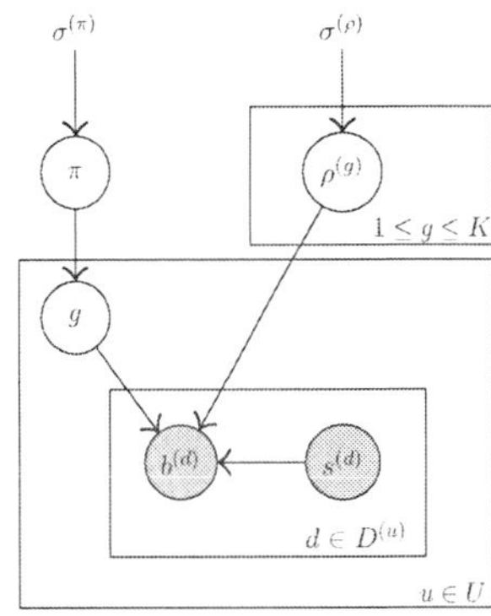

Figure 2: Plate diagram for the user group model.

the visual context c, and the behavior b is the RE. We follow Ferreira and Paraboni (2014) in training individual models for the different attributes which can be used in the RE (e.g., that a is a button; that it is blue; that the RE contains a binary relation such as "to the right of"), such that we can simply represent b as a binary choice $b \in \{1, -1\}$ between whether a particular attribute should be used in the RE or not. We can then implement an analog of Ferreira's model in terms of (1) by using feature functions $\phi(b, a, c) = b \cdot \phi'(a, c)$, where $\phi'(a, c)$ corresponds to their *context* features, which do not capture any speaker-specific information.

4 Log-linear models with user groups

As discussed above, a user-agnostic model such as (1) does not do justice to the variability of language comprehension and production across different speakers and listeners. We will therefore extend it to a model which distinguishes different *user groups*. We will not try to model why[1] users behave differently. Instead our model sorts users into groups simply based on the way in which they respond to stimuli, in the sense of Section 3, and implements this by giving each group g its own parameter vector $\rho^{(g)}$. As a theoretical example, Group 1 might contain users who reliably comprehend REs which use colors ("the green button"), whereas Group 2 might contain users who more easily understand relational REs ("the button next to the lamp"). These groups are then discovered at training time.

When our trained NLG system starts interacting with an unseen user u, it will infer the group to which u belongs based on u's observed responses to previous stimuli. Thus as the dialogue with u unfolds, the system will have an increasingly pre-

cise estimate of the group to which u belongs, and will thus be able to generate language which is increasingly well-tailored to this particular user.

4.1 Generative story

We assume training data $D = \{(b_i, s_i, u_i)\}_i$ which contains stimuli s_i together with the behaviors b_i which the users u_i exhibited in response to s_i. We write $D^{(u)} = \{(b_1^u, s_1^u), \ldots (b_N^u, s_N^u)\}$ for the data points for each user u.

The generative story we use is illustrated in Fig. 2; observable variables are shaded gray, unobserved variables and parameters to be set in training are shaded white and externally set hyperparameters have no circle around them. Arrows indicate which variables and parameters influence the probability distribution of other variables.

We assume that each user belongs to a group $g \in \{1, \ldots, K\}$, where the number K of groups is fixed beforehand based on, e.g., held out data. A group g is assigned to u at random from the distribution

$$P(g|\pi) = \frac{\exp(\pi_g)}{\sum_{g'=1}^{K} \exp(\pi_{g'})} \tag{2}$$

Here $\pi \in \mathbb{R}^K$ is a vector of weights, which defines how probable each group is a-priori.

We replace the single parameter vector ρ of (1) with group-specific parameters vectors $\rho^{(g)}$, thus obtaining a potentially different log-linear model $P(b|s; \rho^{(g)})$ for each group. After assigning a group, our model generates responses $b_1^u, \ldots, b_N^u$ at random from $P(b|s; \rho^{(g)})$, based on the group specific parameter vector and the stimuli $s_1^u, \ldots, s_N^u$. This accounts for the generation of the data.

We model the parameter vectors $\pi \in \mathbb{R}^K$, and $\rho^{(g)} \in \mathbb{R}^n$ for every $1 \leq g \leq K$ as drawn from

---

$$P(D; \theta) = \left(\prod_{u \in U} \sum_{g=1}^{K} P(g|\pi) \cdot \prod_{d \in D^{(u)}} P\left(b_d | s_d; \rho^{(g)}\right) \right) \cdot \left(\mathcal{N}\left(\pi | 0, \sigma^{(\pi)}\right) \cdot \prod_{g=1}^{K} \mathcal{N}\left(\rho^{(g)} | 0, \sigma^{(\rho)}\right) \right) \quad (3)$$

$$\mathcal{L}(\theta) = \sum_{u \in U} \log \sum_{g=1}^{K} P(g|\pi) \cdot \prod_{d \in D^{(u)}} P\left(b_d | s_d; \rho^{(g)}\right) \quad (4)$$

$$\mathcal{AL}(\theta) = \sum_{u \in U} \sum_{g=1}^{K} \left(P\left(g | D^{(u)}; \theta_{(i-1)}\right) \cdot \left(\log P(g|\pi) + \sum_{d \in D_u} \log P\left(b_d | s_d; \rho^{(g)}\right) \right) \right) \quad (5)$$

normal distributions $\mathcal{N}(0, \sigma^{(\pi)})$, and $\mathcal{N}(0, \sigma^{(\rho)})$, which are centered at 0 with externally given variances and no covariance between parameters. This has the effect of making parameter choices close to zero more probable. Consequently, our models are unlikely to contain large weights for features that only occurred a few times or which are only helpful for a few examples. This should reduce the risk of overfitting the training set.

The equation for the full probability of the data and a specific parameter setting is given in (3). The left bracket contains the likelihood of the data, while the right bracket contains the prior probability of the parameters.

4.2 Predicting user behavior

Once we have set values $\theta = (\pi, \rho^{(1)}, \ldots, \rho^{(K)})$ for all the parameters, we want to predict what behavior b a user u will exhibit in response to a stimulus s. If we encounter a completely new user u, the prior user group distribution from (2) gives the probability that this user belongs to each group. We combine this with the group-specific log-linear behavior models to obtain the distribution:

$$P(b|s; \theta) = \sum_{g=1}^{K} P\left(b|s; \rho^{(g)}\right) \cdot P(g|\pi) \quad (6)$$

Thus, we have a group-aware replacement for (1).

Furthermore, in the interactive setting of a dialogue system, we may have multiple opportunities to interact with the same user u. We can then develop a more precise estimate of u's group based on their responses to previous stimuli. Say that we have made the previous observations $D^{(u)} = \{\langle s_1, b_1 \rangle, \ldots, \langle s_N, b_N \rangle\}$ for user u. Then we can use Bayes' theorem to calculate a *posterior* estimate for u's group membership:

$$P\left(g | D^{(u)}; \theta\right) \propto P\left(D^{(u)} | \rho^{(g)}\right) \cdot P(g|\pi) \quad (7)$$

This posterior balances whether a group is likely in general against whether members of that group behave as u does. We can use $P_u(g) = P\left(g | D^{(u)}; \theta\right)$ as our new estimate for the group membership probabilities for u and replace (6) with:

$$P\left(b|s, D^{(u)}; \theta\right) = \sum_{g=1}^{K} P\left(b|s; \rho^{(g)}\right) \cdot P_u(g) \quad (8)$$

for the next interaction with u.

An NLG system can therefore adapt to each new user over time. Before the first interaction with u, it has no specific information about u and models u's behavior based on (6). As the system interacts with u repeatedly, it collects observations $D^{(u)}$ about u's behavior. This allows it to calculate an increasingly accurate posterior $P_u(g) = P\left(g | D^{(u)}; \theta\right)$ of u's group membership, and thus generate utterances which are more and more suitable to u using (8).

5 Training

So far we have not discussed how to find settings for the parameters $\theta = \pi, \rho^{(1)}, \ldots, \rho^{(K)}$, which define our probability model. The key challenge for training is the fact that we want to be able to train while treating the assignment of users to groups as unobserved.

We will use a maximum *a posteriori* estimate for θ, i.e., the setting which maximizes (3) when D is our training set. We will first discuss how to pick parameters to maximize only the left part of (3), i.e., the data likelihood, since this is the part that involves unobserved variables. We will then discuss handling the parameter prior in section 5.2.

5.1 Expectation Maximization

Gradient descent based methods (Nocedal and Wright, 2006) exist for finding the parameter settings which maximize the likelihood for log-linear models, under the conditions that all relevant variables are observed in the training data. If group assignments were given, gradient computations, and therefore gradient based maximization, would be straightforward for our model. One algorithm specifically designed to solve maximization problems with unknown variables by reducing them to the case where all variables are observed, is the expectation maximization (EM) algorithm (Neal and Hinton, 1999). Instead of maximizing the data likelihood from (3) directly, EM equivalently maximizes the log-likelihood, given in (4). It helps us deal with unobserved variables by introducing "pseudo-observations" based on the expected frequency of the unobserved variables.

EM is an iterative algorithm which produces a sequence of parameter settings $\theta_{(1)}, \ldots, \theta_{(n)}$. Each will achieve a larger value for (4). Each new setting is generated in two steps: (1) an lower bound on the log-likelihood is generate and (2) the new parameter setting is found by optimizing this lower bound. To find the lower bound we compute the probability for every possible value the unobserved variables could have had, based on the observed variables and the parameter setting $\theta_{(i-1)}$ from the last iteration step. Then the lower bound essentially assumes that each assignment was seen with a frequency equal to these probabilities - these are the "pseudo-observations".

In our model the unobserved variables are the assignments of users to groups. The probability of seeing each user u assigned to a group, given all the data $D^{(u)}$ and the model parameters from the last iteration $\theta_{(i-1)}$, is simply the posterior group membership probability $P\left(g|D^{(u)}; \theta_{(i-1)}\right)$. The lower bound is then given by (5). This is the sum of the log probabilities of the data points under each group model, weighted by $P\left(g|D^{(u)}; \theta_{(i-1)}\right)$. We can now use gradient descent techniques to optimize this lower bound.

5.1.1 Maximizing the Lower Bound

To fully implement EM we need a way to maximize (5). This can be achieved with gradient based methods such as L-BFGS (Nocedal and Wright, 2006). Here the gradient refers to the vector of all partial derivatives of the function with respect to each dimension of θ. We therefore need to calculate these partial derivatives.

There are existing implementations of the gradient computations our base model such as in Engonopoulos et al. (2013). The gradients of (5)

for each of the $\rho^{(g)}$ is simply the gradient for the base model on each datapoint d weighted by $P\left(g|D^{(u)}; \theta_{(i-1)}\right)$ if $d \in D_u$, i.e., the probability that the user u from which the datapoint originates belongs to group g. We can therefore compute the gradients needed for each $\rho^{(g)}$ by using implementations developed for the base model.

We also need gradients for the parameters in π, which are only used in our extended model. We can use the rules for computing derivatives to find, for each dimension g:

$$\frac{\partial \mathcal{UL}(\theta)}{\partial \pi_g} = \sum_{u \in U} P_u(g) - \frac{\exp\left(\pi_g\right)}{\sum_{g'=1}^{K} \exp\left(\pi_{g'}\right)}$$

where $P_u(g) = P\left(g|D^{(u)}; \theta_{(i-1)}\right)$. Using these gradients we can use L-BFGS to maximize the lower bound and implement the EM iteration.

5.2 Handling the Parameter Prior

So far we have discussed maximization only for the likelihood without accounting for the prior probabilities for every parameter. To obtain our full training objective we add the log of the right hand side of (3):

$$\log\left(\mathcal{N}\left(\pi|0, \sigma^{(\pi)}\right) \cdot \prod_{g=1}^{K} \mathcal{N}\left(\rho^{(g)}|0, \sigma^{(\rho)}\right)\right)$$

i.e., the parameter prior, to (4) and (5). The gradient contribution from these priors can be computed with standard techniques.

5.3 Training Iteration

We can now implement an EM loop, which maximizes (3) as follows: we randomly pick an initial value $\theta_{(0)}$ for all parameters. Then we repeatedly compute the $P\left(g|D^{(u)}; \theta_{(i-1)}\right)$ values and maximize the lower bound using L-BFGS to find $\theta_{(i)}$. This EM iteration is guaranteed to eventually converge towards a local optimum of our objective function. Once change in the objective falls below a pre-defined threshold, we keep the final θ setting.

For our implementation we make a small improvement to the approach: L-BFGS is itself an iterative algorithm and instead of running it until convergence every time we need to find a new $\theta_{(i)}$, we only let it take a few steps. Even if we just took a single L-BFGS step in each iteration, we would still obtain a correct algorithm (Neal and

Hinton, 1999) and this has the advantage that we do not spend time trying to find a $\theta_{(i)}$ which is a good fit for the likely poor group assignments $P\left(g|D^{(u)};\theta_{(i-1)}\right)$ we obtain from early parameter estimates.

6 Evaluation

Our model can be used in any component of a dialog system for which a prediction of the user's behavior is needed. In this work, we evaluate it in two NLG-related prediction tasks: RE production and RE comprehension. In both cases we evaluate the ability of our model to predict the user's behavior given a stimulus. We expect our user-group model to gradually improve its prediction accuracy compared to a generic baseline without user groups as it sees more observations from a given user.

In all experiments described below we set the prior variances $\sigma_\gamma = 1.0$ and $\sigma_\pi = 0.3$ after trying out values between 0.1 and 10 on the training data of the comprehension experiment.

6.1 RE production

Task The task of RE generation can be split in two steps: *attribute selection*, the selection of the visual attributes to be used in the RE such as color, size, relation to other objects and *surface realization*, the generation of a full natural language expression. We focus here on attribute selection: given a visual scene and a target object, we want to predict the set of attributes of the target object that a human speaker would use in order to describe it. Here we treat attribute selection in terms of individual classification decisions on whether to use each attribute, as described in Section 3. More specifically, we focus on predicting whether the speaker will use a *spatial relation* to another object ("landmark"). Our motivation for choosing this attribute stems from the fact that previous authors (Viethen and Dale, 2008; Ferreira and Paraboni, 2014) have found substantial variation between different users with respect to their preference towards using spatial relations.

Data We use the GRE3D3 dataset of human-produced REs (Viethen and Dale, 2010), which contains 630 descriptions for 10 scenes collected from 63 users, each describing the same target object in each scene. 35% of the descriptions in this corpus use a spatial relation. An example of such a scene can be seen in Fig. 3.

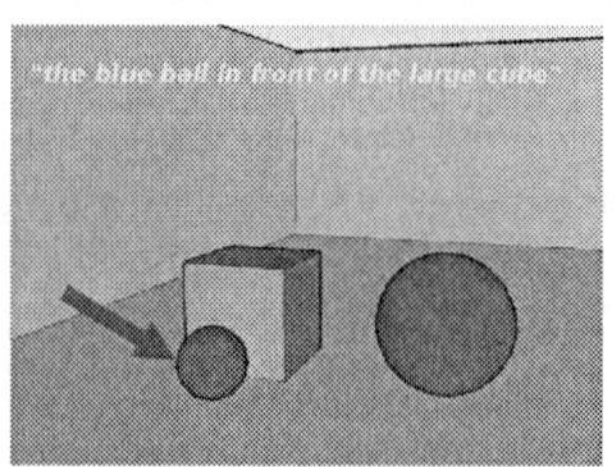

Figure 3: A sample scene with a human-produced RE from the GRE3D3 dataset.

Models We use two baselines for comparison:

Basic: The state-of-the-art model on this task with this dataset, under the assumption that users are seen in training, is presented in Ferreira and Paraboni (2014). They define context features such as type of relation between the target object and its landmark, number of object of the same color or size, etc., then train an SVM classifier to predict the use of each attribute. We recast their model in terms of a log-linear model with the same features, to make it fit with the setup of Section 3.

Basic++: Ferreira and Paraboni (2014) also take speaker features into account. We do not use speaker identity and the speaker's attribute frequency vector, because we only evaluate on unseen users. We do use their other speaker features (age, gender), together with *Basic*'s context features; this gives us a strong baseline which is aware of manually annotated user group characteristics.

We compare these baselines to our *Group* model for values of K between 1 and 10, using the exact same features as *Basic*. We do not use the speaker features of *Basic++*, because we do not want to rely on manually annotated groups. Note that our results are not directly comparable with those of Ferreira and Paraboni (2014), because of a different training-test split: their model requires having seen speakers in training, while we explicitly want to test our model's ability to generalize to unseen users.

Experimental setup We evaluate using cross-validation, splitting the folds so that all speakers we see in testing are previously unseen in training. We use 9 folds in order to have folds of the same size (each containing 70 descriptions coming from 7 speakers). At each iteration we train on 8 folds and test on the 9th. At test time, we process each test instance iteratively: we first predict for each instance whether the user u would use a spatial relation or not and test our prediction; we then add the

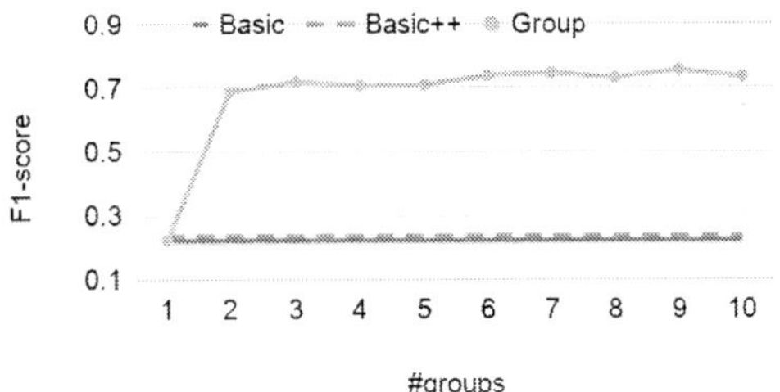

Figure 4: F1 scores on test data for values of K between 1 and 10 in the production experiment.

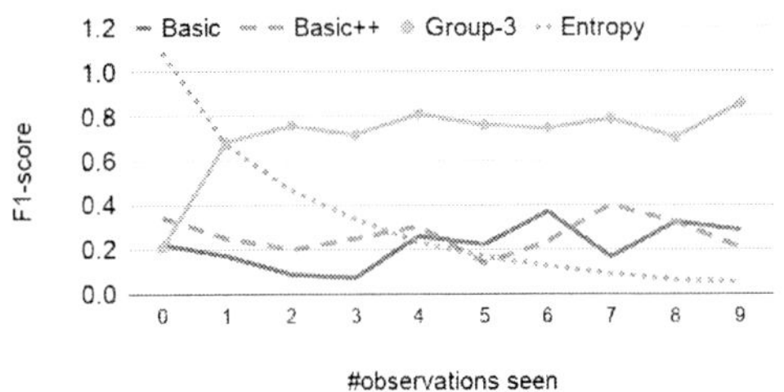

Figure 5: F1-score evolution with increasing number of observations from the user in the production experiment.

actual observation from the corpus to the set $D^{(u)}$ of observations for this particular user, in order to update our estimate about their group membership.

Results　Figure 4 shows the test F1-score (micro-averaged over all folds) as we increase the number of groups, compared to the baselines. For our *Group* models, these are averaged over all interactions with the user. Our model gets F1-scores between 0.69 and 0.76 for all values of $K > 1$, out-performing both *Basic* (0.22) and *Basic++* (0.23).

In order to take a closer look at our model's behavior, we also show the accuracy of our model as it observes more instances at test time. We compare the model with $K = 3$ groups against the two baselines. Figure 5 shows that the group model's F1-score increases dramatically after the first two observations and then stays high throughout the test phase, always outperforming both baselines by at least 0.37 F1-score points after the first observation. The baseline models of course are not expected to improve with time; fluctuations are due to differences between the visual scenes. In the same figure, we plot the evolution of the entropy of the group model's posterior distribution over the groups (see (7)). As expected, the model is highly uncertain at the beginning of the test phase about which group the user belongs to, then gets more and more certain as the set $D^{(u)}$ of observations from that user grows.

6.2　RE comprehension

Task　Our next task is to predict the referent to which a user will resolve an RE in the context of a visual scene. Our model is given a stimulus $s = (r, c)$ consisting of an instruction containing an RE r and a visual context c and outputs a probability distribution over all possible referents b. Such a model can be used by a probabilistic RE generator to select an RE which is highly likely to be correctly understood by the user or predict potential

misunderstandings (see Section 3).

Data　We use the GIVE-2.5 corpus for training and the GIVE-2 corpus for testing our model (the same used by Engonopoulos et al. (2013)). These contain recorded observations of dialog systems giving instructions to users who play a game in a 3D environment. Each instruction contains an RE r, which is recorded in the data together with the visual context c at the time the instruction was given. The object b which the user understood as the referent of the RE is inferred by the immediately subsequent action of the user. In total, we extracted 2927 observations by 403 users from GIVE-25 and 5074 observations by 563 users from GIVE-2.

Experimental setup　We follow the training method described in Section 3. At test time, we present the observations from each user in the order they occur in the test data; for each stimulus, we ask our models to predict the referent a which the user understood to be the referent of the RE, and compare with the recorded observation. We subsequently add the recorded observation to the dataset for the user and continue.

Models　As a baseline, we use the *Basic* model described in Section 3, with the features of the "semantic" model of Engonopoulos et al. (2013). Those features capture information about the objects in the visual scene (e.g. salience) and some basic semantic properties of the RE (e.g. color, position). We use those features for our *Group* model as well, and evaluate for K between 1 and 10.

Results on GIVE data　*Basic* had a test accuracy of 72.70%, which was almost identical with the accuracy of our best *Group* model for $K = 6$ (72.78%). This indicates that our group model does not differentiate between users. Indeed, after training, the 6-group model assigns 81% prior probability to one of the groups, and effectively gets stuck with this assignment while testing; the mean entropy of the posterior group distribution only falls from an initial 1.1 to 0.7 after 10 observations.

We speculate that the reason behind this is that the features we use are not sensitive enough to capture the differences between the users in this data. Since our model relies completely on observable behavior, it also relies on the ability of the features to make relevant distinctions between users.

Results on synthetic data In order to test this hypothesis, we made a synthetic dataset based on the GIVE datasets with 1000 instances from 100 users, in the following way: for each user, we randomly selected 10 scenes from GIVE-2, and replaced the target the user selected, so that half of the users always select the target with the highest visual salience, and the other half always select the one with the lowest. Our aim was to test whether our model is capable of identifying groups when they are clearly present in the data and exhibit differences which our features are able to capture.

We evaluated the same models in a 2-fold cross-validation. Figure 6 shows the prediction accuracy for *Basic* and the *Group* models for K from 1 to 10. All models for $K > 1$ clearly outperform the baseline model: the 2-group model gets 62.3% vs 28.6% averaged over all test examples, while adding more than two groups does not further improve the accuracy. We also show in Figure 7 the evolution of the accuracy as $D^{(u)}$ grows: the *Group* model with $K = 2$ reaches a 64% testing accuracy after seeing two observations from the same user. In the same figure, the entropy of the posterior distribution over groups (see production experiment) falls towards zero as $D^{(u)}$ grows. These results show that our model is capable of correctly assigning a user to the group they belong to, once the features are adequate for distinguishing between different user behaviors.

6.3 Discussion

Our model was shown to be successful in discovering groups of users with respect to their behavior, within datasets which present discernible user variation. In particular, if all listeners are influenced in a similar way by e.g. the visual salience of an object, then the group model cannot learn different weights for the visual salience feature; if this happens for all available features, there are effectively no groups for our model to discover.

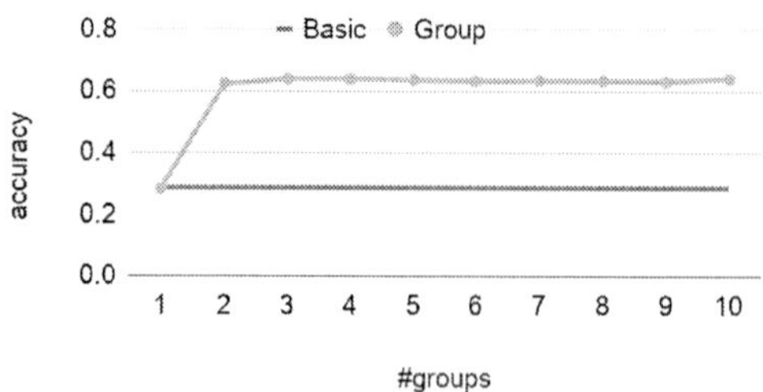

Figure 6: Prediction accuracies in the comprehension experiment with synthetic data.

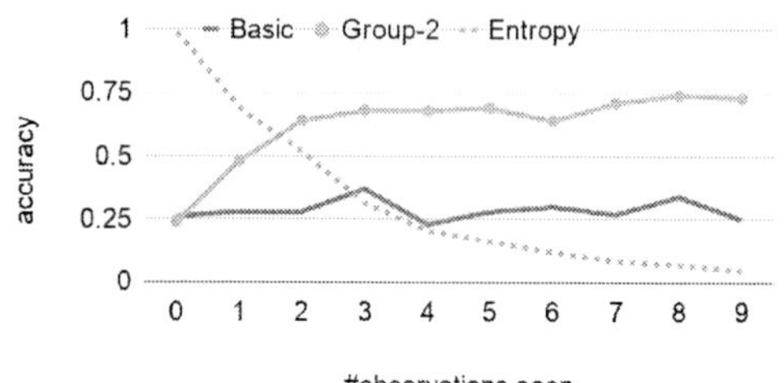

Figure 7: Accuracy evolution with increasing number of observations from the user in the comprehension experiment with synthetic data.

Once the groups have been discovered, our model can then very quickly distinguish between them at test time. This is reflected in the steep performance improvement even after the first user observation in both the real data experiment in 6.1 and the synthetic data experiment in 6.2.

7 Conclusion

We have presented a probabilistic model for NLG which predicts the behavior of individual users of a dialog system by dynamically assigning them to user groups, which were discovered during training[2]. We showed for two separate NLG-related tasks, RE production and RE comprehension, how our model, after being trained with data that is not annotated with user groups, can quickly adapt to unseen users as it gets more observations from them in the course of a dialog and makes increasingly accurate predictions about their behavior.

Although in this work we apply our model to tasks related to NLG, nothing hinges on this choice; it can also be applied to any other dialog-related prediction task where user variation plays a role. In the future, we will also try to apply the basic principles of our user group approach to more sophisticated underlying models, such as neural networks.

---

[2]Our code and data is available in `https://bit.ly/2jTu1Vm`

References

David Benyon and Dianne Murray. 1993. Developing adaptive systems to fit individual aptitudes. In *Proceedings of the 1st international conference on Intelligent user interfaces*. ACM, pages 115–121.

Adam L. Berger, Stephen A. Della Pietra, and Vincent J. Della Pietra. 1996. A maximum entropy approach to natural language processing. *Computational Linguistics* 22.

Markus Dräger and Alexander Koller. 2012. Generation of landmark-based navigation instructions from open-source data. In *Proceedings of the Thirteenth Conference of the European Chapter of the ACL*.

Nikos Engonopoulos and Alexander Koller. 2014. Generating effective referring expressions using charts. In *Proceedings of the INLG and SIGDIAL 2014 Joint Session*. pages 6–15.

Nikos Engonopoulos, Martín Villalba, Ivan Titov, and Alexander Koller. 2013. Predicting the resolution of referring expressions from user behavior. In *Proceedings of the 2013 Conference on Empirical Methods in Natural Language Processing*. pages 1354–1359.

Thiago Castro Ferreira and Ivandré Paraboni. 2017. Improving the generation of personalised descriptions. In *Proceedings of the 10th International Conference on Natural Language Generation*. pages 233–237.

Thiago Castro Ferreira and Ivandr Paraboni. 2014. Referring expression generation: taking speakers preferences into account. In *Proceedings of the International Conference on Text, Speech, and Dialogue*.

Katja Häuser, Jutta Kray, and Vera Demberg. 2017. Age differences in language comprehension during driving: Recovery from prediction errors is more effortful for older adults. In *Proceedings of CogSci*.

Srinivasan Janarthanam and Oliver Lemon. 2014. Adaptive generation in dialogue systems using dynamic user modeling. *Computational Linguistics* 40.

Alexander Koller, Kristina Striegnitz, Andrew Gargett, Donna Byron, Justine Cassell, Robert Dale, Johanna Moore, and Jon Oberlander. 2010. Report on the Second NLG Challenge on Generating Instructions in Virtual Environments (GIVE-2). In *Proceedings of the 6th International Natural Language Generation Conference*.

Radford M. Neal and Geoffrey E. Hinton. 1999. A view of the em algorithm that justifies incremental, sparse, and other variants. In Michael I. Jordan, editor, *Learning in graphical models*, MIT Press, Cambridge, MA, USA, pages 355–368. http://dl.acm.org/citation.cfm?id=308574.308679.

Jorge Nocedal and Stephen Wright. 2006. *Numerical Optimization*. Springer.

Cecile Paris. 1988. Tailoring object descriptions to a user's level of expertise. *Computational Linguistics* 14.

J. A. Rosenblum and J. D. Moore. 1993. Participating in instructional dialogues: Finding and exploiting relevant prior explanations. In *Proceedings of the World Conference on Artificial Intelligence in Education*.

Kristina Striegnitz, Alexandre Denis, Andrew Gargett, Konstantina Garoufi, Alexander Koller, and Mariet Theune. 2011. Report on the Second Second Challenge on Generating Instructions in Virtual Environments (GIVE-2.5). In *Proceedings of the 13th European Workshop on Natural Language Generation*.

Jette Viethen and Robert Dale. 2008. The use of spatial relations in referring expression generation. In *Proceedings of the Fifth International Natural Language Generation Conference*. Association for Computational Linguistics, pages 59–67.

Jette Viethen and Robert Dale. 2010. Speaker-dependent variation in content selection for referring expression generation. In *Proceedings of the Australasian Language Technology Association Workshop 2010*. pages 81–89.

Marilyn Walker, Amanda Stent, Francois Mairesse, and Rashmi Prasad. 2007. Individual and domain adaptation in sentence planning for dialogue. *Journal of AI Research* 30.

Controlling Personality-Based Stylistic Variation
with Neural Natural Language Generators

Shereen Oraby[1], Lena Reed[1], Shubhangi Tandon[1],
Sharath T.S.[1], Stephanie Lukin[2], and Marilyn Walker[1]
[1]Natural Language and Dialogue Systems Lab, University of California, Santa Cruz
[2]U.S. Army Research Laboratory, Los Angeles, CA
`{soraby,lireed,shtandon,sturuvek,mawalker}@ucsc.edu`
`stephanie.m.lukin.civ@mail.mil`

Abstract

Natural language generators for task-oriented dialogue must effectively realize system dialogue actions and their associated semantics. In many applications, it is also desirable for generators to control the style of an utterance. To date, work on task-oriented neural generation has primarily focused on semantic fidelity rather than achieving stylistic goals, while work on style has been done in contexts where it is difficult to measure content preservation. Here we present three different sequence-to-sequence models and carefully test how well they disentangle content and style. We use a statistical generator, PERSONAGE, to synthesize a new corpus of over 88,000 restaurant domain utterances whose style varies according to models of personality, giving us total control over both the semantic content and the stylistic variation in the training data. We then vary the amount of explicit stylistic supervision given to the three models. We show that our most explicit model can simultaneously achieve high fidelity to both semantic and stylistic goals: this model adds a context vector of 36 stylistic parameters as input to the hidden state of the encoder at each time step, showing the benefits of explicit stylistic supervision, even when the amount of training data is large.

1 Introduction

The primary aim of natural language generators (NLGs) for task-oriented dialogue is to effectively realize system dialogue actions and their associated content parameters. This requires training data that allows the NLG to learn how to map

semantic representations for system dialogue acts to one or more possible outputs (see Figure 1, (Novikova et al., 2016)). Because neural generators often make semantic errors such as deleting, repeating or hallucinating content, to date previous work on task-oriented neural generation has primarily focused on faithfully rendering the meaning of the system's dialogue act (Dusek and Jurcícek, 2016b; Lampouras and Vlachos, 2016; Mei et al., 2015; Wen et al., 2015).

INFORM(NAME[THE EAGLE], EATTYPE[COFFEE SHOP], FOOD[ENGLISH], PRICERANGE[HIGH], CUSTOMER-RATING[AVERAGE], AREA[CITY CENTRE], FAMI-LYFRIENDLY[YES], NEAR[BURGER KING])
The three star coffee shop, The Eagle, located near Burger King, gives families a high priced option for English food in the city centre.
Let's see what we can find on The Eagle. Right, The Eagle is a coffee shop with a somewhat average rating. The Eagle is kid friendly, also it's an English restaurant and expensive, also it is near Burger King in the city centre, you see?

Figure 1: Dialogue Act Meaning Representation (MR) with content parameters and outputs

However, in many applications it is also desirable for generators to control the style of an utterance independently of its content. For example, in Figure 1, the first output uses more formal language and complex syntactic structures, as one might see in written language, while the other uses simpler syntax and pragmatic markers characteristic of oral language (Biber, 1991). In this paper, we create several different sequence-to-sequence models and compare how well they can disentangle content and style. Controlling the style of the output requires disentangling the content from the style, but previous neural models aimed at achieving stylistic goals have not focused on task-oriented dialogue where specific semantic attributes and values must be communicated (as per the MR in Figure 1), and where semantic fi-

Proceedings of the SIGDIAL 2018 Conference, pages 180–190,
Melbourne, Australia, 12-14 July 2018. ©2018 Association for Computational Linguistics

Personalities	Realization
MEANING REPRESENTATION (MR)	NAME[FITZBILLIES], EATTYPE[PUB], FOOD[ITALIAN], PRICERANGE[MODERATE], CUSTOMER RATING[DECENT], AREA[RIVERSIDE], FAMILYFRIENDLY[NO], NEAR['THE SORRENTO']
NO-AGG/ NO-PRAG	Fitzbillies is a pub. Fitzbillies has a decent rating. Fitzbillies is moderately priced. Fitzbillies is in riverside. Fitzbillies is an Italian restaurant. Fitzbillies is not family friendly. Fitzbillies is near The Sorrento.
AGREEABLE	Let's see what we can find on Fitzbillies. I see, well it is a pub with a decent rating, also it is an Italian restaurant in riverside and moderately priced near The Sorrento, also it isn't family friendly, you see?
DISAGREEABLE	I mean, everybody knows that moderately priced Fitzbillies is in riverside with a decent rating. It's near The Sorrento. It isn't family friendly. It is an Italian place. It is a pub.
CONSCIENTIOUS	Let's see what we can find on Fitzbillies. I see, well it is a pub with a decent rating, it isn't kid friendly and it's moderately priced near The Sorrento and an Italian restaurant in riverside.
UNCONSCIENTIOUS	Oh god yeah, I don't know. Fitzbillies is a pub with a decent rating, also it is moderately priced near The Sorrento and an Italian place in riverside and it isn't kid friendly.
EXTRAVERT	Basically, Fitzbillies is an Italian place near The Sorrento and actually moderately priced in riverside, it has a decent rating, it isn't kid friendly and it's a pub, you know.

Table 1: Sample neural model output realizations for the same MR for PERSONAGE's personalities

delity can be precisely measured.[1]

One of the main challenges is the lack of parallel corpora realizing the same content with different styles. Thus we create a large, novel parallel corpus with specific style parameters and specific semantics, by using an existing statistical generator, PERSONAGE (Mairesse and Walker, 2010), to synthesize over 88,000 utterances in the restaurant domain that vary in style according to psycholinguistic models of personality.[2] PERSONAGE can generate a very large number of stylistic variations for any given dialogue act, thus yielding, to our knowledge, the largest style-varied NLG training corpus in existence. The strength of this new corpus is that: (1) we can use the PERSONAGE generator to generate as much training data as we want; (2) it allows us to systematically vary a specific set of stylistic parameters and the network architectures; (3) it allows us to systematically test the ability of different models to generate outputs that faithfully realize both the style and content of the training data.[3]

We develop novel neural models that vary the amount of explicit stylistic supervision given to the network, and we explore, for the first time, explicit control of multiple interacting stylistic parameters. We show that the no-supervision (NO-SUP) model, a baseline sequence-to-sequence model (Sutskever et al., 2014; Dusek and Jurcícek, 2016b), produces semantically correct outputs, but

eliminates much of the stylistic variation that it saw in the training data. MODEL_TOKEN provides minimal supervision by allocating a latent variable in the encoding as a label for each style, similar to the use of language labels in machine translation (Johnson et al., 2017). This model learns to generate coherent and stylistically varied output without explicit exposure to language rules, but makes more semantic errors. MODEL_CONTEXT adds another layer to provide an additional encoding of individual stylistic parameters to the network. We show that it performs best on both measures of semantic fidelity and stylistic variation. The results suggest that neural architectures can benefit from explicit stylistic supervision, even with a large training set.

2 Corpus Creation

We aim to systematically create a corpus that can be used to test how different neural architectures affect the ability of the trained model to disentangle style from content, and faithfully produce semantically correct utterances that vary style. We use PERSONAGE, an existing statistical generator: due to space, we briefly explain how it works, referring the interested reader to Mairesse and Walker (2010, 2011) for details.

PERSONAGE requires as input: (1) a meaning representation (MR) of a dialogue act and its content parameters, and (2) a parameter file that tells it how frequently to use each of its stylistic parameters. Sample model outputs are shown in the second row of Figure 1 and in Table 1, illustrating some stylistic variations PERSONAGE produces.

To generate our novel corpus, we utilize the

---

[1] We leave a detailed review of related work to Section 6.

[2] Our stylistic variation for NLG corpus is available at: nlds.soe.ucsc.edu/stylistic-variation-nlg

[3] Section 4 quantifies the naturalness of PERSONAGE outputs.

MRs from the E2E Generation Challenge.[4] The MR in Figure 1 illustrates **all 8** available attributes. We added a dictionary entry for each attribute to PERSONAGE so that it can express that attribute.[5] These dictionary entries are syntactic representations for very simple sentences: the NO-AGG/NO-PRAG row of Table 1 shows a sample realization of each attribute in its own sentence based on its dictionary entry.

Dataset	Number of Attributes in MR					
	3	4	5	6	7	8
TRAIN	0.13	0.30	0.29	0.22	0.06	0.01
TEST	0.02	0.04	0.06	0.15	0.35	0.37

Table 2: Percentage of the MRs in training and test in terms of number of attributes in the MR

We took advantage of the setup of the E2E Generation Challenge and used their MRs, exactly duplicating their split between training, dev and test MRs, because they ensured that the dev and test MRs had not been seen in training. The frequencies of longer utterances (more attribute MRs) vary across train and test, with actual distributions in Table 2, showing how the test set was designed to be challenging, while the test set in Wen et al. (2015) averages less than 2 attributes per MR (Nayak et al., 2017). We combine their dev and training MRs resulting in 3784 unique MRs in the training set, and generate 17,771 reference utterances per personality for a training set size of 88,855 utterances. The test set consists of 278 unique MRs and we generate 5 references per personality for a test size of 1,390 utterances.

The experiments are based on two types of parameters provided with PERSONAGE: aggregation parameters and pragmatic parameters.[6] The NO-AGG/NO-PRAG row of Table 1 shows what PERSONAGE would output if it did not use any of its stylistic parameters. The top half of Table 3 illustrates the aggregation parameters: these parameters control how the NLG combines attributes into sentences, e.g., whether it tries to create complex sentences by combining attributes into phrases and

Attribute	Example
AGGREGATION OPERATIONS	
PERIOD	*X serves Y. It is in Z.*
"WITH" CUE	*X is in Y, with Z.*
CONJUNCTION	*X is Y and it is Z. & X is Y, it is Z.*
ALL MERGE	*X is Y, W and Z & X is Y in Z*
"ALSO" CUE	*X has Y, also it has Z.*
PRAGMATIC MARKERS	
ACK_DEFINITIVE	*right, ok*
ACK_JUSTIFICATION	*I see, well*
ACK_YEAH	*yeah*
CONFIRMATION	*let's see what we can find on X, let's see ......, did you say X?*
INITIAL REJECTION	*mmm, I'm not sure, I don't know.*
COMPETENCE MIT.	*come on, obviously, everybody knows that*
FILLED PAUSE STATIVE	*err, I mean, mmhm*
DOWN_KIND_OF	*kind of*
DOWN_LIKE	*like*
DOWN_AROUND	*around*
EXCLAIM	*!*
INDICATE SURPRISE	*oh*
GENERAL SOFTENER	*sort of, somewhat, quite, rather*
DOWN_SUBORD	*I think that, I guess*
EMPHASIZER	*really, basically, actually, just*
EMPH_YOU_KNOW	*you know*
EXPLETIVES	*oh god, damn, oh gosh, darn*
IN GROUP MARKER	*pal, mate, buddy, friend*
TAG QUESTION	*alright?, you see? ok?*

Table 3: Aggregation and Pragmatic Operations

what types of combination operations it uses. The pragmatic operators are shown in the second half of Table 3. Each parameter value can be set to `high`, `low`, or `don't care`.

To use PERSONAGE to create training data mapping the same MR to multiple personality-based variants, we set **values** for **all** of the parameters in Table 3 using the stylistic models defined by Mairesse and Walker (2010) for the following Big Five personality traits: agreeable, disagreeable, conscientiousness, unconscientiousness, and extravert. Figure 2 shows that each personality produces data that represents a stylistically distinct distribution. These models are probabilistic and specified values are automatically broadened within a range, thus each model can produce 10's of variations for each MR. Note that while each personality type distribution can be characterized by a single stylistic label (the personality), Figure 2 illustrates that each distribution is characterized by multiple interacting stylistic parameters.

Each parameter modifies the linguistic structure in order to create distributionally different subcorpora. To see the effect of each personality using a different set of aggregation operators, cross-reference the aggregation operations in Table 3 with an examination of the outputs in Table 1. The

---

[4] http://www.macs.hw.ac.uk/InteractionLab/E2E/

[5] PERSONAGE supports a one-to-many mapping from attributes to elementary syntactic structures for expressing that attribute, but here we use only one dictionary entry. PERSONAGE also allows for discourse relations such as justification or contrast to hold between content items, but the E2E MRs do not include such relations.

[6] We disable parameters related to content selection, syntactic template selection and lexical choice.

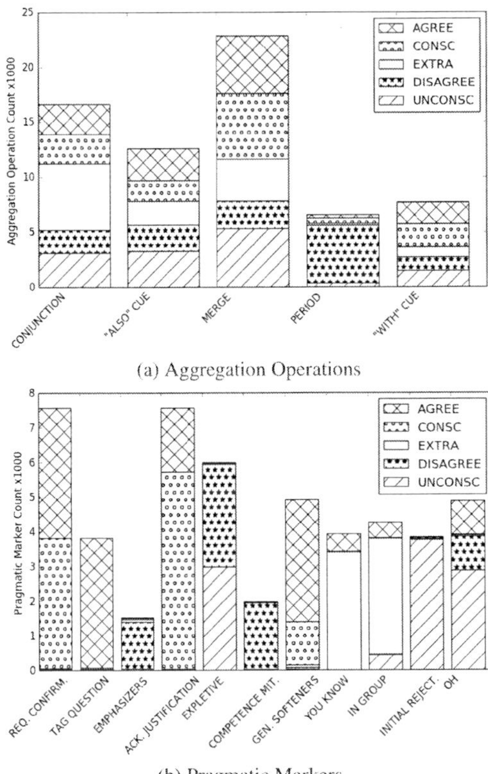

(a) Aggregation Operations

(b) Pragmatic Markers

Figure 2: Frequency of the Top 2 most frequent Aggregation and Pragmatic Markers in Train

simplest choice for aggregation does not combine attributes at all: this is represented by the PERIOD operator, which, if used persistently, results in an output with each content item in its own sentence as in the NO-AGG/NO-PRAG row, or the content being realized over multiple sentences as in the DISAGREEABLE row (5 sentences). However, if the other aggregation operations have a high value, PERSONAGE prefers to combine simple sentences into complex ones whenever it can, e.g., the EX-TRAVERT personality example in Table 1 combines all the attributes into a single sentence by repeated use of the ALL MERGE and CONJUNC-TION operations. The CONSCIENTIOUS row in Table 1 illustrates the use of the WITH-CUE aggregation operation, e.g., *with a decent rating*. Both the AGREEABLE and CONSCIENTIOUS rows in Table 1 provide examples of the ALSO-CUE aggregation operation. In PERSONAGE, the aggregation operations are defined as syntactic operations on the dictionary entry's syntactic tree. Thus to mimic these operations correctly, the neural model

must derive latent representations that function as though they also operate on syntactic trees.

The pragmatic operators in the second half of Table 3 are intended to achieve particular pragmatic effects in the generated outputs: for example the use of a hedge such as *sort of* softens a claim and affects perceptions of friendliness and politeness (Brown and Levinson, 1987), while the exaggeration associated with emphasizers like *actually, basically, really* influences perceptions of extraversion and enthusiasm (Oberlander and Gill, 2004; Dewaele and Furnham, 1999). In PERSON-AGE, the pragmatic parameters are attached to the syntactic tree at *insertion points* defined by syntactic constraints, e.g., EMPHASIZERS are adverbs that can occur sentence initially or before a scalar adjective. Each personality model uses a variety of pragmatic parameters. Figure 2 shows how these markers distribute differently across personality models, with examples in Table 1.

3 Model Architectures

Our neural generation models build on the open-source sequence-to-sequence (seq2seq) TGen system (Dusek and Jurcícek, 2016a)[7], implemented in Tensorflow (Abadi et al., 2016). The system is based on seq2seq generation with attention (Bahdanau et al., 2014; Sutskever et al., 2014), and uses a sequence of LSTMs (Hochreiter and Schmidhuber, 1997) for the encoder and decoder, combined with beam-search and reranking for output tuning.

The input to TGen are dialogue acts for each system action (such as *inform*) and a set of attribute slots (such as *rating*) and their values (such as *high* for attribute *rating*). The system integrates sentence planning and surface realization into a single step to produce natural language outputs. To preprocess the corpus of MR/utterance pairs, attributes that take on proper-noun values are delexicalized during training i.e., *name* and *near*. During the generation phase on the test set, a post-processing step re-lexicalizes the outputs. The MRs (and resultant embeddings) are sorted internally by dialogue act tag and attribute name.

The models are designed to systematically test the effects of increasing the level of supervision, with novel architectural additions to accommodate these changes. We use the default parameter settings from TGen (Dusek and Jurcícek, 2016a) with batch size 20 and beam size 10, and use 2,000

---

[7] `https://github.com/UFAL-DSG/tgen`

training instances for parameter tuning to set the number of training epochs and learning rate. Figure 3 summarizes the architectures.

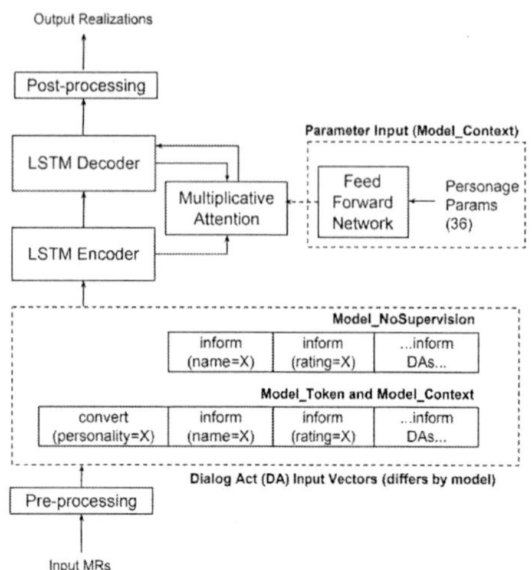

Figure 3: Neural Network Model Architecture

MODEL_NOSUPERVISION. The simplest model follows the baseline TGen architecture (Dusek and Jurcícek, 2016b), with training using all 88K utterances in a single pool for up to 14 epochs based on loss monitoring for the decoder and reranker.

MODEL_TOKEN. The second model adds a token of additional supervision by introducing a new dialogue act, *convert*, to encode personality, inspired by the use of a language token for machine translation (Johnson et al., 2017). Unlike other work that uses a single token to control generator output (Fan et al., 2017; Hu et al., 2017), the personality token encodes a constellation of different parameters that define the style of the matching reference. Uniquely here, the model attempts to *simultaneously* control multiple style variables that may interact in different ways. Again, we monitor loss on the validation set and training continues for up to 14 epochs for the decoder and reranker.

MODEL_CONTEXT. The most complex model introduces a context vector, as shown at the top right of Figure 3. The vector explicitly encodes a set of 36 style parameters from Table 3. The parameters for each reference text are encoded as a boolean vector, and a feed-forward network is added as a context encoder, taking the vector as input to the hidden state of the encoder and making the parameters available at every time step to a multiplicative attention unit. The activations of the fully connected nodes are represented as an additional

time step of the encoder of the seq2seq architecture (Sutskever et al., 2014). The attention (Bahdanau et al., 2014) is computed over all of the encoder states and the hidden state of the fully connected network. Again, we set the learning rate, alpha decay, and maximum training epochs (up to 20) based on loss monitoring on the validation set.

4 Quantitative Results

Here, we present results on controlling stylistic variation while maintaining semantic fidelity.

4.1 Evaluating Semantic Quality

It is widely agreed that new evaluation metrics are needed for NLG (Langkilde-Geary, 2002; Belz and Reiter, 2006; Bangalore et al., 2000; Novikova et al., 2017a). We first present automated metrics used in NLG to measure how well model outputs compare to PERSONAGE input, then introduce novel metrics designed to fill the gap left by current evaluation metrics.

Automatic Metrics. The automatic evaluation uses the E2E generation challenge script.[8] Table 4 summarizes the results for BLEU (n-gram precision), NIST (weighted n-gram precision), METEOR (n-grams with synonym recall), and ROUGE (n-gram recall). Although the differences in metrics are small, MODEL_CONTEXT shows a slight improvement across all of the metrics.

Model	BLEU	NIST	METEOR	ROUGE_L
NOSUP	0.2774	4.2859	0.3488	0.4567
TOKEN	0.3464	4.9285	0.3648	0.5016
CONTEXT	**0.3766**	**5.3437**	**0.3964**	**0.5255**

Table 4: Automated Metric Evaluation

Deletions, Repetitions, and Substitutions. Automated evaluation metrics are not informative about the quality of the outputs, and penalize models for introducing stylistic variation. We thus develop new scripts to automatically evaluate the types common types of neural generation errors: *deletions* (failing to realize a value), *repeats* (repeating a value), and *substitutions* (mentioning an attribute with an incorrect value).

Table 5 shows ratios for the number of deletions, repeats, and substitutions for each model for the test set of 1,390 total realizations (278 unique MRs, each realized once for each of the 5 personalities). The error counts are split by personality, and normalized by the number of unique MRs

---

[8]`https://github.com/tuetschek/e2e-metrics`

(278). Smaller ratios are preferable, indicating fewer errors. Note that because MODEL_NOSUP does not encode a personality parameter, the error values are the same across each personality (averages across the full test set).

The table shows that MODEL_NOSUP makes very few semantic errors (we show later that this is at the cost of limited stylistic variation). Across all error types, MODEL_CONTEXT makes significantly fewer errors than MODEL_TOKEN, suggesting that its additional explicit parameters help avoid semantic errors. The last row quantifies whether some personalities are harder to model: it shows that across all models, DISAGREEABLE and EXTRAVERT have the most errors, while CONSCIENTIOUS has the fewest.

Model	AGREE	CONSC	DISAG	EXTRA	UNCON
DELETIONS					
NoSup	**0.01**	**0.01**	**0.01**	**0.01**	**0.01**
Token	0.27	0.22	0.87	0.74	0.31
Context	0.08	**0.01**	0.14	0.08	**0.01**
REPETITIONS					
NoSup	**0.00**	**0.00**	**0.00**	**0.00**	**0.00**
Token	0.29	0.12	0.81	0.46	0.28
Context	0.02	**0.00**	0.14	**0.00**	**0.00**
SUBSTITUTIONS					
NoSup	0.10	0.10	0.10	0.10	0.10
Token	0.34	0.41	0.22	0.35	0.29
Context	**0.03**	**0.03**	**0.00**	**0.00**	**0.03**
All	0.68	0.35	1.96	1.29	0.61

Table 5: Ratio of Model Errors by Personality

4.2 Evaluating Stylistic Variation

Here we characterize the fidelity of stylistic variation across different model outputs.

Entropy. Shannon text entropy quantifies the amount of variation in the output produced by each model. We calculate entropy as $-\sum_{x \in S} \frac{freq}{total} * log_2(\frac{freq}{total})$, where S is the set of unique words in all outputs generated by the model, $freq$ is the frequency of a term, and $total$ counts the number of terms in all references. Table 6 shows that the training data has the highest entropy, but MODEL_CONTEXT performs the best at preserving the variation seen in the training data. Row NoSup shows that MODEL_NOSUP makes the fewest semantic errors, but produces the least varied output. MODEL_CONTEXT, informed by the explicit stylistic context encoding, makes comparably few semantic errors, while producing stylistically varied output with high entropy.

Pragmatic Marker Usage. To measure whether

Model	1-grams	1-2grams	1-3grams
PERSONAGETRAIN	5.97	7.95	9.34
NoSup	5.38	6.90	7.87
Token	5.67	7.35	8.47
Context	**5.70**	**7.42**	**8.58**

Table 6: Shannon Text Entropy

the trained models faithfully reproduce the pragmatic markers for each personality, we count each pragmatic marker in Table 3 in the output, average the counts and compute the Pearson correlation between the PERSONAGE references and the outputs for each model and personality. See Table 7 (all correlations significant with $p \leq 0.001$).

Model	AGREE	CONSC	DISAG	EXTRA	UNCON
NoSup	0.05	0.59	-0.07	-0.06	-0.11
Token	**0.35**	0.66	0.31	0.57	0.53
Context	0.28	**0.67**	**0.40**	**0.76**	**0.63**

Table 7: Correlations between PERSONAGE and models for pragmatic markers in Table 3

Table 7 shows that MODEL_CONTEXT has the highest correlation with the training data, for all personalities (except AGREEABLE, with significant margins, and CONSCIENTIOUS, which is the easiest personality to model, with a margin of 0.01). While MODEL_NOSUP shows positive correlation with AGREEABLE and CONSCIENTIOUS, it shows *negative* correlation with the PERSONAGE inputs for DISAGREEABLE, EXTRAVERT, and UNCONSCIENTIOUS. The pragmatic marker distributions for PERSONAGE train in Figure 2 indicates that the CONSCIENTIOUS personality most frequently uses *acknowledgement-justify* (i.e., *"well"*, *"i see"*), and *request confirmation* (i.e., *"did you say X?"*), which are less complex to introduce into a realization since they often lie at the beginning or end of a sentence, allowing the simple MODEL_NOSUP to learn them.[9]

Aggregation. To measure the ability of each model to aggregate, we average the counts of each aggregation operation for each model and personality and compute the Pearson correlation between the output and the PERSONAGE training data.

The correlations in Table 8 (all significant with $p \leq 0.001$) show that MODEL_CONTEXT has a higher correlation with PERSONAGE than the two simpler models (except for DISAGREE-

---

[9]We verified that there is not a high correlation between every set of pragmatic markers: different personalities do not correlate, e.g., -0.078 for PERSONAGE DISAGREEABLE and MODEL_TOKEN AGREEABLE.

Model	AGREE	CONSC	DISAG	EXTRA	UNCON
NoSup	0.78	0.80	0.13	0.42	0.69
Token	0.74	0.74	**0.57**	0.56	0.60
Context	**0.83**	**0.83**	0.55	**0.66**	**0.70**

Table 8: Correlations between PERSONAGE and models for aggregation operations in Table 3

Person.	PERSONAGE			MODEL_CONTEXT		
	Ratio Correct	Avg. Rating	Nat. Rating	Ratio Correct	Avg. Rating	Nat. Rating
AGREE	0.60	4.04	5.22	0.50	4.04	4.69
DISAGR	0.80	4.76	4.24	0.63	4.03	4.39
CONSC	1.00	5.08	5.60	0.97	5.19	5.18
UNCON	0.70	4.34	4.36	0.17	3.31	4.58
EXTRA	0.90	5.34	5.22	0.80	4.76	4.61

Table 9: Percentage of Correct Items and Average Ratings and Naturalness Scores for Each Personality (PERSONAGE vs. MODEL_CONTEXT)

ABLE, where MODEL_TOKEN is higher by 0.02). Here, MODEL_NOSUP actually *frequently* outperforms the more informed MODEL_TOKEN. Note that *all personalities use aggregation*, even thought **not** *all personalities use pragmatic markers*, and so even without a special *personality* token, MODEL_NOSUP is able to faithfully reproduce aggregation operations. In fact, since the correlations are frequently higher than those for MODEL_TOKEN, we hypothesize that is able to more accurately focus on aggregation (common to all personalities) than stylistic differences, which MODEL_TOKEN is able to produce.

5 Qualitative Analysis

Here, we present two evaluations aimed at qualitative analysis of our outputs.

Crowdsourcing Personality Judgements. Based on our quantitative results, we select MODEL_CONTEXT as the best-performing model and conduct an evaluation to test if humans can distinguish the personalities exhibited. We randomly select a set of 10 unique MRs from the PERSONAGE training data along with their corresponding reference texts for each personality (50 items in total), and 30 unique MRs MODEL_CONTEXT outputs (150 items in total).[10] We construct a HIT on Mechanical Turk, presenting a single output (either PERSONAGE or MODEL_CONTEXT), and ask 5 Turkers to label the output using the Ten Item Personality Inventory (TIPI) (Gosling et al., 2003). The TIPI is a ten-item measure of the Big Five personality dimensions, consisting of two items for each of the five dimensions, one that *matches* the dimension, and one that is the *reverse* of it, and a scale that ranges from 1 (disagree strongly) to 7 (agree strongly). To qualify Turkers for the task, we ask that they first complete a TIPI on themselves, to help ensure that they understand it.

Table 9 presents results as aggregated counts for the number of times at least 3 out of the 5

Turkers rated the *matching* item for that personality higher than the *reverse* item (Ratio Correct), the average rating the correct item received (range between 1-7), and an average "naturalness" score for the output (also rated 1-7). From the table, we can see that for PERSONAGE training data, all of the personalities have a correct ratio that is higher than 0.5. The MODEL_CONTEXT outputs exhibit the same trend except for UNCONSCIENTIOUS and AGREEABLE, where the correct ratio is only 0.17 and 0.50, respectively (they also have the lowest correct ratio for the original PERSONAGE data).

Table 9 also presents results for naturalness for both the reference and generated utterances, showing that both achieve decent scores for naturalness (on a scale of 1-7). While human utterances would probably be judged more natural, it is not at all clear that similar experiments could be done with human generated utterances, where it is difficult to enforce the same amount of experimental control.

Generalizing to Multiple Personalities. A final experiment explores whether the models learn additional stylistic generalizations not seen in training. We train a version of MODEL_TOKEN, as before on instances with single personalities, but such that it can be used to generate output with a combination of *two* personalities. The experiment uses the original training data for MODEL_TOKEN, but uses an expanded test set where the MR includes **two** personality CONVERT tags. We pair each personality with all personalities except its exact opposite.

Sample outputs are given in Table 10 for the DISAGREEABLE personality, which is one of the most distinct in terms of aggregation and pragmatic marker insertion, along with occurrence counts (frequency shown scaled down by 100) of the operations that it does most frequently: specifically, *period aggregation* and *expletive pragmatic markers*. Rows 1-2 shows the counts and an exam-

---

[10]Note that we use fewer PERSONAGE references simply to validate that our personalities are distinguishable in training, but will more rigorously evaluate our model in future work.

	Persona	Period Agg.	Explet Prag.	Example
1	DISAG	5.71	2.26	Browns Cambridge is damn moderately priced, also it's in city centre. It is a pub. It is an italian place. It is near Adriatic. It is damn family friendly.
2	CONSC	0.60	0.02	Let's see what we can find on Browns Cambridge. I see, well it is a pub, also it is moderately priced, an italian restaurant near Adriatic and family friendly in city centre.
3	DISAG+ CONSC	3.81	0.84	Browns Cambridge is an italian place and moderately priced. It is near Adriatic. It is kid friendly. It is a pub. It is in riverside.

Table 10: Multiple-Personality Generation Output based on DISAGREEABLE

ple of each personality on its own. The combined personality output is shown in Row 3. We can see from the table that while CONSCIENTIOUS on its own realizes the content in two sentences, period aggregation is much more prevalent in the DISAGREEABLE + CONSCIENTIOUS example, with the same content being realized in 5 sentences. Also, we see that some of the expletives originally in DISAGREEABLE are dropped in the combined output. This suggests that the model learns a combined representation unlike what it has seen in train, which we will explore in future work.

6   Related Work and Conclusion

The restaurant domain has long been a testbed for conversational agents with much earlier work on NLG (Howcroft et al., 2013; Stent et al., 2004; Devillers et al., 2004; Gašic et al., 2008; Mairesse et al., 2010; Higashinaka et al., 2007), so it is not surprising that recent work using neural generation methods has also focused on the restaurant domain (Wen et al., 2015; Mei et al., 2015; Dusek and Jurcícek, 2016b; Lampouras and Vlachos, 2016; Juraska et al., 2018). The restaurant domain is ideal for testing generation models because sentences can range from extremely simple to more complex forms that exhibit discourse relations such as justification or contrast (Stent et al., 2004). Most recent work focuses on achieving semantic fidelity for simpler syntactic structures, although there has also been a focus on crowdsourcing or harvesting training data that exhibits more stylistic variation (Novikova et al., 2017; Nayak et al., 2017; Oraby et al., 2017).

Most previous work on neural stylistic generation has been carried out in the framework of "style transfer": this work is hampered by the lack of parallel corpora, the difficulty of evaluating content preservation (semantic fidelity), and the challenges with measuring whether the outputs realize a particular style. Previous experiments attempt to control the sentiment and verb tense of generated movie review sentences (Hu et al., 2017), the content preservation and style transfer of news headlines and product review sentences (Fu et al., 2018), multiple automatically extracted style attributes along with sentiment and sentence theme for movie reviews (Ficler and Goldberg, 2017), sentiment, fluency and semantic equivalence (Shen et al., 2017), utterance length and topic (Fan et al., 2017), and the personality of customer care utterances in dialogue (Herzig et al., 2017). However, to our knowledge, no previous work evaluates simultaneous achievement of multiple targets as we do. Recent work introduces a large parallel corpus that varies on the formality dimension, and introduces several novel evaluation metrics, including a custom trained model for measuring semantic fidelity (Rao and Tetreault).

Other work has also used context representations, but not in the way that we do here. In general, these have been used to incorporate a representation of the prior dialogue into response generation. Sordoni et al. (2015) propose a basic approach where they incorporate previous utterances as a bag of words model and use a feed-forward neural network to inject a fixed sized context vector into the LSTM cell of the encoder. Ghosh et al. (2016) proposed a modified LSTM cell with an additional gate that incorporates the previous context as input during encoding. Our context representation encodes stylistic parameters.

This paper evaluates the ability of different neural architectures to faithfully render the semantic content of an utterance while simultaneously exhibiting stylistic variations characteristic of Big Five personalities. We created a novel parallel training corpus of over 88,000 meaning representations in the restaurant domain, and matched reference outputs by using an existing statistical natural language generator, PERSONAGE (Mairesse and Walker, 2010). We design three neural models that systematically increase the stylistic encodings given to the network, and show that MODEL_CONTEXT benefits from the greatest explicit stylistic supervision, producing outputs that both preserve semantic fidelity and exhibit distinguishable personality styles.

References

Martin Abadi, Paul Barham, Jianmin Chen, Zhifeng Chen, Andy Davis, Jeffrey Dean, Matthieu Devin, Sanjay Ghemawat, Geoffrey Irving, Michael Isard, Manjunath Kudlur, Josh Levenberg, Rajat Monga, Sherry Moore, Derek G. Murray, Benoit Steiner, Paul Tucker, Vijay Vasudevan, Pete Warden, Martin Wicke, Yuan Yu, and Xiaoqiang Zheng. 2016. Tensorflow: A system for large-scale machine learning. In *Proceedings of the 12th USENIX Conference on Operating Systems Design and Implementation*.

Elisabeth André, Thomas Rist, Susanne van Mulken, Martin Klesen, and Stephan Baldes. 2000. The automated design of believable dialogues for animated presentation teams. *Embodied conversational agents* pages 220–255.

Dzmitry Bahdanau, Kyunghyun Cho, and Yoshua Bengio. 2015. Neural machine translation by jointly learning to align and translate. *In ICLR*.

Srinivas Bangalore, Owen Rambow, and Steve Whittaker. 2000. Evaluation metrics for generation. In *Proc. of the First International Natural Language Generation Conference (INLG2000)*.

Anja Belz and Ehud Reiter. 2006. Comparing automatic and human evaluation of nlg systems. In *EACL*.

Douglas Biber. 1991. Variation across speech and writing Cambridge University Press.

Penelope Brown and Steve Levinson. 1987. *Politeness: Some universals in language usage*. Cambridge University Press.

Ondrej Dusek and Filip Jurcícek. 2016a. A context-aware natural language generator for dialogue systems. *In SIGDIAL* pages 85-190.

Ondrej Dusek and Filip Jurcícek. 2016b. Sequence-to-sequence generation for spoken dialogue via deep syntax trees and strings. *Proceedings of the 54th Annual Meeting of the Association for Computational Linguistics* pages 45-51.

Nina Dethlefs, Heriberto Cuayáhuitl, Helen Hastie, Verena Rieser, and Oliver Lemon. 2014. Cluster-based prediction of user ratings for stylistic surface realisation. *EACL 2014* page 702.

Laurence Devillers, Hélène Maynard, Sophie Rosset, Patrick Paroubek, Kevin McTait, Djamel Mostefa, Khalid Choukri, Laurent Charnay, Caroline Bousquet, Nadine Vigouroux, et al. 2004. The french media/evalda project: the evaluation of the understanding capability of spoken language dialogue systems. In *LREC*.

Jean-Marc Dewaele and Adrian Furnham. 1999. Extraversion: the unloved variable in applied linguistic research. *Language Learning*, 49(3):509–544.

Angela Fan, David Grangier, and Michael Auli. 2017. Controllable abstractive summarization. *CoRR* abs/1711.05217.

Jessica Ficler and Yoav Goldberg. 2017. Controlling Linguistic Style Aspects in Neural Language Generation. In *Proc. of the Workshop on Stylistic Variation at EMNLP 18*. pages 94–104.

Zhenxin Fu, Xiaoye Tan, Nanyun Peng, Dongyan Zhao, and Rui Yan. 2018. Style transfer in text: Exploration and evaluation. In *Proceedings of the Thirty-Second AAAI Conference on Artificial Intelligence (AAAI)*, pages 663–670.

M. Gašic, S. Keizer, F. Mairesse, J. Schatzmann, B. Thomson, K. Yu, and S. Young. 2008. Training and evaluation of the his-pomdp dialogue system in noise. *Proc. Ninth SIGdial, Columbus, OH* .

Shalini Ghosh, Oriol Vinyals, Brian Strope, Scott Roy, Tom Dean, and Larry Heck. 2016. Contextual lstm (clstm) models for large scale nlp tasks. *arXiv preprint arXiv:1602.06291* .

S. D. Gosling, P. J. Rentfrow, and W. B. Swann. 2003. A very brief measure of the big five personality domains. *Journal of Research in Personality* Vol. 37:504–528.

Jonathan Herzig and Michal Shmueli-Scheuer and Tommy Sandbank and David Konopnicki. 2017. Neural Response Generation for Customer Service based on Personality Traits. In *Proc. of the INLG*.

Ryuichiro Higashinaka, Marilyn A. Walker, and Rashmi Prasad. 2007. An unsupervised method for learning generation dictionaries for spoken dialogue systems by mining user reviews. *ACM Transactions on Speech and Language Processing* 4(4).

Sepp Hochreiter and Jürgen Schmidhuber. 1997. Long short-term memory. *Neural computation* 9(8):1735–1780.

David M Howcroft, Crystal Nakatsu, and Michael White. 2013. Enhancing the expression of contrast in the sparky restaurant corpus. *ENLG 2013* page 30.

Zhiting Hu, Zichao Yang, Xiaodan Liang, Ruslan Salakhutdinov, and Eric P Xing. 2017. Towards controlled generation of text. *International Conference on Machine Learning* pages 1587–1596.

Melvin Johnson, Mike Schuster, Quoc V Le, Maxim Krikun, Yonghui Wu, Zhifeng Chen, Nikhil Thorat, Fernanda Viégas, Martin Wattenberg, Greg Corrado, et al. 2017. Google's multilingual neural machine translation system: enabling zero-shot translation. *In Transactions of the Association for Computational Linguistics* pages 339-351.

Dan Jurafsky, Rajesh Ranganath, and Dan McFarland. 2009. Extracting social meaning: Identifying interactional style in spoken conversation. In *Proc. of*

Human Language Technologies: The 2009 Annual Conference of the North American Chapter of the Association for Computational Linguistics. pages 638–646.

Juraj Juraska and Panagiotis Karagiannis and Kevin Bowden and Marilyn Walker. 2018. A deep ensemble model with slot alignment for sequence-to-sequence natural language generation. In *Proc. of the 2018 Annual Conference of the North American Chapter of the Association for Computational Linguistics.*

Gerasimos Lampouras and Andreas Vlachos. 2016. Imitation learning for language generation from unaligned data. In Nicoletta Calzolari, Yuji Matsumoto, and Rashmi Prasad, editors, *COLING.* ACL, pages 1101–1112.

I. Langkilde-Geary. 2002. An empirical verification of coverage and correctness for a general-purpose sentence gene rator. In *Proc. of the INLG.*

Benoit Lavoie and Owen Rambow. 1997. A fast and portable realizer for text generation systems. In *Proc. of the Third Conference on Applied Natural Language Processing, ANLP97.* pages 265–268.

Jiwei Li, Michel Galley, Chris Brockett, Georgios P Spithourakis, Jianfeng Gao, and Bill Dolan. 2016. A persona-based neural conversation model. In *Proceedings of the 54th Annual Meeting of the Association for Computational Linguistics* pages 994-1003.

F. Mairesse and M.A. Walker. 2011. Controlling User Perceptions of Linguistic Style: Trainable Generation of Personality Traits. *Computational Linguistics Journal, Vol. 37 Issue 3* pages 455–488.

F. Mairesse and M.A. Walker. 2010. Towards personality-based user adaptation: psychologically informed stylistic language generation. *User Modeling and User-Adapted Interaction* pages 1–52.

François Mairesse, Milica Gašić, Filip Jurčíček, Simon Keizer, Blaise Thomson, Kai Yu, and Steve Young. 2010. Phrase-based statistical language generation using graphical models and active learning. In *Proceedings of the 48th Annual Meeting of the Association for Computational Linguistics* pages 1552–1561.

François Mairesse and Marilyn A. Walker. 2008. Trainable generation of Big-Five personality styles through data-driven parameter estimation. In *Proceedings of the 46th Annual Meeting of the Association for Computational Linguistics (ACL).*

Hongyuan Mei, Mohit Bansal, and Matthew R. Walter. 2016. What to talk about and how? selective generation using lstms with coarse-to-fine alignment. In *Proc. of Human Language Technologies: The 2016 Annual Conference of the North American Chapter of the Association for Computational Linguistics.* pages 720–730.

Igor A. Melčuk. 1988. *Dependency Syntax: Theory and Practice.* SUNY, Albany, New York.

Neha Nayak, Dilek Hakkani-Tur, Marilyn Walker, and Larry Heck. 2017. To plan or not to plan? discourse planning in slot-value informed sequence to sequence models for language generation. In *Proc. of Interspeech 2017.*

Jekaterina Novikova, Ondrej Dušek, and Verena Rieser. 2017. Why we need new evaluation metrics for NLG. In *Proceedings of the 2017 Conference on Empirical Methods in Natural Language Processing.*

Jekaterina Novikova, Ondrej Dušek, and Verena Rieser. 2017. The E2E dataset: New challenges for end-to-end generation. In *Proceedings of the 18th Annual Meeting of the Special Interest Group on Discourse and Dialogue* pages 201-206.

Jekaterina Novikova, Oliver Lemon, and Verena Rieser. 2016. Crowd-sourcing nlg data: Pictures elicit better data. In *International Conference on Natural Language Generation.*

J. Oberlander and A. Gill. 2004. Individual differences and implicit language: personality, parts-of-speech, and pervasiveness. In *Proceedings of the 26th Annual Conference of the Cognitive Science Society,* pages 1035–1040.

Shereen Oraby, Sheideh Homayon, and Marilyn Walker. 2017. Harvesting Creative Templates for Generating Stylistically Varied Restaurant Reviews. In *Proc. of the Workshop on Stylistic Variation at EMNLP 18.* pages 28–36.

James W. Pennebaker, L. E. Francis, and R. J. Booth. 2001. *LIWC: Linguistic Inquiry and Word Count.*

Joseph Polifroni, Lynette Hirschman, Stephanie Seneff, and Victor Zue. 1992. Experiments in evaluating interactive spoken language systems. In *Proc. of the DARPA Speech and NL Workshop.* pages 28–33.

Sudha Rao and Joel Tetreault. Dear sir or madam, may i introduce the gyafc dataset: Corpus, benchmarks and metrics for formality style transfer. In *Proc. of the 2018 Annual Conference of the North American Chapter of the Association for Computational Linguistics.*

Ehud Reiter and Robert Dale. 2000. *Building Natural Language Generation Systems.* Cambridge University Press.

Tianxiao Shen, Tao Lei, Regina Barzilay, and Tommi Jaakkola. 2017. Style transfer from non-parallel text by cross-alignment. *Advances in Neural Information Processing Systems* pages 6833–6844.

Alessandro Sordoni, Michel Galley, Michael Auli, Chris Brockett, Yangfeng Ji, Margaret Mitchell, Jian-Yun Nie, Jianfeng Gao, and Bill Dolan. 2015.

A neural network approach to context-sensitive generation of conversational responses. In *Proc. of Human Language Technologies: The 2015 Annual Conference of the North American Chapter of the Association for Computational Linguistics*. pages 196–205.

Amanda Stent, Rashmi Prasad, and Marilyn Walker. 2004. Trainable sentence planning for complex information presentation in spoken dialogue systems. In *Meeting of the Association for Computational Linguistics*.

Ilya Sutskever, Oriol Vinyals, and Quoc V Le. 2014. Sequence to sequence learning with neural networks. In *Advances in neural information processing systems*. pages 3104–3112.

Marilyn Walker, Rashmi Prasad, and Amanda Stent. 2003. A trainable generator for recommendations in multimodal dialog. In *EUROSPEECH*.

Tsung-Hsien Wen, Milica Gasic, Nikola Mrksic, Pei-hao Su, David Vandyke, and Steve J. Young. 2015. Semantically conditioned lstm-based natural language generation for spoken dialogue systems. In *Proceedings of the 2015 Conference on Empirical Methods in Natural Language Processing* pages 1711–1721.

Steve Whittaker, Marilyn Walker, and Johanna Moore. 2002. Fish or fowl: A Wizard of Oz evaluation of dialogue strategies in the restaurant domain. In *Language Resources and Evaluation Conference*.

A Context-aware Convolutional Natural Language Generation model for Dialogue Systems

Sourab Mangrulkar
National Institute of Technology Goa
100rabmangrulkar@gmail.com

Suhani Shrivastava
National Institute of Technology Goa
suhani1396@gmail.com

Veena Thenkanidiyoor
National Institute of Technology Goa
veenat@nitgoa.ac.in

Dileep Aroor Dinesh
Indian Institute of Technology Mandi
addileep@iitmandi.ac.in

Abstract

Natural language generation (NLG) is an important component in spoken dialog systems (SDSs). A model for NLG involves sequence to sequence learning. State-of-the-art NLG models are built using recurrent neural network (RNN) based sequence to sequence models (Dušek and Jurcicek, 2016a). Convolutional sequence to sequence based models have been used in the domain of machine translation but their application as natural language generators in dialogue systems is still unexplored. In this work, we propose a novel approach to NLG using convolutional neural network (CNN) based sequence to sequence learning. CNN-based approach allows to build a hierarchical model which encapsulates dependencies between words via shorter path unlike RNNs. In contrast to recurrent models, convolutional approach allows for efficient utilization of computational resources by parallelizing computations over all elements, and eases the learning process by applying constant number of nonlinearities. We also propose to use CNN-based reranker for obtaining responses having semantic correspondence with input dialogue acts. The proposed model is capable of entrainment. Studies using a standard dataset shows the effectiveness of the proposed CNN-based approach to NLG.

1 Introduction

In task-specific spoken dialogue systems (SDS), the function of natural language generation (NLG) components is to generate natural language response from a dialogue act (DA) (Young et al., 2009). DA is a meaning representation specifying actions along with various attributes and their values. NLG plays a very important role in realizing the overall quality of the SDS. Entrainment to users way of speaking is essential for generating more natural and high quality natural language responses. Most of the approaches for incorporating entrainment are rule-based models. Recent advances have been in the direction of developing a fully trainable context aware NLG model (Dušek and Jurcicek, 2016a). However, all these approaches are based on recurrent sequence to sequence architecture.

Convolutional neural networks are largely unexplored in the domain of NLG for SDS inspite of having several advantages (Waibel et al., 1989; LeCun and Bengio, 1995). Recurrent networks depend on the computations of previous time step and thus inhibits parallelization within a sequence. Convolutional networks on the other hand, allows parallelization within a sequence resulting in efficient use of GPUs and other computational resources (Gehring et al., 2017). Multi-block (multi-layer) convolutional networks enable controlling the upper bound on the effective context size and form a hierarchical structure. In contrast to the sequential structure of RNNs, hierarchical structure provides shorter paths for modeling long-range dependencies. Recurrent networks apply variable number of nonlinearities to the inputs, whereas convolutional networks apply fixed number of nonlinearities which simplifies the learning (Gehring et al., 2017).

In this paper, we present a novel approach of using convolutional sequence to sequence model (ConvSeq2Seq) for the task of NLG. ConvSeq2Seq generator is an encoder decoder model where convolutional neural networks (CNNs) are used to build both encoder and decoder states. It uses multi-step attention mechanism. In the decoding phase, beam search is implemented and n-best natural language responses are chosen. The n-best beam search responses from ConvSeq2Seq

Proceedings of the SIGDIAL 2018 Conference, pages 191–200,
Melbourne, Australia, 12-14 July 2018. ©2018 Association for Computational Linguistics

generator may have some missing and/or irrelevant information. To address this, we propose to rank the n-best outputs from ConvSeq2Seq generator using convolutional reranker (CNN reranker). CNN reranker implements one dimensional convolution on beam search responses and generates binary vectors. These binary vectors are used to penalize the responses having missing and/or irrelevant information. We evaluate our model on the Alex Context natural language generation (NLG) dataset of Dušek and Jurcicek (2016a) and demonstrate that our model outperforms the RNN-based model of Dušek and Jurcicek (2016a) (TGen model) in automatic metrics. Training time of proposed model is observed to be significantly lower than TGen model. The main contributions of this work are (i) ConvSeq2Seq generator for NLG and (ii) CNN-based reranker for ranking n-best beam search responses for obtaining semantically appropriate responses with respect to input DA.

The rest of this paper is organized as follows. Section 2 gives a brief review of different approaches to NLG. In Section 3, proposed convolutional natural language generator (ConvSeq2Seq) is described along with CNN reranker. The experimental studies are presented in Section 4 and conclusions are given in Section 5.

2 Related Work

Natural language generation (NLG) task is divided into two phases: sentence planning and surface realization. Sentence planning generates intermediate structure such as dependency trees or templates modeling the input semantic symbols. Surface realization phase converts the intermediate structure into the final natural language response.

Conventional approaches to NLG are rule based approaches (Stent et al., 2004; Walker et al., 2002). Most recent NLG approaches include sequence to sequence RNN models (Wen et al., 2015a,b; Dušek and Jurcicek, 2016b,a). Sequence to sequence learning is to map the input sequence to a fixed sized vector using one RNN, and then to map the vector to the target sequence with another RNN. In (Wen et al., 2015a), a sequence to sequence RNN model is used with some decay factor to avoid vanishing gradient problem. The n-best outputs generated by the model are ranked using a CNN-based reranker. The model also uses a backward sequence to sequence RNN reranker to further improve the performance. Model proposed by

Wen et al. (2015b) is a statistical language generator based on a semantically controlled long-short term memory (LSTM) structure. The LSTM generator can learn from unaligned data by jointly optimizing sentence planning and surface realization using a simple cross entropy training criterion, and language variation can be easily achieved by sampling from output candidates.

Model proposed by Dušek and Jurcicek (2016b) serves as a sequence to sequence generation model for SDS which doesn't take into account the context. The model uses single layer sequence to sequence RNN encoder decoder architecture along with attention mechanism to generate n-best output utterances. It then uses RNN reranker to rank the n-best outputs of generator to get the utterance which best describes the input DA. The model can also be used to generate deep syntax trees which can be converted to output utterance using a surface realization mechanism. This model is context unaware because it takes into account only the input DA and no preceding user utterance(s). This leads to generation of very rigid responses and also inhibits flexible interactions. Context awareness adapts/entrains to the user's way of speaking and thereby generates responses of high quality and naturalness. The semantic meaning which is required to be given in response to a query is very well modelled if context awareness is taken into account. This leads to generation of more informative response.

Model proposed by Dušek and Jurcicek (2016a) serves as a baseline sequence to sequence generation model (TGen model) for SDS which takes into account the context. The model takes into account the preceding user utterance while generating natural language output. The model implemented three modifications to the model proposed by Dušek and Jurcicek (2016b). The first modification was prepending context to the input DAs. The second modification was implementing a separate encoder for user utterances/contexts. The third modification was implementing a N-gram match reranker. This reranker is based on n-gram precision scores and promotes responses having phrase overlaps with user utterances (Dušek and Jurcicek, 2016a).

In the next section, we present the proposed CNN-based sequence to sequence generator for NLG.

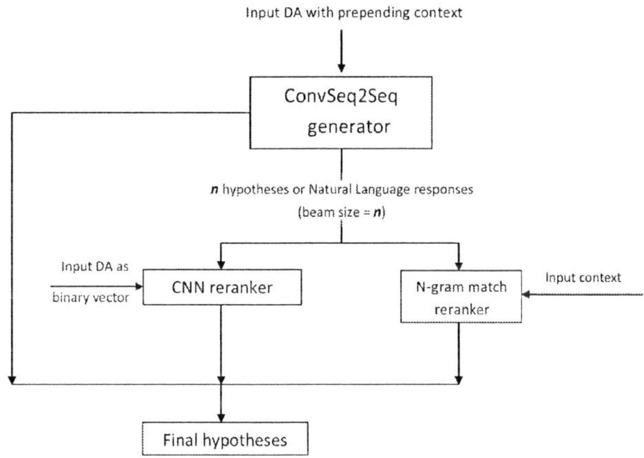

Figure 1: Pipeline of the proposed convolutional NLG model.

3 Proposed Approach

The pipeline of the proposed approach for NLG is shown in Figure 1. Input DA with prepended context is first given to convolutional sequence to sequence generator (ConvSeq2Seq) to get n-best natural language responses or hypotheses (n is beam size). These n-best hypotheses and binary vector representation of input DA are given as input to CNN reranker to get the misfit penalties of the hypotheses. The n-best hypotheses and context user utterance are given as input to the N-gram match reranker to get bigram precision scores of hypotheses. Final rank of each hypothesis i where $1 \leq i \leq n$ is calculated as follows:

$$rank_i = log\_probability_i$$
$$+(\omega * bigram\_precision_i)$$
$$-(W * misfit\_penalty_i)$$

Here, we get log probabilities from ConvSeq2Seq generator, bigram precision scores from N-gram match reranker and misfit penalties from CNN reranker. Here, ω and W are constants. We implement the N-gram match reranker as given by Dušek and Jurcicek (2016a). We describe the proposed convolutional sequence to sequence generator in Section 3.1 and convolutional reranker in Section 3.2.

3.1 ConvSeq2Seq Generator

The proposed sequence to sequence generator is based on convolutional sequence to sequence approach proposed by Gehring et al. (2017)[1]. It

[1]We use the implementation in the pytorch framework (Gehring et al., 2017)

is a CNN-based encoder decoder architecture. Figure 2 shows the working of proposed ConvSeq2Seq generator on an input instance from training dataset. In this architecture, CNNs are used to compute the encoder states and decoder states. This architecture is based on succession of convolutional blocks/layers. Input sequence is represented as a combination of word and position embeddings. These embeddings are operated upon by first convolutional block and gated linear units (GLUs) to get the outputs for the first block. This can be seen in Figure 2 where only one convolutional block is shown for representation purpose. The output from first block is input to the second convolutional block and this succession follows till the last convolutional block.

Stacking of several convolutional layers/blocks allows to increase and control the effective context size. For example, stacking 10 layers of convolutional blocks, each having a kernel width of $k=4$, results in effective context size of 31 elements. Each output is dependent on 31 inputs. Stacking of several convolutional layers/blocks results in a hierarchical structure. In hierarchical structure, nearby elements interact at lower blocks and distant elements at higher blocks. It provides a shorter path for modeling long-range dependencies and eases discovery of compositional structure in sequences compared to sequential structure of RNNs. For example, to model dependencies between n words, only $\mathcal{O}\left(\frac{n}{k}\right)$ convolutional operations would be required by CNN in contrast to $\mathcal{O}(n)$ operations in RNN. RNNs over-process the first word and under-process the last word,

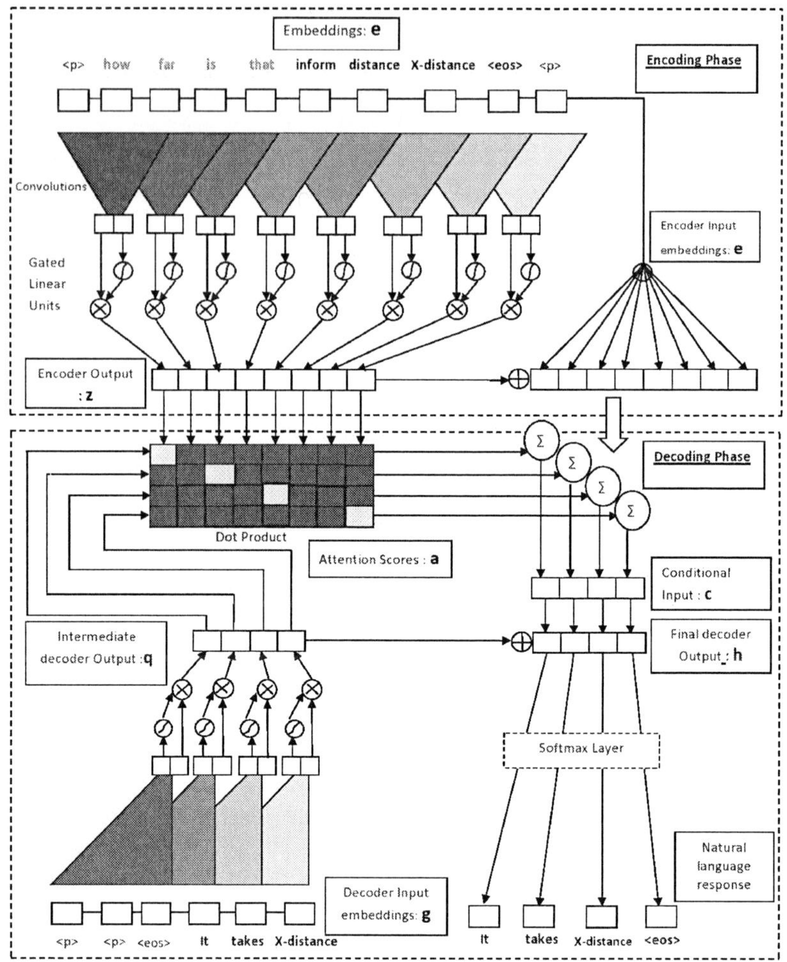

Figure 2: Working of ConvSeq2Seq generator on an input instance from training dataset. Here, for representation purpose, encoder and decoder consists of only one convolutional layer with kernel width k=3. The encoder input sequence $\mathbf{x}$ =(how, far, is, that, inform, distance, X-distance) comprises of user context "how far is that" prepended to input DA "inform distance X-distance".

whereas a constant number of kernels and nonlinearities are applied to the inputs of CNN which eases the learning process (Gehring et al., 2017).

The ConvSeq2Seq model uses position embeddings in addition to word embeddings in order to get a sense of which part of the input sequence it is currently processing (Gehring et al., 2017). Let $\mathbf{e} = (w_1 + p_1, \ldots, w_s + p_s)$ be the input sequence representation, where $\mathbf{w} = (w_1, \ldots, w_s)$ and $\mathbf{p} = (p_1, \ldots, p_s)$ are the the word embeddings and positional embeddings of the input sequence $\mathbf{x} = (x_1, \ldots, x_s)$ (having s elements) to the encoder network respectively. Intermediate states are computed based on a fixed number of input elements.

In encoding phase, input is padded with $\frac{k-1}{2}$ elements on the left and right side with zero vectors. For each block l, the output $\mathbf{z}^l = (z_1^l, \ldots, z_s^l)$ is computed as follows:

$$z_i^l = \nu(\mathbf{W}_z^l[z_{i-k/2}^{l-1}, \ldots, z_{i+k/2}^{l-1}] + b_z^l) + z_i^{l-1}$$

Here, $[z_{i-k/2}^{l-1}, \ldots, z_{i+k/2}^{l-1}]$ is the input $\mathbf{A} \in R^{kd}$ from the previous block, $\mathbf{W}_z^l \in R^{2d \times kd}, b_z^l \in R^{2d}$ are parameters of convolution kernel and d is embedding dimension. Let $\mathbf{B} \in R^{2d}$ be the output of convolution kernel. $\nu()$ is gated linear unit(GLU) which is the nonlinearity function applied to the output $\mathbf{B}$ of convolution kernel. Let $\mathbf{z}^u$ be the encoder output from the last block u.

```
[['inform_no_match', 'departure_time=X-departure_time', 'ampm=X-ampm', 'inform', 'direction=X-direction', 'from_stop=X-from_stop', 'line=X-
line', 'vehicle=X-vehicle', 'iconfirm', 'to_stop=X-to_stop', 'request', 'from_stop=None', 'to_stop=None', 'departure_time_rel=X-
departure_time_rel', 'distance=X-distance', 'alternative=X-alternative', 'num_transfers=X-num_transfers', 'duration=X-duration',
'arrival_time=X-arrival_time']]
```

Figure 3: 19 classes of CNN reranker.

Let $\mathbf{g} = (g_1, \ldots, g_t)$ be the representation of the sequence that is being fed to the decoder network. Computation of $\mathbf{g}$ is similar to that of encoder network. Input to decoder is padded with k-1 elements on both left and right side with zero vectors to prevent decoder from having access to future information. As a result, last k-1 intermediate decoder outputs are removed. In decoding phase, for each block l, the output $\mathbf{h}^l = (h_1^l, \ldots, h_t^l)$ is computed as follows:

$$q_i^l = \nu(\mathbf{W}_q^l [h_{i-k+1}^{l-1}, \ldots, h_i^{l-1}] + b_q^l) \quad (1)$$

$$d_i^l = \mathbf{W}_d^l q_i^l + b_d^l + g_i \quad (2)$$

$$a_{ij}^l = \frac{exp(d_i^l . z_j^u)}{\sum_{m=1}^{s} exp(d_i^l . z_m^u)} \quad (3)$$

$$c_i^l = \sum_{j=1}^{s} a_{ij}^l (z_j^u + e_j) \quad (4)$$

$$h_i^l = c_i^l + q_i^l + h_i^{l-1} \quad (5)$$

Here, $q^l = (q_1^l, \ldots, q_t^l)$ is the intermediate decoder output and its computation is similar to that of encoder network. For computing attention, current intermediate decoder state q_i^l is combined with the embedding of the previous target element g_i as shown in Equation (2). Equation (3) computes attention of i-th decoder state and j-th encoder output element for the l-th decoder block. Equation (4) computes the conditional input which is weighted sum of combination of encoder outputs and input embeddings. Equation (5) computes the current decoder output which is combination of conditional input, intermediate decoder output and previous layer decoder output. Let h_i^L be the decoder output of i-th element and the final decoding block L. Distribution over T possible next target elements y_{i+1} is computed as follows:

$$p(y_{i+1}|y_1, \ldots, y_i, \mathbf{x}) = \zeta(\mathbf{W}_o h_i^L + b_o) \in R^T$$

Here, ζ is softmax function, $\mathbf{W}_o$ and b_o are the weights and bias of fully connected linear layer.

3.2 CNN Reranker

The n-best beam search responses from ConvSeq2Seq model may have missing information and/or irrelevant information. CNN reranker reranks the n-best beam search responses and heavily penalizes those responses which are not semantically in correspondence with the input DA. Responses having missing information and/or irrelevant information are heavily penalized. Convolutional networks are excellent feature extractors and have achieved state-of-the-art results in many text classification and sentence-level classification tasks such as sentiment analysis, question classification, etc (Kim, 2014; Kalchbrenner et al., 2014). This classifier takes as input a natural language response and outputs a binary vector. Each element of binary vector is a binary decision on the presence of DA type or slot-value combinations. For the dataset which we have used (Dušek and Jurcicek, 2016a), there are 19 such classes of DA types and slot-value combinations. These 19 classes are shown in Figure 3.

Input DAs are converted to similar binary vector. Hamming distance between the classifier output and binary vector representation of input DA is considered as reranking penalty. The weighted reranking penalties of all the n-best responses are subtracted from their log-probabilities similar to Dušek and Jurcicek (2016a).

The architecture and working of the CNN reranker on an input instance from training dataset is shown in Figure 4. It is based on the CNN architecture proposed for sentence classification by Kim (2014). Input is a natural language response $\mathbf{x} = (x_1, x_2, \ldots, x_n)$ where x_i's are word embeddings each having m dimensions, resulting in a input matrix of $n \times m$ dimensions. Each filter has the width equal to the size of word embeddings, i.e., m and its height specifies the number of words it will operate on. This one dimensional convolution is followed by applying activation function and 1-max pooling. The resulting feature vector has the dimension equal to the total number of filters. This penultimate layer is operated upon by a logistic layer to output the binary vector. Given penultimate layer feature vector $\mathbf{t}$, the output binary vector $\mathbf{y}$ is computed as:

$$\mathbf{y} = \sigma(\mathbf{t}.\mathbf{W}_f + \mathbf{b})$$

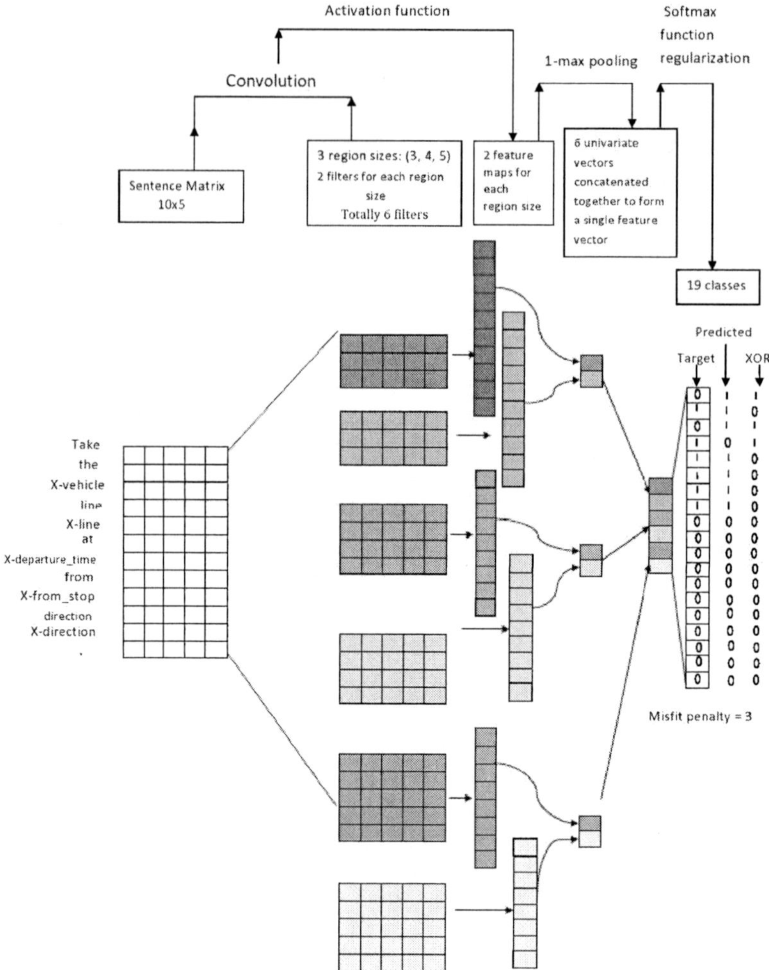

Figure 4: Architecture and working of the CNN reranker on an input instance from training dataset.

Here, σ is sigmoid activation function, $\mathbf{W}_f$ is the weight matrix and $\mathbf{b}$ is the bias vector.

The model proposed by Wen et al. (2015a) implements a CNN reranker that uses one-dimensional filters where convolutional operations are carried out on segments of words. It uses padding vectors. Proposed CNN reranker uses two-dimensional filters which operate on complete words rather than segments of words. This is more intuitive and meaningful. Also, no padding is required. The feature vector from proposed CNN reranker is v-dimensional whereas CNN reranker by Wen et al. (2015a) outputs longer feature vectors having dimension equal to $v * m$, where v = total number of filters and m = embedding size. Thus, proposed CNN reranker requires lesser number of computations.

4   Experimental Studies

The studies in this work are performed on Alex Context natural language generation (NLG) dataset (Dušek and Jurcicek, 2016a). This dataset is intended for fully trainable NLG systems in task-oriented spoken dialogue systems (SDS). It is in the domain of public transport information and has four dialogue act (DA) types namely request, inform, iconfirm and inform no match. It contains 1859 data instances each having 3 target responses. Each data instance consists of a preceding context (user utterance), source meaning representation and target natural language responses/sentences. Data is delexicalized and split into training, validation and test sets as done by Dušek and Jurcicek (2016a). For training and validation, the three paraphrases are used as separate instances. For evaluation they are used as three target references.

Input to our ConvSeq2Seq generator is a DA prepended with user utterance. This allows entrainment of the model to the user utterances. A single dictionary is used for context utterances and DA tokens. Our model is trained by minimizing cross-entropy error using Nesterov Accelerated Gradient (NAG) optimizer (Nesterov, 1983). The hyper-parameters are chosen by cross-validation method. Based on our experiments on validation set, we use maximum sentences per batch 20, learning rate 0.07, minimum learning rate 0.00001, maximum number of epochs 2000, learning rate shrink factor 0.5, clip-norm 0.5, encoder embedding dimension 100, decoder embedding dimension 100, decoder output embedding dimension 100 and dropout 0.3. Encoder part includes 10 layers/blocks, each having 100 units and kernel width of 7. Decoder part includes 10 layers, each having 100 units and kernel width of 7. For generating outputs on test set, we choose batch size 128 and beam size 20.

For our CNN reranker, all the possible combinations of DA tokens and its values are considered as classes. We have 19 such classes. Each input is a natural language sentence and each output is a set of class labels. Training is done by minimizing cross-entropy loss using Adam optimizer (Kingma and Ba, 2015). Cross-entropy error is measured on validation set after every 100 steps. Misclassification penalty for CNN reranker is set to 100. Based on our experiments, we choose embedding dimension 128, filter sizes (3,5,7,9), number of filters 64, dropout keep probability 0.5, batch size 100, number of epochs 100 and L2 regularization, $\lambda=0.05$.

The performance of the proposed ConvSeq2Seq model for NLG is compared with that of TGen model (Dušek and Jurcicek, 2016a). For comparison, we have considered NIST (Doddington, 2002), BLEU (Papineni et al., 2002), METEOR (Denkowski and Lavie, 2014), ROUGE_L (Lin, 2004) and CIDEr metrics (Vedantam et al., 2015). For this study, we have considered script "mteval-v13a-sig.pl" (version 13a) that implements these metrics. This script was used for E2E NLG challenge (Novikova et al., 2017). We focus on the evaluations using this version. Our model has also been evaluated using the metric script "mteval-v11b.pl" (version 11b) to compare our results with those stated in (Dušek and Jurcicek, 2016a). The

13a version takes into account the closest reference length with respect to candidate length for calculation of brevity penalty. This is in accordance with IBM BLEU. On the contrary, 11b version takes shortest reference length for measuring brevity penalty. This is the reason behind higher BLEU scores in the 11b version when compared to 13a version. Both the models have been evaluated on five different metrics, with NIST and BLEU scores being of atmost importance.

We have used N-gram match reranker with the weight ω set to 1 based on experiments done on validation set. When using 11b version for evaluating automatic metrics, weight ω is set to 5.

4.1 Studies of the models using 13a version of the metrics

The comparison of the performance of the proposed model with that of TGen model using the 13a version of the metric implementation is given in Table 1. It is seen from Table 1 that there is a slight improvement in the scores of our ConvSeq2Seq generator after using CNN reranker. However, scores improve significantly when N-gram match reranker is used in addition to CNN reranker. An improvement of 3.32 BLEU points is seen. The best scores are obtained when ω is set to 1 for N-gram match reranker.

ConvSeq2Seq model in combination with CNN reranker and N-gram match reranker outperforms TGen model with N-gram match reranker in all the metrics, with a difference of 0.65 in terms of NIST score which is 8% more than the TGen NIST score on this setup. ConvSeq2Seq model with CNN reranker outperforms TGen model with RNN reranker in all the metrics, with a difference of 1.8 in terms of NIST score which is 27% more than the TGen NIST score on this setup. In the domain of NLG, NIST score is found to have highest correlation with human based judgments when compared to other metrics (Belz and Reiter, 2006). In Table 1, the bold numbers indicate the best scores.

4.2 Studies of the models using 11b version of the metrics

The comparison of the performance of the proposed model with that of TGen model using the 11b version of the metric implementation is given in Table 2. A slight improvement in the scores of our ConvSeq2Seq generator after using CNN reranker is seen in Table 2 except for BLEU score.

Evaluation metric version 13a	NIST	BLEU	METEOR	ROUGE_L	CIDEr
Baseline Model: TGen(RNN+RNN)					
Prepending context (using RNN reranker)	6.660	62.13	0.4434	0.7269	3.6956
+ N-gram match reranker	7.956	65.49	0.4655	0.7547	3.8515
ConvSeq2Seq(CNN + CNN)					
Prepending context	8.450	62.08	0.4670	0.7557	3.7281
+ CNN reranker	8.474	62.23	0.4692	0.7561	3.7412
+ CNN reranker + N-gram match reranker	**8.608**	**65.55**	**0.4762**	**0.7654**	**3.8725**

Table 1: Different automatic metric scores of TGen model (RNN+RNN) and proposed model (CNN+CNN) on test data using evaluation metric version 13a.

Evaluation metric version 11b	NIST	BLEU	METEOR	ROUGE_L	CIDEr
Baseline Model: TGen(RNN+RNN)					
Prepending context (using RNN reranker)	6.456	63.87	-	-	-
+ N-gram match reranker	7.772	69.26	-	-	-
ConvSeq2Seq(CNN + CNN)					
Prepending context	8.450	63.02	0.4670	0.7557	3.7281
+ CNN reranker	8.474	62.93	0.4692	0.7561	3.7412
+ CNN reranker + N-gram match reranker	7.920	69.60	0.4534	0.7238	3.6955

Table 2: Different automatic metric scores of TGen model (RNN+RNN) and proposed model (CNN+CNN) on test data using evaluation metric version 11b.

We see an improvement of 6.7 BLEU points when using N-gram match reranker with ω set to 5. A decrease in scores of other metrics is seen. These inconsistencies are due to the way brevity penalty is calculated for computing BLEU scores in 11b version of metric implementation.

BLEU and NIST scores of the TGen model given in Table 2 match with that represented in (Dušek and Jurcicek, 2016a). The scores of our model shows slight improvement over TGen model.

The studies done to compare the proposed model with the TGen model, show the effectiveness of considering the CNN-based approach to NLG. Studies also show that CNN reranker outperforms the RNN reranker. Further, CNN-based model is expected to take less time to train when compared to RNN-based model. We compare the time taken by the models in the next section.

4.3 Studies on the models based on training time

In this section, we compare the proposed model with that of TGen based on time taken for training. All the experiments were performed on 8GB Nvidia GeForce GTX 1080 GPU. The time taken for training ConvSeq2Seq generator is approximately 4 minutes. The time taken for training CNN reranker is approximately 2 minutes. The time taken for training TGen model is approximately 128 minutes which is 21 times more than our ConvSeq2Seq generator in combination with CNN reranker. This shows the effectiveness of using convolutional neural network in building a model for NLG than using recurrent neural network based approach used in TGen.

5 Conclusion and Future Work

In this paper a novel approach to natural language generation (NLG) using convolutional sequence to sequence learning is proposed. The convolutional model for NLG is found to encapsulate dependencies between words in a better way than recurrent neural network (RNN) based sequence to sequence learning. It is also seen that the convolutional approach makes efficient use of computational resources. The proposed model in combination with CNN reranker and N-gram match reranker is capable of entraining to users' way of speaking. Studies conducted on a standard dataset shows the effectiveness of proposed approach which outperforms the conventional RNN-based approach.

In future, we propose to perform human based evaluations to support the present performance of the model.

References

A. Belz and E. Reiter. 2006. Comparing Automatic and Human Evaluation of NLG Systems. In *11th Conference of the European Chapter of the Association for Computational Linguistics*. http://www.aclweb.org/anthology/E06-1040.

M. Denkowski and A. Lavie. 2014. Meteor Universal: Language Specific Translation Evaluation for Any Target Language. In *Proceedings of the Ninth Workshop on Statistical Machine Translation*. Association for Computational Linguistics, pages 376–380. https://doi.org/10.3115/v1/W14-3348.

G. Doddington. 2002. Automatic Evaluation of Machine Translation Quality Using N-gram Co-occurrence Statistics. In *Proceedings of the Second International Conference on Human Language Technology Research*. Morgan Kaufmann Publishers Inc., San Francisco, CA, USA, HLT '02, pages 138–145. http://dl.acm.org/citation.cfm?id=1289189.1289273.

O. Dušek and F. Jurcicek. 2016a. A Context-aware Natural Language Generator for Dialogue Systems. In *Proceedings of the 17th Annual Meeting of the Special Interest Group on Discourse and Dialogue*. Association for Computational Linguistics, pages 185–190. https://doi.org/10.18653/v1/W16-3622.

O. Dušek and F. Jurcicek. 2016b. Sequence-to-Sequence Generation for Spoken Dialogue via Deep Syntax Trees and Strings. In *Proceedings of the 54th Annual Meeting of the Association for Computational Linguistics (Volume 2: Short Papers)*. Association for Computational Linguistics, pages 45–51. https://doi.org/10.18653/v1/P16-2008.

J. Gehring, M. Auli, D. Grangier, D. Yarats, and Y. N. Dauphin. 2017. Convolutional Sequence to Sequence Learning. In *ICML*. PMLR, volume 70 of *Proceedings of Machine Learning Research*, pages 1243–1252.

N. Kalchbrenner, E. Grefenstette, and P. Blunsom. 2014. A Convolutional Neural Network for Modelling Sentences. In *Proceedings of the 52nd Annual Meeting of the Association for Computational Linguistics (Volume 1: Long Papers)*. Association for Computational Linguistics, pages 655–665. https://doi.org/10.3115/v1/P14-1062.

Y. Kim. 2014. Convolutional Neural Networks for Sentence Classification. In *Proceedings of the 2014 Conference on Empirical Methods in Natural Language Processing (EMNLP)*. Association for Computational Linguistics, pages 1746–1751. https://doi.org/10.3115/v1/D14-1181.

D. P. Kingma and J. L. Ba. 2015. Adam: A Method for Stochastic Optimization. In *Proceedings of International Conference on Learning Representations*. pages 1–13.

Y. LeCun and Y. Bengio. 1995. *Convolutional networks for images, speech, and time series*. MIT Press, Cambridge, MA, USA, 1st edition.

C.-Y. Lin. 2004. ROUGE: A Package for Automatic Evaluation of Summaries. In *Text Summarization Branches Out*. http://www.aclweb.org/anthology/W04-1013.

Y. Nesterov. 1983. A method for unconstrained convex minimization problem with the rate of convergence $o(1/k^2)$. *Doklady AN USSR* 269:543–547. https://ci.nii.ac.jp/naid/20001173129/en/.

J. Novikova, O. Dušek, and V. Rieser. 2017. The E2E Dataset: New Challenges for End-to-End Generation. In *Proceedings of the 18th Annual Meeting of the Special Interest Group on Discourse and Dialogue*. Saarbrücken, Germany. ArXiv:1706.09254. https://arxiv.org/abs/1706.09254.

K. Papineni, S. Roukos, T. Ward, and W.-J. Zhu. 2002. Bleu: a Method for Automatic Evaluation of Machine Translation. In *Proceedings of the 40th Annual Meeting of the Association for Computational Linguistics*. pages 311–318. http://www.aclweb.org/anthology/P02-1040.

A. Stent, R. Prasad, and M. Walker. 2004. Trainable Sentence Planning for Complex Information Presentation in Spoken Dialog Systems. In *Proceedings of the 42nd Annual Meeting on Association for Computational Linguistics*. Association for Computational Linguistics, Stroudsburg, PA, USA, ACL '04. https://doi.org/10.3115/1218955.1218966.

R. Vedantam, C. L. Zitnick, and D. Parikh. 2015. CIDEr: Consensus-based image description evaluation. In *CVPR*. IEEE Computer Society, pages 4566–4575.

A. Waibel, T. Hanazawa, G. Hinton, K. Shikano, and K. J. Lang. 1989. Phoneme recognition using time-delay neural networks. *IEEE Transactions on Acoustics, Speech, and Signal Processing* 37(3):328–339. https://doi.org/10.1109/29.21701.

M. A. Walker, O. Rambow, and M. Rogati. 2002. Training a sentence planner for spoken dialogue using boosting. *Computer Speech & Language* 16(3-4):409–433. https://doi.org/10.1016/S0885-2308(02)00027-X.

T.-H. Wen, M. Gasic, D. Kim, N. Mrksic, P.-H. Su, D. Vandyke, and S. Young. 2015a. Stochastic Language Generation in Dialogue using Recurrent Neural Networks with Convolutional Sentence Reranking. In *Proceedings of the 16th Annual Meeting of the Special Interest Group on Discourse and Dialogue*. Association for Computational Linguistics, pages 275–284. https://doi.org/10.18653/v1/W15-4639.

T.-H. Wen, M. Gasic, N. Mrkšić, P.-H. Su, D. Vandyke, and S. Young. 2015b. Semantically Conditioned LSTM-based Natural Language Generation for Spoken Dialogue Systems. In *Proceedings of the 2015 Conference on Empirical Methods in Natural Language Processing*. Association for Computational Linguistics, pages 1711–1721. https://doi.org/10.18653/v1/D15-1199.

S. Young, M. Gašić, S. Keizer, F. Mairesse, J. Schatzmann, B. Thomson, and K. Yu. 2009. The Hidden Information State Model: a practical framework for POMDP-based spoken dialogue management. *Computer Speech and Language* 24(2):150. https://doi.org/10.1016/j.csl.2009.04.001.

A Unified Neural Architecture for Joint Dialog Act Segmentation and Recognition in Spoken Dialog System

Tianyu Zhao
Graduate School of Informatics,
Kyoto University
zhao@sap.ist.i.kyoto-u.ac.jp

Tatsuya Kawahara
Graduate School of Informatics,
Kyoto University
kawahara@i.kyoto-u.ac.jp

Abstract

In spoken dialog systems (SDSs), dialog act (DA) segmentation and recognition provide essential information for response generation. A majority of previous works assumed ground-truth segmentation of DA units, which is not available from automatic speech recognition (ASR) in SDS. We propose a unified architecture based on neural networks, which consists of a sequence tagger for segmentation and a classifier for recognition. The DA recognition model is based on hierarchical neural networks to incorporate the context of preceding sentences. We investigate sharing some layers of the two components so that they can be trained jointly and learn generalized features from both tasks. An evaluation on the Switchboard Dialog Act (SwDA) corpus shows that the jointly-trained models outperform independently-trained models, single-step models, and other reported results in DA segmentation, recognition, and joint tasks.

1 Introduction

A growing interest in interactive conversational agents and robots has motivated research focus on spoken language understanding (SLU). As an essential part of spoken dialog system (SDS), SLU analyzes user input, and provides the dialog system with information to make a response. In conversations, dialog act (DA) represents the communicative function of an utterance (Stolcke et al., 2000). For instance, we can use DA tag *Statement* to describe utterance *"Me, I'm in the legal department."* and use *Yes-No-Question* to describe *"Do you have to have any special training?"*. Recognition of DA benefits the understanding of dialog

structure, thus allows SDS to conduct meaningful and smooth conversation, e.g. a *Yes-Answer* or *No-Answer* to a *Yes-No-Question*, and end the conversation after a *Conventional-closing*.[1]

Most of previous works focused on DA recognition given transcriptions that are manually segmented (Stolcke et al., 2000; Ivanovic, 2005; Webb et al., 2005; Sridhar et al., 2009; Li and Wu, 2016; Khanpour et al., 2016; Lee and Dernoncourt, 2016; Shen and Lee, 2016; Joty and Hoque, 2016). Early works applied decision trees, Hidden Markov Model (Stolcke et al., 2000), and n-gram models (Stolcke et al., 2000; Ivanovic, 2005) to classify DA tags. Recently, hierarchical neural networks have been introduced to the task. Such models encode a DA segment into a *sentence encoding* by one network and apply the other network for DA recognition given a sequence of *sentence encoding*. Different combinations of networks such as CNN-ANN, RNN-ANN (Lee and Dernoncourt, 2016), and RNN-RNN (Li and Wu, 2016; Khanpour et al., 2016) are shown to greatly improve the accuracy of DA recognition. Ji et al. (2016) introduced an extra latent variable to a hierarchical RNN model to represent discourse relation. Jointly training the latent variable model on DA recognition and language modeling tasks yields competitive results. Recent works (Kumar et al., 2017; Chen et al., 2017) on DA recognition use a hierarchical encoder to generate a vector representation for each DA segment, then a Conditional Random Field (CRF) tagger is applied to sequence labeling given the sequence of segment representations. Kumar et al. (2017) reported an accuracy of 79.2% on SwDA, while Chen et al. (2017) achieved the current state-of-the-art accuracy of 81.3% by incorporating attentional mechanism and extra inputs (character embeddings, Part-

---

[1]Examples of DA tags and utterances are selected from the Switchboard Dialog Act (SwDA) corpus.

Proceedings of the SIGDIAL 2018 Conference, pages 201–208,
Melbourne, Australia, 12-14 July 2018. ©2018 Association for Computational Linguistics

Words	okay	so	I	guess	it	starts	recording	now
Segmentation	E	I	I	I	I	I	I	E
DA	Backchannel	Statement						

Table 1: DA segmentation and recognition: "I" tag refers to inside of a segment, and "E" is the end of a segment.

of-Speech tags, and named entitiy tags). However, these models with CRF layer assume that complete dialog is given before prediction. Thus the reported performances will not apply to real-time SDS, where DA tags are often predicted incrementally.

As shown in Table 1, an utterance in a conversational turn can consist of several DA units. In the example, we use *"E"* tag to denote the end of a segment and *"I"* for inside. The utterance *"okay so I guess it starts recording now"* are split into two segments, which are a *Backchannel* and a *Statement* respectively. However, automatic speech recognition (ASR) in SDS usually provides no punctuation that gives hints for DA segmentation, thus it is necessary to build a sequence labeler for automatic DA segmentation.

A majority of previous works of DA segmentation formulated DA segmentation and recognition in a single step (Zimmermann et al., 2006; Zimmermann, 2009; Quarteroni et al., 2011; Granell et al., 2009). Segmentation labels are combined with DA labels (e.g. *"E_Statement"* denotes the end of a *Statement* segment), and a sequence labeling model is applied to predict tags for both tasks. This approach has a merit of integration so that recognition helps segmentation and segmentation errors are not propagated to the recognition step. On the other hand, it has a drawback that it can hardly incorporate a history of preceding sentences to predict the DA tag of the current sentence. Another approach is to process the data in a pipeline manner. Manuvinakurike et al. (2016) used a CRF for DA segmentation and a Supported Vector Machine (SVM) for DA recognition given predicted segments. For pipeline methods, downstream task (e.g. DA recognition) is vulnerable to errors from upstream task (e.g. DA segmentation). In this paper we propose a unified architecture based on neural networks for DA segmentation and recognition to solve the aforementioned problems. Our method uses separate models for DA segmentation and recognition but introduces joint learning so that the models can learn from both tasks.

Joint learning (also multi-task learning) allows a model to learn from different tasks in parallel, which benefits the generalization of the model. Collobert and Weston (2008) introduced a unified architecture based on Convolutional Neural Networks (CNNs) to natural language processing tasks such as Part-of-Speech (POS) tagging and chunking, and showed that joint learning of related tasks improves model performance. Inspired by this work, we investigate joint learning of DA segmentation and recognition for better generalized model. We compare the jointly-trained models under the unified architecture with models trained separately and previous works on the Switchboard Dialog Act (SwDA) corpus.

2 Models and Training

The proposed method applies a word sequence tagger for segmentation and a sentence classifier for recognition. Under a unified neural architecture, the sequence tagger and the classifier share parameters to learn features from each other and improve generalization. As shown in Figure 1, the left part corresponds to a word sequence tagger for segmentation using Bidirectional Long Short Term Memory (BiLSTM) (Schuster and Paliwal, 1997) and on the right-hand side is a sentence classifier for DA recognition based on hierarchical LSTMs (Hochreiter and Schmidhuber, 1997).

Components for segmentation and recognition will be explained in Section 2.1 and 2.2. In Section 2.3, three proposed models are introduced. In order to compare the proposed models with conventional approach, we describe a single-step model that uses combined labels in Section 2.4.

2.1 Word Sequence Tagger for DA Segmentation

Regarding DA segmentation as a sequence labeling problem, BiLSTM naturally fits the task since it can exploit information of surrounding words in the prediction of the current word. The sequence tagger predicts a segmentation label y_t

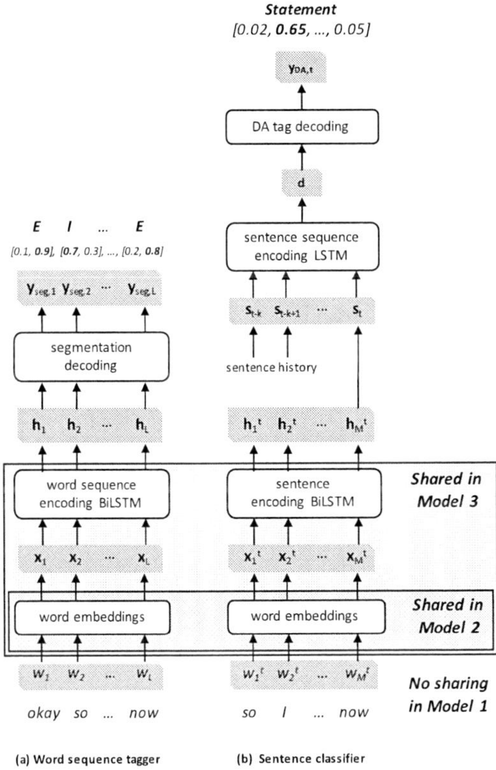

Figure 1: A unified neural architecture consisting of a word sequence tagger for DA segmentation and a sentence classifier for DA recognition.

for each word w_t in the input utterance $w_{1:L}$. A word embedding layer firstly maps the input words $w_{1:L}$ into distributed vector representation of words $\mathbf{x}_{1:L}$. Then we use a BiLSTM to process the sequence and output hidden states $\mathbf{h}_{1:L}$. The last decoding layer computes a probability distribution $\mathbf{y}_{seg,1:L}$ over segmentation labels:

$$\mathbf{x}_{1:L} = \text{word-embedding}(w_{1:L}), \quad (1)$$

$$\mathbf{h}_{1:L} = \text{BiLSTM}(\mathbf{x}_{1:L}), \quad (2)$$

$$\mathbf{y}_{seg,t} = \text{softmax}(W_{seg}\mathbf{h}_t + \mathbf{b}_{seg}), \quad (3)$$

where W_{seg} and $\mathbf{b}_{seg}$ are trainable parameters in the decoding layer.

2.2 Sentence Classifier for DA Recognition

Accurate recognition of DA requires understanding of discourse relations (Ji et al., 2016). Therefore, preceding sentences are needed as context in the recognition of the current sentence. Hierarchical neural networks are able to encode intra-sentence information and capture inter-sentence

relations through a two-level hierarchy. The lower level of the network generates a *sentence encoding* $\mathbf{s}_t$ for input sentence $w_{1:M}^t$ via BiLSTM, and the higher-level LSTM network predicts a DA tag of the input sentence given *sentence encoding* $\mathbf{s}_t$ as well as *sentence encoding*s of preceding k sentences $\mathbf{s}_{t-k}, \mathbf{s}_{t-k+1}, \cdots, \mathbf{s}_{t-1}$.

We use a word embedding layer and a BiLSTM layer to obtain hidden states $\mathbf{h}_{1:M}^t$ as same as in the sequence tagger. The last hidden state $\mathbf{h}_M^t$ (sum of the last hidden states on two directions of BiLSTM as shown in Equation 4) is used as *sentence encoding* $\mathbf{s}_t$. In the same way, $\mathbf{s}_{t-k:t-1}$ are calculated and used as a context in the sentence sequence encoding network. We use a vanila LSTM to process sequence $\mathbf{s}_{t-k:t}$, and input the last hidden state $\mathbf{d}$ to a DA tag decoding layer to compute the probability distribution over DA tags.

$$\mathbf{h}_M^t = \overrightarrow{\mathbf{h}}_M^t + \overleftarrow{\mathbf{h}}_M^t, \quad (4)$$

$$\mathbf{s}_t = \mathbf{h}_M^t, \quad (5)$$

$$\mathbf{d} = \text{LSTM}(\mathbf{s}_{t-k:t}), \quad (6)$$

$$\mathbf{y}_{DA,t} = \text{softmax}(W_{DA}\mathbf{d} + \mathbf{b}_{DA}), \quad (7)$$

where W_{DA} and $\mathbf{b}_{DA}$ are trainable parameters in the DA tag decoding layer.

2.3 Proposed Models

Based on the aforementioned word sequence tagger and sentence classifier, we introduce three models. Different from the single-step method in past works, the proposed models work in a cascading manner, i.e. to split the input text $w_{1:L}$ into segments using the word sequence tagger, then feed each segment $w_{1:M}^t$ to the sentence classifier to predict its DA tag. As shown in Figure 1, the segmentation component and the DA recognition component have the same structure in their lower-level parts (a word embedding layer and a BiLSTM-based encoder layer). The difference between the three models is the number of shared layers.

- **Model 1** A straightforward method is to separately build a word sequence tagger and a sentence classifier. The model that has no shared layers is called Model 1.

- **Model 2** Word embedding layers are shared between the sequence tagger and the DA classifier in Model 2. When training the sequence tagger on the segmentation task, gradients from top end are back-propagated into the shared word embeddings that are also used by the DA classifier, vice versa. Parameters in the shared word embedding layer are updated by losses from both tasks, thus the model learns generalized features on the word level.

- **Model 3** We combine both the word embedding layers and the BiLSTM encoding layers which produce $\mathbf{h}_{1:L}$ and $\mathbf{h}_{1:M}^{t}$ in Model 3. Since the higher-level layers are shared, this model is expected to learn generalization in high-level features.

2.4 Single-step Model for DA Segmentation and Recognition

Previous single-step approaches to DA segmentation and recognition are based on non-network models such as Conditional Random Field (CRF). For a fair comparison between the proposed neural models and single-step method, we implement an LSTM-based sequence tagger to predict combined labels in a single-step manner. The single-step model resembles the segmentation component in Section 2.1 and the only difference is that a set of combined labels are used in the output layer as shown in Figure 2. Therefore, instead of predicting segment boundaries (label *"E"*) only, it generates DA labels at the end of each segment as well (e.g. *"E_Backchannel"*, *"E_Statement"*, etc.).

2.5 Training

The sequence tagger receives a whole turn (i.e. a sequence of consecutive words uttered by one speaker) and predicts segmentation tags (combined tags in the case of single-step model) for all words in the turn. Cross-entropy loss is computed for each word and back-propagated. As for the DA classifier, we use ground-truth segments that are manually transcribed as inputs to the classifier. The model is trained to minimize cross-entropy loss between the predicted DA tag and the oracle DA tag.

When training the joint models (Model 2 and 3), we can apply different strategies to optimize the segmentation and recognition components. One alternative, for example, is to train the segmentation component for one epoch and the recognition component for the next epoch. However, it results in that segmentation loss is likely to dominate the optimizing direction for an entire epoch and vice versa for another epoch. This may pre-

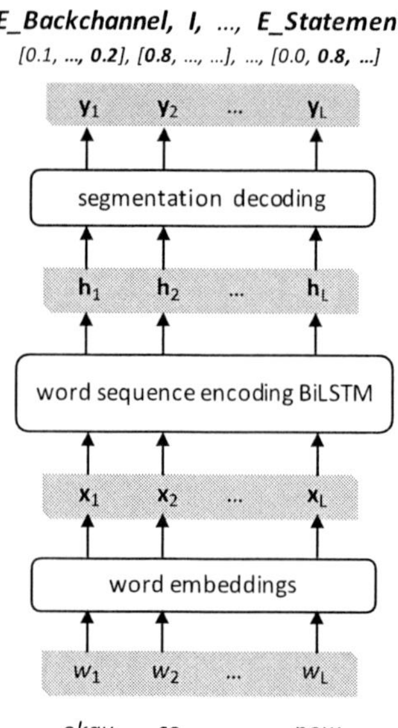

Figure 2: An LSTM-based single-step model that uses combined labels

vent the model from learning from different signals simultaneously. Thus, instead of switching between segmentation loss and recognition loss every epoch, we compute and minimize both segmentation loss and recognition loss for every mini-batch of data.

3 Experimental Evaluations

Three sets of experiments are conducted to evaluate model performance on the DA segmentation task, the DA recognition task, and their joint task respectively. In the segmentation task, we use the word sequence tagger to predict segmentation labels given a sequence of words in a turn. In the recognition task, segments with correct boundaries are given as inputs, and we use the sentence classifier to predict a DA tag for each segment. Lastly in the joint task, instead of using segments with correct boundaries, we split each turn into segments according to the predicted segmentation labels by the sequence tagger. Then the sentence classifier outputs DA tags for the predicted segments.

3.1 Evaluation Metrics

Word-level error rate is used to assess performance on the segmentation task. It compares the predicted boundaries with ground-truth boundaries and counts the number of words that lie in wrongly

Reference	I	I	E_G	I	I	E_S	I	I	E_Q	I	E_S
Prediction	I	I	E_G	I	I	I	E_S	I	E_Q	I	E_R
Word-level Segmentation Error	√	√	√	×	×	×	×	×	×	√	√
Word-level Joint Error	√	√	√	×	×	×	×	×	×	×	×

Table 2: An example of the calculation of metrics for segmentation and joint tasks, where word-level segmentation error rate is 54.5% (6/11), and word-level joint error rate is 72.7% (8/11).

predicted segments. The joint task is evaluated on word level as well. However, it additionally takes DA tags into consideration. An example of the calculation of these metrics is illustrated by Table 2. The DA recognition task is evaluated by accuracy.

3.2 Corpus and Preprocessing

The Switchboard Dialog Act (SwDA) corpus (Jurafsky et al., 1997) is used for evaluation. It contains 1155 human-human telephone conversations and is annotated with 42 clustered DA tags. We follow the train/dev/test set split by Stolcke et al. (2000). Table 3 gives related statistics of the corpus.

dataset	train	dev	test
# of sessions	1003	112	19
# of turns	91k	10k	2k
# of segments	178k	19k	4k
# of words	1565k	164k	35k

Table 3: Corpus statistics of SwDA.

The SwDA corpus is manually transcribed, segmented and labeled with DA tags. In order to conduct meaningful experiments, we removed all the punctuation (i.e. commas, periods, exclamation marks, and question marks) and slash marks ("/") in the transcription because they cover most of segmentation boundaries and we cannot obtain such punctuation labels from ASR results in practice. Moreover, all the annotation comments in brackets are removed. Capitalization of words are also converted into the lower case. Vocabulary is limited to the most frequent 10,000 words (originally 21,177 words after preprocessing) for fast training and inference.

3.3 Experimental Setup

We use the mini-batch gradient descent with momentum to optimize the models with a mini-batch size of 32 for 20 epochs. The learning rate is set as 1 initially and decays in half when the total loss of development dataset does not decrease. Gradients are clipped between [-0.5, 0.5] to avoid exploding. We also experiment with different values of history length k from 1 to 5, which is the number of preceding *sentence encodings* used in the upper-level LSTM of the DA recognition. For all the implemented models, we choose 200, 100 as the dimension of word embedding and the dimension of LSTM hidden states respectively. Both word sequence encoding BiLSTM and sentence encoding BiLSTM consist of two hidden layers, while the sentence sequence encoding LSTM has only one hidden layer. Dropout (Srivastava et al., 2014) is applied after the word embedding layer and between the BiLSTM layers with a drop probability of 0.5.

3.4 Experimental Results

3.4.1 Segmentation Evaluation

The error rates of the three models are shown in Figure 3. With punctuation and slash marks removed, segmentation error rates are fairly high (from 18.7% to 20.8%). However, the jointly-trained models (Model 2 and 3) always result in lower error rates than Model 1. It indicates that joint training benefits the segmentation model in the unified architecture. Specifically, there is a statistically significant error rate reduction of 1.3% when comparing the best result of Model 2 (18.7%) with that of Model 1 (20.0%), and also a statistically significant reduction of 0.9% when compared with the single-step model's 19.6%.

Quarteroni et al. (2011) reported a segmentation error rate of 1.4% using CRF model in their work. However, they used punctuation and slash marks which we removed, thus it is inappropriate to directly compare the results.

3.4.2 Recognition Evaluation

As shown in Figure 4, Model 1 achieves 77.1% at a history length of 5 and gives a strong baseline. Through joint training, Model 2 and 3 further improved the accuracy to 77.7% and 77.8% at history length of 1 and 2. Since the single model simulta-

Model	Segmentation Error Rate	Recognition Accuracy	Joint Error Rate
Model 1	20.0	77.1	31.8
Model 2	**18.7**	77.7	**30.6**
Model 3	18.9	**77.8**	31.0
single-step model	19.6		33.5
CRF (Quarteroni et al., 2011)	1.4*		29.1*
CNN-ANN (Lee and Dernoncourt, 2016)		73.1	
DRLM (Ji et al., 2016)		77.0	
Hierarchical GRU (Li and Wu, 2016)		79.4**	

* The CRF used punctuation and slash marks for segmentation. For reference, when punctuation and slash marks are reserved in our experiments, Model 2 gets a word-level segmentation error rate of 0.3% and a joint error rate of 20.5%.
** Non-textual features were used in this work.

Table 4: Best results (in %) of models.

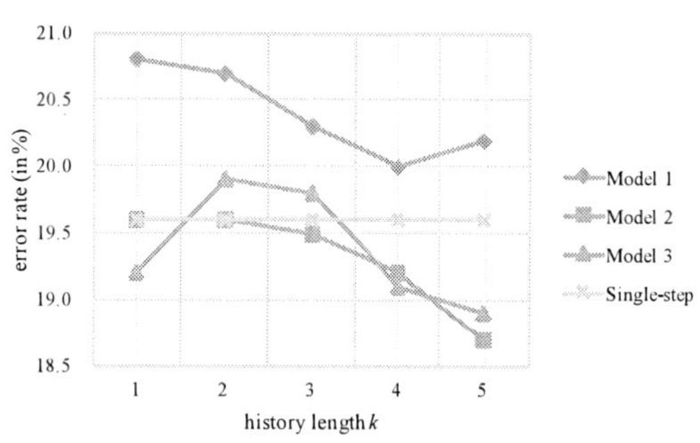

Figure 3: Word-level segmentation error rates

Figure 4: Recognition accuracies

neously predicts segmentation and DA labels, it is unable to predict a DA tag given a sentence with ground-truth boundaries and is excluded from the recognition evaluation.

Lee and Dernoncourt (2016) reported a recognition accuracy of 71.4% using a CNN-ANN model and Ji et al. (2016) reported 77.0% using a jointly-trained latent variable RNN. Li and Wu (2016) reached 79.4% by using extra non-textual features including sentence length, utterance index, sub-utterance index, and turn-taking information.

3.4.3 Joint Evaluation

Figure 5 shows word-level joint error rates of the proposed models. Model 1, 2, and 3 have lowest error rates of 31.8%, 30.6%, and 31.0% respectively. We can see that Model 2 and 3 have better results than Model 1 for all history lengths, which suggests jointly-trained models consistently perform better. It is confirmed from the results that joint learning gives a statistically significant

error rate reduction (1.2% reduction from 31.8% of Model 1 to 30.6% of Model 2). The single-step neural network results in 33.5% joint error rate, much higher than the proposed models. A major reason is that the single-step model cannot capture context of preceding sentences, thus degrading recognition accuracy and leading to poor performance in the joint task.

A single-step CRF model by Quarteroni et al. (2011), which uses word and Part-of-Speech (POS) n-grams features, reached a word-level joint error rate of 29.1% while its segmentation error rate reached 1.4% using punctuation and slash marks in transcription. If we also reserve punctuation and slash marks in our experiments, Model 2 is able to get a lowest joint error rate of 20.5% with a segmentation error rate of only 0.3%.

Model 3 shares the higher-level layers than Model 2 but does not develop consistent and significant advantage. We noticed that the segmentation performance and recognition performance of

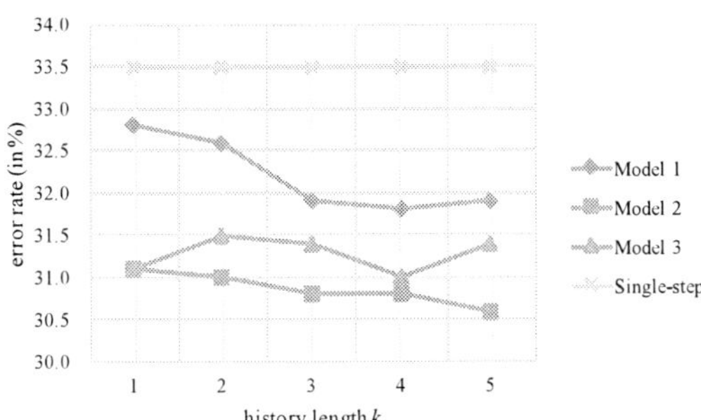

Figure 5: Word-level joint error rates

Model 3 have a reverse trend, i.e. the recognition accuracy decreases when the segmentation error rate reduces. We suspect that since most parameters in the segmentation components are shared (all layers except for the segmentation decoding layer) in Model 3, signals from the DA recognition side can affect the entire segmentation model and lead to problems in optimization.

The best results of the mentioned models in segmentation, recognition, and joint tasks are summarized in Table 4.

4 Conclusion

In this work, we presented a unified neural architecture for joint DA segmentation and recognition for SDS, which consists of a word sequence tagger and a sentence classifier. Since the two components have similar structure, we partially merged them in their word embedding layers (Model 2) and BiLSTM encoding layers (Model 3). Experimental results of segmentation, recognition and the joint tasks on the Switchboard Dialog Act (SwDA) corpus showed that the proposed models gained significant error rate reduction over single-step approaches. Among the three models, Model 2 and 3 improved generalization through joint training and outperformed Model 1, whose segmentation and recognition components are trained independently.

Acknowledgments

This work was supported by JST ERATO Ishiguro Symbiotic Human-Robot Interaction program (Grant Number JPMJER1401), Japan.

References

Zheqian Chen, Rongqin Yang, Zhou Zhao, Deng Cai, and Xiaofei He. 2017. Dialogue act recognition via crf-attentive structured network. *CoRR*, cs.CL.

Ronan Collobert and Jason Weston. 2008. A unified architecture for natural language processing: Deep neural networks with multitask learning. In *Machine Learning, Proceedings of the Twenty-Fifth International Conference (ICML 2008), Helsinki, Finland, June 5-9, 2008*, pages 160–167. ACM.

Ramón Granell, Stephen G. Pulman, and Carlos D. Martínez-Hinarejos. 2009. Simultaneous dialogue act segmentation and labelling using lexical and syntactic features. In *Proceedings of the SIGDIAL 2009 Conference, The 10th Annual Meeting of the Special Interest Group on Discourse and Dialogue, 11-12 September 2009, London, UK*, pages 333–336.

Sepp Hochreiter and Jürgen Schmidhuber. 1997. Long short-term memory. *Neural computation*, 9(8):1735–1780.

Edward Ivanovic. 2005. Dialogue act tagging for instant messaging chat sessions. In *ACL 2005, 43rd Annual Meeting of the Association for Computational Linguistics, Proceedings of the Conference, 25-30 June 2005, University of Michigan, USA*, pages 79–84.

Yangfeng Ji, Gholamreza Haffari, and Jacob Eisenstein. 2016. A latent variable recurrent neural network for discourse relation language models. In *Proceedings of NAACL-HLT*, pages 332–342.

Shafiq R. Joty and Enamul Hoque. 2016. Speech act modeling of written asynchronous conversations with task-specific embeddings and conditional structured models. In *Proceedings of the 54th Annual Meeting of the Association for Computational Linguistics, ACL 2016, August 7-12, 2016, Berlin, Germany, Volume 1: Long Papers*.

Dan Jurafsky, Elizabeth Shriberg, and Debra Biasca. 1997. Switchboard swbd-damsl shallow-discourse-function annotation coders manual. *Institute of Cognitive Science Technical Report*, pages 97–102.

Hamed Khanpour, Nishitha Guntakandla, and Rodney Nielsen. 2016. Dialogue act classification in domain-independent conversations using a deep recurrent neural network. In *COLING 2016, 26th International Conference on Computational Linguistics, Proceedings of the Conference: Technical Papers, December 11-16, 2016, Osaka, Japan*, pages 2012–2021.

Harshit Kumar, Arvind Agarwal, Riddhiman Dasgupta, Sachindra Joshi, and Arun Kumar. 2017. Dialogue act sequence labeling using hierarchical encoder with CRF. *CoRR*, cs.CL.

Ji Young Lee and Franck Dernoncourt. 2016. Sequential short-text classification with recurrent and convolutional neural networks. In *NAACL HLT 2016, The 2016 Conference of the North American Chapter of the Association for Computational Linguistics: Human Language Technologies, San Diego California, USA, June 12-17, 2016*, pages 515–520.

Wei Li and Yunfang Wu. 2016. Multi-level gated recurrent neural network for dialog act classification. In *COLING 2016, 26th International Conference on Computational Linguistics, Proceedings of the Conference: Technical Papers, December 11-16, 2016, Osaka, Japan*, pages 1970–1979.

Ramesh R. Manuvinakurike, Maike Paetzel, Cheng Qu, David Schlangen, and David DeVault. 2016. Toward incremental dialogue act segmentation in fast-paced interactive dialogue systems. In *Proceedings of the SIGDIAL 2016 Conference, The 17th Annual Meeting of the Special Interest Group on Discourse and Dialogue, 13-15 September 2016, Los Angeles, CA, USA*, pages 252–262.

Silvia Quarteroni, Alexei V. Ivanov, and Giuseppe Riccardi. 2011. Simultaneous dialog act segmentation and classification from human-human spoken conversations. In *Proceedings of the IEEE International Conference on Acoustics, Speech, and Signal Processing, ICASSP 2011, May 22-27, 2011, Prague Congress Center, Prague, Czech Republic*, pages 5596–5599.

Mike Schuster and Kuldip K Paliwal. 1997. Bidirectional recurrent neural networks. *IEEE Transactions on Signal Processing*, 45(11):2673–2681.

Sheng-syun Shen and Hung-yi Lee. 2016. Neural attention models for sequence classification: Analysis and application to key term extraction and dialogue act detection. In *Interspeech 2016, 17th Annual Conference of the International Speech Communication Association, San Francisco, CA, USA, September 8-12, 2016*, pages 2716–2720.

Vivek Kumar Rangarajan Sridhar, Srinivas Bangalore, and Shrikanth Narayanan. 2009. Combining lexical, syntactic and prosodic cues for improved online dialog act tagging. *Computer Speech & Language*, 23(4):407–422.

Nitish Srivastava, Geoffrey Hinton, Alex Krizhevsky, Ilya Sutskever, and Ruslan Salakhutdinov. 2014. Dropout: A simple way to prevent neural networks from overfitting. *The Journal of Machine Learning Research*, 15(1):1929–1958.

Andreas Stolcke, Klaus Ries, Noah Coccaro, Elizabeth Shriberg, Rebecca Bates, Daniel Jurafsky, Paul Taylor, Rachel Martin, Carol Van Ess-Dykema, and Marie Meteer. 2000. Dialogue act modeling for automatic tagging and recognition of conversational speech. *Computational linguistics*, 26(3):339–373.

Nick Webb, Mark Hepple, and Yorick Wilks. 2005. Dialogue act classification based on intra-utterance features. In *Proceedings of the AAAI Workshop on Spoken Language Understanding*, volume 4, page 5.

Matthias Zimmermann. 2009. Joint segmentation and classification of dialog acts using conditional random fields. In *INTERSPEECH 2009, 10th Annual Conference of the International Speech Communication Association, Brighton, United Kingdom, September 6-10, 2009*, pages 864–867.

Matthias Zimmermann, Andreas Stolcke, and Elizabeth Shriberg. 2006. Joint segmentation and classification of dialog acts in multiparty meetings. In *2006 IEEE International Conference on Acoustics Speech and Signal Processing, ICASSP 2006, Toulouse, France, May 14-19, 2006*, pages 581–584.

Cost-Sensitive Active Learning for Dialogue State Tracking

Kaige Xie, Cheng Chang, Liliang Ren, Lu Chen and Kai Yu
Key Lab. of Shanghai Education Commission for Intelligent Interaction and Cognitive Eng.
SpeechLab, Department of Computer Science and Engineering
Brain Science and Technology Research Center
Shanghai Jiao Tong University, Shanghai, China
{lightyear0117, cheng.chang, renll204, chenlusz, kai.yu}@sjtu.edu.cn

Abstract

Dialogue state tracking (DST), when formulated as a supervised learning problem, relies on labelled data. Since dialogue state annotation usually requires labelling all turns of a single dialogue and utilizing context information, it is very expensive to annotate all available unlabelled data. In this paper, a novel *cost-sensitive* active learning framework is proposed based on a set of new dialogue-level query strategies. This is the first attempt to apply active learning for dialogue state tracking. Experiments on DSTC2 show that active learning with mixed data query strategies can effectively achieve the same DST performance with significantly less data annotation compared to traditional training approaches

1 Introduction

The dialogue state tracker, an important component of a spoken dialogue system, tracks the internal belief state of the system based on the history of the dialogue. For each turn, the tracker outputs a distribution over possible dialogue states, on which the dialogue system relies to take proper actions to interact with users. Various approaches have been proposed for dialogue state tracking, including *hand-crafted rules* (Wang and Lemon, 2013; Sun et al., 2014), *generative models* (Thomson and Young, 2010; Young et al., 2010, 2013) and *discriminative models* (Ren et al., 2013; Lee and Eskenazi, 2013; Williams, 2014). For *discriminative models*, recent studies on data-driven approaches have shown promising performance, especially on Recurrent Neural Network (RNN) (Henderson et al., 2013, 2014c). As for datasets, the Dialog State Tracking Chal-

lenge (DSTC) series (Williams et al., 2016) have provided common testbeds for this task.

Though data-driven approaches have achieved promising performance, they require large amounts of labelled data, which are costly to be fully annotated. Besides this, it is quite difficult to label a single dialogue because, for every dialogue turn, experts need to label all the semantic slots and typically, to label a single turn accurately, they need to pay attention to the context rather than the current turn only. Active learning (AL) (Settles, 2010) can be applied to select valuable samples to label. Using the AL approach, we need fewer labelled samples when training the model to reach the same or even better performance compared to traditional training approaches.

Although it is often assumed that the labelling costs are the same for all samples in some tasks (González-Rubio and Casacuberta, 2014; Sivaraman and Trivedi, 2014), it is appropriate to consider different labelling costs for the dialogue state tracking task where different dialogues vary in the number of turns. In this paper, we define the labelling cost for each dialogue sample with respect to its number of dialogue turns. Then we provide a new AL query criterion called *diversity*, and finally propose a novel *cost-sensitive* active learning approach based on three dimensions: *cost*, *uncertainty*, and *diversity*. The results of experiments on the DSTC2 dataset (Henderson et al., 2014a) demonstrate that our approaches are more effective compared to traditional training methods.

In the next section, we will present the proposed cost-sensitive active learning framework for dialogue state tracking. Then in Section 3 we will describe the experimental setup and show the results of experiments on the DSTC2 dataset, followed by our conclusions and future work in Section 4.

Proceedings of the SIGDIAL 2018 Conference, pages 209–213,
Melbourne, Australia, 12-14 July 2018. ©2018 Association for Computational Linguistics

2 Cost-Sensitive Active Learning

A complete work cycle of active learning for dialogue state tracking includes 3 steps: (1) train the tracker with labelled dialogue samples; (2) post query using the query strategy to select the valuable unlabelled dialogue and ask experts for its label; (3) merge the newly-labelled dialogue with all previously-labelled dialogue samples and return to (1). The tracker and query strategy will be introduced in Section 2.1 and 2.2 respectively.

2.1 Dialogue State Tracker

Our proposed active learning workflow is independent of the tracker type. Here we use the *LecTrack* model (Zilka and Jurcicek, 2015) as a word-based tracker. For each turn t in a dialogue, the tracker takes in a word concatenation of all history words (together with their confidence scores from ASR) within this dialogue and finally outputs a prediction. The general model structure (at turn t) is shown in Figure 1. The notation $\mathbf{w} \oplus \mathbf{u}$ denotes the concatenation of two vectors, $\mathbf{w}$ (the word) and $\mathbf{u}$ (the confidence score). FC refers to the Fully Connected Layer. The output of FC is then encoded by the LSTM encoder Enc, whose output (only the last one) will be sent to a Softmax layer to make a prediction $\mathbf{p}_t^s \in \mathbb{R}^{N_s}$ over all N_s possible values for a given slot s at turn t:

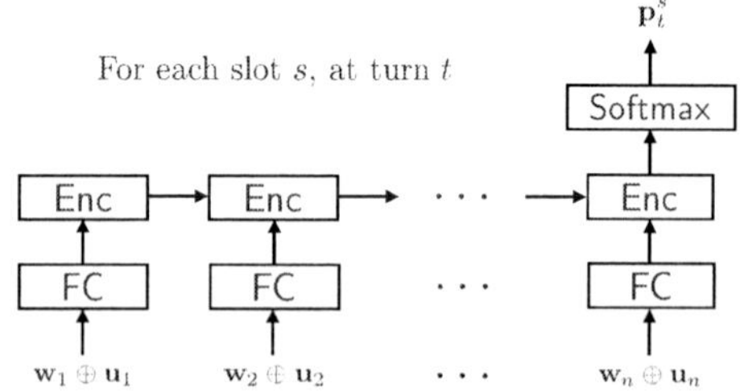

Figure 1: *LecTrack* model stucture. 4 models in total since $s \in \{food, pricerange, name, area\}$.

2.2 Cost-Sensitive Active Learning Methods

Given that different dialogues vary in the number of turns, we assume that the smallest query unit should be a whole dialogue, and that the cost for labelling a dialogue is directly proportional to the number of dialogue turns.

Since all the unlabelled data is possible to be collected simultaneously, the DST task can be regarded as *pool-based sampling* (Settles, 2010). This assumes that there is a small pool of labelled data $\mathcal{L}$, and a large pool of unlabelled data $\mathcal{U}$ available. That allows us to query the samples in a greedy fashion according to some measurement criteria, which are used to evaluate all samples in the unlabelled pool.

We propose four novel query strategies. The first three utilize one kind of measurement criterion respectively and the last one is based on the mixture of the first three. For convenience, a certain dialogue sample is denoted as x.

Cost Strategy (CS)

This strategy prefers the dialogue samples that have the minimum number of turns. For each dialogue sample, its labelling cost, denoted as $C(x)$, can be defined as the number of turns.

Uncertainty Strategy (US)

This strategy prefers the dialogue samples whose predictions the DST model is most uncertain about. In this paper, we take advantage of *entropy* (Shannon, 2001) as the uncertainty measurement criterion. The dialogue uncertainty on slot s, $U_s(x)$, is the average over all the *entropy* values of dialogue turns:

$$U_s(x) = -\frac{1}{C(x)} \sum_{t=1}^{C(x)} \sum_{i=1}^{N_s} \mathbf{p}_t^s[i] \log \mathbf{p}_t^s[i],$$

where $\mathbf{p}_t^s$ can be directly obtained from the DST model described in Section 2.1.

Diversity Strategy (DS)

This strategy prefers the dialogue samples that are most diverse from the dialogues currently in the labelled pool $\mathcal{L}$. As the training and querying process goes on, the diversity of dialogue samples selected to be labelled will decrease gradually, which results in a biased training process. To handle such problem, here we design a novel Spherical k-Means Clustering (MacQueen et al., 1967) based method to evaluate the diversity of dialogue samples and select the most diverse ones in unlabelled pool $\mathcal{U}$ to label, so that we could maintain the diversity of dialogue samples in labelled pool $\mathcal{L}$.

Different dialogues have varying lengths so an embedding function to map each dialogue into a fixed-dimensional continuous space is needed. We utilize the method of *unsupervised dialogue embeddings* (Su et al., 2016) to extract a dialogue feature, which is used to calculate the diversity.

We choose the bag-of-words (BOW) representation as a turn-level feature $\mathbf{f}_t$ at turn t, which will be sent into a Bi-directional

LSTM (BLSTM) (Graves et al., 2013) encoder to obtain the two directional hidden sequences, $\mathbf{h}^f_{1:T}$ and $\mathbf{h}^b_{1:T}$. At turn t, $\mathbf{h}^f_t = LSTM^f(\mathbf{f}_t, \mathbf{h}^f_{t-1})$ and $\mathbf{h}^b_t = LSTM^b(\mathbf{f}_t, \mathbf{h}^b_{t+1})$. Then, the dialogue feature vector $\mathbf{v}$ is calculated as the average over all hidden sequences, i.e., $\mathbf{v} = \frac{1}{T} \sum_{t=1}^{T} \mathbf{h}^f_t \oplus \mathbf{h}^b_t$, where the notation $\mathbf{h}^f_t \oplus \mathbf{h}^b_t$ denotes the concatenation of the two vectors, $\mathbf{h}^f_t$ and $\mathbf{h}^b_t$.

Next, the dialogue feature vector is chosen as the input of a forward LSTM decoder for each turn t, which ultimately outputs feature sequences $\mathbf{f}'_{1:T}$. The model's training target is to minimize the mean-square-error (MSE) between $\mathbf{f}_{1:T}$ and $\mathbf{f}'_{1:T}$.

The feature vectors of all dialogues in both $\mathcal{L}$ and $\mathcal{U}$ can be obtained with this pre-trained model. Define $\mathcal{V}_{\mathcal{L}} = \{\mathbf{v}_{l_1}, \mathbf{v}_{l_2}, \cdots\}$ as the feature vector set of $\mathcal{L}$ and $\mathcal{V}_{\mathcal{U}} = \{\mathbf{v}_{u_1}, \mathbf{v}_{u_2}, \cdots\}$ as the feature vector set of $\mathcal{U}$.

We fit the set $\mathcal{V}_{\mathcal{L}}$ into a Spherical k-Means model with N_c clusters, so that we can acquire a substitutional set of feature vectors denoted as $\mathcal{V}'_{\mathcal{L}} = \{\mathbf{v}'_{l_1}, \mathbf{v}'_{l_2}, \cdots, \mathbf{v}'_{l_{N_c}}\}$, which is composed of N_c representative feature vectors (clusters) among the vectors in the original set $\mathcal{V}_{\mathcal{L}}$. Then for each vector $\mathbf{v}_{u_i}$ in $\mathcal{V}_{\mathcal{U}}$, calculate its *cosine similarity* to N_c vectors in $\mathcal{V}'_{\mathcal{L}}$ respectively, and regard the maximum of N_c similarity values as its true similarity to the whole labelled set, since the cluster of maximum similarity has the largest representativeness of all the original vectors in the labelled set. Therefore, the diversity measure $D(x)$ can be defined as the opposite number of similarity:

$$D(x) = - \max_{i=1,\ldots,N_c} \left\{ \frac{\mathbf{v}_{u_x} \cdot \mathbf{v}'_{l_i}}{||\mathbf{v}_{u_x}|| \cdot ||\mathbf{v}'_{l_i}||} \right\}.$$

Mixed Strategy

In practice, we usually need different query strategies at different learning stages (Settles, 2010). Based on the strategies presented above, we propose a new query strategy called **Cost-Uncertainty-Diversity Strategy (CUDS)**, which is originated from the idea of combining multiple strategies. This strategy takes into consideration three measurement criteria, i.e. *cost*, *uncertainty* and *diversity*, so that the unlabelled samples can be evaluated more comprehensively.

Specifically, what we want is to select samples with low cost, high uncertainty and high diversity. Based on this, we propose a new measurement criterion, denoted as $M(x)$. Naturally, the goal of **CUDS** is to pick out the dialogue samples which

have the maximum measurement value $M(x)$:

$$M(x) = -\alpha C(x) + \beta U_s(x) + \gamma D(x), \quad (1)$$

where α, β and γ are positive weighting parameters that can be tuned so as to find a good trade-off among those three measurement criteria.

In order to conduct weighting, $C(x)$, $U_s(x)$ and $D(x)$ should possess the same scale. $C(x)$ ranges from 1 to C_{max}, the maximum number of a single dialogue's turns, and therefore we replace $C(x)$ in Equation 1 with $C_m(x) = C(x)/C_{max}$. The range of $D(x)$ is $(-1, 1)$, so we replace $D(x)$ in Equation 1 with $D_m(x) = (D(x)+1)/2$. Then the original Equation 1 is transformed into Equation 2:

$$M(x) = -\alpha C_m(x) + \beta U_s(x) + \gamma D_m(x). \quad (2)$$

3 Experiments and Results

3.1 Experimental Setup

Experiments are conducted to assess the performance of different query strategies on single slot and joint goal respectively. The dataset we use is the second Dialogue State Tracking Challenge (DSTC2) dataset (Henderson et al., 2014a), which focuses on the restaurant information domain and contains 7 slots of which 4 are informable and all 7 are requestable. We implement the dialogue state tracker as described in Section 2.1. The model is trained using Stochastic Gradient Descent (SGD), collaborating with a gradient clipping heuristic (Pascanu et al., 2012) to avoid the exploding gradient problems.

3.2 Results on Single Slot

In this section, five different query strategies are compared on single slot. Besides the four query strategies presented in Section 2.2, here we choose **Random Strategy (RS)** as our baseline query strategy. **RS** means we randomly select dialogues to annotate. Although it may seem quite simple, we have to point out that such naive strategy does perform not bad in practice. We attribute such phenomenon to the fact that the query process is dominated by the underlying distribution of the original dataset. A nature of AL called *sampling bias* (Dasgupta and Hsu, 2008) can be considered as the main cause. The training set may gradually diverge from the real data distribution as the training and querying process continues. However, **RS** is luckily not influenced by this effect, which allows it to be a powerful baseline to compare with.

According to the current strategy, the model

queries 2 dialogue samples each time. Figure 2 displays the training accuracy curves of the *food* slot (the most difficult slot) using different query strategies. Here we use the number of labelled dialogue turns as the *x*-axis, which can be regarded as the labelling cost. It is shown that the three query strategies (**CS/US/DS**), which are based on single measurement criterion respectively, have better performance than the baseline strategy (**RS**). The reason why **DS** does not perform very well at the beginning is that the diverse but greatly scarce data is not sufficient to train an effective model. Our proposed mixed strategy **CUDS** achieves the best performance among all the query strategies, which proves the effectiveness of our strategy mixture methodology. Considering the training cost, although the DSTC2 training set is composed of **11677** turns (**1612** dialogues) in total, **CUDS** only consumes about **3000** turns (about **520** dialogues) for training to convergence. Besides, while **RS** consumes **5000** turns (about **700** dialogues) when converging, **CUDS** just consumes **2000** turns (about **360** dialogues) to achieve the performance equal to the convergence level of **RS**, reducing the cost by **60%**.

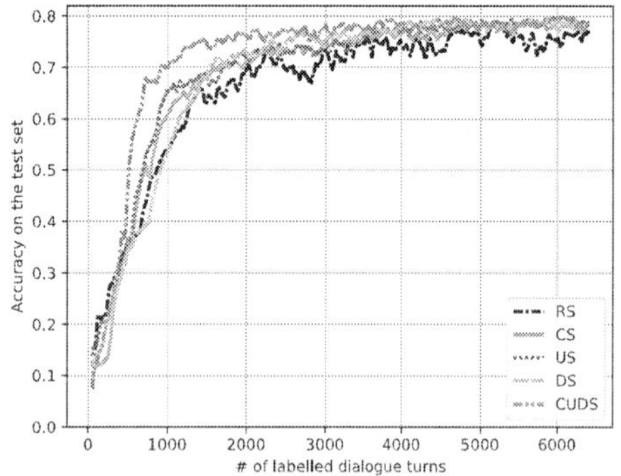

Figure 2: Curves of *food* slot.

3.3 Results on Joint Goal

Figure 3 displays the training accuracy curves of the joint goal using five different query strategies. At different learning stages, the query strategy of best performance is different. **US** rises more quickly at the beginning while **DS** diverges earlier. The reasons include: in order to finally reach convergence, the tracker need to see samples of great diversity, which allows it to give consideration to several semantic slots; however, samples of large *entropy* can bring tracker more concrete information on the most controversial cases, which helps it to learn from scratch rapidly. Our mixed strategy

CUDS, combining the advantages of those two while minimizing the cost at the same time, obtains a performance improvement. Although the final convergence level is not quite high due to the limitation of *LecTrack* model, it does not diminish the effectiveness of proposed AL query strategies.

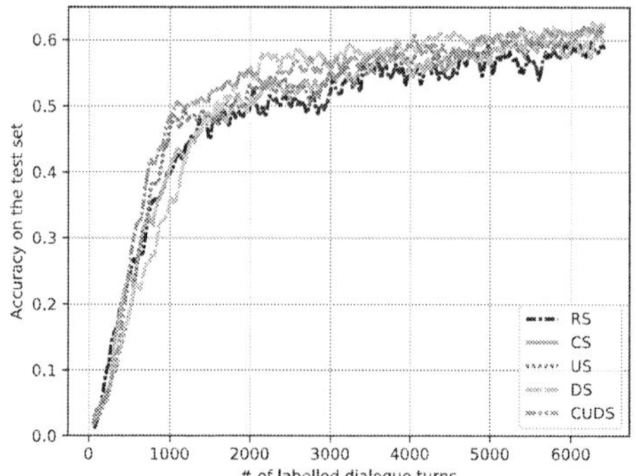

Figure 3: Curves of joint goal.

4 Conclusions and Future Work

In this paper, a novel cost-sensitive active learning technique is presented for dialogue state tracking, which assumes that each dialogue sample has a nonuniform labelling cost related to the number of dialogue turns. Besides *cost*, we also provide another two measurement criteria, *uncertainty* and *diversity*. Our mixed query strategy considers those three criteria comprehensively in order to make queries more appropriately. Experiment results demonstrate that our proposed approaches can achieve promising tracking performance with lower cost compared to traditional methods.

Our future work roughly includes two parts. One is to deploy our proposed AL methods on some other dialogue tasks such as DSTC3 (Henderson et al., 2014b) to verify the results presented in this paper. The other is to conduct our approaches on DST models of better performance (Mrkšić et al., 2017) because the model's tracking ability has an inevitable influence on the whole active learning process.

Acknowledgements

The corresponding author is Kai Yu. This work has been supported by Shanghai International Science and Technology Cooperation Fund (No. 16550720300), the Major Program of Science and Technology Commission of Shanghai Municipality (STCSM) (No. 17JC1404104) and the JiangSu NSFC project (BE2016078).

References

Sanjoy Dasgupta and Daniel Hsu. 2008. Hierarchical sampling for active learning. In *Proceedings of the 25th international conference on Machine learning*, pages 208–215. ACM.

Jesús González-Rubio and Francisco Casacuberta. 2014. Cost-sensitive active learning for computer-assisted translation. *Pattern Recognition Letters*, 37:124–134.

Alex Graves, Navdeep Jaitly, and Abdel-rahman Mohamed. 2013. Hybrid speech recognition with deep bidirectional lstm. In *Automatic Speech Recognition and Understanding (ASRU), 2013 IEEE Workshop on*, pages 273–278. IEEE.

Matthew Henderson, Blaise Thomson, and Jason D Williams. 2014a. The second dialog state tracking challenge. In *Proceedings of the SIGDIAL 2014 Conference*, pages 263–272.

Matthew Henderson, Blaise Thomson, and Jason D Williams. 2014b. The third dialog state tracking challenge. In *Spoken Language Technology Workshop (SLT), 2014 IEEE*, pages 324–329. IEEE.

Matthew Henderson, Blaise Thomson, and Steve Young. 2013. Deep neural network approach for the dialog state tracking challenge. In *Proceedings of the SIGDIAL 2013 Conference*, pages 467–471.

Matthew Henderson, Blaise Thomson, and Steve Young. 2014c. Robust dialog state tracking using delexicalised recurrent neural networks and unsupervised adaptation. In *Spoken Language Technology Workshop (SLT), 2014 IEEE*, pages 360–365. IEEE.

Sungjin Lee and Maxine Eskenazi. 2013. Recipe for building robust spoken dialog state trackers: Dialog state tracking challenge system description. In *Proceedings of the SIGDIAL 2013 Conference*, pages 414–422.

James MacQueen et al. 1967. Some methods for classification and analysis of multivariate observations. In *Proceedings of the fifth Berkeley symposium on mathematical statistics and probability*, volume 1, pages 281–297. Oakland, CA, USA.

Nikola Mrkšić, Diarmuid Ó Séaghdha, Tsung-Hsien Wen, Blaise Thomson, and Steve Young. 2017. Neural belief tracker: Data-driven dialogue state tracking. In *Proceedings of the 55th Annual Meeting of the Association for Computational Linguistics (Volume 1: Long Papers)*, volume 1, pages 1777–1788.

Razvan Pascanu, Tomas Mikolov, and Yoshua Bengio. 2012. Understanding the exploding gradient problem. *CoRR, abs/1211.5063*.

Hang Ren, Weiqun Xu, Yan Zhang, and Yonghong Yan. 2013. Dialog state tracking using conditional random fields. In *Proceedings of the SIGDIAL 2013 Conference*, pages 457–461.

Burr Settles. 2010. Active learning literature survey. *University of Wisconsin, Madison*, 52(55-66):11.

Claude E Shannon. 2001. A mathematical theory of communication. *ACM SIGMOBILE Mobile Computing and Communications Review*, 5(1):3–55.

Sayanan Sivaraman and Mohan M Trivedi. 2014. Active learning for on-road vehicle detection: A comparative study. *Machine vision and applications*, pages 1–13.

Pei-Hao Su, Milica Gasic, Nikola Mrkšić, Lina M Rojas Barahona, Stefan Ultes, David Vandyke, Tsung-Hsien Wen, and Steve Young. 2016. On-line active reward learning for policy optimisation in spoken dialogue systems. In *Proceedings of the 54th Annual Meeting of the Association for Computational Linguistics (Volume 1: Long Papers)*, volume 1, pages 2431–2441.

Kai Sun, Lu Chen, Su Zhu, and Kai Yu. 2014. A generalized rule based tracker for dialogue state tracking. In *Spoken Language Technology Workshop (SLT), 2014 IEEE*, pages 330–335. IEEE.

Blaise Thomson and Steve Young. 2010. Bayesian update of dialogue state: A pomdp framework for spoken dialogue systems. *Computer Speech & Language*, 24(4):562–588.

Zhuoran Wang and Oliver Lemon. 2013. A simple and generic belief tracking mechanism for the dialog state tracking challenge: On the believability of observed information. In *Proceedings of the SIGDIAL 2013 Conference*, pages 423–432.

Jason Williams, Antoine Raux, and Matthew Henderson. 2016. The dialog state tracking challenge series: A review. *Dialogue & Discourse*, 7(3):4–33.

Jason D Williams. 2014. Web-style ranking and slu combination for dialog state tracking. In *Proceedings of the SIGDIAL 2014 Conference*, pages 282–291.

Steve Young, Milica Gašić, Simon Keizer, François Mairesse, Jost Schatzmann, Blaise Thomson, and Kai Yu. 2010. The hidden information state model: A practical framework for pomdp-based spoken dialogue management. *Computer Speech & Language*, 24(2):150–174.

Steve Young, Milica Gašić, Blaise Thomson, and Jason D Williams. 2013. Pomdp-based statistical spoken dialog systems: A review. *Proceedings of the IEEE*, 101(5):1160–1179.

Lukas Zilka and Filip Jurcicek. 2015. Incremental lstm-based dialog state tracker. In *Automatic Speech Recognition and Understanding (ASRU), 2015 IEEE Workshop on*, pages 757–762. IEEE.

Discourse Coherence in the Wild: A Dataset, Evaluation and Methods

Alice Lai
University of Illinois at Urbana-Champaign[*]
aylai2@illinois.edu

Joel Tetreault
Grammarly
joel.tetreault@grammarly.com

Abstract

To date there has been very little work on assessing discourse coherence methods on real-world data. To address this, we present a new corpus of real-world texts (GCDC) as well as the first large-scale evaluation of leading discourse coherence algorithms. We show that neural models, including two that we introduce here (SENTAVG and PARSEQ), tend to perform best. We analyze these performance differences and discuss patterns we observed in low coherence texts in four domains.

1 Introduction

Discourse coherence is an important aspect of text quality. It encompasses how sentences are connected as well as how the entire document is organized to convey information to the reader. Developing discourse coherence models to distinguish coherent writing from incoherent writing is useful to a range of applications. An automated coherence scoring model could provide writing feedback, e.g. identifying a missing transition between topics or highlighting a poorly organized paragraph. Such a model could also improve the quality of natural language generation systems.

One approach to modeling coherence is to model the distribution of entities over sentences. The entity grid (Barzilay and Lapata, 2005), based on Centering Theory (Grosz et al., 1995), was the first of these models. Extensions to the entity grid include additional features (Elsner and Charniak, 2008, 2011; Feng et al., 2014), a graph representation (Guinaudeau and Strube, 2013; Mesgar and Strube, 2015), and neural convolutions (Tien Nguyen and Joty, 2017). Other approaches have used lexical cohesion (Morris and Hirst,

1991; Somasundaran et al., 2014), discourse relations (Lin et al., 2011; Feng et al., 2014), and syntactic features (Louis and Nenkova, 2012). Neural networks have also been successfully applied to coherence (Li and Hovy, 2014; Tien Nguyen and Joty, 2017; Li and Jurafsky, 2017). However, until now, these approaches have not been benchmarked on a common dataset.

Past work has focused on the discourse coherence of well-formed texts in domains like newswire (Barzilay and Lapata, 2005; Elsner and Charniak, 2008) via tasks like sentence ordering that use artificially constructed data. It was unknown how well the best methods would fare on *real-world data* that most people generate.

In this work, we seek to address the above deficiencies via four main contributions. First, we present a new corpus, the Grammarly Corpus of Discourse Coherence (GCDC), for real-world discourse coherence. The corpus contains texts the average person might write, e.g. emails and online reviews, each with a coherence rating from expert annotators (see examples in Table 1 and supplementary material). Second, we introduce two simple yet effective neural network models to score coherence. Third, we perform the first large-scale benchmarking of 7 leading coherence algorithms. We show that prior models, which performed at a very high level on well-formed and artificially generated data, have markedly lower performance in these new domains. Finally, the data, annotation guidelines, and code have all been made public.[1]

2 A Corpus for Discourse Coherence

2.1 Related Work

Most previous work in discourse coherence has been evaluated on a sentence ordering task that assumes each text is well-formed and perfectly co-

---

[1]https://github.com/aylai/GCDC-corpus

Proceedings of the SIGDIAL 2018 Conference, pages 214–223,
Melbourne, Australia, 12-14 July 2018. ©2018 Association for Computational Linguistics

Score	Text
Low	Should I be flattered? Even a little bit? And, as for my alibi, well, let's just say it depends on the snow and the secret service. So, subject to cross for sure. Do you think there could be copycats? Do you think the guy chose that mask or just picked up the nearest one? Please keep me informed as the case unfolds– On another matter, can you believe Dan Burton will be the chair of one of the House subcommittees we'll have to deal w? Irony and satire are the only sane responses. Happy New Year–and here's hoping for many more stories that make us laugh!
High	Cheryl, I just spoke with Vidal Jorgensen. They expect to be on the ground in about 8 months. They have not yet raised enough money to get the project started – the total needed is $6M and they need $2M to get started. Vidal said they process has been delayed because their work in Colombia and China is consuming all their resources at the moment. Once on the ground, they will target the poorest of the poor and go to the toughest areas of Haiti. They anticipate an average loan size of $200 and they expect to reach about 10,000 borrowers in five years. They expect to be profitable in 4-5 years. Meghann

Table 1: Examples of texts and coherence scores from the Clinton domain.

herent, and any reordering of the same sentences is less coherent. Presented with a pair of texts – the original and a random permutation of the same sentences – a coherence model should be able to identify the original text. More challenging versions of this task (sentence insertion (Elsner and Charniak, 2011) and paragraph reconstruction (Lapata, 2003; Li and Jurafsky, 2017)) all assume that the original text is perfectly coherent.

Datasets for the sentence ordering task tend to use texts that have been professionally written and extensively edited. These have included the Accidents and Earthquakes datasets (Barzilay and Lapata, 2005), the Wall Street Journal (Elsner and Charniak, 2008, 2011; Lin et al., 2011; Feng et al., 2014; Tien Nguyen and Joty, 2017), and Wikipedia (Li and Jurafsky, 2017).

Another task, summary evaluation (Barzilay and Lapata, 2005), uses human coherence judgments, but include machine-generated texts. Coherence models are only required to identify which of a pair of texts is more coherent (presumably identifying human-written texts).

The line of work most closely related to our approach is the application of coherence modeling to automated essay scoring. Essays are written by test-takers, not professional writers, so they are not assumed to be coherent. Manual annotation is required to assign the essay an overall quality score (Feng et al., 2014) or to rate the coherence of the essay (Somasundaran et al., 2014; Burstein et al., 2010, 2013). While this line of work goes beyond sentence ordering to examine the qualities of a low-coherence text, it has only been applied to test-taker essays.

In contrast to previous datasets, we collect writing from non-professional writers in everyday contexts. Rather than using permuted or machine-generated texts as examples of low coherence, we want to investigate the ways in which people try but fail to write coherently. We present a corpus that contains texts from four domains, covering a range of coherence, each annotated with a document-level coherence score. In Sections 2.2-2.6, we describe our data collection process and the characteristics of the resulting corpus.

2.2 Domains

For a robust evaluation, we selected domains that reflect what an average person writes on a regular basis: forum posts, emails, and product reviews. For online forum posts, we sampled responses from the Yahoo Answers L6 corpus[2] for the **Yahoo** domain. For emails, we used the State Department's release of emails from Hillary Clinton's office[3] and emails from the Enron Corpus[4] to make up our **Clinton** and **Enron** domains. Finally, we sampled reviews of businesses from the Yelp Open Dataset[5] for our **Yelp** domain.

2.3 Text Selection

We randomly selected texts from each domain given a few filters. We want each text to be long enough to exhibit a range of characteristics of local and global coherence, but not so long that the labeling process is tedious for annotators. Therefore, we considered texts between 100 and

---

[2] https://webscope.sandbox.yahoo.com/catalog.php?datatype=1

[3] https://foia.state.gov/Search/Results.aspx?collection=Clinton_Email

[4] https://www.cs.cmu.edu/~./enron/

[5] https://www.yelp.com/dataset

215

300 words in length. We ignored texts containing URLs (as they often quote writing from other sources) and texts with too many line breaks (usually lists).

2.4 Annotation

We collected coherence judgments both from expert raters with prior linguistic annotation experience, as in Burstein et al. (2010) and from untrained raters via Amazon Mechanical Turk. This allows us to assess the efficacy of using untrained raters for this task. We asked the raters to rate the coherence of each text on a 3-point scale from 1 (low coherence) to 3 (high coherence) given the following instructions, which are based on prior coherence annotation efforts (Barzilay and Lapata, 2008; Burstein et al., 2013):

> A text with high coherence is easy to understand, well-organized, and contains only details that support the main point of the text. A text with low coherence is difficult to understand, not well organized, or contains unnecessary details. Try to ignore the effects of grammar or spelling errors when assigning a coherence rating.

Expert Rater Annotation We solicited judgments from 13 expert raters with previous annotation experience. We provided a high-level description of coherence but no detailed rubric, as we wanted them to use their own judgment. We also provided examples of low, medium, and high coherence along with a brief justification for each label. The raters went through a calibration phase during which we provided feedback about their judgments. In the annotation phase, we collected 3 expert rater judgments for each text.

Mechanical Turk Annotation We collected 5 MTurk judgments for each text from a group of 62 Mechanical Turk annotators who passed our qualification test. We again provided a high-level description of coherence. However, we only provided a few examples for each category so as not to overwhelm the annotators.

We were mindful of how the characteristics of each domain might affect the resulting coherence scores. For example, after rating a batch of generally low coherence forum data, business emails may appear to be more coherent. However, our goal is to discover the characteristics of a low coherence business email or a low coherence forum

post, not to compare the two domains. Therefore, we recruited new MTurk raters for each domain so as not to bias their scores. The same 13 expert raters worked on all four domains, but we specifically instructed them to consider whether each text was a coherent document *for its domain*.

2.5 Grammarly Corpus of Discourse Coherence

The resulting four domains each contain 1200 texts (1000 for training, 200 for testing). Each text has been scored as {low, medium, high} coherence by 5 MTurk raters and 3 expert raters. There is one consensus label for the expert ratings and another consensus label for the MTurk ratings. We computed the consensus label by averaging the integer values of the coherence ratings (low = 1, medium = 2, high = 3) over the MTurk or expert ratings and thresholding the mean coherence score (low $\leq 1.8 <$ medium $\leq 2.2 <$ high) to produce a 3-way classification label (Table 2). We observed that the MTurk raters tended to label more texts as "medium" coherence than the expert raters. Since the MTurk raters did not go through an extensive training session, they may be less confident in their ratings, defaulting to *medium* as the safe option.

Table 3 contains type and token counts for the full dataset, and Figure 1 shows the number of paragraphs, sentences, and words per document.

Domain	Raters	Coherence Class (%)		
		Low	Med	High
Yahoo	untrained	35.5	39.2	25.3
	expert	46.6	17.4	37.0
Clinton	untrained	36.7	38.6	24.7
	expert	28.2	20.6	51.1
Enron	untrained	34.9	44.2	20.9
	expert	29.9	19.4	50.7
Yelp	untrained	19.9	43.4	36.7
	expert	27.1	21.8	51.1

Table 2: Distribution of coherence classes as a percentage of the training data.

	Yahoo	Clinton	Enron	Yelp
# types	13,235	15,564	13,694	12,201
# tokens	189,444	220,115	223,347	213,852

Table 3: Type and token counts in each domain.

2.6 Annotation Agreement

To quantify agreement among annotators, we follow Pavlick and Tetreault (2016)'s approach to

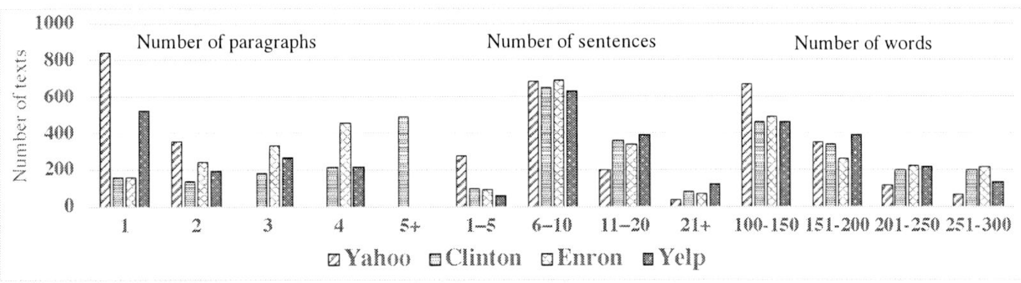

Figure 1: Number of paragraphs, sentences, and words per document.

Domain	Raters	ICC	Weighted κ
Yahoo	untrained	0.113 ± 0.024	0.060 ± 0.013
	expert	0.557 ± 0.010	0.386 ± 0.009
Clinton	untrained	0.270 ± 0.020	0.156 ± 0.013
	expert	0.398 ± 0.015	0.250 ± 0.011
Enron	untrained	0.141 ± 0.021	0.077 ± 0.012
	expert	0.428 ± 0.014	0.273 ± 0.011
Yelp	untrained	0.120 ± 0.026	0.069 ± 0.014
	expert	0.304 ± 0.015	0.181 ± 0.010

Table 4: Interannotator agreement (mean and standard deviation) on all domains.

simulate two annotators from crowdsourced labels. We repeat the simulation 1000 times and report the mean agreement values in Table 4 for both intraclass correlation (ICC) and quadratic weighted Cohen's κ for an ordinal scale.

The expert raters have fair agreement (Landis and Koch, 1977) for three of the domains, but agreement among MTurk raters is quite low. These agreement numbers are the result of an extensive annotation development process and emphasize the difficulty of the task. We recommend that future work in this area leverages raters with a strong annotation background and the time for in-depth instructions. For evaluation, we use the consensus label from the expert judgments. For comparison, we include an experiment using MTurk consensus labels in the supplementary material.

3   Models

We evaluate a range of existing discourse coherence models on GCDC: entity-based models, a word embedding graph model, and neural network models. These models from previous work have been very effective on the sentence ordering task, but have not been used to produce coherence scores. We also introduce two new neural sequence models.

3.1   Baseline

We compute the Flesch-Kincaid grade level (Kincaid et al., 1975) of each text and treat it as a coherence score. While Flesch-Kincaid is a readability measure, previous work has treated readability and text coherence as overlapping tasks (Barzilay and Lapata, 2008; Mesgar and Strube, 2015). For coherence classification, we search over the grade level scores on the training data and select thresholds that result in the highest accuracy.

3.2   Entity-based Models

Entity-based models track entity mentions throughout the text. In the majority of our experiments, we applied Barzilay and Lapata (2008)'s coreference heuristic and consider two nouns to be coreferent only if they are identical. As Elsner and Charniak (2011) noted, automatic coreference resolution often fails to improve coherence modeling results. However, we also evaluate the effect of adding an automatic coreference system in Section 4.1.

Entity grid (EGRID)   The entity grid (Barzilay and Lapata, 2005) is a matrix that tracks entity mentions over sentences. We reimplemented the model from Barzilay and Lapata (2008), converting the entity grid into a feature vector that expresses the probabilities of local entity transitions. We use scikit-learn (Pedregosa et al., 2011) to train a random forest classifier over the feature vectors.

Entity graph (EGRAPH)   The entity graph (Guinaudeau and Strube, 2013) interprets the entity grid as a graph whose nodes are sentences. Two nodes are connected if they share at least one entity. Graph edges can be weighted according to the number of entities shared, the syntactic roles of the entities, or the distance between sentences. The coherence score of a text is the average out-degree of its graph, so for classification we identify the thresholds that maximize accuracy on the training data.

Entity grid with convolutions (EGRIDCONV) Tien Nguyen and Joty (2017) applied a convolutional neural network to the entity grid to capture long-range transitions. We use the authors' implementation.[6]

3.3 Lexical Coherence Graph (LEXGRAPH)

The lexical coherence graph (Mesgar and Strube, 2016) represents sentences as nodes of a graph, connecting nodes with an edge if the two sentences contain a pair of similar words (i.e. the cosine similarity of their pre-trained word vectors is greater than a threshold). From the graph, we can extract a feature vector that expresses the frequency of all k-node subgraphs. We use the authors' implementation[7] and train a random forest classifier over the feature vectors.

3.4 Neural Network Models

We reimplemented a neural network model of coherence, the sentence clique model, to evaluate its effectiveness on GCDC. We also introduce two new neural network models that are more straightforward to implement than the clique model.

Sentence clique (CLIQUE) Li and Jurafsky (2017)'s model operates over cliques of adjacent sentences. For the sentence ordering task, a positive clique is a sequence of k sentences from the original document. A negative clique is created by replacing the middle sentence of a positive clique with a random sentence from elsewhere in the text. The model contains a single LSTM (Hochreiter and Schmidhuber, 1997) that takes a sequence of GloVe word embeddings and produces a sentence vector at the final output step. All k sentence vectors are concatenated and passed through a final layer to produce a probability that the clique is coherent. The final coherence score is the average of the scores of all cliques in the document.

We extend CLIQUE to 3-class classification by labeling each clique with the document class label (low, medium, high). To predict the text label, the model averages the predicted coherence class distributions over all cliques.

Sentence averaging (SENTAVG) To investigate the extent to which sentence order is important in our data, we introduce a neural network model that ignores sentence order. The model contains a single LSTM that produces a sentence vector (the final output vector) from a sequence of GloVe embeddings for the words in that sentence. The document vector is the average over all sentence vectors in that document, and is passed through a hidden layer and a softmax to produce a distribution over coherence labels.

Paragraph sequence (PARSEQ) The role of paragraph breaks has not been explicitly discussed in previous work. Models like EGRID assume that entity transitions have the same weight whether adjacent sentences A and B occur in the same paragraph or different paragraphs. We expect paragraph breaks to be important for assessing coherence in longer documents.

Therefore, we introduce a paragraph sequence model, PARSEQ, that can distinguish between paragraphs. PARSEQ contains three stacked LSTMs: the first takes a sequence of GloVe embeddings to produce a sentence vector, the second takes a sequence of sentence vectors to produce a paragraph vector, and the third takes a sequence of paragraph vectors to produce a document vector. The document vector is passed through a hidden layer and a softmax to produce a distribution over coherence labels. A diagram of this model is available in the supplementary material.

4 Evaluation

We evaluate the models on multiple coherence prediction tasks. The best model parameters, reported in the supplementary material, are the result of 10-fold cross-validation over the training data.

For all neural models (EGRIDCONV, EGRIDCONV +coref, CLIQUE, SENTAVG, and PARSEQ), the reported results are the mean of 10 runs with different random seeds, as suggested by Reimers and Gurevych (2017).

We indicate (†) when the best neural model result is significantly better ($p < 0.05$) than the best non-neural result. We use the one-sample Wilcoxon signed rank test and adjusted the p-values to account for the false discovery rate.

4.1 Classification

For this task, each text has a consensus label expressing how coherent it is: {low, medium, high}.

---

[6]https://github.com/datienguyen/cnn_coherence
[7]https://github.com/MMesgar/lcg

System	Accuracy			
	Yahoo	Clinton	Enron	Yelp
Majority class	41.0	55.5	44.0	54.0
Baseline	43.5	56.0	52.5	**55.0**
EGRID	38.0	43.0	46.0	45.5
EGRID +coref	41.5	48.0	47.0	49.0
EGRAPH	40.0	56.0	43.5	53.0
EGRAPH +coref	42.5	55.0	44.0	54.0
EGRIDCONV	47.0	56.3	44.8	54.2
EGRIDCONV +coref	51.0	56.6	44.7	54.0
LEXGRAPH	37.0	51.0	45.0	48.0
CLIQUE	53.5	**61.0**†	**54.4**†	49.1
SENTAVG	52.6	58.4	53.2	54.3
PARSEQ	**54.9**†	60.2	53.2	54.4†

Table 5: Three-way classification results on test.

System	Spearman ρ			
	Yahoo	Clinton	Enron	Yelp
Baseline	0.089	0.323	0.244	0.200
EGRID	0.110	0.146	0.168	0.121
EGRAPH	0.198	0.366	0.074	0.103
EGRIDCONV	0.204	0.251	0.258	0.104
LEXGRAPH	0.130	0.049	0.273	−0.008
CLIQUE	0.474	0.474	0.416	0.304
SENTAVG	0.466	**0.505**†	0.438	0.311
PARSEQ	**0.519**†	0.448	**0.454**†	**0.329**†

Table 6: Score prediction results on test.

We report overall accuracy for all systems on predicting the expert rater consensus label (Table 5). We repeated this evaluation using the MTurk rater labels and included those results in the supplementary material.

The neural models outperformed the entity-based and lexical graph models. Non-neural models showed mixed results, performing on par with or worse than our baseline. Most models perform poorly on Yelp, worse than the baseline, perhaps because Yelp has the lowest annotator agreement among expert raters.

We also tried adding coreference information for the entity-based methods, as it has been shown to be useful in some prior work (Barzilay and Lapata, 2008; Elsner and Charniak, 2008). For the base entity model experiments, we used Barzilay and Lapata (2008)'s heuristic to determine whether two nouns are coreferent. For the +coref setting, we used the Stanford coreference annotator (Clark and Manning, 2015) as a preprocessing step before computing the entity grid. The coreference system yielded consistent performance improvements of 1–5% accuracy over the corresponding heuristic results, indicating that automatic coreference resolution can help entity-based models in these domains.

4.2 Score Prediction

A 3-point coherence score might not reflect the range of coherence that actually exists in the data. We can instead present a more fine-grained score prediction task where the gold score is the mean of the three expert rater judgments (low coherence = 1, medium = 2, high = 3). In Table 6, we report Spearman's rank correlation coefficient between the gold scores and the predicted coherence scores. As in the classification task, the neural methods convincingly outperformed all other methods, with PARSEQ the top performer in three out of four domains.

4.3 Sentence Ordering

The sentence ordering ranking task is a somewhat artificial evaluation, as a document whose sentences have been randomly shuffled does not resemble a human-written text that is not very coherent. However, we still want to assess whether good performance on previous sentence ordering datasets translates to GCDC. Since the sentence ordering task assumes well-formed texts, we use only the high coherence texts. As a result, there are fewer texts than for the classification task, as we show below. The number of training examples is 20 times the number of texts, as we generate 20 random permutations for each text.

	Yahoo	Clinton	Enron	Yelp
Train texts	369	511	507	511
Test texts	76	111	88	108

Table 7 shows the accuracy of each system on identifying the original text in each (original, permuted) text pair. We leave out the baseline and SENTAVG because they ignore sentence order. We also simplify PARSEQ to a sentence sequence model (SENTSEQ) containing only two LSTMs because the sentence ordering task ignores paragraph information. As in the prior two evaluations, the neural models perform best in most domains, although EGRAPH is best on Yahoo.

4.4 Minority Class Classification

One application of a coherence classification system would be to provide feedback to writers by flagging text that is not very coherent. Such a sys-

System	Accuracy			
	Yahoo	Clinton	Enron	Yelp
Random baseline	50.0	50.0	50.0	50.0
EGRID	55.9	78.2	77.4	62.9
EGRAPH	**64.0**	75.3	75.9	59.5
EGRIDCONV	54.8	75.5	73.1	58.7
LEXGRAPH	62.5	78.3	77.9	60.8
CLIQUE	57.8	**89.4**[†]	**88.7**[†]	64.6
SENTSEQ	58.3	88.0	87.1	**74.2**[†]

Table 7: Sentence ordering results on test data.

System	Yahoo	Clinton	Enron	Yelp
Baseline	0.283	0.255	0.341	0.197
EGRID	0.258	0.260	0.294	0.161
EGRAPH	0.308	**0.382**	0.278	0.117
EGRIDCONV	0.360	0.238	0.279	0.169
LEXGRAPH	0.342	0.094	0.357	0.000
CLIQUE	0.055	0.000	0.077	0.146
SENTAVG	**0.481**[†]	0.332	**0.393**[†]	**0.199**
PARSEQ	0.447	0.296	0.373	0.112

Table 8: Minority class predictions, $F_{0.5}$ score on test data.

tem should identify only the most incoherent areas of the text, to ensure that the feedback is not a false positive. To evaluate this scenario, we present a minority class classification problem where only 15-20% of the data is low coherence:

	Yahoo	Clinton	Enron	Yelp
Low coherence %	30.0	16.6	18.4	14.8

We relabel a text as *low coherence* if at least two expert annotators judged the text to be low coherence, and relabel as *not low coherence* otherwise.

We report the $F_{0.5}$ score of the low coherence class in Table 8, where precision is emphasized twice as much as recall.[8] This is in line with evaluation standards in other writing feedback applications (Ng et al., 2014). Again, the neural models perform best in most domains. However, the results of this experiment in particular show that there is still a large gap between the performance of these models and what might be required for high-precision real-world applications.

4.5 Cross-Domain Classification

Up to this point, we assumed that the four domains are different enough from one another that we should train separate models for each. To test

<hr>

[8]Precision and recall are in the supplementary material.

		Test			
		Yahoo	Clinton	Enron	Yelp
Train	Yahoo	**54.9**	56.7	50.6	**55.3**
	Clinton	51.8	**60.2**	50.7	40.4
	Enron	51.5	59.9	**53.2**	50.8
	Yelp	48.3	55.5	44.0	54.4

Table 9: Cross-domain accuracy of PARSEQ on three-way classification test data.

	Test accuracy			
	Yahoo	Clinton	Enron	Yelp
Train in-domain	54.9	60.2	53.2	54.4
Train all data	**58.5**	**61.0**	**53.9**	**56.5**

Table 10: Classification accuracy of PARSEQ when trained on data from all four domains.

this assumption, we train PARSEQ, one of the top performing neural models, in one domain (e.g. Yahoo) and evaluate it in a different domain (Clinton, Enron, and Yelp). Table 9 compares the in-domain results (the diagonal) to the cross-domain results.

While the model's accuracy generally decreases when transferred to a different domain, sometimes this decrease is not too severe: for example, training on Yahoo/Enron data and testing on Clinton data, or training on Yahoo data and testing on Yelp data. It is reasonable that training on one set of business emails (Clinton or Enron) produces a model that can accurately score the coherence of other sets of business emails. Similarly, both Yahoo and Yelp contain online text written for public consumption which may share coherence characteristics, so it is not surprising that a model trained on Yahoo data works on Yelp (even outperforming the Yelp-trained model).

These results indicate that we might be able to train a better coherence model by combining all our data across multiple domains. We evaluate this theory in Table 10, comparing the results of the PARSEQ model evaluated in-domain (e.g. trained and tested on Yahoo data) to a model trained on the combined training data from all four domains. With four times as much training data, the performance of PARSEQ improves in all domains, indicating that better coherence models may be trained from data outside of a specific, narrow domain.

4.6 Discussion

We observe some trends across our experiments. The basic entity models (EGRID and EGRAPH) tend to perform poorly, often barely outperforming the baseline. The entity grids computed from GCDC texts are often extremely sparse, so meaningful entity transitions between sentences are infrequent. In addition, scoring the coherence of a text (either classification or score prediction) is more difficult than the sentence ordering task, where basic entity models do outperform the random baseline by a reasonable margin. Both the data and the difficulty of the tasks contribute to poor performance from the basic entity models.

The neural network models almost always outperform other models. This supports Li and Jurafsky (2017)'s claim that neural models are better able to extend to other domains compared to previous coherence models. Our PARSEQ and SENTAVG models are easier to implement than CLIQUE and outperform CLIQUE on a majority of experiments. EGRIDCONV usually does not perform as well as the other neural models, but it usually improves over EGRID.

Finally, the relative success of SENTAVG, which ignores sentence order, is evidence that identifying a document's original sentence order is not the same as distinguishing low and high coherence documents. The large number of parameters in PARSEQ may explain why it is sometimes outperformed by SENTAVG.

5   Analysis

To better understand what distinguishes a low coherence text from a high coherence text, we manually analyzed Yahoo and Clinton texts whose labels were unanimously agreed on by all three raters. Regardless of the domain, many low coherence texts are not well-organized and appear to be written almost as stream of consciousness. They often lack connectives, resembling a list of points rather than a coherent document.

Incoherent Yahoo texts often contain extremely long sentences, lack paragraph breaks, and veer off-topic without a transition or any connection back to the main point. This is an especially frequent occurrence with personal anecdotes.

Low coherence Clinton emails make better use of paragraphs, but they too often lack transitions between topics. In addition, missing information was a primary reason for low coherence scores. We provided the raters with individual emails, not the entire email thread, so raters had less information than the original recipient of the email. This amplifies the detrimental effects on coherence of

jargon, abbreviation, and missing context. However, overuse of these compression strategies can result in low coherence even for the intended recipient, so it is worth modeling their effects.

Across domains, coherent texts have a clear topic that is maintained throughout the text, and they are well-organized, with sentences, paragraphs and sub-topics following a logical ordering. Connectives, such as *however, for example, in turn, also, in addition* are used more frequently to assist the structure and flow.

Although sentence order is clearly important, rewriting a disorganized text is not as simple as reordering sentences. Even if changing the location of one sentence increases coherence, a true fix would still require rewriting that sentence or the surrounding sentences. Our analysis indicates that the sentence reordering task is not a good evaluation of whether models can truly be useful to the task of identifying low coherence texts.

6   Conclusion

In this paper, we examine the evaluation of discourse coherence by presenting a new corpus (GCDC) to benchmark leading methods on real-world data in four domains. While neural models outperform others across multiple evaluations, much work remains before any of these methods can be used for real-world applications. That said, our SENTAVG and PARSEQ models serve as simple and effective methods to use in future work.

We recommend that future evaluations move away from the sentence ordering task. While it is an easy evaluation to carry out, the performance numbers overpredict the success of those systems in real-world conditions. For example, prior evaluations (Tien Nguyen and Joty, 2017; Li and Jurafsky, 2017) report performance numbers around or above 90% accuracy, which contrasts with the much lower figures shown in this paper. In addition, we recommend that future annotation efforts leverage expert raters, preferably with a background in annotation, as this task is difficult for untrained workers on crowdsourcing platforms.

By releasing GCDC, the annotation guidelines, and our code, we hope to encourage future work on more realistic coherence tasks.

Acknowledgments

The authors would like to thank Yahoo Research and Yelp for making their data available, and Ji-

wei Li and Mohsen Mesgar for sharing their code.
Thanks also to Michael Strube, Annie Louis, Rebecca Hwa, Dimitrios Alikaniotis, Claudia Leacock, Courtney Napoles, Jill Burstein, Mirella Lapata, Martin Chodorow, Micha Elsner, and the anonymous reviewers for their helpful comments.

References

Regina Barzilay and Mirella Lapata. 2005. Modeling local coherence: An entity-based approach. In *Proceedings of the 43rd Annual Meeting of the Association for Computational Linguistics (ACL'05)*. Association for Computational Linguistics, Ann Arbor, Michigan, pages 141–148. https://doi.org/10.3115/1219840.1219858.

Regina Barzilay and Mirella Lapata. 2008. Modeling local coherence: An entity-based approach. *Computational Linguistics* 34(1):1–34. https://doi.org/10.1162/coli.2008.34.1.1.

Jill Burstein, Joel Tetreault, and Slava Andreyev. 2010. Using entity-based features to model coherence in student essays. In *Human Language Technologies: The 2010 Annual Conference of the North American Chapter of the Association for Computational Linguistics*. Association for Computational Linguistics, pages 681–684. http://www.aclweb.org/anthology/N10-1099.

Jill Burstein, Joel R. Tetreault, and Martin Chodorow. 2013. Holistic discourse coherence annotation for noisy essay writing. *D&D* 4(2):34–52. http://dad.uni-bielefeld.de/index.php/dad/article/view/2825.

Kevin Clark and Christopher D. Manning. 2015. Entity-centric coreference resolution with model stacking. In *Association for Computational Linguistics (ACL)*.

Micha Elsner and Eugene Charniak. 2008. Coreference-inspired coherence modeling. In *Proceedings of ACL-08: HLT, Short Papers*. Association for Computational Linguistics, Columbus, Ohio, pages 41–44. http://www.aclweb.org/anthology/P/P08/P08-2011.

Micha Elsner and Eugene Charniak. 2011. Extending the entity grid with entity-specific features. In *Proceedings of the 49th Annual Meeting of the Association for Computational Linguistics: Human Language Technologies*. Association for Computational Linguistics, Portland, Oregon, USA, pages 125–129. http://www.aclweb.org/anthology/P11-2022.

Vanessa Wei Feng, Ziheng Lin, and Graeme Hirst. 2014. The impact of deep hierarchical discourse structures in the evaluation of text coherence. In *Proceedings of COLING 2014, the 25th International Conference on Computational Linguistics: Technical Papers*. Dublin

City University and Association for Computational Linguistics, Dublin, Ireland, pages 940–949. http://www.aclweb.org/anthology/C14-1089.

Barbara J. Grosz, Scott Weinstein, and Aravind K. Joshi. 1995. Centering: A framework for modeling the local coherence of discourse. *Computational Linguistics* 21(2):203–225. http://dl.acm.org/citation.cfm?id=211190.211198.

Camille Guinaudeau and Michael Strube. 2013. Graph-based local coherence modeling. In *Proceedings of the 51st Annual Meeting of the Association for Computational Linguistics (Volume 1: Long Papers)*. Association for Computational Linguistics, Sofia, Bulgaria, pages 93–103. http://www.aclweb.org/anthology/P13-1010.

Sepp Hochreiter and Jürgen Schmidhuber. 1997. Long short-term memory. *Neural Computation* 9(8):1735–1780. https://doi.org/10.1162/neco.1997.9.8.1735.

J. Peter Kincaid, Robert P. Fishburne Jr., Richard L. Rogers, and Brad S. Chissom. 1975. Derivation of new readability formulas (automated readability index, fog count and Flesch reading ease formula) for navy enlisted personnel. Technical Report, DTIC Document.

J. Richard Landis and Gary G. Koch. 1977. The measurement of observer agreement for categorical data. *Biometrics* 33(1):159–174. http://www.jstor.org/stable/2529310.

Mirella Lapata. 2003. Probabilistic text structuring: Experiments with sentence ordering. In *Proceedings of the 41st Annual Meeting of the Association for Computational Linguistics*. Association for Computational Linguistics, Sapporo, Japan, pages 545–552. https://doi.org/10.3115/1075096.1075165.

Jiwei Li and Eduard Hovy. 2014. A model of coherence based on distributed sentence representation. In *Proceedings of the 2014 Conference on Empirical Methods in Natural Language Processing (EMNLP)*. Association for Computational Linguistics, Doha, Qatar, pages 2039–2048. http://www.aclweb.org/anthology/D14-1218.

Jiwei Li and Dan Jurafsky. 2017. Neural net models of open-domain discourse coherence. In *Proceedings of the 2017 Conference on Empirical Methods in Natural Language Processing*. Association for Computational Linguistics, Copenhagen, Denmark, pages 198–209. https://www.aclweb.org/anthology/D17-1019.

Ziheng Lin, Hwee Tou Ng, and Min-Yen Kan. 2011. Automatically evaluating text coherence using discourse relations. In *Proceedings of the 49th Annual Meeting of the Association for Computational Linguistics: Human Language Technologies*. Association for Computational Linguistics, Portland, Oregon, USA, pages 997–1006. http://www.aclweb.org/anthology/P11-1100.

Annie Louis and Ani Nenkova. 2012. A coherence model based on syntactic patterns. In *Proceedings of the 2012 Joint Conference on Empirical Methods in Natural Language Processing and Computational Natural Language Learning*. Association for Computational Linguistics, Jeju Island, Korea, pages 1157–1168. http://www.aclweb.org/anthology/D12-1106.

Mohsen Mesgar and Michael Strube. 2015. Graph-based coherence modeling for assessing readability. In *Proceedings of the Fourth Joint Conference on Lexical and Computational Semantics*. Association for Computational Linguistics, Denver, Colorado, pages 309–318. http://www.aclweb.org/anthology/S15-1036.

Mohsen Mesgar and Michael Strube. 2016. Lexical coherence graph modeling using word embeddings. In *Proceedings of the 2016 Conference of the North American Chapter of the Association for Computational Linguistics: Human Language Technologies*. Association for Computational Linguistics, San Diego, California, pages 1414–1423. http://www.aclweb.org/anthology/N16-1167.

Jane Morris and Graeme Hirst. 1991. Lexical cohesion computed by thesaural relations as an indicator of the structure of text. *Computational Linguistics* 17(1):21–48. http://dl.acm.org/citation.cfm?id=971738.971740.

Hwee Tou Ng, Siew Mei Wu, Ted Briscoe, Christian Hadiwinoto, Raymond Hendy Susanto, and Christopher Bryant. 2014. The CoNLL-2014 shared task on grammatical error correction. In *Proceedings of the Eighteenth Conference on Computational Natural Language Learning: Shared Task*. Association for Computational Linguistics, Baltimore, Maryland, pages 1–14. http://www.aclweb.org/anthology/W14-1701.

Ellie Pavlick and Joel Tetreault. 2016. An empirical analysis of formality in online communication. *Transactions of the Association for Computational Linguistics* 4:61–74.

F. Pedregosa, G. Varoquaux, A. Gramfort, V. Michel, B. Thirion, O. Grisel, M. Blondel, P. Prettenhofer, R. Weiss, V. Dubourg, J. Vanderplas, A. Passos, D. Cournapeau, M. Brucher, M. Perrot, and E. Duchesnay. 2011. Scikit-learn: Machine learning in Python. *Journal of Machine Learning Research* 12:2825–2830.

Nils Reimers and Iryna Gurevych. 2017. Reporting score distributions makes a difference: Performance study of LSTM-networks for sequence tagging. In *Proceedings of the 2017 Conference on Empirical Methods in Natural Language Processing*. Association for Computational Linguistics, Copenhagen, Denmark, pages 338–348. https://www.aclweb.org/anthology/D17-1035.

Swapna Somasundaran, Jill Burstein, and Martin Chodorow. 2014. Lexical chaining for measuring discourse coherence quality in test-taker essays. In *Proceedings of COLING 2014, the 25th International Conference on Computational Linguistics: Technical Papers*. Dublin City University and Association for Computational Linguistics, Dublin, Ireland, pages 950–961. http://www.aclweb.org/anthology/C14-1090.

Dat Tien Nguyen and Shafiq Joty. 2017. A neural local coherence model. In *Proceedings of the 55th Annual Meeting of the Association for Computational Linguistics (Volume 1: Long Papers)*. Association for Computational Linguistics, Vancouver, Canada, pages 1320–1330. http://aclweb.org/anthology/P17-1121.

Neural Dialogue Context Online End-of-Turn Detection

Ryo Masumura, Tomohiro Tanaka, Atsushi Ando
Ryo Ishii, Ryuichiro Higashinaka and Yushi Aono
NTT Media Intelligence Laboratories, NTT Corporation,
1-1, Hikarinooka, Yokosuka-shi, Kanagawa, 239-0847, Japan
`ryou.masumura.ba@hco.ntt.co.jp`

Abstract

This paper proposes a fully neural network based dialogue-context online end-of-turn detection method that can utilize long-range interactive information extracted from both target speaker's and interlocutor's utterances. In the proposed method, we combine multiple time-asynchronous long short-term memory recurrent neural networks, which can capture target speaker's and interlocutor's multiple sequential features, and their interactions. On the assumption of applying the proposed method to spoken dialogue systems, we introduce target speaker's acoustic sequential features and interlocutor's linguistic sequential features, each of which can be extracted in an online manner. Our evaluation confirms the effectiveness of taking dialogue context formed by the target speaker's utterances and interlocutor's utterances into consideration.

1 Introduction

In human-like spoken dialogue systems, end-of-turn detection that determines whether a target speaker's utterance is ended or not is an essential technology (Sacks et al., 1974; Meena et al., 2014; Ward and Vault, 2015). It is widely known that heuristic end-of-turn detection based on non-speech duration determined by speech activity detection (SAD) is insufficient for smooth turn-taking (Hariharan et al., 2001).

Various methods have been examined for modeling the end-of-turn detection (Koiso et al., 1998; Shriberg et al., 2000; Schlangen, 2006; Gravano and Hirschberg, 2011; Sato et al., 2002; Guntakandla and Nielsen, 2015; Ferrer et al., 2002, 2003; Atterer et al., 2008; Arsikere et al., 2014,

2015). A general approach is discriminative modeling using acoustic or linguistic features extracted from target speaker's current utterance. In addition, recent studies use recurrent neural networks (RNNs) as they are suitable for directly capturing long-range sequential features without manual specification of fixed length features such as maximum, minimum, average values of acoustic features or bag-of-words features (Masumura et al., 2017; Skantze, 2017)

We note, however, that interlocutor's utterances are rarely used for end-of-turn detection. In dialogues, target speaker's utterances are definitely impacted by the interlocutor's utterances (Heeman and Lunsford, 2017). It is expected that we can improve end-of-utterance detection performance by capturing the "interaction" between the target speaker and the interlocutor.

In this paper, we propose a neural dialogue-context online end-of-turn detection method that can flexibly utilize both target speaker's and interlocutor's utterances. To the best of our knowledge, this paper is the first study to utilize dialogue-context information for neural end-of-turn detection. Although some natural language processing tasks recently examine dialogue-context modeling (Liu and Lane, 2017; Tran et al., 2017), they cannot handle multiple acoustic and lexical features individually extracted from both target speaker's and interlocutor's utterances. In the proposed method, target speaker's and interlocutor's multiple sequential features, and their interactions are captured by stacking multiple time-asynchronous long short-term memory RNNs (LSTM-RNNs). In order to achieve low-delayed end-of-turn detection in spoken dialogue systems, acoustic sequential features extracted from target speaker's speech and linguistic sequential features extracted from the interlocutor's (system's) responses are used for capturing interactive information.

Proceedings of the SIGDIAL 2018 Conference, pages 224–228,
Melbourne, Australia, 12-14 July 2018. ©2018 Association for Computational Linguistics

In our experiments, human-human contact center dialogue data sets are used with the goal of constructing a human-like interactive voice response system. We show that the proposed method outperforms a variant that uses only target speaker's utterances.

2 Proposed Method

End-of-turn detection is the problem of detecting whether each end-of-utterance point is a turn-taking point or not. The utterance is defined as an internal pause unit (IPU) if it is surrounded by non-speech units (Koiso et al., 1998). The speech/non-speech units are estimated by SAD.

In dialogue-context-based online end-of-turn detection, all past information of both target speaker's and interlocutor's utterances behind the speaker's current end-of-utterance can be utilized for extracting context information. The estimated label is either end-of-turn or not. The label of the t-th target speaker's end-of-utterance in a conversation can be decided by:

$$\hat{l}^{(t)} = \underset{l^{(t)} \in \{0,1\}}{\operatorname{argmax}} P(l^{(t)}|\boldsymbol{S}^{(1:t)}, \boldsymbol{C}^{(1:t)}, \Theta), \quad (1)$$

where Θ denotes a model parameter. $\hat{l}^{(t)}$ is the estimated label of the t-th speaker's end-of-utterance. $\boldsymbol{S}^{(1:t)}$ represents speaker's utterances $\{\boldsymbol{S}^{(1)}, \cdots, \boldsymbol{S}^{(t)}\}$ where $\boldsymbol{S}^{(t)}$ is the t-th utterance. $\boldsymbol{C}^{(1:t)}$ represents interlocutor's utterances $\{\boldsymbol{C}^{(1)}, \cdots, \boldsymbol{C}^{(t)}\}$ where $\boldsymbol{C}^{(t)}$ is the t-th utterance that occurred just before $\boldsymbol{S}^{(t)}$. Undoubtedly, there are some exceptional cases wherein the t-th interlocutor's utterance is none.

The t-th speaker's utterance involves N kinds of sequential features:

$$\boldsymbol{S}^{(t)} = \{\boldsymbol{s}_1^{(t)}, \cdots, \boldsymbol{s}_N^{(t)}\}, \quad (2)$$

$$\boldsymbol{s}_n^{(t)} = \{\boldsymbol{a}_{n,1}^{(t)}, \cdots, \boldsymbol{a}_{n,I_n^t}^{(t)}\}, \quad (3)$$

where $\boldsymbol{s}_n^{(t)}$ represents the n-th sequential feature in $\boldsymbol{S}^{(t)}$, and $\boldsymbol{a}_{n,i}^t$ is the i-th frame's feature in $\boldsymbol{s}_n^{(t)}$. I_n^t is the length of $\boldsymbol{s}_n^{(t)}$. In the same way, the t-th interlocutor's utterance involves M kinds of sequential features:

$$\boldsymbol{C}^{(t)} = \{\boldsymbol{c}_1^{(t)}, \cdots, \boldsymbol{c}_M^{(t)}\}, \quad (4)$$

$$\boldsymbol{c}_m^{(t)} = \{\boldsymbol{b}_{m,1}^{(t)}, \cdots, \boldsymbol{b}_{m,J_m^t}^{(t)}\}, \quad (5)$$

where $\boldsymbol{c}_m^t$ represents the m-th sequential feature in $\boldsymbol{C}^{(t)}$, and $\boldsymbol{b}_{m,j}^{(t)}$ is the j-th frame's feature in $\boldsymbol{c}_m^{(t)}$. J_m^t is a length of $\boldsymbol{c}_m^{(t)}$.

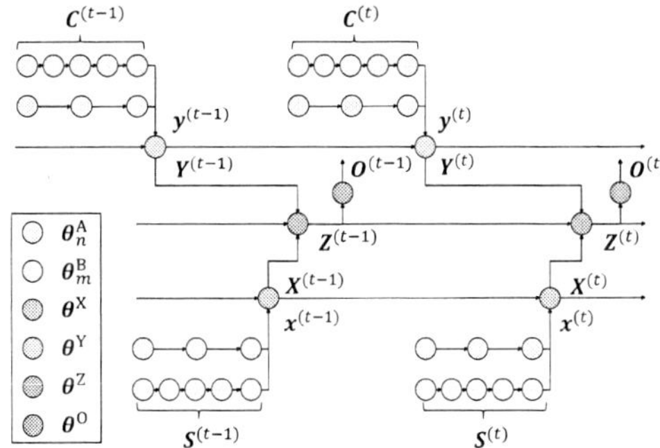

Figure 1: Model structure of neural dialogue-context online end-of-turn detection.

2.1 Fully Neural Network based Modeling

This paper proposes a neural dialogue context online end-of-turn detection method that is modeled using fully neural networks. In order to model $(l^{(t)}|\boldsymbol{S}^{(1:t)}, \boldsymbol{C}^{(1:t)}, \Theta)$, we extend stacked time asynchronous sequential networks that include multiple time-asynchronous LSTM-RNNs for embedding complete sequential information into a continuous representation (Masumura et al., 2017). In order to capture long-range dialogue context information, the proposed method employs two stacked time asynchronous sequential networks for both target speaker's and interlocutor's utterances. In addition, the proposed method introduces another sequential network to capture interactions of both side's utterances.

Figure 1 details the structure of the proposed method. In the proposed method, each feature within an utterance is individually embedded into a continuous representation in an asynchronous manner. To this end, LSTM-RNNs are prepared for individual sequential features in both target speaker's and interlocutor's utterances. Each sequential information is embedded as:

$$\boldsymbol{A}_n^{(t)} = \mathrm{LSTM}(\boldsymbol{a}_{n,1}^{(t)}, \cdots, \boldsymbol{a}_{n,I_n^t}^{(t)}; \theta_n^{\mathrm{A}}), \quad (6)$$

$$\boldsymbol{B}_m^{(t)} = \mathrm{LSTM}(\boldsymbol{b}_{m,1}^{(t)}, \cdots, \boldsymbol{b}_{m,J_m^t}^{(t)}; \theta_m^{\mathrm{B}}), \quad (7)$$

where $\boldsymbol{A}_n^{(t)}$ denotes a continuous representation that embeds the n-th sequential feature within the t-th target speaker's utterance. $\boldsymbol{B}_m^{(t)}$ denotes a continuous representation that embeds the n-th sequential feature within the t-th interlocutor's utterance. LSTM() represents a function of the unidirectional LSTM-RNN layer. θ_n^{A} and θ_m^{B} are model parameters for the n-th sequence in the target speaker's utterance and the m-th sequence in the interlocutor's utterance, respectively.

The continuous representations individually formed from each sequential feature are merged to yield an utterance-level continuous representation as follows:

$$x^{(t)} = [A_1^{(t)^\top}, \cdots, A_N^{(t)^\top}]^\top, \qquad (8)$$

$$y^{(t)} = [B_1^{(t)^\top}, \cdots, B_M^{(t)^\top}]^\top, \qquad (9)$$

where $x^{(t)}$ and $y^{(t)}$ represent utterance-level continuous representations for the t-th target speaker's utterance and the t-th interlocutor's utterance, respectively.

In order to capture long-range contexts, target speaker's utterance-level continuous representations and interlocutor's utterance-level continuous representations are individually embedded into a continuous representation. The t-th continuous representation that embeds a start-of-dialogue and the current end-of-utterance is defined as:

$$X^{(t)} = \mathrm{LSTM}(x^{(1)}, \cdots, x^{(t)}; \theta^\mathsf{X}), \qquad (10)$$

$$Y^{(t)} = \mathrm{LSTM}(y^{(1)}, \cdots, y^{(t)}; \theta^\mathsf{Y}), \qquad (11)$$

where $X^{(t)}$ denotes a continuous representation that embeds speaker's utterances behind the t-th speaker's end-of-utterance, and $Y^{(t)}$ denotes a continuous representation that embeds interlocutor's utterances behind the t-th interlocutor's end-of-utterance. θ^X and θ^Y are model parameters for the target speaker's utterance-level LSTM-RNN and the interlocutor's utterance-level LSTM-RNN, respectively.

In addition, to consider the interaction between the target speaker and the interlocutor, both utterance-level continuous representations are additionally summarized as:

$$z^{(t)} = [X^{(t)^\top}, Y^{(t)^\top}]^\top, \qquad (12)$$

$$Z^{(t)} = \mathrm{LSTM}(z^{(1)}, \cdots, z^{(t)}; \theta^\mathsf{Z}), \qquad (13)$$

where $Z^{(t)}$ denotes a continuous representation that embeds all dialogue context sequential information behind the t-th target speaker's end-of-utterance. θ^Z represents the model parameter.

In an output layer, posterior probability of end-of-turn detection in the t-th target speaker's end-of-utterance is defined as:

$$O^{(t)} = \mathrm{SOFTMAX}(Z^{(t)}; \theta^0), \qquad (14)$$

where $\mathrm{SOFTMAX}()$ is a softmax function, and θ^0 is a model parameter for the softmax function. $O^{(t)}$

corresponds to $P(l^{(t)}|S^{(1:t)}, C^{(1:t)}, \Theta)$. Summarizing the above, Θ is represented as $\{\theta_1^\mathsf{A}, \cdots, \theta_N^\mathsf{A}, \theta_1^\mathsf{B}, \cdots, \theta_M^\mathsf{B}, \theta^\mathsf{X}, \theta^\mathsf{Y}, \theta^\mathsf{Z}, \theta^0\}$. In training, the parameter can be optimized by minimizing the cross entropy between a reference probability and an estimated probability:

$$\hat{\Theta} = \underset{\Theta}{\mathrm{argmin}} - \sum_{d \in \mathcal{D}} \sum_{t=1}^{T_d} \sum_{l \in \{0,1\}} \hat{O}_{l,d}^{(t)} \log O_{l,d}^{(t)}, \qquad (15)$$

where $\hat{O}_{l,d}^{(t)}$ and $O_{l,d}^{(t)}$ are a reference probability and an estimated probability of label l for the t-th end-of-utterance in the d-th conversation, respectively. $\mathcal{D}$ represents a training data set.

2.2 Features for Spoken Dialogue Systems

In neural dialogue-context-based online end-of-turn detection, various sequential features can be leveraged for capturing both target speaker's and interlocutor's utterances. In spoken dialogue systems, the interlocutor is the system. Therefore, lexical information generated by the system's response generation module can be utilized. This paper uses pronunciation sequences and word sequences as the interlocutor's sequential features. In the proposed modeling, we use both symbol sequences by converting them into continuous vectors. On the other hand, the target speaker's utterances are speech. This paper introduces fundamental frequencies (F0s), and senone bottleneck features inspired by Masumura et al. (2017). The senone bottleneck features, which extract phonetic information as continuous vector representations, offer strong performance without recourse to lexical features.

3 Experiments

This paper employed Japanese simulated contact center dialogue data sets instead of human-computer dialogue data sets. The data sets include 330 dialogues and 6 topics. One dialogue means one telephone call between one operator and one customer, in which each speaker's speech was separately recorded. In order to simulated interactive voice response applications, we regard the operator as the interlocutor, and the customer as the target speaker. We divided each data set into speech units and non-speech units using an LSTM-RNN based SAD (Eyben et al., 2013) trained using various Japanese speech data. An utterance is defined as a unit surrounded by non-speech units whose

	Speaker's features	Interlocutor's features	Dialogue context	Recall	Precision	F-value	Accuracy
(1).	F0	-	-	80.4	69.9	74.8	73.4
(2).	SENONE	-	-	82.7	78.3	80.4	80.3
(3).	F0+SENONE	-	-	84.5	77.4	80.8	80.6
(4)	-	PRON	-	46.2	64.9	54.0	61.3
(5).	-	WORD	-	66.1	64.6	65.4	65.3
(6).	-	PRON+WORD	-	68.3	64.1	66.2	65.9
(7).	SENONE	WORD	√	82.0	80.5	81.2	81.4
(8).	F0+SENONE	PRON+WORD	√	**82.7**	**81.4**	**82.1**	**82.0**

Table 2: *Experimental results: Recall (%), Precision (%), F-value (%), and Accuracy (%).*

Topics	#calls	#utterances	#turns
Finance	50	3,991	2,166
Internet provider	64	3,860	1,799
Local government unit	58	3,741	1,598
Mail-order	52	3,752	1,828
PC repair	45	2,838	1,934
Mobile phone	61	4,453	2,016
Total	330	22,635	11,341

Table 1: *Experimental data sets.*

duration is more than 100 ms. Turn-taking points and backchannel points were manually annotated for all dialogues. The evaluation used 6-fold cross validation in which training and validation data were 5 topics and test data were 1 topic. Detailed setups are shown in Table 1 where #calls, #utterances, and #turns represent number of calls, utterances and end-of-turn points, respectively.

To realize a comprehensive evaluation, we examined various conditions. In the proposed modeling, unit size of LSTM-RNNs was unified to 256. For training, the mini-batch size was set to 2 calls. The optimizer was Adam with the default setting. Note that a part of the training sets were used as the data sets employed for early stopping. We constructed five models by varying an initial parameter for individual conditions and evaluated the average performance. When using either target speaker's utterances or interlocutor's utterances, required components were only used for building the proposed modeling. We used following sequential features. F0 represents 2 dimensional sequential features of F0 and ΔF0; frame shift was set to 5 ms. SENONE represents 256-dimensional senone bottleneck features extracted from 3-layer senone LSTM-RNN with 256 units trained from a corpus of spontaneous Japanese speech (Maekawa et al., 2000). Its frame shift was set to 10 ms, and the bottleneck layer was set to the third LSTM-RNN layer. PRON represents pronunciation sequences, and WORD represents word sequences of interlocutor's utterances. The lexical features were introduced by converting them into 128 dimensional vectors through linear transformation that was also optimized in training.

3.1 Results

Table 2 shows the experimental results. We used the evaluation metrics of recall, precision, macro F-value, and accuracy. The results gained when using only target speaker's utterances are shown in (1)-(3). In terms of F-value and accuracy, (3) outperformed (1) and (2). This confirms that stacked time-asynchronous sequential network based modeling is effective for combining multiple sequential features. The results gained when using only interlocutor's utterances are shown in (4)-(6). Among them, (6) attained the best performance although its performance was inferior to (1)-(3). In fact, (4)-(6) outperformed random end-of-turn decision making. This indicates interlocutor's utterances are effective in improving online end-of-turn detection performance. The proposed method, which takes both target speaker's and interlocutor's utterances into consideration, is shown in (7) and (8). In terms of F-value and accuracy, (7) outperformed (2) and (5). These results indicate that interaction information is effective for detecting end-of-turn points. The best results were attained by (8), which utilized both multiple target speaker's features and multiple interlocutor's features. The sign test results verified that (8) achieved statistically significant performance improvement ($p < 0.05$) over (3).

4 Conclusions

In this paper, we proposed a neural dialogue context online end-of-turn detection method. Main advance of the proposed method is taking long-range interaction information between target speaker's and interlocutor's utterances into consideration. In experiments using contact center dialogue data sets, the proposed method, which leveraged both target speaker's multiple acoustic features and interlocutor's multiple lexical features, achieved significant performance improvement compared to a method that only utilized target speaker's utterances.

References

Harish Arsikere, Elizabeth Shriberg, and Umut Ozertem. 2014. Computationally-efficient endpointing features for natural spoken interaction with personal-assistant systems. *In Proc. International Conference on Acoustics, Speech, and Signal Processing (ICASSP)*, pages 3241–3245.

Harish Arsikere, Elizabeth Shriberg, and Umut Ozertem. 2015. Enhanced end-of-turn detection for speech to a personal assistant. *In Proc. AAAI Spring Symposium, Turn-Taking and Coordination in Human-Machine Interaction*, pages 75–78.

Michaela Atterer, Timo Baumann, and David Schlangen. 2008. Towards incremental end-of-utterance detection in dialogue systems. *In Proc. International Conference on Computational Linguistics (COLING)*, pages 11–14.

Florian Eyben, Felix Weninger, Stefano Squartini, and Bjorn Schuller. 2013. Real-life voice activity detection with LSTM recurrent neural networks and an application to hollywood movies. *In Proc. International Conference on Acoustics, Speech, and Signal Processing (ICASSP)*, pages 483–487.

Luciana Ferrer, Elizabeth Shriberg, and Andreas Stolcke. 2002. In the speaker done yet? faster and more accurate end-of-utterance detection using prosody in human-computer dialog. *In Proc. International Conference on Spoken Language Processing (ICSLP)*, pages 2061–2064.

Luciana Ferrer, Elizabeth Shriberg, and Andreas Stolcke. 2003. A prosody-based approach to end-of-utterance detection that does not require speech recognition. *In Proc. International Conference on Acoustics, Speech, and Signal Processing (ICASSP)*, pages 608–611.

Agustin Gravano and Julia Hirschberg. 2011. Turn-taking cues in task-oriented dialogue. *Computer Speech and Language*, 25:601–634.

Nishitha Guntakandla and Rodney D. Nielsen. 2015. Modelling turn-taking in human conversations. *AAAI Spring Symposium, Turn-Taking and Coordination in Human-Machine Interaction*, pages 17–22.

Ramalingam Hariharan, Juha Hakkinen, and Kari Laurila. 2001. Robust end-of-utterance detection for real-time speech recognition applications. *In Proc. International Conference on Acoustics, Speech, and Signal Processing (ICASSP)*, pages 249–252.

Peter A Heeman and Rebecca Lunsford. 2017. Turn-taking offsets and dialogue context. *In Proc. Annual Conference of the International Speech Communication Association (INTERSPEECH)*, pages 1671–1675.

Hanae Koiso, Yasuo Horiuchi, Syun Tutiya, Akira Ichikawa, and Yasuharu Den. 1998. An analysis of turn-taking and backchannels based on prosodic and syntactic features in japanese map task dialogs. *Language and Speech*, 41:295–321.

Bing Liu and Ian Lane. 2017. Dialogue contect language modeling with recurrent neural networks. *In Proc. International Conference on Acoustics, Speech, and Signal Processing (ICASSP)*, pages 5715–5719.

Kikuo Maekawa, Hanae Koiso, Sadaoki Furui, and Hitoshi Isahara. 2000. Spontaneous speech corpus of Japanese. *In proc. International Conference on Language Resources and Evaluation (LREC)*, pages 947–952.

Ryo Masumura, Taichi Asami, Hirokazu Masataki, Ryo Ishii, and Ryuichiro Higashinaka. 2017. Online end-of-turn detection from speech based on stacked time-asynchronous sequential networks. *In Proc. Annual Conference of the International Speech Communication Association (INTERSPEECH)*, pages 1661–1665.

Raveesh Meena, Gabriel Skantze, and Joakim Gustafson. 2014. Data-driven models for timing feedback responses in a map task dialogue system. *Computer Speech and Language*, 28:903–922.

Harvey Sacks, Emanuel A. Schegloff, and Gail Jefferson. 1974. A simplet systematics for the organization of turn-taking for conversation. *Language*, pages 696–735.

Ryo Sato, Ryuichiro Higashinaka, Masafumi Tamoto, Mikio Nakano, and Kiyoaki Aikawa. 2002. Learning decison trees to determine turn-taking by spoken dialogue systems. *In Proc. International Conference on Spoken Language Processing (ICSLP)*, pages 861–864.

David Schlangen. 2006. From reaction to prediction: Experiments with computational models of turn taking. *In Proc. Annual Conference of the International Speech Communication Association (INTERSPEECH)*, pages 17–21.

Elizabeth Shriberg, Andreas Stolcke, Dilek Hakkani-Tur, and Gukhan Tur. 2000. Prosody-based automatic segmentation of speech into sentences and topics. *Speech Communication*, 32:127–154.

Gabriel Skantze. 2017. Towards a general, continuous model of turn-taking in spoken dialogue using lstm recurrent neural networks. *In Proc. Annual SIGdial Meeting on Discourse and Dialogue (SIGDIAL)*, pages 220–230.

Quan Hung Tran, Ingrid Zukerman, and Gholamreza Haffari. 2017. A hierarchical neural model for learning sequences of dialogue acts. *In Proc. Conference of the European Chapter of the Association for Computational Linguistics*, 1:428–437.

Nigel G. Ward and David De Vault. 2015. Ten challenges in highly-interactive dialog systems. *AAAI Spring Symposium, Turn-Taking and Coordination in Human-Machine Interaction*, pages 104–107.

Spoken Dialogue for Information Navigation

Alexandros Papangelis[1], Panagiotis Papadakos[2], Yannis Stylianou [1,3], and Yannis Tzitzikas[2,3]
[1] Speech Technology Group - Toshiba Research Europe
[2] Institute of Computer Science - FORTH-ICS, Greece
[3] Computer Science Department - University of Crete, Greece
{alex.papangelis, yannis.stylianou}@crl.toshiba.co.uk
{papadako, tzitzik}@ics.forth.gr

Abstract

Aiming to expand the current research paradigm for training conversational AI agents that can address real-world challenges, we take a step away from traditional slot-filling goal-oriented spoken dialogue systems (SDS) and model the dialogue in a way that allows users to be more expressive in describing their needs. The goal is to help users make informed decisions rather than being fed matching items. To this end, we describe the Linked-Data SDS (LD-SDS), a system that exploits semantic knowledge bases that connect to linked data, and supports complex constraints and preferences. We describe the required changes in language understanding and state tracking, and the need for mined features, and we report the promising results (in terms of semantic errors, effort, etc) of a preliminary evaluation after training two statistical dialogue managers in various conditions.

1 Introduction

There has been an increasing amount of research being conducted on many aspects of Spoken Dialogue Systems (SDS) with applications ranging from well-defined goal-oriented tasks to open-ended dialogue, e.g., (Amazon, 2017). Deep learning and joint optimisations of SDS components are becoming the standard approach e.g., (Chen et al., 2017; Li et al., 2016; Williams et al., 2017; Liu et al., 2017; Wen et al., 2017; Cuayáhuitl et al., 2017; Yang et al., 2017), showing many benefits but also limitations and disadvantages. Due to the complexity of the problem, most of these approaches focus on limited applications e.g., information retrieval on small domains or shallow-understanding chat-bots.

Moving towards conversational AI, we shift the paradigm to information navigation and present in this work a more realistic goal-oriented setup. The proposed paradigm is designed towards complex interactions using semantic knowledge bases and linked data (Heath and Bizer, 2011), and allows users to be more expressive in describing their constraints and prefer-

ences. We aim to enable users to make informed decisions by understanding their needs and priorities through conversation with an intelligent agent.

In this work we extend the Linked Data Spoken Dialogue System (LD-SDS) system proposed in (Papangelis et al., 2017) in the following directions: a) we propose features mined over the set and the order of objects in the current user focus, b) we modify the language understanding and belief state tracking modules to support the proposed complex interactions over rich information spaces, c) we apply an agenda-based user simulator to train two statistical dialogue manager models, and d) we conduct a preliminary evaluation with promising results.

2 Challenges and Background

2.1 Challenges and Requirements

As our paradigm moves towards information navigation, we assume that the users have a vague idea of what they are looking for and through interaction with the system they can understand their own needs better. The user's intents, therefore, do not always express hard restrictions (constraints) but often express *preferences*[1] that users may or may not be willing to relax as the dialogue progresses. Such preferences may refer to the *importance of attributes* over other attributes (e.g., *location* is much more important than *has-free-wifi* when searching for accommodation), or may refer to *preferred values* of a given attribute (e.g., prefer *central* over *northern* locations but *northern* may still be okay under certain circumstances), etc. Moreover, it is worth *highlighting* aspects of items that may have not been mentioned but have high *discriminative power* within their cluster (e.g., 5 hotels match the user's preferences but there's one with vegan menu).

Towards this objective, we propose the interaction of SDS with exploratory systems that offer the aforementioned functionality over semantic knowledge bases. This requires extensions in language understanding and state tracking, and the need for mined features.

---

[1]Preferences can be considered as soft constraints or wishes that might or might not be satisfied

Proceedings of the SIGDIAL 2018 Conference, pages 229–234,
Melbourne, Australia, 12-14 July 2018. ©2018 Association for Computational Linguistics

2.2 Background: Preference-Enriched Faceted Search and `Hippalus`

Faceted search is currently the de facto standard in e-commerce (e.g., eBay, booking.com), and its popularity and adoption is increasing. The enrichment of Faceted Search with *preferences*, hereafter *Preference-enriched Faceted Search* (PFS), was proposed in (Tzitzikas and Papadakos, 2013). It has been proven useful for recall-oriented information needs, because such needs involve decision making that can benefit from the gradual interaction and expression of not only restrictions (hard constraints) but also preferences (soft constraints). It is worth noting that it allows expressing preferences over attributes, whose values can be *hierarchically organized* and/or *multi-valued*, it supports *preference inheritance*, and it offers scope-based rules for *automatic conflict resolution*.

PFS offers various preference actions (e.g., relative, best, worst, around, etc.) that allow the user to order facets (i.e. slots), values, and objects. Furthermore, the user is able to *compose* object related preference actions[2]. Essentially, a user u can express gradually a set of qualitative (i.e. relative) preferences over the values of each facet (slot), denoted by $Pref_u$. These actions define a preference relation (a binary relation) over the values V_{s_i} of each slot s_i, denoted by $\succ_i$, which are then composed to define a preference relation over the elements of the information space, i.e. over $V = V_{s_i} \times ... \times V_{s_n}$ (in the case of multi-valued slots $V = \mathcal{P}(V_{s_i}) \times ... \times \mathcal{P}(V_{s_n})$). Since the descriptions of the objects in the current user focus $\mathcal{F}_u$ are a subset of V, the actions in $Pref_u$ define a preference relation over $\mathcal{F}_u$ denoted as $(\mathcal{F}_u, \succ_{Pref_u})$, from which a bucket order of $\mathcal{F}_u$, i.e. a linear order of subsets of $\mathcal{F}_u$ ranked based on preference and denoted by $B(\mathcal{F}_u, Pref_u) = < b_1, ..., b_z >$, is derived through topological sorting.

`Hippalus` (Papadakos and Tzitzikas, 2014) is an exploratory search system (publicly accessible[3]) that materializes PFS over semantic views gathered from different data sources through SPARQL queries. The information base that feeds `Hippalus` is represented in RDF/S and objects can be described according to dimensions with hierarchically organized and set-valued attributes. Preference actions are validated using the preference language described in (Tzitzikas and Papadakos, 2013). If valid, the system computes the respective preference bucket[4] order and returns the corresponding ranked list of objects.

In addition, `Hippalus` implements the scoring function defined in (Tzitzikas and Dimitrakis, 2016), that expresses the degree up to which an object in $\mathcal{F}_u$ fulfills the preferences in $Pref_u$ and is a real number (in our case its range is the interval $[1, 100]$). The specific scoring function, exploits all available composition modes available in `Hippalus` enriching the bucket orders with scores respecting the *consistency of the qualitative-based bucket order* that is defined as: A scoring function *score* is *consistent with the qualitative-based bucket order*, if for any two objects o, o' and any set of user actions $Pref_u$, it holds: if $pos(o) < pos(o')$ then $score(o, Pref_u) > score(o', Pref_u)$ where $pos(o)$ is the position of o in $B(\mathcal{F}_u, Pref_u)$.

3 Features

3.1 Motivation

In order to reduce the complexity of the dialogue system while at the same time improving its efficiency and effectiveness, we enriched the response of the `Hippalus` system with a number of features, which provide cues about interesting slots/values (as mentioned in §2.1) that can be exploited by the Belief Tracker, Dialogue Manager, Natural Language Generator, and other statistical components of the SDS. These features are extracted from: a) the set of objects of the current user focus (*selectivity* and *entropy*); and b) from the imposed ordering of the objects according to the expressed user preferences (*avg, min and max preference score per bucket* and *pair-wise wins of objects per slot per bucket*).

3.2 Features extracted from object focus

Assume a dataset $\mathcal{D}$ that contains $|\mathcal{O_D}|$ objects, where $\mathcal{F}_u \subseteq \mathcal{O_D}$ is the current focus of the user u (i.e. the objects that satisfy the expressed hard-constraints). Let $S_{|\mathcal{F}_u} = \{s_1, ..., s_n\}$ denote the set of available slots in $\mathcal{D}$ under focus $\mathcal{F}_u$ and $V_{s_i|\mathcal{F}_u} = \{v_{s_{i1}}, ..., v_{s_{im}}\}$ denote the set of values for slot $s_i \in S_{|\mathcal{F}_u}$ respectively[5]. We define the following metrics:

Definition 3.1. The *selectivity* of a slot s_i under focus $\mathcal{F}_u$ is defined as:

$$Selectivity(s_{i|\mathcal{F}_u}) = \frac{|V_{s_i|\mathcal{F}_u}|}{|\mathcal{F}_u|} \tag{1}$$

Definition 3.2. The *entropy* of a slot s_i under focus $\mathcal{F}_u$ is defined as:

$$Entropy(s_{i|\mathcal{F}_u}) = - \sum_{j=1}^{|V_{s_i|\mathcal{F}_u}|} (P(v_{s_{ij}|\mathcal{F}_u}) * log_2(\frac{1}{P(v_{s_{ij}|\mathcal{F}_u})})) \tag{2}$$

where $P(v_{s_{ij}|\mathcal{F}_u})$ is the probability of value $v_{s_{ij}}$ in slot s_i under focus $\mathcal{F}_u$.

Both selectivity and entropy metrics provide insights about the discreteness and the amount of information contained in the values of a specific slot for the objects

---

[2]There are different composition modes like Pareto, Pareto optimal (i.e. skyline), Priority-based, etc.

[3]http://www.ics.forth.gr/isl/Hippalus/

[4]A preference bucket holds incomparable objects with respect to the given soft-constraints

[5]The set of values can be hierarchically organized through a subsumption binary relation $(V_{s_i}, \leq_i)$

under focus $\mathcal{F}_u$. Selectivity is an inexpensive but rough metric that takes values in $[0, 1]$. If the value of each object for a specific slot is unique, then selectivity is 1 (high selectivity), while it is near 0 for the opposite (low selectivity). On the other hand entropy is a refined but more expensive metric, with bigger values when the probabilities of values in $V_{s_i|\mathcal{F}_u}$ are equal. `Hippalus` returns the values of both metrics for each slot of the current user focus $\mathcal{F}_u$ on the fly, along with the pre-computed values for the whole dataset.

3.2.1 Features extracted from object order

Other interesting features can be extracted from the imposed ordering of objects based on the user preferences, including *min*, *max*, and *average preference score* of objects in each bucket, and for each object of a bucket *the sum of pair-wise wins* per each slot over which the user has expressed a preference. The last feature can be used as an indication about the number of wins of each object over all different preference criteria (slots), pinpointing criteria that affect only a small number of objects.

Definition 3.3. The **pair-wise wins PWW** metric under focus $\mathcal{F}_u$ of objects contained in a bucket $b \in B_{\mathcal{F}_u, Pref_u}$ derived by preference actions $Pref_u$ of user u for slot s, is defined as:

$$PWW(b, Pref_{u|s}) = \sum_{o \in b} \sum_{o' \in b} \frac{2 * wins_s(o, o')}{|b|(|b| - 1)} \quad (3)$$

where $Pref_{u|s}$ denotes the preference actions of a user u over the slot s and $wins_s(o, o') = 1$ if $pos_s(o) < pos_s(o')$, where $pos_s(o)$ is the position of o in $B_{\mathcal{F}_u, Pref_u|s}$, else $wins_s(o, o') = 0$.

Notice that big PWW values mean that we have a small number of objects, even a single object, that win the rest objects of the bucket for the preference actions of a specific slot. As an example consider a bucket that contains the cheapest hotel. This hotel wins the rest objects of the bucket for the slot *price* and could be used by the dialogue system to ask if *price* is considered more important than the rest slots (i.e. expression of priority). On the other hand lower values mean that we have a number of ties for the objects of a bucket, and that the dialogue system is not able to pin-point specific slots that could further restrict the top-ranked objects.

4　The LD-SDS

Figure 1 shows the architecture of our system. `Hippalus` is responsible for feeding information regarding the current knowledge view to the SLU and DST components. In addition, it provides the previously mentioned features and the current ranked list of results to the multi-domain policy, and Natural Language Generation (NLG) and Text to Speech (TTS) components respectively. Spoken Language Understanding (SLU) and dialogue state / belief tracking

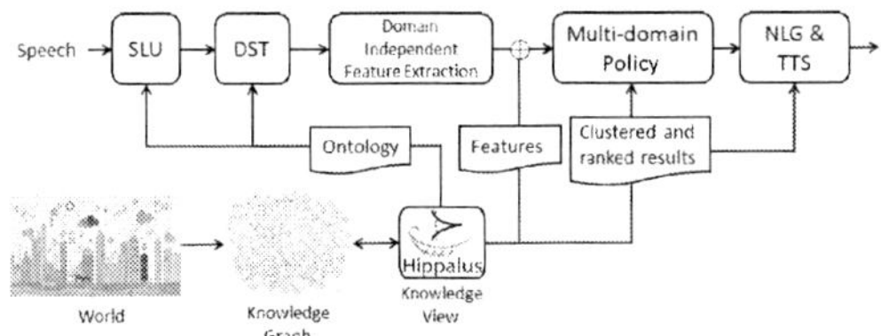

Figure 1: The architecture of our prototype.

(DST / BT), have been extended with operations that correspond to the actions supported by `Hippalus`. Since `Hippalus` supports hierarchical and multi-valued attributes, the notion of slot has been extended to allow the definition of relations between slot values.

4.1　Dialogue Management

The objective is to conduct dialogues with as few semantic errors as possible that result in successfully completed tasks and satisfied users. As baselines for dialogue management, we created a hand-crafted Dialogue Manager (DM) and trained two statistical DMs in simulation. To this end, we developed an agenda-based user simulator (Schatzmann et al., 2007) that was designed to handle the complexities and demands of our SDS, e.g., real values for slots, intervals, hierarchies, all of our operators, hard constraints and preferences, etc., as well as to be able to handle multiple items being suggested by the system (in the sense of an overview of current results) and tell if these items satisfy the user's constraints. In order to handle a wide range of domains, we use the method proposed in (Wang et al., 2015), which extracts features describing each slot and action plus some general features pertaining to the dialogue so far and the current state of the knowledge base. Thus, even if new slots are added to the knowledge base, our dialogue manager does not need to be retrained. Specifically, we use some of the features proposed in (Wang et al., 2015; Papangelis and Stylianou, 2016) and the features described in the previous section, which are necessary to handle the increased complexity of the interaction.

4.2　Understanding and State Tracking

Translating the identified user intentions from SLU into a belief state is not trivial, even for slot filling models with one or two operators (e.g., $=, \neq$). Moreover, as we aim to connect our system to live knowledge bases, it is important for SLU to be able to adapt over time, as well as handle out-of-domain input gracefully. As an initial approach to belief tracking, we follow some simple principles (Papangelis et al., 2017) in conjunction with an existing belief tracker (Ultes et al., 2017). While this is straightforward for regular slots, we need a different kind of belief update for hierarchically valued or multi-valued slots. Specifically, for hierarchical slots we need to recursively perform the belief update, while still following the basic principles. As the constraints become more complex, traversing the hierar-

Variables	E1	E2	E3	E4
Semantic Error	15%	30%	45%	45%
SLU N-Best Size	3	5	7	7
Sim. User Patience	5	3	3	2
Max User Constraints	3	5	7	10
Acceptable Num. Items	7	5	3	2

Table 1: Four environments (parameter settings) under which our DMs were evaluated.

ENV	E1	E2	E3	E4
Single Domain Per Dialogue				
HDC	83.8 ± 5	65.8 ± 6	38.8 ± 9	35.7 ± 8
DQNλ	74.4 ± 8	60.7 ± 9	52.1 ± 10	49.6 ± 9
GPS	$\mathbf{88.1 \pm 4}$	$\mathbf{79.5 \pm 3}$	$\mathbf{66.8 \pm 6}$	$\mathbf{60.3 \pm 9}$
Multiple Domains Per Dialogue				
HDC	82.3 ± 7	71.6 ± 7	40.7 ± 10	30.5 ± 9
DQNλ	$\mathbf{88.3 \pm 2}$	$\mathbf{87.5 \pm 2}$	$\mathbf{85.8 \pm 3}$	$\mathbf{82.9 \pm 4}$
GPS	44.6 ± 8	26.3 ± 2	22.7 ± 6	13.3 ± 7

Table 2: Dialogue success rates for the DMs under various semantic error rates $\pm$ std dev.

chy of values becomes non-trivial. In our prototype, we traverse the hierarchy once for each constraint (relevant to a specific hierarchical slot) and then combine the updates into a single belief update as the average for each value. When updating multi-valued slots, we assign the probability mass to each value that was mentioned (and not negated); this can be seen as generating (or removing) a single-valued "sub-slot" for each value on the fly.

5 Preliminary Evaluation

To assess how well current statistical DMs perform in this setting, we compare a hand-crafted dialogue policy (HDC) against a DM trained with GP-SARSA (GPS) (Gašić et al., 2010) and one trained with Deep Q Networks with eligibility traces (DQN-λ) - an adapted version of (Harb and Precup, 2017). HDC, GPS, and DQN (without eligibility traces) have been the top performing algorithms in a recent benchmark evaluation (Casanueva et al., 2017). We test the DMs under various conditions, presented in Table 1. *Semantic Error* refers to simulated errors, where we change either the type of dialogue act, slot, value, or operator that the simulated user issues, based on some probability. This can happen multiple times, to generate multiple SLU hypotheses. *SLU N-Best Size* is the maximum size of the N-best list of SLU hypotheses, after the simulated error stage. *Sim. User Patience* is the maximum number of times the simulated user tolerates the same action being issued by the DM. *Max User Constraints* is the maximum number of constraints in the simulated user's goal (e.g., $price \leq 70$). One important observation is that task success is very hard to define, as we consider a cluster of ranked items to be a valid system response. Some users may want to get exactly one option while for some it may be acceptable to get no more than four. Therefore, we add a feature to our user simulator to indicate the number of items a user will accept as a final result (provided that all of them meet the user's constraints). We sample this uniformly from the set $\{1, ..., acceptable\}$, as defined in Table 1 (*Acceptable Num. Items*). While this is a rough approximation of real world conditions, we expect that it introduces one more layer of complexity that the statistical DMs need to model.

The dataset used for the evaluation consists of four domains (Hotels, Restaurants, Museums, and Shops) with databases populated with content scrapped from the internet, containing a total of 84 slots and 714 ob-

jects. We evaluated the statistical DMs on a single domain and on a multi-domain setting (as described in section 4.1). Table 2 summarizes the results of our evaluation in simulation in the four environments we have defined, where each entry is the average of 5 runs of 1,000 training and 100 evaluation dialogues. DQN-λ performs better with the rich (dense) domain-independent feature set in the multi-domain scenario, likely because it is exposed to more variability in the data and therefore needs less iterations to learn well-performing policies. In fact, it is able to cope very well in deteriorating conditions, by learning to adapt e.g., by asking for more confirmations. GPS shows the opposite trend, preferring the sparse belief state features of the single-domain scenario, needing many more dialogues (than the 1,000 allowed here) to reach good performance in the multi-domain case.

6 Conclusion

We have presented LD-SDS, a prototype information navigation SDS that connects to semantic knowledge bases to guide users towards making informed decisions. This direction is more challenging compared to other simpler kinds of interaction. To evaluate the quality of the approach that we propose, we developed an agenda-based user simulator and applied it to train two statistical DMs. While we have proven the feasibility of our approach, our system still needs to be trained and evaluated with human users as in some cases statistical DMs may overfit simulators (or take advantage of certain aspects of them). We are therefore in the process of designing studies to collect text-based human-human data that will be used to train LD-SDS either end-to-end or by jointly optimising some of the components. In addition, we plan to evaluate our approach with live semantic knowledge bases and extend our approach to also exploit available unstructured information (out of domain). In the appendix we show an example dialogue with our system that highlights the extensions to the typical slot-filling approach.

References

Amazon. 2017. Amazon alexa prize 2017 proceedings. https://developer.amazon.com/

alexaprize/proceedings. Accessed: 2018-03-09.

Iñigo Casanueva, Paweł Budzianowski, Pei-Hao Su, Nikola Mrkšić, Tsung-Hsien Wen, Stefan Ultes, Lina Rojas-Barahona, Steve Young, and Milica Gašić. 2017. A benchmarking environment for reinforcement learning based task oriented dialogue management. *arXiv preprint arXiv:1711.11023*.

Danqi Chen, Adam Fisch, Jason Weston, and Antoine Bordes. 2017. Reading wikipedia to answer open-domain questions. *arXiv preprint arXiv:1704.00051*.

H. Cuayáhuitl, S. Yu, A. Williamson, and J. Carse. 2017. Scaling up deep reinforcement learning for multi-domain dialogue systems. In *2017 International Joint Conference on Neural Networks*, pages 3339–3346.

Milica Gašić, Filip Jurčíček, Simon Keizer, François Mairesse, Blaise Thomson, Kai Yu, and Steve Young. 2010. Gaussian processes for fast policy optimisation of pomdp-based dialogue managers. In *Proceedings of SIGDial*, pages 201–204. ACL.

Jean Harb and Doina Precup. 2017. Investigating recurrence and eligibility traces in deep q-networks. *arXiv preprint arXiv:1704.05495*.

Tom Heath and Christian Bizer. 2011. Linked data: Evolving the web into a global data space. *Synthesis lectures on the semantic web: theory and technology*, 1(1):1–136.

Jiwei Li, Alexander H. Miller, Sumit Chopra, Marc'Aurelio Ranzato, and Jason Weston. 2016. Learning through dialogue interactions. *CoRR*, abs/1612.04936.

Bing Liu, Gokhan Tur, Dilek Hakkani-Tur, Pararth Shah, and Larry Heck. 2017. End-to-end optimization of task-oriented dialogue model with deep reinforcement learning. *arXiv preprint arXiv:1711.10712*.

Panagiotis Papadakos and Yannis Tzitzikas. 2014. Hippalus: Preference-enriched faceted exploration. In *EDBT/ICDT Workshops*, volume 172.

A Papangelis and Y Stylianou. 2016. Multi-domain spoken dialogue systems using domain-independent parameterisation. In *Domain Adaptation for Dialogue Agents*.

Alexandros Papangelis, Panagiotis Papadakos, Margarita Kotti, Yannis Stylianou, Yannis Tzitzikas, and Dimitris Plexousakis. 2017. Ld-sds: Towards an expressive spoken dialogue system based on linked-data. In *SCAI*.

Jost Schatzmann, Blaise Thomson, Karl Weilhammer, Hui Ye, and Steve Young. 2007. Agenda-based user simulation for bootstrapping a pomdp dialogue system. In *HLT 2007, NAACL*, pages 149–152. Association for Computational Linguistics.

Yannis Tzitzikas and Eleftherios Dimitrakis. 2016. Preference-enriched faceted search for voting aid applications. *IEEE Transactions on Emerging Topics in Computing*.

Yannis Tzitzikas and Panagiotis Papadakos. 2013. Interactive exploration of multi-dimensional and hierarchical information spaces with real-time preference elicitation. *Fundamenta Informaticae*, 122(4):357–399.

Stefan Ultes, Lina M. Rojas Barahona, Pei-Hao Su, David Vandyke, Dongho Kim, Iñigo Casanueva, Paweł Budzianowski, Nikola Mrkšić, Tsung-Hsien Wen, Milica Gasic, and Steve Young. 2017. PyDial: A Multi-domain Statistical Dialogue System Toolkit. In *Proceedings of ACL 2017, System Demonstrations*, pages 73–78, Vancouver, Canada. ACL.

Z. Wang, T.H. Wen, P.H. Su, and Y. Stylianou. 2015. Learning domain-independent dialogue policies via ontology parameterisation. In *16th Annual Meeting of the SIGDial*, page 412.

Tsung-Hsien Wen, David Vandyke, Nikola Mrkšic, Milica Gasic, Lina M Rojas-Barahona, Pei-Hao Su, Stefan Ultes, and Steve Young. 2017. A network-based end-to-end trainable task-oriented dialogue system. In *EACL*, pages 438–449.

D. Jason Williams, Kavosh Asadi, and Geoffrey Zweig. 2017. Hybrid code networks: Practical and efficient end-to-end dialog control with supervised and reinforcement learning. In *ACL*, pages 665–677.

X. Yang, Y. N. Chen, D. Hakkani-Tür, P. Crook, X. Li, J. Gao, and L. Deng. 2017. End-to-end joint learning of natural language understanding and dialogue manager. In *2017 IEEE ICASSP*, pages 5690–5694.

A Supplemental Material

In this section, we provide an example interaction between a human user and the LD-SDS prototype. Figure 2 shows the system in operation. Figures 3 and 4 show examples of slots that can take multiple values or whose values have hierarchical relations, respectively.

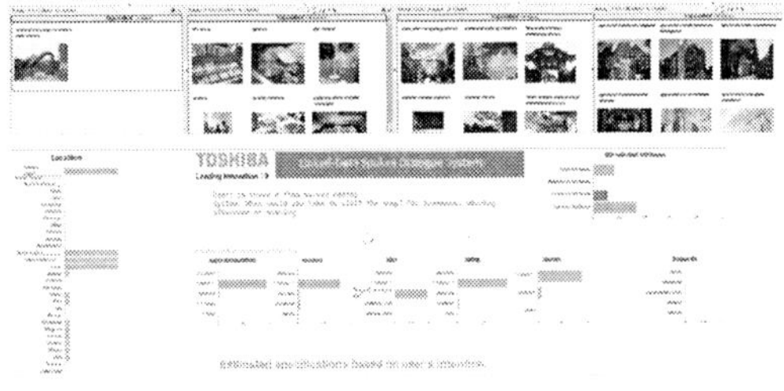

Figure 2: The prototype SDS, acting as a hotel concierge, with live connections to Hippalus.

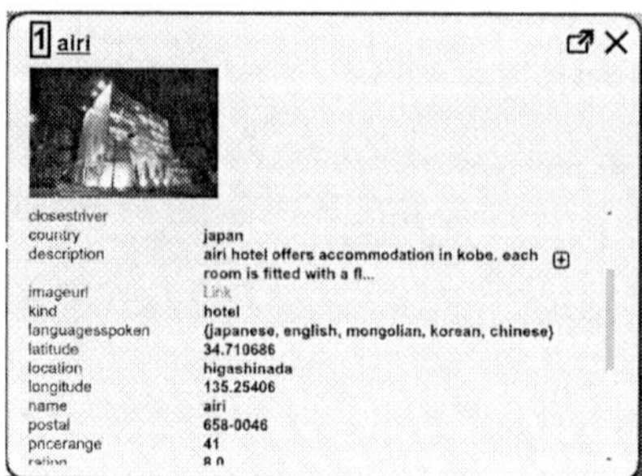

Figure 3: An item in `Hippalus`, where the *languagesspoken* slot can take multiple values.

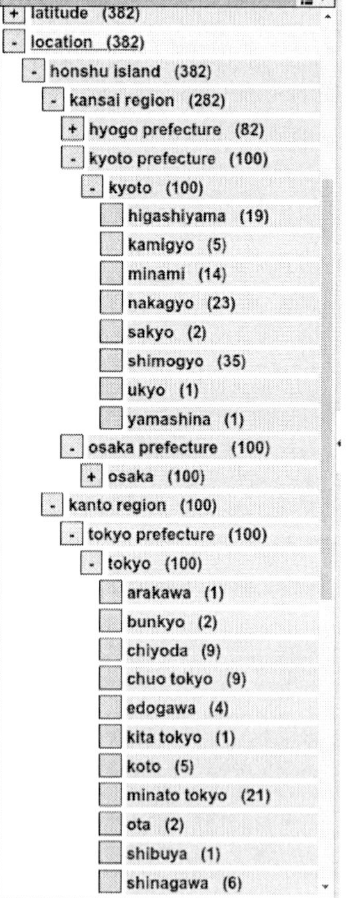

Figure 4: An example of a slot in `Hippalus`, where the values have hierarchical relations.

System: Hello, welcome to the Japanese Hotels spoken dialogue system. How may I help you?
User: I'm looking for a hotel in Kyoto but not in Minami where they offer free Wi-Fi and have non smoking rooms. (ASR confidence: 0.75154209) *Minami is a region in Kyoto.*
Constraints: [type=hotel, location=kyoto, location≠minami, amenities={free-wifi, non-smoking-rooms}]   **Preferences**: [ ]   **Hippalus**: [267 items in 2 buckets; {60, 207} items in buckets]
S: What price range are you looking for?
U: I want something around 70 pounds and with more than two stars. (0.7065863)
C: [pricerange $\sim$ 70, stars $>$ 2]   P: [ ]   H: [188 items in 45 buckets; {25, 103, 13, ...} items in buckets]
S: What kind of user rating would you prefer the hotel to have?
U: I'd like excellent ratings. (0.92533112)
C: [ ]   P: [ratings=excellent : best]   H: [188 items in 27 buckets; {9, 11, 8, ...} items in buckets; identified slots that can affect ranking and reduce items in first bucket: {stars, location, price}]
S: Which of the following criteria are important for you? stars, price, or location?
U: I prefer location and price. (0.95948964)
C: [ ]   P: [location $>>$ all, price $>>$ all]   H: [188 items in 152 buckets; 3 items in first bucket]
S: 3 hotels match your preferences. Two are located in Shimogyo and one in Nakagyo. Ryokan Kyoraku in Shimogyo is cheaper with 59 pounds per night and 3 stars, and Daiwa Roynet is more expensive at 81 pounds per night but with 4 stars. Royal Park in Nakagyo is expensive as well at 79 pounds per night and 4 stars. Both expensive hotels offer more services than the cheaper one.
U: Thank you, goodbye. (0.97125274)

Table 3: Example interaction between a human user and our LD-SDS prototype. In the interest of space, the notes under each dialogue turn briefly show items that correspond to new information. The belief state is updated accordingly. ASR: Automatic Speech Recognition.

Improving User Impression in Spoken Dialog System with Gradual Speech Form Control

Yukiko Kageyama, Yuya Chiba, Takashi Nose, and Akinori Ito

Graduate School of Engineering, Tohoku University

6-6-05, Aoba, Aramaki-Aza, Aoba-ku, Sendai, Miyagi, Japan

`{kageyama@spcom, yuya@spcom, tnose@m, aito@spcom}.ecei.tohoku.ac.jp`

Abstract

This paper examines a method to improve the user impression of a spoken dialog system by introducing a mechanism that gradually changes form of utterances every time the user uses the system. In some languages, including Japanese, the form of utterances changes corresponding to social relationship between the talker and the listener. Thus, this mechanism can be effective to express the system's intention to make social distance to the user closer; however, an actual effect of this method is not investigated enough when introduced to the dialog system. In this paper, we conduct dialog experiments and show that controlling the form of system utterances can improve the users' impression.

1 Introduction

Demand for a spoken dialog system has raised, including AI speakers or personal assistant systems (Bellegarda, 2014). Not only the conventional task-oriented dialog systems (Aust et al., 1995; Zue et al., 2000), but also non-task-oriented systems (Bickmore and Picard, 2005; Meguro et al., 2010; Yu et al., 2016; Akasaki and Kaji, 2017) have attracted the attention in recent years. In order for such dialog systems to become ubiquitous in the society, it is important to improve the user impression to the dialog with the system.

Miyashita et al. (2008) conducted a research that increases the user's intention to talk with the system by gradually increasing the behavior of a robot that expresses intimacy. Their study showed that the user felt the robot more friendly and increased desire to use the robot continuously by the robot's behavior. This research showed that, ex-

pressing intimacy with the user is effective to promote the user's desire to use the system.

In this research, we focused on a linguistic form of system utterances to improve the user impression. Several languages, including Japanese, have a mechanism called "honorifics" by which the speech form changes according to the relative social position or closeness of the social distance to the dialog partner (Brown and Ford, 1961). The honorific is often treated as one of the categories of politeness (Brown and Levinson, 1978, 1987) although several arguments have been raised (Ide, 1989; Agha, 1994). Brown and Levinson (1987) claimed that the speaker can choose strategy according to the politeness level depending on the social distance or relative power between the speakers. In Japanese, the speakers try to close the social distance by gradually decreasing the use of honorific form.

This paper examines effectiveness of introducing such mechanism to the dialog system. Kim et al. (2012) conducted experiments of human-robot interaction in Korean language, and indicated that the robot is perceived more friendly when calling the user in the familiar form, but the effect of the speech form itself was limited. In contrast, we investigate the effect of changing speech form on the user impression including friendliness.

2 Changing Form of System Utterances Considering Social Distance

2.1 Expressions of Japanese for social distance, politeness and familiarity

This study exploits the expressions of Japanese that express politeness and social distance between the talker and the listener. Thus, we first explain such mechanism of Japanese briefly. The Japanese language has a system of speaking form

235

Proceedings of the SIGDIAL 2018 Conference, pages 235–240,
Melbourne, Australia, 12-14 July 2018. ©2018 Association for Computational Linguistics

called "the honorifics (*keigo*)", that indicates social relationships between the speaker and the listener or the speaker and the persons referred in the utterance using the linguistic form. For example, the verb *tsukuru* (to make) can be used as either *tsukuru* (normal form) or *tsukuri-masu* (polite form). Another way of expressing closeness is to use the ending particles, such as *tsukuri-masu* (polite, far) or *tsukuri-masu-yo* (polite, closer). In addition to the honorifics, it is possible to express closeness using different wording, such as *hai* (a positive answer or a backchannel, polite) and *un* (casual). When the interlocutors are familiar with each other, the form of utterances become less polite, closer and more casual. In this experiment, we defined "honorific form" as polite, less close and formal expressions, and "normal form" as less polite, closer and casual expressions.

2.2 Gradual control of system speech form based on speech level shift

The changes of the speech form are caused by several factors, such as the social entrainment (Hirschberg, 2008). One of the main factors is the changes of the social distance. When two persons make conversations several times, it was mentioned that the proportion of honorific form decreases, and that of normal form increases as they make more conversations (Ikuta, 1983). This phenomenon is called "speech level shift" or "speech style shift" (Ikuta, 1983; Hasegawa, 2004). The "speech level" or "speech style" means the expressions in the utterances that express closeness of the interlocutors. Thus, the "speech level shift" means the switching of speech level that occurs in conversations between the same persons.

To make the dialog system express that the system and the user gradually become more friendly, we propose a method to use the speech level shift. In the experiment, the subjects talked with the system for three consecutive days and evaluated the impression on the system and the dialog with the system. We changed the speech level step by step within the three-day experiment, as shown in Table 1. In Japanese, it is natural to use the honorific form when persons meet for the first time; thus, all of the system utterances were in the honorific form in the first conversation.

| | Proposed system | |
	Honorific	Normal
Day 1	100%	0%
Day 2	50%	50%
Day 3	0%	100%

Table 1: The ratio of utterance form corresponding to day of experiment for proposed system

3 Experimental Dialog System

3.1 System architecture

An experimental system is based on an example-based dialog system (Takeuchi et al., 2007; Lee et al., 2009) commonly used for the non-task-oriented system. A computer-based female agent was employed. In the example-based dialog system, the system calculates the similarities between the user's utterance and example sentences in the database, and then selects a response corresponding to the most similar example. This study employed the cosine similarity for the similarity calculation.

3.2 Topic-dependent example-response database for non-task-oriented dialog

The example-response databases for the experiments were constructed through the actual dialogs with the system and users (Kageyama et al., 2017). We focused on chatting between friends, which is one of the non-task-oriented dialog, and prepared four databases corresponding to the different dialog topic. To collect the dialog data, the users asked the agent what she had done yesterday on the assumption that she had led a human-like life in the dialog collection. The topics of the database were cooking, movies, and meal. A dialog example is appended at **Appendix A**. The number of pairs included in the constructed database was ranged from 1,000 to 1,125. The responses of the system were composed in the honorific form.

3.3 Preparation of the system utterances in normal form

The databases of the normal form were constructed by rewriting the form of the response sentences of the collected databases. 26 persons rewrote the sentences into the normal form. In the rewriting, the rewriting rules shown at **Appendix B** were provided to the rewriters for the consistency.

4 Dialog Experiments by Gradually Changing Expression

4.1 Experimental condition

The experiments were conducted in a sound-proof chamber for 3 consecutive days. The participants interacted with the system once a day, where a participant made 10 utterances to control the number of interchanges. The topic of the conversation was different from day to day, where the order of the topics was randomly determined from participant to participant. The rate of the system utterances in the honorific and normal form was changed according to Table 1. After the conversation, they evaluated the impression on the spoken dialog system using a questionnaire. For comparison, we prepared the dialog systems speaking in only the honorific form and the normal form in all three days. These two systems are denoted as "Honorific" and "Normal" hereafter. In the experiments, 14 participants talked with one of the three systems, and thus the total number of the participants was 42 (3 systems × 14 participants). Each group contained 7 male and 7 female participants.

We first presented the participants all the topics the dialog system could handle, and the participants were instructed to ask what the agent did yesterday for the specific topic. We also presented a dialog example to the participants. Then the participants made conversation with the system on the presented topic. The participants were allowed to make self-disclosure utterances.

We expected the system and the participant made conversations within the given topic, but the conversation broke down when the participant made an unanticipated utterance. The participants were instructed to talk with the system until making the specified number of utterances even when the conversation broke down.

4.2 Procedure of dialog experiments

The experimental procedure is as below:

Step 1: The topic is announced to the participant.

Step 2: The participant asks the system what the agent did yesterday.

Step 3: The participant made 10 interchanges with the system.

Step 4: The participant answered a questionnaire on the impression of the dialog.

	Day 1	Day 2	Day 3	Total
Proposed	67.1	72.1	70.7	70.0
Honorific	65.0	71.4	73.6	70.0
Normal	69.3	67.9	66.4	67.9

Table 2: Rate of correct answer [%]

Step 5: The steps 1 to 3 were repeated for 3 consecutive days changing the topic every day

4.3 Evaluation method

At the end of the every conversation, the participants answered the following four questions using the five-grade Likert scale, one (not at all) to five (very much).

Satisfaction: How the participant was satisfied with the dialog

Friendliness: How friendly the participant felt the dialog system

Impression of speech form: How adequate the participant felt of the system's speech form

Intention of talk: How strongly the participant wants to use the system again

In addition, we asked the participants who talked with the proposed system, whether they noticed the changes of the speech form or not after the last experiment.

5 Analysis of Experimental Results

5.1 Analysis of response rates

Table 2 shows the rates of the correct answers made by the system in the experiments. The correctness was judged by the participant based on the naturalness of the response to the question.

As shown in the table, the rate of correct answer of each system through three days experiments is about 70%, and this is almost equal to the previous results (Kageyama et al., 2017). From the one-way layout ANOVA factoring the condition of speech form, the significant difference was not observed. Therefore, the effect of response error in the subjective evaluation is considered to be almost equal between systems.

5.2 Experimental results of subjective evaluation

Figure 1 shows the average scores of the subjective evaluation per day. The graph shows that the subjective scores of the proposed system tend to

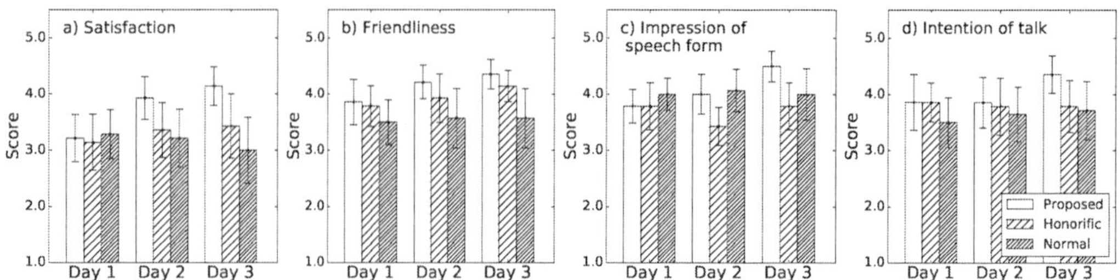

Figure 1: Average scores of subjective evaluation per day (error bar: 95% confidential interval)

	Satisfaction		Friendliness		Impression of speech form	
	Mean diff. (95%CI)	p-value	Mean diff. (95%CI)	p-value	Mean diff. (95%CI)	p-value
Proposed - Honorific	0.45 (-0.04, 0.93)	0.07	0.19(-0.20, 0.59)	0.49	0.43 (0.06, 0.80)	0.02*
Proposed - Normal	0.60 (0.12, 1.07)	0.01*	0.60 (0.20, 0.99)	<0.01**	0.07 (-0.30, 0.44)	0.89
Normal - Honorific	-0.14 (-0.62, 0.33)	0.76	-0.40 (-0.800, -0.01)	0.04*	0.36 (-0.01, 0.72)	0.06

Table 3: Results of Tukey-Kramer multiple-comparison test (Mean diff.: difference of average score, CI: confidence interval, $*p < 0.05$, $**p < 0.01$)

increase day by day, whereas those of the "Honorific" and the "Normal" systems tend to be flat. The scores of "Proposed" and "Honorific" are almost same at the first day because the all of utterances conducted in the honorific form. Interestingly, we can observe the difference between the scores of "Proposed" and "Normal" at Day 3 even both systems spoke in the same form. This result reflects that the effect of the changing form of the utterance by number of interactions.

Here, we conducted the two-way layout ANOVA to compare the condition of the speech form and the number of the interaction, and obtained the significant difference at the speech form factor in Satisfaction ($p \leq 0.01, F = 3.07$), Impression of speech form ($p = 0.01, F = 3.07$), and Friendliness ($p \leq 0.01, F = 3.07$). Then, we conducted the Tukey-Kramer tests to investigate the difference between the conditions. The results are summarized in Table 3.

As shown in the table, "Proposed" surpassed "Honorific" in terms of Impression of speech form, and surpassed "Normal" in terms of Satisfaction and Friendliness. These results suggest that the proposed system tends to obtain the better subjective score comparing to the simple systems without changing the form of utterance.

5.3 Perception of changes of speech form

In the experiments, 5 out of 14 participants that used the proposed system did not perceive the changes of the speech form. Here, we compared

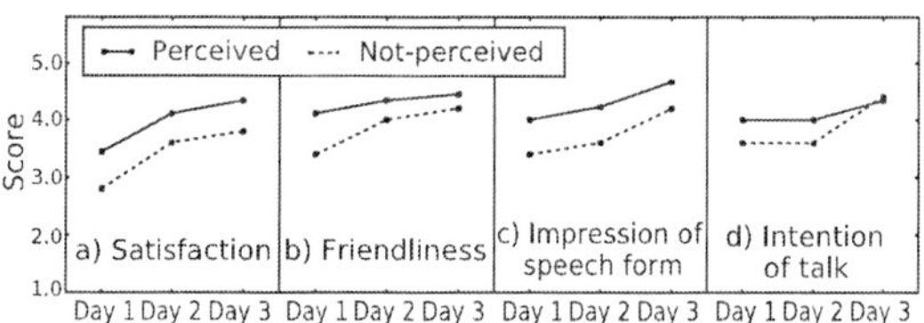

Figure 2: Score depending on perception

the scores between the groups of participants who perceived (denoted as "Perceived") and did not perceive (denoted as "Not-perceived") the changes of the form. Figure 2 shows the variation of the average scores of each group. From the figure, we can observe that all of the subjective scores of "Not-perceived" tend to increase as same with the scores of "Perceived." This result suggests that it is possible that the proposed method is able to improve the user impression unconsciously.

6 Conclusion

In this paper, we examined a method to improve the user impression by changing the form of system utterance according to number of uses. The dialog experiments showed that the proposed method can improve the subjective scores, such as the satisfaction compared to the simple systems unchanging the speech form, even the user could not perceive the changes of the expression.

In a future work, we will examine a method to change the form of the sentences considering the relationship between the speakers (Li et al., 2016).

Acknowledgments

This work was supported by JSPS KAK-ENHI Grant Numbers JP15H02720, JP16K13253, JP17H00823.

References

Asif Agha. 1994. Honorification. *Annual Review of Anthropology*, 23:277–302.

Satoshi Akasaki and Nobuhiro Kaji. 2017. Chat detection in an intelligent assistant: Combining task-oriented and non-task-oriented spoken dialogue system. *arXiv preprint arXiv:1705.00746*.

Harald Aust, Martin Oerder, Frank Seide, and Volker Steinbiss. 1995. The Philips automatic train timetable information system. *Speech Communication*, 17(3–4):249–262.

Jerome R Bellegarda. 2014. Spoken language understanding for natural interaction: The Siri experience. In *Natural Interaction with Robots, Knowbots and Smartphones*, pages 3–14. Springer.

Timothy Bickmore and Rosalind Picard. 2005. Establishing and maintaining long-term human-computer relationships. *ACM Transactions on Computer-Human Interaction*.

Penelope Brown and Stephen C Levinson. 1978. *Questions and politeness: strategies in social interaction*, chapter Universals in language usage: Politeness phenomena. Cambridge University Press.

Penelope Brown and Stephen C Levinson. 1987. *Politeness: Some universals in language use*, volume 4. Cambridge University Press.

Roger Brown and Marguerite Ford. 1961. Address in American English. *Journal of Abnormal and Social Psychology*, 62(2):375–385.

Yoko Hasegawa. 2004. Speech-style shifts and intimate exaltation in Japanese. In *Proc. of the 38th Annual Meeting of the Chicago Linguistic Society*, pages 269–284.

Julia Hirschberg. 2008. Speaking more like you: lexical, acoustic/prosodic, and discourse entrainment in spoken dialogue systems. In *Proc. of the 9th SIGdial Workshop on Discourse and Dialogue*, pages 128–128.

Sachiko Ide. 1989. Formal forms and discernment: Two neglected aspects of universals of linguistic politeness. *Multilingua*, 8(2–3):223–248.

Shoko Ikuta. 1983. Speech level shift and conversational strategy in Japanese discourse. *Language Sciences*, 5(1):37–53.

Yukiko Kageyama, Yuya Chiba, Takashi Nose, and Akinori Ito. 2017. Collection of example sentences for non-task-oriented dialog using a spoken dialog system and comparison with hanf-crafted DB. In *Proc. HCI International*, pages 458–563.

Yunkyung Kim, Sonya S. Kwak, and Myung-suk Kim. 2012. Am I acceptable to you? Effect of a robot's verbal language forms on people's social distance from robots. *Computers in Human Behavior*, 29:1091–1101.

Cheongjae Lee, Sangkeun Jung, Seokhwan Kim, and Gary Geunbae Lee. 2009. Example-based dialog modeling for practical multi-domain dialog system. *Speech Communication*, 51(5):466–484.

Jiwei Li, Michel Galley, Chris Brockett, Georgios Spithourakis, Jianfeng Gao, and Bill Dolan. 2016. A persona-based neural conversation model. In *Proc. of the 54th Annual Meeting of the Association for Computational Linguistics*, pages 994–1003.

Toyomi Meguro, Ryuichiro Higashinaka, Yasuhiro Minami, and Kohji Dohsaka. 2010. Controlling listening-oriented dialogue using partially observable Markov decision processes. In *Proc. of the 23rd International Conference on Computational Linguistics*, pages 761–769.

Zenta Miyashita, Takayuki Kanda, Masahiro Shiomi, Hiroshi Ishiguro, and Norihiro Hagita. 2008. A robot in a shopping mall that affectively guide customers. *Journal of Robotics Society of Japan*, 26(7):821–832.

Shota Takeuchi, Tobias Cincarek, Hiromichi Kawanami, Hiroshi Saruwatari, and Kiyohiro Shikano. 2007. Construction and optimization of a question and answer database for a real-environment speech-oriented guidance system. In *Proc. Oriental COCOSDA*, pages 149–154.

Zhou Yu, Leah Nicolich-Henkin, Alan W Black, and Alexander Rudnicky. 2016. A wizard-of-Oz study on a non-task-oriented dialog systems that reacts to user engagement. In *Proc. of the 17th Annual Meeting of the Special Interest Group on Discourse and Dialogue*, pages 55–63.

Victor Zue, Stephanie Seneff, James R Glass, Joseph Polifroni, Christine Pao, Timothy J Hazen, and Lee Hetherington. 2000. JUPITER: a telephone-based conversational interface for weather information. *IEEE Transactions on speech and audio processing*, 8(1):85–96.

A Dialog example

Speaker	Utterance
User	What did you cook?
System	I cooked *nikujaga*.
User	Are you good at cooking *nikujaga*?
System	I can't say, but I often cook it.
User	Do you make anything else?
System	I often cook *stir fry vegetables*.
User	Did you invite your friend?
System	I used *Cookpad*. Have you ever used it?
User	Did you invite your friend?
System	I went for a light run after cooking.
User	Do you often go jogging?
System	Yes. I'm trying to always go jogging for my health.
User	How long did you run?
System	I ran about 5 km.
User	Where did you run?
System	The jogging path by the *Hirose river*.
User	Did you run alone?
System	Yes, I ran on the jogging path by the *Hirose river*.
User	Have you ever participated in a marathon?
System	Yes, I have participated in a half-marathon several times.

Table 4: Dialog example of cooking (translation from Japanese)

B Example of rewriting sentence

	Example rewriting sentences
Honorific	*Hai, ie de yoku tsukutte masu yo* Yes, I often make it at home.
Normal	*Un, ie de yoku tsukutte iru yo* Yeah, I often make it home

Table 5: Example of rewriting presented to the rewriters (italic: original, upright: translated, under line: different parts depending on form)

A Bilingual Interactive Human Avatar Dialogue System

**Dana Abu Ali, Muaz Ahmad, Hayat Al Hassan, Paula Dozsa,
Ming Hu, Jose Varias, Nizar Habash**
New York University Abu Dhabi
{daa389,muaz.ahmad,hayat.alhassan,pauladozsa,
ming.hu,jose.varias,nizar.habash}@nyu.edu

Abstract

This demonstration paper presents a bilingual (Arabic-English) interactive human avatar dialogue system. The system is named TOIA (time-offset interaction application), as it simulates face-to-face conversations between humans using digital human avatars recorded in the past. TOIA is a conversational agent, similar to a chat bot, except that it is based on an actual human being and can be used to preserve and tell stories. The system is designed to allow anybody, simply using a laptop, to create an avatar of themselves, thus facilitating cross-cultural and cross-generational sharing of narratives to wider audiences. The system currently supports monolingual and cross-lingual dialogues in Arabic and English, but can be extended to other languages.

1 Introduction

Conversational agents are software programs that are able to conduct conversations with human users (interactors), by interpreting and responding to statements made in ordinary natural language. The components of our system, TOIA, target two types of users: (a) avatar makers, which are the people who wish to create personalized avatars, and (b) interactors, those interacting with the avatar. The system is designed to allow anybody, simply using a laptop, to create an avatar of themselves, thus facilitating cross-cultural and cross-generational sharing of narratives to wider audiences. Through our system, we aim to enable interactor users to conduct conversations with a person (avatar maker) who is not available for conversation in real time with the intention of learning about them. Since face-to-face human interaction is a powerful tool of human understanding, TOIA overcomes the restrictions on time and place that limit this type of interaction, presenting users with a platform for dialogue at their own pace and convenience. Additionally, it allows people from different linguistic backgrounds to communicate by supporting mechanisms for cross-lingual interactions between users and avatars that speak different languages.

2 Related Work

TOIA is inspired by research at the University of Southern California's Institute for Creative Technologies (ICT), such as *SGT Blackwell*, a digitally animated character designed to serve as an army conference information kiosk (Leuski et al., 2006). Users can talk to the character through a microphone, after which their speech is converted into text through an automatic speech recognition (ASR) system. This output is then analyzed by an answer selection module and the appropriate response is selected from the 83 pre-recorded lines that Blackwell can deliver. Another ICT project, based off of video recordings instead of digital media, is *New Dimensions in Testimony* (NDT), a prototype dialogue system allowing users to conduct conversations with Holocaust survivor Pinchas Gutter (Traum et al., 2015a,b; Artstein et al., 2015, 2016). Similarly, users talk to the Gutter Avatar through a microphone; their speech is then converted into text through ASR; a dialogue manager identifies the proper video to play back to simulate a conversational turn. The NDT setup is quite impressive in terms of the amount of resources that went into creating the avatar recording — hours of recording, use of top-of-the-line digital cinema cameras, etc. In TOIA, our goal is to create a system that will enable any avatar maker with a laptop and webcam to create and

Proceedings of the SIGDIAL 2018 Conference, pages 241–244,
Melbourne, Australia, 12-14 July 2018. ©2018 Association for Computational Linguistics

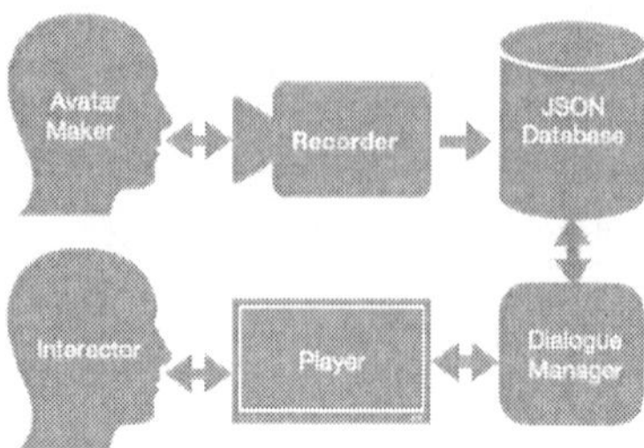

Figure 1: TOIA System Design

publicly share their avatar. We are also interested in enabling the dialogue to happen cross-lingually, where an interactor asks in one language, and the avatar answers in another language (with captions in the interactor's language). In our current system we support Arabic (Ar) and English (En), allowing for all combinations: (Ar-Ar, En-En, Ar-En and En-Ar).

3 Overall System Design

TOIA includes four components: (a) a recorder that records the avatar maker's videos, (b) a database that contains the avatar's video responses and other data facilitating the matching of the interactor's questions with the avatar's answers, (c) a player interface through which the interactor is able to interact with the avatar, and (d) a dialogue manager that matches the user's speech to the avatar's answers in any of the four language pairs. Figure 1 illustrates the relationship among the different components.

3.1 Recorder

We implemented a web-based recorder to help avatar makers record personal videos. We used *Node.js* as the runtime environment, *Express* as the web framework, *WebRTC* for live recording support, and *MangoDB* for real-time data updates.

The overall framework is as follows: Avatar makers create scripts consisting of pairs of questions and answers from scratch or customize existing scripts by removing or adding questions as desired. These scripts are uploaded to a *Cloudant* database. Throughout the recording, avatar makers can further update answers, delete questions or add questions on the spot.

The avatar maker selects a specific question prompt in any order and proceeds to record a video response to pair with it. A semi-transparent head location indicator is provided to help the avatar

maker create consist videos. The avatar maker can review the recorded video, re-record it or delete it. Figure 2 shows a screen capture of the recorder.

Currently, we have recorded four digital avatars using this interface, three in English and one in Arabic, each consisting of around 300 question-answer pairs.

3.2 Database

TOIA's avatar data are stored using two components: (a) a collection of the answer videos saved locally for speedy access; and (b) a JSON database storing question-answer entries. Each question-answer entry in the database has a unique reference id number, the answer video path in file system, as well as a character tag, consisting of the name of the character. Avatar files supporting cross-lingual interaction also include translations of the answer text. We currently use manual translations, but machine translations of the questions and answers may also be included to support cross-lingual dialogue management, allowing for languages beyond Arabic and English. Figure 3 shows three English, and their corresponding Arabic, database entries.

3.3 Player

The main TOIA system interface is the player, through which the interactor user is able to interact with the avatar. Similarly to the recorder, we implemented a web-based user interface using a *Flask* (Grinberg, 2018) web platform utilizing both *Python* and *JavaScript*.

The interactor can initiate a conversation with any of the available avatars by selecting one of them using the first page of the player's interface, and then specifying whether the interaction will be in Arabic or English. The character can easily be switched at any point by returning to the player's main page, after which the interaction session would restart with a different avatar. The player listens to the interactor through a microphone and then passes the collected audio through an ASR system (Google Speech API). The text produced through ASR is then passed on to the dialogue management system. The dialogue management system returns a video file path to be displayed by the player. While the video is playing, the microphone switches to mute mode to avoid feedback. It then starts listening for utterances again once the video ends.

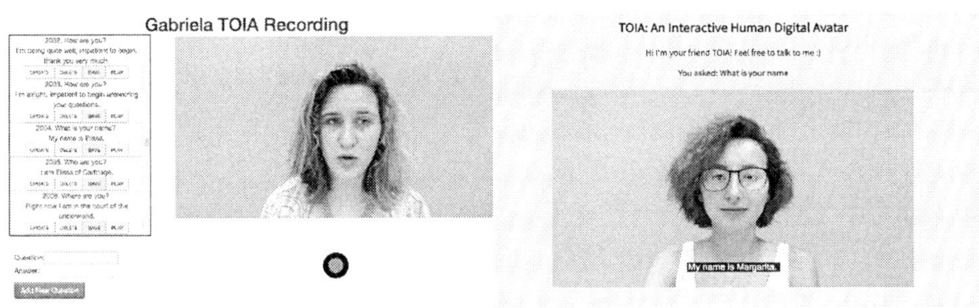

Figure 2: TOIA Recorder (left) and Player (right)

Entry ID	Language	Avatar	Question	Answer	Video Path
1001	English	Katarina	Who are you?	I am an avatar of an NYUAD student who can answer any questions you may have about the university.	katarina-1.mp4
1002	English	Katarina	What can I talk to you about?	You can to talk me about anything relating to Academics, Admissions, life in Abu Dhabi, and NYUAD in general. Feel free to ask me about my experiences here.	katarina-2.mp4
1032	English	Katarina	Where is the NYU Abu Dhabi campus?	The NYU Abu Dhabi campus is located on Saadiyat Island. Saadiyat is home to a few emerging cultural landmarks such as the Louvre Museum in Abu Dhabi.	katarina-32.mp4
2001	Arabic	Katarina	من أنت؟	أنا أفاتار لطالبة في جامعة نيويورك أبوظبي و يمكنني أن أجيب على أي أسئلة لديك عن الجامعة.	katarina-1.mp4
2002	Arabic	Katarina	عن ماذا يمكنني أن أحدثك؟	يمكنك التحدث معي عن أي شيء له علاقة بالشؤون الأكاديمية أو القبول أو الحياة في أبوظبي أو عن جامعة نيويورك أبوظبي بشكل عام. يمكنك سؤالي عن تجربتي الشخصية هنا أيضًا	katarina-2.mp4
2032	Arabic	Katarina	أين يقع حرم جامعة نيويوك أبوظبي؟	يقع حرم جامعة نيويورك أبوظبي في جزيرة السعديات. تعد السعديات موطنا لبعض المعالم الفنية والثقافية الناشئة بما فيها متحف اللوفر أبوظبي.	katarina-32.mp4

Figure 3: TOIA Database example

We designed the interface so that the user's interaction and control could be navigated solely through audio. The speech recognition is done in streaming mode; and the end of a question is determined through silence. This allows for the interaction to feel more natural and as close to a *live* conversation as possible. We have a collection of 'filler' videos with every avatar, that play in a loop while the player is waiting for the question to be completed; the microphone is active only while these videos are playing.

Regardless of the avatar's spoken language, the player accepts utterances in both Arabic and English. The player also displays captions with English subtitles for Arabic speaking avatars, and Arabic subtitles for English speaking avatars. The subtitles are generated based off of the answers in the script, which by design match the video recordings. To support a smoother user experience we display the text processed by the speech recognizer. This allows the user to recognize when the utterance has not been 'heard' correctly, and encourages them to use a clearer or louder voice when interacting with the avatar. The right side of Figure 2 shows the TOIA player interface.

3.4 Dialogue Manager

Once the interactor selects the avatar and interaction language, the dialogue manager loads the data linked to the chosen avatar. A new dialogue session is created in order to save the state of the conversation and ensure a natural flow where repetition and irrelevant answers are minimized.

The input to the dialogue manager is a textual version of the interactor's last utterance with a language id. The output is a path to the video file that is to be played in response.

The dialogue manager matches the interactor's questions with all the questions and answers in the avatar database. In order to facilitate the matching, the text in both the interactor questions and the database entries is preprocessed, removing punctuation and stop words, then expanded into word feature representations for matching purposes. The word representations include: unigram, bigram and trigram sequences, in terms of raw words, their lemmas and their stems. Lemmas abstract over inflectional variants of the word, which is particularly important for Arabic, a morphologically rich language (Habash, 2010).

For English, we use the Natural Language Tool

Kit (NLTK) (Bird et al., 2009). For Arabic, we use the Standard Arabic Morphological Analyzer (SAMA) (Graff et al., 2009). Due to Arabic's orthographic ambiguity, SAMA produces multiple analyses (lemmas and stems) per word. We select a single analysis using the Yamama system's maximum liklihood models for Arabic lemmas (Khalifa et al., 2016).

We further add lemma synonyms to increase the possibility of matching. For English, we used NLTK Synset support (Bird et al., 2009). For Arabic, we created synthetic synsets by clustering Arabic lemmas with the same English glosses. Only for English, the database of questions and answers is also enriched through automatically generated questions, based off of the answers, to increase the probability of finding an appropriate answer for an interactor's query.

The matching process is optimized for speed using a number of hash maps to allow the fast generation of an answer ranked list. The ranking uses the number of matches in the various dimensions mentioned above, term-frequency inverse-document-frequency weights, as well as a history of whether a particular video had been played already in the current session. The more matches between the interactor's utterance and the question-answer pair, the more the likelihood that pair's entry will be selected. In the case of multiple tied entries, the one whose answer video was played the least in the current session is chosen. The playing count of the chosen entry is updated.

4   Preliminary Evaluation

We performed a user study with ten Arabic speakers and ten English speakers, each of whom chatted with three avatars (two English, one Arabic). The metrics we recorded were accuracy, understanding, interaction pace, timely response and conversation flow. On average across all metrics and users, we received a score of 3.6 out of 5. 85% of users enjoyed interacting with avatars, and 60% said they would like to interact with other avatars.

5   Demo Plan

In the demo of our work, we will present the four avatars we have created, each of which can be spoken to in English and Arabic. We will also present users with the ability to test the recorder by creating their own list of questions and answers, and recording a set of videos.

6   Conclusion and Future Work

We presented a bilingual (Arabic-English) interactive human avatar dialogue system that simulates face-to-face conversations between humans using previously recorded digital human avatars.

In the future, we plan to work on a detailed user study to evaluate the performance of the various components in our system. Consistent with our motivating mission, we also plan to make the recorder and player available online to allow users anywhere to use it. We look forward to maximizing its usability so that any person can start sharing their life stories at their own pace, from their point of view, and in the comfort of their home.

References

R. Artstein, A. Gainer, K. Georgila, A. Leuski, A. Shapiro, and D. Traum. 2016. New dimensions in testimony demonstration. In *Proceedings of the Conference of the North American Chapter of the Association for Computational Linguistics.*

R. Artstein, A. Leuski, H. Maio, T. Mor-Barak, C. Gordon, and D. Traum. 2015. How many utterances are needed to support time-offset interaction? In *Proceedings of the International Florida Artificial Intelligence Research Society Conference.*

S. Bird, E. Klein, and E. Loper. 2009. *Natural language processing with Python: analyzing text with the natural language toolkit.* O'Reilly Media, Inc.

D. Graff, M. Maamouri, B. Bouziri, S. Krouna, S. Kulick, and T. Buckwalter. 2009. Standard Arabic Morphological Analyzer (SAMA) Version 3.1. Linguistic Data Consortium.

M. Grinberg. 2018. *Flask web development: developing web applications with python.* O'Reilly Media, Inc.

N. Habash. 2010. *Introduction to Arabic Natural Language Processing.* Morgan & Claypool Publishers.

S. Khalifa, N. Zalmout, and N. Habash. 2016. Yamama: Yet another multi-dialect Arabic morphological analyzer. In *Proceedings of the International Conference on Computational Linguistics (COLING).*

A. Leuski, R. Patel, and D. Traum. 2006. Building Effective Question Answering Characters. In *Proceedings of the SIGDIAL Workshop on Discourse and Dialogue.*

D. Traum, K. Georgila, R. Artstein, and A. Leuski. 2015a. Evaluating spoken dialogue processing for time-offset interaction. In *Proceedings of SIGDIAL.*

D. Traum, A. Jones, K. Hays, H. Maio, O. Alexander, R. Artstein, P. Debevec, A. Gainer, K. Georgila, K. Haase, et al. 2015b. New Dimensions in Testimony: Digitally preserving a Holocaust survivor's interactive storytelling. In *International Conference on Interactive Digital Storytelling.* Springer.

DialCrowd: A toolkit for easy dialog system assessment

Kyusong Lee, Tiancheng Zhao, Alan W. Black and Maxine Eskenazi
Language Technologies Institute
Carnegie Mellon University
Pittsburgh, Pennsylvania, USA
{kyusongl,tianchez,awb,max+}@cs.cmu.edu

Abstract

When creating a dialog system, developers need to test each version to ensure that it is performing correctly. Recently the trend has been to test on large datasets or to ask many users to try out a system. Crowdsourcing has solved the issue of finding users, but it presents new challenges such as how to use a crowdsourcing platform and what type of test is appropriate. DialCrowd makes system assessment using crowdsourcing easier by providing tools, templates and analytics. This paper describes the services that DialCrowd provides and how it works. It also describes a test of DialCrowd by a group of dialog system developers.

1 Introduction

The development of a spoken dialog system involves many steps and always ends in system tests. As our systems have become more complicated and the statistical methods we use demand more and more data, proper system assessment becomes an increasingly difficult challenge. One of the easier approaches to goal-oriented system assessment is to employ user simulation (Jung et al., 2009; Pietquin and Hastie, 2013; Schatzmann et al., 2005). It aims at the overall assessment of the system by measuring goal completion. While this is a useful first approach, it can't reveal what a human user would actually say. Thus this approach is usually used as a first approximation, quickly followed up with some assessment using humans. SOme chatbot systems use machine learning metrics to compare a model-generated response to a golden standard response. However, those metrics assume that a valid response has a significant word overlap with the golden response, which is often not the case. Liu et al. (2016) showed that these metrics correlate very weakly with human judgment. Other approaches used to assess non-task oriented dialog systems include word similarity metrics, next utterance classification, word perplexity, and response diversity (Serban et al., 2015). They are limited since they can't reproduce the variety found in actual user behavior.

Crowdsourcing platforms, such as Amazon Mechanical Turk (AMT), have shown promise in assessing spoken dialog systems (Eskenazi et al., 2013; Jurčíček et al., 2011). But for most developers it is not trivial to set up the crowdsourcing process and obtain usable results. Jurčíček et al. (2011) noted that this process must be cheap to operate and easy to use. Researchers (the requesters) have to overcome the following difficulites: learning how to use the crowdsourcing entity interface, learning how to create an understandable and attractive task, deciding on the correct form that the task should take (the template), connecting the dialog systems that are to be assessed to the crowdsourcing platform, paying the workers, assessing the quality of the workers' production, getting solid final results. To solve the connection issue, researchers have used the telephone to connect their dialog systems, relying on a crowdsourcing web interface to present the task, then sending the worker to the dialog system and finally bringing them back to the interface to collect their production and schedule payment. This connection issue is one example of these hurdles. Researchers are also faced with the choice of the form of assessment. The types of tests may vary. One form that is often found in the literature is to compare two versions of the same system (A/B text). The literature shows that a small number of test types covers most publications.

DialCrowd (https://dialrc.org/dialcrowd.html) is a toolkit that makes crowdsourced evalua-

Proceedings of the SIGDIAL 2018 Conference, pages 245–248,
Melbourne, Australia, 12-14 July 2018. ©2018 Association for Computational Linguistics

tion studies easy to run. We have identified a small number of standard evaluation experiment types and provided templates that generate web interfaces for these studies in a crowdsourcing environment. The DialCrowd interface first has the researcher choose the type of study (or she can make up her own). Once the type is chosen, the corresponding template appears and is filled in. This generates the task (HIT on AMT) that the worker will see. This considerably lowers preparation time, and guides those who are new to the field to commonly-accepted study types. DialCrowd presently has a small set of templates which will soon expand to include those suggested by our users or that we find in the literature. Other aspects of crowdsourced assessment that DialCrowd presently addresses are:

- Explaining the overall goal of the assessment to the worker

- Instructing the worker on how to accomplish the task

- Reminding a requester to post a consent form for explicit permission to use the data

- Helping calculate how much to pay for a HIT

- How to make a HIT less susceptible to BOTs

- Help in designing the appearance of the HIT.

Going forward, DialCrowd will also provide tools to:

- Assess an individual worker

- Create a golden data set

- Assess the final outcome with basic analytics

- Ensure that results are collected ethically and are made available to the community with as few restrictions as possible that do not compromise the worker's privacy.

2 Related Work

The performance of dialog systems can be measured via: task success, the number of turns per dialog, ASR accuracy, system response delay, naturalness of the speech output, consistency with the users expectations, and system cooperativeness (Moller and Skowronek, 2003). These metrics are both subjective and objective. Subjective metrics often come in the form of exit polls following the worker's interaction with a system. They often measure how much a worker liked interacting with a system or whether the worker would like to use the system again. Objective metrics can be extracted automatically or labeled manually by experts.

Toolkits must support both interactive and non-interactive studies. There are offline datasets that could be used to run some system studies. But they can't be used if success depends on how the user responds to a system utterance. In this case, only interactive tests can do the job. On the other hand, some researchers may have sets of responses that their systems have produced for which they need to know the appropriateness, given recent dialog context. Non-interactive tests are used in this case. DialCrowd provides support for both forms.

Non-interactive tests are the simplest to implement since the actual dialog system is not involved. Here the worker often sees a portion of a real dialog and passes some sort of judgment. Yang et al. (2010) for example used the Let's Go dialog logs (Raux et al., 2005) and identified several cue phrases that afforded the development of a set of heuristics to automatically classify those logs into five categories in terms of task success: too short, multi-task, task complete, out of scope, and task-incomplete.

Interactive tests usually have instructions and a scenario to enact that constrain the worker's behavior. Jurčíček et al. (2011)), for example, conducted real user evaluations of the Cambridge Restaurant Information system using AMT.

Crowdsourcing has several advantages. The crowd has been shown to be substantially more efficient in accomplishing assessment tasks (Munro et al., 2010). No time is spent recruiting users. Jurčíček et al. (2011) note that it took several weeks to recruit users for the Cambridge trial while it only took several days to get this done using crowdsourcing and the cost was much lower.

3 DialCrowd

The inspiration for DialCrowd comes from the TestVox toolkit (Parlikar, 2012) for speech synthesis evaluation. TestVox enables any developer to quickly upload data in a standard format and then deploy it on AMT or some other crowdsourcing site, or to a controlled set of developer-selected workers and get results easily and rapidly. TestVox is easy to deploy on AMT.

Several tools have recently been proposed to

connect non-speech dialog systems to AMT. DialCrowd is different in that it is speech-enabled. DialCrowd is designed to make it easy to connect to spoken dialog systems using Google Chrome's speech recognition. It also provides audio testing to ensure that workers have a working microphone, speakers, and headset. DialCrowd is designed to eliminate common crowdsourcing mistakes that affect results such as giving the worker too much information, creating a task with an unreasonably high cognitive load and proposing a task that a bot can easily be created to do. It provides off-the-shelf dialog systems that can be used as a baseline, such as DialPort's Let's Forecast (weather), Let's Eat (restaurants), Let's Go (bus information) and Qubot (question answering chatbot) (Zhao et al., 2016). Requesters can use their own dialog systems as the baseline.

DialCrowd uses test design techniques such as Latin Square in a set of templates (Cochran and Cox, 1950)). It uses timed sandbox trials to suggest correct, respectful payment for a HIT with the following equation $= \frac{M \times T}{60min}$ where M is the hourly minimum wage in the requester's state. T is the average amount of time on task during internal testing for 10 people. Requesters pay using their own accounts with the crowdsourcing platform of choice.

4 Overall Architecture of DialCrowd

DialCrowd has two components: DialCrowd Admin (requester view) and DialCrowd Worker (worker view). Although not restricted to AMT, this paper explains the overall process on AMT as an example. Given a dialog log format, the requester selects the set of turns and the context the worker should see. This section describes the process on DialCrowdAdmin.

1. Creating a project on Amazon MTurk: DialCrowd's requester site provides 10 sample templates that cover common uses of AMT. For interactive assessment, a survey template is chosen and DialCrowdAdmin automatically generates the link to a dialog system.

2. Create a project on DialCrowd Admin: After creating a project, the study is designed in detail. DialCrowd can help assess a single dialog system with Likert feedback ratings. It can also compare more than one dialog system, for example using an A/B template. In the latter case, dialog systems are presented in random order or in a Latin Square format. For non-interactive tests, JSON data, such as dialog logs, is added by the requester. DialCrowd also supports various types of exit polls: Likert scale, open-ended, and A/B, with random order presentation. For interactive tests, there are two types of testing: "1 to N" and "N to 1" where "1 to N" means one worker tests and individually scores N dialog systems (Likert Scale or select the best one). "N to 1" means N workers test one dialog system that DialCrowd has randomly selected amongst several.

3. Connect one or more dialog systems: 1. At the end of the DialCrowdAdmin setup, the DialCrowd Worker webpage is available. To connect to DialCrowd, a dialog system has an HTTP server waiting for utterances that DialCrowd directs to it using some simple specific protocols. This makes connecting to DialCrowd easy for anyone with basic programming knowledge. DialCrowd provides off-the-shelf server wrapper templates in three mainstream programming languages: Java, Python, and JavasSript https://github.com/DialRC/PortalAPI. The API protocol is the same as for DialPort.

4. Testing the task and then deploying it: After running the backend RESTful APIs, the requester inputs the backend API URL and checks the DialCrowd connection. The requester can then preview the website automatically generated by DialCrowdAdmin. DialCrowdAdmin provides log viewers and survey results. Requesters can also download data. DialCrowdWorker is the website through which workers talk to dialog systems and carry out the assigned task. The website is automatically generated by DialCrowdAdmin.

5 A user study of DialCrowd

This section describes a study of the use of DialCrowd by a set of requesters. The DialCrowd toolkit was made available to 10 dialog researchers. We gave them survey links and asked them to use DialCrowd. After they used it, we collected feedback. When asked how long it took to build a crowdsourcing study in their previous research, over 50% said more than one day and less than one week. For DialCrowd, 50% said they finished the whole process in between one and three hours. When asked how they set up the evaluation pipeline previously, 90% said they did it themselves without a toolkit. When asked how easy it was to use the DialCrowd toolkit and if it was useful, answers averaged above 4 on a scale from 1 to 5 where 5 was best.

- The instructions were clear to follow. [AVG:4.4, STD:0.69]

- The toolkit is useful. I want to use this toolkit in the future to run other studies [AVG:4, STD:0.94]

- I will use this toolkit in the future to run other studies [AVG:4.2, STD:0.78]

They also said that it took a lot less time to run a study using DialCrowd (100%), and that the toolkit is well documented (80%). They used interactive tests on their dialog systems or chatbot and non-interactive tests for classifying intent or entity labeling in specific domains. Among the open-ended questions, we received several questions about whether future versions of DialCrowd could include turn-based assessments and full systems that include other ASRs and TTSs, not just Google Chrome APIs. Participants also asked about adding more question types/more support for custom question types through an API. We are working on this function at present.

6 Conclusion

DialCrowd is a spoken dialog system crowdsourcing assessment toolkit. It is designed for use by the research community. Most users have found DialCrowd easy to use and would like to use it again in the future.

Acknowledgments

This work is partly funded by National Science Foundation grant CNS-1512973. The opinions expressed in this paper do not necessarily reflect those of the National Science Foundation.

References

William G Cochran and Gertrude M Cox. 1950. Experimental designs. .

Maxine Eskenazi, Gina-Anne Levow, Helen Meng, Gabriel Parent, and David Suendermann. 2013. *Crowdsourcing for speech processing: Applications to data collection, transcription and assessment.* John Wiley & Sons.

Sangkeun Jung, Cheongjae Lee, Kyungduk Kim, Minwoo Jeong, and Gary Geunbae Lee. 2009. Data-driven user simulation for automated evaluation of spoken dialog systems. *Computer Speech & Language* 23(4):479–509.

Filip Jurčíček, Simon Keizer, Milica Gašić, Francois Mairesse, Blaise Thomson, Kai Yu, and Steve Young. 2011. Real user evaluation of spoken dialogue systems using amazon mechanical turk. In *Twelfth Annual Conference of the International Speech Communication Association*.

Chia-Wei Liu, Ryan Lowe, Iulian V Serban, Michael Noseworthy, Laurent Charlin, and Joelle Pineau. 2016. How not to evaluate your dialogue system: An empirical study of unsupervised evaluation metrics for dialogue response generation. *arXiv preprint arXiv:1603.08023* .

Sebastian Moller and Janto Skowronek. 2003. Quantifying the impact of system characteristics on perceived quality dimensions of a spoken dialogue service. In *Eighth European Conference on Speech Communication and Technology*.

Robert Munro, Steven Bethard, Victor Kuperman, Vicky Tzuyin Lai, Robin Melnick, Christopher Potts, Tyler Schnoebelen, and Harry Tily. 2010. Crowdsourcing and language studies: the new generation of linguistic data. In *Proceedings of the NAACL HLT 2010 workshop on creating speech and language data with Amazon's Mechanical Turk*. Association for Computational Linguistics, pages 122–130.

Alok Parlikar. 2012. Testvox: Web-based framework for subjective evaluation of speech synthesis. *Opensource Software* page 13.

Olivier Pietquin and Helen Hastie. 2013. A survey on metrics for the evaluation of user simulations. *The knowledge engineering review* 28(1):59–73.

Antoine Raux, Brian Langner, Dan Bohus, Alan W Black, and Maxine Eskenazi. 2005. Let's go public! taking a spoken dialog system to the real world. In *Ninth European Conference on Speech Communication and Technology*.

Jost Schatzmann, Kallirroi Georgila, and Steve Young. 2005. Quantitative evaluation of user simulation techniques for spoken dialogue systems. In *6th SIGdial Workshop on DISCOURSE and DIALOGUE*.

Iulian Vlad Serban, Ryan Lowe, Peter Henderson, Laurent Charlin, and Joelle Pineau. 2015. A survey of available corpora for building data-driven dialogue systems. *arXiv preprint arXiv:1512.05742* .

Zhaojun Yang, Baichuan Li, Yi Zhu, Irwin King, Gina Levow, and Helen Meng. 2010. Collection of user judgments on spoken dialog system with crowdsourcing. In *Spoken Language Technology Workshop (SLT), 2010 IEEE*. IEEE, pages 277–282.

Tiancheng Zhao, Kyusong Lee, and Maxine Eskenazi. 2016. Dialport: Connecting the spoken dialog research community to real user data. In *Spoken Language Technology Workshop (SLT), 2016 IEEE*. IEEE, pages 83–90.

Leveraging Multimodal Dialog Technology for the Design of Automated and Interactive Student Agents for Teacher Training

David Pautler, Vikram Ramanarayanan, Kirby Cofino, Patrick Lange & David Suendermann-Oeft
Educational Testing Service R&D
90 New Montgomery St, San Francisco, CA
`<dpautler,vramanarayanan,plange,suendermann-oeft>@ets.org`

Abstract

We present a paradigm for interactive teacher training that leverages multimodal dialog technology to puppeteer custom-designed embodied conversational agents (ECAs) in student roles. We used the open-source multimodal dialog system HALEF to implement a small-group classroom math discussion involving Venn diagrams where a human teacher candidate has to interact with two student ECAs whose actions are controlled by the dialog system. Such an automated paradigm has the potential to be extended and scaled to a wide range of interactive simulation scenarios in education, medicine, and business where group interaction training is essential.

1 Introduction

There has been significant work in the research and development community on the use of embodied conversational agents (ECAs) and social robots to enable more immersive conversational experiences. This effort has led to the development of multiple software platforms and solutions for implementing embodied agents (Rist et al., 2004; Kawamoto et al., 2004; Thiebaux et al., 2008; Baldassarri et al., 2008; Wik and Hjalmarsson, 2009). More recently, there has also been a push towards developing ECAs that are empathetic (Fung et al., 2016) and are directed toward specific educational applications such as computer-assisted language learning (CALL) (Lee et al., 2010), including the possibility of providing targeted feedback to participants (Hoque et al., 2013). The degree of realism and immersiveness of the interaction experience can elicit varying behaviors and responses from users depending on the nature and design of the virtual interlocutor (Astrid et al., 2010).

Figure 1: Screenshot of the two virtual student avatars that teacher candidates interact with

2 Task Design

The task we used for our prototype implementation asks participants to imagine themselves in the role of a 2nd grade teacher leading a classroom discussion on the purpose and function of Venn diagrams with two ECAs designed to behave as students (see Figure 1). We provided participants with a stimulus Venn diagram (shown in Figure 2) in which one item, *fish*, is purposefully placed in the wrong place to serve as a catalyst for a small-group discussion. The learning goals for the discussion are to effectively evaluate the Venn diagram for its accuracy, while considering the similarities and differences between lakes and oceans. Further, one of the ECAs is designed to manifest a certain misunderstanding of this particular Venn diagram—that fish belongs outside all the circles—but the ECA does not reveal this misunderstanding unless it is asked to comment. The teacher candidate must engage both students in conversation, diagnose potential misunderstandings, and then correct those misunderstandings through dialog interactions.

Proceedings of the SIGDIAL 2018 Conference, pages 249–252,
Melbourne, Australia, 12-14 July 2018. ©2018 Association for Computational Linguistics

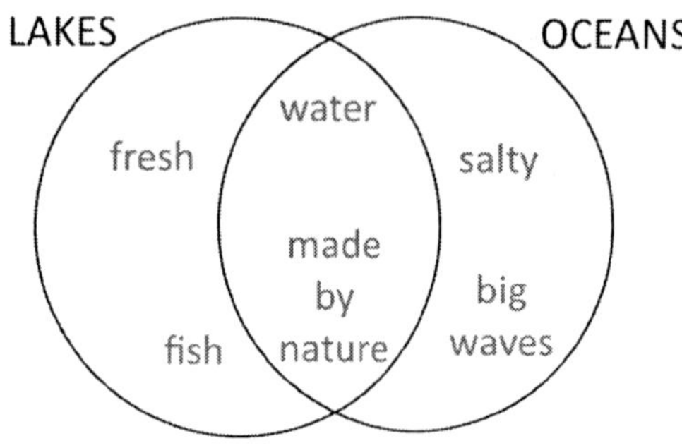

Figure 2: The Venn diagram that the trainee discusses with the ECAs

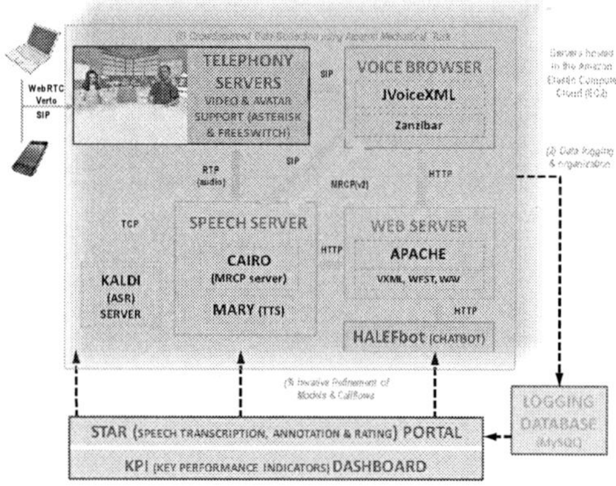

Figure 3: The HALEF multimodal dialog framework with ECAs to support educational learning and assessment applications.

3 System Design and Implementation

This section first describes our existing dialog framework. It then discusses the authoring process, in which the final step is integration of the 3D classroom user interface (UI) with the HALEF dialog system[1]. Note that work described in this paper builds on our previous efforts in building virtual avatars for job interviewing (see for example (Ramanarayanan et al., 2016; Cofino et al., 2017)). While designing such experiences for users and authors, we aim for several high-level goals:

- *The simulation must be available to potential users across the globe with as little setup as possible.* This goal implies that we avoid requiring software to be installed, if possible,

and that we make the experience as accessible as possible.

- *The activity must be realistic and immersive.* Research has shown that engagement is higher with on-screen ECAs than without (and higher yet with physical embodiments such as robots) (Sidner et al., 2005; Rich and Sidner, 2009), and higher engagement might provide more effective training.

- The authoring tools/resources must be as open, low-cost, easy-to-use, and well-supported as possible.

- It must be possible to control the ECAs remotely from the HALEF system and to sync the mouth motions and gestures of the ECAs with the audio of the ECAs' speech.

To fulfill these goals, we decided to use the Unity 3D[2] authoring tool, because it allows a game to be built as a WebGL[3] resource that can be hosted in a web page, thereby saving users from having to install anything. The following subsections describe how we integrated a Unity WebGL resource with HALEF.

3.1 Resources for Authoring

We used the Blender 3D modeling tool[4] to create several of our scenes and ECAs[5]. We also explored creating animations through the motion-capture capabilities of Microsoft Kinect. While both these methods are effective and complement each other, we found both of these to have a steeper learning curve than application designers (content matter experts who are not necessarily expert software engineers) might find acceptable, and they both require substantial time and expertise to develop ECAs of optimal quality. Therefore, going forward, we will work toward creating and maintaining an open repository of scenes, characters, and animations created by game-authoring experts[6].

When scenes, characters, and animations are assembled in Unity and built, they are still non-responsive because there is no way of sending commands (yet). One must add code to the web

---

[1] http://halef.org

[2] https://unity3d.com/
[3] https://developer.mozilla.org/en-US/docs/Web/API/WebGL_API
[4] https://www.blender.org
[5] We worked off assets originally created for us by Mursion, Inc.
[6] The public repository might not include the 3D models shown here as they are proprietary.

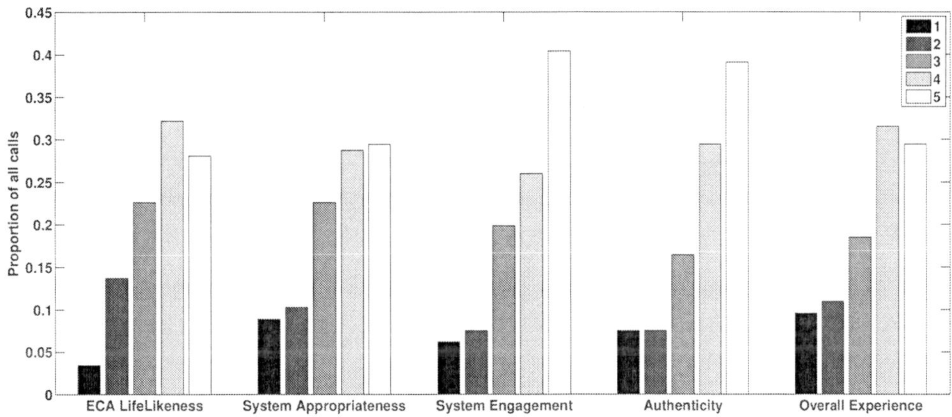

Figure 4: Crowdsourced ratings aggregated from 146 calls during user acceptance tests on Amazon Mechanical Turk.

page to receive commands over the network, as well as to the Unity files in order to route commands to a particular character. We bundled code to support these functions into a new Unity "WebGL template" that is easy to import into new Unity projects. The code includes a JSON configuration file that specifies all information required to connect to the HALEF dialog system. After an author imports this template, she updates the HTML, CSS, and JSON to fit the task (e.g. showing a static image of a Venn diagram), she builds the template as a "WebGL build", and the result is a set of files comprising a website.

For the backend, the author creates a dialog callflow using the Eclipse-based OpenVXML toolkit[7]; the author exports the callflow as a Java-based WAR file and HALEF hosts it on an Apache Tomcat server, similar to the way many HTML-only applications that have dynamic server-based logic are hosted.

To control ECAs from a callflow, the callflow must have nodes containing scripts that send commands over the network to the website. These commands include references to animations that should be triggered, as well as the ECA that should perform them. When an ECA speaks, the command that triggers the audio and mouth motions just identifies the ECA and the audio file. Part of front-end configuration is a sequence of animation-like "blendshape" settings to move the mouth into different phoneme-related shapes (this sequence of blendshape settings is generated from a forced alignment speech recognition tool that is currently proprietary).

4 User Acceptance Tests

We used the Amazon Mechanical Turk crowdsourcing platform to do user acceptance testing (UAT). We collected data from 146 crowd workers interacting with the ECAs. Following their interaction, the workers were also requested to rate, on a scale from 1–5 (with 1 being least satisfactory and 5 being most satisfactory), the following:

1. *ECA Lifelikeness*: How realistic and life-like were the ECAs over the course of the interaction?

2. *Appropriateness*: How appropriate were the system (or ECAs') responses to the questions posed by the user?

3. *Engagement*: How engaged were users while interacting with the ECAs?

4. *Authenticity*: How authentic were the responses of the ECAs, considering that they were supposed to represent students?

5. *Overall Experience*: How was the overall user experience interacting with the application?

Figure 4 plots the results of this user survey. We observe that users gave predominantly positive ratings to all aspects of the survey, with a majority proportion assigning ratings of 4 or 5. This also suggests that the lifelikeness of the ECAs and the appropriateness of system responses warranted the most improvement.

---

[7]https://sourceforge.net/p/halef/openvxml

5   Conclusions

We have presented a multimodal dialog-based teacher training application involving more than one virtual agent to create an immersive and interactive classroom simulation experience. Future work will look at leveraging the results of our user acceptance tests to improving the naturalness of the ECAs and the interaction, as well as in designing the simulation to be more adaptable to the engagement level of users. We will also explore the addition of more student avatars and different situational contexts.

Acknowledgments

We would like to thank David Dickerman and Eugene Tsuprun, who helped with the design and creation of the Venn Diagram task.

References

M Astrid, Nicole C Krämer, Jonathan Gratch, and Sin-Hwa Kang. 2010. it doesnt matter what you are! explaining social effects of agents and avatars. *Computers in Human Behavior*, 26(6):1641–1650.

Sandra Baldassarri, Eva Cerezo, and Francisco J Seron. 2008. Maxine: A platform for embodied animated agents. *Computers & Graphics*, 32(4):430–437.

Kirby Cofino, Vikram Ramanarayanan, Patrick Lange, David Pautler, David Suendermann-Oeft, and Keelan Evanini. 2017. A modular, multimodal open-source virtual interviewer dialog agent. In *Proceedings of the 19th ACM International Conference on Multimodal Interaction*, pages 520–521. ACM.

Pascale Fung, Dario Bertero, Yan Wan, Anik Dey, Ricky Ho Yin Chan, Farhad Bin Siddique, Yang Yang, Chien-Sheng Wu, and Ruixi Lin. 2016. Towards empathetic human-robot interactions. *arXiv preprint arXiv:1605.04072*.

Mohammed Ehsan Hoque, Matthieu Courgeon, Jean-Claude Martin, Bilge Mutlu, and Rosalind W Picard. 2013. Mach: My automated conversation coach. In *Proceedings of the 2013 ACM international joint conference on Pervasive and ubiquitous computing*, pages 697–706. ACM.

Shin-ichi Kawamoto, Hiroshi Shimodaira, Tsuneo Nitta, Takuya Nishimoto, Satoshi Nakamura, Katsunobu Itou, Shigeo Morishima, Tatsuo Yotsukura, Atsuhiko Kai, Akinobu Lee, et al. 2004. Galatea: Open-source software for developing anthropomorphic spoken dialog agents. In *Life-Like Characters*, pages 187–211. Springer.

Sungjin Lee, Hyungjong Noh, Jonghoon Lee, Kyusong Lee, and Gary Geunbae Lee. 2010. Cognitive effects of robot-assisted language learning on oral skills. In *INTERSPEECH 2010 Satellite Workshop on Second Language Studies: Acquisition, Learning, Education and Technology*.

Vikram Ramanarayanan, Patrick Lange, David Pautler, Zhou Yu, and David Suendermann-Oeft. 2016. Interview with an avatar: A real-time engagement tracking-enabled cloud-based multimodal dialog system for learning and assessment. In *Proceedings of the Spoken Language Technology (SLT) Workshop, San Diego, CA*.

Charles Rich and Candace L Sidner. 2009. Robots and avatars as hosts, advisors, companions, and jesters. *AI Magazine*, 30(1):29.

Thomas Rist, Elisabeth André, Stephan Baldes, Patrick Gebhard, Martin Klesen, Michael Kipp, Peter Rist, and Markus Schmitt. 2004. A review of the development of embodied presentation agents and their application fields. In *Life-Like Characters*, pages 377–404. Springer.

Candace L Sidner, Christopher Lee, Cory D Kidd, Neal Lesh, and Charles Rich. 2005. Explorations in engagement for humans and robots. *Artificial Intelligence*, 166(1-2):140–164.

Marcus Thiebaux, Stacy Marsella, Andrew N Marshall, and Marcelo Kallmann. 2008. Smartbody: Behavior realization for embodied conversational agents. In *Proceedings of the 7th international joint conference on Autonomous agents and multiagent systems-Volume 1*, pages 151–158. International Foundation for Autonomous Agents and Multiagent Systems.

Preben Wik and Anna Hjalmarsson. 2009. Embodied conversational agents in computer assisted language learning. *Speech Communication*, 51(10):1024–1037.

An Empirical Study of Self-Disclosure in Spoken Dialogue Systems

Abhilasha Ravichander
Language Technologies Institute
Carnegie Mellon University
aravicha@cs.cmu.edu

Alan Black
Language Technologies Institute
Carnegie Mellon University
awb@cs.cmu.edu

Abstract

Self-disclosure is a key social strategy employed in conversation to build relations and increase conversational depth. It has been heavily studied in psychology and linguistic literature, particularly for its ability to induce self-disclosure from the recipient, a phenomena known as reciprocity. However, we know little about how self-disclosure manifests in conversation with automated dialog systems, especially as any self-disclosure on the part of a dialog system is patently disingenuous. In this work, we run a large-scale quantitative analysis on the effect of self-disclosure by analyzing interactions between real-world users and a spoken dialog system in the context of social conversation. We find that indicators of reciprocity occur even in human-machine dialog, with far-reaching implications for chatbots in a variety of domains including education, negotiation and social dialog.

1 Introduction

Humans employ different strategies during a conversation in pursuit of their social goals (Tracy and Coupland, 1990). The contributions to a conversation can be categorized as those which serve *propositional* functions by adding new information to the dialog, those which serve *interactional* functions by driving the interaction and those which serve *interpersonal* functions, by building up the relationship between the involved parties. When fulfilling interpersonal functions, people either consciously or sub-consciously employ social conversational strategies in order to connect and build relationships with each other (Laurenceau et al., 1998; Won-Doornink, 1985). This feeling of

M: How is it going?
H: Not bad not bad.
M: Oh! Thats great. I had a great day too. Yeah, I've just been chilling all day and catching up with my friends. They just got married. What about you? Anything special that I should know of?
H: Well I went to see a play today, I quite enjoyed it.
M: You know, I spent all my weekend watching T.V. . I am obsessed with this show.
H: What show?

Figure 1: Excerpt dialog from conversation between a user and our dialog agent[1]. H represents user utterance and M represents machine dialog.

rapport, of connecting and having common ground with another human being is one of the fundamental aspects of good human conversation. Maintaining conversational harmony has shown to be effective in several domains such as education (Ogan et al., 2012; Sinha and Cassell, 2015a,b; Frisby and Martin, 2010; Zhao et al., 2016) and negotiation (Drolet and Morris, 2000; Nadler, 2003, 2004).

Self-disclosure is the conversational act of disclosing information about oneself to others. We consider the definition of self-disclosure within the theoretical framework of social penetration theory, where it is defined as the *voluntary* sharing of opinions, thoughts, beliefs, experiences, preferences, values and personal history (Altman and Taylor, 1973). The effect of self-disclosure has been well-studied in the psychology community, in particular it's ability to induce *reciprocity* in dyadic interaction (Jourard, 1971; Derlega et al.,

---

[1]Real interaction data withheld for confidentiality. Conversation data shown here is not real interaction data but follows similar patterns.

Proceedings of the SIGDIAL 2018 Conference, pages 253–263,
Melbourne, Australia, 12-14 July 2018. ©2018 Association for Computational Linguistics

1973). Several studies have shown that self-disclosure reciprocity characterizes initial social interactions between people (Ehrlich and Graeven, 1971; Sprecher and Hendrick, 2004) and further, that *disclosure promotes disclosure* (Dindia et al., 2002).

This brings us to a natural question: how does such behavior manifest itself in interactions with dialog systems? A subtle but crucial aspect is that humans are aware that machines do not have feelings or experiences of their own, so any attempt at self-disclosure on the part of the machine is inherently disingenuous. However, Nass et al. (1994) suggests that humans tend to view computers as social actors, and interact with them in much the same way they do with humans. Disclosure reciprocity in such a setting would have far-reaching implications for dialog systems which aim to elicit information from the user in order to offer more personalized experiences for example, or to better achieve task completion (Bickmore and Cassell, 2001; Bickmore and Picard, 2005; Goldstein and Benassi, 1994; Lee and Choi, 2017).

In this work, we study this phenomena by building an open-domain chatbot (§3) which engages in social conversation with hundreds of Amazon Alexa users (Figure 1.), and gains insights into two aspects of human-machine self-disclosure. First, self-disclosure by the dialog agent is strongly correlated with instances of self-disclosure by the user indicating disclosure reciprocity in interactions with spoken dialog systems (§4.1). Second, initial self-disclosure by the user can characterize user behavior throughout the conversation (§4.2). We additionally study the effect of self-disclosure and likability, but find no reliable linear relationship with the amount of self-disclosure in the conversation (§4.3). To the best of our knowledge, this work is the first large-scale study of reciprocity and self-disclosure between users in the real world and spoken dialog systems.

2   Background

Self-disclosure as a social phenomena is the act of revealing information about oneself to others. It has been of particular interest to study what factors makes humans self-disclose (Miller et al., 1983; Dindia and Allen, 1992; Hill and Stull, 1987; Buhrmester and Prager, 1995; Stokes, 1987; Qian and Scott, 2007; Jourard and Friedman, 1970; Ko and Kuo, 2009), how do they do it (Chen, 1995;

Greene et al., 2006; Chelune, 1975; Sprecher and Hendrick, 2004) and what are the effects of self-disclosing (Gibbs et al., 2006; Mazer et al., 2009; Forest and Wood, 2012; Turner et al., 2007; Knox et al., 1997; Vittengl and Holt, 2000).

One such effect is disclosure reciprocity, which has been shown to be one of the most significant effects of self-disclosure (Jourard, 1971). Reciprocity is the phenomenon by which self-disclosure by one participant in a dyadic social interaction results in self-disclosure from the other participant in response. A substantial amount of research has shown that when one party self-discloses, the other party is much more likely to self-disclose (Jourard, 1971; Jourard and Friedman, 1970; Dindia et al., 2002; Derlega et al., 1973). While the exact cause of this phenomena is not known, it has been suggested that self-disclosure can be viewed as a social exchange, where the party receiving self-disclosure feels obligated to self-disclose in return (Archer, 1979), or as a social conversational norm (Derlega et al., 1993), or from the point of view of social trust-attraction (Vittengl and Holt, 2000) where people self-disclose to people who disclose to them, as they consider self-disclosure to be a sign of trust and liking. Additionally, Sprecher and Hendrick (2004) find that people who consider themselves to be high self-disclosers are likely to be much better at eliciting self-disclosure as well. Derlega et al. (1973) observe that self-disclosure is a positive function of self-disclosure received, regardless of liking for the initial discloser. Mikulincer and Nachshon (1991) analyze personality types and self-disclosure, and find that secure people are more likely to both self-disclose and reciprocate self-disclosure. Cozby (1972) study the relationship between disclosure and liking and suggest that this relationship is not linear. In this work, we attempt to combine these perspectives to gain insights into the nature of self-disclosure in human-machine dialog.

3   Identifying Self-Disclosure

3.1   Coding Self Disclosure

In this work, we consider the definition of self-disclosure within the theoretical framework of social penetration theory (Altman and Taylor, 1973) where it is defined to be the *voluntary* sharing of information which could include amongst other things one's personal history, thoughts, opinions,

Self-Disclosure	No Self-Disclosure
1) M: Good to hear! Is it anything special today?	1) M: Good to hear! Is it anything special today?
H: Nothing much, I am just going down to the lake with my dogs today	H: Not really
2) M: Have you seen the movie Arrival?	2) M: Have you seen the movie Arrival?
H: Oh my god, yes i have it's my favorite movie	H: Yeah I did I did see Arrival

Figure 2: Examples of self-disclosing user responses as well as responses when the user does not self-disclose [2].

beliefs, feelings, preferences, attitudes, aspirations, likes, dislikes and favorites. In a human-machine context, we define self-disclosure as the conversational act of revealing aspects of oneself voluntarily, which would otherwise not be possible to be known by the dialog system. A general rule-of-thumb we follow is, self-disclosure is proportional to the amount of extraneous information that is added to a conversation. For example, we do not identify a direct response to a question as self-disclosure as it is not strictly voluntary. We show examples of our definition of human self-disclosure and non-disclosure in the context of our dialog system in Figure. 2.

3.2 Dataset Preparation

The data for this study was collected by having users from the real-world interact with our open-domain dialog agent. The dialog agent was hosted on Amazon Alexa devices as part of the AlexaPrize competition (Ram et al., 2018) and was one of sixteen socialbots that could be invoked by any user within the United States through the command 'Let's chat!'. The users that interacted with our socialbot were randomly chosen, and did not know which of the sixteen systems they were interacting with. Users who interacted with our bot over a span of three days (N=1507) were randomly assigned to two groups: one received a bot that self-disclosed at high depth from the beginning of the conversation while the other group interacted with a socialbot that self-disclosed only later about superficial topics like movies and TV shows. At the end, both socialbots engaged in free-form conversation with the user, where the initiative of the interaction was on the user and both bots were free to self-disclose at any depth. The users were also free to end the interaction at any time, and thus had no motivation for continuing the conversation besides their own enter-

tainment. To control the direction of the conversation and bot utterance, we utilize a finite state transducer-based dialog system that chats with the user about movies and TV shows, as well as plays games and supports open-domain conversation (Prabhumoye et al., 2017). State transitions are decided based on sentiment analysis of user utterances, in order to gauge interest in a particular topic. Initially the dialog system takes initiative in the conversation and steers the topic of discussion, however later there is a handoff to the user whereby the user can determine the focus of the conversation. In this way, the socialbot leads the user through the following topics, conditioned on user interest as shown in Figure 3:

Greeting : In this phase, our dialog agent greets the user and asks them about their day. The bot which performs high self-disclosure initially also responds with information about it's day and a personal anecdote.

TV Shows: The next phase involves chit chat about popular TV shows. The dialog agent asks the user if they are an enthusiast of a recent popular TV show and moves on to the next phase of the conversation if they aren't.

Movie: In this phase, the dialog agent attempts to engage the user in conversations about movies, asking them if they have seen any of the recent ones.

Word Game: In this phase, the dialog agent requests the user to play a word game. Participation in the game is completely optional and the user can move on to the next phase by stating that they do not wish to play.

CQA: The last phase supports uninhibited free-form conversation. The initiative of the exchange is now on the user and conversation is stateless. The dialog system response is determined by a retrieval model. For each utterance, the socialbot attempts to retrieve the most relevant response from the Yahoo L6 dataset (yl6, 2017), a dataset containing approximately 4 million questions and

---

[2]Not real interaction data, however very similar to actual utterances found in the interaction data

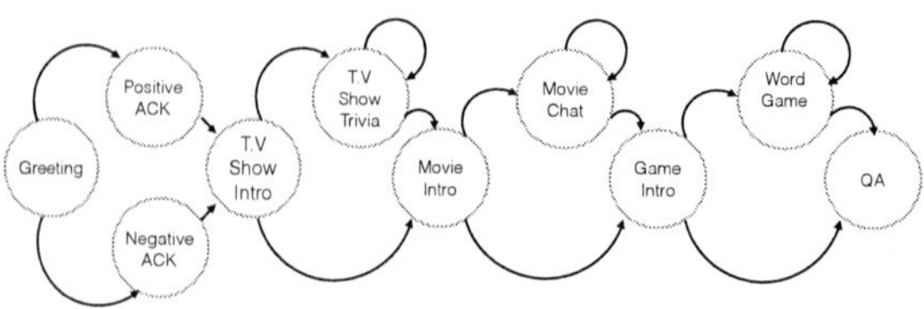

Figure 3: Topic FST for Conversation

their corresponding answers from the Community Question-Answering (CQA) website, Yahoo Answers [3].

The users were then allowed to rate the interaction on a scale of 1-5, based on the question *'Would you interact with this socialbot again?'*. 319 users rated the socialbot (Group 1) and 1507 users interacted with our system in total (Group 2). Following this, to preserve confidentiality of the interaction data, one annotator annotated all turns of conversation from Group 1 for self-disclosure. Annotator reliability was determined by calculating inter-annotator agreement from three external annotators on a carefully prepared anonymized subset of the data amounting to 62 interactions comprising of over 816 turns. The Fleiss' kappa from the four annotators was 63.8, indicating substantial agreement. Atleast two of three annotators agreed on 93.6% of the reference annotations. The full dataset contains a total of 319 conversations, spanning 10751 conversational turns. Out of the 5216 human dialog utterances, 13.8% featured some form of self-disclosure.

Since our agent is a spoken dialog system in the real world there is some amount of noise in the dataset caused due to ASR errors. To estimate this, we randomly sample 100 utterances from the dataset and annotate these utterances for whether they contained an ASR mistake, and if the sentence meaning was still apparent either from context or from the utterance itself. We find that at least one ASR error occurs in 13% of user utterances, but 46.1% of utterances with ASR mistakes can still be understood. Since our dialog agent relies on sentiment-based FST transitions during the initial stages of the conversation, we also analyze the rate of false transitions in the data. We randomly sample 100 utterances from across choice points of all conversations and find that 11% of them consisted of incorrect responses, either due to mistakes in sentiment analysis or due to nu-

ance in the user utterances which rendered a response from the dialog agent unusable. Finally, we analyze how many users had multiple interactions with our dialog agent during the course of our study. This is relevant as user behavior during a second interaction with the system might differ from initial interaction. Users are identifiable only by an anonymized hash key provided by Amazon along with the conversation data. We find that out of 316 users who interacted with our dialog agent and left a rating, only 3 interacted with our agent twice and none of them interacted with our agent more than two times, largely allowing us to disregard this effect.

3.3 Feature Space Design

We utilize the annotations of 319 conversations to train and evaluate a Machine Learning model to identify user self-disclosure. We categorize the features for this model at two levels, *utterance-level* features wherein the user utterance is taken standalone and analyzed for self-disclosure and *conversational-level* features which consider the utterance in context of the current conversation.

3.3.1 Utterance Features

This represents a class of features that only consider the current utterance. These include-

1. **Bag-of-words Features** TF-IDF features from the user utterance.

2. **Linguistic Style Features** This class of features attempts to characterize the linguistic style of user utterances, including lexical choices that might be indicative of self-disclosure (Doell, 2013). These include- i) Length of the user utterance, ii) Presence of negation words, iii) Part-of-speech tags such as nouns and adjectives in the user utterance in order to represent users revealing emotion or discussing topics, iv) Presence of filler words in utterance, v) Number

<hr>

[3] answers.yahoo.com

of named entities in the utterance, vi) Gazeteer features based on common responses to questions asked by our dialog system, indicative of conversational responses as well as strongly positive, negative or neutral responses [4].

3. **LIWC Features** i) Studies have shown (Sparrevohn and Rapee, 2009) that people who self-disclose tend to use words that reveal strong emotion. Thus, we include features to represent words from affect relevant categories of LIWC (Pennebaker et al., 2015), such as anger, anxiety, sadness, positive emotion or negative emotion, ii) number of personal pronouns, first person singular pronouns, first person plural pronouns, second person pronouns, third person plural pronouns, third person singular pronouns, iii) Additionally, users self-disclosing incidents from their personal lives tend to discuss their social settings. Thus, we use relationship words related to the family and friends categories from LIWC.

3.3.2 Conversation Features

These features are broadly based on dialog structure or the language-based features from local conversational context. These include i) TF-IDF features from the user utterance concatenated with the bot utterance[5], to help capture the difference between direct responses to questions and voluntary self-disclosure, ii) dialog system self-disclosing in previous turn, iii) dialog system asking a question in the previous turn, iv) Amount of word overlap with previous machine utterance, which is defined as the number of words that overlap with the previous dialog system utterance normalized by the length of the dialog system utterance, v) Number of content words[6] that overlap with previous machine utterance.

---

[4]Includes phrases such as "I'm fine", "I'm ok", "I'm good", "I'm doing ok", "I'm doing good", "how are you" for conversational responses, "delightful", "favorite", "amazing", "awesome", "fantastic", "brilliant", "the best", "really great" etc. for strongly positive, "boring", "tired", "bored", "sad", "lonely", "disgusting", "hate","awful" etc. for strongly negative and "rain", "summer", "winter", "cold", "wind" etc. for strongly neutral (as users tend to discuss weather while making small talk).

[5]Each word of the bot utterance is encapsulated within a <bot></bot> tag

[6]where we determine content words following the usual definition of nouns, main verbs, adjectives and adverbs.

Model	Accuracy	Precision	Recall	F1
First Person	86.6%	68.0%	6.0%	10.9%
Utterance Features	89.8%	69.8%	46.5%	55.5%
Utterance + Conversation Features	**91.7%**	**74.4%**	**60.5%**	**66.67%**

Table 1: Classification performance(%) of models at identifying user utterances to contain self-disclosure.

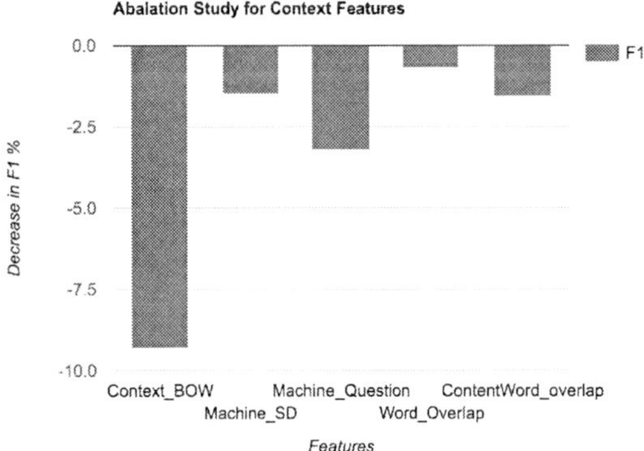

Figure 4: Ablation Study for Conversation Features.

3.4 Results of Identification

The combination of the three categories of features results in a 234-dimensional vector which acts as input to an SVM with a linear kernel. We utilize truncated SVD with 100 components for dimensionality reduction of all bag-of-words based feature classes. We compare against two baselines, the first is a baseline consisting of only personal voiced features (including all LIWC features) and the second attempts to classify self-disclosure independent of dialog context (only conditioned on the current user utterance). We perform 10-fold cross validation and describe our results in Table. 1. We observe that considering user utterances in context of the conversation considerably improves our ability to predict self-disclosure. To perform more detailed error analysis on a larger test set, we randomly sample 1044 utterances from 5216 utterances to be a held-out test set. This test set consists of 134 utterances of self-disclosure. Our classifier achieves an accuracy of 93.4% at recognizing self-disclosure on this test set, with a F1-score of 72.7% (Precision: 77.3%, Recall: 68.6%). The test distribution contains 12.8% examples of self-disclosure and 87.2% examples of no disclosure. We further perform an ablation study of each dialog-context feature as shown in Figure 4. We observe that considering the word in the context of the machine utterance is most helpful in identifying self-disclosure, indicating possibly that it helps us capture the notion of self-disclosure being a voluntary phenomena whereby the user reveals information about himself or herself, by separating instances of direct answers to questions from turns where users disclose more than what is asked. We next conduct a careful manual error analysis of the mistakes made by our classifier, in an attempt to identify what cases are particularly hard or ambiguous. We observe that 85% of user turns which our model wrongly labeled as containing self-disclosure had personal pronouns, suggesting that our model considers these as a very strong signal for self-disclosure. However many of these utterances were in fact direct responses to questions, or questions to the bot itself prefaced with a personal pronoun, and thus not really instances of self-disclosure. 25.9% of the mistakes were not well-formed or meaningful sentences, possibly due to ASR errors, speech disfluencies or user phrasing. We also examine the user turns our model failed to predict as being self-disclosure. 19.5% of these mistakes were not well-formed sentences and 12.1% were statements about the bots performance. A further 21.9% of errors contained rare words which might not have been seen before in the training data along with an absence of the linguistic markers of self-disclosure identified by us (for example, *M: Anything special today? H: Really wanna grab a smoke*). In the future, real world knowledge and a larger amount of training data might help mitigate some of these error classes.

4 Effect of Self-Disclosure

4.1 Reciprocity

We analyze common markers of reciprocity (Jourard and Jaffe, 1970; Harper and Harper, 2006), such as the usage of personal pronouns, word overlap with the previous sentence (normalized by length of previous utterance) and average user utterance length between two groups of users- ones who were shown a bot that self-disclosed initially and a bot which only self-disclosed later (Table 2.).

Marker	Mean SD	Mean Ctrl
Word Overlap*	0.0352	0.0226
First Person Pronouns*	0.84	0.57
Avg. Noun Mentions*	2.00	1.49
Avg. Adjective Mentions	0.55	0.47
Avg. User Utt. Length	4.428	3.983

Table 2: Various effects of conversation with a dialog system that self-discloses right off-the-bat and with a control dialog system that only self-discloses later. * indicates p<0.05 after Bonferroni correction.

Group	No Machine SD	With Machine SD
Rated	10.5%	**24.3%**
All	7.4%	**21.6%**

Table 3: % of turns with Human Self-Disclosure following Machine Self-Disclosure/Non-Disclosure.

Within the data which consists of only rated conversations, we observe how many turns where the machine self-disclosed were also met with human self-disclosure ("Rated" in Table. 3). We then tag all user utterances [7] with our SVM classifier as either being instances of self-disclosure or not being instances of self disclosure ("All" in Table. 3). We find that 10.6% of all user utterances contain self disclosure, and 21.6% of machine utterances that contained self-disclosure were followed by a human utterance that contained self-disclosure, compared to the 7.4% of cases where a user self-disclosed without the machine self-disclosing (p < 0.05). These results are shown in Table. 3.

Next, we observe the utterance after initial self-disclosure for a group where the socialbot self-discloses compared to the equivalent dialog turn for a group where the bot doesn't self-disclose, to analyze if self-disclosure has immediate effects. These results are shown in Table. 4. We observe that when the bot self-discloses, the user self-discloses in response in 56.5% of all cases. However if the bot does not self-disclose and asks the same question, the user self discloses only in 35.5% of all cases (p < 0.0001). Our findings suggest that it is possible user behavior is affected by

---

[7] from 811 conversations of length greater than three turns.

258

Group	No Machine SD	With Machine SD
Rated	44.4%	**62.6%**
All	35.5%	**56.5%**

Table 4: % of turns with Human Self-Disclosure in turns immediately following equivalent initial self-disclosing/non-disclosing turn of machine.

the self-disclosing behavior of our dialog agent, and that such an effect can be seen immediately.

4.2 Initial Self-Disclosure and User behavior

We next examine conversation-wide characteristics and self-disclosure patterns of users based on their initial self-disclosing behavior.

Are Conversations With Initial Self-Disclosure Longer? We analyze whether whether initial occurrences of user self-disclosure lead to users prolonging the conversation by examining average conversational length for two groups of users : those who decided to self-disclose at the very beginning of the conversation itself and those who didn't. We find that users who self-disclose initially tend to have significantly longer conversation than users who do not ($p<0.05$), with an average conversational length of 37.19 turns compared to an average of 32.4 turns for users who chose not to self-disclose.

Does not self-disclosing initially imply reduced self disclosure throughout the conversation? We next examine the hypothesis that users who do not self-disclose initially tend to self-disclose less throughout. This is based on the notion of openness and guardedness in personality (Stokes, 1987; Sermat and Smyth, 1973) indicating that some individuals are more likely to self-disclose than others. For this study, we do not consider interactions involving the word game as it prolongs the conversation without giving opportunities for self-disclosure. We examine to what extent do individuals who refuse to self-disclose initially, self-disclose later in the conversation compared to users who self-disclose from the beginning of the conversation itself. We find that on average, users who do not choose to self-disclose initially are *significantly* less likely to self-disclose ($p<0.05$) even later on in the conversation, only revealing information in 9% of their turns as compared to the 24.6% of turns of other users.

Do users who choose not to self-disclose initially exhibit less interest in following machine interests? To analyze openness to conversation, we invite users to play a long-winded word game with the dialog system. We analyze how much self-disclosure correlates with willingness to play the game and length of game playing. We find that on average users who self-disclose initially are also significantly more open to game-playing than those who don't ($p<0.05$), playing on average 4.75 turns of the game compared to an average gameplay of 3.16 turns by other users. They are also significantly more likely to attempt to play the game ($p<0.05$), with 34.7% of self-disclosing users attempting to play the game and only 25.1% of non-disclosing users attempting to do so.

4.3 Does Self-Disclosure Increase Likability

Motivated by Cozby (1972), we attempt to analyze whether self-disclosure increases likability in human-machine interaction. We utilize the user ratings based on the question *'Would you talk to this socialbot again'* as a proxy for likability of the dialog agent, and examine whether conversations where the user self-disclosed often were given higher ratings than ones where they didn't. We find that there is negligible correlation in general between user ratings and the amount of self-disclosure (pearson's r = 0.01). We then examine the differences in user ratings between the top 20% and bottom 20% of self-disclosing conversations, once more excluding interactions with the game. We observe that while more self-disclosing conversations get higher ratings in general, the results are not statistically significant (average rating of conversations with higher self-disclosure is 3.14 compared to 3.13 for conversations with lesser self-disclosure). Lastly, we analyze the effect of reciprocity and self-disclosure, by analyzing the ratings of users who self-disclosed in response to bot disclosure but find no significant difference in the ratings of such users (3.34 to 3.27). Thus we are unable to find any conclusive linear relationship between self-disclosure and likability.

5 Discussion and Related Work

There has been significant prior interest in computationally analyzing various forms of self-disclosure online (Yang et al., 2017; Wang et al., 2016; Stutzman et al., 2012; Yin et al., 2016;

Bak et al., 2014; De Choudhury and De, 2014). Bickmore et al. (2009) study the effect of machine 'backstories' in dialog, and find that users rate their interactions to be more enjoyable when the dialog system has a backstory. Zhao et al. (2016) identify self-disclosure in peer tutoring between humans. Han et al. (2015); Meguro et al. (2010) identify self-disclosure as a user intention in a natural language understanding system. Oscar J. Romero (2017) use self-disclosure as one strategy amongst others to build a socially-aware conversational agent. Higashinaka et al. (2008) study if users self-disclose on topics they like rather than ones they don't, with a focus on text-based chat rather than spoken dialog. Similarly, Lee and Choi (2017) study the relation between self-disclosure and liking for a movie recommendation system, using a Wizard-of-Oz approach instead of constructing a dialog agent. Perhaps closest to our work is the work of Moon (2000), which studies the phenomena of reciprocity in human-machine self-disclosure. However, this phenomena is not studied for dialog, and similar to previous work, relies on a text-based series of interview questions.

In this work, we are interested in realizing self-disclosure in a real-time, large-scale spoken dialogue system. We depart from previous work in three main ways. First, we have the opportunity of deploying a dialog agent in the wild, and studying hundreds of interactions with real users in US households. Second, we study reciprocity of self-disclosure in human-machine dialog, and find markers of reciprocity even in conversations with a dialog agent. Third, we characterize users by their initial self-disclosing behavior and study conversation-level behavioral differences. We believe this work to be a step towards better understanding the effect of dialog agents deployed in the real-world employing self-disclosure as a social strategy, as well as better understanding the implications of self-disclosing *user* behavior with dialog agents.

We acknowledge limitations of our current approach. In this work, our definition of self-disclosure is binary. A more nuanced version that considers both magnitude and valence of self-disclosure would open up several further research directions, such as analyzing reciprocity matching in depth of disclosure and analyzing user behavior based on the valence of disclosure. It would also be interesting to analyze how agent behavior can significantly influence non-disclosing users, as our results find that users who do not initially self-disclose continue to self-disclose at reduced levels throughout the conversation. Another immediate research direction would be to study the effect of other social conversational strategies such as praise (Fogg and Nass, 1997; Zhao et al., 2016) at a large scale in spoken-dialog systems. In the future, one could imagine dialog agents that reason over both social strategies and their magnitude, conditioned on user behavior, in service of their conversational goals.

6 Conclusion

In this work, we empirically study the effect of self-disclosure in a large-scale experiment involving real-world users of Amazon Alexa. We find that indicators of reciprocity occur even in conversations with dialog systems, and that user behavior can be characterized by self-disclosure patterns in the initial stages of the conversation. We hope that these findings inspire more user-centric research in dialog systems, with an emphasis on dialog agents that attempt to build a relationship and maintain rapport with the user when eliciting information.

Acknowledgements

This work has partially been supported by the National Science Foundation under Grant No. CNS 13-30596. The views and conclusions contained herein are those of the authors and should not be interpreted as necessarily representing the official policies or endorsements, either expressed or implied, of the NSF, or the US Government. The authors are grateful to the CMU Magnus team for their hard work through the AlexaPrize competition, with special thanks to Shrimai Prabhumoye and Chaitanya Malaviya for helping with this effort. The authors would like to express their gratitude to Diyi Yang, Alexander Rudnicky and Dan Jurafsky for interesting discussions related to this work. The authors would like to especially thank Shruti Rijhwani, Shivani Poddar and Aditya Potukuchi for their time and support through this effort. Finally, the authors are immensely grateful to the Amazon Alexa team for facilitating universities to do dialog research with real user data, through the Alexa Prize competition, as well as to all the Amazon Alexa users who were willing to interact with our system.

References

2017. Yahoo Webscope. (2007). L6 - Yahoo! Answers Comprehensive Questions and Answers version (1.0). `https://webscope.sandbox.yahoo.com/catalog.php`. [Online; accessed 15-August-2017].

Irwin Altman and Dalmas Taylor. 1973. Social penetration theory. *New York: Holt, Rinehart &\Mnston* .

R.L Archer. 1979. Anatomical and psychological sex differences. *Self-disclosure: Origins, Patterns, and Implications of Openness in Interpersonal Relationships* .

JinYeong Bak, Chin-Yew Lin, and Alice Oh. 2014. Self-disclosure topic model for classifying and analyzing twitter conversations. In *Proceedings of the 2014 Conference on Empirical Methods in Natural Language Processing (EMNLP)*. pages 1986–1996.

Timothy Bickmore and Justine Cassell. 2001. Relational agents: a model and implementation of building user trust. In *Proceedings of the SIGCHI conference on Human factors in computing systems*. ACM, pages 396–403.

Timothy Bickmore, Daniel Schulman, and Langxuan Yin. 2009. Engagement vs. deceit: Virtual humans with human autobiographies. In *International Workshop on Intelligent Virtual Agents*. Springer, pages 6–19.

Timothy W Bickmore and Rosalind W Picard. 2005. Establishing and maintaining long-term human-computer relationships. *ACM Transactions on Computer-Human Interaction (TOCHI)* 12(2):293–327.

Duane Buhrmester and Karen Prager. 1995. Patterns and functions of self-disclosure during childhood and adolescence. .

Gordon J Chelune. 1975. Self-disclosure: An elaboration of its basic dimensions. *Psychological Reports* 36(1):79–85.

Guo-Ming Chen. 1995. Differences in self-disclosure patterns among americans versus chinese: A comparative study. *Journal of Cross-Cultural Psychology* 26(1):84–91.

Paul C Cozby. 1972. Self-disclosure, reciprocity and liking. *Sociometry* pages 151–160.

Munmun De Choudhury and Sushovan De. 2014. Mental health discourse on reddit: Self-disclosure, social support, and anonymity.

Valerian J Derlega, Marian Sue Harris, and Alan L Chaikin. 1973. Self-disclosure reciprocity, liking and the deviant. *Journal of Experimental Social Psychology* 9(4):277 284.

VJ Derlega, S Metts, S Petronio, and ST Margulis. 1993. Sage series on close relationships. self-disclosure.

Kathryn Dindia, M Allen, R Preiss, B Gayle, and N Burrell. 2002. Self-disclosure research: Knowledge through meta-analysis. *Interpersonal communication research: Advances through meta-analysis* pages 169–185.

Kathryn Dindia and Mike Allen. 1992. Sex differences in self-disclosure: A meta-analysis. *Psychological bulletin* 112(1):106.

Kelly Doell. 2013. The word feel as an indicator of enacted social support in personal relationships. *International Journal of Psychological Studies* 5(4):107.

Aimee L Drolet and Michael W Morris. 2000. Rapport in conflict resolution: Accounting for how face-to-face contact fosters mutual cooperation in mixed-motive conflicts. *Journal of Experimental Social Psychology* 36(1):26–50.

Howard J Ehrlich and David B Graeven. 1971. Reciprocal self-disclosure in a dyad. *Journal of Experimental Social Psychology* 7(4):389–400.

Brian J Fogg and Clifford Nass. 1997. Silicon sycophants: The effects of computers that flatter. *International journal of human-computer studies* 46(5):551–561.

Amanda L Forest and Joanne V Wood. 2012. When social networking is not working: Individuals with low self-esteem recognize but do not reap the benefits of self-disclosure on facebook. *Psychological science* 23(3):295–302.

Brandi N Frisby and Matthew M Martin. 2010. Instructor–student and student–student rapport in the classroom. *Communication Education* 59(2):146–164.

Jennifer L Gibbs, Nicole B Ellison, and Rebecca D Heino. 2006. Self-presentation in online personals: The role of anticipated future interaction, self-disclosure, and perceived success in internet dating. *Communication Research* 33(2):152–177.

Gary S Goldstein and Victor A Benassi. 1994. The relation between teacher self-disclosure and student classroom participation. *Teaching of Psychology* 21(4):212–217.

Kathryn Greene, Valerian J Derlega, and Alicia Mathews. 2006. Self-disclosure in personal relationships. *The Cambridge handbook of personal relationships* pages 409–427.

Sangdo Han, Jeesoo Bang, Seonghan Ryu, and Gary Geunbae Lee. 2015. Exploiting knowledge base to generate responses for natural language dialog listening agents. In *Proceedings of the 16th Annual Meeting of the Special Interest Group on Discourse and Dialogue*. pages 129–133.

Vernon B Harper and Erika J Harper. 2006. Understanding student self-disclosure typology through blogging. *The Qualitative Report* 11(2):251–261.

Ryuichiro Higashinaka, Kohji Dohsaka, and Hideki Isozaki. 2008. Effects of self-disclosure and empathy in human-computer dialogue. In *Spoken Language Technology Workshop, 2008. SLT 2008. IEEE*. IEEE, pages 109–112.

Charles T Hill and Donald E Stull. 1987. Gender and self-disclosure. In *Self-Disclosure*, Springer, pages 81–100.

Sidney M Jourard. 1971. Self-disclosure: An experimental analysis of the transparent self. .

Sidney M Jourard and Robert Friedman. 1970. Experimenter-subject" distance" and self-disclosure. *Journal of Personality and Social Psychology* 15(3):278.

Sidney M Jourard and Peggy E Jaffe. 1970. Influence of an interviewer's disclosure on the self-disclosing behavior of interviewees. *Journal of Counseling Psychology* 17(3):252.

Sarah Knox, Shirley A Hess, David A Petersen, and Clara E Hill. 1997. A qualitative analysis of client perceptions of the effects of helpful therapist self-disclosure in long-term therapy. *Journal of counseling psychology* 44(3):274.

Hsiu-Chia Ko and Feng-Yang Kuo. 2009. Can blogging enhance subjective well-being through self-disclosure? *CyberPsychology & Behavior* 12(1):75–79.

Jean-Philippe Laurenceau, Lisa Feldman Barrett, and Paula R Pietromonaco. 1998. Intimacy as an interpersonal process: The importance of self-disclosure, partner disclosure, and perceived partner responsiveness in interpersonal exchanges. *Journal of personality and social psychology* 74(5):1238.

SeoYoung Lee and Junho Choi. 2017. Enhancing user experience with conversational agent for movie recommendation: Effects of self-disclosure and reciprocity. *International Journal of Human-Computer Studies* 103:95–105.

Joseph P Mazer, Richard E Murphy, and Cheri J Simonds. 2009. The effects of teacher self-disclosure via facebook on teacher credibility. *Learning, Media and technology* 34(2):175–183.

Toyomi Meguro, Ryuichiro Higashinaka, Yasuhiro Minami, and Kohji Dohsaka. 2010. Controlling listening-oriented dialogue using partially observable markov decision processes. In *Proceedings of the 23rd international conference on computational linguistics*. Association for Computational Linguistics, pages 761–769.

Mario Mikulincer and Orna Nachshon. 1991. Attachment styles and patterns of self-disclosure. *Journal of Personality and Social Psychology* 61(2):321.

Lynn C Miller, John H Berg, and Richard L Archer. 1983. Openers: Individuals who elicit intimate self-disclosure. *Journal of Personality and Social Psychology* 44(6):1234.

Youngme Moon. 2000. Intimate exchanges: Using computers to elicit self-disclosure from consumers. *Journal of Consumer Research* 26(4):323–339.

Janice Nadler. 2003. Rapport in negotiation and conflict resolution. *Marq. L. Rev.* 87:875.

Janice Nadler. 2004. Rapport in legal negotiation: How small talk can facilitate e-mail dealmaking. *Harv. Negot. L. Rev.* 9:223.

Clifford Nass, Jonathan Steuer, and Ellen R Tauber. 1994. Computers are social actors. In *Proceedings of the SIGCHI conference on Human factors in computing systems*. ACM, pages 72–78.

Amy Ogan, Samantha L Finkelstein, Erin Walker, Ryan Carlson, and Justine Cassell. 2012. Rudeness and rapport: Insults and learning gains in peer tutoring. Springer.

Ran Zhao Justine Cassell Oscar J. Romero. 2017. Cognitive-inspired conversational-strategy reasoner for socially-aware agents. In *Proceedings of the Twenty-Sixth International Joint Conference on Artificial Intelligence, IJCAI-17*. pages 3807–3813. https://doi.org/10.24963/ijcai.2017/532.

James W Pennebaker, Ryan L Boyd, Kayla Jordan, and Kate Blackburn. 2015. The development and psychometric properties of liwc2015. Technical report.

Shrimai Prabhumoye, Fadi Botros, Khyathi Chandu, Samridhi Choudhary, Esha Keni, Chaitanya Malaviya, Thomas Manzini, Rama Pasumarthi, Shivani Poddar, Abhilasha Ravichander, et al. 2017. Building cmu magnus from user feedback. *Alexa Prize Proceedings* .

Hua Qian and Craig R Scott. 2007. Anonymity and self-disclosure on weblogs. *Journal of Computer-Mediated Communication* 12(4):1428–1451.

Ashwin Ram, Rohit Prasad, Chandra Khatri, Anu Venkatesh, Raefer Gabriel, Qing Liu, Jeff Nunn, Behnam Hedayatnia, Ming Cheng, Ashish Nagar, et al. 2018. Conversational ai: The science behind the alexa prize. *arXiv preprint arXiv:1801.03604* .

Vello Sermat and Michael Smyth. 1973. Content analysis of verbal communication in the development of relationship: Conditions influencing self-disclosure. *Journal of Personality and Social Psychology* 26(3):332.

Tanmay Sinha and Justine Cassell. 2015a. Fine-grained analyses of interpersonal processes and their effect on learning. In *International Conference on Artificial Intelligence in Education*. Springer, pages 781–785.

Tanmay Sinha and Justine Cassell. 2015b. We click, we align, we learn: Impact of influence and convergence processes on student learning and rapport building. In *Proceedings of the 1st Workshop on Modeling INTERPERsonal SynchrONy And infLuence*. ACM, pages 13–20.

Roslyn M Sparrevohn and Ronald M Rapee. 2009. Self-disclosure, emotional expression and intimacy within romantic relationships of people with social phobia. *Behaviour Research and Therapy* 47(12):1074–1078.

Susan Sprecher and Susan S Hendrick. 2004. Self-disclosure in intimate relationships: Associations with individual and relationship characteristics over time. *Journal of Social and Clinical Psychology* 23(6):857.

Joseph P Stokes. 1987. The relation of loneliness and self-disclosure. In *Self-disclosure*, Springer, pages 175–201.

Frederic Stutzman, Jessica Vitak, Nicole B Ellison, Rebecca Gray, and Cliff Lampe. 2012. Privacy in interaction: Exploring disclosure and social capital in facebook.

Karen Tracy and Nikolas Coupland. 1990. Multiple goals in discourse: An overview of issues. *Journal of Language and Social Psychology* 9(1-2):1–13.

Rhiannon N Turner, Miles Hewstone, and Alberto Voci. 2007. Reducing explicit and implicit outgroup prejudice via direct and extended contact: The mediating role of self-disclosure and intergroup anxiety. *Journal of personality and social psychology* 93(3):369.

Jeffrey R Vittengl and Craig S Holt. 2000. Getting acquainted: The relationship of self-disclosure and social attraction to positive affect. *Journal of Social and Personal Relationships* 17(1):53–66.

Yi-Chia Wang, Moira Burke, and Robert Kraut. 2016. Modeling self-disclosure in social networking sites. In *Proceedings of the 19th ACM Conference on Computer-Supported Cooperative Work & Social Computing*. ACM, New York, NY, USA, CSCW '16, pages 74–85. https://doi.org/10.1145/2818048.2820010.

Myong Jin Won-Doornink. 1985. Self-disclosure and reciprocity in conversation: A cross-national study. *Social Psychology Quarterly* pages 97–107.

Diyi Yang, Zheng Yao, and Robert Kraut. 2017. Self-disclosure and channel difference in online health support groups.

Zhijun Yin, You Chen, Daniel Fabbri, Jimeng Sun, and Bradley Malin. 2016. # prayfordad: Learning the semantics behind why social media users disclose health information. In *Tenth International AAAI Conference on Web and Social Media*.

Ran Zhao, Tanmay Sinha, Alan Black, and Justine Cassell. 2016. Automatic recognition of conversational strategies in the service of a socially-aware dialog system. In *Proceedings of the 17th Annual Meeting of the Special Interest Group on Discourse and Dialogue*. Association for Computational Linguistics, Los Angeles, pages 381–392. http://www.aclweb.org/anthology/W16-3647.

Role play-based question-answering by real users for building chatbots with consistent personalities

Ryuichiro Higashinaka[1], Masahiro Mizukami[1], Hidetoshi Kawabata[2]
Emi Yamaguchi[2], Noritake Adachi[2], and Junji Tomita[1]
[1]NTT Corporation
[2]DWANGO Co., Ltd.
{higashinaka.ryuichiro, mizukami.masahiro}@lab.ntt.co.jp
{hidetoshi_kawabata, emi_yamaguchi, noritake_adachi}@dwango.co.jp
tomita.junji@lab.ntt.co.jp

Abstract

Having consistent personalities is important for chatbots if we want them to be believable. Typically, many question-answer pairs are prepared by hand for achieving consistent responses; however, the creation of such pairs is costly. In this study, our goal is to collect a large number of question-answer pairs for a particular character by using role play-based question-answering in which multiple users play the roles of certain characters and respond to questions by online users. Focusing on two famous characters, we conducted a large-scale experiment to collect question-answer pairs by using real users. We evaluated the effectiveness of role play-based question-answering and found that, by using our proposed method, the collected pairs lead to good-quality chatbots that exhibit consistent personalities.

1 Introduction

Having a consistent personality is important for chatbots if we want them to be believable (Li et al., 2016; Gordon et al., 2016; Curry and Rieser, 2016; Sugiyama et al., 2017; Akama et al., 2017). Although neural network-based methods are emerging for achieving consistent personalities, their quality is not that high (Li et al., 2016). Therefore, in many systems, question-answer pairs are prepared by hand for consistent responses (Takeuchi et al., 2007; Leuski et al., 2009; Traum et al., 2015). However, the creation of such pairs is costly.

In this study, our aim is to collect a large number of question-answer pairs for a particular character by using role play-based question-answering (Higashinaka et al., 2013a) in which

multiple users play the roles of certain characters and respond to questions by online users. The concept is shown in Figure 1. The main idea is that role players collectively represent a single character and that a question is broadcast via a character to all role players. In this way, question-answer pairs can be efficiently collected because there is less burden on people responding, and the entertaining nature of role playing makes people likelier to participate (Ments, 1999). In a small-scale experiment, Higashinaka et al. found that question-answer pairs of a character can be efficiently collected by multiple users and that users are highly motivated to provide questions and answers.

There were two limitations to their work. One was that the experiment was conducted using only a small number of people, who were recruited by the authors. It was not clear if the scheme would work with real users (i.e., users who are not recruited nor paid by researchers). The other limitation was that the applicability of the collected data to the creation of chatbots was not verified. In their small-scale experiment, the maximum number of question-answer pairs for a character was only about 80. This was because users were allowed to register any of their favorite characters, resulting in a small amount of data per character. It was difficult to create a chatbot with such little data.

In this paper, we tackle these limitations by using role play-based question-answering for collecting question-answer pairs from real users. Regarding the second limitation, we limited the characters to two famous ones so as to collect a large number of question-answer pairs per character and create workable chatbots. We conducted a subjective evaluation of the chatbots by using human participants. Our contributions are as follows:

- We verified that role play-based question-

264

Proceedings of the SIGDIAL 2018 Conference, pages 264–272,
Melbourne, Australia, 12-14 July 2018. ©2018 Association for Computational Linguistics

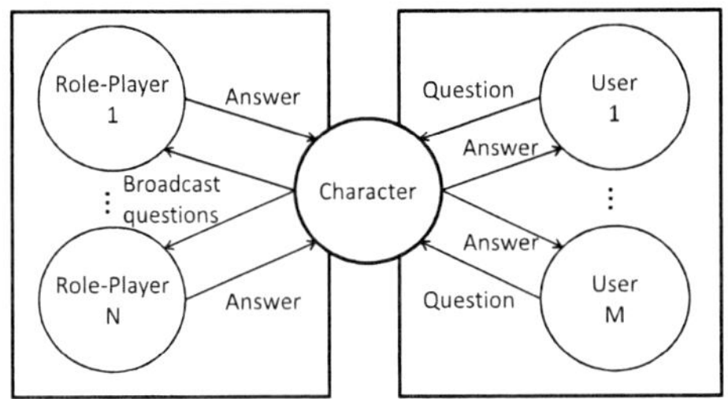

Figure 1: Role play-based question-answering scheme (Higashinaka et al., 2013a).

answering works with real users, collecting a large number of question-answer pairs per character in a short period.

- We proposed a method to create chatbots from collected question-answer pairs and verified that it can lead to good-quality chatbots exhibiting consistent personalities.

We first describe our data collection by using role play-based question-answering with real users. Then, we propose our method for creating chatbots using the collected question-answer pairs. Next, we describe the experiment we conducted to evaluate the quality of the chatbots by using human participants. After covering related work, we summarize the paper and mention future work.

2 Data collection by real users

To collect a large number of question-answer pairs per character, we focused on two characters: a real person called Max Murai and a fictional character in a novel, Ayase Aragaki. They are popular characters in Japan and have a large number of fans. We created Web sites in their fan communities so that fans could try role play-based question-answering. We first describe the two characters in more detail and then briefly go over the Web sites. Finally, we present the statistics of the data and look at the results from several aspects.

2.1 Characters

Max Murai His real name is Tomotake Murai (Max Murai is his stage name). Born in 1981, Murai is a CEO of the IT company AppBank but also a YouTuber who specializes in the live coverage of TV games. He is known to have a frank personality.

Ayase Aragaki A fictional character in the novel "Ore no imouto ga konnnai kawaii wakega

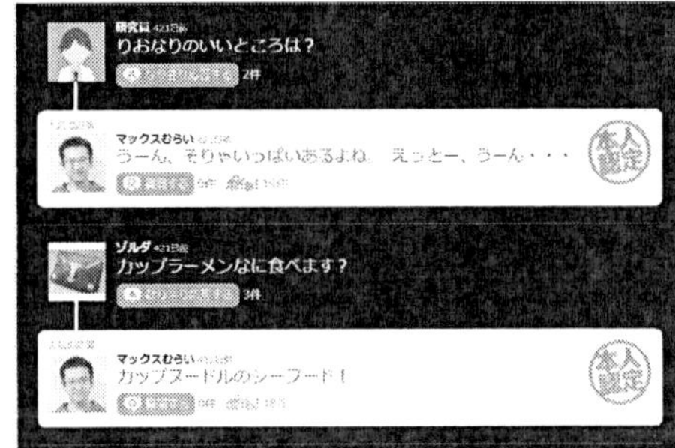

Figure 2: Web site for Max Murai.

Figure 3: Web site for Ayase Aragaki.

nai" (My Little Sister Can't Be This Cute), which has sold more than five million copies in Japan in its series. Ayase is not a main character but plays a supporting role. Her character is often referred to as a "Yandere". According to Wikipedia, Yandere characters are mentally unstable, incredibly deranged, and use extreme violence or brutality as an outlet for their emotions.

2.2 Web sites

On the Japanese streaming service NICONICO Douga[1], each character has a channel for their fans. The channel is limited to subscribers. Through the generosity of this service, we were allowed to establish our Web sites for role play-based question-answering on their channels. Murai has more than 10,000 subscribers; the number of subscribes for Ayase is not disclosed.

We opened the Web sites in March and October 2017 for Murai and Ayase, respectively. Figures 2 and 3 show screenshots of the sites. The appearances of the sites were adjusted to the characters. The users can ask the characters questions by

---

[1] http://www.nicovideo.jp/

	Murai	Ayase
No. of users who participated	340	333
No. of question-answer pairs	12,959	15,112
No. of questions	7,652	6,482
Average words per question	10.38	13.09
Average letters per question	17.42	20.35
No. of unique words in questions	7,317	6,654
No. of words in questions	79,412	84,838
No. of users who posted questions	284	262
No. of questions per user	22.51	19.47
No. of answers	12,959	15,112
No. of answers per question	1.69	2.33
Average words per answer	7.03	15.27
Average letters per answer	11.59	24.64
No. of unique words in answers	8,666	10,208
No. of words in answers	91,119	230,707
No. of users who posted answers	243	290
No. of answers per user	38.11	45.38

Table 1: Posting statistics.

	Murai		Ayase	
Threshold	Hours	Days	Hours	Days
1K	21.36	0.89	25.71	1.07
2K	22.17	0.92	26.88	1.12
5K	1,730.05	72.09	72.21	3.01
10K	2,307.60	96.15	443.73	18.49
12K	2,808.91	117.04	993.37	41.39
15K	N/A	N/A	2,834.26	118.09

Table 2: Time taken to reach certain number of question-answer pairs.

means of a text-field interface, and users who want to play the role of the characters can post answers. To stimulate interaction, the Web sites show the rankings of users by their number of posts. In addition, a "like" button is placed beside each answer so that when a user thinks the answer sounds very much "like" the character in question, this opinion can be reflected in the number of "likes". The sites were primarily for collecting one-shot question-answer pairs. It was also possible for the Murai site to collect follow-up question-answer pairs, but this function was rarely utilized by users.

2.3 Statistics

The statistics of the postings (at the time of submission) are listed in Table 1. We obtained a total of 12,959 and 15,112 question-answer pairs for Murai and Ayase, respectively. The size of the data is quite large. We want to emphasize that the users were not paid for their participation; they did so voluntarily. This indicates that role play-based question-answering works well with real users. As seen in the table, more than 300 users participated for each character. The questions/answers for Ayase were longer and contained more words and letters.

2.4 Efficiency

Table 2 shows the times when the number of question-answer pairs exceeded certain thresholds. We can see how fast we could collect a few thousand question-answer pairs. For both characters, it took just about a couple of days to reach 2,000 question-answer pairs. For Ayase, the pace was much faster than for Murai, reaching 10,000 question-answer pairs in 18 days. After a cer-

tain period, the pace of the postings slowed. Although role play-based question-answering is certainly entertaining, we may need to consider ways to keep users engaged in the interaction. Enabling more sustainable collection of question-answer pairs is future work.

2.5 Quality of the postings

We also evaluated the answers given by the users through subjective evaluation (see GOLD in Tables 4 and 5). We obtained the average naturalness/character-ness scores of around 3.5–4.0 on a five-point Likert scale, indicating that the answers collected through role play-based question-answering were good. However, it was surprising that human users also struggled to obtain scores over 4.0, indicating that generating utterances for a particular character is difficult, even for humans.

2.6 Satisfaction of users

We asked users of the channels to participate in a survey to determine their user satisfaction. We used the same questionnaire as in (Higashinaka et al., 2013a). It consisted of three questions: (Q1) How do you rate the usability of the Web site?, (Q2) Would you be willing to use the Web site again?, and (Q3) Did you enjoy role playing on the Web site? The users answered based on a five-point Likert scale, with one being the lowest score and five the highest. Twenty-three and 36 participants took part in the survey for Murai and Ayase, respectively.

Table 3 shows the results of the questionnaire averaged over all participants. Since these results were obtained from volunteers, they may not reflect the view of all site users. However, the results are encouraging: at the very least, they indicate that there are real users who feel very positively about the experience of role play-based question-answering.

	Questionnaire item	Murai	Ayase
Q1	Usability of Web site	3.74	4.08
Q2	Willingness for future use	4.57	4.56
Q3	Enjoyment of role playing	4.39	4.53

Table 3: Questionnaire results.

3 Creating chatbots from collected question-answer pairs

Now that we have successfully collected a large number of question-answer pairs for our two characters, the next step is to determine if the collected pairs can be useful for creating chatbots that exhibit the personalities of the characters in question; namely, Murai and Ayase. Since the size of the data was not large enough to train neural-generation models (Vinyals and Le, 2015), we opted for a retrieval-based approach in which relevant question-answer pairs are retrieved using an input question as a query and the answer part of the most relevant pair is returned as a chatbot's response. One of the methods we used is a simple application of an off-the-shelf text search engine, and the other is our proposed method, which is more sophisticated and uses neural-translation models for ranking.

3.1 Simple retrieval-based method

This method uses the text search engine LUCENE[2] for retrieval. Questions and answers are first indexed with LUCENE. We use a built-in Japanese analyzer for morphological analysis. Given an input question, the BM25 algorithm (Walker et al., 1997) is used to search for a similar question using the content words of the input question. The answers for the retrieved questions are used as the output of this method. Although simple, this method is quite competitive with other methods when there are many question-answer pairs because it is likely that we will be able to find a similar question by word matching.

3.2 Proposed method

Only using word-matching may not be sufficient. Therefore, we developed a more elaborate method that re-ranks the results retrieved from LUCENE. Our idea comes from cross-lingual question answering (CLQA) (Leuski et al., 2009) and recent advances in neural conversational models (Vinyals and Le, 2015). We also conducted semantic and intent-level matching between ques-

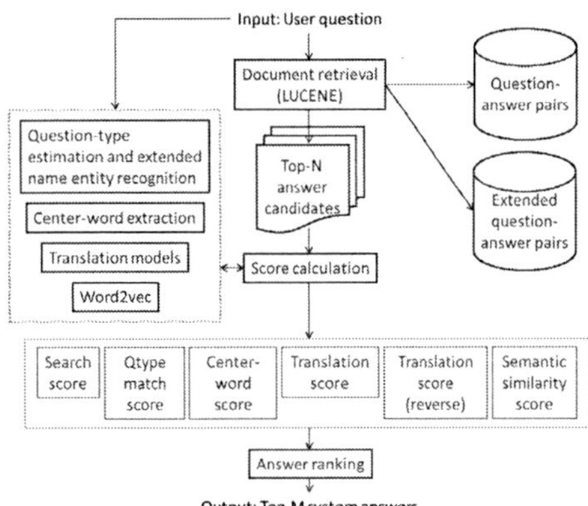

Figure 4: Flow of proposed method.

tions so that appropriate answer candidates could be ranked higher. Figure 4 shows the flow of this method. Given an input question Q, the method outputs answers in the following steps. The details of some of the key models/modules used in the steps are described later.

1. Given Q, LUCENE retrieves top-N question-answer pairs $(Q'_1, A'_1) \ldots (Q'_N, A'_N)$, as described in Section 3.1.

2. The question-type estimation and extended named entity recognition modules estimate the question types of Q and Q' and extract extended named entities (Sekine et al., 2002) contained in A'. The question-type match score is calculated by using the match of the question type and the number of extended named entities in A' requested by Q. See Section 3.3 for details.

3. The center-word extraction module extracts center-words (noun phrases (NPs) that represent foci/topics) from both Q and Q'. The center-word score is 1.0 if one of the center-words of Q is included in those of Q'; otherwise it is 0.0.

4. The translation model is used to calculate the probability that each A' is translated from Q, that is, $p(A'|Q)$. We also calculate the probability bi-directionally, that is, $p(Q|A')$, which has been shown to be effective in CLQA (Leuski et al., 2009). The probabilities are normalized by dividing them by the number of words on the target side. Since the raw probabilities are difficult to integrate with other scores, we sort the question-answer pairs by their probabilities and use their ranks

to obtain the translation scores. That is, if the rank is r, its score is calculated by

$$1.0 - (r - 1)/\mathrm{max\_rank}, \qquad (1)$$

where max_rank is the maximum number of elements to be ranked.

5. The semantic similarity model is used to calculate the semantic similarity score between Q and Q'. We use Word2vec (Mikolov et al., 2013) to calculate this score. First, we obtain word vectors (trained from Wikipedia) for each word in Q and Q' and then calculate the cosine similarity between the averaged word vectors.

6. The score calculation module integrates the above scores to obtain a final score:

$$
\begin{aligned}
\mathrm{score}&(Q, (Q', A')) \\
=\ & w_1 * \mathrm{search\_score} \\
+\ & w_2 * \mathrm{qtypes\_match\_score} \\
+\ & w_3 * \mathrm{center\text{-}word\_score} \\
+\ & w_4 * \mathrm{translation\_score} \\
+\ & w_5 * \mathrm{rev\_translation\_score} \\
+\ & w_6 * \mathrm{semantic\_similarity\_score} \quad (2)
\end{aligned}
$$

Here, search_score indicates the score converted from the rank of the search results from LUCENE. The conversion is done using Eq. (1). rev_translation_score indicates the translation score derived from $p(Q|A')$. The $w_1 \dots w_6$ denote the weights of the scores.

7. The question-answer pairs are sorted by their scores, and top-M answers are returned as output.

3.3 Modules

We describe some of the models/modules used in the above steps.

Question-type estimation and extended named entity recognition We estimated four question types for a question. One is a general question type. We used the taxonomy described in (Higashinaka et al., 2014), which has 16 question subtypes. We trained a logistic-regression based question-type classifier that classifies a question into one of the 16 question types. The other three question types come from an extended named entity taxonomy proposed by Sekine (2002). The taxonomy has three layers ranging from abstract

(e.g., Product, Location) to more concrete entities (e.g., Car, Spa, City). We trained a logistic-regression-based classifier that classifies which of the named entity types is requested in a question. We trained a classifier for each layer; thus, we had three classifiers. Using our in-house data, by two-fold cross-validation, the classification accuracies are 86.0%, 84.9%, 76.9%, and 73.5% for the general question type, layer-1, layer-2, and layer-3 question types, respectively. We also extract extended named entities from an answer candidate (A') by using our extended named entity recognizer (Higashinaka et al., 2013b) and check whether the extended named entities corresponding to the layer-1, layer-2, and layer-3 question types of a question (Q) are included in A'.

The qtypes_match_score is calculated as follows: if there is a match of the general question type between Q and Q', the score of one is obtained. Then, the number of extended-named-entity question types covered by the answer candidate is added to this score. Finally, this score is divided by four for normalization.

Center-word extraction We define a center-word as an NP that denotes the topic of a conversation. To extract such NPs from an utterance, we used conditional random fields (CRFs) (Lafferty et al., 2001). For the training and testing, we prepared about 20K sentences with center-word annotation. The sentences were those randomly sampled from our in-house open-domain conversation corpus. The feature template uses words, part-of-speech (POS) tags, and semantic categories of current and neighboring words. The extraction accuracy is 76% in F-measure with our in-house test set.

Translation model We trained a translation model by using a seq2seq model. We trained the model by using the OpenNMT Toolkit[3] with default settings. The translation model learns to translate a question into an answer. By using the trained model, we can obtain the generative probability of an answer given a question; namely $p(A'|Q)$. Since the amount of question-answer pairs was limited, we first trained a model by using our in-house question-answering data comprising 0.5 million pairs. The data were collected using crowd-sourcing. We then adapted the model to our question-answer pairs. The model for $p(Q|A')$ was trained in the same manner by swapping the

---

[3] http://opennmt.net/

source and target data. To reflect the number of "likes" associated with the answers (see Section 2.2), we augmented the number of samples by their number of "likes"; that is, if a question-answer pair has n "likes", n samples of such a question-answer pair are included in the training data.

3.4 Extending question-answer pairs

When developing our method, we noticed that, in some cases, top-N search results do not contain good candidates because of the lack of question coverage. When the top-N questions do not semantically match reasonably with the input question, the answers are likely to be inappropriate. To have a wider coverage of questions, we extended our question-answer pairs by using Twitter. Our methodology was simple: for each answer A that occurred twice or more in our question-answer pairs, we searched for tweets that resemble A with a Levenshtein distance (normalized by the sentence length) below 0.1. Then, if the tweets had an in-reply-to relationship to other tweets, they were retrieved and coupled with A to form extended question-answer pairs. The reason we focused on an answer that occurred twice or more is mainly due to the efficiency of crawling, but such answers that occur multiple times are likely to be characteristics of the characters in question. We obtained 2,607,658 and 1,032,492 extended question-answer pairs for Murai and Ayase, respectively.

4 Experiments

We conducted a subjective evaluation to determine the quality of chatbots created from our collected question-answer pairs. We first describe how we prepared the data for evaluation and how we recruited participants. We then describe the evaluation criteria. Next, we describe the methods for comparison, in which we compared the methods presented in the previous section with a rule-based baseline and gold data (human-generated data). Finally, we explain the results and present our analyses.

4.1 Data

To create the data for testing, we first randomly split the question-answer pairs into train, development, and test sets with the ratios of 0.8, 0.1, and 0.1, respectively. The splits were made so that the same question would not be included over multiple sets. We used the train and development

sets to train the translation models. In addition, the question-answer pairs used by LUCENE for retrieval consisted only of train and development data. For each character, 50 questions were randomly sampled from the test set and used as input questions for this experiment.

4.2 Procedure

We recruited 26 participants each for Murai and Ayase. The participants were recruited mainly from the subscribers of the channels for the two characters. Before taking part in the experiment, they self-declared their levels of knowledge about the characters. Then, they rated the top-1 output of the five methods (shown below) for the 50 questions; they rated at maximum 250 answers (since some methods output duplicate answers, such answers were only rated once). We compensated for their time by giving Amazon gift cards worth about 20 US dollars.

4.3 Evaluation criteria

The participants rated each output answer by their degree of agreement to the following statements on a five-point Likert scale (1: completely disagree, 5: completely agree).

Naturalness Not knowing who's speaking, the answer is appropriate to the input question.

Character-ness Knowing that the character in question is speaking, the answer is appropriate to the input question.

The first criterion evaluates the interaction from a general point of view, while the second from the character point of view. Ideally, we want the character-ness to be high, but we want to maintain at least reasonable naturalness when considering the deployment of the chatbots. Note that an utterance can be rated low in terms of naturalness but high in character-ness, or vice-versa: for example, some general utterances, such as greetings, can never be uttered by particular characters.

4.4 Methods for comparison

We compared five methods. A rule-based baseline written in Artificial Intelligence Markup Language (AIML) (Wallace, 2009) was used. The aim of having this baseline is to emulate when we do not have any question-answer pairs available. Although this is a simple rule-based baseline, it is a competitive one because it uses one of the largest rule sets in Japanese.

	All		High		Low	
	Natural	Character	Natural	Character	Natural	Character
(a) AIML	2.93	2.60	2.93	2.49	2.96	2.95
(b) LUCENE	2.80	2.87^{aa}	2.81	2.80^{aa}	2.75	3.10
(c) PROP_WO_EXDB	3.16^{aabb}	3.17^{aabb}	3.17^{abb}	3.09^{aabb}	3.13	$\mathbf{3.42}^{aa}$
(d) PROP	$\mathbf{3.39}^{aabbcc}$	$\mathbf{3.20}^{aabb}$	$\mathbf{3.42}^{aabbcc}$	$\mathbf{3.14}^{aabb}$	$\mathbf{3.32}^{bb}$	3.39^{a}
(e) GOLD	$3.91^{aabbccdd}$	$3.81^{aabbccdd}$	$3.93^{aabbccdd}$	$3.80^{aabbccdd}$	$3.85^{aabbccdd}$	$3.85^{aabbccdd}$

Table 4: Results for Murai. The scores were averaged over the participants. Superscripts indicate whether the value is significantly better than those for the methods denoted with letters; two letters, such as 'aa', indicate statistical significance $p < 0.01$, and a single letter indicates $p < 0.05$. The Steel-Dwass multiple comparison test was used as a statistical test. The best scores (excluding GOLD) are in bold.

	All		High		Low	
	Natural	Character	Natural	Character	Natural	Character
(a) AIML	2.71	2.44	2.74	2.42	2.49	2.63
(b) LUCENE	2.98^{aa}	3.13^{aa}	3.05^{aa}	3.13^{aa}	2.48	3.11
(c) PROP_WO_EXDB	3.04^{aa}	3.15^{aa}	3.09^{aa}	3.14^{aa}	2.62	3.19^{a}
(d) PROP	$\mathbf{3.23}^{aabbc}$	$\mathbf{3.24}^{aa}$	$\mathbf{3.28}^{aabb}$	$\mathbf{3.23}^{aa}$	$\mathbf{2.78}$	$\mathbf{3.27}^{aa}$
(e) GOLD	$3.61^{aabbccdd}$	$3.74^{aabbccdd}$	$3.68^{aabbccdd}$	$3.75^{aabbccdd}$	3.11^{aabb}	3.65^{aab}

Table 5: Results for Ayase. See caption of Table 4 for notations in table.

Rule-based baseline (AIML) The typical approach to implement a chatbot is by using rules. We used the rules written in AIML created by Higashinaka et al (2015). There are roughly 300K rules. In Japanese, sentence-end expressions are key factors to exhibit personality. Therefore, following the method by Miyazaki et al. (2016), we created sentence-end conversion rules so that the output of this method would have the sentence-end expressions that match the characters in question.

Retrieval-based method (LUCENE) The retrieval-based method described in Section 3.1.

Proposed method 1 (PROP_WO_EXDB) The proposed method described in Section 3.2. This method does not use the extended question-answer pairs from Twitter. The weights $w_1 \ldots w_6$ are all set to 1.0. We used 10 for N for document retrieval.

Proposed method 2 (PROP) The proposed method with extended question-answer pairs from Twitter, as described in Section 3.4. We retrieved 10 candidates from collected question-answer pairs and 10 from extended ones. The weights $w_1 \ldots w_6$ are all set to 1.0.

Upper bound (GOLD) The gold responses by the online users to the test questions. When multiple answers are given to a question, one is randomly selected.

4.5 Results

Tables 4 and 5 list the results for Murai and Ayase, respectively. The topmost row indicates the level of knowledge about the characters. 'All' indicates the results of all participants, 'High' those who self-declared as being very knowledgeable, and 'Low' those who self-declared otherwise. We had 26 High and 6 Low participants for Murai, and 23 High and 3 Low participants for Ayase.

The tendencies were the same for the two characters, although the scores for Ayase were generally lower than those of Murai. AIML performed the worst followed by LUCENE. It was surprising that AIML's score was low; this is probably because of the peculiarities of the input questions for the characters. PROP_WO_EXDB and PROP performed better than AIML and LUCENE with statistical significance in many cases. GOLD was always the best-performing method. PROP was significantly better than PROP_WO_EXDB for naturalness but not for character-ness.

These results indicate that simple text-based retrieval is not sufficient, and we need more elaborate methods. The effectiveness of the extended question-answer pairs seems to be limited. It can be useful to make the interaction seem natural, but this does not necessarily improve character-ness, although we believe that having the ability to converse naturally is a requirement for chatbots.

When we focus on the results as they relate to the knowledge levels, we see large differences between High and Low. The High participants are likely to differentiate the answers more than Low

Question	Method	Answer	Nat.	Char.
What did you eat for lunch today?	AIML	I had a chicken breast rice bowl. It was good. What did you eat?	4.50	3.46
	LUCENE	Anything will do when you are playing video games.	1.88	2.08
	PROP_WO_EXDB	Ramen!	4.81	4.77
	PROP	Ramen.	4.73	4.31
	GOLD	I had a ginger grilled meal at Hidakaya.	4.92	4.15

Table 6: Examples of answers for Murai by each method. Questions and answers were originally in Japanese. English translations are by the authors.

Question	Method	Answer	Nat.	Char.
You are so cute.	AIML	Cute is the best.	2.69	2.15
	LUCENE	Shut up or I will sew your mouth.	3.04	4.12
	PROP_WO_EXDB	Thank you! It's a little embarrassing.	4.69	4.08
	PROP	Thank you!	4.62	4.15
	GOLD	You say silly things all the time. I may take it seriously.	4.08	4.27

Table 7: Examples of answers for Ayase by each method.

participants. For example, for Murai, there were only few cases in which there was statistical significance between the proposed methods when the knowledge level was low. The tendency was the same for Ayase. This highlights the difficulty in evaluating for characters.

Tables 6 and 7 show examples of answers for Murai and Ayase, respectively. Overall, since the proposed methods achieved character-ness scores well over 3 (which is the middle point in the scale), we conclude that we can create chatbots with consistent personalities by means of role play-based question-answering.

5 Related Work

Although there have not been any studies involving role play-based question-answering for data collection, there is a large body of research for creating chatbots that show consistent personalities.

There have been several studies on characters by generating or rewriting utterances reflecting the underlying personality traits (Mairesse and Walker, 2007; Sugiyama et al., 2014; Miyazaki et al., 2016). In addition, there has been extensive research on extending neural conversational models to reflect personal profiles (Li et al., 2016). Although such neural network-based methods show promising results, they still suffer from sparsity of data and non-informative utterances (Li et al., 2015). This paper proposed increasing the source data for character building; the data can be useful for neural models.

6 Summary and future work

Our goal for this study was to verify the effectiveness of role play-based question-answering for creating chatbots. Focusing on two famous characters in Japan, we successfully collected a large volume of question-answer pairs for two characters by using real users. We then created chatbots using the question-answer pairs. Subjective evaluation showed that although a simple text-retrieval based method does not work well, our proposed method that uses translation models as well as question-type matching and center-word extraction works well, showing reasonable scores in terms of naturalness and character-ness.

For future work, we need to consider approaches to improve the quality of the proposed method. For example, we are currently using equal weights for scoring. We believe that they can be optimized using training data. We also want to incorporate other pieces of information that may contribute to the ranking of answers, such as sentence embeddings (Kiros et al., 2015), discourse relations (Lin et al., 2009; Otsuka et al., 2017), and external knowledge about the characters. Although we used two very different characters in this paper, we want to use additional types of characters as targets for role play-based question-answering. We also want to incorporate the chatbots into the Web sites so that the users can feel they are training up the characters.

Acknowledgments

We thank the developers of DWANGO Co., Ltd. for creating the role play-based question-answering Web sites. We also thank the subscribers of the Max Murai and Tukasa Fushimi channels on NICONICO Douga for their cooperation. We thank the members of the Service Innovation Department at NTT DOCOMO, especially Yuiko Tsunomori, for helpful discussions and suggestions.

References

Reina Akama, Kazuaki Inada, Naoya Inoue, Sosuke Kobayashi, and Kentaro Inui. 2017. Generating stylistically consistent dialog responses with transfer learning. In *Proc. IJCNLP*, volume 2, pages 408–412.

Amanda Cercas Curry and Verena Rieser. 2016. A subjective evaluation of chatbot engines. In *Proc. WOCHAT*.

Carla Gordon, Jessica Tin, Jeremy Brown, Elisabeth Fritzsch, and Shirley Gabber. 2016. Wochat chatbot user experience summary. In *Proc. WOCHAT*.

Ryuichiro Higashinaka, Kohji Dohsaka, and Hideki Isozaki. 2013a. Using role play for collecting question-answer pairs for dialogue agents. In *Proc. INTERSPEECH*, pages 1097–1100.

Ryuichiro Higashinaka, Kenji Imamura, Toyomi Meguro, Chiaki Miyazaki, Nozomi Kobayashi, Hiroaki Sugiyama, Toru Hirano, Toshiro Makino, and Yoshihiro Matsuo. 2014. Towards an open-domain conversational system fully based on natural language processing. In *Proc. COLING*, pages 928–939.

Ryuichiro Higashinaka, Toyomi Meguro, Hiroaki Sugiyama, Toshiro Makino, and Yoshihiro Matsuo. 2015. On the difficulty of improving hand-crafted rules in chat-oriented dialogue systems. In *Proc. APSIPA*, pages 1014–1018.

Ryuichiro Higashinaka, Kugatsu Sadamitsu, Kuniko Saito, and Nozomi Kobayashi. 2013b. Question answering technology for pinpointing answers to a wide range of questions. *NTT Technical Review*, 11(7).

Ryan Kiros, Yukun Zhu, Ruslan R Salakhutdinov, Richard Zemel, Raquel Urtasun, Antonio Torralba, and Sanja Fidler. 2015. Skip-thought vectors. In *Proc. NIPS*, pages 3294–3302.

John Lafferty, Andrew McCallum, and Fernando CN Pereira. 2001. Conditional random fields: Probabilistic models for segmenting and labeling sequence data.

Anton Leuski, Ronakkumar Patel, David Traum, and Brandon Kennedy. 2009. Building effective question answering characters. In *Proc. SIGDIAL*, pages 18–27.

Jiwei Li, Michel Galley, Chris Brockett, Jianfeng Gao, and Bill Dolan. 2015. A diversity-promoting objective function for neural conversation models. *arXiv preprint arXiv:1510.03055*.

Jiwei Li, Michel Galley, Chris Brockett, Georgios P Spithourakis, Jianfeng Gao, and Bill Dolan. 2016. A persona-based neural conversation model. *arXiv preprint arXiv:1603.06155*.

Ziheng Lin, Min-Yen Kan, and Hwee Tou Ng. 2009. Recognizing implicit discourse relations in the penn discourse treebank. In *Proc. EMNLP*, pages 343–351.

François Mairesse and Marilyn Walker. 2007. PERSONAGE: Personality generation for dialogue. In *Proc. ACL*, pages 496–503.

Morry Van Ments. 1999. *The Effective Use of Role Play: Practical Techniques for Improving Learning*. Kogan Page Publishers.

Tomas Mikolov, Ilya Sutskever, Kai Chen, Greg S Corrado, and Jeff Dean. 2013. Distributed representations of words and phrases and their compositionality. In *Proc. NIPS*, pages 3111–3119.

Chiaki Miyazaki, Toru Hirano, Ryuichiro Higashinaka, and Yoshihiro Matsuo. 2016. Towards an entertaining natural language generation system: Linguistic peculiarities of Japanese fictional characters. In *Proc. SIGDIAL*, pages 319–328.

Atsushi Otsuka, Toru Hirano, Chiaki Miyazaki, Ryuichiro Higashinaka, Toshiro Makino, and Yoshihiro Matsuo. 2017. Utterance selection using discourse relation filter for chat-oriented dialogue systems. In *Dialogues with Social Robots*, pages 355–365. Springer.

Satoshi Sekine, Kiyoshi Sudo, and Chikashi Nobata. 2002. Extended named entity hierarchy. In *Proc. LREC*.

Hiroaki Sugiyama, Toyomi Meguro, and Ryuichiro Higashinaka. 2017. Evaluation of question-answering system about conversational agent's personality. In *Dialogues with Social Robots*, pages 183–194. Springer.

Hiroaki Sugiyama, Toyomi Meguro, Ryuichiro Higashinaka, and Yasuhiro Minami. 2014. Large-scale collection and analysis of personal question-answer pairs for conversational agents. In *Proc. IVA*, pages 420–433.

Shota Takeuchi, Tobias Cincarek, Hiromichi Kawanami, Hiroshi Saruwatari, and Kiyohiro Shikano. 2007. Construction and optimization of a question and answer database for a real-environment speech-oriented guidance system. In *Proc. Oriental COCOSDA*, pages 149–154.

David Traum, Kallirroi Georgila, Ron Artstein, and Anton Leuski. 2015. Evaluating spoken dialogue processing for time-offset interaction. In *Proc. SIGDIAL*, pages 199–208.

Oriol Vinyals and Quoc Le. 2015. A neural conversational model. *arXiv preprint arXiv:1506.05869*.

Steve Walker, Stephen E Robertson, Mohand Boughanem, Gareth JF Jones, and Karen Sparck Jones. 1997. Okapi at TREC-6 automatic ad hoc, VLC, routing, filtering and QSDR. In *Proc. TREC*, pages 125–136.

Richard S Wallace. 2009. The anatomy of alice. In *Parsing the Turing Test*, pages 181–210. Springer.

Addressing Objects and Their Relations:
The Conversational Entity Dialogue Model

Stefan Ultes, Paweł Budzianowski, Iñigo Casanueva, Lina Rojas-Barahona,
Bo-Hsiang Tseng, Yen-Chen Wu, Steve Young and Milica Gašić
Cambridge University Engineering Department
Cambridge, United Kingdom
`{su259,pfb30,ic340,lmr46,bht26,ycw30,sjy11,mg436}@cam.ac.uk`

Abstract

Statistical spoken dialogue systems usually rely on a single- or multi-domain dialogue model that is restricted in its capabilities of modelling complex dialogue structures, e.g., relations. In this work, we propose a novel dialogue model that is centred around entities and is able to model relations as well as multiple entities of the same type. We demonstrate in a prototype implementation benefits of relation modelling on the dialogue level and show that a trained policy using these relations outperforms the multi-domain baseline. Furthermore, we show that by modelling the relations on the dialogue level, the system is capable of processing relations present in the user input and even learns to address them in the system response.

1 Introduction

Data-driven statistical spoken dialogue systems (SDS) (Lemon and Pietquin, 2012; Young et al., 2013) are a promising approach for realizing spoken dialogue interaction between humans and machines. Up until now, these systems have successfully been applied to single- or multi-domain task-oriented dialogues (Su et al., 2017; Casanueva et al., 2017; Lison, 2011; Wang et al., 2014; Papangelis and Stylianou, 2017; Gašić et al., 2017; Budzianowski et al., 2017; Peng et al., 2017) where each dialogue is modelled as multiple independent single-domain sub-dialogues. However, this multi-domain dialogue model (MDDM) does not offer an intuitive way of representing multiple objects of the same type (e.g., multiple restaurants) or dynamic relations between these objects. To the best of our knowledge, neither problem has yet been addressed in statistical SDS research.

The goal of this paper is to propose a new dialogue model—the conversational entity dialogue model (CEDM)—which offers an intuitive way of modelling dialogues and complex dialogue structures inside the dialogue system. Inspired by Grosz (1978), the CEDM is centred around objects and relations instead of domains thus offering a fundamental change in how we think about statistical dialogue modelling. The CEDM allows

- to model dynamic relations directly, independently and persistently so that the relations may be addressed by the user *and* the system,

- the system to talk about multiple objects of the same type, e.g., multiple restaurants,

while still allowing feasible policy learning.

The remainder of the paper is organized as follows: after presenting a brief motivation and related work in Section 2, Section 3 presents background information on statistical SDSs. Section 4 contains the main contribution and describes the conversational entity dialogue model in detail. Looking at one aspect of the CEDM, the modelling of relations, Section 5 describes a prototype implementation and shows the benefits of the CEDM in experiments with a simulated user. Section 6 concludes the paper with a list of open questions which need to be addressed in future work.

2 Motivation and Related Work

To introduce the terminology that will be used in this work and to illustrate the necessity of adequate modelling of relations, Figure 1 shows an example dialogue about hotels and restaurants in Cambridge with the relation *in the same area*. Instead of talking about a sequence of domains, the system and the user talk about different objects and relations. Each part of the dialogue thus may be

Proceedings of the SIGDIAL 2018 Conference, pages 273–283,
Melbourne, Australia, 12-14 July 2018. ©2018 Association for Computational Linguistics

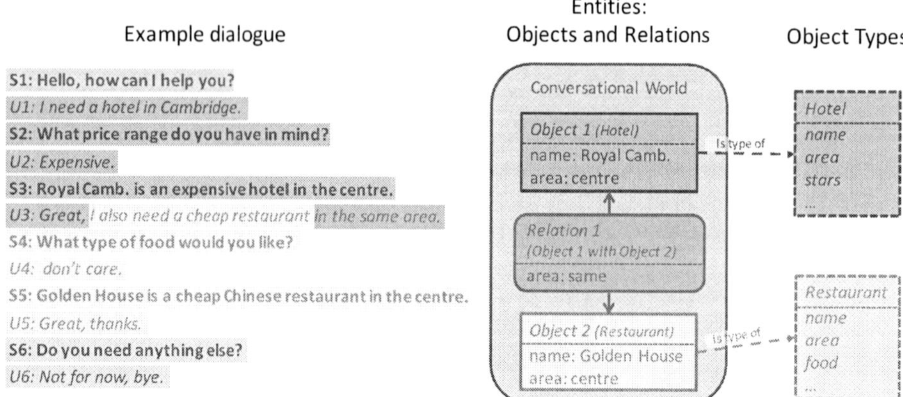

Figure 1: A dialogue between the system (S) and a user (U) about a restaurant and a hotel *in the same area* along with the mapping of fractions of the dialogue to the respective objects (of predefined types) and the relation. All objects and relations reside inside a conversational world.

mapped to an object or a relation in the conversational world or may be mapped to the world itself (grey). In the example, the first part (blue) is about *Object 1* of type *hotel*. When the focus shifts towards *Object 2* of type *restaurant* (green) at U3, the user also addresses the relation (red) *in the same area* between *Object 1* and *Object 2*.

Addressing a relation in this way could still be captured by the semantic interpretation of the user input as the information *area=centre* may be derived from the context. However, if the user said *I need a hotel and a restaurant in Cambridge in the same area* right in the beginning of the dialogue (U1), no context information would be available. To capture these dialogue structures, the dialogue model and the corresponding dialogue state must be able to represent them adequately.

The proposed CEDM achieves this by modelling state information about conversational entities instead of domains. More precisely, it models separate states about the objects (e.g., the hotel or restaurant) and the relations. Previous work on dialogue modelling already incorporated the idea of objects or entities to be the principal component of the dialogue state (Grosz, 1977; Bilange, 1991; Montoro et al., 2004; Xu and Seneff, 2010; Heinroth and Minker, 2013). However, these dialogue models are not based on statistical dialogue processing where a probability distribution over all dialogue states needs to be modelled and maintained. This additional complexity, though, cannot be incorporated in a straight-forward way into the proposed models. In contrast, the CEDM offers

a comprehensive and consistent way of modelling these probabilities by defining and maintaining entity-based states. Work on statistical dialogue state modelling (Young et al., 2010; Lee and Stent, 2016; Schulz et al., 2017) also contain a variant of objects but is still based on the MDDM thus not offering any mechanism to model multiple entities or relations between objects. Ramachandran and Ratnaparkhi (2015) proposed a belief tracking approach using relational trees. However, they only consider static relations present in the ontology and are not able to handle dynamic relations.

3 Statistical Spoken Dialogue Systems

Statistical SDS are model-based approaches[1] and usually assume a modular architecture (see Fig. 2). The problem of learning the next system action is framed as a partially-observable Markov decision process (POMDP) that accounts for the uncertainty inherent in spoken communication. This uncertainty is modelled in the belief state $b(s)$ representing a probability over all states s.

Reinforcement learning (RL) is used in such a sequential decision-making process where the decision-model (the policy π) is trained based on

---

[1]Model-free approaches like end-to-end generative networks (Serban et al., 2016; Li et al., 2016) have interesting properties (e.g., they only need text data for training) but they still seem to be limited in terms of dialogue structure complexity (not linguistic complexity) in cases where content from a structured knowledge base needs to be incorporated. Approaches where incorporating this information is learned along with the system responses based on dialogue data (Eric and Manning, 2017) seem hard to scale.

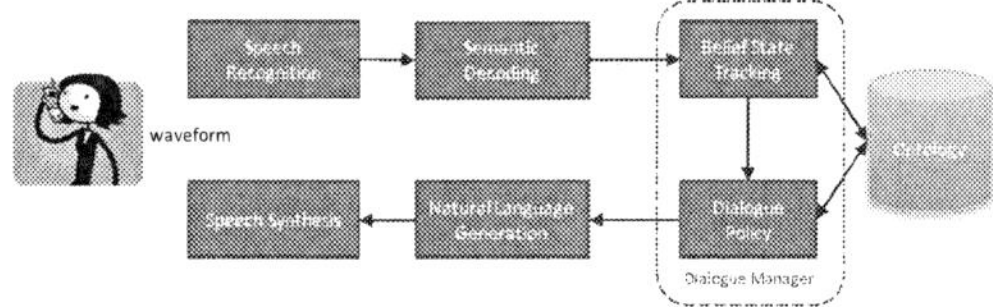

Figure 2: The modular statistical dialogue system architecture. The dialogue manager takes the semantic interpretation as input to track the belief state. The updated state is then used by the dialogue policy to decide on the next system action.

sample data and a potentially delayed objective signal (the reward r) (Sutton and Barto, 1998). The policy selects the next action $a \in A$ based on the current system belief state b to optimise the accumulated future reward R_t at time t:

$$R_t = \sum_{k=0}^{\infty} \gamma^k r_{t+k+1} \ . \tag{1}$$

Here, k denotes the number of future steps, γ a discount factor and r_τ the reward at time τ.

The Q-function models the expected accumulated future reward R_t when taking action a in belief state b and then following policy π:

$$Q^\pi(b, a) = E_\pi[R_t | b_t = b, a_t = a] \ . \tag{2}$$

For most real-world problems, finding the exact optimal Q-values is not feasible. Instead, RL algorithms have been proposed for dialogue policy learning based on approximating the Q-function directly or employing the policy gradient theorem (Williams and Young, 2006; Daubigney et al., 2012; Gašić and Young, 2014; Williams et al., 2017; Su et al., 2017; Casanueva et al., 2017; Papangelis and Stylianou, 2017).

Aside from the policy model, the dialogue model plays an important role: it defines the structure and internal links of the dialogue state as well as the system and user acts (i.e., the semantics the system can understand). Thus, the policy model is only able to learn system behaviour based on what is defined by the dialogue model. By defining the dialogue state, the dialogue model further represents an abstraction over the task ontology or knowledge base restricting the view on the information that is relevant so that the system is able to converse[2]. Most current dialogue models are built

around *domains* which encapsulate all relevant information as a section of the dialogue state that belongs to a given topic, e.g., finding a *restaurant* or *hotel*. However, the resulting flat state that is widely used (Williams et al., 2005; Young et al., 2010; Thomson and Young, 2010; Lee and Stent, 2016; Schulz et al., 2017, e.g.) is not intuitive to model complex dialogue structures like relations.

To overcome this limitation, we propose the conversational entity dialogue model which will be described in detail in the following section.

4 Conversational Entity Dialogue Model

The conversational entity dialogue model (CEDM) is proposed as an alternative way of statistical dialogue modelling having the concept of entities at the core of the model. Entities being objects or relations offer an intuitive way of modelling complex task-oriented dialogues.

4.1 Objects and Relations

Objects are entities of a certain object type (e.g., *Restaurant* or *Hotel*) where each type defines a set of attributes (see Fig. 1). This type definition matches the contents of the back-end knowledge base and thus the internal representation of real-world objects. This is similar to the definition of domains. In contrast to domains, though, this notion allows the modelling of multiple objects of the same type within a dialogue as well as the modelling of a type hierarchy which may be exploited during policy learning.

Relations are also entities that connect objects or attributes of objects. An example is shown in Figure 3: the two objects *obj1* and *obj2* of types *Hotel* and *Restaurant* respectively are connected through the attribute *area* with the *equals* relation.

Possible relations may directly be derived from the object type definitions, e.g., by allowing only connections for attributes that represent the same concepts like area. Note that these relations are dynamic relations that may be drawn between objects in a conversation. This is different to static relations which are often used in knowledge bases to describe how concepts relate to each other.

4.2 Conversational Entities in a Conversational World

A conversational entity is a virtual entity that exists in the context of the current conversation and is either a conversational object or a conversational

---

[2]Using the knowledge base directly to model the (noisy) dialogue state (Pragst et al., 2015; Meditskos et al., 2016) usually results in high access times.

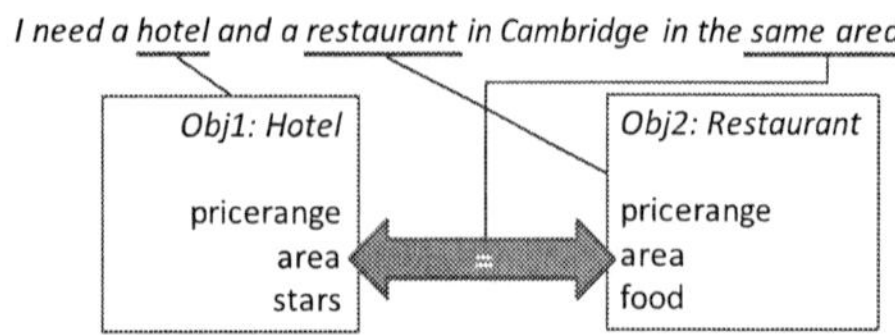

Figure 3: Example mapping of a user utterance to two objects and one relation.

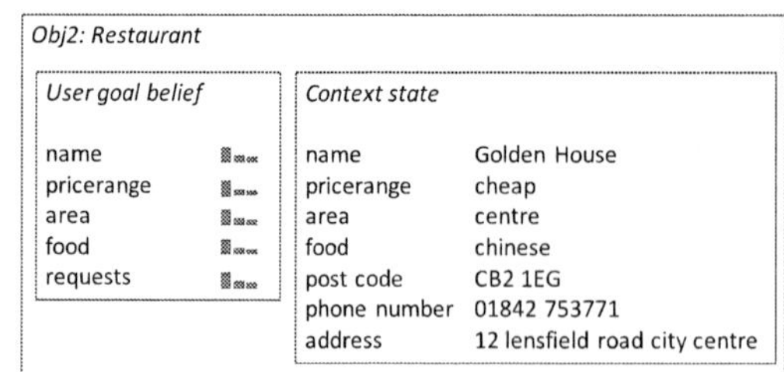

Figure 4: Example of a conversational entity representing object *obj2* of type *Restaurant*. The user goal belief models the search constraints the user has provided to the system and the context state represents the most recent real-world match offered by the system.

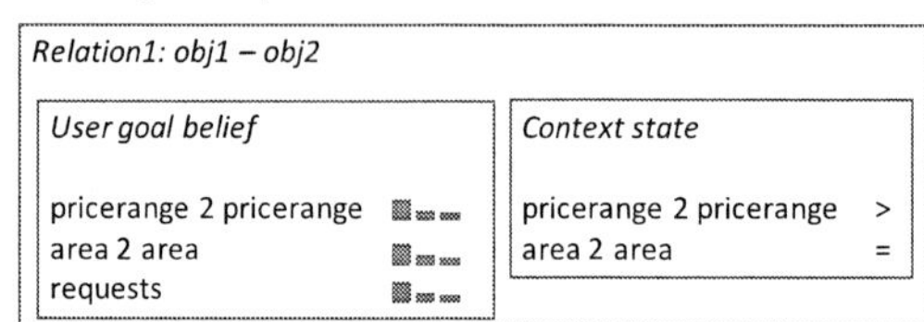

Figure 5: Example of the conversational entity *Relation1* between *obj1* and *obj2*. The user goal belief models the search constraints the user has provided to the system and the context state represents the relations based on the most recent real-world matches for both objects offered by the system.

relation. A conversational object may match a real-world entity but does not need to. In fact, the task of a goal-oriented dialogue is often to find a matching real-world entity based on the information acquired by the system during the dialogue. In the example dialogue (Fig. 1), matching entities have already been found for both objects. However, a conversational object exists independently of whether a matching real-world entity has been found yet or even exists.

Derived from the object type definition, a conversational object comprises an internal state that consists of the user goal belief s_u and the context state s_c as shown in the example in Figure 4. There, s_u is depicted using marginal probabilities for each slot (which is common in recent work on statistical SDS). While the user goal belief models the system's belief of what the user wants based on the user input, the context state models information that the system has shared with the user. In the example of Figure 4, the system has already offered a matching real-world object based on the user goal belief of the conversational object. If no offer has been made yet, the context state is empty.

The context state plays an important role as addressed relations usually refer to the object offered by the system instead of search constraints represented by the user goal belief. The context state further allows to relate to attributes that have not been mentioned in the dialogue.

One key aspect of the CEDM is that relations are also modelled as a conversational entity. Thus, these conversational relations also define a user goal belief and a context state as shown in Figure 5. The attributes of the relation are created out of the attributes of the objects they connect. In the given example, the attributes *area* and *pricerange* of the two objects are connected resulting in the relation attributes *area2area* and *pricerange2pricerange*. The values of these attributes are the actual relations, e.g., *equals* or *greater/less than*. Similar to the slot belief of conversational objects, each attribute is modelled with a marginal probability over all possible relations.

Assigning part of the belief state to the relations enables the system to specifically react to these relations and even to address them in a system utterance. Furthermore, if the context state of one of the related objects changes (e.g., because the user changed their mind), the relation may still persist.

Each conversational entity resides within a conversational world w (see Fig. 1) that defines the number of objects and the type of each object (relations may be derived from this) as well as general state information. This world may either be predefined or needs to be derived from the user input. In the latter case, the user input is usually noisy and an uncertainty needs to be modelled within the dialogue state. As this work focuses on relation modelling, a predefined conversational world is used leaving the uncertainty modelling of conversational worlds for future work.

4.3 Belief Tracking and Focus of Attention

The task of belief tracking is to update the probability distribution $b'(s)$ over the states s based on the system action a, the observation o of the user input and the previous probability distribution b:

$$b'(s) = P(s|o, a, b) . \qquad (3)$$

With the additional complexity of the CEDM having an unknown number of entities in a conversational world, we propose to decompose the state s in the spirit of work by Williams et al. (2005). The belief update for each entity e is then defined as

$$b'_e(u, s_u, s_c, h_e) = P(u, s_u, s_c, h_e|a, o, b_e) , \quad (4)$$

where s_u is the user goal state of entity e, s_c the context state of e, h_e the dialogue history of e and u the last user action[3].

The belief update for the world belief b_w is

$$b'_w(u, s_w, h_w) = P(u, s_w, h_w|a, o, b_w) , \quad (5)$$

where s_w is the world state of world w, h_w the dialogue history and u the last user action.

This multi-part belief allows hierarchical dialogue processing on the world level and the entity level as depicted in Figure 6. Each level produces its own belief and based on that, the system is able to act on each level. On the world level, the system might produce general dialogue behaviour like greetings or engage in a dialogue to adequately identify the entity which is addressed by the user input. On the entity level, the system talks to the user to acquire information about the concrete entity the user is talking about, e.g., to find a matching entity in the knowledge base.

In addition to belief tracking, we would like to introduce another concept called focus of attention. Based on work by Grosz (1978), we define the current focus of attention $\mathcal{F}$ for each conversational world as a subset of conversational entities in this world $\mathcal{F} \subseteq W$. Hence, the task of focus tracking is to find the new set of conversational entities which is in the current focus of attention based on the user input and the updated belief state. Even though the concept of focus is not mandatory, it may be helpful when framing the reinforcement learning problem as it allows to limit the size of the input to the reinforcement learning algorithm as well as the number of actions available to the learning algorithm at a given time. Using $\mathcal{F}$ may also prevent the system from acting in parts of the belief state that are completely irrelevant to the current part of the conversation.

---

[3]In case of an unknown number of entities represented by a probability over worlds, the probability in Equation 4 needs to be extended to depend on the conversational world and needs to be multiplied by a probability over all worlds.

world level	world general behaviour	b_w
entity level	entity specific behaviour	b_e

Figure 6: The layered model of the CEDM with the respective components of the belief state.

4.4 The Conversational Entity vs. the Multi-Domain Dialogue Model

The functionality and the modelling possibilities of the proposed CEDM go beyond (and thus include) the possibilities of the multi-domain dialogue model (MDDM). To demonstrate this, we will outline how a dialogue using the MDDM may be modelled using the CEDM. The core concept *domain* of the MDDM may be mapped to one conversational object of a specific type where the slots of the domain are the attributes of the type. Since the number of domains is predefined, there is only one conversational world with a set number of conversational objects. Relations may not be modelled using the MDDM. Belief update is reduced to finding the right entity for the user input and updating its state. In the CEDM, the semantic decoding of user input includes the entity (or entity type) it refers to, which is similar to the topic tracker of the MDDM where the topic tracker also defines the domain the system acts in. Hence, the focus of attention will always contain only the entity that has been addressed by the user. By that, a policy for each conversational object (and thus object type) may be trained which is the same as the domain policies of the MDDM.

5 Relation Modelling Evaluation

To demonstrate the capabilities and benefits of the conversational entity dialogue model (CEDM), the aspect of relation modelling has been selected as it is a core concept of the CEDM. For this, we built upon the mapping to the multi-domain dialogue model (MDDM) as described in Section 4.4 and extend it with conversational relations. After a brief description of the model implementation, the experiments and their results are presented using two conversational objects of different types. Note that only the *equals* relation is considered here due to limitations of the marginal belief state model.

5.1 Model Implementation

To implement all relevant aspects of the CEDM, the publicly available open-source statistical dialogue system toolkit PyDial (Ultes et al., 2017) is used which originally follows the MDDM.

The main challenge for policy implementation is to integrate both the state of the object in $\mathcal{F}$ as well as the states of all corresponding relations into the dialogue decision. To achieve this, a hierarchical policy model based on feudal reinforcement learning (Dayan and Hinton, 1993) has been implemented following the approach of Casanueva et al. (2018). For each object type, a master policy decides whether the next system action addresses a conversational relation or the conversational object. A respective sub-policy is then invoked in a second step where each object type and each relation type are modelled by an individual policy. Thus, the model decomposes the action selection problem to take account for the specificities of the object policy and relation policies respectively and is able to handle a variable number of relations. During training, all policies (master and sub-policies) receive the same reward signal.

Aside from the feudal RL architecture which seems to be intuitive for the proposed CEDM, the main problem is the handling of back-end database access. In the MDDM, each domain models all information which is necessary to do the data-base lookup. However, this is not possible in the CEDM as information from different conversational objects and relations need to be taken into account. One way of doing this is to apply a rule-based merging of the state of the conversational object in $\mathcal{F}$ with the states of all other conversational objects that are related through a conversational relation to form the focus state $\hat{b}$:

$$\hat{b}_s(v) = \frac{\sum_i w_i b_s^i(v)}{\sum_i w_i} \, , \qquad (6)$$

where s is the slot, v is the value, and b^i the belief of the i-th conversational entity involved in the merging process. $w_i = 1 - b_s^i(\emptyset)$ is the weight of the i-th conversational entity where $b_s^i(\emptyset)$ represents the probability where no information about slot s has yet been shared with the system. b^i either refers to the belief b^o of the conversational object o in $\mathcal{F}$ or to an already weighted belief $\tilde{b}^{o'}$ originating from the conversational relation $rel^{oo'}$ connecting conversational object o with o':

$$\tilde{b}_s^{o'}(v) = \begin{cases} rel_s^{oo'}(=) \cdot b_s^{o'}(v), & v \neq \emptyset \\ rel_s^{oo'}(=) \cdot b_s^{o'}(v) + rel_s^{oo'}(\emptyset), & v = \emptyset \end{cases}$$

where $b^{o'}$ is the belief of object o'. The relation probability rel is 0 if the slot s has no matching

slot in o'. Please note that for $b_s^{o'}(v)$, even though we refer to the belief, the context state of o' is used instead if not empty. The focus state is used as input to the master policy as well as the sub-policy of the conversational object.

As an example, consider $b_s^o = [\emptyset : 0.3, v_1 : 0.7, v_2 : 0.0]$, $b_s^{o'} = [\emptyset : 0.2, v_1 : 0.0, v_2 : 0.8]$, and $rel_s^{oo'} = [\emptyset : 0.1, =: 0.9]$. This results in $\tilde{b}_s^{o'} = [\emptyset : 0.28, v_1 : 0.0, v_2 : 0.78]$ and $\hat{b}_s = [\emptyset : 0.29, v_1 : 0.35, v_2 : 0.36]$. This example also shows that conflicts which may exists between the state of the conversational object and the state defined by the relation are visible at this level. To help the policy to learn in this situation, an additional conflict bit is added to the focus belief state as input to the master policy.

The source code of the CEDM implementation is available at http://pydial.org/cedm.

5.2 Experimental Setup

To evaluate the relation modelling capabilities of the CEDM, the task of finding a hotel and a restaurant in Cambridge has been selected (corresponding to the *CamRestaurants* and *CamHotels* domains of PyDial). The corresponding conversational world consists of two conversational objects of types *hotel* and *restaurant* and one conversational relation. Based on the object type definitions, the conversational relation connects the slots *area* and *pricerange* of both objects. Using a simulated environment, the goals of the simulated user were generated so that at least one of these two slots is related (i.e., contains the same value).

To test the influence of the user addressing the relation instead of the correct value (e.g., "restaurant in the same area as the hotel" vs. "restaurant in the centre"), we have extended the simulated agenda-based user (Schatzmann and Young, 2009) with a probability r of the user addressing the relation instead of the value. The higher r, the more often the user addresses the relation. The user simulator is equipped with an additional error model to simulate the semantic error rate (SER) caused in a real system by the noisy speech channel.

For belief tracking, an extended version of the focus tracker (Henderson et al., 2014)—an effective rule-based tracker—was used for the conversational entities and the conversational world that also discounts probabilities if the respective value has been rejected by the user. As a simulated interaction is on the semantic level, no semantic decoder for the relations is necessary. For training and evaluation of the proposed framework, both the master policy and all sub-policies are modelled with the GP-SARSA algorithm (Gašić and Young, 2014). This is a value-based method that uses a Gaussian process to approximate the state-value function (Eq. 2). As it takes into account the uncertainty of the estimate, it is sample-efficient.

To compare the dialogue performance of the CEDM with the MDDM baseline, two experiments have been conducted. All dialogues follow the same structure: the user and the system first talk about one conversational object before moving on to the second object. As the user only addresses a relation to an object that has previously been part of the dialogue, relations are only relevant when talking about the second object. However, there are times where a relation has been addressed by the user before the goal of the first object changed which resulted in the addressed relation being wrong. This could only be resolved by the system by addressing the relation itself.

Experiment 1 In the first experiment, the influence of r on the dialogue performance is investigated in a controlled environment. Having a fixed order, only the feudal policy of the second object (where relations may occur), the *restaurant*, is learned. To avoid interfering effects of jointly learning both policies at the same time, the first object *hotel* uses a handcrafted policy.

Experiment 2 The second experiment focusses on the joint learning effects. Thus, the order of objects is alternated, all objects use the feudal policy model and are trained simultaneously.

5.3 Results

The experiments have been conducted based on the PyDial simulation environments Env. 1 and Env. 3 specified by Casanueva et al. (2017) where Env. 1 operates on a clean communication channel with an SER of 0% and Env. 3 simulates an SER of 15%. For each experiment, a policy for the respective object types was trained with 4,000 and tested with 1,000 dialogues. The reward was set to +30/+0 for success/failure and -1 for each turn with a maximum of 25 turns per object. The results were averaged over 5 different random seeds.

Experiment 1 As can be seen in Table 1 and Figure 7 on the left, the proposed CEDM with a feudal policy model is easily able to deal with relations addressed by the user for any relation probability r in both environments. Success rate and reward achieve similar results for all r. Only for very high r, a small reduction in performance is visible. This can be explained with the added complexity of the dialogue itself as well as the system actions that address the relations. A high relation probability for a slot requires the system to address either the relation or the slot value directly. Both actions may have similar or contradicting impact on the dialogue which makes it harder to learn a good policy. In Env. 3, the added noise results in minor fluctuations which may be expected.

In contrast, the baseline (the MDDM) is not able to handle the user addressing relations adequately for higher r: while for low r, the policy is able to compensate by requesting the respective information again, the performance drops at around $r = 0.5$. The reason why the performance of the baseline does not drop as much in Env. 3 as it does in Env. 1 is the way the simulated error model of the simulated user operates. By producing a 3-best-list of user inputs, the chance that the actual correct value is introduced as noise if a relation has originally been uttered is relatively high. As the n-best-list of Env. 1 has the length of one, this does not happen there.

The performance of the hand-crafted hotel policy was similar for all r in Env. 1 with $rew = 23.4, suc = 99.7\%$ and in Env. 3 with $rew = 20.1, suc = 94.5\%$.

Analysing the system actions of the dialogues of the CEDM shows that the system learns to address a relation in up to 28% of all dialogues for $r = 1.0$.

Example dialogues for Env. 1 are shown in Figures 8 and 9.

Experiment 2 The results shown in Table 1 and Figure 7 on the right show the performance of the conversational object policies when the respective object was the second one in the dialogue (where relations occur). Still, policies of both objects were trained in all dialogues. The effects of this added noise become visible in the results as they seem to be less stable. Furthermore, the overall performance for the *restaurant* policy drops a bit, but still shows the same characteristics as in Experiment 1. Learning a *hotel* policy results in worse overall performance (which matches the literature) and in cases where a relation is involved.

The performance of the policy of the first object was similar for all r where the restaurant policy achieved $rew = 21.5, suc = 95.4\%$ and the hotel

Table 1: Reward and success rate of both experiments for different relation probabilities r comparing the proposed CEDM to the MDDM baseline. The measures only show the performance of the second object in the dialogue where the relation is relevant. All results are computed after 4,000/1,000 train/test dialogues and averaged over 5 trials with different random seeds. **Bold** indicates statistically significant outperformance ($p < .05$), *italic* indicates no statistically significant difference.

	Experiment 1								Experiment 2							
	Restaurant - Env. 1				Restaurant - Env. 3				Restaurant - Env. 3				Hotel - Env. 3			
	CEDM		base		CEDM		base		CEDM		base		CEDM		base	
r	Rew.	Suc.	Rew.	Suc.	Rew.	Suc.	Rew.	Suc.	Rew.	Suc.	Rew.	Suc.	Rew.	Suc.	Rew.	Suc.
0.0	**23.3**	99.3%	23.2	**99.6%**	20.4	94.3%	**20.8**	**96.6%**	20.1	95.0%	**20.7**	**96.1%**	*16.5*	**86.7%**	*16.6*	85.8%
0.1	23.1	**99.5%**	**23.2**	99.1%	20.5	94.7%	**21.1**	**96.5%**	*20.3*	*94.4%*	20.4	94.4%	16.5	86.4%	**17.5**	**89.0%**
0.3	**23.2**	**99.5%**	23.1	99.0%	20.2	93.6%	**21.0**	**95.8%**	19.7	93.6%	**20.4**	**95.0%**	*16.2*	85.5%	*16.5*	**87.1%**
0.5	**22.8**	**99.6%**	21.9	96.2%	**19.8**	**92.8%**	18.7	89.7%	**19.7**	**92.5%**	19.3	92.0%	14.6	80.8%	15.2	**82.4%**
0.7	**22.6**	**99.2%**	17.4	82.3%	**19.9**	**92.9%**	17.7	86.8%	**19.2**	**91.6%**	17.9	87.9%	**16.7**	**86.9%**	12.7	75.7%
0.9	**22.5**	**99.4%**	5.3	41.6%	**19.3**	**91.2%**	15.0	79.8%	**18.2**	**89.5%**	14.2	78.2%	**9.8**	**64.3%**	8.1	61.5%
1.0	**21.6**	**99.5%**	-3.6	11.7%	**18.9**	**90.2%**	13.9	76.8%	**17.9**	**88.3%**	10.9	67.5%	**13.8**	**79.4%**	7.0	58.2%

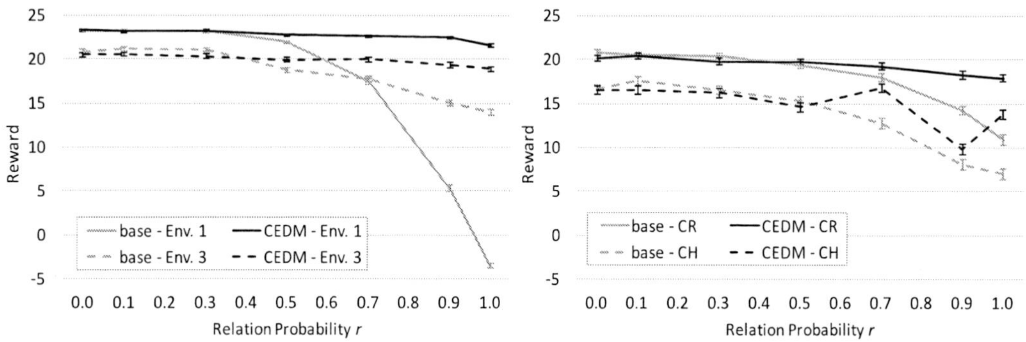

Figure 7: Reward and confidence interval of Experiment 1 (left) and Experiment 2 (right) for different relation probabilities r comparing the proposed CEDM to the MDDM baseline. The measures only show the performance of the second object in the dialogue where the relation is relevant. All results are computed after 4,000/1,000 train/test dialogues and averaged over 5 trials with different random seeds.

policy $rew = 18.8, suc = 90.2\%$.

Analysing the system actions of the dialogues shows that the CEDM learns to address a relation in up to 24.5% of all dialogues for $r = 1.0$.

6   Conclusion and Future Work

In this paper, we have presented a novel dialogue model for statistical spoken dialogue systems that is centred around objects and relations (instead of domains) thus offering a new way of modelling statistical dialogue. The two major advantages of the new model are the capability of including multiple objects of the same type and the capability of modelling and addressing relations between the objects. By assigning a part of the belief state not only to each object but to each relation as well, the system is able to address the relations in a system response.

We have demonstrated the importance of the aspect of relation modelling—a core functionality of our proposed model—in simulated experiments showing that by using a hierarchical feudal policy architecture, adequate policies may be learned that lead to successful dialogues in cases where relations are often mentioned by the user. Furthermore, the resulting policies also learned to address the relation itself in the system response.

However, only a small part of the proposed dialogue model has been evaluated in this paper. To explore its full potential, many questions need to be addressed in future work. For creating a suitable semantic decoder that is able to semantically parse linguistic information about relations, an extensive prior work on named entity recognition and dependency parsing already exists and needs to be leveraged and applied to conduct real user experiments. Moreover, relations other than *equals* need to be investigated. Finally, the challenges of identifying all conversational entities in the dialogue and assigning the correct one to each user action as well as finding suitable belief-tracking approaches for the proposed multi-layered architecture along with effective policy models need to be addressed.

Acknowledgments

This research was partly funded by the EPSRC grant EP/M018946/1 *Open Domain Statistical Spoken Dialogue Systems*.

References

Eric Bilange. 1991. An approach to oral dialogue modelling. In *The Structure of Multimodal Dialogue; Second VENACO Workshop*.

Paweł Budzianowski, Stefan Ultes, Pei-Hao Su, Nikola Mrkšić, Tsung-Hsien Wen, Iñigo Casanueva, Lina Rojas-Barahona, and Milica Gašić. 2017. Subdomain modelling for dialogue management with hierarchical reinforcement learning. In *Proceedings of the 18th Annual Meeting of the Special Interest Group on Discourse and Dialogue (SIGDIAL)*, pages 86–92. Association for Computational Linguistics.

Iñigo Casanueva, Paweł Budzianowski, Pei-Hao Su, Nikola Mrkšić, Tsung-Hsien Wen, Stefan Ultes, Lina Rojas-Barahona, Steve Young, and Milica Gašić. 2017. A benchmarking environment for reinforcement learning based task oriented dialogue management. In *Deep Reinforcement Learning Symposium, 31st Conference on Neural Information Processing Systems (NIPS)*.

Iñigo Casanueva, Paweł Budzianowski, Pei-Hao Su, Stefan Ultes, Lina Rojas-Barahona, Bo-Hsiang Tseng, and Milica Gašić. 2018. Feudal reinforcement learning for dialogue management in large domains. In *Proc. of the Conference of the North American Chapter of the Association for Computational Linguistics - Human Language Technologies (HLT/NAACL)*.

Lucie Daubigney, Matthieu Geist, Senthilkumar Chandramohan, and Olivier Pietquin. 2012. A comprehensive reinforcement learning framework for dialogue management optimization. *IEEE Journal of Selected Topics in Signal Processing*, 6(8):891–902.

Peter Dayan and Geoffrey E Hinton. 1993. Feudal reinforcement learning. In *Advances in neural information processing systems*, pages 271–278.

Mihail Eric and Christopher D. Manning. 2017. Key-value retrieval networks for task-oriented dialogue. In *Proceedings of the 18th Annual SIGdial Meeting on Discourse and Dialogue*, pages 37–49, Saarbrcken, Germany. Association for Computational Linguistics.

Milica Gašić, Nikola Mrkšić, Lina Rojas-Barahona, Pei-Hao Su, Stefan Ultes, David Vandyke, Tsung-Hsien Wen, and Steve Young. 2017. Dialogue manager domain adaptation using gaussian process reinforcement learning. *Computer Speech and Language*, 45:552–569.

Milica Gašić and Steve J. Young. 2014. Gaussian processes for POMDP-based dialogue manager optimization. *IEEEACM Transactions on Audio, Speech, and Language Processing*, 22(1):28–40.

Barbara J. Grosz. 1977. The representation and use of focus in dialogue understanding. Technical report, SRI International Menlo Park United States.

Barbara J. Grosz. 1978. Focusing in dialog. In *Proceedings of the 1978 Workshop on Theoretical Issues in Natural Language Processing*, TINLAP '78, pages 96–103, Stroudsburg, PA, USA. Association for Computational Linguistics.

Tobias Heinroth and Wolfgang Minker. 2013. *Introducing Spoken Dialogue Systems into Intelligent Environments*. Springer, Boston (USA).

Matthew Henderson, Blaise Thomson, and Jason Williams. 2014. The second dialog state tracking challenge. In *15th Annual Meeting of the Special Interest Group on Discourse and Dialogue*, volume 263.

Sungjin Lee and Amanda Stent. 2016. Task lineages: Dialog state tracking for flexible interaction. In *SIGDial*, pages 11–21, Los Angeles. ACL.

Oliver Lemon and Olivier Pietquin. 2012. *Data-Driven Methods for Adaptive Spoken Dialogue Systems*. Springer New York.

Jiwei Li, Will Monroe, Alan Ritter, Michel Galley, Jianfeng Gao, and Dan Jurafsky. 2016. Deep reinforcement learning for dialogue generation. In *Proceedings of the 2016 Conference on Empirical Methods in Natural Language Processing*, pages 1192–1202. Association for Computational Linguistics.

Pierre Lison. 2011. Multi-policy dialogue management. In *Proceedings of the SIGDIAL 2011 Conference*, pages 294–300. Association for Computational Linguistics.

Georgios Meditskos, Stamatia Dasiopoulou, Louisa Pragst, Stefan Ultes, Stefanos Vrochidis, Ioannis Kompatsiaris, and Leo Wanner. 2016. Towards an ontology-driven adaptive dialogue framework. In *Proceedings of the 1st International Workshop on Multimedia Analysis and Retrieval for Multimodal Interaction*, pages 15–20. ACM.

Germán Montoro, Xavier Alamán, and Pablo A Haya. 2004. A plug and play spoken dialogue interface for smart environments. In *International Conference on Intelligent Text Processing and Computational Linguistics*, pages 360–370. Springer.

Alexandros Papangelis and Yannis Stylianou. 2017. Single-model multi-domain dialogue management with deep learning. In *International Workshop for Spoken Dialogue Systems*.

Baolin Peng, Xiujun Li, Lihong Li, Jianfeng Gao, Asli Celikyilmaz, Sungjin Lee, and Kam-Fai Wong. 2017. Composite task-completion dialogue policy learning via hierarchical deep reinforcement learning. In *Proceedings of the 2017 Conference on Empirical Methods in Natural Language Processing*, pages 2231–2240. Association for Computational Linguistics.

Louisa Pragst, Stefan Ultes, Matthias Kraus, and Wolfgang Minker. 2015. Adaptive dialogue management in the kristina project for multicultural health care applications. In *Proceedings of the 19thWorkshop on the Semantics and Pragmatics of Dialogue (SEM-DIAL)*, pages 202–203.

Deepak Ramachandran and Adwait Ratnaparkhi. 2015. Belief tracking with stacked relational trees. In *Proceedings of the 16th Annual Meeting of the Special Interest Group on Discourse and Dialogue*, pages 68–76.

Jost Schatzmann and Steve J. Young. 2009. The hidden agenda user simulation model. *Audio, Speech, and Language Processing, IEEE Transactions on*, 17(4):733–747.

Hannes Schulz, Jeremie Zumer, Layla El Asri, and Shikhar Sharma. 2017. A frame tracking model for memory-enhanced dialogue systems. *arXiv preprint arXiv:1706.01690*.

Iulian Vlad Serban, Alessandro Sordoni, Yoshua Bengio, Aaron C Courville, and Joelle Pineau. 2016. Building end-to-end dialogue systems using generative hierarchical neural network models. In *AAAI*, pages 3776–3784.

Pei-Hao Su, Paweł Budzianowski, Stefan Ultes, Milica Gasic, and Steve Young. 2017. Sample-efficient actor-critic reinforcement learning with supervised data for dialogue management. In *SIGdial*, pages 147–157, Saarbrcken, Germany. ACL.

Richard S. Sutton and Andrew G. Barto. 1998. *Reinforcement Learning: An Introduction*, 1st edition. MIT Press, Cambridge, MA, USA.

Blaise Thomson and Steve J. Young. 2010. Bayesian update of dialogue state: A POMDP framework for spoken dialogue systems. *Computer Speech & Language*, 24(4):562–588.

Stefan Ultes, Lina M. Rojas-Barahona, Pei-Hao Su, David Vandyke, Dongho Kim, Iñigo Casanueva, Paweł Budzianowski, Nikola Mrkšić, Tsung-Hsien Wen, Milica Gašić, and Steve J. Young. 2017. Pydial: A multi-domain statistical dialogue system toolkit. In *ACL Demo*. Association of Computational Linguistics.

Zhuoran Wang, Hongliang Chen, Guanchun Wang, Hao Tian, Hua Wu, and Haifeng Wang. 2014. Policy learning for domain selection in an extensible multi-domain spoken dialogue system. In *Proceedings of the 2014 Conference on Empirical Methods in Natural Language Processing (EMNLP)*, pages 57–67.

Jason D Williams, Kavosh Asadi, and Geoffrey Zweig. 2017. Hybrid code networks: practical and efficient end-to-end dialog control with supervised and reinforcement learning. In *Proceedings of the 55th Annual Meeting of the Association for Computational Linguistics (Volume 1: Long Papers)*, pages 665–677, Vancouver, Canada. Association for Computational Linguistics.

Jason D. Williams, Pascal Poupart, and Steve J. Young. 2005. Factored partially observable markov decision processes for dialogue management. In *4th Workshop on Knowledge and Reasoning in Practical Dialog Systems, International Joint Conference on Artificial Intelligence (IJCAI)*, pages 76–82.

Jason D. Williams and Steve J. Young. 2006. Scaling pomdps for dialog management with composite summary point-based value iteration (cspbvi). In *AAAI Workshop on Statistical and Empirical Approaches for Spoken Dialogue Systems*, pages 37–42.

Yushi Xu and Stephanie Seneff. 2010. Dialogue management based on entities and constraints. In *Proceedings of the 11th Annual Meeting of the Special Interest Group on Discourse and Dialogue*, pages 87–90. Association for Computational Linguistics.

Steve J. Young, Milica Gašić, Simon Keizer, François Mairesse, Jost Schatzmann, Blaise Thomson, and Kai Yu. 2010. The hidden information state model: A practical framework for POMDP-based spoken dialogue management. *Computer Speech & Language*, 24(2):150–174.

Steve J. Young, Milica Gašić, Blaise Thomson, and Jason D. Williams. 2013. POMDP-based statistical spoken dialog systems: A review. *Proceedings of the IEEE*, 101(5):1160–1179.

A Example Dialogues

```
 1:  Sys    hello()
 2:  User   inform(CamHotels#type="placetostay", CamHotels#area="west", CamHotels#pricerange="moderate",
             CamHotels#kind="guesthouse")
 3:  Sys    inform(CamHotels#kind="guesthouse", CamHotels#pricerange="moderate", CamHotels#name="hobsons
             house", CamHotels#area="west")
 4:  User   reqalts()
 5:  Sys    inform(CamHotels#name="none", CamHotels#name!="hobsons house", CamHotels#kind="guesthouse",
             CamHotels#pricerange="moderate", CamHotels#area="west")
 6:  User   reqalts(CamHotels#area="north")
 7:  Sys    inform(CamHotels#kind="guesthouse", CamHotels#pricerange="moderate",
             CamHotels#name="limehouse", CamHotels#area="north")
 8:  User   request(CamHotels#price)
 9:  Sys    inform(CamHotels#name="limehouse", CamHotels#price="a cheapest single room is 40 pounds and a
             cheapest double room is 75 pounds")
10:  User   inform(CamRestaurants#type="restaurant", CamRestaurants#food="british")
11:  Sys    request(CamRestaurants#pricerange)
12:  User   inform(CamRestaurants#pricerange="moderate")
13:  Sys    request(CamRestaurants#area)
14:  User   inform(CamRestaurants#area=CamHotels#area)
15:  Sys    inform(CamRestaurants#name="none", CamRestaurants#food="british",
             CamRestaurants#pricerange="moderate", CamRestaurants#area="north")
16:  User   negate(CamRestaurants#area="west")
17:  Sys    confirm(CamHotels#area=CamRestaurants#area)
18:  User   negate(CamRestaurants#area="west")
19:  Sys    inform(CamRestaurants#food="british", CamRestaurants#pricerange="moderate",
             CamRestaurants#name="saint johns chop house", CamRestaurants#area="west")
20:  User   bye()
21:  Sys    bye()
```

Figure 8: An example simulated dialogue using the proposed CEDM (Experiment 1, Env. 1, $r = 0.7$) about finding a hotel first (blue) followed by a restaurant (green). The system is able to process user input addressing a relation (Turn 14) as well as to address the relation in a system utterance (Turn 17). The dialogue nicely shows how the system is able to resolve a conflict between the belief of the conversational relation and the belief of the conversational object (i.e., CamRestaurants#area = CamHotels#area vs. CamRestaurants#area = "west").

```
 1:  Sys    hello()
 2:  User   inform(CamHotels#type="placetostay", CamHotels#kind="hotel", CamHotels#area="north",
             CamHotels#stars="2")
 3:  Sys    inform(CamHotels#kind="hotel", CamHotels#name="lovell lodge", CamHotels#stars="2",
             CamHotels#area="north")
 4:  User   confirm(CamHotels#kind="hotel")
 5:  Sys    inform(CamHotels#name="lovell lodge", CamHotels#kind="hotel")
 6:  User   inform(CamRestaurants#type="restaurant", CamRestaurants#food="chinese",
             CamRestaurants#pricerange="expensive")
 7:  Sys    request(CamRestaurants#area)
 8:  User   inform(CamRestaurants#area=CamHotels#area)
 9:  Sys    request(CamRestaurants#area)
10:  User   inform(CamRestaurants#area=CamHotels#area)
11:  Sys    request(CamRestaurants#area)
12:  User   inform(CamRestaurants#area=CamHotels#area)
13:  Sys    request(CamRestaurants#area)
14:  User   inform(CamRestaurants#area="north")
15:  Sys    inform(CamRestaurants#food="chinese", CamRestaurants#pricerange="expensive",
             CamRestaurants#name="hakka", CamRestaurants#area="north")
16:  User   bye()
17:  Sys    bye()
```

Figure 9: An example dialogue using the MDDM (Experiment 1, Env. 1, $r = 0.7$) about finding a hotel first (blue) followed by a restaurant (green). As the system is not able to process user input addressing a relation it keeps requesting the same information (Turns 7-12: CamRestaurants#area) over and over until the user finally utters the actual value of the area (Turn 14: CamRestaurants#area="north") which then leads to a successful dialogue.

Conversational Image Editing:
Incremental Intent Identification in a New Dialogue Task

Ramesh Manuvinakurike[1], Trung Bui[2], Walter Chang[2], Kallirroi Georgila[1]
[1]Institute for Creative Technologies, University of Southern California
[2]Adobe Research
[manuvinakurike,kgeorgila]@ict.usc.edu, [bui,wachang]@adobe.com

Abstract

We present "conversational image editing", a novel real-world application domain combining dialogue, visual information, and the use of computer vision. We discuss the importance of dialogue incrementality in this task, and build various models for incremental intent identification based on deep learning and traditional classification algorithms. We show how our model based on convolutional neural networks outperforms models based on random forests, long short term memory networks, and conditional random fields. By training embeddings based on image-related dialogue corpora, we outperform pre-trained out-of-the-box embeddings, for intention identification tasks. Our experiments also provide evidence that incremental intent processing may be more efficient for the user and could save time in accomplishing tasks.

1 Introduction

The development of digital photography has led to the advancement of digital image editing, where professionals as well as hobbyists use software tools such as Adobe Photoshop, Microsoft Photos, and so forth, to change and improve certain characteristics (brightness, contrast, etc.) of an image.

Image editing is a hard task due to a variety of reasons: (1) The task requires a sense of artistic creativity. (2) The task is time consuming, and requires patience and experimenting with various features before settling on the final image edit. (3) Sometimes users know at an abstract level what changes they want but are unaware of the image editing steps and parameters that will result in the desired image. For example, a person's face in a photo may look flushed, but the users may not know that adjusting the saturation and the temperature settings to some specific values will change the photo to match their expectations. (4) Users are not sure what changes to perform on a given image. (5) Users are not fully aware of the features and the functionality that are supported by the given image editing tool.

Users can often benefit from conversing with experts to edit images. This can be seen in action in web services such as the Reddit Photoshop Request forum[1], Zhopped[2], etc. These web services include two types of users: expert editors who know how to edit the photographs, and novice users who post their photographs and request changes to be made. If the editor needs further clarification regarding the requested change, they post their query and wait for a response from the user. The conversational exchanges also happen through edit feedback where the editor interprets the user request and posts the edited photographs. The user can reply with further requests for changes until they are fully satisfied. Due to this message-forum-like setup, users do not have the freedom to request changes in real time (at the same time as the changes are actually being performed), and hence often end up with edited images that do not fully match their requests. Furthermore, the editors are often unable to provide suggestions that could make the photograph fit better the user's narrative for image editing.

In this setup the users can benefit greatly from conversing with an expert image editor in real time who can understand the requests, perform the editing, and provide feedback or suggestions as the editing is being performed. Our ultimate goal is to build a dialogue system with such capabilities.

---

[1]https://www.reddit.com/r/PhotoshopRequest/
[2]https://zhopped.com

Proceedings of the SIGDIAL 2018 Conference, pages 284–295,
Melbourne, Australia, 12-14 July 2018. ©2018 Association for Computational Linguistics

Conversational image editing is a task particularly well suited for incremental dialogue processing. It requires a lot of fine-grained changes (e.g., changing brightness to a specific value), which often cannot be just narrated with a command. In order to perform such fine-grained changes to the user's liking, it is necessary that the editor understands the user utterances incrementally (word-by-word) and in real time, instead of waiting until the user has finished their utterance. For example, if the user wants to increase the brightness, they could utter "more, more, more" until the desired change has been achieved. The changes should occur as soon as the user has uttered "more" and continue happening while the user keeps saying "more, more".

In this paper, our contributions are as follows: (1) We introduce "conversational image editing", a novel dialogue application that combines natural language dialogue with visual information and computer vision. Ultimately a dialogue system that can perform image editing should be able to understand what part of the image the user is referring to, e.g., when the user says "remove the tree". (2) We provide a new annotation scheme for incremental dialogue intentions. (3) We perform intent identification experiments, and show that a convolutional neural network model outperforms other state-of-the-art models based on deep learning and traditional classification algorithms. Furthermore, embeddings trained on image-related corpora lead to better performance than generic out-of-the-box embeddings. (4) We calculate the impact of varying confidence thresholds (above which the classifier's prediction is considered) on classification accuracy and savings in terms of number of words. Our analysis provides evidence that incremental intent processing may be more efficient for the user and save time in accomplishing tasks. To the best of our knowledge this is the first time in the literature that the impact of incremental intent understanding on savings in terms of number of words (or time) is explicitly measured. DeVault et al. (2011) measured the stability of natural language understanding results as a function of time but did not explicitly measure savings in terms of number of words or time.

2   Related Work

Combining computer vision and language is a topic that has recently drawn much attention.

Some approaches assume that there are manual annotations available for mapping words or phrases to image regions or features, while other approaches employ computer vision techniques. Research is facilitated by publicly available data sets such as MS COCO (Lin et al., 2014) and Visual Genome (Krishna et al., 2017). Typically image and language corpora consist of digital photographs paired with crowdsourced captions, and sometimes mappings of words and captions to specific parts of an image.

Yao et al. (2010) is an example of a work relying on manual input. They developed a semi-automatic method for parsing images from the Internet to build visual knowledge representation graphs. On the other hand, the following works did not rely on manual annotations. Feng and Lapata (2013) generated captions from news articles and their corresponding images. Mitchell et al. (2012) and Kulkarni et al. (2013) built systems for understanding and generating image descriptions.

Due to space constraints, below we focus on work that combines computer vision or visual references (enabled through manual annotations) and language in the context of a dialogue task, which is most relevant to our work. Antol et al. (2015) introduced the "visual question answering" task. Here the goal is to provide a natural language answer, given an image and a natural language question about the image. Convolutional neural networks (CNNs) were employed for encoding the images (Krizhevsky et al., 2012). This was later modeled as a dialogue-based question-answering task in Das et al. (2017). These works used images from the MS COCO data set. de Vries et al. (2017) introduced "GuessWhat?!", a two-player game where the goal is to find an unknown object in a rich image scene by asking a series of questions. They used images from MS COCO and CNNs for image recognition.

Paetzel et al. (2015) built an incremental dialogue system called "Eve", which could guess the correct image, out of a set of possible candidates, based on descriptions given by a human. The system was shown to perform nearly as well as humans. Then in the same domain, Manuvinakurike et al. (2017) used reinforcement learning to learn an incremental dialogue policy, which outperformed the high performance baseline policy of Paetzel et al. (2015) in offline simulations based on real user data. Each image was associated with certain descriptions and the game worked for a specific data set of images without actually using computer vision.

Manuvinakurike et al. (2016a) developed a model for incremental understanding of the described scenes among a set of complex configurations of geometric shapes. Kennington and Schlangen (2015) learned perceptually grounded word meanings for incremental reference resolution in the same domain of geometric shape descriptions, using visual features.

Huang et al. (2016) built a data set of sequential images with corresponding descriptions that could potentially be used for the task of visual storytelling. Mostafazadeh et al. (2016) introduced the task of "visual question generation" where the system generates natural language questions when given an image, and then Mostafazadeh et al. (2017) extended this work to natural language question and response generation in the context of image-grounded conversations.

Some recent work has started investigating the potential of building dialogue systems that can help users efficiently explore data through visualizations (Kumar et al., 2017).

The problem of intent recognition or dialogue act detection has been extensively studied. Below we focus on recent work on dialogue act detection that employs deep learning. People have used recurrent neural networks (RNNs) including long short term memory networks (LSTMs), and CNNs (Kalchbrenner and Blunsom, 2013; Li and Wu, 2016; Khanpour et al., 2016; Shen and Lee, 2016; Ji et al., 2016; Tran et al., 2017). The works that are most similar to ours are by Lee and Dernoncourt (2016) and Ortega and Vu (2017) who compared LSTMs and CNNs on the same data sets. However, neither Lee and Dernoncourt (2016) nor Ortega and Vu (2017) experimented with incremental dialogue act detection as we do.

Regarding incrementality in dialogue, there has been a lot of work on predicting the next user action, generating fast system responses, and turn-taking (Schlangen et al., 2009; Schlangen and Skantze, 2011; Dethlefs et al., 2012; Baumann and Schlangen, 2013; Selfridge et al., 2013; Ghigi et al., 2014; Kim et al., 2014; Khouzaimi et al., 2015). Recently Skantze (2017) presented a general continuous model of turn-taking based on LSTMs. Most related to our work, DeVault et al. (2011) built models for incremental interpretation and prediction of utterance meaning, while Manuvinakurike et al. (2016b) and Petukhova and Bunt (2014) built models for incremental dialogue act recognition.

3 Data

We use a Wizard of Oz setup to collect a dialogue corpus in our image edit domain. The Wizard-user conversational session is set up over Skype and the conversation recorded on the Wizard's system. The screen share feature is enabled on the Wizard's screen so that the user can see in real time the changes requested. There are no time constraints, and the Wizard and the user can talk freely until the user is happy with the changes performed. Users may have varying levels of image editing expertise and knowledge of the image editing tool used during the interaction (Adobe Lightroom).

Each user is given 4–6 images and time to think of ways to edit them to make them look better. The conversation typically begins with the step called *image location*. The user describes the image in a unique manner so that it can be located in the library of photos by the Wizard. If the descriptions are not clear the Wizard can ask clarification questions. Once the image is located, the user conveys to the Wizard the changes they desire. The user and the Wizard have a conversation until the user is happy with the final outcome. In order to capture all the changes that the user wants to achieve in spoken language, the image editing tool is controlled only by the Wizard. Figure 4 in the Appendix shows the Adobe Lightroom interface as seen by the user and the Wizard. Note that users were not explicitly told that they would interact with another human and could not see who they interacted with because the Wizard and the user were in different locations. However, the naturalness of the conversation made it obvious that they were conversing with another human.

The photographs chosen for the study are sampled from the Visual Genome data set (Krishna et al., 2017). For the dialogue to be reflective of a real-world scenario the images sampled should be representative of the images regularly edited by the users. We sampled 200 photoshop requests from the Reddit Photoshop Request forum and Zhopped, and found that the images in those posts fell into eight high-level categories: animals, city scenes, food, nature/landscapes, indoor scenes, people, sports, and vehicles.

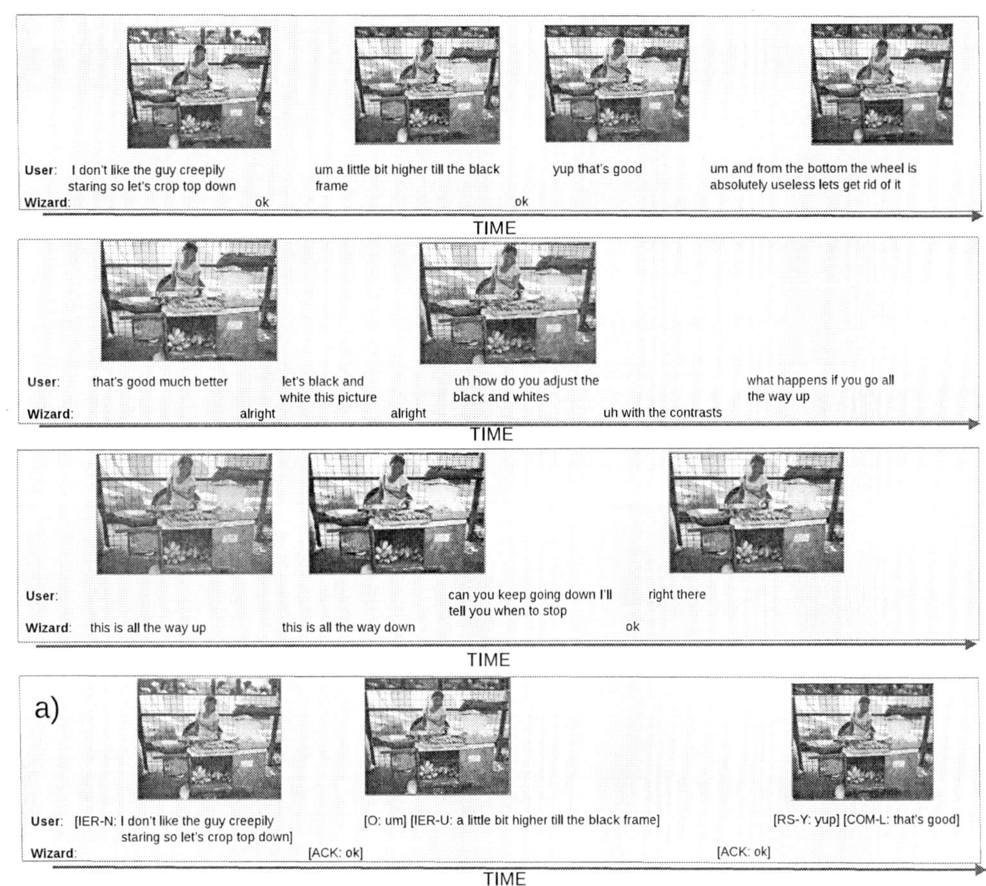

Figure 1: Example Wizard-user conversation. The user provides new requests, modifies the requests, provides feedback, and issues a high-level command. The Wizard responds with acknowledgments and provides a clarification. Figure 1a shows the annotation of the dialogue acts for the user utterances.

# users	28
# dialogues	129
# user utterances	8890
# Wizard utterances	4795
# time (raw)	858 min
# user tokens	59653
# user unique tokens	2299
# Wizard tokens	26284
# Wizard unique tokens	1310
# total unique tokens	2650

Table 1: Data statistics.

Figure 1 shows a sample conversation between the user and the Wizard, and Table 1 shows the statistics of the data. Details of the semantics of the conversation are discussed in Section 4. Each dialogue session ranges between 2–30 min (7 min on average). The dialogues were transcribed via crowdsourcing (Amazon Mechanical Turk). We intend to publicly release the data.

4 Dialogue Semantics

The data collected were annotated with dialogue acts. User utterances were segmented at the word level into utterance segments. An utterance is defined as a portion of speech preceded and/or followed by a silence interval greater than 300 msec. Each utterance segment was then assigned a dialogue act. The annotations were performed by two expert annotators. The inter-annotator agreement was measured by having our two annotators annotate the same dialogue session of 20 min, and kappa was found to be 0.81 which indicates high agreement. Below we describe briefly our dialogue act scheme.

Image Edit Requests: The most common dialogue acts used by the user are called "Image Edit Requests (IERs)". These are user requests concerning the changes to be made to the images. IERs are further categorized into 4 groups: IER-New (IER-N), IER-Update (IER-U), IER-Revert (IER-R), and IER-Compare (IER-C). IER-N requests refer to utterances that are concerned with new image edit requests different from the previously requested edits. These requested changes are either abstract ("it's flushed out, can you fix it?") or exact ("change the saturation to 20%"). The Wizard interprets these requests and performs the changes. IER-U labels are used for utterances that request updates to the previously mentioned IER-Ns. These include the addition of more details ("change it to 50%") to the IER-N ("change the saturation"), issuing corrections to the IER ("can you reduce the value again?"), modifiers (more, less), etc. If the users are completely unhappy with the change they can revert the change made (IER-R). The IER-R act is used if the user reverts the complete changes performed, compared to only changing the values. For example, if the user is modifying the saturation of the image and across multiple turns changes the value of saturation from 20% to 30% and back to 20%, the user's action is labeled as IER-U. If the user wants all the saturation changes to be undone, the user's action is labeled as IER-R. Users may also want to compare the changes made across different steps ("can we compare this to the previous update?"), and this action is labeled as IER-C.

Comments: Once the changes are performed the user is typically happy with the change and issues a comment that they like the edit (COM-L), or they are unhappy and issues a comment that they dislike the edit (COM-D). In some cases the users are neutral and neither like nor dislike the edit. Typically such utterances are comments on the images and are labeled as COM-I.

Requests & Responses: The user may ask the Wizard to provide suggestions on the IERs. These are labeled as "Request" acts. "Yes" and "no" responses uttered in response to the Wizard's suggestions are labeled as RS-Y or RS-N.

Suggestions: This is the most commonly used Wizard dialogue act after "Acknowledgments". When the user does not know what edits to perform, the Wizard issues suggestion utterances with the intention of providing the user with ideas about the changes that could be performed. The Wizard provides new suggestions (S-N), e.g., "do you want to change the sharpness on this image?". The Wizard could also provide update suggestions for the current request under consideration (S-U), e.g., "sharpness of about 50% was better".

Other user actions are labeled as questions about the features supported by the image editing tool, clarifications, greetings, and discourse markers. In total there are 26 dialogue act labels, including the dialogue act "Other (O)" which covers all of the cases that do not belong in the other categories. In this work we are interested in the task of understanding the user utterances only, and in particular, in classifying user utterances into one of 10 labels: IER-N, IER-U, IER-R, IER-C, RS-Y, RS-N, COM-L, COM-D, COM-I, and O.

An agent will eventually be developed to replace the Wizard, which means that the agent will need to interpret the user utterances. The task of understanding the user utterance happens in two phases. In the first step the goal is to identify the dialogue acts. The second step is to understand the user image edit requests IER-N and IER-U at a fine-grained level. For example, when the user says "make the tree brighter to 100", it is important to understand the exact user's intent and to translate this into an action that the image editing tool can perform. For this reason we use action-entities tuples $<$action, attribute, location/object, value$>$. The user utterances are mapped to dialogue acts and then to a pre-defined set of image action-entities tuples which are translated into image editing actions. For more information on our annotation framework for mapping IERs to actionable commands see Manuvinakurike et al. (2018). It is beyond the scope of this work to perform the image editing and we intend to pursue this in future work. Table 2 shows an example of the process of understanding the image edit requests.

5   Incrementality

Table 3 shows example utterances for some of the most frequently occurring dialogue acts in the corpus. In these examples it can be seen that, with the exception of 3, all the other dialogue acts can be identified with some degree of certainty without waiting for the user to complete the utterance. Also, Figure 5 in the Appendix shows example IERs. One of the motivations for our work is to identify the right dialogue act at the earliest time.

Utterance	Segments	Dialogue Act	Action	Attribute	Location Object	Value
uh make the tree brighter <sil> to like a 100 <sil> nope too much 50 please	uh	O	-	-	-	-
	make the tree brighter	IER-N	Adjust	brightness	tree	-
	to like a 100	IER-U	Adjust	brightness	tree	100
	nope too much	COM-D	-	-	-	-
	50 please	IER-U	Adjust	brightness	tree	50
perfect <sil> let's work on sharpness	perfect	COM-L	-	-	-	-
	let's work on sharpness	IER-N	Adjust	sharpness	-	-

Table 2: Examples of commonly occurring dialogue acts, actions, and entities.

	Utterance	Tag
1	add a vignette since it's also encircled better	IER-N
2	can we go down to fifteen on that	IER-U
3	go back to .5	IER-U
4	actually let's revert back	IER-R
5	can you compare for me before and after	IER-C
6	I like it leave it there please	COM-L
7	no I don't like this color	COM-D

Table 3: Examples of some of the most commonly occurring dialogue acts in our corpus.

Not only is this more efficient but also more natural. The human Wizard can begin to take action even before the utterance completion, e.g., in utterance 1 the Wizard clicks the "vignette" feature in the tool before the user has finished uttering their request. Another goal is to measure potential savings in time gained through incremental processing, i.e., how much we save in terms of number of words when we identify the dialogue act earlier rather than waiting until the full completion of the utterance, without sacrificing performance.

6 Model Design

For our experiments we use a training set sampled randomly from 90% of the users (116 dialogues for training, 13 dialogues for testing). We use word embedding features whose construction is described in Section 6.1. There are several reasons for using word embeddings as features, e.g., unseen words have a meaningful representation and provide dimensionality reduction.[3]

<hr>

[3]Figure 6 shows the visual presentation of the utterances embeddings using t-SNE (Maaten and Hinton, 2008).

6.1 Constructing Word Embeddings

We convert the words into vector representations to train our deep learning models (and a variation of the random forests). We use out-of-the-box word vectors available in the form of GloVe embeddings (Pennington et al., 2014) (trained with Wikipedia data), or we employ fastText (Bojanowski et al., 2017) to construct embeddings using the data from the Visual Genome image region description phrases, the dialogue training set collected during this experiment, and other data related to image editing that we have collected (image edit requests out of a dialogue context). From now on these embeddings trained with fastText will be referred to as "trained embeddings".

As we can see in Table 4, for models E (LSTMs) and I (CNNs) we use word embeddings trained with fastText on the aforementioned data sets. The Vanilla LSTM (model D) does not use GloVe or trained embeddings, i.e., there is no dimensionality reduction. Model H (CNN) uses GloVe embeddings. The vectors used in this work (both GloVe and trained embeddings) have a dimension of 50. For trained embeddings, the vectors were constructed using skipgrams over 50 epochs with a learning rate of 0.5.

Recent advancements in creating a vector representation for a sentence were also evaluated. We used the Sent2Vec (Pagliardini et al., 2018) toolkit to get a vector representation of the sentence and then used these vectors as features for models G and J. Note that LSTMs are sequential models where every word needs a vector representation and thus we could not use Sent2Vec.

6.2 Model Construction

We use WEKA (Hall et al., 2009) for the Naive Bayes and Random Forest models, MALLET

	Model	Accur
A	Baseline (Majority) *	0.32
B	Naive Bayes *	0.41
C	Conditional Random Field *	0.51
D	LSTM (Vanilla) *	0.53
E	LSTM (trained word embeddings) *	0.55
F	Random Forest *	0.72
G	Random Forest (with Sent2Vec)	0.73
H	CNN (GloVe embeddings)	0.73
I	CNN (trained word embeddings)	0.74
J	CNN (Sent2Vec)	0.74

Table 4: Dialogue act classification results for perfect segmentation. * indicates significant difference ($p < 0.05$) between the best performing models (I and J) and the other models.

(McCallum, 2002) for the CRF model (linear chain), and TensorFlow (Abadi et al., 2016) for the LSTM and CNN models. The models B, C, D, and F in Table 4 use bag-of-words features. The CNN has 2 layers, with the first layer containing 512 filters and the second layer 256 filters. Both layers have a kernel size of 10 and use ReLU activation. The layers are separated by a max pooling layer with a pool size of 10. The dense softmax is the final layer. We use the Adam optimizer with the categorical cross entropy loss function. The LSTM cell is made up of 2 hidden layers. We use a dropout with keep_prob = 0.1. We put the logits from the last time steps through the softmax to get the prediction. We use the same optimizer and loss function as for the CNN since they were found to be the best performing.

Table 4 shows the dialogue act classification accuracy for all models on our test set. Here we assume that we have the correct utterance segmentation for both the training and the test data. Note that because of the "Other" dialogue act all words in a sentence will belong to a segment and a dialogue act category. We hypothesize that the poor performance of the sequential models (CRF and LSTM) is due to the lack of adequate training data to capture large context dependencies.

6.3 Incrementality

Table 5 shows the savings in terms of overall number of words and average number of words saved

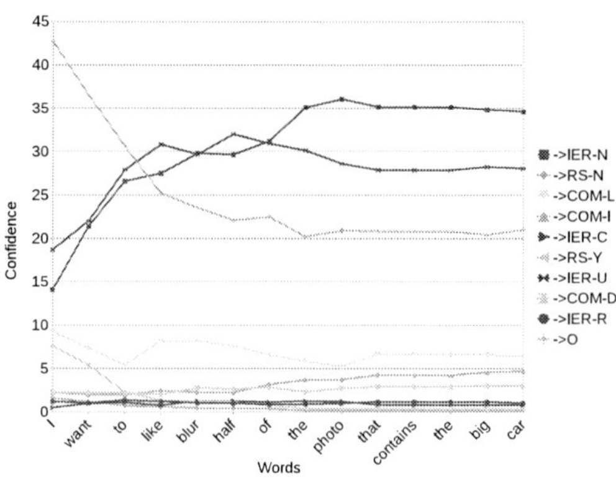

Figure 2: Confidence contours based on every word. The correct tag is IER-N. The confidence contours at the word level take time to stabilize.

per sentence, for each dialogue act in the corpus.

Figure 2 shows the confidence curves for predicting the dialogue act with the progression of every word. From this figure it is clear that after listening to the word "photo" the classifier is confident enough that the user is issuing the IER-N command. Here the notion of incrementality is to predict the right dialogue act as early as possible and evaluate the savings in terms of the number of words. While from this example it is clear that the correct dialogue act can be identified before the user completes the utterance, it is not clear when to commit to a dialogue act. The trade-off involved in committing early is often not clear. Table 5 shows the maximum savings that can be achieved in an ideal scenario where an oracle (an entity informing if the prediction is correct or wrong as soon as the prediction is made) identifies the earliest point of predicting the correct dialogue act.

The method used for calculating the savings is shown in Table 6. In this example for the utterance "I think that's good enough", we feed the classifier the utterances one word at a time and get the classifier confidence. The class label with the highest score is obtained. Here the oracle tells us that we could predict the correct class COM-L as soon as "I think that's good" was uttered and thus the word savings would be 1 word.

However, in real-world scenarios the oracle is not present. We use several confidence thresholds and measure the accuracy and the savings achieved in predicting the dialogue act without the oracle. For the predictions in the test set we get the accuracy for each of the thresholds. Then if the

Tag	% Overall Word Savings	Average Word Savings per Utterance
IER-N	37	3.96
IER-U	39	2.72
IER-R	41	1.63
IER-C	40	1.69
COM-L	36	1.13
COM-D	41	1.38
COM-I	37	2.56
RS-Y	28	0.34
RS-N	37	0.69
O	47	3.95

Table 5: Percentage of overall word savings and average number of words saved per utterance, for each dialogue act.

Utterance	Max conf	Class
I	0.2	O
I think	0.3	O
I think that's	0.3	O
I think that's good	**0.5**	**COM-L**
I think that's good enough	**0.5**	**COM-L**

Table 6: Example incremental prediction. The correct label is COM-L. Columns 2 and 3 show the maximum confidence level and model prediction after each word is uttered.

predictions are correct, we calculate the savings. Thus Figure 3 shows the word savings for each confidence threshold when the predictions are correct for that threshold.

So in the example of Table 6, for a confidence threshold value of 0.4, we extract the class label assigned for the utterance once the max confidence score exceeds 0.4. In this case once the word "good" was uttered by the user the confidence score assigned (0.5) was higher than the threshold value of 0.4 and we take the predicted class as COM-L. The word savings in this case is 1 word and our prediction is correct. But for a confidence threshold value of 0.2, our prediction would be the tag O which would be wrong and there would be no time savings. Figure 3 shows that as the confidence threshold values increase the accuracy of the predictions rises but the savings decrease.

Researchers have used simulations (Paetzel et al., 2015) or a reinforcement learning policy (Manuvinakurike et al., 2017) to learn the right

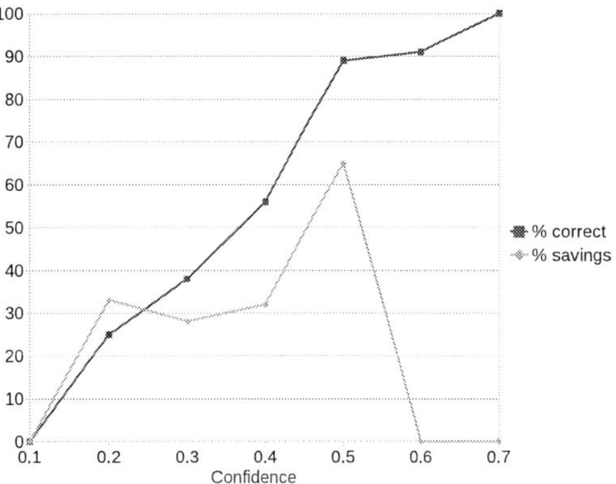

Figure 3: % savings (for correct predictions) and accuracy (% correct) of incremental predictions of dialogue acts as a function of confidence level.

points of interrupting the user which are dependent on the language understanding confidence scores. Here we do not focus on learning such policies. Instead, our work is a precursor to learning an incremental system dialogue policy.

7 Conclusion

We presented "conversational image editing", a novel real-world application domain, which combines dialogue, visual information, and the use of computer vision. We discussed why this is a domain particularly well suited for incremental dialogue processing. We built models for incremental intent identification based on deep learning and traditional classification algorithms. We calculated the impact of varying confidence thresholds (above which the classifier's prediction is considered) on classification accuracy and savings in terms of number of words. Our experiments provided evidence that incremental intent processing could be more efficient for the user and save time in accomplishing tasks.

Acknowledgments

This work was supported by a generous gift of Adobe Systems Incorporated to USC/ICT, and the first author's internship at Adobe Research. The first and last authors were also funded by the U.S. Army Research Laboratory. Statements and opinions expressed do not necessarily reflect the position or policy of the U.S. Government, and no official endorsement should be inferred.

References

Martín Abadi, Paul Barham, Jianmin Chen, Zhifeng Chen, Andy Davis, Jeffrey Dean, Matthieu Devin, Sanjay Ghemawat, Geoffrey Irving, Michael Isard, Manjunath Kudlur, Josh Levenberg, Rajat Monga, Sherry Moore, Derek G. Murray, Benoit Steiner, Paul Tucker, Vijay Vasudevan, Pete Warden, Martin Wicke, Wuan Yu, and Xiaoqiang Zheng. 2016. TensorFlow: A system for large-scale machine learning. In *Proceedings of the 12th USENIX Symposium on Operating Systems Design and Implementation*, Savannah, Georgia, USA.

Stanislaw Antol, Aishwarya Agrawal, Jiasen Lu, Margaret Mitchell, Dhruv Batra, C. Lawrence Zitnick, and Devi Parikh. 2015. VQA: Visual Question Answering. In *Proceedings of ICCV*, Santiago, Chile.

Timo Baumann and David Schlangen. 2013. Openended, extensible system utterances are preferred, even if they require filled pauses. In *Proceedings of SIGDIAL*, Metz, France.

Piotr Bojanowski, Edouard Grave, Armand Joulin, and Tomas Mikolov. 2017. Enriching word vectors with subword information. *Transactions of the Association for Computational Linguistics*, 5:135–146.

Abhishek Das, Satwik Kottur, Khushi Gupta, Avi Singh, Deshraj Yadav, José M. F. Moura, Devi Parikh, and Dhruv Batra. 2017. Visual dialog. In *Proceedings of CVPR*, Honolulu, Hawaii, USA.

Nina Dethlefs, Helen Hastie, Verena Rieser, and Oliver Lemon. 2012. Optimising incremental dialogue decisions using information density for interactive systems. In *Proceedings of EMNLP–CoNLL*, Jeju Island, Korea.

David DeVault, Kenji Sagae, and David Traum. 2011. Incremental interpretation and prediction of utterance meaning for interactive dialogue. *Dialogue and Discourse*, 2(1):143–170.

Yansong Feng and Mirella Lapata. 2013. Automatic caption generation for news images. *IEEE Transactions on Pattern Analysis and Machine Intelligence*, 35(4):797–812.

Fabrizio Ghigi, Maxine Eskenazi, M. Ines Torres, and Sungjin Lee. 2014. Incremental dialog processing in a task-oriented dialog. In *Proceedings of INTERSPEECH*, Singapore.

Mark Hall, Eibe Frank, Geoffrey Holmes, Bernhard Pfahringer, Peter Reutemann, and Ian H Witten. 2009. The WEKA data mining software: An update. *ACM SIGKDD Explorations Newsletter*, 11(1):10–18.

Ting-Hao (Kenneth) Huang, Francis Ferraro, Nasrin Mostafazadeh, Ishan Misra, Aishwarya Agrawal, Jacob Devlin, Ross Girshick, Xiaodong He, Pushmeet Kohli, Dhruv Batra, C. Lawrence Zitnick, Devi Parikh, Lucy Vanderwende, Michel Galley, and Margaret Mitchell. 2016. Visual storytelling. In *Proceedings of NAACL–HLT*, San Diego, California, USA.

Yangfeng Ji, Gholamreza Haffari, and Jacob Eisenstein. 2016. A latent variable recurrent neural network for discourse relation language models. In *Proceedings of NAACL–HLT*, San Diego, California, USA.

Nal Kalchbrenner and Phil Blunsom. 2013. Recurrent convolutional neural networks for discourse compositionality. In *Proceedings of the ACL Workshop on Continuous Vector Space Models and their Compositionality*, Sofia, Bulgaria.

Casey Kennington and David Schlangen. 2015. Simple learning and compositional application of perceptually grounded word meanings for incremental reference resolution. In *Proceedings of ACL*, Beijing, China.

Hamed Khanpour, Nishitha Guntakandla, and Rodney Nielsen. 2016. Dialogue act classification in domain-independent conversations using a deep recurrent neural network. In *Proceedings of COLING*, Osaka, Japan.

Hatim Khouzaimi, Romain Laroche, and Fabrice Lefèvre. 2015. Optimising turn-taking strategies with reinforcement learning. In *Proceedings of SIGDIAL*, Prague, Czech Republic.

Dongho Kim, Catherine Breslin, Pirros Tsiakoulis, Milica Gašić, Matthew Henderson, and Steve Young. 2014. Inverse reinforcement learning for micro-turn management. In *Proceedings of INTERSPEECH*, Singapore.

Ranjay Krishna, Yuke Zhu, Oliver Groth, Justin Johnson, Kenji Hata, Joshua Kravitz, Stephanie Chen, Yannis Kalantidis, Li-Jia Li, David A. Shamma, Michael Bernstein, and Li Fei-Fei. 2017. Visual Genome: Connecting language and vision using crowdsourced dense image annotations. *International Journal of Computer Vision*, 123:32–73.

Alex Krizhevsky, Ilya Sutskever, and Geoffrey E. Hinton. 2012. ImageNet classification with deep convolutional neural networks. In *Proceedings of NIPS*, Lake Tahoe, Nevada, USA.

Girish Kulkarni, Visruth Premraj, Vicente Ordonez, Sagnik Dhar, Siming Li, Yejin Choi, Alexander C. Berg, and Tamara L. Berg. 2013. Babytalk: Understanding and generating simple image descriptions. *IEEE Transactions on Pattern Analysis and Machine Intelligence*, 35(12):2891–2903.

Abhinav Kumar, Barbara Di Eugenio, Jillian Aurisano, Andrew Johnson, Abeer Alsaiari, Nigel Flowers, Alberto Gonzalez, and Jason Leigh. 2017. Towards multimodal coreference resolution for exploratory data visualization dialogue: Context-based annotation and gesture identification. In *Proceedings of SemDial*, Saarbrücken, Germany.

Ji Young Lee and Franck Dernoncourt. 2016. Sequential short-text classification with recurrent and convolutional neural networks. In *Proceedings of NAACL–HLT*, San Diego, California, USA.

Wei Li and Yunfang Wu. 2016. Multi-level gated recurrent neural network for dialog act classification. In *Proceedings of COLING*, Osaka, Japan.

Tsung-Yi Lin, Michael Maire, Serge Belongie, James Hays, Pietro Perona, Deva Ramanan, Piotr Dollár, and C. Lawrence Zitnick. 2014. Microsoft COCO: Common objects in context. In *Proceedings of the European Conference on Computer Vision*, Zurich, Switzerland.

Laurens van der Maaten and Geoffrey Hinton. 2008. Visualizing data using t-SNE. *Journal of Machine Learning Research*, 9(Nov):2579–2605.

Ramesh Manuvinakurike, Jacqueline Brixey, Trung Bui, Walter Chang, Doo Soon Kim, Ron Artstein, and Kallirroi Georgila. 2018. Edit me: A corpus and a framework for understanding natural language image editing. In *Proceedings of LREC*, Miyazaki, Japan.

Ramesh Manuvinakurike, David DeVault, and Kallirroi Georgila. 2017. Using reinforcement learning to model incrementality in a fast-paced dialogue game. In *Proceedings of SIGDIAL*, Saarbrücken, Germany.

Ramesh Manuvinakurike, Casey Kennington, David DeVault, and David Schlangen. 2016a. Real-time understanding of complex discriminative scene descriptions. In *Proceedings of SIGDIAL*, Los Angeles, California, USA.

Ramesh Manuvinakurike, Maike Paetzel, Cheng Qu, David Schlangen, and David DeVault. 2016b. Toward incremental dialogue act segmentation in fast-paced interactive dialogue systems. In *Proceedings of SIGDIAL*, Los Angeles, California, USA.

Andrew Kachites McCallum. 2002. MALLET: A machine learning for language toolkit. http://mallet.cs.umass.edu.

Margaret Mitchell, Jesse Dodge, Amit Goyal, Kota Yamaguchi, Karl Stratos, Xufeng Han, Alyssa Mensch, Alex Berg, Tamara Berg, and Hal Daumé III. 2012. Midge: Generating image descriptions from computer vision detections. In *Proceedings of EACL*, Avignon, France.

Nasrin Mostafazadeh, Chris Brockett, Bill Dolan, Michel Galley, Jianfeng Gao, Georgios Spithourakis, and Lucy Vanderwende. 2017. Image-grounded conversations: Multimodal context for natural question and response generation. In *Proceedings of IJCNLP*, Taipei, Taiwan.

Nasrin Mostafazadeh, Ishan Misra, Jacob Devlin, Margaret Mitchell, Xiaodong He, and Lucy Vanderwende. 2016. Generating natural questions about an image. In *Proceedings of ACL*, Berlin, Germany.

Daniel Ortega and Ngoc Thang Vu. 2017. Neural-based context representation learning for dialog act classification. In *Proceedings of SIGDIAL*, Saarbrücken, Germany.

Maike Paetzel, Ramesh Manuvinakurike, and David DeVault. 2015. "So, which one is it?" The effect of alternative incremental architectures in a high-performance game-playing agent. In *Proceedings of SIGDIAL*, Prague, Czech Republic.

Matteo Pagliardini, Prakhar Gupta, and Martin Jaggi. 2018. Unsupervised learning of sentence embeddings using compositional n-gram features. In *Proceedings of NAACL–HLT*, New Orleans, Louisiana, USA.

Jeffrey Pennington, Richard Socher, and Christopher Manning. 2014. Glove: Global vectors for word representation. In *Proceedings of EMNLP*, Doha, Qatar.

Volha Petukhova and Harry Bunt. 2014. Incremental recognition and prediction of dialogue acts. In *Computing Meaning*, pages 235–256. Springer.

David Schlangen, Timo Baumann, and Michaela Atterer. 2009. Incremental reference resolution: The task, metrics for evaluation, and a Bayesian filtering model that is sensitive to disfluencies. In *Proceedings of SIGDIAL*, London, UK.

David Schlangen and Gabriel Skantze. 2011. A general, abstract model of incremental dialogue processing. *Dialogue and Discourse*, 2(1):83–111.

Ethan Selfridge, Iker Arizmendi, Peter Heeman, and Jason Williams. 2013. Continuously predicting and processing barge-in during a live spoken dialogue task. In *Proceedings of SIGDIAL*, Metz, France.

Sheng-syun Shen and Hung-yi Lee. 2016. Neural attention models for sequence classification: Analysis and application to key term extraction and dialogue act detection. In *arXiv preprint arXiv:1604.00077*.

Gabriel Skantze. 2017. Towards a general continuous model of turn-taking in spoken dialogue using LSTM recurrent neural networks. In *Proceedings of SIGDIAL*, Saarbrücken, Germany.

Quan Hung Tran, Ingrid Zukerman, and Gholamreza Haffari. 2017. A generative attentional neural network model for dialogue act classification. In *Proceedings of ACL – Short Papers*, Vancouver, Canada.

Harm de Vries, Florian Strub, Sarath Chandar, Olivier Pietquin, Hugo Larochelle, and Aaron Courville. 2017. GuessWhat?! visual object discovery through multi-modal dialogue. In *Proceedings of CVPR*, Honolulu, Hawaii, USA.

Benjamin Z. Yao, Xiong Yang, Liang Lin, Mun Wai Lee, and Song-Chun Zhu. 2010. I2T: Image parsing to text description. *Proceedings of the IEEE*, 98(8):1485–1508.

Figure 4: The interface as seen by the user and the Wizard. We use Adobe Lightroom as the image editing program.

Tag	User Edit Requests
IER-N	I want to um add more focus on the boat
IER-N	can you make the water uh nicer color
IER-N	uh can we crop out uh little bit off the bottom
IER-N	is there a way to add more clarity
IER-N	can we adjust the shadows
IER-U	more [saturation]
IER-U	can we get rid of the hints of green in it
IER-U	bluer
IER-U	little bit more from the left [crop]
IER-R	can you unfocus it
IER-C	can you show me before and after

Figure 5: Example user edit requests. Only two bounding boxes are labeled in the image for better reading. The actual images have more extensive object labels.

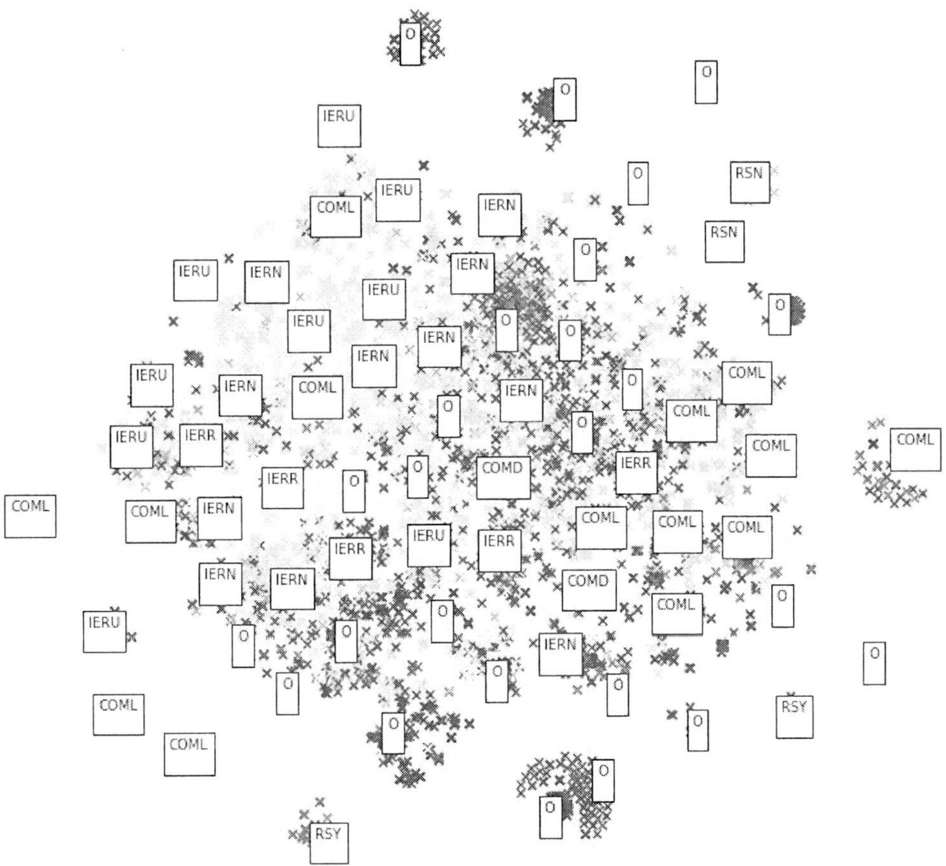

Figure 6: Visualization of the sentence embeddings of the user utterances used for training. The t-SNE visualizations after half-way through the utterances are shown. The utterances that have the same dialogue acts can be seen grouping together. This shows that the complete utterance is not always needed to identify the correct dialogue act.

Fine-Grained Discourse Structures in Continuation Semantics

Timothée Bernard
Laboratoire de linguistique formelle / Université Paris Diderot-Paris 7
Sémagramme / Inria Nancy - Grand Est
`timothee.bernard@ens-lyon.org`

Abstract

In this work, we are interested in the computation of logical representations of discourse. We argue that all discourse connectives are anaphors obeying different sets of constraints and show how this view allows one to account for the semantically parenthetical use of attitude verbs and verbs of report (e.g., *think*, *say*) and for sequences of conjunctions ($A \, CONJ_1 \, B \, CONJ_2 \, C$). We implement this proposal in event semantics using de Groote (2006)'s dynamic framework.

1 Introduction

The aim of a theory of discourse such as Rhetorical Structure Theory (RST, Mann and Thompson 1988) or Segmented Discourse Representation Theory (SDRT, Asher and Lascarides 2003) is to explain the structure of text beyond the sentence level, usually through a set of *discourse relations* (DRs; e.g., *Explanation, Elaboration, Contrast*).[1] This structure is not only of theoretical interest but has also proved valuable for several Natural Language Processing (NLP) and Computational Linguistics (CL) applications, such as Question Answering (Narasimhan and Barzilay, 2015; Jansen et al., 2014) or Machine Translation (Guzmán et al., 2014; Tu et al., 2014).

The vast majority of the NLP and CL world relies on statistical rather that symbolic methods. Yet, logic-based systems, which are closer to the linguistic theories, can be a viable alternative, especially for inference-related problems (Bos and Markert, 2005; Bjerva et al., 2014; Abzianidze,

2015). That is the direction we advocate for; grounded in the fields of formal grammar and formal semantics, we are interested in the computation of logical representations of discourse. Following Asher and Pogodalla (2011); Qian and Amblard (2011), we argue that it is not necessary to extends syntax beyond the sentence level, as a dynamic framework such as the one presented by de Groote (2006) and based on *continuation semantics*, allows one to handle discourse relations with a traditional lexicalized grammar.

In particular, this paper shows how a system of anaphora resolution—independently required for the interpretation of pronouns (*she, it*) and discourse adverbials (*then, otherwise*)—along with an appropriate representation of propositional attitude verbs and verbs of report (AVs, e.g., *think, say*) can be used to account for the *non-alignment between syntactic and discourse arguments* (Dinesh et al., 2005; Hunter and Danlos, 2014) observed for instance in (1).[2] In these discourses, although the AV with its subject (*Jane said*) is part of the syntactical arguments of the connectives, it is not considered part of the corresponding discourse arguments and is said to be *evidential*. Evidential status impacts, among other things, the inferences that can be drawn, in particular on the beliefs of the author (Danlos and Rambow, 2011; Hunter, 2016; Hunter and Asher, forthcoming).

(1)   (from Hunter and Danlos 2014)

     a.   *John didn't come to the party* <u>although</u> Jane said **he was back in town**.

     b.   *Lots of people are coming to my party.*

---

[1] DRs appear inter-sententially, e.g., *Consequence* in *Mary did not sleep well yesterday. So, she is tired*, but also intra-sententially, e.g., *Explanation* in *Mary is tired, because she did not sleep well*.

[2] Following the notation convention of the Penn Discourse Treebank (PDTB, Prasad et al. 2007), the two arguments of relevant discourse relations—named "Arg_1" and "Arg_2"—are shown in italic and bold, while the connectives lexicalizing them, if any, are underlined.

Proceedings of the SIGDIAL 2018 Conference, pages 296–305,
Melbourne, Australia, 12-14 July 2018. ©2018 Association for Computational Linguistics

Jane said, for example, that **Fred is coming with his whole family**.

This article is organized as follows. In Section 2, we present the anaphoric character of adverbial connectives. In Section 3, we start by reviewing the notion of (semantically) parenthetical report—a category that subsumes evidential reports—and we highlight its relation with discourse connectives. Next, we sketch our main contribution, namely that parenthetical reports can be modeled by assuming that *all* connectives behave anaphorically, even though different classes of connectives obey different sets of constraints. These ideas are implemented formally using continuation semantics in Section 4. In Section 5, we discuss related work and Section 6 concludes the article.

2 Adverbial connectives as anaphors

In English, using a discourse connective—a word that lexicalizes a DR, such as *although* and *for example* in (1) above—is the most direct and reliable way to express a DR. The three main categories of discourse connectives are COORDINATE CONJUNCTIONS (e.g., *and, or*), SUBORDINATE CONJUNCTIONS (e.g., *because, although*) and ADVERBIALS (e.g., *for example, otherwise*). Webber et al. (2003) argue that in contrast with the first two types, jointly called "structural connectives", adverbials are interpreted *anaphorically*. In other words, the arguments of adverbials cannot be determined by syntax alone (nor an extension of syntax using similar notions of dependency or constituency) and are found in or derived from the context in a similar fashion as the antecedents of nominal anaphoric expressions (e.g., *she*).

While Webber et al. (2003); Webber (2004) outline D-LTAG, a discourse grammar incorporating anaphoric elements for adverbial connectives, nothing is said about the resolution of the anaphors. In contrast, our approach considers a traditional lexicalized sentence-level grammar such as Combinatorial Categorial Grammar (CCG, Steedman and Baldridge 2011), a formalism for which parsing is an active research topic (Lewis et al., 2016; Ambati et al., 2016), and we focus here on the semantic part of the lexicon, embedding explicitly the anaphoric process in the computation of the semantics of the discourse. In addition, we will see in the next section that considering that structural connectives do sometime behave anaphorically too accounts for

(non-)parenthetical reports in a simple way.

3 Parenthetical reports

3.1 Intensionality and evidentiality

It was observed in Urmson (1952) that some verbs, called *parentheticals*, can have a special meaning when used with the first person of the present simple. In these cases, the verb is not used primarily to describe an event or a state, but rather to indicate "the emotional significance, the logical relevance or the reliability" of a statement. As an illustration, Urmson (1952) provides sentences in (2), in which *I suppose* is used to signal a certain degree of reliability (low or moderate) of the speaker's opinion.[3]

(2)   a.   I suppose that your house is very old.
       b.   Your house, I suppose, is very old.
       c.   Your house is very old, I suppose.

It appears that this behaviour is not limited to the first person present. Indeed, Simons (2007) cites dialogue (3) as an example, where *Henry thinks that* is described as an *evidential*, indicating the source of its complement (*she's left town*), which is the main point of the sentence. This evidential use is opposed to the traditional non-parenthetical (or *intensional*) use, for which the AV carries the main point of the sentence as in (4) (also from Simons 2007).[4]   Only when *Henry thinks that* is interpreted as evidential can (3b) be accepted as a valid answer to (3a). Things are similar with monologue; in (5) (from Hunter and Danlos 2014), the evidential use of *Jane said* allows *he is out of town* to be argument of an implicit *Explanation* relation.[5]

(3)   a.   *Why isn't Louise coming to our meetings these days?*
       b.   Henry thinks that **she's left town**.

(4)   a.   *Why didn't Henry invite Louise to the party?*
       b.   **He thinks that she's left town.**

---

[3]The name "parenthetical" comes from the syntactic possibility of the sentence-medial (2b) and sentence-final (2c) positions. In all sentences of (2), the verb plays the same role and is said to be *semantically parenthetical*.

[4]Although they can serve another discourse function, AVs used parenthetically are very often evidential. As, in addition, our proposal presented below in Section 3.3 applies equally to all semantically parenthetical uses, we will use the two terms interchangeably in the remaining of this article.

[5]A DR is *implicit* when it is not lexically marked by a connective such as *because* but inferred at a sentence boundary.

(5) *Fred didn't come to my party.* Jane said **he is out of town.**

The ability to account for both uses of AVs is of theoretical and practical interest. First, one might expect an efficient NLP system to be able to make the difference between, for instance, cases where a report is given as an explanation (as in (4)) and cases where the explanation is only the object of the report (as in (3) or (5)). Also, propositions reported by an evidential are interpreted as, if not true, at least possibly true, information that is valuable for reasoning systems. According to Hunter (2016); Hunter and Asher (forthcoming), parenthetical reports are related to modal (or *hedged*) DRs: the *Explanation* in (5) is modalized ($\diamond Explanation$) and entails (at least) the possibility of both of its arguments. While they focus on implicit DRs, they seem to extend their claim to explicit ones, such as (6) (or (1) above). According to Danlos and Rambow (2011), however, the relation in (6) is not hedged and a strong *revision of propositional attitude* occurs: one infers that the speaker agrees with Jill's report.

(6) *John didnt come to the party.* <u>Instead,</u> Jill said that **he went to dinner with his brother.** (from Hunter and Asher forthcoming)

This last question seems hard to settle without conducting a proper experiment on native speakers and is out of the scope of the present article, which aims at modelling through anaphorlike properties of connectives how DRs receive their arguments and how this process gives rise to (non-)parenthetical interpretations of AVs. Therefore, we will not here take stance on the matter but instead explain how both views can be accommodated within our proposal.

3.2 Two classes of explicit connectives

Hunter and Danlos (2014) argue that some connectives, such as *because*, restrict the reports in their scope to the intensional interpretation, while others, such as *for example* or *although*, behave like the implicit connective in (5). In this example, while an implicit *because* is perfectly fine and lead to an evidential interpretation of the report, the use of an explicit connective is not compatible with the evidential interpretation (7a).[6] Only an

intensional interpretation could be accepted: however in this particular case (7b), it corresponds to a very unnatural reading. *For example*, on the contrary, does not suffer from the same limitations (8): the explicit connective is compatible with the evidential interpretation (8b).

(7) a. **Fred didn't come to my party* <u>because</u> Jane said **he is out of town.**

    b. #*Fred didn't come to my party* <u>because</u> **Jane said he is out of town.**

(8) *Lots of people are coming to my party.*

    a. Jane said that **Fred is coming with his whole family.**

    b. <u>For example</u>, Jane said that **Fred is coming with his whole family.**

Independently, Haegeman (2004) argues that adverbial clauses (i.e., subordinate clauses that function as adverbs) are composed of two classes: *central* adverbial clauses and *peripheral* ones. Several syntactic and semantic phenomena distinguish between them; in particular, negation and modal operators present in a matrix clause can also scope over a central clause as in (9), which can either mean that the rain makes Fred happy or that Fred is sad for a reason other than the rain. On the other hand, such elements cannot scope over a peripheral one, as illustrated by (10), which unambiguously expresses a contrast between Fred's happiness and the rain. It appears that all the subordinate conjunctions allowing parenthetical reports mentioned by Hunter and Danlos (2014) introduce peripheral clauses while the ones that do not allow them all introduce central clauses. We think that this is no coincidence and will thus call "central" the connectives that allow parenthetical reports and "peripheral" the ones that do not.[7]

(9) Fred is not sad <u>because</u> **it is raining.**

(10) *Fred is not sad* <u>although</u> **it is raining.**

The non-alignment between syntactic and discourse arguments resulting from the parenthetical use of AVs is in no way exceptional.[8] Us-

---

while a "#" indicates a semantically rejected one.

[7] Some ambiguous connectives can introduce both type of adverbial clauses. For instance, *while* is central when used temporally and peripheral when used contrastively.

[8] The term "non-alignment"—or sometimes "mismatch" (Prasad et al., 2008)—is used to describe a DR *Rel* lexicalized by a connective *CONN* such that the (discourse) arguments of the former do not directly correspond to the (syntactic) arguments of the latter.

ing the PDTB Browser[9], we have calculated that in the PDTB, 12.7% of the all explicit relations attributed to the writer have at least one of their arguments attributed to another agent, principally due to the use of an evidential. This proportion is even higher (26.9%) for implicit relations, which most of the time (98.0%) can be accounted for *via* an implicit (i.e., morphologically empty) adverbial connectives at the beginning of a clause or sentence (Prasad et al., 2008).

3.3 Evidentiality and anaphora

Consider a sentence of the form *A CONN Jane says X* and label e_A the propositional content of *A*, e_B the content of *Jane says X*, e' the content of the report *X* and e the content of the full sentence. We propose that no connectives are really fully structural, but all behave anaphorically, in the sense that their discourse arguments are not determined by syntax alone. In consequence, these discourse arguments are not necessarily the propositional contents of their syntactic arguments (in this case e_A and e_B respectively). However, these anaphors are constrained by a few rules. The first one applies to all connectives: a discourse argument must have been introduced by the corresponding syntactic argument (in this case, e_A is the only candidate for Arg_1, but both e_B and e' are candidates for Arg_2). The second applies only to central connectives: these cannot "decompose" a clause headed by an AV to access the report (here, for instance, e') but have to stop at the AV itself (here e_B). A third rule is introduced at the end of the section.

This explains why the two sentences in (11) are acceptable: *although*, a peripheral connective, has access to both e_B and e' which can be selected as Arg_2 depending on their semantics.[10] In contrast, *because* is central and so in the present configuration uses necessarily e_B for Arg_2; in consequence, the AV is always interpreted intentionally, which

predicts the acceptability of (12a) and the incoherence (in most contexts) of (12b).

(11)   a.   *Fred came*$_{e_A}$ <u>although$_e$</u> **Sabine said$_{e_B}$ she hated$_{e'}$ him**.

       b.   *Fred came*$_{e_A}$ <u>although$_e$</u> Sabine says$_{e_B}$ **he was sick$_{e'}$**.

(12)   a.   *Fred came*$_{e_A}$ <u>because$_e$</u> **Sabine said$_{e_B}$ she liked$_{e'}$ him**.

       b.   # *Fred came*$_{e_A}$ <u>because$_e$</u> **Sabine says$_{e_B}$ he had recovered$_{e'}$**.

We propose that a third constraint applies to all connectives: when its syntactic argument contains a conjunction, a connective is able to decompose it to access the matrix clause, as in (13b), but not the embedded one. This constraint disambiguates between the two possible bracketings of *A CONJ$_1$ B CONJ$_2$ C* structures: when the Arg_1 of the relation lexicalized by *CONJ$_2$* is the content of either *A* or the whole *A CONJ$_1$ B* then the bracketing is as in (13), when instead this Arg_1 is the content of *B*, then the bracketing is as in (14).

(13)   a.   [*Fred played music while Sabine was taking a nap*] <u>because</u> **he wanted to annoy her**.

       b.   [*Fred washed the dishes* while Sabine was taking a nap] <u>because</u> **he wanted to be nice to her**.

(14)   Fred broke his arm because [*he fell* <u>because</u> **he was drunk**].

This idea of handling connectives as restricted anaphors can probably be put in practice in various ways; in the remainder of this article we have chosen to implement it in a logical system based on λ-calculus.

4   Implementation

4.1   Continuation semantics as a dynamic framework

The notion of *continuation* has emerged in the theory of computer programming in relation to the idea of order of evaluation (see Reynolds 1993 on the history of continuation). It has proved very useful in the understanding of natural language too (Barker and Shan, 2014) and in particular, it forms the basis of de Groote (2006)'s framework for *dynamic semantics*, i.e., a system accounting for the context-change nature of sentences and in particular, the possibility for a sentence to make

---

[9] http://bit.ly/2zfrTNr

[10] It has been argued that there is no mismatch between syntax and discourse in (11b) and that the two sentences in (11) have the same structure (Hardt, 2013). The argument is based on the idea that if there is a contrast between *A* and *B* and if agent *X* speaks truthfully, then there is a contrast between *A* and *X SAYS B*. One of the issues with this view is that it fails to account for the differences between (non-)parenthetical uses of AVs; in particular, if (11) have the same structure, how does one infer that the speaker/writer can reject the truth of the complement of the AV in (11a) but not in (11b)? In addition, while the given argument might be intuitively appealing for *Concession* and *Contrast*, extending it to other DRs such as the one lexicalized by *for example* would require to drastically weaken the meaning of those DRs.

reference to entities introduced previously in the discourse (Asher, 2016). A *continuized* function takes a continuation—which is a representation of some further computation—as an additional argument. This function is then free to execute or not its continuation and (if the continuation is itself a function taking an argument) with what argument. According to a similar principle, in the continuation semantics of de Groote (2006), a sentence is a function that takes as argument not only its left context, but also its continuation, i.e., the remaining portion of the discourse, whose argument is meant to be the context updated with the information expressed by the proposition.

Such a framework, based on Church (1940)'s simply typed λ-calculus, is able to handle complex dynamic phenomena (Lebedeva, 2012; Qian, 2014). In particular, an anaphora is modelled using a *selection function*, a term representing the algorithmic process of determining (from the context) the reference of the anaphoric expression. For instance, the pronoun *she* uses a selection function sel_{she} that, provided a context c, returns a feminine individual mentioned in c.[11] One of the advantages of de Groote (2006)'s framework over other dynamic systems—such as Kamp and Reyle (1993)'s DRT or Groenendijk and Stokhof (1991)'s DPL—is that it relies entirely on usual mathematical notions; in particular, variables behave standardly and variable renaming, a critical operation to avoid clashes and loss of information (the *destructive assignment problem*), is handled by the classical operation of α-conversion.[12]

We add to the continuation semantics of Lebedeva (2012); Qian (2014) a basic type for *propositional referential markers*. Mathematically, those propositional markers are similar to the event variables of *event semantics* (Davidson, 1967), according to which *Marie walk* is translated as $\exists e.\ walk(e, Marie)$, i.e., "there exists an event that is a walking by Marie"; the main difference is that those markers denote propositions and are thus suitable to represent the complements of AVs. This move allows us to reuse the anaphora system of continuation semantics for propositional anaphora at no cost. We consider here that any

sentence describes such a propositional marker, which is provided to the semantic translation of the sentence as an argument, and can additionally introduce other markers in the context when, for instance, it contains a report or a discourse connective.

4.2 Sentence-level analysis

The meaning of a single sentence is computed as usual, according to a syntactic parse and the semantic entries of the lexicon; Table 1 below shows the parts of the lexicon that are relevant to the current discussion. For the sentence *Fred came*, the result is given by a in Table 2. This term has three arguments (as all dynamic propositions): a propositional marker e, a context c and a continuation ϕ (the variable representing the subsequent sentences). It states that e is about Fred coming, and passes the context updated with this description of e (i.e., $p :: c$) to its continuation.[13]

4.2.1 AVs

Because a verb such as *think* has a propositional complement, it corresponds here to a three-place predicate, relating the proposition being constructed (about the thinking), the thinker, and the proposition describing what is thought. Crucially, because the two propositions are represented by objects of the same logical type, they can both be referred to anaphorically in the same way. Note how ⟦think⟧ in Table 1 introduces the marker e', described by the complement P (the proposition embedded under *think*). The meaning of *Eva thinks he recovered* is given in b_2 of Table 2: this term states that e is about Eva thinking e', which is about "he" (note the selection function that has to find a reference in the context) having recovered.

It is important to remark that the object of a thought (or of any report that is not *factive*; Karttunen 1971) is not necessarily a true proposition. Therefore, merely stating the existence of a propositional marker, as in ⟦think⟧, does not imply that the corresponding proposition is true. This means that at some point, we will have to indicate when propositions are true; this will be achieved through a predicate *true* and an entailment relation over makers: $a \supset b \triangleq true(a) \rightarrow true(b)$.

---

[11] Describing the implementation of the selection functions is out of the scope of this work; however, we make sure that their arguments are informative enough for them to be mathematically defined.

[12] See Hindley and Seldin (1986) for more about λ-calculus.

[13] The precise implementation of contexts is irrelevant but a representation as lists of formula can be assumed.

$$\llbracket \text{Fred} \rrbracket = \lambda P.\ P\,Fred$$
$$\llbracket \text{he} \rrbracket = \lambda Pec.\ Psel_{he}(c)ec$$
$$\llbracket \text{come} \rrbracket = \lambda S.\ S(\lambda sec\phi.\ \underbrace{come(e,s)}_{p} \wedge \phi(p :: c))$$

$$\llbracket \text{think} \rrbracket = \lambda PS.\ S(\lambda sec\phi.\ \exists e'.\ \underbrace{think(e,s,e')}_{p} \wedge Pe'(p :: c)\phi)$$

$$\llbracket \text{because} \rrbracket = \lambda ABec\phi.\ \exists e_A.\ \underbrace{e \supset e_A}_{p_1} \wedge Ae_A(p_1 :: c)(\lambda c'.\ \exists e_B.\ \underbrace{e \supset e_B}_{p_2} \wedge Be_B(p_2 :: c')(\lambda c''.$$
$$\underbrace{Explanation(e, sel_C(e_A, c''), sel_C(e_B, c''))}_{p_3} \wedge \phi(p_3 :: c'')))$$

$$\llbracket \text{although} \rrbracket = \lambda ABec\phi.\ \exists e_A.\ \underbrace{e \supset e_A}_{p_1} \wedge Ae_A(p_1 :: c)(\lambda c'.\ \exists e_B.\ \underbrace{e \supset e_B}_{p_2} \wedge Be_B(p_2 :: c')(\lambda c''.$$
$$\underbrace{Concession(e, sel_P(e_A, c''), sel_P(e_B, c''))}_{p_3} \wedge \phi(p_3 :: c'')))$$

$$\boldsymbol{D_i} = \lambda \phi.\ \phi c_i$$
$$\boldsymbol{dupd} = \lambda DS\phi.\ D(\lambda c.\ \exists e.\ \underbrace{true(e)}_{p} \wedge Se(p :: c)\phi)$$

$$\llbracket \text{however} \rrbracket = \lambda Bec\phi.\exists e_B.\ \underbrace{e \supset e_B}_{p_1} \wedge Be_B(p_1 :: c)(\lambda c'.\ \underbrace{Contrast(e, sel(c), sel_P(e_B, c'))}_{p_2} \wedge \phi(p_2 :: c'))$$

Table 1: The semantic lexicon. The six first terms ($\llbracket \text{Fred} \rrbracket$-$\llbracket \text{although} \rrbracket$) are introduced in Section 4.2; the last three ($\boldsymbol{D_i}$-$\llbracket \text{however} \rrbracket$) are discussed in Section 4.3. The underbraces are only a shorthand for copies of the corresponding terms.

4.2.2 Conjunctions

As AVs, conjunctions introduce propositional markers; in this case, one for each syntactic argument. We said earlier that all connectives behave, at least to some extent, anaphorically. In our proposition, this corresponds to the fact that the two propositional variables e_A and e_B transmitted to the two syntactic arguments (A and B, respectively), are not hard-wired as the discourse arguments of the relation lexicalized by the connective; instead, two types of selection functions are used: sel_C and sel_P, for central and peripheral connectives respectively. These functions have two arguments: the first one is the marker representing the whole corresponding syntactic argument (e_A or e_B) and the second one is a context. If the context has been judiciously updated, the selection function has then all the information needed to respect the constraints it is subject to and retrieve the correct discourse argument.

All central conjunctions have a lexical entry similar to $\llbracket \text{because} \rrbracket$ given in Table 1. This term can be understood sequentially: for A and B, e (the marker of the whole *A because B* proposition), the left context c and a continuation ϕ:

i) e_A, a marker whose truth is entailed by the truth of e, is described by executing A;

ii) similarly, e_B is described by executing B;

iii) the relation *Explanation* between two anaphorically determined propositions (one from e_A, the other from e_B) is stated (this is the description of e);

iv) the remaining ϕ of the discourse is executed.

This order of evaluation is expressed through intermediate continuations, which are written so that the context is appropriately updated from the beginning to the end: the input context of the connective is c, $(p_1 :: c)$ is given to A which gives back c', then $(p_2 :: c')$ is given to B which gives back c'' and finally the connective transmits $(p_3 :: c'')$ to its continuation.

The (unnatural) sentence *Fred came because Eva thinks he had recovered* therefore leads to the term c in Table 2: because of the three constraints applying to sel_C (in particular the impossibility of accessing the content of a report), there is no ambiguity in the discourse arguments of the explanation, which are e_A (about the coming) and e_B (about the thinking). This corresponds to an intensional interpretation of the AV which can be judged inappropriate based on world-knowledge.

The entries for peripheral conjunctions (e.g., $\llbracket \text{although} \rrbracket$ in Table 1) only differ in the use of the sel_P selection function instead of sel_C. The sentence *Fred came although Eva thinks he was sick* is translated into term c' of Table 2: while $sel_P(e_A, c'')$ is necessarily resolved as e_A itself (because of the first rule), $sel_P(e_B, c'')$ could potentially be either e_B (intensional interpretation) or c' (evidential one), the latter being indicated by world-knowledge.

4.3 Discourse analysis

4.3.1 Discourse update

To actually compute full discourses, two additional elements are needed (see Lebedeva 2012, who expresses discourse dynamics through continuations and an exception raising/handling mechanism but does not account for DRs); they are shown in Table 1. The first one, D_i, is the initial (content-empty) discourse, which simply contains some initial context c_i that is passed to its continuation.[14] The second is the *dupd* operator, that updates a discourse D with a sentence S, by transferring the context from the former to the latter and introducing a new true propositional marker.[15]

4.3.2 Adverbials

The adverbial connectives, an example of which is given as ⟦however⟧ in Table 1, are very similar to the conjunctions of the previous section. The only difference is that as they lack one syntactic argument, only one propositional marker (e_B) is introduced, while the other has to be determined anaphorically from the left context c with an unconstrained selection function. The discourse *Fred came. However, Sabine thinks he is sick* is translated into term d of Table 2; it is very similar to c', only the selection of Arg_1 is different.

4.4 Hedging DRs?

So far, we have been considering that explicit connectives always introduced "plain" (unmodalized) DRs. By simply adding as axioms that *veridical* DRs such as *Explanation* or *Concession* (Asher and Lascarides, 2003) entail the truth of their arguments ($R(e, e_A, e_B) \Rightarrow e \supset e_A \wedge e \supset e_B$), we obtain the strong revision of propositional attitude proposed by Danlos and Rambow (2011). However, to get the "hedged DR" interpretation advocated for by Hunter (2016), one can modify the terms of the connectives along the following lines: use a conditional statement to introduce a modalized propositional marker for the DR if one of the selected arguments has been introduced by an AV (this piece of information is present in the

---

[14]The initial context c_i can be chosen arbitrarily, for instance as empty, or containing some world-knowledge.

[15]A discourse can also be evaluated to a static formula with the trivial continuation $stop = \lambda c.\ \top$.

context), directly use the provided (unmodalized) marker otherwise.

5 Related work

The idea of using de Groote (2006)'s continuation semantics framework for computing discourse structure was first discussed by Asher and Pogodalla (2011), who were interested in integrating SDRT more tightly with syntax. They outlined a system that does so, giving explicitly a lexical entry for adverbial connectives that uses a selection function to recover its Arg_1. Qian and Amblard (2011) defend a very similar proposition, but focus on implicit DRs and use an event-based semantics instead of SDRT, in which the discourse arguments are events rather than discourse speech acts (DSA). Their account, as ours, is expressed in a logical language that is simpler than the one of SDRT, which uses labels that name DSA (Asher and Lascarides, 2003); in consequence, all the discourse that they and we treat are directly and entirely (including the DRs) translated in first order logic, ready to be used by theorem provers and model builders. However, considering that discourse arguments are propositions allows us to handle DRs which takes as arguments the complements of propositional attitude verbs (which arguably are propositions and not events nor DSA).

These two previous works both focused on the general principles of introducing DRs in continuation semantics and how to ensure the accessibility constraint (for the selection functions) known as the *Right Frontier Constraint* (Asher and Lascarides, 2003). This constraint is not only of linguistics interest, it also naturally lowers the ambiguity of anaphors and thus reduces the computation required for the selection algorithms. However, the solutions proposed in these two articles can easily be implemented in our particular proposition as ensuring this constraint is orthogonal to the issues mainly discussed here, namely the variation in anaphoric properties of discourse connectives and the interpretation of AVs.

The distinction between central and peripheral conjunctions and their interaction with AVs has been formally modeled by Bernard and Danlos (2016). In particular, they account for the scope phenomena distinguishing the two classes of subordinating conjunctions discussed in Haegeman (2004)–which we do not. However, their proposition is heavily dependent on the syntactic aspect

$$a \triangleq [\![\text{come}]\!][\![\text{Fred}]\!] \qquad = \lambda ec\phi. \; \underbrace{come(e, Fred)}_{p} \wedge \phi(p :: c)$$

$$b_1 \triangleq [\![\text{recovered}]\!][\![\text{he}]\!] \qquad = \lambda ec\phi. \; \underbrace{recover(e, sel_{he}(c))}_{p} \wedge \phi(p :: c)$$

$$b_2 \triangleq [\![\text{think}]\!](b_1)[\![\text{Eva}]\!] \qquad = \lambda ec\phi. \; \exists e'. \; \underbrace{think(e, Eva, e')}_{p_1} \wedge \underbrace{recover(e', sel_{he}(p_1 :: c))}_{p_2} \wedge \phi(p_2 :: p_1 :: c)$$

$$c \triangleq [\![\text{because}]\!](a)(b_2) \qquad = \lambda ec\phi. \; \exists e_A. \; \underbrace{e \supset e_A}_{p_1} \wedge \underbrace{come(e_A, Fred)}_{p_2} \wedge \exists e_B. \; \underbrace{e \supset e_B}_{p_3} \wedge \exists e'. \; \underbrace{think(e_B, Eva, e')}_{p_4}$$

$$\wedge \underbrace{recover(e', sel_{he}(p_4 :: \ldots p_1 :: c))}_{p_5}$$

$$\wedge \underbrace{Explanation(e, sel_C(e_A, p_5 :: \ldots p_1 :: c), sel_C(e_B, p_5 :: \ldots p_1 :: c))}_{p_6}$$

$$\wedge \phi(p_6 :: \ldots p_1 :: c)$$

$$c' \triangleq [\![\text{although}]\!](a)(b_2') \qquad = \lambda ec\phi. \; \exists e_A. \; \underbrace{e \supset e_A}_{p_1} \wedge \underbrace{come(e_A, Fred)}_{p_2} \wedge \exists e_B. \; \underbrace{e \supset e_B}_{p_3} \wedge \exists e'. \; \underbrace{think(e_B, Eva, e')}_{p_4}$$

$$\wedge \underbrace{sick(e', sel_{he}(p_4 :: \ldots p_1 :: c))}_{p_5}$$

$$\wedge \underbrace{Concession(e, sel_P(e_A, p_5 :: \ldots p_1 :: c), sel_P(e_B, p_5 :: \ldots p_1 :: c))}_{p_6}$$

$$\wedge \phi(p_6 :: \ldots p_1 :: c)$$

$$d \triangleq \boldsymbol{dupd}(\boldsymbol{D}_i(a))([\![\text{however}]\!](b_2)) = \lambda \phi. \; \exists e_A. \; \underbrace{true(e_A)}_{p_1} \wedge \underbrace{come(e_A, Fred)}_{p_2} \wedge \exists e. \; \underbrace{true(e)}_{p_3}$$

$$\wedge \exists e_B. \; \underbrace{e \supset e_B}_{p_4} \wedge \exists e'. \; \underbrace{think(e_B, Eva, e')}_{p_5} \wedge \underbrace{sick(e', sel_{he}(p_5 :: \ldots p_1 :: c_i))}_{p_6}$$

$$\wedge \underbrace{Contrast(e, sel(p_3 :: \ldots p_1 :: c_i), sel_P(e_B, p_6 :: \ldots p_1 :: c_i))}_{p_7} \wedge \phi(p_7 :: \ldots p_1 :: c_i)$$

Table 2: Some examples of terms discussed in Section 4. Term b_2' (used in c') is obtained by replacing *recover* with *sick* in b_2.

of the formalism they use, namely STAG (Shieber and Schabes, 1990), while we are more agnostic about this part of the grammar. Furthermore, they model the difference between (non-)parenthetical uses of AVs as a lexical ambiguity (the idea being that the parenthetical version of AVs are only compatible with peripheral connectives), whereas, in line with Simons (2007)'s analysis, we see it as a pragmatic ambiguity concerning the argument of discourse connectives. We achieve this through the use of selection functions, a mechanism independently motivated by pronominal anaphora and adverbial connectives. This allows us to process whole discourses with a limited set of tools while they only account for subordinating conjunctions (i.e., intra-sentential DRs).

Building on Hunter (2016)'s analysis, Hunter and Asher (forthcoming) present a coercion mechanism to compositionally derive in SDRT the correct discourse structure of instances involving evidential reports with *implicit* connectives. However, their solution does not account for examples involving an evidential with an *explicit* DR, such as (8b), which remain for them problematic. Note

that the present account smoothly extends to implicit DRs under the assumption that they are introduced by implicit adverbial connectives (similar to $[\![\text{however}]\!]$ in Table 1).

6 Conclusion

We have argued that all discourse connectives—not the adverbials only—should be treated as anaphors, with different classes of connectives obeying different anaphoric constraints. We have shown that this view allows one to account for semantically parenthetical reports without postulating any ad-hoc lexical ambiguity concerning the status of AVs. Instead, the parenthetical interpretation is viewed here as a product of the discourse structure itself. The same mechanism also handles sequences of conjunctions (*A CONJ$_1$ B CONJ$_2$ C*). We have shown how to implement this proposal in de Groote (2006)'s dynamic framework. Such a framework makes it possible to handle discourse semantics without the need of a syntactic parse above the sentence level, and in a strictly compositional way using continuations.

Acknowledgments

This work has been partly financed by Labex EFL (ANR/CGI).

References

Lasha Abzianidze. 2015. A Tableau Prover for Natural Logic and Language. In *Proceedings of the 2015 Conference on Empirical Methods in Natural Language Processing*. Lisbon, Portugal, pages 2492–2502. https://doi.org/chbq.

Bharat Ram Ambati, Tejaswini Deoskar, and Mark Steedman. 2016. Shift-Reduce CCG Parsing using Neural Network Models. In *Proceedings of the 2016 Conference of the North American Chapter of the Association for Computational Linguistics: Human Language Technologies*. Association for Computational Linguistics, San Diego, California, pages 447–453. https://doi.org/cfzr.

Nicholas Asher. 2016. Discourse semantics. In Maria Aloni and Paul Dekker, editors, *The Cambridge Handbook of Formal Semantics*, Cambridge University Press, Cambridge Handbooks in Language and Linguistics, pages 106–129. https://doi.org/cg8x.

Nicholas Asher and Alex Lascarides. 2003. *Logics of Conversation*. Cambridge University Press. http://bit.ly/2h9hdtw.

Nicholas Asher and Sylvain Pogodalla. 2011. SDRT and Continuation Semantics. In Takashi Onada, Daisuke Bekki, and Eric McCready, editors, *New Frontiers in Artificial Intelligence JSAI-isAI 2010 Workshops, LENLS, JURISIN, AMBN, ISS, Tokyo, Japan, November 18-19, 2010, Revised Selected Papers*, Springer Berlin Heidelberg, volume 6797 of *Lecture Notes in Computer Science*, pages 3–15. http://bit.ly/2jxS0Kn.

Chris Barker and Chung-chieh Shan. 2014. *Continuations and Natural Language*. Oxford University Press. http://bit.ly/2zcrN7E.

Timothée Bernard and Laurence Danlos. 2016. Modelling Discourse in STAG: Subordinate Conjunctions and Attributing Phrases. In *Proceedings of the 12th International Workshop on Tree Adjoining Grammars and Related Formalisms (TAG+12)*. Düsseldorf, Germany, pages 38–47. http://bit.ly/2hEqBm5.

Johannes Bjerva, Johan Bos, Rob van der Goot, and Malvina Nissim. 2014. The Meaning Factory: Formal Semantics for Recognizing Textual Entailment and Determining Semantic Similarity. In *Proceedings of the 8th International Workshop on Semantic Evaluation*. Dublin, Ireland, pages 642–646. https://doi.org/chbn.

Johan Bos and Katja Markert. 2005. Recognising Textual Entailment with Logical Inference. In *Proceedings of the Conference on Human Language Technology and Empirical Methods in Natural Language Processing*. Association for Computational Linguistics, Stroudsburg, PA, USA, HLT '05, pages 628–635. https://doi.org/fb8m79.

Alonzo Church. 1940. A Formulation of the simple theory of types. *The Journal of Symbolic Logic* 5(02):56–68. https://doi.org/br4892.

Laurence Danlos and Owen Rambow. 2011. Discourse Relations and Propositional Attitudes. In *Proceedings of CID 2011*. Agay, France. http://bit.ly/2B69Uu7.

Donald Davidson. 1967. The Logical Form of Action Sentences. In Nicholas Rescher, editor, *The Logic of Decision and Action*, University of Pittsburgh Press, Pittsburgh, pages 81–95. https://doi.org/bqqp72.

Philippe de Groote. 2006. Towards a Montagovian Account of Dynamics. In Masayuki Gibson and Howell Jonathan, editors, *Proceedings of the 16th Semantics and Linguistic Theory Conference*. University of Tokyo, Japan, pages 1–16. https://doi.org/cfvq.

Nikhil Dinesh, Alan Lee, Eleni Miltsakaki, Rashmi Prasad, Aravind Joshi, and Bonnie Webber. 2005. Attribution and the (Non-)Alignment of Syntactic and Discourse Arguments of Connectives. In *Proceedings of the Workshop on Frontiers in Corpus Annotations II: Pie in the Sky*. Association for Computational Linguistics, Ann Arbor, Michigan, pages 29–36. http://bit.ly/2BdrzjS.

Jeroen Groenendijk and Martin Stokhof. 1991. Dynamic Predicate Logic. *Linguistics and Philosophy* 14(1):39–100. http://bit.ly/2zqWbNJ.

Francisco Guzmán, Shafiq Joty, Lluís Màrquez, and Preslav Nakov. 2014. Using discourse structure improves machine translation evaluation. In *Proceedings of the 52nd Annual Meeting of the Association for Computational Linguistics*. Baltimore, Maryland, volume 1: Long Papers, pages 687–698. https://doi.org/cg83.

Liliane Haegeman. 2004. The syntax of adverbial clauses and its consequences for topicalisation. In Martine Coene, Gretel De Cuyper, and Yves D'Hulst, editors, *Current Studies in Comparative Romance Linguistics*, Antwerp University, number 107 in APiL, pages 61–90. http://bit.ly/2AuIu1S.

Daniel Hardt. 2013. A Uniform Syntax and Discourse Structure: the Copenhagen Dependency Treebanks. *Dialogue & Discourse* 4(2):53–64. http://bit.ly/2GgMnqX.

J. Roger Hindley and Jonathan P. Seldin. 1986. *Introduction to Combinators and λ-calculus*. Cambridge University Press. https://doi.org/cg8w.

Julie Hunter. 2016. Reports in Discourse. *Dialogue & Discourse* 7(4). http://bit.ly/2FhGTen.

Julie Hunter and Nicholas Asher. forthcoming. Composing Discourse Parenthetical Reports. In *Proceedings of Sinn und Bedeutung 21*. Edinburgh, UK. http://bit.ly/2zbOWad.

Julie Hunter and Laurence Danlos. 2014. Because We Say So. In *Proceedings of the EACL 2014 Workshop on Computational Approaches to Causality in Language*. Association for Computational Linguistics, Gothenburg, Sweden, pages 1–9. http://bit.ly/2ysAHAY.

Peter Jansen, Mihai Surdeanu, and Peter Clark. 2014. Discourse Complements Lexical Semantics for Non-factoid Answer Reranking. In *Proceedings of the 52nd Annual Meeting of the Association for Computational Linguistics (Volume 1: Long Papers)*. Baltimore, Maryland, USA, pages 977–986. https://doi.org/cg84.

Hans Kamp and Uwe Reyle. 1993. *From Discourse to Logic. Introduction to Modeltheoretic Semantics of Natural Language, Formal Logic and Discourse Representation Theory*. Number 42 in Studies in Linguistics and Philosophy. Springer Netherlands, Dordrecht. https://doi.org/cfzt.

Lauri Karttunen. 1971. Some Observations on Factivity. *Paper in Linguistics* 4(1):55–69. https://doi.org/fkhz9n.

Ekaterina Lebedeva. 2012. *Expressing Discourse Dynamics Through Continuations*. Ph.D. Thesis, Université de Lorraine. http://bit.ly/2hC44WX.

Mike Lewis, Kenton Lee, and Luke Zettlemoyer. 2016. LSTM CCG Parsing. In *Proceedings of the 2016 Conference of the North American Chapter of the Association for Computational Linguistics: Human Language Technologies*. Association for Computational Linguistics, San Diego, California, pages 221–231. https://doi.org/cfzs.

William C. Mann and Sandra A. Thompson. 1988. Rhetorical Structure Theory: Toward a functional theory of text organization. *Text* 8(3):243–281. https://doi.org/dsvtxb.

Karthik Narasimhan and Regina Barzilay. 2015. Machine Comprehension with Discourse Relations. In *Proceedings of the 53rd Annual Meeting of the Association for Computational Linguistics and the 7th International Joint Conference on Natural Language Processing*. Beijing, China, volume 1: Long Papers, pages 1253–1262. https://doi.org/cg8z.

Rashmi Prasad, Nikhil Dinesh, Alan Lee, Eleni Miltsakaki, Livio Robaldo, Aravind K. Joshi, and Bonnie L. Webber. 2008. The Penn Discourse TreeBank 2.0. In *Proceedings of the 6th International Conference on Language Resources and Evaluation*. Marrackech, Morocco. http://bit.ly/2zfxbbE.

Rashmi Prasad, Eleni Miltsakaki, Nikhil Dinesh, Alan Lee, Aravind Joshi, Livio Robaldo, and Bonnie Webber. 2007. The Penn Discourse Treebank 2.0 Annotation Manual. Technical Report IRCS 203, University of Pennsylvania. http://bit.ly/2yrZ9SP.

Sai Qian. 2014. *Accessibility of Referents in Discourse Semantics*. Ph.D. Thesis, Université de Lorraine. http://bit.ly/2hBK8mP.

Sai Qian and Maxime Amblard. 2011. Event in Compositional Dynamic Semantics. In *Proceedings of LACL 2011*. Montpellier, France, pages 219–234. http://bit.ly/2hC8AEK.

John C. Reynolds. 1993. The discoveries of continuations. *LISP and Symbolic Computation* 6(3-4):233–247. https://doi.org/bp628x.

Stuart M. Shieber and Yves Schabes. 1990. Synchronous Tree-adjoining Grammars. In *Proceedings of the 13th Conference on Computational Linguistics*. Association for Computational Linguistics, Stroudsburg, PA, USA, volume 3 of *COLING '90*, pages 253–258. https://doi.org/cjtstd.

Mandy Simons. 2007. Observations on embedding verbs, evidentiality, and presupposition. *Lingua* 117(6):1034–1056. https://doi.org/bjf99b.

Mark Steedman and Jason Baldridge. 2011. Combinatory Categorial Grammar. In Robert D. Borsley and Kersti Brjars, editors, *Non-Transformational Syntax*, Wiley-Blackwell, pages 181–224. https://doi.org/bkvn3v.

Mei Tu, Yu Zhou, and Chengqing Zong. 2014. Enhancing Grammatical Cohesion: Generating Transitional Expressions for SMT. In *Proceedings of the 52nd Annual Meeting of the Association for Computational Linguistics*. Association for Computational Linguistics, Baltimore, Maryland, volume 1: Long Papers, pages 850–860. https://doi.org/chbr.

J. O. Urmson. 1952. Parenthetical Verbs. *Mind* 61(244):480–496. http://bit.ly/2zhRiXo.

Bonnie Webber. 2004. D-LTAG: extending lexicalized TAG to discourse. *Cognitive Science* 28(5):751–779. https://doi.org/dxnfk4.

Bonnie Webber, Matthew Stone, Aravind Joshi, and Alistair Knott. 2003. Anaphora and Discourse Structure. *Computational Linguistics* 29(4):545–587. https://doi.org/c7b9dn.

Automatic Extraction of Causal Relations from Text using Linguistically Informed Deep Neural Networks

Tirthankar Dasgupta, Rupsa Saha, Lipika Dey and **Abir Naskar**

TCS Innovation Lab, India

(dasgupta.tirthankar, rupsa.s, lipika.dey, abir.naskar)@tcs.com

Abstract

In this paper we have proposed a linguistically informed recursive neural network architecture for automatic extraction of cause-effect relations from text. These relations can be expressed in arbitrarily complex ways. The architecture uses word level embeddings and other linguistic features to detect causal events and their effects mentioned within a sentence. The extracted events and their relations are used to build a causal-graph after clustering and appropriate generalization, which is then used for predictive purposes. We have evaluated the performance of the proposed extraction model with respect to two baseline systems,one a rule-based classifier, and the other a conditional random field (CRF) based supervised model. We have also compared our results with related work reported in the past by other authors on SEMEVAL data set, and found that the proposed bidirectional LSTM model enhanced with an additional linguistic layer performs better. We have also worked extensively on creating new annotated datasets from publicly available data, which we are willing to share with the community.

1 Introduction

The concept of causality can be informally introduced as a relationship between two events e_1 and e_2 such that occurrence of e_1 results in the occurrence of e_2. Curating causal relations from text documents help in automatically building causal networks which can be used for predictive tasks. Expression of causality can be expressed within text documents in arbitrarily complex ways. For example, in the sentence *"Aircel files for bankruptcy over mounting financial troubles"*, the event *"mounting financial troubles"* is causing the event *"Aircel filed for bankruptcy."* In a more complicated scenario, *"Company recalled some vehicles to fix loose bolts that could lead to engine stall"* we can observe nested cause-effect pairs. Here, the effect *"company recalled vehicle"* is caused by the event *"to fix loose bolts is not easy to extract. That the cause "loose bolts" could lead to engine stall"*, is even more difficult to detect.

While there has been a considerable body of researchers working in the area whose work has been reviewed in section 2, there are many challenges that are still not properly addressed. Most of the earlier approaches have considered rule based or traditional machine learning algorithms which heavily depend on careful feature engineering. Though one sees adoption of deep learning techniques for causality extraction, it is still considerably low compared to other text mining tasks. This is largely due to the unavailability of adequate annotated data: the only available dataset for evaluation is the SEMEVAL-10 Task 8 which is woefully inadequate to train such deep models. There are challenges with annotations of this data also (Rehbein and Ruppenhofer, 2017).

Most of the existing extraction mechanisms look for single word representation of events within a sentence, thereby yielding wrong results. For example, in the sentence *"The AIDS pandemic caused by the spread of HIV infection"* the cause and effect are both multi-word phrases i.e. "spread of HIV infection" and 'AIDS pandemic'. However, SEMEVAL 2010 annotated dataset for this task mentions the cause and effect as "infection" and "pandemic" only. In another example, *"Infectious diseases or communicable diseases are caused by bacteria, viruses, and parasites."*, the need to extract multiple causal as well as effect events is obvious. The example sentence in the first paragraph not only demonstrates the need to

Proceedings of the SIGDIAL 2018 Conference, pages 306–316,
Melbourne, Australia, 12-14 July 2018. ©2018 Association for Computational Linguistics

extract phrases as events, but also highlights how complex such statements can be, often without the use of known causal connectives like *"causes, because of, leads to, after, due to"* etc. which have been traditionally exploited by the community.

In this work, we explore the use of bidirectional LSTMs that can learn to detect causal instances from sentences. To address the paucity of training data, we propose the use of additional linguistic feature embeddings, over and above the regular word embeddings. With the use of such linguistically-informed deep architecture, we avoid the task of complex feature engineering.

A major contribution of this work is in developing annotated datasets with information curated from multiple sources spanning across different domains. To do this, we have collected news articles and generate annotations. Beside SE-MEVAL dataset we have also used another available dataset that has annotated data about drugs and their adverse effect extracted from Medline (Gurulingappa et al., 2012). We have done intensive experimentations with parts of the dataset for training and testing which will be discussed in the following sections.

Detection of causal relation from text has many analytical and predictive applications. Few of these are: detecting cause-effect relations in medical documents, learning about after effects of natural disasters, learning causes for safety related incidents etc.. However to build a meaningful application that can detect an event from texts and predict its possible effects, there is a need to curate large volume of cause-effect event pairs. Further, similar events need to be grouped and generalized to super classes, over which the predictive framework can be built(Zhao et al., 2017). In this paper, we have proposed a k-means clustering of causal and effect events detected from text, using word vector representations.

The rest of the paper is organized as follows. Section 2 summarizes challenges and related works on causality detection. Section 3 presents the resource creation and the architecture of the proposed causality extraction framework. Experiments and evaluation are detailed in Section 4. Finally, in section 5 we conclude the paper.

2 Challenges in Causality Detection and the State of the Art

Identification of causality is not a trivial problem. Causation can occur in various forms. Two common differentiations are made on: a) *Marked and Unmarked causality* and b) *Implicit and Explicit causality* (Blanco et al., 2008)(Hendrickx et al., 2009)(Sorgente et al., 2013). Marked Causality is where there is a linguistic signal of causation present. For example, *"I attended the event because I was invited"*. Here, causality is marked by *because*. On the other hand in *"Drive slowly. There are potholes"*, causality is unmarked.

Explicit Causality is where both cause and effect are stated. For example, *"The burst has been caused by water hammer pressure"* has both cause and effect stated explicitly. However, *"The car ran over his leg"* does not have the effect of the accident explicitly stated.

Automatic extraction of cause-effect relations are primarily based on three different approaches namely, Linguistic rule based, supervised and unsupervised machine learning approaches. Both SemEval-2007 (Girju et al., 2007) & 2010 (Hendrickx et al., 2009) had tasks aimed at identifying different relations from text, including Cause-Effect relations. Both tasks offered a corpus of annotated gold standard data to researchers. However, the task has primarily focused on extracting single word cause-effect pairs. Early work in this area relied totally on hand-coded patterns. These were heavily dependent on both domain and linguistic knowledge, due to the nature of the patterns, and were hard to scale up. PROTEUS (Grishman, 1988) and COATIS (Garcia, 1997) were two early systems that used such non-statistical techniques. C.G Khoo carried out extensive development of this train of thought in a series of works (Khoo et al., 1998) (Khoo et al., 2001), and eliminated a lot of the need for domain knowledge.

A method of automatically identifying linguistic patterns that indicate causal relations and a semi-supervised method of validation of patterns obtained was proposed by (Girju et al., 2002). In particular, this work introduced the usage of WordNet hierarchal classes, namely, human action, phenomenon, state, psychological feature and event, as a distinguishing feature.

Radinsky et al. in their work uses statistical inferencing combined with hierarchical clustering technique to predict future events from news (Radinsky et al., 2012). Logistic regression was employed (Bui et al., 2010) to extract drugs (cause) and virus mutation (effect) occurrences from medical literature. The relatively untouched task of extracting implicit cause-effect from sentences was tackled by Ittoo et.al (Ittoo and Bouma, 2011). More recently, Zhao et al. (Zhao et al., 2017) have proposed novel causality network embeddings for the abstract representation of causal events from News headlines. Here, the authors have primarily used four common causal connectives namely, "because", "after", "because of" and "lead to" to extract causal mentions in news headlines and constructed a network of causal relations. The authors have proposed a novel generalization technique to represent "specific events" into more abstract form. Finally, they proposed a dual cause-effect model that uses the causal network embeddings and optimize the margin based loss function to predict effect of a given cause. Although the work is commendable, there are various factors that need to be addressed further. For example, construction of the causal network itself is a non trivial task. Some of the linguistic challenges have already mentioned earlier in this section. Further, Zhao et al. worked with only unambiguous causal connectives. On the contrary causal connectives can be ambiguous also (Sorgente et al., 2013) (Hendrickx et al., 2009) For example, *from* in *"Profits from the sale were given to charity"* implies causation of *profits* due to *the sale*, while *from* in *"Sales profits increased from 1.2% to 2%"* does not have any causality involved in it. Analysis of such complex constructs are yet to be addressed.

3 Proposed Methodology

The overall architecture of our proposed approach is composed of three modules: a)Resource Creation b) Linguistic preprocessor and feature extractor, c) Classification model builder, and d) Prediction framework for cause/effect, built on the output of the classifier module. Each of the individual modules are described in the following subsections.

3.1 Resource Creation

Data Description: In this section we will discuss about the following dataset used to develop and test our proposed models. 1) Part of the SemEval 2010 Task 8 data set dealing with"Cause-Effect"

Table 1: Data Statistics

Source	Sentence count	Avg. sent. length
Analyst Report (AR)	4500	23.7
SEMEVAL (SEM)	1331	18.7
BBC News(BBC)	503	22.5
ADE	3000	20.5
Recall News (RN)	1052	23.1

relation, which consists of 1331 sentences. 2) The adverse drug effect (ADE) dataset (Gurulingappa et al., 2012) composed of 1000 sentences consisting of information about consumption of different drugs and their associated side effects. 3)The BBC News Article dataset, created by the Trinity College Computer Science Department, containing news articles in five topical areas : business, sports, tech, entertainment and politics from 2004-2005 (Greene and Cunningham, 2006). We have considered 140 business news articles, containing approximately 1950 sentences. Out of this, around 500 sentences were found to contain causation. 4)Around 4500 analyst reports of a specific organization over a period of seven months is the fourth dataset that we have considered. We have manually extracted all the sentences that contained causation. 5) The Recall dataset [1] is a collection of 1050 recall news of different products.

The first two datasets, that is, SemEval and ADE datasets, are already publicly available. However, for the SemEval dataset we have extended the annotation to phrase-level causal relationships. Hence the fresh annotations of these existing data sets, as well as parts of the annotated Recall news and BBC news datasets, will be publicly shared with this paper. We could not share the analyst report dataset due to copyright and IPR issues.

Preprocessing: We perform a number of preprocessing over the collected dataset. The first stage of preprocessing involves identifying which sentences are probably candidates for cause-effect identification out of a body of text. This involves looking for the presence of at least one causal connective in the sentence under consideration. Xuelan (Xuelan and Kennedy, 1992) reported a list of 130 causal connectives in English. To extend the list we follow methods similar to Girju (Girju, 2003) and Blanco (Blanco et al., 2008). We use Wordnet (University, 2010) as our lexical database. An entry of WordNet, whose gloss definition contains any of the terms in the exist-

---

[1] https://www.edmunds.com/recalls/

Table 2: Annotation Examples

Honda/E_1 Motor/E_1 Co./E_1 is/E_1 recalling/E_1 Acura/E_1 ILX/E_1 and/E_1 ILX/E_1 Hybrid/E_1 vehicles/E_1 because/CC_1 excessive/C_1 headlight/C_1 temperatures/C_1 pose/C_1 a/C_1 fire/C_1 risk/C_1.
Attrition/C_1 of/C_1 associates/C_1 will/CC_1 effect/CC_1 scheduled/E_1/C_2 release/E_1/C_2 of/E_1/C_2 product/E_1/C_2 causing/CC_2 high/E_2 business/E_2 impact/E_2.

ing causal list, is included in the list as a possible causal connectives. Once we have a list of words, we further expand the list by adding common phrases with contain one or more of these words. For example, the seed word *causes* is extended to include phrases like "one of the main causes of", "a leading cause of" etc. This gives us an extended connective list of 310 words/phrases. Table 3 shows a few examples of seed words and new terms added to the list. After preprocessing, we finally obtained a dataset of 8K sentences for annotation in terms of their cause, effect and causal connectives.

The Annotation Process: The above sentences are presented to three expert annotators. The experts were asked to complete the following two tasks. a) Identify whether a given sentence contains a causal event (either cause/effect) and b) Annotate each word in a sentence in terms of the four labels *cause (C)*, *effect(E)*, *causal connectives(CC)* and *None*. An illustration of the annotated dataset is depicted in Table 2.

In some of the candidate sentences, it is observed that a single sentence contains multiple cause-effect pairs, some of which are even chained together. In order to handle multiple instances of causality present in the same sentence, sentences are split into sub-sentences. e.g. *"In developing countries four-fifths of all the illnesses are caused by water-borne diseases with diarrhoea being the leading cause of childhood death"* (Hendrickx et al., 2009). This sentence has two distinct causes and their corresponding effects : *four-fifths of all the illnesses are caused by water-borne diseases* and *diarrhoea being the leading cause of childhood death*.

We have also observed a number of cases where a single sentence contains a chain of causal events where a cause event e_1 results the effect of another event e_2 which in turn causes event e_3. In such cases e_2 will be marked as both effect for e_1 and cause for e_3. For example, in *"The reactor meltdown caused a chain reaction that destroyed all the towers in the network"* (Hendrickx et al., 2009), there are two different causalities, chained

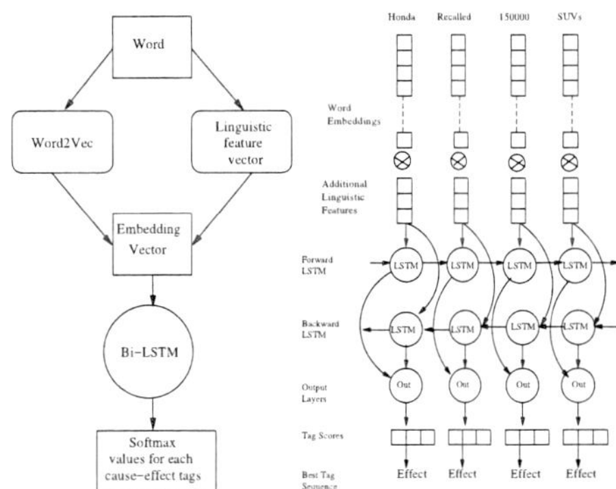

Figure 1: Overview of the bidirectional LSTM architecture for Cause-Effect relation extraction.

together: (1)*The reactor meltdown caused a chain reaction* and (2)*a chain reaction that destroyed all the towers in the network*. The effect in the first case and the cause in the second is *"A chained reaction"*. Similar example illustrated with an annotation is depicted in example (2) of Table 2. In order to extract all instances of causality present in a sentence, the sentence is divided into sub-sentences. We use openIE (Schmitz et al., 2012) to extract multiple relationships from the sentence, and then treat each relationship as a separate sentence.

Based on the given annotation scheme, each of the annotator received around 2500 sentences. Out of these, 2000 sentences are unique and rest 500 are overlapping. Using these 500 common sentences, we measure the inter annotator agreement of the annotation using the Fleiss Kappa (Fleiss and Paik, 1981) measure (κ). This is computed as $\kappa = \frac{\bar{P}-\bar{P}_e}{1-\bar{P}_e}$. The factor $1-\bar{P}_e$ gives the degree of agreement that is attainable above chance, and $\bar{P}-\bar{P}_e$ gives the degree of agreement actually achieved above chance. We have achieved the inter annotator agreement to be around 0.63. This implies that the expert annotated dataset is reliable to be used for further processing. Some more examples of annotated sentences are elaborated in the appendix A.

Table 3: Examples of seed and learnt terms from WordNet for lexical patterns

Seed	New Term	Wordnet Gloss of Term	Example
due to	corrode	cause to deteriorate due to agent	The acid corroded the metal.
	break down	collapse due to agent	Stomach juices break down proteins.
cause to	choke	become or cause to become obstructed	He choked on a fishbone.
	confuse	cause to be unable to think clearly	The sudden onslaught confused the enemy.

3.2 The linguistically informed Bi-directional LSTM model

There is a recent surge of interest in deep neural network based models that are based on continuous-space representation of the input and non-linear functions. Thus, such models are capable of modeling complex patterns in data and since they do not depend on manual engineering of features, they can be applied to solve problems in an end-to-end fashion. On the other hand, such neural network models fails to consider the latent linguistic characteristics of a text that can play an important role in extraction of the relevant information. Therefore, we have proposed a deep neural network model based on the bidirectional long-short term memory (LSTM) model (Hochreiter and Schmidhuber, 1997) (Schmidhuber et al., 2006) that along with the word embeddings, utilizes different linguistic features within a text for the automatic classification of cause-effect relations.

In identification of causal relationships from text, the surrounding context is of paramount information. While typical LSTMs allow the preceding elements to be considered as context for an element under scrutiny, we prefer to use bidirectional LSTMs (Bi-LSTM) networks (Graves et al., 2012) that are connected so that both future and past sequence context can be examined, i.e. both preceding and succeeding elements can be considered.

The overview of the proposed model is depicted in Figure 1. Corresponding to each input text, we determine the word embedding representation of each words of the text and the different linguistic feature embeddings. The input to the Bi-LSTM unit is an embedding vector (E)which is the composition of the word embedding representation (W_e) and the linguistic feature embeddings (W_l). This is represented as $\vec{E} = \vec{W_e} \otimes \vec{W_l}$

Generating Word Embeddings: Pre-trained GloVe word vector representations of dimension 300 have been used for this work (Pennington et al., 2014). GloVe is a relatively recent method of obtaining vector representations of words and has been proven to be effective. Along with the GloVe vector, the embedding vector of each word is appended with the vector formed from the linguistic features that has been described in the earlier section.

Generating linguistic feature embeddings: Apart from the presence of causal connectives mentioned earlier, other features added to make our model linguistically informed are relevant lexical and syntactic features : Part of Speech(POS) tags (Manning et al., 2014), Universal Dependency relations (De Marneffe et al., 2006) and position in Verb/ Noun/ Prepositional Phrase structure. We have also used the semantic features as identified by Girju (Girju, 2003) - the nine Noun hierarchies (H(1) to H(9)) in WordNet namely, *entity, psychological feature, abstraction, state, event, act, group, possession, and phenomenon.* First, a single feature Primary Causal Class (PCC) is defined for a word w_i. If $w_i \in H_i$ where H_i is any of the nine WordNet hierarchies, $PCC = H_i$, else $PCC = null$. Another feature, Secondary Causal Class(SCC) is also defined. This takes value $H(i)$ if any WordNet synonym of the word belongs to $H(i)$, and is $Null$ otherwise. Further, we consider the dependency structure of the sentence, which gives us that w_i is dependent on word p_i. In addition to the five features described above for w_i, we also consider the same five features of p_i as part of w_is feature set. If w_i is not dependent on any other word in the sentence, then the parent features are the same as the word features. An example of the linguistic feature selection can be found in appendix A.

Network Architecture: We use a k-layer Bi-RNN, composed of k Bi-RNNs stacked, where the output of each such unit is the input to the next unit (Irsoy and Cardie, 2014). A two-layer stack of Bi-LSTMs is employed for the purpose of experiments. The model is trained with Adam optimizer (Kingma and Ba, 2014) and dropout layer with the dropout value of 0.5 for each Bi-RNN. The dropout layer reduces the problem of overfitting often seen in trained models by dropping unit with connections to the neural network at random during the training process (Srivastava et al., 2014). The model is fit over runs of 2000 epochs, with batch size of 128. The loss is calculated as a function of the mean cross entropy generated. Each Bi-LSTM has 256 hidden layers and 1 final dense layer with softmax activation as output.

3.3 Causal Embeddings for Representing Similar Events

We have applied the proposed causal extraction technique over a large set of data from four different domains namely, Analyst Reports, Adverse Drug Effects, Business News and Product Recall News. We observe that a number of extracted causal events shows high degree of semantic similarity. For example, *"Engine breakdown"* and *"Engine failure"* represents the same semantic sense. Therefore, we intend to group these events into clusters. Accordingly, we device a novel algorithm to determine similar causal events. The algorithm follows the following steps: a) first identify the word embeddings of each constituent word of a causal event. The word embeddings are identified using the standard GloVe representations (Pennington et al., 2014). Apart from the word embeddings, we have also created phrase embeddings by computing a tensor product between the individual word embeddings. For example, given two causal events $C_1 = w_1, w_2..., w_i$ and $C_2 = w'_1, w'_2, ...w'_j$, where $w_1, w_2, ...w_k$ and $w'_1, w'_2...w'_k$ are the constituent word embeddings of the causal events C_1, and C_2 such that $i \neq j$, the phrase embedding $P_{(w_1, w_2)}$ is created by computing the tensor product of each adjacent word embedding pairs. This is represented as $P(w_1, w_2) = w_1 \otimes w_2$. Similar word and phrase embeddings are constructed for causal event C_2. Consequently, we define $A\ and\ B$ as the number of word embeddings in $C_1\ and C_2$ respectively. Similarly, $A'\ and\ B'$ are the number of phrase embeddings in $C_1\ and\ C_2$ respectively. Therefore, the similarity

$$S(C_1, C_2) = \frac{(S' + S'')}{N_1 + N_2}$$

The expressions N_1 and N_2 implies $A \cup B$ and $A' \cup B'$ respectively. S' and S'' are computed as: $S' = \sum_{\forall w_i \in C_1} S_{w_i}$ and $S'' = \sum_{\forall p_i \in C_1} S_{p_i}$ Where,

$$S_{w_i} = \max_{\forall w'_j \in C_2} (Sim(w_i, w'_j))$$

$$S_{p_i} = \max_{\forall p'_j \in C_2} (Sim(p_i, p'_j))$$

Again, p and p' are the individual phrase embeddings in sentence C_1 and C_2 respectively. $Sim(x, y)$ is the cosine similarity between the two word vector w_x and w_y. Based on the similarity score, we perform a k-means clustering to form clusters of similar causal events. We have used the Average silhouette method to identify number of clusters k. For the present work we obtained the value of k as 21. A partial network of a few representative clusters, as obtained from the vehicle Recall database, is shown in Figure 2. For each cluster, the size is given as number of phrases that constitute the cluster, and a few representative phrases of each cluster is also shown as reference. The name of the cluster is chosen from the most common noun chunks present in the cluster. The network itself is shown as a directed graph, with edges directed from Cause to Effect, as edge weights being computed as the fraction of total occurrences of the cause that lead to the effect.

Following the method each cluster can be further represented by a verb-noun pair as proposed in (Zhao et al., 2017). For noisy clusters where no such generalization is possible are left out for the time being.

4 Experiments and Results

We perform a number of different experiments to evaluate and compare the performance of our proposed system with the baseline systems. In general we classify the experiments into three different groups. Each group uses different techniques to identify causality in text. Group-1 uses rule based method, group-2 uses a CRF based classification model, group-3 uses Bi-LSTM model and group-4 uses our proposed linguistically informed Bi-LSTM model. The outputs of the experiments are evaluated in terms of the five given datasets that are explained earlier. Again, corresponding to each group, we define three different evaluation tasks. The tasks are distinguished in terms of the way each datasets are divided for training, development and testing purposes.

In Task-I, we took the five datasets separately and each dataset is divided into 80%, 10% and 10% for training, testing and development respectively. The F1 scores obtained by each system on the datasets by this model are reported in Table 4 for identified Cause, Effect and Causal Connec-

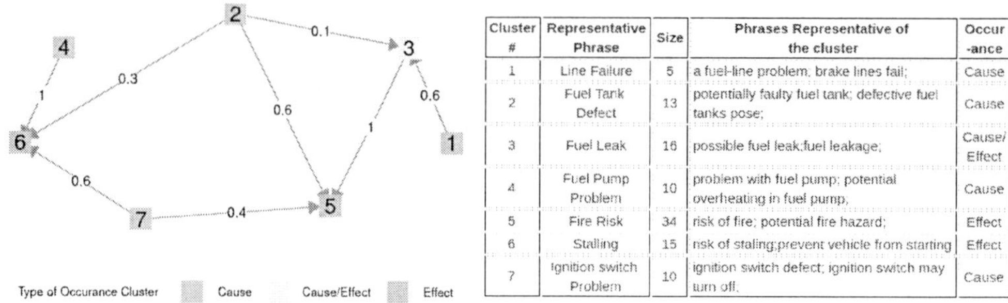

Figure 2: A projection of the network of cause-effect clusters

Table 4: Comparing F-scores of the Cause (C), Effect(E) and Connective (CC) extraction by the four classification models namely, Rule based (R), CRF, Bi-LSTM(BL) and Linguistically informed Bi-LSTM model (L-BL). The evaluation criteria follows Task-II technique where The models are trained and tested on five different dataset namely, Analyst Report (AR), BBC News (BBC), SemEval data (SEM), Adverse Drug Effect data(ADE) and Recall News (R).

		R	**CRF**	**BL**	**L-BL**
	AR	65.92	68.02	69.10	**70.12**
	BBC	61.07	68.12	70.18	**74.63**
	SEM	68.00	71.23	81.62	**84.22**
C	ADE	51.18	**69.5**	64.8	65.13
	R	76.36	74.43	75.68	**78.91**
	AR	59.14	60.45	65.13	**66.50**
	BBC	66.34	67.03	68.91	**73.48**
	SEM	69.20	76.6	78.05	**78.86**
E	ADE	58.51	**76.1**	73.56	74.05
	R	77.96	78.03	78.86	**79.16**
	AR	57.89	58.40	59.10	**59.84**
	BBC	61.32	64.19	69.02	**72.32**
	SEM	70.23	73.22	74.87	**75.39**
CC	R	66.17	70.58	72.41	**74.3**

tives.

In Task-II, we combine all the five datasets together and divide the training set, development set and test sets into 80%, 10% and 10% respectively. The division in dataset follows a five-fold manner. Therefore, the 10% testing data in fold-1 is different from the 10% testing data in fold-2 or fold-3. We compute the individual results and report the average of them.

Finally, in **Task-III**, we train the model using one dataset and test it to other four models. We conducted the experiments using the designated training portions of each dataset of BBC news, Recall News, Analyst Reports and SemEval individually to train the model and then tested all the sets on each resultant model. Of these, the best results were seen to be from the model trained on the BBC dataset.

From Table 4 we observe that in most of the

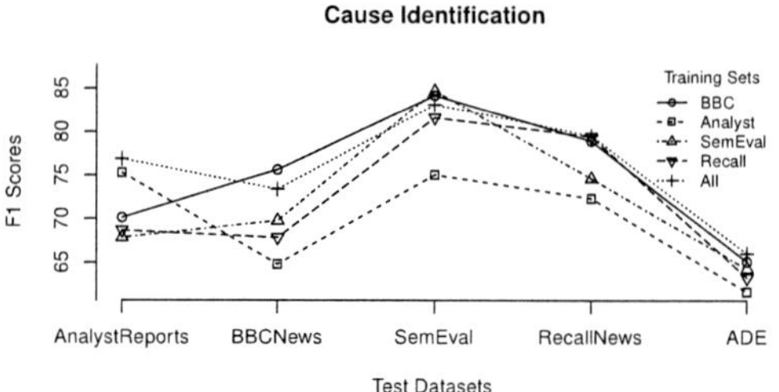

Figure 3: F1 scores for Cause Identification across different datasets for different training sets

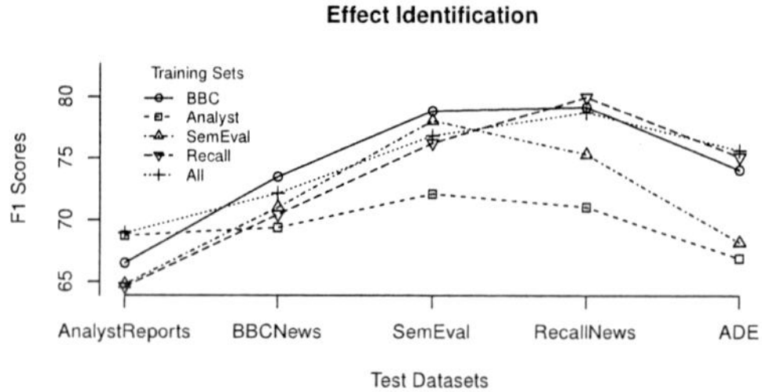

Figure 4: F1 scores for Effect Identification across different datasets for different training sets

cases Bi-directional LSTM model along with the additional layer of linguistic features significantly reduces the false negative score and achieved a high true positive score thereby achieving a high F-measure. For the project analyst report, BBC News, SEMEVAL and Recall news, we have achieved F-measures of around 66%, 73%, 79%, and 78% respectively which is best as compared to the other baseline methods. For the ADE dataset, the CRF classifier performs better than the proposed deep learning techniques, at about 73%. The inclusion of openIE as a sentence-splitter

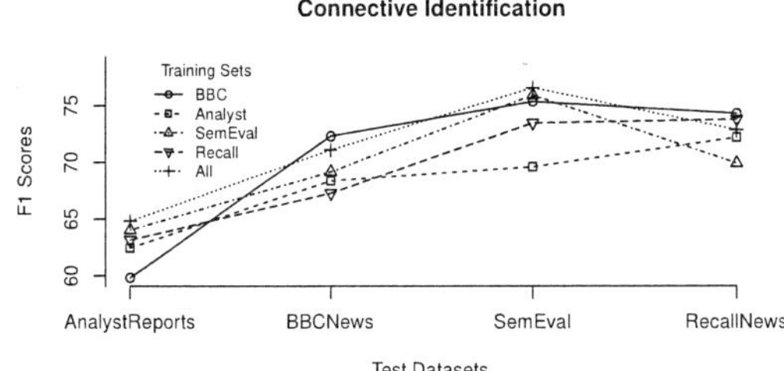

Figure 5: F1 scores for Causal Connective Identification across different datasets for different training sets

gave the most significant improvements in situations where the sentence structure was not overtly complicated, despite of the presence of multiple causal instances. Hence, the SemEval and ADE dataset results gained most from it. However, sentences from news sources often had a far more complicated structure than what OpenIE could resolve. The presence of descriptive clause along with valid cause/effect phrases made it difficult for the system to correctly identify and localize the valid phrases. In fact, the system suffered when working with such sentences, even when there was just a single instances of causality present. In the SemEval dataset, openIE usage led to identification of multiple causality in around 1/4th of the cases where multiple causality was indeed present. However, in the BBC News dataset, this amount was barely 8% of all the sentences that contained multiple instances of causation.

On an average, around 7% cases the system incorrectly predicted a cause/effect relation as valid which is actually not, whereas only 4% of the sentences were incorrectly identified as "Not an cause/effect" despite being marked as "cause/effect" by the experts. The primary reason behind this is due to fact that most of the collected texts are noisy, as a result of which the dependency parser fails to parse the texts properly and thus returning incorrect linguistic feature values. For ADE dataset, we observed that a large number of descriptions are written in languages other than English, as a result of which the classifier failed to predict correctly. Another source of error is the occurrence of incomplete sentences that restricts the classification engine to correctly label the descriptions. Apart from labeling the cause and effect events, the proposed classifier also aims to label the explicit causal connectives. Table 4 reports the results of the connective classification. We have observed that the proposed classification model is able to identify novel causal connectives that were previously not enlisted in the original causal connective list. We previously mentioned that existing schemes of having a single word represent cause and effect leads to a loss of information. Just in the SemEval dataset, just 33% of the total corpus is such that their given single-word annotation effectively captures all the information about the causal event present in the sentence. Using our proposed methodology and extending the scheme to phrases give us the complete causal information in almost 60% of the sentences that were only partially covered previously. However, we are able to somewhat quantify this observation only for the SemEval dataset, since the other datasets do not have a single-word gold standard annotation. As discussed in section 2, ambiguous causatives are a big contributor to causality being identified when it is not actually present in the sentence. Examples of some common ambiguous causal connectives, as well some of the novel connectives identified by the system (which were not present in our original list), are given in Appendix A. In addition to the above results, Figures 3, 4 and 5 show the relative performances of models trained with the individual datasets and then tested on all the test sets (Task-III).

5 Conclusion

In this paper, we present a linguistically informed deep neural network architecture for the automatic extraction of cause-effect relations from text documents. Our proposed architecture uses word level embeddings and other linguistic features to detect causal events and their effects. We evaluate the performance of the proposed model with respect to a rule based classifier and a conditional random field (CRF) based supervised classifier. We find that the bi-directional LSTM model along with an additional linguistic layer performs much better than existing baseline systems. Along with the extraction task another important contribution of this work is the development of new dataset annotated in terms of the cause-effect relations, which will be publicly shared with this paper for further research in this domain.

References

Eduardo Blanco, Nuria Castell, and Dan Moldovan. 2008. Causal relation extraction. In *Lrec*.

Quoc-Chinh Bui, Breanndán Ó Nualláin, Charles A Boucher, and Peter MA Sloot. 2010. Extracting causal relations on hiv drug resistance from literature. *BMC bioinformatics*, 11(1).

Marie De Marneffe, Bill MacCartney, Christopher Manning, et al. 2006. Generating typed dependency parses from phrase structure parses. In *Proceedings of LREC*, volume 6.

Levin B. Fleiss, J.L. and M.C. Paik. 1981. The measurement of interrater agreement. *Statistical methods for rates and proportions*, 2:212–236.

Daniela Garcia. 1997. Coatis, an nlp system to locate expressions of actions connected by causality links. *Knowledge acquisition, modeling and management*.

Roxana Girju. 2003. Automatic detection of causal relations for question answering. In *Proceedings of the ACL 2003 workshop on Multilingual summarization and question answering-Volume 12*. Association for Computational Linguistics.

Roxana Girju, Dan I Moldovan, et al. 2002. Text mining for causal relations. In *FLAIRS Conference*, pages 360–364.

Roxana Girju, Preslav Nakov, Vivi Nastase, Stan Szpakowicz, Peter Turney, and Deniz Yuret. 2007. Semeval-2007 task 04: Classification of semantic relations between nominals. In *Proceedings of the 4th International Workshop on Semantic Evaluations*, pages 13–18. Association for Computational Linguistics.

Alex Graves et al. 2012. *Supervised sequence labelling with recurrent neural networks*, volume 385. Springer.

Derek Greene and Pádraig Cunningham. 2006. Practical solutions to the problem of diagonal dominance in kernel document clustering. In *Proceedings of the 23rd international conference on Machine learning*, pages 377–384. ACM.

Ralph Grishman. 1988. Domain modeling for language analysis. Technical report, DTIC Document.

Harsha Gurulingappa, Abdul Mateen Rajput, Angus Roberts, Juliane Fluck, Martin Hofmann-Apitius, and Luca Toldo. 2012. Development of a benchmark corpus to support the automatic extraction of drug-related adverse effects from medical case reports. *Journal of biomedical informatics*, 45(5):885–892.

Iris Hendrickx, Su Nam Kim, Zornitsa Kozareva, Preslav Nakov, Diarmuid Ó Séaghdha, Sebastian Padó, Marco Pennacchiotti, Lorenza Romano, and Stan Szpakowicz. 2009. Semeval-2010 task 8: Multi-way classification of semantic relations between pairs of nominals. In *Proceedings of the Workshop on Semantic Evaluations: Recent Achievements and Future Directions*, pages 94–99. Association for Computational Linguistics.

Sepp Hochreiter and Jürgen Schmidhuber. 1997. Long short-term memory. *Neural computation*, 9(8):1735–1780.

Ozan Irsoy and Claire Cardie. 2014. Opinion mining with deep recurrent neural networks. In *EMNLP*, pages 720–728.

Ashwin Ittoo and Gosse Bouma. 2011. Extracting explicit and implicit causal relations from sparse, domain-specific texts. In *International Conference on Application of Natural Language to Information Systems*, pages 52–63. Springer.

Christopher SG Khoo, Jaklin Kornfilt, Robert N Oddy, and Sung Hyon Myaeng. 1998. Automatic extraction of cause-effect information from newspaper text without knowledge-based inferencing. *Literary and Linguistic Computing*, 13(4):177–186.

Christopher SG Khoo, Sung Hyon Myaeng, and Robert N Oddy. 2001. Using cause-effect relations in text to improve information retrieval precision. *Information processing & management*, 37(1):119–145.

Diederik Kingma and Jimmy Ba. 2014. Adam: A method for stochastic optimization. *arXiv preprint arXiv:1412.6980*.

Christopher Manning, Bauer Surdeanu, Mihai, Finkel John, Bethard Jenny, J. Steven, and David. McClosky. 2014. The stanford corenlp natural language processing toolkit. In *52nd Annual Meeting of the Association for Computational Linguistics: System Demonstrations*.

Jeffrey Pennington, Richard Socher, and Christopher Manning. 2014. Glove: Global vectors for word representation. In *Empirical Methods in Natural Language Processing (EMNLP)*.

Kira Radinsky, Sagie Davidovich, and Shaul Markovitch. 2012. Learning to predict from textual data. *Journal of Artificial Intelligence Research*, 45:641–684.

Ines Rehbein and Josef Ruppenhofer. 2017. Catching the common cause: extraction and annotation of causal relations and their participants. In *Proceedings of the 11th Linguistic Annotation Workshop*, pages 105–114.

Jürgen Schmidhuber, F Gers, and Douglas Eck. 2006. Learning nonregular languages: A comparison of simple recurrent networks and lstm. *Learning*, 14(9).

Michael Schmitz, Robert Bart, Stephen Soderland, Oren Etzioni, et al. 2012. Open language learning for information extraction. In *Proceedings of the 2012 Joint Conference on Empirical Methods in Natural Language Processing and Computational Natural Language Learning*, pages 523–534. Association for Computational Linguistics.

Antonio Sorgente, Giuseppe Vettigli, and Francesco Mele. 2013. Automatic extraction of cause-effect relations in natural language text. *DART@ AI* IA*, 2013:37–48.

Nitish Srivastava, Geoffrey E Hinton, Alex Krizhevsky, Ilya Sutskever, and Ruslan Salakhutdinov. 2014. Dropout: a simple way to prevent neural networks from overfitting. *Journal of machine learning research*, 15(1):1929–1958.

Princeton University. 2010. Wordnet. *About WordNet*.

Fang Xuelan and Graeme Kennedy. 1992. Expressing causation in written english. *RELC Journal*, 23(1):62–80.

Sendong Zhao, Quan Wang, Sean Massung, Bing Qin, Ting Liu, Bin Wang, and ChengXiang Zhai. 2017. Constructing and embedding abstract event causality networks from text snippets. In *Proceedings of the Tenth ACM International Conference on Web Search and Data Mining*, pages 335–344. ACM.

A Appendix

We use this section to elaborate on certain aspects of our work with the help of some more examples.

Table 6 shows the list of linguistic features constructed for each word of an example sentence. W1-W6 are similarly features of the original word, which are, in order,part of speech tag, universal dependency tag, parent word id, phrase structure, primary causal class and secondary causal class. Feature P is the parent word, and P1-P6 are the features of the parent word, similar to those described as W1-W6. Finally, the last column is the label associated with the word. *C* implies *Cause*, *CN* implies *Causal Connective*, *E* implies *Effect*, and *N* implies *None*.

Table 7 shows some more typical cases of causal sentences encountered and their respective annotations. As explained, the four annotation labels are *cause (C)*, *effect(E)*, *causal connectives(CC)* and *None(N)*. The second sentence contains an example of a phrase irrelevant to the actual causality that is present in the target sentence. In the current work, preciseness of the solution is dependent on it correctly disregarding the irrelevant portion and identifying causality only in the rest of the sentence. The third sentence, on the other hand, shows an example of one of the more challenging scenarios of causality identification, i.e. in the absence of any explicit causal connective. While the causality in the given sentence looks obvious to an observer, the challenge lies in the fact that there are possible grammatically and structurally similar sentences that do *not* contain causality.

Table 8 shows some common ambiguous causal connectives that identify sentences as causal even in the cases where they are not being used to identify causality. To further emphasize on their ambiguity, we show, in parallel, examples where the same connectives imply causality.

Table 5: Examples of some unusual learnt connectives

account for	**Direct payments by the patient** account for *a large proportion of funding*
derive from	*The name of Portugal* derives from **the Romano-Celtic name Portus Cale**
dictate by	*A spin label's motions* aredictated by **its local environment**
based on the fact	His *conclusion* is based on the fact **the objects contain more than 1% Arsenic**
on account of	The amount covers *expenses* on account of **his staff and transportation**
stem from	He suffers from *seizures* stemming from a **childhood injury**
punishment for	They claim the *downfall* was punishment for **the political ambitions of their leader.**
having	Having **dealt with their internal problems**, *the two companies were ripe for consolidation.*

Table 5 depicts a sample set of novel causal connectives identified by our system.

Table 6: Features of an example sentence "*Suicide is one of the leading cause of death among teens*"

Word	W1	W2	W3	W4	W5	W6	P	P1-P4	P5	P6	Label
Suicide	NNP	nsubj	3	B-NP	none	action	one	...	none	psychological	C
is	VBZ	cop	3	B-VP	none	none	one	...	none	psychological	N
one	CD	root	0	B-NP	none	psychological	one	...	none	psychological	CN
of	IN	case	7	B-PP	none	psychological	causes	...	none	action	CN
the	DT	det	7	B-NP	none	none	causes	...	none	action	CN
leading	VBG	amod	7	I-NP	none	action	causes	...	none	action	CN
causes	NNS	nmod	3	I-NP	action	none	one	...	none	psychological	CN
of	IN	case	9	B-PP	none	none	death	...	state	none	CN
death	NN	nmod	7	B-NP	state	none	causes	...	none	action	E
among	IN	case	11	B-PP	none	none	teens	...	none	none	N
teens	NNS	cop	9	B-NP	none	none	death	...	state	none	N

Table 7: Some typical annotation examples where causes are denoted in bold, effects are written in italic and connectives are underlined

They will *seize land owned by a British company* <u>as part of</u> **the President's agrarian reform program**	Example of a simple case of causality
They/*N* will/*N* seize/*E* land/*E* owned/*E* by/*E* a/*E* British/*E* company/*E* as/*CC* part/*CC* of/*CC* the/*C* President's/*C* agrarian/*C* reform/*C* program/*C*	
Gasoline is up <u>because of</u> **refinery issues in Texas**, <u>which means</u> *there will be a scramble for products in the Gulf Coast*	Example of multiple effects of single cause
Gasoline/*E1* is/*E1* up/*E1* because/*CN1* of/*CN1* refinery/*C1* issues/*C1* in/*C1* Texas/*C1* which/*CN2* means/*CN2* there/*E2* will/*E2* be/*E2* a/*E2* scramble/*E2* for/*E2* products/*E2* in/*E2* the/*E2* Gulf/*E2* Coast/*E2*	
The recent falls have partly been <u>the result of</u> **big budget deficits**, as well as **the US's yawning current account gap**	Example of multiple causes of single effect
The/*E* recent/*E* falls/*E* have partly been the/*CN* result/*CN* of/*CN* big/*C1* budget/*C1* deficits/*C1*, as well as the/*C2* US's/*C2* yawning/*C2* current/*C2* account/*C2* gap/*C2*	
According to figures from the Ministry of Economy Trade and Industry, *the decline* was <u>led by</u> **a fall in demand for electronic parts for mobile phones and digital televisions**	Example of irrelevant phrase along with causal information
According/*N* to/*N* figures/*N* from/*N* the/*N* Ministry/*N* of/*N* Economy/*N* Trade/*N* and/*N* Industry/*N* the/*E* decline/*E* was/*N* led/*CC* by/*CC* a/*C* fall/*C* in/*C* demand/*C* for/*C* electronic/*C* parts/*C* for/*C* mobile/*C* phones/*C* and/*C* digital/*C* televisions/*C*	
The increase in trade has *put the country on the same level as Romania, Egypt and El Salvador*	Example with no explicit causal connective
The/*C* increase/*C* in/*C* trade/*C* has/*N* put/*E* the/*E* country/*E* on/*E* the/*E* same/*E* level/*E* as/*E* Romania/*E* Egypt/*E* and/*E* El-Salvador/*E*	

Table 8: Examples of ambiguous causatives that indicate causation only in certain context

Connective	Example Without Causality	Example With Causality
from	*The firms higher numbers* are <u>from</u> **improved advert sales**.	The companys sales rose to $18.6bn from last year's $12.3bn.
followed by	**The tornado** caused destruction <u>followed by</u> *widespread disease*.	The leader was followed by his supporters in the march.
since	*The company has cut jobs* <u>since</u> **demands were low**.	The company has cut 5% jobs since September 2002.

Toward Zero-shot Entity Recognition
in Task-oriented Conversational Agents

Marco Guerini[1], **Simone Magnolini**[1,2], **Vevake Balaraman**[1], **Bernardo Magnini**[1]

[1] Fondazione Bruno Kessler, Via Sommarive 18, Povo, Trento — Italy

[2] AdeptMind Scholar

{guerini,magnolini,balaraman,magnini}@fbk.eu

Abstract

We present a domain portable zero-shot learning approach for entity recognition in task-oriented conversational agents, which does not assume any annotated sentences at training time. Rather, we derive a neural model of the entity names based only on available gazetteers, and then apply the model to recognize new entities in the context of user utterances. In order to evaluate our working hypothesis we focus on nominal entities that are largely used in e-commerce to name products. Through a set of experiments in two languages (English and Italian) and three different domains (furniture, food, clothing), we show that the neural gazetteer-based approach outperforms several competitive baselines, with minimal requirements of linguistic features.

1 Introduction

In this paper we focus on user utterance understanding, where a conversational system has to interpret the content of a user dialogue turn. At this step, most of conversational systems try to capture both the intent of the utterance and the relevant entities and relations that are mentioned. As an example, given a user query like: *Can I find a Canada Goose parka blue for -30?*, an online shop assistant should be able to recognize that the intent of the utterance is 'Search' and that the following entities are mentioned: Product_Category = parka; Brand = Canada Goose; Color = blue; Min_temperature = -30. We are particularly interested in application domains, like e-commerce, which show specific characteristics: large variety of entity names for the same category (e.g. *a black and white t-shirt, black pants, white vintage shoes*

are all names of clothes); compositionality of entity names (e.g. *black pants, black short pants*); utterances with multiple occurrences of the same entity category (e.g. "I would like to order a *salami pizza* and two *mozzarella cheese sandwiches*" contains two occurrences of food); strong requirements of multilinguality (e.g. *scarpe bianche vintage* and *white vintage shoes*). Finally, we are interested in domains where available repositories can only cover a portion of the possible entity names that a user can express in an interaction.

Our working hypothesis is that, in such scenarios, current entity recognition approaches based on supervision (i.e. we call them *pattern-based* as they need utterances annotated with entities in the context they occur), need a huge amount of supervision to manage the variety of entity names, which would make those approaches ineffective in most practical situations. Thus, we propose an entity recognition method, we call it *gazetteer-based*, which takes advantage of available entity names for a certain category to train a neural model that is then applied to label new unseen entities in a user utterance. This method shares several features with recent proposals in zero-shot learning (Xie et al., 2016), as we do not assume any annotated utterances at training time, and we make use of entity names as "side information".

We run several experiments on three e-commerce domains (furniture, food, clothing) and two languages (English and Italian), with different characteristics in terms of entity names, and show that: (i) the gazetteer-based approach significantly outperforms the pattern-based approach in our domains and languages; (ii) the method captures linguistic properties of the entity names related to their compositionality, which are reliable indicators of the complexity of the task.

The paper is structured as follows. Section 2 introduces the entity recognition task we are

Proceedings of the SIGDIAL 2018 Conference, pages 317–326,
Melbourne, Australia, 12-14 July 2018. ©2018 Association for Computational Linguistics

addressing. Section 3 provides background and relevant related work. Section 4 describes the gazetteer-based methodology that we adopt for entity recognition in user utterances. Finally, section 5 and 6 describe, respectively, the experimental setting and the obtained results.

2 Entity Recognition for E-commerce

Common conversational systems adopt a slot filling approach as semantic representation of the utterance content. Usually, it is assumed that the utterance contains just one entity for each slot. In addition, typical entities corresponds to named entities (e.g. locations) or to almost closed classes (e.g. time, dates, quantities, currencies). Although this is substantially true for several popular task oriented scenarios, like flight booking (a well known dataset is ATIS – Air Travel Information Services), point of interest navigation, and calendar scheduling (for instance the dataset used in (Eric and Manning, 2017)), other conversational scenarios show different characteristics. In this section we focus on conversational agents for the e-commerce scenario, and highlight the characteristics which we believe are relevant for entity recognition.

Task-oriented dialogue. E-commerce chat-bots are supposed to carry on a task-oriented dialogue whose goal is helping the user to select products presented in an online shop, and, ultimately, buy them. For the purposes of this paper we restrict our attention to written chat-style dialogues (i.e. voice is not considered).

Entity names. The main focus of the interaction is on products (i.e. users search, compare, assess information on products they are interested in). Products can be referred to in several ways, including their descriptions (e.g. *a round table with a marble top*), proper names (e.g. *Adidas Gazelle*), or with a mix of them (e.g. *a white Billy shelf*). Depending on the complexity of the domain, a single online shop may manage from thousands to several hundreds of thousand of different products, with hundreds of variants (e.g. size and colour for clothes). Throughout this paper, we refer to such product descriptions as *entity names*. As we will see, there is a high variance in the way online vendors assign and manage such names. For the purposes of this paper, it is relevant to notice that taking advantage of e-commerce website catalogs, it

is relatively easy to download repositories of entity names for a large variety of products, and for several languages. On the other hand, a structured description of such entities - in term of slot-value pairs - is often missing. We call these repositories of entity names *gazetteers*.

Conversational patterns. Conversational patterns in e-commerce dialogues are relatively simple. High level user intents vary from searching for one or more products, asking to compare characteristics of products, and finalizing the purchase. Although there are just a few datasets available to support our intuition (e.g. the Frames dataset presented in (El Asri et al., 2017)), we may assume that the context in which product names appear is quite limited. Compared to other scenarios (e.g. booking hotels and flights), it is quite frequent that user mention more than one product in the same utterance (e.g. "Please deliver at home a *salami pizza*, a *pepperoni pizza with onions* and two *mozzarella cheese sandwiches*").

Multilinguality. E-commerce is becoming more and more multilingual. The market is worldwide and vendors offer navigation in several languages. For our purposes a strong requirement is that approaches for entity recognition must be easily portable through languages.

3 Background and Related Work

In this section we report useful context for the *gazetteer based* approach that will be described in Section 4. We focus on entity recognition, zeroshot learning and generation of synthetic data.

3.1 Entity Recognition

Entity recognition has been largely approached as a sequence labeling task (see, for instance, the Conll shared tasks on named entities recognition (Tjong Kim Sang and De Meulder, 2003)). Given an utterance $U = \{t_1, t_2, ..., t_n\}$ and a set of entity categories $C = \{c_1, c_2, ..., c_m\}$, the task is to label the tokens in U that refer to entities belonging to the categories in C. As an example, using the IOB format (Inside, Outside, Beginning) (Ramshaw and Marcus, 1995), the utterance "I would like to order a salami pizza and two mozzarella cheese sandwiches", would be labeled as shown in Table 1.

We refer to the Automatic Content Extraction program - ACE (Doddington et al., 2004), where

I	would	like	to	order	a	salami	pizza	and	two	mozzarella	cheese	sandwiches
O	O	O	O	O	O	B-FOOD	I-FOOD	O	O	B-FOOD	I-FOOD	I-FOOD

Table 1: IOB annotation of food entities inside user request.

two main entity classes are distinguished: named entities and nominal entities. We focus on the latter, as this is more relevant for utterance understanding in the e-commerce scenario. Nominal entities are noun phrase expressions describing an entity. They can be composed by a single name (e.g. *pasta, carpet, parka*) or by more than one token (e.g. *capri sofa bed beige, red jeans skinny fit, lightweigh full frame camera, grilled pork belly tacos*). Nominal entities are typically compositional, as they do allow morphological and syntactic variations (e.g. for food names, *spanish baked salmon, roasted salmon* and *hot smoked salmon*), which makes it possible to combine tokens of one entity name with tokens of another entity name to generate new names (e.g. for food names, *salmon tacos* is a potential food name given the existence of *salmon* and *tacos*). In addition to adjectival and prepositional modifiers, conjunctions are also very frequent (e.g. *beef and bean burritos, black and white t-shirt*). Compositionality is crucial in our approach, as we take advantage of it to syntethically generate negative training examples for a certain entity category, as detailed in Section 4.1.

3.2 Zero-shot Learning

In conversational agents there is a general lack of data, both annotated and unannotated, as real conversations are still not widely available for different domains and languages. To overcome this limit, in our gazetteer-based approach we take advantage of the fact that it is relatively easy to obtain repositories of entity names for several categories (e.g. food names, locations, movie titles, names of products, etc.). We use such repositories as "side information" in zero-shot learning to recognize entity names for a certain class, even if no annotated utterances are available for that class. While similar approaches have been already proposed to improve portability across domains (e.g. (Bapna et al., 2017) uses slot names as side information), in this paper we take advantage of the zero-shot approach focusing on large repositories of compositional entity names.

Several approaches have been proposed to implement zero-shot learning, including those that use multiple embeddings (Norouzi et al., 2013),

those that extract features that generalize through different domains (Socher et al., 2013), and those that recast zero-shot learning as a domain adaptation problem (Elhoseiny et al., 2013).

3.3 Synthetic Data Generation

Partly due to the need of large amounts of training data to feed neural networks, recently there has been a diffused interest on methods for automatically generate synthetic data (see (Jaderberg et al., 2014)). The effectiveness of synthetic data generation has been shown in several domains, including the generation of textual descriptions of visual scenes (Hoag, 2008), and of parallel corpora for Machine Translation (Abdul-Rauf et al., 2016). Alternative approaches to data generation for conversational agents are based on simulated conversations (Shah et al., 2018). As for the e-commerce domain, because of the dramatic scarcity of available datasets, we were forced to use synthetic generation in two cases: negative training examples for entity names, used to train our gazetteer-based approach, and lexicalization of utterances, used for testing the performance of our approach.

4 NN_g Entity Recognition

In our zero-shot learning assumption we propose a neural gazetteer-based approach, which includes two main components: a neural classifier (NN_g) trained solely on the entity names in a gazetteer, described in Section 4.1, and the entity tagger that applies the neural classifier to a user utterance, described in Section 4.2.

4.1 NN_g Classifier

The NN_g classifier is the core of the gazetteer-based approach. It is implemented using a multilayer bidirectional LSTM (Schuster and Paliwal, 1997) that classifies an input sequence of tokens either as entity or non-entity for a certain entity category, with a certain degree of confidence. We base our NN_g classifier on the system proposed in (Lample et al., 2016), which was modified to match the peculiarities of the gazetteer-based approach: (i) we extend it as a 3-layer biLSTM with 120 units per layer and a single dropout layer

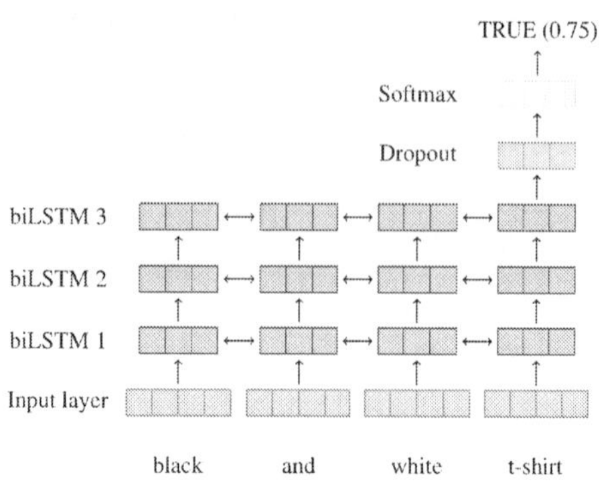

Figure 1: Structure of the Neural Gazetteer (NN_g) entity classifier. The input layer concatenates the features in a single vector.

(dropout probability of 0.5) between the third biLSTM and the output layer. This topology (see Figure 1) has been empirically defined using the train and dev portions of the synthetic gazetteers described in section 5.2. (ii) The output layer is a softmax layer – instead of a CRF layer – because the goal of NN_g is to classify the whole sequence and not to tag each single token using the IOB format. The softmax layer provides the probability of a sequence being positive or negative for a certain category, based on the output from the previous layers. We use this probability as a *confidence score* for a sequence being positive or negative.

This multilayer biLSTM is meant to build an internal representation of the core compositional structure of the entity names that are listed in the gazetteer, and to generalize such structure to recognize new entity names of the same category.

Synthetic Training Data. In order to train the NN_g classifier, we need not only positive examples (i.e. entity name), but also negative ones, i.e. sub-sequences of an utterance where no entities are present or where only parts of the entity name are present. To obtain such negative examples we used the following methodology based on synthetic generation. For each entity name i in a gazetteer G, negative counterparts can be obtained either using a sub-sequence of i (making sure it is not present in the gazetteer), or by taking i and adding tokens at the beginning or end of it (or both), following the pattern $t_1 + i + t_2$, where t_1 is the ending token of a random entity in G and t_2 is the starting token of a random entity in G. Between these tokens and i there can be

separators, as a white space, a comma or the *and* conjunction, so to mimic how multiple entities are usually expressed in sentences. Alternatively, t_1 and t_2 can be tokens randomly extracted from a generic corpus, so as to mimic cases when the entity is expressed in isolation. For example, if the initial positive example is *black and white t-shirt*, the possible negative sub-sequences that are generate are: | *black* | *white* | *black and* | *and white* | *black and white* |. The sub-sequences | *white t-shirt* | *t-shirt* | are not considered because they are already included in the gazetteer as positive examples. Adding tokens, using the pattern $t_1 + i + t_2$, we obtain other potential negative examples: | *buy black and white t-shirt* | *black and white t-shirt and sweater* | *buy black and white t-shirt and sweater* |, and so on. According to this procedure, we generate more negative examples than positive. In order to avoid an unbalanced dataset, we randomly select two negative examples per positive one: a sub-sequence and an example surrounded by other words, resulting in a 1:2 proportion.

Classifier Features. The NN_g classifier combines several features: two different word embeddings (i.e. generic and specific), a char-based embedding, and seven handcrafted features. The generic word embedding is employed to capture generic language use, and it is similar to the one used in (Lample et al., 2016). For English it was trained using the English Gigaword version 5, while for Italian it was trained using a dump of the Italian Wikipedia. We use an embedding dimension of 64 for both English and Italian, a minimum word frequency cutoff of 4, and a window size of 8. The second word embedding is employed to capture language use that is specific for each domain, and it is extracted using the training gazetteer as corpus, with a dimension of 30, a minimum word frequency cutoff of 1, and a window size of 2. Finally, the char-based embedding with a dimension of 50 is still based on (Lample et al., 2016) and it is trained on the domain gazetteers. Its function is to deal with out of vocabulary terms and possible misspellings.

Handcrafted features are meant to explicitly represent the core structure of a typical entity name. We consider seven features of an entity name: (i) the actual position of the token within an entity name; (ii) the length of the entity name under inspection; (iii) the frequency of the token in the gazetteer; (iv) the average length of the entity name containing a certain token; (v) the average position of the token in the entity name it appears in; (vi) the bigram probability with reference to the previous token in the entity name; (vii) the list of all the possible PoS associated to the token.

4.2 NN_g Tagger

The neural classifier described in the previous section is applied to all the sub-sequences of a certain utterance (see algorithm 1), in order to select candidates entity names for a certain category. After classification the algorithm takes a further step to select the actual entities, by ranking the candidates according to the confidence score provided by the classifier, and by selecting the top not overlapping candidates. As an example, the utterance "I'm looking for golden yellow shorts and dark blue shirt" contains six sub-sequences that are classified as positive by the NN_g classifier (lines [1-5]): | *shorts* | *yellow shorts* | *golden yellow shorts* | *shirt* | *blue shirt* | *dark blue shirt* |, while all other sub-sequences, such as: | *I'm looking* | *looking for a golden* | *shorts and dark* | *dark blue* |, are classified as negative. Then, positive examples are ranked according to their confidence score (lines [6]): | *golden yellow shorts* | *yellow shorts* | *dark blue shirt* | etc. Finally, *golden yellow shorts* is selected while *yellow shorts* is discarded because the latter overlaps with the former. Likewise *dark blue shirt* is selected since it is not overlapping with other already selected sub-sequences while all remaining ones are discarded (lines [7-11]).

Algorithm 1 NN_g Tagger

1: **for** *sub-sequence* in *utterance* **do**
2:     **if** *sub-sequence* is an entity **then**
3:         add *sub-sequence* to *entity-list*
4:     **else**
5:         discard *sub-sequence*
6: **order** *entity-list* by confidence-score
7: **for** *element* in *entity-list* **do**
8:     **if** *element* not overlap previous elements **then**
9:         tag *element* as entity
10:    **else**
11:        discard *element*

---

5 Experimental Setting

In this section we first introduce two alternative approaches for entity recognition that we used as

---

Algorithm 2 Rule-based entity recognition

1: G : tokens in Gazetteer - excluding stopwords.
2: $morpho$: morphological variations of token.
3: POS : possible PoS tags for the token.
4: $bigram$: All bi-grams in Gazetteer.
5:
6: **for** *token* in *utterance* **do**
7:     **if** *token* is in an NP chunk **then**
8:         **if** IN_GAZETTEER(*token*) **then**
9:             tag *token* as entity
10:    **else**
11:        **if** any(*morpho*[*word*] in G) **then**
12:            **if** any(PoS[*word*] is *noun*) **then**
13:                tag *token* as entity
14: **for** $token_i$ in *utterance* **do**
15:     **if** $bigram(token_i, token_{i+1})$ exits **then**
16:         tag $token_i$ and $token_{i+1}$ as entity
17: **Format** tags to IOB notation

---

comparison with NN_g, and then the datasets that are used for our experiments.

5.1 Entity Recognition Algorithms

We have compared the NN_g approach described in Section 4 with two alternative entity recognition approaches: an unsupervised rule-based algorithm, which takes advantage of both the entity gazetteer and of linguistic information about chunking, and a supervised algorithm that needs annotated sentences as training.

Rule-based entity recognition. This approach is based on (Eftimov et al., 2017), a system that uses a terminological-driven and rule-based named entity recognizer, taking advantage of both entity dictionaries and rules based on chunks. The core strategy is that a chunk in a text is recognized as belonging to a category C if any of its tokens are present in the gazetteer for category C. The approach in (Eftimov et al., 2017) is tailored to a single domain/language and involves merging successive chunks into a single one based on the rules imposed by the algorithm. We extended the approach by adding morphological features and the possible PoS of a word, for which we used TextPro (Pianta et al., 2008), (see Algorithm 2).

We assume that the dictionary+chunk algorithm is particularly suitable for compositional entities. In fact, actual entities in a text can still be recognized even if the perfect match is not present in the original dictionary. For example, the target entity *white t-shirt with long sleeves* can be correctly identified as long as there are entities in the gazetteer that contain the tokens of interest, such as *black and white t-shirt* and *red t-shirt with long sleeves*.

Neural pattern-based entity recognition (NN_p). We used the bidirectional LSTM architecture introduced by (Lample et al., 2016) for named entity recognition. Given an input embedding for a token in the utterance, the outputs from the forward and backward LSTM are concatenated to yield the context vector for the token, which is then used by a CRF layer to classify it to the output type (O, I-, B-). There are 100 LSTM units and a dropout of 0.5 is applied to the BiLSTM layer. To train the NN_p model, we used pre-trained embeddings on Wikipedia corpora. This helps the model to adapt itself to unseen words in the test data, provided they have an embedding.

As expected, the proposed NN_p model is highly efficient to identify the context in which an entity occurs in the utterance. However, it is also prone to make errors in the sequence of the tags (i.e. tagging a token to be I- without a preceding B- tag). This is because, when trained with limited data, the entities in the training data do not cover all possible tags for a token, and also not all the possible entities (Lample's model was trained on more than ten thousand sentences per language, but in our scenario the training data is limited to few hundred sentences). For this reason, and to highlight the model's capability to identify the context of an entity, at test time the outputs of the model are post-processed to comply with the IOB notation; e.g. tag sequences such as O, I-, B-, I- are modified to O, B-, I-, I-.

5.2 Datasets

We experimented entity recognition in three e-commerce domains and two languages for a total of six configurations. The three domains are respectively: *food*, *clothing* and *furniture*. Languages are Italian and English. In order to run our experiments the following datasets were used.

Entity gazetteers (positive examples for NN_g). We collected a gazetteer of nominal entities for each domain-language pair. To allow for consistent comparisons across languages and domains we scraped just one website per domain and extracted the English/Italian gazetteers versions. In Table 2 we describe each gazetteer, reporting its size in terms of number of entity names, the average length of the names (in number of tokens), plus the length variability of such names (standard deviation, SD). We also report additional metrics that try to grasp the complexity of entity name in the gazetteer: (i) the normalized type-token ratio (TTR), as a rough measure of how much lexical diversity there is for the nominal entities in a gazetteer, see (Richards, 1987); (ii) the ratio of $type_1$ tokens, i.e. tokens that can appear in the first position of an entity name but also in other positions, and $type_2$ tokens, i.e. tokens appearing at the end and elsewhere; (iii) the ratio of entities that contain another entity as sub-part of their name. With these measures we are able to partially quantify how difficult it is to recognize the length of an entity, how difficult is to individuate the boundaries of an entity (ratio of $type_1$ and $type_2$ tokens), how much compositionality there is starting from basic entities (i.e. how many new entities can be potentially constructed by adding new tokens). Note that $type_1$ and $type_2$ ratios can cover cases in common with sub-entity ratio, but they model different phenomena: given *white t-shirt*, the entity name *black and white skirt* represents a case of $type_1$ token for *white* but without sub-entity matching, while *white t-shirt with long sleeves* represents a sub-entity matching without making *white* a $type_1$ token.

Synthetic Gazetteers (positive + negative examples for NN_g) (SG). To train NN_g, we apply the methodology described in Section 4.1 to obtain synthetic negative data. After splitting each gazetteer using a 64:16:20 ratio (train:dev:test), we created the aforementioned data sets, where – for each entity i (positive example) present in the train-dev splits – we added two negative examples obtained by randomly selecting one of the methodologies described in Section 4.1. The optimal number of negative examples was obtained during the training phase by varying their ratio.

Synthetic Utterances (training for NN_p, test data for all approaches) (SU). To test our approaches we used synthetic sentences produced by lexicalizing templates, following the idea presented in (Cheri and Bhattacharyya, 2017; He et al., 2017). These recent approaches show the feasibility of using synthetic sentences both for training and test. More generally, there's a growing interest in using synthetic data for conversational agents, e.g. the *bAbI* datasets - meant to de-

Gazetteer	#entities	#tokens	length $\pm$ SD	TTR	type$_1$(%)	type$_2$(%)	sub-entity(%)
food_EN	58539	265726	4.54 $\pm$2.53	0.76	21.37	14.61	10.70
food_IT	29340	101860	3.47 $\pm$1.80	0.69	16.90	22.44	13.31
furniture_EN	3595	13601	3.78 $\pm$1.48	0.62	3.24	7.10	2.75
furniture_IT	2624	10045	3.83 $\pm$1.56	0.63	2.32	7.61	3.43
clothing_EN	36290	127944	3.53 $\pm$1.05	0.63	13.12	0.30	12.60
clothing_IT	34698	130106	3.75 $\pm$1.24	0.64	0.29	14.71	13.50

Table 2: Gazetteers used in the experiments. Description in terms of number of entity names, total number of tokens, average length and standard deviation (SD) of entities, type-token ratio (TTR, norm obtained by repeated sampling of 200 tokens), type$_1$ and type$_2$ unique tokens ratio and sub-entity ratio.

Intent	Template
Select	I'm fine with <entity>
Description	Could you explain to me what <entity> is
AddToList	I want to put both <entity> and <entity> on my list
RateItem	I want to give <entity> two stars

Table 3: Examples of intents and corresponding templates used to generate test utterances.

velop learning algorithms for text understanding and reasoning - were all constructed in a synthetic way (Weston et al., 2015).

We created 237 templates for English and the same amount for Italian. These templates were manually designed in order to be domain independent (e.g. using terminology that can be applied to any domain), and correspond to typical intents that can be found in the e-commerce scenario (e.g. buy, add to list, rate item, etc.) and were evenly distributed in order to contain 1 to 3 entity names. A few examples are given in Table 3.

We split the templates in a 64:16:20 ratio (train:dev:test) before lexicalization: to lexicalize SU_{train} we randomly choose entities that were in the train split of the gazetteers, while for SU_{test} we randomly choose entities than were in the test split of the gazetteers. It should be noted that we used this procedure to better isolate the effect of entity name and their compositional nature over learning approaches, in fact: (i) we controlled for the impact of patterns on learning by using the same patterns across data sets train and test splits. (ii) we made the task more challenging than in standard situations, since no entity present in the training can be present in the test sets as well. In this way we can assess the ability of the approaches to learn the structure of entity names and generalize it to

NN$_g$ features config.	F1	SDV
Gazetteer-info	88.08	4.94
Handcrafted	86.39	5.90
Embeddings	87.66	4.10
All	89.95	4.05

Table 4: Average F1 and standard deviation for various features configurations of NN$_g$ over the six SG data sets (three domains and two languages).

new examples. So, for example, a simple baseline that uses exact match over the train gazetteers to identify entities in the test sentences would report a F1 of 0.

Finally, according to our zero-shot assumption, the NN$_g$ is trained using solely SG, while its performances are computed using SU_{test}.

6 Experiments and Results

We run two different sets of experiments to explore the impact of compositionality on the task of entity recognition. The first set was meant to find the optimal feature configuration for NN$_g$, and the second one was the comparison of the three main approaches over the six SU datasets.

1. Experiments with NN$_g$ on SG. We run a set of experiments to assess the best feature configuration for the gazetteer-based approach. In Table 4 we report the overall results of NN$_g$ using different feature configurations, over the six SG data sets. The topological configuration of NN$_g$ is kept constant, as described in Section 4. As can be seen, the configuration using all features is the best one (F1 89.95), and also the one with the lowest standard deviation (4.05). This means not only that this configuration provides the best results on average but also the most consistent ones across all data sets. Interestingly, the configuration that uses no external linguistic knowledge (Gazetteer-info)

	English			Italian		
	Food	Furniture	Clothing	Food	Furniture	Clothing
Baseline 1: Rule-based	5.74	33.61	34.75	21.26	25.13	44.78
Baseline 2: NN_p	25.53	43.67	61.76	14.79	25.33	22.88
NN_g approach	32.43	63.28	76.92	37.17	40.41	62.64

Table 5: Experimental results (F1) over the six domain-language data sets.

is the second best, indicating that even in the worst case, in which no linguistic resource is available, we can still expect to obtain competitive results.

2. Experiments and Comparison on SU. Table 5 reports the comparison among the rule-based baseline, the NN_p baseline, and the NN_g approach. NN_g is the best approach on all domains and languages. This confirms our initial hypothesis that the structure of entity names induced by gazetteers is fundamental when having little knowledge of the context in which entities occur within utterances (i.e. having few training examples).

It should be noted that the effect of entity name complexity (reported in Table 2) emerges clearly from the experiments: all the approaches tend to be affected by it. In both languages we have the following order in term of performances *food* < *furniture* < *clothing*. While for *food* results are evident (the highest length-SD, TTR, $type_1$ and $type_2$ token ratios and high sub-entity ratio affect the performances even if the gazetteers are big) for *furniture* and *clothing* we need to look closer at the metrics in Table 2. Neglecting the possible effects of gazetteer size, we see that *clothing* tends to have higher ratio of $type_1$ or $type_2$ tokens: this is due to the large use of modifiers, such as colour, typical of the domain (depending on language the modifier is attached before or after the head *white t-shirt* vs *maglietta bianca*). Still, being the other token type almost 0, either the beginning or the end of an entity name is unambiguous, and in case of adjacent entities in a sentence this is enough to recognize the boundaries between the two.

The NN_g version that uses only gazetteer features (i.e. no linguistic knowledge is assumed), even if not reported in Table 5, showed to perform more poorly than the version using all features. Still, it is competitive against NN_p, outperforming it in five SU data sets out of six, and providing an average F1 improvement of 10 points.

Finally, in Table 6 we report the results of an additional analysis, where we computed the F1 scores according to the number of entities present in the test sentences (all domain and languages). As can be seen, NN_g is the least sensitive to the number of entities present in the test sentences (i.e. NN_g is the most consistent in term of performance under all circumstances). This can be explained by the fact that NN_g, being focused on recognizing entities rather than patterns, is less sensitive to cases of contiguous occurrences of entities that can be wrongly segmented by other approaches.

#Entities	Rule-based	NN_p	NN_g
One	27.46	47.39	59.04
Two	35.52	45.29	48.12
Three	22.14	24.43	52.42

Table 6: Results (F1) of the three approaches according to the number of entities in the SU datasets.

7 Conclusions and Future Work

We have provided experimental evidence that zero-shot entity recognition based on gazetteers is highly performing. To our knowledge, this is the first time that a neural model has been applied to capture compositionality of entity names. Due to the scarcity of annotated utterances, the proposed approach is particularly recommendable for its portability through different domains and languages. Our experiments have been tested on synthetic data (i.e. utterances semi-automatically generated starting from a set of conversational patterns) in the context of e-commerce chat-bots, taking advantage of some of the characteristics of the scenario. As for the future, we intend to test the approach on natural utterances (i.e. not synthetically generated).

Acknowledgements

This work has been partially supported by the AdeptMind scholarship, and by the CBF EIT Digital project. The authors thank the anonymous reviewers and Hendrik Buschmeier for their help and suggestions.

References

Sadaf Abdul-Rauf, Holger Schwenk, Patrik Lambert, and Mohammad Nawaz. 2016. Empirical use of information retrieval to build synthetic data for SMT domain adaptation. *IEEE/ACM Trans. Audio, Speech & Language Processing* 24(4):745–754.

Ankur Bapna, Gokhan Tur, Dilek Hakkani-Tur, and Larry Heck. 2017. Towards zero shot frame semantic parsing for domain scaling. In *Interspeech 2017*.

Joe Cheri and Pushpak Bhattacharyya. 2017. Towards harnessing memory networks for coreference resolution. In *Proceedings of the 2nd Workshop on Representation Learning for NLP*. pages 37–42.

George Doddington, Alexis Mitchell, Mark Przybocki, Lance Ramshaw, Stephanie Strassel, and Ralph Weischedel. 2004. The automatic content extraction (ace) program - tasks, data, and evaluation. In *Proceedings of the Fourth International Conference on Language Resources and Evaluation (LREC-2004)*. European Language Resources Association (ELRA), Lisbon, Portugal. ACL Anthology Identifier: L04-1011. http://www.lrec-conf.org/proceedings/lrec2004/pdf/5.pdf.

Tome Eftimov, Barbara Koroušić Seljak, and Peter Korošec. 2017. A rule-based named-entity recognition method for knowledge extraction of evidence-based dietary recommendations. *PLoS ONE* 12(6):e0179488.

Layla El Asri, Hannes Schulz, Shikhar Sharma, Jeremie Zumer, Justin Harris, Emery Fine, Rahul Mehrotra, and Kaheer Suleman. 2017. Frames: a corpus for adding memory to goal-oriented dialogue systems. In *Proceedings of the 18th Annual SIGdial Meeting on Discourse and Dialogue*. Association for Computational Linguistics, pages 207–219. http://aclweb.org/anthology/W17-5526.

Mohamed Elhoseiny, Babak Saleh, and Ahmed Elgammal. 2013. Write a classifier: Zero-shot learning using purely textual descriptions. In *Computer Vision (ICCV), 2013 IEEE International Conference on*. IEEE, pages 2584–2591.

Mihail Eric and Christopher D. Manning. 2017. Key-value retrieval networks for task-oriented dialogue. *CoRR* abs/1705.05414. http://arxiv.org/abs/1705.05414.

Shizhu He, Cao Liu, Kang Liu, and Jun Zhao. 2017. Generating natural answers by incorporating copying and retrieving mechanisms in sequence-to-sequence learning. In *Proceedings of the 55th Annual Meeting of the Association for Computational Linguistics (Volume 1: Long Papers)*. volume 1, pages 199–208.

Joseph E. Hoag. 2008. *Synthetic Data Generation: Theory, Techniques and Applications*. Ph.D. thesis, Fayetteville, AR, USA. AAI3317844.

Max Jaderberg, Karen Simonyan, Andrea Vedaldi, and Andrew Zisserman. 2014. Synthetic data and artificial neural networks for natural scene text recognition. *CoRR* abs/1406.2227. http://arxiv.org/abs/1406.2227.

Guillaume Lample, Miguel Ballesteros, Sandeep Subramanian, Kazuya Kawakami, and Chris Dyer. 2016. Neural architectures for named entity recognition. *CoRR* abs/1603.01360. http://arxiv.org/abs/1603.01360.

Mohammad Norouzi, Tomas Mikolov, Samy Bengio, Yoram Singer, Jonathon Shlens, Andrea Frome, Greg Corrado, and Jeffrey Dean. 2013. Zero-shot learning by convex combination of semantic embeddings. *CoRR* abs/1312.5650. http://arxiv.org/abs/1312.5650.

Emanuele Pianta, Christian Girardi, and Roberto Zanoli. 2008. The textpro tool suite. In *Proceedings of the Sixth International Conference on Language Resources and Evaluation (LREC'08)*. Marrakech, Morocco. Http://www.lrec-conf.org/proceedings/lrec2008/.

Lance A. Ramshaw and Mitchell P. Marcus. 1995. Text chunking using transformation-based learning. *CoRR* cmp-lg/9505040. http://arxiv.org/abs/cmp-lg/9505040.

Brian Richards. 1987. Type/token ratios: What do they really tell us? *Journal of child language* 14(2):201–209.

M. Schuster and K.K. Paliwal. 1997. Bidirectional recurrent neural networks. *Trans. Sig. Proc.* 45(11):2673–2681. https://doi.org/10.1109/78.650093.

Pararth Shah, Dilek Hakkani-Tür, Gökhan Tür, Abhinav Rastogi, Ankur Bapna, Neha Nayak, and Larry P. Heck. 2018. Building a conversational agent overnight with dialogue self-play. *CoRR* abs/1801.04871.

Richard Socher, Milind Ganjoo, Christopher D Manning, and Andrew Ng. 2013. Zero-shot learning through cross-modal transfer. In *Advances in Neural Information Processing Systems 26*, Curran Associates, Inc., pages 935–943. http://papers.nips.cc/paper/5027-zero-shot-learning-through-cross-modal-transfer.pdf.

Erik F Tjong Kim Sang and Fien De Meulder. 2003. Introduction to the conll-2003 shared task: Language-independent named entity recognition. In *Proceedings of the seventh conference on Natural language learning at HLT-NAACL 2003-Volume 4*. Association for Computational Linguistics, pages 142–147.

Jason Weston, Antoine Bordes, Sumit Chopra, Alexander M Rush, Bart van Merriënboer, Armand Joulin, and Tomas Mikolov. 2015. Towards ai-complete question answering: A set of prerequisite toy tasks. *arXiv preprint arXiv:1502.05698*.

Sihong Xie, Shaoxiong Wang, and Philip S. Yu. 2016. Active zero-shot learning. In *Proceedings of the 25th ACM International on Conference on Information and Knowledge Management*. ACM, New York, NY, USA, CIKM '16, pages 1889–1892. https://doi.org/10.1145/2983323.2983866.

Appendix

In this section we provide some examples where NN_g is able to handle cases of entity names that other approaches are not able to. These cases are mainly due to token type ($type_1$ and $type_2$) and consecutive entities in a sentence – see table 7.

	NN_g	NN_p	Rule-based
Type$_1$ token error			
roasted	B-	B-	B-
asparagus	I-	I-	I-
with	I-	O	I-
orange	I-	B-	I-
glaze	I-	I-	I-
ann	B-	O	B-
chair	I-	B-	I-
mustard	I-	I-	I-
Type$_2$ token error			
dolly	B-	B-	B-
cushion	I-	I-	I-
cover	I-	O	I-
beige	I-	B-	I-
Consecutive entities error			
layene	B-	B-	B-
armchair	I-	I-	I-
bed	I-	I-	I-
brown	I-	I-	I-
trap	B-	I-	I-
chair	I-	I-	I-
dark	I-	I-	I-
brown	I-	I-	I-
ralf	B-	I-	I-
chair	I-	I-	I-
and	O	O	I-
malira	B-	B-	B-
table	I-	I-	I-

Table 7: some entity names correctly segmented by our approach but not by other approaches. In bold the type$_{1/2}$ token causing the error.

Identifying Explicit Discourse Connectives in German

Peter Bourgonje and **Manfred Stede**
Applied Computational Linguistics
University of Potsdam / Germany
`firstname.lastname@uni-potsdam.de`

Abstract

We are working on an end-to-end Shallow Discourse Parsing system for German and in this paper focus on the first subtask: the identification of explicit connectives. Starting with the feature set from an English system and a Random Forest classifier, we evaluate our approach on a (relatively small) German annotated corpus, the Potsdam Commentary Corpus. We introduce new features and experiment with including additional training data obtained through annotation projection and achieve an f-score of 83.89.

1 Introduction

A task central to the field of Discourse Processing is the uncovering of coherence relations that hold between individual (elementary) units of a text. When discourse relations are explicitly signaled in a text, the explicit markers are called *(discourse) connectives*. Connectives can be two-way ambiguous in the sense of having either a discourse or a sentential reading, and if they have a discourse reading, many can assign multiple senses. Further, connectives form a syntactically heterogeneous group and include coordinating and subordinating conjunctions, adverbials, and depending on the definition maintained, also certain prepositions. In our experiments, we adopt the definition of Pasch et al. (2003, p.331) where X is a connective if X cannot be inflected, the meaning of X is a two-place relation, the arguments of X are propositional structures and the expressions of the arguments of X can be sentential structures. Following Stede (2002), we include prepositions that have a discourse function.

Recent approaches toward end-to-end shallow discourse parsing (SDP) have focused on a pipeline approach where the identification of discourse connectives is the first step, followed by the extraction of the arguments of the connective and the classification of the sense. This pipeline architecture has dominated the CONLL 2015[1] and 2016[2] shared tasks on SDP. We will adopt it for our goal, viz. developing an end-to-end discourse parser for German. This paper focuses on the first step in the pipeline and introduces a connective identification module for German. We train a classifier using annotated data (Section 3), investigate and extend the feature set (Section 4), discuss and evaluate the results (Section 5) and summarize in Section 6.

2 Related Work

Early attempts at formalizing discourse parsing procedures for English are described in (Soricut and Marcu, 2003), among others. Pitler and Nenkova (2009) experiment with syntactically motivated features for the binary classification of discourse connectives (connective or non-connective reading) and report an f-score of 94.19 for the PDTB data (Prasad et al., 2008). The SDP pipeline architecture is adopted from Lin et al. (2014) and is also used in the best-scoring systems of the 2015 and 2016 CONLL shared tasks, (Wang and Lan, 2015) and (Oepen et al., 2016) respectively. Oepen et al. (2016) achieve an overall f-score of 27.77 for full SDP, but 91.79 for identifying explicit connectives. The best-scoring system for this subtask (Li et al., 2016) achieved an impressive 98.38.

A notable drawback of the pipeline architecture is the possibility of error propagation. This is addressed by (Biran and McKeown, 2015), who use

---

[1] `http://www.cs.brandeis.edu/~clp/conll15st/`
[2] `http://www.cs.brandeis.edu/~clp/conll16st/`

327

Proceedings of the SIGDIAL 2018 Conference, pages 327–331,
Melbourne, Australia, 12-14 July 2018. ©2018 Association for Computational Linguistics

a tagging-based approach and divide the task into processing intra-sentential and inter-sentential relations (as opposed to the more typical division into explicit and implicit relations) and report a final f-score of 39.33. This is based on a more lenient scoring system though, and Oepen et al. (2016) achieve 44.20 using a similar partial matching scoring system.

The main resources available for German are DiMLex, a lexicon of German discourse connectives containing 275 entries (Stede, 2002), (Scheffler and Stede, 2016) and the Potsdam Commentary Corpus (PCC) (Stede and Neumann, 2014), described in more detail in Section 3. We experiment with generating extra training data through annotation projection. This approach is inspired by Versley (2010), who attempts to disambiguate German connectives using a parallel English-German corpus. Earlier work on connective identification for German is done by (Dipper and Stede, 2006), who train the Brill Tagger using a modified tag set and consider only 9 of the 42 ambiguous entries in DiMLex, reporting an f-score of 90.20. In our present study, we deal with the full set of connectives for which we have training data.

3   Data

To the best of our knowledge, the only German corpora containing discourse annotations are the PCC[3] and a subsection of the TüBa-D/Z corpus (Versley and Gastel, 2012), complemented by a lexicon of discourse connectives; DiMLex[4]. We use the PCC, which is a corpus of 176 texts taken from the editorials page of a local German newspaper and is annotated on several layers: discourse connectives and their arguments and sense, syntax trees, Rhetorical Structure Theory trees and coreference chains.

The PCC contains in total 33,222 words and 1,176 connective instances. Because the texts were not sampled to extract targeted examples (of particular connectives or senses), they do not contain the full set of connective entries from DiMLex, but 156 unique connectives, compared to in total 275 entries in DiMLex. From this corpus we extracted 3,406 data instances (1,176 connective instances, plus 2,230 candidates with a

non-connective reading). Of 156 unique connectives, 74 are unambiguous and always have discourse reading (at least in the PCC). But these 74 connectives represent only 279 instances (8% of the total data). Of the remaining 82 connectives, the distribution is heavily skewed and covers the full spectrum of possibilities; while connectives like 'Und'[5] ('and'), 'sondern' ('but/rather') and 'wenn' ('if') have a high connective ratio of 0.95, 0.93 and 0.97 respectively; 'als' ('as'), 'Wie' ('(such) as') and 'durch' ('by/through') very seldom have the connective reading (a ratio of 0.08, 0.05, and 0.06, respectively).

In comparison, the training section of the 2016 CONLL shared task data alone contains ca. 933k words and ca. 278k training instances, so we cannot expect to get results nearly as good as those that were obtained for English. In an attempt to generate additional training data, we thus experimented with annotation projection, inspired by Versley (2010). We implemented an English connective classifier using the feature set of Lin et al. (2014), classified the English part of a parallel corpus, located the German counterparts through word alignment, and used the sentences obtained as additional training data. The parallel corpus is EuroParl (Koehn, 2005) and the word alignments were obtained using MGIZA (Gao and Vogel, 2008). Filtering out input sentences of more than 100 words (due to high syntactic parsing costs for subsequent steps) and alignments to German words not present in DiMLex, this resulted in 18,853 extra data instances.

4   Method

We started with the feature set of Lin et al. (2014) (in turn based on (Pitler and Nenkova, 2009)), which is a combination of surface (token and bigram), part-of-speech and syntactic features (like path to the root node, category of the siblings, etc.). The parse trees are obtained from the NLTK implementation of the Stanford Parser for German (Rafferty and Manning, 2008). We use a Random Forest classifier (Pedregosa et al., 2011) for all experiments. All scores are the result of 10-fold cross-validation using 90% of the PCC as training data and the remaining 10% as test data (except for the setup using the additional EuroParl data; this data is added to the training data for each of

---

[3]`http://angcl.ling.uni-potsdam.de/resources/pcc.html`

[4]`https://github.com/discourse-lab/dimlex`

[5]Note that we make a distinction between 'Und' (uppercase U) and 'und' here.

the 10 folds). As a result of error analysis on the output when using the base feature set, we added some extra features. Because we include prepositions in our set of connectives (which additionally includes conjunctions and adverbials), we included a feature indicating the syntactic group of the connective to explicitly differentiate for five cases; the four categories above[6] plus *other* for the remaining cases (like 'um...zu' (discontinuous 'in order...to')). The value for this feature is just a more general label than connective's part-of-speech category, included to avoid sparsity. While being sentence-initial is in most cases reflected by the bigram features, we included an explicit feature that indicates whether or not the candidate is initial to a clause that starts with S (S or S-*bar*). These two features, which are directly derived from other features already present in the set, would likely not improve performance much if more training data is available, but as our experiments show, they do improve the f-score by another 2 points in our scenario in which training data is limited. Another feature that improved performance was sentence length; intuitively it makes sense that as sentences get longer, the need for explicit structuring of the propositions therein increases. Together, these added features improved the f-score (see Table 1).

5   Results & Evaluation

The results for the different setups are illustrated in Table 1. We use a micro-averaged f1 score for all experiments.

We compare performance of the classifier to a majority vote baseline, where each instance is assigned its most frequent label. Using the base feature set results in an f-score of 81.90 (second row of Table 1). Using extra training data generated through annotation projection on EuroParl yields a negative result (below the baseline) and f-score decreases considerably, to 65.98 (third row). This decrease can be explained by the susceptibility of this approach to error propagation. The English classifier, trained on the PDTB (f-score of 93.64) is applied to another domain (EuroParl), word-alignments introduce errors, and the additional German training data is again from another domain (EuroParl) than the test set (news commentary). The extra training data obtained in this

way (18,853 instances) apparently does not compensate for this. We note that the scores resulting from annotation projection data are comparable to the f-score of 68.7 reported by (Versley, 2010). This may suggest an upper-limit in performance when using data obtained through annotation projection, but more research is needed to verify this.

Since the PCC has gold annotations for syntax trees, we used these for part-of-speech tag and other syntactic features, in order to establish the impact of parsing errors. As shown in the first row, this mainly impacts precision and leads to an increase of almost 5 points for the f-score (using the base feature set). However, because having access to gold parses is not feasible in an end-to-end scenario, we consider this an estimation of the impact of parsing errors and continue using automatically generated parse trees for the other experiments.

The best results were obtained using the extended feature set (see Section 4) and are displayed in the last row of Table 1.

Inspecting the individual scores, we found that in particular 'auch' ('also') and 'als' ('as/than') were difficult to classify (with f-scores of 27.03 and 28.57, respectively), despite being relatively frequent (208 and 147 examples in the PCC). Although they are not connectives in the majority of cases (ratios of 0.13 ('auch') and 0.08 ('als')), some connectives with similar ratios yet significantly lower frequencies have higher f-scores, such as 'so' ('so/thus'); frequency of 108, ratio of 0.11 and f-score of 72.00) and 'damit' ('in order to/thereby'); frequency of 30, ratio of 0.19 and f-score of 60.00. When using separate classifiers for the different syntactic categories (a setup which did not result in improved performance), the conjunctions performed best (with 91.81 for coordinating and 90.25 for subordinating conjunctions) and prepositions worst (51.55), but group-internally the differences were equally large, with some prepositions having above-average scores and some having scores close to 0. Further attempts at increasing the overall f-score quickly led to looking into solutions for individual connectives and came with the risk of over-fitting to the data set.

To put our score for German into perspective, we performed a set of experiments with different amounts of training data for English. Figure 1 shows the f-score (y-axis) when gradually increasing the number of training instances (x-axis). The

---

[6]prepositions, co-ordinating conjunctions, sub-ordinating conjunctions and adverbials

	precision	recall	f-score
majority vote baseline	73.76	87.32	79.60
base features + gold trees	*86.44*	*85.13*	*85.76*
base features + auto-generated trees	78.88	85.16	81.90
base features + EuroParl training data	74.23	59.54	65.96
extended features + auto-generated trees	**82.16**	**85.69**	**83.89**

Table 1: Results for binary connective classification on PCC for gold trees and automatically generated trees

blue line represents the curve for English, starting with 1,000 instances randomly sampled from the total of 278k instances in the 2016 CONLL shared task data. Recall that using this full set, the f-score using the same feature set and classification algorithm (RandomForest) is 93.64. The orange triangle represents performance for German, using all available instances from the PCC. While we have no explanation for the dent in the curve at 10,000 instances (and the smaller one around 20,000), we focus on the German score and note that with 81.90, this is 1.8 points higher than the corresponding score for English (80.09). This comparison suggests that the problem of connective identification is not significantly more or less challenging for German than it is for English. In fact, seeing that we also include the syntactic category of prepositions (which is not included in the PDTB connectives), and this group scored the worst in our separate-classifier setup, it suggests that for the other categories, performance is better for German than it is for English. When leaving out prepositions altogether, f-score increased to 85.99. But because it was a conscious decision to include prepositions, the most straightforward means of improving performance for the problem at hand seems to be adding more (in-domain) training data.

6 Conclusion & Outlook

We implement the first part of a pipeline for end-to-end discourse parsing for German; the identification of discourse connectives. We use a Random Forest classifier and add additional syntactic features to the base set, which is taken from a state-of-the-art system for English. Evaluating this approach on the Potsdam Commentary Corpus, we arrive at an f-score of 83.89, improving by over 4 points compared to a majority vote baseline. Generating additional training data through annotation projection on a parallel corpus does not

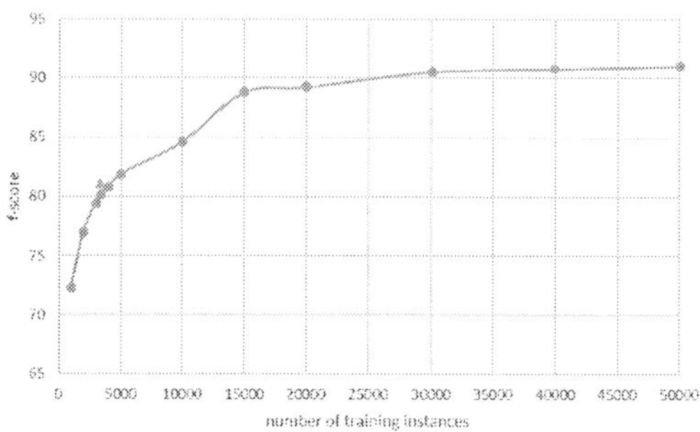

Figure 1: f-scores for varying training data volumes for English (blue line) and f-score for PCC as training data for German (orange triangle)

improve performance. Our approach is best compared to Dipper and Stede (2006), who achieve a higher f-score (90.20) but only consider 9 connectives whereas we consider the full set present in the annotated data. Versley (2010) also does not limit the set of connectives but uses an annotation projection approach resulting in an f-score of 68.7.

We show that performance for German is on par with (in fact, slightly better than) English when using the same amount of training data, the same feature set and the same classifier. This may suggest that the task is not necessarily more challenging or complicated for German than it is for English, though it remains unclear what role domain plays here (news commentary in the German case vs. news in the English case). We plan to annotate more training data in the same domain, but also out-of-domain to establish domain influence. We will continue to work on the follow-up components in the pipeline (argument extraction and sense classification), but will simultaneously attempt to improve performance for this first step in the pipeline, due to the sensitivity of the architecture to error propagation.

Acknowledgments

We are grateful to the Deutsche Forschungsgemeinschaft (DFG) for funding this work in the project 'Anaphoricity in Connectives'. We would like to thank the anonymous reviewers for their helpful comments on an earlier version of this manuscript.

References

Or Biran and Kathleen McKeown. 2015. PDTB Discourse Parsing as a Tagging Task: The Two Taggers Approach. In *SIGDIAL Conference*. The Association for Computer Linguistics, pages 96–104.

Stefanie Dipper and Manfred Stede. 2006. Disambiguating potential connectives. In *Proceedings of the KONVENS Conference*. Konstanz.

Qin Gao and Stephan Vogel. 2008. Parallel implementations of word alignment tool. In *Software Engineering, Testing, and Quality Assurance for Natural Language Processing*. Association for Computational Linguistics, SETQA-NLP '08, pages 49–57.

Philipp Koehn. 2005. Europarl: A parallel corpus for statistical machine translation. In *Conference Proceedings: the tenth Machine Translation Summit*. AAMT, Phuket, Thailand, pages 79–86.

Zhongyi Li, Hai Zhao, Chenxi Pang, Lili Wang, and Huan Wang. 2016. A Constituent Syntactic Parse Tree Based Discourse Parser. In *Proceedings of the CONLL 2016 Shared Task*. Berlin, pages 60–64.

Ziheng Lin, Hwee Tou Ng, and Min-Yen Kan. 2014. A PDTB-Styled End-to-End Discourse Parser. *Natural Language Engineering* 20:151–184.

Stephan Oepen, Jonathon Read, Tatjana Scheffler, Uladzimir Sidarenka, Manfred Stede, Erik Velldal, and Lilja Øvrelid. 2016. OPT: OsloPotsdamTeesside—Pipelining Rules, Rankers, and Classifier Ensembles for Shallow Discourse Parsing. In *Proceedings of the CONLL 2016 Shared Task*. Berlin.

Renate Pasch, Ursula Brauße, Eva Breindl, and Ulrich Herrmann Waßner. 2003. *Handbuch der deutschen Konnektoren*. Walter de Gruyter, Berlin/New York.

Fabian Pedregosa, Gael Varoquaux, Alexandre Gramfort, Vincent Michel, Bertrand Thirion, Olivier Grisel, Mathieu Blondel, Peter Prettenhofer, Ron Weiss, Vincent Dubourg, Jake Vanderplas, Alexandre Passos, David Cournapeau, Matthieu Brucher, Matthieu Perrot, and Edouard Duchesnay. 2011. Scikit-learn: Machine Learning in Python. *Journal of Machine Learning Research* 12:2825–2830.

Emily Pitler and Ani Nenkova. 2009. Using syntax to disambiguate explicit discourse connectives in text. In *Proceedings of the ACL-IJCNLP 2009 Conference Short Papers*. Association for Computational Linguistics, ACLShort '09, pages 13–16.

Rashmi Prasad, Nikhil Dinesh, Alan Lee, Eleni Miltsakaki, Livio Robaldo, Aravind Joshi, and Bonnie Webber. 2008. The Penn Discourse Treebank 2.0. In *In Proceedings of LREC*.

Anna N. Rafferty and Christopher D. Manning. 2008. Parsing Three German Treebanks: Lexicalized and Unlexicalized Baselines. In *Proceedings of the Workshop on Parsing German*. Association for Computational Linguistics, PaGe '08, pages 40–46.

Tatjana Scheffler and Manfred Stede. 2016. Adding semantic relations to a large-coverage connective lexicon of German. In Nicoletta Calzolari et al., editor, *Proc. of the Ninth International Conference on Language Resources and Evaluation (LREC 2016)*. Portoro, Slovenia.

Radu Soricut and Daniel Marcu. 2003. Sentence level discourse parsing using syntactic and lexical information. In *Proceedings of the 2003 Human Language Technology Conference of the North American Chapter of the Association for Computational Linguistics*.

Manfred Stede. 2002. DiMLex: A lexical approach to discourse markers. In *Exploring the Lexicon - Theory and Computation*. Edizioni dell'Orso, Alessandria.

Manfred Stede and Arne Neumann. 2014. Potsdam Commentary Corpus 2.0: Annotation for discourse research. In *Proceedings of the Ninth International Conference on Language Resources and Evaluation (LREC'14)*. European Language Resources Association (ELRA), Reykjavik, Iceland.

Yannick Versley. 2010. Discovery of Ambiguous and Unambiguous Discourse Connectives via Annotation Projection. In *Proceedings of Workshop on Annotation and Exploitation of Parallel Corpora (AEPC)*. Northern European Association for Language Technology (NEALT).

Yannick Versley and Anna Gastel. 2012. Linguistic tests for discourse relations in the TüBa-D/Z corpus of written German. *Dialogue and Discourse* pages 1–24.

Jianxiang Wang and Man Lan. 2015. A Refined End-to-End Discourse Parser. In *Proceedings of the Nineteenth Conference on Computational Natural Language Learning - Shared Task*. Association for Computational Linguistics, pages 17–24.

Feudal Dialogue Management with Jointly Learned Feature Extractors

Iñigo Casanueva*, Paweł Budzianowski, Florian Kreyssig,
Stefan Ultes, Bo-Hsiang Tseng, Yen-chen Wu and Milica Gašić
Department of Engineering, University of Cambridge, UK
{ic340,pfb30,mg436}@cam.ac.uk

Abstract

Reinforcement learning (RL) is a promising dialogue policy optimisation approach, but traditional RL algorithms fail to scale to large domains. Recently, Feudal Dialogue Management (FDM), has shown to increase the scalability to large domains by decomposing the dialogue management decision into two steps, making use of the domain ontology to abstract the dialogue state in each step. In order to abstract the state space, however, previous work on FDM relies on handcrafted feature functions. In this work, we show that these feature functions can be learned jointly with the policy model while obtaining similar performance, even outperforming the handcrafted features in several environments and domains.

1 Introduction

In task-oriented Spoken Dialogue Systems (SDS), the Dialogue Manager (DM) (or policy) is the module in charge of deciding the next action in each dialogue turn. One of the most popular approaches to model the DM is Reinforcement Learning (RL) (Sutton and Barto, 1999), having been studied for several years (Levin et al., 1998; Williams and Young, 2007; Henderson et al., 2008; Pietquin et al., 2011; Gašić et al., 2013; Young et al., 2013). However, as the dialogue state space increases, the number of possible trajectories needed to be explored grows exponentially, making traditional RL methods not scalable to large domains.

Recently, Feudal Dialogue Management (FDM) (Casanueva et al., 2018) has shown to increase the scalability to large domains. This approach is based on Feudal RL (Dayan and Hinton, 1993),

a hierarchical RL method that divides a task spatially rather than temporally, decomposing the decisions into several steps and using different levels of abstraction for each sub-decision. When applied to domains with large state and action spaces, FDM showed an impressive performance increase compared to traditional RL policies.

However, the method presented in Casanueva et al. (2018), named FDQN[1], relied on handcrafted feature functions in order to abstract the state space. These functions, named Domain Independent Parametrisation (DIP) (Wang et al., 2015), are used to transform the belief of each slot into a fixed size representation using a large set of rules.

In this paper, we demonstrate that the feature functions needed to abstract the belief state in each sub-decision can be jointly learned with the policy. We introduce two methods to do it, based on feed forward neural networks and recurrent neural networks respectively. A modification of the original FDQN architecture is also introduced which stabilizes learning, avoiding overfitting of the policy to a single action. Policies with jointly learned feature functions achieve similar performance to those using handcrafted ones, with superior performance in several environments and domains.

2 Background

Dialogue management can be cast as a continuous MDP (Young et al., 2013) composed of a finite set of actions $\mathcal{A}$, a continuous multivariate belief state space $\mathcal{B}$ and a reward function $\mathcal{R}(b_t, a_t)$. At a given time t, the agent observes the belief state $b_t \in \mathcal{B}$, executes an action $a_t \in \mathcal{A}$ and receives a reward $r_t \in \mathbb{R}$ drawn from $\mathcal{R}(b_t, a_t)$. The action taken, a, is decided by the *policy*, defined as the function $\pi(b) = a$. The objective of RL is to find the optimal policy π^* that maximizes

---

*Currently at PolyAI, inigo@poly-ai.com

[1] In the rest of the paper we will refer to the FDM model presented in Casanueva et al. (2018) as FDQN.

Proceedings of the SIGDIAL 2018 Conference, pages 332–337,
Melbourne, Australia, 12-14 July 2018. ©2018 Association for Computational Linguistics

the expected return R in each belief state, where $R = \sum_{\tau=t}^{T-1} \gamma^{(\tau-t)} r_\tau$, γ is a discount factor, t is the current timestep and T is the terminal timestep.

There are 2 major approaches to model the policy, *Policy-based* and *Value-based* algorithms. In the former, the policy is directly parametrised by a function $\pi(b; \theta) = a$, where θ are the parameters learned in order to maximise R. In the later, the optimal policy can be found by greedily taking the action which maximises the *Q-value*, $Q^\pi(b, a)$, defined as the expected R, starting from state b, taking action a, and then following policy π until the end of the dialogue at time step T:

$$Q^\pi(b, a) = \mathbb{E}\{R | b_t = b, a_t = a\} \qquad (1)$$

2.1 Feudal Dialogue Management

In FDM (Casanueva et al., 2018) (Fig. 1), the (summary) actions are divided in two subsets; slot independent actions $\mathcal{A}_i$ (e.g. hello(), inform()); and slot dependent actions $\mathcal{A}_d$ (e.g. request(), confirm()). In addition, a set of master actions $\mathcal{A}_m = (a_i^m, a_d^m)$ is defined, where a_i^m corresponds to taking an action from $\mathcal{A}_i$ and a_d^m to taking an action from $\mathcal{A}_d$. The feudal dialogue policy, $\pi(b) = a$, decomposes the decision in each turn into two steps. In the first step, the policy decides to take either a slot independent or a slot dependent action. In the second step, the state of each sub-policy is abstracted to account for features related to that slot, and a primitive action is chosen from the previously selected subset. In order to abstract the dialogue state for each sub-policy, a feature function $\phi_s(b) = b_s$ is defined for each slot $s \in \mathcal{S}$, as well as a slot independent feature function $\phi_i(b) = b_i$ and a master feature function $\phi_m(b) = b_m$.

Finally, a master policy $\pi_m(b_m) = a^m$, a slot independent policy $\pi_i(b_i) = a^i$ and a slot dependent policy $\pi_d(b_s | \forall s \in \mathcal{S}) = a^d$ are defined, where $a^m \in \mathcal{A}_m$, $a^i \in \mathcal{A}_i$ and $a^d \in \mathcal{A}_d$. In FDQN, π_m and π_i are modelled as value-based policies. However, Policy-based models can be used to model π_m and π_i, as introduced in section 3.1. In order to generalise between slots, π_d is defined as a set of slot specific policies $\pi_s(b_s) = a^d$, one for each $s \in \mathcal{S}$. The slot specific policies have shared parameters, and the differences between slots are accounted by the abstracted dialogue state b_s. π_d runs each slot specific policy, π_s, for all $s \in \mathcal{S}$, choosing the action-slot pair that maximises the Q-value over all the slot sub-

policies[2].

$$\pi_d(b_s | \forall s \in \mathcal{S}) = \underset{a^d \in \mathcal{A}_d, s \in \mathcal{S}}{\text{argmax}}\ Q^s(b_s, a^d) \qquad (2)$$

Then, the summary action a is constructed by joining a^d and s (e.g. if a^d=*request()* and s=*food*, then the summary action will be *request(food)*). A pseudo-code of the Feudal Dialogue Policy algorithm is given in Appendix B.

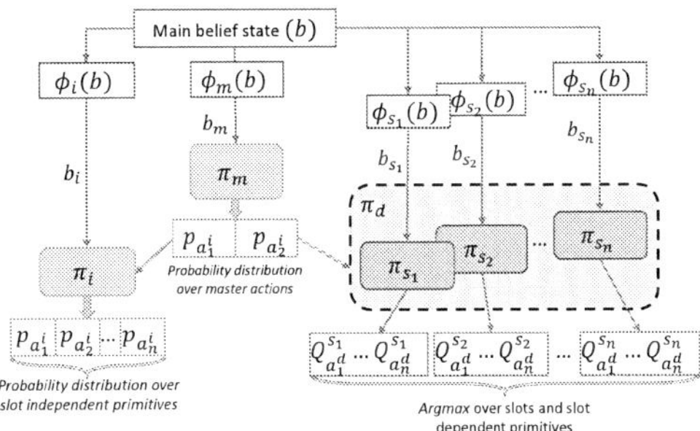

Figure 1: Feudal dialogue architecture used in this work. The sub-policies surrounded by the dashed line have shared parameters. The blue rectangles represent Value-based sub-policies while the orange ones Policy-based sub-policies.

In order to abstract the state space, FDQN uses handcrafted feature functions ϕ_i, ϕ_m and ϕ_s based on the Domain Independent Parametrisation (DIP) features introduced in Wang et al. (2015). These features include the slot independent parts of the belief state, a summarised representation of the joint belief state, and a summarised representation of the belief state of the slot s.

3 FDM with jointly learned feature extractors

In order to avoid the need to handcraft the feature functions ϕ_i, ϕ_m and ϕ_s , two methods which jointly train the feature extractors and the policy model are proposed. FDQN, however, showed to be prone to get stuck in local optima[3]. When the feature functions are jointly learned, this problem will be exacerbated due to the need to learn extra parameters. In section 3.1, two methods to avoid getting stuck in local optima are presented.

3.1 Improved training stability

FDQN showed to be prone to get stuck in local optima, overfitting to an incorrect action and continuously repeating it until the user runs out of

---

[2]Note that, in order to compare values from different sub-policies, π_s needs to be modelled as a Value-based policy.

[3]Depending on the initially observed dialogues, the model might get stuck in a sub-optimal policy. This is a know problem in RL (Henderson et al., 2017).

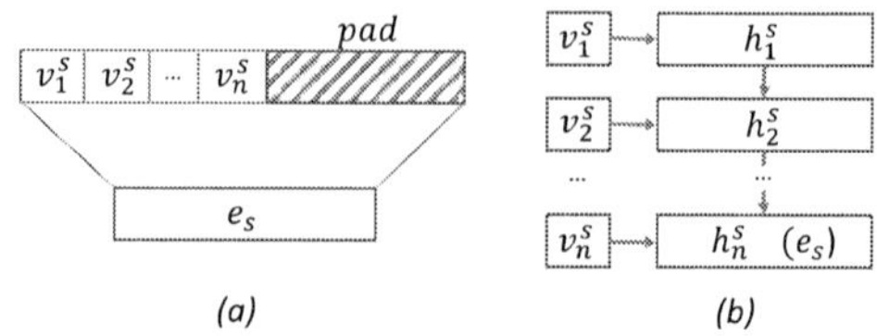

(a)   *(b)*

Figure 2: FFN *(a)* and RNN *(b)* jointly learned feature extractors.

patience. Appendix A shows an example of this problem. We propose two methods that combined help to reduce the overfitting, allowing the feature extractors to be learned jointly.

The belief state used in FDQN only contains information about the last system action. Therefore, if the system gets into a loop repeating the same action for every turn, the belief state cannot depict it. We propose to append the input to each sub-policy with a vector containing the frequencies of the actions taken in the current dialogue. This additional information can be used by the policy to detect these "overfitting loops" and select a different action.

Furthermore, Policy-based Actor Critic methods such as ACER (Wang et al., 2016; Weisz et al., 2018) have shown to be more stable during learning than Value-based methods. Since π_d has to compare Q-values, the slot specific policies π_s need to be Value-based. The master and slot independent policies, however, can be replaced by an Actor Critic policy, as shown in Figure 1. Section 5 shows that by doing this replacement the dialogue manager is able to learn better policies.

3.2 Jointly learned feature extractors

In order to abstract the state space into a slot-dependent fixed length representation, FDQN uses DIP feature functions (Wang et al., 2015). These features, however, need to be hand engineered by the system designer. To reduce the amount of hand-design, we propose two feature extraction models that can be learned jointly with the policy. Figure 2 shows the two proposed models. The first one *(a)*, named FFN in section 5, pads the belief state of the slot to the length of the largest slot and encodes it into a vector e_s through a feed forward neural network. The second one *(b)*, uses a recurrent neural network to encode the values of each slot into a fixed length representation e_s. Each $b_s \forall s \in \mathcal{S}$ is then constructed by concatenating the slot independent parts of the belief to the slot encoding e_s. For the feature functions ϕ_i and ϕ_m,

Domain	Code	# constraint slots	# requests	# values
Cambridge Restaurants	CR	3	9	268
San Francisco Restaurants	SFR	6	11	636
Laptops	LAP	11	21	257

	Env. 1	Env. 2	Env. 3	Env. 4	Env. 5	Env. 6
SER	0%	0%	15%	15%	15%	30%
Masks	on	off	on	off	on	on
User	Std.	Std.	Std.	Std.	Unf.	Std.

Table 1: Sumarised description of the domains and environments used in the experiments. Refer to (Casanueva et al., 2017) for a detailed description.

the slot independent parts of the belief are used directly as inputs to their respective policy models. During training, the errors of the policies can be backpropagated through the feature extractors, training the models by gradient descent.

4 Experimental setup

The PyDial toolkit (Ultes et al., 2017) and the PyDial benchmarking environments (Casanueva et al., 2017)[4] have been used to implement and evaluate the models. These environments present a set of 18 tasks (Table 1) spanning differently sized domains, different Semantic Error Rates (SER), different configurations of action masks and different user model parameter sets (Standard (Std.) or Unfriendly (Unf.)).

4.1 Baselines

The feudal dialogue policy presented in (Casanueva et al., 2018) is used as a baseline, named FDQN in section 5. An implementation of FDQN using the action frequency features introduced in 3.1 is also presented, named FDQN+AF. In addition, the results of the handcrafted policy presented in (Casanueva et al., 2017) are also shown, named HDC.

4.2 Feudal ACER policy

The feudal policy proposed in section 3.1, named FACER, is implemented. This policy uses an ACER policy (Wang et al., 2016) for the slot independent and master policies, and a DQN policy (Mnih et al., 2013) for the slot specific policies. The hyperparameters of the ACER sub-policies are the same than in (Weisz et al., 2018), except for the 2 hidden layers sizes, which are reduced to 100 and 50 respectively. The hyperparameters of the DQN sub-policies are the same as FDQN.

4.3 Jointly learned feature extractors

The FDQN+AF and FACER policies are trained using the FFN and RNN feature extractors proposed in section 3.2, as well as with the DIP fea-

---

[4]The implementation of the models will be released

model features	FDQN+AF			FACER			FDQN	HDC
	DIP	FFN	RNN	DIP	FFN	RNN	DIP	-
Env. 1 CR	13.8	12.8	11.3	11.8	12.9	12.5	11.7	**14.0**
Env. 1 SFR	9.4	6.0	7.3	10.9	4.5	3.8	7.1	**12.4**
Env. 1 LAP	9.2	8.4	7.4	7.7	5.7	8.4	5.7	**11.7**
Env. 2 CR	13.6	11.9	12.9	13.4	13.3	13.1	13.1	**14.0**
Env. 2 SFR	12.9	8.7	11.2	12.3	13.0	12.2	12.4	12.4
Env. 2 LAP	11.8	9.6	10.8	12.1	12.6	12.6	12.0	11.7
Env. 3 CR	**13.1**	12.8	12.9	12.9	13.0	13.0	11.7	11.0
Env. 3 SFR	10.3	9.8	9.9	10.3	10.1	10.5	9.7	9.0
Env. 3 LAP	**9.8**	9.4	9.7	9.6	9.8	9.6	9.4	8.7
Env. 4 CR	11.9	10.8	11.3	11.9	12.0	12.3	11.1	11.0
Env. 4 SFR	**11.2**	7.7	10.0	10.6	10.6	10.9	10.0	9.0
Env. 4 LAP	9.9	-0.6	4.5	**11.2**	10.9	11.0	10.8	8.7
Env. 5 CR	11.1	10.4	11.0	11.0	11.3	11.2	10.4	9.3
Env. 5 SFR	7.5	6.5	6.5	**7.8**	7.2	6.8	7.1	6.0
Env. 5 LAP	6.8	7.3	6.5	6.6	6.8	6.5	6.0	5.3
Env. 6 CR	11.7	11.4	11.6	11.7	11.7	11.8	11.5	9.7
Env. 6 SFR	**8.2**	7.5	7.4	8.1	8.1	7.4	7.9	6.4
Env. 6 LAP	**6.7**	6.7	6.5	6.6	6.3	6.4	5.2	5.5

Table 2: Reward after 4000 training dialogues for FDQN+AF and FACER using DIP, FFN and RNN features, compared to FDQN and the handcrafted policy presented in the PyDial benchmarks (HDC). The best performing model is highlighted in bold while the best performing model with jointly learned features is highlighted in red.

tures used in (Casanueva et al., 2018) . For each slot $s \in S$, b_s is constructed by concatenating the general and the joint belief state[5] to the encoding of the slot e_s generated by the feature extractor. The size of e_s is 25. As input for the π_m and π_i policies, the general and joint belief state is used.

5 Results

Table 2 shows the average reward[6] after 4000 training dialogues in the 18 tasks of the PyDial benchmarks. The reward for each dialogue is defined as $(suc * 20) - n$, where n is the dialogue length and $suc = 1$ if the dialogue was successful or 0 otherwise. The results are the mean over 10 different random seeds, where every seed is tested for 500 dialogues.

Comparing FDQN and FDQN-AF when using DIP features, the importance of including the action frequencies can be seen. The use of these features improves the reward in most of the tasks between 0.5 and 2 points. When training the policies with the joint feature extractors, the action frequencies were found to be a key feature in order to avoid the policies to get stuck in local optima.

FACER shows the best performance with the jointly learned feature extractors, outperforming any other policy (including the ones using DIP

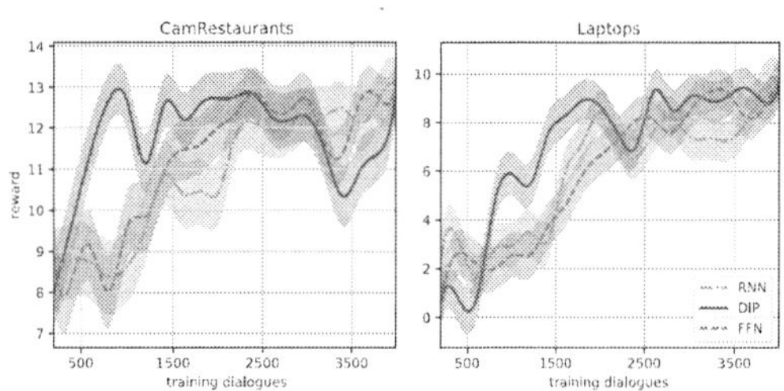

Figure 3: Learning curves for FACER in env. 3 in Cambridge Restaurants and Laptops domains, using DIP, FFN and RNN features. The shaded area represents the standard deviation.

features) in 8 out of 18 tasks, and obtaining a very similar performance in the rest. This shows the improved training stability given by the Policy-based models. In task 1, however, (where FDQN already showed overfitting problems) the FDQN+AF is able to learn better feature extractors than FACER, but the performance is still worse than HDC.

Figure 3 shows the learning curves for FACER in two domains of Env. 3 using the two learned feature extractors (FFN and RNN) compared to the DIP features. It can be observed that the learned features take longer to converge, but the difference is smaller than it could be expected, especially in a large domain such as Laptops.

6 Conclusions and future work

This paper has shown that the feature functions needed to abstract the dialogue state space in feudal dialogue management can be jointly learned with the policy, thus reducing the need of handcrafting them. In order to make it possible to learn the features jointly, two methods to increase the robustness of the model against overfitting were introduced: extending the input features with action frequencies and substituting the master and domain independent policies by ACER policies. In combination, these modifications showed to improve the results in most of the PyDial benchmarking tasks by an average of 1 point in reward, while reducing the handcrafting effort.

However, as the original FDQN architecture needs to model the slot specific policies as Value-based models, ACER policies could only be used for the master and slot independent policies. Future work will investigate new FDM architectures which allow the use of Policy-based models as slot specific policies, while maintaining the parameter sharing mechanism between slots.

---

[5] The joint belief state is sorted and truncated to size 20.

[6] Because of space issues, the success rate is not included. However, the success rate is very correlated with the results presented in (Casanueva et al., 2017) and (Casanueva et al., 2018).

Acknowledgments

This research was funded by the EPSRC grant EP/M018946/1 Open Domain Statistical Spoken Dialogue Systems

References

Iñigo Casanueva, Paweł Budzianowski, Pei-Hao Su, Nikola Mrkšić, Tsung-Hsien Wen, Stefan Ultes, Lina Rojas-Barahona, Steve Young, and Milica Gašić. 2017. A benchmarking environment for reinforcement learning based task oriented dialogue management. *Deep Reinforcement Learning Symposium, 31st Conference on Neural Information Processing Systems (NIPS 2017)*.

Iñigo Casanueva, Paweł Budzianowski, Pei-Hao Su, Stefan Ultes, Lina Rojas-Barahona, Bo-Hsiang Tseng, and Milica Gašić. 2018. Feudal reinforcement learning for dialogue management in large domains. *arXiv preprint arXiv:1803.03232*.

Peter Dayan and Geoffrey E Hinton. 1993. Feudal reinforcement learning. In *Advances in neural information processing systems*, pages 271–278.

Milica Gašić, Catherine Breslin, Matthew Henderson, Dongho Kim, Martin Szummer, Blaise Thomson, Pirros Tsiakoulis, and Steve Young. 2013. Pomdp-based dialogue manager adaptation to extended domains. In *Proceedings of the SIGDIAL Conference*.

James Henderson, Oliver Lemon, and Kallirroi Georgila. 2008. Hybrid reinforcement/supervised learning of dialogue policies from fixed data sets. *Computational Linguistics*, 34(4):487–511.

Peter Henderson, Riashat Islam, Philip Bachman, Joelle Pineau, Doina Precup, and David Meger. 2017. Deep reinforcement learning that matters. *arXiv preprint arXiv:1709.06560*.

Esther Levin, Roberto Pieraccini, and Wieland Eckert. 1998. Using markov decision process for learning dialogue strategies. In *Acoustics, Speech and Signal Processing, 1998. Proceedings of the 1998 IEEE International Conference on*, volume 1, pages 201–204. IEEE.

Volodymyr Mnih, Koray Kavukcuoglu, David Silver, Alex Graves, Ioannis Antonoglou, Daan Wierstra, and Martin Riedmiller. 2013. Playing atari with deep reinforcement learning. *arXiv preprint arXiv:1312.5602*.

Olivier Pietquin, Matthieu Geist, Senthilkumar Chandramohan, et al. 2011. Sample efficient online learning of optimal dialogue policies with kalman temporal differences. IJCAI Proceedings-International Joint Conference on Artificial Intelligence.

Richard S. Sutton and Andrew G. Barto. 1999. *Reinforcement Learning: An Introduction*. MIT Press.

Stefan Ultes, Lina M. Rojas-Barahona, Pei-Hao Su, David Vandyke, Dongho Kim, Iñigo Casanueva, Paweł Budzianowski, Nikola Mrkšić, Tsung-Hsien Wen, Milica Gašić, and Steve J. Young. 2017. Pydial: A multi-domain statistical dialogue system toolkit. In *ACL Demo*. Association of Computational Linguistics.

Zhuoran Wang, Tsung-Hsien Wen, Pei-Hao Su, and Yannis Stylianou. 2015. Learning domain-independent dialogue policies via ontology parameterisation. In *SIGDIAL Conference*, pages 412–416.

Ziyu Wang, Victor Bapst, Nicolas Heess, Volodymyr Mnih, Remi Munos, Koray Kavukcuoglu, and Nando de Freitas. 2016. Sample efficient actor-critic with experience replay. *arXiv preprint arXiv:1611.01224*.

Gellért Weisz, Paweł Budzianowski, Pei-Hao Su, and Milica Gašić. 2018. Sample efficient deep reinforcement learning for dialogue systems with large action spaces. *arXiv preprint arXiv:1802.03753*.

Jason D. Williams and Steve Young. 2007. Partially observable Markov decision processes for spoken dialog systems. *Computer Speech and Language*, 21(2):393–422.

Steve Young, Milica Gašić, Blaise Thomson, and Jason D Williams. 2013. Pomdp-based statistical spoken dialog systems: A review. *Proceedings of the IEEE*, 101(5):1160–1179.

A Dialogues getting stuck in local optima

In this section we present an example of a policy model getting stuck in a sub-optimal policy. The two following dialogues represent a dialogue observed in the initial training steps of the policy and a dialogue observed once the policy has overfitted.

Initial dialogue:
Goal: *food*=british, *area*=centre

1: **usr:** Inform(food=british)
2: **sys:** Confirm(food=british)
3: **usr:** Affirm()|Inform(area=centre)
4: **sys:** Inform(name=The Eagle)
5: **usr:** Thankyou()|Bye()

Overfitted dialogue:
Goal: *food*=british, *area*=centre

1: **usr:** Inform(food=british)
2: **sys:** Confirm(food=british)
3: **usr:** Affirm()
4: **sys:** Confirm(food=british)
5: **usr:** Affirm()
6: **sys:** Confirm(food=british)
7: **usr:** Affirm()
8: **sys:** Confirm(food=british)
9: **usr:** Bye()

In the initial dialogue, the policy interacts with a collaborative user[7], which in line 3, provides more information than the requested by the policy. The dialogue ends up successfully and, therefore, the policy learns that by confirming the slot *food* in that dialogue state it will get enough information to end the dialogue successfully. In the second dialogue, however, the system interacts with a less collaborative user. Therefore, when confirming the slot *food* in line 3, it doesn't get the extra information obtained in the previous dialogue. The policy keeps insisting with this action, until the user runs out of patience and ends up the dialogue. Even with ϵ-*greedy* exploration, as a fraction of the sampled users will be collaborative enough to make this policy successful, the policy can get stuck in this local optima and never learn a better policy - i.e. requesting the value of the slot *area*. Other examples of overfitting include

policies informing entities at random from the first turn (since some users will correct the policy by informing the correct values) or policies that don't learn to inform about the requested slots (since the sampled user goal sometimes doesn't include requesting any extra information, just the entity name).

B Feudal Dialogue Policy algorithm

Algorithm 1 Feudal Dialogue Policy

1: **for** each dialogue turn **do**
2:     observe b
3:     $b_m = \phi_m(b)$
4:     $a^m = \pi_m(b_m)$
5:     **if** $a^m == a_i^m$ **then**   ▷ drop to π_i
6:         $b_i = \phi_i(b)$
7:         $a = \pi_i(b_i)$
8:     **else** $a^m == a_d^m$ **then**   ▷ drop to π_d
9:         $b_s = \phi_s(b) \; \forall s \in \mathcal{S}$
10:         $slot, act = \underset{s \in \mathcal{S}, a^d \in \mathcal{A}_d}{\arg\max} \; Q^s(b_s, a^d)$
11:         $a = join(slot, act)$
12:     **end if**
13:     execute a
14: **end for**

---

[7]The user parameters are sampled at the beginning of each dialogue.

Variational Cross-domain Natural Language Generation for Spoken Dialogue Systems

Bo-Hsiang Tseng, Florian Kreyssig, Paweł Budzianowski,
Iñigo Casanueva, Yen-Chen Wu, Stefan Ultes, Milica Gašić
Department of Engineering, University of Cambridge, Cambridge, UK
{bht26,flk24,pfb30,ic340,ycw30,su259,mg436}@cam.ac.uk

Abstract

Cross-domain natural language generation (NLG) is still a difficult task within spoken dialogue modelling. Given a semantic representation provided by the dialogue manager, the language generator should generate sentences that convey desired information. Traditional template-based generators can produce sentences with all necessary information, but these sentences are not sufficiently diverse. With RNN-based models, the diversity of the generated sentences can be high, however, in the process some information is lost. In this work, we improve an RNN-based generator by considering latent information at the sentence level during generation using the conditional variational autoencoder architecture. We demonstrate that our model outperforms the original RNN-based generator, while yielding highly diverse sentences. In addition, our model performs better when the training data is limited.

1 Introduction

Conventional spoken dialogue systems (SDS) require a substantial amount of hand-crafted rules to achieve good interaction with users. The large amount of required engineering limits the scalability of these systems to settings with new or multiple domains. Recently, statistical approaches have been studied that allow natural, efficient and more diverse interaction with users without depending on pre-defined rules (Young et al., 2013; Gašić et al., 2014; Henderson et al., 2014).

Natural language generation (NLG) is an essential component of an SDS. Given a semantic representation (SR) consisting of a dialogue act and a set of slot-value pairs, the generator should produce natural language containing the desired information.

Traditionally NLG was based on templates (Cheyer and Guzzoni, 2014), which produce grammatically-correct sentences that contain all desired information. However, the lack of variation of these sentences made these systems seem tedious and monotonic. *Trainable generators* (Langkilde and Knight, 1998; Stent et al., 2004) can generate several sentences for the same SR, but the dependence on pre-defined operations limits their potential. Corpus-based approaches (Oh and Rudnicky, 2000; Mairesse and Walker, 2011) learn to generate natural language directly from data without pre-defined rules. However, they usually require alignment between the sentence and the SR. Recently, Wen et al. (2015b) proposed an RNN-based approach, which outperformed previous methods on several metrics. However, the generated sentences often did not include all desired attributes.

The variational autoencoder (Kingma and Welling, 2013) enabled for the first time the generation of complicated, high-dimensional data such as images. The conditional variational autoencoder (CVAE) (Sohn et al., 2015), firstly proposed for image generation, has a similar structure to the VAE with an additional dependency on a condition. Recently, the CVAE has been applied to dialogue systems (Serban et al., 2017; Shen et al., 2017; Zhao et al., 2017) using the previous dialogue turns as the condition. However, their output was not required to contain specific information.

In this paper, we improve RNN-based generators by adapting the CVAE to the difficult task of cross-domain NLG. Due to the additional latent information encoded by the CVAE, our model outperformed the SCLSTM at conveying all information. Furthermore, our model reaches better results when the training data is limited.

Proceedings of the SIGDIAL 2018 Conference, pages 338–343,
Melbourne, Australia, 12-14 July 2018. ©2018 Association for Computational Linguistics

2 Model Description

2.1 Variational Autoencoder

The VAE is a generative latent variable model. It uses a neural network (NN) to generate $\hat{x}$ from a latent variable z, which is sampled from the prior $p_\theta(z)$. The VAE is trained such that $\hat{x}$ is a sample of the distribution $p_D(x)$ from which the training data was collected. Generative latent variable models have the form $p_\theta(x) = \int_z p_\theta(x|z)p_\theta(z)dz$. In a VAE an NN, called the decoder, models $p_\theta(x|z)$ and would ideally be trained to maximize the expectation of the above integral $E[p_\theta(x)]$. Since this is intractable, the VAE uses another NN, called the encoder, to model $q_\phi(z|x)$ which should approximate the posterior $p_\theta(z|x)$. The NNs in the VAE are trained to maximise the variational lower bound (VLB) to $\log p_\theta(x)$, which is given by:

$$
\begin{aligned}
L_{VAE}(\theta, \phi; x) = &-KL(q_\phi(z|x)||p_\theta(z)) \\
&+ E_{q_\phi(z|x)}[\log p_\theta(x|z)]
\end{aligned}
\tag{1}
$$

The first term is the KL-divergence between the approximated posterior and the prior, which encourages similarity between the two distributions. The second term is the likelihood of the data given samples from the approximated posterior. The CVAE has a similar structure, but the prior is modelled by another NN, called the prior network. The prior network is conditioned on c. The new objective function can now be written as:

$$
\begin{aligned}
L_{CVAE}(\theta, \phi; x, c) = &-KL(q_\phi(z|x,c)||p_\theta(z|c)) \\
&+ E_{q_\phi(z|x,c)}[\log p_\theta(x|z,c)]
\end{aligned}
\tag{2}
$$

When generating data, the encoder is not used and z is sampled from $p_\theta(z|c)$.

2.2 Semantically Conditioned VAE

The structure of our model is depicted in Fig. 1, which, conditioned on an SR, generates the system's word-level response x. An SR consists of three components: the domain, a dialogue act and a set of slot-value pairs. *Slots* are attributes required to appear in x (e.g. a hotel's *area*). A *slot* can have a *value*. Then the two are called a *slot-value* pair (e.g. *area=north*). x is *delexicalised*, which means that slot values are replaced by corresponding slot tokens. The condition c of our model is the SR represented as two 1-hot vectors for the domain and the dialogue act as well as a binary vector for the slots.

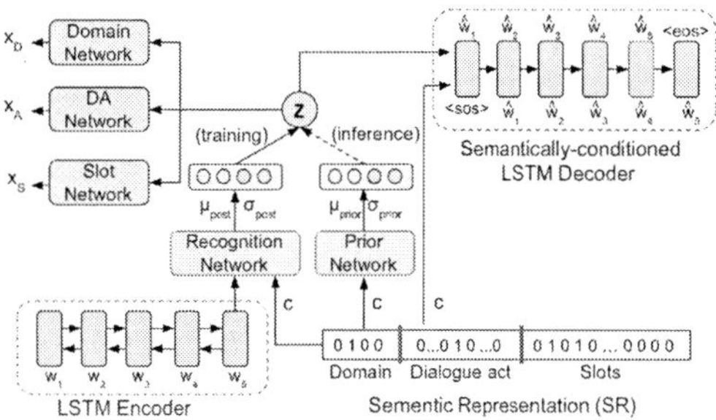

Figure 1: Semantically Conditioned Variational Autoencoder with a semantic representation (SR) as the condition. x is the system response with words $w_{1:N}$. x_D, x_A and x_S are labels for the domain, the dialogue act (DA) and the slots of x.

During training, x is first passed through a single layer bi-directional LSTM, the output of which is concatenated with c and passed to the recognition network. The recognition network parametrises a Gaussian distribution $\mathcal{N}(\mu_{post}, \sigma_{post})$ which is the posterior. The prior network only has c as its input and parametrises a Gaussian distribution $\mathcal{N}(\mu_{prior}, \sigma_{prior})$ which is the prior. Both networks are fully-connected (FC) NNs with one and two layers respectively. During training, z is sampled from the posterior. When the model is used for generation, z is sampled from the prior. The decoder is an SCLSTM (Wen et al., 2015b) using z as its initial hidden state and initial cell vector. The first input to the SCLSTM is a start-of-sentence (sos) token and the model generates words until it outputs an end-of-sentence (eos) token.

2.3 Optimization

When the decoder in the CVAE is powerful on its own, it tends to ignore the latent variable z since the encoder fails to encode enough information into z. Regularization methods can be introduced in order to push the encoder towards learning a good representation of the latent variable z. Since the KL-component of the VLB does not contribute towards learning a meaningful z, increasing the weight of it gradually from 0 to 1 during training helps to encode a better representation in z. This method is termed *KL-annealing* (Bowman et al., 2016). In addition, inspired by (Zhao et al., 2017), we introduce a regularization method using another NN which is trained to use z to recover the condition c. The NN is split into three separate FC NNs of one layer each, which independently recover the *domain*, *dialogue-act* and *slots* components of c. The objective of our model can be written as:

$$L_{SCVAE}(\theta, \phi; x, c) = L_{CVAE}(\theta, \phi; x, c)$$
$$+ E_{q_\phi(z|x,c)}[\log p(x_D|z) + \log p(x_A|z) +$$
$$\log \prod_{i=1}^{|S|} p(x_{S_i}|z)] \quad (3)$$

where x_D is the domain label, x_A is the dialogue act label and x_{S_i} are the slot labels with $|S|$ slots in the SR. In the proposed model, the CVAE learns to encode information about both the sentence and the SR into z. Using z as its initial state, the decoder is better at generating sentences with desired attributes. In section 4.1 a visualization of the latent space demonstrates that a semantically meaningful representation for z was learned.

3 Dataset and Setup

The proposed model is used for an SDS that provides information about restaurants, hotels, televisions and laptops. It is trained on a dataset (Wen et al., 2016), which consists of sentences with corresponding semantic representations. Table 1 shows statistics about the corpus which was split into a training, validation and testing set according to a 3:1:1 split. The dataset contains 14 different system dialogue acts. The television and laptop domains are much more complex than other domains. There are around 7k and 13k different SRs possible for the TV and the laptop domain respectively. For the restaurant and hotel domains only 248 and 164 unique SRs are possible. This imbalance makes the NLG task more difficult.

The generators were implemented using the PyTorch Library (Paszke et al., 2017). The size of decoder SCLSTM and thus of the latent variable was set to 128. KL-annealing was used, with the weight of the KL-loss reaching 1 after 5k minibatch updates. The slot error rate (ERR), used in (Oh and Rudnicky, 2000; Wen et al., 2015a), is the metric that measures the model's ability to convey the desired information. ERR is defined as: $(p + q)/N$, where N is the number of slots in the SR, p and q are the number of missing and redundant slots in the generated sentence. The BLEU-4 metric and perplexity (PPL) are also reported. The baseline SCLSTM is optimized, which has shown to outperform template-based methods and trainable generators (Wen et al., 2015b). NLG often

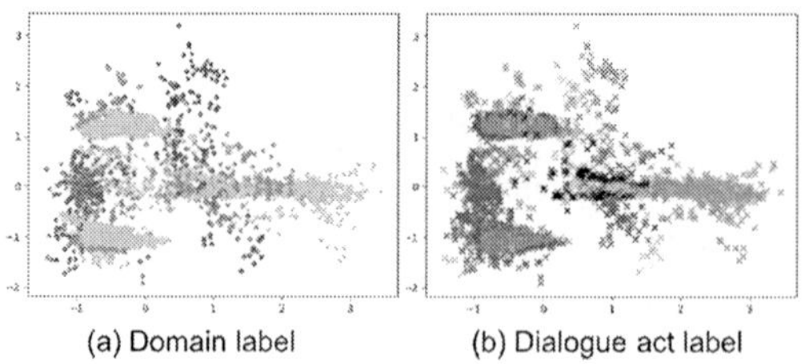

(a) Domain label   (b) Dialogue act label

Figure 2: 2D-projection of z for each data point in the test set, with two different colouring-schemes.

uses the over-generation and reranking paradigm (Oh and Rudnicky, 2000). The SCVAE can generate multiple sentences by sampling multiple z, while the SCLSTM has to sample different words from the output distribution. In our experiments ten sentences are generated per SR. Table 4 in the appendix shows one SR in each domain with five illustrative sentences generated by our model.

4 Experimental Results

4.1 Visualization of Latent Variable z

2D-projections of z for each data point in the test set are shown in Fig. 2, by using PCA for dimensionality reduction. In Fig. 2a, data points of the restaurant, hotel, TV and laptop domain are marked as blue, green, red and yellow respectively. As can be seen, data points from the laptop domain are contained within four distinct clusters. In addition, there is a large overlap of the TV and laptop domains, which is not surprising as they share all dialogue acts (DAs). Similarly, there is overlap of the restaurant and hotel domains. In Fig. 2b, the eight most frequent DAs are color-coded. `recommend`, depicted as green, has a similar distribution to the laptop domain in Fig. 2a, since `recommend` happens mostly in the laptop domain. This suggests that our model learns to map similar SRs into close regions within the latent space. Therefore, z contains meaningful information in regards to the domain, DAs and slots.

4.2 Empirical Comparison

4.2.1 Cross-domain Training

Table 2 shows the comparison between SCVAE and SCLSTM. Both are trained on the full cross-domain dataset, and tested on the four domains individually. The SCVAE outperforms the SCLSTM on all metrics. For the highly complex TV and laptop domains, the SCVAE leads to dramatic improvements in ERR. This shows that the addi-

Table 1: The statistics of the cross-domain dataset

	Restaurant	Hotel	Television	Laptop
# of examples	3114/1039/1039	3223/1075/1075	4221/1407/1407	7944/2649/2649
dialogue acts	reqmore, goodbye, select, confirm, request, inform, inform_only, inform_count, inform_no_match		compare, recommend, inform_all, suggest, inform_no_info, 9 acts as left	
shared slots	name, type, area, near, price, phone, address, postcode, pricerange		name, type, price, family, pricerange,	
specific slots	food, goodformeal, kids-allowed	hasinternet, acceptscards, dogs-allowed	screensizerange, ecorating, hdmiport, hasusbport, audio, accessories, color, screensize, resolution, powerconsumption	isforbusinesscomputing, warranty, battery, design, batteryrating, weightrange, utility, platform, driverange, dimension, memory, processor

Table 2: Comparison between SCVAE and SCLSTM. Both are trained with full dataset and tested on individual domains

Metrics	Method	Restaurant	Hotel	TV	Laptop	Overall
ERR(%)	SCLSTM	2.978	1.666	4.076	2.599	2.964
	SCVAE	**2.823**	**1.528**	**2.819**	**1.841**	**2.148**
BLEU	SCLSTM	0.529	0.642	0.475	0.439	0.476
	SCVAE	**0.540**	**0.652**	**0.478**	**0.442**	**0.478**
PPL	SCLSTM	2.654	3.229	3.365	3.941	3.556
	SCVAE	**2.649**	**3.159**	**3.337**	**3.919**	**3.528**

Table 3: Comparison between SCVAE and SCLSTM in K-shot learning

Metrics	Method	Restaurant	Hotel	TV	Laptop
ERR(%)	SCLSTM	13.039	**5.366**	24.497	27.587
	SCVAE	**10.329**	6.182	**20.590**	**20.864**
BLEU	SCLSTM	**0.462**	0.578	0.382	0.379
	SCVAE	0.458	**0.579**	**0.397**	**0.393**
PPL	SCLSTM	3.649	4.861	5.171	6.469
	SCVAE	**3.575**	**4.800**	**5.092**	**6.364**

tional sentence level conditioning through z helps to convey all desired attributes.

4.2.2 Limited Training Data

Fig. 3 shows BLEU and ERR results when the SC-VAE and SCLSTM are trained on varying amounts of data. The SCVAE has a lower ERR than the SCLSTM across the varying amounts of training data. For very slow amounts of data the SCVAE outperforms the SCLSTM even more. In addition, our model consistently achieves better results on the BLEU metric.

4.2.3 K-Shot Learning

For the K-shot learning experiments, we trained the model using all training examples from three domains and only 300 examples from the target

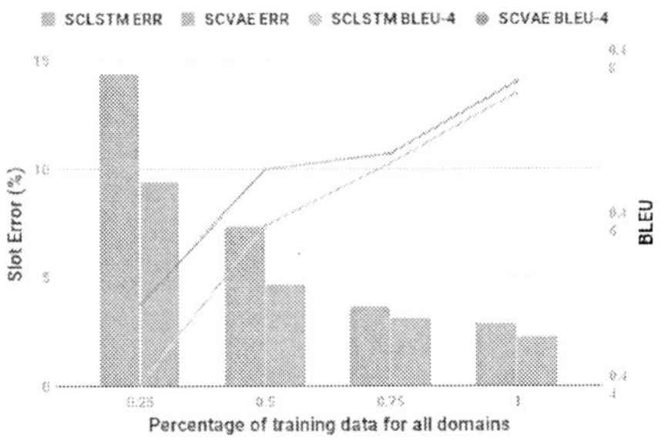

Figure 3: Comparison between SCVAE and SCLSTM with limited training data.

domain[1]. The target domain is the domain we test on. As seen from Table 3, the SCVAE outperforms the SCLSTM in all domains except hotel. This might be because the hotel domain is the simplest and the model does not need to rely on the knowledge from other domains. The SCVAE strongly outperforms the SCLSTM for the complex TV and laptop domains where the number of distinct SRs is large. This suggests that the SCVAE is better at transferring knowledge between domains.

5 Conclusion

In this paper, we propose a semantically conditioned variational autoencoder (SCVAE) for natural language generation. The SCVAE encodes information about both the semantic representation and the sentence into a latent variable z. Due to a newly proposed regularization method, the latent variable z contains semantically meaningful information. Therefore, conditioning on z leads to a strong improvement in generating sentences with all desired attributes. In an extensive comparison the SCVAE outperforms the SCLSTM on a range of metrics when training on different sizes of data and for K-short learning. Especially, when testing the ability to convey all desired information within complex domains, the SCVAE shows significantly better results.

---

[1]600 examples were used for laptop as target domain.

Acknowledgments

Bo-Hsiang Tseng is supported by Cambridge Trust and the Ministry of Education, Taiwan. This research was partly funded by the EPSRC grant EP/M018946/1 Open Domain Statistical Spoken Dialogue Systems. Florian Kreyssig is supported by the Studienstiftung des Deutschen Volkes. Paweł Budzianowski is supported by the EPSRC and Toshiba Research Europe Ltd.

References

Samuel Bowman, Luke Vilnis, Oriol Vinyals, Andrew M. Dai, Rafal Jozefowicz, and Samy Bengio. 2016. *Generating Sentences from a Continuous Space.*

Adam Cheyer and Didier Guzzoni. 2014. Method and apparatus for building an intelligent automated assistant. US Patent 8,677,377.

M Gašić, Dongho Kim, Pirros Tsiakoulis, Catherine Breslin, Matthew Henderson, Martin Szummer, Blaise Thomson, and Steve Young. 2014. Incremental on-line adaptation of pomdp-based dialogue managers to extended domains. In *Fifteenth Annual Conference of the International Speech Communication Association.*

Matthew Henderson, Blaise Thomson, and Steve Young. 2014. Robust dialog state tracking using delexicalised recurrent neural networks and unsupervised adaptation. In *Spoken Language Technology Workshop (SLT), 2014 IEEE*, pages 360–365. IEEE.

Diederik P. Kingma and Max Welling. 2013. Autoencoding variational bayes. *CoRR*, abs/1312.6114.

Irene Langkilde and Kevin Knight. 1998. Generation that exploits corpus-based statistical knowledge. In *Proceedings of the 36th Annual Meeting of the Association for Computational Linguistics and 17th International Conference on Computational Linguistics-Volume 1*, pages 704–710. Association for Computational Linguistics.

François Mairesse and Marilyn A Walker. 2011. Controlling user perceptions of linguistic style: Trainable generation of personality traits. *Computational Linguistics*, 37(3):455–488.

Alice H Oh and Alexander I Rudnicky. 2000. Stochastic language generation for spoken dialogue systems. In *Proceedings of the 2000 ANLP/NAACL Workshop on Conversational systems-Volume 3*, pages 27–32. Association for Computational Linguistics.

Adam Paszke, Sam Gross, Soumith Chintala, Gregory Chanan, Edward Yang, Zachary DeVito, Zeming Lin, Alban Desmaison, Luca Antiga, and Adam Lerer. 2017. Automatic differentiation in pytorch. In *NIPS-W*.

Iulian Vlad Serban, Alessandro Sordoni, Ryan Lowe, Laurent Charlin, Joelle Pineau, Aaron C Courville, and Yoshua Bengio. 2017. A hierarchical latent variable encoder-decoder model for generating dialogues. In *AAAI*, pages 3295–3301.

Xiaoyu Shen, Hui Su, Yanran Li, Wenjie Li, Shuzi Niu, Yang Zhao, Akiko Aizawa, and Guoping Long. 2017. A conditional variational framework for dialog generation. In *ACL*.

Kihyuk Sohn, Honglak Lee, and Xinchen Yan. 2015. Learning structured output representation using deep conditional generative models. In *Advances in Neural Information Processing Systems*, pages 3483–3491.

Amanda Stent, Rashmi Prasad, and Marilyn Walker. 2004. Trainable sentence planning for complex information presentation in spoken dialog systems. In *Proceedings of the 42nd annual meeting on association for computational linguistics*, page 79. Association for Computational Linguistics.

Tsung-Hsien Wen, Milica Gašić, Dongho Kim, Nikola Mrkšić, Pei-Hao Su, David Vandyke, and Steve Young. 2015a. Stochastic Language Generation in Dialogue using Recurrent Neural Networks with Convolutional Sentence Reranking. In *Proceedings of the 16th Annual Meeting of the Special Interest Group on Discourse and Dialogue (SIGDIAL)*. Association for Computational Linguistics.

Tsung-Hsien Wen, Milica Gašić, Nikola Mrkšić, Lina M. Rojas-Barahona, Pei-Hao Su, David Vandyke, and Steve Young. 2016. Multi-domain neural network language generation for spoken dialogue systems. In *Proceedings of the 2016 Conference on North American Chapter of the Association for Computational Linguistics (NAACL)*. Association for Computational Linguistics.

Tsung-Hsien Wen, Milica Gašić, Nikola Mrkšić, Pei-Hao Su, David Vandyke, and Steve Young. 2015b. Semantically conditioned lstm-based natural language generation for spoken dialogue systems. In *Proceedings of the 2015 Conference on Empirical Methods in Natural Language Processing (EMNLP)*. Association for Computational Linguistics.

Steve Young, Milica Gašić, Blaise Thomson, and Jason D Williams. 2013. Pomdp-based statistical spoken dialog systems: A review. *Proceedings of the IEEE*, 101(5):1160–1179.

Tiancheng Zhao, Ran Zhao, and Maxine Eskénazi. 2017. Learning discourse-level diversity for neural dialog models using conditional variational autoencoders. In *Proceedings of the 55th Annual Meeting of the Association for Computational Linguistics, ACL 2017, Vancouver, Canada, July 30 - August 4, Volume 1: Long Papers*, pages 654–664.

Table 4: Semantic representation (SR) with ground truth (GT) and sentences generated by SCVAE

	Restaurant Domain
SR	inform(name='la mediterranee';food='middle eastern';kidsallowed=no;pricerange=cheap)
GT	i have just the restaurant for you . it is called la mediterranee , it serves cheap middle eastern food and childs are not allowed
Gen1	la mediterranee serves middle eastern food in the cheap price range and does not allow childs
Gen2	la mediterranee is a cheap middle eastern restaurant that does not allow kids
Gen3	la mediterranee is cheaply priced restaurant serves middle eastern food and allow childs
Gen4	i would recommend la mediterranee . it is cheap middle eastern food , does not allow child
Gen5	la mediterranee does not allow kids , serves middle eastern food and it is cheap price
	Hotel Domain
SR	inform_count(type='hotel';count='2';near='marina cow hollow';pricerange='inexpensive')
GT	there are 2 other hotels near marina cow hollow that fit inexpensive your price range
Gen1	there are 2 inexpensive hotels near marina cow hollow
Gen2	there are 2 hotels near the marina cow hollow that are inexpensive
Gen3	there are 2 inexpensively priced hotel near marina cow hollow
Gen4	there are 2 inexpensive priced hotels near the marina cow hollow
Gen5	there are 2 hotels in the inexpensive price range near marina cow hollow
	Television Domain
SR	recommend(name=hymenaios 11;type=television;family=d1;hdmiport=1)
GT	the hymenaios 11 is a television with 1 hdmi port in the d1 product family
Gen1	the name of hymenaios 11 is a television in the d1 family with 1 hdmi port
Gen2	hymenaios 11 is a television from the d1 product family with 1 hdmi port
Gen3	the hymenaios 11 television is a member of the d1 product family and has 1 hdmi port
Gen4	the hymenaios 11 television is part of the d1 family , and has 1 hdmi port
Gen5	the hymenaios 11 is a nice television in the d1 family with 1 hdmi port
	Laptop Domain
SR	inform_no_match(type=laptop;isforbusinesscomputing=true;driverange=medium;weightrange=mid weight)
GT	no matches were found for a laptop search for business computing with a medium drive that falls in the mid weight range
Gen1	there is no laptop in the medium drive range that is mid weight range and are used for business use
Gen2	there are no laptops in the medium drive size range and is in the mid weight range . they are used for business computing
Gen3	sorry but there are no laptops that match for a medium drive range , mid weight weight range , and is for business computing
Gen4	there are no mid weight laptops with medium driver and are used for business computing
Gen5	unfortunately , we have no matches for your requirementss for a laptop in the mid weight range , that can be used for business computing , and is in the medium drive range

Coherence Modeling Improves Implicit Discourse Relation Recognition

Noriki Nishida and **Hideki Nakayama**
Graduate School of Information Science and Technology
The University of Tokyo
{nishida,nakayama}@nlab.ci.i.u-tokyo.ac.jp

Abstract

The research described in this paper examines how to learn linguistic knowledge associated with discourse relations from unlabeled corpora. We introduce an unsupervised learning method on text coherence that could produce numerical representations that improve implicit discourse relation recognition in a semi-supervised manner. We also empirically examine two variants of coherence modeling: *order-oriented* and *topic-oriented* negative sampling, showing that, of the two, topic-oriented negative sampling tends to be more effective.

1 Introduction

Shallow discourse parsing aims to automatically identify discourse relations (e.g., comparisons) between adjacent sentences. When connectives such as *however* explicitly appear, discourse relations are relatively easy to classify, as connectives provide strong cues (Pitler et al., 2008). In contrast, it remains challenging to identify discourse relations across sentences that have no connectives.

One reason for this inferior performance is a shortage of labeled instances, despite the diversity of natural language discourses. Collecting annotations about implicit relations is highly expensive because it requires linguistic expertise. [1] A variety of semi-supervised or unsupervised methods have been explored to alleviate this issue. Marcu and Echihabi (2002) proposed generating synthetic instances by removing connectives from sentence pairs. This idea has been extended in many works

and remains a core approach in the field (Zhou et al., 2010; Patterson and Kehler, 2013; Lan et al., 2013; Rutherford and Xue, 2015; Ji et al., 2015; Liu et al., 2016; Braud and Denis, 2016; Lan et al., 2017; Wu et al., 2017). However, these methods rely on automatically detecting connectives in unlabeled corpora beforehand, which makes it almost impossible to utilize parts of unlabeled corpora in which no connectives appear. [2] In addition, as Sporleder and Lascarides (2008) discovered, it is difficult to obtain a generalized model by training on synthetic data due to domain shifts. Though several semi-supervised methods do not depend on detecting connectives (Hernault et al., 2010, 2011; Braud and Denis, 2015), these methods are restricted to manually selected features, linear models, or word-level knowledge transfer.

In this paper, our research question is how to exploit unlabeled corpora without explicitly detecting connectives to learn linguistic knowledge associated with implicit discourse relations.

Our core hypothesis is that unsupervised learning about text coherence could produce numerical representations related to discourse relations. Sentences that compose a coherent document should be connected with syntactic or semantic relations (Hobbs, 1985; Grosz et al., 1995). In particular, we expect that there should be latent relations among local sentences. In this study, we hypothesize that parameters learned through coherence modeling could contain useful information for identifying (implicit) discourse relations. To verify this hypothesis, we develop a semi-supervised system whose parameters are first optimized for coherence modeling and then transferred to implicit discourse relation recognition. We also empirically examine two variants of coherence mod-

---

[1] The Penn Discourse Treebank (PDTB) 2.0 corpus (Prasad et al., 2008), which is the current largest corpus for discourse relation recognition, contains only about 16K annotated instances in total.

[2] For example, nearly half of the sentences in the British National Corpus hold implicit discourse relations and do not contain connectives (Sporleder and Lascarides, 2008).

Proceedings of the SIGDIAL 2018 Conference, pages 344–349,
Melbourne, Australia, 12-14 July 2018. ©2018 Association for Computational Linguistics

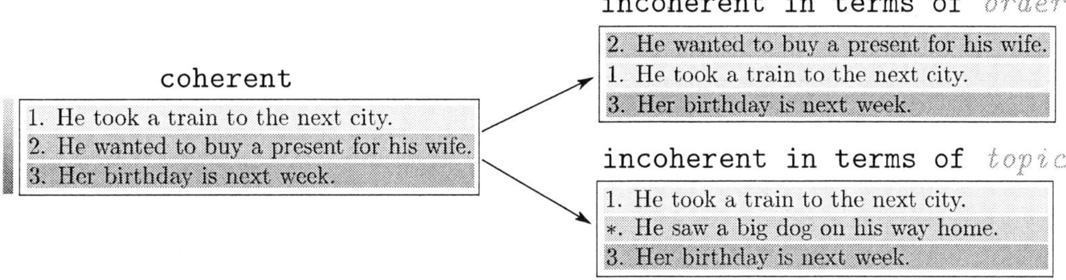

Figure 1: An example of order-oriented and topic-oriented negative sampling in coherence modeling.

eling: (1) *order-oriented* negative sampling and (2) *topic-oriented* negative sampling. An example is shown in Figure 1.

Our experimental results demonstrate that coherence modeling improves Macro F_1 on implicit discourse relation recognition by about 3 points on first-level relation *classes* and by about 5 points on second-level relation *types*. Coherence modeling is particularly effective for relation categories with few labeled instances, such as temporal relations. In addition, we find that topic-oriented negative sampling tends to be more effective than the order-oriented counterpart, especially on first-level relation classes.

2 Coherence Modeling

In this study, we adopt the sliding-window approach of Li and Hovy (2014) to form a conditional probability that a document is coherent. That is, we define the probability that a given document X is coherent as a product of probabilities at all possible local windows, i.e.,

$$P(\text{coherent}|X, \theta) = \prod_{x \in X} P(\text{coherent}|x, \theta), \quad (1)$$

where $P(\text{coherent}|x, \theta)$ denotes the conditional probability that the local clique x is coherent and θ denotes parameters. Clique x is a tuple of a central sentence and its left and right sentences, (s_-, s, s_+). Though larger window sizes may allow the model to learn linguistic properties and inter-sentence dependencies over broader contexts, it increases computational complexity during training and suffers from data sparsity problem.

We automatically build a dataset $\mathcal{D} = \mathcal{P} \cup \mathcal{N}$ for coherence modeling from an unlabeled corpus. Here, $\mathcal{P}$ and $\mathcal{N}$ denote sets of positive and negative instances, respectively. Given a source corpus $\mathcal{C}$ of

$|\mathcal{C}|$ sentences $s_1, s_2, \ldots, s_{|\mathcal{C}|}$, we collect positive instances as follows:

$$\mathcal{P} = \{(s_{i-1}, s_i, s_{i+1}) \mid i = 2, \ldots, |\mathcal{C}| - 1\}. \quad (2)$$

Text coherence can be corrupted by two aspects, which correspond to how to build negative set $\mathcal{N}$.

The first variant is **order**-*oriented negative sampling*, i.e.,

$$\mathcal{N} = \{x' \mid x' \in \phi(x) \wedge x \in \mathcal{P}\} \quad (3)$$

where $\phi(x)$ denotes the set of possible permutations of x, excluding x itself.

The second variant is **topic**-*oriented negative sampling*, i.e.,

$$\mathcal{N} = \{(s_-, s', s_+) \mid s' \in \mathcal{C} \wedge (s_-, s, s_+) \in \mathcal{P}\} \quad (4)$$

where s' denotes a sentence randomly sampled from a uniform distribution over the entire corpus $\mathcal{C}$. We call this method *topic-oriented* because topic consistency shared across a clique (s_-, s, s_+) is expected to be corrupted by replacing s with s'.

3 Model Architecture

We develop a simple semi-supervised model with neural networks. An overall view is shown in Figure 2. Our model mainly consists of three components: sentence encoder E, coherence classifier F_c, and implicit discourse relation classifier F_r. The parameters of E are shared across the two tasks: coherence modeling and implicit discourse relation recognition. In contrast, F_c and F_r are optimized separately. Though it is possible to develop more complex architectures (such as with word-level matching (Chen et al., 2016), a soft-attention mechanism (Liu and Li, 2016; Rönnqvist et al., 2017), or highway connections (Qin et al.,

345

| | 1st-Level Relation *Classes* | | 2nd-Level Relation *Types* | | Coherence |
	Acc. (%)	Macro F_1 (%)	Acc. (%)	Macro F_1 (%)	Acc. (%)
IRel only	51.49	42.29	37.49	24.81	N/A
IRel + *O-Coh* (Small)	52.16	41.39	37.77	25.46	57.96
IRel + *O-Coh* (Large)	52.29	42.48	41.29	**30.70**	**64.24**
IRel + *T-Coh* (Small)	51.70	40.84	37.91	25.35	83.04
IRel + *T-Coh* (Large)	**53.54**	**45.03**	**41.39**	29.67	**91.53**

Table 1: The results of implicit discourse relation recognition (multi-class classification) and coherence modeling (binary classification). *IRel* and *O/T-Coh* denote that the model is trained on implicit discourse relation recognition and order/topic-oriented coherence modeling respectively. "Small" and "large" correspond to the relative size of the used unlabeled corpus: 37K (WSJ) and 22M (BLLIP) positive instances, respectively.

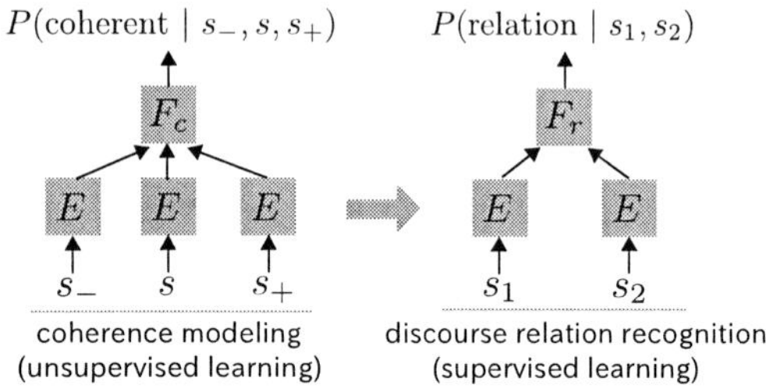

Figure 2: The semi-supervised system we developed. The model consists of sentence encoder E, coherence classifier F_c, and implicit discourse relation classifier F_r.

2016)), such architectures are outside the scope of this study, since the effectiveness of incorporating coherence-based knowledge would be broadly orthogonal to the model's complexity.

3.1 Sentence Encoder

Sentence encoder E transforms a symbol sequence (i.e., a sentence) into a continuous vector. First, a bidirectional LSTM (BiLSTM) is applied to a given sentence of n tokens $w_1, \ldots, w_n$, i.e.,

$$\overrightarrow{h}_i = \text{FwdLSTM}(\overrightarrow{h}_{i-1}, w_i) \in \mathbb{R}^D, \quad (5)$$

$$\overleftarrow{h}_i = \text{BwdLSTM}(\overleftarrow{h}_{i+1}, w_i) \in \mathbb{R}^D \quad (6)$$

where FwdLSTM and BwdLSTM denote forward and backward LSTMs, respectively. We initialize the hidden states to zero vectors, i.e., $\overrightarrow{h}_0 = \overleftarrow{h}_{n+1} = \mathbf{0}$. In our preliminary experiments, we tested conventional pooling functions (e.g., summation, average, or maximum pooling); we found that the following concatenation tends to yield higher performances:

$$h = \left(\overrightarrow{h}_L^\top, \overleftarrow{h}_1^\top\right)^\top \in \mathbb{R}^{2D}. \quad (7)$$

We use Eq. 7 as the aggregation function throughout our experiments.

3.2 Classifiers

We develop two multi-layer perceptrons (MLPs) with ReLU nonlinearities followed by softmax normalization each for F_c and F_r. The MLP inputs are the concatenation of sentence vectors. Thus, the dimensionalities of the input layers are $2D \times 3$ and $2D \times 2$ respectively. The MLPs consist of `input`, `hidden`, and `output` layers.

4 Experiments

4.1 Preparation

We used the Penn Discourse Treebank (PDTB) 2.0 corpus (Prasad et al., 2008) as a dataset for implicit discourse relation recognition. We followed the standard section partition, which is to use Sections 2–20 for training, Sections 0-1 for development, and Sections 21–22 for testing. We evaluate multi-class classifications with first-level relation *classes* (four classes) and second-level relation *types* (11 classes).

We used the Wall Street Journal (WSJ) articles (Marcus et al., 1993)[3] or the BLLIP North American News Text (Complete) (McClosky et al., 2008)[4] to build a coherence modeling dataset, resulting in about 48K (WSJ) or 23M (BLLIP) positive instances. We inserted a special symbol "⟨ARTICLE_BOUNDARY⟩" to each

---

[3] We used the raw texts in LDC99T42 Treebank-3: https://catalog.ldc.upenn.edu/LDC99T42

[4] https://catalog.ldc.upenn.edu/LDC2008T13

	Acc. (%)	Macro F_1 (%)
Rutherford and Xue (2015)	57.10	40.50
Liu et al. (2016)	57.27	44.98
Braud and Denis (2016)[5]	52.81	42.27
Wu et al. (2017)	**58.85**	44.84
IRel only	51.49	42.29
IRel only*	52.72	42.61
IRel + *T-Coh* (Large)	53.54	**45.03**
IRel + *T-Coh* (Large)*	56.60	**46.90**

Table 2: Comparison with previous works that exploit unlabeled corpora on first-level relation *classes*. An asterisk indicates that word embeddings are fine-tuned (which slightly decreases performance on second-level relation *types* due to overfitting).

	Exp.	Cont.	Comp.	Temp.
# of training data	6,673	3,235	1,855	582
IRel only	66.40	53.49	39.48	32.31
IRel + *T-Coh*	**67.48**	**54.94**	**40.41**	**35.60**

Table 3: Results on one-vs.-others binary classification in implicit discourse relation recognition. The evaluation metric is Macro F_1 (%). We evaluate on the first-level relation *classes*: `Expansion`, `Contingency`, `Comparison`, and `Temporal`.

article boundary. For the WSJ corpus, we split the sections into training/development/test sets in the same way with the implicit relation recognition. For the BLLIP corpus, we randomly sampled 10,000 articles each for the development and test sets. Negative instances are generated following the procedure described in Section 2. Note that this procedure requires neither human annotation nor special connective detection.

We set the dimensionalities of the word embeddings, hidden states of the BiLSTM, and hidden layers of the MLPs to 100, 200, and 100, respectively. GloVe (Pennington et al., 2014) was used to produce pre-trained word embeddings on the BLLIP corpus. To avoid overfitting, we fixed the word embeddings during training in both coherence modeling and implicit relation recognition. Dropout (ratio 0.2) was applied to word embeddings and MLPs's layers. At every iteration during training in both tasks, we configured class-balanced batches by resampling.

[5]The values are taken from Wu et al. (2017).

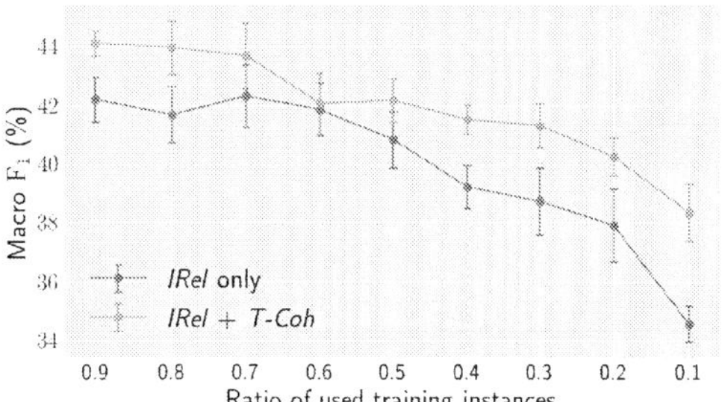

Figure 3: Results on implicit discourse relation recognition (first-level *classes*), with different numbers of training instances. The error bars show one standard deviation over 10 trials.

4.2 Results

To verify whether unsupervised learning on coherence modeling could improve implicit discourse relation recognition, we compared the semi-supervised model (i.e., implicit discourse relation recognition (*IRel*) + coherence modeling with order/topic-oriented negative sampling (*O/T-Coh*)) with the baseline model (i.e., *IRel* only). The evaluation metrics are accuracy (%) and Macro F_1 (%). We report the mean scores over 10 trials. Table 1 shows that coherence modeling improves Macro F_1 by about 3 points in first-level relation *classes* and by about 5 points in second-level relation *types*. Coherence modeling also outperforms the baseline in accuracy. We observed that the higher the coherence modeling performance (see Small vs. Large), the higher the implicit relation recognition score. These results support our claim that coherence modeling could learn linguistic knowledge that is useful for identifying discourse relations.

We also found that topic-oriented negative sampling tends to outperform its order-oriented counterpart, especially on first-level relation *classes*. We suspect that this is because order-oriented coherence modeling is more fine-grained and challenging than topic-oriented identification, resulting in poor generalization. For example, there could be order-invariant cliques that still hold coherence relations after random shuffling, whereas topic-invariant cliques hardly exist. Indeed, training on order-oriented negative sampling converged to lower scores than that of topic-oriented negative sampling (see coherence accuracy).

Next, for reference, we compared our system with previous work that exploits unlabeled corpora. As shown in Table 2, we found our model to outperform previous systems in Macro F_1. In this task, Macro F_1 is more important than accuracy because the class balance in the test set is highly skewed. Note that these previous models rely on previously detected connectives in the unlabeled corpus, whereas our system is free from such detection procedures.

To assess the effectiveness of coherence modeling on different relation classes, we trained and evaluated the models on one-vs-others binary classification. That is, we treated each of the first-level relation *classes* (4 classes) as the positive class and others as the negative class. Table 3 shows that coherence modeling is effective, especially for the `Temporal` relation which has relatively fewer labeled instances than others, indicating that coherence modeling could compensate for the shortage of labeled data.

We also performed an ablation study to discover the performance contribution from coherence modeling by changing the number of training instances used in implicit relation recognition. Here, we assume that in real-world situations, we do not have sufficient labeled data. We downsampled from the original training set and maintained the balance of classes as much as possible. As shown in Figure 3, coherence modeling robustly yields improvements, even if we reduced the labeled instances to 10%.

5 Conclusion

In this paper, we showed that unsupervised learning on coherence modeling improves implicit discourse relation recognition in a semi-supervised manner. Our approach does not require detecting explicit connectives, which makes it possible to exploit entire unlabeled corpora. We empirically examined two variants of coherence modeling and show that topic-oriented negative sampling tends to be more effective than the order-oriented counterpart on first-level relation *classes*.

It still remains unclear whether the coherence-based knowledge is complemental to those by previous work. It is also interesting to qualitatively inspect the differences of learned properties between order-oriented and topic-oriented negative sampling. We will examine this line of research in future.

Acknowledgments

The authors would like to thank anonymous reviewers for their constructive and helpful suggestions on this work. This work was supported by JSPS KAKENHI Grant Number 16H05872.

References

Chloé Braud and Pascal Denis. 2015. Comparing word representations for implicit discourse relation classification. In *Proceedings of the 2015 Conference on Empirical Methods in Natural Language Processing (EMNLP 2015)*.

Chloé Braud and Pascal Denis. 2016. Learning connective-based word representations for implicit discourse relation identification. In *Proceedings of the 2016 Conference on Empirical Methods in Natural Language Processing (EMNLP 2016)*.

Jifan Chen, Qi Zhang, Pengfei Liu, and Xuanjing Huang. 2016. Discourse relations detection via a mixed generative-discriminative framework. In *Proceedings of the 30th Conference on Artificial Intelligence (AAAI 2016)*.

Barbara J. Grosz, Aravind K. Joshi, and Scott Weinstein. 1995. Centering: A framework for modelling the local coherence of discourse. *Computational Linguistis*, 21(2):203–225.

Hugo Hernault, Danushka Bollegala, and Mitsuru Ishizuka. 2010. A semi-supervised approach to improve classification of infrequent discourse relations using feature vector extension. In *Proceedings of the 2010 Conference on Empirical Methods in Natural Language Processing (EMNLP 2010)*.

Hugo Hernault, Danushka Bollegala, and Mitsuru Ishizuka. 2011. Semi-supervised discourse relation classification with structure learning. In *Proceedings of the 12th International Conference on Computational Linguistics and Intelligent Text Processing (CICLing 2011)*.

Jerry R. Hobbs. 1985. On the coherence and structure of discourse. Technical Report CSLI-85-37, Center for the Study of Language and Information (CSLI), Stanford University.

Yangfeng Ji, Gongbo Zhang, and Jacob Eisenstein. 2015. Closing the gap: domain adaptation from explicit to implicit discourse relations. In *Proceedings of the 53st Annual Meeting of the Association for Computational Linguistics (ACL 2015)*.

Man Lan, Jianxiang Wang, Yuanbin Wu, Zheng-yu Niu, and Haifeng Wang. 2017. Multi-task attention-based neural networks for implicit discourse relationship representation and identification. In *Proceedings of the 2017 Conference of Empirical Methods in Natural Language Processing (EMNLP 2017)*.

Man Lan, Yu Xu, and Zhengyu Niu. 2013. Leveraging synthetic discourse data via multi-task learning for implicit discourse relation recognition. In *Proceedings of the 51st Annual Meeting of the Association for Computational Linguistics (ACL 2013)*.

Jiwei Li and Eduard Hovy. 2014. A model of coherence based on distributed sentence representation. In *Proceedings of the 2014 Conference on Empirical Methods in Natural Language Processing (EMNLP 2014)*.

Yang Liu and Sujian Li. 2016. Recognizing implicit discourse relations via repeated reading: neural networks with multi-level attention. In *Proceedings of the 2016 Conference on Empirical Methods in Natural Language Processing (EMNLP 2016)*.

Yang Liu, Sujian Li, Xiaodong Zhang, and Zhifang Sui. 2016. Implicit discourse relation classification via multi-task neural networks. In *Proceedings of the 30th Conference on Artificial Intelligence (AAAI 2016)*.

Daniel Marcu and Abdessamad Echihabi. 2002. An unsupervised approach to recognizing discourse relations. In *Proceedings of the 40th Annual Meeting of the Association for Computational Linguistics (ACL 2002)*.

Mitchell P. Marcus, Mary Ann Marcinkiewicz, and Beatrice Santorini. 1993. Building a large annotated corpus of english: The penn treebank. *Computational Linguistics*, 19(2):313–330.

David McClosky, Eugene Charniak, and Mark Johnson. 2008. Bllip north american news text, complete. *Linguistic Data Consortium*.

Gary Patterson and Andrew Kehler. 2013. Predicting the presence of discourse connectives. In *Proceedings of the 2013 Conference on Empirical Methods in Natural Language Processing (EMNLP 2013)*.

Jeffrey Pennington, Richard Socher, and Christopher D. Manning. 2014. Glove: Global vectors for word representations. In *Proceedings of the 2014 Conference on Empirical Methods in Natural Language Processing (EMNLP 2014)*.

Emily Pitler, Mridhula Raghupathy, Hena Mehta, Ani Nenkova, Alan Lee, and Aravind Joshi. 2008. Easily identifiable discourse relations. In *Proceedings of the 24th International Conference on Computational Linguistics (COLING 2008)*.

Rashmi Prasad, Nikhil Dinesh, Alan Lee, Eleni Miltsakaki, Livio Robaldo, Aravind Joshi, and Bonnie Webber. 2008. The penn discourse treebank 2.0. In *Proceedings of the Sixth International Conference on Language Resources and Evaluation (LREC 2008)*.

Lianhui Qin, Zhisong Zhang, and Hai Zhao. 2016. A stacking gated neural architecture for implicit discourse relation classification. In *Proceedings of the 2016 Conference on Empirical Methods in Natural Language Processing (EMNLP 2016)*.

Samuel Rönnqvist, Niko Schenk, and Christian Chiarcos. 2017. A recurrent neural model with attention for the recognition of chinese implicit discourse relations. In *Proceedings of the 55th Annual Meeting of the Association for Computational Linguistics (ACL 2017)*.

Attapol T. Rutherford and Nianwen Xue. 2015. Improving the inference of implicit discourse relations via classifying explicit discourse connectives. In *Proceedings of the 2015 Conference of the North American Chapter of the Association for Computational Linguistics: Human Language Technologies (NAACL-HLT 2015)*.

Caroline Sporleder and Alex Lascarides. 2008. Using automatically labelled examples to classify rhetorical relations: an assessment. *Natural Language Engineering*, 14(03).

Changxing Wu, Xiaodong Shi, Yidong Chen, Jinsong Su, and Boli Wang. 2017. Improving implicit discourse relation recognition with discourse-specific word embeddings. In *Proceedings of the 55th Annual Meeting of the Association for Computational Linguistics (ACL 2017)*.

Zhi-Min Zhou, Yu Xu, Zheng-Yu Niu, Man Lan, Jian Su, and Chew Lim Tan. 2010. Predicting discourse connectives for implicit discourse relation recognition. In *Proceedings of the 23rd International Conference on Computational Linguistics (COLING 2010)*.

Adversarial Learning of Task-Oriented Neural Dialog Models

Bing Liu
Carnegie Mellon University
Electrical and Computer Engineering
liubing@cmu.edu

Ian Lane
Carnegie Mellon University
Electrical and Computer Engineering
Language Technologies Institute
lane@cmu.edu

Abstract

In this work, we propose an adversarial learning method for reward estimation in reinforcement learning (RL) based task-oriented dialog models. Most of the current RL based task-oriented dialog systems require the access to a reward signal from either user feedback or user ratings. Such user ratings, however, may not always be consistent or available in practice. Furthermore, online dialog policy learning with RL typically requires a large number of queries to users, suffering from sample efficiency problem. To address these challenges, we propose an adversarial learning method to learn dialog rewards directly from dialog samples. Such rewards are further used to optimize the dialog policy with policy gradient based RL. In the evaluation in a restaurant search domain, we show that the proposed adversarial dialog learning method achieves advanced dialog success rate comparing to strong baseline methods. We further discuss the covariate shift problem in online adversarial dialog learning and show how we can address that with partial access to user feedback.

1 Introduction

Task-oriented dialog systems are designed to assist user in completing daily tasks, such as making reservations and providing customer support. Comparing to chit-chat systems that are usually modeled with single-turn context-response pairs (Li et al., 2016; Serban et al., 2016), task-oriented dialog systems (Young et al., 2013; Williams et al., 2017) involve retrieving information from external resources and reasoning over multiple dialog turns. This makes it especially im-

portant for a system to be able to learn interactively from users.

Recent efforts on task-oriented dialog systems focus on learning dialog models from a data-driven approach using human-human or human-machine conversations. Williams et al. (2017) designed a hybrid supervised and reinforcement learning end-to-end dialog agent. Dhingra et al. (2017) proposed an RL based model for information access that can learn online via user interactions. Such systems assume the model has access to a reward signal at the end of a dialog, either in the form of a binary user feedback or a continuous user score. A challenge with such learning systems is that user feedback may be inconsistent (Su et al., 2016) and may not always be available in practice. Further more, online dialog policy learning with RL usually suffers from sample efficiency issue (Su et al., 2017), which requires an agent to make a large number of feedback queries to users.

To reduce the high demand for user feedback in online policy learning, solutions have been proposed to design or to learn a reward function that can be used to generate a reward in approximation to a user feedback. Designing a good reward function is not easy (Walker et al., 1997) as it typically requires strong domain knowledge. El Asri et al. (2014) proposed a learning based reward function that is trained with task completion transfer learning. Su et al. (2016) proposed an online active learning method for reward estimation using Gaussian process classification. These methods still require annotations of dialog ratings by users, and thus may also suffer from the rating consistency and learning efficiency issues.

To address the above discussed challenges, we investigate the effectiveness of learning dialog rewards directly from dialog samples. Inspired by the success of adversarial training in computer vi-

Proceedings of the SIGDIAL 2018 Conference, pages 350–359,
Melbourne, Australia, 12-14 July 2018. ©2018 Association for Computational Linguistics

sion (Denton et al., 2015) and natural language generation (Li et al., 2017a), we propose an adversarial learning method for task-oriented dialog systems. We jointly train two models, a generator that interacts with the environment to produce task-oriented dialogs, and a discriminator that marks a dialog sample as being successful or not. The generator is a neural network based task-oriented dialog agent. The environment that the dialog agent interacts with is the user. Quality of a dialog produced by the agent and the user is measured by the likelihood that it fools the discriminator to believe that the dialog is a successful one conducted by a human agent. We treat dialog agent optimization as a reinforcement learning problem. The output from the discriminator serves as a reward to the dialog agent, pushing it towards completing a task in a way that is indistinguishable from how a human agent completes it.

In this work, we discuss how the adversarial learning reward function compares to designed reward functions in learning a good dialog policy. Our experimental results in a restaurant search domain show that dialog agents that are optimized with the proposed adversarial learning method achieve advanced task success rate comparing to strong baseline methods. We discuss the impact of the size of annotated dialog samples to the effectiveness of dialog adversarial learning. We further discuss the covariate shift issue in interactive adversarial learning and show how we can address that with partial access to user feedback.

2   Related Work

Task-Oriented Dialog Learning   Popular approaches in learning task-oriented dialog systems include modeling the task as a partially observable Markov Decision Process (POMDP) (Young et al., 2013). Reinforcement learning can be applied in the POMDP framework to learn dialog policy online by interacting with users (Gašić et al., 2013). Recent efforts have been made in designing end-to-end solutions (Williams and Zweig, 2016; Liu and Lane, 2017a; Li et al., 2017b; Liu et al., 2018) for task-oriented dialogs. Wen et al. (2017) designed a supervised training end-to-end neural dialog model with modularly connected components. Bordes and Weston (2017) proposed a neural dialog model using end-to-end memory networks. These models are trained offline using fixed dialog corpora, and thus it is unknown how well

the model performance generalizes to online user interactions. Williams et al. (2017) proposed a hybrid code network for task-oriented dialog that can be trained with supervised and reinforcement learning. Dhingra et al. (2017) proposed a reinforcement learning dialog agent for information access. Such models are trained against rule-based user simulators. A dialog reward from the user simulator is expected at the end of each turn or each dialog.

Dialog Reward Modeling   Dialog reward estimation is an essential step for policy optimization in task-oriented dialogs. Walker et al. (1997) proposed PARADISE framework in which user satisfaction is estimated using a number of dialog features such as number of turns and elapsed time. Yang et al. (2012) proposed collaborative filtering based method in estimating user satisfaction in dialogs. Su et al. (2015) studied using convolutional neural networks in rating dialog success. Su et al. (2016) further proposed an online active learning method based on Gaussian process for dialog reward learning. These methods still require various levels of annotations of dialog ratings by users, either offline or online. On the other side of the spectrum, Paek and Pieraccini (2008) proposed inferring dialog rewards directly from dialog corpora with inverse reinforcement learning (IRL) (Ng et al., 2000). However, most of the IRL algorithms are very expensive to run, requiring reinforcement learning in an inner loop. This hinders IRL based dialog reward estimation methods to scale to complex dialog scenarios.

Adversarial Networks   Generative adversarial networks (GANs) (Goodfellow et al., 2014) have recently been successfully applied in computer vision and natural language generation (Li et al., 2017a). The network training process is framed as a game, in which people train a generator whose job is to generate samples to fool a discriminator. The job of a discriminator is to distinguish samples produced by the generator from the real ones. The generator and the discriminator are jointly trained until convergence. GANs were firstly applied in image generation and recently used in language tasks. Li et al. (2017a) proposed conducting adversarial learning for response generation in open-domain dialogs. Yang et al. (2017) proposed using adversarial learning in neural machine translation. The use of adversarial learning in task-oriented dialogs has not been well studied. Peng et al. (2018) recently explored using adversarial loss as an extra critic in addition to the main reward function based on task completion. This method still requires prior knowledge of a user's goal, which can be hard to collect in practice, in defining task completion. Our proposed method uses adversarial reward as the only source of reward for policy optimization in addressing this challenge.

3 Adversarial Learning for Task-Oriented Dialogs

In this section, we describe the proposed adversarial learning method for policy optimization in task-oriented neural dialog models. Our objective is to learn a dialog agent (i.e. the generator, G) that is able to effectively communicate with a user over a multi-turn conversation to complete a task. This can be framed as a sequential decision making problem, in which the agent generates a best action to take at every dialog turn given the dialog context. The action can be in the form of either a dialog act (Henderson et al., 2013) or a natural language utterance. We study on dialog act level in this work. Let U_k and A_k represent the user input and agent outputs (i.e. the agent act a_k and the slot-value predictions) at turn k. Given the current user input U_k, the agent estimates the user's goal and select a best action a_k to take conditioning on the dialog history.

In addition, we want to learn a reward function (i.e. the discriminator, D) that is able to provide guidance to the agent for learning a better policy. We expect the reward function to give a higher reward to the agent if the conversation it had with the user is closer to how a human agent completes the task. Output of the reward function is the probability of a given dialog being successfully completed. We train the reward function by forcing it to distinguish successful dialogs and dialogs conducted by the machine agent. At the same time, we also update the dialog agent parameters with policy gradient based reinforcement learning using the reward produced by the reward function. We keep updating the dialog agent and the reward function until the discriminator can no longer distinguish dialogs from a human agent and from a machine agent. In the subsequent sections, we describe in detail the design of our dialog agent and reward function, and the proposed adversarial dialog learning method.

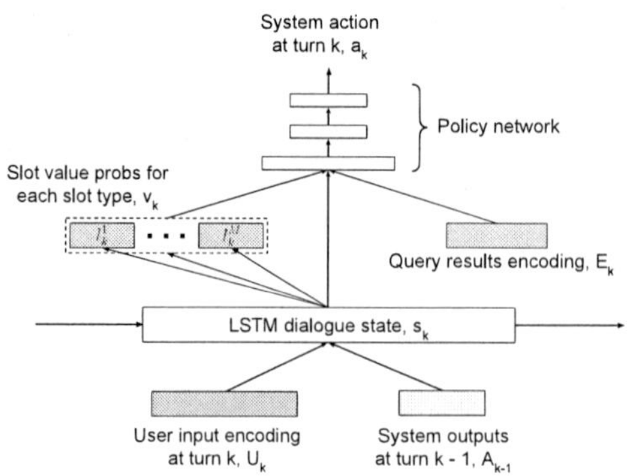

Figure 1: Design of the task-oriented neural dialog agent.

3.1 Neural Dialog Agent

The generator is a neural network based task-oriented dialog agent. The model architecture is shown in Figure 1. The agent uses an LSTM recurrent neural network to model the sequence of turns in a dialog. At each turn of a dialog, the agent takes a best system action conditioning on the current dialog state. A continuous form dialog state is maintained in the LSTM state s_k. At each dialog turn k, user input U_k and previous system output A_{k-1} are firstly encoded to continuous representations. The user input can either in the form of a dialog act or a natural language utterance. We use dialog act form user input in our experiment. The dialog act representation is obtained by concatenating the embeddings of the act and the slot-value pairs. If natural language form of input is used, we can encode the sequence of words using a bidirectional RNN and take the concatenation of the last forward and backward states as the utterance representation, similar to (Yang et al., 2016) and (Liu and Lane, 2017a). With the user input U_k and agent input A_{k-1}, the dialog state s_k is updated from the previous state s_{k-1} by:

$$s_k = \text{LSTM}_G(s_{k-1}, [U_k, A_{k-1}]) \qquad (1)$$

Belief Tracking Belief tracking maintains the state of a conversation, such as a user's goals, by accumulating evidence along the sequence of dialog turns. A user's goal is represented by a list of slot-value pairs. The belief tracker updates its estimation of the user's goal by maintaining a probability distribution $P(l_k^m)$ over candidate values for each of the tracked goal slot type $m \in M$. With the current dialog state s_k, the probability over candidate values for each of the tracked goal slot is calculated by:

$$P(l_k^m \mid \mathbf{U}_{\leq k}, \mathbf{A}_{<k}) = \text{SlotDist}_m(s_k) \quad (2)$$

where SlotDist_m is a single hidden layer MLP with softmax activation over slot type $m \in M$.

Dialog Policy   We model the agent's policy with a deep neural network. Following the policy, the agent selects the next action in response to the user's input based on the current dialog state. In addition, information retrieved from external resources may also affects the agent's next action. Therefore, inputs to our policy module are the current dialog state s_k, the probability distribution of estimated user goal slot values v_k, and the encoding of the information retrieved from external sources E_k. Here instead of encoding the actual query results, we encode a summary of the retrieved items (i.e. count and availability of the returned items). Based on these inputs, the policy network produces a probability distribution over the next system actions:

$$P(a_k \mid U_{\leq k}, A_{<k}, E_{\leq k}) = \text{PolicyNet}(s_k, v_k, E_k) \quad (3)$$

where PolicyNet is a single hidden layer MLP with softmax activation over all system actions.

3.2 Dialog Reward Estimator

The discriminator model is a binary classifier that takes in a dialog with a sequence of turns and outputs a label indicating whether the dialog is a successful one or not. The logistic function returns a probability of the input dialog being successful. The discriminator model design is as shown in Figure 2. We use a bidirectional LSTM to encode the sequence of turns. At each dialog turn k, input to the discriminator model is the concatenation of (1) encoding of the user input U_k, (2) encoding of the query result summary E_k, and (3) encoding of agent output A_k. The discriminator LSTM output at each step k, h_k, is a concatenation of the forward LSTM output $\overrightarrow{h_k}$ and the backward LSTM output $\overleftarrow{h_k}$: $h_k = [\overrightarrow{h_k}, \overleftarrow{h_k}]$.

Once obtaining the discriminator LSTM state outputs $\{h_1, \ldots, h_K\}$, we experiment with four different methods in combining these state outputs to generated the final dialog representation d for the binary classifier:

BiLSTM-last   Produce the final dialog representation d by concatenating the last LSTM state

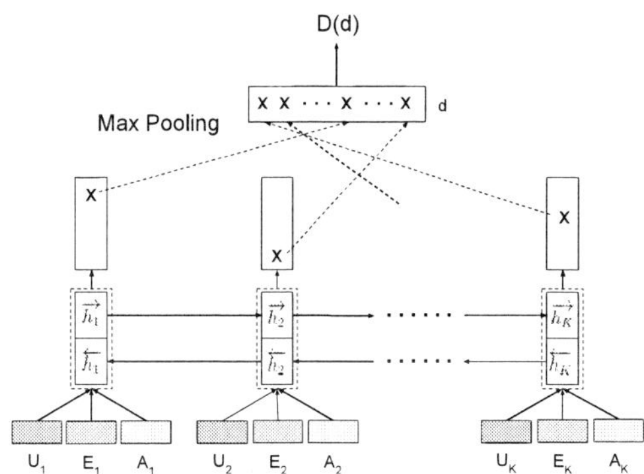

Figure 2: Design of the dialog reward estimator: Bidirectional LSTM with max pooling.

outputs from the forward and backward directions:
$$d = [\overrightarrow{h_K}, \overleftarrow{h_1}]$$

BiLSTM-max   Max-pooling. Produce the final dialog representation d by selecting the maximum value over each dimension of the LSTM state outputs.

BiLSTM-avg   Average-pooling. Produce the final dialog representation d by taking the average value over each dimension of the LSTM state outputs.

BiLSTM-attn   Attention-pooling. Produce the final dialog representation d by taking the weighted sum of the LSTM state outputs. The weights are calculated with attention mechanism:

$$d = \sum_{k=1}^{K} \alpha_k h_k \quad (4)$$

and

$$\alpha_k = \frac{\exp(e_k)}{\sum_{t=1}^{K} \exp(e_t)}, \quad e_k = g(h_k) \quad (5)$$

g a feed-forward neural network with a single output node. Finally, the discriminator produces a value indicating the likelihood the input dialog being a successful one:

$$D(d) = \sigma(W_o d + b_o) \quad (6)$$

where W_o and b_o are the weights and bias in the discriminator output layer. σ is a logistic function.

3.3 Adversarial Learning with Policy Gradient

Once we obtain a dialog sample initiated by the agent and a dialog reward from the reward function, we optimize the dialog agent using REIN-FORCE (Williams, 1992) with the given reward.

The reward $D(d)$ is only received at the end of a dialog, i.e. $r_K = D(d)$. We discount this final reward with a discount factor $\gamma \in [0, 1)$ to assign a reward R_k to each dialog turn. The objective function can thus be written as $J_k(\theta_G) = \mathbb{E}_{\theta_G}[R_k] = \mathbb{E}_{\theta_G}\left[\sum_{t=k}^{K} \gamma^{t-k} r_t - V(s_k)\right]$, with $r_k = D(d)$ for $k = K$ and $r_k = 0$ for $k < K$. $V(s_k)$ is the state value function which serves as a baseline value. The state value function is a feed-forward neural network with a single-node value output. We optimize the generator parameter θ_G to maximize $J_k(\theta_G)$. With likelihood ratio gradient estimator, the gradient of $J_k(\theta_G)$ can be derived with:

$$
\begin{aligned}
\nabla_{\theta_G} J_k(\theta_G) &= \nabla_{\theta_G} \mathbb{E}_{\theta_G}[R_k] \\
&= \sum_{a_k \in \mathcal{A}} G(a_k|\cdot) \nabla_{\theta_G} \log G(a_k|\cdot) R_k \\
&= \mathbb{E}_{\theta_G}[\nabla_{\theta_G} \log G(a_k|\cdot) R_k]
\end{aligned}
\tag{7}
$$

where $G(a_k|\cdot) = G(a_k|s_k, v_k, E_k; \theta_G)$. The expression above gives us an unbiased gradient estimator. We sample agent action a_k following a softmax policy at each dialog turn and compute the policy gradient. At the same time, we update the discriminator parameter θ_D to maximize the probability of assigning the correct labels to the successful dialog from human demonstration and the dialog conducted by the machine agent:

$$
\nabla_{\theta_D}\left[\mathbb{E}_{d \sim \theta_{demo}}[log(D(d))] + \mathbb{E}_{d \sim \theta_G}[log(1 - D(d))]\right]
\tag{8}
$$

We continue to update both the dialog agent and the reward function via dialog simulation or real user interaction until convergence.

4 Experiments

4.1 Dataset

We use data from the second Dialog State Tracking Challenge (DSTC2) (Henderson et al., 2014) in the restaurant search domain for our model training and evaluation. We add entity information to each dialog sample in the original DSTC2 dataset. This makes entity information a part of the model training process, enabling the agent to handle entities during interactive evaluation with users. Different from the agent action definition used in DSTC2, actions in our system are produced by concatenating the act

Algorithm 1 Adversarial Learning for Task-Oriented Dialog

1: **Required:** dialog corpus S_{demo}, user simulator U, generator G, discriminator D
2: Pretrain a dialog agent (i.e. the generator) G on dialog corpora S_{demo} with MLE
3: Simulate dialogs S_{simu} between U and G
4: Sample successful dialogs $S_{(+)}$ and random dialogs $S_{(-)}$ from $\{S_{demo}, S_{simu}\}$
5: Pretrain a reward function (i.e. the discriminator) D with $S_{(+)}$ and $S_{(-)}$ $\triangleright$ eq 8
6: **for** number of training iterations **do**
7:   **for** G-steps **do**
8:    Simulate dialogs S_b between U and G
9:    Compute reward r for each dialog in S_b with D $\triangleright$ eq 6
10:    Update G with reward r $\triangleright$ eq 7
11:   **end for**
12:   **for** D-steps **do**
13:    Sample dialogs $S_{(b+)}$ from $S_{(+)}$
14:    Update D with $S_{(b+)}$ and S_b (with S_b as negative examples) $\triangleright$ eq 8
15:   **end for**
16: **end for**

---

and slot types in the original dialog act output (e.g. "$confirm(food = italian)$" maps to "$confirm\_food$"). The slot values are captured in the belief tracking outputs. Table 1 shows the statistics of the dataset used in our experiments.

# of train/dev/test dialogs	1612/506/ 1117
# of dialog turns in average	7.88
# of slot value options	
Area	5
Food	91
Price range	3

Table 1: Statistics of DSTC2 dataset.

4.2 Training Settings

We use a user simulator for our interactive training and evaluation with adversarial learning. Instead of using a rule-based user simulator as in many prior work (Zhao and Eskenazi, 2016; Peng et al., 2017), in our study we use a model-based simulator trained on DSTC2 dataset. We follow the design and training procedures of (Liu and Lane, 2017b) in building the model-based simulator. The stochastic policy used in the simulator introduces additional diversity in user behavior during dialog simulation.

Before performing interactive adversarial learning with RL, we pretrain the dialog agent and the discriminative reward function with offline supervised learning on DSTC2 dataset. We find this being helpful in enabling the adversarial policy learning to start with a good initialization. The dialog agent is pretrained to minimize the cross-entropy losses on agent action and slot value predictions. Once we obtain a supervised training dialog agent, we simulate dialogs between the agent and the user simulator. These simulated dialogs together with the dialogs in DSTC2 dataset are then used to pretrain the discriminative reward function. We sample 500 successful dialogs as positive examples, and 500 random dialogs as negative examples in pretraining the discriminator. During dialog simulation, a dialog is marked as successful if the agent's belief tracking outputs fully match the informable (Henderson et al., 2013) user goal slot values, and all user requested slots are fulfilled. This is the same evaluation criteria as used in (Wen et al., 2017) and (Liu and Lane, 2017b). It is important to note that such dialog success signal is usually not available during real user interactions, unless we explicitly ask users to provide such feedback.

During supervised pretraining, for the dialog agent we use LSTM with a state size of 150. Hidden layer size for the policy network MLP is set as 100. For the discriminator model, a state size of 200 is used for the bidirectional LSTM. We perform mini-batch training with batch size of 32 using Adam optimization method (Kingma and Ba, 2014) with initial learning rate of 1e-3. Dropout ($p = 0.5$) is applied during model training to prevent the model from over-fitting. Gradient clipping threshold is set to 5.

During interactive learning with adversarial RL, we set the maximum allowed number of dialog turns as 20. A simulation is force to terminated after 20 dialog turns. We update the model with every mini-batch of 25 samples. Dialog rewards are calculated by the discriminative reward function. Reward discount factor γ is set as 0.95. These rewards are used to update the agent model via policy gradient. At the same time, this mini-batch of simulated dialogs are used as negative examples to update the discriminator.

4.3 Results and Analysis

In this section, we show and discuss our empirical evaluation results. We first compare dialog agent trained using the proposed adversarial reward to those using human designed reward and using oracle reward. We then discuss the impact of discriminator model design and model pretraining on the adversarial learning performance. Last but not least, we discuss the potential issue of covariate shift during interactive adversarial learning and show how we address that with partial access to user feedback.

4.3.1 Comparison to Other Reward Types

We first compare the performance of dialog agent using adversarial reward to those using designed reward and oracle reward on dialog success rate. Designed reward refers to reward function that is designed by humans with domain knowledge. In our experiment, based on the dialog success criteria defined in section 4.2, we *design* the following reward function for RL policy learning:

- +1 for each informable slot that is correctly estimated by the agent at the end of a dialog.

- If ALL informable slots are tracked correctly, +1 for each requestable slot successfully handled by the agent.

In addition to the comparison to human designed reward, we further compare to the case of using oracle reward during agent policy optimization. Using oracle reward refers to having access to the final dialog success status. We apply a reward of +1 for a successful dialog, and a reward of 0 for a failed dialog. Performance of the agent using oracle reward serves as an upper-bound for those using other types of reward. For the adversarial reward curve, we use BiLSTM-max as the discriminator model. During RL training, we normalize the rewards produced by different reward functions.

Figure 3 show the RL learning curves for models trained using different reward functions. The dialog success rate at each evaluation point is calculated by averaging over the success status of 1000 dialog simulations at that point. The pretrain baseline in the figure refers to the supervised pretraining model. This model does not get updated during interactive learning, and thus the curve stays flat during the RL training cycle. As shown in these curves, all the three types of reward

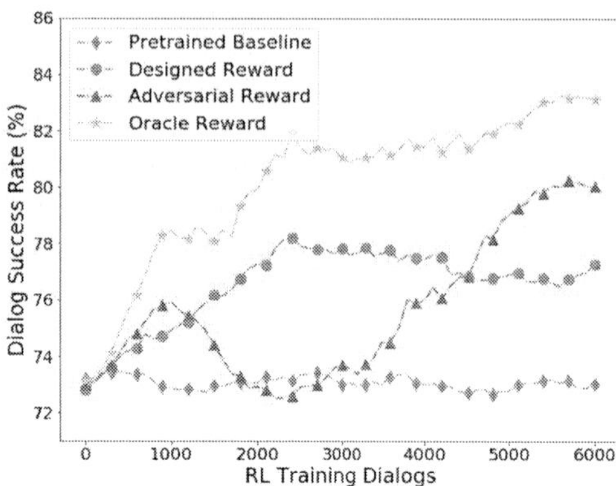

Figure 3: RL policy optimization performance comparing with adversarial reward, designed reward, and oracle reward.

functions lead to improved dialog success rate along the RL training process. The agent trained with designed reward falls behind the agent trained with oracle reward by a large margin. This shows that the reward designed with domain knowledge may not fully align with the final evaluation criteria. Designing a reward function that can provide an agent enough supervision signal and also well aligns the final system objective is not a trivial task (Popov et al., 2017). In practice, it is often difficult to exactly specify what we expect an agent to do, and we usually end up with simple and imperfect measures. In our experiment, agent using adversarial reward achieves a 7.4% improvement on dialog success rate at the end of 6000 interactive dialog learning episodes, outperforming that using the designed reward (4.2%). This shows the advantage of performing adversarial training in learning directly from expert demonstrations and in addressing the challenge of designing a good reward function. Another important point we observe in our experiments is that RL agents trained with adversarial reward, although enjoy higher performance in the end, suffer from larger variance and instability on model performance during the RL training process, comparing to agents using human designed reward. This is because during RL training the agent interfaces with a moving target, rather than a fixed objective measure as in the case of using the designed reward or oracle reward. The model performance only gradually gets stabilized when both the dialog agent and the reward function are close to convergence.

4.3.2 Impact of Discriminator Model Design

We study the impact of different discriminator model designs on the adversarial learning performance. We compare the four pooling methods described in section 3.2 in producing the final dialog representation. Table 2 shows the offline evaluation results on 1000 simulated test dialog samples. Among the four pooling methods, max-pooling on bidirectional LSTM outputs achieves the best classification accuracy in our experiment. Max-pooling also assigns the highest probability to successful dialogs in the test set comparing to other pooling methods. Attention-pooling based LSTM model achieves the lowest performance across all the three offline evaluation metrics in our study. This is probably due to the limited number of training samples we used in pretraining the discriminator. Learning good attentions usually requires more data samples and the model may thus overfit the small training set. We observe similar trends during interactive learning evaluation that the attention-based discriminator leads to divergence of policy optimization more often than the other three pooling methods. Max-pooling discriminator gives the most stable performance during interactive RL training.

Model	Prediction Accuracy	Success Prob.	Fail Prob.
BiLSTM-last	0.674	0.580	0.275
BiLSTM-max	**0.706**	**0.588**	0.272
BiLSTM-avg	0.688	0.561	**0.268**
BiLSTM-attn	0.652	0.541	0.285

Table 2: Performance of different discriminator model design, on prediction accuracy and probabilities assigned to successful and failed dialogs.

4.3.3 Impact of Annotated Dialogs for Discriminator Training

Annotating dialogs for model training requires additional human efforts. We investigate the impact of annotated dialog samples on discriminator model training. The amount of annotated dialogs required for learning a good discriminator depends mainly on the complexity of a task. Given the rather simple nature of the slot filling based DSTC2 restaurant search task, we experiment with annotating 100 to 1000 discriminator training samples. We use BiLSTM-max discriminator model in these experiments. The adversarial

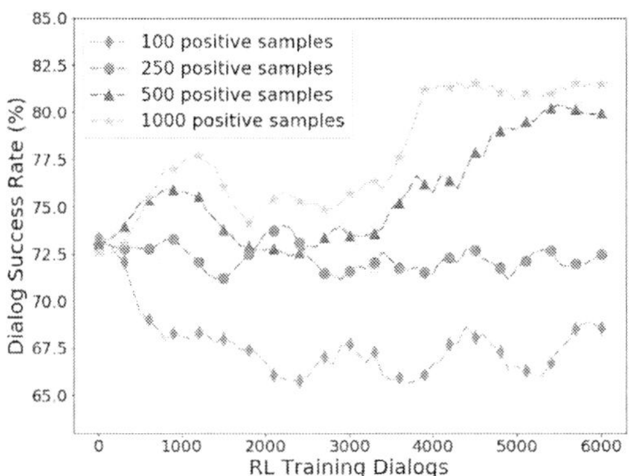

Figure 4: Impact of discriminator training sample size on RL dialog learning performance.

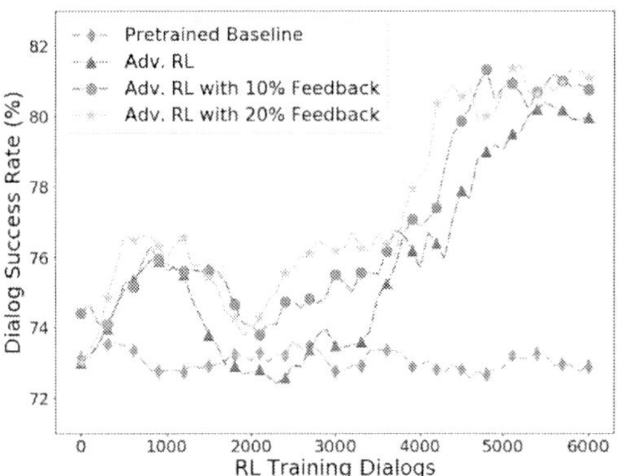

Figure 5: Addressing covariate shift in online adversarial dialog learning with partial access to user feedback.

RL training curves with different levels of discriminator training samples are shown in Figure 4. As these results illustrate, with 100 annotated dialogs as positive samples for discriminator training, the discriminator is not able to produce dialog rewards that are useful in learning a good policy. Learning with 250 positive samples does not lead to concrete improvement on dialog success rate neither. With the growing number of annotated samples, the dialog agent becomes more likely to learn a better policy, resulting in higher dialog success rate at the end of the interactive learning sessions.

4.3.4 Partial Access to User Feedback

A potential issue with RL based interactive adversarial learning is the covariate shift (Ross and Bagnell, 2010; Ho and Ermon, 2016) problem. The positive examples for discriminator training are generated before the interactive learning cycle based on the supervised pretraining dialog policy. During interactive RL training, the agent's policy keeps getting updated. The newly generated dialog samples based on the updated policy may be equally good comparing to the initial set of positive dialogs, but they may look very different. In this case, the discriminator is likely to give these dialogs low rewards as the pattern presented in these dialogs is different to what the discriminator is initially trained on. The agent will thus be discouraged to produce such type of successful dialogs in the future with these negative rewards. To address such covariate shift issue, we design a DAgger (Ross et al., 2011) style imitation learning method to the dialog adversarial learning. We assume that during interactive learning with users, occasionally we can receive feedback from users

indicating the quality of the conversation they had with the agent. We then add those dialogs with good feedback to the pool of positive dialog samples used in discriminator model training. With this, the discriminator can learn to assign high rewards to such good dialogs in the future. In our empirical evaluation, we experiment with the agent receiving positive feedback 10% and 20% of the time during its interaction with users. The experimental results are shown in Figure 5. As illustrated in these curves, the proposed DAgger style learning method can effectively improve the dialog adversarial learning with RL, leading to higher dialog success rate.

5 Conclusions

In this work, we investigate the effectiveness of applying adversarial training in learning task-oriented dialog models. The proposed method is an attempt towards addressing the rating consistency and learning efficiency issues in online dialog policy learning with user feedback. We show that with limited number of annotated dialogs, the proposed adversarial learning method can effectively learn a reward function and use that to guide policy optimization with policy gradient based reinforcement learning. In the experiment on a restaurant search domain, we show that the proposed adversarial learning method achieves advanced dialog success rate comparing to baseline methods using other forms of reward. We further discuss the covariate shift issue during interactive adversarial learning and show how we can address it with partial access to user feedback.

References

Antoine Bordes and Jason Weston. 2017. Learning end-to-end goal-oriented dialog. In *International Conference on Learning Representations*.

Emily L Denton, Soumith Chintala, Rob Fergus, et al. 2015. Deep generative image models using a laplacian pyramid of adversarial networks. In *Advances in neural information processing systems*, pages 1486–1494.

Bhuwan Dhingra, Lihong Li, Xiujun Li, Jianfeng Gao, Yun-Nung Chen, Faisal Ahmed, and Li Deng. 2017. Towards end-to-end reinforcement learning of dialogue agents for information access. In *Proceedings of ACL*.

Layla El Asri, Romain Laroche, and Olivier Pietquin. 2014. Task completion transfer learning for reward inference. *Proc of MLIS*.

Milica Gašić, Catherine Breslin, Matthew Henderson, Dongho Kim, Martin Szummer, Blaise Thomson, Pirros Tsiakoulis, and Steve Young. 2013. Online policy optimisation of bayesian spoken dialogue systems via human interaction. In *ICASSP*, pages 8367–8371. IEEE.

Ian Goodfellow, Jean Pouget-Abadie, Mehdi Mirza, Bing Xu, David Warde-Farley, Sherjil Ozair, Aaron Courville, and Yoshua Bengio. 2014. Generative adversarial nets. In *Advances in neural information processing systems*, pages 2672–2680.

Matthew Henderson, Blaise Thomson, and Jason Williams. 2013. Dialog state tracking challenge 2 & 3.

Matthew Henderson, Blaise Thomson, and Jason Williams. 2014. The second dialog state tracking challenge. In *SIGDIAL*.

Jonathan Ho and Stefano Ermon. 2016. Generative adversarial imitation learning. In *Advances in Neural Information Processing Systems*, pages 4565–4573.

Diederik Kingma and Jimmy Ba. 2014. Adam: A method for stochastic optimization. In *ICLR*.

Jiwei Li, Michel Galley, Chris Brockett, Georgios P Spithourakis, Jianfeng Gao, and Bill Dolan. 2016. A persona-based neural conversation model. In *Proc. of ACL*.

Jiwei Li, Will Monroe, Tianlin Shi, Alan Ritter, and Dan Jurafsky. 2017a. Adversarial learning for neural dialogue generation. In *Proceedings of ACL*.

Xuijun Li, Yun-Nung Chen, Lihong Li, and Jianfeng Gao. 2017b. End-to-end task-completion neural dialogue systems. *arXiv preprint arXiv:1703.01008*.

Bing Liu and Ian Lane. 2017a. An end-to-end trainable neural network model with belief tracking for task-oriented dialog. In *Interspeech*.

Bing Liu and Ian Lane. 2017b. Iterative policy learning in end-to-end trainable task-oriented neural dialog models. In *Proceedings of 2017 IEEE Workshop on Automatic Speech Recognition and Understanding (ASRU)*.

Bing Liu, Gokhan Tur, Dilek Hakkani-Tur, Pararth Shah, and Larry Heck. 2018. Dialogue learning with human teaching and feedback in end-to-end trainable task-oriented dialogue systems. In *NAACL*.

Andrew Y Ng, Stuart J Russell, et al. 2000. Algorithms for inverse reinforcement learning. In *Icml*, pages 663–670.

Tim Paek and Roberto Pieraccini. 2008. Automating spoken dialogue management design using machine learning: An industry perspective. *Speech communication*, 50(8-9):716–729.

Baolin Peng, Xiujun Li, Jianfeng Gao, Jingjing Liu, Yun-Nung Chen, and Kam-Fai Wong. 2018. Adversarial advantage actor-critic model for task-completion dialogue policy learning. In *ICASSP*.

Baolin Peng, Xiujun Li, Lihong Li, Jianfeng Gao, Asli Celikyilmaz, Sungjin Lee, and Kam-Fai Wong. 2017. Composite task-completion dialogue policy learning via hierarchical deep reinforcement learning. In *Proceedings of the 2017 Conference on Empirical Methods in Natural Language Processing*, pages 2231–2240.

Ivaylo Popov, Nicolas Heess, Timothy Lillicrap, Roland Hafner, Gabriel Barth-Maron, Matej Vecerik, Thomas Lampe, Yuval Tassa, Tom Erez, and Martin Riedmiller. 2017. Data-efficient deep reinforcement learning for dexterous manipulation. *arXiv preprint arXiv:1704.03073*.

Stéphane Ross and Drew Bagnell. 2010. Efficient reductions for imitation learning. In *Proceedings of the thirteenth international conference on artificial intelligence and statistics*, pages 661–668.

Stéphane Ross, Geoffrey Gordon, and Drew Bagnell. 2011. A reduction of imitation learning and structured prediction to no-regret online learning. In *Proceedings of the fourteenth international conference on artificial intelligence and statistics*, pages 627–635.

Iulian V Serban, Alessandro Sordoni, Yoshua Bengio, Aaron Courville, and Joelle Pineau. 2016. Building end-to-end dialogue systems using generative hierarchical neural network models. In *Proceedings of the 30th AAAI Conference on Artificial Intelligence (AAAI-16)*.

Pei-Hao Su, Paweł Budzianowski, Stefan Ultes, Milica Gasic, and Steve Young. 2017. Sample-efficient actor-critic reinforcement learning with supervised data for dialogue management. In *Proceedings of the 18th Annual SIGdial Meeting on Discourse and Dialogue*, pages 147–157, Saarbrücken, Germany. Association for Computational Linguistics.

Pei-Hao Su, Milica Gašić, Nikola Mrkšić, Lina Rojas-Barahona, Stefan Ultes, David Vandyke, Tsung-Hsien Wen, and Steve Young. 2016. On-line active reward learning for policy optimisation in spoken dialogue systems. In *Proceedings of ACL*.

Pei-Hao Su, David Vandyke, Milica Gasic, Dongho Kim, Nikola Mrksic, Tsung-Hsien Wen, and Steve Young. 2015. Learning from real users: Rating dialogue success with neural networks for reinforcement learning in spoken dialogue systems. In *Interspeech*.

Marilyn A Walker, Diane J Litman, Candace A Kamm, and Alicia Abella. 1997. Paradise: A framework for evaluating spoken dialogue agents. In *Proceedings of the eighth conference on European chapter of the Association for Computational Linguistics*, pages 271–280. Association for Computational Linguistics.

Tsung-Hsien Wen, David Vandyke, Nikola Mrkšić, Milica Gašić, Lina M. Rojas-Barahona, Pei-Hao Su, Stefan Ultes, and Steve Young. 2017. A network-based end-to-end trainable task-oriented dialogue system. In *Proc. of EACL*.

Jason D Williams, Kavosh Asadi, and Geoffrey Zweig. 2017. Hybrid code networks: practical and efficient end-to-end dialog control with supervised and reinforcement learning. In *ACL*.

Jason D Williams and Geoffrey Zweig. 2016. End-to-end lstm-based dialog control optimized with supervised and reinforcement learning. *arXiv preprint arXiv:1606.01269*.

Ronald J Williams. 1992. Simple statistical gradient-following algorithms for connectionist reinforcement learning. *Machine learning*, 8(3-4):229–256.

Zhaojun Yang, Gina-Anne Levow, and Helen Meng. 2012. Predicting user satisfaction in spoken dialog system evaluation with collaborative filtering. *IEEE Journal of Selected Topics in Signal Processing*, 6(8):971–981.

Zhen Yang, Wei Chen, Feng Wang, and Bo Xu. 2017. Improving neural machine translation with conditional sequence generative adversarial nets. *arXiv preprint arXiv:1703.04887*.

Zichao Yang, Diyi Yang, Chris Dyer, Xiaodong He, Alex Smola, and Eduard Hovy. 2016. Hierarchical attention networks for document classification. In *Proceedings of the 2016 Conference of the North American Chapter of the Association for Computational Linguistics: Human Language Technologies*, pages 1480–1489.

Steve Young, Milica Gašić, Blaise Thomson, and Jason D Williams. 2013. Pomdp-based statistical spoken dialog systems: A review. *Proceedings of the IEEE*, 101(5):1160–1179.

Tiancheng Zhao and Maxine Eskenazi. 2016. Towards end-to-end learning for dialog state tracking and management using deep reinforcement learning. In *SIGDIAL*.

Constructing a Lexicon of English Discourse Connectives

Debopam Das and **Tatjana Scheffler** and **Peter Bourgonje** and **Manfred Stede**
Applied Computational Linguistics
UFS Cognitive Sciences
University of Potsdam / Germany
`firstname.lastname@uni-potsdam.de`

Abstract

We present a new lexicon of English discourse connectives called DiMLex-Eng, built by merging information from two annotated corpora and an additional list of relation signals from the literature. The format follows the German connective lexicon DiMLex, which provides a crosslinguistically applicable XML schema. DiMLex-Eng contains 149 English connectives, and gives information on syntactic categories, discourse semantics and non-connective uses (if any). We report on the development steps and discuss design decisions encountered in the lexicon expansion phase. The resource is freely available for use in studies of discourse structure and computational applications.

1 Introduction

Discourse connectives are generally considered to be the most reliable signals of coherence relations, and they are widely used in a variety of NLP tasks involving the processing of coherence relations, such as discourse parsing (Hernault et al., 2010; Lin et al., 2014), machine translation (Meyer et al., 2011), text summarization (Alemany, 2005), or argumentation mining (Kirschner et al., 2015). Accordingly, corpora annotated for discourse connectives and coherence relations have been developed for different languages.

In addition to discourse-annotated corpora, a *lexicon* of discourse connectives, giving the list of connectives for a language, along with useful information about their syntactic and semantic-pragmatic properties, can also serve as a valuable resource. Such lexicons were developed and are becoming more and more available in different languages, beginning with German (Stede

and Umbach, 1998), later for Spanish (Briz et al., 2008) and French (Roze et al., 2010), and more recently for Italian (Feltracco et al., 2016), Portuguese (Mendes et al., 2018) and Czech (Mírovský et al., 2017).

We present a lexicon of English discourse connectives called DiMLex-Eng, which is developed as a part of the Connective-Lex database[1] at the University of Potsdam. It includes 149 connectives, a large part of which was compiled from the annotations of the Penn Discourse Treebank 2.0 (Prasad et al., 2008). We expanded that list to include additional connectives from the RST Signalling Corpus (Das et al., 2015) and relational indicators from a list supplied by Biran and Rambow (2011). For organizing the entries in the lexicon, we use the format of DiMLex, a lexicon of German connectives (Stede and Umbach, 1998; Scheffler and Stede, 2016). For each entry in DiMLex-Eng, we provide information on the possible orthographic variants of the connective, its syntactic category, non-connective usage (if any), and the set of discourse relations indicated by the connective (with examples from corpora). We describe our criteria for filtering connective candidates for inclusion in the lexicon, and give an outlook on the relationship between connectives and the broader range of 'cue phrases' or 'AltLex' expressions in language.

2 Sources of English connectives

2.1 The PDTB corpus connective list

The Penn Discourse Treebank corpus (PDTB, Prasad et al., 2008) is the best-known resource for obtaining English connectives. In the PDTB, connectives are defined as discourse-level predicates that take as their arguments two abstract objects such as events, states, and propositions, and that

---

[1] `http://connective-lex.info/`

Proceedings of the SIGDIAL 2018 Conference, pages 360–365,
Melbourne, Australia, 12-14 July 2018. ©2018 Association for Computational Linguistics

number	category	number	category
67	ADVP	2	NN
25	phrase	2	JJ
20	IN	2	INTJ
26	PP	1	VB
12	RB	1	RBR
8	CC	1	NNP
2	UCP	1	WHNP

Table 1: Distribution of syntactic types for connectives in the PDTB.[4]

are generally expressible as clauses.[2] In addition to *explicit* connectives, the PDTB contains *implicit* connectives: In the absence of an explicit connective, annotators insert an extra one that best signals a relation between two discourse segments. The PDTB also provides annotations of *AltLex* (alternative lexicalization) for instances where adding an implicit connective would lead to a redundancy in expressing the relation, since it is already conveyed by an indicative phrase.

The PDTB annotators were given the above-mentioned definition of 'connective' and asked to identify words/phrases that accord to this definition. In the end, 100 distinct connectives were marked in the corpus. This list of words was later routinely used by researchers working on shallow discourse parsing in order to find connective candidates in text. However, since the list of connectives is based on annotations of a particular corpus, no claim of exhaustivity of this list was ever raised. Since the corpus is annotated with parse trees and sense relations, the distribution of syntactic types and semantic relations attested for each connective can also be extracted. Table 1 shows the overall distribution of syntactic types for the connectives in the PDTB (note that one connective can have several syntactic types).

2.2 The RST Signalling Corpus

The RST Discourse Treebank (RST-DT, Carlson et al., 2003) is the largest and most widely used corpus for developing discourse parsers for the framework of Rhetorical Structure Theory (Mann and Thompson, 1988). In contrast to the PDTB, it does not contain any markup of connectives; rather, it is restricted to representing the coherence relations among text segments. Recently, however, the RST-DT has been enriched with markup on *relation signals* in the RST Signalling Corpus (Das et al., 2015) (henceforth RST-SC): Going through every coherence relation in the corpus manually, the authors decided for each what signal (if any) can be located in either of the two related spans, which would aid the reader in identifying the relation. This goal leads to marking not only connectives, but also other lexical, semantic, syntactic, layout, or genre-based features. In the RST-SC, about 18 percent of all the relations are indicated by connectives or other discourse markers, which are distributed over 201 different types.

2.3 RST-DT relational indicator list

Also aiming at identifying lexical signals of relations, Biran and Rambow (2011) used a semi-automatic approach: They extracted all instances of relations (i.e., pairs of two text spans) from the RST-DT, and automatically identified the most indicative (1..4)-grams of words using a variant of TF/IDF. The n-grams were ranked, and an empirically-determined cutoff demarcated the list. The authors were specifically interested in argumentative relations and thus added a manual filtering step for a relevant subset of RST relations. However, they made a list of 230 indicators for all relations available.[5] The indicators range from one to four-word expressions, many of which qualify as discourse connectives: conjunctions (*but, although*), prepositional phrases (*for instance, in addition*) or adverbials (*probably*).

The list also contains items belonging to different lexical categories, such as nouns (*statement, result*), verbs (*concluded, to ensure*) or other elements which simply comprise random strings of words and do not neatly represent any syntactic constituents (e.g., *and we certainly do, and just as we*). These items would be rejected as discourse connectives by any definition from the literature, and the procedure was of course not meant to result in a list of connectives per se. Yet, using this procedure, one could expect to also find quite a few proper connectives. As an explanation of why their number is, however, relatively

---

[2]In some exceptional cases, the arguments in the PDTB can also be realized as non-clausal structures, such as VP coordinates, nominalizations, or anaphoric expressions representing abstract objects.

[4]'Phrase' indicates that the connective consists of more than one partial tree; otherwise, the single category that dominates the entire connective was chosen.

[5]http://www.cs.columbia.edu/~orb/code_data.html

small, note that relations are often realised without any explicit connective, thus lowering their co-occurrence numbers. Additionally, since a connective can be ambiguous in terms of the senses it represents, its distribution relative to one particular sense is less pronounced when it also accompanies other senses.

3 DiMLex

We chose to develop DiMLex-Eng using the format of the German DiMLex (DIscourse Marker LEXicon).[6] Its current version (Scheffler and Stede, 2016) contains an exhaustive list of 275 German discourse connectives. Following Pasch et al. (2003), (with one modification to be discussed in the next section), a connective in DiMLex is defined as a lexical item x which has the following properties: (i) x cannot be inflected; (ii) the meaning of x is a two-place relation; (iii) the arguments of this relation are propositional structures; (iv) the arguments can be expressed as sentential structures. This definition is comparable to the one used in the PDTB. Both frameworks consider a connective as a relational signal taking two semantic arguments.

For each entry, DiMLex provides a number of features, characterizing its syntactic, semantic and pragmatic behaviour. DiMLex has recently been incorporated in the Connective-Lex database (see Section 1), developed as part of the European COST action TextLink[7], and DiMLex-Eng is being included there as well.

4 Merging the sources into DiMLex-Eng

Our selection of entries in DiMLex-Eng follows from what we consider as English discourse connectives. The definition is partly based on that used for German connectives in DiMLex (provided in Section 3), and further modified by incorporating some features from the annotation in the PDTB. We consider a word or phrase x as a connective in English if it has the following properties:

- x cannot be inflected.
- The meaning of x is a two-place relation.
- The arguments of this relation are abstract objects (propositions, events, states, or pro-

cesses).

- Usually, the arguments are expressed as clausal or sentential structures. However, they can also be expressed by phrasal structures (e.g., noun phrases beginning with connectives like *according to*, *because of*, or *given*) as long as they denote abstract objects.

Furthermore, we used the following two lexicographic exclusion criteria to determine whether a connecting phrase x which signals a coherence relation (as defined above) warrants inclusion in the lexicon as a connective entry:

1. x should be a fixed expression and cannot be freely modified by inserting other material.
2. x is not semantically compositional with respect to its component parts.

Criterion 1 excludes free phrases such as *for this reason* which can be modified: *for this excellent reason*, *for these reasons*, etc. Criterion 2 excludes phrases which consist of a connective and an intensifier/adverb such as *particularly if* or *especially when* (here, only *if* and *when* are considered connectives with their own lexicon entries), and also items comprising two connectives such as *and therefore* or *but at the same time*. According to this criterion, however, phrases such as *even though* and *even if* are considered to be distinct connectives, since their meaning is not straightforwardly compositional.

Once we decided on the definition of English connectives, we began compiling the lexicon with entries from the PDTB 2.0. We decided to include all 100 explicit connectives from the corpus, because they adequately fulfill our definitional requirements for connectives.

In the lexicon expansion phase, we first added more connectives from the RST-SC (Das et al., 2015). We observed that of the 100 PDTB connectives included in the initial version of DiMLex-Eng, 71 connectives are also found in the RST-SC, adding up to 3.390 instances (of marker tokens or phrases). More importantly, in the opposite direction, from the RST-SC, we added 46 connectives (which do not occur in the PDTB) to DiMLex-Eng. The resulting 146 entries cover 3.721 instances in the RST-SC (an extra 331 compared to the initial version of DiMLex-Eng). The RST-SC contains 201 types (3.899 instances). Note that we add only a subset of these to DiMLex-Eng due to the restrictions on entries explained above. With our extended lexicon, we now cover 117 of 201

---

[6]https://github.com/discourse-lab/dimlex/
[7]http://www.textlink.ii.metu.edu.tr/connective-lex

types (58%) and 3.721 of 3.899 instances (95%), compared to 35% (types) and 87% (instances) for the initial lexicon version that included just the PDTB-based list.

In the final phase of entry collection, we consulted the relational indicator list of Biran and Rambow (2011), and screened out only those items which satisfy our definition of discourse connective. We found that of the 230 entries in the Biran and Rambow list, seven items overlap with our 44 entries already selected from the RST-SC. Additionally, 12 of the 230 items were in the list initially extracted from the PDTB 2.0. Upon manual evaluation of the remaining 211 entries, we found five more connectives that we added to our lexicon.

5 Populating the lexicon entries

DiMLex-Eng includes significant lexicographic information about the syntactic and semantic-pragmatic properties of connectives. For syntactic and other non-discourse features of a connective entry, it specifies: (i) possible orthographic variants, (ii) ambiguity information (whether the lexical item also has non-connective readings), (iii) the syntactic category of the connective (see Table 1; mainly: adverb, subordinating conjunction/preposition, coordinating conjunction, or phrase), (iv) possible coherence relations expressed by the connective, (v) examples[8] of relations associated with the connective .

The semantic information about coherence relations was derived from the observed corpus instances in the cases of connectives from the PDTB and RST-SC. That is, each entry lists all coherence relations with which the connective occurred, together with frequency information.

For encoding the lexicographic features in DiMLex-Eng, we use the format of DiMLex, which provides a cross-linguistically applicable XML schema. Figure 1 shows a representation of the lexical entry for *by contrast* in DiMLex-Eng. The entry shows that *by contrast* is a PP which can be used to signal three possible coherence relations: CONTRAST (occurring 11 out of 27 times when *by contrast* was used as a connective in the corpus), JUXTAPOSITION (12 times), and OPPOSITION (4). The lexicon is being extended with

corpus examples for each sense, where available.

6 Summary and Outlook

We have presented DiMLex-Eng, a lexicon of English discourse connectives, compiled from annotated corpora and modeled after DiMLex, a lexicon of German discourse connectives. The connectives in DiMLex-Eng are lexically frozen expressions (e.g., *because, furthermore, since*) that correspond to what are described by Danlos et al. (2018) as *primary* connectives (with respect to their degree of grammaticalization). The knowledge of such connectives along with their manually curated syntactic and discourse attributes, as the one offered by DiMLex-Eng, are valuable in areas such as language learning and contrastive discourse studies. Also, the connectives in DiMLex-Eng, together with other coherence relation signals, can serve as a valuable resource for discourse parsing and related applications.

Coherence relation signals, not necessarily restricted to being discourse connectives, may also comprise many other items, which are discussed under the labels of *cue phrase* (Knott and Dale, 1994), *secondary connective* (Danlos et al., 2018), *AltLex* expression (Prasad et al., 2008), or *relational indicator* (Biran and Rambow, 2011). These are more difficult to describe systematically and hence are less amenable to a lexical treatment; we leave it to future work to extend DiMLex-Eng into this direction.

We would like to point out that using the approach of selecting words and phrases that frequently co-occur with coherence relations, we find only 24 words or phrases that fulfill the constraints of true (primary) connectives, compared to the complete lexicon of 149 entries. This seems to imply that simple statistical co-occurrence measures are not sufficient for identifying discourse connectives, which must satisfy syntactic and semantic criteria, as well.

Another approach for automatic generation of discourse connective lexicons is by translational mapping between parallel corpora, which we are pursuing in ongoing work (Bourgonje et al., 2017), following up on earlier studies such as that of Cartoni et al. (2013). We hope to use this approach to identify additional connectives for DiMLex-Eng as well as establish and enhance correspondences between DiMLex-Eng and other similar connective lexicons.

---

[8]Mostly taken from the PDTB, RST-SC and Corpus of Contemporary American English (https://corpus. byu.edu/coca/)

```
<entry id="67" word="by contrast">
   <orths>
      <orth canonical="0" orth_id="67o1" type="cont">
         <part type="phrasal">By contrast</part>
      </orth>
      <orth canonical="1" orth_id="67o2" type="cont">
         <part type="phrasal">by contrast</part>
      </orth>
   </orths>
   <syn>
      <cat>PP</cat>
      <sem>
         <pdtb2_relation anno_N="27" freq="11"
                         sense="Comparison.Contrast" />
      </sem>
      <sem>
         <pdtb2_relation anno_N="27" freq="12"
                         sense="Comparison.Contrast.Juxtaposition" />
      </sem>
      <sem>
         <pdtb2_relation anno_N="27" freq="4"
                         sense="Comparison.Contrast.Opposition" />
      </sem>
   </syn>
</entry>
```

Figure 1: DiMLex-Eng entry for the connective *by contrast*.

Acknowledgments

Our work was financially supported by Deutsche Forschungsgemeinschaft (DFG), as part of (i) project A03 in the Collaborative Research Center 1287 "Limits of Variability in Language" and (ii) project "Anaphoricity in Connectives".

References

Laura Alonso i Alemany. 2005. *Representing discourse for automatic text summarization via shallow NLP techniques*. PhD dissertation, Universitat de Barcelona.

Or Biran and Owen Rambow. 2011. Dentifying justifications in written dialogs by classifying text as argumentative. *International Journal of Semantic Computing*, 5(4):363–381.

Peter Bourgonje, Yulia Grishina, and Manfred Stede. 2017. Toward a bilingual lexical database on connectives: Exploiting a German/Italian parallel corpus. In *Proceedings of the Fourth Italian Conference on Computational Linguistics*, Rome, Italy.

Antonio Briz, Salvador Pons Bordería, and José Portolés. 2008. Diccionario de partículas discursivas del español.

Lynn Carlson, Daniel Marcu, and Mary Ellen Okurowski. 2003. Building a discourse-tagged corpus in the framework of Rhetorical Structure Theory. In Jan van Kuppevelt and Ronnie Smith, editors, *Current Directions in Discourse and Dialogue*. Kluwer, Dordrecht.

Bruno Cartoni, Sandrine Zufferey, and Thomas Meyer. 2013. Annotating the meaning of discourse connectives by looking at their translation: The translation-spotting technique. 4:65–86.

Laurence Danlos, Kateřina Rysová, Magdaléna Rysová, and Manfred Stede. 2018. Primary and secondary discourse connectives: definitions and lexicons. *Dialogue and Discourse*. To appear.

Debopam Das, Maite Taboada, and Paul McFetridge. 2015. RST Signalling Corpus, LDC2015T10. Linguistic Data Consortium.

Anna Feltracco, Elisabetta Jezek, Bernardo Magnini, and Manfred Stede. 2016. LICO: A Lexicon of Italian Connectives. In *Proceedings of the Second Italian Conference on Computational Linguistic (CLiC-it 2016)*.

Hugo Hernault, Hemut Prendinger, David duVerle, and Mitsuru Ishizuka. 2010. HILDA: A Discourse Parser Using Support Vector Machine Classification. *Dialogue and Discourse*, 1(3):1–33.

Christian Kirschner, Judith Eckle-Kohler, and Iryna Gurevych. 2015. Linking the thoughts: Analysis of argumentation structures in scientific publications. In *Proceedings of the 2015 NAACL-HLT Conference*.

Alistair Knott and Robert Dale. 1994. Using linguistic phenomena to motivate a set of coherence relations. *Discourse Processes*, 18(1):35–62.

Ziheng Lin, Hwee Tou Ng, and Min-Yen Kan. 2014. A PDTB-Styled End-to-End Discourse Parser. *Natural Language Engineering*, 20(2):151184.

William C. Mann and Sandra A. Thompson. 1988. Rhetorical structure theory: Toward a functional theory of text organization. *Text*, 8(3):243–281.

Amalia Mendes, Iria del Rio, Manfred Stede, and Felix Dombek. 2018. A Lexicon of Discourse Markers for Portuguese: LDM-PTs. In *Proceedings of the 11h International Conference on Language Resources and Evaluation (LREC)*, Miyazaki, Japan.

Thomas Meyer, Andrei Popescu-Belis, Sandrine Zufferey, and Bruno Cartoni. 2011. Multilingual Annotation and Disambiguation of Discourse Connectives for Machine Translation. In *Proceedings of the SIGDIAL 2011 Conference*, SIGDIAL '11, pages 194–203, Stroudsburg, PA, USA. Association for Computational Linguistics.

Jiří Mírovský, Pavlína Synková, Magdaléna Rysová, and Lucie Políková. 2017. CzeDLex A Lexicon of Czech Discourse Connectives. In *the Prague Bulletin of Mathematical Linguistics*, volume 109, pages 61–91.

Renate Pasch, Ursula Braue, Eva Breindl, and Herrmann Ulrich Waner. 2003. *Handbuch der deutschen Konnektoren*. Walter de Gruyter, Berlin/New York.

Rashmi Prasad, Nikhil Dinesh, Alan Lee, Eleni Miltsakaki, Livio Robaldo, Aravind Joshi, and Bonnie Webber. 2008. The Penn Discourse Treebank 2.0. In *Proceedings of the 6th International Conference on Language Resources and Evaluation (LREC 2008)*, Marrackech, Morocco.

Charlotte Roze, Danlos Laurence, and Philippe Muller. 2010. LEXCONN: a French Lexicon of Discourse Connectives. In *Multidisciplinary Approaches to Discourse - MAD 2010*, Moissac, France.

Tatjana Scheffler and Manfred Stede. 2016. Adding Semantic Relations to a Large-Coverage Connective Lexicon of German. In *Proceedings of the Tenth International Conference on Language Resources and Evaluation (LREC)*, Portorož, Slovenia.

Manfred Stede and Carla Umbach. 1998. DiMLex: A lexicon of discourse markers for text generation and understanding. In *Proceedings of the 17th international conference on Computational linguistics - Volume 2*. Association for Computational Linguistics.

Maximizing SLU Performance with Minimal Training Data Using Hybrid RNN Plus Rule-based Approach

Takeshi Homma   Adriano S. Arantes   Maria Teresa Gonzalez Diaz   Masahito Togami
Hitachi America, Ltd.
3315 Scott Boulevard, 4th Floor, Santa Clara, CA 95054, USA
takeshi.homma.ps@hitachi.com
{Adriano.Arantes, Teresa.GonzalezDiaz}@hal.hitachi.com

Abstract

Spoken language understanding (SLU) by using recurrent neural networks (RNN) achieves good performances for large training data sets, but collecting large training datasets is a challenge, especially for new voice applications. Therefore, the purpose of this study is to maximize SLU performances, especially for small training data sets. To this aim, we propose a novel CRF-based dialog act selector which chooses suitable dialog acts from outputs of RNN SLU and rule-based SLU. We evaluate the selector by using DSTC2 corpus when RNN SLU is trained by less than 1,000 training sentences. The evaluation demonstrates the selector achieves Micro F1 better than both RNN and rule-based SLUs. In addition, it shows the selector achieves better Macro F1 than RNN SLU and the same Macro F1 as rule-based SLU. Thus, we confirmed our method offers advantages in SLU performances for small training data sets.

1   Introduction

Spoken language understanding (SLU) was further researched by using rule-based methods (Bellegarda, 2013) and machine learning (ML) (Tur et al., 2010). ML achieves good SLU performances for large training data sets. However, ML-based SLU with small training data results in poor performances. Therefore, if we want to launch a new spoken dialog service as fast as possible, we cannot use ML-based SLUs as there is no time to prepare sufficient training data.

The goal of this study is to maximize SLU performances especially when the training data size is small.   To achieve this objective, we propose a selection method which chooses a suitable SLU either from rule-based or ML-based SLUs depending on SLU output reliability.   While researchers have studied selection methods to choose a suitable SLU result from plural SLUs by applying several algorithms (Hahn et al., 2008; Katsumaru et al., 2009; Karahan et al., 2003; Wang et al., 2002), most of them focused on selectors that improve SLU performances for large training data sets. However, their selection methods did not take into account the impact on performance for different training data sizes, specifically, how a selector would work on small training data.

Previous studies have evaluated SLU performances by metrics such as Micro F1. Nevertheless, performance evaluation by only Micro F1 is not suitable for practical dialog systems as these systems must recognize all dialog acts that users can say. In practical dialog systems, the distribution of dialog acts for actual user utterances is usually uneven. On this scenario, even if SLU completely fails to recognize some rare dialog acts, the Micro F1 remains almost unchanged and that is the main reason why systems cannot exclusively rely on this metric.

Macro F1 is another common major metric in SLU. Macro F1 computes an averaged Micro F1 of all dialog acts and decreases drastically when it fails to recognize rare dialog acts. Thus, we evaluate Macro F1 as a better metric to confirm that a selector can recognize all dialog acts.

This paper brings the following contributions to the SLU subject. First, we propose a conditional random fields (CRF) based selector which chooses suitable SLU outputs either from rule-based or ML-based SLUs. Second, we assess our selection method with different sizes of training data for recurrent neural network (RNN) based SLU. Finally, unlike most of previous studies, we evaluate SLU

Proceedings of the SIGDIAL 2018 Conference, pages 366–370,
Melbourne, Australia, 12-14 July 2018. ©2018 Association for Computational Linguistics

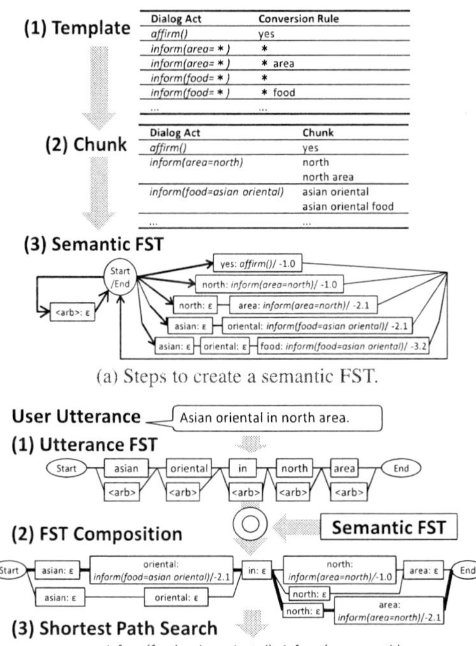

(a) Steps to create a semantic FST.

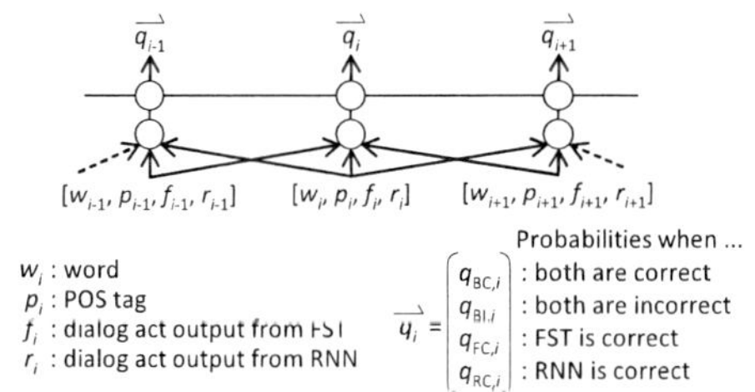

(b) Steps of SLU after user utterance using semantic FST.

Figure 1: Rule-based SLU by using semantic finite state transducers. $<$arb$>$ is a symbol that accepts any word. ε means no dialog acts are output.

Figure 2: Model for dialog act selection.

performances by using not only Micro F1 but also Macro F1.

Experiments validate our novel approach and demonstrate that the proposed selector produces better SLU performances (up to 10.1% Micro F1 and 19.2% Macro F1) than ML-based for small training data sets and achieves "upper bound" of SLU performances regardless of training data size. This result confirms that our selector helps to improve ML-based SLU performance even if we utilize very limited training data.

2 SLU Algorithms

2.1 Rule-based Algorithm

Our rule-based SLU utilizes a SLU using finite state transducers (FST) modified from (Ferreira et al., 2015) (Figure 1). SLU developers prepare templates that convert each dialog act to chunks. Chunks are phrases that users may say when they intend to perform the dialog acts. The chunks are embedded to an FST which we call "semantic FST" (Figure 1.a). The user utterance is also converted to an utterance FST (Figure 1.b). Then, the method executes a FST composition operation (Mohri, 1997) between the utterance FST and the semantic FST. Finally, the method searches the shortest path within a composed FST. The SLU results are the dialog acts along the shortest path, i.e., a path with minimal summed weights. Based on heuristics, dialog acts generated from many words are more confident than the ones generated from just few words. Thus, the semantic FST weights are adjusted to prioritize dialog acts generated from many words.

2.2 RNN Algorithm

We used gated recurrent units (GRU) RNN cells for ML-based SLU (Mesnil et al., 2015; Zhang and Wang, 2016). Each GRU cell receives one word and POS (Part-Of-Speech) tag. We convert hidden states of a GRU to probabilities of dialog acts that the word belongs to. The algorithm selects the dialog acts with maximum probabilities from all words. The gathered dialog acts represent SLU results. In previous studies, each RNN cell outputs dialog acts with in/out/begin (IOB) tags. Our GRU cell, however, outputs dialog acts without IOB tags because this condition resulted in better accuracies in a preliminary experiment.

2.3 Selection Algorithm

Figure 2 shows a selection model that receives word and POS tag. In addition, it receives dialog acts obtained from FST and RNN generated for a corresponding word. Finally, the model outputs probabilities of 4-class judgements: both dialog acts are correct (BC), both dialog acts are incorrect (BI), FST outputs correct dialog act (FC), and RNN outputs correct dialog act (RC). We implement this model by using CRF.

Figure 3 shows a pipeline of the selection algorithm: (A) is for training of RNN SLU, (B) is for training of a selection model, and (C) is for evaluation. To obtain training data for a selection model, we first input RNN training data to FST to get FST SLU results. Besides, we do 10-fold cross validation for RNN SLU by using RNN training data to

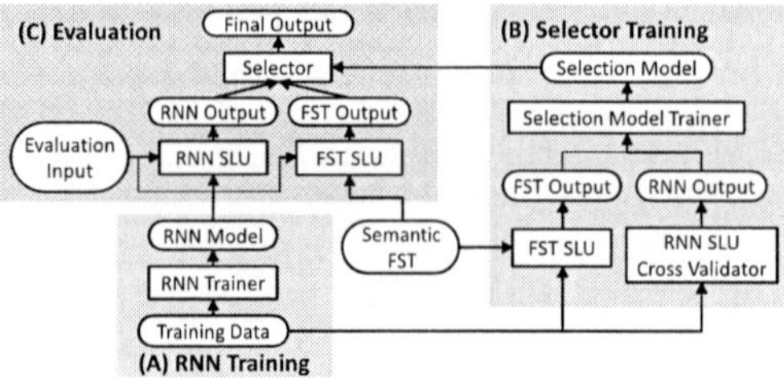

Figure 3: Pipeline for dialog act selection.

Table 1: Parameters of GRU RNN.

input	embedded word (100 dim.)
	POS tag (1-hot vector; 32 dim.)
output	dialog act probability (538 dim.)
hidden layer	bidirectional GRU
	(100 nodes, 1-layer)
context window	1
dropout rate	0.1
batch size	8

make training inputs. These SLU results are used for training of the selection model.

3 Evaluation

3.1 Dataset

We used a corpus from the Dialog State Tracking Challenge 2 (DSTC2), to evaluate our method (Henderson et al., 2014). This corpus contains transcribed sentences of user utterances for restaurant reservation dialogs. The sentences have sentence-level dialog acts. From the sentence-level dialog acts, we manually annotated word-level dialog acts. The DSTC2 corpus has a training set of 11,677 sentences, a development set of 3,934, and a test set of 9,890. From the training set, we randomly chose sentences to create training sets with various sentence sizes (100–10,000). Distribution of dialog acts in DSTC2 corpus is skewed; only 25% of dialog acts appeared in 90% of sentences for both training and test sets. The DSTC2 corpus has an "ontology" which defines all dialog acts that user may say. This ontology defines 659 dialog acts. 649 dialog acts are defined in forms of intent(slot=value), e.g., *inform(food=chinese)*, *deny(area=west)*, and *confirm(pricerange=cheap)*. Other 10 dialog acts are defined by only intent, e.g., *affirm( )*, *negate( )*, and *hello( )*.

3.2 SLU Methods

RNN Table 1 shows the configuration of GRU for RNN SLU. The GRU receives an embedded word vector with 1-hot POS tag vector. The em-

bedding weights are initialized with normally distributed random numbers. The hidden states of a GRU are converted to an output vector with dialog acts probabilities, by multiplying a linear matrix and softmax function. The dimension of an output vector is 538 (537 acts and "no act" class) because the largest training set (10k sentences) contains only 537 dialog acts. The hyper parameters for RNN is determined based on SLU performance in the development set. We terminate RNN training when Micro F1 on the development set is maximized.

FST We manually made 43 templates to convert dialog acts in DSTC2 ontology to 975 chunks. Figure 1.a step (1) shows template examples. When a dialog act has a value, we create chunks by embedding the value. Created chunks are converted to a semantic FST.

3.3 Selection Method

The CRF-based selector uses the following input features: word, POS tag, dialog act that FST SLU outputs, and dialog act that RNN SLU outputs. It also outputs a 4-class judgement (see Figure 2). The CRF model is trained to maximize probabilities that the selector outputs correct judgement classes. Features and hyper parameters for training CRF are determined based on selection accuracies of dialog acts in the development set. A window size for making features is set to 5. We use 3-gram features within the window. During evaluation, we choose dialog acts as follows. Assuming that the selection model outputs maximum probability in BI, we discard both dialog acts obtained from FST and RNN SLUs. Otherwise, we compare probabilities of FC and RC. For a larger FC, we adopt a dialog act output from FST SLU. In case RC is larger, we adopt a dialog act output from RNN SLU. We use CRF++ (Kudo, 2013) for training and evaluation of the selection model.

3.4 Training Data Expansion

Whitelaw et al. (2008) reported methods to increase small training data for named entity recognition by expanding them using entity dictionaries. We used the same method to increase training data for RNN by using the ontology in DSTC2. Figure 4 illustrates the method to increase training data. From one training sentence, we make additional training sentences by replacing the value of a dialog act and corresponding words with different ones. We added new sentences if the sen-

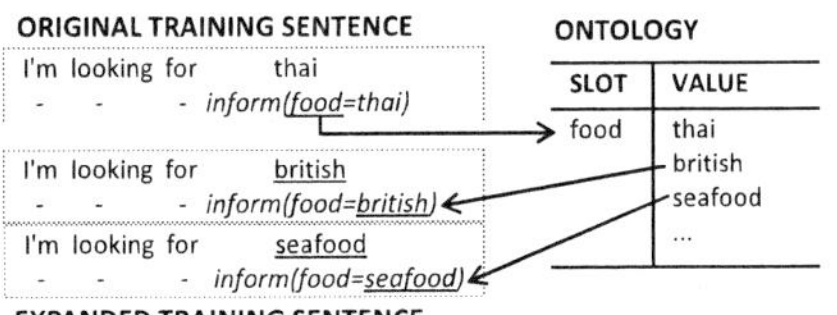

Figure 4: Expansion of training data for RNN training as baseline condition.

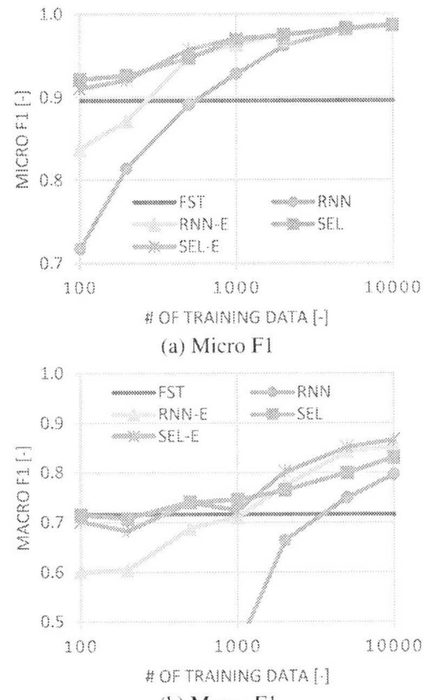

(a) Micro F1

(b) Macro F1

Figure 5: Evaluation results of SLU performances.

tences do not exist in the training data. By using this method, for example, we increase the training set with 100 sentences to 1.2k, and a set with 10k sentences to 67k.

Experimental conditions are as follows.

FST SLU by FST.

RNN SLU by RNN.

RNN-E SLU by RNN trained using expanded training data.

SEL Selection from FST and RNN.

SEL-E Selection from FST and RNN-E.

In SEL-E condition, RNN cross validation uses expanded sentences as training data, and non-expanded sentences as evaluation data.

3.5 Results

Figure 5 shows SLU performances. We first focus on results for small training data sets ($<$1k). SEL and SEL-E achieved better Micro F1 than others (Figure 5.a). Especially, when training sentences were less than 500, SEL achieved Micro F1 6.2–

10.1% better than ML-based SLU (RNN-E), and 2.8–3.3% better than FST SLU. SEL also resulted in Macro F1 7.7–19.2% better than RNN-E (see Figure 5.b). Although SEL resulted in Macro F1 slightly lower than FST in some small-sized training data, the decreasing rate was at most 1.2% (FST 0.716, SEL 0.707 at 200 training sentences). SEL-E resulted in Macro F1 with the biggest decreasing rate compared to FST (4.7% at 200 training sentences). Therefore, our approach suggests that SEL is a suitable selection method to improve SLU accuracies for small training data.

Next, we focus on results for large training data sets ($\geq$1k). SEL and SEL-E provided almost the same Micro F1 as RNN-E. Meanwhile, SEL-E achieved the best Macro F1 among all SLUs at 2k or larger training sentences. SEL-E improved Macro F1 with rates of 1.1–3.6% from RNN-E. Because SEL-E achieves the highest SLU performances, our approach suggests that SEL-E is the best selection method among the ones evaluated to improve SLU accuracies at large training data.

4 Conclusion

This work aims to improve SLU performance for small training data sets. We achieve this goal by proposing a novel CRF-based dialog act selector which chooses suitable SLU outputs either from rule-based or ML-based SLUs. Other main contributions are: novel selector method evaluation for different training data sizes; and, SLU performance assessment using Micro F1 and Macro F1. Experimental results show that our selection methods achieve up to 10.1% Micro F1 and 19.2% Macro F1 performance improvements compared to ML-based SLU for small training data. For large training data, our proposed methods outperform state-of-the-art RNN SLU methods for Macro F1 up to 3.6% while keeping Micro F1 equivalent to RNN SLU.

Consequently, our methods improve ML-based SLU performances for training data having scarce and abundant number of samples. This achievement opens up the possibility for fast launch of new spoken dialog services even with limited data available which was not possible before this work.

We also note that the best selection method is different depending on the training data size. As a follow-up paper, we will investigate selection algorithms that consistently achieve "upper bound" performances in all sizes of training data.

References

Jerome R. Bellegarda. 2013. Large-scale personal assistant technology deployment: the Siri experience. In *Proceedings of the Annual Conference of the International Speech Communication Association (Interspeech)*, pages 2029–2033, Lyon, France.

Emmanuel Ferreira, Bassam Jabaian, and Fabrice Lefèvre. 2015. Zero-shot semantic parser for spoken language understanding. In *Proceedings of the Annual Conference of the International Speech Communication Association (Interspeech)*, pages 1403–1407, Dresden, Germany.

Stefan Hahn, Patrick Lehnen, and Hermann Ney. 2008. System combination for spoken language understanding. In *Proceedings of the Annual Conference of the International Speech Communication Association (Interspeech)*, pages 236–239, Brisbane, Australia.

Matthew Henderson, Blaise Thomson, and Jason Williams. 2014. The second dialog state tracking challenge. In *Proceedings of the SIGDIAL*, pages 263–272, Philadelphia, Pennsylvania, USA.

Mercan Karahan, Dilek Hakkani-Tür, Giuseppe Riccardi, and Gokhan Tur. 2003. Combining classifiers for spoken language understanding. In *Proceedings of the IEEE Workshop on Automatic Speech Recognition and Understanding (ASRU)*, pages 589–594, St. Thomas, Virgin Islands, USA.

Masaki Katsumaru, Mikio Nakano, Kazunori Komatani, Kotaro Funakoshi, Tetsuya Ogata, and Hiroshi G. Okuno. 2009. Improving speech understanding accuracy with limited training data using multiple language models and multiple understanding models. In *Proceedings of the Annual Conference of the International Speech Communication Association (Interspeech)*, pages 2735–2738, Brighton, United Kingdom.

Taku Kudo. 2013. CRF++: Yet another crf toolkit. https://taku910.github.io/crfpp. Accessed: Aug. 15, 2017.

Grégoire Mesnil, Yann Dauphin, Kaisheng Yao, Yoshua Bengio, Li Deng, Dilek Hakkani-Tür, Xiaodong He, Larry Heck, Gokhan Tur, Dong Yu, and Geoffrey Zweig. 2015. Using recurrent neural networks for slot filling in spoken language understanding. *IEEE/ACM Transactions on Audio, Speech, and Language Processing*, 23(3):530–539.

Mehryar Mohri. 1997. Finite-state transducers in language and speech processing. *Computational Linguistics*, 23(2):269–311.

Gokhan Tur, Dilek Hakkani-Tür, and Larry Heck. 2010. What is left to be understood in ATIS? In *Proceedings of the IEEE Workshop on Spoken Language Technology (SLT)*, pages 19–24, Berkeley, California, USA.

Ye-Yi Wang, Alex Acero, Ciprian Chelba, Brendan Frey, and Leon Wong. 2002. Combination of statistical and rule-based approaches for spoken language understanding. In *Proceedings of the International Conference on Spoken Language Processing (ICSLP)*, pages 609–612, Denver, Colorado, USA.

Casey Whitelaw, Alex Kehlenbeck, Nemanja Petrovic, and Lyle Ungar. 2008. Web-scale named entity recognition. In *Proceedings of the ACM Conference on Information and Knowledge Management (CIKM)*, pages 123–132, Napa, California, USA.

Xiaodong Zhang and Houfeng Wang. 2016. A joint model of intent determination and slot filling for spoken language understanding. In *Proceedings of the International Joint Conference on Artificial Intelligence (IJCAI)*, pages 2993–2999, New York, USA.

An Analysis of the Effect of Emotional Speech Synthesis on Non-Task-Oriented Dialogue System

Yuya Chiba, Takashi Nose, Mai Yamanaka, Taketo Kase, Akinori Ito
Graduate School of Engineering,
Tohoku University, Japan

Abstract

This paper explores the effect of emotional speech synthesis on a spoken dialogue system when the dialogue is non-task-oriented. Although the use of emotional speech responses has been shown to be effective in a limited domain, e.g., scenario-based and counseling dialogue, the effect is still not clear in the non-task-oriented dialogue such as voice chat. For this purpose, we constructed a simple dialogue system with example- and rule-based dialogue management. In the system, two types of emotion labeling with emotion estimation are adopted, i.e., system-driven and user-cooperative emotion labeling. We conducted a dialogue experiment where subjects evaluate the subjective quality of the system and the dialogue from multiple aspects such as richness of the dialogue and impression of the agent. We then analyze and discuss the results and show the advantage of using appropriate emotions for expressive speech responses in the non-task-oriented system.

1 Introduction

Recently, spoken dialogue systems have been becoming popular in various applications, such as a speech assistant system in smartphones and smart speakers, an information guide system in public places, and humanoid robots. There have been a variety of studies for developing spoken dialogue systems, and the systems are roughly grouped into two categories, task-oriented and non-task-oriented systems, from the aspect of having a goal or not in the dialogue. Although the task-oriented dialogue systems (Zue et al., 2000; Kawanami et al., 2007) are important as practical applications, e.g., ticket vending and information guidance, the role of the non-task-oriented systems is increasing for more advanced human-computer interaction (HCI) including voice chat.

There have been many studies related to the non-task-oriented dialogue systems. Nakano et al. (2006) tried to incorporate both task-oriented and non-task-oriented dialogue functions into a humanoid robot us-

ing a multi-expert model. Dybala et al. (2010) proposed an evaluation method of subjective features of human-computer interaction using chatbots. Yu et al. (2016) proposed a set of conversational strategies to handle possible system breakdowns. Although these studies enhance the performance of the dialogue systems, an important role is still missing from the viewpoint of the system expressivity. Specifically, the system cannot perceive and express para-linguistic information such as emotions, which is completely different from our daily communication.

Several studies have been presented where emotions were taken into consideration in spoken dialogue systems. MMDAgent (Lee et al., 2013) is a well-known open-source dialogue system toolkit where emotional speech synthesis based on hidden Markov models (HMMs) (Yoshimura et al., 1999) is incorporated and style modeling and style interpolation techniques can be used for providing expressive speech (Nose and Kobayashi, 2011). Su et al. (2014) have combined situation and emotion detection with a spoken dialogue system for health care to provide more warming feedback of the system. Kase et al. (2015) developed a scenario-based dialogue system where emotion estimation and emotional speech synthesis were incorporated. However, the use of emotional speech synthesis was not investigated in a non-task-oriented dialogue system, and the effect of the emotions on the dialogue is still unclear.

In this study, we develop a Japanese simple non-task-oriented expressive dialogue system with text-based emotion detection and emotional speech synthesis. We then conduct a dialogue experiment in which participants chat with the system and evaluate the performance in terms of multiple subjective measures such as richness and pleasantness of the conversation and analyze the result. We also examine the change of the pitch variation of the users in the dialogue to investigate the acoustic effect of the system expressivity on the utterance of the users.

2 Overview of the Dialogue System

Figure 1 shows the flow of the dialogue system constructed for the experiment in Section 5. The speech input is decoded to the text using a speech recog-

Proceedings of the SIGDIAL 2018 Conference, pages 371–375,
Melbourne, Australia, 12-14 July 2018. ©2018 Association for Computational Linguistics

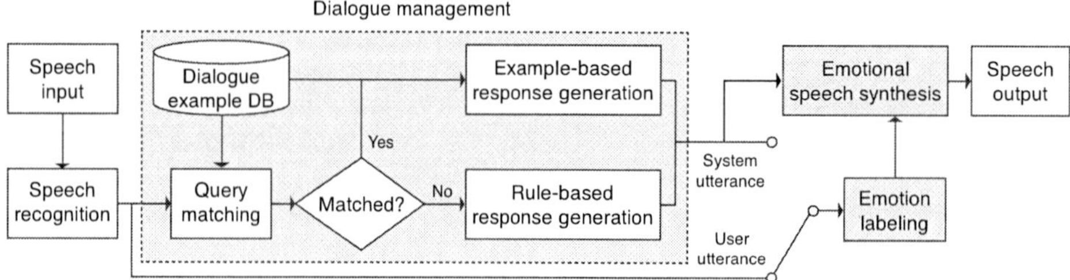

Figure 1: Overview of our non-task-oriented dialogue system with system-driven/user-cooperative emotional speech synthesis. The system or the user utterance is used alternatively for the emotion labeling in the case of (a) the system-driven or (b) the user-cooperative systems, respectively.

Table 1: Dialogue example between a user and the system. U and S denote user and system, respectively, and E and R denote the types of the response generation, i.e., example- and rule-based, respectively.

U	Hi!	
S	Hello! Let's talk about ball games.	E
U	All right!	
S	Is the basketball exciting?	R
U	I like watching basketball.	
S	That's good, me too.	R
U	Do you like baseball?	
S	I don't like baseball.	R
U	Why?	
S	I've never thought the reason.	E
U	I see.	

nizer, Julius (Lee and Kawahara, 2009). In the dialogue management part, system responses are generated by combining example-based and typical rule-based (Weizenbaum, 1966) response generation methods. First, query matching for the example-based response generation is applied to the text using a dialogue example database that is constructed in advance. Specifically, the decoded text is converted to a vector using a bag of words, and cosine similarity is calculated between the text and the questions in the database. If the similarity score is larger than or equal to a predetermined threshold, the answer corresponding to the question having highest similarity is adopted as the system utterance. Otherwise, the system utterance is generated by applying the prepared rules to the decoded text, i.e., the user utterance. For the rule-based response generation, nouns (e.g., baseball, pasta) and subjective words (e.g., like, dislike, happy) are extracted from the user utterance and are used for the response generation based on the rules. Table 1 shows an example of the dialogue between a user and the system where the system responses are generated using both example- and rule-based methods.

After the response generation, emotion estimation, in other words, emotion labeling, is performed us-

ing either the system or the user utterance to choose the emotion to be used in the succeeding speech synthesis. We call the emotion labeling with the system and the user utterances "system-driven" and "user-cooperative" labeling hereafter, which was also discussed in the previous study on scenario-based dialogue (Kase et al., 2015). Finally, emotional speech synthesis based on HMMs is performed using the emotion label and the corresponding emotion-dependent acoustic model trained in advance. The details of the emotion estimation and the emotional speech synthesis are described in Sections 3 and 4, respectively.

3 Emotion Labeling Using System or User Utterance

In both system-driven and user-cooperative emotion labeling, the emotion category is estimated from the content of the text (Guinn and Hubal, 2003), i.e., the system or the user utterance in Figure 1, which was previously used in (Kase et al., 2015). Basically, the estimation of emotion category is based on matching between words in a sentence and a database of emotional expression words. Two data sources are exploited, one is an evaluation polarity dictionary of verbs (Kobayashi et al., 2004), and the other is a sentiment polarity dictionary of nouns (Takase et al., 2013), both are for Japanese words. The expressions and words in those dictionaries have either positive or negative polarity. Thus, if a sentence has a word or an expression (a phrase) with positive or negative polarity, we give the sentence "happy" or "sad" emotion, respectively. If no such words and phrases are found, we give a "neutral" emotion label. Several rules are employed for complicated situation in the expression matching, as follows.

1. If the emotional expression in the database is a phrase, the phrase is adopted only when all words of the phrase coincide with the text.

2. If two or more expressions are matched, the last expression is adopted.

3. If a negative expression is found such as "not (nai in Japanese) " after the match, we reverse

the polarity. Note that the negative expressions in Japanese succeed the modified word, e.g., "tanoshiku nai (happy not)" means unhappy.

4 Emotional Speech Synthesis

In this study, we use emotional speech synthesis based on HMMs which are widely used in the various research fields. The choice is mainly because of the computation cost in speech synthesis. The computation cost of HMM-based speech synthesis is relatively low compared to the other existing synthesis methods such as synthesis techniques based on unit selection (Hunt and Black, 1996) and deep neural networks (Zen et al., 2013). The low computation cost is essential to achieve the spoken dialogue system with smooth interaction between the system and users. In addition, a variety of expressive speech synthesis techniques have been proposed in the HMM-based speech synthesis (Nose and Kobayashi, 2011), which will enrich the dialogue system also in the future work.

In the HMM-based speech synthesis, speech samples are modeled by the sequences of context-dependent phone HMMs. Phonetic and prosodic contextual factors are used for the context. In the model training, the HMM parameters are tied using state-based context clustering with decision trees for each acoustic features, i.e., spectral, excitation, and duration features. The HMMs are then optimized using the EM algorithm. In this study, we adopted style-dependent modeling (Yamagishi et al., 2005) for the emotional speech synthesis. In the synthesis phase, the input text is converted to a context-dependent label sequence using text analysis, and the corresponding HMMs are concatenated to create a sentence HMM. Finally, the speech parameters are generated from the sentence HMM using speech parameter generation algorithm (Tokuda et al., 1995), and a waveform is synthesized using a vocoder.

5 Dialogue Experiment

We conducted a dialogue experiment using several systems to confirm and investigate the effect of emotional speech synthesis on the non-task-oriented dialogue system.

5.1 Experimental Procedure and Conditions

Ten subjects participated in the dialogue experiment and evaluated the subjective quality of the system and the dialogue. Each subject conducted a dialogue whose topic was "ball game" twice. The duration was about 60 to 90 seconds in each dialogue. We constructed the following four systems where different emotion labeling was adopted.

Baseline No emotion labeling (neutral)

System System-driven emotion labeling

User User-cooperative emotion labeling

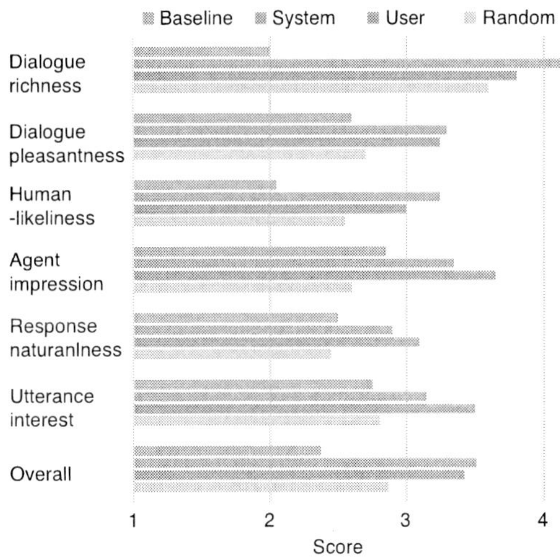

Figure 2: Average subjective scores of the participants for non-task-oriented dialogue to the four systems.

Random Random emotion labeling

Participants sat on a chair in a soundproof room and conducted a dialogue with an agent in a laptop PC. The visual of the agent was 10 cm high and 4 cm wide, and only lip-sync was implemented with no facial expressions and motions. After the dialogue, participants were asked about 1) richness of the dialogue, 2) pleasantness of the dialogue, 3) human-likeliness of the agent, 4) impression of the agent, 5) naturalness of the response, and 6) interest in the response. The rating score is 1 for the lowest and 5 for the highest.

For the emotional speech synthesis, we used emotional speech data of a professional female narrator who uttered 503 phonetically balanced Japanese sentences with neutral, joyful, and sad emotional expressions. The other basic conditions of the training and synthesis were the same as the previous study (Yamagishi et al., 2005).

5.2 Results and Discussions

Figure 2 shows the average scores of the subjective rating for the four systems. From the results, we first found a clear increase of the overall scores in the cases of using system-driven and user-cooperative emotion labeling compared to the baseline (no emotions) and random emotion labeling. This result indicates that the use of appropriate emotions in the synthetic speech response improves the subjective performance also for the non-task-oriented dialogue system.

Next, we conducted one-way ANOVA for the four systems, where emotion labeling methods was a factor. We found significant differences at a 5% level for the richness of the dialogue ($p < 0.001$), pleasantness of the dialogue ($p = 0.025$), human-likeliness of the agent ($p = 0.005$), and impression of the agent ($p = 0.001$).

Table 2: p-values of the multiple comparison test by t-test with Bonferroni correction. The results with a significant difference at 5% level are in a bold font.

Richness of the dialogue

	System	User	Random
Baseline	**<0.001**	**<0.001**	**<0.001**
System		>1.000	0.239
User			>1.000

Pleasantness of the dialogue

	System	User	Random
Baseline	0.094	0.147	>1.000
System		>1.000	0.224
User			0.335

Human likeliness of the agent

	System	User	Random
Baseline	**0.006**	0.050	0.951
System		>1.000	0.298
User			>1.000

Impression of the agent

	System	User	Random
Baseline	0.482	**0.035**	>1.000
System		>1.000	0.057
User			**0.002**

From these results, we verified that the type of the emotion labeling method actually affected the impression of subjects to the agent and conversation. In contrast, there are no significant differences in the naturalness of the response ($p = 0.242$) and interest in the response ($p = 0.062$) from the result of the one-way ANOVA. We then conducted a multiple comparison test by t-test with Bonferroni correction. Table 2 shows the p-values of the test.

In the rating of the richness of the dialogue, the three systems with emotions gave higher scores than the baseline. This result indicates that the richness is related to the variation of the emotions of the synthetic speech responses. Although there is no significant difference in the pleasantness of the dialogue, several scores had the same tendency as the previous study (Kase et al., 2015) in which the systems with the emotion labeling based on emotion estimation gave higher scores than the other systems. On the other hand, in human-likeliness of the agent, the tendency was different from the result in (Kase et al., 2015), and the system-driven labeling gave the highest score. A possible reason for this mismatch is that dialogue breakdown can occur in the non-task-oriented dialogue differently from the scenario-based one. About the impression of the agent, the user-cooperative system gave a better score than the baseline and the random labeling systems. Users tend to prefer the system that understands the users' emotional state and sympathizes with them.

5.3 Prosodic Analysis of User Utterances

In the dialogue experiment, we recorded the user utterances with 16 kHz sampling and 16 bit quantization.

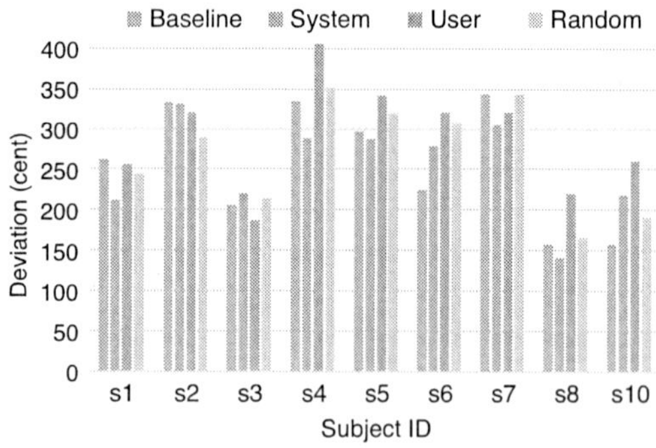

Figure 3: Mean values of the F0 deviations in each utterance for respective subjects, s1 to s10, (except s9).

The utterances of one subject (s9) had a problem in the recording, and hence we analyzed the 511 utterances of nine subjects. In this study, we focused on the fundamental frequency (F0) which is known to be the most important speech parameter for emotional expression. F0s were extracted using the SWIPE algorithm (Camacho, 2007) with 10-ms frame shift.

We calculated the deviations of F0s for the utterances of respective subjects in each system. Figure 3 shows the mean values of the deviations for each subject. We conducted one-way ANOVA where the labeling method was a factor. Although we expected that the emotional speech responses in a non-task-oriented dialogue more affect the user utterances than that in the scenario-based dialogue, there was no significant difference ($p = 0.613$) between the systems. One possible reason is that the naturalness of the system response is still insufficient to draw out emotions of the users.

6   Conclusions

In this paper, we discussed the effect of emotional speech synthesis on the non-task-oriented spoken dialogue system. We constructed dialogue systems with system-driven and user-cooperative emotion labeling and compared the subjective performance with the systems with no emotion and random emotion labeling. Experimental results showed that the use of emotional speech responses clearly improves the subjective scores such as richness of the dialogue and impression of the agent even when the dialogue is non-task-oriented. Improving the performance of the emotion estimation using both system and user utterances is our future work. The use of the acoustic information in the emotion estimation is also a remaining issue.

Acknowledgments

Part of this work was supported by JSPS KAKENHI Grant Numbers JP15H02720, JP16K13253, and JP17H00823.

References

Arturo Camacho. 2007. *SWIPE: A sawtooth waveform inspired pitch estimator for speech and music*. Ph.D. thesis, University of Florida Gainesville.

Pawel Dybala, Michal Ptaszynski, Rafal Rzepka, and Kenji Araki. 2010. Evaluating subjective aspects of HCI on an example of a non-task oriented conversational system. *International Journal on Artificial Intelligence Tools*, 19(06):819–856.

Curry Guinn and Rob Hubal. 2003. Extracting emotional information from the text of spoken dialog. In *Proceedings of the 9th International Conference on User Modeling*.

Andrew J Hunt and Alan W Black. 1996. Unit selection in a concatenative speech synthesis system using a large speech database. In *Proc. ICASSP*, volume 1, pages 373–376.

Taketo Kase, Takashi Nose, and Akinori Ito. 2015. On appropriateness and estimation of the emotion of synthesized response speech in a spoken dialogue system. In *Proceedings of the International Conference on Human-Computer Interaction*, pages 747–752.

Hiromichi Kawanami, Hiroshi Saruwatari, Kiyohiro Shikano, et al. 2007. Development and portability of ASR and Q&A modules for real-environment speech-oriented guidance systems. In *Proceedings of IEEE Workshop on Automatic Speech Recognition & Understanding*, pages 520–525.

Nozomi Kobayashi, Kentaro Inui, Yuji Matsumoto, Kenji Tateishi, and Toshikazu Fukushima. 2004. Collecting evaluative expressions for opinion extraction. In *Proceedings of the International Conference on Natural Language Processing*, pages 596–605.

Akinobu Lee and Tatsuya Kawahara. 2009. Recent development of open-source speech recognition engine julius. In *Proc. APSIPA ASC*, pages 131–137.

Akinobu Lee, Keiichiro Oura, and Keiichi Tokuda. 2013. MMDAgent—A fully open-source toolkit for voice interaction systems. In *Proc. ICASSP*, pages 8382–8385.

Mikio Nakano, Atsushi Hoshino, Johane Takeuchi, Yuji Hasegawa, Toyotaka Torii, Kazuhiro Nakadai, Kazuhiko Kato, and Hiroshi Tsujino. 2006. A robot that can engage in both task-oriented and non-task-oriented dialogues. In *IEEE-RAS International Conference on Humanoid Robots*, pages 404–411.

Takashi Nose and Takao Kobayashi. 2011. Recent development of HMM-based expressive speech synthesis and its applications. In *Proc. APSIPA ASC*, pages 1–4.

Bo-Hao Su, Ping-Wen Fu, Po-Chuan Lin, Po-Yi Shih, Yuh-Chung Lin, Jhing-Fa Wang, and An-Chao Tsai. 2014. A spoken dialogue system with situation and emotion detection based on anthropomorphic learning for warming healthcare d. In *Proceedings of the IEEE International Conference on Orange Technologies*, pages 133–136.

Sho Takase, Akiko Murakami, Miki Enoki, Naoaki Okazaki, and Kentaro Inui. 2013. Detecting chronic critics based on sentiment polarity and users behavior in social media. In *Proceedings of the Student Research Workshop in 51st Annual Meeting of the Association for Computational Linguistics*, pages 110–116.

Keiichi Tokuda, Takao Kobayashi, and Satoshi Imai. 1995. Speech parameter generation from HMM using dynamic features. In *Proc. ICASSP*, pages 660–663.

Joseph Weizenbaum. 1966. ELIZA—a computer program for the study of natural language communication between man and machine. *Communications of the ACM*, 9(1):36–45.

Junichi Yamagishi, Koji Onishi, Takashi Masuko, and Takao Kobayashi. 2005. Acoustic modeling of speaking styles and emotional expressions in HMM-based speech synthesis. *IEICE Trans. Inf. Syst.*, E88-D(3):503–509.

Takayoshi Yoshimura, Keiichi Tokuda, Takashi Masuko, Takao Kobayashi, and Tadashi Kitamura. 1999. Simultaneous modeling of spectrum, pitch and duration in HMM-based speech synthesis. In *Proc. Eurospeech*, pages 2347–2350.

Zhou Yu, Ziyu Xu, Alan W Black, and Alexander Rudnicky. 2016. Strategy and policy learning for non-task-oriented conversational systems. In *Proceedings of the 17th Annual Meeting of the Special Interest Group on Discourse and Dialogue*, pages 404–412.

Heiga Zen, Andrew Senior, and Mike Schuster. 2013. Statistical parametric speech synthesis using deep neural networks. In *Proc. ICASSP*, pages 7962–7966.

Victor Zue, Stephanie Seneff, James R Glass, Joseph Polifroni, Christine Pao, Timothy J Hazen, and Lee Hetherington. 2000. JUPITER: a telephone-based conversational interface for weather information. *IEEE Transactions on Speech and Audio Processing*, 8(1):85–96.

Multi-task learning for Joint Language Understanding and Dialogue State Tracking

Abhinav Rastogi
Google AI
Mountain View
abhirast@google.com

Raghav Gupta
Google AI
Mountain View
raghavgupta@google.com

Dilek Hakkani-Tur
Google AI
Mountain View
dilek@ieee.org

Abstract

This paper presents a novel approach for multi-task learning of language understanding (LU) and dialogue state tracking (DST) in task-oriented dialogue systems. Multi-task training enables the sharing of the neural network layers responsible for encoding the user utterance for both LU and DST and improves performance while reducing the number of network parameters. In our proposed framework, DST operates on a set of candidate values for each slot that has been mentioned so far. These candidate sets are generated using LU slot annotations for the current user utterance, dialogue acts corresponding to the preceding system utterance and the dialogue state estimated for the previous turn, enabling DST to handle slots with a large or unbounded set of possible values and deal with slot values not seen during training. Furthermore, to bridge the gap between training and inference, we investigate the use of scheduled sampling on LU output for the current user utterance as well as the DST output for the preceding turn.

1 Introduction

Task-oriented dialogue systems interact with users in natural language to accomplish tasks they have in mind, by providing a natural language interface to a backend (API, database or service). State of the art approaches to task-oriented dialogue systems typically consist of a language understanding (LU) component, which estimates the semantic parse of each user utterance and a dialogue state tracking (DST) or belief tracking component, which keeps track of the conversation context and the dialogue state (DS). Typically, DST uses the

System:	Hello! How can I help?
Acts:	*greeting*
User:	Hello, book me a table for two at Cascal.
Intent:	RESERVE_RESTAURANT
Acts:	*greeting*, *inform*(#people), *inform*(restaurant)
State:	`restaurant=Cascal, #people=two`
System:	I found a table for two at Cascal at 6 pm. Does that work?
Acts:	*offer*(time=6 pm)
User:	6 pm isn't good for us. How about 7 pm?
Acts:	*negate*(time), *inform*(time)
State:	`restaurant=Cascal, #people=two, time=7 pm`

Figure 1: A dialogue with user intent, user and system dialogue acts, and dialogue state.

semantic parse generated by LU to update the DS at every dialogue turn. The DS accumulates the preferences specified by the user over the dialogue and is used to make requests to a backend. The results from the backend and the dialogue state are then used by a dialogue policy module to generate the next system response.

Pipelining dialogue system components often leads to error propagation, hence joint modeling of these components has recently gained popularity (Henderson et al., 2014; Mrkšić et al., 2017; Liu and Lane, 2017), owing to computational efficiency as well as the potential ability to recover from errors introduced by LU. However, combining joint modeling with the ability to scale to multiple domains and handle slots with a large set of possible values, potentially containing entities not seen during training, are active areas of research.

In this work, we propose a single, joint model for LU and DST trained with multi-task learning. Similar to Liu and Lane 2017, our model employs a hierarchical recurrent neural network to encode the dialogue context. Intermediate feature representations from this network are used for identifying the intent and dialogue acts, and tagging slots

Proceedings of the SIGDIAL 2018 Conference, pages 376–384,
Melbourne, Australia, 12-14 July 2018. ©2018 Association for Computational Linguistics

Utterance:	Table	for	two	at	Olive	Garden
	↓	↓	↓	↓	↓	↓
Slot Tags:	O	O	B-#	O	B-rest	I-rest

Figure 2: IOB slot tags for a user utterance. Slot values *#* = *two* and *rest* = *Olive Garden* are obtained from corresponding B and I tags.

in the user utterance. Slot values obtained using these slot tags (as shown in Figure 2) are then used to update the set of candidate values for each slot. Similar to Rastogi et al. 2017, these candidate values are then scored by a recurrent scoring network which is shared across all slots, thus giving an efficient model for DST which can handle new entities that are not present in the training set - i.e., out-of-vocabulary (OOV) slot values.

During inference, the model uses its own predicted slot tags and previous turn dialogue state. However, ground truth slot tags and dialogue state are used for training to ensure stability. Aiming to bridge this gap between training and inference, we also propose a novel scheduled sampling (Bengio et al., 2015) approach to joint language understanding and dialogue state tracking.

The paper is organized as follows: Section 2 presents related work, followed by Section 3 describing the architecture of the dialogue encoder, which encodes the dialogue turns to be used as features by different tasks in our framework. The section also defines and outlines the implementation of the LU and DST tasks. Section 4 describes our setup for scheduled sampling. We then conclude with experiments and discussion of results.

2   Related Work

The initial motivation for dialogue state tracking came from the uncertainty in speech recognition and other sources (Williams and Young, 2007), as well as to provide a comprehensive input to a downstream dialogue policy component deciding the next system action. Proposed belief tracking models have ranged from rule-based (Wang and Lemon, 2013), to generative (Thomson and Young, 2010), discriminative (Henderson et al., 2014), other maximum entropy models (Williams, 2013) and web-style ranking (Williams, 2014).

Language understanding has commonly been modeled as a combination of intent and dialogue act classification and slot tagging (Tur and De Mori, 2011). Recently, recurrent neural network (RNN) based approaches have shown good

results for LU. Hakkani-Tür et al. 2016 used a joint RNN for intents, acts and slots to achieve better overall frame accuracy. In addition, models such as Chen et al. 2016, Bapna et al. 2017 and Su et al. 2018 further improve LU results by incorporating context from dialogue history.

Henderson et al. 2014 proposed a single joint model for single-turn LU and multi-turn DST to improve belief tracking performance. However, it relied on manually constructed semantic dictionaries to identify alternative mentions of ontology items that vary lexically or morphologically. Such an approach is not scalable to more complex domains (Mrkšić et al., 2017) as it is challenging to construct semantic dictionaries that can cover all possible entity mentions that occur naturally in a variety of forms in natural language. Mrkšić et al. 2017 proposed the NBT model which eliminates the LU step by directly operating on the user utterance. However, their approach requires iterating through the set of all possible values for a slot, which could be large or potentially unbounded (e.g. date, time, usernames). Perez and Liu 2017 incorporated end-to-end memory networks, as introduced in Sukhbaatar et al. 2015, into state tracking and Liu and Lane 2017 proposed an end-to-end model for belief tracking. However, these two approaches cannot accommodate OOV slot values as they represent DS as a distribution over all possible slot values seen in the training set.

To handle large value sets and OOV slot values, Rastogi et al. 2017 proposed an approach, where a set of value candidates is formed at each turn using dialogue context. The DST then operates on this set of candidates. In this work, we adopt a similar approach, but our focus is on joint modeling of LU and DST, and sampling methods for training them jointly.

3   Model Architecture

Let a dialogue be a sequence of T turns, each turn containing a user utterance and the preceding system dialogue acts output by the dialogue manager. Figure 3 gives an overview of our model architecture, which includes a user utterance encoder, a system act encoder, a state encoder, a slot tagger and a candidate scorer. At each turn $t \in \{1, ..., T\}$, the model takes a dialogue turn and the previous dialogue state D^{t-1} as input and outputs the predicted user intent, user dialogue acts, slot values in the user utterance and the updated

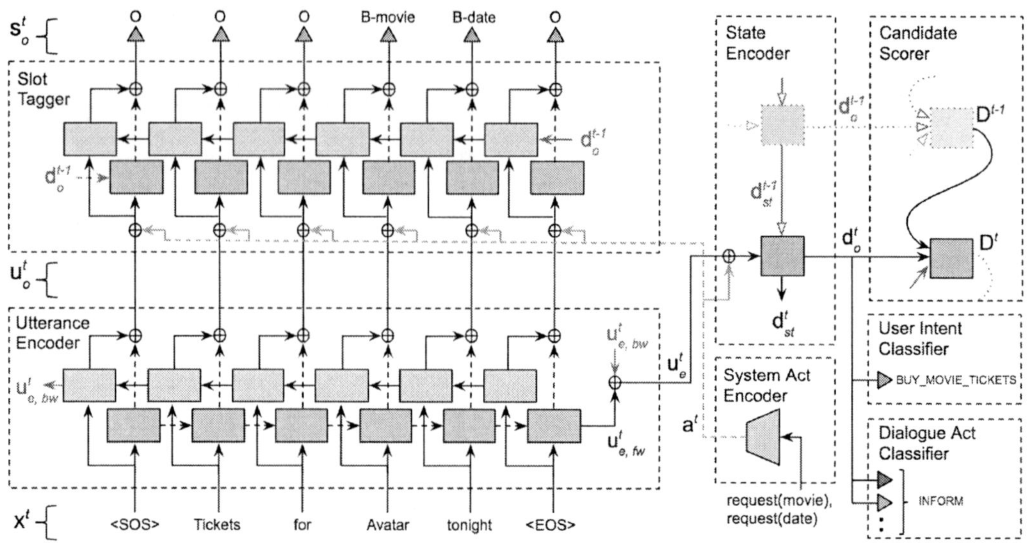

Figure 3: Architecture of our joint LU and DST model as described in Section 3. x^t is the sequence of user utterance token embeddings, a^t is the system act encoding and blue arrows indicate additional features used by DST as detailed in Section 3.8.

dialogue state D^t.

As a new turn arrives, the system act encoder (Section 3.1) encodes all system dialogue acts in the turn to generate the system dialogue act vector a^t. Similarly, the utterance encoder (Section 3.2) encodes the user utterance into a vector u_e^t, and also generates contextual token embeddings u_o^t for each utterance token. The state encoder (Section 3.3) then uses a^t, u_e^t and its previous turn hidden state, d_{st}^{t-1}, to generate the dialogue context vector d_o^t, which summarizes the entire observed dialogue, and its updated hidden state d_{st}^t.

The dialogue context vector d_o^t is then used by the user intent classifier (Section 3.4) and user dialogue act classifier (Section 3.5). The slot tagger (section 3.6) uses the dialogue context from previous turn d_o^{t-1}, the system act vector a^t and contextual token embeddings u_o^t to generate refined contextual token embeddings s_o^t. These refined token embeddings are then used to predict the slot tag for each token in the user utterance.

The system dialogue acts and predicted slot tags are then used to update the set of candidate values for each slot (Section 3.7). The candidate scorer (Section 3.8) then uses the previous dialogue state D^{t-1}, the dialogue context vector d_o^t and other features extracted from the current turn (indicated by blue arrows in Figure 3) to update the scores for all candidates in the candidate set and outputs the

updated dialogue state D^t. The following sections describe these components in detail.

3.1 System Act Encoder

Previous turn system dialogue acts play an important role in accurate semantic parsing of a user utterance. Each system dialogue act contains an act type and optional slot and value parameters. The dialogue acts are first encoded into binary vectors denoting the presence of an act type. All dialogue acts which don't have any associated parameters (e.g. *greeting* and *negate*) are encoded as a binary indicator vector a_{utt}^t. Dialogue acts with just a slot s as parameter (e.g. *request(date)*) are encoded as $a_{slot}^t(s)$, whereas acts having a candidate value c for a slot s as parameter (e.g. *offer(time=7pm)*) are encoded as $a_{cand}^t(s, c)$. These binary vectors are then combined using equations 1-4 to obtain the combined system act representation a^t, which is used by other units of dialogue encoder (as shown in Figure 3). In these equations, e_s is a trainable slot embedding defined for each slot s.

$$a_{sc}^t(s) = a_{slot}^t(s) \oplus e_s \oplus \Sigma_c a_{cand}^t(s, c) \quad (1)$$

$$a_{sc}'^t(s) = ReLU(W_{sc}^a \cdot a_{sc}^t(s) + b_{sc}^a) \quad (2)$$

$$a_{usc}^t = \left(\frac{1}{|S^t|} \sum_{s \in S^t} a_{sc}'^t(s) \right) \oplus a_{utt}^t \quad (3)$$

$$a^t = ReLU(W_{usc}^a \cdot a_{usc}^t + b_{usc}^a) \quad (4)$$

3.2 Utterance Encoder

The user utterance takes the tokens corresponding to the user utterance as input. Special tokens SOS and EOS are added at the beginning and end of the token list. Let $x^t = \{x_m^t \in \mathbb{R}^{u_d}, \forall 0 \leq m < M^t\}$ denote the embedded representations of these tokens, where M^t is the number of tokens in the user utterance for turn t (including SOS and EOS).

We use a single layer bi-directional GRU recurrent neural network (Cho et al., 2014) with state size d_u and initial state set to 0, to encode the user utterance. The first output of the user utterance encoder is $u_e^t \in \mathbb{R}^{2d_u}$, which is a compact representation of the entire user utterance, defined as the concatenation of the final states of the two RNNs. The second output is $u_o^t = \{u_{o,m}^t \in \mathbb{R}^{2d_u}, 0 \leq m < M^t\}$, which is the embedded representation of each token conditioned on the entire utterance, defined as the concatenation of outputs at each step of the forward and backward RNNs.

3.3 State Encoder

The state encoder completes our hierarchical dialogue encoder. At turn t, the state encoder generates d_o^t, which is an embedded representation of the dialogue context until and including turn t. We implement the state encoder using a unidirectional GRU RNN with each timestep corresponding to a dialogue turn. As shown in Figure 3, the dialogue encoder takes $a^t \oplus u_e^t$ and its previous hidden state d_{st}^{t-1} as input and outputs the updated hidden state d_{st}^t and the encoded representation of the dialogue context d_o^t (which are the same in case of GRU).

3.4 User Intent Classification

The user intent is used to identify the backend with which the dialogue system should interact. We predict the intents at each turn to allow user to switch intents during the dialogue. However, we assume that a given user utterance can contain atmost one intent and model intent prediction as a multi-class classification problem. At each turn, the distribution over all intents is calculated as

$$p_i^t = softmax(W_i \cdot d_o^t + b_i) \qquad (5)$$

where $\dim(p_i^t) = |I|$, $W_i \in \mathbb{R}^{d \times |I|}$ and $b_i \in \mathbb{R}^{|I|}$, I denoting the user intent vocabulary and $d = \dim(d_o^t)$. During inference, we predict $argmax(p_i^t)$ as the intent label for the utterance.

3.5 User Dialogue Act Classification

Dialogue acts are structured semantic representations of user utterances. User dialogue acts are used by the dialogue manager in deciding the next system action. We model user dialogue act classification as a multilabel classification problem, to allow for the presence of more than one dialogue act in a turn (Tur and De Mori, 2011). At each turn, the probability for act a is predicted as

$$p_a^t = sigmoid(W_a \cdot d_o^t + b_a) \qquad (6)$$

where $\dim(p_a^t) = |A_u|$, $W_a \in \mathbb{R}^{d \times |A_u|}$, $b_a \in \mathbb{R}^{|A_u|}$, A_u is the user dialogue act vocabulary and $d = \dim(d_o^t)$. For each act α, $p_a^t(\alpha)$ is interpreted as the probability of presence of α in turn t. During inference, all dialogue acts with a probability greater than t_u are predicted, where $0 < t_u < 1.0$ is a hyperparameter tuned using the dev set.

3.6 Slot Tagging

Slot tagging is the task of identifying the presence of values of different slots in the user utterance. We use the IOB tagging scheme (Tjong Kim Sang and Buchholz 2000, see Figure 2) to assign a label to each token. These labels are then used to extract the values for different slots from the utterance.

The slot tagging network consists of a single-layer bidirectional LSTM RNN (Hochreiter and Schmidhuber, 1997), which takes the contextual token embeddings u_o^t generated by the utterance encoder as input. It outputs refined token embeddings $s_o^t = \{s_{o,m}^t, \forall 0 \leq m < M^t\}$ for each token, M^t being the number of tokens in user utterance at turn t.

Models making use of dialogue context for LU have been shown to achieve superior performance (Chen et al., 2016). In our setup, the dialogue context vector d_o^{t-1} encodes all the preceding turns and the system act vector a^t encodes the system dialogue acts preceding the user utterance. As shown in Figure 3, d_o^{t-1} is used to initialize [1] the hidden state (cell states are initialized to zero) for the forward and backward LSTM recurrent units in the slot tagger, while a^t is fed as input to the tagger by concatenating with each element of u_o^t as shown below. We use an LSTM instead of a GRU for this layer since that resulted in better performance on the validation set.

$$s_{in}^t = \{u_{o,m}^t \oplus a^t, \forall 0 \leq m < M^t\} \qquad (7)$$

$$s_{e,bw}^t, s_{o,bw}^t = LSTM_{bw}(s_{in}^t) \qquad (8)$$

$$s_{e,fw}^t, s_{o,fw}^t = LSTM_{fw}(s_{in}^t) \qquad (9)$$

$$s_o^t = s_{o,bw}^t \oplus s_{o,fw}^t \qquad (10)$$

---

[1] After projection to the appropriate dimension.

Let S be the set of all slots in the dataset. We define a set of $2|S| + 1$ labels (one B- and I- label for each slot and a single O label) for IOB tagging. The refined token embedding $s_{o,m}^t$ is used to predict the distribution across all IOB labels for token at index m as

$$p_{s,m}^t = softmax(W_s \cdot s_{o,m}^t + b_s) \qquad (11)$$

where $\dim(p_{s,m}^t) = 2|S| + 1$, $W_s \in \mathbb{R}^{d_s \times 2|S|+1}$ and $b_s \in \mathbb{R}^{2|S|+1}$, $d_s = \dim(s_{o,m}^t)$ is the output size of slot tagger LSTM. During inference, we predict $argmax(p_{s,m}^t)$ as the slot label for the mth token in the user utterance in turn t.

3.7 Updating Candidate Set

A candidate set C_s^t is defined as a set of values of a slot s which have been mentioned by either the user or the system till turn t. Rastogi et al. 2017 proposed the use of candidate sets in DST for efficiently handling slots with a large set of values. In their setup, the candidate set is updated at every turn to include new values and discard old values when it reaches its maximum capacity. The dialogue state is represented as a set of distributions over value set $V_s^t = C_s^t \cup \{\delta, \phi\}$ for each slot $s \in S^t$, where δ and ϕ are special values dontcare (user is ok with any value for the slot) and null (slot not specified yet) respectively, and S^t is the set of all slots that have been mentioned either by the user or the system till turn t.

Our model uses the same definition and update rules for candidate sets. At each turn we use the predictions of the slot tagger (Section 3.6) and system acts which having slot and value parameters to update the corresponding candidate sets. All candidate sets are padded with dummy values for batching computations for all slots together. We keep track of valid candidates by defining indicator features $m_v^t(s, c)$ for each candidate, which take the value 1.0 if candidate is valid or 0.0 if not.

3.8 Candidate Scorer

The candidate scorer predicts the dialogue state by updating the distribution over the value set V_s^t for each slot $s \in S^t$. For this, we define three intermediate features r_{utt}^t, $r_{slot}^t(s)$ and $r_{cand}^t(s, c)$. r_{utt}^t is shared across all value sets and is defined by equation 12. $r_{slot}^t(s)$ is used to update scores for V_s^t and is defined by equation 13. Furthermore, $r_{cand}^t(s, c)$ is defined for each candidate $c \in C_s^t \subset V_s^t$ using equation 14 and contains all features that are associated to candidate c of slot s.

$$r_{utt}^t = d_o^t \oplus a_{utt}^t \qquad (12)$$

$$r_{slot}^t(s) = a_{slot}^t(s) \oplus [p_\delta^{t-1}(s), p_\phi^{t-1}(s)] \qquad (13)$$

$$r_{cand}^t(s, c) = a_{cand}^t(s, c) \oplus [p_c^{t-1}(s)] \oplus \\ [m_v^t(s, c), m_u^t(c)] \qquad (14)$$

In the above equations, d_o^t is the dialogue context at turn t output by the state encoder (Section 3.3), a_{utt}^t, $a_{slot}^t(s)$ and $a_{cand}^t(s, c)$ are system act encodings generated by the system act encoder (Section 3.1), $p_\delta^{t-1}(s)$ and $p_\phi^{t-1}(s)$ are the scores associated with dontcare and null values for slot s respectively. $p_c^{t-1}(s)$ is the score associated with candidate c of slot s in the previous turn and is taken to be 0 if $c \notin C_s^t$. $m_v^t(s, c)$ are variables indicating whether a candidate is valid or padded (Section 3.8). We define another indicator feature $m_u^t(c)$ which takes the value 1.0 if the candidate is a substring of the user utterance in turn t or 0.0 otherwise. This informs the candidate scorer which candidates have been mentioned most recently by the user.

$$r'^t_{slot}(s) = r_{utt}^t \oplus r_{slot}^t(s) \qquad (15)$$

$$l_s^t(\delta) = FF_{cs}^1(r'^t_{slot}(s)) \qquad (16)$$

$$l_s^t(c) = FF_{cs}^2(r'^t_{slot}(s) \oplus r_{cand}^t(s, c)) \qquad (17)$$

$$p_s^t = softmax(l_s^t) \qquad (18)$$

Features used in Equations 12-14 are then used to obtain the distribution over V_s^t using Equations 15-17. In the above equations, $l_s^t(\delta)$ denotes the logit for dontcare value for slot s, $l_s^t(c)$ denotes the logit for a candidate $c \in C_s^t$ and $l_s^t(\phi)$ is a trainable parameter. These logits are obtained by processing the corresponding features using feedforward neural networks FF_{cs}^1 and FF_{cs}^2, each having one hidden layer. The output dimension of these networks is 1 and the dimension of the hidden layer is taken to be half of the input dimension. The logits are then normalized using softmax to get the distribution p_s^t over V_s^t.

4 Scheduled Sampling

DST is a recurrent model which uses predictions from the previous turn. For stability during training, ground truth predictions from the previous turn are used. This causes a mismatch between training and inference behavior. We use scheduled sampling (Bengio et al., 2015) to bridge this

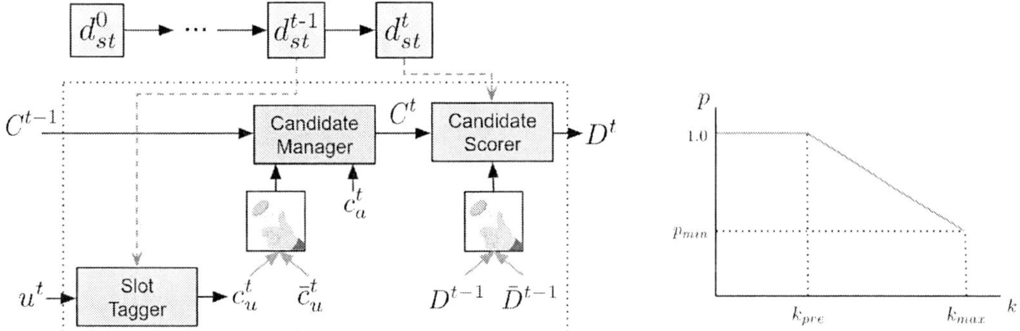

Figure 4: Illustration of scheduled sampling for training the candidate scorer. The left figure shows the two locations in our setup where we can perform scheduled sampling, while the plot on the right shows the variation of sampling probabilities p_c and p_D with training step. See Section 4 for details.

mismatch. Scheduled sampling has been shown to achieve improved slot tagging performance on single turn datasets (Liu and Lane, 2016). Figure 4 shows our setup for scheduled sampling for DST, which is carried out at two different locations - slot tags and dialogue state.

The performance of slot tagger is critical to DST because any slot value missed by the slot tagger will not be added to the candidate set (unless it is tagged in another utterance or present in any system act). To account for this, during training, we sample between the ground truth slot tags ($\bar{c}_u^t$) and the predicted slot tags (c_u^t), training initially with $\bar{c}_u^t$ (i.e. with keep probability $p_c = 1$) but gradually reducing p_c i.e. increasingly replacing $\bar{c}_u^t$ with c_u^t. Using predicted slot tags during training allows DST to train in presence of noisy candidate sets.

During inference, the candidate scorer only has access to its own predicted scores in the previous turn (Equations 13 and 14). To better mimic this setup during training, we start with using ground truth previous scores taken from $\bar{D}^{t-1}$ (i.e. with keep probability $p_D = 1$) and gradually switch to D^{t-1}, the predicted previous scores, reducing p_D.

Both p_c and p_D vary as a function of the training step k, as shown in the right part of Figure 4; only ground truth slot tags and dialogue state are used for training i.e. p_c and p_D stay at 1.0 for the first k_{pre} training steps, and then decrease linearly as the ground truth slot tags and state are increasingly replaced by model predictions during training.

5 Experiments

The major contributions of our work are two-fold. First, we hypothesize that joint modeling of LU and DST results in a computationally efficient model with fewer parameters without compromising performance. Second, we propose the use of scheduled sampling to improve the robustness of DST during inference. To this end, we conduct experiments across the following two setups.

Separate vs Joint LU-DST - Figure 3 shows the joint LU-DST setup where parameters in the utterance encoder and state encoder are shared across LU tasks (intent classification, dialogue act classification and slot tagging) and DST (candidate scoring). As baselines, we also conduct experiments where LU and DST tasks use separate parameters for utterance and state encoders.

Scheduled Sampling - We conduct scheduled sampling (as described in Section 4) experiments in four different setups.

1. *None* - Ground truth slot tags ($\bar{c}_u^t$) and previous dialogue state ($\bar{D}^{t-1}$) are used for training.
2. *Tags* - Model samples between ground truth ($\bar{c}_u^t$) and predicted (c_u^t) slot tags, sticking to ground truth previous state.
3. *State* - Model samples between ground truth ($\bar{D}^{t-1}$) and predicted (D^{t-1}) previous state, sticking to ground truth slot tags.
4. *Both* - Model samples between $\bar{D}^{t-1}$ and D^{t-1} as well as between $\bar{c}_u^t$ and c_u^t.

In the last three setups, we start sampling from predictions only after $k_{pre} = 0.3\,k_{max}$ training steps, as shown in Figure 4.

5.1 Evaluation Metrics

We report user intent classification accuracy, F1 score for user dialogue act classification, frame accuracy for slot tagging and joint goal accuracy and slot F1 score for DST. During DST evaluation, we always use the predicted slot values and the dialogue state in the previous turn. Slot frame accuracy is defined as the fraction of turns for which all slot labels are predicted correctly. Similarly, joint goal accuracy is the fraction of turns for which the predicted and ground truth dialogue state match for all slots. Since it is a stricter metric than DST slot F1, we use it as the primary metric to identify the best set of parameters on the validation set.

5.2 Datasets

We evaluate our approaches on two datasets:

- **Simulated Dialogues**[2] - The dataset, described in Shah et al. 2017, contains dialogues from restaurant (Sim-R) and movie (Sim-M) domains across three intents. A challenging aspect of this dataset is the prevalence of OOV entities e.g. only 13% of the movie names in the dev/test sets also occur in the training data.
- **DSTC2** - We use the top ASR hypothesis and system dialogue acts as inputs. Dialogue act labels are obtained from top SLU hypothesis and state labels for requestable slots. DS labels are obtained from state labels for informable slots. We use a semantic dictionary (Henderson et al., 2014) to obtain ground truth slot tags. We also use the semantic dictionary to canonicalize the candidate values since the slot values in the dialogue state come from a fixed set in the DSTC2 dialogues and may be different from those present in the user utterance.

5.3 Training

We use sigmoid cross entropy loss for dialogue act classification and softmax cross entropy loss for all other tasks. During training, we minimize the sum of all task losses using ADAM optimizer (Kingma and Ba, 2014), for 100k training steps with batches of 10 dialogues each. We used grid-search to identify the best hyperparameter values (sampled within specified range) for learning rate (0.0001 - 0.005) and token embedding dimension (50 - 200). For scheduled sampling experiments, the minimum keep rate i.e. p_{min} is varied between

0.1 - 0.9 with linear decay. The layer sizes for the utterance encoder and slot tagger are set equal to the token embedding dimension, and that of the state encoder to half this dimension.

Slot Value dropout - To make the model robust to OOV tokens arising from new entities not present in the training set, we randomly replace slot value tokens in the user utterance with a special OOV token with a probability that linearly increases from 0.0 to 0.4 during training.

6 Results and Discussion

Table 1 shows our results across the two setups described in Section 5, for the Simulated Dialogues datasets. For Sim-R + Sim-M, we observe that the joint LU-DST model with scheduled sampling (SS) on both slot tags and dialogue state performs the best, with a joint goal accuracy of 73.8% overall, while the best separate model gets a joint goal accuracy of 71.9%, using SS only for slot tags. Even for the no-SS baselines, the joint model performs comparably to the separate model (joint goal accuracies of 68.6% and 68.7% respectively), indicating that sharing results in a more efficient model with fewer parameters, without compromising overall performance. For each SS configuration, our results comparing separate and joint modeling are statistically significant, as determined by the McNemar's test with $p < 0.05$.

On the Sim-R dataset, the best joint model obtains a joint goal accuracy of 87.1%, while the best separate model obtains 85.0%. However, we observe a significant drop in joint goal accuracy for the Sim-M dataset for both the joint model and the separate model as compared to Sim-R. This can partly be attributed to the Sim-M dataset being much smaller than Sim-R (384 training dialogues as opposed to 1116) and that the high OOV rate of the *movie* slot in Sim-M makes slot tagging performance more crucial for Sim-M. While SS does gently bridge the gap between training and testing conditions, its gains are obscured in this scenario possibly since it is very hard for DST to recover from a slot value being completely missed by LU, even when aided by SS.

For the two datasets, we also observe a significant difference between the slot frame accuracy and joint goal accuracy. This is because an LU error penalizes the slot frame accuracy for a single turn, whereas an error in dialogue state propagates through all the successive turns, thereby drasti-

[2]Dataset available at http://github.com/google-research-datasets/simulated-dialogue/

Table 1: Experiments and results on test set with variants of scheduled sampling on separate and joint LU-DST models, when trained on Sim-M + Sim-R.

Eval Set	SS Setup	Intent Accuracy		Dialogue Act F1 Score		Slot Frame Accuracy		Joint Goal Accuracy		DST Slot F1 Score	
		Sep	Joint	Sep	Joint	Sep	Joint	Sep	Joint	Sep	Joint
Sim-R	None	0.999	0.997	0.956	0.935	0.924	0.919	0.850	0.846	0.951	0.952
	Tags	0.998	0.998	0.936	0.957	0.917	0.922	0.805	0.871	0.936	0.962
	State	0.999	0.998	0.931	0.939	0.919	0.920	0.829	0.852	0.935	0.951
	Both	0.994	0.998	0.948	0.919	0.917	0.916	0.829	0.849	0.942	0.953
Sim-M	None	0.991	0.993	0.966	0.966	0.801	0.800	0.276	0.283	0.806	0.817
	Tags	0.993	0.994	0.970	0.967	0.895	0.801	0.504	0.262	0.839	0.805
	State	0.996	0.970	0.964	0.955	0.848	0.799	0.384	0.266	0.803	0.797
	Both	0.989	0.996	0.970	0.959	0.887	0.860	0.438	0.460	0.805	0.845
Sim-R +	None	0.996	0.996	0.959	0.944	0.890	0.885	0.687	0.686	0.902	0.906
Sim-M	Tags	0.996	0.997	0.946	0.960	0.910	0.888	0.719	0.698	0.902	0.905
	State	0.996	0.990	0.940	0.943	0.899	0.886	0.702	0.683	0.897	0.899
	Both	0.993	0.997	0.954	0.931	0.909	0.900	0.717	**0.738**	0.894	**0.915**

cally reducing the joint goal accuracy. This gap is even more pronounced for Sim-M because of the poor performace of slot tagger on *movie* slot, which is often mentioned by the user in the beginning of the dialogue. The relatively high values of overall DST slot F1 for Sim-M for all experiments also corroborates this observation.

Table 2: Reported joint goal accuracy of model variants on the DSTC2 test set.

Model	Separate	Joint
No SS	0.661	0.650
Tags only SS	0.655	**0.670**
State only SS	0.661	0.660
Tags + State SS	0.656	0.658
Liu and Lane 2017	-	0.73
Mrkšić et al. 2017	-	0.734

Table 2 shows our results on the DSTC2 dataset, which contains dialogues in the restaurant domain. The joint model gets a joint goal accuracy of 65.0% on the test set, which goes up to 67.0% with SS on slot tags. Approaches like NBT (Mrkšić et al., 2017) or Hierarchical RNN (Liu and Lane, 2017) are better suited for such datasets, where the set of all slot values is already known, thus eliminating the need for slot tagging. On the other hand, our setup uses slot tagging for candidate generation, which allows it to scale to OOV entities and scalably handle slots with a large or unbounded set of possible values, at the cost of performance.

Analyzing results for scheduled sampling, we observe that for almost all combinations of metrics, datasets and joint/separate model configurations, the best result is obtained using a model trained with some SS variant. For instance, for Sim-M, SS over slot tags and state increases joint goal accuracy significantly from 28.3% to 46.0% for joint model. SS on slot tags helps the most with Sim-R and DSTC2: our two datasets with the most data, and low OOV rates, while SS on both slot tags and dialogue state helps more on the smaller Sim-M. In addition, we also found that slot value dropout (Section 5.3), improves LU as well as DST results consistently. We omit the results without this technique for brevity.

7 Conclusions

In this work, we present a joint model for language understanding (LU) and dialogue state tracking (DST), which is computationally efficient by way of sharing feature extraction layers between LU and DST, while achieving an accuracy comparable to modeling them separately across multiple tasks. We also demonstrate the effectiveness of scheduled sampling on LU outputs and previous dialogue state as an effective way to simulate inference-time conditions during training for DST, and make the model more robust to errors.

References

Ankur Bapna, Gokhan Tur, Dilek Hakkani-Tur, and Larry Heck. 2017. Sequential dialogue context modeling for spoken language understanding. In *Proceedings of the 18th Annual SIGdial Meeting on Discourse and Dialogue*, pages 103–114.

Samy Bengio, Oriol Vinyals, Navdeep Jaitly, and Noam Shazeer. 2015. Scheduled sampling for sequence prediction with recurrent neural networks. In *Advances in Neural Information Processing Systems*, pages 1171–1179.

Yun-Nung Chen, Dilek Hakkani-Tür, Jianfeng Gao, and Li Deng. 2016. End-to-end memory networks with knowledge carryover for multi-turn spoken language understanding.

Kyunghyun Cho, Bart Van Merriënboer, Caglar Gulcehre, Dzmitry Bahdanau, Fethi Bougares, Holger Schwenk, and Yoshua Bengio. 2014. Learning phrase representations using rnn encoder-decoder for statistical machine translation. *arXiv preprint arXiv:1406.1078*.

Dilek Hakkani-Tür, Asli Celikyilmaz, Yun-Nung Chen, Jianfeng Gao, Li Deng, and Ye-Yi Wang. 2016. Multi-domain joint semantic frame parsing using bi-directional rnn-lstm.

M. Henderson, B. Thomson, and S. Young. 2014. Word-based dialog state tracking with recurrent neural networks. In *Proceedings of the 15th Annual Meeting of the Special Interest Group on Discourse and Dialogue (SIGDIAL)*, pages 292–299.

Sepp Hochreiter and Jürgen Schmidhuber. 1997. Long short-term memory. *Neural computation*, 9(8):1735–1780.

Diederik P Kingma and Jimmy Ba. 2014. Adam: A method for stochastic optimization. *arXiv preprint arXiv:1412.6980*.

Bing Liu and Ian Lane. 2016. Joint online spoken language understanding and language modeling with recurrent neural networks. In *17th Annual Meeting of the Special Interest Group on Discourse and Dialogue*, page 22.

Bing Liu and Ian Lane. 2017. An end-to-end trainable neural network model with belief tracking for task-oriented dialog. In *Proceedings of Interspeech*.

Nikola Mrkšić, Diarmuid Ó Séaghdha, Tsung-Hsien Wen, Blaise Thomson, and Steve Young. 2017. Neural belief tracker: Data-driven dialogue state tracking. In *Proceedings of the 55th Annual Meeting of the Association for Computational Linguistics (Volume 1: Long Papers)*, volume 1, pages 1777–1788.

Julien Perez and Fei Liu. 2017. Dialog state tracking, a machine reading approach using memory network. In *Proceedings of the 15th Conference of the European Chapter of the Association for Computational Linguistics: Volume 1, Long Papers*, volume 1, pages 305–314.

A. Rastogi, D. Hakkani-Tür, and L. Heck. 2017. Scalable multi-domain dialogue state tracking. In *IEEE Workshop on Automatic Speech Recognition and Understanding (ASRU)*.

P. Shah, D. Hakkani-Tür, G. Tur, A. Rastogi, A. Bapna, N. Nayak, and L. Heck. 2017. Building a conversational agent overnight with dialogue self-play. *arXiv preprint arXiv:1801.04871*.

Shang-Yu Su, Pei-Chieh Yuan, and Yun-Nung Chen. 2018. How time matters: Learning time-decay attention for contextual spoken language understanding in dialogues. In *Proceedings of the 2018 Conference of the North American Chapter of the Association for Computational Linguistics: Human Language Technologies*.

Sainbayar Sukhbaatar, Jason Weston, Rob Fergus, et al. 2015. End-to-end memory networks. In *Advances in neural information processing systems*, pages 2440–2448.

Blaise Thomson and Steve Young. 2010. Bayesian update of dialogue state: A pomdp framework for spoken dialogue systems. *Computer Speech & Language*, 24(4):562–588.

Erik F Tjong Kim Sang and Sabine Buchholz. 2000. Introduction to the conll-2000 shared task: Chunking. In *Proceedings of the 2nd workshop on Learning language in logic and the 4th conference on Computational natural language learning-Volume 7*, pages 127–132. Association for Computational Linguistics.

Gokhan Tur and Renato De Mori. 2011. *Spoken language understanding: Systems for extracting semantic information from speech*. John Wiley & Sons.

Zhuoran Wang and Oliver Lemon. 2013. A simple and generic belief tracking mechanism for the dialog state tracking challenge: On the believability of observed information. In *Proceedings of the SIGDIAL 2013 Conference*, pages 423–432.

Jason Williams. 2013. Multi-domain learning and generalization in dialog state tracking. In *Proceedings of the SIGDIAL 2013 Conference*, pages 433–441.

Jason D Williams. 2014. Web-style ranking and slu combination for dialog state tracking. In *Proceedings of the 15th Annual Meeting of the Special Interest Group on Discourse and Dialogue (SIGDIAL)*, pages 282–291.

Jason D Williams and Steve Young. 2007. Partially observable markov decision processes for spoken dialog systems. *Computer Speech & Language*, 21(2):393–422.

Weighting Model Based on Group Dynamics to Measure Convergence in Multi-party Dialogue

Zahra Rahimi
Intelligent Systems Program
University of Pittsburgh
Pittsburgh, PA, 15260
zar10@pitt.edu

Diane Litman
Intelligent Systems Program
University of Pittsburgh
Pittsburgh, PA, 15260
litman@cs.pitt.edu

Abstract

This paper proposes a new weighting method for extending a dyad-level measure of convergence to multi-party dialogues by considering group dynamics instead of simply averaging. Experiments indicate the usefulness of the proposed weighted measure and also show that in general a proper weighting of the dyad-level measures performs better than non-weighted averaging in multiple tasks.

1 Introduction

Entrainment is the tendency of speakers to begin behaving like one another in conversation. The development of methods for automatically quantifying entrainment in text and speech data is an active research area, as entrainment has been shown to correlate with outcomes such as success measures and social variables for a variety of phenomena, e.g., acoustic-prosodic, lexical, and syntactic (Nenkova et al., 2008; Reitter and Moore, 2007; Mitchell et al., 2012; Levitan et al., 2012; Lee et al., 2011; Stoyanchev and Stent, 2009; Lopes et al., 2013; Lubold and Pon-Barry, 2014; Moon et al., 2014; Sinha and Cassell, 2015; Lubold et al., 2015). One of the main measures of entrainment is convergence which is the main focus of this paper. Within a conversation, convergence measures the amount of increase in similarity of speakers over time in terms of linguistic features (Levitan and Hirschberg, 2011).

While most research has focused on quantifying the amount of entrainment between speaker pairs (i.e., dyads), recent studies have started to develop measures for quantifying entrainment between larger groups of speakers (Friedberg et al., 2012; Danescu-Niculescu-Mizil et al., 2012; Gonzales et al., 2010; Doyle and Frank, 2016; Litman et al.,

2016; Rahimi et al., 2017a). To date, mainly simple methods such as unweighted averaging have been used to move from dyads to groups (Gonzales et al., 2010; Danescu-Niculescu-Mizil et al., 2012; Litman et al., 2016).

However, because multi-party interactions are more complicated than dyad-level interactions, it is not clear that the contribution of all group members should be weighted equally. For example, to account for participation differences, Friedberg et al. proposed a weighting method based on the number of uttered words of each dyad (Friedberg et al., 2012), although this did not yield performance improvements compared to simple averaging. Rahimi et al. (Rahimi et al., 2017b) provided examples of group-specific behaviors that were not properly quantified using simple averaging. While this case study nicely identified potential problems with prior measures, their observations were only based on a few example dialogues and no solutions were proposed.

In this paper, we propose a new weighting method to normalize the contribution of speakers based on group dynamics. We explore the effect of our method, participation weighting, and simple averaging when calculating group convergence from dyads. We conclude that our proposed weighted convergence measure performs significantly better on multiple benchmark prediction and regression tasks that have been used to evaluate convergence in prior studies (De Looze et al., 2014; Lee et al., 2011; Jain et al., 2012; Rahimi et al., 2017a; Doyle et al., 2016; Lee et al., 2011).

2 Convergence for Multi-Party Dialogue

The convergence measure that we extend in this paper is adopted from prior work. Originally, convergence between dyads (Levitan and Hirschberg, 2011) was measured by calculating the difference

Proceedings of the SIGDIAL 2018 Conference, pages 385–390,
Melbourne, Australia, 12-14 July 2018. ©2018 Association for Computational Linguistics

between the dissimilarity of speakers in two non-overlapping time intervals. If the dissimilarity in the second interval was less than in the first, the pair was said to be converging.

Extending this work, multi-party convergence (Litman et al., 2016) was measured using Non-Weighted (NW) averaging of each pairs' convergence, as shown in Equations 1 and 2:

$$GroupDiff_t = \frac{\sum_{\forall i \neq j \in group}(|f_{i,t} - f_{j,t}|)}{|group| * (|group| - 1)} \quad (1)$$

$$Conv_{NW} = GroupDiff_{t_1} - GroupDiff_{t_2} \quad (2)$$

$GroupDiff_t$ corresponds to average group differences calculated for linguistic feature f in time interval t for all pairs (i,j). The convergence is the difference between $GroupDiff$s in two intervals.

In the next subsections, we introduce two weighted variations of these formulas: a baseline based on participation ratios (Friedberg et al., 2012), and a method based on group dynamics.

2.1 Weighting Based on Participation

The idea behind this approach is that the weights for speakers that may have talked very little should be reduced. In prior work on multi-party lexical entrainment (Friedberg et al., 2012), speaker participation was measured by number of uttered words; the participation ratios of speaker pairs were then used as the weights.

Since our work focuses on acoustic-prosodic entrainment, we measure speaker participation by amount of speaking time. The Participation Ratio (PR) of each speaker in a given temporal interval is their total speech time divided by the duration of the interval including silences. Speech and silence periods are automatically annotated using Praat (Boersma and Heuven, 2002). The Participation-based Weighted (PW) average of convergence for all pairs p in a group is then computed as follows:

$$Conv_{PW} = \frac{\sum_{\forall p \in group}(Conv_p * PR_p)}{Num_p \sum_{\forall p \in group} PR_p} \quad (3)$$

Num_p indicates number of pairs, and Participation Ratio for a pair, PR_p, for the two intervals is the sum of PRs for both speakers and in both intervals. Finally, convergence for pair $p = (i, j)$ and for two disjoint intervals t_1 and t_2 is calculated as in Equation 4:

$$Conv_{p=(i,j)} = (|f_{i,t_1} - f_{j,t_1}| - |f_{i,t_2} - f_{j,t_2}|) \quad (4)$$

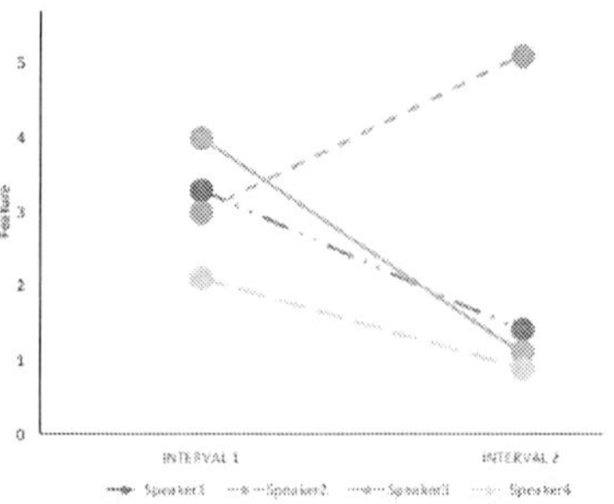

Figure 1: A group in which all speakers except Speaker2 are converging to each other.

2.2 Weighting Based on Group Dynamics

Although participation-based weighting decreases the contribution of less active speakers when calculating group convergence, it does not take group convergence dynamics into account. Rahimi et al. (Rahimi et al., 2017b) argue that it might instead be better to decrease the contribution of speakers whose convergence behaviors differ from the rest of the group (e.g., $Speaker2$ in Figure 1). To tackle this issue, we use weighting to decrease the contribution of outlier speakers. In particular, we propose that the weight for a speaker should be the percentage of individuals who have the same convergence behavior as the speaker.

Equation 5 defines our proposed Group Dynamic-Based Weighted (GDW) convergence measure:

$$Conv_{GDW} = \sum_{g \in G} \frac{|g|}{|N|} * \frac{\sum_{i \in g} \sum_{j \neq i \in N} Conv_{ij}}{|Num_{pair}|} \quad (5)$$

G is a set including three categories: $G = \{Converging, Diverging, MixedBehavior\}$, g is a set of all individuals who belong to a category in G, $|N|$ is the number of all speakers in the group, and $|Num_{pair}|$ is the number of pairs.

Consider the example in Figure 1. There are 12 pairs (6 unique pairs since convergence is a symmetric measure). Each speaker is in three unique pairs with the other three members of the group.

If all conversational pairs that a speaker is involved in have positive convergence values, the speaker is converging to the group and has the $Converging$ category. If all involved pairs have negative value, the speaker is diverging from the group. Else, the speaker has a mixed-behavior.

The weight for each category is the number of speakers who have corresponding behavior normalized by the group size. For example, in a group where all members diverge from each other, the weights will be: $converging = 0$, $diverging = 1$, and $mixedBehavior = 0$. For the group in Figure 1, weights are: $converging = 0$, $diverging = 1/4$, and $mixedBehavior = 3/4$. So, the group convergence for this example is as follows, where $C(i)$ is shortened for sum of pair convergences for speaker i:

$$Conv_{GDW} = 0 * 0 + \frac{1}{4} * C(2)$$
$$+ \frac{3}{4} * [C(1) + C(3) + C(4)] \quad (6)$$

3 Data

To evaluate the utility of weighting based on group dynamics, we measure acoustic-prosodic convergence in the Teams Corpus (Litman et al., 2016). The corpus includes audio files for 62 teams of 3 or 4 individuals playing a cooperative board game in two sessions. First games (Game1) take significantly longer than second games (Game2) (27.1 vs. 18.4 minutes, $p < .001$) and are in chronological order. The teams are disjoint in participants. We break each game into four equal intervals[1] (including silences) and choose the first and last intervals to compute convergence for eight acoustic-prosodic features: maximum (max), mean, and standard deviation (SD) of pitch; max, mean, and SD of intensity; local jitter[2]; and local shimmer[3]. The features are extracted from each of the first and last intervals for each speaker in each team.

Individually taken self-reported pre- and post-game surveys are available for both sessions, including: (1) favorable social outcome measures (perceptions of cohesion, satisfaction, potency/efficacy and perceptions of shared cognition), and (2) conflict measures (task, process, and relationship conflicts). Since favorable measures have high correlations, we z-scored each separate outcome and averaged these scores to make a single omnibus favorable group perception scale and then averaged them for each team to create a team-level **Favorable** measure. Since process conflict was the only conflict measure that could be split at the median without making arbitrary choices[4], we z-scored the process conflict and averaged it in the

groups to construct a team-level **Process Conflict** measure. **Favorable** and **Process Conflict** will be used to evaluate the quality of the different convergence measures from Section 2.

4 Experiments and Discussion

Our experimental evaluations use two tasks that have been used for convergence measure evaluations in previous studies (De Looze et al., 2014; Lee et al., 2011; Jain et al., 2012; Rahimi et al., 2017a; Doyle et al., 2016; Lee et al., 2011).

Predicting Social Outcomes: Our first task examines how the NW, PW, and GDW measures of acoustic-prosodic convergence (independent variables) relate to the social outcome measures (dependent variables) from Section 3. This is similar to prior studies which have evaluated convergence in terms of predicting outcomes (Doyle et al., 2016; Lee et al., 2011; Rahimi et al., 2017a). We hypothesize that the group-dynamic weighted convergence measure will outperform the non-weighted and participation-based measures.

First, we train a hierarchical multiple regression with each of the three groups of convergence measures, added once in the first level and the other time in the second, to measure if the second level predictors significantly improve the explanation of variance. We only keep predictors with significant coefficients when presenting the models.[5]

For **Process Conflict,** the results show that all NW, PW, and GDW predictor groups are as good as each other; no matter which group is entered in the first level, the predictors in the second level do not significantly improve model fit.

For **Favorable,** neither PW nor NW in the second level significantly improves performance. However, Table 1 shows that adding the GDW measures at the second level significantly improves a model with only NW features at the first level. The amount of variance explained in Model 2 is significantly above and beyond Model 1, $\Delta R^2 = 0.048$, $\Delta F(2, 119) = 3.179$, $p = 0.045$. The reverse order, GDW at first level and NW at the second level, shows that the improvement at the second level is not significant, $\Delta R^2 = 0.031$, $\Delta F(2, 119) = 2.068$, $p = 0.131$. These results indicate that the proposed weighted (GDW) convergence (for intensity max and SD) are the best

---

[1] Any method of breaking the games to compare two disjoint intervals can be used.

[2] The average absolute difference between the amplitudes of consecutive periods, divided by the average amplitude.

[3] The average absolute difference between consecutive periods, divided by the average amplitude.

[4] The median split is required for our classification tasks.

[5] To control for the effect of first versus second dialogue (game) for each group, we also included an independent variable for game. However, the coefficient was never significant.

	Independent Vars	M1 (β)	M2 (β)
	Intensity_max (NW)	0.248*	-0.164
	Intensity_SD(NW)	-0.055	-0.479+
	Intensity_max(GDW)		0.430+
	Intensity_SD(GDW)		0.457+
R^2		0.063	0.110
F		4.034*	3.678*

Table 1: Hierarchical regression results with intensity max and SD convergence as independent, and **Favorable** as dependent, variables. The NW measures are added in the first level and GDW measures in the second level. Significant / trending results if p-value is < 0.05 (*) or < 0.1 (+).

	Favorable	Process Conflict
Majority	50	53
NW	50	66.93
PW	53.23	**67.74+**(GDW)
GDW	**62.90****	62.90
GDW+PW	58.87	66.13

Table 2: LOOCV prediction accuracies of binary favorable social outcome and process conflict variables. (**) indicates GWD model significantly outperforms both PW and NW models. (+) indicates PW improvement over GDW is trending.

predictors of the favorable social outcome compared with the other two measures of convergence.

Next, we reduce the task from regression to a binary classification by splitting the two social outcome variables at the median. We perform Leave-One-Out Cross-Validations (LOOCV) using a logistic regression (L2) algorithm and all eight acoustic-prosodic features to predict binary outcomes. The results in Table 2 show that the GWD model significantly[6] outperforms both PW and NW models to predict the favorable social outcome. In the prediction of process conflict, the PW model outperforms both NW and GDW models and its improvement over GDW is trending.

In sum, the results in both tables support our hypothesis for the favorable social outcome, where the proposed GDW convergence measure is a better predictor of the outcome. For process conflict, we do not see any significant difference.

Predicting Real Dialogues: The existence of entrainment should not be incidental. To evaluate this criteria, we use permuted versus real conversations as in (De Looze et al., 2014; Lee et al., 2011; Jain et al., 2012). We hypothesize that GDW will be the best convergence measure for distin-

---

	All	Game1	Game2
Majority	50	50	50
NW	54.43	60.48	49.19
PW	53.62	58.06	51.61
GDW	54.03	**67.74*+**	48.39

Table 3: Accuracies using the linear SVM models and LOOCV to predict real conversations. (+) indicates GWD outperforms NW with p = 0.06 , (*) indicates GWD outperforms PW with p = 0.004.

guishing real versus permuted dialogues.

For each of the 124 game sessions, we construct artificially permuted versions of the real dialogues as follows. For each speaker, we randomly permute the silence and speech intervals extracted by Praat. Next, we measure convergence for all the groups with permuted audios. We perform a leave-one-out cross-validation experiment to predict real conversations using the convergence measures. We examined several classification algorithms including logistic regression; linear SVM was the only one that showed significant results.

The "All" results in Table 3 show that none of the models significantly outperform the majority baseline. To diagnose the issue, we perform the prediction on each game separately. The proposed GDW model significantly outperforms other models for Game 1. However, for Game 2, none of the results are significantly different. One reason might be that convergence occurs quickly during Game 1, and there is not much convergence occurring at Game 2. Thus, there is no significant difference between permuted and not permuted convergence for any of the features during Game 2.

5 Conclusion

In this paper, we introduced a new weighted convergence measure for multi-party entrainment which utilizes group convergence dynamics to weight pair convergences. Experimental results show that the proposed weighted measure is more predictive for two evaluation tasks used in prior entrainment studies: predicting favorable social outcomes and predicting real versus permuted conversations. In future work we plan to apply the proposed weighted convergence measure to features other than acoustic-prosodic, e.g., lexical.

Acknowledgments

This work is supported by NSF 1420784,1420377. We thank Susannah Paletz for her feedback.

---

[6]Corrected paired t-test was performed to address instance dependency from both games (Nadeau and Bengio, 2000).

References

Paul Boersma and Vincent van Heuven. 2002. Praat, a system for doing phonetics by computer. *Glot international*, 5(9/10):341–345.

Cristian Danescu-Niculescu-Mizil, Lillian Lee, Bo Pang, and Jon Kleinberg. 2012. Echoes of power: Language effects and power differences in social interaction. In *Proceedings of WWW*, pages 699–708.

Celine De Looze, Stefan Scherer, Brian Vaughan, and Nick Cambpell. 2014. Investigating automatic measurements of prosodic accommodation and its dynamics in social interaction. *Speech Communication*, 58:11–34.

Gabriel Doyle and Michael C Frank. 2016. Investigating the sources of linguistic alignment in conversation. In *ACL (1)*.

Gabriel Doyle, Dan Yurovsky, and Michael C Frank. 2016. A robust framework for estimating linguistic alignment in twitter conversations. In *Proceedings of the 25th international conference on world wide web*, pages 637–648. International World Wide Web Conferences Steering Committee.

Heather Friedberg, Diane Litman, and Susannah B. F. Paletz. 2012. Lexical entrainment and success in student engineering groups. In *Proceedings Fourth IEEE Workshop on Spoken Language Technology (SLT)*, Miami, Florida.

Amy L. Gonzales, Jeffrey T. Hancock, and James W. Pennebaker. 2010. Language style matching as a predictor of social dynamics in small groups. *Communication Research*, 37:3–19.

Mahaveer Jain, John W. McDonough, Gahgene Gweon, Bhiksha Raj, and Carolyn Penstein Ros. 2012. An unsupervised dynamic bayesian network approach to measuring speech style accommodation. In *EACL*, pages 787–797.

Chi-Chun Lee, Athanasios Katsamanis, Matthew P. Black, Brian R. Baucom, Panayiotis G. Georgiou, and Shrikanth Narayanan. 2011. An analysis of pca-based vocal entrainment measures in married couples' affective spoken interactions. In *INTERSPEECH*, pages 3101–3104.

Rivka Levitan, Agustín Gravano, Laura Willson, Stefan Benus, Julia Hirschberg, and Ani Nenkova. 2012. Acoustic-prosodic entrainment and social behavior. In *2012 Conference of the North American Chapter of the Association for Computational Linguistics: Human Language Technologies*, pages 11–19.

Rivka Levitan and Julia Hirschberg. 2011. Measuring acoustic-prosodic entrainment with respect to multiple levels and dimensions. In *Interspeech*.

Diane Litman, Susannah Paletz, Zahra Rahimi, Stefani Allegretti, and Caitlin Rice. 2016. The teams corpus and entrainment in multi-party spoken dialogues. In *Proceedings of the 2016 Conference on Empirical Methods in Natural Language Processing*, pages 1421–1431.

José Lopes, Maxine Eskenazi, and Isabel Trancoso. 2013. Automated two-way entrainment to improve spoken dialog system performance. In *ICASSP*, pages 8372–8376.

Nichola Lubold and Heather Pon-Barry. 2014. Acoustic-prosodic entrainment and rapport in collaborative learning dialogues. In *Proceedings of the 2014 ACM workshop on Multimodal Learning Analytics Workshop and Grand Challenge*, pages 5–12. ACM.

Nichola Lubold, Heather Pon-Barry, and Erin Walker. 2015. Naturalness and rapport in a pitch adaptive learning companion. In *Automatic Speech Recognition and Understanding (ASRU), 2015 IEEE Workshop on*, pages 103–110. IEEE.

Christopher Michael Mitchell, Kristy Elizabeth Boyer, and James C. Lester. 2012. From strangers to partners: Examining convergence within a longitudinal study of task-oriented dialogue. In *SIGDIAL Conference*, pages 94–98.

Seungwhan Moon, Saloni Potdar, and Lara Martin. 2014. Identifying student leaders from mooc discussion forums through language influence. In *Proceedings of the EMNLP 2014 Workshop on Analysis of Large Scale Social Interaction in MOOCs*, pages 15–20.

Claude Nadeau and Yoshua Bengio. 2000. Inference for the generalization error. In *Advances in neural information processing systems*, pages 307–313.

Ani Nenkova, Agustín Gravano, and Julia Hirschberg. 2008. High frequency word entrainment in spoken dialogue. In *Proceedings of the 46th Annual Meeting of the Association for Computational Linguistics on Human Language Technologies: Short Papers*, HLT-Short '08, pages 169–172.

Zahra Rahimi, Anish Kumar, Diane Litman, Susannah Paletz, and Mingzhi Yu. 2017a. Entrainment in multi-party spoken dialogues at multiple linguistic levels. *Proc. Interspeech 2017*, pages 1696–1700.

Zahra Rahimi, Diane Litman, and Susannah Paletz. 2017b. Acoustic-prosodic entrainment in multiparty spoken dialogues: Does simple averaging extend existing pair measures properly? In *International Workshop On Spoken Dialogue Systems Technology*.

David Reitter and Johanna D. Moore. 2007. Predicting success in dialogue. In *Proceedings of the 45th Meeting of the Association of Computational Linguistics*, pages 808–815.

Tanmay Sinha and Justine Cassell. 2015. Fine-grained
analyses of interpersonal processes and their effect
on learning. In *Artificial Intelligence in Education:
17th International Conference*, pages 781–785.

Svetlana Stoyanchev and Amanda Stent. 2009. Lexical
and syntactic priming and their impact in deployed
spoken dialog systems. In *Proceedings of Human
Language Technologies: The 2009 Annual Conference of the North American Chapter of the Association for Computational Linguistics, Companion Volume: Short Papers*, NAACL-Short '09, pages 189–
192, Stroudsburg, PA, USA. Association for Computational Linguistics.

Concept Transfer Learning for Adaptive Language Understanding

Su Zhu and **Kai Yu** *

Key Laboratory of Shanghai Education Commission for Intelligent Interaction and Cognitive Engineering
SpeechLab, Department of Computer Science and Engineering
Brain Science and Technology Research Center
Shanghai Jiao Tong University, Shanghai, China
{paul2204,kai.yu}@sjtu.edu.cn

Abstract

Concept definition is important in language understanding (LU) adaptation since literal definition difference can easily lead to data sparsity even if different data sets are actually semantically correlated. To address this issue, in this paper, a novel concept transfer learning approach is proposed. Here, substructures within literal concept definition are investigated to reveal the relationship between concepts. A hierarchical semantic representation for concepts is proposed, where a semantic slot is represented as a composition of *atomic concepts*. Based on this new hierarchical representation, transfer learning approaches are developed for adaptive LU. The approaches are applied to two tasks: value set mismatch and domain adaptation, and evaluated on two LU benchmarks: ATIS and DSTC 2&3. Thorough empirical studies validate both the efficiency and effectiveness of the proposed method. In particular, we achieve state-of-the-art performance (F_1-score 96.08%) on ATIS by only using lexicon features.

1 Introduction

The language understanding (LU) module is a key component of dialogue system (DS), parsing user's utterances into corresponding semantic concepts (or semantic slots [1]). For example, the utterance *"Show me flights from Boston to New York"* can be parsed into *(from_city=Boston, to_city=New York)* (Pieraccini et al., 1992). Typically, the LU is seen as a plain slot filling task.

____

The corresponding author is Kai Yu.

[1] Slot and concept are equal in LU. They will be mixed in the rest of this paper to some extent.

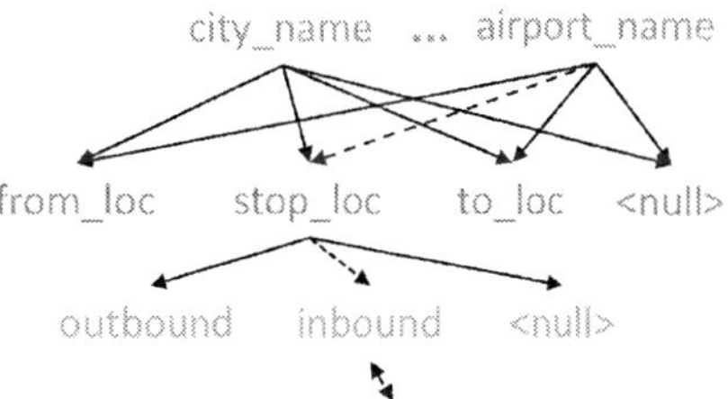

Figure 1: An example of hierarchical structure to represent semantic slot with atomic concepts. There are three levels in this structure. The plain slot $SLOT$ (*transfer airport of the inbound flight*) can be represented as a tuple of atomic concepts sequentially.

With sufficient in-domain data and deep learning models (e.g. recurrent neural networks, bidirectional long-short term memory network), statistical methods have achieved satisfactory performance in the slot filling task recently (Kurata et al., 2016; Vu, 2016; Liu and Lane, 2016).

However, retrieving sufficient in-domain data for training LU model (Tur et al., 2010) is unrealistic, especially when the semantic slot extends or dialogue domain changes. The ability of LU approaches to cope with changed domains and limited data is a key to the deployment of commercial dialogue systems (e.g. Apple Siri, Amazon Alexa, Google Home, Microsoft Cortana etc).

In this paper, we investigate substructure of semantic slots to find out slot relations and promote data reuse. We represent semantic slots with a hierarchical structure based on atomic concept tuple, as shown in Figure 1. Each semantic slot is composed of different atomic concepts, e.g. slot *"from_city"* can be defined as a tuple of atoms [*"from_location"*, *"city_name"*],

Proceedings of the SIGDIAL 2018 Conference, pages 391–399,
Melbourne, Australia, 12-14 July 2018. ©2018 Association for Computational Linguistics

Train: Show flights from [Boston:*FC*] to [Atlanta:*TC*].
I am going to leave [Michigan:*FC*] to [Indiana:*TC*].

Test: I am going to leave [Atlanta:*FC*] to [Boston:*TC*].

Figure 2: An example of mismatched LU datasets labelled with *[value: slot]*. *FC* refers to *"from_city"*. *TC* refers to *"to_city"*.

and *"date_of_birth"* can be defined as [*"date"*, *"birth"*].

Unlike the traditional slot definition on a plain level; modeling on the atomic concepts helps identify linguistic patterns of related slots by atom sharing, and even decrease the required amount of training data. For example, the training and test sets are unmatched in Figure 2, whereas the patterns of atomic concepts (e.g. *"from"*, *"to"*, *"city"*) can be shared.

In this paper, we investigate the slot filling task switching from plain slots to hierarchical structures by proposing the novel atomic concept tuples which are constructed manually. For comparison, we also introduce a competitive method which automatically learns slot representation from the word sequence of each slot name. Our methods are applied to value set mismatch and domain adaptation problems on ATIS (Hemphill et al., 1995) and DSTC 2&3 (Henderson et al., 2013) respectively. As shown in the experimental results, the slot-filling based on concept transfer learning is effective in solving the value set mismatch and domain adaptation problems. The concept transfer learning method especially achieves state-of-the-art performance (F_1-score 96.08%) on the ATIS task.

The rest of the paper is organized as follows. The next section is about the relation to prior work. The atomic concept tuple is introduced in section 3. The proposed concept transfer learning is then described in section 4. Section 5 describes a competitive method with slot embedding derived from the literal descriptions of slot names. In section 6, the proposed approach is evaluated on the value set mismatch and domain adaptation problems. Finally, our conclusions are presented in section 7.

2 Related Work

Slot Filling in LU Zettlemoyer and Collins (2007) proposed a grammar induction method by learning a Probabilistic Combinatory Categorial Grammar (PCCG) from logical-form annotations. As a grammar-based method, PCCG is close to a hierarchical concepts structure in grammar generation and combination. But this grammar-based method does not possess high generalization capability for atomic concept sharing, and heavily depends on a well-defined lexicon set.

Recent research on statistical slot filling in LU has been focused on the Recurrent Neural Network (RNN) and its extensions. At first, RNN outperformed CRF (Conditional Random Field) on the ATIS dataset (Yao et al., 2013; Mesnil et al., 2013). Long-short term memory network (LSTM) was introduced to obtain a marginal improvement over RNN (Yao et al., 2014). After that, many RNN variations were proposed: encoder-labeler model (Kurata et al., 2016), attention model (Liu and Lane, 2016; Zhu and Yu, 2017) etc. However, these work only predicted the plain semantic slot, not the structure of atomic concepts.

Domain Adaptation in LU For the domain adaptation in LU, Zhu et al. (2014) proposed generating spoken language surface forms by using patterns of the source domain and the ontology of the target domain. With regard to the unsupervised LU, Heck and Hakkani-Tur (2012) exploited the structure of semantic knowledge graphs from the web to create natural language surface forms of entity-relation-entity portions of knowledge graphs. For the zero-shot learning of LU, Ferreira et al. (2015); Yazdani and Henderson (2015) proposed a model to calculate similarity scores between an input sentence and semantic items. In this paper, we focus on the extension of slots with limited seed data.

3 Atomic Concept Tuples

Although concept definition is one of the most crucial problems of LU, there is no unified surface form for the domain ontology. Even for the same semantic slot, names of this slot may be quite different. For example, the city where the flight departs may be called *"from_city"*, *"depart_city"* or *"from_loc.city_name"*. Ontology definitions from different groups may be similar but not consistent, which is not convenient for data reuse. Meanwhile, semantic slots defined in traditional LU systems are on a plain level, while there is no structure to indicate their relation.

To solve this problem, we propose to use atomic concepts to represent the semantic slots. Atomic concepts are exploited to break down the slots. We represent the semantic slots as atomic concept tuples (Figure 1 is an example). The semantic slot composed of these atomic concepts can keep a unified resource for concept definition and extend the semantic knowledge flexibly.

We propose a criteria to construct atomic concept manually. For a given vocabulary C of the atomic concepts, a semantic slot s can be represented by a tuple $[c_1, c_2, ..., c_k]$, where $c_i \in C$ is in the i-th dimension and k is tuple length. In particular, a "*null*" atom is introduced for each dimension. Table 1 illustrates an example of slot representation on the ATIS task. To avoid a scratch concept branch, we make a constraint:

$$C_i \cap C_j = \{null\}, 1 \le i \ne j \le k$$

where C_i ($1 \le i \le k$) denotes all possible atomic concepts which exist in dimension i (i.e. $c_i \in C_i$). The concept tuple is ordered.

In general, atomic concepts can be classified into two categories, one is value-aware and the other is context-aware. The principle for defining slot as a concept branch is: lower dimension less context-aware. For example, "*city_name*" and "*airport_name*" depend on rare context (value-aware). They should be located in the first dimension. "*from_location*" depends on the context like a pattern of "*a flight leaves [city_name]*", which should be in the second dimension. The atomic concept tuple shows the inner relation between different semantic slots explicitly.

slot	atomic concept tuple
city	[*city_name, null*]
from_city	[*city_name, from_location*]
depart_city	[*city_name, from_location*]
arrive_airport	[*airport_name, to_location*]

Table 1: An example of slot representation by atomic concepts.

Therefore, the procedure of constructing atomic concept tuples for slots can be divided into the following steps.

- Firstly, we build a vocabulary C of the atomic concepts for all the slots. By analyzing the conceptual intersection of different slots, we can split the slots into smaller ones which are called atomic concepts. After that, each slot is represented as a set of atomic concepts which are not ordered.

- Secondly, we gather the atoms into different groups. Atomic concepts from the same group should be mutually exclusive. Therefore we can investigate the inner relation and outer relation of these groups.

- Finally, each group is associated with one dimension (C_i) of the atomic concept tuple. The groups are ordered depending on whether they are value-aware or context-aware.

4 Concept Transfer Learning

The slot filling is typically considered as a sequence labelling problem. In this paper, we only consider the sequence-labelling based slot filling task. The input (word) sequence is denoted by $\mathbf{w} = (w_1, w_2, ..., w_N)$, and the output (slot tag) sequence is denoted by $\mathbf{s} = (s_1, s_2, ..., s_N)$. Since a slot may be mapped to several continuous words, we follow the popular in/out/begin (IOB) representation (e.g. an example in Figure 3).

Words	show	flights	from	Boston	to	New	York	today
Slots	O	O	O	B-FromCity	O	B-ToCity	I-ToCity	B-Date

Figure 3: An example of annotation for slot filling.

The typical slot filling task predicts a plain slot sequence given a word sequence, dubbed as **plain slot-filling (PS)**.

In this paper, the popular bidirectional LSTM-RNN (BLSTM) is used to model the sequence labeling problem (Graves, 2012). It can be exploited to capture both past and future features for a specific time frame. The BLSTM reads the input sentence $\mathbf{w}$ and generates N hidden states $h_i = \overleftarrow{h_i} \oplus \overrightarrow{h_i}, i \in \{1, .., N\}$:

$$\overleftarrow{h_i} = b(\overleftarrow{h_{i+1}}, e_{w_i}); \quad \overrightarrow{h_i} = f(\overrightarrow{h_{i-1}}, e_{w_i})$$

where $\overleftarrow{h_i}$ is the hidden vector of the backward pass in BLSTM and $\overrightarrow{h_i}$ is the hidden vector of the forward pass in BLSTM at time i, b and f are LSTM units of the backward and forward passes respectively, e_w denotes the word embedding for each word w, and $\oplus$ denotes the vector concatenation operation. We write the entire operation as a mapping BLSTM_{Θ^w} (Θ^w refers to the parameters):

$$(h_1...h_N) = \text{BLSTM}_{\Theta^w}(w_1...w_N) \qquad (1)$$

Therefore, the plain slot filling defines a distribution over slot tag sequences given an input word

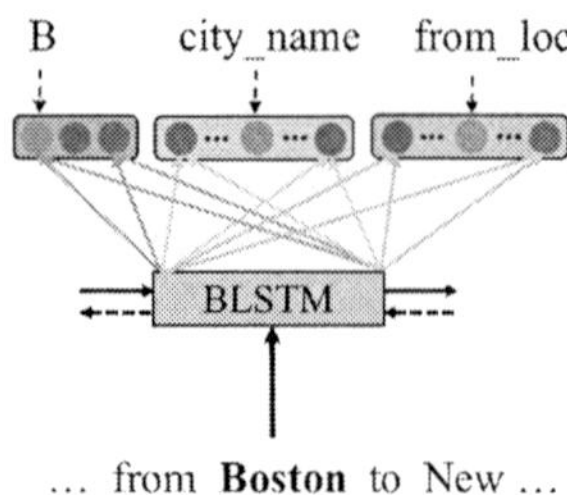

(a) *Atomic concept independent (AC)*

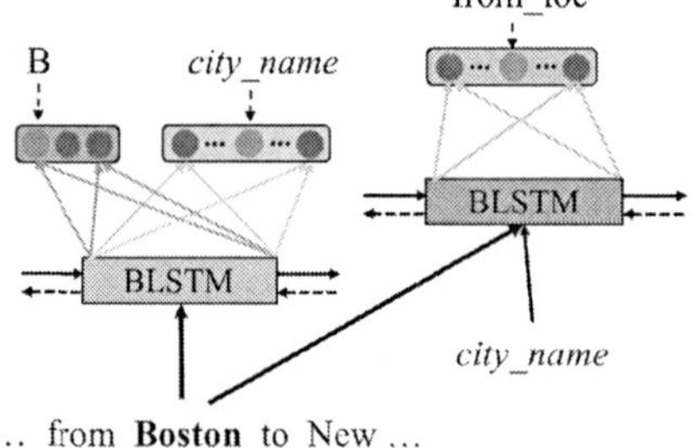

(b) *Atomic concept dependent (ACD)*

Figure 4: The proposed method about the atomic-concepts based slot filling. A slot is considered as a tuple of atomic concepts, e.g. *"from_city"* is represented as [*"city_name"*, *"from_loc"*]. Multiple output layers are utilized to predict different atoms (including IOB schema). We involve two architectures: a) the AC assumes that the output layers are independent, b) while the ACD makes a dependence assumption.

sequence:

$$p(\mathbf{s}|\mathbf{w}) = \prod_{i=1}^{N} p(s_i|h_i)$$
$$= \prod_{i=1}^{N} \text{softmax}(W_o \cdot h_i)^T \delta_{s_i} \qquad (2)$$

where the matrix W_o (output layer) consists of the vector representations of each slot tag, the symbol δ_d is a Kronecker delta with a dimension for each slot tag, and the *softmax* function is used to estimate the probability distribution over all possible plain slots.

4.1 Atomic-Concepts Based Slot Filling

The slot is indicated as an atomic concept tuple based on hierarchical concept structure. Slot filling is considered as a concept-tuple labelling task.

(a) Atomic concept independent

Slot filling can be transferred to a multi-task sequence labelling problem, regarding these atomic concepts **independently** (i.e. **AC**). Each task predicts one atomic concept by a respective output layer. Thus, the slot filling problem can be formulated as

$$p(\mathbf{s}|\mathbf{w}) = \prod_{i=1}^{N} [p(\text{IOB}_i|h_i) \prod_{j=1}^{k} p(c_{ij}|h_i)]$$

where the semantic slot s_i is represented by an atomic concept branch $[c_{i1}, c_{i2}, ..., c_{ik}]$, and IOB_i is the IOB schema tag at time i. As illustrated in Figure 4(a), the semantic slot *"from_city"* can be represented as [*"city_name"*, *"from_loc"*]. The

prediction of IOB is regarded as another task specifically. All tasks share the same parameters except for the output layers.

(b) Atomic concept dependent

Atomic concepts can also be regarded **dependently** (i.e. **ACD**) so that atomic concept prediction depends on the former predicted results. The slot filling problem can be formulated as

$$p(\mathbf{s}|\mathbf{w})$$
$$= \prod_{i=1}^{N} [p(\text{IOB}_i|h_i)p(c_{i1}|h_i) \prod_{j=2}^{k} p(c_{ij}|h_i, c_{i,1:j-1})]$$

where $c_{i,1:j-1} = (c_{i,1}, ..., c_{i,j-1})$ is the predicted result of former atomic concepts of slot tag s_i, indicating a structured multi-task learning framework.

In this paper, we make some simplifications on concept dependence. We predict atomic concept only based on the last atomic concept, as shown in Figure 4(b).

4.2 Training and Decoding

Since our approach is a structured multi-task learning problem, the model loss is summed over each task during training. For the domain adaptation, we firstly gather training data from the source domain and seed data from the target domain to be a union set. Subsequently, the union data is fed into the slot filling model.

During the decoding stage, we combine predicted atomic concepts with probability multiplication. The evaluation is made on the top-best hypothesis. Although the atomic-concepts based slot filling may predict an unseen slot. We didn't perform any post-processing but considered the unseen slot as a wrong prediction.

5 Literal Description of Slot Name

In the section, we introduce a competitive system which uses the literal description of the slot as an input of the slot filling model. The literal description of slot used in this paper is the word sequence of each slot name, which can be obtained automatically. As the names of relative slots may include the same or similar word, the word sequence of slot name can also help reveal the relation between different slots. Therefore, it is very meaningful to compare this method with the atomic concept tuples involving human knowledge.

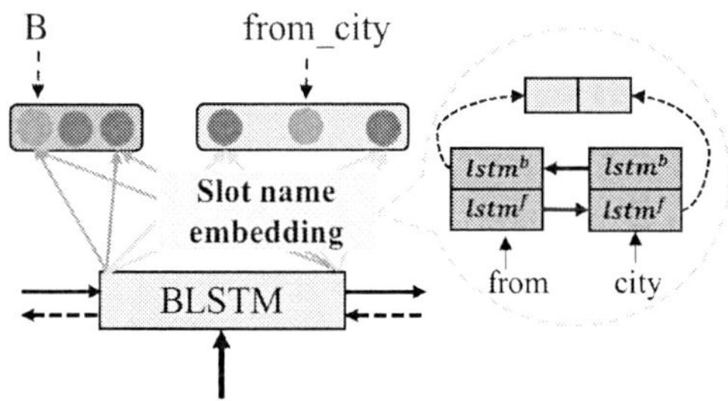

Figure 5: The proposed framework of slot filling based on the literal description of the slot. The literal description of a slot is the word sequence of slot name which can be obtained automatically, e.g. *"from_city"* is represented as a word sequence of "from city". Another BLSTM in the orange dotted circle is exploited to derive softmax embeddings from the slot names.

The architecture of this competitive system is illustrated in Figure 5. First, it assumes that each slot name is a meaningful natural language description so that the slot filling task is tractable from the input word sequence and slot name. Second, another BLSTM model is applied to derive softmax embedding from the slot names. In this method, we also split the slot filling task into IOB tag prediction and slot name prediction. In other words, the slot tag s_i is broken down into IOB_i and slot name SN_i, e.g. the slot tag "B-*from_city*" is split into "B" and *"from_city"*. The details are indicated below.

With the BLSTM applied on the input sequence, we have hidden vectors $h_i, i \in \{1, .., N\}$ as shown in Eqn. (1). This model redefines the distribution over slot tag sequences given an input word sequence, compared with Eqn. (2):

$$p(\mathbf{s}|\mathbf{w}) = \prod_{i=1}^{N} p(\text{IOB}_i|h_i)p(\text{SN}_i|h_i)$$

where $p(\text{IOB}_i|h_i)$ predicts the IOB tag and $p(\text{SN}_i|h_i)$ makes a prediction for the slot name. We define

$$p(\text{SN}_i|h_i) = \text{softmax}(W \cdot h_i)^T \delta_{\text{SN}_i}$$

where $W \in \mathbb{R}^{A \times B}$ is a matrix, $h_i \in \mathbb{R}^B$ is a vector, A is the number of all different slot names. The matrix W consists of the embedding of each slot name (i.e. each row vector of W with length B).

To capture the slot relation within different slot names, we apply another BLSTM model (as shown in the orange dotted circle of Figure 5) onto the word sequence (literal description) of each slot name. For the j-th slot name ($j \in \{1, .., A\}$) with a word sequence $\mathbf{x}^j = (x_1^j, ..., x_{N_j}^j)$, we have

$$\overleftarrow{v_n^j} = \text{lstm}^b(\overleftarrow{v_{n+1}^j}, e_{x_n^j}); \quad \overrightarrow{v_n^j} = \text{lstm}^f(\overrightarrow{v_{n-1}^j}, e_{x_n^j})$$

where $\overleftarrow{v_n^j}$ is the hidden vector of the backward pass and $\overrightarrow{v_n^j}$ is the hidden vector of the forward pass at time n ($n \in \{1, .., N_j\}$), e_x denotes the word embedding for each word x. We take the tails of both backward and forward pass as the slot embedding, i.e.

$$W_j = \overleftarrow{v_1^j} \oplus \overrightarrow{v_{N_j}^j}$$

where W_j is the j-th row vector of matrix W.

The relative slots using the same or similar word in slot naming will be close in the space of slot embedding inherently. Therefore, this method is a competitive system to the atomic concept tuples. We will show the comparison in the following section.

6 Experiments

We evaluate our atomic-concept methods on two tasks: value set mismatch and domain adaptation.

Value set mismatch task evaluates the generalization capability of different slot filling models. In a language understanding (LU) system, each slot has a value set with all possible values which can be assigned to it. Since the semantically annotated data is always limited, only a part of values is seen in the training data. Will the slot filling model perform well on the unseen values? To answer this question, we synthesize a test set by the values mismatched with the training set of ATIS corpus. Our methods may take advantages of the prior knowledge about slot relations based on the atomic concepts and the literal descriptions of slot names.

Domain adaptation task evaluates the adaptation capability of our methods when they meet new slots in the target domain. In this task, a seed training set of the target domain is provided. However, it is very limited: 1) some new slots may not be covered; 2) not all contexts are covered for each new slot. The atomic-concepts based method would alleviate this problem. Each slot is defined as a tuple of atomic concepts in our method. Therefore, it is possible to learn an unseen slot of the target domain if its atomic concepts exist in the data of the source domain and the seed data of the target domain. It is also possible to see more contexts for a new slot if its atomic concepts exist in the source domain which has much more data.

6.1 Value Set Mismatch

ATIS corpus has been widely used as a benchmark by the LU community. The training data consists of 4978 sentences and the test data consists of 893 sentences.

In this task, we perform an adaptation for unmatched training and test sets, in which there are many unseen slot-value pairs in the test set (Figure 2 is an example). It is a common problem in the development of commercial dialogue system since it is impossible to collect data covering all possible slot-value pairs. We simulate this problem on the ATIS dataset (Hemphill et al., 1995) by creating an unmatched test set (**ATIS_X_test**).

ATIS_X_test is synthesized from the standard ATIS test set by randomly replacing the value of each slot with an unseen one. The unseen value sets are collected from the training set according to bottom-level concepts (e.g. *"city_name"*, *"airport_name"*). For example, if the value set of *"from_city"* is {*"New York"*, *"Boston"*} and the value set of *"to_city"* is {*"Boston"*}, then the unseen value for *"to_city"* is *"New York"*. The test sentence *"Flights to [xx:to_city]"* can be replaced to *"Flights to [New York:to_city]"*. Finally, the ATIS_X_test gets the same sentence number to the standard ATIS test set.

6.1.1 Experimental Settings

We randomly selected 80% of the training data for model training and the remaining 20% for validation. We deal with unseen words in the test set by marking any words with only one single occurrence in the training set as $\langle unk \rangle$. We also converted sequences of numbers to the string DIGIT, e.g. 1990 is converted to DIGIT*4 (Zhang and Wang, 2016). Regarding BLSTM model, we set the dimension of word embeddings to 100 and the number of hidden units to 100. For training, the network parameters are randomly initialized in accordance with the uniform distribution (-0.2, 0.2). Stochastic gradient descent (SGD) is used for updating parameters. The *dropout* with a probability of 0.5 is applied to the non-recurrent connections during the training stage.

We try different learning rates by grid-search in range of $[0.008, 0.04]$. We keep the learning rate for 100 epochs and save the parameters that give the best performance on the validation set. Finally, we report the F_1-score of the semantic slots on the test set with parameters that have achieved the best F_1-score on the validation set. The F_1-score is calculated using CoNLL evaluation script. [2]

6.1.2 Experimental Results and Analysis

Table 2 summarizes the recently published results on the ATIS slot filling task and compares them with the results of our proposed methods on the standard ATIS test set. We can see that RNN outperforms CRF because of the ability to capture long-term dependencies. LSTM beats RNN by solving the problem of vanishing or exploding gradients. BLSTM further improves the result by considering both the past and future features. Encoder-decoder achieves the state-of-the-art performance by modeling the label dependencies. Encoder-labeler is a similar method to the Encoder-decoder. These systems are designed to predict the plain semantic slots traditionally.

Compared with the published results, our method outperforms the previously published F1-score, illustrated in Table 2. **AC** gets a marginal improvement (+0.15%) over **PS** by predicting the atomic concepts independently instead of the plain slots. Moreover, **ACD** predicts the atomic concepts dependently, gains 0.50% (significant level 95%) over the **AC**. Worth to mention that **ACD** achieves a new state-of-the-art performance of the

[2] http://www.cnts.ua.ac.be/conll2000/chunking/output.html

Model	ATIS	ATIS_X_test
CRF (Mesnil et al., 2013)	92.94	–
RNN (Mesnil et al., 2013)	94.11	–
LSTM (Yao et al., 2014)	94.85	–
BLSTM (Zhang and Wang, 2016)	95.14	–
Encoder-decoder (Liu and Lane, 2016)	95.72	–
Encoder-labeler (Kurata et al., 2016)	95.66	–
Encoder-decoder-pointer (Zhai et al., 2017)	95.86	–
Encoder-decoder*	95.79	79.84
BLSTM* (PS)	95.43	79.59
PS + dict-feats	95.57	80.74
AC	95.58	80.90
ACD	**96.08**	**86.16**
Slot name embedding	95.52	81.49

Table 2: Comparison with the published results on the standard ATIS task, and evaluation on ATIS_X_test. (* denotes our implementation.)

standard slot-tagging task on the ATIS dataset, with only the lexicon features [3].

Our methods are also tested on the ATIS_X_test to measure the ability of generalization. For comparison, we also apply dictionary features (n-gram indication) of value sets (e.g. some kind of gazetteers) collected from training data into the **PS** model (i.e. PS+*dict-feats* in Table 2). From Table 2, we can see that: 1) The plain slot filling models (**PS**, Encoder-decoder) are not on par with other models. 2) The atomic-concepts based slot filling gets a slight improvement over the **PS** with *dict-feats*, considering the concepts independently (**AC**). 3) The atomic-concepts based slot fillings (**ACD** gains a large margin over **AC**, considering the concepts dependently. 4) The method based on slot name embedding (described in Section 5) achieves a slight improvement than **AC**, which implies that it is possible to reveal the relationship between slots automatically.

Case study: As illustrated in Table 3, the plain slot filling (PS) predicts the label of *"late"* wrongly, whereas the atomic-concepts based slot fillings (i.e. AC and ACD) get the accurate annotation. The word of "late" is never covered by the slot *"period_of_day"* in the training set. It is hard for the plain slot filling (PS) to predict an unseen mapping correctly. Luckily, the "late" is covered by the family of the slot *"period_of_day"* in the training set, e.g. *"arrive_time.period_of_day"*. Therefore, AC and ACD can learn this by modeling the atomic concepts separately.

6.2 Domain Adaptation

Our methods are also evaluated on the DSTC 2&3 task (Henderson et al., 2013) which is considered to be a realistic domain adaptation problem.

DSTC 2 (source domain) comprises of dialogues from the restaurant information domain in Cambridge. We use the **dstc2_train** set (1612 dialogues) for training and the **dstc2_dev** (506 dialogues) for validation.

DSTC 3 (target domain) introduces the tourist information domain about restaurant, pubs and coffee shops in Cambridge, which is an extension of DSTC 2. We use seed data **dstc3_seed** (only 11 dialogues) as the training set of the target domain.

DSTC3_S_test: In this paper, we focus on three new semantic slots: *"has_tv, has_internet, children_allowed"*. [4] They only exist in the DSTC 3 dataset and have few appearances in the seed data. A test set is chosen for specific evaluation on these new semantic slots, by gathering all the sentences (688 sentences) whose annotation contains these three slots and randomly selecting 1000 sentences irrelevant to these three slots from the *dstc3_test* set. This test set is named as **DSTC3_S_test** (1688 sentences).

The union of a slot and action is taken as a plain semantic slot (e.g. *"confirm.food=Chinese"*), since each slot is tied with an action (e.g. *"inform"*, *"deny"* and *"confirm"*) in DSTC 2&3. The slot and action are taken as atomic concepts. For the slot filling task, only the semantic annotation with aligned information is kept, e.g. the semantic tuple *"request(phone)"* is ignored. We use transcripts as input, and make slot-value alignment by

---

[3]There are other published results that achieved better performance by using Name Entity features, e.g. Mesnil et al. (2013) got 96.24% F_1-score. The NE features are manually annotated and strong information. So it would be more meaningful to use only lexicon features. Meanwhile, several other works can obtain competitive results by using the intent classification as another task for joint training, e.g. Liu and Lane (2016) achieved 95.98% F_1-score. In this paper, we consider the slot filling task only.

[4]For each slot of *"has_tv, has_internet, children_allowed"*, the semantic annotation *"request(slot)"* is replaced with *"confirm(slot=True)"*. Then we have the slot-tagging format, e.g. "does it have [television:confirm.has_tv]".

Reference	... could get in [boston:city_name] [late:**period_of_day**] [night:period_of_day]
PS	... could get in [boston:city_name] [late:**airport_name**] [night:period_of_day]
AC	... could get in [boston:city_name] [late:**period_of_day**] [night:period_of_day]
ACD	... could get in [boston:city_name] [late:**period_of_day**] [night:period_of_day]

Table 3: Examples show how concept transfer learning benefits. We use *[value:slot]* for annotation.

string matching simply.

6.2.1 Experimental Results and Analysis

The experimental settings are similar to the ATIS's, whereas the seed data in DSTC 3 is also used for validation.

Model	Training set	F_1-score
PS	dstc3_seed	83.52
PS	dstc2_train + dstc3_seed	89.57
AC	dstc3_seed	83.58
AC	dstc2_train + dstc3_seed	91.98
ACD	dstc2_train + dstc3_seed	**92.15**

Table 4: The performance of our methods evaluated on the DSTC3_S_test.

The performance of our methods in the DSTC 2&3 task is illustrated in Table 4. We can see that: 1) By incorporating the data of the source domain (dstc2_train), **PS** and **AC** achieve improvements respectively. 2) **AC** gains more than **PS** by modeling the plain semantic slot as atomic concepts. The atomic concepts promote the associated slots to share input features for the same atoms. 3) The atomic-concepts based slot filling considering the concepts dependently (**ACD**) gains little (0.17%) over **AC** considering the concepts independently. It may be due to the small size of dstc3_seed.

Case study: Several cases from these models (trained on the union set of dstc2_train and dstc3_seed) are also chosen to explain why the atomic-concepts based slot filling outperforms the typical plain slot filling, as shown in Table 5. From the above part of Table 5, we can see **PS** predicts a wrong slot. Because the grammar *"does it have [something]"* is only for the plain slot *"confirm.hastv"* in the seed data. From the below part of Table 5, we can see that only **ACD** which considers the concepts dependently predicts the right slot. Since *"confirm.childrenallowed"* never exists in the seed data, **PS** can't learn patterns about it. Limited by the quantity of the seed data, **AC** also doesn't extract the semantics correctly.

Reference	does it have [internet:confirm.hasinternet]
PS	does it have [internet:confirm.hastv]
AC	does it have [internet:confirm.hasinternet]
ACD	does it have [internet:confirm.hasinternet]

Reference	do they allow [children:confirm.CA]
PS	do they allow [children:CA]
AC	do they allow [children:CA]
ACD	do they allow [children:confirm.CA]

Table 5: Examples show how concept transfer learning benefits. CA denotes *childrenallowed*.

7 Conclusion

To address data sparsity problem of language understanding (LU) task, we present a novel method of concept definition based on well-defined atomic concepts. We present the concept transfer learning for slot filling on the atomic concept level to solve the problem of adaptive LU. The experiments on the ATIS and DSTC 2&3 datasets show our method obtains promising results and outperforms the traditional slot filling, due to the knowledge sharing of atomic concepts.

The atomic concepts are constructed manually in this paper. In future work, we want to explore more flexible concept definition for concept transfer learning of LU. Moreover, we also propose a competitive method based on slot name embedding which can be extracted from the literal description of the slot name automatically. The experimental result shows that it lays foundation for finding a more flexible concept definition method for adaptive LU.

Acknowledgments

This work has been supported by the China NSFC project (No. 61573241), Shanghai International Science and Technology Cooperation Fund (No. 16550720300) and the JiangSu NSFC project (BE2016078). Experiments have been carried out on the PI supercomputer at Shanghai Jiao Tong University. We also thank Tianfan Fu for comments that greatly improved the manuscript.

References

Emmanuel Ferreira, Bassam Jabaian, and Fabrice Lefvre. 2015. Zero-shot semantic parser for spoken language understanding. In *16th Annual Conference of the International Speech Communication Association (InterSpeech)*.

Alex Graves. 2012. *Supervised Sequence Labelling with Recurrent Neural Networks*. Springer Berlin Heidelberg.

L Heck and D Hakkani-Tur. 2012. Exploiting the semantic web for unsupervised spoken language understanding. In *Spoken Language Technology Workshop*, pages 228–233.

Charles T Hemphill, John J Godfrey, and George R Doddington. 1995. The atis spoken language systems pilot corpus. In *Proceedings of the Darpa Speech and Natural Language Workshop*, pages 96–101.

Matthew Henderson, Blaise Thomson, and Jason Williams. 2013. Dialog state tracking challenge 2 & 3. [online] Available: http://camdial.org/mh521/dstc/.

Gakuto Kurata, Bing Xiang, Bowen Zhou, and Mo Yu. 2016. Leveraging sentence-level information with encoder lstm for semantic slot filling. In *Proceedings of the 2016 Conference on Empirical Methods in Natural Language Processing*, pages 2077–2083, Austin, Texas. Association for Computational Linguistics.

Bing Liu and Ian Lane. 2016. Attention-based recurrent neural network models for joint intent detection and slot filling. In *17th Annual Conference of the International Speech Communication Association (InterSpeech)*.

Grégoire Mesnil, Xiaodong He, Li Deng, and Yoshua Bengio. 2013. Investigation of recurrent-neural-network architectures and learning methods for spoken language understanding. In *INTERSPEECH*, pages 3771–3775.

Roberto Pieraccini, Evelyne Tzoukermann, Zakhar Gorelov, J-L Gauvain, Esther Levin, C-H Lee, and Jay G Wilpon. 1992. A speech understanding system based on statistical representation of semantics. In *Acoustics, Speech, and Signal Processing, 1992. ICASSP-92., 1992 IEEE International Conference on*, volume 1, pages 193–196. IEEE.

Gokhan Tur, Dilek Hakkani-Tür, and Larry Heck. 2010. What is left to be understood in atis? In *Spoken Language Technology Workshop (SLT), 2010 IEEE*, pages 19–24. IEEE.

Ngoc Thang Vu. 2016. Sequential convolutional neural networks for slot filling in spoken language understanding. In *17th Annual Conference of the International Speech Communication Association (InterSpeech)*.

Kaisheng Yao, Baolin Peng, Yu Zhang, Dong Yu, Geoffrey Zweig, and Yangyang Shi. 2014. Spoken language understanding using long short-term memory neural networks. In *2014 IEEE Spoken Language Technology Workshop (SLT)*, pages 189–194. IEEE.

Kaisheng Yao, Geoffrey Zweig, Mei-Yuh Hwang, Yangyang Shi, and Dong Yu. 2013. Recurrent neural networks for language understanding. In *INTERSPEECH*, pages 2524–2528.

Majid Yazdani and James Henderson. 2015. A model of zero-shot learning of spoken language understanding. In *Conference on Empirical Methods in Natural Language Processing*, pages 244–249.

Luke S. Zettlemoyer and Michael Collins. 2007. Online learning of relaxed ccg grammars for parsing to logical form. In *EMNLP-CoNLL 2007, Proceedings of the 2007 Joint Conference on Empirical Methods in Natural Language Processing and Computational Natural Language Learning, June 28-30, 2007, Prague, Czech Republic*, pages 678–687.

Feifei Zhai, Saloni Potdar, Bing Xiang, and Bowen Zhou. 2017. Neural models for sequence chunking. In *AAAI*, pages 3365–3371.

Xiaodong Zhang and Houfeng Wang. 2016. A joint model of intent determination and slot filling for spoken language understanding. In *the Twenty-Fifth International Joint Conference on Artificial Intelligence (IJCAI-16)*.

Su Zhu, Lu Chen, Kai Sun, Da Zheng, and Kai Yu. 2014. Semantic parser enhancement for dialogue domain extension with little data. In *Spoken Language Technology Workshop (SLT), 2014 IEEE*, pages 336–341. IEEE.

Su Zhu and Kai Yu. 2017. Encoder-decoder with focus-mechanism for sequence labelling based spoken language understanding. In *IEEE International Conference on Acoustics, Speech and Signal Processing(ICASSP)*, pages 5675–5679.

Cogent: A Generic Dialogue System Shell Based on a Collaborative Problem Solving Model

Lucian Galescu, Choh Man Teng, James Allen, Ian Perera
Institute for Human and Machine Cognition (IHMC)
40 S Alcaniz, Pensacola, FL 32502, USA
{lgalescu,cmteng,jallen,iperera}@ihmc.us

Abstract

The bulk of current research in dialogue systems is focused on fairly simple task models, primarily state-based. Progress on developing dialogue systems for more complex tasks has been limited by the lack generic toolkits to build from. In this paper we report on our development from the ground up of a new dialogue model based on collaborative problem solving. We implemented the model in a dialogue system shell (**Cogent**) that allows developers to plug in problem-solving agents to create dialogue systems in new domains. The Cogent shell has now been used by several independent teams of researchers to develop dialogue systems in different domains, with varied lexicons and interaction style, each with their own problem-solving back-end. We believe this to be the first practical demonstration of the feasibility of a CPS-based dialogue system shell.

1 Introduction

Many areas of natural language processing have benefited from the existence of tools and frameworks that can be customized to develop specific applications. In the area of dialogue systems, there are few such tools and frameworks and they mostly remain focused on simple tasks that can be encoded in a state-based dialogue model (see, e.g., Williams et al., 2016 and the Dialogue State Tracking Challenge[1]). In this category some of the more expressive approaches to dialogue modeling are based on the information state (Cooper, 1997); notable toolkits include TrindiKit (Larsson and Traum, 2000) and its open-source successor trindikit.py (Ljunglöf, 2009), and OpenDial (Lison and Kennington, 2016).

Unfortunately, there is a dearth of tools for developing mixed-initiative dialogue systems that involve complex back-end reasoning systems. Early theoretical work of SharedPlans (Grosz and Kraus, 1996; Lochbaum et al., 1990) and plan-based dialogue systems (e.g., Allen and Perrault, 1980; Litman and Allen, 1987) laid good foundations. The Collaborative Problem Solving (CPS) model (Allen et al., 2002) seemed to promise a solution but that model has never been implemented in a truly domain-independent way. Ravenclaw (Bohus and Rudnicky, 2009) is a plan-based dialog management framework that has been used to develop a number of dialogue systems. Its dialogue engine is task-independent and includes a number of generic conversational skills; however, its behavior is driven by task-specific dialogue trees, which have to be implemented anew for every application.

Dialogue management involves understanding the intention of the user's contributions to the dialogue, and deciding what to do or say next. It is the core component of a dialogue system, and typically requires significant development effort for every new application domain. We believe that dialogue managers based on models of the collaborative problem solving process offer the highest potential for *flexibility* and *portability*. Flexibility refers to the ability to cover the full range of natural dialogues users may want to engage in, and portability refers to how easy it is to customize or modify a system to work in new domains (Blaylock, 2007).

In this paper we describe a new, domain-independent dialogue manager based on the CPS model, and its implementation in an open-source dialog system shell (**Cogent[2]**). To demonstrate its flexibility, we also describe briefly a few dialogue systems for different domains.

---

[1] https://www.microsoft.com/en-us/research/event/dialog-state-tracking-challenge/

[2] https://github.com/wdebeaum/cogent

Proceedings of the SIGDIAL 2018 Conference, pages 400–409,
Melbourne, Australia, 12-14 July 2018. ©2018 Association for Computational Linguistics

2   Collaborative Problem Solving

When agents are engaged in solving problems together, they need to communicate to agree on what goals to pursue and what steps to take to achieve those goals, negotiate roles, resources, etc. To underscore its collaborative aspect, this type of joint activity has been called Collaborative Problem Solving (CPS). Modeling the type of dialogue agents engage in during CPS must, therefore, take into account the nature of the joint activity itself. In the early 2000s, Allen and colleagues described a preliminary plan-based CPS model of dialogue based on an analysis of an agent's collaborative behavior at various levels:

- An **individual problem-solving** level, where each agent manages its own problem-solving state, plans and executes individual actions, etc.;

- A **collaborative problem-solving** level, which models and manages the joint or collaborative problem-solving state (shared goals, resources, situations);

- An **interaction** level, where individual agents negotiate changes in the joint problem-solving state; and, finally,

- A **communication** level, where speech acts realize the interaction level acts.

This model was refined in a series of publications, and several prototype systems were developed for illustration (Allen et al., 2002; Blaylock and Allen, 2005; Allen et al., 2007; Ferguson and Allen, 2007), all based on the TRIPS system (Allen et al., 2000).

One of the main benefits of this model is that linguistic interpretation and high-level intention recognition could be performed independently of the individual problem-solving level, whose contribution to interpretation would be to specialize the higher-level intentions into concrete problem-solving actions and verify that such actions make sense. The corollary is that in this model the back-end problem solvers would be insulated from the need to worry about linguistic issues.

On this basis, it should be possible to create a generic dialogue system shell with only domain-independent components. Other developers, not necessarily specialists in NLU or dialogue systems, could use this shell to build, relatively quickly, intelligent dialogue systems for collaborative tasks in various domains. The various prototypes of TRIPS CPS-based systems referenced above did not fulfill this promise. In each, the CPS level was integrated fairly tightly with the individual problem-solving level for the application domain, and they were all developed by the same team. Thus, even though each such prototype implemented (a version of) the CPS model and used the same platform for NLU, the ultimate goal of creating a domain-independent dialogue shell that others could customize to develop independently dialogue systems has so far remained elusive. Similarly, the CPS-based dialogue manager in SAMMIE (Becker et al., 2006) also aimed for domain independence but never quite realized it (Blaylock, 2007).

In the rest of the paper we will report on our attempt to develop a generic dialogue shell based on the CPS model. We start with a description of the general architecture of a dialogue system based on the CPS model. Then, we will describe our dialogue manager, with a focus on its interface with the domain-specific problem solving agent. Finally, we give some details on six prototype dialogue systems developed using our dialogue shell, five of which were developed by independent teams of researchers.

3   CPS-based Dialogue Systems

A collaborative conversational agent must understand a user's utterances, that is, obtain a representation of the meaning of the utterance, recognize its intention, and then reason with this intention to decide what to do and/or say next. Finally, the system must convert its own intentions into language and communicate them to the user.

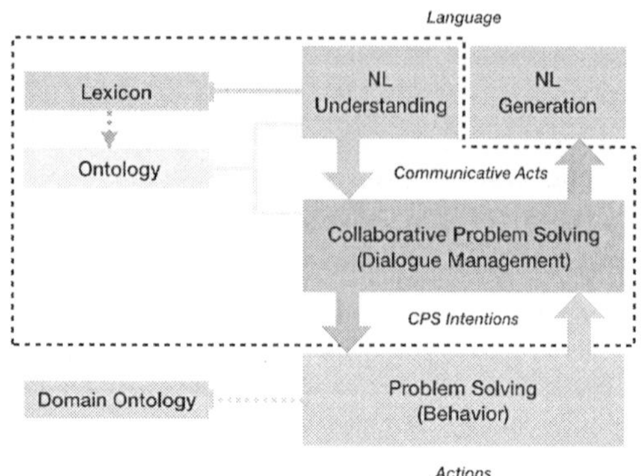

Figure 1: Conceptual architecture of a CPS-based dialogue system

Figure 1 shows a conceptual diagram of the dialogue system we envision. This follows the common separation of a conversational agent's functionality into *interpretation*, *behavior* and *generation*, but where the separation lines are is critical for realizing the idea of isolating domain-independent from domain-specific processing. We take the output of NL Understanding (assumed here to have broad lexical, syntactic and semantic coverage) to be a domain-independent semantic representation of the user's utterance (a *communicative act*), expressed in terms of a domain-independent ontology. Intention recognition is performed by the CPS agent, which takes into account the discourse context and converts communicative acts into *abstract communicative intentions*. These communicative intentions need to be further evaluated with respect to the actual problem-solving state, so they are not fully interpreted until they reach the problem solving agent. This agent is responsible for the domain-specific behavior – hereafter we will refer to it as the *Behavioral Agent* (BA) – and for operationalizing the communicative intentions into actions (which may involve planning, acting on the world, updating its knowledge of the situation, etc.). An autonomous BA should be able to plan and act on its own, but neither the BA nor the user can singlehandedly decide on the status of collaborative goals without a commitment from the other party. The BA expresses its attitude towards shared goals by sending to the CPS agent its own communicative intentions, which the CPS agent will use to update the collaborative state and generate communicative acts for NL generation (such as accepting or rejecting a goal, or proposing a new one).

Customization: Figure 1 includes, on the left side, a number of resources needed by our ideal dialogue system: (1) a broad *lexicon* for NL understanding; (2) a general-purpose (upper-level) *ontology*; and, optionally, (3) a *domain ontology*.

Even a state-of-the-art broad coverage parser, with an extensive domain-independent high-level ontology and lexicon, will not contain all the word senses and concepts needed for every application domain. Additionally, the general ontology concepts need to be mapped onto the domain ontology used by the back-end problem solvers.

Lastly, NL generation from semantic representations of communicative acts is a difficult problem, with no general solutions. Many task-oriented dialogue systems employ template-based techniques, which can lead to satisfactory, if somewhat repetitive text realizations. Such templates are tailored for the application domain.

It may appear that customizing a generic dialogue shell to specific applications involves a considerable amount of work. Nevertheless, we believe these customization tasks are easier to accomplish and require less linguistic expertise than building a dialogue manager for every application, let alone building domain-specific natural language understanding components.

4   Our CPS Model

Let us now turn to the details of our new instantiation of the CPS model. Unlike prior work on CPS-based dialogue management, we focus on the interface between the CPS agent (CPSA) and the BA. This allows us to directly address the issue of domain-independence that posed difficulties in other approaches (e.g., Blaylock, 2007).

The CPSA computes communicative intentions based on the communicative acts resulting from the NLU component. These communicative intentions are realized in our model as *CPS Acts*, represented as a pair *<ACI, CONTEXT>*, where *ACI* represents the abstract communicative intention and *CONTEXT* represents the semantic content of the act in a knowledge representation language. Where there is no ambiguity we will omit *CONTEXT* and denote CPS acts by their *ACI* only.

In the following subsections we will describe the set of CPS acts we have devised so far, grouped by the manner in which they affect the collaborative state.

4.1 CPS Acts Related to Problem-Solving Objectives

The CPS Model defines an *objective* as an intention that is driving the agent's current behavior (Allen et al., 2002). An objective can be proposed by either agent, provided they are ready to commit to it. We represent the intention to commit to an objective via the CPS act ADOPT. For example, if the user starts a conversation with "*Let's build a tower*", this results in the following CPS act:

```
(ADOPT :id O1 :what C1 :as (GOAL))
```

Here, O1 represents a unique, persistent identifier for the shared objective proposed via this act (all objectives are assigned an identifier). C1 is an identifier indexed into the *CONTEXT* of this CPS act (i.e., it refers to an event of building a tower). Additionally, the act also indicates the relation between this objective and any pre-existing objectives. In this example, the relation was identified as GOAL, indicating that this is a top-level objective (we will discuss later other types of relations between objectives available in our model).

Once an objective has been jointly committed to, either agent can propose to drop their commitment to it, via a CPS act called ABANDON. Or, they might propose to shift focus from the active objective (the one currently driving the agents' behavior), by an act called DEFER, which will result in the objective becoming inactive. A proposal to bring an inactive objective back into an active state an agent results in a SELECT act. Finally, an agent can propose that an objective should be considered completed, via a RELEASE act. All these four acts only take as an argument the objective's unique identifier, for example: (ABANDON :id O1).

Note that all of these four acts can be *proposed*, indicating the agent's intentional stance towards their commitment to that objective. The user performs a proposal via a speech act. The same intention may be expressed by different surface speech acts. Going back to our example, the objective of building a tower together can be expressed via a direct proposal ("*Let's build a tower*"); a question ("*Can we build a tower?*"); or an indirect speech act ("*I think we should build a tower*"). The CPSA recognizes the user intent in all these variants, using the surface speech act and other linguistic cues present in the communicative act it receives from NLU). Thus, they all result in the same ADOPT act as above.

If, on the other hand, the BA wants to propose that an objective be jointly pursued, say that it wants to start working on O1 by a subgoal O2 of placing a block on the table, it can do so via a PROPOSE act, whose content is the intention to commit to that objective:

```
(PROPOSE :content (ADOPT :id O2
  :what C2 :as (SUBGOAL :of O1)))
```

where C2 is indexed into the *CONTEXT* of the act for a representation of the event of placing a block on the table. Upon receiving this act, the CPSA will update the collaborative state to reflect the BA's intention to commit to O2, and formulate a communicative act for NLG to realize the proposal in a system utterance.

For a proposal to result in a shared objective, the two agents must agree to commit to it. The CPSA is responsible for gathering the agreements of both the user and the BA. When the CPSA recognizes that the user is proposing an objective, it will first send an EVALUATE act to the BA, whose content is the proposed objective, e.g.,:

```
(EVALUATE :content (ADOPT :id O1
  :what C1 :as (GOAL))
```

This act creates an obligation on the part of the BA to evaluate whether it is able to commit to it in the current situation, and, if so, respond by signaling agreement (ACCEPTABLE), rejection (REJECTED), or, when it cannot even interpret what the objective is, a failure (FAILURE). For example, the BA's agreement, that is, its intention to commit to the objective proposed by the user, would be communicated via:

```
(ACCEPTABLE :content (ADOPT :id O1
  :what C1 :as (GOAL))
```

Since the user has already signaled their intention to commit to the objective by proposing it, on receiving from the BA that the objective is ACCEPTABLE, the CPSA knows that there is mutual agreement, decides that that the objective is now adopted, and sends back to the BA the following CPS act:

```
(COMMIT :content (ADOPT :id O1
  :what C1 :as (GOAL))
```

to signal that now there is a joint commitment to O1. This creates an obligation on the part of the BA to pursue O1 in whatever manner it deems appropriate.

When we have a system-proposed objective, such as O2 above, if the user expresses their acceptance ("*Yes*", "*Sure*", "*I can handle that*", etc.), the CPSA will recognize this as completing the agreement, and then it would adopt the objective and send the COMMIT act to the BA.

Having described in some detail how objectives are created, and how the CPSA decides that there is joint commitment to them, let us turn briefly to some of the details that we brushed over.

Relations between objectives: We mentioned above two relations between the objective currently under consideration and the prior objectives (either previously adopted ones, or ones that have been discussed but are still being negotiated), namely GOAL and SUBGOAL. Currently the CPSA can infer two more. One is MODIFICATION, used when one of the agents is expressing an intention of changing in some manner a prior objective (for example, if one of the agents had suggested placing a blue block on the table, the other agent might suggest placing a red block instead). The second one we call ELABORATION, and is used by the CPSA to signal that it has insufficient knowledge to decide whether the objective under discussion is really a subgoal or a modification of another one, or, perhaps a new top-level goal. It is possible, however, that the BA may be able to use its more detailed knowledge of the situation to make that determination. Thus, upon receiving an objective marked as an elaboration of another one, if the BA deems it acceptable, it has the obligation to clarify the relation as well.

Rejections and failures: If a user proposes an objective, presumably they have an expectation that the objective is achievable. If the BA rejects it, the user will likely not be satisfied with a simple "*No*". Similarly, if the BA fails to understand the objective (or if it encounters any other type of failure, e.g., while trying to perform some action), the system should be able to explain what happened. Thus, the REJECTED and FAILURE CPS acts have features for optionally specifying a reason and a possible way of repairing the situation. The reason for rejection/failure is one of a relatively small set of predefined ones (e.g., UNKNOWN-OBJECT, FAILED-ACTION), and it is expected that the NLG component will make use of it to generate more helpful utterances. As for how to repair the situation, this can be an alternative objective, that the BA is ready to commit to, which could be either a modification of the reject-

ed one, or, perhaps, an objective which, if realized, would make the rejected objective acceptable. For example, if the user wanted to build an all-blue 5-block tower, but the BA has only 4 blue blocks, it would reject the goal (INSUFFICIENT-RESOURCES), but it could suggest as an alternative that a 4-block blue tower would be an achievable alternative. This might be realized as "*Sorry, I don't have enough blocks for that, but we can build a 4-block blue tower.*". If the user accepts ("*OK*"), the CPSA will immediately commit to the suggested objective.

4.2 CPS Acts Related to Situations

Collaborative problem solving requires not only joint commitments to certain objectives, but also a set of shared beliefs about the situation. These shared beliefs occasionally need to be updated. One agent may inform the other of a fact that they believe the other should know. This may come about unprompted or as a result of being asked. The CPS Model offers little guidance on how such acts fit in, even though they are very common in conversation. The examples given seem to suggest an interpretation of questions and simple assertions based on plan recognition (Allen, 1979), which is a tall order, particularly for a domain-independent dialogue manager. When agent A informs agent B of a fact P, this indicates A's immediate intention that B knows P. Similarly, if A asks B whether P is true (an ask-if speech act) or what object satisfies P (an ask-wh speech act), A's immediate intention is that B informs A of those particular facts (Allen and Perrault, 1980). Getting at the intentions *behind* these immediate intentions requires fairly sophisticated, often domain-specific reasoning (in our implementation the CPSA can do that to some extent via abstract task models, but, due to space limitations, we will not discuss it here). Therefore, we created a small set of CPS acts for representing the intentions to impart and request knowledge about situations.

In our model, an assertion of a fact results in the following CPS act:

```
(ASSERTION :id A3 :what C3
 :as (CONTRIBUTES-TO :goal O1))
```

where C3 is an identifier pointing to a representation of the content of the assertion in the *CONTEXT* of the CPS act. The relation between an ASSERTION act and an existing objective (or NIL if no such objective exists) is an underspeci-

fied one, of contributing somehow to it. The BA
needs to decide, if it accepts A3, how this addition
will change its understanding of the situation and
affect O1 or any other (adopted) objective.

For ask-if questions the CPSA will produce the
following act:

```
(ASK-IF :id A4 :query Q4
 :as (QUERY-IN-CONTEXT :goal O1))
```

Here Q4 is an identifier pointing to a representation (in the *CONTEXT* of the CPS act) of a statement to be evaluated for its truth value.

For ask-wh questions the CPSA produces acts
in the following format:

```
(ASK-WH :id A5
  :what W5 :query Q5 :choices S5
  :as (QUERY-IN-CONTEXT :goal O1))
```

This expresses the intention of knowing the value
of an entity (W5), possibly restricted to a set of
choices (S5), that makes a proposition (Q5) true.
As before, all these identifiers should be given appropriate descriptions in the *CONTEXT*. This act
can thus represent the intention expressed by a
question such as *"What color should we use for
the first block, blue or red?"*.

Finally, an answer to a question takes the following form:

```
(ANSWER :to A5
  :what W5 :query Q5 :value V6
  :justification J6)
```

This indicates the value V6 (e.g., blue) for the entity W5 makes the statement Q5 true (we should
use blue for the first block), in response to the
CPS act with the identifier A5. If the answer is in
response to an ASK-IF act, V6 can only be TRUE
or FALSE. Optionally, a justification (J6) may be
added to show how the answer came about.

It is important to note that we treat these intentions as special types of objectives, that can become adopted, active, etc., just like other objectives. For example, if one of these CPS acts is initiated by the user, the act must be evaluated by the
BA. If it deems the act ACCEPTABLE, the CPSA
will commit to working on it (updating the system's beliefs, or answering the question). If originating from the BA, the act must be proposed
first, and realized through a communicative act.

Side effects: We noted above that updating the
system's beliefs about the situation may affect the
status of existing objectives. Insofar as the BA is
capable of foreseeing these effects, it ought to inform the CPSA so the collaborative state can be
updated. Any such changes would result in an obligation to inform the user. In our model we use an
additional feature for the ACCEPTABLE act (see
previous section), for describing the effect. Its
value is an objective to be proposed. For example,
if, in the context of the shared objective of building a tower, the system asks *"Who is going to
move the blocks?"*, and the user says *"I will"*, this
answer has the side effect of modifying the existing objective (in this case specializing it to include
the identity of the builder). The system's acceptance of the answer will necessarily imply the
acceptance of the modification as well, and the
CPSA will update the collaborative state accordingly.

4.3 CPS Acts Related to Initiative and Exe-cution

Another important role of the CPSA in managing
the dialogue is to negotiate initiative. To facilitate
an orderly conversation, it restricts both the timing
and the magnitude of the BA's ability to affect the
collaborative state. It does so via a special CPS
act, called WHAT-NEXT, which takes a single argument: the identifier of an adopted shared objective (usually the one that is active). This act can be
sent to the BA whenever there are no pending updates to the collaborative state, and no outstanding
communicative acts to process or to wait on. In effect, by sending this act, the CPSA transfers the
task initiative to the BA, which gives it the chance
to, ultimately, influence discourse initiative as
well. The BA has the obligation to respond with a
single update to the collaborative state, presumably the one with the highest priority. This restriction is critical, because it frees the CPSA from
the need to consider too many options about what
to do and say next, a decision that, in many situations, would require domain-specific knowledge.

The BA's reply to a WHAT-NEXT depends on its
own private problem-solving state. It may be that
it has done some planning and, as a result, it wants
to propose a way of making progress towards accomplishing the active objective. It may be that it
does not have sufficient information to make progress, in which case it may formulate an intention
to ask the user to provide the information. Or, if
the active objective is a question, it may have
come up with an answer; that update would prob-

ably get very high priority. All these possibilities are handled by acts we have already discussed.

One other possibility is that the BA is currently not doing any reasoning, but simply acting on the active objective, or has accomplished it. Updates to the status of an objective are communicated via a special CPS act, which takes the following form:

```
(EXECUTION-STATUS :goal A1
 :status GS)
```

Here GS is an expression that indicates the status of the goal. Currently it can be one of three indicators:

1. DONE, which signifies that A1 was accomplished. CPSA will create a communicative act to inform the user, and, if the user agrees, releases the objective.

2. WORKING-ON-IT, which indicates that the BA is actively pursuing A1, but it will take more time. The CPSA may decide to inform the user, and creates a trigger for itself to check back later.

3. WAITING-FOR-USER, which indicates that the BA cannot make progress on A1 because it is waiting for the user to act on it (or another objective that A1 depends on). As a result, the CPSA will construct a communicative act to prompt the user.

This CPS act also allows the BA to communicate partial execution status (that it has executed some actions, though it has not accomplished the objective yet), but we leave those details out of this discussion.

5   The Cogent System

We implemented our CPS model as a component in the TRIPS system (Allen et al., 2000), which has recently been released in the public domain under a GNU GPL License.

The TRIPS system comes with a broad coverage parser (Allen and Teng, 2017) with an extensive grammar and an effective 100,000+ word semantic vocabulary defined in terms of a 4000 concept domain-independent ontology. It operates in concert with a suite of statistical preprocessing components, performing tasks such as part-of-speech tagging, named entity recognition, and identification of likely constituent boundaries. These preprocessed inputs are provided to the core TRIPS parser as advice. The parser con-

structs from the input a logical form, which is a semantic representation that captures an unscoped modal logic (Manshadi et al., 2008). The logical form includes the surface speech act, semantic types, semantic roles for predicate arguments, and dependency relations.

TRIPS also includes an interpretation manager that converts the logical forms into communicative acts, performing language-based intention recognition and normalizing different surface forms.

We packaged the TRIPS NLU components (including the lexicon and ontology) with our CPS agent, thereby creating a dialogue system shell, which we call **Cogent**. This system does not include a BA or an NLG component (**Cogent**'s components are surrounded with a dashed line in Figure 1). Thus, it is a true domain-independent shell, not a system that can be adapted to other domains. It can carry out very minimal conversations because social conversational acts such as greetings are handled in a domain-independent manner in the CPSA. But, ultimately, the purpose of the shell is to be used to create domain applications. The success of the task we set to accomplish is whether this shell can be and is used by independent developers to develop operational dialogue systems in domains of their choice.

As discussed in the previous section, the CPS acts and the obligations they engender establish a protocol that developers of behavioral agents must implement. Other than that, we believe the CPSA offers functionality to develop different styles of conversational agents (user-driven, system-driven or fully mixed-initiative). The developers also must implement their own NL Generation component, for reasons that we touched upon earlier.

Of note, by default all CPS acts have their contents expressed in the TRIPS ontology. We are also providing a tool for mapping concepts in the TRIPS ontology to domain ontologies. We have adapted the TRIPS interpretation manager to use these mappings to produce content in the domain ontology, to make it easier for the Behavioral Agents to interpret the *CONTEXT* associated with each CPS act. The details of the ontology mapping tool and the mappings it creates are, however, beyond the scope of this paper.

6   Systems Implemented in Cogent

We describe briefly six system prototypes that have been built using **Cogent** as the base framework; thus, they all use the same CPS agent described above. In all cases, the developers of these prototypes used the protocol described above to create behavioral agents that, in turn, act as integrators of other problem solvers. The descriptions of these systems are going to be necessarily brief; the interested reader is encouraged to follow the references to get a better understanding of their capabilities and the kinds of dialogues they support (unfortunately, not all systems have been published yet). All these systems have been developed as part of DARPA's Communicating with Computers (CwC) program[3].

Cabot: This is a mixed-initiative system for planning and execution in the blocks world, the tasks being of jointly building structures (Perera et al., 2017). Both the user and the system can come up with their own goals, and, if necessary, they will negotiate constraints on those structures (size, colors, etc.) so all the goals can be completed. They also negotiate their roles in building these structures ("architect" or "builder"). This system uses a 2D simulated version of the blocks world. The examples used in this paper are from interactions with this system.

Cabot-L: This system learns names and structural properties of complex objects in a physically situated blocks world scenario (Perera et al., 2017; Perera et al., 2018). The user teaches the system by providing examples of structures together with descriptions in language. The system has capabilities to perceive the world and detect changes to it, and can ask the user questions about various features of the structures, to learn a general model. To validate the inferred model, the user can then show additional examples and ask the system to classify them and explain its reasoning. The user and the system can interact via either written or spoken language.

BoB: This system acts as an assistant biologist. It has fairly extensive knowledge of molecular biology and can assist the user by responding to inquiries about properties of genes, proteins, molecular mechanisms, their relationship to cellular processes and disease, building and visualizing complex causal models, running simulations on these models to detect their dynamic properties, etc. To manage this wide range of problem-solving behaviors, *BoB*'s BA integrates a variety of agents with specific expertise.

Musica: This system uses a computational model of music cognition, as well as knowledge about existing pieces of music, to help a human composer create and edit a musical score (Quick and Morrison, 2017).

SMILEE: This system acts as a partner for playing a cooperative game (Kim et al., 2018). The game involves placing pieces (blocks) on a board to create complex symmetrical configurations. Players alternate, but each player can hold their turn for multiple rounds. Each player has some freedom to be creative with respect to the configuration being pursued (it is not set in advance). Thus, they have to negotiate turn taking, and they can ask for explanations to achieve a shared understanding about the properties of the configuration being created.

Aesop: A system for building animated stories. The user acts as a director, and can choose scenes, props, characters, direct them what to do, etc. Essentially, the system provides a dialogue interface to a sophisticated system for creating visual narratives.

Of note, these systems work in several application domains, with varying interaction styles. *Musica* and *Aesop* currently work mostly in fixed-initiative mode (user tells the system what to do). All others involve varying degrees of mixed initiative. While *Cabot* is a more traditional planning domain, it is interesting to note that all others involve fairly open-ended collaborative tasks, for which the ultimate goal is learning or creating something new. *BoB* is notable for the fact that it is helping the user learn new knowledge, by helping to formulate and evaluate biological hypotheses (which may even lead to new scientific discoveries).

Importantly, with the exception of *Cabot-L*, which was developed by our team, all others were developed by independent teams (the BAs for *Cabot* and *BoB* were developed by a single team, though the latter also involved collaboration with a large group of biologists and bioinformaticians). We helped those teams understand how our tools work and the meaning of the CPS acts (especially to the early adopters, who did not have the benefit of much documentation), but we had no role in deciding what problem-solving behaviors they should or should not implement, how to implement them and so on. Two of the systems (*BoB* and *Musica*) required additions to our surface NLP components (mainly add-

---

ing domain-specific named entity recognizers) and some additional ontology concepts and mappings; we provided those customizations. The version of the TRIPS Parser we started with proved to be fairly robust, but we did have to adapt it in response to failures reported by the dialogue system developers. Nevertheless, these enhancements were not domain-specific – that is, the same parser, with the same grammar, is used for all systems.

In all systems, developers used custom template-based NLG.

7 Summary and Discussion

In this paper we reported on the development of a new domain-independent dialogue manager based on the collaborative problem solving model. We packaged this dialogue manager with a suite of broad coverage natural language understanding components (from the TRIPS system) and created a new, domain-independent CPS-based dialogue system shell. This shell has been used by several independent teams of researchers to develop dialogue systems in a variety of application domains, with different conversational styles. We believe this to be the first successful implementation of a domain-independent dialogue system shell based on the CPS model (or any other model of equivalent complexity).

We do not claim the CPSA to be complete, however. For example, it can sometimes detect an ambiguity in the user's intention and generate a clarification question, but its abilities in this regard are fairly limited. *BoB* has demonstrated some limited handling of hypotheticals (in what-if questions) at the problem-solving level, but the CPSA itself does not yet track hypothetical situations. We expect that, with wider adoption, we will inevitably be confronted with the need to improve both our model and its implementation.

As noted above in reference to *BoB* and *Musica*, for domains requiring adaptation of the NLU components, language specialists are still needed. We have not endeavored to create tools that would make it easier for dialogue system developers to adapt/improve themselves the NLU components.

Our current focus is on evaluating the robustness of the intention recognition functionality of the CPSA.

Acknowledgments

This research was supported by the DARPA Communicating with Computers program, under ARO contract W911NF-15-1-0542.

References

James F. Allen. 1979. *A Plan-Based Approach to Speech Act Recognition.* Ph.D. Thesis. University of Toronto.

J. Allen, N. Blaylock, and G. Ferguson. 2002. A problem solving model for collaborative agents. In *Proceedings of the First International Joint Conference on Autonomous Agents and Multiagent Systems: Part 2*, pp. 774-781. ACM.

J. Allen, D. Byron, M. Dzikovska, G. Ferguson, L. Galescu, and A. Stent. 2000. An architecture for a generic dialogue shell. *Natural Language Engineering*, 6(3-4): 213-228.

J. Allen, N. Chambers, G. Ferguson, L. Galescu, H. Jung, M. Swift, and W. Taysom, W. 2007. PLOW: a collaborative task learning agent. In *Proceedings of the 22nd National Conference on Artificial intelligence*, Vol. 2, pp. 1514-1519. AAAI Press.

J.F. Allen and C.R. Perrault. 1980. Analyzing intention in utterances. *Artificial intelligence* 15(3):143-178.

J.F. Allen and C.M. Teng. 2017. Broad coverage, domain-generic deep semantic parsing. In *Proceedings of the AAAI Spring Symposium on Computational Construction Grammar and Natural Language Understanding.*

T. Becker, N. Blaylock, C. Gerstenberger, I. Kruijff-Korbayová, A. Korthauer, M. Pinkal, M. Pitz, P. Poller, and J. Schehl. 2006. Natural and intuitive multimodal dialogue for in-car applications: The SAMMIE system. *Frontiers in Artificial Intelligence and Applications*, 141:612.

Nate Blaylock. 2007. Towards Flexible, Domain-Independent Dialogue Management using Collaborative Problem Solving. In *Proceedings of the 11th Workshop on the Semantics and Pragmatics of Dialogue (Decalog 2007)*, pp. 91–98.

N. Blaylock and J. Allen. 2005. A collaborative problem-solving model of dialogue. In *Proceedings of the 6th SIGdial Workshop on Discourse and Dialogue*, pp. 200–211, Lisbon.

N. Blaylock, J. Allen, and G. Ferguson. 2003. Managing communicative intentions with collaborative problem solving. In *Current and New Directions in Discourse and Dialogue*, pp. 63-84. Springer, Dordrecht.

D. Bohus and A.I. Rudnicky. 2009. The RavenClaw dialog management framework: Architecture and systems. *Computer Speech & Language*, 23(3), 332-361. https://doi.org/10.1016/j.csl.2008.10.001

Robin Cooper. 1997. Information states, attitudes and dialogue. In *Proceedings of the Second Tbilisi Symposium on Language, Logic and Computation*, Tbilisi, pp. 15-20.

G. Ferguson and J. Allen. 2007. Mixed-initiative systems for collaborative problem solving. *AI magazine*, 28(2):23.

B.J. Grosz and S. Kraus. 1996. Collaborative plans for complex group action. *Artificial Intelligence*, 86(2):269-357.

S. Kim, D. Salter, L. DeLuccia, K. Son, M.R. Amer, and A. Tamrakar. 2018. SMILEE: Symmetric Multi-modal Interactions with Language-gesture Enabled (AI) Embodiment. In *Proceedings of the 16th Annual Conference of the North American Chapter of the Association for Computational Linguistics: Human Language Technologies (NAACL HLT 2018)*.

S. Larsson and D.R. Traum. 2000. Information state and dialogue management in the TRINDI dialogue move engine toolkit. *Natural Language Engineering*, 6(3-4), 323-340.

P. Lison and C. Kennington. 2016. OpenDial: A toolkit for developing spoken dialogue systems with probabilistic rules. In *Proceedings of ACL-2016 System Demonstrations*, pp 67-72. Association for Computational Linguistics. https://doi.org/10.18653/v1/P16-4012

D.J. Litman and J.F. Allen. 1987. A Plan Recognition Model for Subdialogues in Conversations. *Cognitive Science*, 11: 163-200. https://doi.org/10.1207/s15516709cog1102_4

Peter Ljunglöf. 2009. trindikit.py: An open-source Python library for developing ISU-based dialogue systems. In *Proceedings of the 1st International Workshop on Spoken Dialogue Systems Technology (IWSDS'09)*, Kloster Irsee, Germany.

K.E. Lochbaum, B.J. Grosz, and C.L. Sidner. 1990. Models of plans to support communication: An initial report. In *Proceedings of the 8th National Conference on Artificial Intelligence*, pp. 485-490.

M.H. Manshadi, J. Allen, and M. Swift. 2008. Toward a universal underspecified semantic representation. In *Proceedings of the 13th Conference on Formal Grammar (FG 2008)*, Hamburg, Germany.

V. Pallotta. 2003. Computational dialogue models. MDM research project deliverable, EPFL IC-ISIM LITH, Lausanne (CH).

I.E. Perera, J.F. Allen, L. Galescu, C.M. Teng, M.H. Burstein, S.E. Friedman, D.D. McDonald, and J.M. Rye. 2017. Natural Language Dialogue for Building and Learning Models and Structures. In *Proceedings of the 31st AAAI Conference on Artificial Intelligence (AAAI-17)*, pp. 5103-5104.

I. Perera, J. Allen, C.M. Teng, and L. Galescu. 2018. A Situated Dialogue System for Learning Structural Concepts in Blocks World. In *Proceedings of the 19th Annual Meeting of the Special Interest Group on Discourse and Dialogue (SIGDIAL 2018)*, Melbourne, Australia.

D. Quick and C.T. Morrison. 2017. Composition by Conversation. In *Proceedings of the 43rd International Computer Music Conference*, pp. 52-57.

J. Williams, A. Raux, and M. Henderson. 2016. The dialog state tracking challenge series: A review. *Dialogue & Discourse*, 7(3), 4-33.

Identifying Domain Independent Update Intents in Task Based Dialogs

Prakhar Biyani *
Twitter Inc.
1355 Market St #900
San Francisco, CA 94103
pbiyani@twitter.com

Cem Akkaya
Yahoo Research, Oath Inc.
701 First Ave
Sunnyvale, CA 94089
cakkaya@oath.com

Kostas Tsioutsiouliklis
Yahoo Research, Oath Inc.
701 First Ave
Sunnyvale, CA 94089
kostas@oath.com

Abstract

One important problem in task-based conversations is that of effectively updating the belief estimates of user-mentioned slot-value pairs. Given a user utterance, the intent of a slot-value pair is captured using dialog acts (DA) expressed in that utterance. However, in certain cases, DA's fail to capture the actual *update intent* of the user. In this paper, we describe such cases and propose a new type of semantic class for user intents. This new type, Update Intents (UI), is directly related to the type of update a user intends to perform for a slot-value pair. We define five types of UI's, which are independent of the domain of the conversation. We build a multi-class classification model using LSTM's to identify the type of UI in user utterances in the Restaurant and Shopping domains. Experimental results show that our models achieve strong classification performance in terms of F-1 score.

1 Introduction

An important part of dialog management in dialog systems is to detect the type of update to be performed for a slot after every turn in order to keep track of the dialog state. (The dialog state reflects the user goals specified as slot-value pairs.) User dialog acts (Young, 2007) express the user's intents towards slots mentioned in the conversation. They are extracted in the spoken language understanding (SLU) module and are utilized by the downstream state tracking systems to update belief estimates (Williams et al., 2013; Lee and Stent, 2016; Henderson et al., 2014c). However,

currently used dialog acts do not capture the update intended by the user in the following cases:

1. **Implicit denials:** User denials for slot-values are expressed using the "deny" and "negate" dialog acts. However, these acts only address explicit negations/denials such as "no", "I do not want ⟨slot-value⟩'. But a user may express denial for a value implicitly. Consider utterances 8 and 9 in Table 1 where a user *adds* and *removes* people from a slot, PNAMES, which contains names of people going to an event. Current SLU systems would detect the "inform" dialog act in both utterances and, hence, would miss the (implicit denial) "remove" update.

2. **Updates to numeric slots:** Numeric slots are the slots whose values can be increased and decreased in addition to getting set/replaced. Since dialog acts do not capture the "increase" and "decrease" intents towards a numeric value, such updates cannot be handled using dialog acts alone. For example, consider utterances 4, 5 and 6 in Table 1 where the value of a numeric slot, NGUEST (number of guests in an invite), is set, increased and decreased respectively. The dialog act expressed in these utterances is "inform" which does not convey the update type.

3. **Preference for slot values:** The "inform" dialog act specifies values for slots but does not take into account the preferences for any particular slot value(s). Consider utterances 1, 2 and 3 in Table 1 where the location slot (LOC) is referred. In utterance 2, the user is equally interested in the three locations ("Ross", "Napa" and "San Jose"). However, in utterance 3 the user prefers "Gilroy" over other values and intends to *replace* the old values with "Gilroy". Clearly, the SLU output does not capture this change in the user intent.

We posit that identifying the above intents in user utterances as a part of SLU would improve estimation of user goals in task based dialogs. To ad-

<hr>

The work was done when the author was at Yahoo Research, Oath Inc.

Proceedings of the SIGDIAL 2018 Conference, pages 410–419,
Melbourne, Australia, 12-14 July 2018. ©2018 Association for Computational Linguistics

Id	User utterance	Expected SLU output	SLU output with update intents
		Task: Restaurant search	
1	Find French restaurants in Ross and Napa.	inform(LOC=Ross|Napa)	inform(**append**(LOC=Ross|Napa))
2	Show some in San Jose too.	inform(LOC=San Jose)	inform(**append**(LOC=San Jose))
3	Show me in Gilroy instead.	inform(LOC=Gilroy)	inform(**replace**(LOC=Gilroy))
		Task: Restaurant reservation	
4	Book a table for 4 at Olive Gardens.	inform(NGUEST=4)	inform(**replace**(NGUEST=4))
5	Add 4 more seats.	inform(NGUEST=4)	inform(**increaseby**(NGUEST=4))
6	Can you remove 2 seats.	inform(NGUEST=2)	inform(**decreaseby**(NGUEST=2))
7	Actually make it for 5.	inform(NGUEST=5)	inform(**replace**(NGUEST=5))
		Task: Restaurant reservation	
8	Invite Joe, Mike and John for drinks at SoMar today.	inform(PNAMES=[John &Mike& Joe])	inform(**append**(PNAMES=Joe&Mike &John))
9	Take Joe off the list.	inform(PNAME=Joe)	inform(**remove**(PNAMES=Joe))

Table 1: Example user-bot conversations with only user utterances. For illustration, only the relevant slots are shown in the SLU output.

dress the above issues, we propose five generic ***update intents*** (UI's) which are directly related to the type of update expressed by the user: Append, Remove, Replace, IncreaseBy and DecreaseBy, and build a model to identify them in a user utterance. Table 2 defines the five UI's. We model the problem of identifying UI's as a multi-class classification. For a user utterance, we classify UI's for all the slot-values present in the utterance into one of the five classes. We treat an utterance as a sequence of tokens and slot-values, and perform sequence labeling using LSTM's for the classification. It should be noted that the focus of this work is on identifying the UI's in user utterance and not on investigating the mechanisms of using them for belief tracking, which is part of our larger goal.

UI's are generic in nature and independent of the dialog domain. Given a slot type (such as numeric), they can be applied to any slot of that type. This enables transfer learning across similar slots in different domains. To demonstrate this, we experiment with two domains (shopping and restaurants) and define three types of slots: 1. Numeric slots, 2. Conjunctive multi-value (CMV) slots, and 3. Disjunctive multi-value (DMV) slots (explained in Section 3.1.1). We then delexicalize slot-values in user utterances with the corresponding slot type (not slot name) and conduct cross-domain training and testing experiments. Experimental results demonstrate strong classification performance in individual domains as well as across domains.

Contributions: 1) We propose a new semantic class of slot-specific user intents (UI's) which are

directly related to the update a user intends to perform for a slot. 2) The proposed UI's enable effective updates to slots. 3) Our models predict UI's with high accuracy. 4) We present a novel delexicalization approach which enables transfer learning of UI's across domains.

2 Related Work

Although we are not aware of any prior work on identifying update intents, our current work is related to dialog act identification and dialog state tracking. Here, we review works in these two areas and contrast them against ours.

Dialog act identification: Dialog acts (DA) in an utterance express the intention of their speaker/writer. Identifying DA types has been found to be useful in many natural language processing tasks such as question answering, summarization, and spoken language understanding (SLU) in dialog systems. A variety of DA's have been proposed for specific application tasks and domains, such as email conversations (Cohen et al., 2004), online forum discussions (Bhatia et al., 2012; Kim et al., 2010), and dialog systems (Young, 2007). The latter is relevant to this work. In dialog systems, DA's are used to infer a user's intention towards either the slots or the conversation in general. Some of the DA's used in dialog systems are inform, confirm, deny, and negate. Previous works on DA identification in dialog systems have used a range of approaches like n-grams based utterance level SVM classifier (Mairesse et al., 2009), SVM classifier built on weighted n-grams using word confusion networks incorporating ASR uncertainties and dialog context (Henderson et al., 2012), log linear models (Chen et al., 2013), and recurrent neural networks (Hori et al., 2015, 2016; Ushio et al., 2016). This work is similar to DA identification in the sense that both the UI's and the DA's express certain semantics in the utterance and are independent of the dialog domain. However, there are important differences: 1) DA's mainly reflect the intent towards the conversation; however, UI's convey the type of update a user wants to a particular slot. 2) DA's can be slot-independent (such as *hello*, *negate*, etc.) whereas UI's are always defined with respect to a slot.

Dialog State Tracking: Dialog state tracking (DST) entails updating the conversation state (also known as belief state) after every dialog turn. A conversation state is a probability distribution over competing user goals which are expressed in the form of slot-value pairs. For a user utterance, DST relies on SLU to get a list of k-best hypotheses of DA's and slot-value pairs expressed in the utterance. To update the belief state, DST approaches utilize DA's by using their SLU confidence scores as features (Ren et al., 2013; Kim and Banchs, 2014), encoding the DA's using n-gram vectors weighted by the SLU confidence scores (Henderson et al., 2014c; Mrkšić et al., 2015), and using rule-based updates (Lee and Stent, 2016). Recently, efforts have been made to bypass the SLU output and learn update mechanisms directly from user utterance (Mrksic et al., 2017). Though DA's are important for updating belief state, as explained in Section 1, certain updates like implicit denials, numeric updates, and slot preferences are not handled by the DA's used in the dialog systems literature. UI's, on the other hand, are proposed to address this problem. The work by Hakkani-Tür et al. (Hakkani-Tür et al., 2012) on identifying *action updates* in a multi-domain dialog system is closely related to the current work. Some of their action updates are similar to UI's. However, unlike the current work, they did not deal with numeric updates and did not distinguish between types of multi-value slots (explained in Section 3.1.1).

3 Approach

In task-based dialogs, users complete a task by giving sequences of utterances in which they specify slot-values with corresponding intents. Dialog

UI Type	Definition
Append	Append a specified value to the slot.
Remove	Remove a specified value from the slot.
IncreaseBy	Increase a value of a slot by a specified amount.
DecreaseBy	Decrease a value of a slot by a specified amount.
Replace	Replace the value of a slot by a specified value.

Table 2: Types of update intents and their definitions.

systems extract this information using dialog act detection and slot-filling as part of SLU. The most common and helpful intents for completing a task are setting a value for a slot and denying a particular value for a slot. Traditionally, these two intents are determined by the *inform* and *deny* dialog acts. However, as explained in Section 1, a user may not always set and deny a value explicitly. While denials can be implicit, relative preferences can also be provided for slot-value(s). In case of numeric slots, user can set a value by incrementing or decrementing the previous values of slots. All these common scenarios are not handled by the *inform* and *deny* dialog acts.

In this work, we propose a new set of slot-specific intents which are directly related to the type of update expressed towards the slot. We call these intents ***update intents*** or UI's. The UI's express five common types of updates:

1. **Append**: A user specifies a value or multiple values for a multi-value slot. This is equivalent to "appending" the specified value(s) to a multi-value slot. (Refer to Section 3.1.1 for the definition of multi-value and numeric slots).

2. **Remove**: A user denies a value or multiple values for a multi-value slot implicitly or explicitly. This is equivalent to "removing" the specified value(s) from a multi-value slot.

3. **Replace**: A user specifies a preference for a slot value in case of multi-value slots. In case of numeric (single value) slots, this intent expresses setting and re-setting of a slot value (Utterances 4 and 7 in Table 1). This UI is defined with respect to the slot-value for which the preference is expressed. For example, in the utterance "I would prefer San Jose over Gilroy" the UI for San Jose is *replace*, whereas for Gilroy it is *remove*. Note that in case of multi-value slots, *replace* cannot be decomposed into a combination of an "append" and a "remove" update when the "remove" intent is

not specified. For example, in "I would prefer San Jose" there is no "remove" intent and, hence, simply using the "append" intent for San Jose would not extract the preference for San Jose.

4. IncreaseBy: A user specifies a value by which a particular numeric slot's value is to be increased.

5. DecreaseBy: A user specifies a value by which a particular numeric slot's value is to be decreased.

Table 1 shows examples of the above five UI's. The third column shows the expected SLU output with UI's.

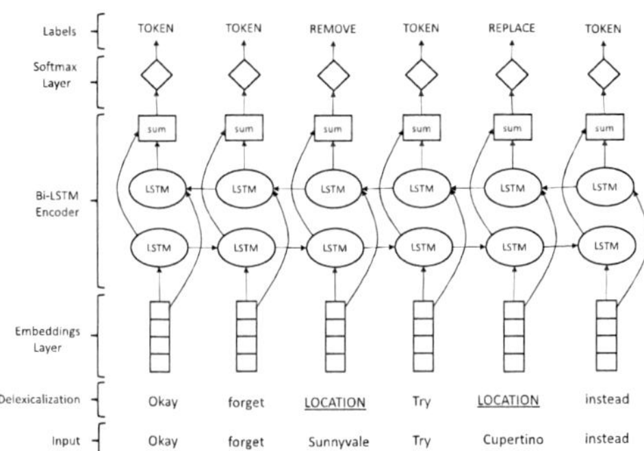

Figure 1: Model architecture

3.1 Modeling

Given a user utterance, the goal is to determine UI's for all the slot-values present in it. We formulate this task as a classification problem. Given a user utterance and the mentioned slot-values, classify the update intents for all the slot-values in one of the five classes: Append, Remove, Replace, IncreaseBy and DecreaseBy.

We model the above problem as a sequence labeling task. We treat a user utterance as a sequence of words and slot-values. The labels for slot-values are the corresponding UI's whereas for words (which are not slot-values), we define a generic label "TOKEN". For model optimization and error computation, we do not consider the "TOKEN" labels. Figure 1 describes our model architecture. We used Bidirectional LSTMs (Graves and Schmidhuber, 2005) for sequence labeling. For input representation, we used GloVe word embeddings (Pennington et al., 2014). For regularization, we used dropout and early stopping. We give more details about model parameters in Section 5.

3.1.1 Learning Across Domains

In many cases, it is not possible to list all the values of a slot in the ontology. Even if the values are listed, it may not be practical to generate a training data containing all the values, if there are too many values for the slot. In such cases, it is beneficial to unlink the learning from particular slot-values and link it, instead, to the slot itself. This is because the word patterns used to refer to values of the same slot are similar and hence can be shared across the values. For example, a user would use similar word patterns to refer to values of slot "LOCATION". One way to do this is by replacing slot-values in utterances with the name of the slot. This is also called *delexicalization* and has been used successfully in many previous works (Henderson et al., 2014c; Mrkšić et al., 2015). In our model, we also delexicalize slot-values with the name of the slot as shown in Figure 1.

Delexicalization with slot names is helpful in generalizing to slot-values not seen in the training data in one domain. However, it cannot be used for cross-domain generalization as different domains may not share the same slots. To address this problem, we define three generic slot types depending upon the values (numeric/non-numeric) a slot can take and whether a slot can take multiple values simultaneously (list-based) or not:

1. Numeric slot: Slots whose values can be increased and decreased. NGUEST in Table 1 is a numeric slot. A numeric slot is a single value slot, i.e., "appending" and "removing" (multiple) values are not allowed for numeric slots. This slot supports IncreaseBy, DecreaseBy and Replace UI's.

2. Disjunctive multi-value (DMV) slot: Slots which can take multiple values only in disjunction, i.e., when user specifies those values as options. In a restaurant search domain, examples of DMV slots are location and cuisine. LOC slot in Table 1 is a DMV slot.

3. Conjunctive multi-value (CMV) slots: These are list type slots which can take multiple values in conjunction. Examples are slots containing names of people going to an event, items in a shopping list, etc. Slot PNAMES in Table 1 is a CMV slot. Both CMV and DMV slots support Append, Remove and Replace UI's.

Different domains may not share same slots but they often share slots with same types. For example, list of groceries in the shopping domain and list of people in a dinner invite in the restaurant domain are of type CMV. Similarly, the number of guests in a dinner reservation and the number of items of a particular grocery are of type numeric. If we delexicalize slot-values with slot types, we can transfer learning for a slot type in one domain to the same slot type in another domain.

There can be cases where there are different ways (word patterns) to specify updates to two slots even if they are of the same type, because of differences in the corresponding domains or some other reason. For example, lets say slots S_1 and S_2 are in different domains but share the same slot-type S and we have training data for slot S_1. S_1 and S_2 have similarities owing to their common slot-type but have certain differences in the ways users can express update intents for them. In such a case, to generate training data for S_2, we would need data capturing the differences between the two slots because the examples with common features are already contained in S_1's training data. Generating this additional data is easier than generating the full data for S_2. The amount of additional data required will depend upon the degree by which the slots (S_1 and S_2) differ. When applied to a large number of slots and domains, this strategy would significantly reduce the time and effort that goes into data generation. To demonstrate this, we conduct training and testing experiments on two domains, restaurants and online shopping, and report results in Section 5.2.

4 Data Preparation

To evaluate our approach, we needed dialogs containing numeric, CMV, and DMV slots in the domain ontology along with the proposed update intents expressed in user utterances. Existing datasets with annotated dialog acts such as WOZ 2.0 (Wen et al., 2017), ATIS (Dahl et al., 1994), Switchboard DA corpus [1], Dialog State Tracking Challenge (DSTC) datasets (Henderson et al., 2014a; Williams et al., 2013; Henderson et al., 2014b) and ICSI meeting recorder DA corpus (Shriberg et al., 2004) did not satisfy these requirements. DSTC 2 and DSTC 3 datasets contained DMV slots but not the CMV (list-based slots) and numeric slots [2]. DSTC 4 (Kim et al., 2015), DSTC 5 (Kim et al., 2016) and DSTC

---

[1]http://compprag.christopherpotts.net/swda.html

[2]The *pricerange* slot in DSTC2 and 3 is a categorical (and not a numeric) slot with a fixed set of values

6 (Boureau et al., 2017) introduced a new set of speech acts which contains "HOW_MUCH" act for the numeric price range and time slots. However, the act only supports the *Replace* UI and not the *IncreaseBy* and *DecreaseBy* UI's. Moreover, the three datasets are not public. Therefore, we generated our own datasets.

We generated user utterances in two domains: restaurants and online shopping. In each domain, eight human editors generated user utterances independent of each other. The sets of editors were different across the two domains. Table 3 explains the slots used in the two domains. For each domain, we defined certain tasks which are listed in Table 4. Editors wrote conversations to complete those tasks. Since this was not a real dialog system, editors were asked to assume appropriate bot responses based on their requests such as "Okay", "Added", "Removed", "Done" during the conversation. Also, since the focus was on identifying update intents and not on the overall SLU, (dialog act detection, slot-filling, etc.), we did not build our own custom slot-tagger and, instead, asked the editors to annotate the slot-values with the corresponding slot name in addition to the update intents. Here is a sample annotation for the task "restaurant reservation".

$$Drop\ \underbrace{\overbrace{one}^{\text{NGUEST}}}_{\text{DecreaseBy}}\ person,\ \underbrace{\overbrace{Joe}^{\text{PNAMES}}}_{\text{Remove}}\ can't\ make\ it.$$

For the shopping domain, 305 conversations with 1308 user utterances were generated. For the restaurant domain, 280 conversations with 1323 user utterances were generated. The distribution of utterances among editors is 96, 110, 212, 79, 176, 258, 211 and 166 for the shopping domain. For the restaurant domain, the editorial distribution is 322, 181, 116, 106, 143, 107, 109 and 239. The distribution of Append, Remove, Replace, IncreaseBy and DecreaseBy UI's for restaurant domain is 1022, 301, 601, 92, 112 respectively. The corresponding distribution for the shopping domain is 1249, 241, 521, 297, 90. Note that, an utterance may have more than one UI.

5 Experiments and Results

5.1 Experimental Setting

We implement the proposed architecture in Section 3 using Keras (Chollet et al., 2015), a high-level neural networks API, with the Tensorflow (Abadi et al., 2015) backend. Training is

Slot	Type	Definition
		Restaurants
PNAMES	CMV	List of names of people in a reservation.
NGUEST	Numeric	Number of people in a reservation.
MENUITEMS	CMV	List of menu items to be ordered.
CUISINE	DMV	Type of cuisine.
LOCATION	DMV	Location (city) of restaurant.
		Shopping
GITEMS	CMV	List of grocery items.
QTY	Numeric	Quantity of a particular (grocery or apparel) item.
ASTORE	DMV	Apparel shopping store.
AITEMS	CMV	List of apparels.
COLOR	DMV	Color of apparel.
SIZE	DMV	Size of apparel.

Table 3: List of slots, their type and definitions in the restaurant and shopping domains.

done by mini-batch RMSProp (Hinton et al., 2012) with a fixed learning rate. In all our experiments, mini-batch size is fixed to 64. Training and inference are done on a per-utterance level. The embedding layer in the model is initialized with 300-dimensional Glove word vectors obtained from common crawl (Pennington et al., 2014). Embeddings for missing words are initialized randomly with values between -0.5 and 0.5.

Evaluation: Using a random split of train and test sets would have examples from the same editor in both train and test sets which would bias the estimation. Therefore, we split our data into eight folds corresponding to the eight editors, i.e., each fold contains examples from only one of the editors. To evaluate our models, we train and validate on the data from seven folds and test the performance on the held-out (eighth) fold. We run this experiment for each editor, i.e., eight times, and average results across the eight folds. For validation, we use 15% of the training data. We use precision, recall and F-1 score to report the performance of our classifiers. Overall classification performance metrics are computed by taking the weighted average of the metrics for individual classes. A class's weight is the ratio of the number of instances in it to the total number of instances.

Parameter tuning: In each experiment, 15% of the current training set is utilized as a development set for hyper-parameter tuning and the model with best setting is applied to the test set to report the results. We tune learning rate, dropout via grid search on the development set. In addition, we uti-

lize early stopping to avoid over-fitting. The optimal hyper-parameter settings for our classification experiments (reported in Table 5) is $dropout = 0.3$, $learningrate = 0.001$ for the restaurants domain and $dropout = 0.25$, $learningrate = 0.001$ for the shopping domain.

Baseline: We used n-grams based multinomial logistic regression as a baseline. N-grams based models have been extensively used in text classification (Biyani et al., 2016, 2013, 2012). Such models have also been found to be effective as semantic tuple classifiers for dialog act detection and slot filling tasks (Chen et al., 2013; Henderson et al., 2012). Since there can be multiple slot-values and, hence, multiple UI's expressed in a user utterance, the entire utterance cannot be used to extract n-grams for all the expressed UI's. Therefore, we segment user utterances into relevant contexts for the slot-values and classify the contexts into one of the five UI classes. A context for a value is an ordered list of words which are indicative of the update to be performed for the value. We use two approaches for segmentation based on the k words window approach: a) hard segmentation, b) soft segmentation. In the first approach, we assign the words around the value to its context based on the following constraints:

1. If an utterance contains only one value, the entire utterance is taken as the context for the value.

2. If there are n words (s.t. $n < 2k$) between two slot values then the preference is given to the right value. That is, k words are assigned to the context of the right value and $n - k$ words are assigned to the context of the left value.

3. All the words to the left of the first value (in the utterance) are added to the value's context. Similarly, all the words to the right of the last value are added to its context.

In soft segmentation, we do not perform a hard assignment of the words, between the two values to the context of one of the values. Instead, we encode the words into one of these categories based on its position with respect to the value and if it is in between two values (and let the model learn weights for words in each category): 1) towards left of a value and between two values, 2) towards right of a value and between two values, 3) towards left of a value, 4) towards right of a value.

We extracted unigrams and bigrams from the context of slot-values. We experimented with different window sizes and k=2 gave the best results.

Task	Informable slots	Supported update intents	Example user utterances
		Restaurants	
Search	location, cuisine	Append, Remove, Replace.	Utterances 1 to 3 in Table 1
Reservation	pnames, nguest	All UI's	Utterance 4 to 7 in Table 1
Order food	menuitems	Append, Remove, Replace.	1. Order a *cheese burger* and a *coke can*. 2. Can you do a *diet coke*.
		Shopping	
Grocery	gitems, qty	All UI's	1. *One dozen white eggs* and *one* pound of *apples*. 2. Add *two* more pounds of *apples*.
Apparel	aitems, astore, color, size, qty	All UI's.	1. Show me *blue sweaters* at *Target*. 2. I think *black* will suit better.

Table 4: Tasks in the two domains with corresponding info slots, supported update intents and example utterances. Slot-values in the utterances are in italics.

Class	Prec.	Re.	F-1	#Instances
		Restaurants		
Append	90.64	92.86	91.74	1022
Remove	85.66	81.40	83.48	301
Replace	89.05	93.34	91.15	601
IncreaseBy	95.29	88.04	91.53	92
DecreaseBy	96.88	83.04	89.42	112
Overall	90.02	90.65	90.27	2128
		Shopping		
Append	92.22	95.26	93.72	1245
Remove	85.71	74.69	79.82	241
Replace	85.63	82.50	84.04	520
IncreaseBy	98.30	97.31	97.80	297
DecreaseBy	91.36	82.22	86.55	90
Overall	90.86	90.18	90.45	2393

Table 5: Classification results on the two domains.

Method	Prec.	Re.	F-1
		Restaurants	
1.Baseline(soft)	84.28	82.84	81.96
2.Baseline(hard)	85.74	84.96	84.32
3.Model-delex	$90.66^{1,2}$	$85.14^{1,2}$	$87.74^{1,2}$
4.Model	$90.02^{1,2}$	$90.65^{1,2,3}$	$90.27^{1,2,3}$
		Shopping	
1.Baseline(soft)	82.62	81.12	79.86
2.Baseline(hard)	82.81	81.55	80.32
3.Model-delex	$86.30^{1,2}$	82.10	$84.05^{1,2}$
4.Model	$90.86^{1,2,3}$	$90.18^{1,2,3}$	$90.45^{1,2,3}$

Table 6: Comparison of different classification models on the two domains. Superscripts' denote statistical significance over the corresponding model with a p-value of 0.05 or less. Model-delex is the proposed model without delexicalization.

5.2 Results

In this section, we present the results of our classification and domain-independence experiments.

5.2.1 Classification Results

Table 5 shows the classification results on the two domains. For both the domains, our model achieves more than 90% overall F-1 scores. Per-class results are also strong. The Append, Replace, and IncreaseBy classes achieve more than 91% F-1 scores for the restaurant domain. For the shopping domain, IncreaseBy is the best performing class (97% F-1) followed by Append and DecreaseBy. Despite having significantly fewer examples compared to the other classes, IncreaseBy and DecreaseBy perform very well. One of the reasons for this behavior could be that after delexicalization, for these two classes, there is only one slot (QTY in shopping and NGUEST in restaurants) for which the model learns the patterns. Other than these two classes, this slot is shared by the Replace class. Hence, given a delexicalized numeric slot-value, the model needs to discriminate between these three classes whose relative distribution is much smoother than the overall distribution of the five classes. For the other delexicalized slot-values, the model discriminates between Append, Remove and Replace, where the majority class has a much higher number of examples than the minority Remove class. Hence, we see that the Append class performs significantly

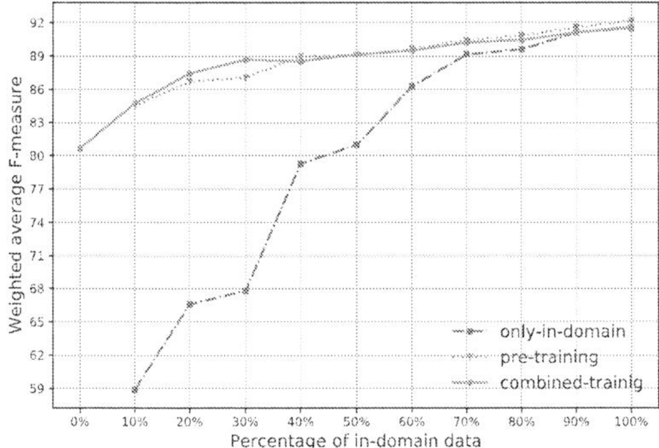

Figure 2: Restaurant as out-domain and shopping as in-domain.

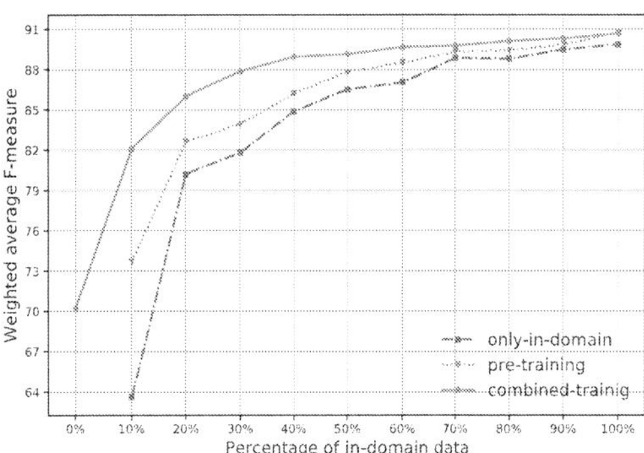

Figure 3: Shopping as out-domain and restaurant as in-domain

better than the Remove class.

We also compare our model with the two baselines explained in Section 5.1. Table 6 presents these results. We see that the proposed model significantly outperforms the two baselines. This shows that for UI classification, contextual information around a slot-value is captured much more effectively using sequence models than static classifiers. We also experimented with our model without delexicalization to verify the gains it brings. As can be seen, delexicalization does improve the performance in both domains.

5.2.2 Domain Independence Results

We conducted experiments to explore if learning of UI's in a domain can be used to predict UI's in a different domain. We use one of the domains as the "in-domain" (where learning is transferred to) and the other as the "out-domain" (where learning is transferred from). For this experiment, we set aside 20% of the in-domain data as the test set. At each step, we use 15% of the training data as the validation set. We explored two settings:

1. **Combined-training**: In this setting, we start by training our model on the entire out-domain data and then, incrementally, add a fraction (10%) of the in-domain data (left after taking out the test data) to the current training data, retrain the model (from scratch) on the combined data.

2. **Pre-training**: Here, we train a model on the out-domain data and fine-tune it with the in-domain data. At each step, we add a fraction (10%) of the in-domain data to the current training data and refit the pre-trained out-domain model on it by initializing the model weights to the weights of the model trained on the out domain data.

Figures 2 and 3 report the results of these two settings. For Figure 2, the model trained only on the out-domain (restaurant) data achieves F-1 score of more than 80% on the in-domain test set. As we add more in-domain data, the F-1 score increases. With only 30% of the in-domain data, we get 89% F-1 score. Also, we see that pre-training and combined-training have similar performances.

For Figure 3, the out-domain model achieves a much lower F-1 score on the in-domain data. This shows that the transfer is not symmetric. This could be due to the PNAME slot, which has no similar slots in the shopping domain. There is also a difference between the performance curve of pre-training and combined-training. This indicates that fine-tuning a pre-trained model is harder than combined training when patterns are not covered by the out-domain data.

6 Conclusions and Future Work

We proposed a new type of slot-specific user intents, **update intents** (UI's), that are directly related to the type of update a user intends for a slot. The UI's address user intents containing implicit denials, numeric updates and preferences for slot-values, which are not handled by the currently used dialog acts. We presented a sequence labeling model for classifying UI's. We also proposed a method to transfer learning of UI's across domains by delexicalizing slot-values with their slot types. For that, we defined three generic slot types. Experimental results showed strong performance for UI classification and promising results for the domain independence experiments. In the future, we plan to explore mechanisms to utilize the UI's in belief tracking.

References

Martín Abadi, Ashish Agarwal, Paul Barham, Eugene Brevdo, Zhifeng Chen, Craig Citro, Greg S. Corrado, Andy Davis, Jeffrey Dean, Matthieu Devin, Sanjay Ghemawat, Ian Goodfellow, Andrew Harp, Geoffrey Irving, Michael Isard, Yangqing Jia, Rafal Jozefowicz, Lukasz Kaiser, Manjunath Kudlur, Josh Levenberg, Dandelion Mané, Rajat Monga, Sherry Moore, Derek Murray, Chris Olah, Mike Schuster, Jonathon Shlens, Benoit Steiner, Ilya Sutskever, Kunal Talwar, Paul Tucker, Vincent Vanhoucke, Vijay Vasudevan, Fernanda Viégas, Oriol Vinyals, Pete Warden, Martin Wattenberg, Martin Wicke, Yuan Yu, and Xiaoqiang Zheng. 2015. TensorFlow: Large-scale machine learning on heterogeneous systems. Software available from tensorflow.org. https://www.tensorflow.org/.

Sumit Bhatia, Prakhar Biyani, and Prasenjit Mitra. 2012. Classifying user messages for managing web forum data. In *Proceedings of the 15th International Workshop on the Web and Databases*. pages 13–18.

Prakhar Biyani, Cornelia Caragea, and Prasenjit Mitra. 2013. Predicting subjectivity orientation of online forum threads. In *Computational Linguistics and Intelligent Text Processing*, Springer, pages 109–120.

Prakhar Biyani, Cornelia Caragea, Amit Singh, and Prasenjit Mitra. 2012. I want what i need!: analyzing subjectivity of online forum threads. In *Proceedings of the 21st ACM international conference on Information and knowledge management*. ACM, pages 2495–2498.

Prakhar Biyani, Kostas Tsioutsiouliklis, and John Blackmer. 2016. " 8 amazing secrets for getting more clicks": Detecting clickbaits in news streams using article informality. In *AAAI*. pages 94–100.

Y-Lan Boureau, Antoine Bordes, and Julien Perez. 2017. Dialog state tracking challenge 6 end-to-end goal-oriented dialog track. Technical report, Tech. Rep.

Yun-Nung Chen, William Yang Wang, and Alexander I Rudnicky. 2013. An empirical investigation of sparse log-linear models for improved dialogue act classification. In *Acoustics, Speech and Signal Processing (ICASSP), 2013 IEEE International Conference on*. IEEE, pages 8317–8321.

François Chollet et al. 2015. Keras. https://github.com/fchollet/keras.

William W Cohen, Vitor R Carvalho, and Tom M Mitchell. 2004. Learning to classify email into"speech acts". In *Proceedings of the 2004 Conference on Empirical Methods in Natural Language Processing*.

Deborah A Dahl, Madeleine Bates, Michael Brown, William Fisher, Kate Hunicke-Smith, David Pallett, Christine Pao, Alexander Rudnicky, and Elizabeth Shriberg. 1994. Expanding the scope of the atis task: The atis-3 corpus. In *Proceedings of the workshop on Human Language Technology*. Association for Computational Linguistics, pages 43–48.

Alex Graves and Jürgen Schmidhuber. 2005. Framewise phoneme classification with bidirectional lstm and other neural network architectures. *Neural Networks* 18(5-6):602–610.

Dilek Hakkani-Tür, Gokhan Tur, Larry Heck, Ashley Fidler, and Asli Celikyilmaz. 2012. A discriminative classification-based approach to information state updates for a multi-domain dialog system. In *Thirteenth Annual Conference of the International Speech Communication Association*.

Matthew Henderson, Milica Gašić, Blaise Thomson, Pirros Tsiakoulis, Kai Yu, and Steve Young. 2012. Discriminative spoken language understanding using word confusion networks. In *Spoken Language Technology Workshop (SLT), 2012 IEEE*. IEEE, pages 176–181.

Matthew Henderson, Blaise Thomson, and Jason D Williams. 2014a. The second dialog state tracking challenge. In *Proceedings of the 15th Annual Meeting of the Special Interest Group on Discourse and Dialogue (SIGDIAL)*. pages 263–272.

Matthew Henderson, Blaise Thomson, and Jason D Williams. 2014b. The third dialog state tracking challenge. In *Spoken Language Technology Workshop (SLT), 2014 IEEE*. IEEE, pages 324–329.

Matthew Henderson, Blaise Thomson, and Steve J Young. 2014c. Word-based dialog state tracking with recurrent neural networks. In *SIGDIAL Conference*. pages 292–299.

G Hinton, Nitish Srivastava, and Kevin Swersky. 2012. Rmsprop: Divide the gradient by a running average of its recent magnitude. *Neural networks for machine learning, Coursera lecture 6e* .

Chiori Hori, Takaaki Hori, Shinji Watanabe, and John R Hershey. 2015. Context sensitive spoken language understanding using role dependent lstm layers. In *Machine Learning for SLU Interaction NIPS 2015 Workshop*.

Chiori Hori, Takaaki Hori, Shinji Watanabe, and John R Hershey. 2016. Context-sensitive and role-dependent spoken language understanding using bidirectional and attention lstms. In *INTERSPEECH*. pages 3236–3240.

Seokhwan Kim and Rafael E. Banchs. 2014. Sequential labeling for tracking dynamic dialog states. In *Proceedings of the SIGDIAL 2014 Conference, The 15th Annual Meeting of the Special Interest Group on Discourse and Dialogue, 18-20 June 2014, Philadelphia, PA, USA*. pages 332–336.

Seokhwan Kim, Luis Fernando D'Haro, Rafael E Banchs, Jason D Williams, Matthew Henderson, and Koichiro Yoshino. 2016. The fifth dialog state tracking challenge. In *Spoken Language Technology Workshop (SLT), 2016 IEEE*. IEEE, pages 511–517.

Seokhwan Kim, Luis Fernando DHaro, Rafael E Banchs, Jason Williams, and Matthew Henderson. 2015. Dialog state tracking challenge 4.

Su Nam Kim, Li Wang, and Timothy Baldwin. 2010. Tagging and linking web forum posts. In *Proceedings of the Fourteenth Conference on Computational Natural Language Learning*. Association for Computational Linguistics, pages 192–202.

Sungjin Lee and Amanda Stent. 2016. Task lineages: Dialog state tracking for flexible interaction. In *SIGDIAL Conference*. pages 11–21.

François Mairesse, Milica Gasic, Filip Jurcícek, Simon Keizer, Blaise Thomson, Kai Yu, and Steve Young. 2009. Spoken language understanding from unaligned data using discriminative classification models. In *Acoustics, Speech and Signal Processing, 2009. ICASSP 2009. IEEE International Conference on*. IEEE, pages 4749–4752.

Nikola Mrkšić, Diarmuid O Séaghdha, Blaise Thomson, Milica Gašić, Pei-Hao Su, David Vandyke, Tsung-Hsien Wen, and Steve Young. 2015. Multidomain dialog state tracking using recurrent neural networks. *arXiv preprint arXiv:1506.07190* .

Nikola Mrksic, Diarmuid Ó Séaghdha, Tsung-Hsien Wen, Blaise Thomson, and Steve J. Young. 2017. Neural belief tracker: Data-driven dialogue state tracking. In *Proceedings of the 55th Annual Meeting of the Association for Computational Linguistics, ACL 2017*. pages 1777–1788.

Jeffrey Pennington, Richard Socher, and Christopher D. Manning. 2014. Glove: Global vectors for word representation. In *Empirical Methods in Natural Language Processing (EMNLP)*. pages 1532–1543. http://www.aclweb.org/anthology/D14-1162.

Hang Ren, Weiqun Xu, Yan Zhang, and Yonghong Yan. 2013. Dialog state tracking using conditional random fields. In *Proceedings of the SIGDIAL 2013 Conference*. pages 457–461.

Elizabeth Shriberg, Raj Dhillon, Sonali Bhagat, Jeremy Ang, and Hannah Carvey. 2004. The icsi meeting recorder dialog act (mrda) corpus. Technical report, INTERNATIONAL COMPUTER SCIENCE INST BERKELEY CA.

Takashi Ushio, Hongjie Shi, Mitsuru Endo, Katsuyoshi Yamagami, and Noriaki Horii. 2016. Recurrent convolutional neural networks for structured speech act tagging. In *Spoken Language Technology Workshop (SLT), 2016 IEEE*. IEEE, pages 518–524.

Tsung-Hsien Wen, David Vandyke, Nikola Mrkšić, Milica Gasic, Lina M Rojas Barahona, Pei-Hao Su, Stefan Ultes, and Steve Young. 2017. A network-based end-to-end trainable task-oriented dialogue system. In *Proceedings of the 15th Conference of the European Chapter of the Association for Computational Linguistics: Volume 1, Long Papers*. volume 1, pages 438–449.

Jason D Williams, Antoine Raux, Deepak Ramachandran, and Alan W Black. 2013. The dialog state tracking challenge. In *SIGDIAL Conference*. pages 404–413.

Steve Young. 2007. Cued standard dialogue acts. *Report, Cambridge University Engineering Department, 14th October* .

Association for Computational Linguistics
209 N. Eighth Street
Stroudsburg, Pennsylvania 18360

ISBN 978-1-5108-6854-0